SOME SUGGESTIONS FOR USING

POPULAR WRITING IN AMERICA

THE INTERACTION OF STYLE AND AUDIENCE

FIFTH EDITION

Donald McQuade
University of California, Berkeley

Robert Atwan

New York Oxford
OXFORD UNIVERSITY PRESS
1993

Oxford University Press

Oxford New York Toronto
Delhi Bombay Calcutta Madras Karachi
Kuala Lumpur Singapore Hong Kong Tokyo
Nairobi Dar es Salaam Cape Town
Melbourne Auckland Madrid

and associated companies in
Berlin Ibadan

Published by Oxford University Press, Inc.
200 Madison Avenue, New York, New York 10016

ISBN 0-19-507308-8 (text)
ISBN 0-19-508283-4 (instructor's manual)

9 8 7 6 5 4 3 2 1

Printed in the United States of America
on acid-free paper

PREFACE

We are grateful to our many colleagues across the country who have suggested specific ways of strengthening the uses of *Popular Writing in America* as a teaching tool and as an occasion for effective student writing. We have tried to include as many of their recommendations as possible in this latest edition of the Teacher's Manual.

As with previous editions, we have tried to make this Teacher's Manual as practical as possible. We have set out, for example, to anticipate any difficulties students might have with our newly added selections, and we have worked hard at making our discussion questions and writing exercises at once as engaging and as productive as possible. And once again we have prepared writing exercises which encourage students to adapt the structures and strategies of what they have read to their own efforts to write more successfully. We have also designed the discussion questions so that they progress from the specific and the factual to the general and the speculative. For example, the questions prepared for the more difficult selections prompt students to understand fully what they have read *before* they are asked to tackle the more complex issues raised by the selection. And in this fifth edition of the Teacher's Manual we have been especially conscious of drafting questions that will help students to discover the unusually rich array of stylistic and thematic interconnections among the selections in *Popular Writing in America*. Our hope is that in working closely with the interactions of style and audience, students will come to appreciate more clearly—and specifically—the interrelations of the seemingly disparate parts of their own verbal lives as readers, thinkers, and writers.

In each of the previous editions of the Teacher's Manual for *Popular Writing in America,* we have noted that a teacher's manual can be an exercise in self-justification. If the editors cannot imagine concretely how a particular selection in their text could be made to work in the classroom, then perhaps they should not have included that piece of writing in the first place. In this manual we have put together sets of questions for each of the advertisements, poems, prose selections, and scripts that appear in this fifth edition of *Popular Writing in America.* We hope that these questions—most of which have already been tried successfully in class—will help enliven discussion and encourage students to think carefully about their reading and writing.

Though the sets of questions are designed to sound like a series of conversational *promptings,* they are also meant to be flexible enough to be useful in creating writing exercises. Obviously, some questions are tougher than others. But the tough ones are not reserved exclusively for the writing that will seem most difficult to students. For some selections, the instructor may want to ask students to respond personally, rather than analytically. When we thought a "personal experience" response would be appropriate to a selection, we added an assignment for that purpose. Finally, only the individual instructor can have a clear sense of which questions and exercises will work best for a particular class.

Tone is always a problem in a teacher's manual. The questions are written for students but are, of course, meant to be read first by their instructors. As a result, our questions may now and then sound peculiarly attuned primarily to the interests of those who have a professional stake in teaching reading and writing. We trust that our colleagues will excuse our lapses into academic idiom, translate these into more accessible terms, and proceed with the business of talking with students reasonably—and encouragingly—about their reading and writing.

Berkeley, Calif. D. McQ.
South Orange, N.J. R. A.
October 1992

CONTENTS

TEXT TABLE OF CONTENTS

AUTOMOBILES

EATING AND DRINKING

MEDIA

INSTITUTIONAL AND CORPORATE ADVERTISING

PRESS 111

CLASSICS 487

SCRIPTS 685

TABLE OF LINKED SELECTIONS

The Myth of Success

American Popular Culture: Some Characters

Coming of Age

Two Declarations of Freedom

The Art of Seeing

Men and Women

The Language of War

The Art of Humor

Questioning America's Values

The American Short Story: A Mini-Anthology

QUESTIONS FOR READING AND WRITING

ADVERTISING

RESPONDING TO THE LANGUAGE AND STRATEGIES OF ADVERTISING: SOME SUGGESTED QUESTIONS

You might find the following questions helpful in generating class discussions or in composing essay assignments on *any* advertisement.

Speaker

1. Read the advertisement aloud. Does the ad sound as if it were being delivered by a particular person or by a group of people (that is, by some kind of corporate personality)?
2. Imagine someone is speaking the words of this ad. How would you describe the sound of the speaker's voice? Does the speaker sound, for example, tough-minded or sentimental, polite or strident, young and impetuous, or experienced and worldly? Do you notice any changes in the way the speaker sounds as the ad progresses? Does the speaker, for example, maintain the same tone? If you think so, find specific examples to substantiate your reading. If not, when and how do these changes occur? How would you describe the various tones? What effect do they have? Have you heard tones such as these before? Where and when? Can you locate the sources of the speaker's diction?
3. Does the speaker's voice sound more appropriate to public speech or to intimate conversation?
4. Does the speaker consider himself or herself essentially different from his or her audience or essentially similar to it? What opinion does the speaker appear to hold of the audience's intelligence and/or its level of education or literacy?
5. Consider carefully the nature of the information given in the ad. Does the speaker appear to expect the audience to be familiar with the information or not? Does the speaker seem to know more about the information than the audience does, or is the speaker simply referring to what is common knowledge?
6. What is the speaker's relation to the subject? Is the speaker, for example, subjective? Objective? At ease with the subject? Emotionally involved? Superior to it? Inferior to it? What is the speaker's attitude toward the subject? Serious? Humorous? Critical? Enthusiastic? Proud? Casual?
7. How reliable is the speaker? Are there any indications that you shouldn't yield readily to his or her statistics? His or her ways of thinking?

Audience

1. To whom is the advertisement addressed? What kind of person do you think the speaker of the ad imagines the reader to be? What kind of person is spoken to in this manner?
2. What specific words and phrases can you point to that give you an indication of the probable level of education, intelligence, age group, social or economic class, sociability, and political beliefs of the audience?
3. What opinion of their own intelligence, sociability, and class status does the ad expect its readers to have? Would you include yourself as part of this audience? Why? Why not?
4. To what needs or desires is the advertisement meant to appeal? Are these appeals directed to the intellect? To the emotions? To "common sense"? To something else? Are there other, more subtle appeals made? Explain.
5. What specific values is the audience expected to hold *before* reading the ad? How does the ad work with these values? Be specific.
6. How does the total "language" of the advertisement (words, picture, layout, tone, etc.) tend to define certain characteristics of its audience?

Some Aspects of Composition

1. Define the kind of response which the ad attempts to provoke in the reader, and show by what verbal means this attempt is made.

2. How does the advertisement attract the reader? Emotion? Fear? Snobbery? Emulation? Feelings of inferiority? Characterize as precisely as you can the nature of the argument used in the advertisement. What is the writer's most prominent mode of persuasion? Does the writer try to convince through logic? Emotional appeal? Association? Irony? Satire? Ridicule? What other techniques of persuasion can you locate in the ad? Does the writer "prove" his or her claims? Which does he or she merely assert? Does he or she use scientific or pseudo-scientific language?
3. How would you describe the sentence structure in the ad? What is the effect of the repetition of this particular structure? Apply some of these same questions to the paragraph structure in the ad and to the general organization of the advertisement.
4. How would you characterize the diction used in the ad? Is it formal or informal? Does it capitalize on colloquial expressions? Slang? The use of dialects and regionalisms? Are any words repeated? Why?
5. Is the language of the ad primarily concrete? Abstract? If the latter, are you always sure that you know what each of these abstractions means? Does the ad's success in some measure depend on a casual lack of precise definition for such abstractions?
6. Describe the figurative language used in the ad. What is the writer's primary source for creating his or her metaphors? Is the figurative language used to reinforce or to qualify what is being argued for in the advertisement? Does the speaker use analogy? Personification? Alliteration? If so, with what effect?

Next to Nature

1. How do the model's clothes and the way she wears her hair relate to the claims for the product made in this ad's copy? Is is important that she holds a flower in her hand? How old do you think the model is supposed to be? (Notice the use of the word "girls'" in the copy's first sentence.) What demographic does Yardley hope to capture with this ad? Is it similar to the readership sought by the Pompeian ad?
2. If a product is designed to make a woman look "natural," why does she need the product at all? What is the implied relationship between artifice and nature in this ad? Is there really such a thing as "natural" beauty? If so, how do you define it? Is it physical? Is a certain lifestyle connected with beauty suggested by the photograph and the language used here? What does the copywriter suggest with the phrase "How to make the most of what you have," highlighted at the bottom of the page? Do you think this ad would be effective with young women today?
3. Read the article "Greenwash" by David Beers and Catherine Capellaro (later in the Advertising section). The rhetoric that corporations use to overcome their reputations as polluters promotes a vision of nature as in need of human assistance. What do the campaigns documented by Beers and Capellaro have in common with Yardley's approach to beauty? Does the woman in the "Next to Nature" ad correlate with the humans who raised the eagles in the Chevron ad (later in the Advertising section), or the eagles, or both?

Madame Rowley's Toilet Mask

1. What is the effect of numbering the list of reasons a potential buyer should use Madame Rowley's mask? Examine the list; does it present any concrete evidence that the mask would be beneficial? Does the pseudo-scientific or medicalized tone of the copy change the way a reader might view this beauty aid? How are the concepts of health and beauty related in this ad?
2. Notice the boldface words in the copy, and those that are capitalized. Read just those words aloud. Does a pattern emerge? What anxieties and reassurances are reflected in this subtext to the ad? Why do you think the paragraph at the bottom of the ad, which seems to summarize the list above it, was included? How would a reader, skimming through a magazine, be drawn in to this ad?
3. What notions of the pursuit of beauty are communicated through the drawing at the center of the page? Does the picture show an average user, one of the "society ladies" endorsing the product, or Madame Rowley herself? Who do you think Madame Rowley is? Can you think of other examples of famous names being connected to products in order to slant their appeal? Would knowing something about the person behind the name influence a reader's interest in the product?

"Mother, Here She Is"

1. Imagine yourself in the position of the woman or man pictured in this ad. Could such a situation occur in your life? How is this advertisement history-bound, in both the conflict it presents and in the language it employs? How might the basic situation presented here be changed to suit today's young female readership? Can you find a similar ad in a current fashion magazine, or on television?

2. What is the position of the man in this narrative? Why do you think he speaks the lines highlighted by the illustration? In some other cosmetics ads, capturing a man's interest is presented as the central reason for using the product. Find such an ad and compare it to this one. How does this ad shift the power relation? Is the man really irrelevant in the world of cosmetics advertising?
3. Compare the gaze of the couple illustrated here to that of the model using Madame Rowley's mask, and that of the model in the Next To Nature ad (earlier in the Advertising section). How do these gazes influence the reader's involvement in and interpretation of the ad? Are the illustrations more important in some ads than others? Which of the three women attracts you more? Which seems most like you? Do the different illustrations reflect shifting attitudes about "woman's place" throughout American history?

WOMEN

Woman's Attractiveness

1. In 1918, the United States was emerging from its involvement in World War I. Reread this ad in the context of that event. Find parallels between the language here used to extoll femininity and that employed in reference to American soldiers and their duties. Contrast this ad with the one for the U.S. Army (*There's something about a soldier, later in this section*). How does that example mirror or contrast with this one?
2. How would you describe the expression on the face of the bride pictured here? Does she display or conceal the power the copy indicates that she possesses? How does her status as a bride affect the message conveyed by the text?
3. List the qualities necessary to fulfill 1918's standard of feminine beauty, as detailed in this ad. How do you think the copywriters decided to highlight certain aspects of appearance over others? Do you think the ad is convincing in its presentation of "a youthful figure" as the most important quality in a woman? Find other texts that present weight and figure control as the feminine consumer's number one priority.

Often a Bridesmaid but Never a Bride

1. Where does the language used to describe "Edna's case" come from? How does the language used in the smaller print differ from that in the larger print? What point is being made by the difference in typography? Comment on the effectiveness of the headline. Have you ever heard this line before? What verbal qualities are at work here?

Should a Gentleman Offer a Tiparillo to a Lab Technician?

1. What stereotype of a woman scientist is the advertisement endorsing? How does the language of the ad indicate this? How does the photograph contradict the image conveyed by the copy? What is the effect of this disparity, and why does the advertiser want it?
2. What is the point of the headline question? Why should it be a question at all? How much does it depend upon innuendo? From an advertiser's point of view, what is the purpose of posing this question? Is it simply to try to get women to smoke little cigars? Explain.

"When I Grow Up, I'm Going to Be a Judge, or a Senator or Maybe President"

1. Why are there so many numbers in the copy? What tone do they establish? Try rewriting the ad avoiding all numbers. How does this diminish its effectiveness? Explain.
2. Why was a black girl chosen as the model for this ad? Note that, though the ad concerns discrimination, the copy does not mention race. What do these choices imply about the social values of the NOW Legal Fund? How might they express the Fund's attitudes toward fairness?
3. Why is there so much copy here? What does the quantity of copy suggest about the ad's intended audience?

"I Know She's a Very Important Person"

1. This is the kind of advertisement that becomes less obvious the longer you consider it. Examine the ad carefully. Who is supposed to be speaking? How can you tell? What are the characters looking at? Why do you suppose the copywriter did not want them looking at each other? What do you imagine is their relationship? Do you think the woman in the ad is the subject of the copy? Discuss the range of possibilities contained in the ad.
2. Examine the language of the ad. Is it intended to be said aloud, or does it reflect someone's thoughts? What qualities go into making someone a "very important person"? Why is the "VIP" said to be "decisive" as well as "charming"? Do these qualities usually go together?
3. Why are the lights on in the office?

A Western Original Wears a Western Original

1. This advertisement shows Jacqueline Phillips Guibora, a Provo Utah police officer, promoting the purchase of Wrangler jeans. Examine carefully the nature of the photograph and describe the image(s) it conveys. What significance do the ad's creators attach to her clothing? What function does the rifle play in the ad? What strategies does the ad invoke to draw the reader's attention to the Wrangler jeans? What role does the police officer's posture play in the success of the ad? What effect(s) are created by having the police officer lean against the front end of the car?
2. Reread the language of the advertisement. In what specific ways does it reinforce (or weaken) the image(s) created in the ad? What are the advantages/disadvantages of the way in which the language of the ad is positioned in relation to its central image(s)?
3. An article in the *New York Times* by Robert Reinhold entitled "Policewoman in Denim Is Betty Grable of Gulf" (January 15, 1991, p. A12) reported that this advertisement was "the favorite pinup picture of American soldiers in the Persian Gulf War." Speculate about the reasons this ad was so widely liked as a "pinup picture" by soldiers in the Gulf War.
4. Look back through issues of *Life* and *Look* magazines during the Second World War. (You might start with issues published during 1943.) In what ways are the ads you find in those magazines (featuring Betty Grable and other female celebrities) like/unlike the one for Wrangler jeans?
5. Read the advertisements entitled "I'm the NRA" and "Help Me Fight the National Rifle Association" (later in the Advertising section). Given their positions, how would Representative Alberto Gutman and Mrs. James S. Brady respond to the ad for Wrangler jeans?

There's Something about a Soldier

1. The language in this advertisement works to reassure women considering an Army post about that choice. What stereotypes does the text seem to be fighting against? How do the two pictures work in relation to the text's message? Why is the photograph of the woman in uniform larger than the one of her in civilian clothes? Why do you think a male companion is included in the second photograph?
2. What kind of person is the imagined speaker of the text? Does the text communicate a sense of authority? If so, how? Why is the phrase "There's something about a soldier" isolated from the rest of the text? Is the rest of the text contradictory to that phrase? How are references to traditional and unconventional feminine attributes kept in balance here?

What If?

1. This ad refers to a specific occurrence that saturated the media in 1991—the Anita Hill/Clarence Thomas hearings. Do you think that in a year's time, the ad might have lost its power? Find other examples of ads that refer to current events to communicate a message. How do these differ from those using historical events or figures, such as the McDonald's advertisement later in the Advertising section.
2. This advertisement uses more text than many included in the Advertising section. Why might a longer message prove more effective in this campaign? How does the phrase "Turn your anger into action" work in relation to the rest of the text? Would you describe the tone of the text as reasonable or forceful? Find examples of other political ad campaigns that have taken a different approach to making an argument.
3. Why do you think the National Women's Political Caucus chose a drawing instead of a staged photograph or a candid from the Anita Hill/Clarence Thomas hearings to illustrate this ad? What visual associations (from other magazines, books, newspapers) does such a line drawing suggest? Examine the expressions on the faces of the women pictured—do they correlate with images of male congress members that you can remember, or are they different? Why do you think the two women on the left end are pictured as smiling? Do you think the racial mix of women pictured is representative of a possible female Senate?

Remember P.E. Class?

1. Four-page advertisements are uncommon in contemporary magazines, although companies such as Benetton, Guess, and Ralph Lauren have also presented such campaigns. How does spreading an ad over several pages change its effect on the reader? How does it change its relationship to the rest of the magazine? How does the storylike language in this ad factor into its presentation? Do the photographs relate directly to the story? How do you connect image and text here?
2. What age do you think the imagined reader of the text is? Is she or he a child or an adult? If she is an adult, why is the effect of the casual, simplistic

language used in the text? How are childhood anxieties used to promote a product here?

3. The italicized words in this text seem to have been selected randomly. Examine those phrases; can any connection be made among them? How does typeface and graphic presentation affect your reading of the text? Do the words "Just Do It" come as a surprise at the end? Do they seem supported by the rest of the text? Why did Nike choose to make the only references to its own product a small logo at the top of the first page and an even smaller toll-free number at the bottom? What is really being marketed here?
4. Consider the discussion of the word "average" in the eighth paragraph. Does this reflect the common definition of the word? To whom might "average" mean "stuck?" What does this paragraph indicate about the demographic Nike hopes to capture with this campaign? Could "average" be used as a positive term in another kind of ad?

Buy What You Want to Buy

1. This advertisement uses relatively little text to convey its message. How does the sentence "Buy what you want to buy" affect your reading of the photograph? of the rest of the ad? Would the image have attracted your attention without this prompting? Imagine another line of copy that could change the meaning of the ad. Why do you think that the copywriter(s) used the imperative form of the verb here?
2. How does the placement of the American Express card influence your response to the ad? What effects are created by positioning the woman's body in relation to the art object and in relation to the American Express card?
3. What is your reaction to the second sentence in the ad: "And no bankcard is going to stop you with a limit set long long ago*"? What is the function of the asterisk at the end of the sentence? In what specific ways does that asterisk reinforce (or subvert) the statement?
4. Reread the third and fourth sentences: "You know what you can afford. You just want to be trusted." What function does the word "just" serve in the fourth sentence? What effect does it have on the sentence? on your response to the ad?
5. What do you make of the final two sentences in the ad: "You're a responsible person. Most of the time." In what specific ways does the final sentence reinforce—or undercut—the substance of the previous sentence? What attitude toward women is apparent in the final sentence?
6. What attitudes toward woman underlie this ad? The model in this ad is typical of advertisements featuring female subjects, such as the "Next to Nature" ad. (See earlier in the Advertising section.) Do you think the American Express Company is aiming for a female or male readership, or both? How would female students respond differently to this image than do males? Examine the ways in which the ad plays with traditional gender roles. More generally, what attitudes toward consumerism underlie this ad?

MEN

We Smash 'Em Hard

1. What connection is there between what the Yank veteran says and what the spokesman for White Owl Cigars says? What word characterizes both the Yank's performance and the cigar's? How does the picture of the White Owl Cigars in the right-hand corner reinforce the thrust of what the Yank is saying?
2. What is the occasion for the Yank's chauvinistic speech? Specifically, to whom is he talking? Would similar language and sentiments appear in a contemporary ad?
3. Discuss the effectiveness of the strategy of using military figures to promote cigarette smoking.
4. The ad for White Owl Cigars would work nicely in class with the often anthologized Thomas Hardy poem "The Man He Killed." Focus on the language and logic of war.

Case 099B

1. What features do you notice about the illustration? What sense of "identity" does it evoke? What details are emphasized in the illustration? Which are underplayed? With what effect(s)? Based on your analysis of the illustration and the language of the copy in the ad, whom do you imagine to be the principal audience for this ad? Men? Women? Both? Point to specific words and phrases to support your reading.
2. Does the image of the man identified in this advertisement depend for its effectiveness more on the illustration than on the language of the advertisement? Explain why?
3. What is the purpose of the headline? What response do the copywriters expect to evoke by using the phrase "Case 099B"? What is the function of the "B" in "Case 099B"? How effective is this headline? What is its psychological effect?
4. Read the advertisement "Often a Bridesmaid but Never a Bride" in the section on Women in Adver-

tising. Discuss the similarities and differences between the two advertisements. Which do you judge to be more effective? Why? In what sense is having ''halitosis'' different—or similar—for the man and the woman pictured in each ad?

How Joe's Body Brought Him Fame Instead of Shame

1. Why do you think this ad has become a classic of the advertising industry? What does it encapsulate?
2. What image of men does the ad endorse? What image of women? Do you think the concerns of the advertisement are dated, or do you find the anxieties it trades on still part of our everyday life?
3. Why do you think the ad was constructed in comic-book format? How is the dramatic situation condensed to the bare essentials? What is the effect of that compression? How does it reinforce the claim that ''only 15 minutes a day'' can make a ''new man''?

The End of the Skinny Body!

1. How convinced are you by the before-after story of Charlie Kemp? What facts are left out? How, for example, have ''a few simple exercises'' turned him into ''a muscular man of vitality?''
2. If you think the ad is far-fetched, try imagining the audience that would be convinced by its argument and evidence. What type of person is the ad appealing to? What expectations would this person have? What sort of things would this person not want to do—for example, why is exercise played down and drinking played up? Does the ad directly promise muscles? How does it suggest muscular development will take place instead of just additional fat?

When Crusher Lizowski Talks about Being a Homemaker, You Listen

1. What is your first reaction to the boldface text at the top of this ad? How does the photograph work with that text? Find examples in the body of the text that play off these initial contradictions. Why did the copywriter choose ''Japanese food'' and ''macrame'' as Crusher's specialties?
2. In the middle of the text, a paragraph begins, ''Being a homemaker is, after all, being an adult.'' This is a serious message. Does the ad effectively communicate this notion, despite its humorous overtones? How does the humor work against stereotypes of homemakers? Would the aforementioned sentence have a different meaning if a traditional woman in an apron, with a name like ''Mary Jones,'' was pictured?
3. Crusher says he cooks and cleans the house ''when I'm not on the road.'' What profession do you imagine takes him away from home? How does his association with that profession further enhance the message of the ad?

''Hello?'' ''How's the Great American Novel Going?''

1. What does this man's occupation—a struggling novelist—imply about his character? Do you suppose he has another occupation as well? What is Paco Rabanne saying about itself by choosing such a man to represent it?
2. Cologne presumably serves a social function: it's something a person uses primarily in the company of others. What logic, then, is there in having an isolated man complain of having used up his cologne?
3. How does gender operate in this ad? How would the appeal of the ad differ if the photo depicted the female character instead of the male character? Imagine their roles reversed, the isolated woman receiving a phone call from a man. How would this make for an effective perfume ad? Explain.
4. Write the opening page of this man's novel.

An American Hero

1. How would you characterize the person in the photograph? What is he carrying—and why? How do these props affect your sense of his personality? In what sense is he a hero? Does he seem courageous? Exceptional? Discuss the meaning of the word *hero* in the context of the ad.
2. The man is obviously a businessman; yet where is the typical briefcase? How does the absence of a briefcase help characterize him? Does it contribute to his heroic qualities?
3. Create a story for this scene. Where is the person going? What is his mood? Is he married or single? How much of what you invent about him is determined by the props in the picture?

Obsession for Men

1. Spend a few minutes examining carefully the photograph in this advertisement for Calvin Klein cologne. Write as full a description as possible of the factual evidence depicted. Consider, for example, the placement—as well as the relationship—of the two bodies shown in the ad. Then consider the

relation of these two bodies to their surroundings. Once you have completed this detailed description, write at least another paragraph in which you draw inferences from the observations you have made.

2. Now consider the sparse language of this ad. Notice, for example, the layout of the six words that appear on the page. What relationship do you notice between the layout of the two sets of three words? What significance do you attach to the ways in which these words are presented to readers of the ad?
3. What range of associations does the word "Obsession" evoke? Which of these associations do you think the copywriters allude to in this ad? With what effect(s)? Is the intended audience for this ad primarily male? female? Explain.
4. In what specific ways do you find this ad to be effective? ineffective? Read through several recent issues of popular magazines (*Esquire, Vanity Fair, Rolling Stone,* for example), and find other examples of ads for Calvin Klein's cologne, "Obsession for Men." In what specific ways are these other ads similar to/different from this one? Which do you judge to be more effective? Why?

When You're Old, and Tired, and Suspicious

1. Examine carefully the design of this two-page advertisement. What are the effects of the two contrasting photos? Describe as accurately as you can the details evident in each of the two photographs. (As you do so try to resist making judgments.) After you have completed that exercise, focus on drawing inferences from what you have observed. What inferences can you reasonably draw from your observations?
2. Consider again the photograph of the younger man. What do you make of the angle used to capture the young man running? In what specific ways does this angle (this point of view) represent the shoes to best advantage? Explain. What sorts of appeals are the copywriters making to readers in this ad? Are these appeals primarily logical? emotional? something else? Explain your answer by referring to specific words and phrases. What, finally, is the basic strategy in selling Nike in this ad?
3. Reread the text of the ad. Who is the "you" identified in the phrase, "When you're old, and tired, and suspicious"? Does the reference for "you" remain consistent throughout the ad? If not, how and when does it change? With what effect(s)? Whom do you imagine speaking the words of this ad? The older man? the younger man? someone else? Verify your response by pointing to specific words and phrases.
4. What are the effects of Nike's referring to its product as "gear" and "shoes"—and not as "sneakers"? Check the meanings of the word "sneakers." Does what you see in this ad lead you to include Nike in this definition of "sneakers"?

In This World of Total Confusion

1. Why should this advertisement for Oaktree clothing be categorized under the section on "Men"? What male desires are being appealed to in this ad? In this regard, compare and contrast the strategies used in this ad with the ones used in the ad for Calvin Klein's "Obsession for Men." Which do you find more effective? Why?
2. What details in the design of the advertisement do you find especially effective? Why? Focus for a few moments on the photograph featured in the ad. What about it strikes you as particularly effective? Why? Is the ad promoting the purchase of the shirt? the pants? both? What details in the evidence of the photograph lead you to your conclusion?
3. Reread the text of the ad. Which words and phrases do you find especially effective? Why? What does the phrase "In This World of Total Confusion" seem to allude to? What is the nature of the "confusion" that the ad seems to trade on?
4. Who do you assume are the people identified in the use of "we" in this ad? What significance do you attach to the use of the word "pretend" in the ad? What is the claim made in the last statement of the ad: "WE WANT IT UNDERSTOOD THAT ONLY **CROSS COLOURS** IS MADE BY TRUE BROTHERS FROM THE HOOD"? What response does the use of the phrase "TRUE BROTHERS" evoke?
5. Examine carefully the text in the lower-left corner of the ad. In what specific ways does the language in what appears to be a label differ from the language used in the label on the shirt? What do you take the phrases "POST HIP HOP NATION" and "ACADEMIC HARDWARE" to mean? What relationship do you understand to exist between the **Cross Colours** label and the use of the name OAKTREE in large letters on the right side of the ad?

ANXIETIES

The Girl with the Clear Skin Wins

1. The main line of text in this advertisement sets up a competition between the two women pictured.

The prize attained by the "clear-skinned girl" may seem obvious. What else, besides the attentions of men, might she have that the other woman lacks? What material fears might such an ad have preyed upon in 1916? Would it be possible to set up the same competition between women today? How might today's version differ?

2. In the second paragraph, this text refers to "nature" as a curative element. How does the use of this term compare to the way it is used in the ads for Madame Rowley's, Pompeian and Next to Nature (see the Introduction to Advertising)? This ad also describes its product as recommended by physicians. How does this appeal to medical authority relate to the anxieties the ad stimulates?
3. In small type to the left and at the end of the main body of the text, other potential uses of Resinol are addressed. Why do you think men and mothers of babies aren't included in the ad's primary imagined readership? What kinds of "competition" could be imagined amongst mothers, that might be addressed in other ads?
4. Compare this advertisement with the Neutrogena ad later in this section. Then compare both of these to the Pompeian and the Next to Nature ads (see the Introduction to Advertising). How do the illustrations differ according to the time periods in which they were published? What changing attitudes about women and beauty might be construed from these differences?

Again She Orders—"A Chicken Salad, Please"

1. What anxiety does the syntax of the initial paragraph prey on? What is the effect of shifting abruptly to a dramatic situation in the second paragraph? Is her order of a chicken salad for the third time "while dining with him" a matter of etiquette? of poor taste?
2. How often are the words "embarrassed" "embarrassment," and "crudities" repeated? To what effect? How do these words define the primary fear the advertisement banks on? Is anyone finally able to escape the dimensions and social pressures implicit in the copywriter's repeated flurries of questions?
3. Describe the syntax in the sixth paragraph. How does it reflect the accumulation and the culmination of the character's anxieties? How does it provide a transition to the promise of a solution to the woman's repeated embarrassments? How does the copywriter establish that the *Book of Etiquette* can become a protection ("armor") from "embarrassment"?
4. What is the effect of shifting from "you" to "we" in the section entitled "Are You Conscious of Your Crudities"?
5. Why are the final two paragraphs in this advertisement set off in smaller print? Are the sentences there merely repetitive? Do you sense any "embarrassment" when the copywriter urges us to "Take advantage of the special bargain offer"? Is the tone of this sentence marked by a lapse into the very "crudities" the speaker exhorts us to avoid?
6. How are we to read "Mail this coupon *now* while you are thinking of it"? Do the implications of this command ensure continued sales for the *Book of Etiquette?* What is the purpose of saying *"The Book of Etiquette* will be sent to you in a plain carton with no identifying marks"?

Shy Person's Guide to a Successful Love Life

1. Compare the layouts of this ad and the "How to Write a Personal Letter" ad below. Why does each have a byline? Why does this one have rules between the columns and justified lines of type? If this ad more closely resembles a newspaper article, how does the layout complement the ad's appeal?
2. How does "P. Woodland-Smith" try to win the confidence of the reader? What associations does the name itself carry? Look at the diction of the copy. How does its informality make the claims of the copy more convincing or less? Explain.
3. After studying the style of this ad's language, rewrite the "How to Spell" ad as P. Woodland-Smith might. How might he appeal to the same anxieties as Garrison Keillor does? Explain how the method of his appeal would be the same.

How to Write a Personal Letter

1. This advertisement might be indistinguishable from a magazine article, if not for certain stylistic choices. How do typeface, photographs, and corporate sponsorship indicate this is an ad? How do those same elements suggest that this ad more closely resembles an article than it does other ads? International Paper Company is trying to sell something here—but what? And to whom? (Please note the box at the bottom of the page in responding to this question.)
2. Other ads in this series have used novelist John Irving ("How to Spell") and other well-known writers. Why would International Paper Company choose these well-known authors as representatives? What are the similarities and differences between this kind of celebrity sponsorship and athletic shoe ads featuring sports heroes? cosmetic ads using famous models or actresses?

3. In this particular ad, Garrison Keillor tells readers something about himself before he actually begins discussing how to write a letter. How does his writing style influence his self-presentation? Find an example from one of Keillor's books, or from his syndicated radio show, and show how this ad fits into the writer's creation of a public image. Why do we trust Keillor's advice on writing a personal letter?
4. ''How to Write a Personal Letter'' describes an activity that most people know how to perform, although they may not engage upon it on a regular basis. How much of what Keillor says is really ''how-to'' talk? How would you categorize the rest of the piece? Why would International Paper contextualize this ad as a form of instruction? Do you find this approach condescending? Why might a reader, leafing through a magazine, find such a text appealing?

LifeStyles Introduces the Strongest Condom Made in America

1. Before the spread of AIDS, condom manufacturers invoked a different anxiety in readers—the risk of pregnancy. Which elements of this ad specifically respond to the fear of AIDS, and which relate more generally to anxieties about sexuality? How does the use of a young male model in the photograph affect the slant of the ad?
2. According to this ad, ''strength'' is the main attribute that makes this brand of condom the best choice. In earlier condom ad campaigns, attributes such as sensitivity or even thinness, have been emphasized. How does this ad's stress on the product's material strength relate to the text's more general message, expressed in phrases such as, ''It is now more important than ever to be careful about relationships.''? Does the ''strength'' mentioned here go beyond the product's material durability?
3. The Distilled Spirits Council's testimony against overdrinking (later in this section) also refers to the potential danger in an activity thought of as ''fun.'' Using that ad as a model, write a new text for this condom ad, emphasizing the responsibilities of safe sex. Is there a difference between stimulating fear and appealing to readers' consciences? What else, besides the strength of a condom, might a safe sex ad campaign emphasize?

I Learned I Was HIV Positive 5 Years Ago

1. How does the lighting and the position of the model in each photograph here substantiate the message of the text? What is your reaction when you look at the top photo? Does that feeling change when you look at the bottom photo? Where does your eye turn first when you see this ad? Where does it linger? Does the ad leave you with a feeling of hope or danger?
2. This ad campaign was one of the first to stress the term ''HIV positive'' in reference to people who have contracted the AIDS virus but not yet developed symptoms of the disease. How might the use of this term change public perception of the epidemic? In this ad, how does the switch to the term ''HIV positive'' mirror the transformation the subject of the ad undergoes?
3. Compare the use of the word ''control'' in this ad to the emphasis on ''strength'' in the Lifestyles condom ad. Can you extrapolate, from these two examples, a developing language of coping with the AIDS epidemic? How do these phrases tie in with the terminology of self-help and recovery movements so popular in America today?

Neutrogena Gives You the Clean-pore Advantage Over Acne

1. The various typefaces and graphic styles used in this advertisement make it resemble a page from the editorial portion of a fashion magazine. What are the differences between this page and the average ''Beauty Tips'' spread in such a magazine? Is the experience of reading such an ad different from reading articles that give similar infomation? Note that this ad promotes several different Neutrogena products. Would it have a different effect if only one product were featured?
2. How does this ad use pseudo-scientific style to sell its product? Examine the use of numbers in the text. What mood is produced through the mix of casual sentences and technical terms? How do the concepts of purity and health figure into this promotion? How does the photograph of the model and of the bar of soap further enforce the ad's general message?
3. Contrast this ad with the one for Pompeian Massage Cream earlier in this section. Does the Neutrogena promotion play on reader anxieties? How has the position of the imaginary product user changed in the newer ad? Why do you think no male presence is included in the Neutrogena illustration?

AUTOMOBILES

''Most Automobiles Are Like Most Men''

1. What female stereotypes does the advertisement introduce? How do the comparisons the women

make reveal some of these stereotypes? What is the copywriter's strategy in connecting these stereotypes to the automobile? Why, for example, does he have Helen say, "It's some funny new spring they've invented . . ."?

2. What is the purpose of Helen's complaint that the car is too useful? Why does her friend compare her to a Socialist because of that complaint? Do you think her complaint undermines the sales strategy or reinforces it? Explain.
3. How is the women's social status revealed entirely through their conversation?

Note: Because this advertisement contains a miniature conversation, it can be helpful in teaching dialogue and characterization through diction and tone. Students can be shown how clear and effective dialogue can be written without continual reliance on the "he said, she said" formula.

Her Habit of Measuring Time

1. In 1924, the automobile and the modern woman were both on the rise in America. This ad appeals to one in order to sell the other. Yet the image of this woman is very different from that of the carefree, daring flapper. Why do you think the Ford Motor Company chose this more conservative scene to promote its new line of closed cars? How might the ad have been pitched differently if leisure, rather than work, were the activity emphasized?
2. Notice the many references to time in this text. Why might an auto company focus on this aspect of working woman's concerns? How does the illustration further stress the importance of technology in ordering a modern woman's life?
3. Were you surprised by this reference to working women from the early part of the century? Find similar examples in other magazines of the time. How do these conform to and contrast from the more traditional image of woman as wife and mother?
4. What image of women is conveyed by this advertisement? Do you think the image is a positive one? Explain why or why not.
5. Describe the language of the advertisement. From what part of life are the words drawn? Point to specific words and phrases to establish your contention. How does the language match the graphics? How does the language characterize the woman pictured in the ad?
6. Compare this ad with the one for Suzuki ("We were cruisin' Highway 34 when Lenny said"). Note the similarities and differences between the two in their depictions of women. Aside from stylistic differences, what broader cultural similarities and differences do you notice? What are their implications for the ways in which women are depicted in each period?
7. What relations between women and automobiles are promoted by such ads as "Her habit of measuring time," "We were cruisin' Highway 34," and "Most Automobiles Are Like Most Men"? How do advertisers profit from these relations? How do these appeals differ from those directed to men?

Lemon

1. What is the illustration meant to suggest? Can you find anything wrong with the car in the picture? Why not? What is the ad pretending to risk by its headline? What is meant to be appealing about this strategy? Explain.
2. How is the phrase "missed the boat" meant to work? What is its figurative meaning? its literal one? Can you find other ads that use language in this way?
3. What "preoccupation with detail" do you find in the copy? What attention to small things? Why, for example, doesn't the copywriter round off the number of men from 3,389 to 3,400? What effect on an audience is such a detail intended to have?

Separates the Men from the Boys

1. How do the placement and angle of the photo support the claims for Toronado's masculinity and uniqueness? Why, for example, is the background blank? Why is the car pointed outward, toward the viewer? How would the photo be less effective if the car were positioned in the middle distance and facing the side of the page?
2. Though the language of the copy sounds tough and simple, it is rather heavily adorned with literary flourishes, such as alliteration, metaphor, balance, and parallel structure. How many of these can you locate? What specific effects do they have?
3. Which of the men depicted in the ads in the Men section would this ad *least* appeal to? Redesign the ad—copy, photo, and layout—so that it would appeal to this man.

Which Man Would You Vote For?

1. Why does the top photograph feature a larger crowd and greater fanfare? Does it make you feel

the Volkswagen is less important? Why would the advertiser want to create that effect? Explain.

2. Consider the layout. What difference would it make if the photo of the ''fancy convertible'' were at the bottom instead of the top? Explain.
3. Do you think this advertisement contains a serious political message? If so, do you think it is inappropriate for a commercial announcement to use political overtones? Explain.
4. Which man do you think will win? How does the ad help determine your answer?

You're Not John Doe, Why Drive His Car?

1. Who is the ''John Doe'' mentioned in the first sentence of this ad? Who is the imagined reader of the ad, and how is that person different from John Doe? By what means does the ad characterize the John Doe figure as negative? Do you think that the ad might not succeed with people who do like to wear beige sweaters, or is the underlying subtext more powerful than the details given?
2. How reasonable is the claim, ''A car isn't just something you drive. It's something you wear''? What shift in thinking must the consumer make in order to think of an automobile as a clothing item? What kind of lifestyle does this kind of rhetoric assume in an imagined reader? Why do you think the ad also makes reference to ''Manhattan studio apartments?''

Marcel Jojola Likes the Saturn SLI So Much, He Had His Customized for Work

1. Notice the proper names used in this Saturn advertisement. What associations do the names Marcel Jojola and Bear Valley evoke? Do you think Officer Jojola really exits, or is a model playing his part? Does the advertiser expect the reader to believe in Officer Jojola? What qualities in a car are represented through the use of a law enforcement officer as an endorser?
2. The ad copy uses an issue familiar to the American public as a selling point for the Saturn. What is that issue? How do politics and style interact in the story the ad copy tells?
3. The last sentence of the third paragraph refers to a ''we.'' Who is the implied speaker? How does the language used in the copy reinforce the sense of a particular individual telling the story? Why do you think the copywriter chose ''we'' instead of ''I''?
4. What does the punchline of this story—that Officer Jojola bought two Saturns—indicate about the product? about Officer Jojola?

We Were Cruisin Highway 34 When Lenny Said

1. This advertisement uses a graphic trick to draw the reader in, decreasing the typeface size as the narrative continues. How does the language used in the first sentence catch the reader's attention? Why do you think ''Lenny'' is mentioned in the third line? When do you discover ''Lenny's'' relationship to the people in the car and his purpose for making the suggestion he makes in the fourth line? Does the action in the story make sense? How does the typeface work with the story to pique readers' curiosity?
2. What qualities in the Suzuki Sidekick are represented by the story of Lenny and his family? Find specific elements in the copy that highlight qualities of the automobile. How does the small paragraph at the end of the story work with the previous text in promoting the Sidekick? Considering the action in the story, and the names and details provided, speculate on the intended market for this car. Do you feel included as an imagined reader of this text? Why?
3. The implied speaker of the story here is a woman driver. Why do you think the copywriter chose her perspective, rather than that of the male navigator's? What qualities of the car that might specifically appeal to the kind of woman presented by the copywriter are highlighted? Would the ad have the same appeal if the speaker were Lenny?
4. What do you think happens directly after the story told here ends? Write a sequel to this ad using a ''further adventures'' theme.
5. How does the slogan ''Everyday vehicles that aren't'' complement the story presented here? Can you think of a different slogan that would work as well?

EATING AND DRINKING

How Would You Put a Glass of Ballantine Ale into Words?

1. Characterize as precisely as you can the sound of Hemingway's voice in this advertisement. Does his tone change in any way as he proceeds in his endorsement of Ballantine Ale? What connections can you establish between the way Hemingway presents himself in the photograph and the way he presents himself in his sentences? How would you characterize his prose style here? Is the structure of his sentences similar to that used in his fiction (see ''Solider's Home'' in ''Classics'')?
2. To whom is the advertisement addressed? What assumptions does Hemingway hold about the so-

cioeconomic level of the readers of this ad? How would you characterize Hemingway's attitude toward his audience? Does he distinguish himself in any way from his readers? Does it seem that he feels superior to his audience? Point to specific evidence in the language of the ad to support your response. What is the purpose of putting Hemingway's testimonial into the form of a typed letter? What effect does this have?

3. To what needs, desires, and fantasies does the ad appeal? Comment on the effectiveness of associating marlin fishing with drinking ale. What specific connections does Hemingway establish between the two activities?
4. How does this advertisement capitalize on traditional American values and ideals? How, specifically, does this ad trade on American notions of hard work and masculinity? What is the effect of saying "you have to work hard to deserve to drink it"? Is the ad more persuasive because Hemingway is the speaker?

"You're Some Tomato . . ." / "You Sweet California Doll . . ."

1. What kind of people are you asked to imagine speaking in this ad? How self-consciously seductive is the language meant to be?
2. What is funny about the line "You're some tomato" used in this context? In what sense do the expressions "You've got taste" and "Rollover" depend on the same basic joke? This particular verbal strategy is often used in advertising. Can you think of some other examples?
3. How would you characterize the diction in these two ads? What popular expressions and clichés do these ads bank on? Does the sound of the voice for the Vodka remain consistent from one ad to the next? What similarities can you locate in the syntax of these two advertisements?
4. Er, well, is any conventional sexual symbolism brought in as part of the fun?

Why Husbands Leave Home

1. What guilt or anxiety does the advertisement trade on? Do you think the ad is targeted more to women or to men? How can you tell which group is being addressed? How seriously is the intended audience expected to respond to the domestic drama? Explain your answer.
2. What is the effect of the "scribbled note"? What does it add to the dramatic situation? How does Jeanette's note allow us to contrast her everyday life to Howie's?
3. What kind of market resistance does Schrafft's anticipate for its frozen food products? How is that resistance seen in the ad? How is the ad designed to counter that resistance?

America

1. Who is the intended audience of this ad? What details in the copy make this clear?
2. Why do you think the ad concentrates more on America than on its product? What identification is the ad looking for? Why do you think the ad directly promotes patriotic feelings? What is in it for the Coca-Cola Company?
3. Read over carefully the paragraph beginning "In fact, all of the good things in this country are real." Why is the copywriter pointing this out? Why does the ad refer to its own advertising? What does it imply its own advertising had done? Explain.
4. How does this ad tie in with television commercials for Coke? What is meant by "start looking up" in the last line? How is looking up related to Coca-Cola both literally and figuratively?

With My Cooking, the Army That Travels on Its Stomach . . .

1. What is the central joke here? The ad is obviously written for an audience other than the U.S. Army. Why do you think the advertisers used this particular strategy?
2. How does the language of the copy reinforce the ad's message? For example, why does the cook use such expressions as "green," "down the drain," "a seasoned veteran"?
3. Consider the expression "I had enough to feed an army." What is the joke here? What is its intended effect? Countless ads use this form of verbal strategy. Find other examples in this section and discuss their use and effect. Why do you think such expressions have become a basic tool of copywriting?

Geraldine Chaplin Talks about Her "First Time"

1. Advertisers use different techniques to appeal to men and women through sex. Explain whether the Campari ad is aimed exclusively at one gender or makes appeals to both. Is it "romantic" at all? If so, in what way?
2. Why is this ad cast in the form of an interview? Suppose it were a monologue. How would this affect Chaplin's credibility or persuasiveness? Explain.

They Gave the Board of Education a Lesson in the Constitution

1. This ad uses a familiar moment in American history to promote a seemingly unrelated product. Determine the connection between the civil rights movement and Burger King. Recall the familiar Burger King slogan not mentioned in this ad. Why do you think that slogan was excluded here? Do you feel that the civil rights movement is trivialized by this association with a fast food chain? If so, in what specific ways? Compare this piece to the McDonald's ad that follows. Which proves more effective? Why?
2. Research the Brown vs. Board of Education case to which this ad refers. In what specific ways do you—or do you not—feel the photograph and text used here accurately represent the circumstances of that case? Which historical elements are highlighted here? Which are excluded? Do you feel the ad serves an educational purpose? How might the ad have approached its historical reference differently? Notice especially the last paragraph in the text. What kind of agency is being attributed to the children pictured here? Why did Burger King tell this story from the children's perspective?
3. How does the photograph reinforce the message of the text. Upon initially viewing the ad, to whom did you think the "they" referred? What appears to be the relationship between the armed guards and the children in the photograph? If you saw the photograph without the text, would you know what it signifies? Find other contexts in which such images have been used from textbooks, magazines, or television. How does the message differ when the text surrounding the photograph changes?

Unless We Keep Living the Dream . . .

1. This McDonald's promotion follows in an advertising tradition that might be called the "public service sponsorship." Find other ads that address social concerns while subtly advertising a product; companies you might explore include Benetton, Esprit, and Ben & Jerry's Ice Cream. What impression of the sponsoring company is established by an association with such serious topics as civil rights, environmental decay or AIDS? Show how this method is used differently by different advertisers.
2. Write a biography for the children pictured here, suggested by the ad copy and photograph. Are these boys McDonald's customers? Does that matter?
3. This ad was produced for a specific holiday, Martin Luther King Day. It refers to a "community" of which McDonald's claims to be a part. Who belongs to that community? Why is no more specific language used here? What social realities are elided by the phrase, "Each and every one of us must do our part?". Is this ad directed to Caucasians, people of color, or both groups?

MEDIA

These Are the Books That Hitler Burned

1. How does the copywriter's association of a product (the Great Books) with a prominent historical event (the burning of the books in Berlin) determine the strategies used in the composition of the advertisement and the assumptions made about the ways in which the readers will respond? Discuss why you think the personality and activities of Adolf Hitler have been associated with the purchase of books.
2. Although you are given a documented photograph, how do you know that "these are the books that Hitler burned"? To what exactly does the demonstrative pronoun *these* refer? Is there any confusion here? If so, is the confusion significant?
3. Do you notice any difference between the words the ad uses when talking about Hitler and those used when talking about the Great Books? Imagine someone is speaking the words of this ad. Do you notice any changes in the way the speaker sounds as the ad progresses? How would you describe these various tones? What effect do they have? Have you heard tones such as these before? Where and when?
4. Do you think the speaker proceeds logically? Are there any significant differences among terms like "truth," "thoughts," "words," and "theories"? Are you always sure you know what these terms mean? In what sense do "ideas" "enlighten," "guide," or "console"? Do ideas *always* do these things? If not, is the ad in any way inconsistent or unconvincing?
5. What kind of person do you think the speaker of the ad imagines the reader to be; in other words, what kind of person is spoken to in this manner? Is the reader supposed to be someone interested merely in purchasing and owning books?

Why Teenage Girls Stick with Their Mouthwash Longer Than Their Boyfriends

1. Examine the photograph carefully. How do the props and the composition help define the audience

as potential buyers of ad space? How many products for consumption are depicted? Why is the model posed in front of a mirror? What activities is she supposed to enjoy? How old does she appear to be?

2. Compare the headline with the body of the copy. Where and how does the copy provide the information promised by the headline? Suppose the word *why* was omitted from the headline. How would this change its tone?
3. What attitude does the copy express toward the readers of *Seventeen?* Are the readers taken to be mindless consumers? Cultivated young adults? Aging, vain women? Compare the strategies of this ad with those of the *Cosmopolitan* ad below, presenting Brooke Shields's reflections on her way of life. Imagine a similar monologue for the model in this ad that would offer the same basic arguments for buying space in *Seventeen* as the existing copy does. Explain how this would make the ad more effective or less.

Some People Are So Opposed to Murder They'll Kill Anyone Who Commits It

1. Notice the angle from which the photo of the chair was taken. How might this be intended to affect the reader? If the photo had been shot from above, how would its effect be different? Suppose a person had been placed in the chair. Would this have made the picture more effective or less?
2. Does this ad seem to favor either side in the debate on the death penalty? If so, how? If not, why? Explain whether you think it is appropriate for a news program to express an opinion on such an issue.
3. Consider the clever phrasing of the headline and the pun at the end of the copy. What, if anything, do these suggest about the relation between the news organization and the issues it reports? To what extent do the reporters take themselves to be entertainers? Explain whether their attitude compromises their ability to report the news.

Can a Girl Be Too Busy?

1. This ad is meant in part to appeal to companies that might consider placing ads in *Cosmopolitan*. Look over all the contemporary ads reproduced in this book. Find three that, on the basis of what you can infer from this ad, might be suited to *Cosmopolitan*'s readers. Write an essay justifying your choices.
2. Consider the implications of the slogan immediately below the photo. Imagine some ways to rephrase it ("My most satisfying relationship is with a magazine," "It's the only magazine that satisfies me," etc.). Discuss how changes might affect its appeal.
3. Just as the photo makes the model appear well-rounded physically, the copy tries to make her seem well-rounded culturally, emotionally, and socially. In your opinion, explain whether there is anything valuable missing from her life as it is depicted here.

The New Traditionalist

1. In this ad, *Good Housekeeping* associates itself with the phrase "New Traditionalist." What does the story and photograph presented here suggest about the "New Traditionalist" movement? How does this movement differ from "old" traditionalism? Which aspects of femininity is *Good Housekeeping* interested in preserving by promoting this world view, and which does it wish to change?
2. This ad presumes a reader's prior knowledge about *Good Housekeeping*. Upon what ground is the "authority" mentioned in the second to last paragraph established? What negative connotations surrounding *Good Housekeeping* does this ad fight against? Compare this ad with the one promoting Future Homemakers of America earlier in the Advertising section. Which do you think is more effective? Why?
3. Compare this ad with the U.S. Army ("There's something about a soldier") ad earlier in the Advertising section. Both confront the changing activities and attitudes of American women, specifically in relation to the workplace. The GI Bill ad directly addressed women considering non-traditional work, reassuring them about aspects of feminine behavior. Does this ad address a similar readership? How does it use elements of reassurance differently? Why do you think this ad addresses the reader indirectly instead of directly?

It Weighs 8,000,000 Pounds Less Than Your Average Library

1. The lead sentence in this ad highlights Sony Bookman's light weight. Yet no one actually carries a library around with them. How does this selling point operate? What concerns underlie the reference to literal weight? How does a "lighter" library better serve a contemporary lifestyle? What kind of consumer would be attracted by the quality of "lightness"?

2. In the photograph, the Sony Bookman rests beside an old-fashioned cartridge pen. What values are represented by the pen? By the Bookman? How does this contrast work to reassure the consumer? Also notice the computer books pictured behind and alongside the Bookman. What kind of library is the one being promoted? To whom might these featured texts appeal?
3. The last sentence of the ad's main copy reads, "Can we carry your books for you?" What does this cliché invoke? How does it contrast or blend in with the rest of the copy? What does it add to the image of the Sony Bookman? Who are the "we" in the sentence? Who is the "you"? Did the sentence make you laugh? Did it make the product seem more appealing to you?

Swimming at Night Had Never Bothered Me Before

1. As you read this advertisement for Mitsubishi Home Theater, consider the effectiveness of running a three-page ad. How often have you seen a three-page ad? What specific strategies did the writers of this ad use to induce you to read the entire ad? How effective did you find each of those strategies? What is your judgment of the effectiveness of choosing not to present an image of the product until the third page in this three-page sequence?
2. As you reread this ad, focus on the identity of the speaker and on the sound of the speaker's voice. What evidence can you point to in order to determine whether the speaker is male or female. Does the gender of the speaker matter? Why? Why not? How would you characterize the speaker's tone of voice? Is the speaker who says ". . . watching a movie such as this on a Mitsubishi Home Theater . . . was not, repeat not, good for my nerves" the same person who says (in the text immediately following the illustration): "Mitsubishi Home Theater brings you an experience so lifelike, you'll feel although you're right there in the middle of the action . . ."? What specific words and phrases can you point to as verification of your reading?
3. What devices do the writers of this ad rely on to create a sense that the experience presented in the language of the ad is "so lifelike"? What effects are produced by the speaker's repetition of "not, repeat not, good for my nerves"? How convincing did you find this speaker's voice to be? In effect, how "lifelike" did you find the ad to be? What do you understand the phrase "TECHNICALLY, ANYTHING IS POSSIBLE" means—in general usage? in the particular context of this ad?

INSTITUTIONAL AND CORPORATE ADVERTISING

Do Something Different around Home

1. From the startling photo to the anecdote about the blizzard to the slogans, this ad promotes the peaceful, good-neighborly image of the National Guard. What does this emphasis imply about the values of the ad's presumed audience? In this regard, how does the ad differ from ads for other services familiar to you?
2. Look at the ads for magazines in the Media section above. In which of those might this ad most successfully run? Explain.
3. Describe the age, position in society, and ambitions of the audience for this advertisement. Does the ad make an emotional appeal to them, a rational one, or a mixture of both? Explain. Rewrite the ad changing the nature of its appeal.

Who Ever Said the Man Who Discovers a Cure for Cancer . . .

1. What is the intention of the headline? Have you ever actually heard anyone say that *only* a white male will discover a cure for cancer? What attitude in its audience does the advertisement count on?
2. What audience is the ad calculated to reach? How does it go about including the audience directly?
3. Why is the word *black* repeated so often in the copy? What effect does it have? Do you think there is any underlying strategy behind this repetition? Explain.

A Word to Smokers/A Word to Nonsmokers

1. The Tobacco Institute is clearly an interested party. How does this fact come out in the ad? Are smokers and nonsmokers addressed differently? Explain.
2. Why do you think the Institute chose the particular image of a wall to show the division between smokers and nonsmokers? What political resonance does the wall suggest? How is its meaning reinforced by the illustration?
3. Why is the difference between smokers and nonsmokers turned into a matter of individual free-

dom? Why does the Institute focus on freedom and government regulation?

4. How does the copy proceed to conciliate nonsmokers? Does it try to argue them into smoking? What characteristics does the copy assume nonsmokers possess? Why does it operate on that assumption rather than attack nonsmokers? Explain the advantages of the copywriter's strategy.

Note: This advertisement can provide a succinct and effective way of showing how different methods of persuasion are designed for different audiences.

If Your Idea of a Good Time Is Listed on This Page, You Ought to Have Your Head Examined

1. Analyze the layout in the upper part of the ad. What would be the effect of printing each of the phrases in a different typeface? Of punctuating with exclamation points instead of periods? Of placing the second phrase first or last?
2. Consider the diction of the language in the copy. How does it differ from the diction of the phrases above? Note the proportion of monosyllabic words to polysyllabic words in the two halves of the ad. What effect is achieved by using more longer words in the lower section?

Reach Out and Touch Someone

1. What concepts of gender are reflected in this ad? Are they traditional ones? How might they be judged offensive? Suppose the father consoled his son by saying, "You'll outgrow *her*." How would this change the ad's appeal? With whom do you suppose the father is speaking on the phone, a male or a female? How does the copy invite you to guess?
2. It might be argued that this ad sells a technological service by linking it with sentiments of "sharing" and "reaching out." Using this as a model write an ad for some other similar service (photocopying or computer systems, for example) that also makes an appeal to the emotions of the audience.

"I'm the NRA"

1. How does Representative Gutman create a political context for his opinion? What does he imply about the direction of our government if strict controls are legislated? Do you think the implied association that gun control equals communism is logical? Explain.
2. Why do you think the NRA finds Gutman a valuable spokesman? What persuasive qualities does he bring to his cause? In your mind, does his support of the NRA enhance the organization's credibility? Explain why or why not.
3. Is Gutman's argument in the second paragraph original, or have you heard it before? Explain his logic. Do you find it sensible, or do you find gaps in his reasoning? Explain why he is pictured carrying a handgun instead of a rifle.

"Help Me Fight the National Rifle Association"

1. Note the names of each rival organization. Would it make any difference if the names were reversed to "The National Handgun Association" and "Rifle Control, Inc."?
2. Examine the differences in persuasive appeal between the two ads. Both use individuals with political identities, but which ad emphasizes political identity more? Why? Which ad focuses more on rights? Which on criminal violence? Explain how each group maintains a different emphasis.
3. Try breaking down this debate into its most essential terms. What are they?

There Are Three Things Everyone Should Read Before Entering College

1. This advertisement promotes a product not usually sold through print advertising—a university education. The copy plays on the fact that this "product" is unlike others marketed by Madison Avenue. Note the specific ways in which the writer contrasts this ad with others promoting education. (See especially paragraphs four through six of the main copy, and paragraph eleven.) Do you find the message here believable, or ironic, or both? What details make this marketing effort different from those selling "sausages or deodorant soap"?
2. Notice the different occupations listed throughout the second page of the advertisement. How does this ad promote the value of a "liberal education" to people interested in those fields? What kind of Adelphi student is implied by the photograph that ends the ad? How might Adelphi present itself differently if it were seeking a different group of students—say, Ivy Leaguers or minority students?
3. Consider the two "masterworks" mentioned in the ad's lead copy—Plato's Republic and the complete works of Aristotle. What vision of a "good education" does the privileging of these works present? In recent years, educators' views have been changing regarding the canon of classic literature; Richard Wright's and Langston Hughes's

fiction are considered by some to be as essential to a complete education as are Shakespeare's plays. Rewrite this ad with these shifts in the literary canon in mind. How would you insure that the ad's basic message still come across? What adjustments might be necessary in the rest of the copy? (Make note of paragraph six on page one.)

Focussing on Education

1. This advertisement asserts that teaching has come to resemble a blue-collar occupation in America. What implied judgment against blue-collar employment is communicated here? What hierarchy of concerns is suggested by the phrase "bread-and-butter issues are not the same as professional issues"? What "bread-and-butter issues" facing our school system (i.e. funding cutbacks, inner city conditions, the rise in illiteracy) does this piece ignore? What does the ad emphasize instead?
2. Analyze the illustration accompanying this advertisement. Does the "worker" pictured resemble your image of a blue-collar employee? Of a teacher? What effect does the image of students as assembly-line products have on the ad, which does not directly address student concerns?
3. In presenting this advertisement, the sponsoring company, Rockwell International, declares its hope that the piece will "encourage informed discussion and debate." How does this stated intention influence the way the ad itself comes across? What impression does it give of the Rockwell corporation, considering that no mention is made of what Rockwell produces? What might be the unstated effect Rockwell hopes to produce with such an ad? How does Rockwell's approach differ from that of the American Paper Company, in that corporation's "public service" presentation earlier in the Advertising section? How is it similar?
4. Doyle says that a shift in metaphors can suggest a structure that would alleviate the problems facing teachers today. Yet when he explains this shift, he also changes the position of the teacher-figure within the metaphor. In the business metaphor, the teacher is the assembly-line worker; in the high-tech image, the teacher becomes management, while "robots" perform on the assembly line. Following this line of reasoning, who becomes the robot? How could this scenario possibly be enacted in the classroom?

Wouldn't You Want to Know if U.S. Territory Was Going to be Invaded?

1. Take several moments to examine the details presented in this advertisement for the Central Intelligence Agency. What do you notice about the people in the photograph? About the buildings? This advertisement appeared in an October 1991 issue of *Ebony* magazine. Go to your college or university library and find a recent issue of *Ebony*. In what ways is this ad similar to/different from the others you've found in *Ebony?*
2. What in your judgment is the purpose of this advertisement? What do you think the C.I.A. hoped to accomplish by printing this advertisement? Is it, for example, an informational ad—one designed to provide African Americans with reliable information about the C.I.A.? Is it designed to recruit African Americans for employment in the C.I.A.? If so, what kind of employment is proposed? What identity does the C.I.A. hope to establish in the minds of the readers of this ad? What image of the C.I.A. emerges from the language of this ad? Point to specific words and phrases to verify your reading.
3. Based on the information presented in this ad, has your view of the Central Intelligence Agency changed? If so, in what specific ways? If not, why not? Read the two-page ad prepared by the Tobacco Institute (printed earlier in this section on "Institutional and Corporate Advertising). What specific strategies do these advertisements share? In what ways are the methods used to present their respective messages different?

Trees Aren't the Only Plants That Are Good for the Atmosphere

1. What are the specific strategies that the copywriters for the U.S. Council for Energy Awareness employ in trying to establish a positive attitude toward the use of nuclear energy? Characterize, for example, the logic of the ad. How is this logic established in the syntax of the ad? Show how the copywriters build an argument from one sentence to the next, from one paragraph to the next. What is the logical conclusion established by the sequence of points made in the ads? How convincing do you find this argument. Explain.
2. Examine the headline. What word(s) in the headline capture your attention? Why? With what effect(s)? How many "plants" can be seen in the photograph? What does the word "good" mean in this sentence? in the overall ad? How does the word "atmosphere" become literalized as the ad proceeds? With what effects?
3. Consider the layout of the ad. What effects do the designers of the ad try to elicit from their readers by emphasizing the tree in the foreground of the photo? What other details in the photograph under-

score this desired effect? What are the results of placing the nuclear power plant in the distance? In what specific ways would the effects of this ad be different had its designers shot the photograph with the nuclear power plant closer to the front?

MARIANNE MOORE
Correspondence with the Ford Motor Company

1. How would you characterize the sound of David Wallace's first letter? Point to particular words and phrases. Does the sound of his voice remain consistent throughout the series of letters? If you think it does, find specific examples to verify your contention. If not, when and how does it change?
2. Is the occasion of addressing a famous poet or the fact that Wallace is announcing the production of a new *line* of automobiles responsible for the way he sounds in these letters? Evidence?
3. How, specifically, does Wallace try to create a tone for his prose that is somehow made equivalent to the dignity he ascribes to this new automobile? Is there any evidence that the seriousness with which Wallace first addresses Marianne Moore gradually gives way to a more light-hearted spiritedness? How do you respond to such phrases as "embarrassing pedestrianism," and "miles short of our ambition"? Examine carefully the close of each letter. Are the changes noted there (moving from "Respectfully" to "Cordially") reflected in an increasing amiability in the text of each letter? Point to some specific examples.
4. How would you describe the sound of Moore's voice in her initial response (dated October 21, 1955) to Wallace's invitation to join the ranks of American advertisers? Does her tone in any way duplicate the sound of Wallace's letters? How, for example, are such phrases as "under advisement," "recruited," "this high matter," "designation," and "quest" meant to be read?
5. In the letter dated November 11, 1955, Wallace's prose seems especially gallant and euphemistically playful. What advantages or disadvantages are implicit in such a strategy, given the context of this exchange of letters?
6. Describe the tone of Wallace's last letter. How does he give himself away? Judging from her responses in these letters, would you say that Moore finds commercialism and popular culture threats to her allegiances to poetry?

Writing Exercises: Marianne Moore's attention to the classical origins of several of the names she suggests for the automobile provides an opportunity to talk about etymology in class and an occasion to have students trace in an essay the origins of a brand name for an automobile or any other product chosen from among the many advertisements included in this book.

Invent a new product or improve on an old one. Work with a category where major differences in the product are not quite so apparent (for example, beer, alcohol, gasoline, paint, soap). Create a single-page advertisement for this product.

Skill in graphics and artwork in general are certainly no prerequisites or even obstacles to completing such an exercise. Simply set off that part of the page which you feel should be an illustration and describe (in that area, if possible) the details of the illustration you envision. You could, of course, cut out and paste in this area appropriate characters, scenes, and so on, from other ads.

They'll Know You've Arrived When You Drive Up in an Edsel

1. How does the pun in the headline function in relation to the entire advertisement? Describe the operation of the pun in detail, analyzing all of the consumer situations it suggests.
2. Compare the Edsel ad to David Wallace's letter to Marianne Moore inviting her to invent a name for the new Ford product (see "Correspondence with the Ford Motor Company"). What qualities and automotive features was the Edsel intended to convey to customers? What verbal and visual devices does the ad use to convey these impressions?
3. What is the strategy behind the copywriter's heavy reliance on the second-person pronoun?

DAVID OGILVY
How to Write Potent Copy

1. What tone of voice does Ogilvy encourage advertising copywriters to adopt? Characterize his own tone in this essay. Does it remain consistent? What happens to the sound of his voice, for example, when he talks about his advertisement of "Puerto Rico's Operation Bootstrap"? Describe Ogilvy's figurative language. What kind of experience does he draw on to create his metaphors? How appropriate are these terms to his subject?
2. Ogilvy quotes Claude Hopkins's view that "fine writing is a distant disadvantage. So is unique literary style. They take attention away from the subject." Select at random ten advertisements from those reprinted in this book, and examine them with this statement in mind.
3. Consider Ogilvy's remarks about the use of clichés in advertising. He encourages copywriters to use

them when "they work." How can you tell if a cliché works? Of what help are they to any writer? Ogilvy demonstrates his own attitude toward clichés by introducing some into the very sentences he writes on them. "Don't turn up your nose . . ." is one example. Find other instances of cliché in his essay, and comment on their effectiveness. Work back over several of the advertisements reprinted in this book and locate clichés in them. Examine these phrases in their specific verbal contexts, and determine if they "work" as Ogilvy suggests they will.

4. When discussing the important features of "Body Copy," Ogilvy appropriates the language of Dr. Charles Edwards when he says, "the more you tell, the more you sell." Show how Ogilvy's own sentences reveal that he is writing the kind of copy he is recommending. How, for example, does he try to make his own copy "enthusiastic," "friendly," and especially "memorable"? What compositional tactics does he use to achieve these goals? How would you describe Ogilvy's characteristic sentence structure? How is that feature of his prose style reinforced by the maxims he creates for advertising? Point to some examples.
5. Ogilvy claims, "When you have written your headline, you have spent eighty cents out of your dollar." What kind of language and what sales strategies does Ogilvy urge copywriters to include in their headlines? Choose any five of the advertisements reprinted in this book, and analyze their headlines in terms of Ogilvy's suggestions. Which seem to follow his advice?
6. Ogilvy talks at some length about "the most powerful words" in advertising. Trace the appearance of several of these words in the ads included on this book. Do these words occur, for example, as often in the older ads as they do in the more recent ones? What do these words tell us about the interests of American readers? Do you notice any trends in the use of these words that Ogilvy claims will "work wonders"? What do these words have in common? How can you group them? Are they, for example, mostly nouns? verbs? adjectives? adverbs? After you have worked out a reasonable response to this question, consider whether your conclusion can tell you anything important about the verbal strategies of advertising.
7. Ogilvy discusses the advantages of including "*emotional* words like DARLING, LOVE, FEAR, PROUD, FRIEND, and BABY." But how does Ogilvy suggest that the copywriter can connect the response elicited by these words to a particular product? He moves on to say that copywriters should "avoid superlatives, generalizations, and platitudes." Select several ads, and analyze them in terms of Ogilvy's dicta.
8. His reader is advised that "Testimonials from celebrities get remarkably high readership." In the testimonial for "How Would You Put a Glass of Ballantine Ale into Words?" how does the copywriter associate a public personality with a particular product? Why *this* person to endorse *this* product? What relation is established between the person and the product? Are there structural similarities in ads that employ testimonials? Are these ads geared to the same audience? Do they use the same tone? Explain.
9. At the "heart" of Ogilvy's own ads there is what he calls a "well-aimed combination of snobbery and economy." How well do these words work together? Is it contradictory, for example, to suggest that someone can have taste and also be frugal? Explain. Using the principles of advertising Ogilvy espouses, examine one of the ads he wrote that is reproduced earlier. (See "At 60 Miles an Hour the Loudest Noise in This New Rolls-Royce Comes from the Electric Clock.") Show how this ad keys on "snobbery" and "economy." Do these terms "work" not only to characterize the appeal of the products Ogilvy advertises but also to serve as a description of his own prose style in this essay?

Additional Writing Exercise: Compare two advertisements that deal with the same product. The products do not necessarily have to be identical; you can compare, say, an ad for Rolls-Royce with an ad for Volkswagen. Write a clearly organized essay in which you analyze the similarities and differences between the two advertisements. Base your analysis on the suggested questions for analyzing ads.

"At 60 Miles an Hour the Loudest Noise in This New Rolls-Royce Comes from the Electric Clock"

1. In what sense does David Ogilvy want his copy to illustrate the same "patient attention to detail" that makes the product the "best car in the world"? What does this attention to detail suggest about the audience Ogilvy has in mind? Compare this ad with the one for Volkswagen.
2. How do the nineteen points made in the copy emphasize both luxury and economy? Why would Ogilvy's audience be concerned with economy? In what sense are both luxury and economy conveyed by the ad's illustration? What part does "The Village Grocer" play in the total effect of the ad?

What is the purpose of showing a woman driving this car?

3. How does the ad meet the criteria Ogilvy establishes for writing ''Potent Copy''?

PATRICIA VOLK
A Word from Our Sponsor

1. Volk's essay appeared in the *New York Times Magazine,* in which a general readership seeks in-depth views of contemporary issues. Her article gives the ''inside story'' of a process that mystifies many people—writing advertising copy. But she also carefully persuades the reader to feel comfortable with the world of advertising. How does Volk use shifts in point-of-view to accomplish this? How does she simultaneously incorporate and explain advertising lingo? By the end of her article, what impression has she given of the advertising industry? Can this article be called a ''critique'' or is it more of an ''homage''?
2. List the fictitious brand names and slogans Volk mentions. How do these color the article's tone? Does the use of humor make the information about advertising that Volk provides easier to understand? Does it make you feel more sympathetic to advertising copywriters?
3. Compare this article with one of the others included in this section that analyzes the advertising phenomenon. How does Volk's point of view contrast with these more critical views of advertising? What contrasting images of advertising executives are presented within these articles? How does Volk work to make an occupation appear attractive, an occupation which a large part of the American public finds as suspicious?

NEIL POSTMAN
The Parable of the Ring

1. Compare Neil Postman's television parables with those in the New Testament. How do these contemporary versions compare to the original texts, from which the term ''parable'' came? Obviously Postman employs irony in his discussion of commercials, but how do his examples resonate on a deeper level? What serious points does he make about society's need for moral or spiritual lessons?
2. How does Postman's tone reinforce his argument? Find words and phrases in his essay that echo Biblical language and/or exegesis.
3. Find examples from current television of the commercial ''parables'' Postman describes. Devise other parables and find examples for them. Does Postman's analysis work for contemporary styles of advertising, which often emphasize images over narrative and sometimes seem to have no story at all? Is there always a story of ''redemption'' underlying television commercials?
4. Postman is one of the leading anti-television critics in the academy. Find other viewpoints on television and its value to or effect on viewers, either in this book (Patricia Volk) or in other magazines or books. Contrast Postman's implied judgment of television with those analyses.

TERESA RIORDAN
Miller Life Guy

1. Teresa Riordan's discussion of the sexist aspects of Miller's ''Beachin' Times'' advertising campaign follows a long tradition of feminist critiques of media. At the library, find other such analyses, from the groundbreaking work of Women Against Violence Against Women (WAVAW) to Naomi Wolf's recent book, *The Beauty Myth.* For a view of how advertising makes an appeal to women, see Rosalind Coward's *Female Desires.* How have feminist critiques changed, in tone and in content, over the years? Where does Riordan's wry commentary fit in? Was Riordan ''hard enough'' on her subject matter? Does sarcasm work in her favor or does it weaken her point?
2. Design a parallel ''Beachin' Times'' that would appeal to women readers. Is it possible to reverse the stereotypes presented in Miller's original ad supplement, so that they apply to males? What would make beer, a product that ostensibly sells better to men, appeal to women? Can you find examples of beer ads that are aimed at women? How do they differ from the one described by Riordan?
3. Look at the pictorial ad that accompanies this article. How does it fit in with Riordan's description of ''Beachin' Times?'' What does the equation of the word ''pilsner'' with the model pictured imply? Look up the word ''pilsner'' in the dictionary. Does its meaning have anything to do with femininity? What leaps of logic must a reader make in order to associate the model pictured with that word?
4. Look through the ''Advertising'' section and find other images of women used to sell advertising. Do other archetypes, besides the ''Babe,'' exist? Which type of feminine figure do advertisers think appeals to which market? For example, see the Nike ad. This ad is indented for a young female audience. How does it operate differently than the Miller ad? Are there any similarities?

She Hardly Gets Noticed

1. What relationship is established between the Miller Lite can and the woman depicted in the photograph? What does the copywriter intend to convey in the first sentence of the ad: "She's the word pilsner, right there on the can"? What is the referent for the word "she"? for the word "pilsner"?
2. What response does the repetition of the word "Pilsner" evoke? How did Miller Lite change "Beer but good, forever"? What are the resonances of the word "good" here? "forever"?
3. What is the referent for the word "she" in the final sentence? What is your overall impression of the effectiveness of this ad? What—more specifically—do you find works well in it? What doesn't work? What do you find offensive about it?

MICHAEL SPECTER
Cigarettes for the Tractor-Pull Generation

1. This news story, using a leaked R.J. Reynolds marketing plan, gives another "inside view" of the process of devising an advertising campaign. The tone of this article is, however, quite different from Patricia Volk's in "A Word from Our Sponsor" (earlier in this section). How does the arrangement of quotations and commentary in Michael Specter's supposedly objective news piece create a point of view regarding its subject? Note especially the article's last two paragraphs. Imagine how the piece might be different, particularly if Volk were to have written it.
2. People outside the advertising profession often are shocked at the objectifying process of defining a marketing group, as R.J. Reynolds did "virile females" for the "Dakota" project. Yet this type of marketing plan is very common. Explore the structure of these plans by doing one of the following activities.

A. Choose one of the promotions appearing in the "Advertising" section and recreate the marketing plan that led to that ad. Is it possible to imagine more than one target audience for some ads?

B. Design a marketing plan for a new product, such as a shampoo targeted at Asian American college students, or a cake mix intended to appeal to working mothers, or an athletic shoe for people who consider themselves out of shape. Detail the same aspects of your projected audience as did R.J. Reynolds for "virile females." Then design an advertisement that fulfills your marketing projections.

C. Create a marketing plan for a product targeted at someone like yourself. Analyse your consumer habits, income, education level, and leisure interests. Devise an advertisement, using your plan, that should appeal to you precisely. Then find an ad that does appeal to you. Are your ad and the real one very much alike? How do they differ?

DAVID BEERS AND CATHERINE CAPELLARO
Greenwash

1. Capellaro and Beers use colloquialisms and puns such as "the emperor has dropped trow" (p. 104) and "lies advertised by slippery oil" to create a particular tone for their article. How would you characterize that tone? How does it influence your view of the corporations cited as polluters? If the article were written in a less colorful style, how would its effect change?
2. On p. 108, Greenpeace media director Peter Dykstra says, "There's a real moral vacuum in how people deal with advertising." This article, with its myriad examples of duplicitous statement-making, enforce Dykstra's point. Do you think there are examples of advertising that do exhibit a moral code? Looking back through the other ads printed in your textbook, can you find others that offend you in this way? Do you think the rhetoric of morality can really be applied to the world of advertising?
3. Compare the "greenwash" ads mentioned by Capellaro and Beers to the "public service" pieces sponsored by International Paper, Burger King, and McDonald's in this section. What do these ads have in common? How do they differ? None of these ads directly promote a product that an individual consumer can purchase. What do they promote? How do the concepts of "consumerism" and "citizenship" connect in these ads?

The Eagle Has Landed

1. With what historical moment do you associate the headline "The eagle has landed"? Comment on the appropriateness of the headline in this instance. How effective was the headline in capturing your attention?
2. Comment on the copywriter's use of a string of fragments at the opening of the ad. What do these fragments contribute to your overall impression of the ad? What, if anything, would you changed in the way the text of this ad is presented?
3. Comment on the effectiveness of evoking images of the first moon landing in this ad. What are your responses to the graphic images in the ad: the egg shell and the eagle's footprint. In what ways do these images contribute to the success of the ad?

PRESS

STAFF CORRESPONDENT
Important. Assassination of President Lincoln

1. What details of language and tone strike you as dated? Make a list of words and phrases you would not expect to find in a modern newspaper. Do these words and phrases have anything in common? How do they contribute to an understanding of the nineteenth-century audience the newspaper was addressed to?
2. Compare this account with the *New York Times* report of Kennedy's assassination. How does each report establish a setting? How do crowds figure in each account? In what sense is the reaction of the crowd an indication of how the reporter imagines his audience will react? Which report do you find more politically oriented and why? Which report aims more at sensational effects?
3. It is important to remember that the newspaper report of Lincoln's assassination was for thousands of people the only source of information they had. On the other hand, those who read of Kennedy's death had the instantaneous reports of radio and television to supplement the newspaper account. Comment on how you think this essential historical difference affects the actual writing of each report in terms of style and coverage.

Additional Writing Exercise: This sequence of writing exercises and class discussions is designed to prompt the class to be more attentive to the specific compositional strategies, problems, and characteristics of newspaper writing. It also provides students with the opportunity to engage in some role-playing in class. Select several students from the class, and ask them to state a specific incident or to engage in an argument about a particular subject. They are encouraged, of course, to choose carefully the particular words, actions, and voices that would be suitable to that occasion. The remainder of the class is directed to function as reporters and observe and listen carefully to what ensues. The class is asked to take notes on what happens. They are then instructed to work up these notes into a newspaper report based on the principles of the "inverted pyramid" outlined in the introduction to "Press." These student-reporters are to work against a very specific deadline. For example, they are to spend no more than an hour in class or at home working on the report. At the next class meeting, each student exchanges his or her essay for another. They must then function as copy editors and reduce the report they have been given to approximately one-quarter to one-third of its original length without sacrificing any important details. This stage of the exercise is completed when each student has written a headline for the story. The final stage involves a class discussion of (1) the original student reports on the incident (to be photocopied), noting the differences in factual information, point of view, omissions, inclusions, inferences, judgments, the writer's attitude toward the event, tone, and so on; and (2) a comparison of some of the original reports with the copy-edited versions.

STEPHEN CRANE
Stephen Crane's Own Story

1. How does Crane through his individual experience suggest something larger about the behavior of men in similar situations? What qualities of behavior does Crane admire in the men on the steamer? What qualities of their language does he focus on?
2. How does Crane's own prose style convey both a sense of heroic activity and a sense of slapstick? Point to examples of both. How does this mixture of tones affect our response to the situation he is describing?
3. "And then by the men on the ten-foot dingy were words said that were still not words—something far beyond words." Comment on this statement as it applies to the language of "The Open Boat," the short story Crane wrote a few months after his newspaper account. Can you point to any other instances in this report which anticipate "The Open Boat"? How does Crane draw on the techniques of fiction in "Stephen Crane's Own Story"?

Personal Experience Exercises: Write a narrative account of "a close call." Describe as accurately as you can the conditions that led to the event, the participants, the extent of injuries or damages, and your reactions at the time. Describe an intense personal experience, and discuss what effect it had on you.

The following options can be offered to students for organizing their essay:

a. Describe the incident. Describe the feelings and accompanying thoughts. Describe other incidents in which the same emotion was experienced. Through comparison, contrast, and analysis, formulate a statement about that particular emotion.

b. Describe the incident. Describe the feelings and accompanying thoughts. Explain what you learned. Compare your new knowledge with your previous ignorance, paying particular attention to what effect your former ignorance and your new knowledge have had. Explain why you think it's good to have this knowledge and why you'll function more efficiently as a result.

c. Describe the incident. Describe the feelings and accompanying thoughts. If others were present during the incident, what were their reactions? If not, what might they have been? How are your reactions to the incident similar to or different from the reactions of others?

FRANCIS PHARCELLUS CHURCH
Is There a Santa Claus?

1. What aspects of Church's language make it seem that he is writing for adults as well as children? How would the essay differ if it were intended exclusively for one or another group?
2. Look at the metaphor in the paragraph second from the end. What sense does it make to you? How does it help express Church's opinion about those who believe only what they can see?
3. Which of the terms, phrases, and attitudes seem outdated? If the essay were published in a newspaper today, how would it differ? Write an updated version.

HEYWOOD BROUN
There Isn't a Santa Claus

1. Look at Broun's use of the terms *myth* and *truth*. Which does he seem to value more? How does he distinguish between them? Compare this with the way Church conflates *truth* and *faith* (or *poetry* and *romance*). Which writer seems more naïve in this regard? Explain.
2. Where is the humor in Broun's essay? Why should he try to be humorous? How does this add to his persuasiveness? Explain whether he succeeds in being humorous. How does humor affect the reader's estimation of the writer?
3. Broun claims that the story of Santa Claus differs from most folk stories in that "a folk story is generally true in spirit no matter how fantastic in details." How might the Santa Claus story be adapted to fit Broun's definition? What audience—besides Broun himself—would be likely to appreciate this adaptation?

JACK LAIT
Dillinger "Gets His"

1. What point of view does Jack Lait adopt in reporting the shooting of John Dillinger? Does he consider himself privileged in some way? Explain. When does he become a factor in the story? Why? To what effect? Does Lait follow the principle of the "inverted pyramid" as outlined in the introduction to "Press"? Lait had gained a reputation as a hard-nosed reporter. By citing specific word choices and sentence patterns, show how this identity is revealed in Lait's style.
2. Reread the opening paragraph of Lait's report carefully several times. What strategies and rhetorical devices does he use to draw readers into his story? How does he create a sense of balance, of justice, in the opening paragraph? How is Dillinger introduced? How does Lait turn each of these characteristics back on Dillinger? Compare the distinguishing features of Dillinger's personality to those of Joey Gallo, as reported in "Death of a Maverick Mafioso" (see "Magazines"). How were these men alike? different?
3. Why does Lait devote so much of his report to a description of Dillinger's body at the morgue? What is the effect of this scene? Does Lait himself take on any of the characteristics of the crowds "milling around the death spot"? Explain. Why does he repeat the word *warm* when describing Dillinger's corpse at the morgue? Does Lait in any way seem resentful of Dillinger's reputation for toughness? For being a "ladies' man"? Cite specific evidence to support your response. Are there any aspects of Lait's portrayal of Dillinger which seem sympathetic? Explain.

Additional Writing Exercise: Compare Lait's account of the shooting of John Dillinger with the following poem: David Wagoner's poem, "The Shooting of John Dillinger Outside the Biograph Theater, July 22, 1934."

DAVID WAGONER

The Shooting of John Dillinger Outside the Biograph Theater, July 22, 1934

1966

Chicago ran a fever of a hundred and one that groggy Sunday.
A reporter fried an egg on a sidewalk; the air looked shaky.
And a hundred thousand people were in the lake like shirts in a laundry.
Why was Johnny lonely?
Not because two dozen solid citizens, heat-struck, had keeled over backward.
Not because those lawful souls had fallen out of their sockets and melted.
But because the sun went down like a lump in a furnace or a bull in the Stockyards.
Where was Johnny headed?
Under the Biograph Theater sign that said, "Our Air is Refrigerated."
Past seventeen FBI men and four policemen who stood in doorways and sweated.
Johnny sat down in a cold seat to watch Clark Gable get electrocuted.
Had Johnny been mistreated?
Yes, but Gable told the D. A. he'd rather fry than be shut up forever.
Two women sat by Johnny. One looked sweet, one looked like J. Edgar Hoover.
Polly Hamilton made him feel hot, but Anna Sage made him shiver.
Was Johnny a good lover?
Yes, but he passed out his share of squeezes and pokes like a jittery masher
While Agent Purvis sneaked up and down the aisle like an extra usher,
Trying to make sure they wouldn't slip out till the show was over.
Was Johnny a fourflusher?
No, not if he knew the game. He got it up or got it back.
But he liked to take snapshots of policemen with his own Kodak,
And once in a while he liked to take them with an automatic.
Why was Johnny frantic?
Because he couldn't take a walk or sit down in a movie
Without being afraid he'd run smack into somebody
Who'd point at his rearranged face and holler, "Johnny!"
Was Johnny ugly?
Yes, because Dr. Wilhelm Loeser had given him a new profile
With a baggy jawline and squint eyes and an erased dimple,
With kangaroo-tendon cheekbones and a gigolo's mustache that should've been illegal.
Did Johnny love a girl?
Yes, a good-looking, hard-headed Indian named Billie Frechette.
He wanted to marry her and lie down and try to get over it,
But she was locked in jail for giving him first-aid and comfort.
Did Johnny feel hurt?
He felt like breaking a bank or jumping over a railing
Into some panicky teller's cage to shout, "Reach for the ceiling!"
Or like kicking some vice president in the bum checks and smiling.
What was he really doing?
Going up the aisle with the crowd and into the lobby
With Polly saying, "Would *you* do what Clark done?" And Johnny saying, "Maybe."
And Anna saying, "If he'd been smart, he'd of acted like Bing Crosby."
Did Johnny look flashy?
Yes, his white-on-white shirt and tie were luminous.
His trousers were creased like knives to the tops of his shoes,
And his yellow straw hat came down to his dark glasses.
Was Johnny suspicious?
Yes, and when Agent Purvis signalled with a trembling cigar,

Johnny ducked left and ran out of the theater,
And innocent Polly and squealing Anna were left nowhere.
Was Johnny a fast runner?
No, but he crouched and scurried past a friendly liquor store
Under the coupled arms of double-daters, under awnings, under stars,
To the curb at the mouth of an alley. He hunched there.
Was Johnny a thinker?
No, but he was thinking more or less of Billie Frechette
Who was lost in prison for longer than he could possibly wait,
And then it was suddenly too hard to think around a bullet.
Did anyone shoot straight?
Yes, but Mrs. Etta Natalsky fell out from under her picture hat.
Theresa Paulus sprawled on the sidewalk, clutching her left foot.
And both of them groaned loud and long under the streetlight.
Did Johnny like that?
No, but he lay down with those strange women, his face in the alley,
One shoe off, cinders in his mouth, his eyelids heavy.
When they shouted questions at him, he talked back to nobody.
Did Johnny lie easy?
Yes, holding his gun and holding his breath as a last trick,
He waited, but when the Agents came close, his breath wouldn't work.
Clark Gable walked his last mile; Johnny ran half a block.
Did he run out of luck?
Yes, before he was cool, they had him spread out on dished-in marble
In the Cook County Morgue, surrounded by babbling people
With a crime reporter presiding over the head of the table.
Did Johnny have a soul?
Yes, and it was climbing his slippery wind-pipe like a trapped burglar.
It was beating the inside of his ribcage, hollering, "Let me out of here!"
Maybe it got out, and maybe it just stayed there.
Was Johnny a money-maker?
Yes, and thousands paid 25¢ to see him, mostly women,
And one said, "I wouldn't have come, except he's a moral lesson,"
And another, "I'm disappointed. He feels like a dead man."
Did Johnny have a brain?
Yes, and it always worked best through the worst of dangers,
Through flat-footed hammerlocks, through guarded doors, around corners,
But it got taken out in the morgue and sold to some doctors.
Could Johnny take orders?
No, but he stayed in the wicker basket carried by six men
Through the bulging crowd to the hearse and let himself be locked in,
And he stayed put as it went driving south in a driving rain.
And he didn't get stolen?
No, not even after his old hard-nosed dad refused to sell
The quick-drawing corpse for $10,000 to somebody in a carnival.
He figured he'd let *Johnny* decide how to get to Hell.
Did anyone wish him well?
Yes, half of Indiana camped in the family pasture,
And the minister said, "With luck, he could have been a minister."
And up the sleeve of his oversized gray suit, Johnny twitched a finger.
Everyone still alive. And some dead ones. It was a new kind of holiday
With hot and cold drinks and hot and cold tears. They planted him in a cemetery
With three unknown vice presidents, Benjamin Harrison, and James Whitcomb Riley,
Who never held up anybody.

DAVID WAGONER

The Shooting of John Dillinger outside the Biograph Theater, July 22, 1934

(see poem on p. 24)

This poem, with its litany of questions and answers about the death of John Dillinger, simultaneously (and paradoxically) turns the story into a kind of myth and demystifies its subject. You will probably want to teach it in conjunction with Jack Lait's "Dillinger Gets His" in the "Press" section. Lait's piece, with its hard-nosed morality, should be a good contrast to Wagoner's, which focuses not so much on the melodrama of the shooting and the morgue as on the oppressive nature of everything about the incident, from the heat to what was on Dillinger's mind to the public's extraordinary response to his death.

1. Suppose that Wagoner had written the poem as a straightforward narrative, omitting the questions that he asks here. How might the poem affect us differently? What sort of person do you imagine asking the questions here? Are they the sort of questions an investigative reporter would ask, for example? What is the effect of the questioner's using "Johnny" rather than "John" or "Dillinger"?
2. What rhymes or half-rhymes can you see here? Do most of the lines contain a complete unit of thought, or do sentences tend to spill over from one line to the next? What is the effect of this? Do the rhymes and the end-stopped lines make the narrative feel more like a ritual recounting of the experience or like a newspaper account? Why might Wagoner want the poem to have this effect?
3. What kind of image does the poem give of Dillinger? Does he seem a daring desperado? A cheap, no-good crook? What lines in the poem can you use to support your answer? How does the picture of Dillinger one finds here differ from that in "Dillinger Gets His" (see "Press")? Which writer is more sympathetic to Dillinger? In which selection does Dillinger seem more human to you?
4. Why doesn't Wagoner end the poem with Dillinger's death? What does the account of what happens after he dies do to our sense of him? Does he seem more heroic? Why or why not? What does this section of the poem tell us about the American public? Why, then, does the poem end as it does? Why does Wagoner specify that the vice-presidents are unknown? What sort of comment about America is he making here?

GEORGE H. MAHAWINNEY

An Invasion from the Planet Mars

1. What is Mahawinney's attitude toward the broadcast? Does he personally feel that people behaved foolishly? Does he believe that the hoax was morally irresponsible? Explain.
2. What kinds of incidents does he select to describe the effect of the broadcast on the nation? Do you think he thinks any of these are comical? How can you tell? Describe the tone of his last two paragraphs. What can this tell you about his professional relation to the news event?

DOROTHY THOMPSON

Mr. Welles and Mass Delusion

1. What difference is there between George Mahawinney's and Dorothy Thompson's approaches to the broadcast? Do their different purposes reflect a difference in tone? Explain. Which writer's attitude toward the event is more indirect, more tongue-in-cheek?
2. Does Thompson see the broadcast as a good joke on the population? Is she amused? Where does she place moral responsibility, on Welles or on his audience? Explain. What kind of interaction does she find in this broadcast between style and audience? Comment on the connections between what she calls "mass politics" and what we have come to know as "mass media."

Additional Writing Exercise: Have you ever been fooled by someone or some organization? Describe the incident and how you discovered that you had been victimized.

Note: For an excerpt from the original broadcast, see "Scripts."

LANGSTON HUGHES

Family Tree

Hughes' dialogue with Simple is anything but simple. In teaching this piece, try to establish how each of the interlocutors exposes the limitations of the other; neither's grasp of reality is wholly satisfactory. Simple, with his commonsense wisdom and bent to digression, is too wrapped up in the particulars of his own life; and the speaker, for all his right motives, is something of a stuffed shirt.

Simple may be a black man from the 1940s, but his attitude toward women is in many ways no different from that of many men today. How often are women still asked, overtly or covertly, to be "both old-fashioned and modern at the same time"?

1. In his first long speech here, Simple seems to wander away from discussing his dubious Indian ancestry to a discussion of women. How does he bring the question of his Indian blood back into the conversation? Where else in the selection does he refer to the topic? Since the selection isn't really about the truth of Simple's claim to be part Cherokee, why does Hughes keep bringing Simple back to the topic?
2. Why are Simple's ideas about women based on outmoded economics? How might the time at which the piece was written have influenced the description of the economic conditions of black women? How might the economic conditions in the time of Simple's youth have been different?
3. Why does Simple say "Cog hell!"? What is his impression of the narrator's language? Who would you guess has had a better formal education, the narrator or Simple? Does the narrator's language suggest any shortcomings in his education?
4. "With me it is personal," says Simple at the end of the essay. How are we to take this statement? Is Simple being too narrow, too locked into his own little world? Or is he exposing a real weakness in the narrator—a sort of bland liberalism that has nothing to do with real people? Or are both speakers somehow partly at fault?

WILLIAM L. LAURENCE
Atomic Bombing of Nagasaki Told by Flight Member

1. How does Laurence justify the use of the atomic bomb? Compare his reasoning with the Yank's in the advertisement for White Owl Cigars ("We Smash 'Em Hard"). Discuss the logic and the morality behind both of these wartime attitudes toward an enemy.
2. What does the atomic bomb mean to Laurence? How does he talk about it before the explosion? afterward? Can you find any elements from science-fiction writing in his account? How do these elements affect your response to the bombing of Nagasaki?

TOM WICKER
Kennedy is Killed by Sniper as He Rides in Car in Dallas

1. Characterize Wicker's tone. How "involved" is it? How emotional does he let his prose become? Find specific examples to substantiate your response. Characterize his sentence structure. Does the shape of Wicker's sentences offer additional evidence to support your answer to the previous question? If so, explain how. When is the passive voice (for example, "It is believed") used in the report? Why? Why would the active voice be less appropriate in such instances?
2. One of Wicker's strengths as a writer is his ability to interweave details into a compelling narrative. Locate some examples of this technique in the report. What happens, however, to Wicker's prose when it comes time to report the specific nature of Kennedy's wounds? What kind of language does he turn to? Compare this aspect of Wicker's story with the report on the assassination of Lincoln. Locate as many instances of "official" language as possible in each story. What does each reporter feel obliged to do to (or with) this kind of language?
3. Contrast the presence of reporters during this momentous event with their presence during the swirl of events surrounding Lincoln's murder. Although none was present (in very close proximity to Lincoln or Kennedy) at the instant the fatal shots were fired, which reporter makes his account sound closer to that of an eyewitness? How is that effect achieved stylistically? Point to specific examples. Which reporter seems removed? How is that reflected in his prose?
4. Trace through particular examples how inferences and judgments find their way into Wicker's report as his account moves farther away from the lead paragraph. What is the effect of ending the report by quoting passages from the speech Kennedy was to have delivered that day in Dallas? An extended analysis of Wicker's coverage of Kennedy's assassination can be found in the introduction to "Press."

TOM WICKER
The Assassination

1. Wicker's essay is a dramatic description of the process of preparing one of the major news stories of this century. Show how Wicker's personal perspective and his own point of view are kept to a minimum in the report the *New York Times* published on President Kennedy's murder.
2. Wicker describes how he hurried about Dallas gathering "bits and pieces" of information that were soon to be worked up into his story for the *Times*. Using the details provided to Wicker by Mel Crouch, a local television reporter, Bob Clark

of ABC, Julian Reade, a presidential staff assistant, Gladwin Hill, another reporter for the *Times*, and the initial statements of the medical staff at Parkland Hospital, show how Wicker incorporated the "information" he gathered into the final, published story. How is each set of details introduced into Wicker's story? At what points? With what effects? Does each or any of these moments seem to be "thrown in" to Wicker's initial efforts to write a 500-word "straight" narrative on what had occurred?

3. How does Wicker's sense of a clearly defined audience (employees of the *New York Times*) help shape the way he writes this report—as opposed to the account the *Times* published on November 23, 1963? Locate moments of comic irony in "The Assassination." Why has Wicker mentioned them?
4. Compare the nature of Wicker's figurative language in this report with the metaphors he creates for the *Times* account. How is the figurative language different? Do they draw on the same sources? Is Wicker's knowledge of his audience in any way a factor in this respect?
5. Wicker talks more than once about the reporter's "instinct," his simply *knowing* that something is "true." Is there any evidence of this instinct in his report for the *Times?* Is this instinct reflected in Wicker's syntax or diction in the final report? Explain. A good deal of what Wicker says in "The Assassination" undercuts the conventional image of the reporter out to get a "scoop." In fact, Wicker's remarks point to an extraordianry sense of esprit de corps among the reporters covering the shooting: "Nobody thought about an exclusive; it didn't seem important." Why wouldn't a scoop, especially about such an important event, be important to a journalist? to a newspaper?
6. When seeing Mrs. Kennedy accompany the coffin from the hospital, Wicker tells us, "That was just about the only eyewitness matter that I got with my own eyes that entire afternoon." How does Wicker's prose create the sense of his having been an eyewitness to all the tumultuous events of that day in Dallas?

Additional Writing Exercise: Describe the process you experienced as you came to discover something new about yourself, someone else, or some object. Were you pursuing someone, some goal? Were you making something? Be as detailed as possible.

THOMAS O'TOOLE
"The Eagle Has Landed": Two Men Walk on the Moon

1. How does the time sequence O'Toole uses to organize his narrative conform to the "inverted pyramid" model discussed in the introduction to "Press"? For example, where does he begin and end his account? Note the number of times the headline quotation ("The Eagle Has Landed") is repeated in the text. What does this repetition tell you about O'Toole's narrative sequence and about the organization of news articles in general?
2. "Their first moments on the moon were truly incredible, but the entire day seemed incredible, as if the scenario for it all had been written by some bizarre science fiction writer." Discuss O'Toole's statement in relation to the substance and tone of his account and to the way the astronauts from their conversation seemed to be responding to the event. *Incredible* is a word O'Toole uses frequently. Comment on the applicability or inapplicability of the term as it appears throughout the report. What is the effect of the word tonally?
3. How is O'Toole's audience determined by the event he is writing about? How does that affect his responses? What attitudes toward the landing, technology, and adventure in general does O'Toole assume his audience shares? Would these attitudes be shared by all "mankind"? Explain.

VIVIAN GORNICK
The Next Great Moment in History Is Theirs

1. Consider the circle of acquaintances that Gornick introduces her readers to in the course of her article. What do they have in common? What does this circle suggest about the type of reader she imagines for her writing? What kind of information will that reader find most interesting? What terminology most familiar? For example, what do words like "aberrated," "neurotic," "aggressive," "symptoms," and "pathology" have in common?
2. How does Gornick dissociate herself ideologically from her circle of friends? Why were her conversations with female friends particularly inadequate? How has her circle of friends helped to determine her sense of an audience? For example, explain how her opening paragraphs create both a sense of controversy and an image of the participants. How does her imagined audience differ from the "general population" that she considers to be "totally unaware of what is happening"?
3. Discuss the effectiveness of introducing her own

personal experience into the essay. Why, for example, does she compare and contrast her youth with her brother's? How does she give her persoanl experiences historical significance?

4. Comment on the effectiveness of Gornick's strategy to begin her essay with a series of specific examples before making her general point. Show how her essay anticipates, includes, and then refutes opposing points of view. How does she define her concept of ''energy''? Is it clear? Why does she compare and contrast women and blacks? Comment on the effectiveness of this tactic. Why does she save the detailed description of the feminist movement until the very end of the essay? Why is that section of the article necessary? In her account of the various organizations within the contemporary feminist movement, how does she avoid the triteness of a middle-of-the-road affiliation?

Personal Experience Exercises: Write about a personal experience—sudden or continuous—that led to your involvement in a social or political movement (e.g., feminism), or to your adoption of an ideology (e.g., liberalism), or to your conversion to a religious group (e.g., the Quakers), or to your decision to affiliate yourself with some sort of collective enterprise (e.g., a club). What had your decision to do with finding out that what you thought were your own individual experiences were shared by others? What prompted this discovery? Did you have any resistance at first to finding out that others felt or wanted the same things you did? explain.

In a well-developed essay, explore your own identity as a woman or a man. Choose a specific incident to discuss, stating what you were expected to do (and by whom) because of your role as a woman or a man. Describe as accurately as you can what you finally chose to do and why.

MIKE ROYKO
Jackie's Debut a Unique Day

1. Mike Royko writes this piece from the perspective of a young boy—himself, thirty years younger. How does he establish the youthful point of view of the narrator? Find specific examples of childlike insights and observations that Royko includes to enforce his position in the story. What effect does the innocent quality of Royko's narrative voice have on the subject he addresses here? Can you imagine a similar piece being written about a significant moment in today's race relations? How does Royko's perspective reflect or shape the historical moment to which he addresses himself?
2. This piece ends with an epiphanic moment, in which an almost miraculous occurrence brings the story's deeper meaning into focus. Such moments can often be found in short stories (James Joyce, in his collection *Dubliners,* solidified the epiphanic style), but ''real life'' doesn't always provide journalists with such convenient devices. Do you believe that Royko really caught Jackie Robinson's baseball? How does the structure of this column resemble that of a short story?
3. Compare this piece with Maya Angelou's account of Joe Louis' championship fight from her autobiography *I Know Why the Caged Bird Sings* (Classics). Angelou's piece also recounts a childhood memory of a crucial moment in race relations and popular culture, but her perspective as an African-American woman differs greatly from that of Royko, a white male. Imagine these texts as two parts of a conversation. What aspects of the issues at hand does Royko highlight? What do you learn from Angelou's account that you cannot learn from Royko's? Compare the endings of the two pieces—Royko's is upbeat, Angelou's apprehensive. What underlying feeling or ideology about race relations is communicated by each story's conclusion?

SUSAN JACOBY
Unfair Game

1. This piece demonstrates a column writer's ability to address social issues in personal terms. Susan Jacoby uses incidents from her own life to illuminate the common occurrence of sexual harrassment. Think of events in your own life that might serve as examples of common problems or phenomena. These occurrences could reflect a number of power relations: between genders or among races; between parent and child; employer and worker; teacher and student. Write an essay, modelled on Susan Jacoby's, that puts your chosen issue into the context of daily life. Note how Jacoby combines commentary and analysis with examples, and also uses irony to get her point across.
2. While more and more examples of sexual harrassment are being discussed in public, some men continue to insist that women overexaggerate the aggressiveness of their advances. Imagine how the men cited in Jacoby's piece might explain their views of the situations described. What assumptions about femininity do these men make? What counter-assumptions does Jacoby make?
3. Who do you think Jacoby imagines as her reader-

ship for this column? What parts of the essay seem to speak to men and which speak to women? If this article had appeared in a feminist magazine such as *Ms.*, do you think Jacoby would have written it differently? What if it had been published in a men's magazine such as *Esquire?*

JIMMY BRESLIN
"Life in a Cage"

1. In this column, Jimmy Breslin combines elements of several different journalistic genres—the obituary, the editorial, and the interview feature—to create a multi-layered commentary on the death of Juan Perez. List which sections of Breslin's piece correspond with these different story styles. What different qualities does the story gain from each element? How would the piece be different if it were a more conventional, or "straight," news story?
2. Find examples of Breslin's use of irony to show his distress at the day-to-day mistreatment of inner city children. Note particularly his brief mention of the fate of the polar bears on p. 181. What impact does the single-sentence paragraph, "The two polar bears were shot," have on the story Breslin is relating?
3. Breslin makes little mention of the polar bears in his story, yet animal rights activists protested their quick execution after Juan Perez' death, saying that the bears were not murderers, just natural predators who reacted to the situation at hand. (The folk singer Phranc has recorded a song, "The Ballad of Lucy + Ted," to commemorate the bears' fate.) Research the events surrounding this event in your library's newspaper room, and write a Breslin-style column from the perspective of the defenders of the polar bears.
4. Examine Breslin's use of quotations in this column. How does he capture the different voices of the people he interviews? How do these voices work to communicate the writer's message?

DEBBIE McKINNEY
Youth's Despair Erupts

1. Although it originally appeared in a daily newspaper, McKinney's article is structured much like a magazine feature. Notice the different sections of the piece and the way in which McKinney builds her narrative. Take each section separately and discuss the "mini-story" it contains. Then analyze how these "mini-stories" come together to form a compelling whole. Are the subheads that lead off each section effective? Does McKinney's introduction set you up for what follows? What overall point is communicated through her conclusion?
2. Employing a sparse, unemotional writing style, McKinney evokes the wasteland of Alaskan village life through the use of meticulous detail. Go through the piece and list the various details McKinney provides, from the various mind-altering substances mentioned in the third paragraph to the listing of Conner's daily routine in jail. What emotions or moods do these facts evoke in the reader?
3. As is noted in the headnote, the series of which McKinney's article was a part won a Pulitzer prize for the *Anchorage Daily News,* and led to some legislative reform regarding Native alcohol use. The piece follows in a long tradition of journalism that seeks to effect social change. In the library, find other examples of this "muckraking" brand of journalism. Progressive publications such as *The Village Voice* and *Mother Jones* are often good places to look. Examine how these pieces use the subject matter at hand to promote political or social causes, to point out society's ills and to press for change. (You might also look for examples for historical subjects as well. The writings of Upton Sinclair, Theodore Dreiser and other muckraking literary figures might compare well to McKinney's article.)

DIANA GRIEGO ERWIN
His Dreams Belong to the Next Generation

1. Note the physical description of Delgado that runs through Erwin's piece. Do you get a mental picture of the man from the writer's words? How does that picture affect your consideration of his words, and of his story?
2. Erwin identifies with Delgado because her father's life experience resembles his. She speaks from a similar position as does the subject of her article. Yet she does not speak for Delgado, allowing his words and the details of his life to hold their own weight. How would this story be different if it were written by Delgado (besides the fact that it would be in Spanish)? What added insights can an outside observer such as Erwin bring to a story?
3. Erwin only uses one Spanish phrase in her story: *como un burro,* like a donkey, which is how Delgado feels Anglos treats him. Judging from the circumstances, Erwin and Delgado's original conversation was undoubtedly in Spanish. Do you feel Erwin should have used more Spanish in her article? What is the effect of putting that particular phrase into its original language? Judging from her

choice of language, what kind of audience do you think Erwin imagines for her piece?

SAMUEL FRANCIS
Rapping Garbage As Art

1. Does Francis provide a thorough analysis of the lines he cites from N.W.A. in paragraph four of this editorial? What does Francis mean by "the metrical wheelchair in which rap moves"? Can you imagine a different way of interpreting these lyrics? If so, explain. Do the standards Francis applies to rap lyrics adequately fit the genre, or is he taking standards from another era and applying them inappropriately? Be specific as possible in your response.
2. Francis chose particular rappers to cite in support of his argument against the music. How do Ice Cube and Schooly D's words reinforce his arguments? Do you feel Francis quoted these artists out of context? Can you think of other rappers who might have said very different things? From recent periodicals such as *Rolling Stone* or *Spin,* find quotations from hip hop artists that might change the cast of Francis' argument.
3. Write an editorial defending rap, employing the same matter-of-fact tone that Francis uses. Can his rhetorical techinque be turned around to support the opposite point of view?

DAVID VON DREHLE
Shaken Survivors Witness Pure Fury

1. David von Drehle mixes simile and detailed description to communicate the experience of surviving a hurricane. Find the various comparisons he makes in the article (example: von Drehle leans into the storm "like a street mime," the sound of the storm reminds him of a dentist's suction tube). Without these phrases, does the story still hold its power? Consider how these similes work in league with factual details to evoke a particular atmosphere.
2. This is a first-person piece, although von Drehle doesn't emphasize his own personality here. How does the writer's identity figure in this article? Does he act purely as a sensual recorder of events? Do you get a sense of von Drehle's emotional state from this piece?
3. Find the various examples of extraordinary occurrences that von Drehle includes in order to show the extremity of Hurricane Hugo. How does he note these phenomena, such as the street sign penetrating the parked car near the end of the piece? To what extent does he succeed in creating a sense of a topsy-turvy world?
4. Find accounts of Hurricane Andrew, which hit Florida in August 1992, and compare them to von Drehle's piece. What issues and stories surrounding a natural disaster does von Drehle ignore in order to focus on his subject?

MICHAEL VENTURA
On Kids and Slasher Movies

1. Ventura uses hyperbole when he compares the boy buying a Halloween mask to dropping the atomic bomb and discovering the German death camps. Then he constructs an argument to support his hyperbole. Do you think he succeeds in proving his point? Why? Why not? How does the extremity of his tone reinforce his argument? Or, to ask the same question in a different way, how did you feel after reading this piece? What emotional state does Ventura evoke through his dramatic writing style?
2. The central argument in this piece is summed up in these two sentences: "No one feels safe anywhere. This has become the very meaning of the 20th century." How does the rest of the piece support this assertion?
3. Compare this piece to Jimmy Breslin's "Life in a Cage" (also in Press). Breslin's article also decries the violent circumstances in which a young boy must live. How do the pieces differ, in language and in structure? How are they similar? Which do you find more convincing?

ANNA QUINDLEN
Fighting the War on Cigs

1. Anna Quindlen provides both sides of the argument for and against sale of cigarettes in her article, although she clearly disapproves of smoking. Note how, in paragraphs five and eight, she offers reasons supporting the cigarette industry. How does she integrate these arguments into a piece that generally supports the opposite point of view? Does she succeed in presenting a balanced picture of the conflict she describes?
2. How does Quindlen characterize Dr. Sullivan? What is her attitude toward his pronouncements? How does she undermine his arguments and then assert her own? Do you find her proposal at the end of the piece plausible? How does her argument lead to that conclusion?
3. Sarcasm plays an important role in this article, reinforcing a sense of the ridiculousness of American governmental policies toward cigarettes. Find examples of how Quindlen uses dry humor to sup-

port her anti-cigarette stance. How does Quindlen characterize smokers? Would a smoker be offended by this piece, or sympathetic? Who do you think Quindlen imagines as her audience?

SCOTT HIGHAM, ANNE BARTLETT, AND JAMES F. McCARTY
A First: Album Ruled Obscene

1. This piece cites a wide variety of people, directly or indirectly involved with the 2 Live Crew case. List the people quoted and what purpose each interviewee's point of view serves in constructing this story. Why, for example, is Alan Dershowitz included here? How do the quotes from various Florida law officers figure in the story? Do you think any of the interviewees should have been given more room to speak in this article?
2. This article attempts to do two things: report on a particular incident and provide commentary about that occurrence and its implications. How are these two elements integrated in the story?
3. Near the article's conclusion, the reporters mention a courtroom scene in which the defense showed evidence of other sexually explicit media, which have not been censored. How is this event described here? Is the reporting sympathetic to the defense? Does Luther Campbell come off as a reasonable man? What about Nick Navarro? Does this piece present an objective or biased view of the 2 Live Crew controversy?

ANCIL DAVIS
National Association of Independent Record Distributors and Manufacturers Meet Tackles Sticky Problems

1. Ancil Davis uses trade lingo throughout this piece as a kind of shorthand, readable by entertainment business insiders. Did the language of this article alienate you? If so, in what specific ways? Could you understand what Davis was reporting? Rewrite the piece for a general audience, as if it were to appear in your local Sunday paper.
2. Tom Silverman invokes Elvis and the Beatles as predecessors of the censored artists being discussed at the National Association of Independent Record Distributors and Manufacturers conference. Using the newspaper room in your library, find primary sources of evidence that those legendary artists also were met by the disapproval of American authorities. How were the arguments made against Elvis and the Beatles different from those made against rappers today? How were they the same? In those cases, how did the artists and their sympathizers respond to protests against them?

TOTTIE ELLIS
Hooray for this Crackdown on Obscenity

1. Why does Ellis put the word "songs" in quotation marks in the third paragraph of her piece? Compare this move with the analysis Sam Francis provides of rap lyrics in "Rapping Garbage as Art" earlier in this section. How does challenging the artistic value of rap music reinforce these writers' arguments against their moral worth? If Ellis considered 2 Live Crew's music worthwhile as art, would her assertion that it is obscene be as convincing?
2. Governor Bob Martinez compares 2 Live Crew's music to an obscene telephone call. In what ways do you—or do you not—think this is a fair comparison? How does the issue of choice factor into Martinez' comparison? How does this argument against 2 Live Crew relate to the testimony of the two Rosenblum boys concerning "dirty lyrics" in the schoolyard in Ancil Davis' report? How would an anti-censorship advocate respond to these assertions?
3. In the penultimate paragraph of this editorial, Ellis lists various credos of civil society. In doing so, she compares the production of "obscenity" to cocaine use and yelling fire in a crowded theatre. Do you think these comparisons are fair? Are they convincing? Why? Why not? What basic social standards does Ellis adhere to, according to this piece?

MONA CHAREN
Much More Nasty Than They Should Be

1. Mona Charen's position regarding 2 Live Crew is similar to Tottie Ellis'; but in subtle ways, her argument differs. What distinguishes Charen's rhetorical style? How does she use examples to build toward her conclusion? Is her own political identity—that of a conservative former Reagan speechwriter—present in this piece?
2. What does Charen mean by the phrase "common culture," which ends her commentary? Whom does she include in this culture? Who might be excluded? How does the concept of "ordered liberty" figure into Charen's perception of "common culture"?
3. Compare Charen's piece to Michael Ventura's article "On Kids and Slasher Movies" (p. 197). Both writers express disgust with current moral standards as expressed through popular culture.

Yet Ventura is a liberal (some might even call him a radical) writing for an alternative newsweekly, and Charen is a conservative writing for a daily paper. How can their positions be so similar, considering their differing backgrounds? Can you think of other examples of writers with very different political views seeming to "come together" on certain points?

4. What leap of logic does Charen make when she compares crack murders to the music of 2 Live Crew? What does she leave out in making this point? How do you think Henry Louis Gates, Jr., would respond to this assertion by Charen?

JUAN WILLIAMS
The Real Crime: Making Heroes of Hate Mongers

1. Juan Williams interviews a different group of people than do the other writers examining the 2 Live Crew case. His "experts" are almost all African American, and he speaks from inside the community at the center of the controversy. How does this approach shift the argument against 2 Live Crew? Does Williams' piece read as more "authentic" or "informed" than do Mona Charen's or Tottie Ellis's? Who from the African American community doesn't get to speak in Williams' article?
2. This article, like many of those in this section, asserts that popular cultural texts have a direct and material effect on the communities to which they are addressed. Another argument would say that these texts speak from already existent conditions; they are symptoms, rather than causes. Which position do you feel is most correct? Support your argument with examples.
3. Compare the lead in Williams' story with that in Anna Quindlen's op ed piece "Winning the War on Cigs" (earlier in the Press section). What techniques do the two share? What is the impact of such a lead on the reader?

HENRY LOUIS GATES, JR.
2 Live Crew, Decoded

1. Henry Louis Gates uses terms from literary criticism, such as "carnivalesque" and "cultural codes," in explaining his view of 2 Live Crew's lyrics. These words communicate a sense of authority, but they also could prove confusing to people unfamiliar with such criticism. Do you think Gates' rhetorical style makes his argument more or less effective? What kind of audience is Gates addressing in this piece? (You might find it useful to remember that it appeared on the "op ed" page of the *New York Times*).
2. Gates suggests that 2 Live Crew's sexism may "cancel itself out" because of its overexaggerated nature. Compare this argument with those raised by the African American women interviewed in Juan Williams' article. Considering their testimony, does Gates' point make sense? What view of the connection between artistic expression and reality does Gates hold?
3. According to Gates, "Rock songs have always been about sex but have used elaborate subterfuges to convey that fact." Can you find examples of this in albums by white artists? Rock, and especially heavy metal, has also come under fire from legal and moral authorities over the years. For example, the British metal band Judas Priest was sued by the parents of a Nevada teenager who had committed suicide; the boy's family stated that he had been pushed into his violent act by the rock group's lyrics. (An excellent documentary on this court case, called *Dream Deceivers,* is available through First Run/Icarus Film at 1-800-876-1710.) Examining the Judas Priest case or other examples of controversial rock music, what commonalities do you discover with the 2 Live Crew case? What specific threats do protestors see in heavy metal, as opposed to those perceived in rap music?

DAVID MILLS
The Judge vs. 2 Live Crew: Is the Issue Obscenity or Young, Black Males?

1. Consider the distinction between "verbal" and "oral" that David Mills makes in section two of this article. Do you agree that music, and other art forms that utilize live performance, need to be analyzed differently from literature? Can you find other examples of performed texts that do not "translate" on the written page?
2. Mills offers several examples of earlier artists upon whom 2 Live Crew have based their work. Seek out some of the texts by these artists ('70s "party" records, blaxploitation films) and compare them to "As Nasty As They Wanna Be." Are the connections that Mills suggests exist between these various artworks really present? Do you think 2 Live Crew has produced "serious art" in this tradition? (Note to teachers: this work tends to be quite explicit. However, to understand the 2 Live Crew controversy and to render a judgment on it, students should hear the music.)
3. Mills calls for "black scholars and intellectuals" to contextualize 2 Live Crew for non-blacks. Besides the writings of Henry Louis Gates, Jr. (whom Mills quotes) can you find work by such thinkers? Look for articles or books by Nelson George, Greg

Tate, Michelle Wallace and Thulani Davis. Did these writers respond to the 2 Live Crew controversy? Reading their words, can you discern a particular African-American cultural criticism developing?

TERI MADDOX
Unsuspecting Parents Can't Believe Their Ears

1. Unlike editorial writers Tottie Ellis and Sam Francis, reporter Teri Maddox does not explicitly state which side she is on in the debate over censorship and artistic freedom. Do you think a particular stance on the issue is communicated through this article? Discuss how choices such as who is interviewed and what is reported in a story influence the way in which "news" is cast. Is there such a thing as an "objective" news report?
2. Bob DeMoss chaims that the media's refusal to publish explicit lyrics in articles that discuss censorship undermines efforts, like his, to "clean up" popular culture. Do you agree with him? Examine the other articles in this section; how do they deal specifically with the content of 2 Live Crew's work? How do different approaches to this material serve different writers' purposes?
3. Maddox begins her story by presenting a visual image of parents' response to explicit material. Going through the rest of this textbook, find other leads that use this technique (for example, Anna Quindlen's in "Fighting the War on Cigs" (see earlier in this section) or David von Drehle, "Shaken Survivors Witness Pure Fury," (also earlier in this section). How do these writers evoke visual images to strengthen the impact of their stories? What varying purposes can visual description serve? How does the use of detail differ from story to story?

LAURA PARKER
How Things Got Nasty in Broward County

1. Laura Parker contextualizes the case of 2 Live Crew by providing a view of Broward County, where the controversy took place. Other pieces in this section on 2 Live Crew contextualize the case differently. Compare Parker's approach to that of Henry Louis Gates, Jr. or Juan Williams. Which do you think tells a more complete version of the story? Is it even possible to compare these approaches, when they are so different? How do they connect? What would a "complete" rendition of the 2 Live Crew controversy include?
2. Parker invokes characters from popular culture in detailing the personal styles of Nick Navarro and Jack Thompson. How would you typify these men, as Parker describes them? How does her characterization of them shed light on the controversy which they have stirred?
3. Why do you think Parker quotes Broward County resident Viola Anderson at the end of her story? Does including the opinion of an "average" citizen increase the feeling of authenticity in her piece? Discuss how "man-or-woman-on-the-street" reporting is used in journalism generally—what is its function? How is it usually performed?

LUTHER CAMPBELL
Today They're Trying to Censor Rap, Tomorrow . . .

1. Campbell makes a series of points supporting his position in this article. Which points do you think are effective, and which are weak? Do you think the article could have been organized differently? If so, in what specific ways? What is the cumulative effect of all these different arguments playing off each other?
2. In the summer of 1992, rapper Ice T experienced a somewhat similar face-off with authorities over the song "Cop Killer," performed by his group, Body Count. Ice T also articulated his own view of the controversy in which he was involved, in magazines including *Rolling Stone* and *Spin*. Find examples of Ice T's response and compare them to Luther Campbell's. What points do they share? what differences?
3. Do you agree with Campbell that the move to censor rap could lead to restrictions on "high" art forms such as theatre or classical music? What other ramifications of this controversy could you imagine? How, for example, does the censorship of rap connect with other moves by legal authorities in connection with the African American community? How does it connect with the public funding of the arts, as viewed through the lens of the conflict over the National Endowment for the Arts in the early 1990s? Researching several different occurrences of censorship or restriction of "obscene" art, come up with a general analysis of censorship in contemporary America—its causes and its effects.

RUSSELL BAKER
Don't Mention It

1. Find the original texts for which Andy Rooney and Jimmy Breslin were censured and, after viewing them, reread Russell Baker's response. Do you agree with his argument? How might his own so-

cial position, gender, and race influence his view? How do you think Henry Louis Gates, Jr. (see Press) would have responded to these same texts? To Baker's argument?

2. Baker uses the terms ''dolt'' and ''geezer'' to describe people such as Breslin and Rooney. These terms might be considered offensive by some people. How does Baker's use of them reinforce or undermine his argument? What kind of subtle point do you think he might be making here?
3. Read this editorial in conjunction with David Savage's article ''Forbidden Words on Campus'' (see Press). Do you agree that liberals who question racist or sexist language choice are similar in their views to conservatives who challenge the music of 2 Live Crew? How do issues of authority and power figure into this debate? Do you think there are times when people speaking or writing publicly should be censored?

ANN POWERS AND NINA SCHUYLER
Censorship in America: Why It's Happening

1. Chart the development of Ann Powers' and Nina Schuyler's analysis of the causes that led to the legislative restraints imposed on the arts in the early 1990s. What do they identify as the major specific factors that led to legislative monitoring of the disbursement of taxpayer funds in the arts. What role, for example, do Powers and Schuyler assign to television programming in the development of this trend toward increasing censorship? What do they say about the impact of radical feminism on government efforts to regulate the arts? Summarize—and then comment on—the charges of racism that surface in their article.
2. Powers and Schuyler open their article by asserting that ''America is caught in a paradox.'' Trace the historical evidence Powers and Schuyler muster in support of their argument that ''newspapers, radio and television—the very symbols of free speech—report new tales about the suppression of free speech.'' What other paradoxes do they note during the course of their analysis of increasing efforts to suppress free speech in contemporary America? What causes do they identify as the sources of these efforts to regulate free speech? What do they envision to be the consequences of such efforts?
3. How do Powers and Schuyler define ''the mainstream''? What organizations claim to represent the mainstream, and what values are associated with this term? Much of the controversy over government regulation of free speech revolves around definitions of ''obscenity.'' Summarize the various definitions of ''obscenity'' offered—explicitly and implicitly—by various groups in this article. Which do you find most reasonable? Why? Which definition do Powers and Schuyler affiliate themselves with?
4. Ann Powers and Nina Schuyler published this article in the *San Francisco Weekly,* an alternative newspaper that ranges far in its weekly coverage of national and local issues in politics and the arts. Compare and contrast this account of censorship in America with any of the newspaper articles that focus on the efforts to silence the rap group 2 Live Crew. (See earlier in the Press section.) In what specific ways does writing for an alternative newsweekly differ from that done for a daily newspaper? What do these pieces have in common? In what ways does this comparison/contrast help you to understand better the meaning of the word ''mainstream''?

GEORGE LAKOFF
Metaphor and War

1. Using George Lakoff's metaphors (the State-As-Person), Clausewitz' metaphor (War as Violent Crime), and the like, interpret a variety of articles that were published during the Gulf War. Do different kinds of publications employ different metaphors? How are these metaphors evident on the level of rhetoric? through narrative structure? How do the photographs accompanying the articles reinforce the metaphors employed?
2. Lakoff distinguishes between ''national interests'' and the particular interests of individuals who live in a particular nation. Can you think of other areas in which ''national interests'' might conflict with personal ones? How can public policy be made, considering the gap between these areas of interest? How does the distinction between ''national'' and personal interests undermine the metaphor of the State-As-Person?
3. The metaphors used in war are not the sole province of the media, but with television and other media so pervasive in distributing information, Lakoff's story is one of mass communication as much as one of national consciousness. Compare this piece to Neil Postman's essay, ''The Parable of the Ring-Around-the-Collar'' (see Advertising). Are the phenomena discussed in these two articles similar? What underlying themes run through both?

DAVID SAVAGE
Forbidden Words on Campus

1. Why do you think the ongoing conflict over ''fighting words'' has centered on college cam-

puses, rather than in corporate workplaces, government offices, or in the press? What in particular about college life makes the issue of personal rhetoric so heated? Can you find examples of similar situations in other environments?

2. ACLU President Nadine Strossen suggests that other means are needed to fight racism and sexism on campus, besides restrictive speech codes. What other methods might deter such activities? Can people's minds be changed through restrictions on their forms of public expression? How do policies such as affirmative action relate to this issue?
3. Have you ever been the victim or the perpetrator of "fighting words"? Can you find examples of this conflict on your own campus? If you have experienced this type of occurrence, how did you respond? Are there "fighting words" that aren't based on gender or race?

MAUREEN DOWD
The Senate and Sexism

1. Maureen Dowd announces in the opening sentence of her report that the case of Anita F. Hill and Clarence Thomas "has offered a rare look into the mechanics of power and decision-making in Washington, a city where men have always made the rules and the Senate remains an overwhelmingly male club." Summarize the major points of Dowd's analysis of these "mechanics of power and decision-making in Washington." Trace how Dowd structures and supports her report by citing women *and* men in Washington. How does Dowd use these quotations to make her point? What are the advantages/disadvantages of relying so heavily on direct quotations?
2. What is the main point of Dowd's report? What point of view does Dowd establish in relation to the events and judgments she recounts? Point to specific words and phrases to verify your points. How "neutral" and "objective" does Dowd seem in her account of the impact of Anita Hill's charges? What evidence led you to your conclusion? How does Dowd's selection of details and quotations suggest what she thinks about Anita Hill? Clarence Thomas? sexual harassment? the Senate?
3. Read the advertisement entitled "What If?" distributed by the National Women's Political Caucus. Consider carefully the substance of the argument presented in this advertisement. What specific convergences do you notice between the position established in the advertisement and Maureen Dowd's account of the impact of Anita Hill's charges of sexual harassment against Clarence Thomas? (It is important to remember that Dowd published her report on the day the Senate decided to postpone its vote on Judge Thomas' confirmation and to hold hearings on her charges of sexual harassment.) Compare and contrast the responses elicited from the readers of the news report and the ad. Which is more effective in making its point(s)? Why?
4. Prepare the first draft of an expository essay, in which you recount your own experience with sexism. How will you handle the matter of direct citation from witnesses? What kind of structure will you set up for your essay? What overall point will you try to make?

PATRICK O'CONNELL
Settlement of America: A Continuing Crime

JEFFREY HART
Feting the Lindbergh of the 15th Century

1. Summarize the main points of each "op-ed" essay. Which do you find more convincing? Why?
2. Reread Patrick O'Connell's "Settlement of America: A Continuing Crime." What sorts of appeals does O'Connell make in his efforts to earn the assent of his readers? Consider the parallels O'Connell draws between Columbus' "discovery" of America and other moments of historical significance. What aspects does he underscore in each comparison? What connections does he establish between and among these events?
3. O'Connell's essay depends for its conviction and impact on invoking the definitions of the word "genocide." Reread the article, identify the instances when O'Connell encourages us to "come to terms with what it means to live in a nation founded on genocide." Offer a judgment on the effectiveness of O'Connell's invoking this term.
4. Contrast the stricture of Jeffrey Hart's essay "Feting the Lindbergh of the 15th Century." Would Hart include O'Connell among the "pushy ideologues and pressure groups [which] have managed to make [Columbus] controversial"? Around what issue—and what word—does Hart structure his argument? How does Hart anticipate the objections of those who view Columbus in far less flattering terms? What happens to Hart's argument when he moves, as he says, "outside political arrangements"? How convincingly does Hart make his case? Explain.

KAREN JURGENSEN
Redskins, Braves: Listen to Those You've Offended

PAUL HEMPHILL
Names Debate Off Target

1. Summarize the major points Jurgensen and Hemphill make in support of and in opposition to the objections of many Native Americans to the continued use of "Braves" as the nickname for Atlanta's major league baseball team and the "Redskins" as the nickname of the Washington entry in the National Football league. What points does each writer offer to support her and his respective position? Which do you find more convincing? Why?
2. What other symbolic names and actions can you identify in the worlds of American sports and entertainment? What other reasons can you think of to support (or oppose) the continued use of such names and actions. Be sure that you emphasize which side you take in this debate—and the reasons that underpin your position.
3. Draft an editorial—for publication in *USA Today*—which offers the readers of that paper your response to the issues raised in Jurgensen and Hemphill's editorials. What specific strategies will you use to convince the people who read that newspaper of the merits of your position. Now redraft the same editorial for publication in your hometown newspaper. What specific changes did you find it necessary to make in adapting the editorial to meet the expectations of the readers of your local newspaper?

MAGAZINES

JACK LONDON
The Story of an Eyewitness

1. What are London's criteria for damage? How do people figure in his account of the earthquake? Do they seem more or less significant than the property? What is the effect of London's descriptions of the possessions people are trying to salvage?
2. Does London show any affection for his native city? Can you find moments in his writing when he sounds dejected or bewildered because of the disaster? What is his purpose in choosing to end his article with the perspective from Nob Hill?

WILLIAM HARD
De Kid Wot Works at Night

1. What assumptions about his audience's attitude toward newsboys and messenger boys seem implicit in Hard's sentences? What conventional images circulate about children "wot work at night"? Locate specific examples of the "popular imagination" of the newsboy in Hard's essay. How does Hard go about dispelling this public image of newsboys? How does he use this tactic in his case for legislative reform? What are the specifics of his proposed legislation?
2. What features of the newsboys' life does Hard focus on? Does the essay suggest that life during the day provides a viable alternative for the boys? What is it, specifically, that Hard finds so attractive in "Jelly"?
3. How is Hard's essay more than a description of the circumstances of the newsboys' lives? Is the essay in any way argumentative? What evidence does he offer to validate his assertions? How does he anticipate, include, and then refute the arguments of opposing points of view? How does he "handle," for example, the issue of the children's education? When does Hard allow political commentary to surface in his essay? With what effect? Does he argue that genuine individual initiative necessitates living outside of the law, outside of legal sanctions? Explain. When do larger social issues appear in the essay?
4. Characterize Hard's sentence structure. When are his sentences short and matter-of-fact? When are they expansive and highly figurative? Why? For example, what is the purpose of having a single, very long opening sentence built on the accumulation of adverbial clauses? Comment on the effectiveness of repeating "When" and "Then it is." How would you characterize the language used in the opening section? What kind of context does this kind of language create for Hard's report on the newsboys? Consider the scene at the movie theater, the "theatorium," as Hard calls it. This is the moment when "Jelly" decides on a new "career" for himself. Characterize the sentence struc-

ture at this point. How is it different from the opening? How can you account for this difference?

5. What is the function of the incident where "Jelly" stabs Mr. Gazzolo? As you reread this section, can you detect any evidence that Hard is parodying the characteristic way newspapers report such an event? Be specific. Locate and discuss other instances in which Hard's essay wavers between parody and extreme social consciousness.

Note: An extended analysis of Hard's "De Kid Wot Works at Night" can be found in the introduction to "Magazines."

PETER HOMANS
The Western: The Legend and the Cardboard Hero

1. Look at the language of the first three paragraphs of the essay, especially their tone, imagery, and grammar. How does it differ from the language of the essay's last few paragraphs? Describe the sense of versatility or adaptability given by Homans's shifting style.
2. Does Homans admire or enjoy Westerns, do you suppose? Does he satirize them in the essay? If the answer to both questions is yes, does that mean Homans contradicts himself? Explain.
3. Explain whether the Western setting and outdated characters are necessary for the embodiment of the "myth" of the Western. How could the paradigms of the Western be adapted to science fiction?
4. Imitating Homans, analyze some other genre familiar to you—a police series on television, a martial-arts film, a romance novel. How do their myths differ from those of the Western? Does the analysis account for the popularity of the genre? How does it account for the enjoyment people receive from the embodiment of the myth in particular films or books? Explain whether one's pleasure is deepened or refined by thinking of Westerns as "puritan morality tales."
5. Homans's article appeared in 1962. Consider some of the changes in typical plots and characters of Westerns since then. In what ways do movies and television programs produced since then diverge from Homans's model? How are these changes related to other changes in American culture? Explain.

TIME STAFF
Death of a Maverick Mafioso

1. Demonstrate how *Time* makes film the predominant environment for its report on the shooting of Joey Gallo. What fantasy of American life does *Time* play on to characterize Gallo? To what figures in American film is Gallo compared? Are these *Time*'s choices? What evidence does *Time* offer to verify its contentions?
2. How would you characterize the language used by Marta Curro and Joan Hackett to describe Gallo? What do their terms have in common? Is *Time*'s own diction consistent with theirs? Explain. Why does *Time* often refer to Gallo and Diopioulis as "Joey" and "Pete"?
3. Compare the description of the murder of Joey Gallo here with "Dillinger 'Gets His'" (see "Press") and the shooting of Don Corleone in Mario Puzo's *The Godfather* (see "Best-Sellers"). How are both gangsters made attractive? How are the criminal activities of both figures given a kind of legitimacy?
4. Compare this report with another *Time* article of your choosing. Is there any consistency in the diction and figurative language from one report to the next? Is the tone of each story in any way the same? Explain. Can you identify some of the components of *Time*'s characteristic style?

N. SCOTT MOMADAY
A First American Views His Land

Momaday's essay is a wonderful account of the feelings of the American Indians for their land. He uses both imaginative narrative and incidents from his own experience to illustrate his point. In discussing the selection with your class, you might want to focus on the ways he illustrates what he says, so that it never remains too long in the realm of the abstract.

The essay will likely lead to a discussion of contemporary attitudes toward our environment. You might ask why Indian values are so different from ours, and what sorts of dangers our values may lead us into. You may want to bring in the selection by Robert Frost ("The Gift Outright" in "Classics"), should the discussion take this turn.

1. Consider Momaday's accounts of the killing of the bison and the deer. Why is the first so detailed and the second so short? What do the details of the killing of the bison contribute to our sense of the contrast between the hunter in New Mexico and the hunter on the Great Lakes, thousands of years later? Why does Momaday emphasize the primitive violence of the first scene?
2. Momaday speculates that the Native American idea that the land is sacred may have arisen from the recognition that the physical world is beautiful. How do you think the Indian sense of beauty is like that of other Americans? In what ways might it be

different? What does Momaday mean when he says that this sense of the physical world is ''a matter of morality''? How does it represent the realization of one's humanity? Do you think he means by *morality* what we usually mean by the word?
3. Explain why Momaday thinks the narrative about the buried woman expresses a love for the land. Why doesn't it matter that the woman has no name? Why is the attention to her dress so significant? How does the feeling for the woman and the dress differ from what we might find on a headstone in a cemetery?
4. How does the Kiowa woman's saying ''It is good that you have come here'' differ from our saying to a visitor, ''How nice of you to drop by''? Explain what you think the woman means by *good*. In what situations, if any, could someone who is not an Indian use *good* in this sense?
5. What is the main difference between the Indian attitude toward the land and that of the rest of American society? In what ways might the Indian attitude be more appropriate for the 1980s? How might having such an attitude help us to survive?
6. Not too many of us have the deep connection with the land that Momaday writes of here, but all of us have some feeling for a place where we have grown up. Write an essay in which you describe your feelings about such a place, using one or more incidents from your past to illustrate that feeling.

TONI MORRISON
Cinderella's Stepsisters

1. By what means does Morrison attempt to appeal to her audience here? Explain whether there is logic and proof in her language or whether Morrison attempts to evoke emotions. If the latter, is she successful? What emotions are brought forth, and how? When she proclaims, ''I want not to *ask* you but to *tell* you not to participate in the oppression of your sisters,'' she might be taken as a bully. Does her language at all contradict this judgment? How?
2. Though published in a magazine, Morrison's essay was originally given as a commencement address at Barnard College in New York. How might this circumstance have determined what aspects of women's relations she would focus on?
3. Imagine you have been chosen to give a commencement address at your college. Following Morrison's example, discuss a fairy tale and try to make it relevant to an audience ''commencing'' their adult lives.

GRETEL EHRLICH
The Solace of Open Spaces

1. Ehrlich explains that residents of Wyoming ''still feel pride because they live in such a harsh place, part of the glamorous cowboy past.'' How does she reveal the harshness of Wyoming's landscape? What stylistic devices does she use to underscore that harshness? In what specific ways does Ehrlich recreate a sense of Wyoming's ''glamorous cowboy past''?
2. What explanation does Ehrlich offer for her decision to settle in Wyoming? What actions does she take to emphasize her recognition that ''life on the sheep ranch woke me up''?
3. How does Ehrlich describe Wyoming's cities and towns? What attitude does she reveal about them? How does she balance her overall presentation of that state? She characterizes the state as ''barren'' and ''desolate,'' yet she also notes that ''there's a coziness to living in this state.'' How does she reconcile this seeming contradiction?
4. What stylistic devices does Ehrlich use to create a sense of the state's vastness, of the ''solace'' of its ''open spaces''?
5. How do westerners convey their thoughts and feelings in a place where solitude and silence prevail? How does Ehrlich account for the shyness—the verbal reticence—of the people of Wyoming?
6. Characterize Ehrlich's attention to the effects of the natural elements—especially the wind and water—on both the land and the people of Wyoming. Identify the metaphors Ehrlich creates for the wind and water. Which strike you as most dramatic? Why?
7. How does Ehrlich distinguish between ''wilderness'' and ''wildness'' in Wyoming? Contrast her depiction of the lives of the Native Americans and the ''sod-busters'' in Wyoming.
8. What does Ehrlich mean when she says, ''The emptiness of the West was for others a geography of possibility''? How is this sense of possibility constricted by the harsh realities of later years? What physical limitations were imposed on this sense of possibility? Explain what Ehrlich means by ''a rage against restraint.'' What does she describe as ''the dark side to the grandeur of these spaces''?

STEPHEN KING
Now You Take ''Bambi'' or ''Snow White''— That's *Scary!*

1. What does King achieve by beginning his essay with a discussion of traditional fairy tales? Sup-

pose the first five paragraphs had been omitted. How would the essay be less persuasive? Explain.

2. Look closely at King's diction and the personal anecdotes he relates. Does he sound like an authority on child rearing? If not, explain whether this detracts from his reliability as an advisor to parents.
3. King suggests that horror stories offer "a chance to enter for a little while a scary yet controllable world where we can express our fears, aggressions and possibly even hostilities." Compare this with the underlying structure of the Tarzan stories and Westerns, as described by Peter Homans. Explain whether all three of these genres are equally popular today. If not, consider whether the differences in popularity can be explained with reference to the "myths" they embody. What myths are most potent or attractive today?
4. Why might children's responses to a narrated fairy tale differ from their responses to a filmed version of the same story? How might the nature of the media—print and film—determine their responses?
5. Read a few traditional fairy tales, paying close attention to their techniques of storytelling. Now rewrite a contemporary horror story adopting the traditional techniques. Would your recomposed version be more suitable for young children to hear? Why?

BOB GREENE
Fifteen

1. Note how the article is broken into sections separated by spacing. Is there any logic to the ordering of the sections? Consider whether there is any sense of randomness in the ordering. How does the sequence of sections determine the effect of the essay?
2. In saying that fifteen is a "weird age to be male," Greene seems to suggest that fifteen-year-olds are caught between childhood and adulthood. How might the essay as a whole support such an opinion?
3. The final paragraph of the essay expresses Greene's affection for the boys he has described. Where and how has he implied such an attitude elsewhere in the essay, or is the reader surprised by the last paragraph?
4. Write an essay on Greene's model that describes a character in a setting familiar to you. Consider whether Greene's method of transcribing conversation and events prevents you from expressing your own views of the characters and setting.

THE SPACE SHUTTLE DISASTER

LANCE MORROW
A Nation Mourns

1. What is the effect of Morrow's use of the phrase "pure heaven" in his opening paragraph? How does he reinforce the image in the remainder of that paragraph? What other references does Morrow make to "purity" in the rest of the essay? With what effect? How, for example, was the shuttle mission "symbolically immaculate"?
2. Note the contrast between Morrow's description of the explosion as "a primal event of physics" and his characterization of the "weird metaphysics of videotape." What does he see as the nature of that metaphysics?
3. What does Morrow mean when he characterizes the role of television in the aftermath of the shuttle disaster? In what sense is television's role "sacramental"?
4. Do you agree with Morrow's assessment that Christa McAuliffe, the teacher-astronaut aboard Challenger, represents "all the right things in America"? Explain.

JERRY ADLER
We Mourn Seven Heroes

1. Compare and contrast Adler's opening paragraph to Morrow's. Which is more engaging? Why? The emphasis in Adler's opening paragraph is on the nation's disbelief in the reality of the Challenger's destruction. What stylistic devices does Adler use to create and reinforce this sense of disbelief?
2. What is the point of Adler's characterizing the shuttle explosion as "a humiliating failure of rocket technology"?
3. What different emphases does Adler create for his discussion of the media's role in the wake of the explosion of the Challenger?
4. Identify and comment on the effectiveness of Adler's use of irony in this essay. Does Adler seem to treat his subject with more or less irony than Morrow? Point to specific words and phrases to verify your response.
5. Compare and contrast the ending of Adler's essay to that of Morrow's. Which ending do you judge to be more effective? Why?

MARTIN GOTTFRIED
Rambos of the Road

Most college students are relatively new drivers. They will not remember a time when, as Martin Gottfried suggests, Americans "were at their finest and most civilized when in their cars.'' Students today are likely to have encountered—or are themselves—these ''Rambos of the Road.''

1. Cars are likely to be a high priority for most of the students in your class. Encourage them to consider the role of the automobile in their own lives, perhaps focusing on its symbolic significance. To what extent is their self-esteem linked to their performance behind the wheel?
2. You might ask your students to examine their own attitudes about the ''anti-social behavior'' Gottfried deplores. Do they accept such behavior as a by-product of the pressures of American living or do they reject it as mere hoodlumism? Can they generate some other views of this phenomenon?
3. Is there an ''ethics'' of driving? Ask your students about ideas on how to improve ''road manners.'' Can such manners be taught in driver's education, or are they learned in other ways altogether? Are a driver's manners necessarily a reflection of that person's manners in general?

SALLIE TISDALE
We Do Abortions Here: A Nurse's Story

Virtually everyone has a carefully thought out position on abortion and as a result of this fact discussion usually ends in a stalemate. When discussing Tisdale's essay, it might be useful to have your students hold their own views on abortion in check until they have ascertained their true responses to the piece.

1. Ask your students if they feel that Tisdale is being entirely honest in her arguments for abortion. As a nurse, how might her views of abortion differ from other people's?
2. Why has the topic of abortion attracted so much national attention? Consider with your class why so many people have developed strong positions? What are the major issues at stake in this debate?
3. Generate as many arguments for and against abortion with your students as possible? Which strike the students as most persuasive? Which of the arguments have a rational basis? Which ones have an emotional basis? Must the arguments with emotional bases be discounted?

RANDY SHILTS
Talking AIDS to Death

Randy Shilts contends that efforts to find a cure for AIDS have been hindered by government indifference and public ignorance. Your students might consider their own attitudes toward the victims of AIDS. Do they believe with Shilts that AIDS victims are still stigmatized? How has their own understanding of the disease increased in the last several years?

1. What kinds of responses to AIDS and its victims have your students encountered? Do your students find themselves agreeing with a majority of these views? How do most of these views hold up against the current facts about AIDS?
2. Ask your students what moral problems have been introduced by the AIDS crisis. Have them prepare a list of ethical dilemmas relating to the prevention, treatment, or spread of AIDS. Through discussion, consider several of these dilemmas and gauge the range of responses. A sample problem for discussion might be: ''Should clean syringes be distributed to IV drug users in order to prevent the spread of disease through shared use of needles?''
3. Have your students consider the number of ways that the AIDS epidemic affects all of us psychologically and socially. How has AIDS changed their attitudes toward relationships and dating?

ANN HODGMAN
No Wonder They Call Me a Bitch

This hilarious essay—one that your students might also describe as ''disgusting''—answers a question many of us may have asked ourselves: what does dog food taste like? ''Is a Gaines-burger really like a hamburger?'' After courageously testing many leading brands of dog food, from Gaines-burgers to Purina Dog Chow, Hodgman concludes that most dog foods—though edible—do not live up to their advertising claims.

1. Why does Hodgman cite so frequently the language of dog food packaging and advertising? To whom is that language directed? Of what importance is that language to her experiment?
2. To what extent do dog food advertisers assume parallels between the eating habits of human beings and dogs? What assumption do people generally make about what dogs prefer to eat? How accurate do you think these assumptions are?
3. Hodgman's essay originally appeared in one of America's leading satirical magazines. In what ways is Hodgman's piece humorous? In what ways in her humor satirical? Against whom is the satire directed?

ELIZABETH F. BROWN AND WILLIAM R. HENDEE
Adolescents and Their Music

The findings of the studies surveyed in this article might be profitably compared to Allen Bloom's speculations (see best sellers) about the effects of rock music on the adolescent mind. Have your students consider whether any of Bloom's charges are borne out by actual research.

1. One of the studies cited maintained that teenagers who watched television were more likely to be part of the mainstream than teenagers who spent more time listening to rock music. In another study, television is linked to aggressive behavior in teenagers. How can these two conclusions be reconciled? Does the fact that these studies seem to conflict undermine the conclusions of the article as a whole?
2. Brown and Hendee's report make reference to a number of cases in which rock music has been adapted for advertising purposes? Ask your students to make a list of other instances where rock is used to sell a product or to promote a cause. Can they think of any uses of rock in advertising where the song's message could be seen as undermining the purpose of the commercial?
3. Ask your students to consider whether the article presupposes that rock music belongs only to youth. Do they feel that the impact of rock can only be understood in generational terms?

LILLIAN ROBINSON
What Culture Should Mean

Your students probably have a good grasp of what constitutes canonical literature already. If not, you may want to talk about specific works and why they have traditionally been included in the college curriculum. Let your students offer some new titles for admission to the canon. What kinds of features do such works tend to have in common?

1. You might want to obtain reading lists for courses in Western civilization and world literature taught at your institution. With your students analyze the professed goals of these courses? Are there any non-Western texts included in the sample?
2. Have your students read Sidney Hook's essay "Civilization and its Malcontents," and ask them to take notice of the common themes addressed by both pieces. In what ways is Hook's essay a response to Robinson?
3. Let your student's imagine that they must recommend texts for a revised first-year curriculum designed to expose new students to works of Western and non-Western cultures alike as well as to works by women, minorities, and homosexuals. Ask them to develop a criterion for selection consistent with the goals of the course.

SIDNEY HOOK
Civilization and Its Malcontents

Before discussing Sidney Hook's analysis of recent educational trends with your students, you might explore with them their own sense of a Western tradition. Do they have a strong sense of larger cultural identity or do they tend to define themselves more along gender or ethnic lines?

1. Ask your students to what extent their own education has been traditionally Western. What other kinds of texts have shaped them intellectually?
2. Consider Hook's tone and style throughout the piece. Given that the magazine in which the essay first appeared is avowedly conservative, toward what kind of audience does Hook direct his argument? What is the author's primary purpose in writing this essay?
3. Does Hook explicitly exclude the possibility of introducing multicultural texts into the Western canon? Consider Lillian Robinson's essay on this question. In what ways is Hook opposed to the view expressed by Robinson? In what ways could he be said to agree with her position?

ISHMAEL REED
Antihero

Your students should already be familiar with the kinds of distortion that occur in the news each day. Before engaging them in a discussion of Reed's article, you might discuss the problem of distortion in the media more generally. Who do they believe is responsible for these distortions? the newscasters themselves? the networks that employ them? What share of the responsibility for inaccurate reporting does the viewing audience bear?

1. Do your students believe that the distortion of information has increased or decreased in recent years? Ask them to provide evidence for their positions?
2. Your students may want to consider the last major political campaign they followed closely. Ask them to describe the relation between the media and the particular campaigns? How in their view should the media cover political campaigns and elections in order not to bias voters?
3. Ishmael Reed is concerned primarily with the depiction of blacks in the news media. What other groups have been negatively or at least incorrectly portrayed by television news? Are your students aware of any public efforts to change the way certain groups have been represented?

JOSH OZERSKY
TV's Anti-Families: Married . . . with Malaise

If they are not already regular viewers of the TV programs examined in Josh Ozersky's opinion piece, they will at least be familiar with most of them. You might begin discussion of the piece by considering, in a more general fashion, the role of TV in our lives. Does it really have the power to affect us to the extent that the author claims it does?

1. Ask your students whether they feel the representation of family on *The Simpsons* is realistic or even whether it is intended to be realistic? To what extent does the status of the program as a cartoon compromise its claims to realism?
2. Do your students feel that Ozersky exaggerates the effects of these sitcoms on the viewing public? At one point, he calls *The Simpsons* "the least ironic" of the sitcoms under scrutiny. Ask your students if they feel this is an accurate statement. What evidence does Ozersky provide for the lack of irony he observes?
3. *Tikkun* describes itself as a progressive magazine. Does Ozersky's piece reflect a progressive/liberal view of culture or does it resist political labels altogether? Would it be incorrect to assume that Ozersky's views are inconsistent with progressive values? Would it be incorrect to assume that Ozersky's views are consistent with conservative values?

JOHN UPDIKE
The Mystery of Mickey Mouse

In this highly entertaining essay, John Updike takes a close look at "the most persistent and pervasive figment of American popular culture in this century"—Mickey Mouse. Demonstrating his noted powers of observation, Updike traces the evolution of Mickey's career and the way it mirrors the profound changes in American social history.

1. What are the most noticeable changes in the early years of Mickey's development? Of what importance were those changes? What was the effect of Disney's alterations and revisions of Mickey's person and character?
2. Why does Updike consider Mickey's connections with African-Americans? How do these connections contribute to your understanding of Mickey? Do you think Updike's characterization is accurate? Or do you see it as far-fetched?
3. How would Updike define the differences between "star" and "icon"? How does one become the other? Do you agree that Mickey has acquired icon status?
4. What problems does Mickey face in the 1990s? Why is Updike optimistic about Mickey's staying power?

ROBERT HUGHES
The Fraying of America

In this trenchant analysis of American culture in the 1990s, the famed art historian Robert Hughes takes on the increasing prevalence of multiculturalism and political correctness in our schools and institutions. Hughes fears that these fashionable trends are leading Americans down the path of serious fragmentation and divisiveness. The essay is passionate and provocative and should lead to heated discussion.

1. If, according to Hughes, America has always been a pluralistic and heterogeneous society, then why is the current emphasis on multiculturalism threatening? What is the basis of America's cohesion in the past?
2. Why have the arts—painting, literature, music, etc.—recently become a battleground for political views? Why does Hughes find this unhealthy? Do you think the politicization of art is intrinsically a bad thing? How might you argue against Hughes's point of view in this matter?
3. How does Hughes's attitude toward the literary canon compare with the views of Lillian Robinson and Sidney Hook? With which writer is Hughes in more agreement?
4. As Hughes puts it, "the word self-esteem has become one of the obstructive shibboleths of education." Why do the advocates of multiculturalism promote "self-esteem" as an educational value? Why is Hughes resistant to this value? What does he think an emphasis on self-esteem leaves out of education?

BEST-SELLERS

HARRIET BEECHER STOWE
Uncle Tom's Cabin

1. How does Stowe create for the reader a sense of slavery as an economic system? What are the levels of transaction that keep that system functioning? How is the audience Stowe imagines for her novel typified by the white tourists on the river boat?
2. "The most dreadful part of slavery, to my mind, is its outrages on the feelings and affections,—the separation of families, for example," says one white woman on the river boat. How is this particular outrage dramatized in the chapter? What standards of domestic conduct does Stowe feel should be maintained by blacks and whites?
3. Discuss the connection between Stowe's political ideology and her strong commitment to the family structure.

P. T. BARNUM
Early Life

The career of P. T. Barnum may be viewed as a quintessential American success story. Since your students are probably familiar with other narratives of this kind, ask them what features are common to such stories. More advanced students might look at some contemporary examples of this genre and examine how it has changed in the light of changing American values.

1. How useful is the term "autobiography" for describing Barnum's account of his early life? What kinds of facts does Barnum provide about this period of his life? What kinds of facts might he want to exclude? In what ways do you suspect the events of his later life have shaped the narrative of his early years?
2. Consider whether Barnum's narrative explicitly links a propensity for mischief with the successful accumulation of material goods? In what ways could the account be said to do so implicitly? Identify passages in which such links are made directly or indirectly. What is the author's attitude toward his childhood misdeeds?
3. Why does Barnum include the anecdote about the church stove? How might the story be reconciled with the rest of Barnum's narrative since it seems to have little directly to do with Barnum himself?

ERNEST LAURENCE THAYER
Casey at the Bat

The Thayer poem can be a good way to lighten things up if you have been studying more serious material for some time; it also provides an accessible and amusing way of discussing narration and diction. Note the efficiency with which the story opens, the building of mood, and the omission of climactic action—all characteristics of ballad tradition. Note, too, the disparity between the diction and the action—a device that goes back to Fielding and Ben Jonson and Chaucer.

1. What is the tone of phrases such as "deep despair" and "that hope which springs eternal" in stanza 2? What other phrases in the stanza lead you to suspect that they should be taken with a grain of salt? How, in other words, does the choice of diction here contribute to the humor? Point out three or four other stanzas where the odd mixture of levels of diction creates a similar effect.
2. Notice where the story starts. How does Thayer's account differ from that of a sportswriter in this respect? Why does he start his account in the ninth inning, neglecting to tell us how and when the runs have been scored?
3. How many stanzas does Thayer take to go from Blake's double to Casey's first strike? What is the effect of this buildup? Do the first two strikes seem to have any significant effect on Casey?
4. What happens to the tense of the verb in the next-to-last stanza? What is the effect of the tense here? What is the effect of the three "and now" phrases in the stanza? What major fact does the narrative omit? Why, given the buildup in the next-to-last stanza, is the omission so effective? Suppose that Thayer had said at this point that Casey missed the ball. What narrative problems might that have entailed? Why, instead, does he switch the scene abruptly away from the ballpark? How does his doing so make the last line more effective?
5. What is the effect of the rhyme here? In class, spend a few minutes writing a prose version of one of the stanzas (have a few people do each stanza). Read the version you have come up with. How does the absence of rhyme make the piece less funny?
6. After watching a game or reading an account of one in the paper, try writing your own short ver-

sion of "Casey at the Bat." Use the principles of narrative that you have observed Thayer using here, and try to vary your diction so that it is at odds with your subject.

7. Take some ordinary event—an evening out with friends, a drive in the country—and try writing an account of it in which your language is puffed up beyond what the event merits.

EDGAR RICE BURROUGHS
Tarzan of the Apes

1. What is appealing about the idea of a human being raised from infancy by animals? What elements of fantasy life does Burroughs capitalize on by creating such a figure? What advantages does this give Tarzan in both the human and the nonhuman worlds he inhabits?
2. Note the similes Burroughs uses to describe Tarzan. What kind of man does the totality of those similes create? In what sense is Burroughs writing a story of heredity and environment? How does Tarzan embody the best of both worlds? Explain. Compare his fictional attributes to those of other heroes of American best-sellers—Mike Hammer of *I, the Jury,* for example.
3. Examine closely the language Burroughts uses to describe the first encounter between Tarzan and Jane. Why is that encounter more explicitly sexual than the rest of their jungle dalliance? Compare the language Burroughs uses to describe that first sexual encounter with the language he uses to describe the battle between Tarzan and Terkoz. Comment on the similarities of those descriptions and the effect they have on a reader.

Additional Writing Exercise: A college English instructor wrote the words "Woman without her man is a savage" on the blackboard and directed his students to punctuate it correctly.

The males wrote: "Woman, without her man, is a savage." The females wrote: "Woman! Without her, man is a savage." Consider the responses of both the males and the females. In a well-developed essay, (1) discuss the differences in the viewpoints expressed, and (2) relate those differences to the larger question of male/female roles.

DALE CARNEGIE
How to Win Friends and Influence People

1. What is Carnegie's fundamental point? Describe as precisely as you can the nature of his argument. What is his basic mode of persuasion? How does he use quotations and anecdotes to support his "case"? Based on the examples he chooses, what would you say Carnegie's own "politics" are?
2. What kind of person do you think Carnegie envisions for his prose? How does this influence his diction, figurative language, and sentence structure? How closely does he identify himself with this audience? How does Carnegie characteristically sound? Does his tone remind you of, for example, a cynic? an "average" citizen? a preacher? a historian? Explain. Does his voice sound more appropriate to a conversation or to a lecture? What assumptions does Carnegie seem to make about the intelligence of his reader?

WILFRED FUNK AND NORMAN LEWIS
Thirty Days to a More Powerful Vocabulary

1. What type of person do Funk and Lweis imagine their reader to be? What social, economic, or educational level is this reader expected to have attained? What does the word *boss* in the opening sentence suggest about the kind of person the writers want to reach? Do their examples suggest anything specific about their imagined audience?
2. Point to uses of language and strategies in this preface that seem to come from advertising. How, for example, is scientific documentation used?
3. Do you agree that "the extent of your vocabulary indicates the degree of your intelligence"? Discuss this assumption. What do you think Funk and Lewis mean by *vocabulary?* What kind of words do they have in mind for their reader to learn? Do you think a reader will be informed about words like *love, hate, kindness, beauty, food?* Do words like these have anything to do with what they call "brain power"? Explain.
4. Assuming their course of vocabulary study is as much "fun" and is as "easy" as Funk and Lewis say it is, then how could a reader feel certain that the people he or she may be competing with for coveted "executive positions" will not themselves be acquiring the same verbal skills in the next thirty days? Explain.

OGDEN NASH
Kindly Unhitch That Star, Buddy

Nash's piece should be a good introduction to poetry. It is certainly not intimidating, so it should allow you to discuss the effects of rhyme and rhythm without having it sound like mumbo-jumbo. Get the class to notice the effects of the feminine rhymes and the long, loose lines. Once you do so, they should be able to figure out why the last line is so effective.

Since the obsession with success practically defines our national character, you may want to teach the poem with any number of other pieces. "Casey at the Bat," for example, treats the subject of failure, and many ads such as that for Edsel help to define what Americans have thought success is.

1. Consider the first two lines of the poem. What does the simile in the second line suggest Nash thinks of our aspirations to succeed? What is the effect here of rhyming "failure" with "azalea"? How does the rhyme help to establish Nash's tone? Point to other rhymes in the poem that seem to you to have a similar effect.
2. Notice that lines 22–24 and lines 25–28 are in effect just two lines, since they rhyme with each other. Does the expectation of a rhyme at the end of line 28 make you want to read the lines more quickly or more slowly? Why, given the subject of lines 25–28, is this effect appropriate? How does it create a contrast with the short last line of the poem?
3. What do you think Nash means when he says that half the people say no and half yes in order to succeed? Do you agree with him that neither method will guarantee success? Do you agree that if everyone were equally successful, people would still be trying to outdo each other?

MICKEY SPILLANE
I, the Jury

1. What is Hammer's attitude toward the law and its official enforcers? What can he do, for example, that Pat Chambers can't do? What popular attitudes toward law and order in America is Spillane appealing to? Explain. How does Hammer compare to other heroes of best-selling novels—say, Don Corleone of *The Godfather?*
2. Imagine someone that Hammer could not talk tough to and get away with it. Would that person necessarily be physically tougher? Explain. Would Spillane include a person like that in the novel? What would be the compositional risk of doing so?
3. What range of slang does Hammer know? How does he use it with people? Discuss the effectiveness of his curses, threats, and gibes. In what sense is Hammer's voice another of his weapons?

GRACE METALIOUS
Peyton Place

1. What is the effect of rendering the community of Peyton Place through Michael Rossi's eyes? What differences between Rossi and the community does Metalious want to emphasize? How does she establish those differences? Whose side is she on? How can you tell?
2. Examine Metalious's description of Rossi. How does this description compare with those of other heroes of best-sellers, Mike Hammer and Tarzan, for example? What advantages does Rossi have in the novel? Would these also be advantages in real life? Explain.

VANCE PACKARD
The Hidden Persuaders

1. What facts and figures in his report does Packard feel will surprise people? Do you find his information surprising or alarming? Explain. Why would people who shop regularly not be aware of the manipulations surrounding them? What is it that they are not paying attention to? Would the kind of mental obliviousness Packard notes in his essay carry over into other areas of life?
2. The connotations of *impulsive* range from a moral irresponsibility to a charming spontaneity. Can you think of a context for each of these meanings? How do supermarket engineers and advertising agencies encourage people to think favorably of impulsive behavior? Find advertisements that encourage and imaginatively reward impulsive behavior (e.g., airlines that want you to fly now, pay later). How is the impulsiveness made appealing? Do people like to be thought of as impulsive? If so, why? Explain how advertising can reinforce an audience's collective self-image.

MARIO PUZO
The Godfather

1. Describe as precisely as you can the code of behavior each member of a "family" is expected to abide by. How, specifically, is someone rewarded for loyalty to this code? What personal standards of behavior does Don Corleone set up for himself? How are these principles tested? By whom?
2. Characterize the way Don Corleone speaks. The narrator tells us, "The old man hated unnecessary flourishes in business matters." Show how this concern is reflected in the Don's particular word choices and his general tone of voice.
3. How much attention is paid to manners in this passage? Evaluate, for example, the formal introductions and initial verbal exchanges between Don Corleone and Virgil "the Turk" Sollozo. How does the prose rhythm at the moments when Sollozo is speaking or when the narrator is talking

about him reflect the tension between him and the Don? Everything seems to be treated as a business venture. Why is all of this lawlessness given a kind of dignity by Puzo?

4. Michael Corleone is described as being "as closemouthed as his father." How is this trait dramatized in Michael's telephone "conversation" with Hagen? How does the term "closemouthed" also serve as a metaphor to characterize Puzo's style when either Don Corleone or Michael is speaking?

ALEX HALEY
Roots

Haley's narrative reveals how point of view contributes to a story's effect. Kunta learns about slavery and the white man by talking to his father and grandmother, so that one discovers with him the fears that pervaded the world of black Africans. By using Kunta's point of view, Haley never has to come out and *say* that slavery was oppressive, that it created a terror at the periphery of every village, every mind.

1. Whose point of view are we closest to in this selection? Why do you think Alex Haley has told the story from his point of view, rather than from that of, say, Omoro? What are the advantages of having Kunta know so little about slavery? How does it help us to understand what it might have been like for an African to discover that the institution of slavery existed?
2. Did slavery exist in the African culture that Haley writes of here? In what ways was a slave in that culture treated differently from one sold to the white men? What do Kunta and Lamin learn from Nyo Boto's story? What do you think each of them is thinking of as they leave her?
3. Who are the toubob? Why is Kunta so curious about them? How do the people in Kunta's culture regard them? Why hasn't Omoro told his sons more about them? What is the effect on us of discovering through Kunta's eyes who the toubob are and what they do? As he learns more about the toubob, do they seem more or less terrifying? Why is it so effective that even Omoro doesn't know what happens to the stolen people?
4. Write a narrative in which you show how a child comes to learn some unpleasant truth about the world: about death, about divorce, about crime. Try to help your reader see through the child's eyes, to discover through the child's questions and observations, how one first attempts to understand such truths. You may want to think back to your own childhood.

BENJAMIN SPOCK
The Common Sense Book of Baby Care

1. How does Spock achieve a tone of "common sense"? Consider his use of illustrations and anecdotes. In what ways do these appeal to the reader's common sense?
2. Look at the sentences that actually contain advice. How do Spock's suggestions differ in tone from those of Dr. John B. Watson, cited in the headnote? How does Spock avoid directly telling the parents what to do? Why?
3. Compare Spock's style of advising with the style of Stephen King ("Magazines"). In what ways do their relations to their readers differ? Which one sounds most like an "expert"? Explain.

RON KOVIC
Born on the Fourth of July [*Wounded*]

Most of your students will be too young to remember very much about the Vietnam conflict or its aftermath. It might be useful to find out what they do know and how they learned about the war. Through what cultural materials (books, movies, music, stories by veterans, etc.) has their knowledge of the war been shaped? How has their reading of Kovic's account influenced their understanding?

1. Why does Kovic begin his autobiography with an account of his being wounded? Why does he begin that account after he has been hit by enemy fire? How would the literary effect of his opening been altered by an account of his activities moments before being shot?
2. Does Kovic attempt to portray himself as a war hero? Consider the episode in which he is awarded the Purple Heart. Why does he include this episode? What effect is achieved by including it?
3. Ron Kovic's narrative is autobiography, though at points it resembles fictional narrative. Examine closely those places in the story where Kovic seems to be using devices commonly found in fiction. Ask your class to consider whether they think Kovic is purposely using such devices.
4. Many of your students may already have seen the Oliver Stone movie based on Kovic's book. You might consider viewing the film together and making note of how the film alters, if at all, the narrative materials offered by the book.

WILLIAM LEAST HEAT MOON
Blue Highways

1. How does your sense of the author change in the course of this passage? Is his relation to the waitress at the beginning different from his relation to characters later in the piece? How are these expressed?
2. As the headnote reports, Moon thinks of writing as a process of discovery. What does he discover in this essay, apart from the town of Nameless? Is Nameless one of the places "where time and men and deeds" connect? Explain.
3. Compare this author's techniques for conducting interviews with those of Bob Greene. Which writer renders his own character most fully? Rewrite one of the essays by those writers as Moon might. What opportunities for characterization does this open up?
4. Imagine that Moon visited your town on his journey. Whom would he have met? What would he have discovered? Write up a record of this visit, in imitation of this essay.

LETITIA BALDRIGE
Letitia Baldrige's Complete Guide to Executive Manners [*A Woman Traveling Alone*]

Perhaps some of the women in your class have been in situations in which they felt vulnerable while traveling alone. Perhaps some of the men in your class have approached women traveling alone. Ask these students to consider their actions and reactions in these situations. At the time of their experience, did they feel there were rules of conduct that governed their actions? Why does the situation examined by Baldrige have repercussions that go beyond issues of rudeness or civility?

1. Compare Baldrige's advice with Susan Jacoby's "Unfair Game." Does Jacoby seem to follow any of the rules of conduct set forth by Baldrige? Do you feel that Baldrige would approve of Jacoby's attitude in this situation? Would she approve of her actions?
2. What kinds of assumptions about interactions between men and women inform both selections? How does Baldrige differ from Jacoby in her attitude toward men's advances? What might account for the difference?

GARRISON KEILLOR
Lake Wobegon Days

1. Characterize the nature of Keillor's humor in this excerpt from *Lake Wobegon Days*. What are the distinguishing features of Keillor's sense of humor?
2. Whom does Keillor seem to imagine as the audience for his fiction? In what specific ways does Keillor seem to play with his readers' expectations? with his sense of shared experience with them?
3. Locate the voice of the narrator in this selection. How would you describe the sound of the narrator's voice? What attitude does the narrator seem to reveal toward the characters in this story?

BARRY LOPEZ
Arctic Dreams

1. How does Lopez's first paragraph contribute to establishing an effective relationship between him and his readers? Based on this paragraph, what assumptions about his readers does Lopez reveal? What opinion, for example, does he hold of their intelligence? What specific values does he assume or expect his audience to hold?
2. Lopez seems to focus early in this selection from *Arctic Dreams* on the "radical changes . . . made in the native way of life" by both the advent of technology and, more specifically, the discovery of oil in Alaska. What exactly are these changes, and how have they affected the native way of life?
3. Lopez talks of the native Alaskans' penchant for making "so few generalized or abstract statements," focusing instead "on the practical, the specific, the concrete." Follow through on this point. Identify as many examples as possible of this native preference for the concrete and specific. Apply this phrase to Lopez's own writing. How accurate a characterization is it of his own intellectual inclinations?
4. Read Jack London's story "To Build a Fire" ("Classics"). How accurate and appropriate a commentary on the Arctic landscape do you think London would judge the following line from Lopez's story to be: "I had the feeling, sometimes, that nothing was hidden"? How might Lopez's point that we all need to promote the "preservation of this capacity to adapt" serve as a commentary on the theme and action of London's story? Compare Lopez's account of the adventures of Comock with London's story of another effort to survive in the Arctic. What similarities do you find in these two very different stories? In what specific ways might Lopez's assertion that Arctic people "lived resolutely in the heart of every moment they found themselves in, disastrous and sublime" also be applied to the character in London's story? In what

ways is this statement an inappropriate gloss on that story?

5. Lopez observes, "A fundamental difference between our culture and Eskimo culture, which can be felt even today in certain situations, is that we have irrevocably separated ourselves from the world that animals occupy." What are the specific differences Lopez identifies between our culture and Eskimo culture? Which does he prefer? Why? Explain how this quotation might serve as a commentary on London's story.
6. Lopez admires Eskimos for being "resilient, practical, and enthusiastic." In what specific ways does he follow up on each of these points? How does Lopez justify his assertion that "they are a good people to know"?

ALLAN BLOOM
The Closing of the American Mind [*Music*]

This essay may be compared productively to the scientific paper by Elizabeth F. Brown, M.D. and William R. Hendee, Ph.D. entitled "Adolescents and Their Music: Insights Into the Health of Adolescents." Ask your students to consider whether any of the dangers enumerated by Allan Bloom in his essay are substantiated by medical or psychological findings. If Bloom's conclusions cannot be verified scientifically in what sense can they be said to have validity?

1. Encourage your students to create their own arguments for or against rock music. Discuss with them the kinds of elements that make for a persuasive argument. Whether or not they agree with Bloom they should examine closely the way he constructs his appeal.
2. Ask your students to consider the role of rock music in their own lives? About how much time do they spend in an average day listening to this music? Is it merely a form of entertainment to them or does it exert a more profound effect on them? How can such an effect be measured?
3. While Bloom believes that rock music has no cultural value, your students might not only disagree but they may also be able to provide examples of songs that exert a positive influence on our culture. Let them offer some suggestions of lyrics to be examined closely in class for their social and cultural value.

AMY TAN
The Joy Luck Club [*Two Kinds*]

Many of us have been subject to a parent's disappointment in our failure to meet expectations. Your students may recall times in their own lives when they fell short of parental expectations. How did they attempt to come to terms with their parent's dissatisfaction? Placed in this context, Tan's story should be easier to discuss in class.

1. Consider with your students how the daughter's narrative helps her to forge her own identity. How does this occur? Does the narrator seem to have a stronger presence at the end than at the beginning of the story?
2. To what extent do the racial issues presented in the story complicate the already complex relationship between mother and daughter. How does the protagonist's ethnic background help to shape her mother's expectation for her?

SUSAN FALUDI
Backlash, the Undeclared War Against American Women [*Blame It on Feminism*]

In one of the most controversial bestsellers of 1991–92, journalist Susan Faludi argues that the apparent gains of the feminist movement are in serious danger of being overturned. Though she examines numerous reasons for this backlash, she especially singles out the media for its irresponsible representations of women and feminist goals.

1. Why does Faludi contend that problems facing women today derive from the push toward equality that was the first goal of feminist politics in the 60s?
2. What phenomena does Faludi cite as proof for her contention that equality for women is an illusion? What real gains does she believe the feminist movement has made since it began in the 1960s? To what extent are those gains, i.e., reproductive rights, equal pay, etc. currently jeopardized?
3. Why does Faludi refer in her title to an "undeclared war against American Women?" Does military terminology recur throughout her essay? What other examples can you find? Do you think she intends her reader to accept the idea of the "war" metaphorically or literally? How important is this term to her argument?

CLASSICS

CHRISTOPHER COLUMBUS
from Michel de Cuneo's Letter on Columbus' Second Voyage

1. How does de Cuneo characterize the natives that the voyagers meet? How does he distinguish among different native groups? What about his description seems factual, and what stereotypical? Why did de Cuneo consider the last-mentioned natives to be "like brothers"?
2. To whom do you think this letter was addressed? What details give away the receiver's position and relation to de Cuneo? How does the intimacy of the letter form provide insight into Columbus' voyages that another form might not?
3. Consider de Cuneo's anecdote about the native woman he encounters on the boat. What does his recollection reveal about his attitudes toward natives, and toward women?

TOM WOLFE
Columbus and the Moon

1. From the first sentence of this essay, Wolfe attempts to demystify the conquests of both Columbus and NASA. How do his word choice and sentence structure reinforce the banal tone of his description? What does Wolfe hope to accomplish by speaking of these explorers in these mundane terms? Does he succeed in "humanizing" his subjects?
2. Read the excerpt from Michel de Cuneo's letter (see Classics) in light of Wolfe's arguments. Can you find evidence for Wolfe's claims in de Cuneo's words? How does each writer use detail to reveal the essence of these voyages?
3. In his penultimate paragraph, Wolfe discusses Columbus' reputation. He calls the voyager "a man with a supernatural sense of destiny, whose true glory is to plunge into the unknown. . . ." Recently, Native Americans and other minority groups have challenged this image of Columbus. What does the current controversy over Columbus' image reflect, in terms of our own historical moment and in relation to the facts of Columbus' life?

THOMAS JEFFERSON
The Declaration of Independence

1. Summarize Jefferson's reasons for America's separation from England in modern terms. What underlying conceptions of citizens' rights are communicated through his complaints? (Note: It might be useful to look at the Bill of Rights in relation to this question.) How reasonable does each of his points strike you? If you haven't thoroughly read this document before, were the arguments over issues you expected to see discussed in this Declaration?
2. Only a small portion of Jefferson's document speaks to universal issues; most of it is a list of particular grievances against the King. What about this text, besides its historical significance, remains fresh in Americans' minds? What does Jefferson say that resonates in the America of the late 20th century?

NATHANIEL HAWTHORNE
My Kinsman, Major Molineux

1. Often, Nathaniel Hawthorne's stories operate like puzzles, with seemingly odd situations slowly becoming clearer to an unknowing protagonist. How is the puzzle of Major Molineux constructed within this tale? How does Hawthorne use Robin's various encounters with the townspeople to build suspense? What insight has Robin gained at the end of the story?
2. The townspeople here represent Hawthorne's view of "we, the people" who sought freedom from Britain in the American Revolution. He offers a less-than-flattering portrait of this milieu. What different aspects of American town life do the various characters represent? How does the clergyman fit into this scheme? Why do you think the clergyman refuses to show Robin to the ferry at the tale's conclusion?
3. As Robin sits and waits to spy his kinsman, he drifts into a reverie on his home and family. How does this scene work in contrast to the rest of the story? Is it written differently? What sense does this contrast add to the tale?

4. Reread the Declaration of Independence (see Classics) and speculate on the reason for Major Molineux's tar-and-feathering. What complaints may the townspeople have against the major? What is Hawthorne's opinion of the town's action against the old gentleman?

FREDERICK DOUGLASS
from Narrative of the Life of Frederick Douglass [*How a Slave Was Made a Man*]

1. Introducing this story, Douglass offers one of the most famous lines from his narrative: "You have seen how a man was made a slave; you shall see how a slave was made a man." How does he fulfill this statement in the anecdote that follows? What qualities, according to Douglass, distinguish slave from man? What actions demonstrate those qualities?
2. What significance does Douglass give his encounter with Sandy, and his taking up of the root? Does Douglass believe in the root's magic powers? Is there a tacit recognition of the root's effect on his mental state? Can you think of other examples in which superstition works to empower people? to weaken them?
3. Douglass describes the threat of his master as a claim that the man would "get hold of him" if he didn't behave. This phrase is a rich metaphor, speaking of more than simple violence. What of Douglass does the master have hold of? How does Douglass "get hold of" Mr. Covey? How does physical violence relate to mental and spiritual oppression in the master-slave relationship, as seen in this passage?

HENRY DAVID THOREAU
Walden

1. Thoreau asserts that he wants to live "Spartan-like." What details of his autobiographical account reinforce this self-image? Does the personality we find in the prose style confirm the Spartan image? Explain.
2. What demands does Thoreau's prose style and allusiveness make on readers? How do these demands reinforce his contempt for and distrust of newspaper writing? What, in particular, do newspapers miss in their attempts to cover people and events? What does Thoreau presumably believe he does *not* miss in his writing?
3. What does Thoreau gain in the last paragraph by imaginatively divesting himself of his intellect? What is the effect of the animal imagery? What has this intellectual divestment to do with Thoreau's sense of reality? Compare the diction, imagery, and intellectual attitudes in this passage from *Walden* with Ike McCaslin's initiation into the wilderness in Faulkner's *The Bear*.

WALT WHITMAN
I Hear America Singing

1. What vision of American experience emerges from reading this poem? On whom does Whitman focus his attention in this poem? What does Whitman admire most about them? What do these people have in common? In what ways are they different? Does Whitman seem to prefer one or more over the others he mentions?
2. What would you say was the theme of this poem? How well—and in what specific ways—does Whitman articulate this theme? What significance does Whitman assign to "singing"? What significance, if any, do you attach to the frequent repetition of the word "as" in the poem?
3. Reread the final three lines in the poem, beginning with "Each singing what belongs to him or her and to none else." How do these lines reinforce the point(s) Whitman makes throughout the poem? If you were invited to revise this poem, would you extend it—perhaps to other, related examples? change it in some important way? something else? Explain. Comment on the overall effectiveness of the poem. What response(s) did the poem elicit from you?

WALT WHITMAN
One's-Self I Sing

1. Examine carefully the title of the poem. What do you make of the juxtaposition of the pronouns "One" and "I" in the same line? What does this juxtaposition suggest about Whitman's overall subject in this poem? What function does the word "Yet" serve in line 2? What paradox does Whitman underscore in the first stanza? How does Whitman extend that paradox in the second stanza?
2. What does the word "Form" refer to in line 4? How does he develop the concept of that word in the lines that follow? How would you characterize Whitman's vision of life in this poem? Point to specific words and phrases to verify your response.
3. This poem is a shorter version of the "Inscription" printed on the frontispiece of the 1867 edition of *Leaves of Grass*. The poem was also reprinted in the "Sands at Seventy" group under the title "Small the Theme of My Chant." Find these two earlier versions of the poem and compare and

contrast them with the version you have before you. Prepare a list of the changes that Whitman made as he moved from one version to the next. With respect to the poem's overall theme and its stylistic effectiveness, what significance can you infer from each of the changes he made?

WALT WHITMAN
A Noiseless Patient Spider

1. Find examples of assonance and alliteration in the first stanza of the poem. How do these complement the image of the spider and its activity?
2. Catalogue the verb forms in the poem. Note the shift from the past tense and past participles to the present tense, present participles, and the future. How might this pattern determine the poem's meaning?
3. Where—and how—does Whitman make any explicit comparisons between the two stanzas, or does he simply juxtapose them? What relation does he imply between his soul and the spider? How would the effect of the poem be changed if the sixth line read "And you O my soul where you stand, resemble the spider . . ."?

HARRIET JACOBS
The Loophole of Retreat

1. To what does the title of this passage, "The Loophole of Retreat," refer? What power does Jacobs gain by drilling the holes in the wall? In what way does this cause her to triumph over Dr. Flint, despite her confinement?
2. When she finds the gimlet, Jacobs says, she is "as rejoiced as Robinson Crusoe." Do you think the comparison to the Defoe character makes sense? What is Jacobs able to make of her tiny attic world? Does she master it, the way Crusoe masters his island?
3. Compare this passage to the excerpt from Frederick Douglass' slave narrative (see Classics). These two writers underwent very different, severe tests during their enslavement. Yet parallels can be drawn between their stories. In what way does Jacobs discover "how a slave is made a woman?" Douglass felt that his resolve to fight back renewed his spirit; what, if anything, renews Jacobs' spirit? How are the differences in their stories connected to their respective genders?

EMILY DICKINSON
After Great Pain

1. What Biblical reference might Dickinson be making with the line "a Wooden way"? How does she connect images of death with references to inanimate objects to paint a portrait of sorrowful numbness?
2. The final image in this poem suggests a state of frostbite. Compare Dickinson's poem with Jack London's story "To Build a Fire" (see Classics). Do these texts refer to a similar process? How do they differ?

EMILY DICKINSON
One Need not Be a Chamber

1. Who is the "cooler host" to which Dickinson refers in line 8? How many different metaphors does she use to describe the self? How do these metaphors relate? Why does she say "a self" and not simply "one's self" in line 11?
2. Read this poem in connection with Charlotte Perkins Gilman's "The Yellow Wallpaper" (see Classics). Both describe a version of madness. How are the process of mental unraveling characterized in each text? What aspects of madness are addressed in Gilman's text, that are not addressed here? What is the source of the mental trouble in this poem?

EMILY DICKINSON
I Felt a Cleaving in My Mind

1. Examine the order of the phrases that begin the second stanza. How does Dickinson's language mimic the mental process she describes? Can you find examples of this structural move in her two other poems included here?
2. What is the effect of the poem's concluding image? Did it strike you as out of place? Does it enact the message of the first stanza? Do you think another image would have been more appropriate?

MARK TWAIN
Old Times on the Mississippi

1. Discuss why Twain is so attracted to the life of steamboatmen. What qualities do they display? What experiences do they have that make them so appealing?
2. To what extent is the steamboatman's appeal based on speech? Go through the selection, and highlight Twain's references to the ways people talk. Comment on the overall significance of these references.
3. Twain criticizes the night watchman for his sentimentality. In what ways is the man sentimental? To what extent is his sentimentality a feature of his

language? Does Twain himself as a storyteller indulge in sentimentality? Explain.

MARK TWAIN
How to Tell a Story

1. According to Twain, why is the humorous story better than the comic one? What, essentially, is the difference? In what sense is the humorous story dependent upon a *persona,* a character who is in dramatic relation to the funny story and is not merely someone who is telling it?
2. How do humorous stories differ from comic or witty ones in their assumptions about an audience? In what way does the story Twain uses for his demonstration model depend for its effect upon an audience that is literally present? Would his story be a funny one if no one were present? How would a joke, in Twain's terms, differ from this?
3. Of what importance is the "pause" to the art of telling in general? Why is it so difficult to get right? What does Twain's insistence on the pause tell us about his sense of language?

CHARLOTTE PERKINS GILMAN
The Yellow Wallpaper

1. When "The Yellow Wallpaper" was "rediscovered" by literary critics in recent decades, the story was hailed as a feminist narrative. How does Gilman's story of a woman's descent into madness reflect feminist ideas and concerns? In what ways does it illustrate some of the points Vivian Gornick makes in "The Next Great Moment of History is Ours" (see Press)?
2. Gilman plays with the first person perspective, using the narrator's distorted vision to conceal her story's "punchline" until the last page. At what point did you begin to suspect that something might be "wrong" with the protagonist? How does the writing style change later in the story to convey the narrator's deteriorating mental state?
3. What is the effect of setting this story at a vacation home? How does Gilman contrast the theme of the summer idyll with her heroine's distress? How is the narrator's confinement similar to Harriet Jacobs' in "The Loophole of Retreat?" Which woman retains stronger agency?

KATE CHOPIN
The Dream of an Hour

1. The impact of Kate Chopin's "The Dream of an Hour" depends on the shock of recognition. For example, as soon as Mrs. Mallard learns of the reported death of her husband, she realizes that the circumstances of her life have suddenly changed greatly. But along with this recognition does she also suddenly realize a great deal more about herself? Explain. Kate Chopin uses setting to tell us more about Mrs. Mallard. After retreating to the privacy of her room to grieve, Mrs. Mallard sinks in a "comfortable, roomy arm-chair." How does what Mrs. Mallard notices in her immediate environment reinforce her new sense of self-awareness? Explain.
2. Consider the title of this story. Is it meant to be taken literally? What, specifically, is Mrs. Mallard's "Dream"? What does the word "Hour" in the title refer to? How does the knowledge that Chopin once changed the title to "The Story of an Hour" affect your response to it? Explain.
3. Comment on the final phrase of the story—"joy that kills." How do you think this phrase should be read? What other possible readings could this phrase lend itself to? What, exactly, is the point of this story? What does this story tell us about self-identity and intimate relationships?
4. Compare Chopin's attitudes toward female identity with those expressed by Vivian Gornick in "The Next Great Moment in History Is Theirs" (see "Press").

STEPHEN CRANE
The Open Boat

1. Compare "The Open Boat" with Crane's newspaper account of the sinking of the *Commodore* in "Press." What literary interest has he taken in this experience? Which incidents of the newspaper account does he drop; which does he expand in his reworking of the tale? Comment, for example, on the effectiveness of Crane's opening his story after the shipwreck. What does he gain or lose with this strategy? Why is Crane's story broken up into three sections? What structural unity is discernible in each section? Among the three? Which features of his journalistic prose style does he seem most intent on retaining for his short story? Why? Discuss the effect of such similes as "many a man ought to have a bathtub larger than the boat which here rode upon the sea," "like carpets on a line in a gale," or "it is easier to steal eggs from under a hen."
2. What aspects of the men's language is Crane most interested in? Of what interest to him, for example, is the men's swearing? How does their speech and silence indicate a "subtle brotherhood of men"? What is the compositional reason for the correspondent's remembering the popular poem? In

what ways are the men intimate with each other without saying so? How is their speech itself given physical dimension?

3. Compare Crane's initial description of the waves to the way he characterizes them as the survivors face the surf. An audience begins to gather to witness their attempts to reach the shore. How does Crane characterize these people? Are there subsequent moments when the survivors become another kind of audience? Explain. Is there any sense of competition between these two groups? Explain.

JACK LONDON
To Build a Fire

1. What mood does London create in the opening paragraph of his story? What stylistic devices does he use to reinforce this mood? How does the mood intensify or change as the story develops? What contrast does London establish in the second paragraph? How does he sustain that contrast throughout the story?
2. What does London tell us about the main character that immediately intensifies the drama? How would you characterize the intellectual disposition of the main character? Is he, for example, more likely to engage in imaginative reverie or to restrict himself to the literal aspects of an experience? something else? Explain.
3. How does London dramatize the extent of the cold in this Arctic scene? What effect does the cold have on the "big native husky" that accompanies the man? What contrast does London establish between the man and the dog?
4. London sees attention to detail as a means to heighten the dramatic effects of his story. One example is his mentioning that the man chews tobacco. How does London's use of this detail intensify the effects of the story's setting? Find other, comparable examples of London's use of details, and identify the effects produced by their use in the story.
5. What narrative devices does London use to accelerate the pace of the action in this story? What strategies does he use to intensify the suspense? What is the role of "inherited knowledge" in the story?
6. London reports that "The man was shocked" after the fire he built was "blotted out" by the avalanchelike crush of snow falling from a tree. How does London increase the drama of the moments that follow? Are the man's actions that follow an expression of shock? something else? What dramatic function does the dog serve in this scene?
7. What devices does London use to quicken the pace of his narrative? Look carefully, for example, at the length and structure of his sentences. How do these factors reinforce the effects he tries to create? How might the phrase "the moment of controlled despair" serve as a summary of the man's response to his predicament?
8. Near the end of the story, London's narrator tells us that the man "entertained . . . the conception of meeting death with dignity." To what extent and in what ways is this conception consistent with his behavior? his other thoughts?
9. Comment on the final sentence in the story. How does London encourage his readers to respond to this line?

ROBERT FROST
Design

1. How does the concept of design operate in this poem? Note that the poem is a sonnet, more particularly an Italian sonnet with an octave and sestet. Compare the tone of these two parts. Where—and how—does it change? How does the speaker answer the questions he poses in the sestet?
2. Look at the rhyme scheme. It is based on only three rhyming sounds (*-ite, -oth, -all*), which is remarkably few for a sonnet. How does the use of rhyme express Frost's notions of design?
3. Reread the final lines. How many meanings are there for *appall?* What is its etymology? How does it relate to the other imagery in the poem? What is the grammatical mood of the last line? How would the meaning of the line—and of the poem—be changed if it read "If design *governs* in a thing so small"?

ROBERT FROST
The Gift Outright

In this quietly patriotic poem, Frost says that Americans did not find a national identity until they let the land possess them. In other words, he upsets the assumption that the land is inert, something to be owned and mastered. In saying that if people are to have an identity they must be rooted in the land they live in, Frost comes surprisingly close to the American Indian sense of the relationship between man and nature that one finds in N. Scott Momaday's piece (see "Magazines"). You may also want to compare the poem to Robinson Jeffers's "Carmel Point," in which the environment so absorbs civilization that humankind becomes insignificant.

1. Read the poem aloud, listening for the "meaning

by sound.'' What sounds do you hear most frequently? How do the sounds in each section of the poem make the lines hold together, although there isn't any rhyme? What other technical features of the poem help it hold together? Is the rhythm, for example, mostly regular or irregular? What is the effect of this? Are the lines of about the same length? What does this contribute to one's sense of the poem?

2. What is the relationship between Americans and their land, according to Frost? What lines of the poem suggest what he thinks this relationship is? What does he mean, for example, when he says that we ''found our salvation in surrender''? What do you think Frost means by saying that we could not be ourselves, be Americans, until we let the land possess us? Does this attitude differ from what you think of as the traditional American attitude toward the land? How? How would N. Scott Momaday respond to this poem? What would Frost think of the American Indian's feelings about the land, as Momaday describes them?
3. What are the ''deeds'' of war to which Frost refers in line 13? How does his sense of this war differ from what you may have learned from history books? Why does he say we gave ourselves ''to the land vaguely realizing westward''? What does his wording tell us about his conception of the settling of the West?
4. Find all the terms in the poem related to ownership and giving. Note how Frost uses these in seemingly paradoxical ways. Are the paradoxes meaningful or mere contradictions? Explain whether it makes sense to say that in order to ''possess'' something one must give something away. What *is* the ''gift'' referred to in the title?
5. Find examples of grammatical balance and parallelism in the poem (for example, lines 6 and 7). How do these embody the meaning of the poem?
6. Compare Frost's ideas about the relation between citizen and country with those in Martin Luther King, Jr.'s speech below. How might King adopt the terminology of this poem to argue for civil rights?

ERNEST HEMINGWAY
Soldier's Home

1. How is Krebs characterized in the first few paragraphs of the story? The narrator calls him ''Krebs,'' not ''Harold Krebs'' or ''Harold.'' What effect does this have? What did Krebs like about being a soldier, according to these paragraphs? What is the significance of his having enlisted for duty and not having waited to be drafted?
2. How does the reader's sense of Krebs change in the scenes involving his family? How does his life at home differ from his life in the war? His family seems to treat him like a child. How does he behave like one?
3. After examining carefully Hemingway's diction, sentence structure, and paragraph structure, write an additional page of this story imitating its style. As Krebs watches his sister play baseball, for example, how would he feel? How, if at all, would he express his feelings?

WILLIAM CARLOS WILLIAMS
The Use of Force

In Williams's story a routine house call becomes a head-on collision between the will of the doctor and that of the young patient. The doctor wins the battle to look at her throat, but to do so he must reduce himself to the stubborn fury that defines the child. Williams never says what prompts the girl to be so bent on hiding the diphtheria, so you should raise the question to the class. What kind of fear, what sense of violation, does she feel?

1. Consider Williams's description of the child in the fourth paragraph. What words and phrases tell us his attitude toward her? Would he say the same things about her at the end of the piece? Is Williams's point of view, then, that of the doctor at this moment, or that of the writer giving an account of the incident some time later?
2. Why is the doctor irritated that the parents use the word ''hurt''? What does he think of the parents' knowledge of child psychology? of his own? Why does he admire the child and have contempt for her parents? Why does the admiration later turn to fury?
3. Why can't the child's parents force her jaws open? Aren't they strong enough? Does the doctor retain his sense of superiority over the parents throughout the story? Why not? In describing what happened to him, what point is Williams making? Have you ever been in a situation where you lost control in a similar way? Do you think that what happens to the doctor could happen to anyone?

E. B. WHITE
Once More to the Lake

1. White's essay has the quality of elegy; how does he evoke a state of mourning throughout? How does his repetition of key phrases further this effect? How does the essay's last line relate to this elegaic quality—is the sting of death that he feels the same, or different, from the melancholy

quality that he has established in the rest of the story?

2. In the middle of the essay, in the paragraph that begins, "Summertime, oh summertime," White shifts from the particulars of his own memory to a generalization about society and summer. What effect does this shift have on the whole of the essay? Does a similar move occur anywhere else in the text? How does White balance particulars and universals throughout his narrative?
3. White addresses the theme of change by talking about the outboard motors that have recently invaded the lake. How does he use this example to explore the differences between his childhood and his son's? What distinctions are made here that aren't made elsewhere in the essay? What does this passage tell us about White?

WILLIAM FAULKNER
The Bear

1. In a conversation about *The Bear* William Faulkner once made the following remark concerning the idea of the "hunt":

> The hunt was simply a symbol of pursuit. Most of anyone's life is a pursuit of something. That is, the only alternative to life is immobility, which is death. . . . And always to learn something of—not only to pursue but to overtake and then to have the compassion not to destroy, to catch, to touch, and then let go because then tomorrow you can pursue again. If you destroy it . . . then it's gone, it's finished. . . . The pursuit is the thing, not the reward, not the gain.

   How is Faulkner's conception of the "hunt" reflected in the style of the story? If we consider the act of writing itself as a hunt, a pursuit of something, an attempt to learn, what is the effect of a particular sentence like the following:

> It did not emerge, appear; it was just there, immobile, fixed in the green and windless noon's hot dappling, not as big as he had dreamed it but as big as he had expected, bigger, dimensionless against the dappled obscurity. . . .

   Where do you get by following such sentences through? Where, for example, does this sentence leave you? How is this particular sentence characteristic of the form of the story—its development, its moment of climax? How does the movement of this sentence resemble the movement of the selection as a whole?
2. How does the word *relinquishment* characterize what both Ike and the reader must learn? What does Ike have to relinquish before he can see the bear? What does each of these items represent? What must the reader give up? How does *relinquishment* describe the effects of Faulkner's style on his reader? What three things must Ike learn before he can see the bear? Are these terms also applicable to your experience of reading the story? Explain.
3. Read the first sentence of *The Bear*. What problems do you encounter? What, for example, does the phrase "this time" mean? What is the purpose of the decidedly abstract language early in the story? Comment on Faulkner's use of negatives. What does the use of negatives keep the reader from doing? What do you make of the repeated images of fluidity and "dissolving"?
4. How is nature depicted? From where does Faulkner get his figurative language to talk about nature? How is civilization characterized? How does Faulkner describe man's relation to the wilderness? Why do men go to nature? What happens to such factors as racial and social distinctions when men are in the wilderness?

Note: For an analysis of the stylistic demands of *The Bear,* see the introduction to "Classics."

RICHARD WRIGHT
Black Boy

1. Richard Wright presents himself to the reader as a writer of "history"—that is, he attempts to describe and interpret something important that actually happened in the past, his discovery of books. Discuss the relation between "reading" one's own life and "reading" literature.
2. What techniques does Wright use to convey his particular point of view toward himself, whites, the South, and American culture in general? Do we learn about Wright's character, his thoughts and feelings, primarily through his own words? Do we also come to know more about him through his dramatic encounters with people? Explain. Does Wright's stylistic strategy emphasize "telling" or "showing"? How immediate does Wright make these scenes? How close does he bring his reader to the situations developed?
3. What effect does the locale, the particular setting for this passage, have on the dimensions of dramatic irony Wright introduces? Point to and discuss the instances of irony in this excerpt. Compare the reactions of the librarian to Wright's "note" with his anticipation of her response. What stylistic tactics does he use to deal with her anticipated response?
4. How does Wright go about distinguishing himself from the other "men on the job"? From other

blacks? From the South in general? What is his method for classifying the other workers? Comment on the applicability of the following statement to the lives of American blacks before and after the movement toward black militancy: "I had seen many Negroes solve the problem of being black by transferring their hatred of themselves to others with a black skin and fighting them."

5. Why, specifically, does Wright assume a "sense of guilt" as he changes his outlook on life? When does that guilt take on "criminal" dimensions? Why?
6. What dramatic incident does Wright use to demonstrate the range of his vocabulary as a youngster? What are his attitudes toward "English grammar"? Why does he prefer to study language and syntax in novels? What does Wright tell us that indicates that he would be particularly drawn to naturalistic and realistic writing? Can you detect the influence of any of the writers Wright mentions on his prose style? Is there any noticeable change in Wright's sentence structure or in the prose rhythm as we move along in this passage? Do the sentences become increasingly self-assertive? Do the prose rhythms seem more fluid? Explain.

Personal Experience Exercises: Describe your recollections of your earliest reading. What were the particular circumstances for that activity? Describe the difficulties you encountered. What were the pleasures you experienced?

Write an essay about a conflict which led to a greater self-awareness and/or new understanding of another person. Describe the situation in which you came into conflict with another person (or persons) and as a result changed your attitude toward yourself or the other(s) involved. Describe the nature of the conflict and the process by which you changed your attitude or ideas.

The exercise asks the student to do two things: (1) describe a particular situation or experience in a way that will make it clear and vivid to the reader, and (2) discuss the growing awareness the experience led to.

FLANNERY O'CONNOR
The Life You Save May Be Your Own

1. What is the source of the story's title? How does the title resemble the kind of language Mr. Shiftlet ordinarily uses? Give examples of his "borrowed" language.
2. In the television version of the story, Mr. Shiftlet changes his mind and returns to the restaurant to pick up Lucynell. Why was the story changed? How does the change reflect the different assumptions both Flannery O'Connor and the television network have about their respective audiences? (One way to approach this revision is to ask what compositional and moral problems are resolved by a "happy ending.")

TILLIE OLSEN
Tell Me a Riddle

Olsen's story is of a mother who, because of ignorance and circumstances, has not given her eldest child the kind of upbringing she needs. It is not, however, self-pitying, nor does it, for all its bleakness, deny the daughter dignity. The mother is apparently addressing a well-intentioned but obtuse social worker, giving him or her a biography of her daughter from the time she was born to age nineteen. It is the story of a relationship that circumstance never let develop, of intentions never fulfilled, but in Emily's gift for pantomime and in her mother's final stoic comment one finds a stubborn will to endure in the face of all the bleakness. In teaching the piece, make sure that students see that the story the mother tells is not simply a string of excuses for her failure to give Emily what she needed.

1. To whom does the speaker of this story seem to be speaking? Why is this person so interested in Emily? Does it seem to you that he or she understands Emily better than the speaker does? What leads you to think so?
2. What does Emily's mother think about the way she has brought her daughter up? In what ways would she have raised Emily differently? What are some of the ways she thinks Emily's upbringing went wrong? Does she blame herself for these mistakes? Who or what, then, is responsible for what happened? What does this suggest about the mother's feelings about her own life?
3. What have the effects of her mother's frequent absences been on Emily? How does she seem to have learned to cope with these separations? What might the separations have to do with her frequent absences from school? with her feeling that the world will soon be destroyed by atomic bombs? with her gift for pantomime? What needs might she be trying to fill by her performing? Do you think they are really filled? What words and phrases in the text lead you to think so? Does Emily's mother think her daughter has found happiness, now that she is such a popular performer? Why or why not?
4. Try putting yourself in your parents' position, and write an account of your life from their point of

view. What went wrong, and what went right, in your upbringing? What mistake might your parents have made? What do you think the effects of your upbringing might be on the way you are now? You may want to talk with your parents before writing the story, and you may want to address it to someone outside your family who knows you, but not too well.

ALLEN GINSBERG
A Supermarket in California

Ginsberg is probably closer to Whitman than most other modern American poets, so this poem might well be taught at the same time as the Whitman poems. What should emerge as you teach the two poems, however, is the enormous, almost tragic, difference in vision. Whitman, in his expansive optimism, can address everyone around him and readers generations hence; Ginsberg, solitary and searching for images, can address only dead poets. One senses Ginsberg striving (self-consciously and awkwardly) for the vision of Whitman, knowing all along that it won't quite do anymore. The address to Whitman becomes, paradoxically, a sign that Whitman's sense of America and of his bond with humankind is no longer possible.

1. Ginsberg says that he went to the supermarket "in my hungry fatigue, and shopping for images." What sort of fatigue do you think he was feeling? What might the fact that he had to go shopping for images have to do with this fatigue? What was Ginsberg looking for in the market besides food?
2. Since Walt Whitman and Garcia Lorca were both dead long before this poem was written, why does Ginsberg address them here? Do the poets—Whitman, especially—seem to belong in the store or not? What words and phrases in the poem lead you to think so? Why, for example, does Ginsberg imagine himself followed by the store detective? Why don't they ever pass the cashier?
3. What is Ginsberg's sense of life in America toward the end of the poem? Why does he turn to a dead poet to accompany him as he walks through this life? Lethe was the river of forgetfulness crossed by the dead in classical mythology. What does Ginsberg's allusion to the river tell us of what he feels about Whitman's vision?

SYLVIA PLATH
Man in Black

1. To whom does the title of this poem refer? What is the man in black's relationship to the places Plath mentions in the poem? How do those place characterizations work to characterize the human figure?
2. Plath was skilled at using onomotapoeia (word sounds that resemble their referents) to strengthen the impact of her poems. Try reading this poem out loud. What effect do phrases such as "shove / and suck of the grey sea" or "snuff-colored sand cliffs rise" have on the poem's meaning? What meaning is conveyed simply through the sounds of the words?

SYLVIA PLATH
The Detective

1. This poem may seem puzzling at first. What mystery is Plath revealing here? What kind of woman is the victim? Read the poem in connection with Charlotte Perkins Gilman's "The Yellow Wallpaper" and Kate Chopin's "The Dream of an Hour" (see Classics). Can you make any connections between and among these texts? Why is it important to know if the women in the poem were "arranging cups"?
2. In the poem's third to last line, Plath makes a literary reference. What famous character is she invoking? Why might she refer to him? In what kind of mystery does this character appear? How does this relate to the themes in Plath's poem?

JOHN UPDIKE
A & P

1. How is the supermarket used as the setting for this story? Is it simply a place where the events happen, or does it play a more functional role in the story? How does the fact that the story is set in a supermarket affect Sammy's style? How does the supermarket provide him with terms, images, and metaphors to describe people and experiences? How are the characters described in relation to supermarket commodities? What effect does this produce? Why do you think the story is titled "A & P" and not something like, say, "Sammy's Rebellion" or "Sammy Strikes Out"?
2. How does Sammy's way of talking differ from that of the other characters in the story? Is Sammy's way of speaking one the girls would approve of?
3. How does Sammy use Queenie's voice to characterize her? What is Queenie's attitude toward Lengel? Is she intimidated, insulted, condescending? Why does Sammy consider himself their "unsuspected hero"?
4. Why is Sammy protective of the girls? Does he "identify" with them in any way? In what sense are the girls like him? Different? Does he regard

Queenie only in sexual ways? Is there something else he admires about her? Explain.

5. How does Queenie's confrontation with Lengel affect Sammy's own behavior?
6. Do you think Sammy's quitting is a genuine act of nonconformity or merely a self-conscious, stagey gesture? Explain.

MARTIN LUTHER KING, JR.
I Have a Dream

1. How does this sermon announce itself to be a spoken, rather than a written, discourse? What aspects of the language are most suited to oral presentation? Rewrite the sermon as if it were a personal letter from King to, say, the governor of Alabama. How would King's tactics change?
2. How does King try to characterize, for a white audience, the movement he represents? What kinds of threat, if any, does he wish to pose to those in power? Does he sound like a violent revolutionary in this speech? If not, how does he avoid sounding this way, and why?
3. Look carefully at the appeals in the first and last paragraphs. What traditions of captivity and struggle does he allude to? What effects do these allusions have? What is the effect of his ending with the words of a spiritual? How does he invite his nonblack audience to identify with the lyrics?

MAYA ANGELOU
I Know Why the Caged Bird Sings

1. Angelou never states explicitly how she and her family and friends felt about Joe Louis, and yet it becomes clear very quickly that they revered him highly. What techniques does she use to express this? Would the effect of the passage be changed if it began with an explicit statement of their attitude? Explain.
2. How does the reader's sense of Angelou's regard for Louis change? What are the implications of the paragraph beginning ''My race groaned . . .''? Evidently, Louis was a towering symbol of blacks, for both blacks and whites. How has the reader been prepared for this revelation earlier?
3. How does the final paragraph complicate the reader's sense of Angelou? If it had been omitted, explain whether she would have seemed less wise or sensitive.
4. Adopting Angelou's techniques for dramatizing memories, write an account of how you, your family, or your community responded to a symbolic event.

NORMAN MAILER
Of a Fire on the Moon

1. Mailer says of the astronauts: ''Their characteristic matter-of-fact response is overcome occasionally by swoops of hyperbole.'' How does this description apply to O'Toole''s *Washington Post* account of the moon landing (see ''Press'')? What do you think prompts the astronauts' changes of tone? When do they occur? Do they have any relation to the astronauts' sense of audience? For example, do the astronauts speak differently when their remarks are addressed to Houston directly and when they are addressing the worldwide TV audience? Explain.
2. Why is Mailer particularly alert to any possible disturbances in the astronauts' sense of time, space, and gravity (e.g., ''Did lunar gravity have power like a drug to shift the sense of time?'')? What is Mailer paying attention to at such moments that O'Toole in his *Washington Post* account isn't? How does the quality of Mailer's attention get translated into a more agile metaphorical language?
3. Which astronaut does Mailer find most interesting? Why? In general, does he find the moon landing an exciting event? Does his writing indicate any shifts between enthusiasm and boredom? Explain.

JOAN DIDION
On the Mall

1. Consider the organization of the essay, especially its segmentation. Is there a logic to the sequence of the segments? How does the organization—or lack of it—reflect Didion's opinion of malls? Explain whether her opinion is refined by the structure or obscured by it.
2. In the first paragraph Didion characterizes malls as ''toy garden cities in which no one lives but everyone consumes, profound equalizers, the perfect fusion of the profit motive and the egalitarian ideal.'' How does she support these claims in the body of the essay?
3. Compare Didion's theories of store layout and the experience of shopping with those of Vance Packard (see ''Best-Sellers''). How does Didion's style differ? Which writer better describes your own opinions and experiences?
4. Summarize the ''shopping-center theory'' offered in the essay, then use it to analyze the layout of a mall familiar to you. How might the theory be modified to better explain the mall you discuss?

MAXINE HONG KINGSTON
from Woman Warrior [*No Name Woman*]

1. In this chapter from her family memoir *The Woman Warrior,* Maxine Hong Kingston combines fictionalization with memory to compose a life story for her shunned aunt. She breaks off her narrative several times and shifts it around, as if the story of the aunt cannot be settled. Why did she not stick to one version of her aunt's biography? What aspects of Chinese village life and tradition does she address in these different stories? Does she come to any conclusion about her aunt?
2. At one point, Kingston writes, "Those of us in the first American generations have had to figure out how the invisible world the emigrants built around our childhoods fit in solid America." Describe how Kingston does this in "No Name Woman."
3. Compare the depiction of the villagers' raid on the family house here with the tar-and-featherings of Major Molineux in Hawthorne's story (see Classics). Both writers depict a crowd's attack upon a victim, but what each describes differs considerably. What do these scenes indicate about the society each author critiques?

WALKER PERCY
The Loss of the Creature

1. Walker Percy uses anecdotes about travelling to introduce his argument about our disconnectedness to the things we encounter. These stories might seem familiar to you. Recount a trip you took which disappointed you for the reasons Percy mentions. Or, describe one in which you felt that you encountered Percy's "it." How can you claim that your experience was "authentic?" What steps led you toward, or away from, that "authentic" encounter?
2. Percy introduces two connected, but differing, ideas here: the loss of the creature, and the loss of sovereignty. Distinguish between the two, and discuss how they are interconnected. How does the theme of possession run through this essay? What does it mean, in Percy's terms, to "own" an experience?
3. Why is it important, according to Percy, for the "genuine research man" to be "a little vague and always humble before the thing?" How does this phrase relate to Percy's larger argument about education? How does this discussion of learning relate to Percy's own process as a writer? In what ways is this essay about Percy, as a writer, himself?

RAYMOND CARVER
What We Talk About When We Talk About Love

1. This story represents a school of writing, called "minimalism," that became popular in the 1970s. This movement also includes such authors as Ann Beattie and Joyce Carol Oates. This style revolves around a narrative in which "nothing happens"—no major disaster or catharsis overwhelms the characters, whose ordinary lives presumably go on as before, once the story ends. Yet a sense of event emanates from Carver's story. How does he use conversation, anecdote and mood to propel his narrative? What is changed at the story's end?
2. Often this style of fiction has been described as having a "journalistic" tone. Compare Carver's story to Debbie McKinney's long article "Youth's Despair Erupts" (see Press). In terms of narrative and rhetorical style, what do they have in common? How, for example, does each use understatement to drive home the power of the narrative?
3. Contesting definitions of love occupy the conversation between Carver's characters. Name the different ways the two couples talk about love. Does the story suggest that any of these definitions is the most accurate? How does the narrative's inconclusive ending relate to its theme of love described?

LEWIS THOMAS
The World's Largest Membrane

1. The first paragraph of this essay offers a vivid image of the earth. Subsequent paragraphs provide scientific explanation of the atmosphere's makeup. What rhetorical effect does this shift from description to explanation accomplish? Throughout the rest of the piece, how does Thomas combine familiar language with technical terminology to inform the reader?
2. Annie Dillard's essay "Total Eclipse" (see the next selection) offers a different view of the wonders of the atmosphere. She also takes a personal approach to the natural world, teaching us about our surroundings while telling a story. What does Dillard include that Thomas does not? Which piece do you find more engaging and why?
3. At the end of this excerpt, Thomas speaks of something the earth does "for our pleasure." Of course, this natural occurrence does not take place because it pleases humans. Why do you think Thomas used this phrase? What is the point of "humanizing" the workings of the atmosphere? How does this phrase relate to the essay's last image, of rain pounding on the roof at night?

ANNIE DILLARD
Total Eclipse

1. Dillard writes in a prose style that not many contemporary authors employ. How would you describe her style? Does this style work to enrich her narrative? What emotional sense is communicated through the language she uses? What kinds of details does she include that work against this language to create tension?
2. Dillard calls the universe "a clockwork of loose spheres flung at stupefying, unauthorized speeds." How does this description contrast to Lewis Thomas' depiction of the atmosphere (see Classics)? Why do you think one author stresses an image of a benign universe while the other emphasizes its seemingly random force? How might the two images connect?
3. What do you make of the "odd thing" that Dillard relates at the end of her piece? Does Dillard provide an explanation for this occurrence? Why do you think she ended her essay here? How do the final three paragraphs contrast and connect to the one that precedes them? What feeling does this essay leave you with?

EUDORA WELTY
The Little Store

1. Look carefully at the essay and try to infer the principles behind Welty's selection and arrangement of details. Note, for example, that near the beginning she lists some of the games she played as a child. How does this express her feelings toward the story? Why should it precede her description of the store itself?
2. Compare Welty's style of reminiscence with that of Maya Angelou. Both writers describe stores, but the stores play different roles in their lives. How do their styles reflect this difference? Which essay gives a clearer picture of the store? To which writer was the store more important? Explain.
3. Following Welty's example, write an essay describing the way a particular store looked to you in your childhood. Fill it with as many specific details as you can, but shape them to give the reader an understanding of attitudes and emotions they called forth from you.

JUNE JORDAN
Nobody Mean More to Me than You and the Future Life of Willie Jordan

1. June Jordan positions herself immediately within this essay, by using the pronoun "our" in reference to the language of African Americans. How does Jordan employ a first-person perspective to enrich her narrative throughout the text? What does this subjective stance mean, in terms of her political message? Does it lend the essay a sense of authority? If so, how so? Why do you think Jordan to take such a personal stance in telling this story?
2. Jordan sees her writing as a form of activism, a political intervention that she hopes will effect the structure of this country and the world. What is "activist" about this essay? How does its structure relate to its political stance? Why does Jordan reprint all of Willie Jordan, Jr.'s essay at the end of her piece? How does that choice connect with her arguments about the purpose of teaching Black English?
3. Does Jordan persuade you that Black English is a legitimate, and indeed crucial, part of a modern American education? How does the story of Reggie Jordan's death enforce her points about Black English? Can you think of other examples of minority groups being silenced, both linguistically and physically, in this country? Look at Maxine Hong Kingston's narrative of her aunt's life (see Classics). How does the subject of silencing enter into that story? How does it differ from Jordan's text? What connects the two stories?

SCRIPTS

ORSON WELLES
The War of the Worlds

1. Why do you think Orson Welles adapted H. G. Wells's novel in precisely this way? In what sense is his performance one of parody? Explain the object of the parody. What was the audience supposed to be responding to? What, in fact, did it respond to?
2. Point to instances of tone, idiom, or procedure that contribute to the effect of authenticity. How does specificity of location contribute to the effect Welles wants to convey? In general, if fiction can *sound* exactly like fact, what criteria can you use to distinguish between them? Explain. What criteria does Dorothy Thompson use in her report on Welles's "triumph" (see "Press")?

3. What aspects of the language make the script seem especially realistic? Which details are most plausible? Which are implausible?
4. How does the speech of Phillips differ from that of the announcer at the beginning? How does Welles represent Phillips's curiosity and apprehensiveness? How does the final announcer's speech differ from previous ones? Does the final speech seem at all frightening to you in its written form? What qualities of tone, diction, and imagery make it frightening?
5. Refer to the essays about this broadcast by Mahawinney and Thompson in the "Press" section. Explain how your reading of these articles at all changes your opinion of the script. The broadcast evidently had a tremendous effect. What aspects of the style of the script account for this?
6. Following Welles's model, write a script for the radio coverage of a fictional catastrophe that might frighten a contemporary audience. What sort of catastrophe would be appropriate? How might advances in technology change the nature of the coverage of the event in the media?

BUD ABBOTT AND LOU COSTELLO
Who's on First

1. To what extent does this dialogue depend on the characters of the comedians? How are their characters created by the language? How can the characters be told apart strictly on the basis of the script?
2. The fundamental joke of this routine could be termed a pun: *who, what,* and so on, are words used in two ways by the characters. What other kinds of puns are there?
3. Who is the best audience for this sketch? Why would people who laugh at other humorists laugh at this? Explain whether there is any cruelty in the humor here.

BATTEN, BARTON, DURSTINE, AND OSBORNE
Ring Around the Collar

1. What images of men and women does this ad depict? Which sex is treated more flatteringly? Explain whether the ad is in any way offensive to you. How is its effectiveness as an advertisement reduced therefore?
2. This is said to be one of the most successful television ads ever produced. How would you account for its success? David Ogilvy, in "How to Write Potent Copy" (Advertising), summarizes some of the common principles of advertising. How does this ad conform to them?
3. Explain whether you find Ogilvy's assessment of such ads accurate or inaccurate. How do you imagine Vance Packard would respond to the ad?

DICK ORKIN AND BERT BERDIS
Puffy Sleeves

1. Compare the style and tactics of this ad with those of other ads depicting contemporary men (see "Advertising"). How does this ad depend for its effects on a listener's knowledge of other ads? How does this ad react against stereotypes or conform to them? Consider that much of the humor derives from the character's fear of humiliation in being taken for a woman or transvestite. Suppose the character were a woman wearing her husband's overcoat. Explain whether there would be any humor left in the ad.
2. In what ways is this specifically a radio script? How do the writers establish the setting and characters? Compare it to a television or film script. Radio can rely more heavily on dialogue; what special opportunities does this offer a radio writer for creating characters?
3. Recompose the ad for Wisk above as Dick and Bert might. How can their principle of portraying everyday life, as explained in the headnote, be applied to the situation given in that ad? Note that there is already an element of embarrassment—which Dick and Bert seem to rely heavily on—in the plot of the Wisk ad. How might they turn the events on the canal into an example of "the little stupid things that everyone does"?

ROBERT GELLER
Hemingway's "Soldier's Home"

1. When addressing the discussion questions, carefully examine and compare Hemingway's first three paragraphs with Geller's first three shots. Decide whether Geller made use of all the visual possibilities Hemingway offers. How has he selected and modified the language borrowed from the story's narrator?
2. The description of the second shot explains that the stock footage should not "editorialize about the war." What does this phrase mean? How does Hemingway editorialize about the war? About anything else? In what ways is Krebs an unusual image of a World War I soldier? Compare him, for example, to the soldier in the White Owl cigar ad (see "Advertising").
3. Hemingway's story gives few indications of how Krebs felt about his life as a soldier or about the people he knew in Europe. How has Geller

amplified these? How has he distorted Krebs's character on this point?

4. Following Geller's model, invent a scene based on a hint in the story. It should contain descriptions of settings, props, actions, and camera shots as well as characteristic lines of dialogue. Explain how a film script opens up more—or fewer—opportunities for expression than prose fiction.

RICHARD ECKHAUS
The Jeffersons—"The Black Out"

1. Reread the comic sequence at the opening of the first act. Which jokes "work" when read in script form, and which ones don't? Why? Mark places in the script where a laugh track might be added. Explain whether these struck you as humorous moments when reading the script initially.
2. Discuss the treatment of economic and social power in the script. In what ways are Con Edison, insurance companies, the police, and the class of store owners shown to be similar? Note how George's role is complicated in relation to these. He is a store owner, but, at the end, he acts against his best interests as one. He is abused by the police and verbally abuses them, yet he relies on them for protection and uses the same term they use—*animals*—to refer to looters. Whose side is George on? How might these complications be appropriate in a character meant to appeal to a wide audience?
3. Look carefully at the closing pages of the script. What specifically convinces George that he should keep his Bronx store open? Compare the roles of the inmate Jackson and the old man. What do they represent? What do they help George see about himself and his world? What does George's final decision express about his character?

Roseanne

Invite your class to examine closely the way the show's dialogue frequently works. You might select several exchanges in Act I, Scene 1, where Rosanne responds to her children's questions about misplaced books, breakfast, bookbags, etc. It would be a good idea to ask several students to act out the dialogue and then analyze its pattern.

1. What do most of these exchanges have in common? What verbal patterns emerge? What do they tell us about the ways in which the show violates traditional values only to reaffirm them?
2. How does the show's writer work humor into these dialogues? What does the humor consist of? Why, for example, does Roseanne answer her daughter's question about where her English book is with the quip "I sold it"? Why does the exchange not end here? Why does Roseanne eventually say "Top of the TV"? What would the show be like if Roseanne didn't offer a responsible answer?
3. Josh Ozersky in "TV's Anti-Families: Married . . . with Malaise" (see *Magazines*) cites *Roseanne* as an example of a show that promotes the image of a dysfunctional family. Do your students agree with this evaluation? What aspects of the show can they point to that affirm traditional family values? What would the show be like if it really did portray serious family dysfunction?
4. In a recent discussion on sitcoms, one of the scriptwriters claimed that "everybody wants to do something a little different, a little progressive, a little controversial. But there are only a few basic jokes, a few basic concepts, and they've all been done before." Invite your class to examine *Roseanne* in light of this statement. Which parts of the show do they consider original? Which parts derivative?

SUGGESTIONS FOR USING *POPULAR WRITING IN AMERICA* TO ORGANIZE A SEMESTER'S WORK

Popular Writing in America facilitates a variety of instructional modes. For courses in popular culture, the book's broad historical sweep, its concern for many of the dominant themes of American life, and its generous amount of reading material make it a source book for students to draw on in coming to terms with the ways in which the most widely read styles of American prose interact with each other and with their audiences to produce that intricate network of artistic and commercial collaboration known as "popular culture." The Table of Linked Selections organizes the reading material into workable units for classroom discussion such as Women and Consumerism, Cars and Self-

Identity, and Success to provide engaging teaching opportunities for discussing some of the most recurrent issues in American social history.

For introductory courses in college composition, we have built into the book at least two distinct approaches to the basic principles of teaching effective prose. One of our basic intentions is to show the effects that a particular medium and a presumed audience have on a writer's style. This is evident from the book's organization: the selections move from writing intended for vast numbers of people (''Advertising,'' ''Press'') to writing designed to appeal to more specific audiences (''Magazines,'' ''Best-Sellers,''), and finally to selections usually regarded as intended for a limited audience (''Classics''). The section on ''Scripts'' focuses on what has become America's most popular form of public discourse. Each section, then, can be treated in the order in which it appears in the book, so that the student progresses from simple to generally more complicated prose styles during the course of a semester. A more detailed description of the assumption underlying this plan for a semester's work follows, along with some suggested reading assignments.

This basic concern for showing the relationship between the writer and his or her audience should make the book easy to work with for teachers who are interested in demonstrating the importance of a rhetorical approach to students of writing. The Rhetorical Table of Contents groups the reading selections under such headings as Exposition, Narration, Description, Argument, and Persuasion. The categories listed in the Rhetorical Table of Contents are supplemented by three syllabi, the first describing some fundamental assumptions and exercises for this approach to writing, the second outlining a semester using the Rhetorical Table of Contents as a basis, and the third, a more detailed course description, providing subjects to be covered on a weekly basis.

The various course descriptions that follow are, of course, not meant to be prescriptive. They do, however, share a basic goal: to strengthen the student's ability to write clearly, efficiently, and accurately about matters of varying intellectual complexity based on working with the most popular forms of public discourse. In effect, the student studies the process of composition—how a writer employs certain stylistic procedures to elicit a specific response from a particular audience. The student is not being asked, however, to reproduce exactly the style of the writer he or she is reading, but if he or she can describe how someone else has achieved certain effects in writing, the student, too, will be composing successfully.

SEQUENTIAL ORGANIZATION

This syllabus attempts to provide students with a clearer sense of the nature and range of their own experiences of literacy, in a way in which most of us have come to encounter and to deal with language in our lives—experiences which, at least initially, are not necessarily dependent on the built-in institutionalized pressures and expectations of educational curricula. The material for this course is intended to represent written language in its widest sense. Reading selections have been drawn from six of the most popular forms of American writing since the middle of the nineteenth century: advertisements, journalism, magazines, best-sellers, ''classics,'' and scripts. This sequence is not necessarily used to suggest gradations in the quality of verbal performance. If works of established literary merit tend to appear later, it is because the organization of the course reflects, in most cases, increasingly complex experiences of literacy. Such a sequence also prepares the student to deal with literature in a more extensive way in a full semester's work in writing about literature.

This format promotes, at least initially, a collaborative context for reading. Students and teachers start out talking about common reading material—using a mutually accessible, shared vocabulary. The book moves from experiences of language that are shared (advertisements, newspapers) to the more personal pleasures and challenges implicit in responding to classic American writing and to America's most popular form of discourse, scripts. At least one benefit of this six-part series is that students are not put in the position where they must struggle to master a special set of critical or even grammatical terms *before* they can talk to a teacher or to each other about what they are reading or planning to write about. But this is not at all to suggest that students will not want to learn those special literary/critical terms. Most students will—simply because they gradually come to recognize the added dimensions of their own verbal abilities and will want to broaden them further.

Given this initial collaborative effort, one that encourages increasing self-confidence, students should become more relaxed with their own writing and less resistant to talking about the more complex but interrelated forms of expression found in successive chapters. They will approach the more demanding writing of the later sections through the more manageable forms of literacy dealt with earlier. Students will be better equipped and trained, then, to deal successfully with the complications of, say, Allen Ginsberg's "A Supermarket in California" as they come to realize that they occasionally respond to the language they ordinarily read in ads, newspapers, and magazines with more verbal resources not necessarily very remote from those that went into the production of Ginsberg's poem. By illustrating the underlying verbal strategies of advertisements, newspaper writing, magazine articles, best-sellers, classics, and scripts, *Popular Writing in America* can become an important resource for developing in its readers the kind of critical awareness and self-confidence that will enable them to approach *any* piece of writing attentively, intelligently, and in the spirit with which it was written.

The subject of the course is not so much advertisements, newspaper articles, or great literature as it is the nature of the *language* used in different forms of literacy and the ways in which that language creates and maintains a reading audience. These demonstrably successful styles of literacy provide a focus for examining the strategies and techniques used by a literate speaker when addressing a large, literate audience. Within such a public context, the student gains a valuable perspective on his or her own performances as a reader and a composer of sentences. We try to have students come to realize how an author (whether of an ad, a newspaper story, a magazine article, a best-selling novel, a poem, a script, or what comes to be considered a classic) uses language to elicit and control an audience's response. This plan should help students to approach their own writing and conversation with an enlivened sense of the possibilities for their producing similar effects in these fundamental, and oftentimes crucial, experiences. By offering a variety of writing styles and points of view—many on the same subject—students are better able to place themselves in a position where they can regard their own experiences from shifting perspectives. Students are encouraged, then, to recognize the possibilities for changing the sound of their own voices without losing track of themselves.

The organization of the syllabus is such that all of the various forms of writing discussed are to be closely interrelated. Through a comparison of subjects, purposes, and styles, students will not only be made aware of the many ways in which language is used by other writers having specific personal and professional interests to serve, but will also gain confidence in their own verbal skills by discovering the broad range of options available to them as talkers and writers. It is hoped that students will also arrive at a clearer understanding of the interrelations of their own, often quite complex, verbal experiences.

The beginning of the semester (weeks 1 and 2) is devoted to some basic but important exercises. Perhaps the best way for students to learn to think and write critically about any subject is for them to develop the habit of attending closely to the language and stylistic strategies of any given text and their effects on an audience. Writing is essentially a social act. Each selection that appears in *Popular Writing in America,* whether it is an advertisement for a cigarette or an automobile, a newspaper report on a murder, a feature story in a magazine on a celebrity, an excerpt from a best-selling novel like *Roots,* a poem by Robert Frost, or a short story by Kate Chopin, quite obviously assumes that there is an audience who can read it and, in some ways, be influenced by it. Yet it is only when we make an effort to measure the responses of an intended audience implicit in a piece of writing against the quality of our own participation that we can assess more comprehensively the interactions between the various styles and audiences within a common culture.

One of the most effective strategies for introducing students to the interaction of a writer's prose style and his or her presumed audience is to lead them in an analysis of different responses to the same subject prepared for different audiences. The instructor works with students in examining selections which interconnect, that is, pieces which can be studied specifically to demonstrate this writer-audience relationship. Possible subjects for comparison and contrast are the excerpt from Mario Puzo's *The Godfather* ("Best-Sellers") with *Time*'s "Death of a Maverick Mafioso" ("Magazines").

Stephen Crane's news account of his own shipwreck (see "Stephen Crane's Own Story" in "Press") with his fictional rendition of the same event, "The Open Boat" ("Classics").

The *Washington Post*'s account of man's first walk on the moon (see "'The Eagle Has Landed': Two Men Walk on the Moon" in "Press") with Norman Mailer's description from *Of a Fire on the Moon* ("Classics").

Tom Wicker's account of the assassination of President John F. Kennedy (see "Kennedy Killed in a Car as He Rides in Dallas" in "Press") with his recollections of the event as described in "The Assassination" (see "Press").

For a complete list of possible interconnections, see the Table of Linked Selections.

Throughout these exercises in the interaction of style and audience, we encourage students to realize the need to adapt their styles to the particular level of interest and ability of different audiences. It is hoped that they will view their own uses of language in a more public context, that they will regard language as commonly shared property and see their own compositional efforts as drawing on and interacting with all the other forms of expression that circulate publicly and that compete for our attention.

In the next section of the syllabus (weeks 3 and 4), students are asked to read, discuss, and write about demonstrably successful examples of writing directed toward the largest possible public—advertisements. Advertisements are a forceful reminder that writing is a public, corporate enterprise. The language and rhetorical strategies of advertising are simply unavoidable. Yet, although they represent some of the most expensive and calculated acts of composition in America, most people react to advertisements in exactly the way advertising agencies would like them to—as consumers, not as critically attentive readers. Assuming, however, that advertising is "a business or words," not necessarily of commodities, it is useful to join students in examining how the language and strategies of advertisements affect the ways we talk and think. For teaching purposes, then, ads constitute a lively repository of American vocabulary, idiom, syntax, metaphor, and style—in short, a fairly reliable index of the state of public discourse.

The business of advertisers is to invent stylistic methods to address large audiences in a language designed to be readily accessible and immediately persuasive. Since the audience and purpose of most ads are so clearly defined, they can become useful exercises to teach students to be alert to their own inclusion in an audience. So, too, advertisements provide teachers and students with an opportunity to discover some of the tactics writers have at their disposal to capture an audience's attention. Whether the instructor decides to work with ads singly or with sets of ads dealing with the same product over a number of decades, working with advertising provides students with the opportunity both to study the techniques of effective writing and to examine changes in American society based on the ways in which the society is addressed in advertisements.

One way to approach the interaction of style and audience in advertising would be to start with a specific ad, say, "Can a Girl Be *Too* Busy?" After working closely with its language and strategy, students may reevaluate the ad in terms of the precepts outlined by David Ogilvy. The framework this professional advertiser creates for the ways people can think about and produce ads could create an interesting context for an extended analysis of any number of advertisements, including ones for the same kind of product or possibly even some of Ogilvy's own ads (see, for example, the Rolls-Royce ad).

The class moves on in weeks 5 and 6 to consider the language of news reporting. Examples chosen for reading, writing, and discussion could range from different styles of headlines (see "Important. Assassination of President Lincoln," "Dillinger 'Gets His'," and "Kennedy Is Killed . . .") through the prose of teletype releases (see the reports on the assassination of President Lincoln and the moonshot) to extended forms of news coverage. Students are invited to examine the stylistic strategies of various kinds of reporting and to observe how the reporters' ways of writing about an event become for their audiences so synonymous with the event that it becomes practically impossible to consider the event independently of the language provided by newspapers. Seen in this way, events become the "products" of newspapers.

Newspaper writing serves as an excellent model for teaching the strategies and techniques of effective prose, especially organization and point of view. The example of the "inverted pyramid" shows one very precise system of ordering readily accessible to students. So, too, they come to realize rather quickly that whatever their particular angle on an event or an issue, they must support it with many details. It is quite obvious that students write best when least intimidated. A relatively simple form of writing such as a newspaper story or an advertisement usually contains enough verbal stimulus and "style" to allow a teacher to introduce a critical discussion of linguistic and compositional strategies based on material students feel comfortable and familiar with. Students who learn analytical techniques by responding to exercises on news reports and ads should feel at least somewhat more secure in their approaches to the more sophisticated and verbally complex forms of writing later on in the semester.

In the following portion of the syllabus (weeks 7 and 8), the class will examine the writing in magazines, which provide examples of widely distributed material written with a very specific readership in mind. The familiar picture of "That Cosmopolitan Girl" is an instructive instance of a magazine's embodying its image in a person or voice that supposedly represents the life-style, or the desired life-style, of its readership. If the writers for magazines can imagine a particular audience, they can also be fairly confident in their assumptions about the interests of their readers and the kinds of material their audiences are capable of understanding and the voices they can respond to.

Magazines might be said to occupy a place between newspapers and books. Magazines capitalize on those contemporary topics of public interest that have already been introduced, and, at the same time, they include between their covers articles, fiction, poetry, and personal essays that eventually find their way into book form. Reading selections for this part of the syllabus might connect, for example, the committee prose of newspaper reports and editorials with a consideration of what happens to the same events when handled in a different form. But this section on writing from magazines obviously should not be limited to examples of news reports. Essays on the same subject from different magazines can be read to determine how different audiences get talked to in different terms. A broad range of subject matter, tone, and format from the many popular periodicals represented in the book could also be introduced into class discussion, specific choices depending, of course, on the particular abilities and interests of each instructor's class. The rhetorical and thematic listings provide ample flexibility for teachers to introduce the appropriate rhetorical strategies by using articles most suitable to their students.

In the next section of the syllabus (weeks 9 and 10), the class will read, discuss, and write about best-selling prose and poetry. The term is used nonpejoratively to refer simply to those works that have had large sales and extensive publicity. It is, for the most part, writing that the academic community has traditionally paid little attention to, yet, because of their massive audiences and their frequent interactions with other forms of media, best-selling books deserve to be attended to by those interested in examining the relationship between their own verbal experiences and those of a literate public.

The success of best-selling writing depends clearly, and rather heavily, on the language, subjects, and strategies of what is current in advertising, newspapers, and magazines. In addition, best-sellers can be used to teach not only tone and metaphor, but also clarity and diction. These aspects of style are particularly apparent in best-selling prose, usually because they are repeated so insistently. But the instructor's selection of specific passages for classroom use should not be made simply to introduce samples of mediocrity—though some best-sellers are obviously better than others—but as illustrations of the various prose styles and themes that have appealed enormously to American audiences.

The writing included in the next portion of the syllabus (weeks 11 and 12) provides students with stylistic alternatives to all the other forms of writing encountered earlier in the syllabus. "Classics" illustrate language used in the most demanding ways possible. Naturally, the authors of works that become classics expect their audiences to have attained a high degree of literacy. In fact, it may be said that these authors require their readers not only to be literate but to be literary as well. That is, readers of classics are asked to engage in difficult, sometimes highly complex verbal experiences, and at the same time are asked, in the act of reading, to refer those verbal experiences to a wider context of accumulated literary responses.

The authors of classics, it should be added, are not necessarily hostile to other, less complicated forms of writing. If anything, they are probably more willing to accommodate the multiplicity of styles and voices surrounding them than are writers who must, because of a greater commercial investment, appeal to quite specific audiences. Journalists, for example, may be reluctant to record the interferences and incursions they may have encountered in their attempted news coverage (they have only a limited amount of space for their stories), just as the authors of best-sellers may not want to (or may not even know how to) risk unsettling their audiences with sudden shifts in tone or point of view, or subtle maneuvers into irony or parody. It is, however, primarily in their consciousness of the literary sources of their material that the writers of what come to be known as classics differ from journalists or the authors of best-sellers. They are more sensitive to the connections their own language or style has to all the other forms of written expression, be they ads, newspaper reports, magazine articles, best-sellers, poems, or even other classics.

Students' reading in this section should include a wide range of styles. For example, Crane, Hemingway, Updike, Percy, and Ginsberg can be assigned for the purpose of showing each author's special attraction to the strategies and themes of other forms of media. So, too, Norman Mailer can be used in class as an example of a writer who is competitively responsive to practically every form of contemporary prose.

In the final weeks (13 and 14) of the course, students remind themselves of the analytic skills they have practiced during the semester by turning to the study of scripts, an increasingly important—and popular—form of writing in America. Yet, because scripts are intended to be heard and not read, they provide a convenient occasion to underscore the interrelations of style and audience. Comparing, for example, Robert Geller's script of "Soldier's Home" with Ernest Hemingway's short story will reveal how the pressures—and pleasures—of writing vary with the different forms of media. And, by closing the semester's work with a detailed analysis of the stylistic and thematic interactions of scripts with the other forms of writing in *Popular Writing in America,* students should be better able to appreciate the specific ways in which writing for television depends on other popular forms of American discourse.

Too often, readers isolate their skills in dealing with literature. It is, for many students, a special subject which demands very special skills. But our sequence of reading and writing exercises tries to point up some of the common stylistic features of ads, newspapers, magazines, best-sellers, classic American writing, and scripts. This plan engenders in students the kind of confidence that will enable them to approach any form of writing with a greater sense of ease; they will see it in the context of the other forms of literacy included in the syllabus. Such a strategy should help minimize the conventional resistance of many students toward reading and encourage students to see the interrelations among the seemingly disparate events in their own verbal lives.

RHETORICAL ORGANIZATION

The following brief description of a semester's work is structured according to the basic rhetorical devices most commonly used to teach effective techniques of writing. Appropriate readings are suggested in the Rhetorical Table of Contents.

Week 1—*Varieties of Diction:* levels of usage, abstractions, suiting the voice to the occasion, clarity, economy, and figurative language.

Week 2—*Writing and Revising Sentences:* various types, subordination, parallelism, variety in sentences, economy and conciseness, emphasis, using details/concreteness.

Weeks 3 and 4—*Arrangement of Material/ Paragraphs:* unity, coherence, emphasis, transitions, and overall organization.

Weeks 5 and 6—*Description:* people, places, objects.

Weeks 7, 8, and 9—*Narration:* factual and historical narration, fictional incidents.

Weeks 10, 11, and 12—*Exposition:* definition, classification, dealing with causes and effects, comparison and contrast, describing a process, etc.

Weeks 13 and 14—*Argument and Persuasion:* types, induction/deduction, generalization, syllogism, fallacies, persuasion by logical argument, persuasion by appeal to emotion, authority, ethics; persuasion by irony, ridicule; persuasion by association, analogy.

SAMPLE COURSE DESCRIPTION

The following course description was originally prepared by George Mandelbaum, Louise Yelin, Gail Edwin, and Lynne Rosenthal as one of the options available to instructors in the writing program at Queens College, City University of New York.

The purpose of this course is to develop the student's competence in the writing of expository prose. While this activity involves the description of people, places, and objects, as well as narration (that is, describing people, places, and objects by moving through time), the primary intention of expository prose is the effective communication of ideas. Presentation of ideas may be—and often is—accomplished in a conversational tone; it may—and often does—involve a description or discussion of personal experiences. But expository prose is neither conversation nor autobiography per se. Rather, it serves to establish and support a thesis either about oneself or about something external to oneself. In other words, this is primarily a course in argumentation.

Although the differences between the ways students present a position while thinking, speaking, and writing are too numerous to mention, certain similarities do exist. In every case, students support generalizations by pointing to particular examples, analyze causes and effects of phenomena, and note similarities and differences. To focus their attention on modes of thinking in which they continually engage, and to clarify how they can use such modes to establish and support a thesis while writing, this syllabus stresses the formal rhetorical models. Each model crystallizes one of these modes; consequently, the model helps students to analyze one mode in detail and encourages them to explore how it can be presented in a clear and interesting way. Through analysis—in essence, through thinking about the very process of thinking—students become conscious of what they continually do unconsciously and can use that consciousness in presenting ideas. By exploring how to establish and support a thesis through one mode while writing, they develop an awareness of the strategies suggested by each model and can use these tactics in writing whatever papers they will present in the future.

Order of Writing Exercises

I. Intense personal experience and effects
II. Four paragraphs
III. Social phenomena and causes
IV. Analyze an essay
V. Polemical essay
VI. Compare and contrast
VII. Resource paper

I. *Describe an intense personal experience and discuss the causes that led to it and the effects it had on you.*

This exercise invites an initial discussion of point of view, dialogue, narrative, and the relationship between writer and reader. It also encourages students to think about cause-effect relationships in their own lives and thoughts and to present such relationships by shaping narrative. The assignment demonstrates that while generalizations are important and necessary, they must be based firmly on specifics. The exercise stresses the analysis of the relationship between cause and effect. This attention to cause-effect relationships is extended in a more rigorous way in writing exercises III and V.

Possible Content: Some aspect of your identity as a man or woman; a major success in some personal activity; recollection of a personal "tragedy"; participation in a newsworthy event; attendance at a music festival; remembrance of some aspect of your youth.

Problems: Students should be encouraged both to come to terms with the assignment and to structure it in whatever way they choose. Developing a structure and moving through analysis to generalizations is made easier in the following three ways because each asks students to note similarities and differences in addition to discussing causes and effects:

1. Describe the incident; describe the feelings and accompanying thoughts; describe other incidents in which the same emotion was felt. Through comparison, contrast, analysis, what statement can you make about the particular emotion?

2. Describe the incident; describe the feelings and accompanying thoughts; explain what you

learned; compare your new knowledge with your previous ignorance, paying special attention to what effect your ignorance had and your new knowledge has or will have; explain why it is beneficial to have the knowledge and why you will function more efficiently as a result of it.

3. Describe the incident; describe the feelings and accompanying thoughts. If others were present during the incident, what were their reactions—if not, what might they have been? How are your reactions similar to or different from those of others? Why do the similarities or differences exist?

Preparation: Advertisements, essays, excerpts from best-sellers, poems, and short stories that emphasize incidents and personal reactions to them. Possible readings include *Advertising:* We Smash 'Em Hard; Often a Bridesmaid, but Never a Bride; The End of the Skinny Body!; Again She Orders—"A Chicken Salad, Please"; Geraldine Chaplin Talks about Her "First Time"; Can a Girl Be *Too* Busy. *Press:* Stephen Crane, "Stephen Crane's Own Story"; George Mahawinney, "An Invasion from the Planet Mars"; William L. Laurence, "Atomic Bombing of Nagasaki Told by Flight Member"; Tom Wicker, "The Assassination"; Vivian Gornick, "The Next Great Moment in History Is Theirs." *Magazines:* Bob Greene, "Fifteen." *Best-Sellers:* Edgar Rice Burroughs, *Tarzan of the Apes;* Mickey Spillane, *I, the Jury." Classics:* Kate Chopin, "The Dream of an Hour"; Henry David Thoreau, *Walden;* Stephen Crane, "The Open Boat"; Richard Wright, *Black Boy;* John Updike, "A & P."

II. *Write four paragraphs of expository prose.*

It's good to move to paragraphs early in the semester for three reasons. First, it's important for the students to understand as quickly as possible the basic structural unit used to present ideas. Second, one can go back to the unit in the future should something go awry in the paragraphs students write. Third, it allows teachers to focus on writing problems that students can easily perceive. If one attends with too much care to such matters as wordiness, simple matters of punctuation, or word choices at the beginning of the semester, students often feel that instructors are "picky" and refuse to see the value of attending to such matters. Students are more likely to understand the negative effects of repeating the same idea four times in one paragraph or of a paragraph that has no topic sentence and therefore wanders aimlessly about. By limiting the number of comments on major problems, instructors are more likely to gain the trust of students and establish themselves as perceptive readers.

The transition of paragraphs revolves around a discussion of the differences among descriptive, narrative, and expository prose. Instructors can prepare students for the assignment by analyzing paragraphs of each kind of writing and by pointing to examples of each in the first paper students wrote. Because a good paragraph of expository prose will invariably move from particulars to generalizations or analyze causes and/or effects or observe differences and similarities, the moves in such paragraphs should be pointed out in class as well.

It's advantageous to assign the first two paragraphs together at one time and the second two a little later.

1. Paragraph with topic sentence at the beginning. Since the presentation of ideas necessitates the continual use of such a paragraph structure, its purpose is self-evident.

Possible Content: As in the other three paragraphs, students may write on an assigned topic or on anything they choose.

Problems: Topic sentence covers either an area broader than that dealt with in the paragraph or an area having nothing to do with it; the idea established in the topic sentence is repeated (with slight variation) throughout the paragraph.

2. Paragraph with topic sentence at the end. Since the reader generally expects the topic sentence at the beginning of a paragraph, this structure teaches students about the suspense and surprise created by upsetting expectations. The instructor can refer to this paragraph when discussing the effect of episodic sentences or holding back on one's thesis and beginning a paper with a particular experience or reaction.

Problems: Students will repeat the topic sentence at the end and at the beginning; the topic sentence will have nothing to do with the rest of the paragraph.

Preparation: Teachers can point to paragraphs they found in reading *Popular Writing in America,* make some up, or create some with students in class.

3. Classify something into two categories in the topic sentence and then discuss each category in turn. This exercise shows students how to deal with two different ideas in the same paragraph (thereby preparing them to compare and contrast) and establishes a basic strategy about structure. Like insomniacs, students toss and turn a great deal. In paragraphs or papers, they often begin with idea "a," move to "b" and "c," go back to

"b," then "c," and so on. Since a fundamental strategy of structuring is to put the same kinds of ideas in the same place, the instructor can go back to this paragraph as a structural model for proceeding this way.

Problems: Students will jump back and forth from one idea to the other for no apparent reason; the two categories suddenly turn into three as the student suddenly remembers something essential.

4. Make a value judgment or assertion and support it. This exercise clarifies for students what value judgments and assertions are, requires them to recognize that these need to be supported, and invites them to explore ways that such support can be given.

Problems: The topic is too broad for one paragraph or is unsupported or is narrative parading as expository prose.

Preparation: Possible reading for class discussion of this sequence of writing exercises can be drawn from almost any of the nonfiction selections in the six sections of the book. "Press" offers, for example, especially useful illustrations of the topic sentence at the beginning of the paragraph, as it does for the exercise on value judgments. (See also, the reportage in the weekly news magazines.)

III. *Describe a social phenomenon and discuss its causes.*

This exercise encourages students to see that social phenomena are not isolated events but rather effects brought about by antecedent events. They come to recognize, too, how causal relationships can be explored and presented.

Since students will already have dealt with causes and effects on a personal level in the first assignment and since any number of paragraphs in the second assignment will deal with such a relationship, the transition to this assignment is fairly easy. Instructors merely need to note that in this paper students reverse the normal time sequence by beginning with the effect and moving back to causes and that students are to focus not on themselves but on the social phenomena. Students should be encouraged to deal with a phenomenon of which they consider themselves a part in order to invite them to move back and forth from the personal to the impersonal.

Possible Content: A few of the many possibilities are increasing popularity of rock music and concerts; growing tendency of women to remain independent and work after graduating from high school or college rather than get married; use of sex in print advertising; specific trends in fashions; American's dependence on automobiles.

Problems: Students have a tendency to choose broad topics like the rise and fall of the Roman Empire; they also tend to confuse description of a phenomenon with its causes or of causes with effects.

Possible Structures:

1. Describe in the first paragraph (or first two or three paragraphs) and then discuss causes, working in examples of own experiences if appropriate.

2. Describe, discuss what others have pointed to as the causes, then either agree or disagree with them, working in examples of own experiences if appropriate.

3. Describe your own experience; note that what is true of yours is also true of others' and then analyze causes, working in how causes affected you.

Preparation: For possible reading, see *Advertising:* any of the seven groups of advertisements. *Press:* assassination (see Lincoln and Kennedy murders), the Orson Welles radio broadcast, the moon landing (see Thomas O'Toole, Norman Mailer), and women's liberation. *Magazines:* child labor (see William Hard) and the various categories listed in the Table of Linked Selections.

IV. *Analyze a piece of writing.*

This exercise encourages students to apply all that they have learned—and what they now learn about tone, diction, and syntax—to an analysis of advertisements, journalism, magazine articles, or the nonfictional best-sellers and classics. Classics, poetry, and best-selling fiction are equally suitable for this exercise. In any event, *Popular Writing in America* provides a wide range of reading possibilities to adapt to the particular level of your class.

Since almost any piece of writing tries to achieve a certain effect on readers or listeners, students can see the writing as a highly complex set of causes that attempt to change the reader's opinion, attitude, or awareness about certain issues. The assignment is therefore similar to assignment III. In both III and IV, students can either vary or follow a pattern in which they begin with effects and move back to causes.

Problems: Students will either summarize what they are to analyze or write down a series of generalizations or personal impressions that are not supported by references to the text.

Possible Structure:

1. Describe the audience that the author is trying to reach and what effect he or she is trying to achieve.

2. Explain how the basic argument, diction,

tone, syntax, and structure help achieve that effect.

3. To conclude, do either of the following: indicate whether the essay had the desired effect on you and explain why it did or did not, or, since you have discussed *what* the author tries to do and *how* he or she does it, make a general statement about the relationship between his or her ends and means. (For example, if the writer forms in and out groups to establish a certain relationship between himself or herself and the reader, make a statement about the formation of such groups that would illuminate why the author chose to make such a move.)

V. *Write a polemical essay.*

Since students now realize that an author chooses words to have a specific impact on a specific audience, and since they know how to analyze causes and effects, they are ready to define an audience, take a position, and attempt to persuade that audience that their position is viable.

The primary purpose of a polemical essay is to argue that a particular course of action should or should not be carried out. The exercise can be varied in a number of ways: by changing the person who will argue the position or by changing the audience that the same person will address. The student's tone, diction, and syntax will, of course, need to be adjusted in each instance, yet the basic strategies of persuasion will have certain similarities. In each case, the students will be required to explore the positive and negative effects of whatever course of action he or she is supporting or arguing against.

Possible Content: The instructor can ask students to take a position on one or more issues defined in class or to take on anything that interests them.

Problems: Students believe that it's enough to just state that whatever they want done should be done or that whatever they define as being good or right actually is so. They also may devote too much time to describing the problem and not enough to defending their solution.

Possible Structures:

1. Describe situation; explain why it is undesirable; offer solution; discuss effect of solution on problem.

2. Describe problem; discuss causes and probable effects of problem; offer solution; show how solution will affect causes, and (if necessary) show that positive effects of solution will outweigh negative ones.

3. Problem; previous solutions; effects of such solutions; own solution; own solution better because effects better.

Preparation:

1. See the entries under "Argument and Persuasion" in the Rhetorical Table of Contents.

2. Since persuasion so often deals with antecedent events, the present situation, and the effect of desirable action, persuasive writing is often structured according to past, present, and future. One can clarify that structure by pointing to political slogans ("Never Again") or advertising ("If he kissed you once, will he kiss you again? Be certain with Certs.")

3. Have students debate some issue.

VI. *Compare and contrast two pieces of writing.*

Two options are possible if the instructor asks students to compare two pieces of writing. Have them analyze the first piece when they analyze an essay in assignment IV, introduce the other at this point, and have them compare the two. Or introduce two entirely different pieces of writing.

Possible Content: Since students so often have difficulty in analyzing one extended piece of writing, they will find it even harder to deal with two. It therefore might be a good idea to deal with relatively short pieces of writing. For example, one can ask students to examine the coverage of the case against 2 Live Crew, the coverage of the space shuttle disaster, Stephen Crane's two versions of being shipwrecked, the different accounts of the moon landing (Thomas O'Toole in "Press" and Norman Mailer in "Classics"), Tom Wicker's newspaper report on the assassination of President Kennedy and his recollections of the event as described in "The Assassination" ("Press"). An instructor could also assign any two essays grouped under a common heading in the Table of Linked Selections as well as those items listed under "Comparison and Contrast" in the Rhetorical Table of Contents.

Problems: Unless students see one essential similarity and difference that affects the word choices and strategies of each piece of writing, their papers will often wander back and forth from one piece to the other or amount to a list. Other problems are described under assignment IV.

Possible Sturcture:

1. Thesis.

2. Indicate what is similar about the effect each writer tries to produce.

3. Explain how that similarity leads to similar stylistic strategies (or similarities in diction, tone, syntax, etc.).

4. Indicate both what is different about the effect each writer tries to produce and what audience he or she tries to reach.

5. Explain how that difference leads to different strategies (or differences in diction, tone, syntax, etc.).

6. To conclude, indicate either which writer had the desired effect on you and why or which writer uses the best means to achieve his or her ends. (An evaluation of the relationship between means and ends can be worked into the body of the paper as well.)

Preparation: Since students have so many problems with this assignment and since they have so many options in dealing with it, the instructor should discuss both works in class and discuss some of the options they have. For example, if they want to stress primarily similarities or differences, the instructor should discuss how they can do so.

VII. *Write a research paper.*

Possible Content:

1. Do research and write a paper on anything that interests the student.

2. Do research on one (or two or three) topics defined by the teacher in consultation with the students.

3. Do research on and rewrite the social phenomena-cause paper or the polemical essay to include it.

Sample Exercise: Most Americans remember what happened on July 4, 1776, or November 22, 1963. The events of these days are etched in our nation's history. But do you know what happened on the day you were born? Trace back through the microfilm copy of the *New York Times* (or any similar newspaper) to the date of your birth. Find some event that day that interests you. After completing the necessary research in the magazines printed at that time and the books published later on that subject, write a detailed analysis of what occurred, including attention to the causes leading to that event and the effects it produced.

POPULAR WRITING IN AMERICA

POPULAR WRITING IN AMERICA

THE INTERACTION OF STYLE AND AUDIENCE

FIFTH EDITION

Donald McQuade
University of California, Berkeley

Robert Atwan

New York Oxford
OXFORD UNIVERSITY PRESS
1993

Oxford University Press

Oxford New York Toronto
Delhi Bombay Calcutta Madras Karachi
Kuala Lumpur Singapore Hong Kong Tokyo
Nairobi Dar es Salaam Cape Town
Melbourne Auckland Madrid

and associated companies in
Berlin Ibadan

Published by Oxford University Press, Inc.
200 Madison Avenue, New York, New York 10016

Library of Congress Cataloging-in-Publication Data
Popular writing in America : the interaction of style and audience /
[compiled by] Donald McQuade, Robert Atwan.—5th ed.
p. cm. ISBN 0-19-507308-8
1. College readers. 2. English language—Rhetoric.
3. American literature. 4. Popular literature—United States.
I. McQuade, Donald. II. Atwan, Robert.
PE1417.P6 1993 808'.0427—dc20 92-22724

9 8 7 6 5 4 3 2 1
Printed in the United States of America
on acid-free paper

Annie Dillard: "Total Eclipse" from *Teaching a Stone to Talk* by Annie Dillard. Copyright © 1982 by Annie Dillard. Reprinted by permission of HarperCollins Publishers.

Maureen Dowd: "The Senate and Sexism," October 8, 1991. Copyright © 1991 by The New York Times Company. Reprinted by permission.

Gretel Ehrlich: "The Solace of Open Spaces," May 1981, *The Atlantic Monthly*. Copyright © 1981 by Gretel Ehrlich.

Susan Faludi: "Blame it on Feminism," from *Backlash: The Undeclared War Against American Women* by Susan Faludi. Copyright © 1991 by Susan Faludi. Reprinted by permission of Crown Publishers, Inc., and the author.

William Faulkner: From *Go Down, Moses,* by William Faulkner. Copyright 1940, 1941, 1942 by William Faulkner. Copyright 1942 by The Curtis Publishing Company. Copyright renewed 1968, 1969, 1970 by Estelle Faulkner and Jim Faulkner Summers. Reprinted by permission of Random House, Inc.

Samuel Francis: From *The Washington Times,* August 24, 1989. Samuel Francis is a columnist and editorial writer for *The Washington Times.*

Robert Frost: "The Gift Outright" and "Design" from *The Poetry of Robert Frost,* edited by Edward Connery Lathem. Copyright 1936, 1942. Copyright © 1964, 1970 by Lesley Frost Ballantine. Copyright © 1969 by Holt, Rinehart and Winston. Reprinted by permission of Henry Holt and Company, Inc., and Jonathan Cape, Ltd.

Wilfred Funk and Norman Lewis: "First Day: Give Us Fifteen Minutes a Day" from *Thirty Days to a More Powerful Vocabulary* by Wilfred Funk and Norman Lewis. Copyright 1942 by Wilfred Funk, Inc. Reprinted by permission of HarperColllins Publishers.

Henry Louis Gates, Jr.: "2 Live Crew, Decoded," June 19, 1990 Op-Ed. Copyright © 1990 by The New York Times Company. Reprinted by permission.

Robert Geller: Television adaptation of Ernest Hemingway's "Soldier's Home." Used by permission of Charles Scribner's Sons, an imprint of Macmillan Publishing Company, and John Hemingway, Patrick Hemingway, and Gregory Hemingway.

Allen Ginsberg: "A Supermarket in California" from *Collected Poems 1947–1980* by Allen Ginsberg. Copyright © 1955 by Allen Ginsberg. Reprinted by permission of HarperCollins Publishers.

Vivian Gornick: Reprinted by permission of the author and *The Village Voice.*

Martin Gottfried: "Rambos of the Road," copyright © 1986, 1991 by Martin Gottfried. Reprinted by permission of the author.

Robert Greene: "Fifteen," from *Esquire,* August 1982. Reprinted by permission of the author.

Alex Haley: From *Roots* by Alex Haley. Copyright © 1976 by Alex Haley. Used by permission of Doubleday, a division of Bantam Doubleday Dell Publishing Group, Inc.

Jeffrey Hart: "Feting the Lindbergh of the 15th Century," Oct. 14, 1991, *The San Francisco Examiner*. Copyright © 1991 King Features. Reprinted by permission.

Ernest Hemingway: "Soldier's Home." Reprinted with permission of Charles Scribner's Sons, an imprint of Macmillan Publishing Company, from *In Our Time* by Ernest Hemingway. Copyright 1925 by Charles Scribner's Sons; renewal copyright 1953 by Ernest Hemingway.

Scott Higham, Anne Bartlett, James F. McCarty: "A First: Album Ruled Obscene," June 7, 1990, *The Miami Herald*. Reprinted with the permission of *The Miami Herald.*

Ann Hodgman: "No Wonder They Call Me a Bitch," *Spy,* June 1989. Reprinted by permission of UFS, Inc. on behalf of *Spy.*

Sidney Hook: "Civilization and Its Malcontents," *National Review,* October 13, 1989. First published in *Measure,* Number 81, August/September 1989, a publication of the University Centers for Rational Alternatives in New York City.

Langston Hughes: Reprinted by permission of the *Chicago Defender.*

Robert Hughes: "The Fraying of America," *Time,* February 3, 1992. Copyright 1992 by Time Inc. Reprinted by permission.

Susan Jacoby: "Unfair Game." Reprinted by permission of Georges Borchardt, Inc. on behalf of the author. Copyright © 1978 by Susan Jacoby.

The Jeffersons: "The Jeffersons" © 1993 CPT Holdings, reprinted courtesy Columbia Pictures Television.

Karen Jurgensen: Copyright © 1991, *USA Today*. Reprinted with permission.

Garrison Keillor: "Sumus Quod Sumus," from *Lake Wobegon Days* by Garrison Keillor. Copyright © 1985 by Garrison Keillor. Used by permission of Viking Penguin, a division of Penguin Books USA Inc.

Jamaica Kincaid: Copyright © 1990 by Jamaica Kincaid. Reprinted with permission of Wylie, Aitken, and Stone.

Martin Luther King, Jr.: "I Have a Dream" speech. Reprinted by permission of the Joan Davies Agency.

Stephen King: "Now You Take 'Bambi' and 'Snow White' . . . That's Scary," June 13, 1981, *TV Guide*. Reprinted with permission from TV Guide® Magazine. Copyright © 1981 by News American Publications Inc.

Maxine Hong Kingston: From *The Woman Warrior* by Maxine Hong Kingston. Copyright © 1975, 1976 by Maxine Hong Kingston. Reprinted by permission of Alfred A. Knopf, Inc.

Ron Kovic: "Wounded" from *Born on the Fourth of July,* by R. Kovic and R. Ritz. Copyright © 1976. Reprinted by permission of McGraw-Hill.

Jack Lait: "Dillinger 'Gets His' " from International News Service, July 23, 1934. Reprinted with special permission of King Features Syndicate.

William Laurence: "Atomic Bombing of Nagasaki Told by Flight Member," September 9, 1945. Copyright © 1945 by The New York Times Company. Reprinted by permission.

Teri Maddox: "Unsuspecting Parents Can't Believe Their Ears," September 30, 1990, the *Belleville Illinois News Democrat,* Belleville, Illinois.

George Mahawinney: Reprinted with permission of the *Philadelphia Inquirer.*

Norman Mailer: From *Of a Fire on the Moon.* Copyright © 1969, 1970 by Norman Mailer. By permission of Little, Brown and Company.

Debbie McKinney: "Youth's Despair Erupts," January 12, 1988, the *Anchorage Daily News.* Used with permission of Deborah McKinney and the *Anchorage Daily News.*

Grace Metalious: From *Peyton Place.* Copyright © 1956 by Grace Metalious. Reprinted by permission of Simon & Schuster, Inc.

David Mills: "The Judge vs. 2 Live Crew: Is the Issue Obscenity or Young, Black Males?" June 25–July 1, 1990, *Washington Post* (National Weekly Edition). Reprinted by permission of the *Washington Post.*

N. Scott Momaday: "A First American Views His Land," July 1976, *National Geographic.* Reprinted by permission of the author.

William Least Heat Moon: "Nameless Tennessee," pp. 26–35 from *Blue Highways: A Journey into America.* Copyright © 1982 by William Least Heat Moon. By permission of Little, Brown, and Company.

Marianne Moore: Permission to reproduce "Correspondence with the Ford Motor Company" by Marianne Moore granted by Marianne Moore, Literary Executor for the Estate of Marianne Moore. All rights reserved. Originally published in *The New Yorker.*

Toni Morrison. "Cinderella's Stepsisters." Reprinted by permission of Toni Morrison. Copyright © 1977 by Toni Morrison.

Lance Morrow: "A Nation Mourns," February 10, 1986, copyright 1972 Time Inc.; and "Blood in the Streets: Subculture of Violence" April 24, 1972, copyright 1986 Time Inc. Reprinted by permission.

Ogden Nash: From *Verses from 1929 On* by Ogden Nash. Copyright 1935 Ogden Nash. By permission of Little, Brown and Company.

Flannery O'Connor: "The Life You Save May Be Your Own" from *A Good Man Is Hard to Find and Other Stories,* copyright 1953 by Flannery O'Connor and renewed 1981 by Mrs. Regina O'Connor, reprinted by permission of Harcourt Brace Jovanovich, Inc.

David Ogilvy: Reprinted with the permission of Atheneum Publishers, an imprint of Macmillan Publishing Company from *Confessions of an Advertising Man* by David Ogilvy. Copyright © 1963, 1987 by David Ogilvy Trustee.

Tillie Olsen. "I Stand Here Ironing," from *Tell Me a Riddle* by Tillie Olsen. Copyright © 1956, 1957, 1960, 1961 by Tillie Olsen. Used by permission of Delacorte Press/Seymour Lawrence, a division of Bantam Doubleday Dell Publishing Group, Inc., and the Elaine Markson Agency on behalf of the author.

Thomas O'Toole: " 'The Eagle Has Landed': Two Men Walk on the Moon" from the *Washington Post,* July 21, 1969. Reprinted by permission of the *Washington Post.*

Laura Parker: "How Things Got Nasty in Broward County," October 21, 1990, the *Washington Post.* Reprinted by permission of the *Washington Post.*

Walker Percy: "The Loss of the Creature" from *The Message in the Bottle* by Walker Percy. Copyright © 1975 by Walker Percy. Reprinted by permission of Farrar, Straus & Giroux, Inc.

Sylvia Plath: From *The Colossus and Other Poems* by Sylvia Plath. Copyright © 1960 by Sylvia Plath. Reprinted by permission of Alfred A. Knopf, Inc. Originally appeared in *The New Yorker.*

Neil Postman: From *Conscientious Objections* by Neil Postman. Copyright © 1988 by Neil Postman. Reprinted by permission of Alfred A. Knopf, Inc.

Mario Puzo: Reprinted by permission from The Putnam Publishing Group from *The Godfather* by Mario Puzo. Copyright © 1969 by Mario Puzo.

Anna Quindlen: "Fighting the War on Cigs," March 4, 1990. Copyright © 1990 by The New York Times Company. Reprinted by permission.

Ishmael Reed: "Antihero," May 1990, *Spin.* Reprinted by permission of *Spin.*

Teresa Riordan: "Miller Life Guy," March 27, 1989, *The New Republic.* Reprinted by permission of *The New Republic* © 1989. The New Republic, Inc.

Lillian Robinson: "What Culture Should Mean," from *The Nation,* September 25, 1989. This article is reprinted from *The Nation* magazine. © 1989 The Nation Company, Inc.

David Savage: "Forbidden Words on Campus," February 12, 1991, *The Los Angeles Times.*

Michael Specter: "Cigarettes for the Tractor-Pull Generation," *Washington Post* (National Weekly Edition), February 26–March 4, 1990. Reprinted by permission of the *Washington Post.*

Mickey Spillane: From *I, the Jury* by Mickey Spillane. Copyright 1947 by E. P. Dutton, renewed © 1975 by Mickey Spillane. Used by permission of the publisher, Dutton, an imprint of New American Library, a division of Penguin Books USA Inc.

Benjamin Spock: "Should Children Play with Guns?" from *Baby and Child Care.* Copyright © 1945, 1946, 1957, 1968, 1976, 1985, by Benjamin Spock, M.D.

Amy Tan: Reprinted by permission of the Putnam Publishing Group from *The Joy Luck Club* by Amy Tan. Copyright © 1989.

Lewis Thomas: "The World's Biggest Membrane," copyright © 1971, 1972, 1973 by The Massachusetts Medical Society, from *The Lives of a Cell* by Lewis Thomas. Used by permission of Viking Penguin, a division of Penguin Books USA Inc.

Dorothy Thompson: "Mr. Welles and Mass Delusion," copyright 1938 by the *New York Herald Tribune.*

Sallie Tisdale: "We Do Abortions Here: A Nurse's Story," October 1987, *Harper's.* Reprinted by permission of the author.

John Updike: From *Pigeon Feathers and Other Stories* by John Updike. Copyright © 1962 by John Updike. Reprinted by permission of Alfred A. Knopf, Inc. Originally appeared in *The New Yorker.*

Michael Ventura: "On Kids and Slasher Movies," November 3, 1989, *L.A. Weekly* [Original title: "The Toy from Hell"]. Copyright © 1989 by Michael Ventura.

David von Drehle: "Shaken Survivors Witness Pure Fury," September 23, 1989, *The Miami Herald.* Reprinted with permission of the *Miami Herald.*

Eudora Welty: From *The Eye of the Story* by Eudora Welty. Copyright © 1975 by Eudora Welty. Reprinted by permission of Random House, Inc.

E. B. White: "Once More to the Lake," from *Essays of E. B. White* by E. B. White. Copyright 1941 by E. B. White. Reprinted by permission of HarperCollins Publishers.

Tom Wicker: "Kennedy Is Killed by Sniper as He Rides in Car in Dallas," November 23, 1963. Copyright © 1963 by the New York Times Company; "The Assassination," December 1963 *(Times Talk).* Copyright © 1963 by The New York Times Company. Reprinted by permission.

Juan Williams: "The Real Crime: Making Heroes of Hate Mongers," June 17, 1990, the *Washington Post.* Reprinted by permission of the *Washington Post.*

William Carlos Williams: "The Farmer's Daughters," copyright 1938 by Williams Carlos Williams. Reprinted by permission of New Directions Publishing Corporation.

Richard Wright: "Discovering Books" from *Black Boy* by Richard Wright. Copyright 1937, 1942, 1944, 1945 by Richard Wright. Reprinted by permission of HarperCollins Publishers, Mrs. Ellen Wright, and Jonathan Cape, Ltd.

For Our Parents

PREFACE

For this fifth edition of *Popular Writing in America,* we made several changes that we expect will enhance the book's overall flexibility and usefulness. In response to instructors who would like to pay more attention to issue-oriented expository writing in class, we revised the sections on "Press" and "Magazines" to include a generous sampling of contemporary essays and articles, covering such topics as abortion, AIDS, censorship, "politically correct" speech codes, racism, feminism, the canon controversy, and multiculturalism. We also happily complied with the requests of many instructors that we feature more literary works by a diversity of authors, both canonical and noncanonical. New to this edition are essays by John Updike, Frederick Douglass, Harriet Jacobs, E. B. White, Maxine Hong Kingston, Walker Percy, Lewis Thomas, Annie Dillard, and June Jordan; we also added new stories by Nathaniel Hawthorne, Charlotte Perkins Gilman, Raymond Carver, and Amy Tan. These new selections will give teachers a wider range of fiction and nonfiction to work with. Instructors will find selections to suit a variety of classroom purposes—prose that will provide provocative topics for class discussion, practical models for student composition, and imaginative texts for literary study.

We have also responded to instructors who asked for more argumentative material by including a large cluster of relatively short selections on the obscenity controversy surrounding the rap group "2 Live Crew." This cluster—consisting largely of newspaper editorials—offers a variety of opinion on a lively issue and should help stimulate classroom discussion that leads to argumentative essays. Since many instructors use the "Advertising" chapter as a convenient way to teach rhetorical and argumentative strategies, we added many new advertisements to that section, along with new essays that discuss in-depth familiar ads and related campaigns. In addition, we have included throughout the book many more discussion questions focusing on the interrelationships between a work's style, subject, and strategy—and its intended audience.

As in previous editions, our choices were guided by a principle of interconnectedness that we believe is one of the most important features of the book: Virtually every selection in *Popular Writing in America* is connected either stylistically or thematically with one or more of the other selections. An expanded "Table of Linked Selections" follows the "Rhetorical Table of Contents" and will encourage teachers and students to discover the different ways the same subject can be treated by different writers or by different media (for example, how staff writers for *Time* and *Newsweek* each handled the space shuttle disaster in January 1986; how a major author like Stephen Crane used his personal experience of a disaster at sea to write both a newspaper report and a classic American short story; how Ernest Hemingway's famous short story, "Soldier's Home," was transformed into a film script).

We want to remind readers that our selections are not meant to serve only as models for student compositions. The selections are intended in part to generate lively and productive discussions about writing and to help students become more analytically familiar with the diversity of styles and strategies that develop within a contemporary system of communications increasingly dependent on corporate enterprise, mass audiences, interlocking media industries, and vast outlays of money. Few acts of writing—and surely student compositions are no exception—exist completely outside of competitive, socioeconomic considerations. We assume that the more conscious students are of the public and commercial pressures behind a piece of writing (pressures that can be felt *in* the writing, whether an advertisement, news item, magazine article, best-seller, or script), the more sensitive they will become to whatever particular commercial or institutional styles or ''voices'' they may inadvertently be endorsing in their own writing. In order to make this particular interaction of style and audience dramatically visible to students, we have added a considerable number of selections dealing with the ways in which mass-media artists and artifacts determine the shape of our consumer culture.

An awareness of how one sounds is crucial for all effective writing. ''Whom or what does the writer sound like here?'' and ''What sort of reader does the writer imagine here?'' are questions worth asking of any kind of writing, be it the work of a professional or a student, be it inspired or required. Many contemporary writers (see for example the selections from Norman Mailer, Joan Didion, and Walker Percy) depend on an audience critically alert to the ways in which their sentences assimilate, parody, and challenge the highly competitive languages of the mass-communication industries. The work of such writers reminds us that practical matters of style and audience remain vital topics in any writing curriculum.

In general, most of the changes we made for this edition—more newspaper editorials and feature articles, a greater range of recent magazine pieces, and more selections from best-selling nonfiction—represent our considered responses to the many instructors throughout the country who have used *Popular Writing in America* and have generously suggested specific ways they thought the book could be improved. We hope that they will be welcomed by those who have worked with the book before as well as by those who will try it for the first time.

ACKNOWLEDGMENTS

The continued success of *Popular Writing in America,* as with any book in its fifth edition, depends on the generous advice of colleagues across the country who work with it in class each year. For this edition, we would like to thank in particular Laura Davis-Clapper of Kent State University (East Liverpool Campus), who supplied us with a comprehensive analysis of the text as well as several sample syllabi and assignments. Her review was especially helpful to us in preparing this revision. We also received ideas and encouragement from several other reviewers, and want to thank: Paul Belgrade of Millersville University, Maury Dean of Suffolk County Community College, Carolyn Howell of Gulf Coast Community College, and Susan Seyfarth of Middle Tennessee State University. We appreciate, too, the solid help we received from Jack Roberts of Rutgers University and Frank Di Cesare of Seton Hall University. Michael McSpedon ably assisted us in the early stages of manuscript production as did Christine McQuade in coordinating the manuscript for *Some Suggestions for Using Popular Writing in America.* In addition, Jennifer Royal provided invaluable and expert research and production assistance throughout the preparation of this new edition. Ann Powers of the

University of California, Berkeley gave most generously of her time, intelligence, and imagination to developing several aspects of the project.

We are grateful for the many suggestions instructors and friends have given to us over the past decade. We have included as many of their recommendations as possible. In particular, we would like to thank Trudy Baltz, Charles Bazerman, Richard Bonomo, Gail Bounds, Addison Bross, Curtis Church, John Clifford, Edward P. J. Corbett, Mary Corboy, Frank D'Angelo, Kenneth O. Danz, Wheeler Dixon, Kent Ekberg, Lyman Fink, Jr., Christine Freeman, David Gaines, Kate Hirsh, R. S. Hootman, Lee A. Jacobus, Ed Joyce, D. G. Kehl, Helene Keyssar, Kay Kier, Henry Knepler, Roberta Kramer, Andrea Lunsford, William Lutz, Richard Mikita, William Miller, Christopher Motley, Helen Naugle, Matthew O'Brien, Paul O'Connell, Ed Quinn, Lori Rath, Harold Schechter, Michael Schudson, Sharon Shaloo, Phillip Shew, Nancy Sommers, Charles Taylor, Victor H. Thompson, Barbara H. Traister, Ruth VandeKieft, Patrick van den Bossche, William Vesterman, Maureen Waters, and Harvey Wiener.

We would like to acknowledge once again those who helped us structure the original text and whose influence is still very much evident in each new edition: Paul Bertram, Anthony Cardoza, Thomas R. Edwards, Christopher Gray, the late Mark Gibbons, Ron Holland, Daniel F. Howard, the late Betsy B. Kaufman, Robert E. Lynch, Robert Lyons, C. F. Main, George Mandelbaum, Barbara Maxwell, Max Maxwell, John McDermott, Kevin McQuade, Charles Molesworth, Frank Moorman, Richard Poirier, Marie Ponsot, Douglas Roehm, the late Sandra Schor, Gary Tate, Thomas Van Laan, Elissa Weaver, and Ridley Whitaker. John Wright, Gerald Mentor, and Jean Shapiro played important roles in the success of earlier editions, and we continue to value that thoughtful assistance.

We are indebted to the kind people at Oxford University Press who made working on this fifth edition at once pleasant and productive. In particular we would like to thank: Liz Maguire, Ruth Sandweiss, Ellie Fuchs, and especially Susan Chang, whose professionalism as well as her gracious and inexhaustible efforts on our behalf made this a better book and a memorably pleasant experience. As always, Helene Atwan and Susanne Batschelet McQuade have helped in innumerable ways.

CONTENTS

AUTOMOBILES

EATING AND DRINKING

MEDIA

INSTITUTIONAL AND CORPORATE ADVERTISING

PRESS 111

BEST-SELLERS 361

CLASSICS 487

SCRIPTS 685

RHETORICAL TABLE OF CONTENTS

DESCRIPTION

PEOPLE

Advertisements

PLACES

Advertisements

OBJECTS

Advertisements

NARRATION

FACTUAL AND HISTORICAL

FICTIONAL

Advertisements

EXPOSITION

DEFINITION

Advertisements

CLASSIFICATION

Advertisements

ILLUSTRATION

Advertisements

COMPARISON AND CONTRAST

Advertisements

ANALOGY

Advertisements

PROCESS ANALYSIS

Advertisements

CAUSE AND EFFECT

Advertisements

ARGUMENT

Advertisements

PERSUASION

Advertisements

Virtually all of them

TABLE OF LINKED SELECTIONS

The Myth of Success

American Popular Culture: Some Characters

Coming of Age

Two Declarations of Freedom

The Art of Seeing

Men and Women

The Language of War

The Art of Humor

Questioning America's Values

The American Short Story: A Mini-Anthology

INTRODUCTION

This book grew out of our commitment to the notion—one that still might seem peculiar to many people—that *any* form of writing can be made the subject of rewarding critical attention. And because we are most interested in the written products of American culture that are continually shaping the ways we think, talk, and feel, our editorial effort has been to include as great a variety of American themes and prose styles as could be managed within a single text. Along with some traditional selections from such classic American writers as Thoreau, Twain, Crane, and Faulkner, we have brought together an assortment of material from scripts, best-sellers, popular magazines, newspapers, and advertisements. One critical principle informs our selections: we want to illustrate through historical sequences, thematic cross-references, and divergent creative intentions precisely how the most widely read forms of American writing interact with each other and with their audiences to produce that intricate network of artistic and commercial collaboration known as popular culture.

Popular Writing in America is divided into six parts. The opening section consists of some of the most successful copywriting in the history of American advertising. We have arranged the ads in clusters dealing with similar products (automobiles, food, clothing, etc.) and gender issues over a number of decades both to provide a brief historical perspective on the language and rhetorical strategies of advertising and to invite speculation on changes in American culture as they are reflected in the ways our society is talked to in its advertisements. In addition, to demonstrate some of the ways advertising is thought about both inside and outside the industry, we have also included essays on the art of copywriting, several critiques of advertising, and a series of delightful letters showing a prominent American poet exercising her imagination and vocabulary in an attempt to invent a suitable name for a new automobile.

The examples of newspaper writing we include in the next chapter range from different styles of headlines through the compressed prose of teletype releases to extended forms of news coverage. Events of such historical magnitude as the Lincoln and Kennedy assassinations and the use of the atom bomb on Japan are interspersed among some of the usual kinds of news stories, feature articles, interviews, and editorials that comprise the substance of the daily American newspaper. Because we want to emphasize in this chapter the stylistic and structural consequences of writing performed under emergency conditions and against competitive deadlines—"Journalism is literature in a hurry," according to Matthew Arnold—we have weighted our selections in favor of the kinds of violence and tragedies that have inspired reporters, made history, and sold newspapers.

Magazines are eclectic by necessity. Represented are a variety of topics from some of the most popular "big" and "little" magazines published in America. With very few exceptions, an article from a particular magazine is intended to be at least fairly typical of the kind of material and tonal quality found in that magazine around the time the article appeared. Our selections in this chapter are limited to nonfiction because much of the fiction in "Best-Sellers" and "Classics" was originally published in magazines. Consequently, an important periodical such as *Scribner's* is not represented by an article in this section but by Stephen Crane's short story that appears in "Classics."

The material reprinted in "Best-Sellers" affords the reader the opportunity to examine some of the most commercially successful prose in American publishing history. It is, for the most part, writing that the academic community has seldom paid serious attention to—selections from best-sellers are rarely made available in textbooks or anthologies. Yet, because of their massive audiences and their frequent interactions with other forms of media, best-sellers deserve to be attended to by readers interested in examining the relationship between their own verbal experiences and those of a literate public. Passages such as Tarzan's rescue of Jane in *Tarzan of the Apes* or the shooting of Don Corleone from *The Godfather* were selected not as specimens of mediocre writing—mediocre, that is, *because* they are from best-sellers—but as examples of writing that has had enormous impact on the American reading public.

The success of many of the best-selling books represented in this section depended, to a great extent, on their public's previous acceptance of similar subjects and verbal strategies in advertisements, newspapers, and magazine articles. To cite but one example, the phenomenal attention Mario Puzo's *The Godfather* received was in large measure the result of the extensive news coverage given to the felonies and frolics of underworld characters. Popular fiction, in turn, affects other forms of media, as can be seen from the account of the murder of Joey Gallo in *Time* magazine, where the report of a ritualistic gangland shooting self-consciously trades on the rendition of a similar event in *The Godfather*. Throughout the book, connections such as this one are signaled in headnotes and discussion questions in order to map out a network of thematic and stylistic interrelations.

Though our emphasis in "Classics" is on short fiction and poetry, we also include essays, excerpts from autobiographies, and other selected nonfiction from some of America's major authors. We have taken the liberty of designating the work of such contemporary writers as John Updike, Norman Mailer, Flannery O'Connor, and Joan Didion as classic because we feel that the quality of their performances and their critical alertness to the present condition of our language entitle them to be viewed in the same historical perspective as Thoreau, Twain, Crane, and Faulkner. *Classic* is a term we adopt for the sake of convenience; it is not intended to suggest writing that is antiquated, writing that is easily dissociated from popular culture because it sounds serious and elevated, but writing that has, so far, stayed around because it has stayed alive. We want to show from our selections that classic authors have not remained socially and intellectually superior to the various ordinary languages of popular culture but have tried to come to terms with those languages by appropriating them, occasionally discarding them, often shaping or extending them so that their writing can reflect the complex interplay between what we call literature and what we recognize as the accents of the life around us.

In "Scripts" we introduce popular language that is heard rather than read. Though surely the most widely responded to form of writing, radio and television scripts are seldom seen and examined by anyone other than professionals. People tend to forget that much of what they *see* in the movies or on television started first with the written word. In some cases, as in the film version of Ernest Hemingway's "Soldier's Home," what is being seen is a transcription of classic literature. Hemingway's story is included in "Classics" so that readers can examine how such adaptations are accomplished and also learn how the shaping of a text for a film audience affects the way the original material is interpreted. Episodes from such popular television series as *The Jeffersons* and *Roseanne* show how writers work to create an interplay of authentic dialogue and believable characters.

It might be argued that this type of book is unnecessary because the abundance of ads, newspapers, magazines, and best-sellers makes them so available as "texts" that there is really no need to collect samples of them in a separate volume. If our texts had been chosen indiscriminately, simply to document different types of writing, that might be the case. But, quite clearly, one way the book can be used is to illustrate a verbal progression from the readily accessible language and strategies of advertising to the more obviously complicated styles of expression that characterize outstanding prose. The risk of this procedure, however, is that it may prove too schematic, may even encourage readers to regard the ads, some of the journalism and magazine articles, and most of the best-sellers as blatantly inferior forms of writing, "straw men" set up to be discarded all too easily in favor of the durable excellence of the "great works." It should be noted, therefore, that our categories and sequence were not especially designed to endorse already entrenched hierarchies by setting up fairly obvious gradations in the quality of several particular types of prose and poetry but were intended to illustrate how various kinds of writing shaped by quite different commercial purposes and intended audiences interact with and modify each other to produce what we can reasonably call a common culture.

It might also be argued that classics have no place in an anthology devoted to popular writing. Classics are among the finest holdings of an educated minority; popular writing belongs to something as repugnant as "mass culture." That is one way to look at it. Another, and one that this book is premised on, is that classics are among the best things we have to share with each other, and they ought to be encountered in all their challenging complexity as opportunities to enliven and, if necessary, toughen the questions we ask of all the other modes of expression we participate in daily. That is why we have included an excerpt from Norman Mailer's *Of a Fire on the Moon* in "Classics." Throughout his comprehensive report on the Apollo expedition, Mailer is critically aware of the ways his own prose interrelates with a variety of other, mainly competing verbal efforts. Mailer's original contract to write about the Apollo XI astronauts was with *Life,* a popular magazine. But Mailer is no ordinary reporter, and for him the moon shot was no ordinary assignment. As a writer, Mailer is so attuned to his own participation in any form of media that it was only natural that his coverage of the moon landing would inform us as much about the special tasks of modern journalism as about one of the great episodes in American history. As it stands, *Of a Fire on the Moon* is a fascinating social document incorporating the many voices of technology, science, and broadcasting that converged at that particular moment in our culture to produce the moon spectacle. Such responsiveness to the shaping influences of our verbal environment is what we want the word *classic* to suggest.

A word about the introduction to each section. A full survey outlining the history of the various forms of printed media that make up our categories would not have been practical. Also, we wanted to avoid introducing such essentially futile, if not paralyzing, questions as "Is the news truly objective?" and "Is advertising an abuse of language?" Instead, we have tried to strike an agreeable balance between saying something general about the type of material in that section and saying something specific about the verbal qualities of a particular passage. Of course, no single excerpt can typify all the writing in a chapter. Yet we have chosen to examine closely, though not at great length, those passages that we feel will conveniently clarify the relations between the distinctive features of an individual style and the kind of reader that style seems directed to. We thought that by providing models of the analytic procedure we want to encourage we would, in fact, be offering something of a consistent critical approach to what might seem a bewildering assortment of material.

Any act of composition presupposes an audience. To read a text attentively is to discover something specific about the characteristics of the people it is intended to appeal to—their interests and the ways of talking they can respond to most readily. Once we ask the question "Whom is this ad or magazine article addressed to?" we invite statements about the traits of large groups of people. Questions such as this one can be best approached not from a reader's preconceived idea of what certain groups of people in America are supposed to be like but from his or her responsiveness to the specific ways in which a society is talked to in print. Our responses to popular writing will be the more attuned to the culture we live in the more our terms can encompass the aesthetic significance of a particular work and the bearings that significance has on our shared social experiences. In the model analysis we provide in each introduction, especially in the one to "Best-Sellers," we try to show that it is only when we make an effort to measure the responses of the audience implicit in a specific passage—an audience, it should be noted, that very often *literally* appears in the work as spectators, witnesses, advertising models, and so on—against the quality of our own participation that we can assess more comprehensively the interactions between the various styles and audiences within a single society.

Popular forms of writing pose special challenges to traditional analytical methods. Popular writing is often, or so it would seem, so opaquely simple and ordinary that a standard critical vocabulary might come across as too labored or too imposing for the occasion. Yet finding an appropriate tone has always been a problem even for traditional literary criticism. It would *sound* wrong to talk about Ernest Hemingway in the highly idiosyncratic critical language of Henry James's "Prefaces" or to take the same psychological approach in a discussion of Allen Ginsberg that we would take for Emily Dickinson. Writers exist for us, unless we know them in other, more personal ways, essentially in the specific qualities of their tone and idiom. This should always be our starting point. If, for example, we try to adopt a standard analytical procedure (e.g., searching for symbols) to discuss *Tarzan of the Apes,* and our method becomes too irritatingly cumbersome, that can be an occasion for testing the critical language we are working with and for reexamining the quality of our literary responses rather than concluding that Tarzan was not worth talking about in the first place.

It should be apparent from our model of analysis in each introduction that we have made an effort to avoid using a language that relies too heavily on the terminology of traditional literary criticism, a terminology that has, for the most part, evolved from allegiances and inveterate responses to only the most highly regarded forms of literature. We certainly do not mean to disqualify any of the standard critical approaches, as we trust our "Rhetorical Table of Contents" will amply indicate, but we want instead to encourage a lively reciprocity between the academically certified terms of serious literary criticism and the ordinary languages of our popular culture. What we hope will come out of such transactions is a resilient critical language applicable to all forms of public discourse. If we cannot adjust our critical vocabularies and find interesting ways to talk about Tarzan, or advertising, or a newspaper item, then it is doubtful we have found the most spirited ways to approach even the best things in our culture.

ADVERTISING

Advertising is a business of words.

DAVID OGILVY

WE are so accustomed to signs, posters, billboards, songs, jingles, graffiti, circulars, placards, announcements, brochures, packages, commercials, and ads in newspapers and magazines that it is difficult for any of us to imagine a world without public and personal advertisements. Ads are practically inescapable; they literally surround us. Few places are remote enough to be completely free from the appeals of advertising. Suppose we picture ourselves on a secluded tropical beach experiencing a dazzling sunset. Even if we have not noticed any discarded packaging or unobtrusively placed signs, we must still recognize the alluring tropical scene itself as one continually promoted by airlines and travel agencies in newspapers, in magazines, and especially on decorative posters. Efforts to escape advertising, to "discover" landscapes removed from the intrusions of advertisements, may be merely another way of participating in the kind of world advertisements typically endorse. No place, no object, no life-style, and certainly no way of talking can be totally exempt from commercialized public notice. The world we live in is an advertised world.

The business of advertising is to invent methods of addressing massive audiences in a language designed to be easily accessible and immediately persuasive. No advertising agency wants to put out an ad that is not clear and convincing to millions of people. But the agencies, though they would agree that ads should be written to sell products, disagree when it comes down to the most effective methods of doing so. Over the years, advertising firms have developed among themselves a variety of distinctive styles based on their understanding of the different kinds of audiences they want to reach. No two agencies would handle the same product identically. To people for whom advertising is an exacting discipline and a highly competitive profession, an ad is much more than a sophisticated sales pitch, an attractive verbal and visual device to serve manufacturers. In fact, for those who examine ads critically or professionally, products may very well be no more than merely points of departure. Ads often outlive their products, and in the case of early advertisements for products that are no longer available, we cannot help but consider the advertisement independently of our responses to those products. The point of examining ads apart from their announced subjects is not that we ignore the product completely but that we try to see the product only as it is talked about and portrayed in the full context of the ad. Certainly, it is not necessary to have tried a particular product to be able to appreciate the technique and design used in its advertisement.

The emphasis of the following section is on the advertisements themselves, not the commodities they promote. To illustrate a variety of American advertising strategies and styles, we have included advertisements from the late nineteenth century to the present. Some ads have been grouped according to their products; that is, there are a number of ads regarding smoking, transportation, cosmetics, and fashions. This arrangement will allow you to observe some of the ways both advertisements and audiences have changed over the past one hundred years. Many of these ads have been selected because they represent important developments in advertising methodology. But our intentions are not exclusively historical. Other ads were chosen to display significant aspects of standard advertising procedures. We wanted to introduce advertisements that were both interesting and typical. Nearly all the ads we reprint have achieved a good deal of professional recognition. Many have been frequently singled out as examples of some of the finest copy in the history of American advertising.

A few of the early ads may strike you as unimaginative and typographically crude. They appeared in newspapers and magazines before printing innovations and marketing research radically altered advertising techniques. Yet, given their frequent inelegance, naïveté, and commandeering tones, many early ads remind us how advertisers have persistently played on certain themes despite noticeable changes in decorum, style, and methods of persuasion. Perhaps the early ads only put very bluntly the promises and claims that later on would be more politely disguised. Consider the advertisement for Madame Rowley's Toilet Mask that first appeared in 1887. This ad makes no attempt to introduce its product in a pleasing manner. The advantages of using the toilet mask are delivered in a decisively impersonal and mechanically repetitive fashion. No effort was spent on setting up an attractive backdrop or atmosphere. The only graphic detail we are allowed is the sketch of the curious toilet device in operation, appearing ingenuously at the center of an imposingly designed typographical layout.

If the advertisement for Madame Rowley's Toilet Mask makes little attempt to attract visually, neither does it try very hard to gratify its audience verbally. Even the name of the product is deliberately and unappealingly direct—no charming or engaging brand name suggests that the mask is anything more than what it announces itself to be. The copywriter uses none of the enticing and intimately sensuous language that advertisers so often turned to later when addressing women on matters of personal hygiene and beauty. Realizing that Madame Rowley's beauty apparatus was almost embarrassingly unstylish, the writer must have decided he could promote his client's product best by sounding unadornedly legalistic and scientific. While the copywriter assumes that facial beauty is desirable, he restricts his copy to "claims," "grounds," and "proofs" of the toilet mask's effectiveness, instead of extolling the advantages of a blemish-free, "cover girl" complexion. Flattering metaphors that would describe the product or its results more sensitively are avoided, apparently so as not to call into question the speaker's assertions. Only once does the idiom anticipate the language of modern cosmetic advertisements. Facial blemishes are said to "vanish from the skin, leaving it soft, clear, brilliant, and beautiful." Future copywriters would capitalize on words, such as *vanish,* that suggest magical and instantaneous remedies. Later ads for skin care would also focus more directly on the personal and social advantages of having a "soft, clear, brilliant, and beautiful" complexion. But in Madame Rowley's day, beauty in itself had not yet become an advertising commodity.

Apparently, Madame Rowley's Toilet Mask did not put the cosmetic industry out of business. As early as 1912, we find an advertisement for makeup using what has since become a familiar merchandising tactic. The claims made by Madame Rowley's copywriter stopped at a "brilliant" complexion. The ad promised women nothing more than that. But for the writer of the Pompeian Massage Cream copy, a blemish-free countenance was not all his product could supply. The Pompeian ad is one of the first ads for women to promise along with its product's "beautifying" benefits the additional advantages of marital love and social acceptance. A beautiful complexion, the ad writer suggests, means little by itself. At the heart of the Pompeian ad lies one of the most important developments in the history of advertising technique—the realization that "grounds" and "claims" restricted to the product alone will not always sell the goods. Since the Pompeian ad, copywriters have concentrated more and more on an audience's psychological needs, its attitudes and anxieties. In the Pompeian ad, the writer promotes not only an effective way to check the wrinkles and blemishes he poetically calls "Time's ravages" but also adopts an attitude toward the nature and effects of feminine appeal: "a beautiful complexion—that greatest aid to woman's power and influence." This comment, obviously made by a male copywriter, is offered after we have been told that a "Pompeian complexion" will win over any man's mother, "as it does in every other instance in social or business life." The ad inadvertently acknowledges that beauty is only skin deep, after all. Deeper than a woman's worry about facial blemishes, the copywriter intimates, is her terror of not being loved and approved.

MADAME ROWLEY'S TOILET MASK

TOILET MASK
OR
FACE GLOVE.

The following are the claims made for Madame Rowley's Toilet Mask, and the grounds on which it is recommended to ladies for Beautifying, Bleaching, and Preserving the Complexion:

TOILET MA
OR
FACE GLOV

First—The **Mask** is **Soft** and **Flexible** in form, and can be **Easily Applied** and **Worn** without **Discomfort** or **Inconvenience.**

Second—It is durable, and does not dissolve or come asunder, but holds its original mask shape.

Third—It has been **Analyzed** by **Eminent Scientists** and **Chemical Experts,** and pronounced **Perfectly Pure** and **Harmless.**

Fourth—With ordinary care the **Mask** will **last for years,** and its VALUABLE PROPERTIES **Never Become Impaired.**

Fifth—The **Mask** is protected by letters patent, and is the **only Genuine** article of the kind.

Sixth—It is **Recommended** by **Eminent Physicians** and **Scientific Men** as a SUBSTITUTE FOR INJURIOUS COSMETICS.

Seventh—The **Mask** is a **Natural Beautifier,** for **Bleaching** and **Preserving** the **Skin** and **Removing Complexional Imperfections.**

Eighth—Its use cannot be detected by the closest scruti and it may be worn with **perfect privacy,** if sired.

Ninth—The **Mask** is sold at a moderate price, and is to PURCHASED BUT ONCE.

The Toilet Mask (or Face Glove) in position to the face.
TO BE WORN THREE TIMES IN THE WEEK

Tenth—Hundreds of dollars uselessly pended for cosmetics, lotions, like preparations, may be saved possessor.

Eleventh—**Ladies** in every section of country are using the **Mask** gratifying results.

Twelfth—It is safe, simple, cleanly, effective for beautifying purpo and never injures the most deli skin.

Thirteenth—While it is intended the **Mask** should be **Worn Dur Sleep,** it may be applied WI EQUALLY GOOD RESULTS **any time** to suit the convenie of the wearer.

Fourteenth—The **Mask** has received the testimony of w known society and professional ladies, who proclaim i be the greatest discovery for beautifying purposes e vouchsafed to womankind.

COMPLEXION BLEMISHES

May be hidden imperfectly by cosmetics and powders, but can only be removed permanently by the Toilet Mask. By its every kind of spots, impurities, roughness, etc., vanish from the skin, leaving it soft, clear, brilliant, and beautiful. It harmless, costs little, and saves its user money. It prevents and removes wrinkles, and is both a complexion preserver a beautifier. Famous Society Ladies, actresses, belles, etc., use it.

VALUABLE ILLUSTRATED TREATISE, WITH PROOFS AND PARTICULARS.

—MAILED FREE BY—

TOILET MASK
OR
FACE GLOVE.

THE TOILET MASK COMPANY,

Send for Descriptive Treatise. } 1164 BROADWAY, { **Send for Descriptive Treatise.**

NEW YORK.

☞ **Mention this paper when you Write.**

TOILET MAS
OR
FACE GLOVE

[1887]

OF all moments the most trying—when the son brings *her* to his mother, of all critics the most exacting. Mother-love causes her to look with penetrating glance, almost *trying* to find flaws. No quality of beauty so serves to win an older woman as a skin smooth, fresh and healthy *in a natural way*, as easily provided by

POMPEIAN MASSAGE CREAM

Where artificial beautifiers—cosmetics and rouges—would only antagonize; and an uncared-for, pallid, wrinkled skin prove a negative influence—the Pompeian complexion immediately wins the mother, as it does in every other instance in social or business life.

You can have a beautiful complexion—that greatest aid to woman's power and influence. A short use of Pompeian will surprise you and your friends. It will improve even the best complexion, and retain beauty and youthful appearance against Time's ravages.

"Don't *envy* a good complexion; use Pompeian and *have* one."

Pompeian is not a "cold" or "grease" cream, nor a rouge or cosmetic, and positively can not grow hair on the face. Pompeian simply affords a natural means toward a complete cleanliness of the facial pores. And in pores that are "Pompeian clean" lies skin health.

All dealers 50c, 75c, $1

TRIAL JAR

sent for 6c (stamps or coin). Find out for yourself, now, why Pompeian is used and prized in a million homes where the value of a clear, fresh, youthful skin is appreciated. Clip coupon now.

Cut along this line, fill in and mail today

The Pompeian Mfg. Co. 36 Prospect St., Cleveland, Ohio

Gentlemen:—Enclosed find 6c (stamps or coin) for a trial jar of Pompeian Massage Cream.

Name..

Address..

City..State................

[1912]

Unlike Madame Rowley's mask, the Pompeian Massage Cream does not appear at the center of its advertisement. To be sure, the brand name (chosen to suggest the shade of red found on the walls of the "preserved" ancient city of Pompeii) has been allowed central prominence, and the illustration of the product is barely squeezed into the bottom left corner of the ad. More important than the actual cream is the rendition of the familiar dramatic situation in which a young lady is first introduced to the wary scrutiny of her suitor's mother: "Of all the moments the most trying—the son brings *her* to his mother, of all critics the most exacting." With a tone and diction borrowed from the melodramatic superlatives of soap opera and best-selling fiction, the copywriter maintains that with so much at stake a young woman cannot risk using a cosmetic that would make her look vulgar and unacceptable to such an "exacting" critic as a potential mother-in-law. The writer offers, in addition, the ultimate emotional reassurance that the massage cream "positively can not grow hair on the face." The ad leaves little doubt, then, that the "beautiful complexion" its product guarantees is not what is finally being promoted. The clear complexion, in this case, ultimately stands for something else, as it did not in the ad for Madame Rowley's Toilet Mask. Pompeian Massage Cream, not of much consequence in itself, merely personifies the real "product" of the ad—a natural, artless appearance that will ensure unqualified social approval.

Cosmetic advertisements, for the most part, avoid the slightest allusion to artificiality. Madame Rowley's Toilet Mask, which must have looked like an odd contrivance even in its own time, was nevertheless introduced as a "natural beautifier." To bring home a girl whose makeup looked artificial was, to the copywriter for Pompeian Massage Cream at least, an undeserving affront to American motherhood. In our final example of cosmetic advertising, the ad for Yardley's Next to Nature, the entire copy depends on the single notion that makeup must allow a woman to appear *natural,* to look, that is, as if she were not wearing any cosmetic at all. Though the ad does not associate its product with a comforting aura of love and matrimony, like the Pompeian ad, it still assumes that a fine complexion is not an end in itself but a means of possessing a particular kind of "look." Throughout the Next to Nature ad, the copywriter insists on the product's naturalness. The brand name itself bears, as Pompeian did not, more than a loose metaphorical relationship to the product: the name suggests not only that the cosmetic formula is literally close to nature but also that the product's use will engender an appearance that will be the next best thing to natural beauty. Since Madame Rowley's time, advertisers have discovered that probably no word of copy works as effectively as *natural.* The copywriter for Next to Nature appropriately avoids gimmicks and artificiality by adopting a casual manner of speaking and by offering a photograph of a demure and innocent-looking woman as evidence of his product's "transparent" purity. Apparently, he does not feel that he need convince us of his honesty by citing indisputable "claims" and "grounds," nor does he bank on his audience's fear of social or parental disapproval. He is confident that his readers will need no more than his own sincere tone to be persuaded that by using Next to Nature they can have "the fresh, wholesome look" of natural beauty.

These three cosmetic advertisements furnish a brief record of some of the major developments of American advertising. A glance at the ads demonstrates vividly the changes in the layout of advertisements brought about by advances in photography and graphic design. The space apportioned for illustration increases substantially. We move from the cameolike sketch of the figure in the toilet mask to the posterlike photograph of an attractive woman which dominates the Next to Nature advertisement and also conveniently eliminates the copywriter's need to write a lengthy description of what the product can do. The size of the headlines

Of all the make-ups on earth, only one is called Next to Nature.™

One of the freshest things that's happened to girls' faces since sunshine and country air: Yardley's Next to Nature Liquid Make-up.
It's made with vitamin A to moisturize, the purest of waters, and all natural colorings. They're blended into a formula so sheer, you can use it generously and still look like a natural beauty.
Try Next to Nature blushers and new Transparent Pressed Powder too.
Because when it comes to giving you the fresh, wholesome look—there's nobody on earth like Yardley.
Yardley
How to make the most of what you have.
©1973, Yardley of London, Inc.
Yardley
Next to Nature
Yardley
Next to Nature
Next to Nature
Next to Nature

[1973]

increases; the style becomes more informal. The headline for Madame Rowley's Toilet Mask is intended to do no more than name the product explicitly. In the Pompeian ad, however, there are actually two headlines. One simply mentions the product by name, while the other invites a reader's response to a fictional scene. In the Next to Nature ad, after the reader is introduced directly to the brand name and the special quality of the product, she is then talked to marginally in a perky and congenial voice. Few ads in Madame Rowley's day would have taken the liberty of speaking to their readers in such a casual and ingratiating fashion. Neither would a nineteenth-century copywriter have violated grammatical decorum by writing the kind of breezy and fragmented sentences that characterize the brisk style of the Next to Nature copy. Quite clearly, the writing in the Next to Nature ad is meant to sound as natural, relaxed, and sincere as the copywriter imagines his audience would like to talk and behave. By examining these advertisements, then, we are introduced not only to three markedly different styles of writing but also to three noticeably different attitudes toward female beauty.

Even though advertisements represent some of the most expensive and calculated acts of composition in America, the audiences they are directed to seldom attend to them analytically. No one would deny that ads exert tremendous economic and social pressures. (See, for example, the essays by Neil Postman in "Advertising" and Vance Packard in "Best-Sellers.") Yet few people, aside from those in the advertising profession, bother to ask how or why a particular advertisement happened to be written and designed in a certain way. The public generally reacts to advertisements exactly the way advertising agencies would like them to—as consumers, not critics. Assuming, however, that "advertising is a business of *words,*" not necessarily of products, we have included examples of successful copy to invite you to consider more carefully *how* the language and strategies of advertisements affect the ways we talk and think. Advertisements constitute a lively repository of American vocabulary, idiom, metaphor, and style, in short a fairly reliable index of the state of public discourse. They create the one verbal environment in which we all participate, willingly or unwillingly.

Woman's Attractiveness
The Power That Moves the World
WOMEN play a most important rôle in the affairs of the world. It is not only their privilege to represent the highest type of beauty—it is their duty to do so.
Men admire women who are attractive mentally as well as physically. Sweetness and amiability are attractive. Add beauty to these and a woman is irresistible.
The power that moves the world is love born of womanly attractiveness. It has been this way since the world began. So it was in the day of fair Helen of Troy. So it is today. So it will always be.
How to acquire and retain beautiful features, a fine complexion, how to be chic, to smile entrancingly, to walk or dance gracefully, to appear generally to advantage—all of these are worthy of every woman's sincere attention.
No matter how well hair, teeth and complexion are cared for, a matronly figure spells age every time. No one is deceived. And yet with intelligent care any type of figure can be made to regain its youthful lines and maintain them even into late life.
To keep the figure youthful your corset must have youthful lines. This depends upon its designer, for no corset is better than its designer's personal conception of beauty. On his sense of beauty depend the figures of the women who wear the corsets he conceives.
MODART
Front-Laced Corsets
All Modart Corsets are front-laced. They are conceived by the highest paid corset designer in the world. They have ease of adjustment. They are put on and off readily. There are no heavy steels in the back to mar gown or suit lines. Instead of the heavy steels used by most makers, a light flexible steel that will not take a permanent bend is used. The finest fabrics are also employed, so that every Modart Corset retains its shape until worn out. Remember that the corset that won't keep its shape won't keep yours. Modarts keep their shape. There is a Modart for every type of figure.
All Modarts are front-laced, but all front-laced corsets are not Modarts. The Modart label is sewn in every genuine Modart Corset.
MODART CORSET COMPANY
553 Fifth Avenue, New York
Factory: Saginaw, Michigan
How to Get a Properly Fitted Corset
THE only real way to get a properly fitted corset is to get the advice of a trained corsetière in a department or woman's specialty store.
These corsetières will advise and fit you with a Modart Corset free of charge. When you consult them you place yourself under no obligation other than that of your own inclination to purchase.
Do this today and see with your own eyes the wonderful improvement a Modart Corset will make in your figure.
H. VALLELY

Often a bridesmaid but never a bride
EDNA'S case was really a pathetic one. Like every woman, her primary ambition was to marry. Most of the girls of her set were married—or about to be. Yet not one possessed more grace or charm or loveliness than she.
And as her birthdays crept gradually toward that tragic thirty-mark, marriage seemed farther from her life than ever.
She was often a bridesmaid but never a bride.
* * *
That's the insidious thing about halitosis (unpleasant breath). You, yourself, rarely know when you have it. And even your closest friends won't tell you.
Sometimes, of course, halitosis comes from some deep-seated organic disorder that requires professional advice. But usually—and fortunately—halitosis is only a local condition that yields to the regular use of Listerine as a mouth wash and gargle. It is an interesting thing that this well-known antiseptic that has been in use for years for surgical dressings, possesses these unusual properties as a breath deodorant.
It halts food fermentation in the mouth and leaves the breath sweet, fresh and clean. Not by substituting some other odor but by really removing the old one. The Listerine odor itself quickly disappears. So the systematic use of Listerine puts you on the safe and polite side.
Your druggist will supply you with Listerine. He sells lots of it. It has dozens of different uses as a safe antiseptic and has been trusted as such for a half a century. Read the interesting little booklet that comes with every bottle. —Lambert Pharmacal Company, Saint Louis, U. S. A.
HALITOSIS
LISTERINE

[1923]

Should a gentleman offer a Tiparillo to a lab technician?

Behind that pocket of pencils beats the heart of a digital computer. This girl has already cross-indexed Tiparillo® as a cigar with a slim, elegant shape and neat, white tip.

She knows that there are two kinds. Regular Tiparillo, for a mild smoke. Or new Tiparillo M with menthol, for a cold smoke.

She knows. She's programmed.

And she's ready.

But how about you? Which Tiparillo are you going to offer? Or are you just going to stand there and stare at her pencils?

[1968]

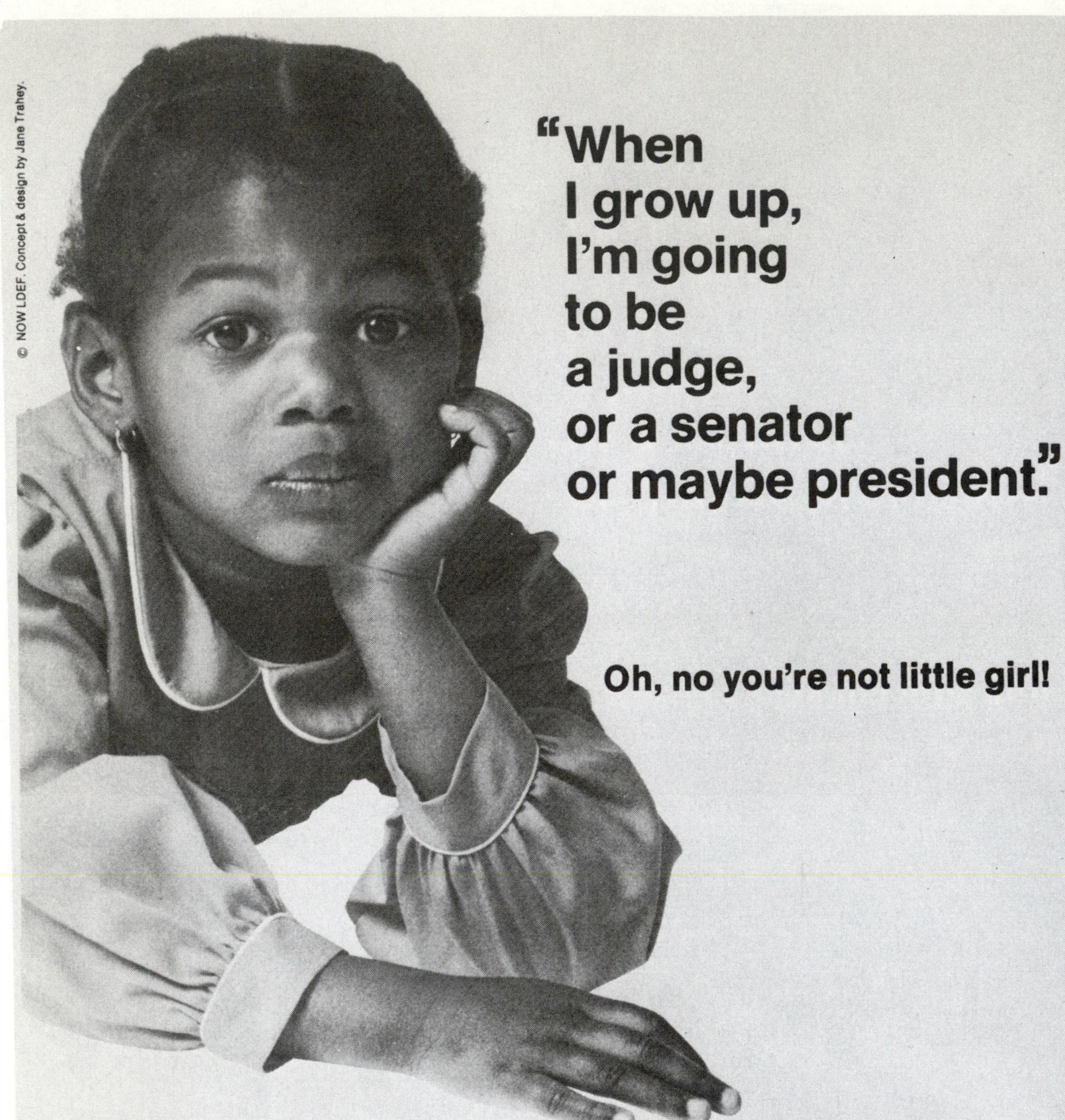

© NOW LDEF. Concept & design by Jane Trahey.
"When
I grow up,
I'm going
to be
a judge,
or a senator
or maybe president."
Oh, no you're not little girl!

Your chances of making it into public office are very slim.
Only 23 of 657 FEDERAL JUDGES are women.
Only 2 of 100 SENATORS are women.
No woman has ever been PRESIDENT.
But you do have a 99% chance to be a NURSE.
(You'll earn less than a tree-trimmer.)
Or a 97% chance to be a TYPIST.
(You'll earn less than the janitor.)
Or a 60% chance to be a SCHOOL TEACHER.
(You'll earn less than a zoo-keeper.)

Concerned mamas and daddies are asking how they can help their female children to get an equal crack at vocational training —training that opens doors to non-stereotypical, better paying jobs. Parents want their female children to get the same kind of coaching in sports and physical education as boys do.

Parents want the kind of counseling that will encourage wider career options for girls. (Most young women graduate without the science and math credits they need to exercise full options for higher education.)
If your female children attend a federally supported public school in this country you can and should help them get a more equal education.

YOU CAN HELP TO CREATE A BETTER FUTURE.
Write NOW Legal Defense & Education Fund (H) 132 W. 43rd Street, N.Y., N.Y. 10036

Space for this message contributed as a public service by Newsweek Inc.

[1980]

"I know she's a very important person. They always send a car around for her when the meetings are over. And it's usually a Lincoln. She's decisive and, actually, quite charming about it. Business has never been better since she took over. She even looks like a very important person."
MARY ANN RESTIVO

[1987]

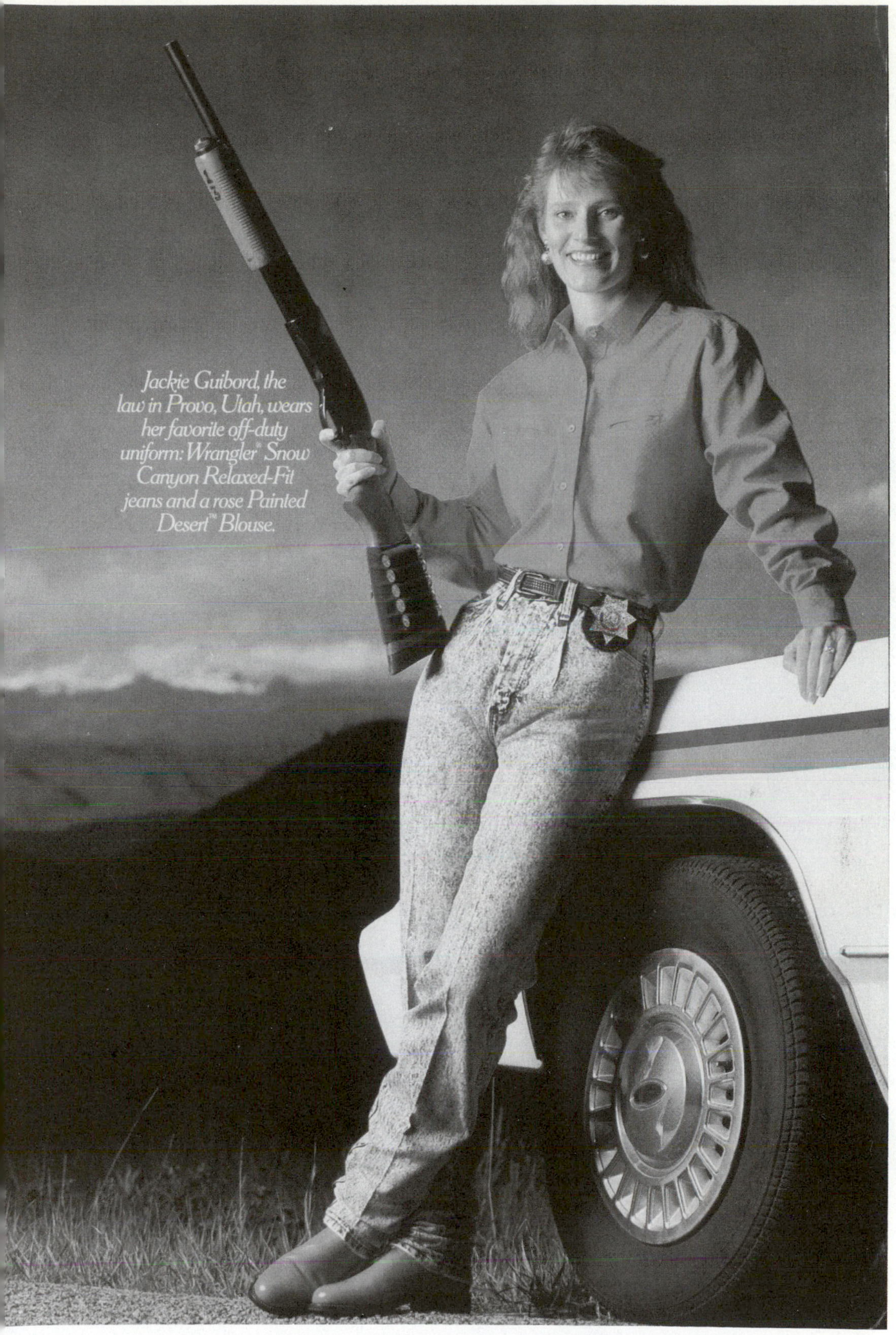
Jackie Guibord, the
law in Provo, Utah, wears
her favorite off-duty
uniform: Wrangler® Snow
Canyon Relaxed-Fit
jeans and a rose Painted
Desert™ Blouse.

[1990]

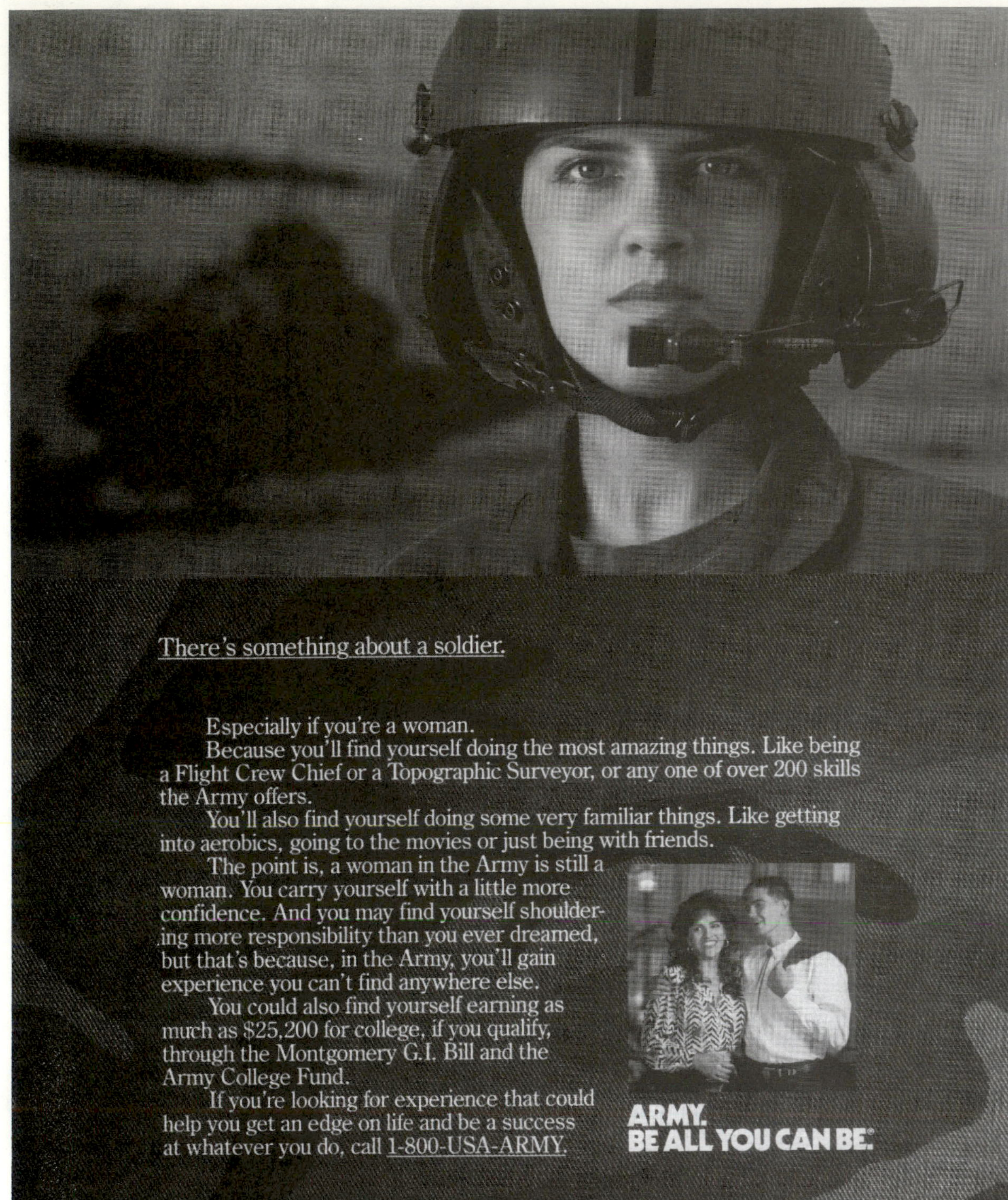
There's something about a soldier.
Especially if you're a woman.
Because you'll find yourself doing the most amazing things. Like being a Flight Crew Chief or a Topographic Surveyor, or any one of over 200 skills the Army offers.
You'll also find yourself doing some very familiar things. Like getting into aerobics, going to the movies or just being with friends.
The point is, a woman in the Army is still a woman. You carry yourself with a little more confidence. And you may find yourself shouldering more responsibility than you ever dreamed, but that's because, in the Army, you'll gain experience you can't find anywhere else.
You could also find yourself earning as much as $25,200 for college, if you qualify, through the Montgomery G.I. Bill and the Army College Fund.
If you're looking for experience that could help you get an edge on life and be a success at whatever you do, call 1-800-USA-ARMY.
ARMY.
BE ALL YOU CAN BE.

[1990]

WHAT IF?

What if 14 women, instead of 14 men, had sat on the Senate Judiciary Committee during the confirmation hearings of Clarence Thomas?

Sound unfair? Just as unfair as fourteen men and no women.

What if even **half** the Senators had been women? Women are, after all, more than half the population. Maybe, just maybe, women's voices would have been heard. Maybe the experiences and concerns of women would not have been so quickly dismissed or ridiculed. And maybe all of America would have benefited.

The behavior and performance of the United States Senate during the Clarence Thomas confirmation hearings demonstrated a stark truth: women are tragically under-represented politically. As long as men make up 98% of the U.S. Senate and 93% of the U.S. House of Representatives, women's voices can be ignored, their experiences and concerns trivialized.

The need for women in public office has never been more obvious. Or essential.

Men control the White House, the Congress, the courthouse and the statehouse. Men have political power over women's lives. It's time that women help make the rules, create the policies, and pass the laws about sexual harassment, day care, affordable health care, and hundreds of decisions that affect American families every day.

The National Women's Political Caucus is determined to even the odds. To hear the voices of women echo in the halls of power.

If you're angry about what you've witnessed in the United States Senate, don't just raise your fist, raise your pen. Join us. The goal of the National Women's Political Caucus is to increase the number of women elected and appointed to public office. We're the only national bi-partisan grassroots organization working across this country to recruit, train and elect women into office at all levels of government.

Turn your anger into action. Join us.

NWPC

Count me in. I want to help the National Women's Political Caucus increase the number of women elected and appointed to public office.

Enclosed is my check payable to NWPC Inc. for:
( )$250 ( )$100 ( )$50 ( )$35 OTHER $____

Name ____________________

Address ____________________

City/State/Zip ____________________

Please bill my ( ) Mastercard ( ) Visa Amount $____

Account Number ____________________ Expiration Date ____________

Signature ____________________ Date ____________

Contributions to NWPC are not tax deductible.

National Women's Political Caucus
1275 K Street, N.W., Suite 750, Washington, D.C. 20005

Paid for by the National Women's Political Caucus

[1991]

Remember P.E. class?

Remember prison ball and jumping jacks and how your P.E. teacher made you try to climb that rope that hung from the ceiling and you never could, *never?*

Or how you had to do chin-ups and see how long you could hang and you could only hang something like 2.5 seconds but that wasn't good enough,

oh no,

you had to hang something like 65 seconds and you could never do that and thank God it was only pass/no pass and you got a pass just for showing up and trying. Which was good.

But then you got older.

And P.E. teachers got smarter. Because now you got graded. You got graded and at least once you got the dreaded C or the equally dreaded C+ and there went your whole grade-point average and speaking of average that's what you were now: *plain-old-just-mediocre-better-luck-next-time-see-ya-later average* and you thought

(continued)

Now wait just a gosh darn minute who, exactly, is average? And the answer came back ringing loud and clear over the top of that chin-up bar: Nobody.

You're not average because average is a lie. You're not average because average means stuck and you're not stuck, you're moving and becoming and trying and you're climbing over every bit of fear or opinion or "no you can't do that" you've ever heard.

So you scoff at average. You laugh. You guffaw. And you run and you play and you move and the more you tell your body that it is a well-oiled machine the more it starts to believe you.

And then one night you have the craziest dream.

You're in the middle of your old gym. Your P.E. teacher is standing there. She is grinning. There is a rope before you. So you climb it. You climb the living heck out of it. You reach the top. And there is absolutely no place to go but up.

Just do it.

[1992]

Buy what you want to buy.
And no bankcard is going to stop you with a limit set long ago.*
You know what you can afford. You just want to be trusted.
You're a responsible person. Most of the time.

THE CARD.
THE AMERICAN EXPRESS CARD.

[1991]

THE SATURDAY EVENING POST

One of the Yank Veterans

"Did I bayonet my first Hun? Sure! How did it feel? It *doesn't* feel! There *he* is. There *you* are. One of you has got to go. I preferred to stay.

"So when sergeant says, 'Smash 'em, boys'—we do. And we go them one better like good old Yankee Doodle Yanks. For bullets and bayonets are the only kind of lingo that a Hun can *understand!*"

* * * *

The *dependable* Yank, whose photograph appears above, first met the *dependable* Owl Cigar while boosting that *dependable* investment—the Liberty Loan.

We didn't tell him about the $2,000,000 stock of leaf that is always aging for Owl and White Owl. Nor the over 100,000,000 Owls and White Owls sold last year. We just swapped him a White Owl for a smile. And it doesn't look like the smile came hard, does it?

Why don't you, too, try an Owl or White Owl—*today?*

DEALERS:
If your distributor does not sell these dependable cigars, write us.
General Cigar Co., Inc., 119 West 40th Street, New York City

TWO DEPENDABLE CIGARS

OWL 6c white OWL 7c

OWL ▾ Square-end 6c

WHITE OWL ▾ Invincible Shape 7c

WHITE OWL

Branded for your Banded protection

[1918]

Case #099 B

George D. Born Portsmouth, N. H., 1883. From Exeter to Yale. Graduated 1906. Brilliant scholar, writer and conversationalist. Two years on New York dailies. First novel "Dreams," 1909, disclosed author's romantic and emotional nature. For some reason, he was not popular with literary set. Engaged, 1911, to daughter of prominent Boston banker. Sensation followed her sudden elopement with another. Paris 1913. Second novel 1914, a failure. Seeking forgetfulness, turned to social life, but met with short-lived welcome. Became recluse until War, in which he served brilliantly. In 1919 produced admirable novel, "Forsaken Gods." Critics, pulpit and press hailed him as genius. Society, however, still refused to accept him. Reported engaged to English actress in fall of 1927. Nothing came of it.

He never knew why

[**REMEMBER—Nothing exceeds halitosis (unpleasant breath) as a social offense. Nothing equals Listerine as a remedy.**]

[1928]

HOW JOE'S BODY BROUGHT HIM FAME INSTEAD OF SHAME

Charles Atlas

—*actual photo of the man who holds the title, "The World's Most Perfectly Developed Man."*

I Can Make YOU A New Man, Too, in Only 15 Minutes A Day!

If YOU, like Joe, have a body that others can "push around"—if you're ashamed to strip for sports or a swim—then give me just 15 minutes a day! I'll PROVE you can have a body you'll be proud of, packed with red-blooded vitality! "*Dynamic Tension.*" That's the secret! That's how I changed myself from a spindle-shanked, scrawny weakling to winner of the title, "World's Most Perfectly Developed Man."

Do you want big, broad shoulders—a fine, powerful chest—biceps like steel—arms and legs rippling with muscular strength—a stomach ridged with bands of sinewy muscle—and a build you can be proud of? Then just give me the opportunity to prove that "*Dynamic Tension*" is what you need.

"Dynamic Tension" Does It!

Using "*Dynamic Tension*" only 15 minutes a day, in the privacy of your own room, you quickly begin to put on muscle, increase your chest measurements, broaden your back, fill out your arms and legs. Before you know it, this easy, NATURAL method will make you a finer specimen of REAL MANHOOD than you ever dreamed you could be! You'll be a New Man!

FREE BOOK

Send NOW for my FREE book. It tells about "*Dynamic Tension,*" shows photos of men I've turned from weaklings into Atlas Champions, tells how I can do it for YOU. Don't put it off! Address me personally: Charles Atlas, Dept. 217B, 115 E. 23 St., New York 10, N. Y.

CHARLES ATLAS, Dept. 217B,
115 East 23rd St., New York 10, N. Y.

I want the proof that your system of "*Dynamic Tension*" will help make a New Man of me—give me a healthy, husky body and big muscular development. Send me your free book, "Everlasting Health and Strength."

Name..
(Please print or write plainly)

Address..

City.................................State..........

☐ Check here if under 16 for Booklet A

[1944]

A NEW JOE WEIDER SCIENTIFIC WEIGHT-GAINING BREAKTHROUGH

The end of the SKINNY BODY!

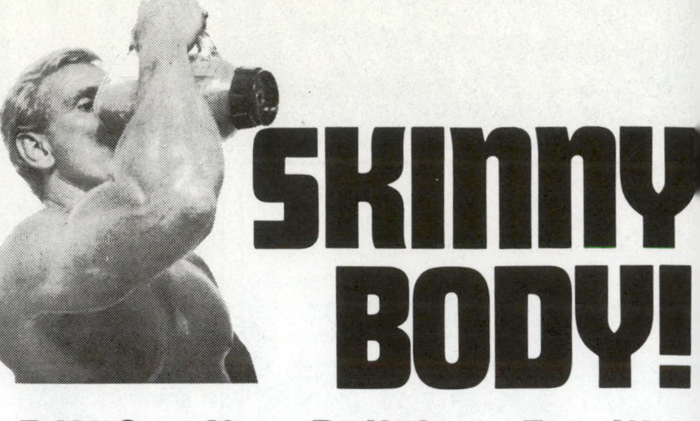

He's "Drinking-On" A-POUND-A-DAY Our New Delicious Fun-Way

Thousands are doing it—Monthly... WHY NOT YOU? Here's a totally new breed of nutritional "wildcat" that's guaranteed to put an end to your muscle-starved, hungry-looking skinny body—through a new, scientifically blended, delicious milkshake-flavored drink. It fills out your body and face—for a fresher, more exciting, fun-going you!

From near death by tuberculosis, emphysema, chronic bronchial asthma, collapsed lungs, alcoholism and drug addiction, this sickly 5′10″ skinny 110-lb. weakling gained 65 pounds of solid muscle—added 12 inches of boulder-sized bulges to his chest, 9½ inches to each arm, 8 inches to each leg, and reduced his waist to 28 inches—to become a body building champion... all through the use of Joe Weider's Trainer of the Champions CRASH-WEIGHT GAIN FORMULA #7 Plan!—That's the **true** story of Charlie Kemp!

A Long History of Physical Weakness Problems

Charlie's trouble started early. All his life he had been frail and sick—by the time he was 10 he had developed asthma, and at 16 his left lung had collapsed. Yet these were only hints of problems that would follow, for during the next three years his left lung collapsed five more times and his right lung collapsed twice—he had cystic emphysema complicated by tuberculosis. This, combined with his sickly appearance, was too much for Charlie's battered ego, and by the time he was 25 he was a bona-fide alcoholic with severe cirrhosis of the liver.

Just when things looked darkest, they got darker. His dismal health brought on narcolepsy, and in order to combat this disease he had to take powerful doses of amphetamines—pep pills. They, in turn, brought on more pernicious complications—loss of appetite and, ironically, insomnia, which required drug depressants. The combination of alcohol and drugs destroyed not only Charlie's physical health but also his mental health, and before long he entered the Seton Psychiatric Institute.

For a full year, psychiatrists bolstered Charlie's psyche, but when he was released, emphysema hit again and his right lung collapsed once more. Was his life really doomed?

Into the hospital again. Surgery curtailed the collapsing of his lungs and removed the diseased portions, and when he was released he found new determination to rebuild his body. But that meant gaining weight—and Charlie, who had to continue taking amphetamines which killed his appetite, began to rely almost entirely on food supplements.

Weider Formula/Method Creates a New Life!

Charlie devoured Joe Weider's CRASH-WEIGHT GAIN FORMULA #7 by the case, altered his eating habits as prescribed for him by Joe Weider, and followed a few simple daily exercises, which helped to turn the weight gains he made into a firmer, more muscular and handsomer body.

His progress was astounding—you see here the gains he made—absolutely phenomenal, especially for a man entering his 40's and a truly great testimonial for the Weider System and Crash Weight Gain Formula #7.

His life changed with him—from a pathetic, undesired, unloved loser whose only companions were dogs—to a prize-winning "Mr. America Physical Achievement Award" body surrounded by the world's most beautiful girls.—This is the miracle of courageous Charlie Kemp!

"Tuberculosis, emphysema, chronic bronchial asthma, collapsed lungs, two lung operations, cirrhosis of the liver, narcolepsy, alcoholic, drug addict, a life in and out of the hospital, psychiatric patient, three packs of cigarettes a day, no SEX desire, unloved—only dogs as companions."

"After years of struggling to stay alive he decided to follow Joe Weider's miraculous Weight-Gaining Plan. The result today is a muscular man of vitality—athletic, handsome, earning $40,000 a year, cured of the sicknesses that used to plague him, and now—surrounded by beautiful girls!"

You Can "Build-Up" Too!

Now, that miracle can be yours. If Charlie Ken who was a hopelessly sick underweight weakli struggling daily to live, could achieve so mu just think what you—underweight but medica fit—can accomplish by using the same milksha flavored drink plan that Charlie used.

Start today to put an end to your skinny bc by following the exact same successful weig Gaining Formula that Charlie Kemp and thc sands of others are using—Monthly! Just dri 4 zestful glasses of delicious CRASH-WEIG GAIN FORMULA #7 daily It's full of calori vitamins, minerals, carbohydrates and tas delicious with your regular meals. It's safe a healthy, made from all-natural nutrients— DRUGS—and does all its work in a relaxed ma ner, piling on pound after pound of handsor weight to flesh out your bones. Combine CRAS WEIGHT GAIN FORMULA #7 with five simp daily exercises, and watch how you fill our yo narrow chest, your skinny arms and spindly le Put an end to your skinny body once, for all in **JUST 14 TO 30 DAYS**! And, oh yes—it al fills out your face for a healthier, more excitir fun-loving you, and that's a lot!

BEFORE AND AFTER MEASUREMENTS

	BEFORE	AFTER	GAINS
Weight	110	175	65 lb
Chest	33	45	12 in
Arms	7½	17	9½ in
Thighs	16	24	8 in
Calves	10	16	6 in
Waist	29	28	Lost 1 in

THE DO-IT-YOURSELF GAIN-A-POUND-A-DAY-KIT

It's a one-day supply of CRASH-WEIGHT, chock full of weight-gaining nutrients that can smash the weight-gaining barrier! You want to gain a pound a day? Half a pound a day? Maybe you just want to add a few pounds here and there. You want it easily—enjoyably—without stuffing yourself with heavy-as-lead foods? Now you can do it! It's as simple as drinking a delicious milkshake.

FREE:

"Valuable Weight-Gaining and Muscle-Building Course." This Illustrated Guide sent FREE with each CRASH-WEIGHT FORMULA #7 Kit. Crammed with step-by-step instructions in muscle-building and weight-gaining basics. Filled with all the latest ideas and how to adapt them for your own personal, fun-going weight gains!

PUT AN END TO YOUR SKINNY BODY!

JOE WEIDER DEPT. P-5
TRAINER OF CHAMPIONS SINCE 1936
21100 ERWIN STREET
WOODLAND HILLS, CALIF. 91364

Dear Joe: I want to put an end to my skinny body and have everyone compliment me on my athletic appearance and muscular gains. Rush me the "Pound-A-Day" CRASH-WEIGHT FORMULA #7 package I have checked below.

Check Plan & Flavor Desired:

- ☐ 7-Day Supply...... $ 8.00) ☐ Chocolate
- ☐ 14-Day Supply...... $14.95) ☐ Vanilla
- ☐ 21-Day Supply...... $20.00) ☐ Strawberry
- ☐ 30-Day Supply...... $25.00) ☐ Butterscotch

Pick any group of flavors desired with 2, 3 or 4-week order. California residents add 5% sales tax. We pay postage.

Name ____________ Age ____

Address ____________

City ________ State ____ Zip ____

(please print clearly)

In Canada: CRASH-WEIGHT, 2875 Bates Rd., Montreal, Quebec

[1973]

When Crusher Lizowski talks about being a homemaker, you listen.

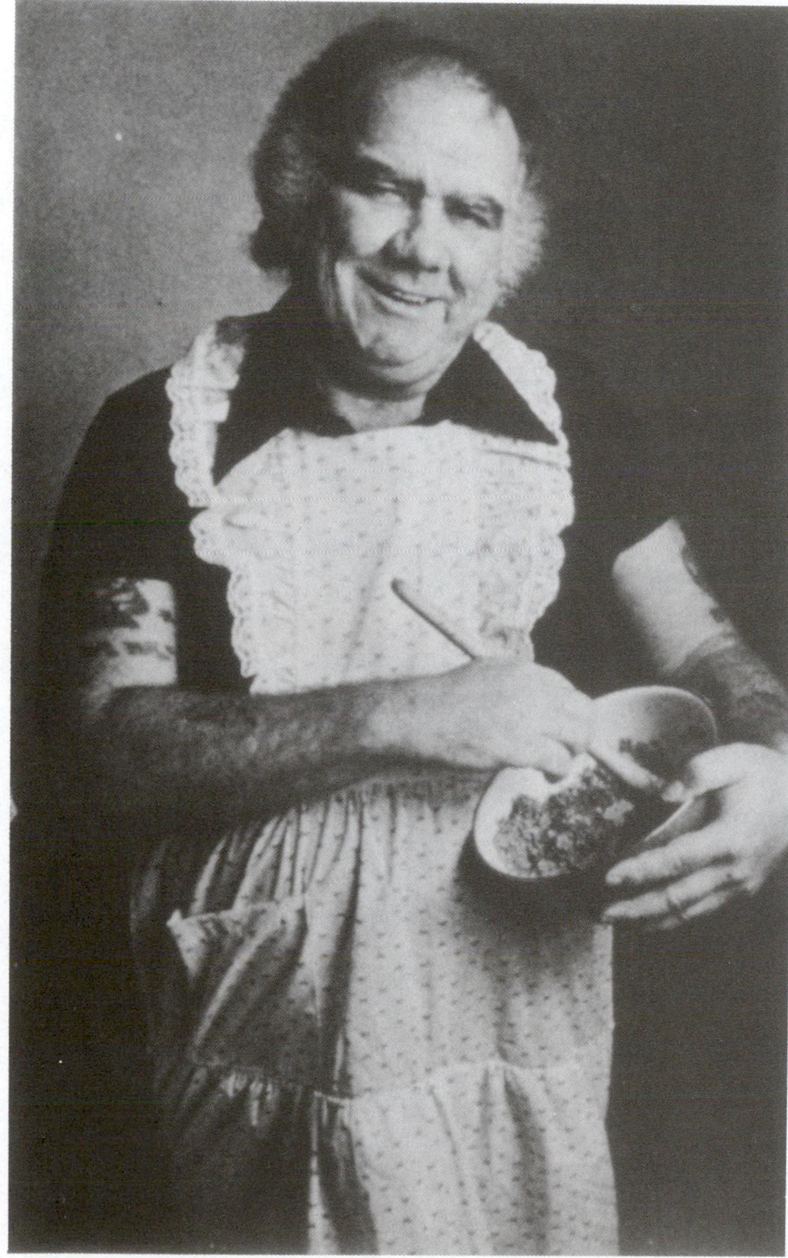

"I like to cook, and I think I'm pretty good at it. My specialty is Japanese dishes. Sushi, tempura, teriyaki, shabu-shabu.

"When I'm not on the road, I do most of the cooking around our house. I'm even teaching my oldest son how to cook.

"My wife and I feel that making a home is sharing. Equally. In the drudgery. In the fun. In everything. Especially in the important things like the care and guidance of our children and in establishing values in our home.

"The point is, I don't believe in the old stereotype about being the lord and master around the house while the little woman raises the kids and cooks the meals.

"I don't see anything unusual in that. Nobody kids me when I put on an apron. Not in front of me at least.

"Being a homemaker is, after all, being an adult. Learning how to manage your life.

"Learning how to give. And how to give yourself to the people you love.

"Another thing I'm into is macrame. I'm learning how to make belts and plant hangers.

"Nobody kids me about that either."

This message about homemaking is brought to you as a public service by Future Homemakers of America and this publication. For more information, write: Future Homemakers of America, 2010 Massachusetts Ave. NW, Washington, DC 20036.

HOMEMAKING
The most misunderstood profession.

[1978]

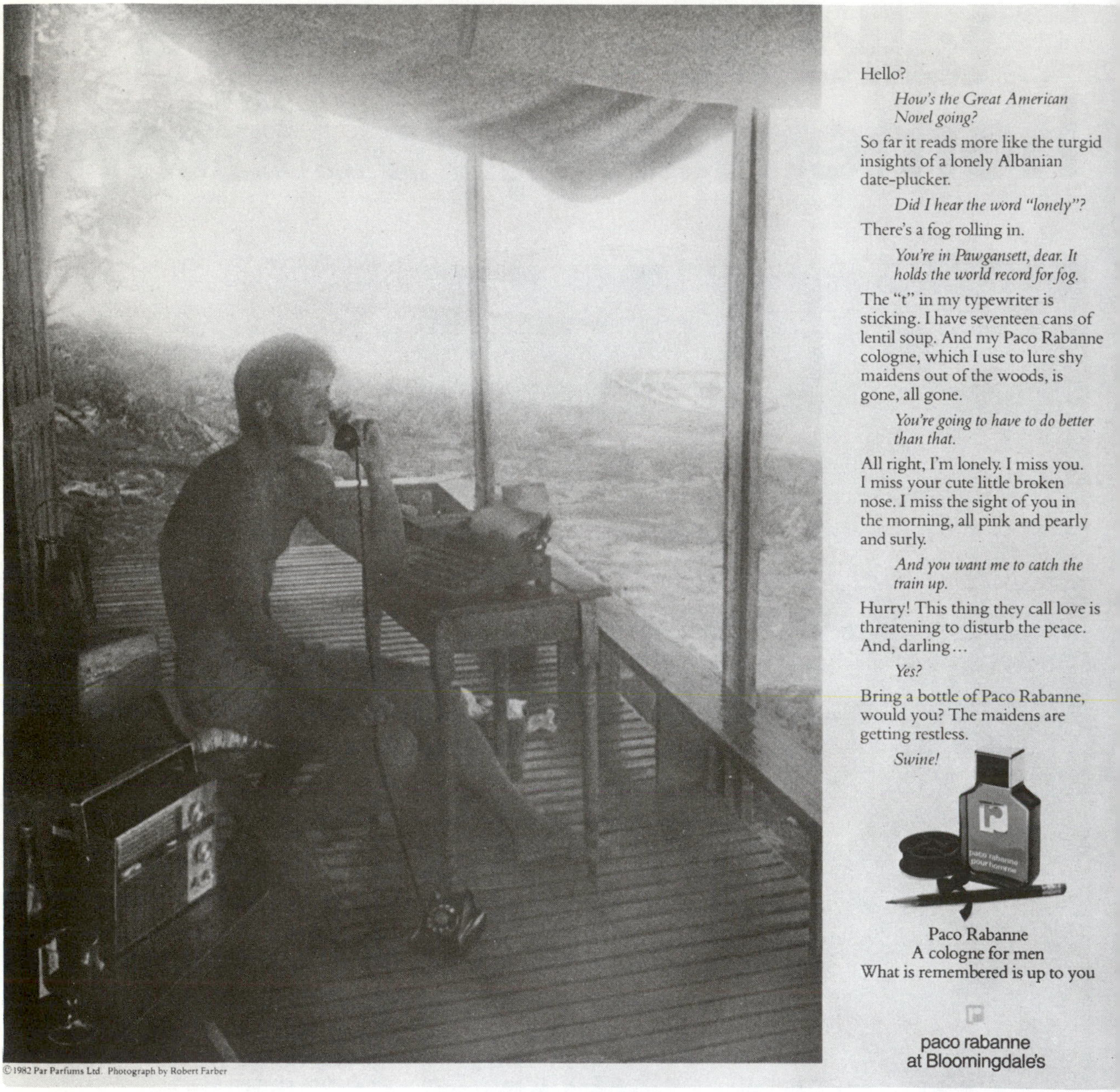

Hello?

How's the Great American Novel going?

So far it reads more like the turgid insights of a lonely Albanian date-plucker.

Did I hear the word "lonely"?

There's a fog rolling in.

You're in Pawgansett, dear. It holds the world record for fog.

The "t" in my typewriter is sticking. I have seventeen cans of lentil soup. And my Paco Rabanne cologne, which I use to lure shy maidens out of the woods, is gone, all gone.

You're going to have to do better than that.

All right, I'm lonely. I miss you. I miss your cute little broken nose. I miss the sight of you in the morning, all pink and pearly and surly.

And you want me to catch the train up.

Hurry! This thing they call love is threatening to disturb the peace. And, darling...

Yes?

Bring a bottle of Paco Rabanne, would you? The maidens are getting restless.

Swine!

Paco Rabanne
A cologne for men
What is remembered is up to you

paco rabanne
at Bloomingdale's

[1982]

aramis
An American Hero
aramis
cologne
The impact never fades
Aramis Inc. 1986

[1986]

OBSESSION
FOR MEN

Calvin Klein
COLOGNE

[1989]

IN THIS WORLD, OF TOTAL CONFUSION
BE CERTAIN Y'ALL 'R NOT DISSED BY ILLUSION.
THE'RE SOME PEOPLE OUT THERE
WHO DON'T EVEN CARE
'BOUT THE MESSAGE *WE* SEND
AND IN THE END, WILL STEAL OUR COLOURS
AND PRETEND.
PRETEND TO BE BROTHERS
BUT WE WANT IT UNDERSTOOD
THAT ONLY *CROSS COLOURS* IS MADE
BY TRUE BROTHERS FROM THE HOOD.
CARL JONES / T.J. WALKER
DESIGNERS & OWNERS
OF
CROSS COLOURS
OAKTREE®
CROSS
POST HIP HOP NATION
CC
ACADEMIC HARDWEAR
COLOURS
YA DIG • YA DIG • YA DIG
®
CLOTHING WITHOUT PREJUDICE

[1992]

When you're old, and tired, and suspicious,

And plagued with doubt, you'll still hear the world calling to you.

You'll wish with all your heart you'd taken the time to listen to it.

And you'll be filled with regret.

Or
maybe
not.
ACG™ STANDS FOR ALL CONDITIONS GEAR BY NIKE, SHOES AND APPAREL DESIGNED FOR ANY ACTIVITY THAT TAKES PLACE OUT IN THE REAL WORLD. SHOWN HERE: THE ACG GRAPHIC WINDSHIRT, DESCHÜTZ SHORT AND AIR MOWABB™ OUTDOOR CROSS-TRAINING SHOES. TO FIND OUT MORE, CALL 1-800-255-8ACG.
NIKE
ACG™

[1992]

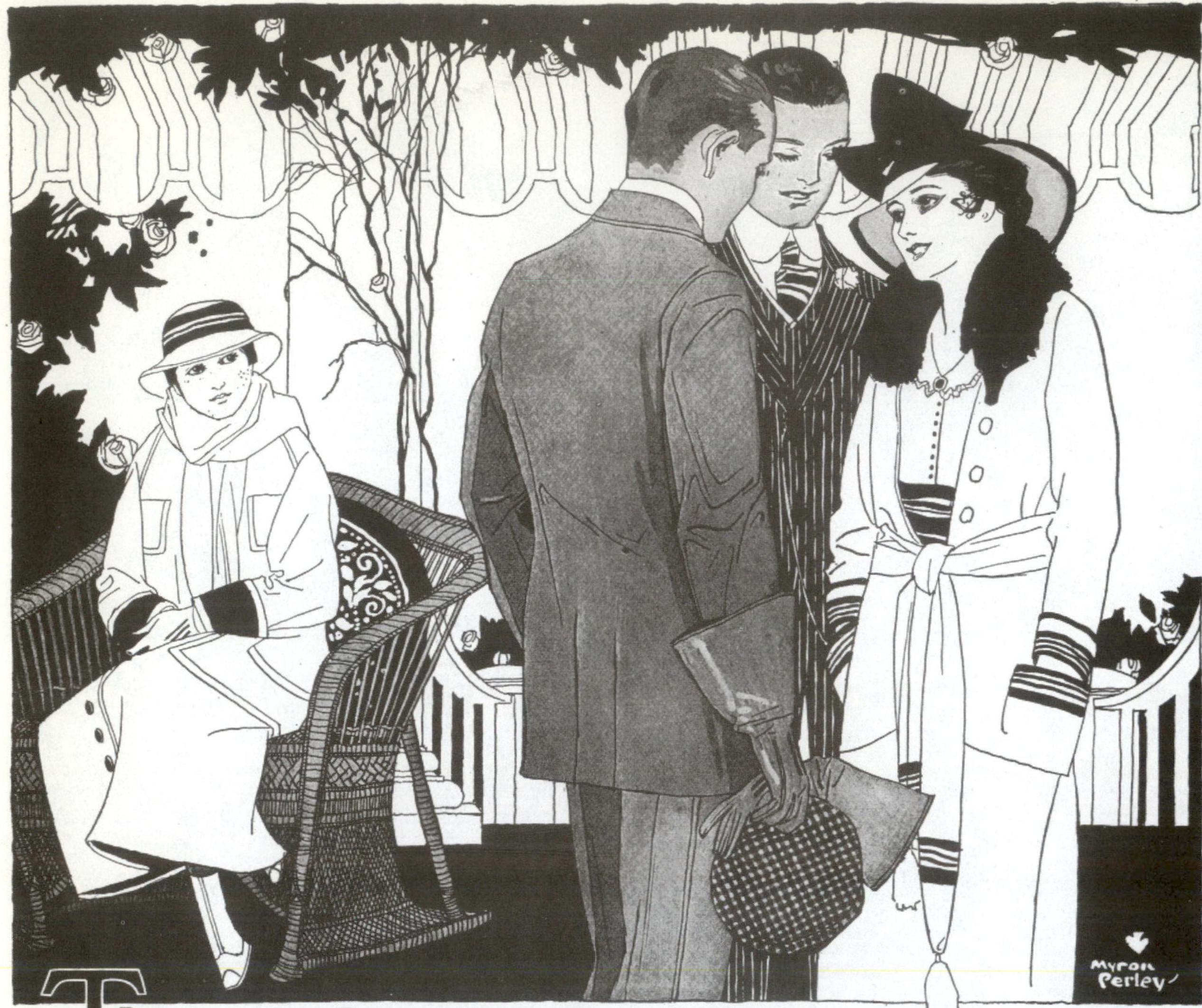

The girl with the clear skin wins

Many an otherwise attractive girl is a social failure because of a poor complexion. If *your* skin is not fresh, smooth and healthy, or has suffered from an unwise use of cosmetics, see if the daily use of Resinol Soap will not greatly improve it.

Resinol Soap is not only unusually cleansing and softening, but its regular use helps *nature* give to the skin and hair that beauty of perfect health which it is impossible to imitate. Tendency to pimples is lessened, redness and roughness disappear, and in a very short time the complexion usually becomes clear, fresh and velvety.

The soothing, restoring influence that makes this possible is the *Resinol* which this soap contains and which physicians have prescribed for over twenty years, in Resinol Ointment, for skin and scalp troubles.

This same gentle medication, together with its freedom from harsh, irritating alkali, adapt Resinol Soap admirably to the care of the hair and of a baby's delicate skin. If the skin is in really bad condition through neglect or improper treatment Resinol Soap should at first be aided by a little Resinol Ointment.

Resinol Soap is sold by all druggists and dealers in toilet goods. In trial-size cake, write to Dept. 5-K, Resinol, Baltimore, Md.

Discriminating men like Resinol Shaving Stick because it soothes and refreshes the face, while supplying a rich, creamy, non-drying lather.

Resinol Soap

[1916]

Again She Orders — "A Chicken Salad, Please"

FOR him she is wearing her new frock. For him she is trying to look her prettiest. If only she can impress him—make him like her—just a little.

Across the table he smiles at her, proud of her prettiness, glad to notice that others admire. And she smiles back, a bit timidly, a bit self-consciously.

What wonderful poise he has! What complete self-possession! If only *she* could be so thoroughly at ease.

She pats the folds of her new frock nervously, hoping that he will not notice how embarrassed she is, how uncomfortable. He doesn't—until the waiter comes to their table and stands, with pencil poised, to take the order.

"A chicken salad, please." She hears herself give the order as in a daze. She hears him repeat the order to the waiter, in a rather surprised tone. Why *had* she ordered that again! This was the third time she had ordered chicken salad while dining with him.

He would think she didn't know how to order a dinner. Well, did she? No. She didn't know how to pronounce those French words on the menu. And she didn't know how to use the table appointment as gracefully as she would have liked; found that she couldn't create conversation—and was actually tongue-tied; was conscious of little crudities which she just knew he must be noticing. She wasn't sure of herself, she didn't *know*. And she discovered, as we all do, that there is only one way to have complete poise and ease of manner, and that is to know definitely what to do and say on every occasion.

Are You Conscious of Your Crudities?

It is not, perhaps, so serious a fault to be unable to order a correct dinner. But it is just such little things as these that betray us—that reveal our crudities to others.

Are you sure of yourself? Do you know precisely what to do and say wherever you happen to be? Or are you always hesitant and ill at ease, never quite sure that you haven't blundered?

Every day in our contact with men and women we meet little unexpected problems of conduct. Unless we are prepared to meet them, it is inevitable that we suffer embarrassment and keen humiliation.

Etiquette is the armor that protects us from these embarrassments. It makes us aware instantly of the little crudities that are robbing us of our poise and ease. It tells us how to smooth away these crudities and achieve a manner of confidence and self-possession. It eliminates doubt and uncertainty, tells us exactly what we want to know.

There is an old proverb which says "Good manners make good mixers." We all know how true this is. No one likes to associate with a person who is self-conscious and embarrassed; whose crudities are obvious to all.

Do You Make Friends Easily?

By telling you exactly what is expected of you on all occasions, by giving you a wonderful new ease and dignity of manner, the Book of Etiquette will help make you more popular—a "better mixer." This famous two-volume set of books is the recognized social authority—is a silent social secretary in half a million homes.

Let us pretend that you have received an invitation. Would you know exactly how to acknowledge it? Would you know what sort of gift to send, what to write on the card that accompanies it? Perhaps it is an invitation to a formal wedding. Would you know what to wear? Would you know what to say to the host and hostess upon arrival?

If a Dinner Follows the Wedding—

Would you know exactly how to proceed to the dining room, when to seat yourself, how to create conversation, how to conduct yourself with ease and dignity?

Would you use a fork for your fruit salad, or a spoon? Would you cut your roll with a knife, or break it with your fingers? Would you take olives with a fork? How would you take celery—asparagus—radishes? Unless you are absolutely sure of yourself, you will be embarrassed. And embarrassment *cannot be concealed*.

Book of Etiquette Gives Lifelong Advice

Hundreds of thousands of men and women know and use the Book of Etiquette and find it increasingly helpful. Every time an occasion of importance arises—every time expert help, advice and suggestion is required—they find what they seek in the Book of Etiquette. It solves all problems, answers all questions, tells you exactly what to do, say, write and wear on every occasion.

If you want always to be sure of yourself, to have ease and poise, to avoid embarrassment and humiliation, send for the Book of Etiquette at once. Take advantage of the special bargain offer explained in the panel. Let the Book of Etiquette give you complete self-possession; let it banish the crudities that are perhaps making you self-conscious and uncomfortable when you should be thoroughly at ease.

Mail this coupon *now* while you are thinking of it. The Book of Etiquette will be sent to you in a plain carton with no identifying marks. Be among those who will take advantage of the special offer. Nelson Doubleday, Inc., Dept. 3911, Garden City, New York.

A Social Secretary for Life!

The Famous Book of Etiquette Nearly 500,000 Sold for $3.50

NOW ONLY $1.98

We have on our shelves at the present time several thousand sets of the Book of Etiquette in the regular $3.50 edition. To clear the shelves quickly and make room for new editions now being printed, Nelson Doubleday, Inc., makes this unusual offer: To the next few thousand people who order the Book of Etiquette, the special bargain price of $1.98 will be extended. In other words, if you act without delay you can secure the complete, two-volume set of the Book of Etiquette at practically *half* the usual cost.

Nelson Doubleday, Inc., Dept. 3911
Garden City, New York

I accept your special bargain offer. You may send me the famous two-volume Book of Etiquette, in a plain carton, for which I will give the postman only $1.98 (plus delivery charges) on arrival—instead of the regular price of $3.50. I am to have the privilege of returning the books within 5 days and having my money refunded if I am not delighted with them.

Name...

[1921]

Sexual Confidence

You can tell when someone's got it the moment they enter a room—the ability to turn people on with just the look in their eyes. And, NOW you can have it too, with the amazing bestseller, SEXUAL CONFIDENCE.

You'll learn: **How to project Sexual Charisma** • Ways to attract new mates • **How to create laughter in the bedroom, and why this will *instantly* triple your capacity for sexual enjoyment** • Touching techniques that help you get intimate right away • **Why "letting-go" during lovemaking will make you a *better* lover** • How to take a "Sexual Holiday" • **Ten techniques for ending sexual anxiety** • How to change your "sexual image" (and why people will suddenly find you far more attractive than ever before) • **Stimulating your lovemate with sensual, new kissing techniques** • A Great Lover's Vocabulary • **And so much more!**

Yes, this revolutionary, 230 page, hardcover bestseller is *fully* guaranteed to make you a better lover. In fact, within just one hour it'll have you radiating Total Sexual Confidence...because from now on you'll know exactly what your lovers want *even before they ask!* Remember, SEXUAL CONFIDENCE has been acclaimed by doctors and therapists as a breakthrough in increasing sexual pleasure. So order today. SEXUAL CONFIDENCE costs far less than a new shirt or blouse, yet it'll bring so many more wonderful people into your love life!

(To order, see coupon at right)

Shy Person's Guide To A Successful Love Life!

A brilliant psychological writer explains how you can conquer shyness literally overnight.

by P. Woodland-Smith

I am a shy person myself.

Yet I could walk into a party tonight and within five minutes be talking, laughing, dancing . . . even making dates with the most attractive people in the room.

I could walk into a restaurant or pub and walk out an hour later with a new acquaintance, a new friend, even a new lover.

Yet the extraordinary thing about all this is that up until recently I was so pathetically shy I often didn't go out for months at a time.

At work I did fine. Socially I was a bust. My lack of dates even became sort of a joke among my friends. Some joke.

Then about six months ago a kindly relative lent me a copy of a book called THE SHY PERSON'S GUIDE TO A HAPPIER LOVE LIFE. The rest is history. In slightly more than two weeks I was dating several new people. And today . . . just six months later . . . I have so many friends and lovers I hardly ever spend an evening home alone. My social life has blossomed to the point that it's started interfering with my work life. Sometimes I actually have to take the phone off the hook to get some of my writing done.

If only I'd known that in two short weeks I'd be able to cure myself of something that had been making me miserable every day of my life. Why, lately I've been having a ball. And I'm absolutely convinced that anyone . . . no matter how incurably shy they *think* they are . . . can do the same.

What THE SHY PERSON'S GUIDE taught me is that there are more people ready to love you than you ever dreamed possible. At work, at school, on the street, in parks, museums, restaurants, *everywhere!* All you have to do is ask. And that's precisely why THE SHY PERSON'S GUIDE can be such a help.

THE SHY PERSON'S GUIDE will show you exactly how to unleash your natural, inborn talent for charming and attracting new people. Imagine how successful you'd be with others if you weren't afraid to speak what was in your heart . . to be as free and as open as you'd like.

Well, THE SHY PERSON'S GUIDE will show you scores of techniques for doing just that: For example, you will discover: **A simple, upfront way of letting someone know you're attracted to them without appearing weak or desperate . . .** a brilliant technique for making someone feel "special" when they're in your company . . . A completely reliable way of telling if someone likes you (you'll be amazed at how many potential lovemates you've been overlooking)...**A simple way to "trick" yourself into being looser and friendlier at parties . . .** How to get invited to more parties and what to do once you get there (not the same old things that make you angry and frustrated with yourself the moment you get home) . . . AND MUCH, MUCH MORE!

The Sooner You Attack Your Shyness, The Easier It Is To Cure

Don't kid yourself into thinking that *next time* you go to a party you'll be braver, more outgoing, That's the classic shy person's trick for *staying* shy. No, if you really want to get better, really want to know the joy of laughing, dancing, meeting people who want to be with you . . . then send for this mind-opening bestseller today.

Alright, maybe you're thinking, *but what if THE SHY PERSON'S GUIDE doesn't work for me.* No problem. Simply return the book and the publisher will send you a complete and immediate refund. No questions asked. Even if you secretly feel the book has done you some good.

But I'm so thoroughly convinced THE SHY PERSON'S GUIDE will change your life, so incredibly *bullish* about its shyness-conquering techniques, I hate to even bring up the guarantee. That's how sure I am this amazing book will work for you.

So send for THE SHY PERSON'S GUIDE TO A HAPPIER LOVE LIFE today. And start enjoying all the love and romance you've been dreaming about. It's out there alright. And it's so darn easy to find, it'd be a crying shame not to get your share.

Free Book

If you order our two bestsellers above we'll send you 100 BEST OPENING LINES, a $6.95 value, absolutely **FREE!** It's filled with 100 humorous, interesting and clever conversation openers, just right for capturing the attention of people you're attracted to. A perfect line for *every* situation—and best of all, it's **FREE!**

100 BEST OPENING LINES

FREE BOOK OFFER!

____ Please send me SEXUAL CONFIDENCE right away. I've enclosed $10.95 plus $2.00 shipping.

____ Please send me the SHY PERSON'S GUIDE TO A HAPPIER LOVE LIFE right away. I've enclosed $11.95 plus $2.00 shipping.

____ Please send me BOTH BOOKS for the low, low price of $22.90 plus $2.00 shipping. I understand I will receive as a bonus, 100 BEST OPENING LINES, a $6.95 value, absolutely FREE!

MasterCard and Visa accepted. Cardholders send card # and exp. date or call toll free anytime: **800-631-2560.** (In NJ call **201-569-8555**). Allow 1-3 weeks.

Name ____________________

Street ____________________

City, State, Zip ____________________

Mail check or money order to: SYMPHONY PRESS, INC. DEPT. NY P.O. BOX 515 TENAFLY, N.J. 07670

All books fully guaranteed for 30 days.

[1983]

LifeStyles introduces the strongest condom made in America.

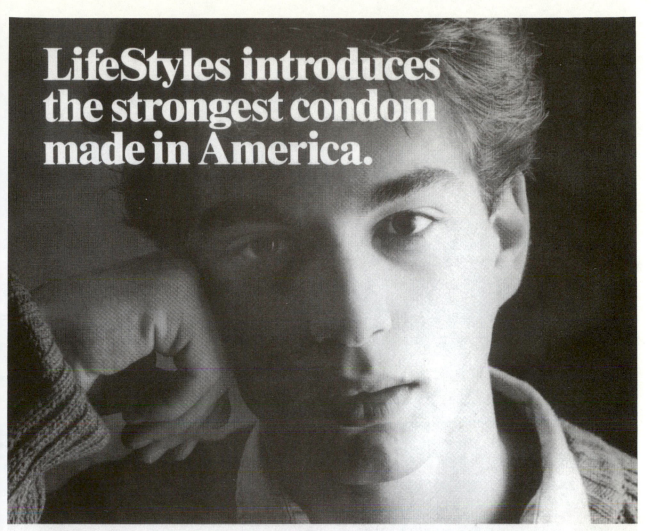

Because unsafe sex, even once, could be tragic.

"AIDS. Every day I hear and read more about it. It kills and there's no cure. And being young is no defense. It is now more important than ever to be careful about relationships."

This is why LifeStyles has introduced the strongest condom made in America. No other condom offers the extra protection of LifeStyles® Extra Strength. No condom is as strong. What's more, no other condom carries a special measure of Nonoxynol-9 inside the tip.

Extra Strength condoms, the newest product of LifeStyles technology, also provide an extremely high degree of sensitivity. With LifeStyles Extra Strength Condoms, properly used, you'll be as sure as you can be that your sex is safer sex. And isn't that what you want?

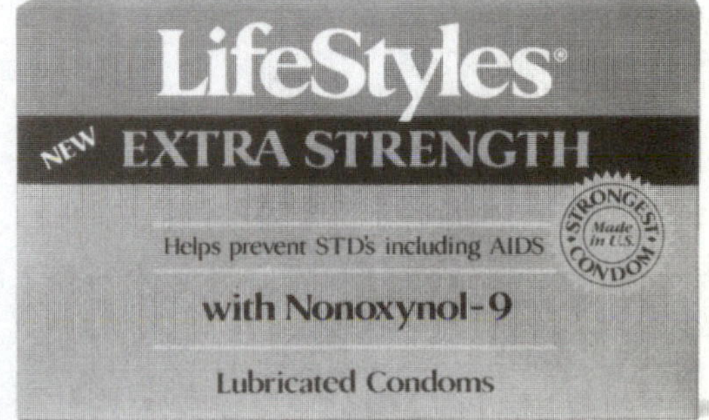

This product combines a latex condom and a spermicidal lubricant. The spermicide, Nonoxynol-9, reduces the number of active sperm, thereby reducing the risk of pregnancy if you lose your erection before withdrawal and some semen spill outside the condom. However, the extent of decreased risk has not been established. This condom should not be used as a substitute for the combined use of a vaginal spermicide and condom.

FROM AMERICA'S LARGEST MANUFACTURER OF CONDOMS, ANSELL INTERNATIONAL, TINTON FALLS, NJ 07724. © 1987 ANSELL, INC.

LifeStyles Extra Strength. Now there's an even stronger reason to use condoms.

[1987]

How to write a personal letter

by Garrison Keillor

International Paper asked Garrison Keillor, author of the best-selling books, Happy to Be Here and Lake Wobegon Days, to tell you how to write a letter that will bring joy into the life of someone you love.

We shy persons need to write a letter now and then, or else we'll dry up and blow away. It's true. And I speak as one who loves to reach for the phone, dial the number, and talk. I say, "Big Bopper here—what's shakin', babes?" The telephone is to shyness what Hawaii is to February, it's a way out of the woods, *and yet*: a letter is better.

Such a sweet gift

Such a sweet gift—a piece of handmade writing, in an envelope that is not a bill, sitting in our friend's path when she trudges home from a long day spent among wahoos and savages, a day our words will help repair. They don't need to be immortal, just sincere. She can read them twice and again tomorrow: *You're someone I care about, Corinne, and think of often and every time I do you make me smile.*

We need to write, otherwise nobody will know who we are. They will have only a vague impression of us as A Nice Person, because frankly, we don't shine at conversation, we lack the confidence to thrust our faces forward and say, "Hi, I'm Heather Hooten, let me tell you about my week." Mostly we say "Uh-huh" and "Oh really." People smile and look over our shoulder, looking for someone else to talk to.

So a shy person sits down and writes a letter. To be known by another person—to meet and talk freely on the page—to be close despite distance. To escape from anonymity and be our own sweet selves and express the music of our souls.

Same thing that moves a giant rock star to sing his heart out in front of 123,000 people moves us to take ball-point in hand and write a few lines to our dear Aunt Eleanor. *We want to be known.* We want her to know that we have fallen in love, that we quit our job, that we're moving to New York, and we want to say a few things that might not get said in casual conversation: *thank you for what you've meant to me, I am very happy right now.*

Skip the guilt

The first step in writing letters is to get over the guilt of *not* writing. You don't "owe" anybody a letter. Letters are a gift. The burning shame you feel when you see unanswered mail makes it harder to pick up a pen and makes for a cheerless letter when you finally do. *I feel bad about not writing, but I've been so busy,* etc. Skip this. Few letters are obligatory, and they are *Thanks for the wonderful gift* and *I am terribly sorry to hear about George's death* and *Yes, you're welcome to stay with us next month,* and not many more than that. Write those promptly if you want to keep your friends. Don't worry about the others, except love letters, of course. When your true love writes *Dear Light of My Life, Joy of My Heart, O Lovely Pulsating Core of My Sensate Life,* some response is called for. Some of the best letters are tossed off in a burst of inspiration, so keep your writing stuff in one place where you can sit down for a few minutes and *Dear Roy, I am in the middle of an essay for International Paper but thought I'd drop you a line. Hi to your sweetie too* dash off a note to a pal. Envelopes, stamps, address book, everything in a drawer so you can write fast when the pen is hot.

A blank

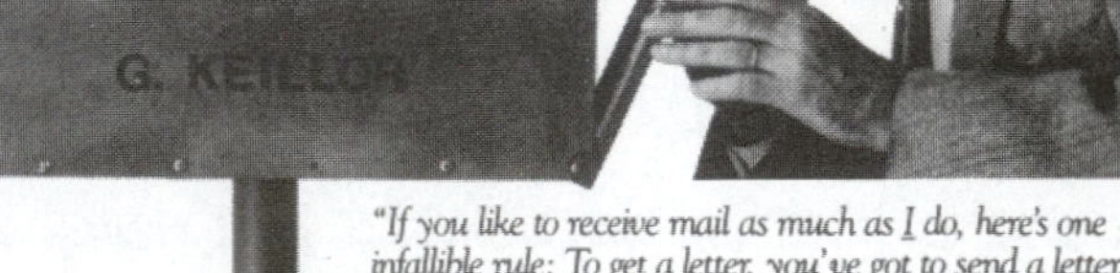

"If you like to receive mail as much as I do, here's one infallible rule: To get a letter, you've got to send a letter."

white 8″ x 11″ sheet can look as big as Montana if the pen's not so hot—try a smaller page and write boldly. Or use a note card with a piece of fine art on the front; if your letter ain't good, at least they get the Matisse. Get a pen that makes a sensuous line, get a comfortable typewriter, a friendly word processor—whichever feels easy to the hand.

Sit for a few minutes with the blank sheet in front of you, and meditate on the person you will write to, let your friend come to mind until you can almost see her or him in the room with you. Remember the last time you saw each other and how your friend looked and what you said and what perhaps was unsaid between you, and when your friend becomes real to you, start to write.

"*Outrage, confusion, love—whatever is in your mind, let it find a way to the page.*"

Tell us what you're doing

Write the salutation—*Dear* You—and take a deep breath and plunge in. A simple declarative sentence will do, followed by another and another and another. Tell us what you're doing and tell it like you were talking to us. Don't think about grammar, don't think about lit'ry style, don't try to write dramatically, just give us your news. Where did you go, who did you see, what did they say, what do you think?

If you don't know where to begin, start with the present moment: *I'm sitting at the kitchen table on a rainy Saturday morning. Everyone is gone and the house is quiet.* Let your simple description of the present moment lead to something else, let the letter drift gently along.

Take it easy

The toughest letter to crank out is one that is meant to impress, as we all know from writing job applications; if it's hard work to slip off a letter to a friend, maybe you're trying too hard to be terrific. A letter is only a report to someone who already likes you for reasons other than your brilliance. Take it easy.

Don't worry about form. It's not a term paper. When you come to the end of one episode, just start a new paragraph. You can go from a few lines about the sad state of rock 'n roll to the fight with your mother to your fond memories of Mexico to your cat's urinary tract infection to a few thoughts on personal indebtedness to the kitchen sink and what's in it. The more you write, the easier it gets, and when you have a True True Friend to write to, a *compadre,* a soul sibling, then it's like driving a car down a country road, you just get behind the keyboard and press on the gas.

Don't tear up the page and start over when you write a bad line—try to write your way out of it. Make mistakes and plunge on. Let the letter cook along and let yourself be bold. Outrage, confusion, love—whatever is in your mind, let it find a way to the page. Writing is a means of discovery, always, and when you come to the end and write *Yours ever* or *Hugs and Kisses,* you'll know something you didn't when you wrote *Dear Pal.*

An object of art

Probably your friend will put your letter away, and it'll be read again a few years from now—and it will improve with age. And forty years from now, your friend's grandkids will dig it out of the attic and read it, a sweet and precious relic of the ancient Eighties that gives them a sudden clear glimpse of you and her and the world we old-timers knew. You will then have created an object of art. Your simple lines about where you went, who you saw, what they said, will speak to those children and they will feel in their hearts the humanity of our times.

You can't pick up a phone and call the future and tell them about our times. You have to pick up a piece of paper.

[1987]

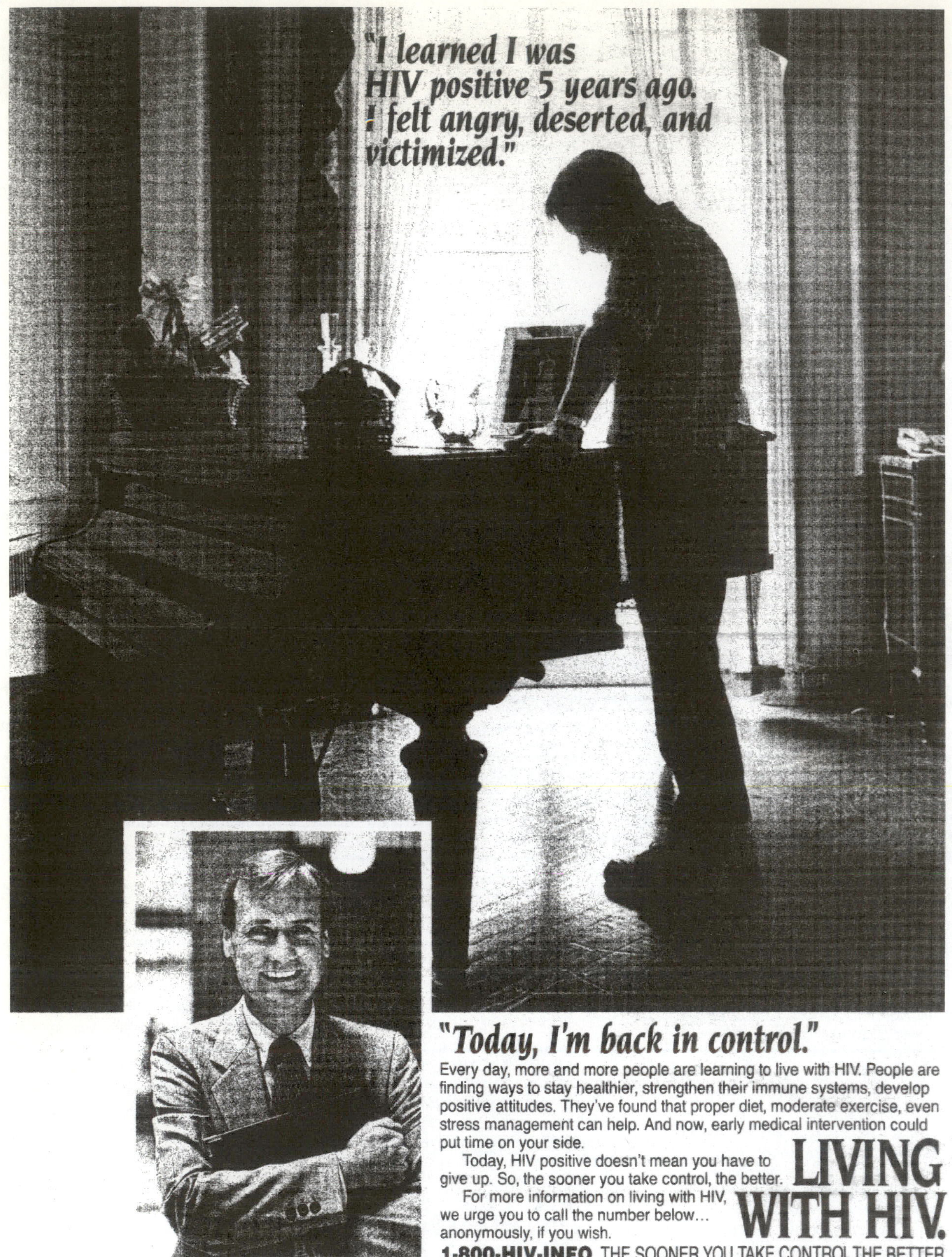

"I learned I was HIV positive 5 years ago. I felt angry, deserted, and victimized."
"Today, I'm back in control."
Every day, more and more people are learning to live with HIV. People are finding ways to stay healthier, strengthen their immune systems, develop positive attitudes. They've found that proper diet, moderate exercise, even stress management can help. And now, early medical intervention could put time on your side.
Today, HIV positive doesn't mean you have to give up. So, the sooner you take control, the better.
For more information on living with HIV, we urge you to call the number below… anonymously, if you wish.
LIVING WITH HIV.
1-800-HIV-INFO THE SOONER YOU TAKE CONTROL THE BETTER.

Brought to you as a public service by the San Francisco Black Coalition on AIDS; and American Academy of Dermatology, American Academy of Family Physicians, American College of General Practitioners in Osteopathic Medicine and Surgery, American Osteopathic Association, American Social Health Association, National Association of People with AIDS; and Burroughs Wellcome Co.

[1991]

Neutrogena® gives you the clean-pore advantage over acne.

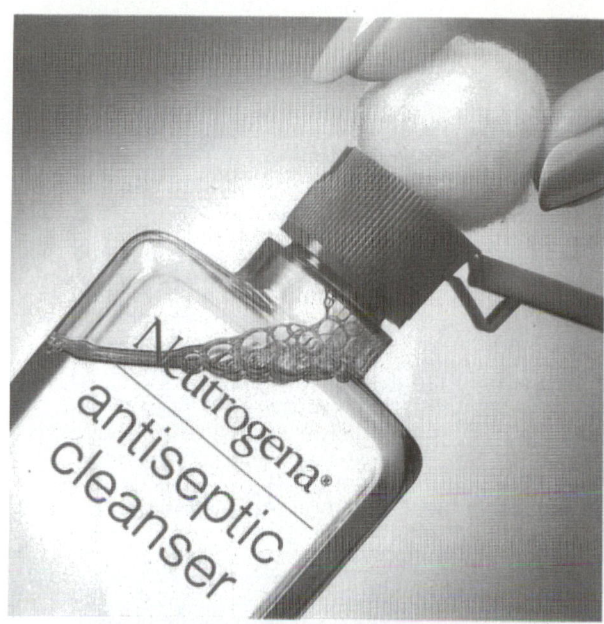

There are about 218,000 pores in your face. If every one of them were perfectly clean, your skin could be noticeably clearer. Which brings us to the Neutrogena® Clean Pore Advantage. It's not a fancy regime. It's simply the result you get when you tackle your skin problems with our four effective products. Use only the ones you need. And see how much easier it is to fight acne with 218,000 clean pores on your side.

AN ANTISEPTIC CLEANSER THAT'S HARD ON DIRT, NOT ON YOUR SKIN. An antiseptic is great for when you can't wash your face or you want even deeper cleansing. But antiseptics with alcohol have the irritating habit of stripping away your skin's natural moisturizers along with dirt and oil, leaving your skin tight and dry. That's why Neutrogena® Antiseptic Cleanser is alcohol-free. So instead of tight and dry, your skin just feels fresh and clean.

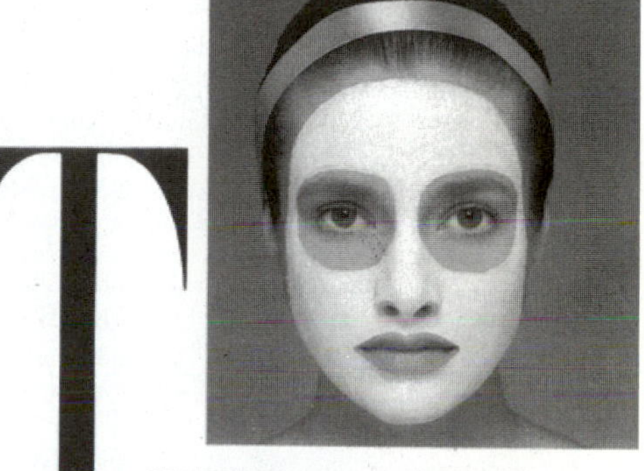

THE 20 MINUTE MASK WITH THE POWER OF AN ALL-DAY ACNE TREATMENT. Benzoyl peroxide may be the strongest acne-fighting medicine you can buy without a prescription. But spending a whole day with it can over-dry. Which is why Neutrogena® Acne Mask does the job in just 20 minutes. Easy to smooth on, easy to rinse off, it combines benzoyl peroxide with the smoothing benefits of clay. So it treats blemishes, cleans pores and leaves your skin healthier.

Clear skin, clear pores, clear bar.

For basic cleansing, choose your weapons carefully, considering what they don't offer as well as what they do. Like Neutrogena® Cleansing Bar for Acne-Prone Skin. Its pure amber formula has no harsh chemicals or irritants. So it gently removes dirt and oil from clogged pores, then rinses away, leaving nothing to interfere with acne medications.

Look for Neutrogena products at your drugstore. For serious acne problems, please consult a dermatologist.

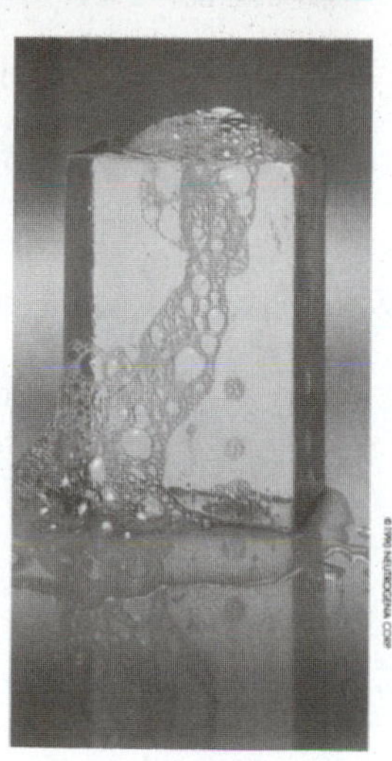

Spot trouble before it breaks out. For zeroing in on acne-prone areas, there's a lot to be said for spot treatments. But some creamy cover-ups can actually block your pores and make matters worse. Put Neutrogena® Drying Gel on the spot instead. Its clear, non-clogging formula dries only where you put it. And no one but you knows it's there.

Neutrogena®

[1992]

"Most Automobiles are like most Men"
"They are either all right or all wrong, but seldom one or the other for long at a time."
"That's probably why they call this a Woman's Car, it's so consistent."
"Your intuition, my dear, is perfect. That's just it. You know, I used to call the last car we had, a 'Cook Four,' because it cost more than it was worth, consumed more than it earned, and was always quitting!"
"And what do you call this?"
"Oh, the Overland is like a first-rate cook—popular with the whole family! This is the first Saturday I've had this car to myself since—"
"Heavens, Helen, you went right into that mudhole!"
"Didn't jar you, did it?"
"No, not at all! But isn't it remarkable for so light a car?"
"Yes. Harry calls it a feather bed on wheels. It's some funny new spring they've invented that lets you down easy when the going's hard. How do you like the tan velour upholstery?"
"Just love it, Helen, it is so restrained. But how about gas?"
"That's restrained, too, my dear. Harry says we're averaging twenty-five miles to the gallon."
"Twenty-five miles?"
"Sounds as incredible as a woman's age, but it's true. In fact, I've only one complaint against this Overland Sedan—it's too useful!"
"Too useful?"
"Yes, too useful. So useful that it points a moral."
"For example?"
"Well, all you ever have to do with this Overland Sedan is to step on it. And that is the fate of all useful things and all useful people. Somebody is always stepping on them!"
"Helen, you talk like a Socialist."
"It's true. This little Overland Sedan is like a household drudge—always working and never through!"
"You'd better hurry, Helen, the train's in. We'll miss Harry."
"Don't worry. He'll wait. There he is now.... oh, Harry!"
"Hello, girls! Have you room for a few bundles and may a husband presume to ride home in his wife's car?"
WILLYS-OVERLAND, INC., TOLEDO, OHIO
Sedans, Coupés, Touring Cars, Roadsters
Willys-Overland, Limited, Toronto, Canada
The John N. Willys Export Corp., New York
Overland

[1921]

Her habit of measuring time in terms of dollars gives the woman in business keen insight into the true value of a Ford closed car for her personal use.

This car enables her to conserve minutes, to expedite her affairs, to widen the scope of her activities. Its low first cost, long life and inexpensive operation and upkeep convince her that it is a sound investment value.

And it is such a pleasant car to drive that it transforms the business call which might be an interruption into an enjoyable episode of her busy day.

TUDOR SEDAN, $590 FORDOR SEDAN, $685 COUPE, $525 (All prices f. o. b. Detroit)

[1924]

Lemon.

This Volkswagen missed the boat.

The chrome strip on the glove compartment is blemished and must be replaced. Chances are you wouldn't have noticed it; Inspector Kurt Kroner did.

There are 3,389 men at our Wolfsburg factory with only one job: to inspect Volkswagens at each stage of production. (3000 Volkswagens are produced daily; there are more inspectors than cars.)

Every shock absorber is tested (spot checking won't do), every windshield is scanned. VWs have been rejected for surface scratches barely visible to the eye.

Final inspection is really something! VW inspectors run each car off the line onto the Funktionsprüfstand (car test stand), tote up 189 check points, gun ahead to the automatic brake stand, and say "no" to one VW out of fifty.

This preoccupation with detail means the VW lasts longer and requires less maintenance, by and large, than other cars. (It also means a used VW depreciates less than any other car.)

We pluck the lemons; you get the plums.

[1960]

Separates the men from the boys.

There are boy-type cars. And there are man-type cars. And Toronado is all man, all the way. Its styling is bold, brawny and massively male. Its handling is authoritative —thanks to the pulling power of front-wheel drive. Its ride is revolutionary, sure, unique—different from any other car.

Its engine is the strongest Rocket ever built: a bigger-than-ever, 455-cubic-inch V-8. Frankly, not everybody is cut out for a Toronado. But, then, who wants to be everybody?

Toronado.
Test drive the front-wheel-drive "youngmobile" from Oldsmobile.

GM

See special Toronado and 4-4-2 models! On display at the New York International Auto Show—now through April 7.

[1969]

Which man would you vote for?

Ah yes, what could be more dazzling than watching the candidates parade about, kissing babies and flashing winning smiles.

Consider the man in the top picture.

He promises to spend your tax dollars wisely.

But see how he spends his campaign dollars.

On a very fancy convertible.

Resplendent with genuine leather seats. A big 425-horsepower engine.

And a price tag that makes it one of the most expensive convertibles you can buy.

Now consider his opponent.

He promises to spend your tax dollars wisely.

But see how he spends his campaign dollars.

On a Volkswagen Convertible.

Resplendent with a hand-fitted top. A warranty and four free diagnostic check-ups that cover you for 24 months or 24,000 miles.*

And a price tag that makes it one of the least expensive convertibles you can buy.

So maybe this year you'll find a politician who'll do what few politicians ever do:

Keep his promises before he's elected.

*If an owner maintains and services his vehicle in accordance with the Volkswagen maintenance schedule any factory part found to be defective in material or workmanship within 24 months or 24,000 miles, whichever comes first (except normal wear and tear and service items), will be repaired or replaced by any U.S. or Canadian Volkswagen Dealer. And this will be done free of charge. See your Volkswagen dealer for details.

[1972]

YOU'RE NOT JOHN DOE. WHY DRIVE HIS CAR? A car isn't just something you drive. It's something you wear. The Mazda MX-3 is a new sports coupe for those of us who'd never be seen driving a beige cardigan. Instead of making a car that everyone would like, Mazda engineers made a car that a few people will love. ❀ So what's to love about the MX-3? For a start, it's the only car of its kind with smooth V6 power. And suspension that lets it change direction quicker than a politician in

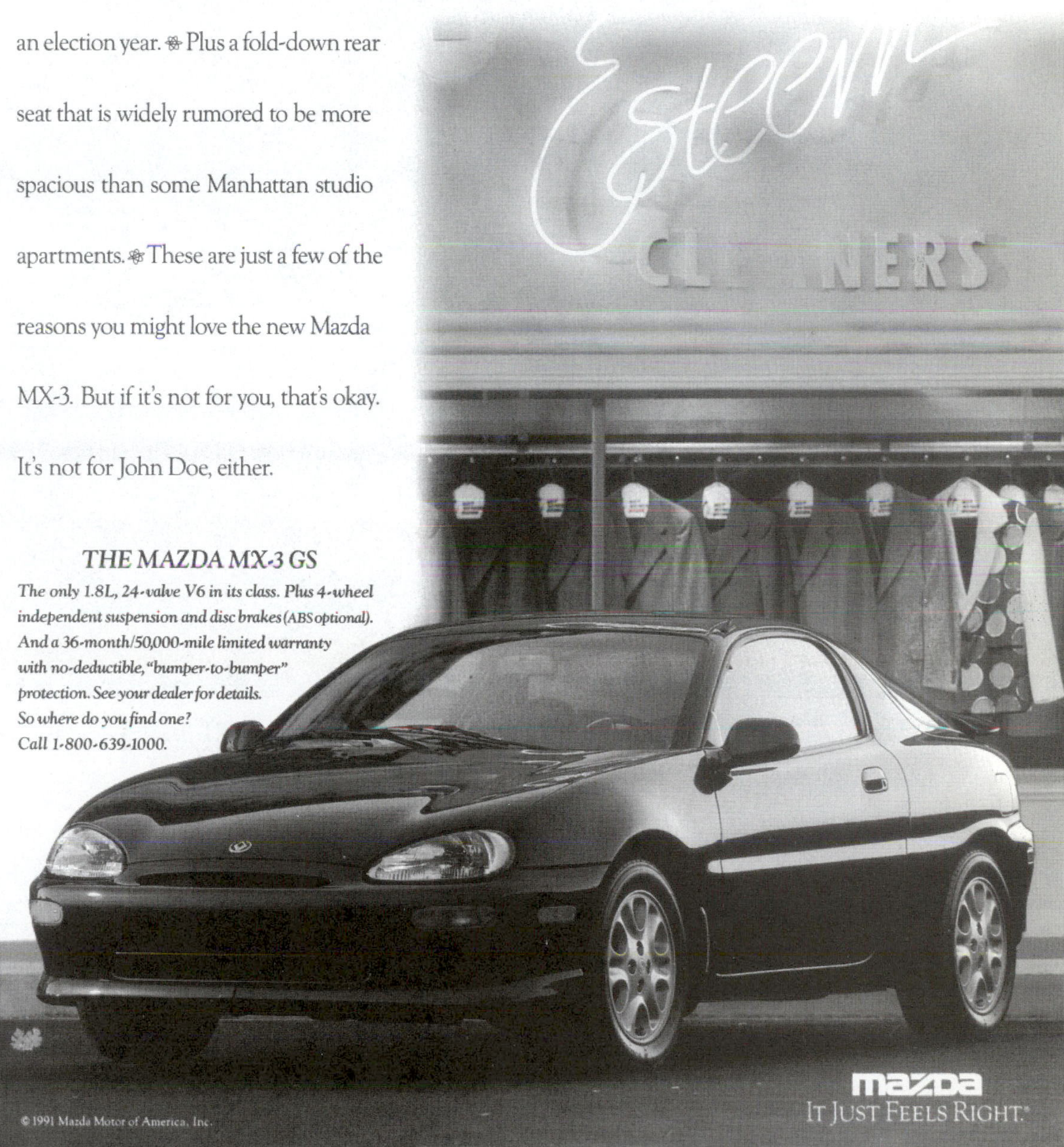
an election year. ❀ Plus a fold-down rear seat that is widely rumored to be more spacious than some Manhattan studio apartments. ❀ These are just a few of the reasons you might love the new Mazda MX-3. But if it's not for you, that's okay.
It's not for John Doe, either.
Esteem
CL NERS
THE MAZDA MX-3 GS
The only 1.8L, 24-valve V6 in its class. Plus 4-wheel independent suspension and disc brakes (ABS optional). And a 36-month/50,000-mile limited warranty with no-deductible, "bumper-to-bumper" protection. See your dealer for details.
So where do you find one?
Call 1-800-639-1000.
© 1991 Mazda Motor of America, Inc.
mazda
IT JUST FEELS RIGHT.

[1991]

MARCEL JOJOLA liked the Saturn SL1 so much, he had his customized for work.

Like a lot of California towns, Bear Valley has budget concerns. And like a lot of Californians, Chief Jojola is a fan of imported cars. He has two Subarus at home, two at the Bear Valley police station, and when they needed a new squad car this year, he just planned on getting another one.

Then someone suggested that perhaps Bear Valley should buy American. Tax dollars, and all. So Marcel, whose most recent experience was all import, wasn't quite sure what to do.

*Base M.S.R.P. including retailer preparation. Tax, license, transportation and options additional. © 1991 Saturn Corporation.

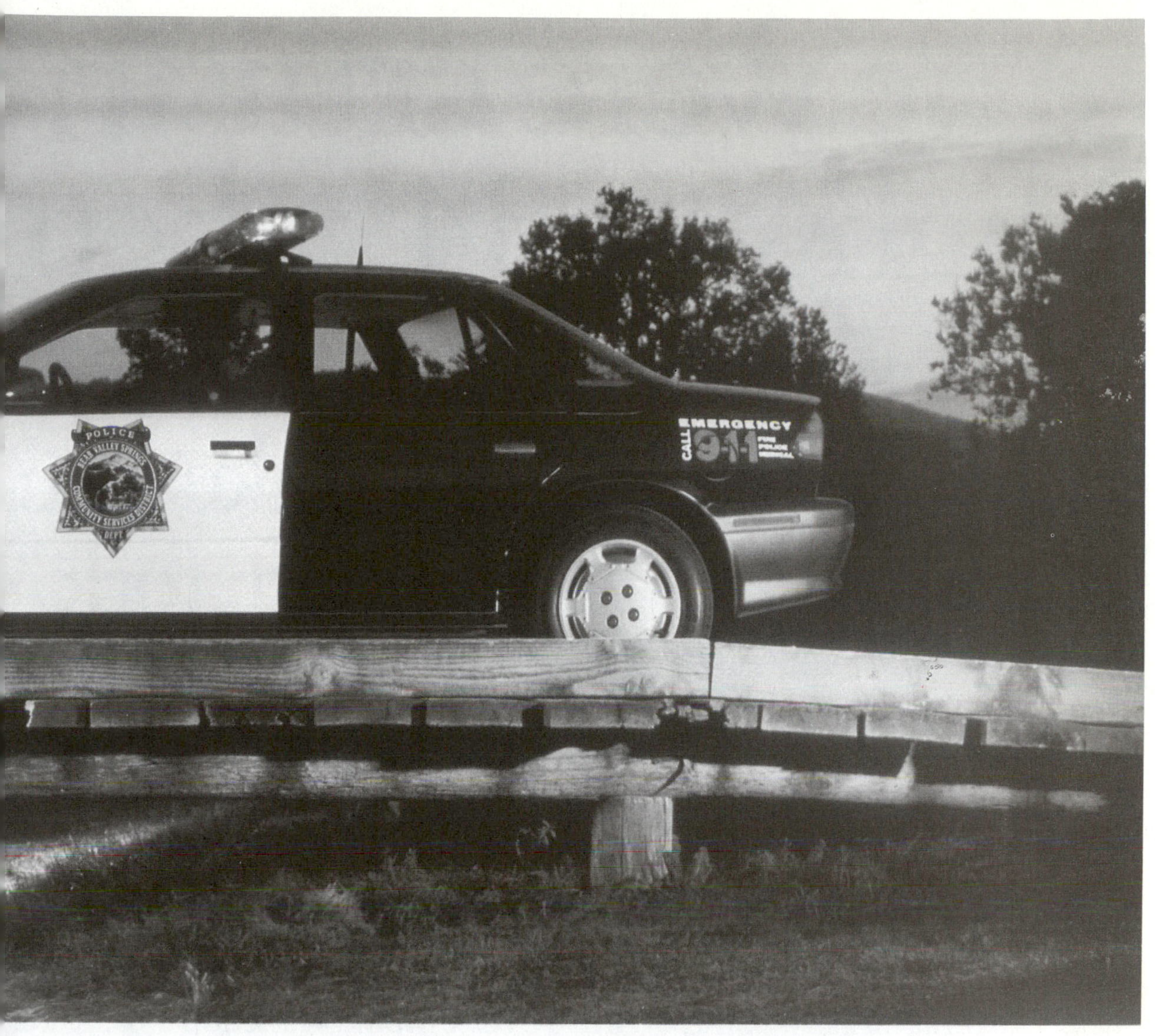

Until the day he ran across a Saturn ad touting the SL1 and its $8995* price tag. Taking along his special police-issue driving gloves, Marcel went for a "law enforcement-style" test drive. (We were pretty relieved to get back to the showroom.)

Anyway, to cut to the chase, the Saturn gave Marcel the performance he was looking for in a patrol car. It's American, which took care of Bear Valley patriotism. And as for the budget folks, they were so happy with the value they were getting with a Saturn, they let Marcel buy two.

SATURN

A DIFFERENT KIND *of* COMPANY. A DIFFERENT KIND *of* CAR.

If you'd like to know more about Saturn, and our new sedans and coupe, please call us at 1-800-522-5000.

[1992]

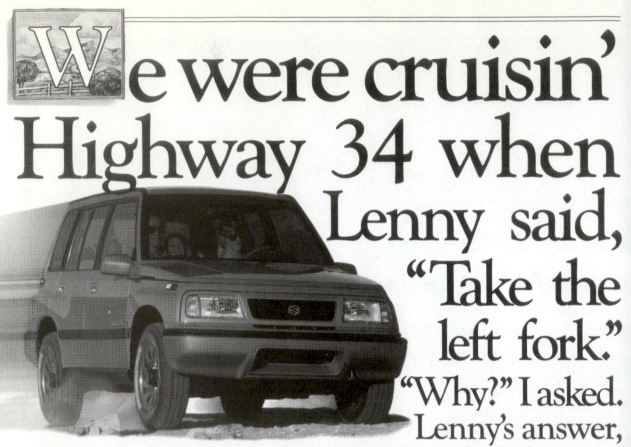

We were cruisin' Highway 34 when Lenny said, "Take the left fork." "Why?" I asked. Lenny's answer,

"Why not?" My husband the navigator. The kids spotted icicles on the shady side of the rocks. More advice from Lenny: "Take the trail between those two big boulders." I was dubious. But Lenny repeated, "Why not?" adding, "the Sidekick® is built to go just about anywhere." So off we went. Four wheelin' uphill. Plenty of power from its 16-valve engine. Lenny was in all his glory. "Go left." An old Doobie Brothers cassette played. A deer bounded by just to our right. I checked the mirror to see if the kids saw her, but they were asleep. "This Sidekick is almost too comfortable," I whispered. Lenny winked at me and said, "Pull over under that tree." I smiled and answered, "Why not?"

THE 4-DR. SIDEKICK 4x4. It has a new, more powerful, 16-valve engine. A new, optional 4-speed electronically-controlled, automatic transmission with lock-up and overdrive. Standard rear anti-lock brake system.[1] Plus, the best gas mileage and one of the lowest sticker prices of any 4-dr. 4x4. So drive it. And live your own adventure. For your nearest Suzuki dealer call 1-800-447-4700.

$12,499[2] 24/26 MPG[3]
CITY HIGHWAY

[1]The rear-wheel anti-lock brake system operates in two-wheel drive mode only.
[2]Manufacturer's suggested retail price. Taxes, title, freight, and license extra. Dealers set own price.
[3]EPA-estimated MPG w/5-sp manual transmission. This vehicle handles differently from ordinary passenger cars. Federal law cautions to avoid sharp turns and abrupt maneuvers. Always wear your seat belt. For specific details, please read your Owner's Manual. Please *Tread Lightly* on public and private land.

SUZUKI.
Everyday vehicles that aren't.™

[1992]

"You're some tomato. California's written all over you.
We could make beautiful Bloody Marys together.
I'm different from those other fellows."

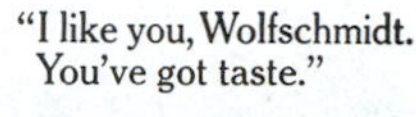

Wolfschmidt in a Bloody Mary is a tomato in triumph. Wolfschmidt has the touch of taste that marks genuine old world vodka. It heightens, accents, brings out the best in every drink.

"You sweet California doll. I appreciate you. I've got taste.
I'll bring out your inner orange. I'll make you famous. Roll over here and kiss me."

"Who was that tomato
I saw you with last week?"

Wolfschmidt in a Screwdriver is an orange in ecstasy. Wolfschmidt has the touch of taste that marks genuine old world vodka. It heightens, accents, brings out the best in every drink.

[1961]

EATING AND DRINKING

ERNEST HEMINGWAY, who has been called the greatest living American writer, is also internationally famous as a deep-sea fisherman. Since publication of *The Sun Also Rises* in 1926, his novels and short stories have enriched the literature of the English language consistently, year after year. His newest book is *The Old Man and the Sea.*

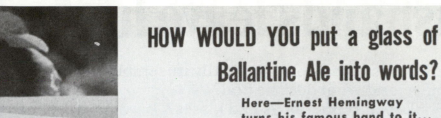

HOW WOULD YOU put a glass of Ballantine Ale into words?

Here—Ernest Hemingway turns his famous hand to it...

Ernest Hemingway

FINCA VIGIA, SAN FRANCISCO DE PAULA, CUBA

Bob Benchley first introduced me to Ballantine Ale. It has been a good companion ever since.

You have to work hard to deserve to drink it. But I would rather have a bottle of Ballantine Ale than any other drink after fighting a really big fish.

We keep it iced in the bait box with chunks of ice packed around it. And you ought to taste it on a hot day when you have worked a big marlin fast because there were sharks after him.

You are tired all the way through. The fish is landed untouched by sharks and you have a bottle of Ballantine cold in your hand and drink it cool, light, and full-bodied, so it tastes good long after you have swallowed it. That's the test of an ale with me: whether it tastes as good afterwards as when it's going down. Ballantine does.

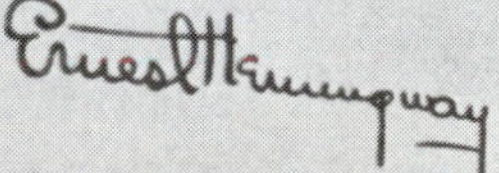

More people like it... More people buy it... than any other ale... ...by Four to One!

BALLANTINE ALE

Since 1840

P. Ballantine & Sons, Newar

[1952]

Why husbands leave home:

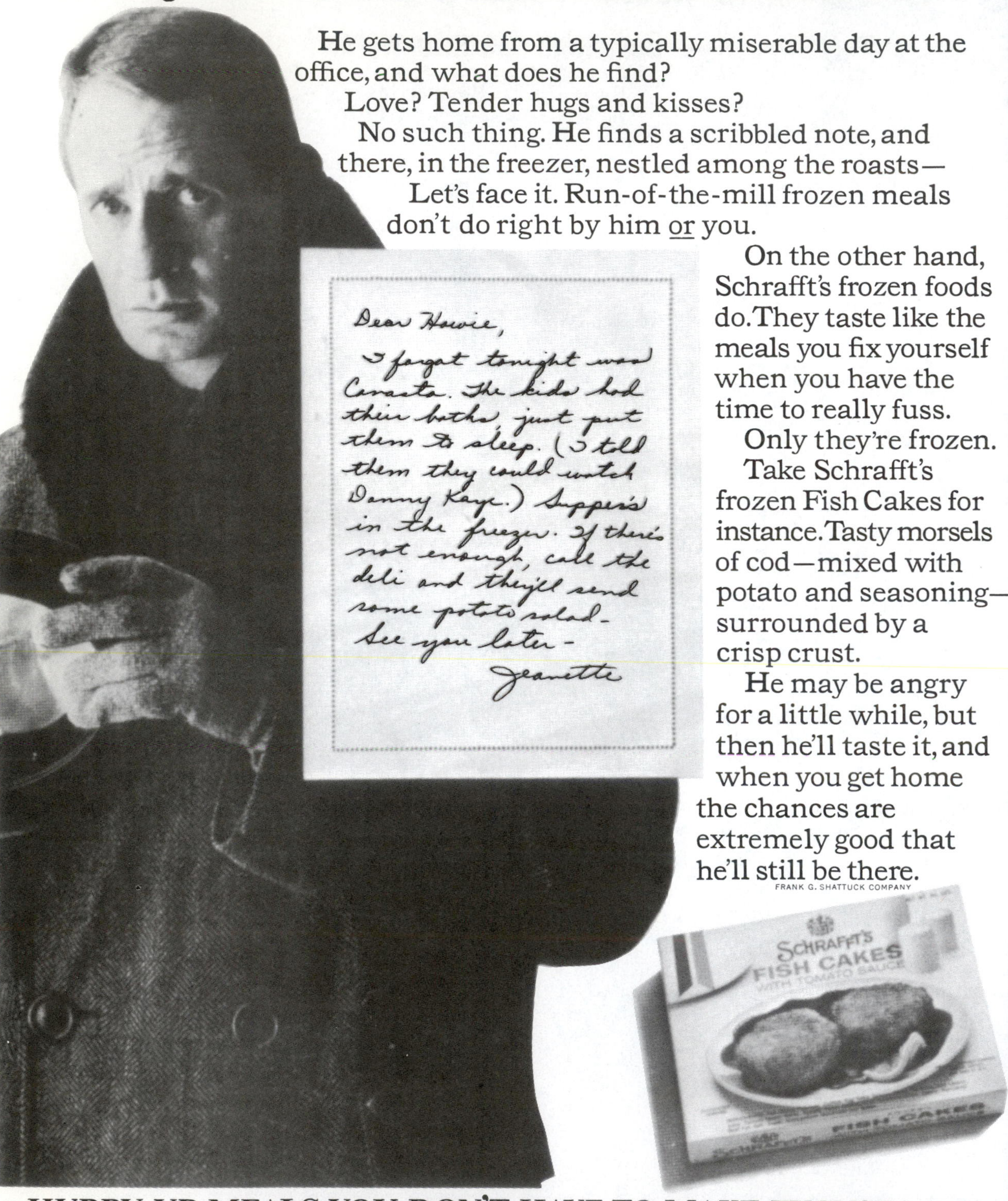

Dear Howie,
I forgot tonight was Canasta. The kids had their baths, just put them to sleep. (I told them they could watch Danny Kaye.) Supper's in the freezer. If there's not enough, call the deli and they'll send some potato salad.
See you later -
Jeanette
SCHRAFFT'S
FISH CAKES
WITH TOMATO SAUCE

He gets home from a typically miserable day at the office, and what does he find?

Love? Tender hugs and kisses?

No such thing. He finds a scribbled note, and there, in the freezer, nestled among the roasts—

Let's face it. Run-of-the-mill frozen meals don't do right by him or you.

On the other hand, Schrafft's frozen foods do. They taste like the meals you fix yourself when you have the time to really fuss.

Only they're frozen.

Take Schrafft's frozen Fish Cakes for instance. Tasty morsels of cod—mixed with potato and seasoning—surrounded by a crisp crust.

He may be angry for a little while, but then he'll taste it, and when you get home the chances are extremely good that he'll still be there.

FRANK G. SHATTUCK COMPANY

HURRY-UP MEALS YOU DON'T HAVE TO MAKE EXCUSES FOR.

SCHRAFFT'S

[1966]

America

If you'll stop and think for just a moment, you'll find we have more of the good things in this country than anywhere else in the world.

Think of this land. From the surf at Big Sur to a Florida sunrise. And all the places in between.

The Grand Canyon . . . the wheat fields of Kansas . . . Autumn in New Hampshire . . .

You could go on forever. But America is more than a place of much beauty. It's a place for good times.

It's Saturday night.

It's a trip down a dirt road in a beat up old jalopy.

It's your team winning. It's a late night movie you could enjoy a thousand times.

And, yes, when you're thirsty, it's the taste of ice- cold Coca-Cola. It's the real thing.

In fact, all of the good things in this country are real. They're all around you, plainly visible. We point to many of them in our advertising. But you can discover many, many more without ever seeing a single commercial for Coke.

So have a bottle of Coke . . . and start looking up.

The Coca-Cola Company

Coca-Cola

Coca-Cola and Coke are registered trade-marks which identify the same product of The Coca-Cola Company

[1975]

With my cooking, the army that travels on its stomach is facing a pretty bumpy road.

As far as being a rookie cook goes, I was as green as the guys who ate what I cooked.

They said my hamburgers tasted like hockey pucks.

They said my chipped beef stuck to their ribs, permanently.

And what they said about my sloppy joes could have gotten them all arrested.

I finally had to face up to it. No one could stomach my cooking. And my brilliant military career would have gone down the drain then and there if it wasn't for McCormick/Schilling.

They're the experts on spice and flavor. And they make all kinds of sauces, seasonings and gravies that can really make things taste good. Even the stuff I cook.

So, I tried their sloppy joes mix. All I had to do was brown 1,000 pounds of ground beef, mix in the McCormick/Schilling seasoning; add tomato paste and 150 gallons of water.

And in no time, I had enough to feed an army.

It was easy. And more important, it was good.

Guys were standing in line for seconds. (Before, they never stuck around for firsts).

Matter of fact, they stopped griping about my cooking long enough for me to finally get my stripes.

And I owe it all to McCormick/Schilling.

I guess you could say that when it comes to cooking, they turned me into a seasoned veteran.

My sloppy joes recipe for 6,000:

Brown 1,000 lbs. of ground beef. Mix in 1,000 packages of McCormick/Schilling Sloppy Joes Mix and blend thoroughly. Stir in 1,000 6-ounce cans of tomato paste and 1,250 cups of water. Bring to a boil. Then reduce heat and simmer 10 minutes, stirring occasionally. Spoon over hamburger buns. Makes 6,000 ½-cup servings. (To get 6 servings, divide by 1,000).

McCormick/Schilling flavor makes all the difference in the world.

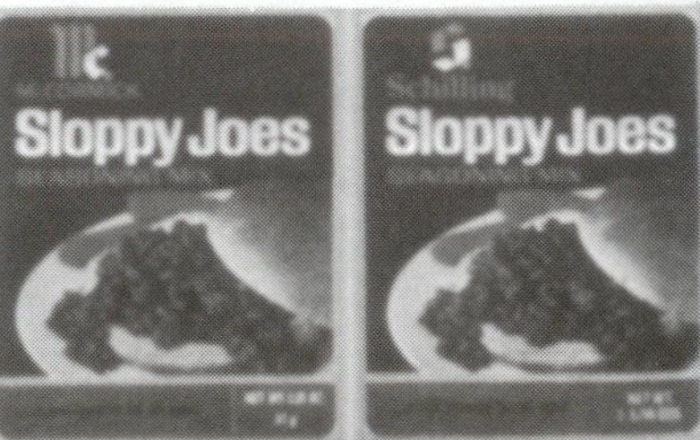

McCormick/Schilling

[1976]

Geraldine Chaplin talks about her 'first time.'

CHAPLIN: To be perfectly blunt, it was a bit disappointing. Oh, it was good... but not at all what I had expected. In fact, I couldn't for the life of me understand why all my friends thought it was such a big deal.

INTERVIEWER: Miss Chaplin, you'd be surprised how many people feel that way. So, don't be embarrassed ... just tell me what happened.

CHAPLIN: It all started at a party in Madrid. I felt a tap on my shoulder and when I turned around there stood this wonderfully attractive young man.

"Campari?" he asked.

"No," I said, "Geraldine."

He laughed and ordered a Campari and soda for me and a Campari and orange juice for himself.

INTERVIEWER: He certainly was a very assertive young man.

CHAPLIN: Yes. You see he turned out to be a cinematographer from Chile and they're like that, you know.

INTERVIEWER: Well? What was it like?

CHAPLIN: A truly bittersweet experience.

INTERVIEWER: Could you be more specific?

CHAPLIN: Yes...it was like eating a mango.

INTERVIEWER: I beg your pardon???

CHAPLIN: Well, I wasn't crazy about them the first time, either. Yet I was so intrigued by their uniqueness, I tried again... then I was a believer.

INTERVIEWER: So now you like it?

CHAPLIN: Love it. There are so many different ways to enjoy it. Once I even tried it on the rocks. But I wouldn't recommend that for beginners.

INTERVIEWER: That's great. Tell me, whatever happened to that handsome young Chilean?

CHAPLIN: We're still very close. But I'll let you in on a secret. That was his first time, too. And to this day, he still hasn't acquired a taste for it.

INTERVIEWER: That's a shame.

CHAPLIN: Yes, it is ... I guess it's because he's never had it a second time.

CAMPARI. THE FIRST TIME IS NEVER THE BEST.

[1981]

THEY GAVE THE BOARD OF EDUCATION A LESSON IN THE CONSTITUTION.
THEY weren't getting a good education, but they were smart enough to know what was right. Right was getting up-to-date textbooks. Right was getting adequate supplies. Right was not being excluded from better schools because their skin was black.
So a group of Kansas children took their cause beyond the school boards, beyond the governors, beyond the legislatures to the Supreme Court. And the nation agreed that the rules were wrong.
Burger King salutes those kids. When they heard they couldn't have the education they deserved, they replied, "Oh, yes we can."
BURGER KING
©1991 BURGER KING CORPORATION

[1992]

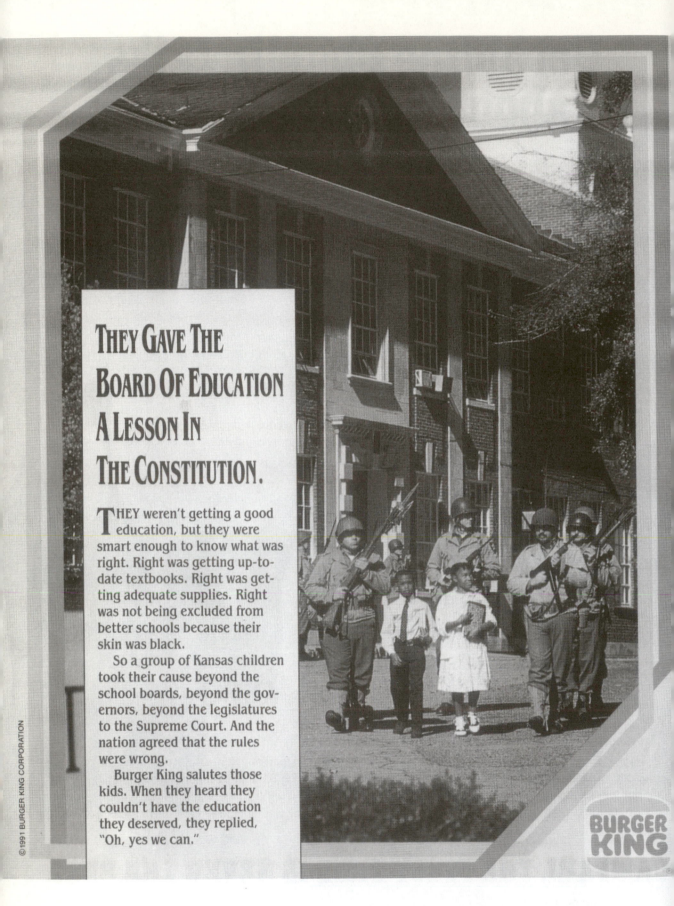

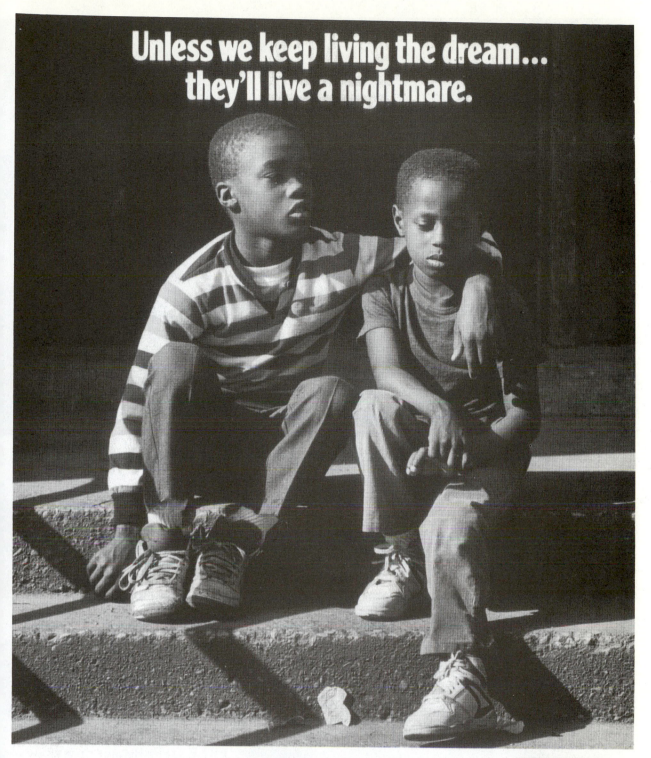

Unless we keep living the dream...
they'll live a nightmare.

Each and every one of us must do our part. And McDonald's® joins the community in dedicating ourselves to keeping Dr. Martin Luther King, Jr.'s dream alive. As we celebrate his birthday, we recognize the fact that the man who leaves the world a better place...never leaves.

[1992]

Keystone Press Agency photograph of the burning of the books, Berlin, May 10, 1933.

These are the books that Hitler burned

He had to.

These books riddle superstition and viciousness with *truth*.

These thoughts and theories built our democracies and broke the chains of bondage.

These words are more powerful than any Gestapo or thought police.

Here, in 54 superbly bound volumes, you'll find the wisdom of Shakespeare, Plato, Thomas Aquinas, Adam Smith, Tolstoy, Darwin and Freud. The truths of Homer, Augustine and many, many more.

No power-hungry madman could stand for long against these books. That's why Hitler burned them.

Now these Great Books can all be yours, 443 works by 74 immortal authors. Yours, in your own home. To enlighten you, console you, to help you guide your children.

The amazing Syntopicon

With Great Books you receive the two-volume Syntopicon, an *idea* index that took 8 years and over a million dollars to build. With the Syntopicon, you can trace every thought in the Great Books as easily as you look up words in your dictionary.

FREE OFFER...act now

Find out more about Great Books. It's free. Just mail in the attached post card for a profusely illustrated 16-page booklet—*free*. Do it today, no postage required. GREAT BOOKS, Dept. 142-J, 425 No. Michigan, Chicago, Illinois 60611.

GREAT BOOKS

54 superb volumes • 74 immortal authors • 443 works

[1966]

Why teenage girls stick with their mouthwash longer than their boyfriends.

Love is different from mouthwash.

Consider: Not too many women aged 20-34 are still going steady with their first boyfriends.

Yet more than one out of every three of them still use the same mouthwash they decided to use as a teenager.

That was one of the findings of a recent major Yankelovich study. Which showed that, besides

mouthwash, girls are about equally loyal to their mascara, packaged goods, and even panty hose.

All this isn't to disparage boyfriends. But it does tend to prove what common sense and we have been saying for some time:

Long before a teenage girl is ready to settle down with the right boy, she is ready to settle down with the right product.

And the place where she does her settling down is Seventeen magazine. Where, each month, over 6,400,000 teenage girls begin lasting relationships.

If you'd like to know more about this new research, please call our Advertising Director, Bob Bunge, at (212) 759-8100.

He'll show you that, when the right one comes along, a girl knows it.

Come to think of it, maybe love isn't very different from mouthwash at all.

seventeen®

Today, she's really 18-34.

[1980]

SOME PEOPLE ARE SO OPPOSED TO MURDER THEY'LL KILL ANYONE WHO COMMITS IT.

"DO YOU WANT THEM DEAD?"

There are now thirty-seven states that stand united behind the death sentence. And a total of five methods by which it's carried out. The electric chair, cyanide gas, hanging, lethal injection and firing squad.

But no matter which method is used, the result is the same. The taking of a human life.

This week, in an Eyewitness News Special Report, Roger Grimsby takes a good hard look at capital punishment.

You'll meet murderers on death row who are waiting to die. And families of their victims. Who can't wait to see them dead.

Watch "Do You Want Them Dead?" Then decide for yourself if the death penalty should become a way of life.

EYEWITNESS NEWS 6PM 7

[1982]

Can a girl be too busy? I'm taking seventeen units at Princeton, pushing on with my career during vacations and school breaks, study singing and dancing when I can, try never to lose track of my five closest chums, steal the time for Michael Jackson and Thomas Hardy, work for an anti-drug program for kids and, oh yes, I hang out with three horses, three cats, two birds and my dog Jack. My favorite magazine says "too busy" just means you don't want to miss anything...don't stop 'til you're gasping. I love that magazine. I guess you could say I'm That COSMOPOLITAN Girl.
© 1984, The Hearst Corporation.
Photographed by Francesco Scavullo
One of my most satisfying relationships is with a magazine.
COSMOPOLITAN®
A PUBLICATION OF THE HEARST CORPORATION

[1984]

THE NEW TRADITIONALIST.

SHE'S A WOMAN WHO LOVES HER JOB – EVEN WHEN ICICLES FORM ON HER HARDHAT.

When winter storms hit the Blue Ridge Mountains, Emily McCoy straps on her tools, and works through the night on high voltage lines.

Nobody said it was easy. Emily trained for the job when she was divorced and a single mother.

But today she's "real happy" about her job, her paycheck and her life with her 8-year-old daughter and her new husband.

Her energy, her attitudes, and her values embody the New Traditionalist movement that now affects almost every aspect of American life.

No magazine can speak to the New Traditionalist with the authority and trust of Good Housekeeping.

That's why there has never been a better time for Good Housekeeping – the Magazine, the Institute, and the Seal.

AMERICA BELIEVES IN GOOD HOUSEKEEPING

THE NEW YORK TIMES MAGAZINE / JUNE 17, 1

[1990]

It weighs 8,000,000 pounds less than your average library.

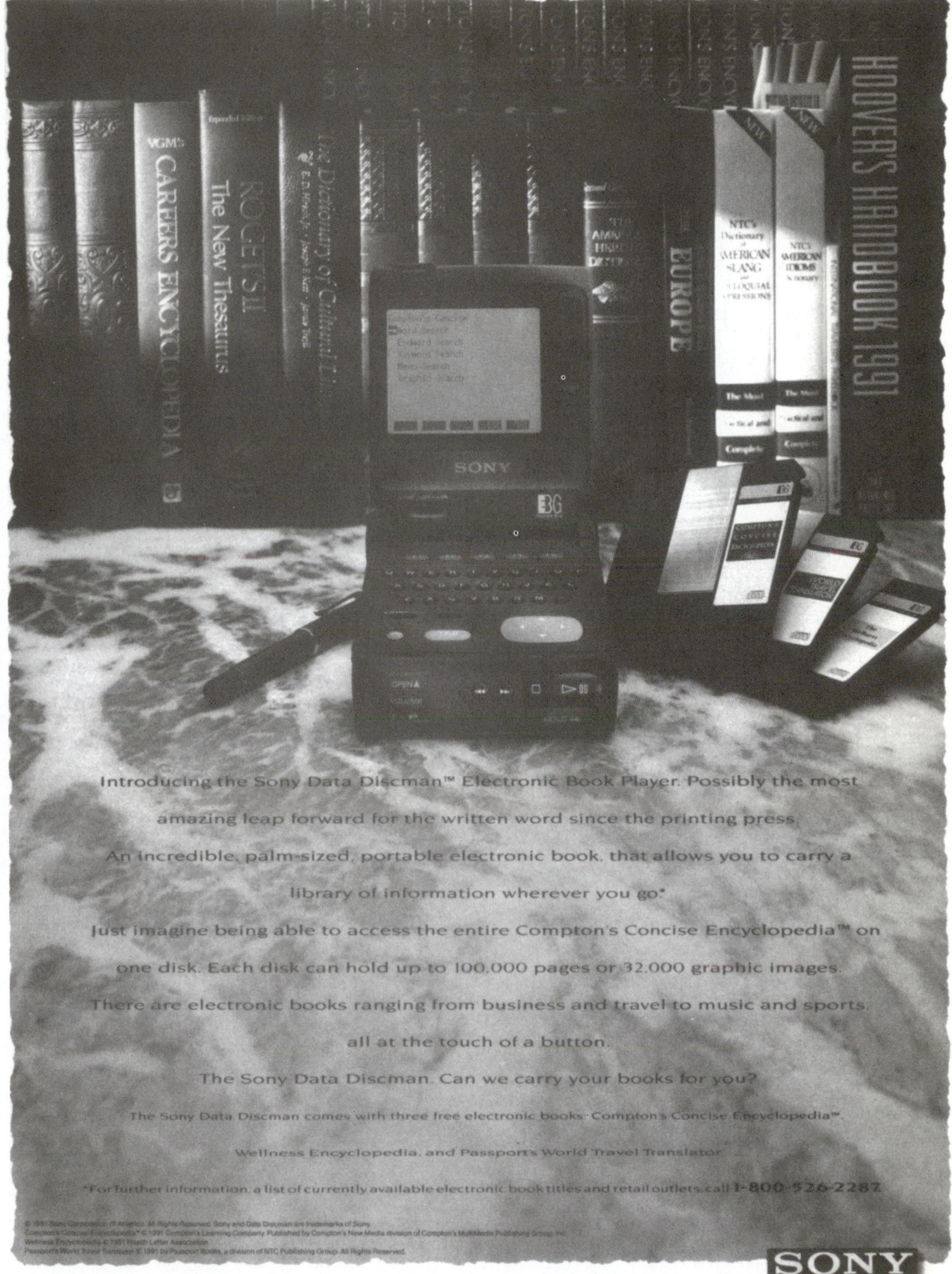

[1992]

Swimming at night had never bothered me before. But as I watched the sun retreat behind the horizon, an overwhelming sense of loneliness swept over me.

I peered into the heavy black water and knew that this was now an alien world, no longer a turquoise playground, but something dark, mysterious, uncaring.

The peaceful murmur of waves and seagulls, sounds I usually found so comforting, had taken on a sinister and mocking air.

Suddenly, there was a splash somewhere off to my right. I turned, but could see nothing. My breath quickened as I heard another ripple, this time behind me.

I was fighting to keep the rush of adrenaline from pushing me into a blind panic when, my God! I felt something brush against the soles of my feet.

As my terror found voice in a bellowing scream I realized it was watching a movie such as this on a Mitsubishi Home Theater with Dolby Surround™ Sound was not, repeat not, good for my nerves.

Mitsubishi's Home Theater brings you an experience so lifelike, you'll feel as though you're right there in the middle of the action. And because we make a whole range of components, you can create the system that suits you best. The example above features the CS-3521R 35-inch direct-view TV, the E-5300 Dolby Surround™ audio system and the HS-U52 Hi-Fi VCR. For your nearest authorized dealer, call (800) 527-8888 ext. 245.

TECHNICALLY, ANYTHING IS POSSIBLE®

[1992]

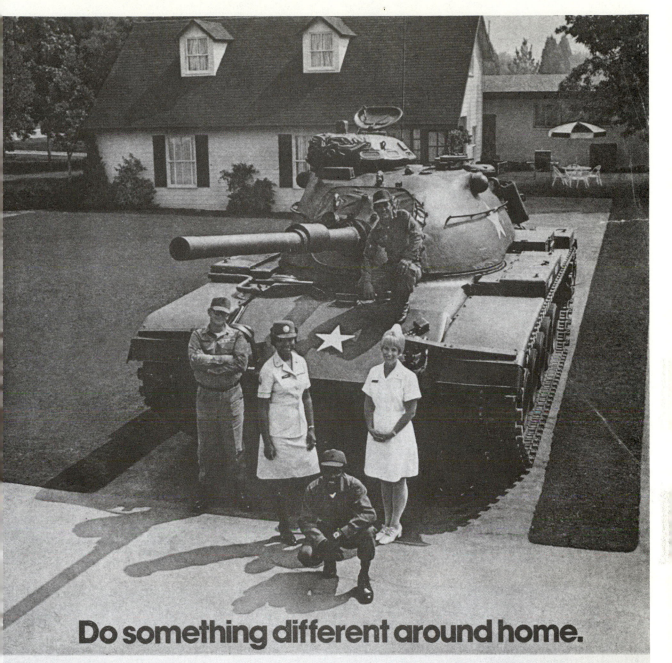

Do something different around home.

You won't have 50 tons of steel parked in your driveway. But it won't be farther away than your local Army National Guard Armory. And that's important. Because you never know when you're going to need it in a hurry.

Last year, for instance, Guard tanks were called out to make war on winter. Hauling 18-wheelers out of snow drifts. Keeping roads open during the blizzards.

And like your tank crews, Guardsmen everywhere use the skills they learn in the Guard to help people in trouble.

What about you? There are a lot of ways you can help your friends and neighbors.

Help Somebody. Including Yourself.

And help yourself while you're at it. The National Guard can teach you valuable career skills. Anything from communications to paramedicine to handling heavy equipment.

Skills that could very well make the difference should disaster strike your town.

It's good work. And the pay's good, too.

So do something that'll make a difference. See your nearest Army Guard recruiter. Or call us, toll free, 800-638-7600. (In Alaska, Hawaii, Puerto Rico or the Virgin Islands, consult your white pages). In Maryland call 301-728-3388.

[1978]

INSTITUTIONAL AND CORPORATE ADVERTISING

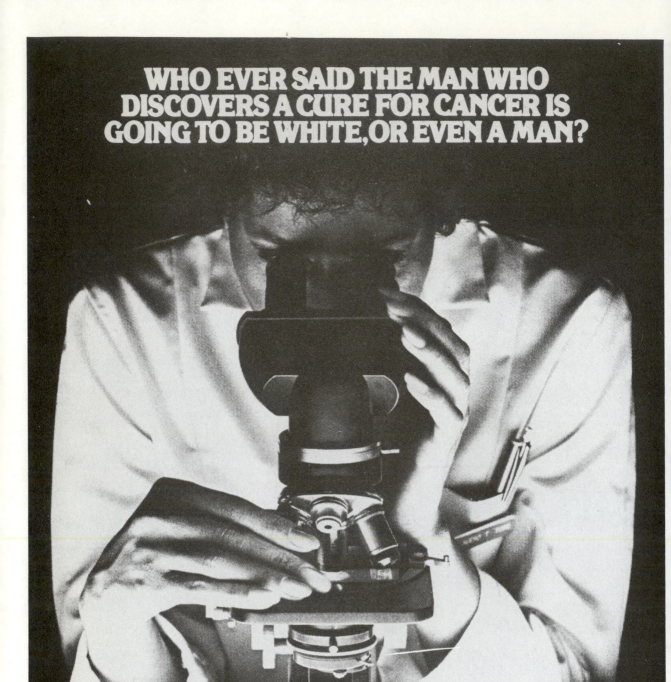

WHO EVER SAID THE MAN WHO DISCOVERS A CURE FOR CANCER IS GOING TO BE WHITE, OR EVEN A MAN?

This black woman could be America's hope...she's a United Negro College Fund graduate who could dedicate her life to finding a cure for cancer. A cure that could save thousands of lives each year. And fill every black person's heart with pride. That's why it's so important that blacks support the United Negro College Fund, 100 percent.

If she discovered the cure, in a sense, it would also be your discovery because the world would recognize it as a major black contribution.

When you give to the United Negro College Fund, you help support 41 private, predominantly black, four-year colleges and universities. Colleges that give us thousands of black graduates each year, who go on to become doctors, lawyers, accountants, engineers and scientists.

So support black education. Because black contributions help make black contributions. Send your check to the United Negro College Fund, Box Q, 500 East 62nd St., New York, N.Y. 10021. We're not asking for a handout, just a hand.

GIVE TO THE UNITED NEGRO COLLEGE FUND.

A mind is a terrible thing to waste.

PHOTOGRAPHER: PACCIONE

A Public Service of This Magazine & The Advertising Council

[1979]

Really tying one on.

Getting s___ faced.

Having one more for the road.

Becoming polluted.

Drinking someone under the table.

Being plastered.

Bragging about the size
of your hangover.

Going out and getting looped.

IF YOUR IDEA OF A GOOD TIME IS LISTED ON THIS PAGE, YOU OUGHT TO HAVE YOUR HEAD EXAMINED.

With the possible exception of sex, no single subject generates as many foolish tales of prowess as the consumption of alcoholic beverages.

But there is a basic difference between the two subjects. Excelling at the former can be highly productive. Excelling at the latter, very destructive.

We, the people who make and sell distilled spirits, urge you to use our products with common sense. If you choose to drink, drink responsibly.

Then the next time someone tells you how lousy he feels because he had "one too many," you can tell him how great you feel because you had "one too few."

That's having a good time.

IT'S PEOPLE WHO GIVE DRINKING A BAD NAME.

Distilled Spirits Council of the U.S. (DISCUS)
1300 Pennsylvania Building, Washington, D.C. 20004

[1979]

A word to smokers
(about people who build walls)

It's no secret that there are some folks these days who are trying to build walls between smokers and nonsmokers.

The theory behind all this is that some smokers annoy nonsmokers and, of course, that can happen.

But if you want to get an idea of the ridiculous lengths that some of the wall-builders would like to go to, you have only to consider this:

In one state alone, it was estimated that the first year's cost of administering and enforcing a proposed anti-smoking law and building the physical walls required was nearly $250,000,000.

The proposal was, of course, defeated — for the plain fact is the one you have observed in your own daily life, that the overwhelming majority of smokers and nonsmokers get along very well and don't need or want to be separated.

This infuriates the wall-builders. Since they cannot have their own way in a world of free choice, they would like to eliminate that world by government fiat, by rules and regulations that would tell you where, and with whom, you may work, eat, play and shop. And the enormous burden that would place on all of us, in higher taxes and costs, does not bother them.

Certainly no one, including smokers, can properly object to the common sense rules of, for instance, banning smoking in crowded elevators, poorly ventilated spaces or, indeed, in any place where it is clearly inappropriate. And individual managers in their own interest should see to the mutual comfort of their smoking and nonsmoking patrons. It is only when the long arm, and notoriously insensitive hands, of government regulators start making these private arrangements for us that we all, smoker and nonsmoker alike, begin to lose our freedom of choice.

In the long run, the wall-builders must fail, and the walls will come tumbling down — if not to the sound of a trumpet, then at least to the slower but surer music of common decency and courtesy practiced on both sides of them.

THE TOBACCO INSTITUTE
1776 K St. N.W., Washington, D.C. 20006
Freedom of choice
is the best choice.

A word to nonsmokers
(about people who build walls)

The chances are that you made up your mind about smoking a long time ago—and decided it's not for you.

The chances are equally good that you know a lot of smokers—there are, after all about 60 million of them—and that you may be related to some of them, work with them, play with them, and get along with them very well.

And finally it's a pretty safe bet that you're open-minded and interested in all the various issues about smokers and nonsmokers—or you wouldn't be reading this.

And those three things make you incredibly important today.

Because they mean that yours is the voice—not the smoker's and not the anti-smoker's—that will determine how much of society's efforts should go into building walls that separate us and how much into the search for solutions that bring us together.

For one tragic result of the emphasis on building walls is the diversion of millions of dollars from scientific research on the causes and cures of diseases which, when all is said and done, still strike the nonsmoker as well as the smoker. One prominent health organization, to cite but a single instance, now spends 28¢ of every publicly-contributed dollar on "education" (much of it in anti-smoking propaganda) and only 2¢ on research.

There will always be some who want to build walls, who want to separate people from people, and up to a point, even these may serve society. The anti-smoking wall-builders have, to give them their due, helped to make us all more keenly aware of the value of courtesy and of individual freedom of choice.

But our guess, and certainly our hope, is that you are among the far greater number who know that walls are only temporary at best, and that over the long run, we can serve society's interests better by working together in mutual accommodation.

Whatever virtue walls may have, they can never move our society toward fundamental solutions. People who work together on common problems, common solutions, can.

THE TOBACCO INSTITUTE
1776 K St. N.W., Washington, D.C. 20006
Freedom of choice
is the best choice.

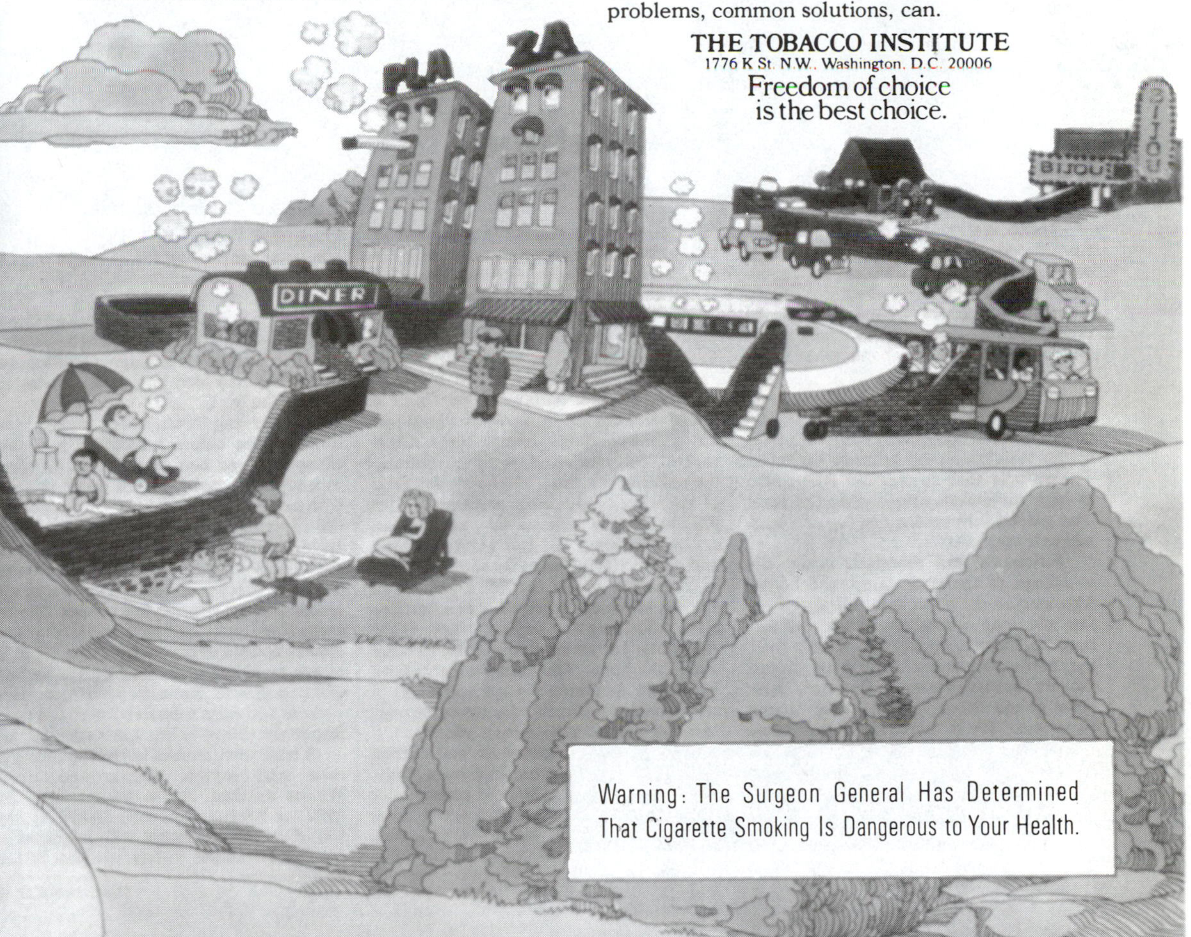

Warning: The Surgeon General Has Determined That Cigarette Smoking Is Dangerous to Your Health.

[1979]

Funny stage they're at: George is older, but somehow he doesn't quite measure up to kid sister Shirley. "It's a stage," Dad consoles his son. "You'll outgrow it." The kids are growing up. Almost too fast. So, be sure to share those little moments, as well as the big, with faraway friends and family. Just reach out with a phone call, and they're sharing your day.
Bell System

Reach out and touch someone.

[1980]

REP. ALBERTO GUTMAN: Florida Legislator, Businessman, Husband, Member of the National Rifle Association.

"Being from a country that was once a democracy and turned communist, I really feel I know what the right to bear arms is all about. In Cuba, where I was born, the first thing the communist government did was take away everybody's firearms, leaving them defenseless and intimidated with fear. That's why our constitutional right to bear arms is so important to our country's survival.

"As a legislator I have to deal with reality. And the reality is that gun control does not work. It actually eliminates the rights of the law-abiding citizen, not the criminal. Criminals will always have guns, and they won't follow gun control laws anyway. I would like to see tougher laws on criminals as opposed to tougher laws on legitimate gun owners. We need to attack the problem of crime at its roots, instead of blaming crime on gun ownership and citizens who use them lawfully.

"It's a big responsibility that we face retaining the right to bear arms. That's why I joined the NRA. The NRA is instrumental in protecting these freedoms. It helps train and educate people, supporting legislation that benefits not only those who bear arms but all citizens of the United States. The NRA helps keep America free."

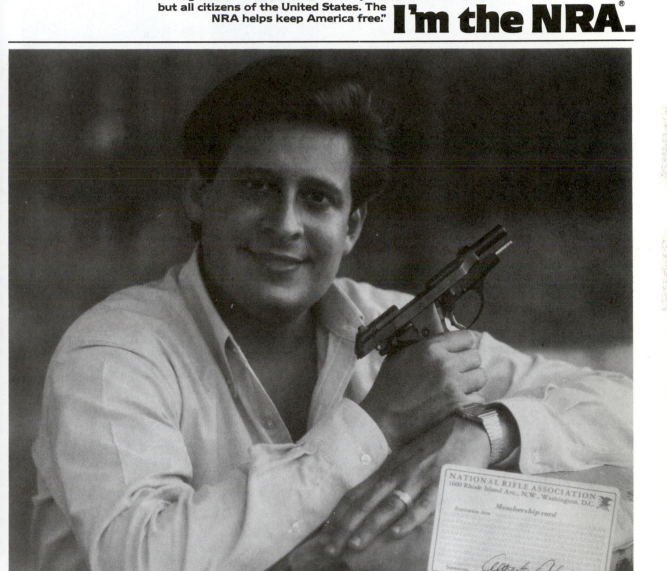

The NRA's lobbying organization, the Institute for Legislative Action, is the nation's largest and most influential protector of the constitutional right to keep and bear arms. At every level of government and through local grassroots efforts, the Institute guards against infringement upon the freedoms of law-abiding gun owners. If you would like to join the NRA or want more information about our programs and benefits, write J. Warren Cassidy, Executive Vice President, P.O. Box 37484, Dept. AG-27, Washington, D.C. 20013.

Paid for by the members of the National Rifle Association of America. Copyright 1987.

[1987]

—Mrs. James S. Brady—

"Help me fight the National Rifle Association."

"Six years ago, John Hinckley pulled a $29 revolver from his pocket and opened fire on a Washington street. He shot the President. He also shot my husband.

I'm not asking for your sympathy. I'm asking for your help.

I've learned from my own experience that, alone, there's only so much you can do to stop handgun violence. But that together, we can confront the mightiest gun lobby—the N.R.A.—and win.

I've only to look at my husband Jim to remember that awful day... the unending TV coverage of the handgun firing over and over... the nightmare panic and fear.

It's an absolute miracle nobody was killed. After all, twenty thousand Americans are killed by handguns every year. Thousands more—men, women, even children—are maimed for life.

Like me, I know you support *stronger* handgun control laws. So does the vast majority of Americans. But the National Rifle Association can spend so much in elections that Congress is afraid to pass an effective national handgun law.

It's time to change that. Before it's too late for another family like mine... a family like yours.

I joined Handgun Control, Inc. because they're willing to take on the N.R.A. Right now we're campaigning for a national waiting period and background check on handgun purchases.

If such simple, basic measures had been on the books six years ago, John Hinckley would never have walked out of that Texas pawnshop with the handgun which came within an inch of killing Ronald Reagan. He lied on his purchase application. Given time, the police could have caught the lie and put him in jail.

Of course, John Hinckley's not the only one. Police report that thousands of known criminals buy handguns right over the counter in this country. We have to stop them.

So, please, pick up a pen. Fill out the coupon. Add a check for as much as you can afford, and mail it to me today.

It's time we kept handguns out of the wrong hands. It's time to break the National Rifle Association's grip on Congress and start making our cities and neighborhoods safe again.

Thank you and God bless you."

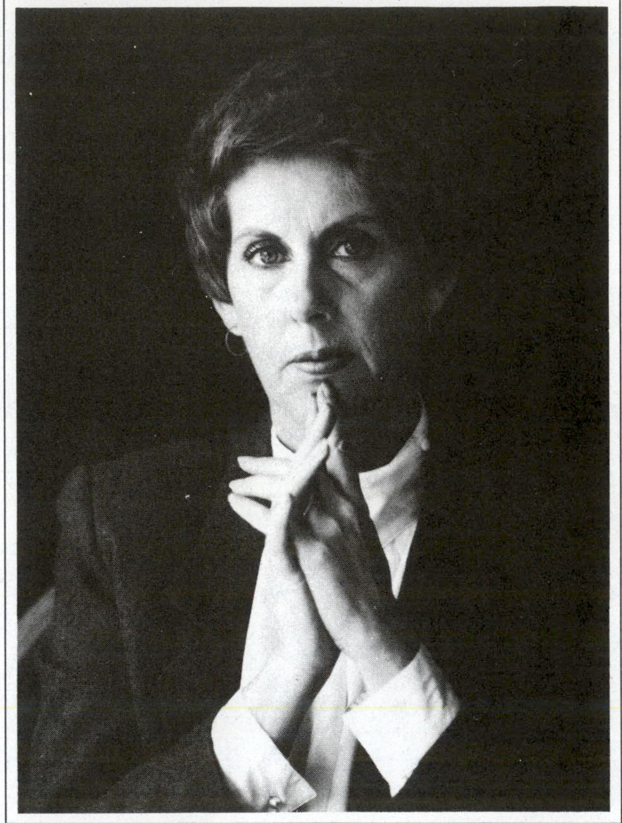

"Together we can win."

Dear Sarah,

It's time to break the N.R.A.'s grip on Congress once and for all. Here's my contribution to Handgun Control, Inc., the million-strong nonprofit citizens' group you help direct:

☐ $15 ☐ $25 ☐ $35 ☐ $50 ☐ $100 or $______.

☐ Tell me more about how I can help.

NAME

ADDRESS

CITY STATE ZIP

HP RS

HANDGUN CONTROL

1400 K Street, N.W., Washington, D.C. 20005, (202) 898-0792

[1987]

FOCUSING ON

EDUCATION

THIS IS THE THIRD IN A SERIES OF PUBLIC-SERVICE ADVERTISEMENTS SPONSORED BY ROCKWELL INTERNATIONAL CORPORATION ABOUT THE NATION'S EDUCATION CRISIS. THEY ARE PUBLISHED TO ENCOURAGE INFORMED DISCUSSION AND DEBATE.

Empowering Teachers

BY DENIS P. DOYLE

EDUCATION "RESTRUCTURING" has captured the imagination of policymakers, business leaders, governors, state legislators, education-association leaders, and citizens at large. Almost everyone in the education business is absorbed with it. Almost everyone, that is, except teachers. Yet without their support and involvement, education restructuring will never be more than a dream.

As we all know, schools can be no better than their teachers. Indeed, given the state of American education, it is a wonder there are so many dedicated and caring teachers, men and women who tolerate bureaucracy, unsatisfactory working conditions, low status, and low wages.

The hard truth is that in many respects teaching looks more like blue-collar than white-collar work. Only in private schools and a handful of the best public schools are teachers treated as professionals, with the opportunities and obligations professionals enjoy. Most teachers must work to the clock, use textbooks adopted by a remote bureaucracy, submit lesson plans for administrative approval, and employ tests and measures imposed by a third party. Other professionals—lawyers, doctors, architects, accountants, clergy—work for themselves. Hospitals and law firms, accounting partnerships and architectural firms employ administrators to do the partners' or senior staff's bidding, not the other way around. Few teachers have access to the simple things other professionals take for granted: a telephone, for example, or a decent faculty lounge where they can have a cup of coffee and share notes with colleagues. Teachers are limited in their choice of opportunities for professional growth and renewal, something most professionals expect routinely. Most important, teachers are not in charge of their professional lives. Unions bargain, but bread-and-butter issues are not the same as professional issues.

What explains this unproductive state of affairs, and what might we do about it? Much of the blame is traceable to a badly out-of-date business metaphor. And the solution lies in a modern, high-tech metaphor.

In the not too distant past, the scientific-management movement, led by people like Frederick Taylor, descended on schools and businesses alike, stopwatches and clipboards in hand. Using a "scientific" approach to management, schools were "teacher-proofed": designed in the hope that they would run whether or not the teachers were any good, echoing similar practices on the nation's assembly lines. The assembly line, it must be remembered, was a triumph of the "dumbing down" of work, making it routine enough for unskilled workers to do. And while no one talks any longer about teacher-proofing the classroom, most teachers in America are familiar with its legacy.

What about the high-tech assembly line? In the most modern manufacturing firms, of course, the routinized work has been so "dumbed down" that robots perform it (and do a better job, because they never get bored or distracted) while the human beings on the line do what they're good at: troubleshooting and problem-solving.

What is the lesson for schools? At least as a trial, we should begin an experiment: teacher-run schools. Teachers can form cooperatives or partnerships or collaboratives or, as Dale Mann of Teachers College recently suggested, teacher ESOPs—Employee Stock Ownership Plans. It works in the business world, why not in schools? This is not an idle question. If teachers are to become true professionals, they must seize the moment and demonstrate to their own satisfaction—as well as their clients'—that they really can do it right.

How to begin such a radical experiment? One step at a time. A great virtue of American federalism is that each state solves its problems its own way; so too can the nation's 15,000 school districts. Bold and visionary schools can experiment and when the evidence is in, the others can follow suit.

Denis P. Doyle is an education analyst and a senior fellow at the Hudson Institute. With David T. Kearns, the deputy secretary of education, he is a co-author of Winning the Brain Race: A Bold Plan to Make Our Schools Competitive *(ICS Press).*

DRAWING BY JEAN-FRANÇOIS ALLAUX

THE VIEWS IN THIS ESSAY ARE THOSE OF THE AUTHOR AND DO NOT NECESSARILY REFLECT THE VIEWS OF ROCKWELL INTERNATIONAL CORPORATION.

[1991]

THERE ARE THREE THINGS EVERYONE SHOULD READ BEFORE ENTERING COLLEGE:

PLATO'S REPUBLIC, THE COMPLETE WORKS OF ARISTOTLE, AND THIS AD.

Not so fast.

If you think you can get away with ignoring the first two works and get right into this ad, stop. Rip this page out and stick it in your sock drawer.

Don't read this ad until you've first savoured Plato. And discovered Aristotle, if not the complete works at least the incomplete collection, maybe the *Ethics* or the *Politics*.

Then you'll be able to deal with the Madison Avenue manipulators who market universities the same way they market sausages or deodorant soap.

Your mind will then be keen enough to dismiss the vapid slogans that university marketers conjure up to attract you, the consumers, who enter the education marketplace each spring. Slogans also designed to soothe parents whose checks enter the universities' treasuries each autumn.

(Used to be a school's slogan would be a nice Latin phrase such as *lux et veritas* or *semper paratus* or *ut omnes te cognoscant*. Now we get corporate gobbledygook like: People making successful people ever more successful, successfully).

If you're heading for business school, for example, you'll not only note the obvious: how many successful graduates in all fields that Adelphi can point to. You'll also investigate what you can learn at Adelphi besides LIFO, FIFO, and the other Principles of Accounting. What is it that a liberal arts environment imparts that a trade school can't?

The same is true of the psychology student or the communications major. Or the pre-law and pre-med students who are, after all, students of the Arts and Sciences, respectively.

When you visit our school, ask to see a dean, even the President. (The President of Adelphi still teaches his philosophy class every Thursday at 5:10 PM. If you drop in with an inquiring mind, he'll welcome you, albeit argumentatively).

The premise of Adelphi is that all students (whether of nursing, psychology, business, the humanities, the physical sciences, education, the fine arts) deserve the opportunity to enrich themselves by exposure to ideas.

Now: will your day-to-day involvement in those ideas make you a better investment banker? Or social worker? Or lawyer? Or high school teacher? Or nurse? Or statesman? Or accountant? Or psychologist? Or doctor? Does a liberal education make a difference in one's ability to make a living in 20th Century America, not to mention 21st Century America?

Yes. And we believe a profound difference. It has done that for 2500 years in every corner of the world. It will be no less efficacious today in the Western Hemisphere, in the United States, on Long Island 45 minutes from Manhattan and a five-block stroll from the Nassau Boulevard station of the Long Island Railroad.

Now that you've removed this ad from your sock drawer, there are three more things to do before entering college. One, give us a call. Two, read our publications and look at our video. And three, visit our campus and say hello.

ADELPHI UNIVERSITY

Garden City, New York 11530. (516) 663-1100.
For application materials and a video, write or call.

[1989]

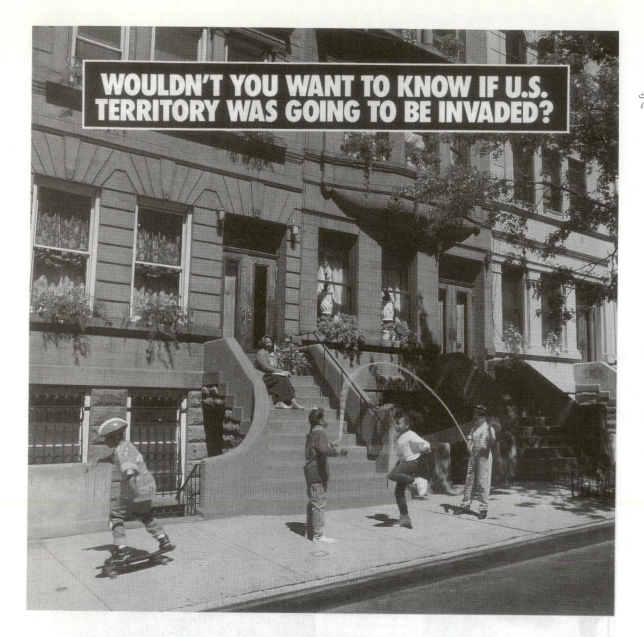

WOULDN'T YOU WANT TO KNOW IF U.S. TERRITORY WAS GOING TO BE INVADED?

The thought of a gang wreaking havoc to your neighborhood is disturbing. Not to mention frightening. Of course you'd want to know if you could stop them way ahead of time.

It's the same way for the President when it comes to America's security. And that's why he depends on the country's largest information network—the Central Intelligence Agency.

We aren't a law enforcement agency. Our job is to collect, analyze and disseminate foreign intelligence information for the United States' policy makers. Officials from the President to members of the National Security Council come to us for an accurate picture of the world.

And to do the best job possible, we not only rely on the most advanced technology around, but the specialized skills and talents of the men and women who work for us.

The result—a much safer home for all of us.

The CIA. Our business is knowing the world's business.

An Equal Opportunity Employer. For information about career opportunities write to: The Central Intelligence Agency, P.O. Box 9065 Dept EB McLean, Va 22102-0065. Applicants must be U.S. citizens with the personal integrity to successfully complete a medical and security background investigation, including a polygraph interview.

[1992]

Trees aren't the only plants that are good for the atmosphere.

Because nuclear plants don't burn anything to make electricity, nuclear plants don't pollute the air.

In fact, America's 111 operating nuclear electric plants displace other power sources and so reduce certain airborne pollutants in the U.S. by more than 19,000 tons every day. Just as important, nuclear plants produce no greenhouse gases.

But more plants are needed—to help satisfy the nation's growing need for electricity without sacrificing the quality of our environment. For a free booklet on nuclear energy, write to the U.S. Council for Energy Awareness, P.O. Box 66080, Dept. HP06, Washington, D.C. 20035.

Nuclear energy means cleaner air.

[1992]

Marianne Moore / Correspondence with the Ford Motor Company

1955

In the following exchange of letters, the distinguished American poet Marianne Moore (1887–1972), a professed "amateur" at the art of copywriting, tries to come up with the best name for a product that the Ford Motor Company thought would revolutionize the automobile industry.

According to Printer's Ink, *the one-time leading advertising trade publication, Ford spent more than $350 million "to create and promote the biggest and most expensive new product ever born."*

OCTOBER 19, 1955

MISS MARIANNE MOORE,
CUMBERLAND STREET,
BROOKLYN 5, NEW YORK

DEAR MISS MOORE:

This is a morning we find ourselves with a problem which, strangely enough, is more in the field of words and the fragile meaning of words than in car-making. And we just wonder whether you might be intrigued with it sufficiently to lend us a hand.

Our dilemma is a name for a rather important new series of cars.

We should like this name to be more than a label. Specifically, we should like it to have a compelling quality in itself and by itself. To convey, through association or other conjuration, some visceral feeling of elegance, fleetness, advanced features and design. A name, in short, that flashes a dramatically desirable picture in people's minds. (Another "Thunderbird" would be fine.)

Over the past few weeks this office has confected a list of three hundred-odd candidates which, it pains me to relate, are characterized by an embarrassing pedestrianism. We are miles short of our ambition. And so we are seeking the help of one who knows more about this sort of magic than we.

As to how we might go about this matter, I have no idea. But, in any event, all would depend on whether you find this overture of some challenge and interest.

Should we be so fortunate as to have piqued your fancy, we will be pleased to write more fully. And, of course, it is expected that our relations will be on a fee basis of an impeccably dignified kind.

Respectfully,
DAVID WALLACE
Special Products Division

OCTOBER 21, 1955

Let me take it under advisement, Mr. Wallace. I am complimented to be recruited in this high matter.

I have seen and admired "Thunderbird" as a Ford designation. It would be hard to match; but let me, the coming week, talk with my brother, who would bring ardor and imagination to bear on the quest.

Sincerely yours,
MARIANNE MOORE

OCTOBER 27, 1955

DEAR MR. WALLACE:

My brother thought most of the names I had considered suggesting to you for your new series too learned or too labored, but thinks I might ask if any of the following approximate the requirements:

THE FORD SILVER SWORD

This plant, of which the flower is a silver sword, I believe grows only on the Hawaiian Island Maui, on Mount Haleakala (House of the Sun); found at an altitude of from 9,500 to 10,000 feet. (The leaves—silver-white—surrounding the individual blossoms—have a pebbled texture that feels like Italian-twist backstitch allover embroidery.)

My first thought was of a bird series—the swallow species—Hirundo, or, phonetically, Aerundo. Malvina Hoffman is designing a device for the radiator of a made-to-order Cadillac, and said in her opinion the only term surpassing Thunderbird would be hurricane; and I then thought Hurricane Hirundo might be the first of a series such as Hurricane Aquila (eagle), Hurricane Accipiter (hawk), and so on. A species that takes its dinner on the wing ("swifts").

If these suggestions are not in character with the car, perhaps you could give me a sketch of its general appearance, or hint as to some of its exciting potentialities—though my brother reminds me that such information is highly confidential.

Sincerely yours,
MARIANNE MOORE

NOVEMBER 4, 1955

DEAR MISS MOORE:

I'm delighted that your note implies that you are interested in helping us in our naming problem.

This being so, procedures in this rigorous business world dictate that we on this end at least document a formal arrangement with provision for a suitable fee or honorarium before pursuing the problem further.

One way might be for you to suggest a figure which could be considered for mutual acceptance. Once this is squared away, we will look forward to having you join us in the continuation of our fascinating search.

Sincerely,
DAVID WALLACE
Special Products Division

NOVEMBER 7, 1955

DEAR MR. WALLACE:

It is handsome of you to consider remuneration for service merely enlisted. My fancy would be inhibited, however, by acknowledgment in advance of performance. If I could be of specific assistance, we could no doubt agree on some kind of honorarium for the service rendered.

I seem to exact participation; but if you could tell me how the suggestions submitted strayed—if obviously—from the ideal, I could then perhaps proceed more nearly in keeping with the Company's objective.

Sincerely yours,
MARIANNE MOORE

NOVEMBER 11, 1955

DEAR MISS MOORE:

Our office philodendron has just benefitted from an extra measure of water as, pacing about, I have sought words to respond to your recent generous note. Let me state my quandary thus. It is unspeakably contrary to procedure to accept counsel—

They'll know you've *arrived* when you drive up in an Edsel

Step into an Edsel and you'll learn where the excitement is this year.

Other drivers spot that classic vertical grille a block away—and never fail to take a long look at this year's most exciting car.

On the open road, your Edsel is watched eagerly for its already-famous performance.

And parked in front of your home, your Edsel always gets even more attention—because it always says a lot about you. It says you chose elegant styling, luxurious comfort and such exclusive features as Edsel's famous Teletouch Drive—only shift that puts the buttons where they belong, on the steering-wheel hub.

Your Edsel also means you made a wonderful buy. For of all medium-priced cars, this one really new car is actually priced the lowest.* See your Edsel Dealer this week.

**Based on comparison of suggested retail delivered prices of the Edsel Ranger and similarly equipped cars in the medium-price field.*

Above: Edsel Citation 2-door Hardtop. Engine: the E-475, with 10.5 to one compression ratio, 345 hp, 475 ft.-lb. torque. Transmission: Automatic with Teletouch Drive. Suspension: Ball-joint with optional air suspension. Brakes: self-adjusting.

EDSEL DIVISION · FORD MOTOR COMPANY

1958 EDSEL

Of all medium-priced cars, the one that's really new is the lowest-priced, too!

[1958]

even needed counsel—without a firm prior agreement of conditions (and, indeed, to follow the letter of things, without a Purchase Notice in quadruplicate and three Competitive Bids). But then, seldom has the auto business had occasion to indulge in so ethereal a matter as this. So, if you will risk a mutually satisfactory outcome with us, we should like to honor your wish for a fancy unencumbered.

As to wherein your earlier suggestions may have "strayed," as you put it—they did not at all. Shipment No. 1 was fine, and we would like to luxuriate in more of same—even those your brother regarded as overlearned or labored. For us to impose an ideal on your efforts would, I fear, merely defeat our purpose. We have sought your help to get an approach quite different from our own. In short, we should like suggestions that we ourselves would not have arrived at. And, in sober fact, have not.

Now we on this end must help you by sending some tangible representation of what we are talking about. Perhaps the enclosed sketches will serve the purpose. They are not IT, but they convey the feeling. At the very least, they may give you a sense of participation should your friend Malvina Hoffman break into brisk conversation on radiator caps.

Sincerely yours,
DAVID WALLACE
Special Products Division

NOVEMBER 13, 1955

DEAR MR. WALLACE:

The sketches. They are indeed exciting; they have quality, and the toucan tones lend tremendous allure—confirmed by the wheels. Half the magic—sustaining effects of this kind. Looked at upside down, furthermore, there is a sense of fish buoyancy. Immediately your word "impeccable" sprang to mind. Might it be a possibility? The Impeccable. In any case, the baguette lapidary glamour you have achieved certainly spurs the imagination. Car-innovation is like launching a ship—"drama."

I am by no means sure that I can help you to the right thing, but performance with elegance casts a spell. Let me do some thinking in the direction of impeccable, symmechromatic, thunderblender. . . . (The exotics, if I can shape them a little.) Dearborn might come into one.

If the sketches should be returned at once, let me know. Otherwise, let me dwell on them for a time. I am, may I say, a trusty confidante.

I thank you for realizing that under contract esprit could not flower. You owe me nothing, specific or moral.

Sincerely,
MARIANNE MOORE

NOVEMBER 19, 1955

Some other suggestions, Mr. Wallace, for the phenomenon:

THE RESILIENT BULLET
or Intelligent Bullet
or Bullet Cloisonné or Bullet Lavolta

(I have always had a fancy for THE INTELLIGENT WHALE—the little first Navy submarine, shaped like a sweet potato; on view in our Brooklyn Yard.)

THE FORD FABERGE

(That there is also a perfume Fabergé seems to me to do no harm, for here allusion is to the original silversmith.)

THE ARC-en-CIEL (the rainbow) ARCENCIEL?

Please do not feel that memoranda from me need acknowledgment. I am not working day and night for you; I feel that etymological hits are partially accidental.

The bullet idea has possibilities, it seems to me, in connection with Mercury (with Hermes and Hermes Trismegistus) and magic (white magic).

Sincerely,
MARIANNE MOORE

NOVEMBER 28, 1955

DEAR MR. WALLACE:

MONGOOSE CIVIQUE

ANTICIPATOR

REGNA RACER (couronne à couronne) sovereign to sovereign

AEROTERRE

Fée Rapide (Aérofée, Aéro Faire, Fée Aiglette, Magi-faire) Comme Il Faire

Tonnerre Alifère (winged thunder)

Aliforme Alifère (wing-slender, a-wing)

TURBOTORC (used as an adjective by Plymouth)

THUNDERBIRD Allié (Cousin Thunderbird)

THUNDER CRESTER

DEARBORN Diamante

MAGIGRAVURE

PASTELOGRAM

I shall be returning the sketches very soon.

M.M.

DECEMBER 6, 1955

DEAR MR. WALLACE:

Regina-rex
Taper Racer Taper Acer
Varsity Stroke

Angelastro
Astranaut

Chaparral

Tir à l'arc (bull's eye)
Cresta Lark
Triskelion (three legs running)

Pluma Piluma (hairfine, feather-foot)

Andante con Moto (description of a good motor?)

My findings thin, so I terminate them and am returning the sketches. Two principles I have not been able to capture: 1, the topknot of the peacock and topnotcher of speed. 2, the swivel-axis (emphasized elsewhere), like the Captain's bed on the whaleship, Charles Morgan—balanced so that it levelled whatever the slant of the ship.

If I stumble on a hit, you shall have it. Anything so far has been pastime. Do not ponder appreciation, Mr. Wallace. That was embodied in the sketches.

M.M.

I cannot resist the temptation to disobey my brother and submit

TURCOTINGA (turquoise cotinga—the cotinga being a South-American finch or sparrow) solid indigo.

(I have a three-volume treatise on flowers that might produce something but the impression given should certainly be unlabored.)

DECEMBER 8, 1955

MR. WALLACE:

May I submit UTOPIAN TURTLE-TOP? Do not trouble to answer unless you like it.

MARIANNE MOORE

DECEMBER 23, 1955

MERRY CHRISTMAS TO OUR FAVORITE TURTLETOPPER.

DAVID WALLACE

DECEMBER 26, 1955

DEAR MR. WALLACE:

An aspiring turtle is certain to glory in spiral eucalyptus, white pine straight from the forest, and innumerable scarlet roses almost too tall for close inspection. Of a temperament susceptible to shock though one may be, to be treated like royalty could not but induce sensations unprecedented august.

Please know that a carfancyer's allegiance to the Ford automotive turtle—extending from the Model T Dynasty to the Wallace Utopian Dynasty—can never waver; impersonal gratitude surely becoming infinite when made personal. Gratitude to unmiserly Mr. Wallace and his idealistic associates.

MARIANNE MOORE

NOVEMBER 8, 1956

DEAR MISS MOORE:

Because you were so kind to us in our early days of looking for a suitable name, I feel a deep obligation to report on events that have ensued.

And I feel I must do so before the public announcement of same come Monday, November 19.

We have chosen a name out of the more than six thousand-odd candidates that we gathered. It fails somewhat of the resonance, gaiety, and zest we were seeking. But it has a personal dignity and meaning to many of us here. Our name, dear Miss Moore, is—Edsel.

I hope you will understand.

Cordially,

DAVID WALLACE

Special Products Division

David Ogilvy / How to Write Potent Copy 1963

David Ogilvy was born in England in 1911 and received his education at Christ Church College, Oxford. His professional experiences have been varied. At one time he served as an apprentice chef in the kitchens of the Hotel Majestic in Paris and at another time as a salesman of kitchen stoves. With the founding of Ogilvy, Benson and Mather in 1948, Ogilvy went on to become one of the leading figures and voices of American advertising. His best-known ads—those for Hathaway shirts, Schweppes tonic, and Rolls-Royce—have focused on distinctive images of Anglo-American sophistication. His most recent book, Ogilvy on Advertising, *was published in 1983.*

''How to Write Potent Copy'' appeared as a chapter in Ogilvy's best-seller, Confessions of an Advertising Man.

I. HEADLINES

The headline is the most important element in most advertisements. It is the telegram which decides the reader whether to read the copy.

On the average, five times as many people read the headline as read the body copy. When you have written your headline, you have spent eighty cents out of your dollar.

If you haven't done some selling in your headline, you have wasted 80 per cent of your client's money. The wickedest of all sins is to run an advertisement *without* a headline. Such headless wonders are still to be found; I don't envy the copywriter who submits one to me.

A change of headline can make a difference of ten to one in sales. I never write fewer than sixteen headlines for a single advertisement, and I observe certain guides in writing them:

(1) The headline is the ''ticket on the meat.'' Use it to flag down the readers who are prospects for the kind of product you are advertising. If you are selling a remedy for bladder weakness, display the words BLADDER WEAKNESS in your headline; they catch the eye of everyone who suffers from this inconvenience. If you want *mothers* to read your advertisement, display MOTHERS in your headline. And so on.

Conversely, do not say anything in your headline which is likely to *exclude* any readers who might be prospects for your product. Thus, if you are advertising a product which can be used equally well by men and women, don't slant your headline at women alone; it would frighten men away.

(2) Every headline should appeal to the reader's *self-interest*. It should promise her a benefit, as in my headline for Helena Rubinstein's Hormone Cream: HOW WOMEN OVER 35 CAN LOOK YOUNGER.

(3) Always try to inject *news* into your headlines, because the consumer is always on the lookout for new products, or new ways to use an old product, or new improvements in an old product.

The two most powerful words you can use in a headline are FREE and NEW. You can seldom use FREE, but you can almost always use NEW—if you try hard enough.

(4) Other words and phrases which work wonders are HOW TO, SUDDENLY, NOW, ANNOUNCING, INTRODUCING, IT'S HERE, JUST ARRIVED, IMPORTANT DEVELOPMENT, IMPROVEMENT, AMAZING, SENSATIONAL, REMARKABLE, REVOLUTIONARY, STARTLING, MIRACLE, MAGIC, OFFER, QUICK, EASY, WANTED, CHALLENGE, ADVICE TO, THE TRUTH ABOUT, COMPARE, BARGAIN, HURRY, LAST CHANCE.

Don't turn up your nose at these clichés. They may be shopworn, but they work.

That is why you see them turn up so often in the headlines of mail-order advertisers and others who can measure the results of their advertisements.

Headlines can be strengthened by the inclusion of *emotional* words, like DARLING, LOVE, FEAR, PROUD, FRIEND, and BABY. One of the most provocative advertisements which has come out of our agency showed a girl in a bathtub, talking to her lover on the telephone. The headline: *Darling, I'm having the most extraordinary experience . . . I'm head over heels in* DOVE.

(5) Five times as many people read the headline as read the body copy, so it is important that these glancers should at least be told what brand is being advertised. That is why you should always include the brand name in your headlines.

(6) Include your selling promise in your headline. This requires long headlines. When the New York University School of Retailing ran headline tests with the cooperation of a big department store, they found that headlines of ten words or longer, containing news and information, consistently sold more merchandise than short headlines.

Headlines containing six to twelve words pull more coupon returns than short headlines, and there is no significant difference between the readership of twelve-word headlines and the readership of three-word headlines. The best headline I ever wrote contained *eighteen* words: *At Sixty Miles an Hour the Loudest Noise in the New Rolls-Royce comes from the electric clock.*[1]

(7) People are more likely to read your body copy if your headline arouses their curiosity; so you should end your headline with a lure to read on.

(8) Some copywriters write *tricky* headlines—puns, literary allusions, and other obscurities. This is a sin.

In the average newspaper your headline has to compete for attention with 350 others. Research has shown that readers travel so fast through this jungle that they don't stop to decipher the meaning of obscure headlines. Your headline must *telegraph* what you want to say, and it must telegraph it in plain language. Don't play games with the reader.

In 1960 the *Times Literary Supplement* attacked the whimsical tradition in British advertising, calling it "self-indulgent—a kind of middle-class private joke, apparently designed to amuse the advertiser and his client." Amen.

(9) Research shows that it is dangerous to use *negatives* in headlines. If, for example, you write OUR SALT CONTAINS NO ARSENIC, many readers will miss the negative and go away with the impression that you wrote OUR SALT CONTAINS ARSENIC.

(10) Avoid *blind* headlines—the kind which mean nothing unless you read the body copy underneath them; most people *don't.*

II. BODY COPY

When you sit down to write your body copy, pretend that you are talking to the woman on your right at a dinner party. She has asked you, "I am thinking of buying a new car. Which would you recommend?" Write your copy as if you were answering that question.

(1) Don't beat about the bush—go straight to the point. Avoid analogies of the "just as, so too" variety. Dr. Gallup has demonstrated that these two-stage arguments are generally misunderstood.

(2) Avoid superlatives, generalizations, and platitudes. Be specific and factual. Be enthusiastic, friendly, and memorable. Don't be a bore. Tell the truth, but make the truth fascinating.

How long should your copy be? It depends on the product. If you are advertising chewing gum, there isn't much to tell, so make your copy short. If, on the other

1. When the chief engineer at the Rolls-Royce factory read this, he shook his head sadly and said, "It is time we did something about that damned clock."

The Rolls-Royce Silver Cloud—$13,550

"At 60 miles an hour the loudest noise in this new Rolls-Royce comes from the electric clock"

What ***makes*** *Rolls-Royce the best car in the world? "There is really no magic about it—it is merely patient attention to detail," says an eminent Rolls-Royce engineer.*

1. "At 60 miles an hour the loudest noise comes from the electric clock," reports the Technical Editor of THE MOTOR. The silence of the engine is uncanny. Three mufflers tune out sound frequencies—acoustically.

2. Every Rolls-Royce engine is run for seven hours at full throttle before installation, and each car is test-driven for hundreds of miles over varying road surfaces.

3. The Rolls-Royce is designed as an *owner-driven* car. It is eighteen inches shorter than the largest domestic cars.

4. The car has power steering, power brakes and automatic gear-shift. It is very easy to drive and to park. No chauffeur required.

5. There is no metal-to-metal contact between the body of the car and the chassis frame—except for the speedometer drive. The entire body is insulated and under-sealed.

6. The finished car spends a week in the final test-shop, being fine-tuned. Here it is subjected to ninety-eight separate ordeals. For example, the engineers use a *stethoscope* to listen for axle-whine.

7. The Rolls-Royce is guaranteed for *three years.* With a new network of dealers and parts-depots from Coast to Coast, service is no longer any problem

8. The famous Rolls-Royce radiator has never been changed, except that when Sir Henry Royce died in 1933 the monogram RR was changed from red to black.

9. The coachwork is given five coats of primer paint, and hand rubbed between each coat, before *fourteen* coats of finishing paint go on.

10. By moving a switch on the steering column, you can adjust the shock-absorbers to suit road conditions. (The lack of fatigue in driving this car is remarkable.)

11. Another switch defrosts the rear window, by heating a network of 1360 invisible wires in the glass. There are two separate ventilating systems, so that you can ride in comfort with all the windows closed. Air conditioning is optional.

12. The seats are upholstered with eight hides of English leather—enough to make 128 pairs of soft shoes.

13. A picnic table, veneered in French walnut, slides out from under the dash. Two more swing out behind the front seats.

14. You can get such optional extras as an Espresso coffee-making machine, a dictating machine, a bed, hot and cold water for washing, an electric razor.

15. You can lubricate the entire chassis by simply pushing a pedal from the driver's seat. A gauge on the dash shows the level of oil in the crankcase.

16. Gasoline consumption is remarkably low and there is no need to use premium gas; a happy economy.

17. There are two separate systems of power brakes, hydraulic and mechanical. The Rolls-Royce is a very *safe* car—and also a very *lively* car. It cruises serenely at eighty-five. Top speed is in excess of 100 m.p.h.

18. Rolls-Royce engineers make periodic visits to inspect owners' motor cars and advise on service.

ROLLS-ROYCE AND BENTLEY

19. The Bentley is made by Rolls-Royce. Except for the radiators, they are identical motor cars, manufactured by the same engineers in the same works. The Bentley costs $300 less, because its radiator is simpler to make. People who feel diffident about driving a Rolls-Royce can buy a Bentley.

PRICE. The car illustrated in this advertisement-f.o.b. principal port of entry—costs **$13,550.**

If you would like the rewarding experience c driving a Rolls-Royce or Bentley, get in touch wit our dealer. His name is on the bottom of this page Rolls-Royce Inc., 10 Rockefeller Plaza, New York, N.Y.

JET ENGINES AND THE FUTURE

Certain airlines have chosen Rolls-Royce turbo-jets for their Boeing 707's and Douglas DC8's. Rolls-Royce prop-jets are in the Vickers Viscount, the Fairchild F.27 and the Grumman Gulfstream.

Rolls-Royce engines power more than half the turbo-jet and prop-jet airliners supplied to or on order for world airlines.

Rolls-Royce now employ 42,000 people and the company's engineering experience does not stop at motor cars and jet engines. There are Rolls-Royce diesel and gasoline engines for many other applications.

The huge research and development resources of the company are now at work on many projects for the future, including nuclear and rocket propulsion.

Special showing of the Rolls-Royce and Bentley at Salter Automotive Imports, Inc., 9009 Carnegie Ave., tomorrow through April 26

[1958]

hand, you are advertising a product which has a great many different qualities to recommend it, write long copy: the more you tell, the more you sell.

There is a universal belief in lay circles that people won't read long copy. Nothing could be farther from the truth. Claude Hopkins once wrote five pages of solid text for Schlitz beer. In a few months, Schlitz moved up from fifth place to first. I once wrote a page of solid text for Good Luck Margarine, with most gratifying results.

Research shows that readership falls off rapidly up to fifty words of copy, but drops very little between fifty and 500 words. In my first Rolls-Royce advertisement I used 719 words—piling one fascinating fact on another. In the last paragraph I wrote, "People who feel diffident about driving a Rolls-Royce can buy a Bentley." Judging from the number of motorists who picked up the word "diffident" and bandied it about, I concluded that the advertisement was thoroughly read. In the next one I used 1400 words.

Every advertisement should be a *complete* sales pitch for your product. It is unrealistic to assume that consumers will read a *series* of advertisements for the same product. You should shoot the works in every advertisement, on the assumption that it is the only chance you will ever have to sell your product to the reader—*now or never*.

Says Dr. Charles Edwards of the graduate School of Retailing at New York University, "The more facts you tell, the more you sell. An advertisement's chance for success invariably increases as the number of pertinent merchandise facts included in the advertisement increases."

In my first advertisement for Puerto Rico's Operation Bootstrap, I used 961 words, and persuaded Beardsley Ruml to sign them. Fourteen thousand readers clipped the coupon from this advertisement, and scores of them later established factories in Puerto Rico. The greatest professional satisfaction I have yet had is to see the prosperity in Puerto Rican communities which had lived on the edge of starvation for four hundred years before I wrote my advertisement. If I had confined myself to a few vacuous generalities, nothing would have happened.

We have even been able to get people to read long copy about gasoline. One of our Shell advertisements contained 617 words, and 22 per cent of male readers read more than half of them.

Vic Schwab tells the story of Max Hart (of Hart, Schaffner & Marx) and his advertising manager, George L. Dyer, arguing about long copy. Dyer said, "I'll bet you ten dollars I can write a newspaper page of solid type and you'd read every word of it."

Hart scoffed at the idea. "I don't have to write a line of it to prove my point," Dyer replied. "I'll only tell you the headline: THIS PAGE IS ALL ABOUT MAX HART."

Advertisers who put coupons in their advertisements *know* that short copy doesn't sell. In split-run tests, long copy invariably outsells short copy.

Do I hear someone say that no copywriter can write long advertisements unless his media department gives him big spaces to work with? This question should not arise, because the copywriter should be consulted before planning the media schedule.

> (3) You should always include testimonials in your copy. The reader finds it easier to believe the endorsement of a fellow consumer than the puffery of an anonymous copywriter. Says Jim Young, one of the best copywriters alive today, "Every type of advertiser has the same problem; namely to be believed. The mail-order man knows nothing so potent for this purpose as the testimonial, yet the general advertiser seldom uses it."

Testimonials from celebrities get remarkably high readership, and if they are honestly written they still do not seem to provoke incredulity. The better known the celebrity, the more readers you will attract. We have featured Queen Elizabeth and Winston Churchill in "Come to Britain" advertisements, and we were able to persuade Mrs. Roosevelt to make television commercials for Good Luck Margarine. When we advertised charge accounts for Sears, Roebuck, we reproduced the credit card of Ted Williams, "recently traded by Boston to Sears."

Sometimes you can cast your entire copy in the form of a testimonial. My first advertisement for Austin cars took the form of a letter from an "anonymous diplomat" who was sending his son to Groton with money he had saved driving an Austin—a well-aimed combination of snobbery and economy. Alas, a perspicacious *Time* editor guessed that I was the anonymous diplomat, and asked the headmaster of Groton to comment. Dr. Crocker was so cross that I decided to send my son to Hotchkiss.

(4) Another profitable gambit is to give the reader helpful advice, or service. It hooks about 75 per cent more readers than copy which deals entirely with the product.

One of our Rinso advertisements told housewives how to remove stains. It was better read (Starch) and better remembered (Gallup) than any detergent advertisement in history. Unfortunately, however, it forgot to feature Rinso's main selling promise—that Rinso washes whiter; for this reason it should never have run.[2]

(5) I have never admired the *belles lettres* school of advertising, which reached its pompous peak in Theodore F. MacManus' famous advertisement for Cadillac, "The Penalty of Leadership," and Ned Jordan's classic, "Somewhere West of Laramie." Forty years ago the business community seems to have been impressed by these pieces of purple prose, but I have always thought them absurd; they did not give the reader a single *fact*. I share Claude Hopkins' view that "fine writing is a distinct disadvantage. So is unique literary style. They take attention away from the subject."

(6) Avoid bombast. Raymond Rubicam's famous slogan for Squibb, "The priceless ingredient of every product is the honor and integrity of its maker," reminds me of my father's advice: when a company boasts about its integrity, or a woman about her virtue, avoid the former and cultivate the latter.

(7) Unless you have some special reason to be solemn and pretentious, write your copy in the colloquial language which your customers use in everyday conversation. I have never acquired a sufficiently good ear for vernacular American to write it, but I admire copywriters who can pull it off, as in this unpublished pearl from a dairy farmer:

Carnation Milk is the best in the land,
Here I sit with a can in my hand.
No tits to pull, no hay to pitch,
Just punch a hole in the son-of-a-bitch.

It is a mistake to use highfalutin language when you advertise to uneducated people. I once used the word OBSOLETE in a headline, only to discover that 43 per cent of housewives had no idea what it meant. In another headline, I used the word INEFFABLE, only to discover that I didn't know what it meant myself.

However, many copywriters of my vintage err on the side of underestimating the educational level of the population. Philip Hauser, head of the Sociology Department at the University of Chicago, draws attention to the changes which are taking place:

> The increasing exposure of the population to formal schooling . . . can be expected to effect important changes in . . . the style of advertis-

2. The photograph showed several different kinds of stain—lipstick, coffee, shoe-polish, blood and so forth. The blood was my own; I am the only copywriter who has ever *bled* for his client.

> ing. . . . Messages aimed at the "average" American on the assumption that he has had less than a grade school education are likely to find themselves with a declining or disappearing clientele.[3]

Meanwhile, all copywriters should read Dr. Rudolph Flesch's *Art of Plain Talk*. It will persuade them to use short words, short sentences, short paragraphs, and highly *personal* copy.

Aldous Huxley, who once tried his hand at writing advertisements, concluded that "any trace of literariness in an advertisement is fatal to its success. Advertisement writers may not be lyrical, or obscure, or in any way esoteric. They must be universally intelligible. A good advertisement has this in common with drama and oratory, that it must be immediately comprehensible and directly moving." [4]

(8) Resist the temptation to write the kind of copy which wins awards. I am always gratified when I win an award, but most of the campaigns which produce *results* never win awards, because they don't draw attention to themselves.

The juries that bestow awards are never given enough information about the *results* of the advertisements they are called upon to judge. In the absence of such information, they rely on their opinions, which are always warped toward the highbrow.

(9) Good copywriters have always resisted the temptation to *entertain*. Their achievement lies in the number of new products they get off to a flying start. In a class by himself stands Claude Hopkins, who is to advertising what Escoffier is to cooking. By today's standards, Hopkins was an unscrupulous barbarian, but technically he was the supreme master. Next I would place Raymond Rubicam, George Cecil, and James Webb Young, all of whom lacked Hopkins' ruthless salesmanship, but made up for it by their honesty, by the broader range of their work, and by their ability to write civilized copy when the occasion required it. Next I would place John Caples, the mail-order specialist from whom I have learned much.

These giants wrote their advertisements for newspapers and magazines. It is still too early to identify the best writers for television.

Patricia Volk / A Word from Our Sponsor 1987

Patricia Volk (b. 1943) has enjoyed a successful career as both an advertising company executive and a writer. She has received numerous awards in each area: The World Beat Press *fiction award for her book* The Yellow Banana *(1984) as well as various* Andy, Clio, *and* Efie *awards for advertising. She has also recently published a collection of her stories,* All It Takes *(1990).*

In the following article, Volk addresses the manipulative uses of language in contemporary advertising—the way in which, for example, "creme" is used to suggest "cream" in a product that lacks it. Examining the craft from the inside out, Volk exposes the tricks of the advertising trade with a delightful sense of humor and leaves us with a serious point: that most American consumers are willing victims of copywriters' purposeful playfulness with language. Volk's article demonstrates that advertisers "twist and twiddle words and understand their power. They make people do things they hadn't thought of doing before."

3. *Scientific American* (October 1962).

4. *Essays Old And New* (Harper & Brothers, 1927). Charles Lamb and Byron also wrote advertisements. So did Bernard Shaw, Hemingway, Marquand, Sherwood Anderson, and Faulkner—none of them with any degree of success.

Linguistically speaking (and that's still the preferred way), there is only one rule in advertising: There are no rules. "We try harder," lacks parallelism. "Nobody doesn't like Sara Lee," is a double negative. And "Modess. Because. . . ." Because . . . why? My friends didn't know. My mother wouldn't tell. My sister said, like Mount Everest, because it was there. The word "creme" on a product means there's no cream in it. "Virtually," as in "Virtually all our cars are tested," means in essence, not in fact. Even a casual "Let's have lunch," said in passing on Mad Ave. means "Definitely, let's not."

Language without rules has little to protect it. Some of the most familiar lines would disappear like ring-around-the-collar if you put a mere "Says who?" after them. "Coke is it." Says who? "Sony. The one and only." Oh, yeah?

Still, one word in advertising has virtually limitless power. It gives "permission to believe." It inspires hope. It is probably (disclaimer) the oldest word in advertising.

What "new" lacks in newness, it makes up for in motivation. Unfortunately, new gets old fast. Legally, it's usable for only six months after a product is introduced. As in, say, "Introducing New Grippies. The candy that sticks to 'the woof of your mouf.' "

Once Grippies are six months old, unlike newlyweds, who get a year, and the New Testament which has gotten away with it for who knows how long, Grippies are reduced to just plain Grippies. That's when you improve them and say "Introducing New Improved Grippies." Now they weally stick like cwazy to that woof.

Had you named your product "New" to start with, as in "New Soap. The soap that cleans like new," you'd never have to worry about your product sounding old. Introduced as "New New Soap," six months down the road it segues into "New Improved New Soap." Or you could avoid the six-month thing entirely and just call it "The Revolutionary New Soap" from day one.

PITCHING GLUE

How do you get the Grippies account in the first place? You "pitch" it in a flurry of work called a "push." A creative team works weekends and sleeps in the office. It's intense.

A successful pitch winds up in a "win," and you've "landed" the account. By the end of the week, everyone in the agency has a free box of Grippies and work begins. This is the "honeymoon period."

Everybody loves everybody else. You take the factory tour. You eat Grippies till your molars roll. And you attend "focus groups," i.e., meetings between researchers and preselected members of your "target audience," the people you hope will love Grippies.

You sit behind a two-way mirror and watch people eat Grippies. You take notes. You start hating the man who scratches the exposed area of his leg between the top of his sock and the bottom of his pants. "Look! He's doing it! He's doing it *again!*" And what you learn in the focus group, you use to build "share," which is the percentage of the population using your *kind* of product that buys yours in particular.

It gives you some idea of how large this country is when you realize that if you can raise Forever Glue's .01 share of market (one person per thousand) to .03, Forever Glue will be a dazzling success. So you do the "Nothing lasts like Forever" campaign, complete with "The Big Idea." You find a small town in a depressed area upstate and glue it back together. Brick by brick, clapboard by clapboard, you actually (favorite ad word) glue a town together and restore it in a classic ''demo'' with ''product as hero.'' You get a corner office and a Tizio lamp.

Forever is stickier. Grippies are grippier. But what if your product is ''parity,'' a ''me-tooer''? What if it has no ''unique selling point'' or ''exclusivity''? What if the world is not waiting for Mega-Bran, the cereal that tastes like Styrofoam pellets and gets soggy in the bowl?

Some folks ''make it sing.'' It's what everybody thinks people in advertising do anyway, as in, ''Oh, you're in advertising! You must write jingles!'' So you write new words to Bon Jovi's ''Never Say Goodbye,'' only the client doesn't want to spend $2 million for the rights. So you check out the P.D.'s, public domain songs, songs with lapsed copyrights that are at least 75 years old. You just have to hope the Mega-Bran lyrics work to the tune of ''Ach, the Moon Climbs High,'' ''Jim Crack Corn,'' or ''Whoopee Ti Yi Yo—Git Along Little Dogies.''

At last the new Mega-Bran campaign is ready to crawl through all the ''loops'' in the ''approval cycle,'' from your client's kids to the network's lawyers. Everybody ''signs off'' on it.

In ''pretest,'' you get ''rich verbatims''—a lot of people who remember everything about your commercial. You go for it. You shoot a finished ''spot.'' You spend $250,000 on production, ''net net,'' and $3 million on network and uh-oh, nobody buys the bran. Your commercial has failed to generate ''trial'' and ''brand awareness.'' It's the Edsel of brans.

Quick, you do another ''execution,'' a celebrity endorsement using someone with a high ''Q'' (familiarity and popularity) score. (Bill Cosby has the highest.) You try ''image advertising,'' which says almost nothing, but leaves the viewer feeling good about your product. (Soft drinks do it all the time.)

Still, no one remembers Mega-Bran. It's a case of ''vampire video''—what people saw in your ad was so strong that it sucked the blood out of your message. The account becomes ''shaky.'' ''Doomers and gloomers'' worry all over your carpet. They ''bail.'' Bailers are people in a room who sniff out with whom the power lies; whatever that person says, the bailer agrees. The fastest bailer I ever knew was an account man who told me every time he was asked his opinion, he saw his mortgage float in front of his eyes.

The account goes from shaky to the ICU. Then it's ''out the door.'' There is no funeral, no period of mourning because every loss presents an opportunity, a chance to roll up your sleeves, grease up your elbow and pitch again.

BODY PARTS

Clients like to find ''niches'' for their products. A niche is a special place no other product can fit. Sometimes you find the niche before you find the product and then you have to find a product to fill the niche you found.

Body parts are always good, though by now almost everything has been spoken for. There are still the navel and the philtrum. If you can do ''exploratories'' and with a little prodding make consumers aware that their philtrums sweat too much, smell funny or have unwanted hair, you're in business. You create a new form of consumer anxiety and cure it in a single stroke. You launch ''Creme de Philtrum,'' with no cream in it, and have ''preemptiveness.'' You're hot.

You don't have to go to school to write great copy. The best writers I know wrap fish in the Elements of Style. Schools say they can teach it, but you either have it or you don't. It's like perfect pitch, good gums, or being able to sit on the floor with your ankles around your neck. They use language to convince, persuade, and, at its best, educate. They twist and twiddle words and understand their power. They make people do things they hadn't thought of doing before. They make them change.

One of the best writers ever had a great line: "The only thing we have to fear is fear itself." It led a whole country out of Depression. Imagine what he could have done with detergent.

Neil Postman / The Parable of the Ring around the Collar

1988

In twentieth-century America, "culture" has leaked through the boundaries of high literature and art to include the newer technological realms of mass media—films, recorded music, and particularly television. Intellectuals have struggled with this shift since it first became evident. From the cautionary writings of Frankfurt school thinkers Walter Benjamin and Theodor Adorno, to the paranoia of "mass culture" critics in the 1950s, to the more accepting and varied responses among postmodern theorists, scholarly assessments of popular culture have unraveled the complexities and "secret meanings" within the images and narratives typical viewers constantly encounter.

Neil Postman's ongoing examination of mass culture, and particularly of television, considers the effects of an ever-growing pool of images on what he views as an increasingly mystified and passive viewing audience. His books, including most notably Teaching as a Subversive Activity *(with Charles Weingartner, 1969),* Crazy Talk, Stupid Talk: Stirring Up Trouble about Language, Technology, and Education *(1976),* Amusing Ourselves to Death: Public Discourse in the Age of Show Business *(1985), and* Conscientious Objections: Stirring Up Trouble about Language, Technology, and Education *(1988), reflect his concern about these developments. A professor at New York University, Postman borrows concepts and terminology from literary criticism and anthropology to elaborate his views. The following article, drawn from* Conscientious Objections, *addresses television commercials as modern spiritual texts. The result is an amusing, unusual view of something most of us hardly think we notice.*

Television commercials are a form of religious literature. To comment on them in a serious vein is to practice hermeneutics, the branch of theology concerned with interpreting and explaining the Scriptures. This is what I propose to do here. The heathens, heretics, and unbelievers may move on to something else.

I do not claim, for a start, that every television commercial has religious content. Just as in church the pastor will sometimes call the congregation's attention to nonecclesiastical matters, so there are television commercials that are entirely secular. Someone has something to sell; you are told what it is, where it can be obtained, and what it costs. Though these may be shrill and offensive, no doctrine is advanced and no theology invoked.

But the majority of important television commercials take the form of religious parables organized around a coherent theology. Like all religious parables, they put forward a concept of sin, intimations of the way to redemption, and a vision of Heaven. They also suggest what are the roots of evil and what are the obligations of the holy.

Consider, for example, the Parable of the Ring around the Collar. This is to television scripture what the Parable of the Prodigal Son is to the Bible, which is to say it is an archetype containing most of the elements of form and content that recur in its genre. To begin with, the Parable of the Ring around the Collar is short, occupying only about thirty seconds of one's time and attention. There are three reasons for this, all obvious. First, it is expensive to preach on television; second, the attention span of the congregation is not long and is highly vulnerable to distraction; and third, a parable does not need to be long—tradition-dictating that its narrative structure be tight, its symbols unambiguous, its explication terse.

The narrative structure of the Parable of the Ring around the Collar is, indeed, comfortably traditional. The story has a beginning, a middle, and an end. A married couple is depicted in some relaxed setting—a restaurant, say—in which they are enjoying each other's company and generally having a wonderful time. But then a waitress approaches their table, notices that the man has a dirty collar, stares at it boldly, sneers with cold contempt, and announces to all within hearing the nature of his transgression. The man is humiliated and glares at his wife with scorn, for she is the source of his shame. She, in turn, assumes an expression of self-loathing mixed with a touch of self-pity. This is the parable's beginning: the presentation of the problem.

The parable continues by showing the wife at home using a detergent that never fails to eliminate dirt around the collars of men's shirts. She proudly shows her husband what she is doing, and he forgives her with an adoring smile. This is the parable's middle: the solution of the problem. Finally, we are shown the couple in a restaurant once again, but this time they are free of the waitress's probing eyes and bitter social chastisement. This is the parable's end: the moral, the explication, the exegesis. From this, we should draw the proper conclusion.

As in all parables, behind the apparent simplicity there are some profound ideas to ponder. Among the most subtle and important is the notion of where and how problems originate. Embedded in every belief system there is an assumption about the root cause of evil from which the varieties of sinning take form. In science, for example, evil is represented in superstition. In psychoanalysis, we find it in early, neurotic transactions with our parents. In Christianity, it is located in the concept of Original Sin.

In television-commercial parables, the root cause of evil is Technological Innocence, a failure to know the particulars of the beneficent accomplishments of industrial progress. This is the primary source of unhappiness, humiliation, and discord in life. And, as forcefully depicted in the Parable of the Ring, the consequences of technological innocence may strike at any time, without warning, and with the full force of their disintegrating action.

The sudden striking power of technological innocence is a particularly important feature of television-commercial theology, for it is a constant reminder of the congregation's vulnerability. One must never be complacent or, worse, self-congratulatory. To attempt to live without technological sophistication is at all times dangerous, since the evidence of one's naïveté will always be painfully visible to the vigilant. The vigilant may be a waitress, a friend, a neighbor, or even a spectral figure—a holy ghost, as it were—who materializes in your kitchen, from nowhere, to give witness to your sluggardly ignorance.

Technological innocence refers not only to ignorance of detergents, drugs, sanitary napkins, cars, salves, and foodstuffs, but also to ignorance of technical machinery such as savings banks and transportation systems. One may, for example, come upon one's neighbors while on vacation (in television-commercial parables, this is always a sign of danger) and discover that they have invested their money in a certain bank of whose special interest rates you have been unaware. This is, of course, a moral disaster, and both you and your vacation are doomed.

As demonstrated in the Ring Parable, there is a path to redemption, but it can be entered only on two conditions. The first requires that you be open to advice or social criticism from those who are more enlightened. In the Ring Parable, the waitress serves the function of counselor, although she is, to be sure, exacting and very close to unforgiving. In some parables, the adviser is rather more sarcastic than severe. But in most parables, as for example in all sanitary napkin, mouthwash, shampoo, and aspirin commercials, the advisers are amiable and sympathetic, perhaps all too aware of their own vulnerability on other matters.

The Innocent are required to accept instruction in the spirit in which it is offered. This cannot be stressed enough, for it instructs the congregation in two lessons simultaneously: One must be eager to accept advice, and just as eager to give it. Giving advice is, so to speak, the principal obligation of the holy. In fact, the ideal religious community may be depicted in images of dozens of people, each in his or her turn giving and taking advice on technological advances.

The second condition involves one's willingness to act on the advice given. As in traditional Christian theology, it is not sufficient to hear the gospel or even preach it. One's understanding must be expressed in good works. In the Ring Parable, the once-pitiable wife acts almost immediately, and the Parable concludes by showing the congregation the effects of her action. In the Parable of the Person with Rotten Breath, of which there are several versions, we are shown a woman who, ignorant of the technological solution to her problem, is enlightened by a supportive roommate. The woman takes the advice without delay, with results we are shown in the last five seconds: a honeymoon in Hawaii. In the Parable of the Stupid Investor, we are shown a man who knows not how to make his money make money. Upon enlightenment, he acts swiftly and, at the parable's end, he is rewarded with a car, or a trip to Hawaii, or something approximating peace of mind.

Because of the compactness of commercial parables, the ending—that is, the last five seconds—must serve a dual purpose. It is, of course, the moral of the story: If one will act in such a way, this will be the reward. But in being shown the result, we are also shown an image of Heaven. Occasionally, as in the Parable of the Lost Traveler's Checks, we are given a glimpse of Hell: Technological Innocents lost and condemned to eternal wandering far from their native land. But mostly we are given images of a Heaven both accessible and delicious: that is, a Heaven that is here, now, on earth, in America, and quite often in Hawaii.

But Hawaii is only a convenient recurring symbol. Heaven can, in fact, materialize and envelop you anywhere. In the Parable of the Man Who Runs through Airports, Heaven is found at a car-rental counter to which the confounded Runner is shepherded by an angelic messenger. The expression of ecstasy on the Runner's face tells clearly that this moment is as close to transcendence as he can ever hope for.

Ecstasy is the key idea here, for commercial parables depict the varieties of ecstasy in as much detail as you will find in any body of religious literature. At the conclusion of the Parable of the Spotted Glassware, a husband and wife assume such ecstatic countenances as can only be described by the word "beatification." Even in the Ring Parable, which at first glance would not seem to pose as serious a moral crisis as spotted glassware, we are shown ecstasy, pure and serene. And where ecstacy is, so is Heaven. Heaven, in brief, is any place where you have joined your soul with the Deity—the Deity, of course, being Technology.

Just when, as a religious people, we replaced our faith in traditional ideas of God with a belief in the ennobling force of Technology is not easy to say. Television commercials played no role in bringing about this transformation, but they reflect the change, document it, and amplify it. They constitute the most abundant literature we possess of our new spiritual commitment. That is why we have a solemn obligation to keep television commercials under the continuous scrutiny of hermeneutics.

Teresa Riordan / Miller Lite Guy 1989

The mass media, and particularly advertising, have been a major focus for feminist writers since the early 1970s. The famous slide shows presented by Women against Violence against Women (WAVAW) revealed just how many images of brutalized, constricted, submissive, and otherwise weakened women permeate today's magazines and television screens. Women demanded the removal of such negative images through boycotts, billboard defacements, and letter-writing campaigns; yet recent books such as Susan Faludi's Backlash *and Naomi Wolf's* Beauty Myth *shows that the objectification of women (or "babes," as Teresa Riordan identifies them here) still works as one of the most powerful tools of the advertising industry.*

Teresa Riordan, a graduate student in the American Civilization Program at the University of Texas at Austin, takes a bemused but highly disapproving look at a recent Miller beer campaign in this opinion piece written for the New Republic. *Through an analysis of the company's 1989 circular* Beachin' Times, *Riordan suggests that even in our more clean and sober times, sex—that is, a masculinist view of sex as female compliance—still seems like the Golden Apple to advertising executives.*

Poor Spuds MacKenzie. Bud Lite's lovable beer-quaffing piebald mutt managed to survive rumors of death by drug overdose and the awful revelation that "he" was in fact a she. But the "Just Say No" campaign proved too much for her. Because groups like the National Association of State Alcohol and Drug Abuse directors accused Budweiser of using Spuds to glamorize drinking for youngsters, she was put in the doghouse, and Bud has begun busily patching up its image. This year Bud's annual spring-break advertising insert, placed in campus newspapers just before the party season, reads as if it were written by the National Safety Council. "Buckle up," it says, "and save the partying for the beaches." Bud is also sponsoring coffee-and-doughnut pit stops for spring-breakers en route to partydom.

Since the '70s, spring break—about ten days of debauch on a beach—has been a prime time to advertise beer to the 18-to-24-year-old crowd, who represent about one-fifth of American beer swillers. Just a few years ago, brewing companies wooed young beer drinkers with activities like beer-chugging contests. But that was back when moderation was for pencil-necked geeks. Today beer companies rely on what Budweiser marketing specialists prefer to call "nonconsumption activities," such as free movies, concerts, or other gimmicks. The marketing emphasis has moved decidedly in the direction of clean living.

At least, for some beer companies it has. The Miller Brewing Company's spring-break ad campaign responded differently to the new zeitgeist. Most beer advertising for college markets has been based on the rock-solid premise that university men have two overriding concerns: (1) getting drunk; (2) getting laid. If you can't promise one. Miller figured, just promise more of the other.

Witness the ad insert Miller recently placed in dozens of campus newspapers at large state universities. The 16-page high-gloss ad is titled *Beachin' Times,* and its theme is "babes"—as in how to "scam" them and "turn spring break into your own personal trout farm." It features cartoons and photographs of naughty blondes wearing bikinis that cling to their firm breasts, usually with bottles of Miller close at hand. In one shot, six Miller cheerleaders excitedly hold up a gigantic longneck bottle of Lite. The caption is "WAY BIG FUN." Miller offers a poster of this photo—and another that is equally way-big-fun—as free course material for "Interior Design 101." And hey, in case you don't catch the drift, a few clues are subtly worked into the text: "These swell posters make an eye-catching addition to your naked walls. . . . Ask for 'em at the Miller Spring Break Oasis. Then study a whole new set of figures."

An article in *Beachin' Times* on Miller's "pro Beach Volleyball" program begins with this catchy lead-in: "Name something you can dink, bump, and poke. Hint—it's not a Babe." Oh, of course—if it's not a babe, it *must* be a volleyball! A Miller public relations manager explained that the advertising insert is meant to be humorous, "to poke fun at things." There's that word again!

Miller has all its bases covered. *Beachin' Times* includes the obligatory cautionary line about drinking and driving. And the Miller Spring Break Oases at Padre Island and Daytona Beach this month feature non-alcoholic stuff like a way-bitchin', gnarly-dude surf simulator and free long-distance phone calls. Moreover, as Miller's p.r. manager pointed out, the company has always been committed to encouraging "responsible" drinking. For example, she says, Miller has long been involved with the campus group BACCHUS. What does that stand for? "Boost Alcohol . . . hmmm, let me see," she says, "Boost Alcohol Consumption. . . . Just a minute . . . I want to make sure I get this right." She returns with the words that had been eluding her: Boost Alcohol *Consciousness* Concerning the Health of University Students.

In settling on flesh as a unifying theme, Rogers Merchandising, the Chicago marketing firm that masterminded *Beachin' Times,* can't be accused of coming up with an original advertising approach. Then again, look at the product it's pushing: an American beer that tastes like any other American beer. That job calls for some old-fashioned image-making. A man's brand of beer, an executive from another brewing company explained not long ago to *Beverage World,* "is like his badge, a symbol. He's saying, 'This beer is a lot like me.' " Which means that if you drink Miller you're the kind of guy who attracts droves of gorgeous, compliant women (you know, "babes"), even if you do happen to be doltish and short.

Miller's sales pitch worked without incident at the first 54 campuses saturated with copies of *Beachin' Times.* But students at the relatively liberal University of Wisconsin, where the publication was most recently distributed, just voted to censure Miller. In view of this and "other objections," says one of Miller's p.r. people, the company has decided not to distribute *Beachin' Times* to the ten schools remaining on its marketing lists. No matter, though. Alienating its female audience wasn't one of the things that Miller executives were worried about when they approved the campaign. The young adult beer market is overwhelmingly male—mainly other-directed fraternity types who need reassurance that they have the red-blooded impulses of any normal guy.

Of course, there are a few women beer drinkers out there. Maybe Miller was trying to appeal to that slice of the market by offering this spring-training tip on the cover of *Beachin' Times,* next to a drawing of a pig in a pink bikini: "Lose weight. Lots of it."

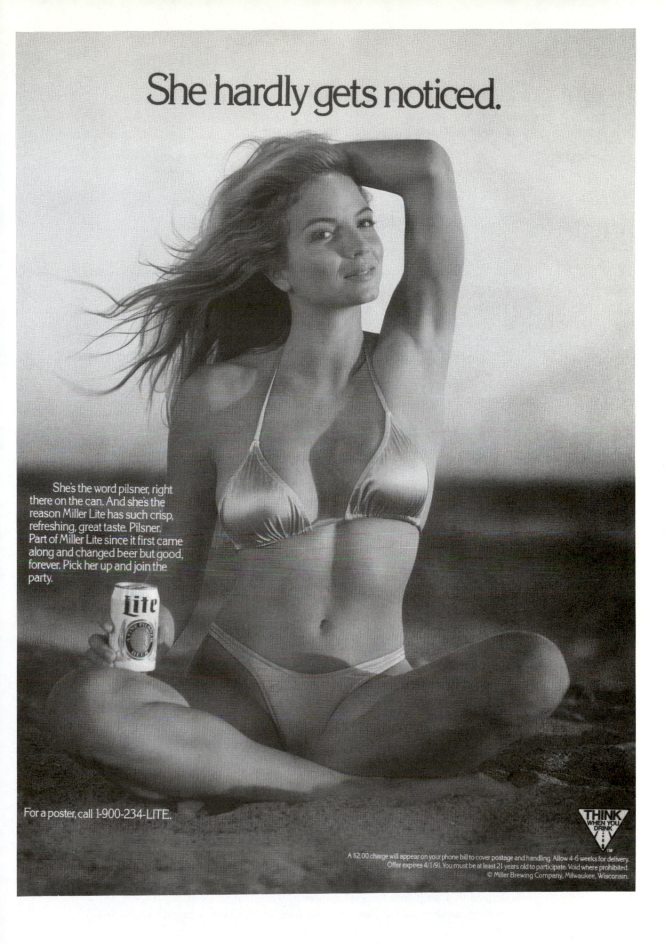

She hardly gets noticed.

She's the word pilsner, right there on the can. And she's the reason Miller Lite has such crisp, refreshing, great taste. Pilsner. Part of Miller Lite since it first came along and changed beer but good, forever. Pick her up and join the party.

Lite

For a poster, call 1-900-234-LITE.

THINK WHEN YOU DRINK™

A $2.00 charge will appear on your phone bill to cover postage and handling. Allow 4-6 weeks for delivery. Offer expires 4/1/91. You must be at least 21 years old to participate. Void where prohibited.

Michael Specter / Cigarettes for the Tractor-Pull Generation

1990

In "Cigarettes for the Tractor-Pull Generation" Michael Specter presents an account of the insensitivity of marketing companies when targeting a specific demographic group for the sale of a product.

Michael Specter is the New York Bureau Chief of the Washington Post. *He was formerly the Science Editor in the Washington office of the* Post.

The R.J. Reynolds Tobacco Co. plans soon to introduce a brand of cigarette that accordingly to the detailed marketing strategy prepared for the company targets young, poorly educated, white women described as "virile females."

Reynolds plans to test the new brand, called "Dakota," this April in Houston. The marketing plan's chief goal is to capture the lucrative market among 18- to 20-year-old women, the only group of Americans whose rate of smoking continues to increase. The competition for that group has become intense.

The marketing campaign focuses on a certain group of women whose favorite pastimes, according to the marketing plan, include "cruising," "partying" and attending "Hot Rod shows" and "tractor pulls" with their boyfriend.

Reynolds officials said in a statement that Dakota is not aimed solely at women. "Different products are designed to different categories of consumers," the statement said. "Dakota is no different. It is not a male brand or a female brand." Reynolds officials would not elaborate, and it could not be determined whether the marketing report, prepared by Promotional Marketing Inc., had been accepted by the tobacco company.

The extensive proposals for "Project V.F.," for virile female, describe the preferred "Dakota" smoker as a woman with no education beyond high school, whose favorite television roles are "Roseanne" and "evening soap opera (bitches)" and whose chief aspiration is "to get married in her early twenties" and spend her free time "with her boyfriend doing whatever he is doing."

Disclosure of the marketing recommendations, dated Sept. 21, 1989, came just three weeks after Reynolds was forced by strong opposition to cancel plans to test market "Uptown," a brand of cigarette aimed at blacks. The marketing study for Dakota shows now the cigarette was designed to "replace Marlboro as the brand of choice among female smokers 18–21."

"It is especially reprehensible to lure young people into smoking and potential lifelong nicotine addiction," said Health and Human Services Secretary Louis W. Sullivan, when asked about the Dakota marketing plan. Sullivan led the fight against Uptown. "And the risk that smoking specifically poses for women adds another tawdry dimension to any cigarette marketing effort aimed at younger women."

Last week, Democratic Senator Edward M. Kennedy of Massachusetts announced plans to seek strict regulation of tobacco products.

Reynolds has acknowledged plans to market Dakota, but reacted angrily to questions about the study.

The marketing study goes into great detail about "positioning Dakota as the choice among YAFS [young adult female smokers] aged 18–24." It estimates that the number of young women who smoke Marlboro is 1,695,006. That figure was derived by multiplying the total number of women aged 18 to 24—14,968,532—by smoking incidence 23.3 percent—and then to Marlboro's market share—48.6 percent.

The plan also outlines future advertising options based on interviews with small groups of potential consumers. ''Cannot be too tough, i.e., bitchy/cold (motorcycle jackets), the memo states. ''Cannot be too cute, giggly. Woman cannot be too submissive (i.e., fawning at man who looks disinterested).

The memo goes on to state that after the ''brand's image is established we can explore greater extremes,'' and says that ''Where smooth comes easy'' is by far the best slogan.

In addition to describing a demographic/psychographic review of the ''virile female'' as one whose ''work is a job: not a career, a way to make money,'' the report describes the person's dress (''jeans, knit tops, sweaters, shorts . . .''), favorite music groups (''all male groups'') and interests (''partying with friends,'' ''dancing'' and ''cruising'').

It also includes many possible promotions that could help stimulate consumer interest in the cigarette. They include creating a rock group called ''Dakota'' to play at special events around the country, the development of ''on-pack'' contests for consumers to select their favorite movies, songs, rock groups, television shows. Others include gambling premiums. ''VP Soap Opera Trivia Videos'' and subscriptions to Soap Opera Digest. A company statement said in reference to test-marketing documents obtained by The Washington Post, ''If they are authentic, they represent stolen, proprietary information belonging to R.J. Reynolds, and which would be of great value to our competitors.''

As millions of better-educated prosperous Americans have quit smoking, tobacco companies have turned their marketing efforts increasingly on the poor, minorities and young women who have become their most solid customers. Targeting sales to specific niches is a common practice in virtually every aspect of American advertising, but it has become extremely controversial when applied to tobacco products aimed at groups at unusually high risk for the fatal diseases caused by smoking.

''All the cigarettes companies are now facing the fact that tobacco is no longer a growth industry,'' says former surgeon general C. Everett Koop, a well-known foe of smoking. ''They are killing several hundred thousand of their customers each year and they need to be replaced. How can they do that? By exploiting foreign markets and young girls, the one group of Americans that have not begun to cut back. It's absolutely deplorable.''

Tobacco use has become the largest preventable cause of death and disease among American women, killing more than 125,000 each year, according to federal health statistics. Recent studies have shown that women who smoke one to four cigarettes a day have two to three times the risk of heart attack as women who do not smoke.

David Beers and Catherine Capellaro / Greenwash 1991

Since the days when Huckleberry Finn fooled his buddies into thinking that the best way to spend an afternoon was with paintbrush in hand, doing Huck's work, the term ''whitewash'' has stood for a trick played on a trusting audience, making them see something much better than what they eventually get. Writing for the progressive monthly magazine Mother Jones, *reporters David Beers and Catherine Capellaro modernize the term and apply it to the deceitful actions of environment-damaging corporations.*

''Greenwash'' details a scenario that combines two major areas of observa-

tion for left-leaning writers today—the worldwide pollution and toxic waste problem and the pull of advertising in shaping our (sometimes inaccurate) perceptions of just how safe a world dominated by corporate interests is. You might want to read this article in conjunction with the advertisement that follows it (''The eagle has landed,'' p. 109) as well as with the other advertisements for corporate consciousness about environmental issues reprinted in the section entitled ''Institutional and Corporate Advertising'' (pp. 69–81). In addition, you might want to contrast Beers and Capellaro's article with the previous experts on cigarette ad campaigns for another view of how the press confronts and exposes the advertisers' ploys.

You're bright, you're ambitious, your finger is on the pulse of Peoria, and ever since you fibbed your way out of your first spanking, you've realized there's a useful vacuum in the part of your brain where shame usually resides. May we suggest a career in greenwashing, the hottest new trend in dissembling for profit?

You gotta be willing to imply that your own dear mother would have liked the way your company clear-cuts redwoods. Louisiana-Pacific's president did it in magazine ads. You gotta be able to write an ad headline like EVERY DAY IS EARTH DAY WITH NUCLEAR ENERGY. It really ran. Let's say a year and a half ago, you immersed a prime San Francisco Bay wetlands area in spilled oil. Could you, without laughing now, or even noticeably perspiring, ceremoniously give the nearest town a bronze statue of John Muir inscribed with your company name? Shell did. Do you have the humongous chutzpah to broadcast the image of wildlife literally clapping for Du Pont, one of the nation's top polluters? How about this extra touch: Beethoven's ''Ode to Joy'' swells in the background. It's been on TV.

The advertising and public-relations industries have long been paid to jujitsu potential anticorporate movements into image builders for their clients. But their attempted co-opting of environmentalism has been so frenzied, so nakedly nineties as to make Orwell's imagination seem stunted. And yet, because most of the media rely on the greenwashers for ad revenue, it's been hard to find anyone who is willing to shout that the emperor has dropped trow. Until now . . .

THE SCRATCH 'N' SNIFF POLLUTION SOLUTION

ARCO shared its clean-air manifesto in a full-page ad in the eco-supplement to *Fortune* right around Earth Day. Under the headline IT'LL HELP CUT OUT AIR POLLUTION, the petroleum giant listed ten things it wants us to do more of, like ''Rideshare'' and ''Combine errands into one trip'' and ''Avoid unnecessary accelerations and braking.'' ARCO printed these on one of those tree-shaped air-fresheners that you hang from your rearview mirror, with a thoughtful dotted line to follow when cutting it out, and the invitation, ''Scratch tree to release scent.'' That'll come in especially handy in the Los Angeles smog belt, where ARCO's Carson refinery has been the second-highest emitter of particulate matter (596 tons), the second-highest of sulfur dioxide (893 tons), and third-highest for total hydrocarbons (1,348 tons). Take the little tree along to Alaska, too, where, in 1985 and 1986 alone, ARCO was cited for 229 excesses of state air-quality standards, most of them involving spewing a particularly foul, black carbon smoke, which the right technology could prevent.

What few realized, until informative ads started appearing, is that without a benevolent hand from big oil, nature itself would get all confused and despondent and just give up. Chevron's ''People Do'' series works this theme especially brazenly, as Justin Lowe, with Hillary Hansen, documented in the *Earth Island Journal* and the *San Francisco Bay Guardian.* Turns out that most of the animal-friendly initiatives that Chevron brags about in its five-to-ten-million-dollar TV and print campaign are required by law, and not voluntary as the ads imply. Example: "On a moonlit California desert, a kit fox senses a prowling coyote," the narrator intones, as we see fox dodge wily coyote by diving into "a cozy den that's designed to keep her snug and safe." Then: "Do people think of things like this just to help an endangered species make it through the night? People do." The artificial-den program is part of Chevron's forced compliance with the Endangered Species Act. When Chevron produced the television ad in 1986, it had only three artificial dens. Two of them were acquired from Gulf Oil when Chevron bought that company, and the third was not so snug: it had been specially built with a cutaway side view for the camera. Producing such a commercial can cost up to $200,000, which would buy a few hundred kit-fox dens. The fox that Chevron filmed, incidentally, was a borrowed and trained captive.

It's hard to pick the boldest lies advertised by slippery oil. In the op-ed-page corner that it rents in the *New York Times,* for example, Mobil asserts, "Just because we get our hands dirty doesn't mean we dirty the environment, too." This is the Mobil that spilled 455,696 gallons of oil from 1984 to 1988, and whose workers contend that lead and benzene at the Beaumont, Texas, plant have been handled so sloppily that they are linked to cancer and birth defects in the area. Mobil's Torrance, California, plant settled a civil complaint in 1989 for hazardous-waste violations.

Still, Texaco deserves a special star. DO IT RIGHT, blares the fat headline over a picture of smiley Texaco senior petroleum engineer Victor Simon and his assurance: "We have a corporate responsibility to do business with a conscience. This includes ensuring that the issues we are all passionate about—the environment and quality of life—are not overlooked. . . . In ever step of our operations, from obtaining emission permits to ensuring on-site safety, simply meeting legislated standards isn't enough. We can and *do* exceed such standards. . . ." Why is this man smiling? In 1989, Texaco was fined $750,000 in the first-ever felony conviction under the Outer Continental Shelf Lands Act, for failing to perform tests of crucial oil-rig blowout-protection equipment, and then fabricating records of those tests. In 1989, Texaco was cited for violations of the Migratory Bird Treaty Act, which protects certain species of birds, including the ones found dead in the oil companies' waste pits. That year, more birds died in oil companies waste pits than from the *Valdez* spill. Also, in 1988, a Texaco subsidiary was ordered to pay the largest settlement ever under California's Hazardous Waste Control Act, $8.95 million for neglecting to properly clean up the area around five thousand corroded, leaking drums of hazardous waste. According to the EPA, Texaco's Port Neches, Texas, refinery poses what may be the highest industrial-site cancer risk in the country.

GARBAGE IN, GARBAGE OUT

Waste Management, Inc., an ad explains, does the favor of "helping the world dispose of its problems." That's green-washspeak for the fact that WMI and its chemical (ChemWaste Management) and nuclear (ChemNuclear) subsidiaries make up the biggest waste-dumping company in the world. Granted, the Waste Management empire didn't create the trillion pounds of toxic waste generated in the United States every year; it just hauls it, burns it, injects it into the earth, and sticks it into landfills. In so doing, it paid out between $20 million and $40 million in environment-related penalties, fines, and settlements in the 1980s. It also was hit with $8.5 million in fines and other settlements for efforts to destroy competitors by price-fixing, etc.

"What sort of a wildlife preserve is this?" asks the narrator for a WMI TV spot, while a soft-focus lens pans over rolling green hills and a butterfly flutters in the foreground. "Part of a scientifically managed sanitary landfill . . . developed by Waste Management." The viewer isn't told that, in 1988, toxics from one WMI landfill leaked into the soil below a canyon occupied by an endangered type of butterfly. Dozens of other landfills tend to endanger hard-strapped communities. In rural, mostly black Emelle, Alabama, CWM has dumped over 3.5 million tons of toxics, and paid one million dollars in environmental penalties. The Emelle hazardous-waste dump—one of the world's largest and still growing—occasionally catches fire, and authorities are resigned to the fact that it will leak into local water sources. Although the data has been challenged, residents say that an independent lab has found toxic chemicals in residents' bodies. Linda Wallace Campbell, an Emelle organizer, says it's no accident that hazardous waste gets dumped in areas like hers, where the average yearly income is nine thousand dollars. "Yeah, they're helping the world dispose of people of color, poor people," says Campbell. "We've got a piece of Love Canal right here."

Another WMI TV classic shows the earth with a list of nasty chemicals scrolling up the screen. Voice-over: "In just three years, we've made over two hundred million pounds of hazardous waste vanish from the face of the earth, destroying it with high-temperature incineration . . . without harm to the environment. We call that making progress." WMI paid a $4,475,000 fine in 1989 because, among other violations, those in charge of its big "state of the art" Chicago incinerator failed to monitor emissions and stop burning deadly PCB wastes when protective scrubbers and stack monitors weren't working. More progress: In 1988, the Illinois EPA temporarily closed the incinerator because (oops) operators disconnected pollution detectors in the stack.

SELL MY MOTHER? HOW MUCH?

"We need everything that's out there. . . . We log to infinity. Because we need it all. It's ours. It's out there, and we need it all. Now." That's what Louisiana-Pacific chairman Harry Merlo, whose company is the biggest producer of redwood, told *Santa Rosa Press Democrat* reporter Mike Geniella a while back. What does a public-relations pro say to a guy like that, especially since, true to his convictions, Merlo has harvested trees faster than they grow, while giving big money to defeat forest-protection initiatives? Get me rewrite!

Here's Merlo in full-page ads that have appeared in *Fortune* and other magazines: "Respect for the environment is nothing new to me. From the time I was a small boy in a poor family of Italian immigrants, I've understood how precious our God-given resources are, and how important it is never to waste them. The lessons I learned from my mother, Clotilde Merlo—lessons of thrift, common sense, hard work, and strength of purpose—I have not forgotten for a single day."

Little Harry also learned from Mrs. Merlo, according to the ad, that "God is in the water." God had better get out and shower off: L-P's Samoa, California, pulp mill, along with the nearby Simpson paper plant, discharges over forty million gallons of effluent into the Pacific Ocean every day. Surfers tired of getting rashes from the resulting "black goo," as they describe it, are, through the Surfrider Foundation, suing. L-P could pay up to seventy-five million dollars if it loses. The judge who denied L-P's motion for dismissal of the suit wrote: "They have essentially exempted themselves from all environmental protection requirements and are therefore free to discharge potential chronically toxic effluent into the waters of the Pacific Ocean with impunity. The position is disingenuous and flies in the face of the Clean Water Act.''

God seems to have forsaken a good portion of Silicon Valley's water, too, since IBM arrived on the scene. The Silicon Valley Toxics Coalition has been documenting IBM's foot-dragging on cleanup of soil and groundwater contamination that they say potentially exposed more than 100,000 residents to chemicals linked to cancer and birth defects. And yet, IBM's denial of this connection may explain its glorious double-pager, which has run in *Scientific American* and other magazines, showing, of all things, a pristine body of water. The headline: IN A CHANGING WORLD, SOME THINGS DESERVE TO REMAIN JUST THE WAY THEY ARE.

Might the ozone layer be one of those deserving things? Well, IBM has promised to phase out its massive chlorofluorocarbon use by 1993, which environmentalists are calling a victory won only after heavy pressure. IBM's San Jose, California, Endicott, New York, and Rochester, Minnesota, facilities were the top three CFC-113 emitters in 1987—over a decade after CFCs were known to shred the ozone layer. Now that IBM is swearing off CFCs, its substitute for washing computer chips will be detergent and distilled water, dried with ultrasound vibration. That technology was around before CFC-113 was introduced. (See *Mother Jones,* December 1989.)

Even if IBM is finally getting around to leaving the ozone alone, Du Pont isn't about to stop messing with it. All those critters on TV applauding to Beethoven are ostensibly jazzed because Du Pont-Conoco is finally double hulling its new oil tankers. Somebody tell the animals that Du Pont is one of the world's largest makers of ozone-shredding chemicals, and plans to continue producing them until at least the year 2000. Du Pont also happened to be the United States' leading toxic polluter in 1988, according to the Citizens Fund report *Poisons in Our Neighborhoods.* Something else to clap about: despite the EPA phaseout of leaded gasoline, Du Pont is still producing lead additives, selling them more and more out of the country. David Schwartzman of Howard University's Geology and Geography department calls these exports ''a crime against children,'' since immature brains and nervous systems are extremely vulnerable to lead poisoning. Now how does ''Ode to Joy'' go again?

FOR THAT GET-UP-AND-GLOW FEELING

POLLUTERS ARE THE REAL ANIMALS. This folksy reminder, scrawled on a sign hoisted by a cute little cartoon bear, adorns a full-page ad for the nuclear industry. Where, then, does that put nuke executives on the food chain? After all, the total accumulation of high-level radioactive waste has nearly doubled since 1980, and will last 250,000 years while we try to solve where to put it. Meanwhile, the volume of low-level radioactive waste has more than doubled, and today bloats three commercial landfills. Nuclear advocates are getting an official ear for their solution: label one-third of it ''below regulatory concern'' and treat it like the coffee grounds in your own trash can. Thus reclassified, low-level radiation could find its way into incinerators, dumps, sewers, and rivers. That could kill up to 250,000 people, a figure based on EPA estimates.

Every day is mishap day with nuclear energy. In fact, the industry has reported 34,300 nuclear ''mishaps,'' nearly ten a day, since 1980. The Nuclear Regulatory Commission concluded that the chances of a severe core meltdown occurring at one of the 112 licensed U.S. plants in the next fifteen years is as high as 45 percent. West German and Swedish scientists have said there is a 70 percent chance of a Chernobyl-scale accident happening in the world every six years. No wonder polls show that U.S. public opposition to nuclear power is at an all-time high.

Which explains those expensive ads trumpeting nuclear power as foe of air pollution and greenhouse gases, and alternative to dependence on messy foreign oil. Just running such ads by nuclear power's propaganda organization, The U.S. Council for Energy Awareness, hasn't afforded enough exposure, as far as the *Wall Street Journal* is concerned. The paper sent reprints to members of Congress, along with a letter, from *WSJ* vice-president for marketing Bernard T. Flanagan, calling them ''informative and thought-provoking.'' Lucrative, too.

The differences between what the greenwashers say and really do is so consistently, as Mrs. Merlo would say, clear cut, that one wonders where they peg the public's gullibility limit. While General Electric trills, ''We bring good things to life,'' it profits from deadly nuclear-weapons work, having helped create the radioactive nightmares at Hanford Nuclear Reservation and the Knolls Atomic Power Lab—hence the on-going boycott of GE. With lovingly rendered animal portraits, GE proudly advertises its sponsorship of National Audubon Society specials on PBS, but neglects to mention that according to Citizens Fund, it ranks number one in Superfund sites and released more cancer-causing chemicals into the environment in 1988 than any other U.S. company. One of the most breathtaking exercises in mock humility is the two-pager taken out by that friend of the environment, the Chemical Manufacturer's Association. The ad literally promises the world: over a picture of the earth runs the headline HANDLE WITH RESPONSIBLE CARE, followed by the group's ''guiding principles,'' like ''To develop and produce chemicals that can be manufactured, transported, used, and disposed of safely.'' Union Carbide, of the Bhopal disaster, is one of the 170 signees.

''It's not that all these ads are untrue. They depict 5 percent of environmental virtue to mask the 95 percent of environmental vice,'' says Greenpeace's media director, Peter Dykstra. ''There's a real moral vacuum in how people deal with advertising.'' Dykstra passes along a prime example of the greenwasher's ethical code, a letter that Greenpeace received from the big New York public relations firm Hill and Knowlton, Inc.

''We need your help. We know from your work that you recognize how critically important it is to reverse the declining quality of our air, land, and water, and to safeguard these resources before they are spoiled forever,'' wrote H&K vice-president Jeffrey L. Christmas, entreating Greenpeace USA's executive director, Peter Bahouth, to help promote a globally televised enviro-concert called Earth '90.

Not long before, the same Hill and Knowlton had written to suspected Mississippi River polluters, warning that Greenpeace might make them a protest target and offering seasoned expertise: ''Hill and Knowlton veterans have worked on almost every major crisis in recent years, including Three Mile Island, Texas Eastern's PCB problem, the dioxin crisis, and Ashland's Ohio River oil spill.'' In case there is any doubt which side H&K represented in all those cases, the letter, leaked by a temp worker, goes on to suggest that firms hire the PR agency to ''develop strategy for counteracting Greenpeace when it reaches [your] facilities. . . .''

H&K's Howard Marder, who wrote the letter, told *Mother Jones* that he sees ''no contradiction'' in the fact that his company tried to make money by both courting and countering Greenpeace. He says that he always advises clients to tell the ''whole truth immediately.'' Did he research the pollution records of any of the companies along the Mississippi before offering to speak for them? No, says Marder, whose letter to one promises: ''We can help select the most effective spokesman to convince the community and media of [your] *credibility*. The *way*

The eagle has landed.

In Oklahoma and Mississippi. Georgia and Alabama. Where few bald eagle nests have produced young in the last 50 years. Using precious eggs and dedicated effort, the Sutton Avian Research Center is successfully raising eaglets from fuzzy to fierce. And releasing them into the habitats bald eagles used to call home. Phillips Petroleum supports this unique program to re-establish our endangered national symbol.

After all, if Man can land an Eagle on the moon, he can surely keep them landing on the earth.

PHILLIPS 66

For more information, contact the George Miksch Sutton Avian Research Center, Inc., P.O. Box 2007, Bartlesville, OK 74005. (918) 336-7778.

[1990]

the message is delivered by the company's spokesman is as important as the message itself.'' The italics are Hill and Knowlton's own. It's an old trick of the trade. Makes a word like credibility seem more credible.

DISCUSSION QUESTIONS

1. Look at the Phillips ad on p. 19 then consider Beers and Capellaro's arguments against the use of such advertising. Does the ad have less power over you after you read the article? Even if you know the facts it hides, does it still prove persuasive on some level? In what specific ways?

2. Do you think the corporations are ethical in presenting such advertisements? When does persuasion become untruth? Compare the ads discussed in this article with any of the product ads in the previous sections. Are one or the other more ''true''?

PRESS

Journalism is literature in a hurry.

MATTHEW ARNOLD

NEWS may be America's best-selling product. Despite the intense competition from radio and television broadcasts, where news is delivered instantaneously and free of charge, well over fifty-eight million Americans are still willing to pay for their daily newspaper. Serving this immense market is an industry built around twenty-three thousand daily and weekly newspapers. The industry ranges from the picturesque one-room office of a country paper, where the news is gathered, written, edited, and printed by a handful of people, to multilevel, worldwide corporate enterprises employing thousands in the strenuous business of compiling, disseminating, and even occasionally making the news. A news item, whether in a two-page rural paper or in that monstrous, practically unfinishable, several-hundred-page Sunday edition of the *New York Times,* needs to be seen, then, as something more than simply a report of current events. To be comprehended fully, the news should be considered in its largest corporate context—as the result of individual and group writing performed under the pressures of advertising revenue, available space, deadlines, audience surveys, ownership policy, editorial selection, and professional competition. The news is not only transmitted information, it is the commodity of newspapers.

The pledge "All the News That's Fit to Print" on the front page of every copy of the *New York Times* reminds us that only news deemed suitable to print has been *selected* for us by editors apparently fastidious in their taste and conscience. The *Times*'s motto, however, once prompted the following slightly cynical parody "All the News That Fits We Print." The joke here works not only at the expense of the *New York Times;* it could easily apply to any large newspaper. A simple experiment shows how relatively small is the percentage of space allotted for what is supposedly a newspaper's main product, news. If you cut out from any newspaper with a fairly large circulation all the commercial and classified advertisements; the theater, movie, radio, and television listings; the national and local gossip; the personal advice columns; the horoscope; the puzzles and games; the cartoons; the letters to the editor; the "human interest" tidbits; and the fillers, you are left with very few of what are, strictly speaking, genuine news items. In short, little of the shape and essence of a modern newspaper remains. The parody of the *Times*'s pledge is right on target. It does seem that readers of most newspapers are given only the news that fits between the spaces reserved for more profitable or entertaining pieces.

To make sure that all the news will fit—in the sense of meeting editorial standards and conforming to the physical confines of the paper—newspapers impose a strictly regulated system of reportorial procedures and conventions. A person who writes for a newspaper must not only contend with tight deadlines but must also satisfy an experienced copy editor whose job is to see to it that the report will conform to the paper's public image and fit easily into its style. The writer must also be aware that the report will compete with all other news and nonnews for prominent display in the layout of each edition. The exigencies of the newspaper business demand that the writer develop a conformable, transferable, and conveniently alterable prose.

Any respected editor will say that clear and concise writing is encouraged. This usually means prose whittled down to short, simple sentences, the sparing use of adjectives and adverbs, a minimal reliance on synonyms, an avoidance of cumbersome syntactical relations, and brief paragraphs with few transitions. Most of the journalism reprinted in this section illustrates writing that conforms to these editorial strictures. Such standards are double-edged: they ensure the kind of writing generally considered to be most appropriate to rendering factual information quickly and precisely, and they guarantee sentences that are uniform and formulaic enough so as to be easily maneuvered into each newspaper's particular editorial requirements and emphases.

A stylistic uniformity for reporting important news stories (feature articles, editorials, and so on, are not so restricted) is enforced even further by a standardized narrative procedure reporters call the inverted pyramid. The opening of a news story conventionally contains all the significant facts—the who, what, when, where, and occasionally the why—and the story tapers off gradually (picture a pyramid upside down), delivering additional facts and embellishments in a diminishing order of importance. Editors assume that their readers will want all the major details of a story right away and that they should have the opportunity to move on to another story as soon as they feel they have absorbed enough information. Consequently, the emphasis in news writing is placed on the "lead," the opening sentences or paragraphs. In writing about a major news event, the reporter is obligated to pack in the principal facts in the first few lines. Because each succeeding sentence becomes less significant and, from an editor's point of view, increasingly dispensable, it is not unusual for reporters to let their prose slacken as their story moves farther away from the top.

By opening the story with its climax, the writer gives up the possibility of sequential development and narrative suspense so that his or her readers can focus on the most important details immediately and the editor can lop off, should he or she need space for something else, the tapered strands of the report without losing any essential points. Therefore, paragraphs in most news stories are not connected to each other within a coherent expository framework. Instead, they can be thought of as self-contained, transferable, and, occasionally, disposable units. As a result, reporters continually face a rather disconcerting problem: they must write in such a manner that enables, even encourages, their audience to stop reading after the main points have been made, and, at the same time, they must make their writing compelling enough so that their readers will want to read on.

Yet reporters contend with more than the difficulties of composition. News stories need to be covered before they can be written. Reporters are men and women often entangled in the intricacies and drawn into the pace of the events they are trying to write about. They compose stories under pressure and in a hurry. To be "on the spot" during an event of some magnitude means most often to get caught up in the uncertain movements of participants and in the prevailing mood of the occasion. The inconveniences are many and unpredictable. One famous reporter, Stephen Crane, accompanying a crew of gun runners headed for Cuba during the insurrection at the close of the last century, was shipwrecked off the coast of Florida (see "Stephen Crane's Own Story") and wound up with a tale far different from the one he had intended to write (see "The Open Boat" in "Classics"). To illustrate most dramatically the kind of difficulties encountered during a strenuous and emotionally trying reportorial assignment, we have included Tom Wicker's recollections of his efforts to cover the assassination of President Kennedy (see "The Assassination").

November 22, 1963, was for Wicker a day of great confusion and physical exhaustion. Though he was on the spot, Wicker was not close enough to the president's car to witness the shooting directly, nor did he even have the opportunity to view the principal characters afterward for more than a few moments. Covering the story of Kennedy's assassination was mainly an ordeal of getting quickly from one good news position to another and of assimilating the disparate and occasionally contradictory details of the event as rapidly as possible. The information came, as Wicker says, "in bits and pieces," and most of the time he had no way of verifying the data. The news story of the assassination was not "out there'' to be copied down leisurely, without risks of inaccuracy. It was a matter of acting on hunches, recovering quickly from wrong turns, finding reliable contacts, getting around physical and bureaucratic obstacles, and all the while trying to put as many details into as coherent a shape as conditions allowed so the story could get to press on time.

Yet the byline report printed in the *New York Times* the next day (see ''Kennedy Is Killed by Sniper'') conveys nothing at all of the frantic pace and exasperating confusions Wicker tells us obstructed his coverage. What Wicker went through that day—whatever public and private significances the event had for him—was not news. The conventions of newspaper reporting are exacting on one point: the reporter must not figure as a main character in his or her own story. If indeed, as Thoreau says, ''It is, after all, always the first person that is speaking,'' we nevertheless need to work quite hard to imagine the ''I'' who is the eyewitness behind Wicker's writing. Not even an effort to read ''between the lines'' could help us reconstruct from his prose alone the tensions of Wicker's day as he hustled around Dallas for the news.

Wicker's report provides us with a fine instance of journalistic workmanship. The assassination was far too important an event for Wicker to take stylistic chances. The *Times* got what it wanted: the straightforward, informative account that is the marrow of news reporting. It saved the expressions of personal grief and the emotional record of the public sentiment appropriate to such occasions for its features and editorials. Part of Wicker's accomplishment in this byline report is his cool, professional manner—he resists the impulse to attract attention to himself as a writer privileged to have been an eyewitness to one of the most sensational news events of the twentieth century. As a narrator, Wicker is never anxious to assure his readers of his presence at the scene. He never pauses in the account to remind us that his perspectives depend on his following the day's developments through several different locations in Dallas. Wicker deliberately avoids commenting on his own emotional connection to an event that we know from his own recollection shocked and grieved him. Nor, as he writes, does he allow himself the liberty of sounding like a worried citizen reflecting on the political and social significance of Kennedy's murder. It is clear that we cannot properly read Wicker's piece as a *personal* account of the assassination. In other words, we can not respond to his writing as if it were—what most of us usually expect writing to be—the disclosure of a particular personality. If Wicker tells us anything at all about himself, it is that he has mastered the discipline of news reporting.

Wicker's prose conforms to all the rules of journalistic style outlined earlier. The writing consists, for the most part, of syntactically simple, declarative sentences. The paragraphs are brief; only one contains as many as five sentences. The first few paragraphs provide the reader with all the crucial information, and the narrative proceeds to register details in what Wicker and his editors presumably considered to be a scale of decreasing importance. Though the narrative procedure would seem to recall the inverted pryamid mentioned above, a closer look at Wicker's prose reveals a movement less narrowing than it would have been had Wicker adhered strictly to that often tyrannizing model. Instead, the narrative proceeds with a spiraling effect, moving from the center outward, moving, that is, away from its lead only to return to it repeatedly, though each time with a new angle and a diminishing emphasis.

Wicker, however, is not fully responsible for the narrative shape the story eventually took. He mentions in his retrospective analysis that he sent off to the *Times* information in ''a straight narrative'' he knew would be cut up by his editors as they decided on the best sequence and appropriate emphases. Although the byline officially recognizes Wicker as the author of the news release, the final report the *Times* printed was, as is usually the case in news writing, the result of a collective activity that included Wicker and several other reporters who assisted him in Dallas, along with a New York staff of rewrite, copy, and managing editors.

While he was writing his report, Wicker must have been acutely conscious of the extensive television coverage given to the assassination. In fact, Wicker tells us that he filled in a few of the gaps in his own report by drawing on some of the information provided by television. Yet, as an antidote to the bewildering discontinuities and the numbing replays of the television reports, Wicker articulated a full, dispassionate recapitulation of the Kennedy assassination, accentuating the official interconnections between people and events rather than the panorama of personalities on location. To illustrate how a journalist responded to a similar incident almost a hundred years earlier, we have included the *New York Herald*'s coverage of President Lincoln's assassination. The April 15, 1865, issue of the *Herald* furnishes us with reportorial styles that were beginning to be conditioned by the invention of the telegraph but were not yet forced into competition with radio and television networks.

Wicker's task as a reporter competing with the live transmission of news was not nearly as problematic as was Thomas O'Toole's assignment for the *Washington Post* to watch and write about the first landing on the moon in July 1969 (see " 'The Eagle Has Landed': Two Men Walk on the Moon"). Given the hermetic nature of such an electronically engineered event as Apollo XI's flight to the moon, O'Toole could not claim a better vantage point for viewing the episode than could anyone else in the world with access to a television set. If the event O'Toole reported was, as he says in his lead, "a show that will long be remembered by the worldwide television audience," then he must have seen his function as that of a television reviewer rather than a privileged eyewitness commentator. In fact, his report makes it clear that the astronauts spent a good deal of their time transforming the moon into a television studio in which they then performed and improvised before the camera. Overshadowed by television, O'Toole's report could be little more than a public transcript of conversations everyone heard and descriptions of what everyone witnessed, punctuated by hyperbolic remarks that could express only the exclamatory mood of millions. Whether viewed as a technological triumph or as a television spectacular, the moon landing came as no special blessing to the newspaper industry. Upstaged by the extensive, unprecedented television coverage, reporters like O'Toole were left with relatively little to do but gather feature stories, collate information from television broadcasts, and turn NASA press releases into intelligible prose.

Each new day does not supply newspapers with a calamity or a triumph—most days newspapers need to find their news in the ordinary occurrences of life. Though a new headline appears daily, it may be merely perfunctory. Given standard newspaper format, one event must always be given more prominence than others. In our selections, we have tried to represent a good portion of the kind of news material you would normally find in American newspapers. We have included many of the standard forms and predominant styles of journalism: headlines, the inverted pyramid of major news stories, the fictional structures of feature stories, the polemical mode of editorials, along with bylines, personal commentaries and columns, interviews, and humorous and whimsical anecdotes. Still, if the subjects for much of the writing that follows strike you as disproportionately unpleasant, that is because the newspaper business generally thrives on the purveyance of "bad news." Pick up any newspaper, and you will be likely to find some account of individual or public violence, organized crime, political scandal, skirmishes with minorities and subcultures, domestic and international conflicts, the catastrophes of floods and earthquakes and fires, and the routine disasters of modern transportation.

The material in this section is not intended as an introduction to the profession of journalism. The texts are meant to be read as examples of the often special language of the reported world. Our purpose is to invite you to consider the compositional procedures and prose styles of various kinds of reporting in order to observe how the reporter's method of writing appropriates public events in a way that makes it especially difficult for any of us to talk or to write about those events independently of the language provided by newspapers.

Staff Correspondent / Important. Assassination of President Lincoln

New York Herald, April 15, 1865

The following series of telegraphic dispatches and reports appeared in the New York Herald *the morning after President Lincoln's assassination.*

IMPORTANT.

•

ASSASSINATION
OF
PRESIDENT LINCOLN.

•

The President Shot at the
Theatre Last Evening.

•

SECRETARY SEWARD
DAGGERED IN HIS BED,
BUT
NOT MORTALLY WOUNDED.

•

Clarence and Frederick Seward Badly Hurt.

•

ESCAPE OF THE ASSASSINS.

•

Intense Excitement in
Washington.

•

Scene at the Deathbed of
Mr. Lincoln.

•

FIRST DISPATCH

Washington, April 14, 1865.

Assassination has been inaugurated in Washington. The bowie knife and pistol have been applied to President Lincoln and Secretary Seward. The former was shot in the throat, while at Ford's theatre to-night. Mr. Seward was badly cut about the neck, while in his bed at his residence.

SECOND DISPATCH

Washington, April 14, 1865.

An attempt was made about ten o'clock this evening to assassinate the President and Secretary Seward. The President was shot at Ford's Theatre. Result not yet known. Mr. Seward's throat was cut, and his son badly wounded.

There is intense excitement here.

DETAILS OF THE ASSASSINATION

Washington, April 14, 1865.

Washington was thrown into an intense excitement a few minutes before eleven o'clock this evening, by the announcement that the President and Secretary Seward had been assassinated and were dead.

The wildest excitement prevailed in all parts of the city. Men, women and children, old and young, rushed to and fro, and the rumors were magnified until we had nearly every member of the Cabinet killed. Some time elapsed before authentic data could be ascertained in regard to the affair.

The President and Mrs. Lincoln were at Ford's theatre, listening to the performance of *The American Cousin,* occupying a box in the second tier. At the close of the third act a person entered the box occupied by the President, and shot Mr. Lincoln in the head. The shot entered the back of his head, and came out above the temple.

The assassin then jumped from the box upon the stage and ran across to the other side, exhibiting a dagger in his hand, flourishing it in a tragical manner, shouting the same words repeated by the desperado at Mr. Seward's house, adding to it, "The South is avenged," and then escaped from the back entrance to the stage, but in his passage dropped his pistol and his hat.

Mr. Lincoln fell forward from his seat, and Mrs. Lincoln fainted.

The moment the astonished audience could realize what had happened, the President was taken and carried to Mr. Peterson's house, in Tenth Street, opposite to the theatre. Medical aid was immediately sent for, and the wound was at first supposed to be fatal, and it was announced that he could not live, but at half-past twelve he is still alive, though in a precarious condition.

As the assassin ran across the stage, Colonel J.B. Stewart, of this city, who was occupying one of the front seats in the orchestra, on the same side of the house as the box occupied by Mr. Lincoln, sprang to the stage and followed him; but he was obstructed in his passage across the stage by the fright of the actors, and reached the back door about three seconds after the assassin had passed out. Colonel Stewart got to the street just in time to see him mount his horse and ride away.

The operation shows that the whole thing was a preconcerted plan. The person who fired the pistol was a man about thirty years of age, about five feet nine, spare built, fair skin, dark hair, apparently bushy, with a large moustache. Laura Keene and the leader of the orchestra declare that they recognized him as J. Wilkes Booth the actor, and a rabid secessionist. Whoever he was, it is plainly evident that he thoroughly understood the theatre and all the approaches and modes of escape to the stage. A person not familiar with the theatre could not have possibly made his escape so well and quickly.

The alarm was sounded in every quarter. Mr. Stanton was notified, and immediately left his house.

All the other members of the Cabinet escaped attack.

Cavalrymen were sent out in all directions, and dispatches sent out to all the fortifications, and it is thought they will be captured.

About half-past ten o'clock this evening a tall, well dressed man made his appearance at Secretary Seward's residence, and applied for admission. He was refused admission by the servant, when the desperado stated that he had a prescription from the Surgeon General, and that he was ordered to deliver it in person. He was still refused, except upon the written order of the physician. This he pretended to show, and pushed by the servant and rushed up stairs to Mr. Seward's room. He was met at the door by Mr. Fred Seward, who notified him that he was master of the house, and would take charge of the medicine. After a few words had passed between them he dodged by Fred Seward and rushed to the Secretary's bed and struck him in the neck with a dagger, and also in the breast.

It was supposed at first that Mr. Seward was killed instantly, but it was found afterwards that the wound was not mortal.

Major Wm. H. Seward, Jr., paymaster, was in the room, and rushed to the defense of his father, and was badly cut in the *melee* with the assassin, but not fatally.

The desperado managed to escape from the house, and was prepared for escape by having a horse at the door. He immediately mounted his horse, and sung out the motto of the State of Virginia, "*Sic Semper Tyrannis!*" and rode cff.

Surgeon General Barnes was immediately sent for, and he examined Mr. Seward and pronounced him safe. His wounds were not fatal. The jugular vein was not cut, nor the wound in the breast deep enough to be fatal.

Washington, April 15—1 A.M.

The streets in the vicinity of Ford's Theatre are densely crowded by an anxious and excited crowd. A guard has been placed across Tenth Street and F and K Streets, and only official persons and particular friends of the President are allowed to pass.

The popular heart is deeply stirred, and the deepest indignation against leading rebels is freely expressed.

The scene at the house where the President lies in *extremis* is very affecting. Even Secretary Stanton is affected to tears.

When the news spread through the city that the President had been shot, the people, with pale faces and compressed lips, crowded every place where there was the slightest chance of obtaining information in regard to the affair.

After the President was shot, Lieutenant Rathbun, caught the assassin by the arm, who immediately struck him with a knife, and jumped from the box, as before stated.

The popular affection for Mr. Lincoln has been shown by this diabolical assassination, which will bring eternal infamy, not only upon its authors, but upon the hellish cause which they desire to avenge.

Vice President Johnson arrived at the White House, where the President lies, about one o'clock, and will remain with him to the last.

The President's family are in attendance upon him also.

As soon as intelligence could be got to the War Department, the electric telegraph and the Signal corps were put in requisition to endeavor to prevent the escape of the assassins, and all the troops around Washington are under arms.

Popular report points to a somewhat celebrated actor of known secession proclivities as the assassin; but it would be unjust to name him until some further evidence of his guilt is obtained. It is rumored that the person alluded to is in custody.

The latest advices from Secretary Seward reveals more desperate work there than at first supposed. Seward's wounds are not in themselves fatal, but, in connection with his recent injuries, and the great loss of blood he has sustained, his recovery is questionable.

It was Clarence A. Seward, instead of William H. Seward, Jr., who was wounded. Fred Seward was also badly cut, as were also three nurses, who were in attendance upon the Secretary, showing that a desperate struggle took place there. The wounds of the whole party were dressed.

One o'clock A.M.

The President is perfectly senseless, and there is not the slightest hope of his surviving. Physicians believe that he will die before morning. All of his Cabinet, except Secretary Seward, are with him. Speaker Colfax, Senator Farwell, of Maine, and many other gentlemen, are also at the house awaiting the termination.

The scene at the President's bedside is described by one who witnessed it as most affecting. He was surrounded by his Cabinet ministers, all of whom were bathed in tears, not even excepting Mr. Stanton, who, when informed by Surgeon General Barnes, that the President could not live until morning, exclaimed, "Oh, no, General; no—no;" and with an impulse, natural as it was unaffected, immediately sat down on a chair near his bedside and wept like a child.

Senator Sumner was seated on the right of the President's couch, near the head, holding the right hand of the President in his own. He was sobbing like a woman, with his head bowed down almost on the pillow of the bed on which the President was lying.

Two o'clock A.M.

The President is still alive, but there is no improvement in his condition.

DISCUSSION QUESTION

1. How does the *Herald* account differ from Wicker's report of President Kennedy's assassination? How is the president described in each? Which account do you think describes the assassination most vividly? Most informatively? With the most feeling?

Stephen Crane / Stephen Crane's Own Story

[*He Tells How the* Commodore *Was Wrecked and How He Escaped*] *New York Press*, January 7, 1897

Though Stephen Crane had not witnessed a single battle before he wrote The Red Badge of Courage *in 1895, the immense popularity of the novel helped to establish a career for him as a leading war correspondent. Crane spent most of his remaining years traveling, despite ill health, to cover the Greco-Turkish, the Boer, and the Spanish American Wars.*

"Stephen Crane's Own Story" details his experiences during the wreck of the Commodore, *a cargo ship carrying guns and ammunition to Cuban insurgents. This account served as the basis for Crane's well-known short story "The Open-Boat" (see "Classics").*

Jacksonville, Fla., Jan. 6.—It was the afternoon of New Year's. The Commodore lay at her dock in Jacksonville and negro stevedores processioned steadily toward her with box after box of ammunition and bundle after bundle of rifles. Her hatch, like the mouth of a monster, engulfed them. It might have been the feeding time of some legendary creature of the sea. It was in broad daylight and the crowd of gleeful Cubans on the pier did not forbear to sing the strange patriotic ballads of their island.

Everything was perfectly open. The Commodore was cleared with a cargo of arms and munition for Cuba. There was none of that extreme modesty about the proceeding which had marked previous departures of the famous tug. She loaded up as placidly as if she were going to carry oranges to New York, instead of

Remingtons to Cuba. Down the river, furthermore, the revenue cutter Boutwell, the old isosceles triangle that protects United States interests in the St. John's, lay at anchor, with no sign of excitement aboard her.

EXCHANGING FAREWELLS

On the decks of the Commodore there were exchanges of farewells in two languages. Many of the men who were to sail upon her had many intimates in the old Southern town, and we who had left our friends in the remote North received our first touch of melancholy on witnessing these strenuous and earnest goodbys.

It seems, however, that there was more difficulty at the custom house. The officers of the ship and the Cuban leaders were detained there until a mournful twilight settled upon the St. John's, and through a heavy fog the lights of Jacksonville blinked dimly. Then at last the Commodore swung clear of the dock, amid a tumult of goodbys. As she turned her bow toward the distant sea the Cubans ashore cheered and cheered. In response the Commodore gave three long blasts of her whistle, which even to this time impressed me with their sadness. Somehow, they sounded as wails.

Then at last we began to feel like filibusters. I don't suppose that the most stolid brain could contrive to believe that there is not a mere trifle of danger in filibustering, and so as we watched the lights of Jacksonville swing past us and heard the regular thump, thump, thump of the engines we did considerable reflecting.

But I am sure that there were no hifalutin emotions visible upon any of the faces which fronted the speeding shore. In fact, from cook's boy to captain, we were all enveloped in a gentle satisfaction and cheerfulness. But less than two miles from Jacksonville, this atrocious fog caused the pilot to ram the bow of the Commodore hard upon the mud and in this ignominious position we were compelled to stay until daybreak.

HELP FROM THE BOUTWELL

It was to all of us more than a physical calamity. We were now no longer filibusters. We were men on a ship stuck in the mud. A certain mental somersault was made once more necessary.

But word had been sent to Jacksonville to the captain of the revenue cutter Boutwell, and Captain Kilgore turned out promptly and generously fired up his old triangle, and came at full speed to our assistance. She dragged us out of the mud, and again we headed for the mouth of the river. The revenue cutter pounded along a half mile astern of us, to make sure that we did not take on board at some place along the river men for the Cuban army.

This was the early morning of New Year's Day, and the fine golden southern sunlight fell full upon the river. It flashed over the ancient Boutwell, until her white sides gleamed like pearl, and her rigging was spun into little threads of gold.

Cheers greeted the old Commodore from passing ship and from the shore. It was a cheerful, almost merry, beginning to our voyage. At Mayport, however, we changed our river pilot for a man who could take her to open sea, and again the Commodore was beached. The Boutwell was fussing around us in her venerable way, and, upon seeing our predicament, she came again to assist us, but this time, with engines reversed, the Commodore dragged herself away from the grip of the sand and again headed for the open sea.

The captain of the revenue cutter grew curious. He hailed the Commodore: "Are you fellows going to sea to-day?"

Captain Murphy of the Commodore called back: "Yes, sir."

And then as the whistle of the Commodore saluted him, Captain Kilgore doffed his cap and said: "Well, gentlemen, I hope you have a pleasant cruise," and this was our last word from shore.

When the Commodore came to enormous rollers that flew over the bar a certain light-heartedness departed from the ship's company.

SLEEP IMPOSSIBLE

As darkness came upon the waters, the Commodore was a broad, flaming path of blue and silver phosphorescence, and as her stout bow lunged at the great black waves she threw flashing, roaring cascades to either side. And all that was to be heard was the rhythmical and mighty pounding of the engines. Being an inexperienced filibuster, the writer had undergone considerable mental excitement since the starting of the ship, and in consequence he had not yet been to sleep and so I went to the first mate's bunk to indulge myself in all the physical delights of holding one's-self in bed. Every time the ship lurched I expected to be fired through a bulkhead, and it was neither amusing nor instructive to see in the dim light a certain accursed valise aiming itself at the top of my stomach with every lurch of the vessel.

THE COOK IS HOPEFUL

The cook was asleep on a bench in the galley. He is of a portly and noble exterior, and by means of a checker board he had himself wedged on this bench in such a manner the motion of the ship would be unable to dislodge him. He woke as I entered the galley and delivered himself of some dolorous sentiments: "God," he said in the course of his observations, "I don't feel right about this ship, somehow. It strikes me that something is going to happen to us. I don't know what it is, but the old ship is going to get it in the neck, I think."

"Well, how about the men on board of her?" said I. "Are any of us going to get out, prophet?"

"Yes," said the cook. "Sometimes I have these damned feelings come over me, and they are always right, and it seems to me, somehow, that you and I will both get out and meet again somewhere, down at Coney Island, perhaps, or some place like that."

ONE MAN HAS ENOUGH

Finding it impossible to sleep, I went back to the pilot house. An old seaman, Tom Smith, from Charleston, was then at the wheel. In the darkness I could not see Tom's face, except at those times when he leaned forward to scan the compass and the dim light from the box came upon his weatherbeaten features.

"Well, Tom," said I, "how do you like filibustering?"

He said "I think I am about through with it. I've been in a number of these expeditions and the pay is good, but I think if I ever get back safe this time I will cut it."

I sat down in the corner of the pilot house and almost went to sleep. In the meantime the captain came on duty and he was standing near me when the chief engineer rushed up the stairs and cried hurriedly to the captain that there was something wrong in the engine room. He and the captain departed swiftly.

I was drowsing there in my corner when the captain returned, and, and going to the door of the little room directly back of the pilot house, he cried to the Cuban leader:

"Say, can't you get those fellows to work. I can't talk their language and I can't get them started. Come on and get them going."

HELPS IN THE FIREROOM

The Cuban leader turned to me and said: "Go help in the fireroom. They are going to bail with buckets."

The engine room, by the way, represented a scene at this time taken from the middle kitchen of hades. In the first place, it was insufferably warm, and the lights burned faintly in a way to cause mystic and grewsome shadows. There was a quantity of soapish sea water swirling and sweeping and swishing among machinery that roared and banged and clattered and steamed, and, in the second place, it was a devil of a ways down below.

Here I first came to know a certain young oiler named Billy Higgins. He was sloshing around this inferno filling buckets with water and passing them to a chain of men that extended up the ship's side. Afterward we got orders to change our point of attack on water and to operate through a little door on the windward side of the ship that led into the engine room.

NO PANIC ON BOARD

During this time there was much talk of pumps out of order and many other statements of a mechanical kind, which I did not altogether comprehend but understood to mean that there was a general and sudden ruin in the engine room.

There was no particular agitation at this time, and even later there was never a panic on board the Commodore. The party of men who worked with Higgins and me at this time were all Cubans, and we were under the direction of the Cuban leaders. Presently we were ordered again to the afterhold, and there was some hesitation about going into the abominable fireroom again, but Higgins dashed down the companion way with a bucket.

LOWERING BOATS

The heat and hard work in the fireroom affected me and I was obliged to come on deck again. Going forward, I heard as I went talk of lowering the boats. Near the corner of the galley the mate was talking with a man.

"Why don't you send up a rocket?" said this unknown man. And the mate replied: "What the hell do we want to send up a rocket for? The ship is all right."

Returning with a little rubber and cloth overcoat, I saw the first boat about to be lowered. A certain man was the first person in this first boat, and they were handing him in a valise about as large as a hotel. I had not entirely recovered from astonishment and pleasure in witnessing this noble deed when I saw another valise go to him.

HUMAN HOG APPEARS

This valise was not perhaps so large as a hotel, but it was a big valise anyhow. Afterward there went to him something which looked to me like an overcoat.

Seeing the chief engineer leaning out of his little window, I remarked to him: "What do you think of that blank, blank, blank?"

"Oh, he's a bird," said the old chief.

It was now that was heard the order to get away the lifeboat, which was stowed on top of the deckhouse. The deckhouse was a mighty slippery place, and with each roll of the ship, the men there thought themselves likely to take headers into the deadly black sea.

Higgins was on top of the deckhouse, and, with the first mate and two colored stokers, we wrestled with that boat, which, I am willing to swear, weighed as much as a Broadway cable car. She might have been spiked to the deck. We could have pushed a little brick schoolhouse along a corduroy road as easily as we could have moved this boat. But the first mate got a tackle to her from a leeward davit, and on the deck below the captain corralled enough men to make an impression upon the boat.

We were ordered to cease hauling then, and in this lull the cook of the ship came to me and said: "What are you going to do?"

I told him of my plans, and he said:

"Well, my God, that's what I am going to do."

A WHISTLE OF DESPAIR

Now the whistle of the Commodore had been turned loose, and if there ever was a voice of despair and death, it was in the voice of this whistle. It had gained a new tone. It was as if its throat was already choked by the water, and this cry on the sea at night, with a wind blowing the spray over the ship, and the waves roaring over the bow, and swirling white along the decks, was to each of us probably a song of man's end.

It was now that the first mate showed a sign of losing his grip. To us who were trying in all stages of competence and experience to launch the lifeboat he raged in all terms of fiery satire and hammerlike abuse. But the boat moved at last and swung down toward the water.

Afterward, when I went aft, I saw the captain standing, with his arm in a sling, holding on to a stay with his one good hand and directing the launching of the boat. He gave me a five-gallon jug of water to hold, and asked me what I was going to do. I told him what I thought was about the proper thing, and he told me then that the cook had the same idea, and ordered me to go forward and be ready to launch the ten-foot dingy.

IN THE TEN-FOOT DINGY

I remember well that he turned then to swear at a colored stoker who was prowling around, done up in life preservers until he looked like a feather bed. I went forward with my five-gallon jug of water, and when the captain came we launched the dingy, and they put me over the side to fend her off from the ship with an oar.

They handed me down the water jug, and then the cook came into the boat, and we sat there in the darkness, wondering why, by all our hopes of future happiness, the captain was so long in coming over to the side and ordering us away from the doomed ship.

The captain was waiting for the other boat to go. Finally he hailed in the darkness: "Are you all right, Mr. Graines?"

The first mate answered: "All right, sir."

"Shove off, then," cried the captain.

The captain was just about to swing over the rail when a dark form came forward and a voice said: "Captain, I go with you."

The captain answered: "Yes. Billy; get in."

HIGGINS LAST TO LEAVE SHIP

It was Billy Higgins, the oiler. Billy dropped into the boat and a moment later the captain followed, bringing with him an end of about forty yards of lead line. The other end was attached to the rail of the ship.

As we swung back to leeward the captain said: "Boys, we will stay right near the ship till she goes down."

This cheerful information, of course, filled us all with glee. The line kept us headed properly into the wind, and as we rode over the monstrous waves we saw upon each rise the swaying lights of the dying Commodore.

When came the gray shade of dawn, the form of the Commodore grew slowly clear to us as our little ten-foot boat rose over each swell. She was floating with such an air of buoyancy that we laughed when we had time, and said "What a gag it would be on those other fellows if she didn't sink at all."

But later we saw men aboard of her, and later still they began to hail us.

HELPING THEIR MATES

I had forgot to mention that previously we had loosened the end of the lead line and dropped much further to leeward. The men on board were a mystery to us, of course, as we had seen all the boats leave the ship. We rowed back to the ship, but did not approach too near, because we were four men in a ten-foot boat, and we knew that the touch of a hand on our gunwale would assuredly swamp us.

The first mate cried out from the ship that the third boat had foundered alongside. He cried that they had made rafts, and wished us to tow them.

The captain said, "All right."

Their rafts were floating astern. "Jump in!" cried the captain, but there was a singular and most harrowing hesitation. There were five white men and two negroes. This scene in the gray light of morning impressed one as would a view into some place where ghosts move slowly. These seven men on the stern of the sinking Commodore were silent. Save the words of the mate to the captain there was no talk. Here was death, but here also was a most singular and indefinable kind of fortitude.

Four men, I remember, clambered over the railing and stood there watching the cold, steely sheen of the sweeping waves.

"Jump," cried the captain again.

The old chief engineer first obeyed the order. He landed on the outside raft and the captain told him how to grip the raft and he obeyed as promptly and as docilely as a scholar in riding school.

THE MATE'S MAD PLUNGE

A stoker followed him, and then the first mate threw his hands over his head and plunged into the sea. He had no life belt and for my part, even when he did this horrible thing, I somehow felt that I could see in the expression of his hands, and in the very toss of his head, as he leaped thus to death, that it was rage, rage, rage unspeakable that was in his heart at the time.

And then I saw Tom Smith, the man who was going to quit filibustering after this expedition, jump to a raft and turn his face toward us. On board the Commodore three men strode, still in silence and with their faces turned toward us. One man had his arms folded and was leaning against the deckhouse. His feet were crossed, so that the toe of his left foot pointed downward. There they stood gazing at us, and neither from the deck nor from the rafts was a voice raised. Still was there this silence.

TRIED TO TOW THE RAFTS

The colored stoker on the first raft threw us a line and we began to tow. Of course, we perfectly understood the absolute impossibility of any such thing; our dingy was within six inches of the water's edge, there was an enormous sea running, and I knew that under the circumstances a tugboat would have no light task in moving these rafts.

But we tried it, and would have continued to try it indefinitely, but that something critical came to pass. I was at an oar and so faced the rafts. The cook controlled the line. Suddenly the boat began to go backward and then we saw this negro on the first raft pulling on the line hand over hand and drawing us to him.

He had turned into a demon. He was wild—wild as a tiger. He was crouched on this raft and ready to spring. Every muscle of him seemed to be turned into an elastic spring. His eyes were almost white. His face was the face of a lost man reaching upward, and we knew that the weight of his hand on our gunwale doomed us.

THE COMMODORE SINKS

The cook let go of the line. We rowed around to see if we could not get a line from the chief engineer, and all this time, mind you, there were no shrieks, no groans, but silence, silence and silence, and then the Commodore sank.

She lurched to windward, then swung afar back, righted and dove into the sea, and the rafts were suddenly swallowed by this frightful maw of the ocean. And then by the men on the ten-foot dingy were words said that were still not words—something far beyond words.

The lighthouse of Mosquito Inlet stuck up above the horizon like the point of a pin. We turned our dingy toward the shore.

The history of life in an open boat for thirty hours would no doubt be instructive for the young, but none is to be told here and now. For my part I would prefer to tell the story at once, because from it would shine the splendid manhood of Captain Edward Murphy and of William Higgins, the oiler, but let it suffice at this time to say that when we were swamped in the surf and making the best of our way toward the shore the captain gave orders amid the wildness of the breakers as clearly as if he had been on the quarter deck of a battleship.

John Kitchell of Daytona came running down the beach, and as he ran the air was filled with clothes. If he had pulled a single lever and undressed, even as the fire horses harness, he could not seem to me to have stripped with more speed. He dashed into the water and dragged the cook. Then he went after the captain, but the captain sent him to me, and then it was that he saw Billy Higgins lying with his forehead on sand that was clear of the water, and he was dead.

Francis Pharcellus Church / Is There a Santa Claus?

New York Sun, December 31, 1897

Francis Pharcellus Church (1839–1906) was not eager to reply to the letter asking for his newspaper's official stance on the existence of Santa Claus, but papers around the world have not been at all reluctant to reprint the editorial Church finally did write. The New York Sun, *which first printed the piece, was noted at the time for its clear, colorful writing—a reputation it owed in large part to Church's prose.*

Thirty-seven years after Church wrote "Yes, Virginia, there is a Santa Claus," Heywood Broun countered with "There isn't any Santa Claus" in the New York World-Telegram. *Broun's editorial* *(see p. 127)* *responds to Church's famous letter and should be contrasted to it.*

We take pleasure in answering at once and thus prominently the communication below, expressing at the same time our great gratification that its faithful author is numbered among the friends of The Sun.

Dear Editor:

I am 8 years old.

Some of my little friends say there is no Santa Claus.

Papa says "If you see it in *The Sun* it's so."

Please tell me the truth, is there a Santa Claus?

Virginia O'Hanlon,
115 West 95th Street

Virginia, your little friends are wrong. They have been affected by the skepticism of a skeptical age. They do not believe except they see. They think that nothing can be which is not comprehensible by their little minds. All minds Virginia, whether they be men's or children's, are little. In this great universe of ours man is a mere insect, an ant, in his intellect, as compared with the boundless world about him, as measured by the intelligence capable of grasping the whole of truth and knowledge.

Yes, Virginia, there is a Santa Claus. He exists as certainly as love and generosity and devotion exist, and you know that they abound and give to your life its highest beauty and joy. Alas! How dreary would be the world if there were no Santa Claus! It would be as dreary as if there were no Virginias. There would be no childlike faith then, no poetry, no romance to make tolerable this existence. We should have no enjoyment, except in sense and sight. The eternal light with which childhood fills the world would be extinguished.

Not believe in Santa Claus! You might as well not believe in fairies! You might get your papa to hire men to watch in all the chimneys on Christmas Eve to catch Santa Claus, but even if they did not see Santa Claus coming down, what would that prove? Nobody sees Santa Claus, but that is no sign that there is no Santa Claus. The most real things in the world are those that neither children nor men can see. Did you ever see fairies dancing on the lawn? Of course not, but that's no proof that they are not there. Nobody can conceive or imagine all the wonders there are unseen and unseeable in the world.

You tear apart the baby's rattle and see what makes the noise inside but there is a veil covering the unseen world which not the strongest man, nor even the united strength of all the strongest men that ever lived, could tear apart. Only faith, fancy, poetry, love, romance, can push aside that curtain and view and picture the supernal beauty and glory beyond. Is it all real? Ah, Virginia, in all this world there is nothing else real and abiding.

No Santa Claus! Thank God he lives and he lives forever. A thousand years from now, Virginia, nay ten times ten thousand years from now, he will continue to make glad the heart of childhood.

Heywood Broun / There Isn't a Santa Claus

New York World-Telegram, December 20, 1934

"After we have shot Santa Claus what can be put in his place?" Heywood Broun asks at the end of his rebuttal to Francis Pharcellus Church's famous editorial, "Is There a Santa Claus?" Though seriously opposed to Church's position, Brown was not the Scrooge his question implies. Writing during the Depression, Broun was as considerate of the disappointment of the poor as Church was of the disillusionment of the innocent.

Broun (1888–1939) was the first president of the American Newspaper Guild and a one-time candidate for Congress on the Socialist Party ticket. He was an important and influential journalist in New York throughout his distinguished career.

Almost any day now *The Sun* will reprint the letter from a little girl about Santa Claus and what the editor said in reply. I am sorry I can't remember the names. This annual tribute to Santa Claus has always left me cold, and I grow more chilly to the piece as the years roll on.

In the first place, the little girl showed a reasonable degree of skepticism. She was just about ready to throw off the shackles of an old myth.

The editor clamped them on again. He didn't tell her the truth. Possibly this bad precedent may account for many editorials on other subjects which have appeared from time to time in various papers.

I am all for legends and fairy stories and ancient customs. A folk story is generally true in spirit no matter how fantastic its details. It is a sort of parable built upon the accumulated wisdom of the ages.

But I have a grievance against the figure called Santa Claus. Unlike most myths, the tale of the old gentleman and his reindeer glorifies an untruth. It warps the minds of the very young with a most pernicious notion. To be sure, the average girl or boy finds out the fake about the age of 3 or 4. The child of 6 who still believes in Santa Claus I would set down as definitely backward.

But even after the literal belief is gone there lingers in the mind a yearning for some other sort of Santa Claus. Oppressed people of various kinds sometimes go from the cradle to the grave without registering any adequate protest against their lot. They are waiting for the sound of the sleigh bells. Santa Claus will come down the chimney and bestow those rights and necessities which they lack. He may be the inspired leader, or he is sent in the guise of some governmental agency or act of legislation.

Naturally, it would be folly to deny that leadership and legislation may nick deeply into many problems, and for my own part I do believe in a paternalistic government. Even so complete reliance should not be placed on any of these three factors or even on them all in combination. There isn't any Santa Claus. Groups of men and women can obtain their hopes and desires only by massing together and going out to fight and agitate for their objectives. It is far more satisfactory to pick an orange directly from the tree than to find it in the toe of your stocking.

Harsh names are hurled at those who go out telling little children that Santa Claus is a fake. These disciples of the whole truth are called cynical and crabbed and spoilsports. But man must find out sooner or later that he stands on his own feet and this information might as well come early rather than late.

If anybody intrusted a baby to my tender care I would spring the truth about Santa Claus the instant the child could walk. I'd say, "And now, fine fellow, you have achieved the art of locomotion. You can go just as far and as fast as your feet will carry you. Forget about the reindeer. They make indifferent draft animals and singularly tough steak. Let me hear no nonsense out of you about Santa Claus. You and I are rational human beings up to the extent of our ability, I hope."

I even wonder whether children do get a great deal of fun out of the old gentleman in the sleigh. No very warm memories linger in my mind. He gave me a wakeful night once a year. Always I waited with rather more fear than anticipation for the sound of his fat belly scraping down the chimney. It gave me a sense of insecurity. If Santa Claus could sneak up on me in that way so might the bogey man, or any evil witch of whom I had read in the fairy books.

As a matter of fact, it was my annual inclination to sell Santa Claus short. My invariable bet was that his gifts would be disappointing. You see, I took the story very literally. It was said that Santa Claus would be lavish and generous with only those children who were very good and had a year's record of complete compliance to all the orders of their elders. No wonder I was bearish on the entire proposition!

In childhood, as in later life, everybody hopes for more than he is likely to get—particularly if the gifts are to be dropped in his lap. The Santa Claus myth has made for more disappointment than joy, if you look over the statistics very carefully. I know of many districts in the large and crowded cities where the old gentlemen couldn't muster as much as a single vote. Of course, from my point of view, it would be better to hold the election the day after Christmas rather than the night before.

The question may be asked, "After we have shot Santa Claus what can be put in his place?" I think we don't need a single figure. How about just centering the spirit of the day around the factor of universal fellowship? Not one Santa Claus but a hundred million!

Jack Lait / Dillinger "Gets His"

International News Service, July 23, 1934

On a steamy July evening in 1934, after having seen Clark Gable and William Powell star in a popular gangster film, Manhattan Melodrama, *John Dillinger, "Public Enemy No. 1," left a run-down movie house on Chicago's East Side and walked into the waiting bullets of federal police forces. By all accounts one of the most notorious criminals of modern times, Dillinger had blazed out a legendary career for himself that had all the earmarks of best-selling detective fiction: daring bank robberies, raids on police arsenals, bloody shoot-outs, bold escapes from prison, along with disguises, blurred fingerprints, and plastic surgery to help him defy what was then described as "the greatest manhunt in contemporary criminal annals." Dillinger eventually found the heat of the limelight deadly. Betrayed by one of the many women he supported, Dillinger finally fell victim to the facts that fed the fictions he provoked.*

Jack Lait, a hard-nosed reporter who later took over as editor of the New York Daily Mirror, *turned out his scoop for the International News Service, an agency set up by William Randolph Hearst in 1909 to offer news items to a network of morning newspapers.*

John Dillinger, ace bad man of the world, got his last night—two slugs through his heart and one through his head. He was tough and he was shrewd, but wasn't as tough and shrewd as the Federals, who never close a case until the end. It took twenty-seven of them to end Dillinger's career, and their strength came out of his weakness—a woman.

Dillinger was put on the spot by a tip-off to the local bureau of the Department of Justice. It was a feminine voice that Melvin H. Purvis, head of the Chicago office, heard. He had waited long for it.

It was Sunday, but Uncle Sam doesn't observe any NRA[1] and works seven days a week.

The voice told him that Dillinger would be at a little third-run movie house, the Biograph, last night—that he went there every night and usually got there about 7:30. It was almost 7:30 then. Purvis sent out a call for all men within reach and hustled all men on hand with him. They waited more than an hour. They knew from the informer that he must come out, turn left, turn again into a dark alley where he parked his Ford-8 coupé.

Purvis himself stood at the main exit. He had men on foot and in parked inconspicuous cars strung on both sides of the alley. He was to give the signal. He had ascertained about when the feature film, *Manhattan Melodrama,* would end. Tensely eying his wrist watch he stood. Then the crowd that always streams out when the main picture finishes came. Purvis had seen Dillinger when he was brought through from Arizona to Crown Point, Indiana, and his heart pounded as he saw again the face that has been studied by countless millions on the front pages of the world.

Purvis gave the signal. Dillinger did not see him. Public Enemy No. 1 lit a cigarette, strolled a few feet to the alley with the mass of middle-class citizens going in that direction, then wheeled left.

A Federal man, revolver in hand, stepped from behind a telegraph pole at the mouth of the passage. "Hello, John," he said, almost whispered, his voice husky with the intensity of the classic melodrama. Dillinger went with lightning right hand for his gun, a .38 Colt automatic. He drew it from his trousers pocket.

But, from behind, another government agent pressed the muzzle of his service revolver against Dillinger's back and fired twice. Both bullets went through the bandit's heart.

He staggered, his weapon clattered to the asphalt paving, and as he went three more shots flashed. One bullet hit the back of his head, downward, as he was falling, and came out under his eye.

Police cleared the way for the police car which was there in a few minutes. The police were there not because they were in on the capture, but because the sight of so many mysterious men around the theater had scared the manager into thinking he was about to be stuck up and he had called the nearest station.

[1]National Recovery Administration, a New Deal Agency that, among other functions, regulated hours of work in industry.

When the detectives came on the run, Purvis intercepted them and told them what was up. They called headquarters and more police came, but with instructions to stand by and take orders from Purvis.

Dillinger's body was rushed to Alexian Brothers' hospital in a patrol wagon. There were no surgeons in it. But the policeman knew he was dead, and at the entrance of the hospital, where a kindly priest in a long cassock had come to the door to see who might be in need of help, the driver was ordered to the morgue.

I was in a taxi that caught up with the police car at the hospital, and we followed across town to the old morgue. No one bothered us, though we went fifty miles an hour.

There was no crowd then. We pulled in. Strong arms carried the limp, light form of the man who had been feared by a great government through that grim door of many minor tragedies. It lay on a rubber stretcher.

In the basement, the receiving ward of the last public hospice of the doomed, they stripped the fearsome remains.

What showed up, nude and pink, still warm, was the body of what seemed a boy, the features as though at rest and only an ugly, bleeding hole under the left eye, such as a boy might have gotten in a street fight. His arms were bruised from the fall and the bumping in the wagon.

But under the heart were two little black, bleeding holes, clean and fresh. These could not have been anything but what they were. That part of John Dillinger did not look as though it was a boy's hurt—it was the fatal finish of a cold-blooded killer and not half of what he had given Officer O'Malley in East Chicago, Indiana, in the bank robbery when he cut the policeman almost in half with a machine gun.

The marks of the garters were still on the skin of his sturdy calves, the only part of him that looked like any part of a strong man. His arms were slender, even emaciated. But his legs were powerful-looking. His feet were neat and almost womanish, after the white socks and dudish white shoes had been taken from them.

His clothes were shabby with still an attempt at smartness. The white shirt was cheap, the gray flannel trousers, and the uninitialed belt buckle were basement-counter merchandise, his maroon-and-white print tie might have cost half a dollar.

In his pockets were $7.70 and a few keys and a watch in which was the picture of a pretty female.

Two women bystanders were caught in the line of fire and wounded slightly as the Federal men blazed away. They were Miss Etta Natalsky, forty-five, and Miss Theresa Paulus, twenty-nine, both residents of the neighborhood.

Miss Natalsky was taken to the Columbus Memorial Hospital with a wound in the leg and Miss Paulus to the Grant Hospital, but her wound, also in the leg, was found to be only superficial.

The notorious desperado had resorted to facial surgery to disguise himself, and it was only by his piercing eyes—described by crime experts as "the eyes of a born killer"—that he was recognized.

In addition to the facial alterations, he had dyed his hair a jet black from its natural sandy shade, and he wore gold-rimmed glasses. Identification of the fallen man was confirmed by Purvis on the spot. Later, at the morgue, an attempt was made to identify the body from fingerprints, but the tips of the fingers had been scarred, as if with acid.

A recent wound in the chest, which had just healed, was revealed in the morgue examination. It was believed this was a memento of a recent bank robbery.

Dr. Charles D. Parker, coroner's physician, remarked on the alteration in the slain man's features. Scars which he carried on each cheek Dillinger had had smoothed out by facial surgery. Purvis, after closely examining the changed features, said:

"His nose, that originally was pronounced 'pug,' had been made nearly straight. His hair had been dyed recently."

Souvenir hunters among the excited crowds that swarmed to the scene of the shooting frantically dipped newspapers and handkerchiefs in the patch of blood left on the pavement.

Traffic became so jammed that streetcars were rerouted, police lines established, and all traffic finally blocked out of the area.

Unsatiated by their morbid milling around the death spot, the crowds a little later rushed to the morgue to view the body. Denied admittance, they battled police and shouted and yelled to get inside. More than two thousand at one time were struggling to force the doors.

I have indisputable proof that the bureau had information that Dillinger had been here for at least three days. It was the first definite location of the hunted murderer since the affray in the Little Bohemia (Wisconsin) lodge.

"We didn't have time to get him then, but we had time enough this time," Purvis said.

Evidently Purvis not only had enough time, but used it with the traditional efficiency of his department. There has always been open rancor between the Chicago police and the Federals, who have several times done them out of rewards. The Federals are not permitted to accept rewards.

But the East Chicago force—Dillinger had slaughtered three of their outfit in two raids, and the "coincidence" of their presence "when the tip came in" is obvious.

That Dillinger suspected nothing is proven by nothing as much as that the safety catch on his magazine gun was set. It was a new, high-type weapon, so powerful that its slugs would penetrate the bulletproof vests of the sort that Dillinger himself had worn in other spots. The number had been filed off. Close examination indicated it had never been fired. It was fully loaded, and a clip of extra cartridges was in a pocket.

He had no other possible instrument of offense or defense, this desperado, except a slender penknife on the other end of a thin chain that held his watch.

All his possessions lay on the marble slab beside the rubber stretcher in the basement of the morgue as the internes pawed his still warm face and body as they threw his head to this side and that, slung him over on his face, and dabbed the still-wet blood from where the bullets had bitten into him.

I wondered whether, a few brief minutes earlier, they would have had the temerity to treat John Dillinger's flesh so cavalierly.

They pointed to the scar on his shinbone, the one which had been so heavily broadcast as maiming and even killing Dillinger. It was a little bit of a thing and looked more like the result of a stone bruise than a volley from the muzzle of outraged society.

They flopped him over on the slab, quite by a clumsy accident, because the body didn't turn easily within the stretcher, what with its gangly, rubbery legs, and its thin, boneless arms. And as what was left of Dillinger clamped like a clod, face down, upon the slab which had held the clay of hoboes and who knows, a still warm but spent hand knocked off the straw hat which had fallen off his head in the alley and been trampled upon. And a good ten-cent cigar. Strangely intact.

The man who had killed him stood two feet away, smoking a cigar of the same brand. I must not mention his name. Purvis says "keep that a trade secret." With John ("Happy Jack") Hamilton and George ("Baby Face") Nelson, Dillinger's lieutenants, still at large, perhaps that is a fair enough precaution.

The Bureau of Identification men were on the job in a jiffy. They proved up the fingerprints, though they had been treated with a biting acid in an effort to obliterate the telltale. But the deltas and cores were unmistakable.

Behind the ears were well-done scars of a face-lifting job by a skillful plastic specialist. A mole on the forehead had been trimmed off rather well. His hair, by rights sandy, had been painted a muddy black with a poor grade of dye.

So had his mustache. The one identifying mark known around the globe as the Dillinger characteristic was there. And even in death he looked just like the Dillinger we all knew from the photographs. Probably the last breath of his ego.

Dillinger was a ladies' man. He didn't want to be picked up and identified by a rube sheriff. But, still, he wanted to whisper to a new sweetie in the confidences of the night:

"Baby, I can trust you—I'm John Dillinger!"

And she would look, and—he was! That mustache!

Having gone to astonishing lengths to change his inconspicuous identifying marks, with the necessary aid and advice of expert medical men, he had still refused to shave off that familiar trade-mark that every newspaper reader could see with eyes shut.

A scar on his chin had been reopened and smoothed up some, but not very convincingly. The droop at the left corner of his mouth was unmistakably intact. But the most striking facial change was in the tightening of the skin on his chin, almost completely killing his dimple, which was almost as widely known as his mustache.

Gold-rimmed eyeglasses fell off his face as he toppled over. These, one of the most amateurish of elements in disguise, did change his appearance decisively, the officers tell me.

The Federal office, as usual, issued contradictory statements and frankly admitted that certain information would not be given out.

Of the twenty-seven men who worked with Purvis, one was Captain Tim O'Neill of East Chicago, and four others were O'Neill's men. Purvis said they were there quite by chance and he had taken them in on the big adventure. A second statement also gave forth that Purvis had seen Dillinger enter as well as leave the theater.

As Dillinger emerged, walking near him were two youngish women, one of them wearing a red dress. Hundreds were leaving the house at the time, and almost any number of women would naturally have been near him. But the one with the red dress hurried up the alley, and four Federals made a formation between her and Dillinger before the first shot was fired. It is my theory that she was with Dillinger and that she was the tip-off party or in league with Purvis.

George M. Mahawinney / An Invasion from the Planet Mars

Philadelphia Inquirer, November 1, 1938

George M. Mahawinney, a rewrite man on duty at the Philadelphia Inquirer *the evening of the famous Orson Welles broadcast of "The War of the Worlds," was besieged by frantic telephone calls seeking information about the invasion from Mars. The* Inquirer, *close to the reputed scene of the Martian landing at Grovers Mill, near Princeton, New Jersey, became the focal point for the nation's coverage of the bizarre results of Welles's broadcast. With America's news services clamoring for reports, Mahawinney wrote the following account in less than an hour. (For an excerpt from the radio broadcast of "The War of the Worlds," See "Scripts.")*

Terror struck at the hearts of hundreds of thousands of persons in the length and breadth of the United States last night as crisp words of what they believed to be a news broadcast leaped from their radio sets—telling of catastrophe from the skies visited on this country.

Out of the heavens, they learned, objects at first believed to be meteors crashed down near Trenton, killing many.

Then out of the "meteors" came monsters, spreading destruction with torch and poison gas.

It was all just a radio dramatization, but the result, in all actuality, was nationwide hysteria.

In Philadelphia, women and children ran from their homes, screaming. In Newark, New Jersey, ambulances rushed to one neighborhood to protect residents against a gas attack. In the deep South men and women knelt in groups in the streets and prayed for deliverance.

In reality there was no danger. The broadcast was merely a Halloween program in which Orson Welles, actor-director of the Mercury Theater on the Air, related, as though he were one of the few human survivors of the catastrophe, an adaptation of H. G. Wells' *The War of the Worlds.*

In that piece of fiction men from Mars, in meteorlike space ships, come to make conquest of earth. The circumstances of the story were unbelievable enough, but the manner of its presentation was apparently convincing to hundreds of thousands of persons—despite the fact that the program was interrupted thrice for an announcement that it was fiction, and fiction only.

For the fanciful tale was broadcast casually, for all the world like a news broadcast, opening up serenely enough with a weather report.

The realism of the broadcast, especially for those who had tuned in after it had started, brought effects which none—not the directors of the Federal Radio Theater Project, which sponsored it, nor the Columbia Broadcasting Company, which carried it over a coast-to-coast chain of 151 stations, nor Station WCAU, which broadcast it locally—could foresee.

Within a few minutes newspaper offices, radio stations, and police departments everywhere were flooded with anxious telephone calls. Sobbing women sought advice on what to do; broken-voiced men wished to know where to take their families.

Station WCAU received more than four thousand calls and eventually interrupted a later program to make an elaborate explanation that death had not actually descended on New Jersey, and that monsters were not actually invading the world.

But calm did not come readily to the frightened radio listeners of the country.

The hysteria reached such proportions that the New York City Department of Health called up a newspaper and wanted advice on offering its facilities for the protection of the populace. Nurses and physicians were among the telephone callers everywhere. They were ready to offer their assistance to the injured or maimed.

Hundreds of motorists touring through New Jersey heard the broadcast over their radios and detoured to avoid the area upon which the holocaust was focused—the area in the vicinity of Trenton and Princeton.

In scores of New Jersey towns women in their homes fainted as the horror of the broadcast fell on their ears. In Palmyra some residents packed up their worldly goods and prepared to move across the river into Philadelphia.

A white-faced man raced into the Hillside, New Jersey, police station and asked for a gas mask. Police said he panted out a tale of "terrible people spraying liquid gas all over Jersey meadows."

A weeping lady stopped Motorcycle Patrolman Lawrence Treger and asked where she should go to escape the "attack."

A terrified motorist asked the patrolman the way to Route 24. "All creation's busted loose. I'm getting out of Jersey," he screamed.

"Grovers Mill, New Jersey," was mentioned as a scene of destruction. In Stockton more than a half-hundred persons abandoned Colligan's Inn after hearing the broadcast and journeyed to Groveville to view the incredible "damage." They had misheard the name of the hypothetical town of "Grovers Mill," and believed it to be Groveville.

At Princeton University, women members of the geology faculty, equipped with flashlights and hammers, started for Grovers Corners. Dozens of cars were driven to the hamlet by curious motorists. A score of university students were phoned by their parents and told to come home.

An anonymous and somewhat hysterical girl phoned the Princeton Press Club from Grovers Corners and said:

"You can't imagine the horror of it! It's hell!"

A man came into the club and said he saw the meteor strike the earth and witnessed animals jumping from the alien body.

The Trenton police and fire telephone board bore the brunt of the nation's calls, because of its geographical location close to the presumed scene of catastrophe. On that board were received calls from Wilmington, Washington, Philadelphia, Jersey City, and Newark.

North of Trenton most of New Jersey was in the midst of a bad scare.

A report spread through Newark that the city was to be the target of a "gas-bomb attack." Police headquarters were notified there was a serious gas accident in the Clinton Hills section of that city. They sent squad cars and ambulances.

They found only householders, with possessions hastily bundled, leaving their homes. The householders returned to their homes only after emphatic explanations by the police.

Fifteen persons were treated for shock in one Newark hospital.

In Jersey City one resident demanded a gas mask of police. Another telephoned to ask whether he ought to flee the area or merely keep his windows closed and hope for the best.

Many New Yorkers seized personal effects and raced out of their apartments, some jumping into their automobiles and heading for the wide-open spaces.

Samuel Tishman, a Riverside Drive resident, declared he and hundreds of others evacuated their homes, fearing "the city was being bombed."

He told of going home and receiving a frantic telephone call from a nephew.

Tishman denounced the program as "the most asinine stunt I ever heard of" and as "a pretty crumby thing to do."

The panic it caused gripped impressionable Harlemites, and one man ran into the street declaring it was the President's voice they heard, advising: "Pack up and go North, the machines are coming from Mars."

Police in the vicinity at first regarded the excitement as a joke, but they were soon hard pressed in controlling the swarms in the streets.

A man entered the Wadsworth Avenue station uptown and said he heard "planes had bombed Jersey and were headed for Times Square."

A rumor spread over Washington Heights that a war was on.

At Caldwell, New Jersey, an excited parishioner rushed into the First Baptist Church during evening services and shouted that a tremendous meteor had fallen, causing widespread death, and that north Jersey was threatened with a shower of meteors. The congregation joined in prayer for deliverance.

Reactions as strange, or stranger, occurred in other parts of the country. In San Francisco, a citizen called police, crying:

"My God, where can I volunteer my services? We've got to stop this awful thing."

In Indianapolis, Indiana, a woman ran screaming into a church.

"New York is destroyed; it's the end of the world," she cried. "You might as well go home to die."

At Brevard College, North Carolina, five boys in dormitories fainted on hearing the broadcast. In Birmingham, Alabama, men and women gathered in groups and prayed. Women wept and prayed in Memphis, Tennessee.

Throughout Atlanta was a wide-spread belief that a "planet" had struck New Jersey, killing from forty to seven thousand persons.

At Pittsburgh one man telephoned a newspaper that he had returned to his home in the middle of the broadcast and found his wife in the bathroom, clutching a bottle of poison.

"I'd rather die this way than like that," she screamed before he was able to calm her.

Another citizen telephoned a newspaper in Washington, Pennsylvania, that a group of guests in his home playing cards "fell down on their knees and prayed," and then hurried home.

At Rivesville, West Virginia, a woman interrupted the pastor's sermon at a church meeting with loud outcries that there had been "an invasion." The meeting broke up in confusion.

Two heart attacks were reported by Kansas City hospitals, and the Associated Press Bureau there received calls of inquiry from Los Angeles, Salt Lake City, Beaumont, Texas, and St. Joseph, Missouri.

Minneapolis and St. Paul police switchboards were deluged with calls from frightened people.

Weeping and hysterical women in Providence, Rhode Island, cried out for officials of the electric company there to "turn off the lights so that the city will be safe from the enemy."

In some places mass hysteria grew so great that witnesses to the "invasion" could be found.

A Boston woman telephoned a newspaper to say she could "see the fire" from her window, and that she and her neighbors were "getting out of here."

The broadcast began at eight P.M. Within a few minutes after that time it had brought such a serious reaction that New Jersey state police sent out a teletype message to its various stations and barracks, containing explanations and instructions to police officers on how to handle the hysteria.

These and other police everywhere had problems on their hands as the broadcast moved on, telling of a "bulletin from the Intercontinental Radio News Bureau" saying there had been a gas explosion in New Jersey.

"Bulletins" that came in rapidly after that told of "meteors," then corrected that statement and described the Mars monsters.

The march of the Martians was disastrous. For a while they swept everything before them, according to the pseudo-bulletins. Mere armies and navies were being wiped out in a trice.

Actually, outside the radio stations, the Martians were doing a pretty good job on the Halloween imaginations of the citizenry. The radio stations and the Columbia Broadcasting Company spent much of the remainder of the evening clearing up the situation. Again and again they explained the whole thing was nothing more than a dramatization.

In the long run, however, calm was restored in the myriad American homes which had been momentarily threatened by interplanetary invasion. Fear of the monsters from Mars eventually subsided.

There was no reason for being afraid of them, anyway. Even the bulletins of the radio broadcast explained they all soon died. They couldn't stand the earth's atmosphere and perished of pneumonia.

Dorothy Thompson / Mr. Welles and Mass Delusion

New York Herald Tribune, November 2, 1938

Dorothy Thompson (1894–1961) remained one of America's most distinguished columnists for more than a generation. Her syndicated reports, "On the Record," appeared three times a week and discussed such contemporary issues as President Roosevelt's New Deal and the emerging Nazi regime—each column marked by her commitment to journalistic candor. In "Mr. Welles and Mass Delusion," Thompson, two days after the Welles broadcast, poignantly depicts the malleability of the national psychology on the eve of another world war and reminds us of the terrifying power of mass media. (For an excerpt from the radio broadcast of "The War of the Worlds," see "Scripts.")

All unwittingly Mr. Orson Welles and the Mercury Theater on the Air have made one of the most fascinating and important demonstrations of all time. They have proved that a few effective voices, accompanied by sound effects, can so convince masses of people of a totally unreasonable, completely fantastic proposition as to create nation-wide panic.

They have demonstrated more potently than any argument, demonstrated beyond question of a doubt, the appalling dangers and enormous effectiveness of popular and theatrical demagoguery.

They have cast a brilliant and cruel light upon the failure of popular education.

They have shown up the incredible stupidity, lack of nerve and ignorance of thousands.

They have proved how easy it is to start a mass delusion.

They have uncovered the primeval fears lying under the thinnest surface of the so-called civilized man.

They have shown that man, when the victim of his own gullibility, turns to the government to protect him against his own errors of judgment.

The newspapers are correct in playing up this story over every other news event in the world. It is the story of the century.

And far from blaming Mr. Orson Welles, he ought to be given a Congressional medal and a national prize for having made the most amazing and important contribution to the social sciences. For Mr. Orson Welles and his theater have made a greater contribution to an understanding of Hitlerism, Mussolinism, Stalinism, anti-Semitism and all the other terrorisms of our times than all the words about them that have been written by reasonable men. They have made the reductio ad absurdum of mass manias. They have thrown more light on recent events in Europe leading to the Munich pact than everything that has been said on the subject by all the journalists and commentators.

Hitler managed to scare all Europe to its knees a month ago, but he at least had an army and an air force to back up his shrieking words.

But Mr. Welles scared thousands into demoralization with nothing at all.

That historic hour on the air was an act of unconscious genius, performed by the very innocence of intelligence.

Nothing whatever about the dramatization of the "War of the Worlds" was in the least credible, no matter at what point the hearer might have tuned in. The entire verisimilitude was in the names of a few specific places. Monsters were depicted of a type that nobody has ever seen, equipped with "rays" entirely fantastic; they were described as "straddling the Pulaski Skyway" and throughout the broadcast they were referred to as Martians, men from another planet.

A twist of the dial would have established for anybody that the national catastrophe was not being noted on any other station. A second of logic would have dispelled any terror. A notice that the broadcast came from a non-existent agency would have awakened skepticism.

A reference to the radio program would have established that the "War of the Worlds" was announced in advance.

The time element was obviously lunatic.

Listeners were told that "within two hours three million people have moved out of New York"—an obvious impossibility for the most disciplined army moving exactly as planned, and a double fallacy because only a few minutes before, the news of the arrival of the monster had been announced.

And of course it was not even a planned hoax. Nobody was more surprised at the result than Mr. Welles. The public was told at the beginning, at the end and during the course of the drama that it *was* a drama.

But eyewitnesses presented themselves; the report became second hand, third hand, fourth hand, and became more and more credible, so that nurses and doctors and National Guardsmen rushed to defense.

When the truth became known the reaction was also significant. The deceived were furious and of course demanded that the state protect them, demonstrating that they were incapable of relying on their own judgment.

Again there was a complete failure of logic. For if the deceived had thought about it they would realize that the greatest organizers of mass hysterias and mass delusions today are states using the radio to excite terrors, incite hatreds, inflame masses, win mass support for policies, create idolatries, abolish reason and maintain themselves in power.

The immediate moral is apparent if the whole incident is viewed in reason: no political body must ever, under any circumstances, obtain a monopoly of radio.

The second moral is that our popular and universal education is failing to train reason and logic, even in the educated.

The third is that the popularization of science has led to gullibility and new superstitions, rather than to skepticism and the really scientific attitude of mind.

The fourth is that the power of mass suggestion is the most potent force today and that the political demagogue is more powerful than all the economic forces.

For, mind you, Mr. Welles was managing an obscure program, competing with one of the most popular entertainments on the air!

The conclusion is that the radio must not be used to create mass prejudices and mass divisions and schisms, either by private individuals or by government or its agencies, or its officials, or its opponents.

If people can be frightened out of their wits by mythical men from Mars, they can be frightened into fanaticism by the fear of Reds, or convinced that America is in the hands of sixty families, or aroused to revenge against any minority, or terrorized into subservience to leadership because of any imaginable menace.

The technique of modern mass politics calling itself democracy is to create a fear—a fear of economic royalists, or of Reds, or of Jews, or of starvation, or of an outside enemy—and exploit that fear into obtaining subservience in return for protection.

I wrote in this column a short time ago that the new warfare was waged by propaganda, the outcome depending on which side could first frighten the other to death.

The British people were frightened into obedience to a policy a few weeks ago by a radio speech and by digging a few trenches in Hyde Park, and afterward led to hysterical jubilation over a catastrophic defeat for their democracy.

But Mr. Welles went all the politicians one better. He made the scare to end scares, the menace to end menaces, the unreason to end unreason, the perfect demonstration that the danger is not from Mars but from the theatrical demagogue.

Langston Hughes / Family Tree — *Chicago Defender*, ca. 1942

The author of more than sixty volumes of fiction, poetry, drama, gospel song-plays, opera lyrics, translations, and children's books, Langston Hughes has also written scores of essays and news reports. Born in Joplin, Missouri, in 1902, Hughes studied at Columbia University and later signed on as a cook's helper aboard a tramp freighter bound for Africa. He also worked as a cook in a Paris night club, as a busboy in a Washington hotel, and, after his writing had been ''discovered'' during the Harlem Renaissance of the late 1920s, served as a correspondent for the Baltimore Afro-American *reporting on the Spanish Civil War.*

Hughes's most popular writing features the exploits, opinions, and musings of Jesse B. Semple (''Simple''), a masterful rendition of a battered but resilient character Hughes had met in a Harlem bar in 1942. Simple tells a story (see Mark Twain's ''How to Tell a Story'' in ''Classics'') with an engaging combination of humor and irony, penetrating wit and realistic observation.

Hughes's conversations with Simple were recorded for more than two decades in the Chicago Defender, *a newspaper addressed to that city's black community, and were subsequently collected in four volumes.*

''Anybody can look at me and tell I am part Indian,'' said Simple.

''I see you almost every day,'' I said, ''and I did not know it until now.''

''I have Indian blood but I do not show it much,'' said Simple. ''My uncle's cousin's great-grandma were a Cherokee. I only shows mine when I lose my temper—then my Indian blood boils. I am quick-tempered just like a Indian. If somebody does something to me, I always fights back. In fact, when I get mad, I am the toughest Negro God's got. It's my Indian blood. When I were a young man, I used to play baseball and steal bases just like Jackie. If the empire would rule me out, I would get mad and hit the empire. I had to stop playing. That Indian temper. Nowadays, though, it's mostly womens that riles me up, especially landladies, waitresses, and girl friends. To tell the truth, I believe in a woman keeping her place. Womens is beside themselves these days. They want to rule the roost.''

''You have old-fashioned ideas about sex,'' I said. ''In fact, your line of thought is based on outmoded economics.''

''What?''

''In the days when women were dependent upon men for a living, you could be the boss. But now women make their own living. Some of them make more money than you do.''

''True,'' said Simple. ''During the war they got into that habit. But boss I am still due to be.''

''So you think. But you can't always put your authority into effect.''

''I can try,'' said Simple. ''I can say, 'Do this!' And if she does something else, I can raise my voice, if not my hand.''

"You can be sued for raising your voice," I stated, "and arrested for raising your hand."

"And she can be annihilated when I return from being arrested," said Simple. "That's my Indian blood!"

"You must believe in a woman being a squaw."

"She better not look like no squaw," said Simple. "I want a woman to look sharp when she goes out with me. No moccasins. I wants high-heel shoes and nylons, cute legs—and short dresses. But I also do not want her to talk back to me. As I said, I am the man. *Mine* is the word, and she is due to hush."

"Indians customarily expect their women to be quiet," I said.

"I do not expect mine to be *too* quiet," said Simple. "I want 'em to sweet-talk me—'Sweet baby, this,' and 'Baby, that,' and 'Baby, you's right, darling,' when they talk to me."

"In other words, you want them both old-fashioned and modern at the same time," I said. "The convolutions of your hypothesis are sometimes beyond cognizance."

"Cog hell!" said Simple. "I just do not like no old loud back-talking chick. That's the Indian in me. My grandpa on my father's side were like that, too, an Indian. He was married five times and he really ruled his roost."

"There are a mighty lot of Indians up your family tree," I said. "Did your granddad look like one?"

"Only his nose. He was dark brownskin otherwise. In fact, he were black. And the womens! Man! They was crazy about Grandpa. Every time he walked down the street, they stuck their heads out the windows and kept 'em turned South—which was where the beer parlor was."

"So your grandpa was a drinking man, too. That must be whom you take after."

"I also am named after him," said Simple. "Grandpa's name was Jess, too. So I am Jesse B. Semple."

"What does the *B* stand for?"

"Nothing. I just put it there myself since they didn't give me no initial when I was born. I am really Jess Semple—which the kids changed around into a nickname when I were in school. In fact, they used to tease me when I were small, calling me 'Simple Simon.' But I was right handy with my fists, and after I beat the 'Simon' out of a few of them, they let me alone. But my friends still call me 'Simple.' "

"In reality, you are Jesse Semple," I said, "colored."

"Part Indian," insisted Simple, reaching for his beer.

"Jess is certainly not an Indian name."

"No, it ain't," said Simple, "but we did have a Hiawatha in our family. She died."

"She?" I said. "Hiawatha was no *she*."

"She was a *she* in our family. And she had long coal-black hair just like a Creole. You know, I started to marry a Creole one time when I was coach-boy on the L. & N. down to New Orleans. Them Louisiana girls are bee-oou-te-ful! Man, I mean!"

"Why didn't you marry her, fellow?"

"They are more dangerous than a Indian," said Simple, "also I do not want no pretty woman. First thing you know, you fall in love with her—then you got to kill somebody about her. She'll make you so jealous, you'll bust! A pretty woman will get a man in trouble. Me and my Indian blood, quick-tempered as I is. No! I do not crave a pretty woman."

"Joyce is certainly not bad-looking," I said. "You hang around her all the time."

"She is far from a Creole. Besides, she appreciates me," said Simple. "Joyce knows I got Indian blood which makes my temper bad. But we take each other as we is. I respect her and she respects me."

"That's the way it should be with the whole world," I said. "Therefore, you and Joyce are setting a fine example in these days of trials and tribulations. Everybody should take each other as they are, white, black, Indians, Creole. Then there would be no prejudice, nations would get along."

"Some folks do not see it like that," said Simple. "For instant, my landlady—and my wife. Isabel could never get along with me. That is why we are not together today."

"I'm not talking personally," I said, "so why bring in your wife?"

"Getting along *starts* with persons, don't it?" asked Simple. "You *must* include my wife. That woman got my Indian blood so riled up one day I thought I would explode."

"I still say, I'm not talking personally."

"Then stop talking," exploded Simple, "because with me it is personal. Facts, I cannot even talk about my wife if I don't get personal. That's how it is if you're part Indian—everything is personal. *Heap much personal.*"

William L. Laurence / Atomic Bombing of Nagasaki Told by Flight Member

New York Times, September 9, 1945

Science dominated the life of William L. Laurence from his early youth. When he was growing up in Lithuania, according to a biographical profile in The New Yorker, *Laurence received as a gift a book "that speculated on the possibility of a civilization on Mars, and young [Laurence] was so impressed that he decided to go to the United States when he was old enough, because from there . . . he might most easily be able to establish contact with that planet."*

He arrived in Hoboken, New Jersey, in 1905 and proceeded to study at Harvard and the Boston University Law School. After five years of reporting for the New York World, *Laurence went to work for the* New York Times, *where he covered some of the most momentous events in the history of twentieth-century science. The only reporter with access to the "top secret" testing and development of the atomic bomb, Laurence also prepared the War Department's press releases on the weapon.*

On August 9, 1945, Laurence flew with the mission to bomb Nagasaki, barely three days after one hundred thousand people had been killed at Hiroshima in what Time *magazine called "The Birth of an Era." Laurence's Pulitzer Prize eyewitness account is underlined by a curious aesthetic sense—one that watches this "thing of beauty" destroy a major Japanese city.*

With the atomic-bomb mission to Japan, August 9 (Delayed)—We are on our way to bomb the mainland of Japan. Our flying contingent consists of three specially designed B-29 Superforts, and two of these carry no bombs. But our lead plane is on its way with another atomic bomb, the second in three days, concentrating in its active substance an explosive energy equivalent to twenty thousand and, under favorable conditions, forty thousand tons of TNT.

We have several chosen targets. One of these is the great industrial and shipping center of Nagasaki, on the western shore of Kyushu, one of the main islands of the Japanese homeland.

I watched the assembly of this man-made meteor during the past two days and was among the small group of scientists and Army and Navy representatives privileged to be present at the ritual of its loading in the Superfort last night, against a background of threatening black skies torn open at intervals by great lightning flashes.

It is a thing of beauty to behold, this "gadget." Into its design went millions of man-hours of what is without doubt the most concentrated intellectual effort in history. Never before had so much brain power been focused on a single problem.

This atomic bomb is different from the bomb used three days ago with such devastating results on Hiroshima.

I saw the atomic substance before it was placed inside the bomb. By itself it is not at all dangerous to handle. It is only under certain conditions, produced in the bomb assembly, that it can be made to yield up its energy, and even then it gives only a small fraction of its total contents—a fraction, however, large enough to produce the greatest explosion on earth.

The briefing at midnight revealed the extreme care and the tremendous amount of preparation that had been made to take care of every detail of the mission, to make certain that the atomic bomb fully served the purpose for which it was intended. Each target in turn was shown in detailed maps and in aerial photographs. Every detail of the course was rehearsed—navigation, altitude, weather, where to land in emergencies. It came out that the Navy had submarines and rescue craft, known as Dumbos and Superdumbos, stationed at various strategic points in the vicinity of the targets, ready to rescue the fliers in case they were forced to bail out.

The briefing period ended with a moving prayer by the chaplain.[1] We then proceeded to the mess hall for the traditional early-morning breakfast before departure on a bombing mission.

A convoy of trucks took us to the supply building for the special equipment carried on combat missions. This included the Mae West, a parachute, a lifeboat, an oxygen mask, a flak suit, and a survival vest. We still had a few hours before take-off time, but we all went to the flying field and stood around in little groups or sat in jeeps talking rather casually about our mission to the Empire, as the Japanese home islands are known hereabouts.

In command of our mission is Major Charles W. Sweeney, twenty-five, of 124 Hamilton Avenue, North Quincy, Massachusetts. His flagship, carrying the atomic bomb, is named *The Great Artiste,* but the name does not appear on the body of the great silver ship, with its unusually long, four-bladed, orange-tipped propellers. Instead, it carries the number 77, and someone remarks that it was "Red" Grange's winning number on the gridiron.

We took off at 3:50 this morning and headed northwest on a straight line for the Empire. The night was cloudy and threatening, with only a few stars here and there breaking through the overcast. The weather report had predicted storms ahead part of the way but clear sailing for the final and climactic stages of our odyssey.

We were about an hour away from our base when the storm broke. Our great ship took some heavy dips through the abysmal darkness around us, but it took these dips much more gracefully than a large commercial air liner, producing a sensation more

1. "Almighty God, Father of all mercies, we pray Thee to be gracious with those who fly this night. Guard and protect those of us who venture out into the darkness of Thy heaven. Uphold them on Thy wings. Keep them safe both in body and soul and bring them back to us. Give to us all the courage and strength for the hours that are ahead; give to them rewards according to their efforts. Above all else, our Father, bring peace to Thy world. May we go forward trusting in Thee and knowing we are in Thy presence now and forever. Amen." Prayer by Chaplain Downey, ending the briefing session preliminary to the bombing of Nagasaki .

in the nature of a glide than a "bump," like a great ocean liner riding the waves except that in this case the air waves were much higher and the rhythmic tempo of the glide was much faster.

I noticed a strange eerie light coming through the window high above the navigator's cabin, and as I peered through the dark all around us I saw a startling phenomenon. The whirling giant propellers had somehow become great luminous disks of blue flame. The same luminous blue flame appeared on the plexiglas windows in the nose of the ship, and on the tips of the giant wings. It looked as though we were riding the whirlwind through space on a chariot of blue fire.

It was, I surmised, a surcharge of static electricity that had accumulated on the tips of the propellers and on the di-electric material of the plastic windows. One's thoughts dwelt anxiously on the precious cargo in the invisible ship ahead of us. Was there any likelihood of danger that this heavy electric tension in the atmosphere all about us might set it off?

I expressed my fears to Captain Bock, who seems nonchalant and unperturbed at the controls. He quickly reassured me.

"It is a familiar phenomenon seen often on ships. I have seen it many times on bombing missions. It is known as St. Elmo's fire."

On we went through the night. We soon rode out the storm and our ship was once again sailing on a smooth course straight ahead, on a direct line to the Empire.

Our altimeter showed that we were traveling through space at a height of seventeen thousand feet. The thermometer registered an outside temperature of thirty-three degrees below zero Centigrade, about thirty below Fahrenheit. Inside our pressurized cabin the temperature was that of a comfortable air-conditioned room and a pressure corresponding to an altitude of eight thousand feet. Captain Bock cautioned me, however, to keep my oxygen mask handy in case of emergency. This, he explained, might mean either something going wrong with the pressure equipment inside the ship or a hole through the cabin by flak.

The first signs of dawn came shortly after five o'clock. Sergeant Curry, of Hoopeston, Illinois, who had been listening steadily on his earphones for radio reports, while maintaining a strict radio silence himself, greeted it by rising to his feet and gazing out the window.

"It's good to see the day," he told me. "I get a feeling of claustrophobia hemmed in in this cabin at night."

He is a typical American youth, looking even younger than his twenty years. It takes no mind reader to read his thoughts.

"It's a long way from Hoopeston," I find myself remarking.

"Yep," he replies, as he busies himself decoding a message from outer space.

"Think this atomic bomb will end the war?" he asks hopefully.

"There is a very good chance that this one may do the trick," I assured him, "but if not, then the next one or two surely will. Its power is such that no nation can stand up against it very long." This was not my own view. I had heard it expressed all around a few hours earlier, before we took off. To anyone who had seen this man-made fireball in action, as I had less than a month ago in the desert of New Mexico, this view did not sound overoptimistic.

By 5:50 it was really light outside. We had lost our lead ship, but Lieutenant Godfrey, our navigator, informs me that we had arranged for that contingency. We have an assembly point in the sky above the little island of Yakushima, southeast of Kyushu, at 9:10. We are to circle there and wait for the rest of our formation.

Our genial bombardier, Lieutenant Levy, comes over to invite me to take his front-row seat in the transparent nose of the ship, and I accept eagerly. From that vantage point in space, seventeen thousand feet above the Pacific, one gets a view of hundreds of miles on all sides, horizontally and vertically. At that height the vast ocean below and the sky above seem to merge into one great sphere.

I was on the inside of that firmament, riding above the giant mountains of white cumulus clouds, letting myself be suspended in infinite space. One hears the whirl of the motors behind one, but it soon becomes insignificant against the immensity all around and is before long swallowed by it. There comes a point where space also swallows time and one lives through eternal moments filled with an oppressive loneliness, as though all life had suddenly vanished from the earth and you are the only one left, a lone survivor traveling endlessly through interplanetary space.

My mind soon returns to the mission I am on. Somewhere beyond these vast mountains of white clouds ahead of me there lies Japan, the land of our enemy. In about four hours from now one of its cities, making weapons of war for use against us, will be wiped off the map by the greatest weapon ever made by man: In one tenth of a millionth of a second, a fraction of time immeasurable by any clock, a whirlwind from the skies will pulverize thousands of its buildings and tens of thousands of its inhabitants.

But at this moment no one yet knows which one of the several cities chosen as targets is to be annihilated. The final choice lies with destiny. The winds over Japan will make the decision. If they carry heavy clouds over our primary target, that city will be saved, at least for the time being. None of its inhabitants will ever know that the wind of a benevolent destiny had passed over their heads. But that same wind will doom another city.

Our weather planes ahead of us are on their way to find out where the wind blows. Half an hour before target time we will know what the winds have decided.

Does one feel any pity or compassion for the poor devils about to die? Not when one thinks of Pearl Harbor and of the Death March on Bataan.

Captain Bock informs me that we are about to start our climb to bombing altitude.

He manipulates a few knobs on his control panel to the right of him, and I alternately watch the white clouds and ocean below me and the altimeter on the bombardier's panel. We reached our altitude at nine o'clock. We were then over Japanese waters, close to their mainland. Lieutenant Godfrey motioned to me to look through his radar scope. Before me was the outline of our assembly point. We shall soon meet our lead ship and proceed to the final stage of our journey.

We reached Yakushima at 9:12 and there, about four thousand feet ahead of us, was *The Great Artiste* with its precious load. I saw Lieutenant Godfrey and Sergeant Curry strap on their parachutes and I decided to do likewise.

We started circling. We saw little towns on the coastline, heedless of our presence. We kept on circling, waiting for the third ship in our formation.

It was 9:56 when we began heading for the coastline. Our weather scouts had sent us code messages, deciphered by Sergeant Curry, informing us that both the primary target as well as the secondary were clearly visible.

The winds of destiny seemed to favor certain Japanese cities that must remain nameless. We circled about them again and again and found no opening in the thick umbrella of clouds that covered them. Destiny chose Nagasaki as the ultimate target.

We had been circling for some time when we noticed black puffs of smoke coming through the white clouds directly at us. There were fifteen bursts of flak in rapid succession, all too low. Captain Bock changed his course. There soon followed eight more bursts of flak, right up to our altitude, but by this time were too far to the left.

We flew southward down the channel and at 11:33 crossed the coastline and headed straight for Nagasaki, about one hundred miles to the west. Here again we circled until we found an opening in the clouds. It was 12:01 and the goal of our mission had arrived.

We heard the prearranged signal on our radio, put on our arc welder's glasses, and watched tensely the maneuverings of the strike ship about half a mile in front of us.

"There she goes!" someone said.

Out of the belly of *The Great Artiste* what looked like a black object went downward.

Captain Bock swung around to get out of range; but even though we were turning away in the opposite direction, and despite the fact that it was broad daylight in our cabin, all of us became aware of a giant flash that broke through the dark barrier of our arc welder's lenses and flooded our cabin with intense light.

We removed our glasses after the first flash, but the light still lingered on, a bluish-green light that illuminated the entire sky all around. A tremendous blast wave struck our ship and made it tremble from nose to tail. This was followed by four more blasts in rapid succession, each resounding like the boom of cannon fire hitting our plane from all directions.

Observers in the tail of our ship saw a giant ball of fire rise as though from the bowels of the earth, belching forth enormous white smoke rings. Next they saw a giant pillar of purple fire, ten thousand feet high, shooting skyward with enormous speed.

By the time our ship had made another turn in the direction of the atomic explosion the pillar of purple fire had reached the level of our altitude. Only about forty-five seconds had passed. Awe-struck, we watched it shoot upward like a meteor coming from the earth instead of from outer space, becoming ever more alive as it climbed skyward through the white clouds. It was no longer smoke, or dust, or even a cloud of fire. It was a living thing, a new species of being, born right before our incredulous eyes.

At one stage of its evolution, covering millions of years in terms of seconds, the entity assumed the form of a giant square totem pole, with its base about three miles long, tapering off to about a mile at the top. Its bottom was brown, its center was amber, its top white. But it was a living totem pole, carved with many grotesque masks grimacing at the earth.

Then, just when it appeared as though the thing had settled down into a state of permanence, there came shooting out of the top a giant mushroom that increased the height of the pillar to a total of forty-five thousand feet. The mushroom top was even more alive than the pillar, seething and boiling in a white fury of creamy foam, sizzling upward and then descending earthward, a thousand Old Faithful geysers rolled into one.

It kept struggling in an elemental fury, like a creature in the act of breaking the bonds that held it down. In a few seconds it had freed itself from its gigantic stem and floated upward with tremendous speed, its momentum carrying it into the stratosphere to a height of about sixty thousand feet.

But no sooner did this happen when another mushroom, smaller in size than the first one, began emerging out of the pillar. It was as though the decapitated monster was growing a new head.

As the first mushroom floated off into the blue it changed its shape into a flower-like form, its giant petals curving downward, creamy white outside, rose-colored inside. It still retained that shape when we last gazed at it from a distance of about two hundred miles. The boiling pillar of many colors could also be seen at that distance, a giant mountain of jumbled rainbows, in travail. Much living substance had gone into those rainbows. The quivering top of the pillar was protruding to a great height through the white clouds, giving the appearance of a monstrous prehistoric creature with a ruff around its neck, a fleecy ruff extending in all directions, as far as the eye could see.

DISCUSSION QUESTIONS

1. How does William Laurence respond to the disastrous event he is covering? Does he include in his report his own feelings about what he is witnessing?

What rhetorical devices characterize his account? What effects do these devices have on your response to his report?

2. Laurence calls the atomic bomb "a thing of beauty." Does he find any other examples of "beauty" on the mission? Explain. How does his use of detail contribute to (or detract from) the aesthetic effects he wants to convey?

3. Does Laurence have any political or moral attitudes toward the bombing? Explain. Point to specific words and phrases to verify your contention. What is the effect of the final image in Laurence's report?

Tom Wicker / Kennedy Is Killed by Sniper as He Rides in Car in Dallas *New York Times,* November 23, 1963

Tom Wicker had a great deal of experience in journalism before he joined the Washington office of the New York Times *in 1960. Born and educated in North Carolina, Wicker worked in his home state as editor of the* Sanhill Citizen *and as managing editor of the* Robesonian. *After serving as copy editor, sports editor, and Washington correspondent for the* Winston-Salem Journal, *Wicker took on the responsibilities of the associate editorship of the* Nashville Tennessean. *After his report on the assassination of President Kennedy, Wicker moved from a featured reporter to columnist and associate editor of the* New York Times. *He has also written several novels. His most recent books include* On Press *(1978),* Unto This Hour *(1984), and* One of Us: Richard Nixon and the American Dream (1991).

Tom Wicker's recollections of his coverage of the tumultuous events of November 22, 1963, follow the report below. They are reprinted from Times Talk, *the monthly report circulated to members of the Times organization.*

KENNEDY IS KILLED BY SNIPER AS HE RIDES IN CAR IN DALLAS; JOHNSON SWORN IN ON PLANE.

Gov. Connally Shot;
Mrs. Kennedy Safe.

•

President Is Struck Down by a Rifle Shot
From Building on Motorcade Route—
Johnson, Riding Behind, Is Unhurt.

DALLAS, Nov. 22—President John Fitzgerald Kennedy was shot and killed by an assassin today.

He died of a wound in the brain caused by a rifle bullet that was fired at him as he was riding through downtown Dallas in a motorcade.

Vice President Lyndon Baines Johnson, who was riding in the third car behind Mr. Kennedy's, was sworn in as the 36th President of the United States 99 minutes after Mr. Kennedy's death.

Mr. Johnson is 55 years old; Mr. Kennedy was 46.

Shortly after the assassination, Lee H. Oswald, who once defected to the Soviet Union and who has been active in the Fair Play for Cuba Committee, was arrested by the Dallas police. Tonight he was accused of the killing.

SUSPECT CAPTURED AFTER SCUFFLE

Oswald, 24 years old, was also accused of slaying a policeman who had approached him in the street. Oswald was subdued after a scuffle with a second policeman in a nearby theater.

President Kennedy was shot at 12:30 P.M., Central Standard Time (1:30 P.M., New York time). He was pronounced dead at 1 P.M. and Mr. Johnson was sworn in at 2:39 P.M.

Mr. Johnson, who was uninjured in the shooting, took his oath in the Presidential jet plane as it stood on the runway at Love Field. The body of Mr. Kennedy was aboard. Immediately after the oath-taking, the plane took off for Washington.

Standing beside the new President as Mr. Johnson took the oath of office was Mrs. John F. Kennedy. Her stockings were spattered with her husband's blood.

Gov. John B. Connally, Jr., of Texas, who was riding in the same car with Mr. Kennedy, was severely wounded in the chest, ribs and arm. His condition was serious, but not critical.

The killer fired the rifle from a building just off the motorcade route. Mr. Kennedy, Governor Connally and Mr. Johnson had just received an enthusiastic welcome from a large crowd in downtown Dallas.

Mr. Kennedy apparently was hit by the first of what witnesses believed were three shots. He was driven at high speed to Dallas Parkland Hospital. There, in an emergency operating room, with only physicians and nurses in attendance, he died without regaining consciousness.

Mrs. Kennedy, Mrs. Connally and a Secret Service agent were in the car with Mr. Kennedy and Governor Connally. Two Secret Service agents flanked the car. Other than Mr. Connally, none of this group was injured in the shooting. Mrs. Kennedy cried, "Oh no!" immediately after her husband was struck.

Mrs. Kennedy was in the hospital near her husband when he died, but not in the operating room. When the body was taken from the hospital in a bronze coffin about 2 P.M., Mrs. Kennedy walked beside it.

Her face was sorrowful. She looked steadily at the floor. She still wore the raspberry-colored suit in which she had greeted welcoming crowds in Fort Worth and Dallas. But she had taken off the matching pillbox hat she wore earlier in the day, and her dark hair was windblown and tangled. Her hand rested lightly on her husband's coffin as it was taken to a waiting hearse.

Mrs. Kennedy climbed in beside the coffin. Then the ambulance drove to Love Field, and Mr. Kennedy's body was placed aboard the Presidential jet. Mrs. Kennedy then attended the swearing-in ceremony for Mr. Johnson.

As Mr. Kennedy's body left Parkland Hospital, a few stunned persons stood outside. Nurses and doctors, whispering among themselves, looked from the window. A larger crowd that had gathered earlier, before it was known that the President was dead, had been dispersed by Secret Service men and policemen.

PRIESTS ADMINISTER LAST RITES

Two priests administered last rites to Mr. Kennedy, a Roman Catholic. They were the Very Rev. Oscar Huber, the pastor of Holy Trinity Church in Dallas, and the Rev. James Thompson.

Mr. Johnson was sworn in as President by Federal Judge Sarah T. Hughes of the Northern District of Texas. She was appointed to the judgeship by Mr. Kennedy in October, 1961.

The ceremony, delayed about five minutes for Mrs. Kennedy's arrival, took place in the private Presidential cabin in the rear of the plane.

About 25 to 30 persons—members of the late President's staff, members of

Congress who had been accompanying the President on a two-day tour of Texas cities and a few reporters—crowded into the little room.

No accurate listing of those present could be obtained. Mrs. Kennedy stood at the left of Mr. Johnson, her eyes and face showing the signs of weeping that had apparently shaken her since she left the hospital not long before.

Mrs. Johnson, wearing a beige dress, stood at her husband's right.

As Judge Hughes read the brief oath of office, her eyes, too, were red from weeping. Mr. Johnson's hands rested on a black, leatherbound Bible as Judge Hughes read and he repeated:

"I do solemnly swear that I will perform the duties of the President of the United States to the best of my ability and defend, protect and preserve the Constitution of the United States."

Those 34 words made Lyndon Baines Johnson, one-time farmboy and schoolteacher of Johnson City, the President.

JOHNSON EMBRACES MRS. KENNEDY

Mr. Johnson made no statement. He embraced Mrs. Kennedy and she held his hand for a long moment. He also embraced Mrs. Johnson and Mrs. Evelyn Lincoln, Mr. Kennedy's private secretary.

"O.K.," Mr. Johnson said. "Let's get this plane back to Washington."

At 2:46 P.M., seven minutes after he had become President, 106 minutes after Mr. Kennedy had become the fourth American President to succumb to an assassin's wounds, the white and red jet took off for Washington.

In the cabin when Mr. Johnson took the oath was Cecil Stoughton, an armed forces photographer assigned to the White House.

Mr. Kennedy's staff members appeared stunned and bewildered. Lawrence F. O'Brien, the Congressional liaison officer, and P. Kenneth O'Donnell, the appointment secretary, both long associates of Mr. Kennedy, showed evidences of weeping. None had anything to say.

Other staff members believed to be in the cabin for the swearing-in included David F. Powers, the White House receptionist; Miss Pamela Turnure, Mrs. Kennedy's press secretary; and Malcolm Kilduff, the assistant White House press secretary.

Mr. Kilduff announced the President's death, with choked voice and red-rimmed eyes, at about 1:36 P.M.

"President John F. Kennedy died at approximately 1 o'clock Central Standard Time today here in Dallas," Mr. Kilduff said at the hospital. "He died of a gunshot wound in the brain. I have no other details regarding the assassination of the President."

Mr. Kilduff also announced that Governor Connally had been hit by a bullet or bullets and that Mr. Johnson, who had not yet been sworn in, was safe in the protective custody of the Secret Service at an unannounced place, presumably the airplane at Love Field.

Mr. Kilduff indicated that the President had been shot once. Later medical reports raised the possibility that there had been two wounds. But the death was caused, as far as could be learned, by a massive wound in the brain.

Later in the afternoon, Dr. Malcolm Perry, an attending surgeon, and Dr. Kemp Clark, chief of neurosurgery at Parkland Hospital, gave more details.

Mr. Kennedy was hit by a bullet in the throat, just below the Adam's apple, they said. This wound had the appearance of a bullet's entry.

Mr. Kennedy also had a massive, gaping wound in the back and one on the right side of the head. However, the doctors said it was impossible to determine immediately whether the wounds had been caused by one bullet or two.

RESUSCITATION ATTEMPTED

Dr. Perry, the first physician to treat the President, said a number of resuscitative measures had been attempted, including oxygen, anesthesia, an indotracheal tube, a tracheotomy, blood and fluids. An electrocardiogram monitor was attached to measure Mr. Kennedy's heart beats.

Dr. Clark was summoned and arrived in a minute or two. By then, Dr. Perry said, Mr. Kennedy was "critically ill and moribund," or near death.

Dr. Clark said that on his first sight of the President, he had concluded immediately that Mr. Kennedy could not live.

"It was apparent that the President had sustained a lethal wound," he said. "A missile had gone in and out of the back of his head causing external lacerations and loss of brain tissue."

Shortly after he arrived, Dr. Clark said, "the President lost his heart action by the electrocardiogram." A closed-chest cardiograph massage was attempted, as were other emergency resuscitation measures.

Dr. Clark said these had produced "palpable pulses" for a short time, but all were "to no avail."

IN OPERATING ROOM 40 MINUTES

The President was on the emergency table at the hospital for about 40 minutes, the doctors said. At the end, perhaps eight physicians were in Operating Room No. 1, where Mr. Kennedy remained until his death. Dr. Clark said it was difficult to determine the exact moment of death, but the doctors said officially that it occurred at 1 P.M.

Later, there were unofficial reports that Mr. Kennedy had been killed instantly. The source of these reports, Dr. Tom Shires, chief surgeon at the hospital and professor of surgery at the University of Texas Southwest Medical School, issued this statement tonight:

"Medically, it was apparent the President was not alive when he was brought in. There was no spontaneous respiration. He had dilated, fixed pupils. It was obvious he had a lethal head wound.

"Technically, however, by using vigorous resuscitation, intravenous tubes and all the usual supportive measures, we were able to raise a semblance of a heartbeat."

Dr. Shires was not present when Mr. Kennedy was being treated at Parkland Hospital. He issued his statement, however, after lengthy conferences with the doctors who had attended the President.

Mr. Johnson remained in the hospital about 30 minutes after Mr. Kennedy died.

The details of what happened when shots first rang out, as the President's car moved along at about 25 miles an hour, were sketchy. Secret Service agents, who might have given more details, were unavailable to the press at first, and then returned to Washington with President Johnson.

KENNEDYS HAILED AT BREAKFAST

Mr. Kennedy had opened his day in Fort Worth, first with a speech in a parking lot and then at a Chamber of Commerce breakfast. The breakfast appearance was a particular triumph for Mrs. Kennedy, who entered late and was given an ovation.

Then the Presidential party, including Governor and Mrs. Connally, flew on to Dallas, an eight-minute flight. Mr. Johnson, as is customary, flew in a separate plane. The President and the Vice President do not travel together, out of fear of a double tragedy.

At Love Field, Mr. and Mrs. Kennedy lingered for 10 minutes, shaking hands with an enthusiastic group lining the fence. The group called itself "Grassroots Democrats."

Mr. Kennedy then entered his open Lincoln convertible at the head of the motorcade. He sat in the rear seat on the right-hand side. Mrs. Kennedy, who appeared to be enjoying one of the first political outings she had ever made with her husband, sat at his left.

In the "jump" seat, directly ahead of Mr. Kennedy, sat Governor Connally, with Mrs. Connally at his left in another "jump" seat. A Secret Service agent was driving and the two others ran alongside.

Behind the President's limousine was an open sedan carrying a number of Secret Service agents. Behind them, in an open convertible, rode Mr. and Mrs. Johnson and Texas's senior Senator, Ralph W. Yarborough, a Democrat.

The motorcade proceeded uneventfully along a 10-mile route through downtown Dallas, aiming for the Merchandise Mart. Mr. Kennedy was to address a group of the city's leading citizens at a luncheon in his honor.

In downtown Dallas, crowds were thick, enthusiastic and cheering. The turnout was somewhat unusual for this center of conservatism, where only a month ago Adlai E. Stevenson was attacked by a rightist crowd. It was also in Dallas, during the 1960 campaign, that Senator Lyndon B. Johnson and his wife were nearly mobbed in the lobby of the Baker Hotel.

As the motorcade neared its end and the President's car moved out of the thick crowds onto Stennonds Freeway near the Merchandise Mart, Mrs. Connally recalled later, "we were all very pleased with the reception in downtown Dallas."

APPROACHING 3-STREET UNDERPASS

Behind the three leading cars were a string of others carrying Texas and Dallas dignitaries, two buses of reporters, several open cars carrying photographers and other reporters, and a bus for White House staff members.

As Mrs. Connally recalled later, the President's car was almost ready to go underneath a "triple underpass" beneath three streets—Elm, Commerce and Main—when the first shot was fired.

That shot apparently struck Mr. Kennedy. Governor Connally turned in his seat at the sound and appeared immediately to be hit in the chest.

Mrs. Mary Norman of Dallas was standing at the curb and at that moment was aiming her camera at the President. She saw him slump forward, then slide down in the seat.

"My God," Mrs. Norman screamed, as she recalled it later, "he's shot!"

Mrs. Connally said that Mrs. Kennedy had reached and "grabbed" her husband. Mrs. Connally put her arms around the Governor. Mrs. Connally said that she and Mrs. Kennedy had then ducked low in the car as it sped off.

Mrs. Connally's recollections were reported by Julian Reade, an aide to the Governor.

Most reporters in the press buses were too far back to see the shootings, but they observed some quick scurrying by motor policemen accompanying the motorcade. It was noted that the President's car had picked up speed and raced away, but reporters were not aware that anything serious had occurred until they reached the Merchandise Mart two or three minutes later.

RUMORS SPREAD AT TRADE MART

Rumors of the shooting already were spreading through the luncheon crowd of hundreds, which was having the first course. No White House officials or Secret

Service agents were present, but the reporters were taken quickly to Parkland Hospital on the strength of the rumors.

There they encountered Senator Yarborough, white, shaken and horrified.

The shots, he said, seemed to have come from the right and the rear of the car in which he was riding, the third in the motorcade. Another eyewitness, Mel Crouch, a Dallas television reporter, reported that as the shots rang out he saw a rifle extended and then withdrawn from a window on the "fifth or sixth floor" of the Texas Public School Book Depository. This is a leased state building on Elm Street, to the right of the motorcade route.

Senator Yarborough said there had been a slight pause between the first two shots and a longer pause between the second and third. A Secret Service man riding in the Senator's car, the Senator said, immediately ordered Mr. and Mrs. Johnson to get down below the level of the doors. They did so, and Senator Yarborough also got down.

The leading cars of the motorcade then pulled away at high speed toward Parkland Hospital, which was not far away, by the fast highway.

"We knew by the speed that something was terribly wrong," Senator Yarborough reported. When he put his head up, he said, he saw a Secret Service man in the car ahead beating his fists against the trunk deck of the car in which he was riding, apparently in frustration and anguish.

MRS. KENNEDY'S REACTION

Only White House staff members spoke with Mrs. Kennedy. A Dallas medical student, David Edwards, saw her in Parkland Hospital while she was waiting for news of her husband. He gave this description:

"The look in her eyes was like an animal that had been trapped, like a little rabbit—brave, but fear was in the eyes."

Dr. Clark was reported to have informed Mrs. Kennedy of her husband's death.

No witnesses reported seeing or hearing any of the Secret Service agents or policemen fire back. One agent was seen to brandish a machine gun as the cars sped away. Mr. Crouch observed a policeman falling to the ground and pulling a weapon. But the events had occurred so quickly that there was apparently nothing for the men to shoot at.

Mr. Crouch said he saw two women, standing at a curb to watch the motorcade pass, fall to the ground when the shots rang out. He also saw a man snatch up his little girl and run along the road. Policemen, he said, immediately chased this man under the impression he had been involved in the shooting, but Mr. Crouch said he had been a fleeing spectator.

Mr. Kennedy's limousine—license No. GG300 under District of Columbia registry—pulled up at the emergency entrance of Parkland Hospital. Senator Yarborough said the President had been carried inside on a stretcher.

By the time reporters arrived at the hospital, the police were guarding the Presidential car closely. They would allow no one to approach it. A bucket of water stood by the car, suggesting that the back seat had been scrubbed out.

Robert Clark of the American Broadcasting Company, who had been riding near the front of the motorcade, said Mr. Kennedy was motionless when he was carried inside. There was a great amount of blood on Mr. Kennedy's suit and shirtfront and the front of his body, Mr. Clark said.

Mrs. Kennedy was leaning over her husband when the car stopped, Mr. Clark said, and walked beside the wheeled stretcher into the hospital. Mr. Connally sat with his hands holding his stomach, his head bent over. He, too, was moved into the hospital in a stretcher, with Mrs. Connally at his side.

Robert McNeill of the National Broadcasting Company, who also was in the reporters' pool car, jumped out at the scene of the shooting. He said the police had taken two eyewitnesses into custody—an 8-year-old Negro boy and a white man—for informational purposes.

Many of these reports could not be verified immediately.

EYEWITNESS DESCRIBES SHOOTING

An unidentified Dallas man, interviewed on television here, said he had been waving at the President when the shots were fired. His belief was that Mr. Kennedy had been struck twice—once, as Mrs. Norman recalled, when he slumped in his seat; again when he slid down in it.

"It seemed to just knock him down," the man said.

Governor Connally's condition was reported as "satisfactory" tonight after four hours in surgery at Parkland Hospital.

Dr. Robert R. Shaw, a thoracic surgeon, operated on the Governor to repair damage to his left chest.

Later, Dr. Shaw said Governor Connally had been hit in the back just below the shoulder blade, and that the bullet had gone completely through the Governor's chest, taking out part of the fifth rib.

After leaving the body, he said, the bullet struck the Governor's right wrist, causing a compound fracture. It then lodged in the left thigh.

The thigh wound, Dr. Shaw said, was trivial. He said the compound fracture would heal.

Dr. Shaw said it would be unwise for Governor Connally to be moved in the next 10 to 14 days. Mrs. Connally was remaining at his side tonight.

TOUR BY MRS. KENNEDY UNUSUAL

Mrs. Kennedy's presence near her husband's bedside at his death resulted from somewhat unusual circumstances. She had rarely accompanied him on his trips about the country and had almost never made political trips with him.

The tour on which Mr. Kennedy was engaged yesterday and today was only quasi-political; the only open political activity was to have been a speech tonight to a fund-raising dinner at the state capitol in Austin.

In visiting Texas, Mr. Kennedy was seeking to improve his political fortunes in a pivotal state that he barely won in 1960. He was also hoping to patch a bitter internal dispute among Texas's Democrats.

At 8:45 A.M., when Mr. Kennedy left the Texas hotel in Fort Worth, where he spent his last night, to address the parking lot crowd across the street, Mrs. Kennedy was not with him. There appeared to be some disappointment.

"Mrs. Kennedy is organizing herself," the President said good-naturedly. "It takes longer, but, of course, she looks better than we do when she does it."

Later, Mrs. Kennedy appeared late at the Chamber of Commerce breakfast in Fort Worth.

Again, Mr. Kennedy took note of her presence. "Two years ago," he said, "I introduced myself in Paris by saying that I was the man who had accompanied Mrs. Kennedy to Paris. I am getting somewhat that same sensation as I travel around Texas. Nobody wonders what Lyndon and I wear."

The speech Mr. Kennedy never delivered at the Merchandise Mart luncheon contained a passage commenting on a recent preoccupation of his, and a subject of much interest in this city, where right-wing conservatism is the rule rather than the exception.

"Voices are being heard in the land," he said, "voices preaching doctrines wholly unrelated to reality, wholly unsuited to the sixties, doctrines which apparently assume that words will suffice without weapons, that vituperation is as good as victory and that peace is a sign of weakness."

The speech went on: "At a time when the national debt is steadily being reduced in terms of its burden on our economy, they see that debt as the greatest threat to our security. At a time when we are steadily reducing the number of Federal employees serving every thousand citizens, they fear those supposed hordes of civil servants far more than the actual hordes of opposing armies.

"We cannot expect that everyone, to use the phrase of a decade ago, will 'talk sense to the American people.' But we can hope that fewer people will listen to nonsense. And the notion that this nation is headed for defeat through deficit, or that strength is but a matter of slogans, is nothing but just plain nonsense."

DISCUSSION QUESTIONS

1. What is the verb tense at the beginning of the headline for Wicker's story? What effect is created by the use of this particular verb form? Does the tense remain consistent with the verb form used in the remainder of the headline? In the text of the story?
2. Compare the headline to this story with that of the *New York Herald* on the assassination of President Lincoln. What can these examples tell you about the language of headlines in general?
3. How is the first paragraph of each story partly determined by the information presented in the headline? Contrast the leads of both news stories. Which do you find most successful? Why? Does each story adhere to the format of the inverted pyramid as described in the introduction to this section?

Tom Wicker / The Assassination *Times Talk,* December 1963

WASHINGTON

I think I was in the first press bus. But I can't be sure. Pete Lisagor of The Chicago Daily News says he *knows* he was in the first press bus and he describes things that went on aboard it that didn't happen on the bus I was in. But I still *think* I was in the first press bus.

I cite that minor confusion as an example of the way it was in Dallas in the early afternoon of Nov. 22. At first no one knew what happened, or how, or where, much less why. Gradually, bits and pieces began to fall together and within two hours a reasonably coherent version of the story began to be possible. Even now, however, I know no reporter who was there who has a clear and orderly picture of that surrealistic afternoon; it is still a matter of bits and pieces thrown hastily into something like a whole.

It began, for most reporters, when the central fact of it was over. As our press bus eased at motorcade speed down an incline toward an underpass, there was a little confusion in the sparse crowds that at that point had been standing at the curb to see the President of the United States pass. As we came out of the underpass, I saw a motorcycle policeman drive over the curb, across an open area, a few feet up a railroad bank, dismount and start scrambling up the bank.

Jim Mathis of The Advance (Newhouse) Syndicate went to the front of our bus and looked ahead to where the President's car was supposed to be, perhaps ten cars ahead of us. He hurried back to his seat.

"The President's car just sped off," he said. "Really gunned away." (How could Mathis have seen that if there had been another bus in front of us?)

But that could have happened if someone had thrown a tomato at the President. The press bus in its stately pace rolled on to the Trade Mart, where the President was to speak. Fortunately, it was only a few minutes away.

At the Trade Mart, rumor was sweeping the hundreds of Texans already eating their lunch. It was the only rumor that I had ever *seen;* it was moving across that crowd like a wind over a wheatfield. A man eating a grapefruit seized my arm as I passed.

"Has the President been shot?" he asked.

"I don't think so," I said. "But something happened."

With the other reporters—I suppose 35 of them—I went on through the huge hall to the upstairs press room. We were hardly there when Marianne Means of Hearst Headline Service hung up a telephone, ran to a group of us and said, "The President's been shot. He's at Parkland Hospital."

One thing I learned that day; I suppose I already knew it, but that day made it plain. A reporter must trust his instinct. When Miss Means said those eight words—I never learned who told her—I knew absolutely they were true. Everyone did. We ran for the press buses.

Again, a man seized my arm—an official-looking man.

"No running in here," he said sternly. I pulled free and ran on. Doug Kiker of The Herald Tribune barreled head-on into a waiter carrying a plate of potatoes. Waiter and potatoes flew about the room. Kiker ran on. He was in his first week with The Trib, and his first Presidential trip.

I barely got aboard a moving press bus. Bob Pierrepoint of C.B.S. was aboard and he said that he now recalled having heard something that could have been shots—or firecrackers, or motorcycle backfire. We talked anxiously, unbelieving, afraid.

Fortunately again, it was only a few minutes to Parkland Hospital. There at its emergency entrance, stood the President's car, the top up, a bucket of bloody water beside it. Automatically, I took down its license number—GG300 District of Columbia.

The first eyewitness description came from Senator Ralph Yarborough, who had been riding in the third car of the motorcade with Vice President and Mrs. Johnson. Senator Yarborough is an East Texan, which is to say a Southerner, a man of quick emotion, old-fashioned rhetoric.

"Gentlemen," he said, pale, shaken, near tears. "It is a deed of horror."

The details he gave us were good and mostly—as it later proved—accurate. But he would not describe to us the appearance of the President as he was wheeled into the hospital, except to say that he was "gravely wounded." We could not doubt, then, that it was serious.

I had chosen that day to be without a notebook. I took notes on the back of my mimeographed schedule of the two-day tour of Texas we had been so near to concluding. Today, I cannot read many of the notes; on Nov. 22, they were as clear as 60-point type.

A local television reporter, Mel Crouch, told us he had seen a rifle being withdrawn from the corner fifth or sixth floor window of the Texas School Book Depository. Instinct again—Crouch sounded right, positive, though none of us knew him. We believed it and it was right.

Mac Kilduff, an assistant White House press secretary in charge of the press on that trip, and who was to acquit himself well that day, came out of the hospital. We gathered round and he told us the President was alive. It wasn't true, we later learned; but Mac thought it was true at that time, and he didn't mislead us about a possible recovery. His whole demeanor made plain what was likely to happen. He also told us—as Senator Yarborough had—that Gov. John Connally of Texas was shot, too.

Kilduff promised more details in five minutes and went back into the hospital. We were barred. Word came to us secondhand—I don't remember exactly how—from Bob Clark of A.B.C., one of the men who had been riding in the press "pool" car near the President's, that he had been lying face down in Mrs. Kennedy's lap when the car arrived at Parkland. No signs of life.

That is what I mean by instinct. That day, a reporter had none of the ordinary means or time to check and double-check matters given as fact. He had to go on what he knew of people he talked to, what he knew of human reaction, what two isolated "facts" added to in sum—above all on what he felt in his bones. I knew Clark and respected him. I took his report at face value, even at second hand. It turned out to be true. In a crisis, if a reporter can't trust his instinct for truth, he can't trust anything.

When Wayne Hawks of the White House staff appeared to say that a press room had been set up in a hospital classroom at the left rear of the building, the group of reporters began struggling across the lawn in that direction. I lingered to ask a motorcycle policeman if he had heard on his radio anything about the pursuit or capture of the assassin. He hadn't, and I followed the other reporters.

As I was passing the open convertible in which Vice President and Mrs. Johnson and Senator Yarborough had been riding in the motorcade, a voice boomed from its radio:

"The President of the United States is dead. I repeat—it has just been announced that the President of the United States is dead."

There was no authority, no word of who had announced it. But—instinct again—I believed it instantly. It sounded true. I knew it was true. I stood still a moment, then began running.

Ordinarily, I couldn't jump a tennis net if I'd just beaten Gonzales. That day, carrying a briefcase and a typewriter, I jumped a chain fence looping around the drive, not even breaking stride. Hugh Sidey of Time, a close friend of the President, was walking slowly ahead of me.

"Hugh," I said, "the President's dead. Just announced on the radio. I don't know who announced it but it sounded official to me."

Sidey stopped, looked at me, looked at the ground. I couldn't talk about it. I couldn't think about it. I couldn't do anything but run on to the press room. Then I told others what I had heard.

Sidey, I learned a few minutes later, stood where he was a minute. Then he saw two Catholic priests. He spoke to them. Yes, they told him, the President was dead. They had administered the last rites. Sidey went on to the press room and spread that word, too.

Throughout the day, every reporter on the scene seemed to me to do his best to help everyone else. Information came only in bits and pieces. Each man who picked up a bit or a piece passed it on. I know no one who held anything out. Nobody thought about an exclusive; it didn't seem important.

After perhaps 10 minutes when we milled around in the press room—my instinct was to find the new President, but no one knew where he was—Kilduff appeared red-eyed, barely in control of himself. In that hushed classroom, he made the official, the unbelievable announcement. The President was dead of a gunshot wound in the brain. Lyndon Johnson was safe, in the protective custody of the Secret Service. He would be sworn in as soon as possible.

Kilduff, composed as a man could be in those circumstances, promised more details when he could get them, then left. The search for phones began. Jack Gertz, traveling with us for A.T. & T., was frantically moving them by the dozen into the hospital, but few were ready yet.

I wandered down the hall, found a doctor's office, walked in and told him I had to use his phone. He got up without a word and left. I battled the hospital switchboard for five minutes and finally got a line to New York—Hal Faber on the other end, with Harrison Salisbury on an extension.

They knew what had happened, I said. The death had been confirmed. I proposed to write one long story, as quickly as I could, throwing in everything I could learn. On the desk, they could cut it up as they needed—throwing part into other stories, putting other facts into mine. But I would file a straight narrative without worrying about their editing needs.

Reporters always fuss at editors and always will. But Salisbury and Faber are good men to talk to in a crisis. They knew what they were doing and realized my problems. I may fuss at them again sometime, but after that day my heart won't be in it. Quickly, clearly, they told me to go ahead, gave me the moved-up deadlines, told me of plans already made to get other reporters into Dallas, but made it plain they would be hours in arriving.

Salisbury told me to use the phone and take no chances on a wire circuit being jammed or going wrong. Stop reporting and start writing in time to meet the deadline, he said. Pay anyone $50 if necessary to dictate for you.

The whole conversation probably took three minutes. Then I hung up, thinking of all there was to know, all there was I didn't know. I wandered down a corridor and ran into Sidey and Chuck Roberts of Newsweek. They'd seen a hearse pulling up at the emergency entrance and we figured they were about to move the body.

We made our way to the hearse—a Secret Service agent who knew us helped us through suspicious Dallas police lines—and the driver said his instructions were to take the body to the airport. That confirmed our hunch, but gave me, at least, another wrong one. Mr. Johnson, I declared, would fly to Washington with the body and be sworn in there.

We posted ourselves inconspicuously near the emergency entrance. Within minutes, they brought the body out in a bronze coffin.

A number of White House staff people—stunned, silent, stumbling along as if dazed—walked with it. Mrs. Kennedy walked by the coffin, her hand on it, her head down, her hat gone, her dress and stockings spattered. She got into the hearse with the coffin. The staff men crowded into cars and followed.

That was just about the only eyewitness matter that I got with my own eyes that entire afternoon.

Roberts commandeered a seat in a police car and followed, promising to "fill" Sidey and me as necessary. We made the same promise to him and went back to the press room.

There, we received an account from Julian Reade, a staff assistant, of Mrs. John Connally's recollection of the shooting. Most of his recital was helpful and it established the important fact of who was sitting in which seat in the President's car at the time of the shooting.

The doctors who had treated the President came in after Mr. Reade. They gave us copious detail, particularly as to the efforts they had made to resuscitate the President. They were less explicit about the wounds, explaining that the body had been in their hands only a short time and they had little time to examine it closely. They conceded they were unsure as to the time of death and had arbitrarily put it at 1 P.M., C.S.T.

Much of their information, as it developed later, was erroneous. Subsequent reports made it pretty clear that Mr. Kennedy probably was killed instantly. His body, as a physical mechanism, however, continued to flicker an occasional pulse and heartbeat. No doubt this justified the doctors' first account. There also was the question of national security and Mr. Johnson's swearing-in. Perhaps, too, there was a question about the Roman Catholic rites. In any case, until a later doctors' statement about 9 P.M. that night, the account we got at the hospital was official.

The doctors hardly had left before Hawks came in and told us Mr. Johnson would be sworn in immediately at the airport. We dashed for the press buses, still parked outside. Many a campaign had taught me something about press buses and I ran a little harder, got there first, and went to the wide rear seat. That is the best place on a bus to open up a typewriter and get some work done.

On the short trip to the airport, I got about 500 words on paper—leaving a blank space for the hour of Mr. Johnson's swearing-in, and putting down the mistaken assumption that the scene would be somewhere in the terminal. As we arrived at a back gate along the airstrip, we could see Air Force One, the Presidential jet, screaming down the runway and into the air.

Left behind had been Sid Davis of Westinghouse Broadcasting, one of the few reporters who had been present for the swearing-in. Roberts, who had guessed right in going to the airport when he did, had been there too and was aboard the plane on the way to Washington.

Davis climbed on the back of a shiny new car that was parked near where our bus halted. I hate to think what happened to its trunk deck. He and Roberts—true to his promise—had put together a magnificent "pool" report on the swearing-in. Davis read it off, answered questions, and gave a picture that so far as I know was complete, accurate and has not yet been added to.

I said to Kiker of The Trib: "We better go write. There'll be phones in the terminal." He agreed. Bob Manning, an ice-cool member of the White House transportation staff, agreed to get our bags off the press plane, which would return to Washington as soon as possible, and put them in a nearby telephone booth.

Kiker and I ran a half-mile to the terminal, cutting through a baggage-handling room to get there. I went immediately to a phone booth and dictated my 500-word lead, correcting it as I read, embellishing it too. Before I hung up, I got Salisbury and asked him to cut into my story whatever the wires were filing on the assassin. There was no time left to chase down the Dallas police and find out those details on my own.

Dallas Love Field has a mezzanine running around its main waiting room; it is equipped with writing desks for travelers. I took one and went to work. My recollection is that it was then about 5 P.M. New York time.

I would write two pages, run down the stairs, across the waiting room, grab a phone and dictate. Miraculously, I never had to wait for a phone booth or to get a line through. Dictating each take, I would throw in items I hadn't written, sometimes whole paragraphs. It must have been tough on the dictating room crew.

Once, while in the booth dictating, I looked up and found twitching above me the imposing mustache of Gladwin Hill. He was the first Times man in and had found me right off; I was seldom more glad to see anyone. We conferred quickly and he took off for the police station; it was a tremendous load off my mind to have that angle covered and out of my hands.

I was half through, maybe more, when I heard myself paged. It turned out to be Kiker, who had been separated from me and was working in the El Dorado room, a bottle club in the terminal. My mezzanine was quieter and a better place to work, but he had a TV going for him, so I moved in too.

The TV helped in one important respect. I took down from it an eyewitness account of one Charles Drehm, who had been waving at the President when he was shot. Instinct again: Drehm sounded positive, right, sure of what he said. And his report was the first real indication that the President probably was shot twice.

Shortly after 7 P.M., New York time, I finished. So did Kiker. Simultaneously we thought of our bags out in that remote phone booth. We ran for a taxi and urged an unwilling driver out along the dark airstrip. As we found the place, with some difficulty, an American Airlines man was walking off with the bags. He was going to ship them off to the White House, having seen the tags on them. A minute later and we'd have been stuck in Dallas without even a toothbrush.

Kiker and I went to The Dallas News. The work wasn't done—I filed a number of inserts later that night, wrote a separate story on the building from which the assassin had fired, tried to get John Herbers, Don Janson, Joe Loftus on useful angles as they drifted in. But when I left the airport, I knew the worst of it was over. The story was filed on time, good or bad, complete or incomplete, and any reporter knows how that feels. They couldn't say I missed the deadline.

It was a long taxi ride to The Dallas News. We were hungry, not having eaten since an early breakfast. It was then that I remembered John F. Kennedy's obituary. Last June, Hal Faber had sent it to me for updating. On Nov. 22, it was still lying on my desk in Washington, not updated, not rewritten, a monument to the incredibility of that afternoon in Dallas.

Thomas O'Toole / "The Eagle Has Landed": Two Men Walk on the Moon *Washington Post,* July 24, 1969

On July 20, 1969, Thomas O'Toole, staff writer for the Washington Post, *covered his story by watching Neil Armstrong and Buzz Aldrin participate in what President Richard Nixon called "the greatest moment in history since the Creation."*

HOUSTON, July 20—Man stepped out onto the moon tonight for the first time in his two-million-year history.

"That's one small step for man," declared pioneer astronaut Neil Armstrong at 10:56 P.M. EDT, "one giant leap for mankind."

Just after that historic moment in man's quest for his origins, Armstrong walked on the dead satellite and found the surface very powdery, littered with fine grains of black dust.

A few minutes later, Edwin (Buzz) Aldrin joined Armstrong on the lunar surface and in less than an hour they put on a show that will long be remembered by the worldwide television audience.

AMERICAN FLAG PLANTED

The two men walked easily, talked easily, even ran and jumped happily so it seemed. They picked up rocks, talked at length of what they saw, planted an American flag, saluted it, and talked by radiophone with the President in the White House, and then faced the camera and saluted Mr. Nixon.

"For every American, this has to be the proudest day of our lives," the President told the astronauts. "For one priceless moment in the whole history of man, all the people on this earth are truly one."

Seven hours earlier, at 4:17 P.M., the Eagle and its two pilots thrilled the world as they zoomed in over a rock-covered field, hovered and then slowly let down on the moon. "Houston, Tranquillity base here," Armstrong radioed. "The Eagle has landed."

At 1:10 A.M. Monday—2 hours and 14 minutes after Armstrong first stepped upon the lunar surface—the astronauts were back in their moon craft and the hatch was closed.

In describing the moon, Armstrong told Houston that it was "fine and powdery. I can kick it up loosely with my toe.

"It adheres like powdered charcoal to the boot," he went on, "but I only go in a small fraction of an inch. I can see my footprint in the moon like fine grainy particles."

Armstrong found he had such little trouble walking on the moon that he began talking almost as if he didn't want to leave it.

"It has a stark beauty all its own," Armstrong said. "It's like the desert in the Southwestern United States. It's very pretty out here."

AMAZINGLY CLEAR PICTURE

Armstrong shared his first incredible moments on the moon with the whole world, as a television camera on the outside of the wingless Eagle landing craft sent back an amazingly clear picture of his first steps on the moon.

Armstrong seemed like he was swimming along, taking big and easy steps on the airless moon despite the cumbersome white pressure-suit he wore.

"There seems to be no difficulty walking around," he said. "As we suspected, it's even easier than the one-sixth G that we did in simulations on the ground."

One of the first things he did was to scoop up a small sample of the moon with a long-handled spoon with a bag on its end like a small butterfly net.

"Looks like it's easy," Aldrin said, looking down from the Lem.

"It is," Armstrong told him. "I'm sure I could push it in farther but I can't bend down that far."

GUIDES ALDRIN DOWN LADDER

At 11:11 P.M., Aldrin started down the landing craft's ten-foot ladder to join Armstrong.

Backing down the nine-step ladder, Aldrin was guided the entire way by Armstrong, who stood at the foot of the ladder looking up at him.

"Okay," Armstrong said, "watch your 'pliss' (PLSS, for portable life support system) from underneath. Drop your pliss down. You're clear. About an inch clear on your pliss."

"Okay," Aldrin said. "You need a little arching of the back to come down."

After he stepped onto the first rung of the ladder, Aldrin went back up to the Lem's "front porch" to partially close the Lem's hatch.

"Making sure not to lock it on my way out," he said in comic fashion. "That's our home for the next couple of hours and I want to make sure we can get back in."

"Beautiful," said Aldrin when he met Armstrong on the lunar surface.

"Isn't that something," said Armstrong. "It's a magnificent sight out here."

While Armstrong watched, Aldrin went through some cautious walking experiments to see how difficult it was in his pressure suit.

"Reaching down is fairly easy," he said. "The mass of the backpack does have some effect on inertia. There's a slight tendency, I can see now, to tip backwards."

Aldrin and Armstrong then both walked around the Lem's 31-foot base, inspecting its four legs and undercarriage at the same time that they began looking over the moon's surface.

"These rocks are rather slippery," Armstrong said. "The powdery surface fills up the fine pores on the rocks, and we tend to slide over it rather easily."

While Armstrong got ready to move the television camera out about 30 feet from the Lem, Aldrin did some more experimental walking.

"If I'm about to lose my balance in one direction," said Aldrin, "recovery is quite natural and easy. You've just got to be careful leaning in the direction you want to go in."

At that, Aldrin apparently spotted an interesting rock.

"Hey, Neil," he said. "Didn't I say we'd find a purple rock?"

"Did you find a purple rock?" Armstrong asked him.

"Yep," replied Aldrin.

The next thing Armstrong did was to change lenses on the television camera, putting a telephoto lens on it for a closeup view of what was happening.

"Now we'll read the plaque for those who haven't read it before," Armstrong said, referring to a small stainless steel plaque that had been placed on one of the landing craft's legs.

"It says," Armstrong said, "Here men from the planet Earth first set foot on the moon. July 1969, A.D. We came in peace for all mankind."

"It has the crew members' signatures," Armstrong said, "and the signature of the President of the United States."

BLEAK BUT BEAUTIFUL

Armstrong next took the television camera out to a spot about 40 feet from the Lem, and placed it on a small tripod.

Incredibly clear, the picture showed a distant Lem, squatting on the bleak but beautiful lunar surface like some giant mechanical toy. It appeared to be perfectly level, not at all tilted on the rough lunar terrain.

When he got the camera mounted correctly, he walked back toward the Lem, with the camera view following him all the way.

Just after 11:30, both men removed a pole, flagstaff and a plastic American flag from one of the Lem's legs. They gently pressed the flag into the lunar surface.

After they saluted the flag, astronaut Bruce McCandless commented on the little ceremony from his perch in the Manned Spacecraft center's mission control room.

"The flag is up now," he said. "You can see the stars and stripes on the lunar surface."

At 11:48 McCandless asked both men to stand together near the flag. "The President of the United States would like to talk to you," McCandless said.

Mr. Nixon spoke to the astronauts for almost two minutes, and when he finished, the two astronauts stood erect and saluted directly at the television camera.

During most of their early time on the moon, astronaut Michael Collins not only didn't see them walking on the moon, but was behind the moon and out of radio touch in his orbiting command craft.

When he finally swung around in front of the moon again, Armstrong and Aldrin had been out almost 30 minutes.

"How's it going?" Collins asked plaintively.

"Just great," McCandless told him.

"How's the television?" he asked.

"Just beautiful," he was told.

Armstrong and Aldrin stayed out on the moon for almost two hours, with Aldrin first back into the Lem just before 1 A.M. Monday.

"Adios, Amigos," he said as he pulled himself easily back up the ladder.

Armstrong started back up the ladder a few minutes after 1 A.M. Monday. He took what seemed like the first four rungs with one huge leap upward. At 1:10 A.M., Armstrong had joined Aldrin inside the cabin. "Okay, the hatch is closed and latched," said Aldrin seconds later.

When both men had repressurized their cabin and taken off their helmets and gloves, Collins reappeared over the lunar horizon in his command craft. At once, he asked how everything had gone.

SLEEP, THEN RENDEZVOUS

"Hallelujah," he said when he was told what had happened.

All three astronauts were due to get their first sleep in almost 24 hours, a sleep that was never more richly deserved.

If nothing went wrong—and nobody was expecting anything would—Armstrong and Aldrin were due to lift back off the surface of the moon at 1:55 P.M. EDT Monday.

Burning their ascent engine full-blast for just over seven minutes, they will start a four-hour flight to rejoin Collins and the command craft 70 miles above the lunar surface.

The majestic moment of man's first steps on the moon came about six hours after Armstrong and Aldrin set their four-legged, wingless landing craft down in the moon's Sea of Tranquillity—precisely at 4:17 P.M. EDT.

"Houston, Tranquillity Base here," Armstrong announced to a breathless world. "The Eagle has landed."

"You did a beautiful job," astronaut Charles Duke said from Houston's Manned Spacecraft Center. "Be advised there's lots of smiling faces down here."

"There's two of them down here," Armstrong replied.

The landing apparently was not an easy one. It was about four miles from the target point in the southwestern edge of the Sea of Tranquillity, almost right on the lunar equator.

"We were coming down in a crater the size of a football field with lots of big rocks around and in it," Armstrong said about five minutes after landing. "We had to fly it manually over the rock field to find a place to land."

"EVERY VARIETY OF SHAPES"

A few minutes later, Aldrin gave a waiting world its first eyewitness description of the moon's surface.

"It looks like a collection of just about every variety of shapes and angularity, every variety of rock you could find," Aldrin said.

"There doesn't appear to be too much color," he went on, "except that it looks as though some of the boulders are going to have some interesting color."

Armstrong then described their landing site in a little detail.

"It's a relatively flat plain," he said, "with a lot of craters of the five- to 50-foot variety. Some small ridges 20 to 30 feet high. Thousands of little one- and two-foot craters. Some angular levees in front of us two feet in size. There is a hill in view ahead of us. It might be a half-mile or a mile away."

Armstrong then described what he said were rocks fractured by the exhaust of Eagle's rocket plume.

"Some of the surface rocks in close look like they might have a coating on them," he said. "Where they're broken, they display a very dark gray interior. It looks like it could be country basalt."

"LIKE BEING IN AN AIRPLANE"

Both men seemed to actually enjoy being in the moon's gravity, which is one-sixth that of earth's.

"It's like being in an airplane," Armstrong said. "It seems immediately natural to move around in this environment."

Armstrong and Aldrin apparently felt fine. Armstrong's heart rate went as high as 156 beats per minute at the time of landing, but dropped down into the nineties 15 minutes later.

The time leading up to the landing is difficult to describe, except to say that it was as dramatic a time as any in memory.

It all began at 3:08 P.M. EDT when Armstrong and Aldrin—flying feet first and face down—fired up their landing craft's descent engine for the first time.

Burning the engine for 27 seconds in what amounted to a braking maneuver to slow it down and start it falling, the two men were behind the moon at the time and out of radio touch with earth.

It was not until 3:47 P.M. that the men at the Manned Spacecraft Center heard that Armstrong and Aldrin were on their way down—and they heard it first from Collins, who flew from behind the moon in the command craft above and in front of the landing craft.

"Columbia, Houston," said Duke from the Center. "How did it go?"

"Listen, Babe," replied an excited Collins. "Everything's going just swimmingly. Beautiful."

Two minutes later, Duke made radio contact with Armstrong and Aldrin.

"We're standing by for your burn report," Duke said.

"The burn was on time," Aldrin told him.

"Rog, copy," Duke said. "Looks great."

At this point, the men in Mission Control bent their backs to the toughest jobs they'd ever have—following the two spacecraft at all times, to give them the guidance they would need for the Eagle's descent to the moon.

"JUST PLAY IT COOL"

Looking around the very quiet Mission Control room, flight director Gene Kranz simply said, "We're off to a good start. Just play it cool."

Flying down and westward across the moon's surface, the Eagle suddenly dropped out of radio contact with earth, but in moments was back in touch again.

"I don't know what the problem was," a totally composed Buzz Aldrin said when he came back on. "We started yawing and we're picking up a little oscillation rate now."

Still falling, the Eagle was coming up over the eastern region of the Sea of Tranquillity at an altitude of 53,000 feet and only minutes away from its second critical maneuver—the powered descent to the lunar surface.

"Five minutes to ignition," Duke radioed up. "You are go for a powered descent."

"Roger," Armstrong replied softly. "Understand."

At 4:05, Armstrong began throttling up the engine to slow the Eagle again, to drop it down toward the lunar surface.

"Light's on," he said. "Descent looks good."

Two minutes later, it was plain to everybody listening that they were indeed on their way down to the moon.

"Show an altitude of 47,000 feet," Armstrong said. "Everything looking good."

Still calm, Aldrin said he noticed a few warning lights coming on inside the spacecraft. "I'm getting some AC voltage fluctuations," he said, "and our position checks downrange show us to be a little long."

"You're looking good to us, Eagle," Duke answered. "You are go to continue powered descent. Repeat. You are go to continue powered descent."

FALLING, SLOWING APPROACH

"Altitude 27,000 feet," Aldrin read off. "This throttle down is better than the simulator."

Down they came, still falling but slowing down at the same time. At 21,000 feet, their speed had fallen to 800 miles an hour.

"You're looking great to us, Eagle," Duke said.

A minute later, it was 500 miles an hour, then it was suddenly down to less than 90 miles an hour.

"You're looking great at eight minutes. . . . You're looking great at nine minutes," Duke told them.

At this point, the two explorers began their final approach to the moon surface, coming in sideways and downwardly only 5200 feet above the moon.

When the Eagle dropped to 4200 feet Duke broke in on the radio, his voice tense and excited.

"Eagle, you are go for landing," he said.

"Roger, understand," a calm Armstrong replied. "Go for landing."

"Eagle, you're looking great," Duke said. "You're go at 1600 feet."

At that, Armstrong began to read off rapidly his altitudes and pitch angles—the angle at which the spacecraft was falling toward the lunar surface.

"Three-hundred feet," he said. "Down three and a half. A hundred feet. Three and a half down. Okay. Seventy-five feet. Looking good. Down a half."

"Sixty seconds," Duke said.

"Lights on," Armstrong replied. "Forty feet. Kicking up some dust. Great shadows.

"Four forward. Drifting to the right a little."

His voice then rose a little, as he turned off the engine for the first time and started free-falling to the moon.

"Okay, engine stop," he said. "Overdrive off. Engine arm off."

There was a pause—then the first voice came from the surface of the moon.

"Houston. Tranquillity Base here," Armstrong announced. "The Eagle has landed."

"You've got a bunch of guys about to turn blue," Duke told him. "Now we're breathing again."

"Okay, standby," Armstrong replied. "We're going to be busy for a minute."

Just then, Collins broke in from his lonesome spot 70 miles above the moon, desperately wanting in on the historic conversation.

"He has landed," Duke informed him. "Eagle has landed at Tranquillity."

"Good show," Collins said. "Fantastic."

Five minutes after touchdown, Duke told them things looked good enough for them to stay there a while.

"We thank you," Armstrong answered.

It was then that Armstrong told Houston he had to fly the spacecraft in manually to avoid a football-sized crater and a large rock field.

COULDN'T PINPOINT LOCATION

"It really was rough over the target area," he said. "It was heavily cratered and some of the large rocks may have been bigger than 10 feet around."

He then said he was not sure of his location on the moon either. "Well," he said, "the guys who said we wouldn't be able to tell exactly where we are are the winners today."

Armstrong reported that the four-legged spacecraft had landed on a level plain and appeared to be tilted at an angle no greater than 4.5 degrees.

Their first moments on the moon were truly incredible, but the entire day seemed incredible, as if the scenario for it all had been written by some bizarre science fiction writer.

"We've done everything humanly possible," Manned Spacecraft Center Director Robert C. Gilruth told one newsman, "but boy is this a tense and unreal time for me."

Preparing for the busiest and most historic day of their lives, the three crewmen hadn't even gotten to sleep until after 1 A.M.—and it was the ground that suggested they all go to bed.

"That really winds things up as far as we're concerned," astronaut Owen Garriott said in Houston. "We're ready to go to bed and get a little sleep."

COLLINS WAKES UP FIRST

"Yeah, we're about to join you," Armstrong replied.

Armstrong and Aldrin were the first to go to sleep, and then Collins finally went to sleep two hours later, at just after 3 A.M.

Four hours later, astronaut Ron Evans was manning the radio in Houston and he put in the first wake-up call.

"Apollo 11, Apollo 11," he said. "Good morning from the black team."

It was Collins who answered first, even though he'd had the least sleep. "Oh my, you guys wake up early," he said.

"You're about two minutes early on the wakeup," Evans conceded. "Looks like you were really sawing them away."

"You're right," said Collins.

Everybody got right down to business then. "Looks like the command module's in good shape," Evans told Collins. "Black team's been watching it real closely for you."

"We sure appreciate that," Collins said, "because I sure haven't."

ACTIVATES LANDING CRAFT

Just after 9:30 A.M., as the three men began their 11th orbit of the moon, Aldrin got into the Eagle for the first time—to power it up, start the oxygen flowing into the spacecraft and make sure everything was in working order. Forty-five minutes later, Armstrong joined him.

On the 13th orbit, Eagle undocked from Columbia, moving off about 40 or 50 feet from the command craft, which Collins was piloting alone.

Like most of the maneuvers they've made, this one was done behind the moon and out of contact with earth—so nobody in Houston knew for almost 45 minutes if the separation had been successful.

At 1:50 P.M., the two spacecraft came over the moon's rim.

"Eagle, we see you on the steerable," said Duke, who had just replaced Evans. "How does it look?"

''Eagle has wings,'' was Armstrong's simple reply.

For a while, all the astronauts did was look each other over, to make sure the two spacecraft were shipshape.

''Check that tracking light, Mike,'' Armstrong told Collins.

''Okay,'' Armstrong said next, ''I'm ready to start my yaw maneuver if it suits you, Mike.''

ELABORATE INSTRUMENT CHECK

Aldrin got on next, reading off what seemed like endless instrument checklists. For 15 minutes, he talked on, never once missing a word, sounding totally composed.

At 2:12 P.M., Collins fired his tiny thruster jets to increase distance between the craft.

''Thrusting,'' Collins said. ''Everything's looking real good.''

The two spacecraft were 1000 feet away from each other within moments. Collins took a radar check on the distance.

''I got a solid lock on it,'' he said. ''It looks like point 27 miles''—about 1400 feet.

''Hey,'' Collins said to Armstrong when he'd looked out his window, ''you're upside down.''

''Somebody's upside down,'' Armstrong replied.

Just then, Collins asked Armstrong: ''Put your tracking light on, please.''

''It's on, Mike,'' answered Aldrin.

''Give us a mark when you're at seven-tenths of a mile,'' Duke said to Collins from the ground.

Moments later, Duke told Collins the big radars on the ground showed the two spacecraft seven-tenths of a mile apart.

''Rog,'' Collins said. ''I'm oscillating between point 69 and seven-tenths.''

At 2:50 P.M. Houston gave the go signal for the first maneuver, the so-called descent orbit insertion burn.

''Eagle,'' Duke said, ''you are go for DOI.''

''Roger,'' replied Aldrin matter-of-factly. ''Go for DOI.''

And while the whole world listened one of the most majestic dramas in mankind's history began to unfold.

DISCUSSION QUESTION

1. Compare Thomas O'Toole's report of the moon landing with Norman Mailer's account in ''Classics.'' How does O'Toole's use of transcripts differ from Mailer's? Why doesn't O'Toole talk about the way the astronauts talk? Why does Mailer do this? What effect does O'Toole want the transcripts to have in his report? What role does television play in his report?

Vivian Gornick / The Next Great Moment in History Is Theirs

[An Introduction to the Women's Liberation Movement]

Village Voice, November 17, 1969

Some pundits say the feminist era is over, but there is no denying the profound influence the women's movement has had on cultural and social shifts in American society over the past twenty-five years. Reading Vivian Gornick's classic early account of the movement's struggles and possibilities is a strange experience today: much of what she describes, such as the offhand oppression of women and their lack of participation in the public sphere, seems dated. Yet the basic struggle among women, to find their voices and places in a rapidly changing world, continues. Gornick's piece, combining autobiography, journalistic accounts, and analysis, serves both as a historical document and a powerful polemic.

Founded in New York in 1955 by free-lance journalist Daniel Wolf, psychologist Edward Fancher, and novelist Norman Mailer, the Village Voice *was the first successful avant-garde, antiestablishment newspaper in what has come to be known as the underground press. Less expensively designed and printed than mass-circulation daily newspapers and with few of their inhibitions or restraints, the* Village Voice *of the late sixties, published weekly with a circulation of well over one hundred thousand, could afford to be eclectic and extensive in its selection and coverage of contemporary events. Today, the* Village Voice *remains one of the most influential alternative publications, offering a forum for writers working from a left, multicultural, and feminist perspective.*

A staff writer for the Voice *for several years, Vivian Gornick has also taught English at Hunter College and at the Stony Brook campus of the State University of New York. In 1971 she edited, together with Barbara K. Moran,* Women in Sexist Society, *an acclaimed collection of essays by professional writers and scholars. She has authored five books, including* Women in Science: Recovering the Life Within *(1983) and* Fierce Attachments: A Memoir *(1987).*

One evening not too long ago, at the home of a well-educated and extremely intelligent couple I know, I mentioned the women's liberation movement and was mildly astonished by the response the subject received. The man said: "Jesus, what *is* all that crap about?" The woman, a scientist who had given up 10 working years to raise her children, said: "I can understand if these women want to work and are demanding equal pay. But why on earth do they want to have children too?" To which the man rejoined: "Ah, they don't want kids. They're mostly a bunch of dykes, anyway."

Again: Having lunch with an erudite, liberal editor, trained in the humanist tradition, I was struck dumb by his reply to my mention of the women's liberation movement: "Ah shit, who the hell is oppressing them?"

And yet again: A college-educated housewife, fat and neurotic, announced with arch sweetness, "I'm sorry, I just don't *feel* oppressed."

Over and over again, in educated, thinking circles, one meets with a bizarre, almost determined, ignorance of the unrest that is growing daily and exists in formally organized bodies in nearly every major city and on dozens of campuses across America. The women of this country are gathering themselves into a sweat of civil revolt, and the general population seems totally unaware of what is happening—if, indeed, they realize *anything* is happening—or that there is a legitimate need behind what is going on. How is this possible? Why is it true? What relation is there between the peculiarly unalarmed, amused dismissal of the women's-rights movement and the movement itself? Is this relation only coincidental, only the apathetic response of a society already benumbed by civil rights and student anarchy and unable to rise to yet one more protest movement? Or is it not, in fact, precisely the key to the entire issue?

Almost invariably, when people set out to tell you there is no such thing as discrimination against women in this country, the first thing they hastily admit to is a *minor* degree of economic favoritism shown toward men. In fact, they will eagerly, almost gratefully, support the claim of economic inequity, as though that will keep the discussion within manageable bounds. Curious. But even on economic grounds or grounds of legal discrimination most people are dismally ignorant of the true proportions of the issue. They will grant that often a man will make as much as $100 more than a woman at the same job, and yes, it *is* often difficult for a woman to be hired when a man can be hired instead, but after all, that's really not so terrible.

This is closer to the facts:

Women in this country make 60 cents for every $1 a man makes.

Women do not share in the benefits of the fair employment practices laws because those laws do not specify "no discrimination on the basis of sex."

Women often rise in salary only to the point at which a man starts.

Women occupy, in great masses, the "household tasks" of industry. They are nurses but not doctors, secretaries but not executives, researchers but not writers, workers but not managers, bookkeepers but not promoters.

Women almost never occupy decision- or policy-making positions.

Women are almost non-existent in government.

Women are subject to a set of "protective" laws that restrict their working hours, do not allow them to occupy many jobs in which the carrying of weights is involved, do not allow them to enter innumerable bars, restaurants, hotels, and other public places unescorted.

Women, despite 100 years of reform, exist in the domestic and marriage laws of our country almost literally as appendages of their husbands. Did you know that rape by a husband is legal but that if a woman refuses to sleep with her husband she is subject to legal suit? Did you know that the word domicile in the law refers to the husband's domicile and that if a woman refuses to follow her husband to wherever he makes his home, legal suit can be brought against her to force her to do so? Did you know that in most states the law imposes severe legal disabilities on married women with regard to their personal and property rights? (As a feminist said to me: "The United Nations has defined servitude as necessarily involuntary, but women, ignorant of the law, put themselves into *voluntary* servitude.")

Perhaps, you will say, these observations are not so shocking. After all, women *are* weaker than men, they do need protection, what on earth is so terrible about being protected, for God's sake! And as for those laws, they're never invoked, no woman is dragged anywhere against her will, on the contrary, women's desires rule the middle-class household, and women can work at hundreds of jobs, in fact, a great deal of the wealth of the country is in their hands, and no woman ever goes hungry.

I agree. These observed facts of our national life are not so shocking. The laws and what accrues from them are not so terrible. It is what's behind the laws that is so terrible. It is not the letter of the law but the spirit determining the law that is terrible. It is not what is explicit but what is implicit in the law that is terrible. It is not the apparent condition but the actual condition of woman that is terrible.

"The woman's issue is the true barometer of social change," said a famous political theoretician. This was true 100 years ago; it is no less true today. Women and blacks were and are, traditionally and perpetually, the great "outsiders" in Western culture, and their erratic swellings of outrage parallel each other in a number of ways that are both understandable and also extraordinary. A hundred years ago a great abolitionist force wrenched this country apart and changed its history forever; many, many radical men devoted a fever of life to wrecking a system in which men were bought and sold; many radical women worked toward the same end; the abolitionist movement contained women who came out of educated and liberal 19th century families, women who considered themselves independent thinking beings. It was only when Elizabeth Cady Stanton and Lucretia Mott were not allowed to be seated at a World Anti-Slavery Conference held in the 1840s that the intellectual abolitionist women suddenly perceived that their own political existence resembled that of the blacks. They raised the issue with their radical men and were denounced furiously for introducing an insignificant and divisive issue, one which was sure to weaken the movement. Let's win this war first, they said, and then we'll see about women's rights. But the women had seen, in one swift visionary moment, to the very center of the truth about their own lives, and they knew that first was *now*, that there would never be a time when men would willingly address themselves to the question of female rights, that to strike out now for women's rights could do nothing but strengthen the issue of black civil rights because it called attention to all instances or rights denied in a nation that prided itself on rights for all.

Thus was born the original Women's Rights Movement, which became known as the Women's Suffrage Movement because the single great issue, of course, was legal political recognition. But it was never meant to begin and end with the vote, just as the abolitionist movement was never meant to begin and end with the vote. Somehow, though, that awful and passionate struggle for suffrage seemed to exhaust both the blacks and the women, especially the women, for when the vote finally came at the end of the Civil War, it was handed to black males—but not to women; the women had to go on fighting for 60 bitterly long years for suffrage. And then both blacks and women lay back panting, unable to catch their breath for generation upon generation.

The great civil rights movement for blacks in the 1950s and '60s is the second wind of that monumental first effort, necessary because the legislated political equality of the 1860s was never translated into actual equality. The reforms promised by law had never happened. The piece of paper meant nothing. Racism had never been legislated out of existence; in fact, its original virulence had remained virtually untouched, and, more important, the black in this country had never been able to shake off the slave mentality. He was born scared, he ran scared, he died scared; for 100 years after legal emancipation, he lived as though it had never happened. Blacks and whites did not regard either themselves or each other differently, and so they in no way lived differently. In the 1950s and '60s the surging force behind the renewed civil rights effort has been the desire to eradicate this condition more than any other, to enable the American black to believe in himself as a whole, independent, expressive human being capable of fulfilling and protecting himself in the very best way he knows how. Today, after more than 15 years of unremitting struggle, after a formidable array of reform laws legislated at the federal, state, and local level, after a concentration on black rights and black existence that has traumatized the nation, it is still not unfair to say that the psychology of defeat has not been lifted from black life. Still (aside from the continuance of crime, drugs, broken homes, and all the wretched rest of it), employers are able to say: "Sure, I'd love to hire one if I could find one who qualified," and while true, half the time it *is*, because black life is still marked by the "nigger mentality," the terrible inertia of spirit that accompanies the perhaps irrational but deeply felt conviction that no matter what one does, one is going to wind up a 35-year-old busboy. This "nigger mentality'' characterizes black lives. It also characterizes women's lives. And it is this, and this alone, that is behind the second wave of feminism now sweeping the country and paralleling precisely, exactly as it does 100 years ago, the black rights movement. The fight for reform laws is just the beginning. What women are really after this time around is the utter eradication of the ''nigger'' in themselves.

Most women who feel ''niggerized'' have tales of overt oppression to tell. They feel they've been put down by their fathers, their brothers, their lovers, their bosses. They feel that in their families, in their sex lives, and in their jobs they have counted as nothing, they have been treated as second-class citizens, their minds have been deliberately stunted and their emotions warped. My own experience with the condition is a bit more subtle, and, without bragging, I do believe a bit closer to the true feminist point.

To begin with, let me tell a little story. Recently, I had lunch with a man I had known at school. He and his wife and I had all been friends at college; they had courted while we were in school and immediately upon graduation they got married. They were both talented art students, and it was assumed both would work in commercial art. But shortly after their marriage she became pregnant, and never did go to work. Within five years they had two children. At first I visited them often; their home was lovely, full of their mutual talent for atmosphere; the wife sparkled, the children flourished; he rose in the field of commercial art; I envied them both their self-containment, and she especially her apparently contented, settled state. But as I had remained single and life took me off in various other directions we soon began to drift apart, and when I again met the husband we had not seen each other in many years. We spoke animatedly of what we had both been doing for quite a while. Then I asked about his wife. His face rearranged itself suddenly, but I couldn't quite tell how at first. He said she was fine, but didn't sound right.

''What's wrong?'' I asked. ''Is she doing something you don't want her to do? Or the other way around?''

''No, no,'' he said hastily. ''I want her to do whatever she wants to do. Anything. Anything that will make her happy. And get her off my back,'' he ended bluntly. I asked what he meant and he told me of his wife's restlessness of the last few years, of how sick she was of being a housewife, how useless she felt, and how she longed to go back to work.

''Well,'' I asked, ''did you object?''

''Of course not!'' he replied vigorously. ''Why the hell would I do that? She's a very talented woman, her children are half grown, she's got every right in the world to go to work.''

''So?'' I said.

''It's *her,*'' he said bewilderedly. ''She doesn't seem able to just go out and get a job.''

''What do you mean?'' I asked. But beneath the surface of my own puzzled response I more than half knew what was coming.

''Well, she's scared, I think. She's more talented than half the people who walk into my office asking for work, but do what I will she won't get a portfolio together and make the rounds. Also, she cries a lot lately. For no reason, if you know what I mean. And then, she can't seem to get up in the morning in time to get a babysitter and get out of the house. This is a woman who was always up at 7 A.M. to feed everybody, get things going; busy, capable, doing 10 things at once.'' He shook his head as though in a true quandary. ''Oh well,'' he ended up. ''I guess it doesn't really matter any more.''

''Why not?'' I asked.

His eyes came up and he looked levelly at me. ''She's just become pregnant again.''

I listened silently, but with what internal churning! Even though the external events of our lives were quite different, I felt as though this woman had been living inside my skin all these years, so close was I to the essential nature of her experience as I perceived it listening to her husband's woebegone tale. I had wandered about the world, I had gained another degree, I had married twice, I had written, taught, edited, I had no children. And yet I knew that in some fundamental sense we were the same woman. I understood exactly—but exactly—the kind of neurotic anxiety that just beset her, and that had ultimately defeated her; it was a neurosis I shared and had recognized in almost every woman I had ever known—including Monica Vitti, having her Schiaparellied nervous breakdown, stuffing her hand into her mouth, rolling her eyes wildly, surrounded by helplessly sympathetic men who kept saying: "Just tell me what's *wrong.*"

I was raised in an immigrant home where education was worshiped. As the entire American culture was somewhat mysterious to my parents, the educational possibilities of that world were equally unknown for both the boy and the girl in our family. Therefore, I grew up in the certainty that if my brother went to college, I too could go to college; and, indeed, he did, and I in my turn did too. We both read voraciously from early childhood on, and we were both encouraged to do so. We both had precocious and outspoken opinions and neither of us was ever discouraged from uttering them. We both were exposed early to unionist radicalism and neither of us met with opposition when, separately, we experimented with youthful political organizations. And yet somewhere along the line my brother and I managed to receive an utterly different education regarding ourselves and our own expectations from life. He was taught many things but what he learned was the need to develop a kind of inner necessity. I was taught many things, but what I learned, ultimately, was that it was the prime vocation of my life to prepare myself for the love of a good man and the responsibilities of homemaking and motherhood. All the rest, the education, the books, the jobs, that was all very nice and of course, why not? I was an intelligent girl, shouldn't I learn? *make* something of myself! but oh dolly, you'll see, in the end no woman could possibly be happy without a man to love and children to raise. What's more, came the heavy implication, if I *didn't* marry I would be considered an irredeemable failure.

How did I learn this? How? I have pondered this question 1000 times. Was it really that explicit? Was it laid out in lessons strategically planned and carefully executed? Was it spooned down my throat at regular intervals? No. It wasn't. I have come finally to understand that the lessons were implicit and they took place in 100 different ways, in a continuous day-to-day exposure to an *attitude,* shared by all, about women, about what kind of creatures they were and what kind of lives they were meant to live; the lessons were administered not only by my parents but by the men and women, the boys and girls, all around me who, of course, had been made in the image of this attitude.

My mother would say to me when I was very young, as I studied at the kitchen table and she cooked: "How lucky you are to go to school! I wasn't so lucky. I had to go to work in the factory. I wanted so to be a nurse! But go be a nurse in Williamsburg in 1920! Maybe you'll be a nurse. . . ." I listened, I nodded, but somehow the message I got was that I was like her and I would one day be doing what she was now doing.

My brother was the "serious and steady" student, I the "erratic and undisciplined" one. When he studied the house was silenced; when I studied, business as usual.

When I was 14 and I came in flushed and disarrayed my mother knew I'd been with a boy. Her fingers gripped my upper arm; her face, white and intent, bent over me: What did he do to you? *Where* did he do it? I was frightened to death. What was she so upset about? What could he do to me? I learned that I was the keeper of an incomparable treasure and it had to be guarded: it was meant to be a gift for my husband. (Later that year when I read "A Rage to Live" I knew without any instruction exactly what all those elliptical sentences were about.)

When I threw some hideous temper tantrum my mother would say: "What a little female you are!" (I have since seen many little boys throw the same tantrums and have noted with interest that they are not told they are little females.)

The girls on the street would talk forever about boys, clothes, movies, fights with their mothers. The 1000 thoughts racing around in my head from the books I was reading remained secret, no one to share them with.

The boys would be gentler with the girls than with each other when we all played roughly; and our opinions were never considered seriously.

I grew up, I went to school, I came out, wandered around, went to Europe, went back to school, wandered again, taught in a desultory fashion, and at last! got married!

It was during my first marriage that I began to realize something was terribly wrong inside me, but it took me 10 years to understand that I was suffering the classic female pathology. My husband, like all the men I have known, was a good man, a man who wanted my independence for me more than I wanted it for myself. He urged me to work, to do something, anything, that would make me happy; he knew that our pleasure in each other could be heightened only if I was a functioning human being too. Yes, yes! I said, and leaned back in the rocking chair with yet another novel. Somehow, I couldn't do anything. I didn't really know where to start, what I wanted to do. Oh, I had always had a number of interests but they, through an inability on my part to stick with anything, had always been superficial; when I arrived at a difficult point in a subject, a job, an interest, I would simply drop it. Of course, what I really wanted to do was write; but that was an altogether ghastly agony and one I could never come to grips with. There seemed to be some terrible aimlessness at the very center of me, some paralyzing lack of will. My energy, which was abundant, was held in a trap of some sort; occasionally that useless energy would wake up roaring, demanding to be let out of its cage, and then I became "emotional"; I would have hysterical depressions, rage on and on about the meaninglessness of my life, force my husband into long psychoanalytic discussions about the source of my (our) trouble, end in a purging storm of tears, a determination to do "something," and six months later I was right back where I started. If my marriage had not dissolved, I am sure that I would still be in exactly that same peculiarly nightmarish position. But as it happened, the events of life forced me out into the world, and repeatedly I had to come up against myself. I found this pattern of behavior manifesting itself in 100 different circumstances; regardless of how things began, they always seemed to end in the same place. Oh, I worked, I advanced, in a sense, but only erratically and with superhuman effort. Always the battle was internal, and it was with a kind of paralyzing anxiety at the center of me that drained off my energy and retarded my capacity for intellectual concentration. It took me a long time to perceive that nearly every woman I knew exhibited the same symptoms, and when I did perceive it, became frightened. I thought, at first, that perhaps, indeed, we were all victims of some biological deficiency, that some vital ingredient had been deleted in the female of the species, that we were a physiological metaphor for human neurosis. It took me a long time to understand, with an understanding that is irrevocable, that we are the victims of culture, not biology.

Recently, I read a marvelous biography of Beatrice Webb, the English socialist. The book is full of vivid portraits, but the one that is fixed forever in my mind is that of Mrs. Webb's mother, Laurencina Potter. Laurencina Potter was a beautiful, intelligent, intellectually energetic woman of the middle 19th century. She knew 12 languages, spoke Latin and Greek better than half the classics-trained men who came to her home, and was interested in everything. Her marriage to wealthy and powerful Richard Potter was a love match, and she looked forward to a life of intellectual companionship, stimulating activity, lively participation. No sooner were they married than Richard installed her in a Victorian fortress in the country, surrounded her with servants and physical comfort, and started her off with the first of the 11 children she eventually bore. He went out into the world, bought and sold railroads, made important political connections, mingled in London society, increased his powers, and relished his life. She, meanwhile, languished. She sat in the country, staring at the four brocaded walls; her energy remained bottled up, her mind became useless, her will evaporated. The children became symbols of her enslavement and, in consequence, she was a lousy mother: neurotic, self-absorbed, increasingly colder and more withdrawn, increasingly more involved in taking her emotional temperature. She became, in short, the Victorian lady afflicted with indefinable maladies.

When I read of Laurencina's life I felt as though I was reading about the lives of most of the women I know, and it struck me that 100 years ago sexual submission was all for a woman, and today sexual fulfillment is all for a woman, and the two are one and the same.

Most of the women I know are people of superior intelligence, developed emotions, and higher education. And yet our friendships, our conversations, our lives, are not marked by intellectual substance or emotional distance or objective concern. It is only briefly and insubstantially that I ever discuss books or politics or philosophical issues or abstractions of any kind with the women I know. Mainly, we discuss and are intimate about our Emotional Lives. Endlessly, endlessly, we go on and on about our emotional "problems" and "needs" and "relationships." And, of course, because we are all bright and well-educated, we bring to bear on these sessions a formidable amount of sociology and psychology, literature and history, all hoked out so that it sounds as though these are serious conversations on serious subjects, when in fact they are caricatures of seriousness right out of Jonathan Swift. Caricatures, because they have no beginning, middle, end, or point. They go nowhere, they conclude nothing, they change nothing. They are elaborate descriptions in the ongoing soap opera that is our lives. It took me a long time to understand that we were talking about nothing, and it took me an even longer and harder time, traveling down that dark, narrow road in the mind, back back to the time when I was a little girl sitting in the kitchen with my mother, to understand, at last, that the affliction was cultural not biological, that it was because we had never been taught to take ourselves seriously that I and all the women I knew had become parodies of "taking ourselves seriously."

The rallying cry of the black civil rights movement has always been: "Give us back our manhood!" What exactly does that mean? Where is black manhood? How has it been taken from blacks? And how can it be retrieved? The answer lies in one word: responsibility; therefore, they have been deprived of self-respect; therefore, they have been deprived of manhood. Women have been deprived of exactly the same thing and in every real sense have thus been deprived of womanhood. We have never been prepared to assume responsibility; we have never been prepared to make demands upon ourselves; we have never been taught to expect the development of what is best in ourselves because no one has ever expected *anything* of us—or for us. Because no one has ever had any intention of turning over any serious work to us. Both we and the blacks lost the ballgame before we ever got up to play. In order to live you've got to have nerve; and we were stripped of our nerve before we began. Black is ugly and female is inferior. These are the primary lessons of our experience, and in these ways both blacks and women have been kept, not as functioning nationals, but rather as operating objects. But a human being who remains as a child throughout his adult life is an object, not a mature specimen, and the definition of a child is: one without reponsibility.

At the very center of all human life is energy, psychic energy. It is the force of that energy that drives us, that surges continually up in us, that must repeatedly spend and renew itself in us, that must perpetually be reaching for something beyond itself in order to satisfy its own insatiable appetite. It is the imperative of that energy that has determined man's characteristic interest, problem-solving. The modern ecologist attests to that driving need by demonstrating that in a time when all the real problems are solved, man makes up new ones in order to go on solving. He must have work, work that he considers real and serious, or he will die, he will simply shrivel up and die. That is the one certain characteristic of human beings. And it is the one characteristic, above all others, that the accidentally dominant white male asserts is not necessary to more than half the members of the race, i.e., the female of the species. This assertion is, quite simply, a lie. Nothing more, nothing less. A lie. That energy is alive in every woman in the world. It lies trapped and dormant like a growing tumor, and at its center there is despair, hot, deep, wordless.

It is amazing to me that I have just written these words. To think that 100 years after Nora slammed the door, and in a civilization and a century utterly converted to the fundamental insights of that exasperating genius, Sigmund Freud, women could still be raised to believe that their basic makeup is determined not by the needs of their egos but by their peculiar child-bearing properties and their so-called unique capacity for loving. No man worth his salt does not wish to be a husband and father; yet no man is raised to be a husband and father and no man would ever conceive of those relationships as instruments of his prime function in life. Yet every woman is raised, still, to believe that the fulfillment of these relationships is her prime function in life and, what's more, her instinctive choice.

The fact is that women have no special capacities for love, and, when a culture reaches a level where its women have nothing to do but "love" (as occurred in the Victorian upper classes and as is occurring now in the American middle classes), they prove to be very bad at it. The modern American wife is not noted for her love of her husband or of her children; she is noted for her driving (or should I say driven?) domination of them. She displays an aberrated, aggressive ambition for her mate and for her offspring which can be explained only by the most vicious feelings toward the self. The reasons are obvious. The woman who must love for a living, the woman who has no self, no objective external reality to take her own measure by, no work to discipline her, no goal to provide the illusion of progress, no internal resources, no separate mental existence, is constitutionally incapable of the emotional distance that is one of the real requirements of love. She cannot separate herself from her husband and children because all the passionate and multiple needs of her being are centered on them. That's why women "take everything personally." It's all they've got to take. "Loving" must substitute for an entire range of feeling and interest. The man, who is not raised to be a husband and father specifically, and who simply loves as a single function of his existence, cannot understand her abnormal "emotionality" and concludes that this is the female nature. (Why shouldn't he? She does too.) But this is not so. It is a result of a psychology achieved by cultural attitudes that run so deep and have gone on for so long that they are mistaken for "nature" or "instinct."

A good example of what I mean are the multiple legends of our culture regarding motherhood. Let's use our heads for a moment. What on earth is holy about motherhood? I mean, why motherhood rather than fatherhood? If anything is holy, it is the consecration of sexual union. A man plants a seed in a woman; the seed matures and eventually is expelled by the woman; a child is born to both of them; each contributed the necessary parts to bring about procreation; each is responsible to and necessary to the child; to claim that the woman is more so than the man is simply not true; certainly it cannot be proven biologically or psychologically (please, no comparisons with baboons and penguins just now—I am sure I can supply 50 examples from nature to counter any assertion made on the subject); all that can be proven is that some*one* is necessary to the newborn baby; to have instilled in women the belief that their child-bearing and housewifely obligations supersede all other needs, that indeed what they fundamentally *want* and need is to be wives and mothers as distinguished from being anything else, is to have accomplished an act of trickery, an act which has deprived women of the proper forms of expression necessary to that force of energy alive in every talking creature, an act which has indeed mutilated their natural selves and deprived them of their womanhood, what*ever* that may be, deprived them of the right to say "I" and have it mean something. This understanding, grasped whole, is what underlies the current wave of feminism. It is felt by thousands of women today, it will be felt by millions tomorrow. You have only to examine briefly a fraction of the women's rights organizations already in existence to realize instantly that they form the nucleus of a genuine movement, complete with theoreticians, tacticians, agitators, manifestos, journals, and thesis papers, running the entire political spectrum from conservative reform to visionary radicalism, and powered by an emotional conviction rooted in undeniable experience, and fed by a determination that is irreversible.

One of the oldest and stablest of the feminist organizations is NOW, the National Organization for Women. It was started in 1966 by a group of professional women headed by Mrs. Betty Friedan, author of *The Feminine Mystique,* the book that was the bringer of the word in 1963 to the new feminists. NOW has more than 3000 members, chapters in major cities and on many campuses all over the country, and was read, at its inception, into the Congressional Record. It has many men in its ranks and it works, avowedly within the system, to bring about the kind of reforms that will result in what it calls a "truly equal partnership between men and women" in this country. It is a true reform organization filled with intelligent, liberal, hardworking women devoted to the idea that America is a reformist democracy and ultimately will respond to the justice of their cause. They are currently hard at work on two major issues: repeal of the abortion laws and passage of the Equal Rights Amendment (for which feminists have been fighting since 1923) which would amend the constitution to provide that "equality of rights under the law shall not be denied or abridged by the United States or by any state on account of sex." When this amendment is passed, the employment and marriage laws of more than 40 states will be affected. Also, in direct conjunction with the fight to have this amendment passed, NOW demands increased child-care facilities to be established by law on the same basis as parks, libraries, and public schools.

NOW's influence is growing by leaps and bounds. It is responsible for the passage of many pieces of legislation meant to wipe out discrimination against women, and certainly the size and number of Women's Bureaus, Women's Units, Women's Commissions springing up in government agencies and legislative bodies all over the country reflect its presence. Suddenly, there are Presidential reports and gubernatorial conferences and congressional meetings—all leaping all over each other to discuss the status of women. NOW, without a doubt, is the best established feminist group.

From NOW we move, at a shocking rate of speed, to the left. In fact, it would appear that NOW is one of the few reformist groups, that mainly the feminist groups are radical, both in structure and in aim. Some, truth to tell, strike a bizarre and puzzling note. For instance, there is WITCH (Women's International Terrorists Conspiracy From Hell), an offshoot of SDS, where members burned their bras and organized against the Miss America Pageant in a stirring demand that the commercially useful image of female beauty be wiped out. There is Valerie Solanas and her SCUM Manifesto, in which Solanas's penetrating observation on our national life was: "If the atom bomb isn't dropped, this society will hump itself to death." There is Cell 55. God knows what they do.

There are the Redstockings, an interesting group that seems to have evolved from direct action into what they call "consciousness-raising." That means, essentially, that they get together in a kind of group therapy session and the women reveal their experiences and feelings to each other in an attempt to analyze the femaleness of their psychology and their circumstances, thereby increasing the invaluable weapon of self-understanding.

And finally, there are the Feminists, without a doubt the most fiercely radical and intellectually impressive of all the groups. This organization was begun a year ago by a group of defectors from NOW and various other feminist groups, in rebellion against the repetition of the hierarchical structure of power in these other groups. Their contention was: women have always been "led"; if they join the rank and file of a feminist organization they are simply being led again. It will still be someone else, even if only the officers of their own interesting group, making the decisions, doing the planning, the executing, and so on. They determined to develop a leaderless society whose guiding principle was participation by lot. And this is precisely what they have done. The organization has no officers, every woman sooner or later performs every single task necessary to the life and aims of the organization, and the organization is willing to temporarily sacrifice efficiency in order that each woman may fully develop all the skills necessary to autonomous functioning. This working individualism is guarded fiercely by a set of rigid rules regarding attendance, behavior, duties, and loyalties.

The Feminists encourage extensive theorizing on the nature and function of a leaderless society, and this has led the organization to a bold and radical view of the future they wish to work for. The group never loses sight of the fact that its primary enemy is the male-female role system which has ended in women being the oppressed and men being the oppressors. It looks forward to a time when this system will be completely eradicated. To prepare for this coming, it now denounces all the institutions which encourage the system, i.e., love, sex, and marriage. It has a quota on married women (only one-third of their number are permitted to be either married or living in a marriage-like situation). It flatly names all men as the enemy. It looks forward to a future in which the family as we know it will disappear, all births will be extra-uterine, children will be raised by communal efforts, and women once and for all will cease to be the persecuted members of the race.

Although a lot of this is hard to take in raw doses, you realize that many of these ideas represent interesting and important turns of thought. First of all, these experiments with a leaderless society are being echoed everywhere: in student radicalism, in black civil rights, in hippie communes. They are part of a great radical lusting after self-determination that is beginning to overtake this country. This is true social revolution, and I believe that feminism, in order to accomplish its aims now, does need revolution, does need a complete overthrow of an old kind of thought and the introduction of a new kind of thought. Secondly, the Feminists are right: most of what men and women now are is determined by the "roles" they play, and love *is* an institution, full of ritualized gestures and positions, and often void of any recognizable naturalness. How, under the present iron-bound social laws, can one know what is female nature and what is female role? (And that question speaks to the source of the whole female pain and confusion.) It *is* thrilling to contemplate a new world, brave or otherwise, in which men and women may free themselves of some of the crippling sexual poses that now circumscribe their lives, thus allowing them some open and equitable exchange of emotion, some release of the natural self which will be greeted with resentment from no one.

But the Feminists strike a wrong and rather hysterical note when they indicate that they don't believe there is a male or female nature, that all is role. I believe that is an utterly wrong headed notion. Not only do I believe there is a genuine male or female nature in each of us, but I believe that what is most exciting about the new world that may be coming is the promise of stripping down to that nature, of the complementary elements in those natures meeting without anxiety, of our different biological tasks being performed without profit for one at the expense of the other.

The Feminists' position is extreme and many of these pronouncements are chilling at first touch. But you quickly realize that this is the harsh, stripped-down language of revolution that is, the language of icy "honesty," of narrow but penetrating vision. (As one Feminist said sweetly, quoting her favorite author: "In order to have a revolution you must have a revolutionary theory.") And besides, you sue for thousands and hope to collect hundreds.

Many feminists, though, are appalled by the Feminists (the in-fighting in the movement is fierce), feel they are fascists, "superweak," annihilatingly single-minded, and involved in a power play no matter what they say; but then again you can find feminists who will carefully and at great length put down every single feminist group going. But there's one great thing about these chicks: if five feminists fall out with six groups, within half an hour they'll all find each other (probably somewhere on Bleecker Street), within 48 hours a new splinter faction will have announced its existence, and within two weeks the manifesto is being mailed out. It's the mark of a true movement.

Two extremely intelligent and winning feminists who are about to "emerge" as part of a new group are Shulamith Firestone, an ex-Redstocking, and Anne Koedt, an ex-Feminist, and both members of the original radical group, New York Radical Women. They feel that none of the groups now going has the capacity to build a broad mass movement among the women of this country and they intend to start one that will. Both are dedicated to social revolution and agree with many of the ideas of many of the other radical groups. Each one, in her own words, comes equipped with "impeccable revolutionary credentials." They come out of the Chicago SDS and the New York civil rights movement. Interestingly enough, like many of the radical women in this movement, they were converted to feminism because in their participation in the New Left they met with intolerable female discrimination. ("Yeah, baby, comes the revolution . . . baby, comes the revolution. . . . Meanwhile, you make the coffee and later I'll tell you where to hand out the leaflets." And when they raised the issue of women's rights with their radical young men, they were greeted with furious denunciations of introducing divisive issues! Excuse me, but haven't we been here before?)

The intention of Miss Firestone and Miss Koedt is to start a group that will be radical in aim but much looser in structure than anything they've been involved with; it will be an action group, but everyone will also be encouraged to theorize, analyze, create; it will appeal to the broad base of educated women; on the other hand, it will not sound ferocious to the timid non-militant woman. In other words . . .

I mention these two in particular, but at this moment in New York, in Cambridge, in Chicago, in New Haven, in Washington, in San Francisco, in East Podunk—yes! believe it!—there are dozens like them preparing to do the same thing. They are gathering fire and I do believe the next great moment in history is theirs. God knows, for my unborn daughter's sake, I hope so.

DISCUSSION QUESTIONS

1. Which of the advertisements reprinted in the "Advertising" section could be used to document the feminist issues in Gornick's essay?

2. In what ways can Gornick's essay be used to establish an ideological context for the situations dramatized in Kate Chopin's "The Dream of an Hour" and Tillie Olsen's "I Stand Here Ironing" (see "Classics")? What attitudes toward the experiences of women do they share? In what ways do they differ?

Mike Royko / Jackie's Debut a Unique Day

Chicago Daily News, October 25, 1972

Mike Royko (b. 1933) writes a 750-word column for the Chicago Sun-Times *five times every week. He did the same for the* Chicago Daily News *for fourteen years. He has been awarded just about every major journalism prize in the business. Author of numerous books, one a longtime resident of the best-seller list, Royko grew up in the tough North Side of Chicago, and his columns have a streetwise slant on the social and political events of that city.*

In "Jackie's Debut a Unique Day," Royko offers a vivid glance at a seminal moment in American race relations. His description of the African Americans who flocked to see—and to cheer—baseball's first nonwhite player, and his poignant account of his own sudden awareness and horror of white racism, throw the light of history on the ethnically diverse arena of today's organized sports.

All that Saturday, the wise men of the neighborhood, who sat in chairs on the sidewalk outside the tavern, had talked about what it would do to baseball.

I hung around and listened because baseball was about the most important thing in the world, and if anything was going to ruin it, I was worried.

Most of the things they said, I didn't understand, although it all sounded terrible. But could one man bring such ruin?

They said he could and he would. And the next day he was going to be in Wrigley Field for the first time, on the same diamond as Hack, Nicholson, Cavarretta, Schmidt, Pafko, and all my other idols.

I had to see Jackie Robinson, the man who was going to somehow wreck everything. So the next day, another kid and I started walking to the ball park early.

We always walked to save the streetcar fare. It was five or six miles, but I felt about baseball the way Abe Lincoln felt about education.

Usually, we could get there just at noon, find a seat in the grandstands, and watch some batting practice. But not that Sunday, May 18, 1947.

By noon, Wrigley Field was almost filled. The crowd outside spilled off the sidewalk and into the streets. Scalpers were asking top dollar for box seats and getting it.

I had never seen anything like it. Not just the size, although it was a new record, more than 47,000. But this was 25 years ago, and in 1947 few blacks were seen in the Loop, much less up on the white North Side at a Cub game.

That day, they came by the thousands, pouring off the northbound Ls and out of their cars.

They didn't wear baseball-game clothes. They had on church clothes and funeral clothes—suits, white shirts, ties, gleaming shoes, and straw hats. I've never seen so many straw hats.

As big as it was, the crowd was orderly. Almost unnaturally so. People didn't jostle each other.

The whites tried to look as if nothing unusual was happening, while the blacks tried to look casual and dignified. So everybody looked slightly ill at ease.

For most, it was probably the first time they had been that close to each other in such great numbers.

We managed to get in, scramble up a ramp, and find a place to stand behind the last row of grandstand seats. Then they shut the gates. No place remained to stand.

Robinson came up in the first inning. I remember the sound. It wasn't the shrill, teen-age cry you now hear, or an excited gut roar. They applauded, long, rolling applause. A tall, middle-aged black man stood next to me, a smile of almost painful joy on his face, beating his palms together so hard they must have hurt.

When Robinson stepped into the batter's box, it was as if someone had flicked a switch. The place went silent.

He swung at the first pitch and they erupted as if he had knocked it over the wall. But it was only a high foul that dropped into the box seats. I remember thinking it was strange that a foul could make that many people happy. When he struck out, the low moan was genuine.

I've forgotten most of the details of the game, other than that the Dodgers won and Robinson didn't get a hit or do anything special, although he was cheered on every swing and every routine play.

But two things happened I'll never forget. Robinson played first, and early in the game a Cub star hit a grounder and it was a close play.

Just before the Cub reached first, he swerved to his left. And as he got to the bag, he seemed to slam his foot down hard at Robinson's foot.

It was obvious to everyone that he was trying to run into him or spike him. Robinson took the throw and got clear at the last instant.

I was shocked. That Cub, a home-town boy, was my biggest hero. It was not only an unheroic stunt, but it seemed a rude thing to do in front of people who would cheer for a foul ball. I didn't understand why he had done it. It wasn't at all big league.

I didn't know that while the white fans were relatively polite, the Cubs and most other teams kept up a steady stream of racial abuse from the dugout. I thought that all they did down there was talk about how good Wheaties are.

Later in the game, Robinson was up again and he hit another foul ball. This time it came into the stands low and fast, in our direction. Somebody in the seats grabbed for it, but it caromed off his hand and kept coming. There was a flurry of arms as the ball kept bouncing, and suddenly it was between me and my pal. We both grabbed. I had a baseball.

The two of us stood there examining it and chortling. A genuine, major-league baseball that had actually been gripped and thrown by a Cub pitcher, hit by a Dodger batter. What a possession.

Then I heard the voice say: "Would you consider selling that?"

It was the black man who had applauded so fiercely.

I mumbled something. I didn't want to sell it.

"I'll give you $10 for it," he said.

Ten dollars. I couldn't believe it. I didn't know what $10 could buy because I'd never had that much money. But I know that a lot of men in the neighborhood considered $60 a week to be good pay.

I handed it to him, and he paid me with ten $1 bills.

When I left the ball park, with that much money in my pocket, I was sure that Jackie Robinson wasn't bad for the game.

Since then, I've regretted a few times that I didn't keep the ball. Or that I hadn't given it to him free. I didn't know, then, how hard he probably had to work for that $10.

But Tuesday I was glad I had sold it to him. And if that man is still around, and has that baseball, I'm sure he thinks it was worth every cent.

Susan Jacoby / Unfair Game

New York Times, February 23, 1978

Susan Jacoby (b. 1946) has a prestigious writing career: she has been education reporter for the Washington Post, *columnist of the "Hers" column for the* New York Times, *and free-lance writer in the Soviet Union between 1969–71. She is author of several books, including, in 1979,* The Possible She.

In "Unfair Game" Jacoby shows how spaces in the public sphere are experienced differently for different people. Using delightful satire, Jacoby speculates on causes for our patterns of social behavior and possibilities for change.

Sexual harassment has become a common term since 1978, when Susan Jacoby wrote this column for the New York Times Magazine. *Years before Anita Hill's confrontation with nominee Clarence Thomas caused tumult in the Supreme Court and sent shock waves across the country, Jacoby examined the double standard of conduct that independent women encounter as they move through their busy lives. Her style in this piece is personal yet extends to address a common social predicament.*

Susan Jacoby's essay appeared as part of the "Hers" column in the New York Times Magazine, *a regular column that expresses a woman's perspective on contemporary social issues. (The column alternates with a masculine version, entitled "About Men.")*

My friend and I, two women obviously engrossed in conversation, are sitting at a corner table in the crowded Oak Room of the Plaza[1] at ten o'clock on a Tuesday night. A man materializes and interrupts us with the snappy opening line, "A good woman is hard to find."

We say nothing, hoping he will disappear back into his bottle. But he fancies himself as our genie and asks, "Are you visiting?" Still we say nothing. Finally my friend looks up and says, "We live here." She and I look at each other, the thread of our conversation snapped, our thoughts focused on how to get rid of this intruder. In a minute, if something isn't done, he will scrunch down next to me on the banquette and start offering to buy us drinks.

"Would you leave us alone, please," I say in a loud but reasonably polite voice. He looks slightly offended but goes on with his bright social patter. I become more explicit. "We don't want to talk to you, we didn't ask you over here, and we want to be alone. Go away." This time he directs his full attention to me—and he is mad. "All right, all right, *excuse me.*" He pushes up the corners of his mouth in a Howdy Doody smile. "You ought to try smiling. You might even be pretty if you smiled once in a while."

At last the man leaves. He goes back to his buddy at the bar. I watch them out of the corner of my eye, and he gestures angrily at me for at least fifteen minutes. When he passes our table on the way out of the room, this well-dressed, obviously affluent man mutters, "Good-bye, bitch," under his breath.

Why is this man calling me names? Because I have asserted my right to set at a table in a public place without being drawn into a sexual flirtation. Because he has been told, in no uncertain terms, that two attractive women prefer each other's company to his.

This sort of experience is an old story to any woman who travels, eats, or drinks—for business or pleasure—without a male escort. In Holiday Inns and at

[1] The famous New York City luxury hotel.

the Plaza, on buses and airplanes, in tourist and first class, a woman is always thought to be looking for a man in addition to whatever else she may be doing. The man who barged in on us at the bar would never have broken into the conversation of two men, and it goes without saying that he wouldn't have imposed himself on a man and a woman who were having a drink. But two women at a table are an entirely different matter. Fair game.

This might be viewed as a relatively small flaw in the order of the universe—something in a class with an airplane losing luggage or a computer fouling up a bank statement. Except a computer doesn't foul up your bank account every month and an airline doesn't lose your suitcase every time you fly. But if you are an independent woman, you have to spend a certain amount of energy, day in and day out, in order to go about your business without being bothered by strange men.

On airplanes, I am a close-mouthed traveler. As soon as the "No Smoking" sign is turned off, I usually pull some papers out of my briefcase and start working. Work helps me forget that I am scared of flying. When I am sitting next to a woman, she quickly realizes from my monosyllabic replies that I don't want to chat during the flight. Most men, though, are not content to be ignored.

Once I was flying from New York to San Antonio on a plane that was scheduled to stop in Dallas. My seatmate was an advertising executive who kept questioning me about what I was doing and who remained undiscouraged by my terse replies until I ostentatiously covered myself with a blanket and shut my eyes. When the plane started its descent into Dallas, he made his move.

"You don't really have to get to San Antonio today, do you?"

"Yes."

"Come on, change your ticket. Spend the evening with me here. I'm staying at a wonderful hotel, with a pool, we could go dancing . . ."

"No."

"Well, you can't blame a man for trying."

I do blame a man for trying in this situation—for suggesting that a woman change her work and travel plans to spend a night with a perfect stranger in whom she had displayed no personal interest. The "no personal interest" is crucial; I wouldn't have blamed the man for trying if I had been stroking his cheek and complaining about my dull social life.

There is a nice postscript to this story. Several months later, I was walking my dog in Carl Schurz Park when I ran into my erstwhile seatmate, who was taking a stroll with his wife and children. He recognized me, all right, and was trying to avoid me when I went over and courteously reintroduced myself. I reminded him that we had been on the same flight to Dallas. "Oh, yes," he said. "As I recall you were going on to somewhere else." "San Antonio," I said. "I was in a hurry that day."

The code of feminine politeness, instilled in girlhood, is no help in dealing with the unwanted approaches of strange men. Our mothers didn't teach us to tell a man to get lost; they told us to smile and hint that we'd be just delighted to spend time with the gentleman if we didn't have other commitments. The man in the Oak Room bar would not be put off by a demure lowering of eyelids; he had to be told, roughly and loudly, that his presence was a nuisance.

Not that I am necessarily against men and women picking each other up in public places. In most instances, a modicum of sensitivity will tell a woman or a man whether someone is open to approaches.

Mistakes can easily be corrected by the kind of courtesy so many people have abandoned since the "sexual revolution." One summer evening, I was whiling away a half hour in the outdoor bar of the Stanhope Hotel. I was alone, dressed up, having a drink before going on to meet someone in a restaurant. A man at the next table asked, "If you're not busy, would you like to have a drink with me?" I told him I was sorry but I would be leaving shortly. "Excuse me for disturbing you," he said, turning back to his own drink. Simple courtesy. No insults and no hurt feelings.

One friend suggested that I might have avoided the incident in the Oak Room by going to the Palm Court[2] instead. It's true that the Palm Court is a traditional meeting place for unescorted ladies. But I don't like violins when I want to talk. And I wanted to sit in a large, comfortable leather chair. Why should I have to hide among the potted palms to avoid men who think I'm looking for something else?

Jimmy Breslin / Life in a Cage

New York Daily News, May 21, 1987

In May 1987, an unusual and disturbing accident occurred at the Prospect Park Zoo in New York: eleven-year-old Juan Perez was eaten alive by two polar bears. The boy had slipped into the polar bear cage on a dare; his two young companions on this adventure, less audacious than Juan, managed to flee the area before the bears got to them. Juan's bizarre death and the subsequent killing of the bears by zoo authorities garnered public notice nationwide as horrified parents argued with animal rights activists over who was at fault and what improvements in the zoo system were needed.

Jimmy Breslin, considered by many to be the quintessential New York columnist, broadens the tale of Juan Perez to include a moral reproof, aimed not against neglectful zoo managers, but against the city of New York in general. Breslin employs his characteristic style—rendering the atmosphere of the city's neighborhoods through detailed descriptions of people's daily lives—to communicate his message: that for many children, a life of poverty is as much of a cage as the one in which Perez met his death.

Jimmy Breslin began his career as a copy boy for the Long Island Press *and later worked for the* Boston Globe, *the Scripps-Howard Syndicate, the* New York Journal-American, *the* New York Herald-Tribune, *the* New York Post, *and the* New York Daily News. *In 1991 he published a biography of Damon Runyon. Jimmy Breslin currently writes a column for* Newsday. *An emotional writer with a hard-boiled sensibility and liberal political leanings, Breslin speaks to a wide audience through his conversational yet pointed prose style.*

That winter, when the landlord didn't give any heat because, as people in the building remember him telling them, he simply forgot to do it, Juan Perez would wake up and go right into the shower. All the time that anybody knew him, the little boy started the day with a shower. All that winter it was a shower with icy water, which made all the other people cringe, he couldn't wait to jump in each morning.

"He came to this apartment in the morning," Frances Tamariz was saying yesterday, "with this wet head. And I would say, Bezoki, that was the name we called him, Bezoki, how can you go around with a wet head when we are all so cold? Did you take a shower? And he would say, 'Yes, I love the cold water.' That was what he was like."

[2] Another restaurant at the Plaza.

Frances Tamariz lives on the second floor and the family of Juan Perez on the first floor of 162 E. 18th St. in Flatbush, a neighborhood of old apartment houses that are packed with people who trace their beginnings from anywhere from south of Virginia to the islands in the last waters of the Caribbean. Frances Tamariz is Peruvian. Just walking along yesterday, on any avenue, down any street, there seemed to be easily more children than can be seen anyplace in the city. Around the corner from the Perez house yesterday, I counted 43 kids on the street, and when I turned the corner and got to number 162, where Juan Perez lived, here was a woman walking into the building who had seven children with her.

The name Juan Perez was the special one yesterday, for on Tuesday night, a raw night for the time of year, he slipped into the polar bear cage at the Prospect Park Zoo a few blocks away and intended to swim in the partially water-filled bear moat. When the other two kids with him were afraid of the water because it was so cold, Juan Perez took their clothes and threw them in the water to make sure they'd have to go in after them. Then, when the two polar bears, aroused and angry, padded toward Juan, the two friends ran, and Juan Perez, in the cold night, stayed and the polar bears caught him in the corner and began to bite him. As Juan Perez did not know how to be afraid, he told his friends to go and get help because the bears were biting him hard.

And so, at age 11, he became a kid living in the middle of teeming Brooklyn who was eaten alive by polar bears. As this was a special death for a young person, the streets of Flatbush were filled with reporters and television people, and everywhere you went yesterday, all along Prospect Park, here were these television microwave trucks with thick cables coiled around light poles, so the signal could be sent clear and strong to stations that cannot wait to get the pictures out. Pictures of anything: the park, the streets, the people. Get them out, get everything out, get anything out, for this was a most startling news story: boy eaten in the heart of Brooklyn by polar bear.

I guess it was a momentous story because of the manner in which the boy died. But at the same time, perhaps somebody should stop just for a paragraph here this morning and mention the fact that there are many children being eaten alive by this bear of a city, New York in the 1980s. To say many is to make an understatement most bland, for there are hundreds of thousands of young in New York who each day have the hope, and thus the life, chewed out of them in a city that feels the bestowing of fame and fortune on landlords is a glorious act, and that all energies and as much money and attention as possible be given to some corporation that threatens to move 40 people to Maryland.

We live in a city, in this New York of the '80s, which makes some builder like Donald Trump into a cheap celebrity, and has a mother who lives with her daughter in a shelter on Catherine Street saying, "You can tell anybody living in a shelter. They all stooped over. All you do is just be sitting all day on the edge of the bed, all hunched over. Nothing to do and no place to go. Just sit there with you little girl and try to amuse her."

And each day in the schools of this city, we stack dead chewed bodies of children up to the classroom ceilings and somebody, somewhere is keeping count and also track of those who are supposed to be in charge or there is no justice anywhere.

The two polar bears were shot.

And now, for the day, we go back to the most thrilling death of a young child, that of Juan Perez. Yesterday, Carmen Perez, the mother, was on the couch in her first-floor apartment, a relative cuddling her head. Others sat in an immaculate living room. The mother cannot speak English and she cannot read or write in any language. But maybe she didn't have time for things like that because she had this apartment on the first floor and there was no way to keep Juan Perez under control. If she walked into the front room, he went out the back window and into an alley and was gone. If she sat in the front room on one of her clean, neat couches and her eyes drooped just a little, Juan Perez was out the window and onto the sidewalk and gone.

"She always would chase him," Frances Tamariz was saying yesterday. "But he could run so fast. All he wanted to do was go out on the street. There was nothing wrong. He always looked nice. The little clothes he had all were clean and pressed. All he wanted to do was run."

"Where was the father?" she was asked.

The father was a drunk, Frances Tamariz, in her proper way of talking, said. "The father was a person who abused alcohol."

"Did he live at home?"

"She got rid of him. He wouldn't work and he lost all hope. He just stayed on the street and drank. When he would come he would try to beat her up. She said to me one day, 'I can take care of myself and my children. I cannot support him.' She threw him out."

"Has he been around today?"

"He died two months ago. He died right out on the street."

"Where?"

"Oh, I don't know. On Church Avenue someplace. By the subway stop. He just died in the street. Then Carmen had to go out and get his body and bury him. He wasn't her husband anymore and she had to bury him. I came home that night with my husband. My husband's name is Fidel. He is a painter. We were coming into the building and Carmen heard us and she opened the door and she told me that her husband died and that she needed money for the funeral. My husband gave her $20. The other people in the building collected money so she could bury her husband."

"How did Juan take it?"

"I saw him when the father died. Juan had on nice black pants and a white shirt. Clean white shirt, all pressed. And he said, 'I saw my father. His face was swollen. But I wasn't afraid. I looked at my father. I wasn't afraid.' "

Debbie McKinney / Youth's Despair Erupts

Anchorage Daily News, January 12, 1988

This harrowing account of a fifteen-year-old boy's bloody rampage and the circumstances surrounding it appeared as part of a Pulitzer Prize–winning series on alcohol's disastrous effects on the native Alaskan population. Debbie McKinney's report begins with a sensational event and then fills in an array of particulars that suggest the symptomatic nature of Chris Conners's seemingly inexplicable act. Rather than preaching the evils of alcohol and drugs, McKinney illustrates in painful detail the effects the abuse of these substances had, not only on Conners, but on the entire village in which he lived. The decay of family life, the inability to find proper work, and an overriding despair about the future connect both as causes and results of drug and alcohol use in Pilot Point and elsewhere in Alaska.

In his acceptance letter to the 1989 Pulitzer Committee, Daily News *managing editor Howard C. Weaver outlined some of the changes resulting from the publication of his paper's series on suicide and self-destruction in Alaska. These pieces managed to effect state legislation on several counts and raised the con-*

sciousness of community leaders about an ongoing and terrible problem. Weaver wrote, "Only a few things can now be said with certainty. The first, and most important, is this: Our series, whatever else its accomplishments, legitimized discussion of the formerly taboo topics of alcoholism—abuse and self-destruction. It galvanized responses in towns, villages and community halls across Alaska. It amplified lonely voices as they cried for help. It brought Alaskans' focus on the future of the Native people into sharp relief."

Reporting such as McKinney's does more than tell a story: it seeks to change the story of communities as they struggle to rectify themselves.

Sophie Larson was the first to be shot. A bullet slammed into her hand, knocking her off the three-wheeler as she and Loren Abyo tried to escape. As she fell, the machine's engine sputtered and died.

Loren ran, but Sophie panicked. She crawled behind the three-wheeler in an attempt to hide. But the gunman kept coming.

It was Sunday, July 31, 1983, in Pilot Point, a fishing village of about 70, surrounded by cold, gray ocean and roads to nowhere on the northern coast of the Alaska Peninsula. The day had begun with a bottle of vodka.

That afternoon, some friends from a neighboring village flew into town with a case of whiskey and six cases of beer, as good a reason as any to party. Someone kicked in marijuana, and a couple of guys shared a gram of cocaine. The group of 10 devoured the drugs and drained the last drop of whiskey at the village airstrip, then topped off the party with a bottle of blackberry brandy.

It was a good time. Then suddenly it wasn't. A fight broke out over one of the women. The blows triggered an explosion deep within the darkest abyss of Chris Conners' mind. The 15-year-old boy, blinded by cocaine, whiskey and a lifetime of hurt that could never be spoken, stormed off and returned with a gun.

In Pilot Point, it's not unusual for children to grow up knowing how to drink. Loren Abyo, 17, and Chris Conners had been drinking together since Chris was in the fifth grade. Now Loren was running for his life and shouting for Sophie to run, too. He sprinted across the tundra and dove over an embankment just as a bullet grazed his back.

Chris Conners then walked up to 19-year-old Sophie, who was crouched behind the three-wheeler. He raised a .357-caliber revolver, aimed and fired. Later she would remember that the bullet burned as it ripped through her neck.

By the time the last shot was fired hours later, three people were dead, four were wounded and the residents of Pilot Point, who had watched Chris Conners grow up cornered by rampant family alcoholism and severe neglect, were left terrified and perplexed at his sudden surge of madness.

His mother, investigators believe, was the last to die. Evelyn Conners was sleeping off a head full of booze when her son walked into her room. Chris was Evelyn's middle son, the son she never could bring herself to love. He pointed a 10-gauge shotgun at her head and squeezed the trigger.

Whatever flipped the switch that day was trivial. The best anyone recalls, Chris tried to kiss Sophie. He thought she wanted him to, but she pushed him away. This was the last rejection he could bear.

Chris was never one to talk about feelings. He never talked about the father who abandoned him. Or the man who killed himself with a bullet through the brain inside his mother's house. Or the way his mother ruined his only hope for a future in the village. After years of burying his emotions, the boy finally broke.

Chris remembers only bits and pieces of what happened that day. Two psychiatrists who examined him believe he was in an alcoholic blackout at the time of the murders. Chris recalls a fight at the airstrip and standing over someone, he doesn't know who, with a gun. He remembers firing a shot at a passing three-wheeler. And he remembers one of the men he wounded saying: ''Chris, what are you going to shoot me for? I never did nothing to you.'' But he doesn't remember shooting the man. He remembers nothing about killing his mother.

His recollection begins on the plane ride to jail, when he looked down at his hands and saw them cuffed and stained with blood.

It wasn't until months later, when Chris saw photographs of his victims, that he fully understood and believed what he had done. As the tears streamed down his face, his emotional suit of armor began to corrode.

For the first time in his life, Chris wanted to talk. The following story is the result of three days of prison interviews with Chris Conners in St. Cloud, Minn., investigators' transcripts, court documents, witnesses' testimony, psychiatrists' reports and telephone interviews with village residents and officials involved in the case.

AN EARLY OUTCAST

Christopher Conners is the product of a summer fling between his mother and a man from a neighboring village. Chris, a mixture of Aleut, Eskimo and Caucasian blood, was born in a cabin in Pilot Point on Feb. 27, 1968. He was the second of three sons born to Evelyn Conners, all of whom had different fathers.

Chris was 10 when he saw his father for the first time. His father had been in the village and was waiting for a plane out when he and Evelyn ran into each other.

Back home, Evelyn told Chris he could go down to the airstrip and take a look at his father. The boy jumped on this three-wheeler and raced off.

The man he saw standing there behind dark, mirrored glasses was tall, broad-shouldered and expressionless. He looked at Chris and Chris looked at him. The boy just kept on riding.

Unlike his two brothers, Chris was extremely overweight as a child, which led to teasing by other children.

Janice Ball, president of the Pilot Point Village Council, said Chris seemed like an outcast for as long as she could recall, particularly with respect to his mother. ''Evelyn would call Chris all kinds of names—not even really treat his as a son,'' she said.

''Christopher could never do anything right, and his mother was always picking on him,'' is the way another villager put it. ''It was just like she treated him like a dog.''

No one can say for sure why Evelyn banished Chris from her heart. Some people say they believe she was so hurt by the father she couldn't bring herself to love the son.

Evelyn Conners was a good woman and a hard worker, village people say. She wouldn't intentionally hurt anyone.

But she was a drunk. Chris remembers hiding bottles from her as a child. When she would drink herself sick, he would throw rags over her vomit.

The alcohol seemed to unlease Evelyn's own anger and frustration at a life that hadn't worked out the way she wanted. Chris remembers times when his mother and grandmother were drinking, and hearing his mother sob: ''Why would you throw me out when it was 20 below zero?'' His grandmother, her head hung, would just say, ''I know, I know.''

Chris and his mother made life hell for each other. That was no secret in the village. Some people talk about the day they saw Chris shouting at his mother, telling her how much he hated her. Others talk about the time Evelyn chewed him out over the CB radio for everyone to hear.

All the drinking, yelling, cursing and slapping became too much. By the time he was 6 years old, Chris refused to live with his mother.

Instead, he lived down the road with his grandparents, Nick and Titianna Meticgoruk. They drank, too, but not nearly as much as his mother. From Chris' perspective, the booze didn't make them mean the way it seemed to with her.

Chris said he didn't mind taking care of them during their occasional binges. He would lend them a steady shoulder as they staggered off to bed and fix hot soup for their hangovers.

Sometimes the binges would last a week or more. During these times, Chris' grandparents would shout at each other. Chris learned that if he just waited it out, eventually peace would return to the house. Then he could look forward to a month or two of them staying sober.

These were Chris' happiest years. His grandparents would hug him when he got home from school, and ask whether any of the kids had been picking on him. He was his grandfather's favorite.

The old man taught Chris to hunt game and smoke fish, and to tell the difference between husky and wolf tracks in the snow. He took Chris out to his trap line and told the boy stories about his days as a reindeer herder up north. At home at night, Chris would climb into his grandfather's lap with a cup of hot chocolate, and together they would indulge in the adventure of Br'er Rabbit on the Uncle Ben Radio Show.

Early on, Chris decided that when he grew up he would become a commercial fisherman like his grandfather had been. Chris' brother, Alan, would inherit his grandfather's fishing permit because he was the oldest. But grandmother's permit would go to him.

THE GOOD TIMES END

The good times in Chris' life ended abruptly when he was 9, at the tail end of one of his grandfather's binges. Chris was about to fix soup for his grandfather's hangover when he walked into the bedroom and found the old man sitting on the floor clinching his teeth and holding his left side. He tried to hide his pain. He slowly stood up, took a few steps into the hallway, stumbled and fell to the floor.

When the village health aides arrived, they suspected a heart attack or stroke, and loaded him into a plane to Dillingham. Chris and his grandmother flew out later. They arrived at the hospital five minutes after he died.

Inside a brightly lit room of stainless steel and sterilized linens, the old man lay still, tubes still poking from his nose and arms. The boy went numb.

That night, a family friend spent half an hour trying to convince Chris it was OK to cry. But Chris couldn't. He had never seen his grandfather cry.

The drinking began early the day of the funeral. Chris' mother, grandmother and other family and friends were at it by 9 or 10 in the morning, mixing alcohol with tears.

At the funeral, Chris' grandmother sat between the boy and his mother. A priest sang and waved a pot of incense, filling the church with a sweet smoke that made Chris queasy. But it wasn't until later, as men lowered the coffin into its grave, that emotion finally punched through. Chris burst into tears, turned and ran.

Back at home, still dressed in a stiff new suit, he lay on his bed and stared at the ceiling. Grieving family and friends returned to the house, and the drinking resumed in the front room. On the other side of a blanket that served as a door, Chris waited for someone to come in to his room, hug him and ask him how he was doing. But nobody came.

Soon after the funeral, Evelyn moved in to help take care of her ailing mother.

Chris didn't want to be home much after that. People in the village gave him a place to sleep when he needed one. If they questioned why a 9-year-old child couldn't bear to be home, they kept it to themselves.

DRUGS AND DRINKING

Six months after his grandfather's death, Chris started smoking marijuana. It made him laugh. Although Chris had been sneaking sips here and there for as long as he could remember, he became a drinker soon thereafter.

The first time Chris drank enough to pass out he was in the fourth grade. He and one of his aunts were in a Ford Capri. Chris helped himself to the large plastic cup of whiskey she placed on the dash, and she was too drunk to notice.

Chris woke up the next morning at a friend's house with a pounding head, unable to remember how the evening had ended. It didn't bother him much; he had learned long ago that hangovers and blackouts were normal.

One night at a friend's house, he wanted to impress a woman who had been flirting with him. She was 26; he was barely 13. He grabbed a bottle of whiskey and chugged it. Ten minutes later he stumbled outside, tripped and passed out with his face in a puddle.

Chris woke up the next morning upstairs, with his clothes gone. Whoever had taken care of him that night had pulled him out of the puddle and tossed his muddy clothes in a heap outside the door. Chris walked home wrapped in a sheet.

As much as Chris was humiliated by his mother's drinking, he was starting to become just like her. She begged him not to. Yet Chris says he occasionally drank with her, beginning at age 13. He says they smoked pot a couple times together, too.

"You know, I think that's what really made her angry at me," said Chris. "I wouldn't listen to her. She would tell me not to drink, and I'd drink anyway. And I believe I drank just to get back at her. That's the way I could get under her skin the most.

"And there was nothing else to do."

'DAD KILLED HIMSELF'

Although Chris said he cared about his mother, he hated the way she was. His resentment carried over to her boyfriends.

Evelyn was with Paul Matsuno back then. Matsuno was an OK guy by Chris' standards, but they still didn't get along. He was a commercial fisherman, part-Aleut, part-Japanese. When he drank, he drank hard, but never raised a hand against the kids.

Chris' 6-year-old brother, Guy, was particularly fond of Matsuno. Guy called him "Dad." Chris tried to, but it didn't feel right.

One winter day in 1980, Chris forgot to stop for the mail on his way home from school. Matsuno was angry; he told Chris to go back and get it. Chris refused. An argument ensued in which Chris said words he would later regret. He called Matsuno something like "a dirty Jap," then stormed out of the house. On his way out, he passed his mother. She was slumped in the seat of a snowmachine, woozy from too much booze. He was so furious, he said he could kill Matsuno.

Later that night, after a drunken argument with Evelyn over a snowmachine, Matsuno picked up a hunting rifle and blew his head all over her living room. Chris' brother Guy was there when he did it; he ran from the house in horror. "Dad killed himself in the face," the boy screamed.

Evelyn silently blamed Chris for Matsuno's suicide, although she said nothing. Chris said nothing. Guy said nothing.

Relatives say Evelyn drank harder than ever after that. Chris did, too. Weekend parties were pretty much the same—drink, pass out, get up, do it again.

The year after Matsuno's death, Evelyn sold her mother's fishing permit—the one that was to have been Chris' inheritance—to her new boyfriend, a white man named Bud Reina. She needed the money. Chris saw the permit as his only chance to make something of himself, to follow in his grandfather's footsteps.

He never talked about it.

ANOTHER NEW HOME

The more Evelyn and Chris drank, the less they could stand each other. Sometimes Evelyn would call Chris' aunt and uncle in Port Heiden, John and Annie Christensen, and ask them to take Chris. They were always willing. Invariably, Evelyn was drunk when she made the calls.

The Christensens got along with Chris. Their home was the epitome of family life, with a constant stream of neighbors, children and dogs through the house. The couple was well respected in the community. John rarely drank, and Annie, like her parents, didn't drink at all. She didn't even allow alcohol in her house.

Chris continued to sneak out and drink once in a while, and a couple of times he got caught. Annie would let him know how much she disapproved and explain why she felt the way she did.

Chris spent two years with John and Annie. In many ways, the Chris Conners who lived in Port Heiden was a different kid from the one his mother knew. In a stable home, he was polite and helpful around the house, Annie says, chopping wood and helping with chores without having to be asked. Back home, his mother couldn't get him to lift a finger.

"He was just like one of my kids, you know," Annie told investigators after the shootings. "He really behaved well here. . . . He didn't ever show any anger when he was talking to me.

"He always seemed concerned and worried about his mom and her drinking. He'd always call and, you know, check on (the family)."

One time, Annie remembers, Chris wanted to go home for his birthday. When he called the village phone, the person who answered told him his family had moved to Anchorage.

"He even started crying, he was so upset over it," Annie recalled. "It was just like he wasn't important. He didn't know (why) they didn't bother to call him and say they were moving."

Chris spent the last couple of years between Pilot Point, Port Heiden and Anchorage. The winter before the murders, while staying with John and Annie, Chris again wanted to be with his family, this time for Christmas. He called his mother; she said she would pay for his brother Alan's plane ticket, but not his.

Chris took the news hard. Although there were presents for him under the tree and Annie had fixed a big turkey dinner, Chris spent all of Christmas Day in bed. He finally got up to pick at some leftovers that evening.

RETURN TO PILOT POINT

Chris quit school that spring and returned to Pilot Point to strike out on his own. He landed a job as a deckhand on a fishing boat, and slept wherever he happened to be—on the boat, at friends' houses, at his mother's place.

One day Chris got drunk and asked to borrow his mother's pickup truck. Although he was told he couldn't, he took it anyway, and blew the engine driving 40 miles an hour in low gear down the beach. It wasn't much of a truck, but Evelyn depended on it to work her setnet site. The two of them screamed it out in front of several villagers.

About a month before the murders, Chris and Evelyn, drinking as usual, started arguing as usual. Out of nowhere, she said what she had been thinking for three years. "*You* killed Paul!" she screamed.

"She was crying," Chris says. "I believe that she really believed I killed him. Maybe what I said did have an effect. I'll never know."

Chris became increasingly agitated as the summer progressed, and people in the village started to notice. Janice Ball said Chris seemed restless. Others said Chris was becoming more and more hot tempered.

Chris earned $5,000 fishing that summer. He bought a couple of three-wheelers—one as a gift for his little brother, Guy—and blew the rest on cocaine, marijuana and booze. He stayed constantly stoned, and on several occasions drank until he blacked out.

Finally, Evelyn had had it. She kept telling people that her son was out of control. The night before the murders, she told Chris she was thinking of putting him in a reform school.

"At that point," Chris said. "I didn't really care what happened to me. I kept telling myself nobody cares about me. I was mad at everyone. I hated everyone."

THE FINAL REJECTION

When Sophie Larson spurned him the next afternoon, the rejection overwhelmed him. When the years of accumulated anger finally burst through, Chris lashed out at everyone—people he cared for, people he hated, people he hardly knew.

According to authorities, the shootings went something like this: After seriously wounding Sophie at the airstrip, Chris took off on his three-wheeler and fired a shot at Sonny Greichen, the man who had hired him to work on his boat. At first, Sonny thought it was a prank, that the gun was loaded with blanks, until a bullet came close enough to his head to make his ears ring.

Chris traded the .357 for a 10-gauge shotgun, then walked into the bedroom of Bud Reina, the man he believed had swindled his mother out of his fishing permit. He blasted Bud in the neck, but he didn't kill him.

By now, word was getting around on the CB that Chris had gone berserk. James Achayok couldn't have known because he had been out riding his three-wheeler. As James' machine rounded the top of a hill, Chris raised the shotgun and fired.

Achayok, age 22, died instantly.

Three pellets from the blast struck the 9-year-old boy who sat hidden behind him. It was Chris' little brother, Guy.

Guy jumped from the three-wheeler, ran a few yards, crumpled to the ground and died.

A schoolteacher was next. Lance Blackwood was home watching "Falcon Crest" when he heard Bud Reina on the CB calling for help. Blackwood grabbed his .44-caliber Magnum, put a handful of bullets in his pocket and headed out the door. As he approached the hill above Evelyn Conners' house, he found James and Guy lying on the ground. He called to them, shook them and tried to get a pulse. Nothing.

He stood over the bodies a long time, not knowing what to do. He finally loaded them into his pickup. As he closed the tailgate, a shotgun pellet struck him in the buttocks, wounding him.

Finally, it was Evelyn's turn.

From a half-mile away, Sonny Greichen watched through binoculars as Chris struggled to load a heavy yellow bundle onto the back of his three-wheeler. The bundle kept sliding off. Sonny saw Chris tie it behind his three-wheeler and drag it across the tundra out of town.

The troopers found Evelyn's body late that night, about a mile from the village. She had been shot in the head, a yellow sheet tied around her neck and bite marks on her face, neck and chest.

Prosecutor Charles Merriner called the murders among the most brutal and senseless he could imagine.

'A SCARED LITTLE BOY'

Chris was like a cornered animal when first brought to McLaughlin Youth Center to await trial for murder, attempted murder and assault. He was described at the time as unemotional, self-centered and volatile.

The murders would be easier to understand if he were psychotic. But psychiatrists who examined him found that wasn't the case.

"When I first heard about this murder, I thought, 'Oh God, I hope I don't get this case because it was so gruesome,' " said Polly Morrow, who did get the case as an investigator for the public defender agency. "When I went to meet him for the first time I expected someone who was sinister, and he was a scared little boy. I think with so many public defender clients, there's no remorse, no sadness about their crimes. This kid was grief-stricken.

"You know the most profound interview I had was with Chris' grandmother, who is now dead. She said to me, 'I don't blame Chris for this. I blame Evelyn.' And this is Evelyn's mother who said this."

Morrow said she believes if someone had intervened earlier, Chris never would have done what he did. She was so moved by her work with him, she left the agency to pursue a master's degree in social work.

The turning point in Chris' attitude came after he was shown photographs of his victims. "I didn't want to accept the fact that I did it," he said. "I knew they were dead, but I didn't want to believe it. After (I saw) those pictures of what I did, I knew I needed somebody to talk to."

After that psychiatrists and counselors started seeing drastic changes. Later evaluations described him as bright, articulate, sensitive and extremely distraught over what he had done.

Psychologist Jon Burke told the court Chris had lived most of his life overwhelmed. In jail, he was finally safe, safe because he didn't have to worry about people being abusive. Only now could he let down his defenses.

Psychiatrist Irvin Rothrock, who originally examined Chris on behalf of the prosecution and found him "cold," was later called to testify for the defense. "I would say he's one of the more favorable people I've seen," he told the court, "more favorable in terms of potential rehabilitation."

Along with these changes came nightmares. Chris would see himself flipping through those pictures, the bodies of his mother, little brother and James. He would wake up in a cold sweat, and be afraid to go back to sleep for fear the images would return.

At one point, he broke the plastic off the light fixture in his cell and slashed a wrist and forearm deep enough to require stitches and leave a trail of scars. During court hearings, Chris threw up as a pathologist summarized autopsy reports.

Before Chris' case could go to trial, the court had to decide whether to try him as a juvenile or an adult. Chris was 15 at the time of the shootings. If he were to remain in the juvenile system, he would be free by his 20th birthday.

Chris' public defenders fought hard to keep the case in juvenile court. They were convinced that he was a "salvageable" human being. Just removing him from his home environment had produced remarkable changes; with extensive counseling, they argued, Chris could turn his life around and pose no threat to society.

Because of the seriousness of the charges, Superior Court Judge Seaborn Buckalew decided Chris should be tried as an adult. That meant he could spend the rest of his life in prison.

The case never went to trial. Instead, Chris pleaded no contest to the charges against him. At this sentencing, Judge Buckalew considered Chris' relationship with his mother and the role of alcohol and neglect. The judge considered the theory that Chris was so drugged he didn't know what he was doing. Buckalew thought, too, about Sophie Larson, hospitalized with bouts of paralysis for months after the shootings. And he thought about those who died.

Despite prosecution pleas that Chris remain behind bars for the rest of his life, Buckalew was persuaded that Chris could be rehabilitated. He gave the boy 55 years to serve.

PAROLE IN 2001?

It has been more than four years since the shootings. Chris is imprisoned in St. Cloud, Minn., but may be returned to Alaska when the new prison in Seward opens. He will be eligible for parole in 2001. Chris said he hopes to get a college education while he is locked up so he can make something of himself once he is free.

Until then, home is a 6-by-9-foot cell with a bed, television, nightstand, fan, toilet and sink. Chris starts each day with a cigarette and a cold shower. He shuffles through his daily routine trying not to think too much. When he does think about what has happened, he becomes intense.

Chris has written to his victims' survivors and those he wounded to say how sorry he is. He doesn't expect them to accept his apology. His older brother, Alan, lost his entire family that night. Chris doesn't expect to ever hear from him again.

"They say time heals all wounds. But I don't think time will heal theirs," Chris said.

He said he plans to sell the shares he holds in his Native corporation, put the money in a savings account to accumulate interest, then give money to those he hurt to help pay medical bills. It's something he said he needs to do to be right with himself.

"To tell you the truth, I will never know why I did what I did. I still have a hard time dealing with it. It's going to be with me all my life. There's no escape from it. Ever."

CIRCLE NEVER ENDS

Back in Pilot Point, the tragedies continue.

Three years after the Conners murders, a volley of shotgun blasts left a 6-year-old boy dead and his stepmother shot in the face. There had been drinking and an argument. The dead boy's 16-year-old brother was charged with the crime.

Loren Abyo, the boy who ran from Chris' bullets at the airstrip four years ago, is dead. He drowned three days after his 21st birthday. He and some friends were drinking on a boat. Loren got tossed off the boat. Nobody on board could swim. His friends just watched him wash out to sea. The man who threw him overboard was convicted of negligent homicide.

"It's just like you're at a dead end or a circle that you never reach the end of," says Janice Ball, one of several people in Pilot Point who don't drink at all. "You just see it happening over and over.

"After all we've been through. . . . You know, you would think they would learn or something. But the drinking just goes on."

Diana Griego Erwin / His Dreams Belong to the Next Generation *Orange County Register,* May 25, 1989

Writers of color often find themselves serving as representatives of their particular ethnic or racial group, particularly when they are columnists. Diana Griego Erwin, a Latina who works for the Orange County Register, *has faced racist treatment as well as the pressures of being a "spokesperson" during her time at the newspaper, but by focusing on a large cross-section of often-overlooked Americans, she has managed to widen her scope to include much beyond her particular community.*

"I prefer to go out into the city or the suburbs, and write about the kinds of things that people are thinking and talking about," Erwin told one interviewer. "I think everyone who works for newspapers sees things from an insider point of view. And so a lot of what I try to do is to represent the common people."

In writing the piece below (which first appeared in the Register *on May 25, 1989), Erwin employed her ability to speak both Spanish and English. As a bilingual journalist, she can cross boundaries that are forever closed to many writers. Erwin uses Spanish only briefly in her piece—in the phrase, "como un burro"—but her choice was carefully considered. She explains: "I wanted to remind readers that all this was in Spanish. It's a very common phrase in Spanish, and readers unfamiliar with Spanish would learn that. So repetition reinforces how he speaks and the problem of language."*

Diana Griego Erwin studied communications and liberal arts at California State University, Fullerton, earning her degree in 1984. Her groundbreaking work at the Denver Post *during the mid-eighties helped that newspaper win a Pulitzer Prize for public service. She continues to write a column for the* Orange County Register. *She is the first Latina(o) winner of the American Society of Newspaper Editors Distinguished Writing Award.*

His brow furrowed and the crow's-feet deepened as he struggled to understand. There was little doubt. He was confused.

The busy information clerk at the Department of Motor Vehicles in Santa Ana didn't notice.

"You need to go over there," she said, pointing across the room to the sea of people waiting. "I already told you."

It was 11 a.m. Her patience was shot for the morning.

The man pulled at the waistband of his beige work pants and scratched his sun-aged face. He stared at her, stalling for time as he tried to understand, but afraid to say he didn't.

He left, returned. The next clerk didn't speak Spanish, either.

"Why can't they learn English?" she grumbled to me, the next in line.

"He probably won't," I said. "But maybe his kids will."

I had to say it. My father had been one of those kids. The ones who learn English although their parents speak Spanish at home. Schools back then didn't offer special programs; some people have told me that nuns rapped their knuckles with a ruler if they spoke Spanish—even on the playground. They learned English quickly and well that way.

But the information clerks didn't know all this, so they couldn't understand the man with the sun-aged face like I did.

I watched as he leaned against a wall where about 15 men waited. Many wore work pants and that same face, deeply lined from too much sun and too many worries.

I asked Luis Manuel Delgado why he waited.

"The lady who speaks Spanish has gone to lunch," he said.

There was no irritation in his voice, no anger at the time wasted. It was simply a fact.

I pointed out that the clerks hadn't treated him very nicely. Didn't that anger him? I wondered.

"I should know how to speak English," he said with a quiet simplicity. "This is the United States."

Delgado, 46, said he works long hours and doesn't leave in time to attend adult English classes.

He came to the United States in 1973 because two brothers and three uncles had migrated here and found better lives than the ones they left in Mexico.

Delgado worked as a bricklayer and saved enough money so his wife and two children could join him after 2½ years. An uncle paid for the other two children to come.

A lifetime renter and a nobody by social standards, Delgado has big dreams for his children. He hopes they are respected by their peers and become property owners. In his old age, maybe he will live comfortably in a house owned by one of his children.

Meanwhile, he works hard and long to educate his kids. They are his future. "I am here for my children," he said proudly.

I was right about Luis Manuel Delgado.

"My kids are very good," he said. "They get good marks in school. They speak English. No accent. One wants to be a doctor.

"When they first came here I told them to study English and learn it well. Don't let them treat you like a donkey like they treat your papa."

I asked him if it didn't hurt, being treated *como un burro,* like he said.

"No, I am not a donkey and my children know it. They know I do all this for them. They are proud of me. Nothing anyone else says or does can make me sad when they have pride in me.

"And they will never be donkeys."

He nodded toward the stressed-out information clerks busily shuffling papers behind the government-issued desk. "And they won't work here," he said. "This is donkey work."

Samuel Francis / Rapping Garbage as "Art"

Washington Times, August 24, 1989

Contemporary editorial writing can often be impersonal in tone, reflecting the sentiments of a media institution rather than an individual writer. Sam Francis's editorials take a different approach to the art. His personality rings through his pieces—his tone is reminiscent of an ultraconservative Harry Truman, employ-

ing "plain speaking" to imbue his writing with a sense of practicality rallying against what he regards as the soggy thinking and pipe dreams of liberals. Francis's writing style creates the illusion that what he says is truth, despite the fact that by the very nature of his task, he is offering opinions.

The following editorial signals Francis's entry into the battle over censorship of rap music. Francis acquired his knowledge of rap by reading articles by fellow Washington Times *writer David Mills. (For an example of Mills's reporting on rap music, see p. 212.) Mills had earlier contributed to the controversies surrounding rap by publishing an interview with Professor Griff of the leading group Public Enemy, in which Griff made anti-Semitic remarks; that interview ignited a furor that turned many former fans against the group and further delineated black nationalist rappers as a group distinct from other supporters of the music. Although Mills is himself African-American, the* Times *is not necessarily considered an advocate of black causes.*

In his editorial, Francis takes a familiar stance regarding controversial art. He questions its merits on artistic grounds, calling it "mediocre" as well as dangerous. He also claims that the music he discusses represents the experience of only a degenerate fraction of the population, substituting a marginalized view for a more democratic picture. Conservatives often employ these tactics when criticizing publicly funded art; hoping that readers will be offended on both aesthetic and moral grounds, they emphasize the most extreme segments of a cultural form and claim that these elements can be read as indicative of the whole.

"Realistic" is the thing to be these days, especially in art. The late Robert Mapplethorpe was "realistic" with his photographs of sodomy and less nameable practices, and last week our David Mills reported on the "realism" of rap music. The lyrics of some rap groups seem to wallow in not-too-critical descriptions of violence, drugs, and sexuality, all in the name of the realities of life for urban blacks. The rappers, say police, parents, and pundits of pop culture, encourage and even incite mayhem.

Whether violent lyrics spark actual violence is one side of the rap record, but there's another that no one hears. The real question about rap, especially the hardcore variety, is whether it says anything worth listening to.

The storm swells over the lyrics of a song called "F—the Police," performed by a group known as N.W.A., which is said to stand for "Niggers With Attitudes." "F— the Police" contains such gems of prosody as

Without a gun and a badge, what you got?
A sucker in a uniform waitin' to get shot
By me, or another nigger
And with a gat, it don't matter if he's smaller or bigger

You've got to admit it's not Rodgers and Hammerstein. In fact, it's barely Mother Goose. But aside from the metrical wheelchairs in which rap moves, the excuse rappers give for their articitic accomplishments is that they're just reflecting reality.

"We call ourselves underground street reporters," says N.W.A.'s Ice Cube. "If everybody did records and all we talked about was the joys of life, and on TV all they showed was rainbows and pastel colors, a kid could go out and get his head blown off and not know why." Rapper "Schooly D" Weaver offers perhaps the most decrepit excuse of the mediocre artist. He says he's expressing "the inner me" and "I write exactly what I feel."

But kids can get their heads blown off and still not know why, even after submerging themselves in Ice Cube's limp doggerel. The rappers' vision of reality is simply vicious. They manage to miss the inner city's other realities—family members working for each other, students trying to elevate themselves, community leaders risking their lives to control the garbage rappers celebrate. The rappers have nothing to say about why the garbage is there, how to clean it up, or even why it stinks—because garbage is all they see and all they want their audiences to see.

Great art always reports on reality. It never disguises it, but neither does it ever surrender to it by merely vomiting up only the ugliness that reality contains. No one will much care about the "inner me" of Schooly D and his buddies if all that's inside them is the ugliness they brag about and all that comes out is the artistic equivalent of diarrhea. After their novelty wears thin, they'll be about as enduring as The Beatles' soup-bowl haircuts in the early '60s.

David von Drehle / Shaken Survivors Witness Pure Fury

Miami Herald, September 23, 1989

How can a reporter wring the truth out of a hurricane? This question was foremost in the mind of Miami Herald *reporter David von Drehle as he headed out to Charleston, South Carolina, to cover the onslaught of Hurricane Hugo. Rather than compiling the usual list of facts—body counts, weather and damage reports—von Drehle decided to immerse himself in the experience of the storm and write a first-person account of his encounter with a natural disaster.*

As von Drehle says, the typical newspaper reader can learn a plethora of facts about a hurricane and still have a basic question: what did it feel like? "Whatever is striking about my story grew out of conversations with a couple of my editors for several years, through a number of hurricane seasons," he recalls. "We would sit around after a hurricane had blown through, and we would talk about how the stories had been good and complete and interesting and all of that, but how hungry we were as readers for a story that just said what it's like to go through one." Von Drehle's sensual description of the storm's horror abandons many newspaper conventions. His innovative approach allows the reader a new level of entry into an often-described occurrence.

After working as a sports reporter at the Denver Post *and at the city desk at the* Miami Herald, *David von Drehle became the New York City correspondent for the* Herald, *a position he still holds.*

CHARLESTON, S.C.—It's noon on Thursday at Folly Beach, a stretch of sand raised a few inches above the surrounding tidal marsh and sprinkled with undistinguished bungalows and weathered seafood shacks.

It's gray, lightly sprinkling. Not unusual for a September afternoon. But big breakers are sending foam over the sea wall and the houses are deserted. The town has the eerie feeling of an unnaturally empty place—like a dusty street in a dime Western just before the bad guys arrive.

Hurricane Hugo is 12 hours away.

Tension grows through the afternoon. Every little gust of air, every spit of rain, every new shade of gray cloud is searched for meaning. With each new breeze, people speed their pace, tighten their jaws.

The streets empty. Traffic jams the roads out of town. Forecasters said gale-force winds might arrive by 3 p.m., but at 5, the palms and elms and oaks are still swaying gently.

At 5:30, as journalists and other thrill-seekers tour the Battery in a gentle rain, visibility drops suddenly. The famous sights from the harbor's edge—like Fort Moultrie, of Revolutionary War fame, and Fort Sumter, where the Civil War began—vanish in the fog.

Then rain comes, warm and straight and thick. The gale arrives next, driving the warm rain ahead of it. A statue honoring the Confederate war dead, a bronze nude brandishing a broadsword, confronts the storm wearing nothing but a fig leaf.

False alarm. The wind and rain die down. But they will be back.

From the television comes the news that Hugo is gaining speed and fury. This will be one of the rare Category 4 storms to hit the United States. Hugo is six hours away.

Sundown, and gray drains from the sky, leaving only black. The tension rises another notch. In the gloaming, the trees ball and buck in the rising winds.

By 9 p.m., the gale is gusting so hard you have to lean into it to make headway, like a street mime.

OUTAGES BLACK OUT AREA

Miami Herald photographer Jon Kral and I hope to make it to hotel rooms near the Charleston airport, 10 miles inland. As we leave downtown, a main power station gives out, and the streets become darker, more menacing.

Water swirls and snakes across the highway as we drive. The rain falls almost horizontally. Broken branches and loose garbage skid over the pavement, and the gusts are now high enough to rock the car as it creeps across Charleston's high bridges.

It's dark in all directions—power failures spread black like it was paint. The failures come quickly and rhythmically, almost as if someone were flipping a row of switches.

The manmade glow is replaced by startling eruptions of muffled light—huge lightning storms showing through the furious shroud.

A rock-and-roll station pledges to stay with us through the hurricane. "Your Hurricane Hugo station!" the DJ cries. Then he announces that the eye of the storm is just two hours away, headed straight for us—"so whatever you do, don't drive!"

Within a few minutes, the station is off the air. The storm becomes too much.

WINDS SHIFT INTO OVERDRIVE

The hotel turns out to be unprepared, but Kral produces a roll of duct tape from his bag and we strip asterisks onto each pane. At 10:30, the room lights go brown, then die, struggle back, then fail for good.

Outside, the air is screaming at the same pitch that wind reaches through a cracked window on an interstate highway. The howl is strangely pleasant, because we make the mistake of thinking that this is about as bad is it will get.

The noise halts briefly, just for a second or two, then comes back at a much higher, much more urgent pitch. After five minutes of that, Hugo clutches and shifts again to an even higher level. The winds step up like a sports car going through the gears—except that Hugo has many more gears.

With each new step, the barometric pressure drops, and we can feel the changes in our ears. At 11:30, we dress to go out into the storm, but quickly change our minds when Hugo jumps three gears in five minutes.

From somewhere inside the shrieking noise come the muffled reports of snapping trees, popping windshields, and sand hitting the windows like pellets.

Water in the toilet bowl rocks and swirls as Hugo howls through the city's sewers. Wind gusts from the light fixtures. The panes pull at their window frames.

A SOUND OF PURE FURY

Frightened families leave their rooms and walk nervously down darkened stairwells to the leaking lobby. At the bottom of one stairwell, we watch as the sucking wind tries to wrench open a double-bolted fire door.

First the air yanks, then slips its fingers into the tiny gap between door and door frame, then strains at the heavy steel structure until the door actually *bends*.

Then the awful clutching silence, and the wind returns, up another impossible gear.

By midnight, as the worst of the fury roars nightmarishly over Charleston, the very walls tremble and quake.

The noise of a killer hurricane has been compared to a passing freight train so many times it has become a sort of journalists' joke. "Let me guess—did it sound like a train?"

But to me, this doesn't sound like a train. It sounds like the harsh intake of a dentist's suction tube, greatly amplified and always increasing. Or the roar of a seashell a billion times over. Or Niagara, if only Niagara cranked up its volume each time your ears got adjusted to it.

Most of all, it sounds like pure fury.

One of Kral's taped windows explodes minutes after we leave the room. When we come back, it's impossible to open the door, the wind is so strong. We have to wait for a pause between gears, then drive with our shoulders.

A TEMPEST IN A MOTEL ROOM

Thick rain is blowing horizontally through the room. Thanks to the duct tape, the shattered glass is in a neat pile on the floor. We shout over the gale.

In the bathroom, the swirling winds have pulled the Sheetrock ceiling away from the walls. For the rest of the tempest, Hugo works on tearing the room apart. Gusts of 25 miles per hour come through the ceiling. The nails and screws groan at the strain.

The winds are much wilder, much more intense than anything I have experienced before. The difference between 100-mph winds and 130-mph winds is so great that they ought to have different names.

At five minutes past midnight, the noise begins gearing down rapidly. By 12:15, it's almost still. Some of us venture outside and inspect the damage by flashlight.

A thick steel flagpole, barely anything to it to resist the wind, is bent at a 60-degree angle. An ancient Pontiac, finned and weighty, has been shoved several feet into a Saab. A Chrysler New Yorker is deposited on the sidewalk.

Along the windward side of the hotel, the windows of the cars are consistently shattered, as if by methodical vandals. "I'll sell this new Honda right now for $9,000," says a distraught owner.

Then he sees his girlfriend's matching car with matching wounds. "Two for $18,000," he says.

COMPLETE STILLNESS

The ground is thick with tree limbs and glass and aluminum and shingles and bits of plastic signs. Bits of Sheraton, bits of McDonald's.

At 12:30, complete stillness. We're in the middle of Hugo's eye. It's still and silent and hot and humid on a landscape covered with debris. It feels like surfacing from a bomb shelter at the end of the world.

"I thought you were supposed to see stars when you're in the eye," someone says.

We all look up. No stars. Then we notice a highway sign, still attached to its pole, jutting up near an old Impala. The sign, we realize, must have been uprooted a quarter-mile away.

It has been driven, like a javelin, through the side of the car, and stuck there as firmly as Excalibur in the stone.

Five minutes pass. Then comes a tiny puff of breeze, so faint as to be imperceptible—except that we are waiting for it so intently. Within a few seconds, a faint drizzle follows. Half a minute after that, the breeze and drizzle are rattling shredded metal like spook-house ghosts.

Then, just before the wind resumes lifting and twirling debris. Orion's belt and a few stars peep through, low in the northern sky. Then disappear.

WIND BLOWS IN OPPOSITE WAY

Back inside, water pours through the lobby ceiling and sloshes on the floor. Now the wind blows the opposite way, drawing the curtains out through Kral's gaping window. They snapped so hard against the adjacent panes we fear they will break, so we rip the curtains from the rods.

By 12:45 Hugo is back near peak fury. Kral points a light into the storm to illuminate the movements of the rain. It zings through the air, up, sideways, diagonally, sometimes downward. It whips and swirls, a true maelstrom.

Now a new row of cars catches the full fury, and new stands of trees. Windshields explode and trees crack like firecrackers. The noise is swallowed in the roar of the storm.

Again, the ears are popping, as the barometric pressure returns. In this respect, Hugo is a lot like flying on a jet—on the *outside.*

The backside of the storm seems to gear up and fade more quickly than the leading edge, but in fact it does not. Time is speeding up. The storm pumped so much adrenaline, and sharpened the senses so acutely, that time slowed, and now it is resuming its normal pace.

The winds drop as Hugo recedes. Almost immediately, it is hard to recall how fiercely it blew. And almost impossible to believe.

Michael Ventura / On Kids and Slasher Movies

L. A. Weekly, November 3, 1989

"Writing a column is like being a jazz musician," says Michael Ventura, whose "Letters at 3 A.M.*" has appeared in the* L. A. Weekly, *off and on, for the past several years. "It's like, I play tenor, and I have this gig, and I know the chords and the theme that I want to play and I just get up and play a set and I get off." Ventura's intense, personal approach to column writing is among the most engaging examples of a style that developed with the rise of alternative newsweeklies such as the* L.A. Weekly, *the* Village Voice, *and the* Boston Phoenix. *Left of center, based on the author's own experiences within a particular cityscape as well as the larger American scene, such writing speaks powerfully to the sophisticated urban dwellers who make up the readership of such publications.*

For Ventura, whose subjects range from his own psychic conflicts and various Los Angeles subcultures to more wide-ranging social and political issues, column writing is, he observes, "a kind of performance piece. Doing it intensely in a short period of time gives it its edge. I think a lot about each column before I do it, and I take notes, but I really do write them around 3 A.M. *I start at around 11 o'clock at night and wind up around 5* A.M."

"It's a question of how you gear up," Ventura says, explaining his method: "You need the right mindset, coming to the thing. When I first started writing for the Austin Sun *when I was 29 years old, I would take two ten-hour days to get my lead. Obviously, I had to find a more efficient way of doing it."*

The following column grew out of one of Ventura's most chilling experiences—having seen a boy purchase a serial killer mask. "I'm a lot more afraid of the need for children to play with that stuff than I am of the atom bomb."

It's a simple thing, really. I shouldn't take it so seriously, I realize that. For it was only a child, a boy of about 10, buying a toy. For Halloween. This was the toy:

A sinister white mask and a quite convincing little rubber meat cleaver. Packaged together in cellophane. It's the "costume" of a maniac killer from one of the slasher movies. The boy wants to play at being a faceless, unstoppable murderer of innocent people (mostly women). At this moment in this Woolworth's, that's the boy's idea of fun.

Understand that I didn't stand there and decide intellectually that this simple and small event is, when all is said and done, the worst thing I've seen. My body decided. My intestines, my knees, my chest. It was only later that I tried to think about it.

This boy's eagerness to "play" maniac killer is an event worse than the Bomb, worse even than Auschwitz. Reduced to its simplest terms, the bomb is a fetish, an object of worship—like other objects of worship before it, it is used as an excuse for arranging the world in a certain fashion, allocating resources, assigning powers. It is insane, but in many ways it is an extension of familiar, even honored, insanities. As for the Nazi camps: The people being murdered knew, as they were being murdered, *that* they were being murdered; the murderers knew they were murdering; and, when the world finally knew, the camps became the measure of ultimate human evil. A crime to scar us all, and our descendants, forever.

There is nothing so clear in the Woolworth's scene. The boy is certainly not committing a crime. The toy's merchandisers are within their rights. To legislate against them would be to endanger most of our freedoms. The mother buying the toy is perhaps making a mistake, perhaps not. Without knowing the boy, and knowing him well, who's to be certain that it isn't better for him to engage in, rather than repress, such play? The mother did not put the desire for the toy in him. Three thousand years of Judeo-Christian culture did that. Nor has the mother the power to take that desire from him. Nobody has that power. If he can want the toy at all, then it almost doesn't matter whether the toy exists or not. Doesn't the boy's need for such play exist with or without the toy?

Nor would I be too quick to blame the boy's desire on television and slasher films. The Nazis who crewed the camps and the scientists who built the bomb did not need television and slasher films to school them in horror. In fact, the worst atrocities from the pharaohs to Vietnam were committed quite ably before the first slasher film was made. Keeping your child away from TV may make *you* feel better, but can any child be protected from the total weight of Western history?

In a world shorn of order, stripped of traditions, molting every decade, every year, a dancing, varicolored snake of a century—pointless violence is evident everywhere, on every level. Professional soldiers are statistically safer than urban women; senseless destruction is visited on trees and on the ozone and on every species of life. No one feels safe anywhere. This has become the very meaning of the 20th century.

So I am in a Woolworth's one day and I feel a sort of final horror as I watch a boy buy a psycho-killer toy so that he can pretend he's an unstoppable maniacal murderer. What is so horrible is that this boy is doing this instinctively, for his very survival. In order to live, in order not to go mad, this boy is acclimating himself to the idea of the killer-maniac, because killer-maniac energy is so present in his world. He's trying to inoculate himself through play, as all children have, everywhere, in every era. He thus lets a little bit of the energy into him—that's how inoculations work. Too little, and he is too afraid of the world—it's too terrifying to feel powerless amid the maniacal that's taken for granted around him; to feel any power at all he needs a bit of it inside him. But if he takes in too much, he could be swamped.

How horrible that he is forced to such a choice. You'd think it would be enough to stop the world in its tracks. And what can we do for him? Struggle for a different world, yes, but that won't change what's already happened to him. What can we do for that boy except be on his side, stand by his choice, and pray for the play of his struggling soul?

Anna Quindlen / Fighting the War on Cigs

New York Times, March 4, 1990

In her fifteen years as a journalist in New York City, Anna Quindlen has earned the title to which countless writers aspire—she is, in many ways, the voice of her generation. Her personal approach to national issues, grounded in her experience as a working mother of three, represents the experience of many "baby boomers" struggling to preserve their liberal values while surviving in a competitive and increasingly conservative America. While "Life in the 30s," the New York Times *column that established her reputation nationwide, concentrated on the particulars of her daily life in Hoboken, Quindlen's current column, "Public and Private" (which appears on the* Times*'s op-ed page), confronts larger issues such as abortion rights, the national debt, and the effects of the Gulf War. The following piece exemplifies the combination of wit, political commitment, and down-to-earth commentary that has made her one of the country's most respected columnists.*

In addition to her work for the New York Times, *Quindlen has written for such publications as* Ms., McCall's, Woman's Day, Vogue, *and* Glamour. *In 1991, she completed her first novel,* Object Lessons, *published by Random House.*

The ad looks like this. There is a woman. She has great clothes, important earrings, big hair, some attitude. There is a white box beneath the woman. The box says, "Smoking Causes Lung Cancer, Heart Disease, Emphysema, And May Complicate Pregnancy." The ad appears to be selling two things: sex and death. Of course, it is really selling cigarettes.

Cigarettes make your drapes smell and your teeth yellow. Oh, and there's the death thing. Americans are now divided into four groups: those who know cigarettes kill you and don't smoke, those who know cigarettes kill you and don't care, those who know cigarettes kill you and can't stop, and young people, who have a deep and abiding belief in their own immortality. There are cigarette manufacturers, too, the only people still willing to defend smoking as though it were freedom of religion. Dr. Louis W. Sullivan has decided to go after them, to go supply-side on cigarettes.

Dr. Sullivan is the Secretary of Health and Human Services, and although he gets his paycheck from those same folks who bring you tobacco subsidies, he has gone on a tear against cigarette manufacturers. First he got angry at them for targeting black smokers with a brand called Uptown. Then he got angry at them for targeting young working-class women—virile females, one overheated marketing plan called them—with a brand called Dakota. Then he got angry at them for sponsoring tennis tournaments.

In sum, Dr. Sullivan does not think cigarette manufacturers should try to sell their product, and especially should not try to sell it to those people most likely to buy it. ''Cigarettes,'' he said, ''are the only legal product that, when used as intended, cause death.''

Can there be any possible rationale for the manufacture and sale of a product that can be (correctly) described that way? Well, yes, but it's a historical, economic and political rationale. Tobacco has been a cash crop in the United States since before it *was* the United States, which can only make you wonder what life would be like if the first settlers had planted coca. The tobacco industry is one of the most profitable in the world.

And as long as there are senators, lobbyists and electoral votes from the Carolinas, cigarettes are certain to remain legal. We know from experience that if tobacco were against the law, an enforcement effort would be expensive and inept. It would be called the War on Cigs.

Dr. Sullivan is waging his war in a way that we've come to expect from government: long on talk, short on action. Take to their rightful conclusions, his arguments lead either to a ban on most cigarette advertising or a call for more socially responsible behavior by those who produce the ads. Since the words ''socially responsible'' and ''cigarette advertising'' rarely appear together outside of a Scrabble board, the latter seems unlikely.

Even an outright advertising ban might not devastate the industry. There would certainly be a drop in use, since cigarette consumers so often die and ads recruit new ones. But there is a theory that advertising and promotion costs are so staggering—more than $2 billion a year, if you want a number to make your eyes pop—that ending cigarette advertising could even benefit some tobacco companies financially. Hurt would be newspapers and magazines, which take in enormous revenues from cigarette ads. This is a quandary. I'm in favor of newspapers and magazines.

I'd be in favor of a War on Cigs, but a real one, with teeth. I don't believe we need to make cigarettes illegal: we should simply act as if they were. Take educational films to high schools showing people in the last stages of lung cancer. Offer free programs to help people quit. Run commercials like the ones now produced by the Partnership for a Drug-Free America, the ones with the egg frying and the words: ''This is your brain. This is drugs. This is your brain on drugs. Any questions?'' Make it *real*.

Senator Edward M. Kennedy has proposed anti-smoking legislation that would provide $50 million for paid advertising and public-service announcements, and add tobacco to school drug-education curriculums. Smokers say such campaigns, as well as smoking bans in public places, make them feel like criminals. Better censure than chemotherapy, I always say.

We need to apply what we've learned from battling crack to battling cigarettes.

The Cartagena statement released at the end of the drug summit meeting took due note of the fact that demand is the twin of supply. Dr. Sullivan shouldn't be wasting his passion focusing on the cigarette companies. He should be persuading the President and the Congress to take real action to cut demand for cigarettes. Supply will follow. Money talks. So does the Secretary. He must do more if there is any hope of waging a war against cigarettes, and of winning it.

DISCUSSION QUESTIONS

1. How does Anna Quindlen's reasoning stand up when the facts laid out in Michael Specter's article "Cigarettes for the Tractor-Pull Generation" (see "Advertising") are considered? Do you agree with Quindlen that education needs to be the main focus of an antismoking campaign, rather than higher taxes on cigarettes or sanctions against tobacco companies? Why? Why not? What other examples of preventative education being used as the main force in combating a public problem can you think of?

2. Compare the assertions put forth by Quindlen with those maintained by the Tobacco Institute in "A Word to Smokers/A Word to Nonsmokers" in "Advertising." What differences emerge in their views of educating the American public about cigarette smoking?

OBSCENITY/THE CASE OF 2 LIVE CREW

Until the early months of 1990, Luther Campbell was just another successful but essentially unknown entrepreneur, serving a small portion of the rap music audience through his group, 2 Live Crew, and his record label, Luke Skyywalker. The music Campbell made followed in a long tradition of "blue" African-American musical artists; from Bessie Smith in the 1920s to Blowfly in the 1980s, such performers have peppered their material with raunchy jokes and sexual references that keep their audiences titillated. For the most part, this "blue" music was largely ignored by the listening public. Then a Florida sheriff, Nick Navarro, got the notion that it was obscene.

The flak over 2 Live Crew's album, As Nasty as They Wanna Be, *reflected more than the high moral standards of Broward County, Florida's legal practitioners. Since the mid-1980s such conservative pressure groups as Tipper Gore's Parents' Music Resource Center and Donald Wildmon's American Family Association had been pushing for legislation to limit the sales and distribution of "adult" cultural products. North Carolina's Senator Jesse Helms successfully introduced legislation restricting the distribution of funds from the National Endowment for the Arts, causing an uproar among artists, with the conflict over an exhibition by the late photographer Robert Mapplethorpe at its center. In the rap world, other artists such as Public Enemy and NWA (Niggers With Attitudes) came under fire for their radical black nationalist or anarchist statements.*

The following section includes a variety of reactions to the 2 Live Crew altercation, ranging from the high-minded moralism of Tottie Ellis in USA Today, *to the Afrocentric logic of academic Henry Louis Gates, Jr. Each of these spins on the 2 Live Crew story highlights a different ingredient in America's ever-shifting social constitution; the affair threw into question such basic issues as freedom of expression, the rights of parents and children, racism, sexism, and the limits of law. Whatever America learned from 2 Live Crew's moment in court, Luther Campbell made the most of the media exposure—one year after their obscenity trial, the group held the number one spot on the syndicated network Video Jukebox for six weeks straight, with the even more explicit (and to some, offensive) video for ''Pop That Coochie.''*

Scott Higham, Anne Bartlett, and James F. McCarty / A First: Album Ruled Obscene *Miami Herald,* June 7, 1990

The following article is a straight new account of the controversy that was already inspiring a growing number of subjective responses from media and public figures around the country. ''A First: Album Ruled Obscene'' introduces several of the key voices in the 2 Live Crew melee: Luther Campbell, Judge Jose A. Gonzalez, Sheriff Nick Navarro, and Florida governor Bob Martinez. Miami Herald *reporters Scott Higham, Anne Bartlett, and James F. McCarty concentrate on outlining the definition of obscenity under contention, deferring to experts such as Professor Bruce Rogow to comment on the events at hand. The writing here, while reaching for objectivity, contains a grain of humor regarding the ''circus'' the 2 Live Crew controversy made of Florida's high court.*

Herald *staff writers Michael Crook, Dexter Filkins and Ronnie Greene contributed to this report.*

A federal judge in Fort Lauderdale ruled Wednesday that 2 Live Crew's album *As Nasty As They Wanna Be* isn't just nasty—it's downright obscene, and police can arrest record shop owners who dare sell in South Florida.

U.S. District Judge Jose A. Gonzalez Jr.'s 62-page decision, the first from the federal bench to brand a musical recording obscene, is expected to have a powerful impact far beyond the three counties he cited—Broward, Dade and Palm Beach.

Gonzalez said the Miami-based band's hot-selling rap record offends community standards and fails the U.S. Supreme Court's litmus test for obscenity. At the same time, he castigated Broward Sheriff Nick Navarro, saying he violated the Constitution by warning record shop owners they could be arrested for selling *Nasty*.

Still, Navarro was delighted by the ruling on the band's sexually graphic album. ''If you sell it, you're going to jail,'' he said.

Luther Campbell, 2 Live Crew's leader, said the ruling didn't matter. ''We'll keep making the same music. We probably won't sell no records in Broward County,'' he said.

Wednesday's ruling provides police and prosecutors with a new tool to target rap bands, rock groups and raunchy performers. Albums by Guns 'N Roses, Eddie Murphy and the rapid-fire, foul-mouthed comic Andrew Dice Clay could be next, civil rights lawyers say.

''It changes the balance of power,'' said Bruce Rogow, a Nova University professor and constitutional law expert who represented 2 Live Crew in the case. ''It's going to give ammunition to those people who want to be repressive.''

Gonzalez said *As Nasty As They Wanna Be* goes too far. The album, which has sold nearly 1.7 million copies nationwide since its release last summer, is laced with explicit, violent lyrics.

''It is quite true that not all speech with sex as its topic is obscene,'' wrote Gonzalez. ''The *As Nasty As They Wanna Be* recording is another matter. . . . It is an appeal directed to 'dirty' thoughts and the loins, not to the intellect and the mind.''

Under the ruling, it would not be illegal to buy or listen to the album. But those convicted of selling it to an adult could spend one year in prison and pay a $1,000 fine, and selling it to a minor could draw a five-year prison term and $5,000 fine, sheriff's spokesman Al Gordon said.

Navarro and his attorney, John Jolly, said sheriff's deputies will stop warning record stores about the record and that Navarro will wait until there's an arrest to put Wednesday's ruling to the test of a criminal trial.

Gonzalez said the album failed a three-part test of obscenity standards set down in a 1973 Supreme Court decision. Before material is banned, the ruling says, an average person applying community standards must find that it appeals to prurient interests, is patently offensive and lacks serious artistic, political or scientific value.

Gonzalez defined the community as Broward, Dade and Palm Beach counties because they share the same geography, culture, news media and transportation network. The judge said he is qualified to comment on the community's standards because he has lived in Broward since 1958.

''It cannot be reasonably argued that the violence, perversion, abuse of women, graphic depictions of all forms of sexual conduct, and microscopic descriptions of human genitalia contained on this recording are comedic art,'' the judge wrote.

Rogow, attorney for the rap group, vowed to appeal. While the ruling's effect is confined to South Florida, he and other legal experts said it is politically powerful, encouraging police and prosecutors elsewhere to test Gonzalez's reasoning.

That's true, said Gov. Bob Martinez, who has crusaded against the album. ''Courts, judges, grand juries and law enforcement officers in communities all over the state have issued similar findings,'' said his spokesman, Jon Peck. ''There's no reason to believe that will stop now.''

Harvard University professor Alan Dershowitz, a liberal constitutional law expert, called the Gonzalez decision ''preposterous,'' predicting it would be overturned by an appeals court.

Gonzalez, he said, misinterpreted the legal meaning of ''obscenity.''

Some police departments in South Florida weren't sure how they would proceed.

West Palm Beach police Sgt. Mike Fulk said he expected most record stores ''will remove it from their shelves because it is a small part of their inventory and they probably do not want to risk arrest.'' Metro-Dade police said they are studying the ruling.

Gonzalez' decision was not a clear victory for Sheriff Navarro, who in March obtained an opinion from Broward Circuit Court Judge Mel Grossman that *Nasty* was probably obscene and that record shop owners could be arrested for selling it.

Gonzalez called Grossman's ruling ''bizarre.''

''This is unusual, since the giving of legal advice is normally the function of lawyers, not judges.''

Once Navarro received the opinion from Grossman, he started to warn record shop owners. Gonzalez called that a violation of the Constitution because it was an ''improper prior restraint of free speech.'' He ordered the sheriff's office to stop the warnings.

Said sheriff's attorney John Jolly: ''The court is clearly saying we're doing it the wrong way. We're going to change our procedures.''

Grossman defended his role.

''I always thought it was better to get an opinion from a neutral judicial officer than rely on a police officer's own personal judgment whether to make an arrest,'' the circuit judge said in an interview Wednesday.

The ruling came nearly three weeks after Gonzalez' courtroom was turned into a X-rated extravaganza, with lawyers for 2 Live Crew showing the judge just how nasty other performers, publishers and movie makers could be. They rolled clips of porn films and produced copies of hard-core magazines.

Their point: Black rap music is being unfairly singled out by Anglo and Hispanic sheriffs and prosecutors who don't understand it.

The controversy will only help 2 Live Crew, said Rogow, their lawyer.

''To have a record declared obscene is a first. It gives the record a much longer life,'' he said.

Band leader Campbell said his band's newest album will be even raunchier. Its title: *Banned In The USA*.

Ancil Davis / National Association of Independent Record Distributors and Manufacturers Meet Tackles Sticky Problems Posed by Stickering

Variety, June 5, 1990

In this brief report by Davis on the annual meeting of music industry leaders, the reader discovers an unusual approach to reporting: the insider's language of the trade magazines. Variety, *the leading trade of the entertainment industry, generally focuses on film and television but covers music and theater news as well. Entertainment professionals read the weekly tabloid religiously, searching for the scoop on hot trends and risky ventures, charting the rise and fall of products released by themselves and their competitors.*

Slang terms such as ''confab'' (gathering), ''prexy'' (president), and ''skedded'' (scheduled) pepper Davis's piece, both quickening the reader's pace and allowing her or him to feel privy to an exclusive language. Writing style, in this context, is transformed into the manipulation of a code shared by all trade writers. The Variety *article is, in many ways, the epitome of the ''quick read''—unprosaic and overflowing with facts, it allows the informed reader easy access to the information he or she requires along with the sense of participating in a community that requires these facts to operate.*

The following piece relates the events of a meeting organized to address the issue of record stickering, an ongoing controversy among music industry professionals. Employing Variety's *usual approach, Davis offers no opinion of his own on the issue: he simply relates the various statements expressed at the meeting, aiming for an ''objective'' account.*

NASHVILLE—The National Association of Independent Record Distributors & Manufacturers (NAIRD), which held its annual confab here for the first time last weekend, grappled with the problems record labeling is expected to pose for indies in light of the March agreement on universal stickering.

At a panel session Friday on ''Dealing With Explicit Lyrics,'' it was clear that both panelists and audience members have made the ''business decision'' to sticker albums. Tom Silverman, prexy of Tommy Boy Records, said the alternative is to issue a ''clean version'' of albums, as done by the Priority and Skyywalker labels. Silverman said that option is unacceptable to Tommy Boy.

Silverman suggested ''grass-roots lobbying'' as an answer for the First Amendment question facing record labels. "It's great to say we're all for the First Amendment," he said, "but who's willing to pay for that right? Maybe what America needs is a path of polarization for six or seven years before it can see how bad it's gotten."

Neil Cooper, head of ROIR Reachout International, and panel member Michael Greene, prexy of the National Academy of Recording Arts & Sciences, attempted to define the parameters a parent should use when selecting material appropriate for children.

Cooper related that he once turned off a questionable tv show his children were watching but felt guilty because he would have continued watching if they hadn't been present.

Greene countered that the industry must now take responsibility for the labeling albums with explicit contents itself. Two young boys, sons of Reiter Records' Stewart Rosenblum, took the microphone to complain about being subjected to "dirty lyrics" on their schoolgrounds.

It was further pointed out that albums from some controversial artists, like Luther Campbell, known as Skyywalker, had been stickered from the beginning. "Children need to define their own generations," said Silverman, "and that's what this is against. There was Elvis and the mop-tops, and now this generation needs to find their own way."

Since NAIRD agreed to the stickering policy, there has been little internal dissension over the decision. However, Alligator Records head Bruce Iglauer, a vocal opponent of the move, had been skedded as a panelist, and he failed to appear.

Subbing for him was Bruce Kaplan, prexy of Flying Fish Records, who suggested following the example of two organizations that implement strong lobbying efforts when faced with legislative decisions that pose threats; the American Booksellers Association, which is directing ads at the upcoming 200th anniversary of the Bill of Rights, and the National Rifle Association, which opposes every "compromise" of the right to bear arms.

Panelist Trish Heimers, v.p. of p.r. for the Recording Industry Assn. of America, proposed members become involved with the recently formed Coalition Against Lyrics Legislation.

It was also pointed out that Louisiana House Bill 154 was passed by a 95-5 vote last week, and Senate hearings are scheduled to begin today.

Greene said a groundswell of support galvanizing the entire music community is needed. "Music retailers," he pointed out, "don't think of themselves as part of the creative community. They were on the front lines when this began, and they were the ones to fold when the first shot was fired."

Overall turnout for the confab was considered a success, with more than 500 people attending.

NAIRD Hall of Fame honorees this year were George Hocutt, founder and charter prexy of the org. and Credence Clearwater Revival.

DISCUSSION QUESTIONS

1. How do the facts laid out in this trade publication feature differ from those highlighted in the *Miami Herald* story by Scott Higham, Anne Bartlett, and James F. McCarty on p. 202? How does language affect the stories told? Which version do you judge more effective? Why?

Tottie Ellis / Hooray for This Crackdown on Obscenity

USA Today, June 12, 1990

USA Today began publishing in the 1980s as America's only nationwide general interest newspaper. Since that time, the paper has come to personify a style of "lite news" that emphasizes large color photographs and personality and entertainment profiles, as well as easy reading while communicating a moderate to conservative political viewpoint.

This editorial typifies USA Today*'s policy of using "ordinary voices" to express political views. Tottie Ellis speaks out against "fuzzy-brained liberals" and champions traditional family values as represented by Broward County sheriff Nick Navarro. She evokes the image of noble lawman Gary Cooper in* High Noon *to drive home her scenario of mythic forces doing battle over the very soul of the American people. This piece stands in contrast to one such as the analysis by Henry Louis Gates, Jr., in the* New York Times *(also in this section), stressing emotionalism over reason, and a unified picture of the American public over a more relativistic, cross-cultural view.*

NASHVILLE, Tenn.—A standing ovation for Sheriff Nick Navarro of Broward County, Fla.

Navarro and his deputies arrested a record store owner for selling a 2 Live Crew album which had been declared obscene after a full-blown trial before federal Judge Jose Gonzalez, a Jimmy Carter appointee.

And, they followed up by arresting two members of the crew itself for violating Florida's obscenity law in their night club performance of some of the "songs" from the album.

The sheriff understood that the store owner and the performers were flouting the law, behaving like anarchists. In fact, they were shaking their fists in the face of the instrument of civilized society. Law without penalty is only advice.

This Florida sheriff was doing both what he was sworn to do and paid to do. I, for one, say well done! Thank heavens somebody is trying to crack down on this grossness in entertainment.

Fuzzy-brained liberals want to switch the issue from obscenity to a First Amendment case. In fact, some go so far as to say there's no such thing as obscenity, which merely begs the question.

This particular album, *As Nasty as They Wanna Be,* contains 600 dirty, sexy, obscene, filthy words, and not one line can be read on the air. Florida Gov. Bob Martinez says, "If you answer the phone one night and the voice on the other end begins to read the lyrics of one of these songs, you'd say you'd received an obscene phone call."

It takes courage and fortitude to enforce the law. Freedom exists only because it can be linked with responsibility. When blatant sexism, racism, hatred, violence and evil are glorified and promoted, society must through checks and balances have the strength to say to even popular rap groups such as 2 Live Crew, "Shut up!"

You can't yell "fire!" in a crowded theater. You can't package garbage and sell it as food. Cocaine is illegal. And the law says obscenity degrades, destroys and debases human relationships and therefore is illegal.

For human beings to be free, we must accept the perils of choice as well as the privilege. But it is wrong to confuse freedom and license. It is as wrong to pollute culture as it is the Earth. When the facts are all in, Sheriff Navarro is going to come out as the sheriff in *High Noon*. Evil is never defeated by a conspiracy of silence.

Mona Charen / Much More Nasty Than They Should Be

Boston Globe, June 16, 1990

In this well-reasoned and forceful argument, syndicated columnist Mona Charen demonstrates the savvy she employed to great success during her years as a Reagan speechwriter. During the president's two terms in office, Charen, along with Patrick Buchanan, directed Reagan's dealings with the media and wrote many of his speeches. Trained as a lawyer, Charen currently syndicates her column twice a week to various conservative publications and also pens an opinion column for the Republican Study Committee Bulletin, *which is circulated among Republican congressional members.*

Disputing the liberal ''freedom of expression'' argument, Charen here contrasts the idea that ''total freedom is anarchy'' with freedom as ''ordered liberty.'' She shows up faults in liberal logic and concludes that culture is only worth protecting if it exhibits a certain modicum of taste. Charen's view assumes a certain shared set of values and terms by which Americans are willing to judge themselves and each other.

I feel like I need a shower. I've just finished listening to ''As Nasty as They Wanna Be'' by 2 Live Crew, the album declared obscene last week by a Florida judge.

How bad is it? Let's put it this way. If the young men on trial in New York for the rape and assault on the Central Park jogger were to become rap music singers, they would sound like 2 Live Crew.

It isn't just that the album is, in the popular euphemism, ''sexually explicit,'' or that it uses gutter language—it is barbarous. The lyrics are disgustingly anti-female. The sexual fantasies of the male singers always include pain and degradation for the ''bitches.''

That could be called social commentary. No doubt someone will call it ''redeeming social value.''

Two members of the 2 Live Crew band were arrested for performing this garbage in Fort Lauderdale, Fla., and now the censorship battle is at full squawk.

The group's lawyer, Bruce Rogow, told the *Washington Post,* ''Put in its historical context, it is a novel and creative use of sound and lyrics. The trouble is, you have a bunch of white folks who don't understand the culture.'' Actually, one of the judges who found this record obscene is black, but that's not really the point. If this trash is an authentic voice of black culture, then one could just as easily argue that the crack murders in the inner city are just the black way of doing business—which white folks don't understand.

Following the arrests, nimble Phil Donahue rushed onto the air to proclaim the liberal First Commandment—Thou shalt not set standards of any kind because when you censor 2 Live Crew, next thing ya know they'll be coming for Phil Donahue.

Why is it that liberals can grasp the fallacy of the slippery-slope argument when the National Rifle Association opposes waiting periods for gun purchases (''Next think ya know they'll be taking away our hunting rifles'') but not when 2 Live Crew seeks shelter beneath the First Amendment?

Censorship is a defining act of civilization. Societies cannot exist without proscribing certain things. When we outlaw racial discrimination or drunken driving or price-fixing, we are defining who we are. And just because we proscribe drunken driving does not mean that we're on the slope to forbidding driving. Only the weak-minded find it impossible to make simple distinctions.

Which brings us to artistic expression—a subject on which liberal thinking has become impacted. People for the American Way is airing radio commercials starring Colleen Dewhurst which ask the listener to imagine a country where artists are persecuted and then say, ''Welcome to America, 1990.''

Dewhurst's point is the stale one about the Mapplethorpe exhibit. Oh pity the photographers whose persecution amounts to being denied a federal subsidy. But are we endangering our liberty by censoring 2 Live Crew?

It's the wrong question. It's wrong because total freedom is not the goal of any society—total freedom is anarchy. The goal of our founders was ''ordered liberty.''

Degrading and decadent entertainment erodes the values on which ordered liberty rests: mutual respect, self-control, sympathy, and civility. It is no answer to say, as does Luther Campbell, that everything described in his songs ''people does.'' People, as he so clearly knows, can be depraved. What he doesn't seem to understand, and perhaps the larger society must teach him, is that people can also be sublime—and will not consent silently to 2 Live Crew polluting our common culture.

Juan Williams / The Real Crime: Making Heroes of Hate Mongers *Washington Post,* June 17, 1990

Award-winning black journalist Juan Williams makes a complicated point in this feature on the cultural ramifications of 2 Live Crew. Outlining some of the problems that have plagued the African American community in modern time—particularly male misogyny and irresponsibility—he suggests that any romanticization of criminal or ''street'' values further endangers an already imperiled black America. Williams argues against aesthetic license in the case of 2 Live Crew because he believes young people do not listen to the music as metaphor—they interpret the music as reality based.

Juan Williams was born in Panama in 1954. He specializes in political analysis for the weekly ''Outlook'' section of the Washington Post *and writes regularly for the* Washington Post Magazine. *He also authored* Eyes on the Prize: America's Civil Rights Years, 1954–1965, *the book that accompanied the renowned PBS series of the same title. Among Williams's numerous awards are the 1990 Art Carter Award of Excellence for Outstanding Local News Reporter and the top prize in Political Commentary from the American Association of University Women.*

Listen to this: Song number one on 2 Live Crew's million-plus seller ''As Nasty as They Wanna Be'' sings the praise of a man acting ''like a dog in heat,'' and taking pride in breaking the walls of a woman's vagina. Song number two again sings about tearing a woman open before having her ''kneel and pray.'' Song number three raps about the joy of a man forcing anal sex on a woman and later making her lick feces.

In Florida a black judge and now a Hispanic judge have ruled that these songs violate that state's obscenity law, prompting a ban on the sale of the record and public performances of the songs in three counties in Florida. In its defense the group's lawyer, Bruce Rogow, argues that the critics may be racists who don't understand black music and that the songs are not meant to be read but danced to by adults who are in a partying mood and appreciate blue humor, and if people don't want to listen to it they don't have to buy it. Luther Campbell, the group's leader, also argues that the lyrics reflect life in America's black neighborhoods. Rogow's ultimate argument is that banning the record amounts to artistic censorship that has resulted in the arrest of record store owners and members of the band.

The lawyer's arguments are more interesting than the profane music, but it's all a fake.

Racism, partying and even censorship are not the issue here. 2 Live Crew's record is hot—in fact getting hotter by all the talk of censorship in one state—and the group is still touring and making plans for another record that Campbell boasts will be "even more obscene."

The real issue is hate-filled music that is abusive of women—especially black women—and an assault on its young audience's budding concepts of good sex, good relationships and good times. Campbell has said he won't let his 7-year-old daughter listen to the music, which routinely refers to women as "bitches."

Making 2 Live Crew champions in a censorship fight or heroes of black America's battle against racial oppression frees the group from responsibility for making millions of dollars by selling pornography to teenagers. The debate over 2 Live Crew is not the same as that surrounding Robert Mapplethorpe and government support for controversial art. 2 Live Crew is cultivating young audiences with the cheap thrill of sex, violence and gold chains.

"Censorship is a red herring in this case," says Jewelle Taylor Gibbs, author of "Young, Black and Male in America: An Endangered Species." "The real issue is values, quality of life. And the real question is how can the black community turn it around. . . .

"With this music," says Gibbs, "I worry most about our young black men who see 2 Live Crew's success and take them as role models—negative, antisocial role models. Their music, their image, is based on degrading women. It extols and romanticizes violence and drugs. Now how can anyone say that is a productive social message for our black kids, especially young males struggling to learn how to become men?"

Gibbs and others concede that it is possible 2 Live Crew may be receiving tougher treatment from the judicial system than a white group would. But they argue that this case is not about race—it is about obscenity. And, specifically, about the impact the group is having on young black people.

In a nation where about half of all black children live in single-parent, female-headed households, the worry is not far-fetched. In a society in which the black family is falling apart, in which teen pregnancy regularly ruins lives and in which the rate of poverty is steadily rising, the urgent concern is that 2 Live Crew is selling corruption—self-hate—to vulnerable young minds in a weak black America.

Dorothy Height, head of the National Council of Negro Women, is particularly concerned with the music's negative impact on young black females. Height says black women are looking for ways to protest the music without making it all the more risqué and attractive to rebellious young people.

"Generally speaking, I favor upholding anyone's First Amendment rights,"

Height says. ''But this music is damaging because it is degrading to women to have it suggested in our popular music that they are to be abused, that it is fun to abuse us, that we like to be abused. . . . This kind of exhibition at a time when all of us are struggling to strengthen our community and deal with problems hurts us badly.

''We are trying to build self-esteem in black women,'' she says, ''Many of our young women do not have a lot of self-respect. . . . We are tired of being put down.''

Marilyn Kern-Foxworth, a professor of journalism at Texas A&M who studies blacks in media, believes 2 Live Crew's lyrics have not prompted a full-fledged opposition from black women because many still deny they are being victimized.

''Too many black women are still saying they see the music as about some other women, not them—no man would treat them like that,'' she says. ''There is a great sense of denial, even though they will tell you these things actually do occur and they complain the black male responsibility toward black women is diminishing.''

2 Live Crew's style and message of abusing women is finding a larger audience than the lewd black comedy and music of the past, which was aimed at adult audiences in nightclubs. ''The young people listen to them and idolize them,'' says Kern-Foxworth. Record store owners nationwide report that teenagers are the big buyers of 2 Live Crew. ''I don't get adults buying this stuff,'' says a record store owner in Northeast Washington. ''This is rap, man—the kids get off on this.''

''The music carries the words into their minds,'' says Kern-Foxworth. ''And the music is now so widespread that the young people can't help but be influenced. They hold the musicians up on a platform so they can't help but want to be like them, to listen to them, to wear the clothes and the gold chains and to do what 2 Live Crew is singing about.

''We are talking about something deviant, aberrant and negative, and kids in the teenaged group do not have the mental ability, the maturity, to sort out what is good and bad for themselves. These musical idols have a tremendous influence.''

The lack of social responsibility exercised by 2 Live Crew is not limited to glorifying abuse, of black women. Although they don't sing about it, a simple look at the group in black baseball caps and layers of gold rope chains reveals their romanticization of the drug culture—featuring the male drug dealer as the hero. The right to use and abuse women is part of being a successful drug dealer.

''The central question,'' says Stanley Crouch, the New York jazz critic and commentator, ''is how the sadistic, misogynic, hateful music adds to the problematic attitudes already burdening the black lower class in America. Listen to it. Women are sex slaves. Materialism is God. The ideal of cool is street-corner narcissism. This is no true vision of black America or black culture, but a slice of the worst of a small element of black culture that is not emblematic of the black community at large.''

In addition, Crouch argues that 2 Live Crew sells whites on the idea that black culture is a base, vulgar entity that starts and stops on a ghetto corner.

''The young people listening to this music don't perceive it as a joke, they don't see it as metaphors about relationships and life,'' he says. ''They see it as reality-based—a way to assert themselves and establish their identity. That is why it is obscene and threatening to black folks beyond what the judge had to say.''

Henry Louis Gates, Jr. / 2 Live Crew, Decoded

New York Times, June 19, 1990

Henry Louis Gates, Jr., is widely regarded as the nation's foremost scholar of African American literature, and he has done much to uncover and champion an ''alternative'' African American cultural tradition that is as rich and deserving of attention as the traditional, Anglo American–based canon. Gates has not limited himself to the archives, however. Besides writing regularly for such publications as the New York Times, *the* Village Voice, *and* Jet, *Gates appeared as a star witness for the defense in the 2 Live Crew obscenity trial, and his testimony proved significant in the acquittal of the rap group. In his testimony, as in the following article, Gates asserts that a careful examination reveals meaning in 2 Live Crew's music that is unseen and unheard by those outside the culture of young African American males. He maintains that the judicial system's lack of knowledge about African American cultural and linguistic traditions severely limits its ability to treat citizens from that community fairly.*

Henry Louis Gates (b. 1950) is currently a professor of English and director of the W. E. B. DuBois Center for African American Studies at Harvard University. His most influential books include Black Literature and Literary Theory *(1984),* The Signifying Monkey: Towards a Theory of Afro-American Literary Criticism *(1988), and* Loose Canons: Notes on the Culture Wars *(1992). Gates also helped create a PBS television series,* The Image of the Black in the Western Imagination.

The rap group 2 Live Crew and their controversial hit recording ''As Nasty as They Wanna Be'' may well earn a signal place in the history of First Amendment rights. But just as important is how these lyrics will be interpreted and by whom.

For centuries, African-Americans have been forced to develop coded ways of communicating to protect them from danger. Allegories and double meanings, words redefined to mean their opposites (''bad'' meaning ''good,'' for instance), even neologisms (''bodacious'') have enabled blacks to share messages only the initiated understand.

Many blacks were amused by the transcripts of Marion Barry's sting operation, which reveals that he used the traditional black expression about one's ''nose being opened.'' This referred to a love affair and not, as Mr. Barry's prosecutors have suggested, to the inhalation of drugs. Understanding this phrase could very well spell the difference (for the Mayor) between prison and freedom.

2 Live Crew is engaged in heavy-handed parody, turning the stereotypes of black and white American culture on their heads. These young artists are acting out, to lively dance music, a parodic exaggeration of the age-old stereotypes of the oversexed black female and male. Their exuberant use of hyperbole (phantasmagoric sexual organs, for example) undermines—for anyone fluent in black cultural codes—a too literal-minded hearing of the lyrics.

This is the street tradition called ''signifying'' or ''playing the dozens,'' which has generally been risqué, and where the best signifier or ''rapper'' is the one who invents the most extravagant images, the biggest ''lies,'' as the culture says. (H. ''Rap'' Brown earned his nickname in just this way.) In the face of racist stereotypes about black sexuality, you can do one of two things: you can disavow them or explode them with exaggeration.

2 Live Crew, like many ''hip-hop'' groups, is engaged in sexual carnivalesque. Parody reigns supreme, from a take-off of standard blues to a spoof of the black

power movement, their off-color nursery rhymes are part of a venerable Western tradition. The group even satirizes the culture of commerce when it appropriates popular advertising slogans (''Tastes great!'' ''Less filling!'') and puts them in a bawdy context.

2 Live Crew must be interpreted within the context of black culture generally and of signifying specifically. Their novelty, and that of other adventuresome rap groups, is that their defiant rejection of euphemism now voices for the mainstream what before existed largely in the ''race record'' market—where the records of Redd Foxx and Rudy Ray Moore once were forced to reside.

Rock songs have always been about sex but have used elaborate subterfuges to convey that fact. 2 Live Crew uses Anglo-Saxon words and is self-conscious about it: a parody of a white voice in one song refers to ''private personal parts,'' as a coy counterpart to the group's bluntness.

Much more troubling than its so-called obscenity is the group's overt sexism. Their sexism is so flagrant, however, that is almost cancels itself out in a hyperbolic war between the sexes. In this, it recalls the inter-sexual jousting in Zora Neale Hurston's novels. Still, many of us look toward the emergence of more female rappers to redress sexual stereotypes. And we must not allow ourselves to sentimentalize street culture: the appreciation of verbal virtuosity does not lessen one's obligation to critique bigotry in all of its pernicious forms.

Is 2 Live Crew more ''obscene'' than, say, the comic Andrew Dice Clay? Clearly, this rap group is seen as more threatening than others that are just as sexually explicit. Can this be completely unrelated to the specter of the young black male as a figure of sexual and social disruption, the very stereotypes 2 Live Crew seems determined to undermine?

This question—and the very large question of obscenity and the First Amendment—cannot even be addressed until those who would answer them become literate in the vernacular traditions of African-Americans. To do less is to censor through the equivalent of intellectual prior restraint—and censorship is to art what lynching is to justice.

David Mills / The Judge vs. 2 Live Crew: Is the Issue Obscenity or Young, Black Males?

Washington Post, National Weekly Edition, June 25–July 1, 1990

David Mills's work as a journalist covering African American popular culture became widely known in 1990, when an interview with Public Enemy's Professor Griff that he conducted for the Washington Times *led to a nationwide controversy regarding that group's anti-Semitic leanings. In the following article, Mills comes to the defense of another highly debated hip-hop group—2 Live Crew—elaborating on Henry Louis Gates, Jr.'s assertions (see p. 211) about black culture and difference through a thumbnail sketch of the cultural tradition that the Florida artists' work reflects, including the adults-only party records of the 1970s of Richard Pryor and ''blaxploitation'' action movies. Mills lets the reader in on a set of reference points that are not evident from a cursory hearing of* As Nasty as They Wanna Be; *in doing so, he makes a strong and detailed case for paying attention to a subculture's particulars when judging its products.*

David Mills writes for the Style section of the Washington Times.

A rap fan in Tennessee sent me a letter last month, before a U.S. District judge in Florida declared the 2 Live Crew's latest album obscene, and before the Crew's leader, Luther Campbell, was arrested and manacled because of words uttered during a nightclub performance, words uttered to an audience of paying adults.

"I do not think that 2 Live Crew is actually on trial," the young man wrote. "I believe that black expression as a whole is on trial. . . . And if 2 Live Crew are found to be obscene, other forms of black expression will be targeted. This could act as the catalyst for anti-black censorship of a much greater scale."

Paranoia? Or does the banning of "As Nasty as They Wanna Be" in southern Florida indeed represent an immediate threat to free speech, especially the speech of African American young men?

Consider the experience of other popular—and foul-mouthed—rappers. Before a 1988 concert in Columbus, Ga., police officers warned Ice-T that he'd be arrested if he uttered certain profane words onstage, he says. Ice-T performed one song and canceled the rest of his show. Last summer, members of N.W.A. (Niggers With Attitudes) were chased out of Detroit's Joe Louis Arena by the police after the rappers, egged on by a chanting crowd, began performing their masterpiece of vituperation, "[Expletive] tha Police." And in Cincinnati, the town that so dutifully tried to protect its citizens from the photographs of Robert Mapplethorpe, a judge fined members of N.W.A. $100 apiece for "offensively coarse utterances" between songs during a Riverfront Coliseum show.

The criminalization of a challenging form of black expressiveness raises urgent questions. Should federal courts be determining the artistic worth of products of the African American culture? Just what artistic worth can there be in a collection of songs as violently raunchy and mean-spirited as 2 Live Crew's "As Nasty as They Wanna Be"?

Where are the black scholars and intellectuals who should be able to place 2 Live Crew in its cultural context and who, must act as the first line of defense when black artists come under attack? And where are the 1.7 million people who have bought "As Nasty as They Wanna Be"? Where is their outrage? It is now a crime in Florida's Broward, Dade and Palm Beach counties to own this album. Anyone who has "Nasty" lying around the house or in the automobile tape deck, is breaking the law. In Florida, possession of obscene material is punishable by up to 60 days in jail and a $500 fine.

E. Ethelbert Miller, director of Howard University's Afro-American Resource Center, says most blacks tend to get alarmed only over the issue of racism, and tend to sit out public debates on such "abstract" matters as artistic freedom. He doesn't think that officials who attack "Nasty" are necessarily "singling out African American art. It's a whole climate out there . . . the right-wing social agenda. And this is where I respect the right wing—they're organized."

"Neither the 'rap' or 'hip-hop' musical genres are on trial," writes U.S. District Judge Jose A. Gonzalez Jr. of Fort Lauderdale in his recent opinion. "The narrow issue before this court is whether the recording entitled 'As Nasty as They Wanna Be' is legally obscene," and therefore unprotected by the First Amendment. "This court's role is not to serve as a censor or an art and music critic."

Despite this declamation, the judge displays a crucial lack of understanding of rap music and its cultural context when he applies the Supreme Court's three tests for obscenity to "As Nasty as They Wanna Be." Let us accept his conclusion that the album meets the first two tests—that it "appeals to the prurient interest" and that, "measured by contemporary community standards, the work depicts or describes, in a patently offensive way, sexual conduct" as defined by state law.

Gonzalez writes that 2 Live Crew's lyrics "are replete with references to female and male genitalia, human sexual excretion, oral-anal contact, fellatio, group sex, specific sexual positions, sado-masochism, the turgid state of the male sexual organ, masturbation, cunnilingus, sexual intercourse, and the sounds of moaning.''

Indeed they are. Luther Campbell has purposefully explored the farthest fringes of comic vulgarity and overblown phallicism. Thus has 2 Live Crew carved out a niche in the highly competitive rap market. Yet all those lascivious lyrics are perfectly permissible under the First Amendment, unless the album, ''taken as a whole, lacks serious literary, artistic, political or scientific value.'' That is the Supreme Court's third test for obscenity. And it gets to the heart of things: What qualifies Judge Gonzalez to assess the artistic value of a rap album?

In the words of Henry Louis Gates, a Duke University English professor and an expert on African American ''vernacular culture'': ''I don't see how people can jump into somebody else's culture, with completely no knowledge of that culture, and then decide what's obscene and what's not.''

The Supreme Court says a work must be judged ''as a whole.'' But Gonzalez goes to great lengths to justify focusing almost exclusively on the dirty words. The judge, citing ''expert testimony,'' writes that ''a central characteristic of 'rap' music is its emphasis on the *verbal* message.'' He concludes that ''it does not significantly alter the message of the 'Nasty' recording to reduce it to a written transcription.''

He is absolutely wrong. Apart from the fact that rap is an outgrowth of funk—that it is fundamentally a dance music—rap is not about the words per se. It's about the rendition of the words. The emphasis is not verbal, it is *oral.* The rappers call it ''flow.'' To misunderstand this is to miss the essence of rap as a vibrant manifestation of the black oral tradition. Only by listening to 2 Live Crew, not by reading its lyrics on a sheet of paper, do you realize that their sexual rants aren't to be taken literally.

2 Live Crew engages in a style of African American ribaldry that is rooted in the inner-city speech heard on street corners and in schoolyards. It's the kind of humor found throughout the '70s on the adults-only ''party records'' of comedians such as Richard Pryor, Richard and Willie and Rudy Ray Moore. (Snippets of their material, not coincidentally, can be found on ''As Nasty as They Wanna Be.'')

In court, the group's main argument was that ''Nasty'' has artistic value as comedy and satire. Gonzalez did not agree: ''It cannot be reasonably argued that the violence, perversion, abuse of women, graphic depictions of all forms of sexual conduct, and microscopic descriptions of human genitalia contained on this recording are comedic art.''

This again demonstrates the danger of a cultural outsider passing judgment on something he doesn't understand. Just as you cannot appreciate a rap song by merely reading its lyrics—disregarding its rhythm tracks, disregarding the nuances of its vocalization—you cannot fully understand this profane style of rapping if you disregard the larger folklore of the streets.

There are fascinating echoes in today's hard-edged rap music not only of black comedy, but of the low-budget ''black exploitation'' action movies of the early '70s and the stylized folk performance-poems, called ''toasts,'' that emanated from the world of pimps and hustlers. ''As Nasty as They Wanna Be'' has real cultural underpinnings.

Comedian Rudy Ray Moore, the spiritual godfather of 2 Live Crew, made a career of recording versions of vulgar, sometimes violent, often sexually exaggerated toasts such as ''Dolemite'' and ''Pimpin' Sam.'' A member of 2 Live Crew drops a nasty couplet about lesbians rubbing belly to belly in ''[Expletive] Almighty''; the same couplet can be found in Moore's version of the ultra-scatological toast ''Dance of the Freaks,'' recorded more than 15 years earlier: and in one written collection of toasts, you can find a version of ''Dance of the Freaks'' recited by a Sing Sing inmate in 1954.

Toasts can be so compelling that one of the legendary, radical Last Poets adopted the style (and the name Lightnin' Rod) for his LP ''Hustler's Convention'' in 1973. Over funky background music from the likes of Kool and the Gang, a criminal flamboyantly spins his underworld tale. ''I was a down stud's dream, a hustler supreme. There wasn't no game that I couldn't play. And if I caught a dude cheatin', I would give him a beatin', and I might even blow him away!'' By the end of the record, after being beaten and shot by the cops and spending years on death row, this ''nickel-and-dime'' hustler has become politicized. About 15 years later, Ice-T released his first album, ''Rhyme Pays,'' a virtual homage to ''Hustler's Convention.''

Between 1972 and 1976, independent film producers and distributors churned out countless action movies with titles such as ''Black Gunn,'' ''Black Caesar,'' ''Black Samson,'' ''Black Fist,'' ''The Black Godfather'' and ''Boss Nigger.'' Designed to appeal, obviously, to the fantasies of young black males, these films were often set in the criminal world.

''In the black community of past decades, the old-style pimp had sometimes been viewed as a folk hero of sorts: a smooth-talking, sexy, hip, moneyed man in control of his destiny,'' writes film historian Donald Bogle in ''Blacks in American Films and Television.'' Describing the 1973 pimp's saga ''The Mack,'' he continues: ''By the 1970s, one might have assumed the pimp would be seen for other things he represented, primarily as an exploiter of women. Instead, young black moviegoers seemed to delight in [the hero's] pretty looks, his firm control over his women, his striking array of material comforts . . . and his tenacious grip on survival.''

To understand 2 Live Crew is to realize the difference between being a lowlife and pretending to be a lowlife, the difference between sick, mean humor and true sickness and meanness. ''A lot of people fail to see that music is acting,'' says Debbie Bennett, spokeswoman for Luke Records. Of 2 Live Crew, she says, ''You won't find four nicer guys.''

But it's their pretense, in all its outrageous sexual explicitness, that fits squarely into the tradition of comedy albums and films that draw upon the rich black folklore of the streets. That is the ''artistic value'' of ''As Nasty as They Wanna Be,'' which entitles it to protection under the First Amendment. That is the context in which 2 Live Crew must be judged. And that is why Judge Gonzalez was wrong to declare the album ''utterly without any redeeming social value,'' and why anyone who is serious about the African American popular culture should be disturbed by his ruling.

Of course, ''just because something comes out of the black culture, just because it has black cultural authenticity, doesn't make it good,'' says Stanley Crouch, noted jazz critic and essayist. Rap in general is ''an expression of a lower aspect of the culture,'' in his view. The members of 2 Live Crew specifically are ''some vulgar street-corner-type clowns,'' ''spiritual cretins,'' ''slime.''

''We're so defensive about ourselves that we feel that we always have to come forward and defend anything that says it represents black authenticity,'' Crouch says. ''We do not have to celebrate the lowest elements in our society. . . . We cannot make a powerful Afro-American culture if we're going to base it on what hustlers and pimps think about the world.''

No doubt. But ''As Nasty as They Wanna Be'' is a piece of entertainment, not a blueprint for living. I don't find the album very entertaining. I am bothered by the meanness of the humor regarding women, just as I am bothered by the jokes of white comedian Andrew Dice Clay. But 2 Live Crew has sold 1.7 million copies of this album, and Clay is packing arenas. Are they driving the culture, or simply reflecting it?

Teri Maddox / Unsuspecting Parents Can't Believe Their Ears

Belleville (Illinois) *News Democrat,* September 30, 1990

In this feature taken from a small-town Illinois newspaper, reporter Teri Maddox records the concerns of church-going parents about the effects of popular media on their children. The article relates the events at a symposium called "A Generation at Risk," sponsored by local church groups, where concerned parents listened to sexually explicit lyrics and saw footage from slasher films and then were counseled on how to discuss such material with its young fans. Maddox records the stunned and angry comments of a selection of symposium participants, creating a sense of unified negative response to the allegedly "obscene" material by piecing together individual reactions. Through this technique, Maddox communicates the general tenor of the event and its ramifications as she experienced it.

The Belleville Democrat *has a circulation of about fifty thousand, serving readers in and around Belleville, a small city located about twenty minutes from St. Louis, Missouri. Maddox is staff writer for the paper's Lifestyle department.*

Parents and grandparents walked out of the Belle-Clair Fairgrounds Exposition Center in a horrified daze.

Moments before, they had gasped at the sexually explicit lyrics by groups such as 2 Live Crew and cringed at scenes from "slasher" films such as "Nightmare on Elm Street 2." Some covered their eyes or looked down at the floor.

They were among about 2,000 area residents at a recent adults-only presentation, "A Generation at Risk," sponsored by several local churches.

"I was weeping," said Belleville resident Diane Patton, 49, a secretary. "I was weeping . . . for our children who are exposed to this."

Collinsville residents Gary Queen, 46, a factory worker, and his wife, Linda, 43, a real-estate agent, said the rap songs were the most shocking and offensive.

Linda Queen said the vast majority of Americans are unaware of how obscene the lyrics are because the traditional media refuses to publish them.

"We're not being informed properly," she said. "I don't think the public should have to come to a place like this to find out what's going on."

The crowd had gathered to hear a presentation by Bob DeMoss, youth specialist for "Focus on the Family," a California-based Christian organization.

DeMoss characterized some Hollywood producers as irresponsible and immoral for selling pre-teenagers albums that glorify rape and other violence.

"We're not talking about Elvis shaking his pelvis, folks," he said. "We've gone from 'I Wanna Hold Your Hand' to 'I Wanna Hold Your Gland.' "

One rap song, "F— tha Police," by N.W.A. describes a plan by young blacks in Los Angeles to "slaughter" police in return for being hassled.

"Suicide Solution" by heavy-metal rocker Ozzy Ozborne is seen by some to portray suicide as a positive alternative to dealing with daily problems.

"Indian Girl (an adult story)" by rapper Slick Rick gives a graphic description of a rape, with the woman crying, *"You're hurting me. Stop."*

"He was playing with her ———. They were soft not lumpy. And then he cracked her legs like Humpty Dumpty. . . ."

"He had no intention of stoppin'. Crazy fun he did not want to leave. . . . She said, 'Stop, stop.' He said, 'Are you talkin' sense or what?' "

DeMoss stopped short of calling for a ban on the music, but said parents need to be aware of it and keep it out of the hands of their children.

Many people believe that the popularity of musicians who record the explicit songs is minimal, he said, but the albums are selling by the millions.

2 Live Crew, whose song on the album, "As Nasty as They Wanna Be" was declared obscene by a Florida judge recently, has sold 1.7 million copies.

DeMoss thinks many of the young fans, including those in elementary school, see the musicians as heroes who will tell them how to be "cool."

"They validate a way of thinking," DeMoss said, noting that a teen-age boy in California committed suicide while listening to the Ozborne song.

Last March in Oklahoma, three teen-agers and a 20-year-old pleaded guilty to beating and repeatedly raping two girls in ninth and 10th grades.

According to the district attorney on the case, the rap song "Gangster of Love" by the Geto Boys was played several times during the violent ordeal.

DeMoss said the lyrics make women seem less than human: *"I like bitches, all kinda bitches, to take off my shirt and pull down my britches."*

"If she's got big ———, I'll squeeze 'em, while she ——— my ——— and ——— my ———. If she's got a friend, I'll ——— her, too! Together, we'll play switcheroo."

The music industry is full of examples of the exploitation of women, Demoss said, which should send those in the feminist movement into action.

On a Guns 'n' Roses album cover is a picture of a woman lying with her underwear pulled down and blood dripping from razor cuts on her exposed breasts.

Alan Brainerd, 28, an interior designer in Belleville, said it was a shock to discover that music had changed so drastically since his teenage years.

As a professional businessman in his 20s, Brainerd said he did not feel "old" or out of touch with the music world. That was before the presentation.

"I couldn't believe it," he said. "I was shocked. Most people don't have a clue that this is going on. I'd say 80 percent of the population is unaware."

Brainerd was offended by the inside cover of a "Dead Kennedys" album. Called "Penis Landscape," it is a close-up of genitals during copulation.

Throughout the presentation, DeMoss told the crowd to "learn to discern" and to teach youngsters to do the same when choosing their entertainment.

The wrong way for parents to react is to burst into the house and demand that all the "offensive" music and posters be destroyed, DeMoss said.

Albums, cassettes and compact discs are expensive, he said, and children will resent the fact that their hard-earned money went for nothing.

DeMoss suggested that families discuss—not argue—and compare different types of music, then set a standard for purchases in the future.

"If you don't have a standard, it's just a shouting match of preferences," he said, noting that the standard in his family is the Bible.

For past purchases, he said, parents could have a "buy-back" agreement to buy back the records that fail to meet the family standard.

DeMoss told the crowd it is wrong to think all modern musicians are bad. "There are a lot of positive things happening in music today," he said.

He played "I Won't Back Down" by Tom Petty, who sings about "knowing what's right" and "standing my ground in a world that's pushing me around."

DeMoss also played the song ''Another Day in Paradise'' by Phil Collins, who encourages people to show kindness to people who are homeless.

DeMoss blames the media, in part, for the lack of public action against the ''bad'' music because it refuses to publish the explicit lyrics, he said.

Teen-agers are the primary consumers, he said. The majority of adults are not exposed to the music and don't know their children listen to it.

DeMoss said he was nearly thrown off the ''Donahue'' show for reading parts of a 2 Live Crew song. Producers felt it would offend their TV viewers.

When testifying at a U.S. Senate hearing on lyrics, DeMoss was reprimanded for using the name of the 2 Live Crew song, ''Me So Horny.''

This does not solve the problem, he said. ''We can sell this stuff to 8-year-olds, yet we adults can't talk about it. Something is wrong, folks.''

On a related topic, DeMoss said youngsters are being desensitized to life-and-death issues because of what they see on television and at theaters.

Hollywood is preoccupied with horror films, he said, and writers and producers are continually trying (and succeeding) to ''outshock the next guy.''

The idols of some children are characters such as ''Freddy Krueger,'' a grotesquely burned serial killer who slices victims with his bladed fingers.

In one film, Krueger murders a woman in a sudsy bathtub by cutting her between the legs. On a poster, he is shown eating the brains of a victim.

In a recent survey of fourth-, fifth- and sixth-graders, half as many of them could identify Abe Lincoln as could identify Krueger, DeMoss said.

In naming their favorite movies, many put the sexually explicit ''Porky's Revenge'' and ''Nightmare on Elm Street'' at the top of their lists.

One boy in the survey said it was fun to see people get their ''heads shot off.'' Another said, ''I like the way people look when they're dead.''

Many parents who think their children are not seeing R-rated films are mistaken, DeMoss said. Some of them watch it on video at a friend's house.

Some cable TV stations run R-rated movies. DeMoss suggested canceling these services and limiting regular television viewing to one hour per day.

He also encouraged people to rearrange their living-room furniture so that couches and chairs are the center of attention instead of the TV set.

In general, he said, parents should talk with their children more often, work at building their self-esteem and arrange to do things as a family.

''We're not telling kids they are important and special,'' he said, and that makes them susceptible to misguided messages about how to be ''cool.''

He pointed to the barrage of magazine and TV advertisements that tell youths, especially girls, that they must change themselves to be sexy and successful.

DeMoss gave examples of ads for products ranging from perfume to makeup to clothes. ''Do your breasts measure up?'' is asked on one cover of *Mademoiselle*.

DeMoss said Madison Avenue executives have managed to ''undermine the self-esteem of young daughters'' and ''sell a warped idea of human sexuality.''

He said many of the ads promote promiscuity, group sex and homosexuality. Those for Calvin Klein perfume show a woman and two men in bed.

Ads in the beauty magazines of today routinely show naked women, DeMoss said, as well as scenes that make smoking and drinking alcohol seem glamorous.

The presentation convinced local residents such as Terry Meyer and the Queens to begin immediately spreading the word to others in the community.

Meyer, 40, a computer programmer in Belleville, plans to ask friends and members of his church to boycott stores that sell pornographic products.

''People have to say, 'We will not do business here unless you take this stuff off the shelves,' '' he said. ''You can say a lot with your pocketbook.''

Linda Queen intends to write letters and make telephone calls to officials. Gary Queen said he will tell his co-workers about the problem.

"I'm angry," he said. "I'm angry at the government. I'm angry at the people doing this. I'm angry at myself—all of us—for letting this happen."

Laura Parker / How Things Got Nasty in Broward County

Washington Post, October 21, 1990

A certain type of newspaper story homes in on the day-to-day life of a locale in the news, illuminating its outstanding qualities as well as its subtler charms. This kind of story provides what is known as "local color"—it fleshes out the context of a news story so that the unfolding details seem more vivid, and often takes a wry view of the "little people" at the periphery of major news events.

Laura Parker's journey through the topless doughnut shops and criminal past of Broward County throws light on a scenario in which "obscenity" is a hotly contested terrain. Parker also fills in the details of Sheriff Nick Navarro's shady past and lawyer Jack Thompson's charismatic present. The article concludes with a classic "local color" parting shot: a bit of advice directed at the main story's famous characters from one of the area's plain folks, 73-year-old Viola Andresen.

Laura Parker is the Miami bureau chief and southern correspondent for the Washington Post.

BROWARD COUNTY, FLA.—Not far from the local sheriff's office, the afternoon regulars bellied up to the counter at one of Broward County's best-known landmarks—the topless doughnut shop tucked in among the fast-food emporiums on South Federal Highway.

Waitress Lisa Kellenberger, clad in a pink ruffled bikini bottom, switched on the tube to the "Geraldo" show, hoping to catch the heavily publicized appearance of County Sheriff Nick Navarro, who was making the rounds of the national talk shows to discuss his obscenity arrest of the rap group 2 Live Crew. The patrons were disappointed. The television station had decided to save the taped appearance for a ballyhooed "special."

Kellenberger shrugged and giggled. Slick Nick, she said, must be getting a percentage of the profits from the soaring record sales that followed his now-famous raid at a Broward nightclub—the first arrests of rappers in the current wave of nationwide publicity over allegedly obscene lyrics.

The spotlight focused on Navarro and 2 Live Crew has finally given this obscure county, lost in Florida's wastelands between the silk-stocking wealth of Palm Beach and the flamingo pink glitz of Miami, the identity it long had sought. "Banned in Broward" was not exactly what the county's promoters had in mind. But although this amorphous sprawl of suburban subdivisions, shopping malls and the occasional porn shop may be an unlikely venue for a looming national battle over free speech vs. obscenity, at least Navarro's dragnet has put it on the map.

"When I came here nine years ago," says Gary Stein, a columnist who writes about Broward for the *Sun-Sentinel* in Fort Lauderdale, Broward's largest city, "the first thing I saw was a topless laundromat and I remember thinking, 'Whoaa, what is this place?' "

Stein chronicles Broward's quirks with glee. Most of Broward's 1.3 million residents are transplanted northerners, many of them retirees, who live in bedroom towns with names such as Coral Springs and Plantation. "Most of Broward is new. There are no neighborhoods like the kind you're used to in Chicago or

Philadelphia,'' he says. ''Everybody who lives here thinks they're just passing through. There is a real feeling of impermanence to the place.''

The impermanence, some say, makes Broward residents more tolerant, which is why the brouhaha over 2 Live Crew seems so out of place. In fact, tolerance has a history in this county. In the 1930s and '40s, Meyer Lansky openly operated numbers rackets here. By the '60s and '70s, college students' wild spring breaks had added new chapters to legends of permissiveness along the Fort Lauderdale beaches.

Even the county's namesake has a story. Napoleon Bonaparte Broward, an early Florida governor, got his start running guns to Cuba on the eve of the Spanish-American War. The past five years have produced an even more imaginative array of businesses: a topless check-cashing service (where, for a generous fee, customers could chat up a topless hostess while waiting for their money), a topless video arcade, and, of course, R-Donuts, which opened in 1985 promising ''pretty girls and the world's best cup of coffee.''

''This was a very exotic, and far-out place for people to come,'' says George Platt, a lawyer and former chairman of the Broward County Democratic Party. ''There was an element of anything goes. This was a place where people came to let their hair down and do things they couldn't do in Newport, Rhode Island.''

If this seems an unreal setting for a national showdown on obscenity, the central players in the drama are even more unlikely—Navarro, a flamboyant sheriff who thrives on publicity; and Jack Thompson, a crusading anti-porn lawyer who likens himself to Batman.

Navarro, who was born in Havana, once coached Al Pacino on the finer points of playing a Cuban drug dealer for the movie ''Scarface'' and auditioned for a television role of his own on ''Miami Vice.'' Even his friends describe him as a combination of southern sheriff and Latin *caudillo,* or strongman. Long before he was elected in 1985, Navarro had a reputation for being audacious. As a chief of the sheriff's department's organized crime division, Navarro and his deputies once ''invaded'' the Bahamas on a drug case, much to the dismay of conventional thinkers in the State Department.

As sheriff, Navarro is Broward's most powerful public official. His style of law enforcement is unusual, and the stories about his escapades are legion. His chemists have manufactured crack in the department's laboratory for use in sting operations. Under court order to relieve overcrowding in his jail, he has angered federal judges by housing prisoners in tents.

He dresses in well-tailored suits and wears a little American flag in his lapel. His office wall is lined with autographed cartoons that lampoon him for his ego and publicity stunts, and he cheerfully tells a visitor that he can't wait to get a recent effort that appeared in the *Miami Herald.* That drawing features him, clutching a billy club and looking like a pit bull, on the cover of a record album titled: NICK NAVARRO: ''As Nasty As He Wanna Be,'' a takeoff on the title of the 2 Live Crew album that started the fuss.

Although Navarro is not one to pass up a headline, lawyer Thompson clearly considers the campaign against rappers to be a moral cause. Thompson says that the lyrics contain violent imagery that encourages abuse of women and children. A soft-spoken lawyer who works out of his Coral Gables home, Thompson is a born-again Christian. He also wears a Batman wristwatch. In sending documents to opponents, he also has been known to attach a photocopy of his driver's license, with a photo of Batman pasted over his own, just to make sure they know who they're dealing with.

''I have sent my opponents pictures of Batman to remind them I'm playing the role of Batman,'' Thompson explains. ''Just like Bruce Wayne helped the police in the movie. I have had to assist the sheriff of Broward County.''

Thompson has, in fact, ''assisted'' all 67 county sheriffs in Florida as well as Republican Gov. Bob Martinez by supplying them late last year with copies of the lyrics of ''As Nasty as They Wanna Be.'' Martinez publicly denounced 2 Live Crew and urged the state attorney's office to use racketeering laws to prosecute the group. The state attorney declined, saying it was a matter for the locals. Enter Navarro.

In February, Navarro went to civil court in search of a judicial opinion on whether the lyrics of 2 Live Crew's album qualified as obscene under state law. Broward County Circuit Judge Mel Grossman found the lyrics ''probably obscene.'' That was enough for Navarro. He dispatched deputies to the county's record stores and warned sales clerks that sale of the offending album could bring arrest. The rappers' lawyers went to work and sued Navarro in federal court.

In a hearing in May, Bruce Rogow, the band's lawyer, introduced into evidence sexually explicit magazines and video tapes purchased from an adult bookstore less than a mile from the judge's court and presented testimony that the rappers' music had artistic value. His case did not succeed, and on June 6, U.S. District Judge Jose A. Gonzalez Jr. found the lyrics obscene.

Four days later, Navarro's deputies staked out a Hollywood, Fla., nightspot, Club Futura, to catch 2 Live Crew's act. The deputies videotaped the performance before an adults-only crowd and swooped down on band members Luther Campbell and Chris Wongwon as the pair drove down Broward's Hollywood Boulevard after the show.

Rogow, who is appealing the federal ruling and fighting the criminal charges, characterizes the episode as ''an aberration.'' He finds consolation that the added publicity has only boosted sales, further thwarting the crusade against 2 Live Crew. Just as ''Banned in Boston'' helped sell books in an earlier era, ''Banned in Broward'' is making 2 Live Crew as hot as they wanna be.

Some Broward residents, who usually forgive their sheriff's yearning for publicity, grumbled that enough was enough. It's not as though Broward had run out of criminals to pursue. There were 115 murders in the county last year and 6,202 aggravated assaults, although not all of those were within the sheriff's jurisdiction.

Some residents are tiring of it all. ''I think Slick Nick should stay at home,'' says Viola Andresen, 73. ''He's just looking for publicity.''

DISCUSSION QUESTIONS

1. Laura Parker uses ''local color'' to cast new light on the 2 Live Crew controversy in this story. Compare her evocation of a particular geographic milieu with the ones created by Debbie McKinney in ''Youth's Despair Erupts'' (p. 182) and Diana Griego Erwin in ''His Dreams Belong to the Next Generation'' (p. 191). What compositional strategies does each writer employ to create a memorable sense of ''place'' in her story? Which do you judge most effective? Why?

2. Parker uses irony and humor to get her point across in this article. Detail the various points where Parker uses the facts at hand to infer a certain viewpoint on the goings-on in Broward County.

Luther Campbell / "Today They're Trying to Censor Rap, Tomorrow . . ." *Los Angeles Times,* November 5, 1990

At the center of one intersecting circle in the current debate over censorship and the arts stands Luther Campbell, Florida resident, small businessman, and leader of the rap group 2 Live Crew. As Nasty as They Wanna Be, *2 Live Crew's second album, became the means for a group of conservative activists (spearheaded by Dade County prosecutor Jack Thompson) to test out laws regarding music censorship in several states. Campbell and his cohorts were themselves arrested, tried, and found innocent of obscenity charges after playing an adults-only show in Dade County. The testimony of music critics and academics, as well as the organized support of the music industry, helped Campbell and the other members of 2 Live Crew avoid conviction, although, as mentioned in the following article, retailers such as Charles Freeman weren't so fortunate.*

This opinion piece from the Los Angeles Times *reveals Campbell as an articulate spokesperson, not for left-wing politics, but for the old-fashioned American Dream. He cites the fact of his success as an entrepreneur as a major reason for attacks on him and declares that freedom to consume whatever products one likes is an inalienable American right. He also mentions the racism involved in targeting black rap groups instead of equally "offensive" white acts and urges his readers to elect officials who will stand up for freedom of expression.*

Luther Campbell continues to reside in Florida, where he makes music with 2 Live Crew and produces other artists for his company, Luke Records.

The First Amendment states that "Congress shall make no law . . . abridging the freedom of speech. . . ." This same clause has been incorporated into the 14th Amendment so that the very same restrictions that apply to Congress apply to the states as well.

In other words, the government has no power to restrict expression because of its message, its ideas, its subject matter or its content. So what's the problem? I write a few songs that are purely for adult entertainment and the whole world is after me.

Either there's a double standard regarding rap music and other entertainment or the Salem witch hunt has returned, and I have been labeled the head warlock.

Today's society is based on sex—just look at how many strip bars and how much pornographic literature is available. Why condemn me—a black artist and entrepreneur—for my particular brand of adult entertainment?

There's a new breed of sheriff turning the music industry upside down. A few right-wing individuals have appointed themselves the judge and jury for what's right and wrong.

It's amazing to me, how during interviews those right-wing individuals neglect to point out that *clean* versions of all my records are geared toward minors and that I voluntarily sticker all of my adult material.

I hope that these people who are pointing fingers are really standing up for the First Amendment and are not using the American flag to hide behind racist motives. I own and operate one of the largest independent recording companies around, and that could be why I was singled out. People need to realize that I'm not in stores with guns to customers' heads forcing them to buy my albums. It's freedom of choice, and that's what America is supposed to be about.

America, the home of the free, and our just legal system, which is supposed to be the finest in the world, helped show the world how organized our judicial system really is. After a week of selecting an unbiased jury and another week of spending taxpayers' money (on a crime that has the same punishment as stealing a hubcap), we were victorious, but at what cost?

It seems to me that our priorities are all in the wrong order. We have an outrageous amount of people sleeping in the streets and without anything to eat, but we find rappers more important.

Our environment is slowly being pulled apart, and we put people in jail for a bunch of words. Kids can't read or write, but that's not enough. We don't want them to think for themselves either. Sometimes I wonder what the starving people in Ethiopia would think about the money we've wasted on taking this to court.

Right now, I don't think we're setting a good example for our future leaders. How can anyone say that an adult can't go into a store and buy what he or she wants? How can anyone say that an adult can't understand what the 2 Live Crew is all about? If anyone can't see that the 2 Live Crew is a comedy group, then I feel sorry for them. We have placed warning stickers on our albums and put out two versions of each album—an adult and a G version—in order to satisfy the public. And as far as I know, we're the only band that does that.

Our victory should be sweeter. Charles Freeman, the Broward County, Fla., record store owner convicted for selling "As Nasty as They Wanna Be" to an adult, should also be celebrating. Freeman only sold "As Nasty as They Wanna Be" to adults. We did our part, and he did his. I do not believe that his conviction is representative of Broward County.

Every day we get calls from people throughout Florida wanting to know what they can do to help. And we tell them the best thing they can do is vote.

A number of the staff members of Luke Records have been deputized to register voters and have made efforts to go to local malls, sports events, flea markets, nightclubs and many other places to encourage young adults to register and vote. Our staff has registered more than 40,000 in Dade and Broward counties alone this year.

And for anyone who says that rap is not black culture, all I have to say is that I'm a black man who has lived in one of the roughest black areas in Miami—Liberty City—and this is my culture. This is a part of what I grew up with. Every day there was some guy trying to outboast another, and the only things off limit were mothers and the deceased. 2 Live Crew's music—and lyrics—is nothing but a group of fellas bragging.

The best thing to come out of this entire fiasco was that the music industry united and stood up for one another. Ads ran in major newspapers and on music networks asking people to prevent censorship. We were heard as a collective musical voice because we know that today they're trying to censor rap and tomorrow it could be classical music or theater or. . . .

DISCUSSION QUESTIONS

1. After reading the other articles in this section on 2 Live Crew, do you trust Luther Campbell as an authority figure? Why? Why not? How does Campbell's voice in this article compare with his portrayal in other articles—such as David Mills's "The Judge vs. 2 Live Crew"? Which do you find more believable? Why?

Russell Baker / Don't Mention It

New York Times, May 30, 1990

The winner of two Pulitzer Prizes (one in 1979 for distinguished commentary, the other in 1982 for Growing Up, *a childhood remembrance), Russell Baker remains one of America's most widely read and respected humorists. After several years of service as a reporter and London bureau chief for the* Baltimore Sun, *Baker joined the Washington bureau of the* New York Times. *In 1962, Baker resigned his reportorial duties ("I just got bored. I had done enough reporting") and began his celebrated column, "Observer."*

"Don't Mention It," which appeared in the New York Times *after Baker's fellow pundits Jimmy Breslin and Andy Rooney both came under fire for publicly using stereotypical terms to discuss ethnic minorities, is not a humor column; rather, it is a well-reasoned defense of Breslin and Rooney and an appeal for greater tolerance of free-speaking Americans.*

The racial diversity of Americans creates a lot of funny language problems, but you can't laugh about them, of course, because it's dangerous these days to laugh about anything that touches on our racial diversity. When the subject is race and somebody laughs, that somebody is inviting denunciation for "insensitivity."

"Insensitivity" is the latest jawbreaker in the ever growing mushmouth vocabulary Americans use to talk about race without, well, without quite talking about race. Laughter at the wrong time is only one of a hundred ways of committing "insensitivity" in talking race. All are to be skirted like minefields.

One may commit an occasional "insensitivity" and escape deadly abuse, but frequent violations can bring down the ultimate epithet from which there is no appeal: "racist."

"Racist" now has a punishing power similar to the power of "Communist" in Red-hunting days when a politician calling you "Communist" expected your boss to fire you immediately. In two recent New York media incidents—involving Andy Rooney and Jimmy Breslin—blacks, gays and Asian-Americans behaved precisely like the old Red hunters by urging that Rooney and Breslin be punished by firings.

Is it amusing to find the forces of liberal egalitarianism carrying on like old-fashioned, bad-guy conservative Joe McCarthy? If so, don't smile too broadly. Being amused here could get you charged with "insensitivity."

It's safer to shift to another target and berate CBS and Newsday because, in briefly benching Rooney and Breslin, both knuckled to the liberals' use of the old Red-hunting tactic. Nothing there to shock anybody, is there? The McCarthy era taught us to expect feeble spines in the media.

"Insensitivity," however, is not so damning as "racism." It may suggest only that the offender is not viciously benighted, but only a dolt too witless to know the score or a geezer perhaps, too old and set in his ways to know what's new in the world.

Such persons may need re-education. If this sounds like the mercy of Chairman Mao, in racial matters it is an old and honorable American custom. In the past generation alone, the country has submitted to immense re-education in the courtesies necessary if it is to flourish in a racially diverse world.

The old ethnic slang terms that were common American household words 40 years ago have almost disappeared from the speech of all but the most primitive citizenry. There was no great problem in getting rid of this old vocabulary; the problem has been in creating new terminology.

Just now, for instance, there is another disagreement about the socially acceptable term for Americans of African ancestry. The term "African-Americans," endorsed by Jesse Jackson, is getting a good bit of use as a replacement for "blacks," which since 1960 has been the word preferred by—well, what shall we call them?

We Americans have re-educated ourselves in racial matters so successfully, you see, that a white (ridiculous word, by the way) may even hesitate to speak of them until supplied with a word officially certified civilized by the parties he wants to discuss.

The old term "people of color," once considered demeaning, is surfacing again in respectable forums. It showed up Monday in the *New York Times* with the chairman of the City University Student Senate saying university enrollment was "65 percent people of color."

Since this number includes students of both African and Hispanic ancestry, "people of color" is obviously an effort to produce a term that will embrace both. But will Hispanics submit to the embrace? It would probably invite charges of "insensitivity" for whites (pinks, tans and grays, actually) to start calling Hispanics "people of color" until we get a more authoritative pronunciamento than a student senate chairman can issue.

What is remarkable is the extreme care almost everybody willingly takes to avoid language that could offend anybody. The bright side of this is that it shows, all the other evidence of our society notwithstanding, that there is still some desire among us to treat each other with common courtesy.

There is also a not-so-bright side. This is the tendency of pressure groups that police the language to insist that it conform to whatever the current orthodoxy may be on racial matters. Trying to destroy nonconformers as heretics can drive the real bigots underground. Under ground is where people like that thrive and multiply.

Ann Powers and Nina Schuyler / Censorship in America: Why It's Happening

San Francisco Weekly, June 20, 1990

After the seemingly free and easy seventies and self-indulgent eighties, American legislators' early-nineties crackdown on controversial artworks came as a shock. But as the following story indicates, a wide variety of social factors contributed to the rise of the new trend toward censorship. Drawing connections between television programming, radical feminism, and racism against blacks, among other things, Powers and Schuyler map out the route that led to the contentious outburst over the public's right to create, distribute, and obtain sexually explicit materials.

"When the forces of Jesse Helms hit San Francisco, the city's art community couldn't believe what was happening," said Powers. "My involvement with the founding of the S.F. Coalition for Freedom of Expression exposed me to a whole group of people who were struggling to understand how the crisis had reached this point. Nina and I started looking into the recent history of censorship in America, at the Meese Commission and related developments, and it became clear that Helms' power tripping wasn't coming from nowhere—he rep-

resented a whole group of powerful people, who felt very threatened by the demographic and political changes this country's been going through.''

The San Francisco Weekly *is an alternative newsweekly that provides challenging coverage of local and national issues and cultural events. Ann Powers is a contributing editor at the* Weekly *and writes a column on ''whatever I want,'' called ''Street Talk.'' Nina Schuyler is a freelance writer and editor.*

America is caught in a paradox. Every day, newspapers, radio and television—our very symbols of free speech—report new tales about the suppression of free speech.

The stories have ranged from the confiscation of albums by Florida's comic rap group 2 Live Crew and the arrests of band members, to corporate boycotts of television shows that present material deemed offensive by Christian fundamentalists, to the assault on the National Endowment for the Arts by right-wing politicians, an attack which may soon result in the elimination of federal funding for artists working outside the commercial mainstream.

The encroachments on basic free speech rights appeared to come out of nowhere. But they didn't. The regulation of the American public by government has gradually been growing stricter over the past 20 years. The battles have been so scattered that it's been difficult to connect them. But they are all part of the conflict between the aging, white, male elite that runs the country and the various groups of emerging subcultures that are changing the face of America. The weapons of choice are self-expression and community-building on the part of women, people of color, gays and lesbians, and even high school kids—and legislation and court decisions on the part of men and a few women that hold the seats of power.

In 1990, America is a baffling place to live. With the specter of Communism reduced to a cartoon rerun, the people for whom politics was defined by the Cold War have nowhere to turn their enemy-seeking eyes but upon their own constituents. There's plenty to disturb them at home: a crack epidemic that has turned nearly every major inner city into a criminal disaster area, a homeless population that continues to grow, an AIDS epidemic that has killed more than 80,000 people. America is in trouble—and Madonna performs live sex acts on stage.

That's how the right wing makes the leap: Artistic freedom, in their eyes, contributes to the decay they see all around them. Sexual images become sexual acts; anti-patriotic symbols (the burning of a flag) are transformed into treasonous betrayals. With this equation in place, it's possible to harbor the belief that regulating people's expressions of dissent from traditional values—the indications of social change—will prevent change from occurring at all.

THE ELUSIVE MAINSTREAM

Those who want to regulate expression claim that their views represent the mainstream. Artists have also been known to use this defense. Yet there is little basis for a definition of the mainstream. ''The whole concept of the mainstream is a mythical construction,'' says David Trend of the San Francisco Bay Area Coalition for Freedom of Expression. ''All these people on the right talk about it; but then they say the mainstream isn't black, Latino, female, gay, young, homeless, sick, addicted . . . you start saying, who's left? The mainstream is an invention that people use to justify social hierarchies.''

The fundamentalist right, which claims to represent the mainstream, rose as a political force in the late 1960s. ''If there was any great thing in society that caused the right to organize, it was the civil rights movement of the sixties,'' says sociologist Barbara Ehrenreich, whose most recent book is a collection of essays called *The Worst Years of Our Lives*. ''The 'sixties still loom very large in these people's minds. They still envision naked hippies invading our cities and countryside; it's the feeling that America is out of control.''

The extreme conservatism of Jesse Helms and his allies might seem comical to more progressive-minded citizens, but their power is significant. ''I don't think of the censorious Christian right as being marginal,'' says Ehrenreich. ''They do have influence, and large numbers of people are willing to hit the streets on their behalf. It's really scary. But on the other hand, I think that any true patriot has to eventually come down on the side of freedom of expression.''

Yet the fear instilled in the American public by rising crime, the government's ''War on Drugs,'' homelessness, and other social ills may be affecting people's attitudes toward civil liberties.

''A new type of threat has arisen,'' said Morton Halperin, director of the National Legislative Office of the American Civil Liberties Union (ACLU). ''That is, the tendency of Congress to declare a full-scale 'war' on something or the other, and to use that as a justification for undermining civil liberties. This is a dangerous trend that so far has brought us 'wars' on drugs, terrorism, and most recently, crime. If it's wartime, so the reasoning goes, civil liberties may be a luxury we can do without.''

THE NEW TELEVISION

The odd bedpartners on the right and left who battled pornography in the early 'eighties had a strong new force to reckon with: technology. The home video boom expanded porn's audience to include those who wouldn't feel comfortable entering a dingy downtown theatre, and the adult film industry shifted its attention to a market based on private consumption. The swinging singles of the 'seventies became the cocooning couples of the 'eighties, and erotic home video entered the yuppie lifestyle.

It's not just pornography, however, that's frightening conservatives through its invasion of the typical American home. Network television has reached new pinnacles of raciness in the past decade, partly due to competition from far less-monitored cable channels. And in what must really frighten conservatives, characters in such programs as *thirtysomething* actually *discuss* their sex lives. Controversial topics that have been raised on prime time television in the past few years include AIDS *(An Early Frost)*, domestic violence *(The Burning Bed)*, cervical cancer *(thirtysomething)*, and nudist colonies *(L.A. Law)*; the list goes on.

Three of the most popular television comedies portray nuclear families with all of their foibles exposed. *Married With Children* (which lost some corporate sponsorship due to a boycott organized by ''concerned mother'' Terry Rakola), *The Simpsons*, and *Roseanne* all present ''typical'' American families fighting, using off-color humor, and struggling through their differences in a manner that's a long way from Ozzie and Harriet. U.S. drug czar William Bennett's recent accusation that cartoon character Bart Simpson is a negative influence on America's youth shows the extent to which conservatives feel threatened by these unapologetic portrayals of family conflict.

Censorship advocates can't stop the flow of controversial programming on television by taking away its funding. But they can, and do, organize boycotts. The Rev. Daniel Wildmon's American Family Association has done much of the legwork in collecting letters to fuel Jesse Helms's fire in the past few months; before this current crusade, his prey was nastiness on television. In the 'eighties, Wildmon organized product boycotts that prompted major corporations including Pepsi (in the famous Madonna ad controversy), Mazda, General Mills and Ralston-Purina to pull advertising from ''offensive'' programs such as *Miami Vice, T.J. Hooker* and *Saturday Night Live*.

THE MEESE COMMISSION

The current battles in Congress over supposedly ''obscene'' art may be rooted in a task force that dealt, not with art, but with pornography. Repulsed with the leniency of a 1970 federal report recommending broad-based sex education and looser laws regulating pornography. Attorney General Edwin Meese appointed an eleven-member commission in 1985 to ''determine the nature, extent and impact on society of pornography.''

To prevent any unwelcome surprises like the 1970 recommendations, Meese stacked the commission with appointees who had well-established records of support for government action against sex books and films.

Not surprisingly, the commission's eventual recommendations included a list of stern measures. According to civil rights leaders, the most ominous conclusion was a dubious correlation between pornography and violence: that certain kinds of violent and ''degrading'' pornography seem to cause certain ill-defined varieties of ''harm.''

''This commission report was just the kind of ammunition that the fundamentalists were waiting for,'' said Leanne Katz, executive director of the National Coalition Against Censorship (NCAC) in New York, a group of forty-one organizations. ''It added fire and legitimacy to their pro-decency movement.''

In fact, the fundamentalist right found some new leaders in several of Meese's commissioners. ''Many of the commissioners are now leading pro-decency organizations in this country,'' said Katz. ''For example, Alan Sears, who was executive director of the commission, heads up the group Citizens for Decency through the Law. Another commissioner, Dr. James Dobson, is president of the conservative organization 'Focus on the Family' and runs a daily radio program to preserve the family through Judeo-Christian values.''

CENSORSHIP AND FEMINISTS

But challenges to free expression are not simply limited to the New Right. Attempts to limit publicly distributed materials have also been perpetrated by people on the left side of the political spectrum. Pornography has been the focus of one protracted struggle concerning censorship and civil liberties among feminists. One of the witnesses who spoke against the sex trade before the Meese commission was Andrea Dworkin, whose books include *Pornography: Men Possessing Women, Women Hating,* and *Intercourse*.

Dworkin and law professor Catharine MacKinnon introduced anti-pornography ordinances in several cities between 1983 and 1985. The ordinances declared that pornography is sex discrimination, and that the women who participate in porn have been denied their civil rights.

Women Against Pornography (WAP) is one organization that continues to fight for Dworkin and MacKinnon's suggested legislation. ''We're not interested in regulating pornography, but in ending it,'' said Norma Ramos of WAP's branch in New York. ''We were (during the time of the Meese Commission) and remain absolutely opposed to obscenity laws.''

WAP opposes the current moves to censor groups like the 2 Live Crew (although Ramos calls their music "incredibly misogynistic material"). Yet, they accuse groups such as the Feminist Anti-Censorship Task Force (FACT) of working against the interests of women. "FACT is a handful of academic women; they're the women involved in the ACLU," says Ramos. "Basically, we say the ACLU fronts for the pornographers, and that FACT fronts for the ACLU."

Feminist anti-porn activists sometimes find themselves, oddly, on the same side as fundamentalists in their struggle to eliminate pornography. But Ramos considers the connection between the two groups to be irrelevant. "The real alliance is between the right wing and the pornographers," she said. "Equality for women isn't a goal of the right wing. They're anti-porn for different reasons. They want to control women's bodies; so do the pornographers."

Feminists can find themselves in a difficult position when confronted with the contrasting agendas of Women Against Pornography and anti-censorship activists. "Especially as a woman, you can be browbeaten into a middle road," said Marianna Beck, co-editor of *Libido,* a journal of erotica for both men and women. "What's politically correct, are you allowed to feel sexual feelings?

"Women Against Pornography testified before the Meese Commission right along the sheriffs who had closed gay bookstores," continued Beck. "Talk about strange and scary alliances!"

Because it is popular among youth, and therefore a harbinger of change, rock music (and rap, the newest strong force in this artistic sphere) has always been considered a threat to the establishment. According to Dave Marsh, publisher of the underground magazine *Rock and Roll Confidential* and the excellent anti-censorship pamphlet *You've Got A Right To Rock: Don't Let Them Take It Away,* there has been a marked increase in organized efforts to prohibit sales of materials deemed "offensive" or "dangerous" in the past decade. The 2 Live Crew controversy, it seems, is only the latest and most extreme drop in the bucket.

You've Got A Right (available for $3 through Box 15052, Long Beach, CA 90815) abounds with details of the gradual erosion of freedom within the world of pop music. In Bound Brook, New Jersey, in 1984, schools banned the wearing of single gloves a la Michael Jackson. In 1989, in Washington D.C., the Transamerica Corporation pulled insurance coverage for G Street Enterprises, a company that stages rap shows, although Transamerica could provide no evidence for its claim that violence at rap concerts was causing G Street to lose money. Between these two extremes lies a spectrum of restrictions on the production and distribution of popular music.

Marsh believes there is an element of racism in the recent attacks against the 2 Live Crew. "The same sexual rhymes are on the first Andrew Dice Clay albums, which are in the same record stores that are now afraid to carry *Nasty as They Wanne Be,*" he notes. He also fears the worst for the group if they're forced to take their case to the higher courts. "If the 2 Live Crew goes to this Supreme Court, it will lose," he predicts. "Antonin Scalia (who provided the swing vote against the recent ban on flag burning) supports the right to controversial political speech, but as far as he's concerned, what's on 2 Live Crew's album isn't political speech."

While efforts continue to limit what kinds of music those under the age of 18 can listen to, the case has been sealed regarding what kids can themselves say in print. In 1988, the Supreme Court stamped an "adults only" label onto the constitution by widening the power of schools to act as censors. The Justices ruled 5–3 in 1988 that public school officials have broad discretion to censor school newspapers.

In the case *Hazelwood* v. *Kuhmeier,* the Court found that high school principal Robert Reynolds was within his rights to delete two pages from the school paper on the grounds that the materials in two stories were ''indecent''—one recounted the experiences of students who had become pregnant and the second dealt with the impact of divorce on students. This overturned a 1969 ruling which said that free speech extended to the classroom.

''The ruling is especially troubling because there was nothing vulgar about the censored articles,'' said the ACLU's Steven Shapiro. ''Here, we are dealing with clearly serious and responsible student speech.''

BANNING BOOKS

One form of censorship with a long history—book banning—has increased dramatically in the past five years. People for the American Way (PAW), a Los Angeles-based constitutional rights group founded by television sit-com producer Norman Lear, reports a 107 percent increase in banning during a five-year period from 1982 to 1987. ''The greatest majority came from California, where there is a disproportionate number of right-wing groups located in Southern California,'' said Michael Hudson, PAW's vice president.

''The roots of current efforts to curb freedom of artistic expression reach back to the early 1980s, when religious fundamentalists and other authoritarians attempted to censor books, films, and television,'' said Ira Glasser, executive director of the ACLU. ''Libraries, museums, schools, theaters, television stations, bookstores, and video shops all came under sustained pressure to restrict the display or availability of images and words felt to offend various self-appointed monitors of morality and taste.''

EYE ON ART

Artists make easy targets, especially in America, where they're treated with at least as much suspicion as respect. ''Unlike many other countries in the world, in this country artists are not held in high regard,'' says David Trend. ''Our government sets aside less money for artists than any other free country in the world. They need their money for defense spending. It's a matter of civic priorities.''

Faced with little financial gains from the sale of their work, an undefined role in the society, and barely any government support, artists have often clung to an outsider's position. ''It's the modernist myth of the individual genius, and it really does undermine us,'' says Trend. ''It promotes an ethos of competition among artists. We end up competing for grants and for sales, rather than working together. It's a very rugged kind of individualism.''

It's an attitude that has sometimes made it hard for artists to organize politically. The art world harbors an elitism that makes alliances with other groups difficult to form. Trend hopes that artists and others concerned with the loss of their civil liberties can form coalitions to fight the highly organized and monied fundamentalist right. ''This situation is following the same progression of events the pro-choice movement followed. If the right to freedom of expression goes to Supreme Court, it'll become a national movement like that one did. It'll be great.''

DISCUSSION QUESTIONS

1. How does the background information in this article differ from that provided by Teri Maddox in her article ''Unsuspecting Parents Can't Believe Their Ears''? Both articles document the history behind a particular historic moment. How do they come to such different conclusions?

2. Compare and contrast Michael Ventura's article, "On Kids and Slasher Movies" (see p. 197), with this one. In what specific ways does writing for an alternative newsweekly differ from that done for a daily newspaper? What do these pieces have in common?

George Lakoff / Metaphor and War

East Bay Express, February 22, 1991

The Gulf War became known to millions through around-the-clock coverage on television and in other media; as those viewers knew, newscasters stayed within certain rules set down by the American government. The result, according to those who opposed the conflict, was a war that resembled a TV miniseries: it had a coherent narrative, a set of heroes and villains, and just the right amount of violence to keep people interested without upsetting them or making them angry.

As CNN and others broadcast this picture-perfect war, alternative voices in the media tried to deconstruct what they viewed as a nearly unstoppable propaganda machine. Some told stories ignored by the mainstream. Others, including Berkeley linguistics professor George Lakoff, closely examined the communicative structures employed by the government in telling the story of the war to itself and the American public. Lakoff describes the various language systems employed in Gulf War rhetoric and speculates on the ways in which they affect both the outcome of the conflict itself and the average person's impressions of it.

George Lakoff has written several books, including Irregularity in Syntax *(1970) and* Women, Fire, and Dangerous Things: What Categories Reveal about the Mind *(1987). He is also the author, along with Mark Johnson, of the highly regarded study* Metaphors We Live By *(1980) and coauthor (with Mark Turner) of* More than Cool Reason: A Field Guide to Poetic Metaphor *(1989). The* East Bay Express *is a weekly alternative source of news and commentary on the arts as well as social and political events for the San Francisco Bay area.*

Metaphors can kill. Secretary of State Baker sees Saddam as "sitting on our economic lifeline." President Bush sees him as having a "stranglehold" on our economy. General Schwartzkopf characterizes the occupation of Kuwait as a "rape." The President says that the US is in the Gulf to "protect freedom, protect our future, and protect the innocent," and that we must "push Saddam Hussein back." Saddam is seen as Hitler. It is vital, literally vital, to understand just what role metaphorical thought is playing in this war.

Metaphorical thought is commonplace and inescapable; in itself, it is neither good nor bad. Abstractions and enormously complex situations are routinely understood via metaphor, so it is not surprising that we use extensive, and mostly unconscious, systems of metaphor to understand the complexities and abstractions of international relations and war. The use of a metaphor, however, becomes pernicious when it hides realities in a harmful way.

It is important to distinguish what is metaphorical from what is not. Pain, dismemberment, death, starvation, and the death and injury of loved ones are not metaphorical. They are real, and in this war they are afflicting hundreds, perhaps thousands, of real human beings.

The Gulf war has been accompanied by systems of metaphor which have been used by military and foreign policy experts and by the public at large. It is important to look at these metaphor systems in order to see the realities they may be obscuring.

THE STATE-AS-PERSON SYSTEM

In international politics, a state is usually conceptualized as a person, engaging in social relations within a world community. Its land-mass is its home. It lives in a neighborhood, and has neighbors, friends, and enemies. States are seen as having inherent dispositions: they can be peaceful or aggressive, responsible or irresponsible, industrious or lazy.

Well-being is wealth. The general well-being of a state is understood in economic terms: its economic health. A serious threat to economic health can thus be seen as a death threat. To the extent that a nation's economy depends on foreign oil, that oil supply becomes a "lifeline" (reinforced by the image of an oil pipeline).

Strength for a state is military strength.

Maturity for the person-state is industrialization. Unindustrialized nations are "underdeveloped," with industrialization as a natural state to be reached. Third World nations are thus immature children, to be taught how to develop properly or disciplined if they get out of line. Nations that fail to industrialize at a rate considered normal are seen as akin to retarded children and judged as "backward" nations.

Morality is a matter of accounting, of keeping the moral books balanced. A wrongdoer incurs a debt, and he must be made to pay. The moral books can be balanced by a return to the situation prior to the wrongdoing, by giving back what has been taken, by recompense, or by punishment. Justice is the balancing of the moral books.

War in this metaphor is a fight between two people, a form of hand-to-hand combat. Thus, the US seeks to "push Iraq back out of Kuwait" or "deal the enemy a heavy blow," or "deliver a knockout punch." A just war is thus a form of combat for the purpose of settling moral accounts.

The most common discourse form in the West where there is combat to settle moral accounts is the classic fairy tale in which people are replaced by states.

THE FAIRY TALE OF THE JUST WAR

Cast of characters: a villain, a victim, and a hero. The victim and the hero may be the same person.

The scenario: A crime is committed by the villain against an innocent victim (typically an assault, theft, or kidnapping). The offense occurs due to an imbalance of power and creates a moral imbalance. The hero either gathers helpers or decides to go it alone. The hero makes sacrifices; he undergoes difficulties, typically making an arduous heroic journey to a treacherous terrain. The villain is inherently evil, perhaps even a monster, and thus reasoning with him is out of the question. The hero is left with no choice but to engage the villain in battle. The hero defeats the villain and rescues the victim. The moral balance is restored. Victory is achieved. The hero, who always acts honorably, has proved his manhood and achieved glory. The sacrifice was worthwhile. The hero receives acclaim, along with the gratitude of the victim and the community.

Experts in international relations have an additional system of metaphors. The principal one is Clausewitz's metaphor:

WAR IS POLITICS PURSUED BY OTHER MEANS

Karl von Clausewitz was a Prussian general who perceived war in terms of political cost-benefit analysis. Each nation-state has political objectives, and war may best serve those objectives. The political "gains" are to be weighed against acceptable "costs." When the costs of war exceed the political gains, the war should cease.

In Clausewitzian terms, war is justified when there is more to be gained by going to war than by not going to war. Morality is absent from the Clausewitzian equation, except when there is a political cost to acting immorally or a political gain from acting morally.

Clausewitz's metaphor only allows war to be justified on pragmatic, not moral, grounds. To justify war on both moral and pragmatic grounds, the Fairy Tale of the Just War and Clausewitz's metaphor must mesh: The "worthwhile sacrifices" of the fairy tale must equal the Clausewitzian "costs" and the "victory" in the fairy tale must equal the Clausewitzian "gains."

Clausewitz's metaphor is the perfect expert's metaphor, since it requires specialists in political cost-benefit calculation. It sanctions the use of the mathematics of economics, probability theory, decision theory, and game theory in the name of making foreign policy rational and scientific.

Clausewitz's metaphor is commonly seen as literally true, but it is, in fact, metaphorical. It uses the State-as-Person metaphor. It turns qualitative effects on human beings into quantifiable costs and gains, thus seeing political action as economics, and it sees war in terms of only one dimension of war, that of political expediency.

To bear in mind what is hidden by Clausewitz's metaphor, we should consider an alternative metaphor that is *not* used by professional strategists or by the general public to understand war as we engage in it:

WAR IS VIOLENT CRIME: MURDER, ASSAULT, KIDNAPPING, ARSON, RAPE, AND THEFT

Here, war is understood only in terms of its moral dimension, and not, say, its political or economic dimension. The metaphor highlights those aspects of war that would otherwise be seen as major crimes.

There is an Us-Them asymmetry in the public use of the War-as-Crime metaphor. The Iraqi invasion of Kuwait is reported in terms of murder, theft, and rape. The American air war or potential ground attack is never discussed in terms of murder, assault, and arson. Allied conduct of the war is seen, in Clausewitzian terms, as rational calculation, while the Iraqi invasion is discussed not as a rational move by Saddam but as the work of a madman. We see Us as rational, moral, and courageous and Them as criminal and insane.

WAR AS A COMPETITIVE GAME

It has long been noted that we understand war as a competitive game, like chess, or as a sport, like football or boxing. It is a metaphor in which there is a clear winner and loser, and a clear end to the game. The metaphor highlights strategic thinking, teamwork, preparedness, the spectators in the world arena, the glory of winning and the shame of defeat.

This metaphor is taken very seriously. There is a long tradition in the West of training military officers in team sports and chess. The military is trained to win. This can lead to a metaphor conflict, as it did in Vietnam, since Clausewitz's metaphor seeks to maximize geopolitical gains, which may or may not be consistent with absolute military victory.

The situation at present is that the public has accepted the rescue scenario of the just war fairy tale as providing moral justification. The President, for internal political reasons, has accepted the competitive game metaphor as taking precedence over Clausewitz's metaphor: If he must choose, he will go for the military win over maximizing geopolitical gains.

Throughout the congressional debate leading up to the war, and in all the expert opinion that has occupied our attention since the war began, the metaphors determining our understanding of the conflict have not been questioned.

IS SADDAM IRRATIONAL?

The villain in the Fairy Tale of the Just War may be cunning, but he cannot be rational. You just do not reason with a demon, nor do you enter into negotiations with him. The logic of the metaphor demands that Saddam be irrational. But is he?

Administration policy is confused on the issue. Clausewitz's metaphor, as used by military strategists, assumes that the enemy is rational: He too is maximizing gains and minimizing costs. Our strategy from the outset has been to "increase the cost" to Saddam. That assumes he is rational and is maximizing his self-interest.

At the same time, he is being called irrational. Our fear of Iraq's possession of nuclear weapons depends on it. If Saddam is rational, he should follow the logic of deterrence. We have thousands of hydrogen bombs in warheads. Israel is estimated to have between 100 and 200 deliverable atomic bombs. The argument that Saddam and the Iraqi military would not be deterred by our nuclear arsenal and by Israel's assumes irrationality.

Saddam is certainly immoral, ruthless, and brutal, but there is no evidence that he is anything but rational. Everything he has done, from assassinating political opponents, to using poison gas against his political enemies, the Kurds, to invading Kuwait, can be seen as furthering his own self-interest.

IS KUWAIT AN INNOCENT VICTIM?

The classical victim is innocent. To the Iraqis, Kuwait was anything but an innocent ingenue. The war with Iran virtually bankrupted Iraq. Kuwait had agreed to help finance the war, but after the war, the Kuwaitis insisted on repayment of the "loan." Kuwaitis had invested hundreds of billions in Europe, America, and Japan, but would not invest in Iraq after the war to help it rebuild. On the contrary, Kuwait began what amounted to economic warfare against Iraq by overproducing its oil quota to hold oil prices down.

In addition, Kuwait had drilled laterally into Iraqi territory in the Rumailah oil field and had extracted oil from Iraqi territory. Kuwait further took advantage of Iraq by buying its currency at extremely low exchange rates. Subsequently, wealthy Kuwaitis used that Iraqi currency on trips to Iraq, where they bought Iraqi goods at bargain rates. Among the things they bought most flamboyantly were liquor and prostitutes—widows and orphans of men killed in the war, who, because of the state of the economy, had no other means of support. All this did not endear Kuwaitis to Iraqis, who were suffering from over seventy percent inflation.

Moreover, Kuwaitis had long been resented for good reason by Iraqis and Muslims from other nations. Capital rich but labor poor, Kuwait imported cheap labor from other Muslim countries to do its least pleasant work. At the time of the invasion, there were 400,000 Kuwaiti citizens living in Kuwait next to 2.2 million foreign laborers who were denied rights of citizenry and treated by the Kuwaitis as lesser beings. In short, to the Iraqis and to other labor-exporting Arab countries, Kuwait is badly miscast as a purely innocent victim.

This does not in any way justify the horrors perpetrated on the Kuwaitis by the Iraqi army. But it is part of what is hidden when Kuwait is cast as an innocent victim. The "legitimate government" that we seek to reinstall is an oppressive monarchy.

IS "VICTORY" POSSIBLE?

In a fairy tale or a game, victory is well-defined. Once it is achieved, the story or game is over. Neither is likely to be the case in the Gulf war, since history continues.

What will constitute "victory" in this war? The President's stated objectives are total Iraqi withdrawal and restoration of the Kuwaiti monarchy. But no one believes the matter will end there, since Saddam would still be in power with a significant part of his forces intact. If, on the other hand, we conquer Iraq, wiping out its military capability, how will Iraq be governed? No puppet government that we could set up will govern effectively since it will be hated by the entire populace. Since Saddam has wiped out all opposition, the only remaining effective government for the country would be his Ba'ath party. Will it count as a victory if Saddam's friends wind up in power? If not, what other choice is there? And if Iraq has no remaining military force, how will it defend itself against Syria and Iran? It will certainly not be a "victory" for us if either of them takes over Iraq.

In all the talk about victory over Iraq, there has been little clarification about what victory would be. And if "victory" cannot be defined, neither can "worthwhile sacrifice."

The metaphors used in the West to conceptualize the Gulf crisis disregard the most powerful political ideas in the Arab world: Arab nationalism and Islamic fundamentalism. The first seeks to form a racially based all-Arab nation, the second, a theocratic all-Islamic state. Though bitterly opposed to one another, they share a great deal. Both are conceptualized in family terms, an Arab brotherhood and an Islamic brotherhood. Both see brotherhoods as more legitimate than existing states. Both are at odds with the State-as-Person metaphor, in which currently existing states are distinct entities with a right to exist in perpetuity.

Also hidden by our metaphors is perhaps the most important daily concern throughout the Arab world: Arab dignity.

Weakness is a major theme in the Arab world, and is often conceptualized in sexual terms, even more than in the West. American officials, in speaking of the "rape" of Kuwait, are conceptualizing a weak, defenseless country as female and a strong militarily powerful country as male. Similarly, it is common for Arabs to conceptualize the colonization and subsequent domination of the Arab world by the West, especially the US, as emasculation.

An Arab proverb that was reported to be popular in Iraq in the days before the war was that "It is better to be a cock for a day than a chicken for a year." The message is clear: It is better to be male, that is, strong and dominant, for a short period of time than to be female, that is, weak and defenseless, for a long time. Much of the popular support for Saddam among Arabs is due to the fact that he is seen as standing up to the US, even if only for a while, and that there is a dignity in this. If upholding dignity is an essential part of what defines Saddam's ''rational self-interest,'' it is vitally important for our government to know this, since he may be willing to continue the war to ''be a cock for a day.''

The US does not have anything like a proper understanding of the issue of Arab dignity. Take the question of whether Iraq will come out of this with part of the Rumailah oil fields and two islands that would give it a port on the Gulf. From Iraq's point of view these are seen as economic necessities if Iraq is to rebuild. President Bush has spoken of this as ''rewarding aggression,'' using a ''Third-World-Countries-As-Children'' metaphor, where the great powers are grown-ups who have the obligation to reward or punish children so as to make them behave properly. This is exactly the attitude that grates on Arabs, who want to be treated with dignity. Instead of seeing Iraq as a sovereign nation that has taken military action for economic purposes, the President treats Iraq as if it were a child gone bad, who has become the neighborhood bully and should be properly disciplined by the grown-ups.

The issue of the Rumailah oil fields and the two islands has alternatively been discussed in the media in terms of ''saving face.'' Saving face is a very different concept than upholding Arab dignity and insisting on being treated as an equal, not an inferior.

Our insistence on using a State-as-Person metaphor, meanwhile, obscures the real and diverse costs of the war. The State-as-Person metaphor highlights the ways in which states act as units, and hides the internal structure of the state. Class structure is hidden by this metaphor, as are ethnic composition, religious rivalry, political parties, the ecology, the influence of the military and of corporations (especially multinational corporations).

Consider the question of our ''national interest.'' It is in a person's interest to be healthy and strong. The State-as-Person metaphor translates this into a ''national interest'' of economic health and military strength. But what is in the ''national interest'' may or may not be in the interest of many ordinary citizens, groups, or institutions, who may become poorer as the GNP rises and weaker as the military gets stronger.

The ''national interest'' is a metaphorical concept, and it is defined in America by politicians and policymakers. For the most part, they are influenced more by the rich than the poor, more by large corporations than small businesses, and more by developers than ecological activists.

When President Bush argues that the war is ''serving our vital national interests,'' he is using a metaphor that hides exactly whose interests are being served and whose are not. For example, poor people, especially blacks and Hispanics, are represented in the military in disproportionately large numbers, and in an extended ground war, they will suffer proportionally more casualties. Thus the war is less in the interest of ethnic minorities and the poor than the white upper classes.

Also hidden are the interests of the military itself, which are served when war is justified. Hopes that, after the Cold War, the military might play a smaller role have been dashed by the President's decision to go to war.

The State-as-Person metaphor has also allowed for a particularly ghoulish cost-benefit analysis about the continuing air war. There is a lot of talk about American deaths in a potential ground war as potential ''costs,'' while Iraqi soldiers killed by the air war count as gains. The cost-benefit accounting leads us to devalue the lives of Iraqis, even when most of those actually killed are not villains at all but simply innocent draftees or reservists or civilians.

The classic fairy tale defines what constitutes a hero: it is a person who rescues an innocent victim and who defeats and punishes a guilty and inherently evil villain, and who does so for moral rather than venal reasons. But in this war, is America functioning as a hero?

It doesn't fit the profile very well.

America appears as classic hero only if you don't look carefully at how the metaphor is applied to the current situation. It is here that the State-as-Person metaphor functions in a way that continues to hide vital truths. The State-as-Person metaphor hides the internal structure of states and allows us to think of Kuwait as a unitary entity, the defenseless maiden to be rescued in the fairy tale. The metaphor hides the monarchical character of Kuwait, and the way Kuwaitis treat women and the vast majority of the people who live in their country. The State-as-Person metaphor also hides the internal structures of Iraq, and thus hides the actual people who are being killed, maimed, or otherwise harmed in this war. The same metaphor also hides the internal structure of the US, and therefore hides the fact that it is the poor and minorities who will make the most sacrifices while not getting any significant benefit from this war. And it hides the main ideas that drive Middle Eastern politics.

Metaphors can kill, and sometimes the first victim is truth.

David G. Savage / Forbidden Words on Campus

Los Angeles, Times, February 12, 1991

David Savage is Supreme Court reporter at the Washington bureau of the Los Angeles Times. *He worked as an education writer from 1981–86 in the Los Angeles bureau of the* Times.

In "Forbidden Words on Campus," David Savage presents a history of speech codes on American colleges to gain insight into today's problems with language and censorship.

WASHINGTON—Campus humor can be a risky business these days.

In December, the editors of the Connector, the student newspaper at the state-run University of Lowell in Massachusetts, published a cartoon mocking what they considered overzealous protesters—both those who favor animal rights and those who favor the death penalty.

One side showed a drawing of an animal rights activist, with the caption: "Some of my best friends are laboratory rats." On the other was a big-bellied death-penalty advocate. "None of his best friends are young, black males," said the legend underneath.

But black students didn't find the cartoon funny and neither did university officials. They promptly charged the student editors with violating the student code by creating a "hostile environment" on campus and other "civil rights" abuses. Eventually, the editors found themselves facing university sanctions that included six months probation and 30 hours of community service and removal from the newspaper's staff.

For decades, denial of free speech has provoked protests on campus. But these days the complaints are on the other side. Today, many students and liberal academics are urging limits on free speech—at least when the topic involves racial or sexual issues.

From Massachusetts to California, more than 200 colleges and universities—

many of them the nation's most elite—have either revised their student codes of conduct or enacted new ''speech codes'' designed to prevent utterances on race, sex, religion, national origin or sexual preference that might offend some students.

''This is the new liberal *cause celebre,''* says U.C. Berkeley law professor Robert C. Post. ''It has forced a wedge between those devoted to civil rights and civil liberties.''

University of Colorado Law School Dean Gene Nichol calls himself an ''old-fashioned, free speech liberal'' but now finds his views unpopular. ''It is no longer 'politically correct' to take the free speech position,'' Nichol laments.

Examples abound:

—The University of Michigan has warned that it will discipline students for comments that ''stigmatize or victimize'' others based on race, sex, sexual orientation, ancestry or religion—including joke-telling or making fun of someone.

—The University of Wisconsin has revised its code of conduct to prohibit ''discriminatory harassment''—including comments that ''demean'' another student or ''create an intimidating, hostile or demeaning environment.''

—The University of California's code prohibits students from making ''personally abusive epithets'' that are ''inherently likely to provoke a violent reaction.'' These include ''derogatory references'' to race, ethnic origin, religion, sex or other characteristics.

Faculties and student bodies alike have split over whether the new limits are needed or wise.

Supporters of the new policies including many law professors, say that the new codes are needed to prevent the spread of ''hate-speech'' on campus—a fear prompted by growing reports of racist incidents including cross-burnings, anonymous hate-mailings and fraternity parties in which white students carried out mock ''slave auctions,'' which onlookers found offensive.

University of Houston law professor Michael Olivas concedes that colleges ideally should be ''enclaves for discussion and free speech'' but argues that racial slurs can prevent young black or Latino students from pursuing their studies.

''These students are extremely vulnerable.'' Olivas contends. ''These comments humiliate and threaten. They don't have anything to do with free speech. The traditional liberals refuse to see that racism warrants special treatment.''

Law professors Mari Matsuda of UCLA and Richard Delgado of the University of Colorado contend that racist comments are a form of assault that can and should be banned on campus.

But others argue that free speech must be protected, even when it is offensive to some listeners. ''I think it is a dangerous precedent to start banning particular words,'' says University of Virginia Prof. Robert O'Neil.

To some, the growth of such ''speech codes'' is part of a historic shift in political attitudes.

In the 1960s, the protesters most often were leftists, who campaigned for civil rights and against the Vietnam War. Conservatives talked of ''law and order'' and of stifling anti-war dissent.

But today, the most vehement street protesters oppose legalized abortion. And it is conservatives who have most visibly taken up the free speech banner.

Whether it is tobacco ads, children's television, anti-abortion demonstrations or racist utterances, ''it is the people on the left who want to regulate speech,'' says University of Chicago law professor Michael McConnell.

What troubles some critics of the new codes is the lengths to which they go in attempting to define improper behavior. Though spurred by incidents of blatant racism, the codes have been used to discipline those whose sins are not as clear-cut.

When the University of Michigan first enacted its speech code, in 1988, it also published a brochure citing examples of "violations."

Among the activities that were included: making jokes about homosexual men and lesbians, displaying a Confederate flag in a dormitory, laughing at a joke about someone who stutters, making derogatory comments about a person's physical appearance, sponsoring entertainment in which a comedian makes jokes about Latinos and uttering classroom remarks such as "Women just aren't as good as men in this field."

Initially, Michigan enforced its new code actively. In 1989, a student hearing board found a graduate student guilty of violations for having publicly characterized homosexuality as a "disease"—though it later refused to impose sanctions, which could have ranged from a formal apology to expulsion from the university.

Later, a black dental student was charged with violating the code for having told a minority instructor that she had heard "minority students had a difficult time in the course" and that they "were not treated fairly."

The instructor filed a complaint of her own because, she said, the student's comment could threaten her chances for tenure. The student eventually was required to write an apology.

In another case, a business student who read "an allegedly homophobic limerick" aloud was required to attend "an educational 'gay rap' session" and write a letter of apology to the campus newspaper.

Still another student was charged with anti-Semitism for having voiced the opinion in class that "Jews used the Holocaust" to justify repression of Palestinians. The case eventually was dismissed, but it provoked protest from free speech advocates.

When several students filed suit, challenging the university's speech code on grounds that it violated the 1st Amendment, U.S. District Judge Avern Cohn struck down the Michigan code as unconstitutional.

As a legal matter, the issue mainly affects state-run universities. Although private schools, such as Stanford University, sometimes impose speech codes as well, they aren't subject to challenge under the 1st Amendment, which only bars the government from restricting free speech and so far has not been applied to private universities.

Dartmouth University recently was the subject of nationwide headlines when it suspended several students who edited an off-campus weekly newspaper that ran articles criticizing a black music professor. Over the years, the publication, the Dartmouth Review, has been castigated for its attacks on women, homosexuals, blacks and Indians.

The U.S. Supreme Court has not spoken on whether racist or sexist comments are protected as free speech. In a 1942 case, Chaplinsky vs. New Hampshire, the high court upheld the conviction of a man who shouted into the face of a policeman that he was a "goddamned racketeer and a damned fascist." Such "fighting words" are not protected by the 1st Amendment, the court declared. More recently, the court has whittled down the "fighting words" exception, but not overruled it.

Two years ago, as many state universities were declaring "demeaning" comments illegal, the Supreme Court declared that burning an American flag, while offensive, was nonetheless legal. "If there is a bedrock principle underlying the 1st Amendment, it is that the government may not prohibit the expression of an idea simply because society finds the idea itself offensive or disagreeable," Justice William J. Brennan Jr. wrote for the court in Texas vs. Johnson.

Judge Cohn cited the flag-burning ruling in striking down the Michigan code.

Since then, universities such as Wisconsin, Stanford and the University of California have revised their codes to punish only the use of so-called ''fighting words.'' They also have decided not to provide examples of words or comments that would violate the codes.

When three Wisconsin students complained that they had been called ''rednecks,'' university officials informed them that the code did not cover that word.

''Redneck is not a demeaning term. It does not have a common meaning,'' said Roger Howard, an assistant dean of students in Madison.

University of California officials in Berkeley and Los Angeles refused to say definitively whether calling a fellow student names ranging from ''nigger'' to ''nerd'' would violate the campus codes.

''We don't have a list of good and bad words,'' says Raymond Goldstone, dean of students at UCLA. ''It is a case-by-case situation.'' Although the University of California's new code took effect in September, 1989, no student has been disciplined because of it.

For traditional liberals, the issue has become a thorny one.

After much hesitation, the American Civil Liberties Union has decided to oppose the new campus codes. Torn between potentially conflicting desires to combat racism and to protect free speech, the ACLU agonized for several years over the issue. But last autumn, the organization issued a new policy statement condemning the new speech codes, while adding that universities are certainly free to punish students for ''acts of harassment, intimidation or invasion of privacy.''

Nadine Strossen, a New York Law School professor who is ACLU's new president, said that the campus speech issue has proved as divisive as championing the rights of neo-Nazis in 1977 to march through a Jewish community of Skokie, Ill.

But Strossen still disparages the new speech codes. ''They are undermining free speech, and they are doing nothing to stop racism and bigotry,'' she says. ''For university administrators, they are a cheap solution to a complex problem.''

Meanwhile, back in Lowell, the controversy continues. Last week, after consulting its attorneys, the university said through a spokesman that it was dropping the charges against the student editors—though it had not yet informed them about the decision.

''We sought a second legal opinion and on the basis of that we're discontinuing any kind of action,'' says Thomas C. Taylor, assistant dean of students, who had signed the initial letters outlining the prescribed punishment.

''We were trying to weigh a lot of issues,'' he explains. ''It was an environmental issue really. We didn't want to have a hostile environment for black students and an atmosphere that would degrade women. That was our intent.''

Ironically, some onlookers believe the black students may have misinterpreted the intent of the cartoon. Although the drawing seems on its face to support claims that they were disproportionately victimized by the death penalty, the students accused the paper of ''racial insensitivity'' for having ''very boldly compared young, black males to a laboratory animals, in particular, rats.''

But Patty Janice, editor of the student newspaper in Lowell, says that she believes her fellow students were made scapegoats for the university's seeming difficulty in attracting black students.

''They have had problems in the past with recruiting black students—the administration has been under the gun,'' she says. ''Attacking us was the easiest way to make it look like they were doing something on that issue.''

DISCUSSION QUESTIONS

1. David G. Savage discusses an aspect of censorship that shares some ground with the issues discussed in this book's section on 2 Live Crew. Often, popular writers draw connections among such disparate, yet related, incidents. Fashion a larger argument about the general state of the First Amendment using material about these different conflicts over freedom of speech.

Maureen Dowd / The Senate and Sexism

New York Times, October 8, 1991

Occasionally, an event will surface that crystallizes a particular set of conflicts foremost in the minds of contemporary Americans. Law professor Anita Hill's charge of sexual harassment against Supreme Court nominee Clarence Thomas was one such occurrence and sent shock waves across the nation. With an ever-rising number of women in the workplace—holding executive as well as menial positions—and with the strong influence of feminism, the American public has been forced to face its own biases regarding gender, sexuality, and respect in the public sphere.

In this article, New York Times *congressional correspondent Maureen Dowd outlines the way in which Ms. Hill's accusations rattled a particular work community: the one on Capitol Hill itself. She gives voice to the congresswomen and female reporters who felt deeply connected with Hill's case and she confronts the old-fashioned views of the "old boys" network that dominates the Senate. Dowd's article was published the day the Senate voted to postpone its vote on Clarence Thomas's confirmation and to conduct public hearings on Ms. Hill's charges. Dowd concludes that Anita Hill was not the only reason that in 1991 that network found itself on shaky ground.*

WASHINGTON, Oct. 7—The bitter "he said, she said" case of Anita F. Hill and Clarence Thomas has offered a rare look into the mechanics of power and decision-making in Washington, a city where men have always made the rules and the Senate remains an overwhelmingly male club.

Even with the facts of the Oklahoma law school professor's accusations of sexual harrassment against Judge Thomas was in dispute, the story of how members of the all-male Judiciary Committee handled the allegations has touched off an angry explosion among women in legal and political circles.

"Once again women and men are watching something unfold through absolutely different sets of eyes and different sets of experiences," said Ann Lewis, a former adviser to Democrats in Washington who is now a political consultant in Boston. She said the case had sent "an electric current of anger through women" and a greater conviction that women must be represented in high places in greater numbers.

SEEKING DELAY IN VOTE

Many female lawmakers and lawyers demanded today, in meetings on Capitol Hill and in petitions, that the Senate delay its vote, arguing that the matter had not been given proper weight by ''the old boy's network,'' that the chairman of the Senate judiciary Committee, Joseph R. Biden Jr. of Delaware, did not fully discuss the accusations with all the panel members and that the committee never questioned Judge Thomas formally and never brought Professor Hill to Washington to hear her side of the story.

Why such a potentially explosive accusation smoldered in the Senate for weeks, then burst into the national press, has now emerged as a central issue.

''They are men, they can't possibly know what it's like to receive verbal harassment, harassment that is fleeting to the man and lasting and demeaning to the woman,'' said Representative Nancy Pelosi, a California Democrat. ''These allegations may not be true. But women in America have to speak up for themselves and say we want to remove all doubt that the person who goes to the Supreme Court has unquestioned respect for women.

''What's the rush? We need a little more time to follow up on allegations so that we can send a signal to women in America that we take sexual harassment seriously.''

Representative Pelosi and other female lawmakers also issued formal statements and petitions to the Senate leaders today urging that the Thomas nomination be re-examined in light of Professor Hill's accusations that, when Judge Thomas was Professor Hill's superior at the Department of Education and the Equal Employment Opportunity Commission in the early 1980's, he first asked her out, and then when she refused, he discussed sexual preferences with her and recounted scenes from pornographic movies he had seen.

''She is not an October surprise,'' Representative Patricia Schroeder, a Colorado Democrat, said of Professor Hill. ''The times they are a' changin' and the boys here don't get it on this issue. They don't really under what sexual harassment is and it's not important to them. They tried simply to dispense with her in short order.

''Why weren't there any questions about his views on pornography by the Senators who had read that F.B.I. report?''

Women contended that the public reaction today of some of the members of the Judiciary Committee showed not only that the men did not give as much weight to the matter as their female counterparts, but that they did not understand the law.

For example, Senator Arlen Specter, a Pennsylvania Republican who is a member of the Judiciary Committee, told reporters that he had privately questioned Judge Thomas before the panel voted on the nomination on Sept. 27 about Professor Hill's accusations and was satisfied. ''The lateness of the allegation, the absence of any touching or intimidation and the fact that she moved with him from one agency to another, I felt I had done my duty and was satisfied with his responses,'' he told The Associated Press.

Asked about his comment later, however, Senator Specter, a former prosecutor, said in an interview that he did understand that touching was not required in a sexual harassment suit, that verbal harassment was also against the law.

ASKED THOMAS BLUNTLY

''I don't want to emphasize the touching thing,'' Mr. Specter said. He added that he had asked Judge Thomas bluntly about Professor Hill's assertions in her affidavit ''that he talked about movies with animals and women having sexual relations and he was aghast.

''I figured why mince words,'' Mr. Specter said. ''He denied ever having asked her out or talked to her about anything like that.''

Many women were angered by Senator Specter's comment defending the nominee, and by comments by Dennis DeConcini, a Democrat from Arizona who defended Judge Thomas today and raised questions about Professor Hill's motivation.

Even some female journalists seemed to have a flash of gender-based anger, when they closely questioned Mr. DeConcini today at a Senate news conference about his remarks challenging Professor Hill's credibility and about why he seemed to automatically believe Judge Thomas and not believe Professor Hill.

A GENDER PROBLEM?

Susan Milligan, a reporter for The New York Daily News who was among those questioning the Senator, noted afterward that "it was a gender and generational problem. He truly did not seem to get it, why we were asking the questions we were asking or what her complaint was.

"Several of us were raising our voices and I think it was because we've all grown up with a heightened sensitivity to women victims of rape and sexual harassment having their characters called into question."

Senator Paul Simon, the Illinois Democrat on the Judiciary Committee who took to the Senate floor tonight to argue that the nomination be delayed, agreed that the matter had "touched a nerve" with women on Capitol Hill, and with some men.

"I think there is, in a body that is 98 males to 2 women, a lack of sensitivity toward women's concerns and black and Hispanic concerns," he said. "If there were 20 women who were members of the Senate we could delay the vote right now."

Katherine T. Bartlett, a law school professor at Duke University who sent a letter to the Senate leadership tonight calling on them to delay the vote and "fully and publicly" investigate Professor Hill's accusations, said she got 70 signatures from women law professors in just hours.

'GAP IN MALE UNDERSTANDING'

"There's an astounding strength of feeling about this," Professor Bartlett said. "There's a sense that there's a gap in male understanding, in the understanding of the people making the decisions. There is a perception that a group of men may not have taken this as seriously as a group of women similarly situated would have taken it."

Judy Lichtman, the head of the Women's Legal Defense Fund, met with Senator George J. Mitchell, the majority leader, in his office this afternoon, along with several prominent black women law professors and lobbyists.

"The Senate was attempting to continue as if it was business in the usual way, when they should have been responding to this extraordinarily serious complaint," Ms. Lichtman said. "This is a microcosm of the the problem, endemic in society, about the way working women are viewed."

Ms. Lichtman and others argued to Senator Mitchell not that Professor Hill was telling the truth, as opposed to Judge Thomas, but simply that her accusations deserved a thorough airing. She said that the criticism of Professor Hill today for coming forth, by Democrats like Mr. DeConcini and respected Republicans like Senator John Danforth of Missouri, who is pressing the White House's political case for its nominee, represented every woman's nightmare about why she does not want to press sexually related charges in the public arena.

"Here is a woman who struggled so with the need to come forward, balancing her need for privacy and putting herself at enormous professional and private risk,'' she said. ''It's an indicator of how women are viewed in society.''

The women and men who talked about the sexual politics of the case today said that the members of the Judiciary Committee may have been suffering from two common responses to accusations of sexual harassment, that it should be treated as a private matter and that it is an uncomfortable, threatening matter for men to deal with.

Ms. Schroeder agreed that her colleagues were made intensely uncomfortable by the explosive nature of Professor Hill's accusations. ''It's a male bonding thing,'' she said. ''They all think of themselves as potential victims, thinking, 'We need to stick together or all these women will come out and make allegations setting us up. We've heard this kind of thing before.' ''

Susan Deller Ross, a professor of law at Georgetown University who signed the letter sent by Professor Bartlett, said that men have a hard time visualizing what it feels like to be ''a vulnerable and trapped female.''

''It's just interesting to think if there had been several strong women on that panel, how they would have reacted to the allegations,'' Professor Ross said. ''We may be going through a societal process of getting men to look at these issues more closely. Now that more women are professionals, they have to take it seriously. They can't ignore it.''

Patrick O'Connell / Settlement of America: A Continuing Crime

San Francisco Examiner, October 14, 1991

Jeffrey Hart / Feting the Lindbergh of the 15th Century

San Francisco Examiner, October 14, 1991

It has been five hundred years since the Nina, Pinta, and Santa Maria stumbled on the middle shores of a continent and the captain of those ships, Christopher Columbus, mistook his landing spot for the Indies. The quincentennial of Columbus's arrival in the New World has generated intense controversy, as Native American and other ethnic groups speak out against genocide while white conservatives struggle to maintain a picture of history that emphasizes progress over oppression. In these dueling op-ed pieces published in the San Francisco Examiner *on October 14, 1991, a representative of each viewpoint has his say. Patrick O'Connell stresses the genocidal heritage—and the present policy—of a nation that has virtually eradicated its native cultures. Dartmouth professor Jeffrey Hart questions the accuracy of a view that removes Columbus's journey from its historical context, and he refuses to see Western culture as positive. The reader, given a choice between two strikingly different viewpoints on a momentous event in American history, can draw her or his own conclusions.*

Columbus began a legacy of genocide that we as a nation had yet to come to terms with. Genocide (defined by federal law as ''specific intent to destroy, in whole or in substantial part, a national, ethnic, racial or religious group,'' or activity that ''subjects the group to conditions of life that are intended to cause the physical destruction of the group in whole or in part'') has been the basic policy of the Europeans toward the indigenous peoples of the land for the past five centuries.

If you are like most Americans, you probably think this genocide ended in the 1890s with the "last Indian wars." But you are mistaken.

The genocide Columbus began almost 500 years ago continues today. But it has become, out of necessity, much more sophisticated and hidden from sight. Today's Indian Wars are carried out under the guise of "settling Indian disputes," "modernizing Indian treaties" and "Indian economic development acts." All these actions are bent on destroying the people under the guise of saving them.

The guilt we feel for the sins of our ancestors, exemplified by the popularity of the film "Dances With Wolves," must be put in perspective to understand where we stand now.

We live in a situation similar to what Germany might face if a new Hitler appeared. To distract people from his current activities, he might remind people of Germany's collective guilt for the crimes of the Third Reich. While whipping up sentimental feelings of guilt, he might institute a new campaign against Jews and other "undesirables."

In our case, though, "Hitler" has never left and the genocidal policy against indigenous peoples continues.

Why is it that we apply the term genocide only to crimes committed by Europeans against other Europeans in the 1930s and '40s? Why is it we never thought such activity was an atrocity when we exterminated an estimated 90 percent of the indigenous population of the Americas and tens of millions of Africans to build this country?

These are things to consider when trying to understand what the moral foundations of our society are and what needs to be changed to make our nation whole.

Until we come to terms with what it means to live in a nation founded on genocide, we will never be whole. It affects our psyche and will continue to destroy our peace of mind until this relationship is made right. This means acknowledging that our basic policy toward the indigenous has been one of continuous genocide.

But acknowledging this is only the first step. We must then act to halt the genocide being carried out in our names today. This means supporting indigenous self-determination, respecting their traditional beliefs and connecting to their land, and supporting them in their struggles to maintain or secure their traditional lands.

With the approach of the 500th anniversary of the landing of Columbus in 1492, it is time we begin to make right this most basic relationship with the indigenous people on whose land we live. Saving the Earth, protecting hard-earned civil rights and fighting all the sicknesses that are destroying the society around us are all necessary to build a better society. But if we hope to reach our potential of a caring and compassionate nation, we must address this most fundamental evil that is destroying the heart of our country—the genocide of the indigenous peoples of this land.

No serious historian doubts that Christopher Columbus was a heroic, though flawed, man of world-historical importance. Yet a few pushy ideologues and pressure groups have managed to make him controversial. As the 500th anniversary of 1492 is celebrated in the coming year, it is quite possible that things will get nasty. Look for some ugly action around Columbus Day.

This columnist just did a TV segment for a Canadian Broadcasting Company show on the Columbus issue. Which boils down to this: Was it a tragedy for Europe to arrive in the New World?

Those who are answering that it was a tragedy are implicitly saying that Western civilization itself is a mistake. They are saying that Europe was evil, and that

America is the culminating evil of Western civilization. They posit a ''golden age'' of pre-Columbian America in which the Indians were in tune with nature, peaceable, and nonpolluting.

All of that is utopian nonsense. The Indians were a stone-age people who had not invented the wheel and had no written language. Some of the Indians were warlike, and ferociously so, while some were pacific and more gentle. All of the tribes are certainly worth studying from a historical or an anthropological point of view.

However, it is ironic that the attack upon Columbus and upon the West is now being mounted at a time when the entire world from Tiananmen Square to Moscow and St. Petersburg is moving relentlessly in a Western direction, indeed in an American direction.

Imagine, a homemade Statute of Liberty in Tiananmen Square. Who thought a year ago that Leningrad would today become St. Petersburg again? The idea of representative government, which is a Western invention, has become the only legitimate form of government as the 20th century draws to its close. Lenin is going to be obliged to get out of his tomb.

And, to move outside political arrangements, are we really supposed to regret the whole culture of the West, from Homer through Einstein? Are we supposed to condemn Michelangelo, Dante, Giotto, Rembrandt, Shakespeare, Newton, Bach?

The fact of the matter is that Columbus was a man of his time, the later 15th century. He certainly had his personal flaws, in which he was not alone. But he was a major figure in what historians call the Age of Exploration, the great westward surge of European peoples.

Historians debate the precise balance of causes for this surge. In part it was the result of advances in navigation, such as the compass and cartography. In part it was because the overland trade routes to China were blocked, and other routes were needed.

I suspect that the westward surge had profounder psychological causes. After all, it washed up in the original 13 colonies, crossed the Mississippi, reached California, went ever Westward to Hawaii and the Philippines, and reached its apogee when Douglas MacArthur signed the surrender document aboard the battleship Missouri in Tokyo Bay.

The westward surge of the Europeans was halted only when it ran up against the reality of China, in Korea and in Vietnam. But the westward surge in ideas and culture continues.

Columbus dared to trust the theories of the early navigators, and, like an astronaut, venture into the unknown. Before him, European captains had reached the Azores, the Canary Islands, and ventured down the coast of Africa. Prince Henry the Navigator surveyed his charts and theorized in his lookout castle in southern Portugal. But, before Columbus, the European seamen were only inching westward.

Columbus pointed his three tiny ships westward, across the great loneliness of the deep unknown.

Columbus was the Lindbergh of the 15th century.

To be sure, the so-called Indians were often treated harshly and did die of disease. But, historically, the history of the world shows great population shifts. The Carthaginians were not pleased to be exterminated by Rome, and the Romans themselves were not delighted by the hordes of vandals and Goths that ended the ''glory'' that was Rome. The Indians lost their war with the Europeans. Don't blame Columbus.

And, by the way, I went to a great university named Columbia. This is ''America''? Who was Amerigo Vespucci anyway?

Karen Jurgensen / Redskins, Braves: Listen to Those You've Offended

USA Today, November 25, 1991

Paul Hemphill / Names Debate off Target

USA Today, November 25, 1991

The Atlanta Braves valiantly, but unsuccessfully, battled the Minnesota Twins in baseball's 1991 World Series, and during this same period the team's management found itself fighting quite a different oppositional force off the field. The American Indian Movement formally protested the use of the name "Braves," as well as the fans' practice of engaging in cartoonish versions of Native American expression such as war whoops and the infamous "tomahawk chop," ostensibly in support of their team. Americans were faced with an image of former radical icon Jane Fonda blithely chopping away next to her husband-to-be, Braves owner Ted Turner, as Native Americans reminded the viewing public of the racial stereotyping and genocide that continue to plague these indigenous groups.

In these concurrent op-ed pieces, Karen Jurgensen, the USA Today *editorial page editor, debates prominent southern writer Paul Hemphill on the issues raised by the tomahawk chop and a controversial name. The pro-and-con format of this pair of articles allows the reader a more expansive view of the issues at hand than would a single piece.*

OUR VIEW

A team's name or a "tomahawk chop" can create problems that might easily be avoided.

The Washington Redskins may be headed for football's Super Bowl, but baseball's Atlanta Braves are ahead in calming anger over the use of Native American names in sports.

The Braves now recognize the problem. The Redskins apparently don't.

Braves officials met last week with the American Indian Movement to discuss the team's name and practices. The reason: Anger over fans' use of the "tomahawk chop" and chants before and during last month's World Series.

Many Native Americans say such acts stereotype them as warring savages or cartoonish characters. Some feel it puts them on the level of animals, a more common source for team names.

Fans may see that reaction as over-sensitive, but there's no doubting the pain is real. It deserves attention.

In recent years, understanding of the problem has led to change. Only six major colleges still use Native American names. Stanford changed long ago from the Indians to the Cardinal; Dartmouth from Indians to Big Green.

Pro sports have baseball's Braves and Cleveland Indians, football's Redskins and Kansas City Chiefs, and hockey's Chicago Blackhawks.

The toughest problem belongs to the Redskins—whose name, like Blackskins or Yellowskins, is flatly offensive and is defined as such by Webster's.

Yet Redskins owner Jack Kent Cooke has refused to meet Native American leaders—a thoughtless response. He might benefit from learning why the name offends the people who inspired it.

Other teams have worthwhile options short of changing names.

Ending offensive practices, like cartoonish mascots, is as easy as consulting with those who might be offended.

Better yet, teams could promote themselves in a way that makes them a source of pride, as the Notre Dame Fighting Irish are to Irish Americans.

Teams with Native American names should follow the Braves' lead. No problem is solved by pretending it doesn't exist.

OPPOSING VIEW

Changing team names does little to change the big problems Native Americans suffer.

When the flap arose over the use of Native American names and artifacts by sport teams—specifically the Atlanta Braves and their fans' "tomahawk chop"—*The New York Times,* crying the loudest over this "political incorrectness," asked Allie Reynolds what he thought.

Reynolds is 3⁄16th Native American, was nicknamed "Superchief" when signed by the Cleveland Indians during World War II and pitched in six World Series for the Yankees. "It looks like they (the American Indian Movement) could find better things to do with their time," he said.

They probably felt the same at the Cherokee Indian Reservation in North Carolina, 150 miles from here, where I've been researching a novel. The 9,000 residents of Cherokee weren't angry about the Braves and the tomahawk chop. They were relieved their namesakes were no longer losers. And they couldn't make toy tomahawks and tom-toms fast enough in the sad little plant that represents their only real industry.

Anyone truly sensitive to the plight of the original Americans should visit a reservation to see what the real problems are. In Cherokee, those problems are 40% unemployment during the tourist off-season, 50% alcoholism among adult males and the malaise that comes from living in a welfare state. If anything, it was a pleasant diversion in Cherokee to see a team named Braves make it to the World Series.

But it has become an issue, and I should think the Braves might be big enough to do their little bit for their brothers in Cherokee. I'm not talking about free tickets or any other public relations gimmick meant to diffuse the situation. Seed money for a bona fide industry—textiles, furniture, whatever would do nicely.

Because baseball is only a game; living on a reservation is anything but.

DISCUSSION QUESTIONS

1. These opposing editorials, like those by Patrick O'Connell and Jeffrey Hart, discuss the effects of symbolic actions on people's material and psychological well-being. Much discussion can be heard today on such issues, ranging from the arguments against cigarette advertising in Anna Quindlen's article (p. 199) to the struggles over 2 Live Crew. What connections do you see between the images we ingest as consumers and the material circumstances of our lives? How does advertising figure in this relationship?

MAGAZINES

I'm obsessed by Time Magazine.
I read it every week.
Its cover stares at me every time I slink past the corner candystore.

ALLEN GINSBERG, "AMERICA"

FROM an early exposé of child labor violations to an analysis of television sitcoms, the following selection of American magazine writing illustrates a variety of prose styles and compositional procedures adopted by writers to address many different levels of reading interest and aptitude.

No magazine is addressed to everyone. Though all magazines are eager to increase their circulation, they nevertheless operate with a fairly limited market in mind. A magazine's image is often as firmly established as the brand image devised by advertisers to ensure a commercially reliable consumer identification with a product. "What Sort of Man Reads *Playboy?*" is, according to that magazine's advertisement, a question easily answered, if not by the details of the photograph in the ad, then certainly by the language describing what the "typical *Playboy* reader is like. Depending on the issue you look at, he may be "urban," "stylish," "his own man," "literate," "free-wheeling," "an individualist." "Can a Girl Be Too Busy" (see "Advertising") offers a further instance, though playfully exaggerated, of a magazine's personification of its public image through characters and voices that supposedly convey the life-style, or desired life-style, of its readers.

Regardless of the ways a magazine goes about promoting its public identity, the type of audience it wants to attract can be seen in the total environment created by such material as the magazine's fiction and nonfiction, advertisements, editorial commentary, paper quality, and overall physical design. An article in *The New Yorker,* for example, is forced to compete for its readers' attention with glossy scenes of high fashion, mixed drinks, and the allure of exotic places. Yet not all magazines imagine or address their readers in quite such fashionable terms. An article appearing in *Good Housekeeping, Harper's, Psychology Today,* or *Scientific American* does not usually take its tone from the modish world that forms the context of magazines such as *The New Yorker, Playboy, Cosmopolitan, Vogue,* and *Esquire.* For example, advertisements for precision instruments, various types of machinery, automobiles, and corporate accountability, along with mathematical games, puzzles, and instructions for home experiments, surround the technical articles published in *Scientific American.* The readers of a magazine like *Good Housekeeping* are expected to be particularly attentive to products, services, and expertise that promise to improve a family's immediate domestic environment.

The ideal reader for a given magazine—the reader as housewife, playboy, academic, outdoorsman—is a vague entity, invented by the magazine more for simple identification than realistic description. No one is *just* a housewife or an academic, even assuming that we know exactly who or what these categories stand for in the first place. Naturally, labels like these suggest different associations to different people. To contend, then, that the audience for *Esquire* is male and to let it go at that is like arguing that the reader of an article in an issue of *TV Guide* can be described solely as someone who has the ability to watch television.

Some affinity surely exists between the readership a magazine commercially promotes and the individual reader a particular article within that magazine assumes. But to characterize more accurately the audience addressed by a particular article, we need to go beyond the conveniently stereotyped reader presupposed by the magazine's title or its public image. For instance, *Everybody's,* a popular magazine first published nationwide in 1903, certainly could not appeal to everyone in America. Like any other magazine, it selected articles that approximated most closely the style of talk and the strategies of persuasion it felt its readers were most accustomed to. For a number of years, *Everybody's* played a prominent role in helping to develop the mode of American journalism that Theodore Roosevelt scornfully christened "muckraking." Along with other leading newspapers and periodicals, *Everybody's* featured a number of successful articles devoted to exposing public scandals and attacking vice and corruption in business and politics. Its readers were assumed to be civic-minded, generally well-informed people concerned with what they felt was a growing network of moral irresponsibility on the part of public administrators and industrial leaders.

William Hard's article "De Kid Wot Works at Night," which appeared in the January 1908 issue of *Everybody's,* was directed to readers already aware of the abuses of child labor and the insidious corruption of urban life through their reading of some of the very newspapers that Hard's young subjects worked so energetically to sell. The boys Hard investigated earned their living out on the streets at night, where they were sadly vulnerable to the sundry temptations of a big city after dark. Hard argued seriously for legislative reform:

> Mr. J. J. Sloan, when he was superintendent of the John Worthy School (which is the local municipal juvenile reformatory), reported that the newsboys committed to his care were, on the average, one-third below the stature and one-third below the strength of average ordinary boys of the same age. In the face of testimony of this kind, which could be duplicated from every city in the United States, it seems absurd to talk about the educative influence of the street. That it has a certain educative influence is undeniable, but it is equally undeniable that the boys who are exposed to this influence should be prevented, by proper legislation, from exposing themselves to it for too many hours a day and should especially be prevented from exposing themselves to it for even a single hour after seven o'clock in the evening.

The facts are certainly unpleasant, and Hard is confident that his readers will be persuaded by the weight of professional testimony and their own natural sympathy for the plight of such unfortunate children.

Yet Hard himself seems not always convinced that his newsboys and messengers are the hopeless victims of a ruthless economic system. It is precisely after seven o'clock in the evening that the children he is writing about come to life. The following description portrays "Jelly," the newsboy Hard chooses as his representative "case," and his little sister in ways not nearly so pathetic as engaging:

> At half past ten he went to an elevated railway station to meet his little sister. She was ten years old. She had dressed herself for the part. From her ragged and scanty wardrobe she had chosen her most ragged and her scantiest clothes.
>
> Accompanied by his sister, "Jelly" then went to a flower shop and bought a bundle of carnations at closing prices. With these carnations he took his sister to the entrance of the Grand Opera House. There she sold the whole bundle to the people coming out from the performance. Her appearance was picturesque and pitiful. Her net profit from the sale of her flowers was usually about thirty-five cents.

Life on the street surely has its "undeniable educative influence." If roaming the streets at night stunted Jelly's growth, it certainly did not cripple his resourcefulness and imagination.

Hard's attitude toward the life-style of Jelly and his associates is ambivalent. The reader of the article is asked to acknowledge the seriousness of the terrible conditions surrounding the lives of impoverished children in the city and, at the same time, to recognize that such circumstances do not always culminate in the melodramatic ruination of their victims. Hard transforms Jelly into an entrepreneur responsive to the fluctuations in the flower market—he buys carnations at "closing prices." Jelly also knows how to profit from the "ragged and scanty wardrobe"of his little sister. She, too, willingly participates in the act, choosing only those clothes that will show her poverty to best advantage. Hard's diction ("dressed . . . for the part," "most ragged," "scantiest," "picturesque") alerts the reader to the theatricality implicit in the attempts of these children to earn a living.

It should be clear from the language of the passage that Hard does not think of Jelly and his sister simply as "pitiful" figures. In fact, the word *pitiful* works not so much to move his readers to compassion for the abject condition of the children as much as to describe the self-conscious ways the children display themselves before a fashionable urban audience. From a sociological standpoint, Jelly and his sister may very well be pitiful, but they are also *acting* pitiful, and the awareness of that distinction is what makes it so difficult for Hard to write a disinterested report wholly committed to immediate legislative reform. Hard's predicament in this article is that the corruption he is striving to eliminate as a reformer sustains the very set of characters he finds, as a writer, so appealing in their verbal energy and playful perseverance.

The attractiveness of the kids who work at night and Hard's reluctance to render them merely in sociological terms prompt him to fictionalize their lives, treating them more like characters in a short story than as subjects to be documented. He takes us beyond the limits of factual observation by vividly imagining many details of the newsboys' behavior in situations that must have been annoyingly inaccessible to him. Whatever *Everybody's* public image and vested interests, Hard's article presupposes a reader attuned to both the need for legislative action and the nuances of parody. The piece exists in a territory somewhere between the reportorial prose of newspapers and the inventions of fiction.

With the exception of highly specialized journals and periodicals, most magazines, despite their commercial or artistic differences, want their articles to be both informative and entertaining, responding to those timely topics the renowned American novelist and magazine editor William Dean Howells once termed "contemporanics." Pick up any popular magazine and you will be sure to come across essays offering information about some subject that is a topic of current public interest. Sex, celebrities, success, catastrophes, scandals, the bizarre—it would be difficult to find a magazine that does not contain a single article with a contemporary slant on one of these perennial subjects. Precisely how these subjects will be rendered in prose most often depends on the vigorous interplay between an author's style and purpose and whatever specific compositional standards or general tone the magazine encourages or requires.

Jack London / The Story of an Eyewitness

[*An Account of the San Francisco Earthquake*]

Collier's Weekly, May 1906

Jack London (1876–1916), a native of San Francisco, happened to be working near the city when the earthquake struck on the evening of April 16, 1906. An internationally prominent novelist, reporter, and social critic, London telegraphed the following vivid eyewitness account of the disaster to Collier's Weekly, *for which he was paid twenty-five cents a word. London's dramatic report, which appeared in an issue devoted entirely to photographs and articles on the earthquake, was perfectly suited to* Collier's *characteristically hard-hitting journalism. With a weekly circulation of more than one million,* Collier's *was the country's leading public affairs magazine and an important precursor of modern photojournalism.*

The earthquake shook down in San Francisco hundreds of thousands of dollars' worth of walls and chimneys. But the conflagration that followed burned up hundreds of millions of dollars' worth of property. There is no estimating within hundreds of millions the actual damage wrought. Not in history has a modern imperial city been so completely destroyed. San Francisco is gone! Nothing remains of it but memories and a fringe of dwelling houses on its outskirts. Its industrial section is wiped out. Its social and residential section is wiped out. The factories and warehouses, the great stores and newspaper buildings, the hotels and the palaces of the nabobs, are all gone. Remains only the fringe of dwelling houses on the outskirts of what was once San Francisco.

Within an hour after the earthquake shock the smoke of San Francisco's burning was a lurid tower visible a hundred miles away. And for three days and nights this lurid tower swayed in the sky, reddening the sun, darkening the day, and filling the land with smoke.

On Wednesday morning at a quarter past five came the earthquake. A minute later the flames were leaping upward. In a dozen different quarters south of Market Street, in the working-class ghetto, and in the factories, fires started. There was no opposing the flames. There was no organization, no communication. All the cunning adjustments of a twentieth-century city had been smashed by the earthquake. The streets were humped into ridges and depressions and piled with debris of fallen walls. The steel rails were twisted into perpendicular and horizontal angles. The telephone and telegraph systems were disrupted. And the great water mains had burst. All the shrewd contrivances and safeguards of man had been thrown out of gear by thirty seconds' twitching of the earth crust.

By Wednesday afternoon, inside of twelve hours, half the heart of the city was gone. At that time I watched the vast conflagration from out on the bay. It was dead calm. Not a flicker of wind stirred. Yet from every side wind was pouring in upon the city. East, west, north, and south, strong winds were blowing upon the doomed city. The heated air rising made an enormous suck. Thus did the fire of itself build its own colossal chimney through the atmosphere. Day and night, this dead calm continued, and yet, near to the flames, the wind was often half a gale, so mighty was the suck.

The edict which prevented chaos was the following proclamation by Mayor E. E. Schmitz:

"The Federal Troops, the members of the Regular Police Force, and all Special Police Officers have been authorized to KILL any and all persons found engaged in looting or in the commission of any other crime.

"I have directed all the Gas and Electric Lighting Companies not to turn on gas or electricity until I order them to do so; you may therefore expect the city to remain in darkness for an indefinite time.

"I request all citizens to remain at home from darkness until daylight of every night until order is restored.

"I warn all citizens of the danger of fire from damaged or destroyed chimneys, broken or leaking gas pipes or fixtures, or any like cause."

Wednesday night saw the destruction of the very heart of the city. Dynamite was lavishly used, and many of San Francisco's proudest structures were crumbled by man himself into ruins, but there was no withstanding the onrush of the flames. Time and again successful stands were made by the fire fighters, and every time the flames flanked around on either side, or came up from the rear, and turned to defeat the hard-won victory.

An enumeration of the buildings destroyed would be a directory of San Francisco. An enumeration of the buildings undestroyed would be a line and several addresses. An enumeration of the deeds of heroism would stock a library and bankrupt the Carnegie medal fund. An enumeration of the dead—will never be made. All vestiges of them were destroyed by the flames. The number of the victims of the earthquake will never be known. South of Market Street, where the loss of life was particularly heavy, was the first to catch fire.

Remarkable as it may seem, Wednesday night, while the whole city crashed and roared into ruin, was a quiet night. There were no crowds. There was no shouting and yelling. There was no hysteria, no disorder. I passed Wednesday night in the part of the advancing flames, and in all those terrible hours I saw not one woman who wept, not one man who was excited, not one person who was in the slightest degree panic-stricken.

Before the flames, throughout the night, fled tens of thousands of homeless ones. Some were wrapped in blankets. Others carried bundles of bedding and dear household treasures. Sometimes a whole family was harnessed to a carriage or delivery wagon that was weighted down with their possessions. Baby buggies, toy wagons, and gocarts were used as trucks, while every other person was dragging a trunk. Yet everybody was gracious. The most perfect courtesy obtained. Never in all San Francisco's history were her people so kind and courteous as on this night of terror.

All the night these tens of thousands fled before the flames. Many of them, the poor people from the labor ghetto, had fled all day as well. They had left their homes burdened with possessions. Now and again they lightened up, flinging out upon the street clothing and treasures they had dragged for miles.

They held on longest to their trunks, and over these trunks many a strong man broke his heart that night. The hills of San Francisco are steep, and up these hills, mile after mile, were the trunks dragged. Everywhere were trunks, with across them lying their exhausted owners, men and women. Before the march of the flames were flung picket lines of soldiers. And a block at a time, as the flames advanced, these pickets retreated. One of their tasks was to keep the trunk pullers moving. The exhausted creatures, stirred on by the menace of bayonets, would arise and struggle up the steep pavements, pausing from weakness every five or ten feet.

Often after surmounting a heart-breaking hill, they would find another wall of flame advancing upon them at right angles and be compelled to change anew the line of their retreat. In the end, completely played out, after toiling for a dozen hours like giants, thousands of them were compelled to abandon their trunks. Here the shopkeepers and soft members of the middle class were at a disadvantage But the workingmen dug holes in vacant lots and back yards and buried their trunks.

At nine o'clock Wednesday evening I walked down through miles and miles of magnificent buildings and towering skyscrapers. Here was no fire. All was in perfect order. The police patrolled the streets. Every building had its watchman at the door. And yet it was doomed, all of it. There was no water. The dynamite was giving out. And at right angles two different conflagrations were sweeping down upon it.

At one o'clock in the morning I walked down through the same section. Everything still stood intact. There was no fire. And yet there was a change. A rain of ashes was falling. The watchmen at the doors were gone. The police had been withdrawn. There were no firemen, no fire engines, no men fighting with dynamite. The district had been absolutely abandoned. I stood at the corner of Kearney and Market, in the very innermost heart of San Francisco. Kearney Street was deserted. Half a dozen blocks away it was burning on both sides. The street was a wall of flame. And against this wall of flame, silhouetted sharply, were two United States cavalrymen sitting on their horses, calmly watching. That was all. Not another person was in sight. In the intact heart of the city two troopers sat on their horses and watched.

Surrender was complete. There was no water. The sewers had long since been pumped dry. There was no dynamite. Another fire had broken out further uptown, and now from three sides conflagrations were sweeping down. The fourth side had been burned earlier in the day. In that direction stood the tottering walls of the Examiner Building, the burned-out Call Building, the smoldering ruins of the Grand Hotel, and the gutted, devastated, dynamited Palace Hotel.

The following will illustrate the sweep of the flames and the inability of men to calculate their spread. At eight o'clock Wednesday evening I passed through Union Square. It was packed with refugees. Thousands of them had gone to bed on the grass. Government tents had been set up, supper was being cooked, and the refugees were lining up for free meals.

At half-past one in the morning three sides of Union Square were in flames. The fourth side, where stood the great St. Francis Hotel, was still holding out. An hour later, ignited from top and sides, the St. Francis was flaming heavenward. Union Square, heaped high with mountains of trunks, was deserted. Troops, refugees, and all had retreated.

It was at Union Square that I saw a man offering a thousand dollars for a team of horses. He was in charge of a truck piled high with trunks from some hotel. It had been hauled here into what was considered safety, and the horses had been taken out. The flames were on three sides of the square, and there were no horses.

Also, at this time, standing beside the truck, I urged a man to seek safety in flight. He was all but hemmed in by several conflagrations. He was an old man and he was on crutches. Said he: "Today is my birthday. Last night I was worth thirty thousand dollars. I bought five bottles of wine, some delicate fish, and other things for my birthday dinner. I have had no dinner, and all I own are these crutches."

I convinced him of his danger and started him limping on his way. An hour later, from a distance, I saw the truckload of trunks burning merrily in the middle of the street.

On Thursday morning, at a quarter past five, just twenty-four hours after the earthquake, I sat on the steps of a small residence of Nob Hill. With me sat Japanese, Italians, Chinese, and Negroes—a bit of the cosmopolitan flotsam of the wreck of the city. All about were the palaces of the nabob pioneers of Forty-nine. To the east and south, at right angles, were advancing two mighty walls of flame.

I went inside with the owner of the house on the steps of which I sat. He was cool and cheerful and hospitable. "Yesterday morning," he said, "I was worth six hundred thousand dollars. This morning this house is all I have left. It will go in fifteen minutes." He pointed to a large cabinet. "That is my wife's collection of china. This rug upon which we stand is a present. It cost fifteen hundred dollars. Try that piano. Listen to its tone. There are few like it. There are no horses. The flames will be here in fifteen minutes."

Outside, the old Mark Hopkins residence, a palace, was just catching fire. The troops were falling back and driving refugees before them. From every side came the roaring of flames, the crashing of walls, and the detonations of dynamite.

I passed out of the house. Day was trying to dawn through the smoke pall. A sickly light was creeping over the face of things. Once only the sun broke through the smoke pall, blood-red, and showing quarter its usual size. The smoke pall itself, viewed from beneath, was a rose color that pulsed and fluttered with lavender shades. Then it turned to mauve and yellow and dun. There was no sun. And so dawned the second day on stricken San Francisco.

An hour later I was creeping past the shattered dome of the City Hall. Than it there was no better exhibit of the destructive force of the earthquake. Most of the stones had been shaken from the great dome, leaving standing the naked framework of steel. Market Street was piled high with the wreckage, and across the wreckage lay the overthrown pillars of the City Hall shattered into short crosswise sections.

This section of the city, with the exception of the Mint and the Post Office, was already a waste of smoking ruins. Here and there through the smoke, creeping warily under the shadows of tottering walls, emerged occasional men and women. It was like the meeting of the handful of survivors after the day of the end of the world.

On Mission Street lay a dozen steers, in a neat row stretching across the street, just as they had been struck down by the flying ruins of the earthquake. The fire had passed through afterward and roasted them. The human dead had been carried away before the fire came. At another place on Mission Street I saw a milk wagon. A steel telegraph pole had smashed down sheer through the driver's seat and crushed the front wheels. The milk cans lay scattered around.

All day Thursday and all Thursday night, all day Friday and Friday night, the flames still raged.

Friday night saw the flames finally conquered, though not until Russian Hill and Telegraph Hill had been swept and three quarters of a mile of wharves and docks had been licked up.

The great stand of the fire fighters was made Thursday night on Van Ness Avenue. Had they failed here, the comparatively few remaining houses of the city would have been swept.

Here were the magnificent residences of the second generation of San Francisco nabobs, and these, in a solid zone, were dynamited down across the path of the fire. Here and there the flames leaped the zone, but these fires were beaten out, principally by the use of wet blankets and rugs.

San Francisco, at the present time, is like the crater of a volcano, around which are camped tens of thousands of refugees. At the Presidio alone are at least twenty thousand. All the surrounding cities and towns are jammed with the homeless ones, where they are being cared for by the relief committees. The refugees were carried free by the railroads to any point they wished to go, and it is estimated that over one hundred thousand people have left the peninsula on which San Francisco stood. The government has the situation in hand, and thanks to the immediate relief given by the whole United States, there is not the slightest possibility of a famine. The bankers and businessmen have already set about making preparations to rebuild San Francisco.

DISCUSSION QUESTIONS

1. Having read London's essay carefully, work back over it once more and note the significant words and phrases that are repeated. What is the purpose of

such repetition? Examine the development of London's sentences. Do they work primarily through logic? Emotion? Accumulation of detail? How does this strategy seem best suited to London's occasion and audience?

2. What terms does London use to measure the disastrous effects of the San Francisco earthquake? Does he see the event from a personal or an objective point of view? Does he use, for example, aesthetic, economic, sociological, or psychological language to define his response?

3. Contrast London's point of view and the effects that perspective elicits from his audience with the eyewitness report of another disaster written by William L. Laurence (see ''Press').

William Hard / De Kid Wot Works at Night

Everybody's Magazine, January 1908

Everybody's Magazine *(1899–1929) was a leading advocate of social, economic, and political reform in the early years of the twentieth century. When William Hard's article appeared, the magazine had more than a half-million readers. Although the self-consciously melodramatic and playful tone of Hard's prose may have surprised an audience accustomed to a more earnest style of social crusading, Hard's article nevertheless accomplished its goal by helping to instigate child labor reform legislation in Illinois.*

When the shades of night look as if they were about to fall; when the atmosphere of Chicago begins to change from the dull gray of unaided local nature to the brilliant white of artificial illumination; when the Loop District, the central crater of the volcano, is filling up rapidly with large numbers of straps [trolley cars] which have been brought downtown from outlying carbarns for the convenience of those who have had enough and who now wish to withdraw; when the sound of the time clock being gladly and brutally punched is heard through every door and window—

When all these things are happening, and, besides—

When all the fat men in the city get to the streetcars first, and all the lean and energetic and profane men have to climb over them to the inner seats; when the salesladies in the department stores throw the night-covers over bargain ormolu clocks just as you pant up to the counter; when the man who has just bought a suburban house stops at the wholesale meat market and carries home a left-over steak in order to have the laugh on the high-priced suburban butcher; when you are sorry your office is on the fifth floor because there are so many people on the eleventh floor and the elevator goes by you without stopping, while you scowl through the glass partition—

When all these things are happening, and, besides—

When the clocks in the towers of the railway stations are turned three minutes ahead so that you will be sure to be on time and so that you will also be sure to drop into your seat with fractured lungs; when the policeman blows his whistle to make the streetcar stop, and the motorman sounds his gong to make the pedestrian stop, and both the motorman and the pedestrian look timorously but longingly at the area of death just in front of the fender; when the streets are full and the straps are full, and the shoes of the motor-cars of the elevated trains are throwing yellow sparks on the shoulders of innocent bystanders; when the reporters, coming back to their offices from their afternoon assignments, are turning about in their doorways to watch the concentrated agony of an American home-going and are thanking God that they go home at the more convenient hour of 1 A.M.—

When all these things are happening, and when, in short, it is between five and six o'clock in the afternoon, the night newsboy and the night messenger boy turn another page in the book of experience and begin to devote themselves once more to the thronging, picturesque, incoherent characters of the night life of a big American city.

Then it is, at just about five o'clock, that the night messenger boy opens the door of his office by pushing against it with his back, turns around and walks sidewise across the floor, throws himself down obliquely on his long, smooth bench, slides a foot or two on the polished surface, comes to a stop against the body of the next boy, and begins to wait for the telegrams, letters and parcels that will keep him engaged till one o'clock the next morning and that may lead his footsteps either to the heavily curtained drawing rooms of disorderly houses in the Red Light district or to the wet planks of the wharves on the Calumet River twelve miles away, where he will curl up under the stars and sleep till the delayed boat arrives from Duluth.

Then it is that the night messenger boy's friend and ally, the night newsboy, gets downtown from school, after having said good-by to his usually mythical "widowed mother," and after having assumed the usually imaginary burden of the support of a "bereaved family." Then it is, at about five o'clock, that he approaches his favorite corner, grins at the man who owns the corner news stand, receives "ten *Choinals*, ten *Murrikins*, ten *Snoozes*, and five *Posts*"; goes away twenty feet, turns around, watches the corner-man to see if he has marked the papers down in his notebook, hopes that he hasn't marked them down, thinks that perhaps he has forgotten just how many there were, wonders if he couldn't persuade him that he didn't give him any "*Murrikins*," calculates the amount of his profit if he should be able to sell the "*Murrikins*" without having to pay the corner-man for them, turns to the street, dodges a frenzied automobile, worms his way into a hand-packed street-car (which is the only receptacle never convicted by the city government of containing short measure), disappears at the car door, comes to the surface in the middle of the aisle, and hands a *News* to a regular customer.

From the time when the arc lamps sputter out bravely against the evening darkness to the time when they chatter and flicker themselves into extinction before the cold, reproving rays of the early morning sun, what does the street-boy do? What does he see? What films in the moving picture of a big American city are unrolled before his eyes? These are questions that are important to every American city, to every mission superintendent, to every desk sergeant, to every penitentiary warden, to every father, to every mother.

Night, in these modern times, is like the United States Constitution. It is an admirable institution, but it doesn't know what is happening beneath it. Night comes down on Chicago and spreads its wings as largely and as comfortably now as when the *Tribune* building was a sand dune. You stand on Madison Street and look upward, through the glare of the arc lamps, and you see old Mother Night still brooding about you, calmly, imperturbably, quite unconscious of the fact that her mischievous children have lined her feathers with electricity, kerosene, acetylene, coal gas, water gas, and every other species of unlawful, unnatural illuminating substance. She still spreads her wings, simply, grandly, with the cosmic unconcern of a hen that doesn't know she is hatching out ducks instead of chickens; and in the morning she rises from her nest and flutters away westward, feeling quite sure that she has fulfilled her duty in an ancient, regular and irreproachable manner.

She would be quite maternally surprised if she could know what her newsboys and messenger boys are doing while she (good, proper mother!) is nodding her head beautifully among the stars.

I do not mean by this remark to disparage the newsboy. He occupies in Chicago a legal position superior to that of the president of a railway company. The president of a railway company is only an employee. He receives a weekly, a monthly, or at least a yearly salary. The newsboy does not receive a salary. He is not an employee. He is a merchant. He buys his papers and then resells them. He occupies the same legal position as Marshall Field & Co. Therefore he does not fall within the scope of the child-labor law. Therefore no rascally paternalistic factory inspector may vex him in his pursuit of an independent commercial career.

At about five o'clock he strikes his bargain with the corner-man. The corner-man owns the corner. It is a strange and interesting system, lying totally without the pale of recognized law. Theoretically, Dick Kelly, having read the Fourteenth Amendment to the Constitution of the United States, and having become conscious of his rights, might try to set up a news stand at the southwest corner of Wabash and Madison. Practically, the Constitution does not follow the flag as far as that corner. Mr. Kelly's news stand would last a wonderfully short time. The only person who can have a news stand at the corner of Wabash and Madison is Mr. Heffner.

Mr. Heffner is the recognized owner, holder, occupant, possessor, etc., of some eighty square feet of sidewalk at that point, and his sovereignty extends halfway down the block to the next corner southward, and halfway down the other block to the next corner westward. When Mr. Heffner has been in business long enough he will deed, convey and transfer his rights to some other man for anywhere between $5 and $1,500.

These rights consist exclusively of the fact that the newspapers recognize the corner-man as their only agent at that particular spot. When the corner-man wishes to transfer his corner to somebody else, he must see that the newspapers are satisfied with his choice of a successor.

The newsboy deals, generally speaking, with the corner-man. The corner-man pays the *Daily News* sixty cents for every hundred copies. He then hands out these hundred copies in "bunches" of, say, ten or fifteen or twenty to the newsboys who come to him for supplies. Each newsboy receives, as a commission, a certain number of cents for every hundred copies that he can manage to sell. This commission varies from five to twenty cents. The profit of the corner-man varies therefore with the commission that he pays the newsboy. The public pays one hundred cents for one hundred copies of the *News*. The *News* itself gets sixty cents; the newsboy gets from five to twenty cents, the corner-man gets what is left, namely, from thirty-five down to twenty cents in net profit.

On the basis of this net profit, plus the gross profit on his own sales made directly by himself to his customers, there is more than one corner-man in Chicago who owns suburban property and who could live on the income from his real-estate investments.

From five o'clock, therefore, on to about half past six, the newsboy flips streetcars and yells "turrible murdur" on commission. But pretty soon the corner-man wants to go home. He then sells outright all the papers left on the stand. . . .

The best specimen of the finished type of newsboy, within my knowledge, is an Italian boy named "Jelly." His father's surname is Cella, but his own name has been "Jelly" ever since he can remember.

"Jelly" was born on the great, sprawly West Side. His father worked during the summer, digging excavations for sewers and gas mains. His mother worked during the winter, making buttonholes in coats, vests, and pants. Neither parent worked during the whole year.

This domestic situation was overlooked by the Hull House investigators. In their report on newsboys they found that the number of paper-selling orphans had been grossly overestimated by popular imagination. Out of 1,000 newsboys in their final tabulation, there were 803 who had both parents living. There were 74 who had only a father living. There were 97 who had only a mother living. There were only 26, out of the whole 1,000, who had neither a father nor a mother to care for them.

But "Jelly" occupied a peculiar position. He had both parents living and yet, from the standpoint of economics, he was a half-orphan, since neither parent worked all the year.

At the age of ten, therefore, "Jelly" began selling papers. His uncle had a news stand on a big important corner not far from "Jelly's" house on the West Side. At the age of ten "Jelly" was selling papers from five to eight in the morning and from five to eight in the evening. He was therefore inclined to go to sleep at his desk when he was receiving his lesson in mental arithmetic in the public school where he was an unwilling attendant. Nevertheless, he showed an extraordinary aptitude for mental arithmetic a few hours later when he was handing out change to customers on his uncle's corner.

"Jelly" was a pretty good truant in those days. There was no money to be made by going to school and it looked like a waste of time. His acquaintance among truant officers came to be broad and thorough. He was dragged back to school an indefinite number of times. Yet, with the curious limitations of a newsboy's superficially profound knowledge of human nature, he has confided to me the fact that every truant officer gets $1 for every boy that he returns to the principal of his school.

Besides being a pretty good truant, "Jelly" became also a pretty good fighter. His very first fight won him the undying gratitude of his uncle.

It happened that at that time the struggle between the circulation departments of the evening newspapers was particularly keen. "Jelly's" uncle allowed himself, unwisely, to be drawn into it. The local circulation experts of the *News* and the *American* noticed that on the news stand kept by "Jelly's" uncle the *Journal* was displayed with excessive prominence and the *News* and the *American* were concealed down below. It was currently reported in the neighborhood that "Jelly's" uncle was receiving $10 a week from the *Journal* for behaving in the manner aforesaid.

In about twenty-four hours the corner owned by "Jelly's" uncle bore a tumultuous aspect. The *News* and the *American* had established a rival stand on the other side of the street. This stand was in charge of a man named Gazzolo. Incidentally, it happened that a man named Gazzolo had beaten and killed a man named Cella in the vicinity of Naples some five years before.

Gazzolo's news stand had confronted Cella's, frowning at it from across the street, for about a week, when it began to be guarded by some six or seven broad-chested persons in sweaters. Meanwhile Cella's news stand had also acquired a few sweaters inhabited by capable young men of a combative disposition.

On the afternoon of the eighth day the sweatered agents of the *News* and the *American* advanced across the street and engaged the willing agents of the *Journal* in a face-to-face and then hand-to-hand combat.

At least three murders have happened in Chicago since that time in similar encounters. "Nigger" Clark, an agent of the *News*, was killed on the South Side, and the Higgins brothers were killed on the Ashland Block corner in the downtown district itself, within view of the worldwide commerce transacted in the heart of Chicago. And a Chicago publisher has told me that these three open murders, recognized by everybody as circulation-department murders, must be supplemented by at least six or seven other clandestine murders before the full story of the homicidal rivalry between the agents of Chicago afternoon newspapers is told.

It was amateur murder before the *American* arrived. Then circulation agents began to be enlisted from the ranks of the pupils in the boxing schools, and since that time the circulation situation has become increasingly pugnacious, until today it has reached the State Attorney's office and has come back to the street in the form of indictments and prosecutions.

Typical of this warfare was the fray that followed when the sweatered agents of the *News* and the *American* came across the street and fell rudely upon the news stand of "Jelly's" uncle.

"Jelly's" uncle had his shoulder-blade broken, but "Jelly" himself, being young and agile, escaped from his pursuers and was instantly and miraculously filled with a beautiful idea.

The agents of the *News* and the *American,* coming across the street to attack "Jelly's" uncle, had left Gazzolo's corner unprotected. "Jelly" traversed the cedar blocks of the street and reached Gazzolo in an ecstatic moment when he was surveying the assault on Cella's shoulder-blade with absorbing glee. Just about one-tenth of a second later Mr. Gazzolo was pierced in the region of the abdomen by the largest blade of a small and blunt pocket-knife in the unhesitating right hand of Mr. Cella's nephew, "Jelly."

It was a slight wound, but in consideration of his thoughtfulness in promptly perceiving Mr. Gazzolo's unprotected situation and in immediately running across the street in order to take advantage of it, "Jelly" was transferred by his uncle to a position of independent responsibility. He was put in charge of a news stand just outside an elevated railway station on the South Side.

Nevertheless, even after this honorable promotion, "Jelly's" father continued to take all his money away from him when he came home at night. And the elder Cella did not desist from this practice till his son had been advanced to the supereminent honor of selling papers in the downtown district.

This final transfer happened to "Jelly" when he was fifteen. He still retained his stand on the South Side, selling papers there from five to ten in the morning, but he also came downtown and sold papers at a stand within the Loop from five to nine at night. His uncle had prospered and had been able to invest $1,000 in a downtown corner, which was on the point of being abandoned by a fellow Italian who desired to return to the hills just south of Naples.

Thereafter, till he was sixteen years old, "Jelly" led a full and earnest life. He rose at four; he reached his South Side stand by five; he sold papers there till ten; he reached the downtown district by eleven; he inspected the five-cent theaters and the penny arcades and the alley restaurants till five in the afternoon; he sold papers for his uncle on commission till half past six; he bought his uncle's left-over papers at half past six and sold them on his own account till nine; and then, before going home at ten in order to get his five hours of sleep, he spent a happy sixty minutes reinspecting the five-cent theaters and the penny arcades and dodging Mr. Julius F. Wengierski.

Mr. Wengierski is a probation officer of the Juvenile Court. At that time he was making nightly tours through the downtown district talking to the children on the streets and trying to induce them to go home. He made a special study of some fifty cases, looking into the home circumstances of each child and gathering notes on the reasons why the child was at work. He was assisted by the agents of a reputable and conscientious charitable society.

In only two instances, out of the whole fifty, was the boy's family in need of the actual necessaries of life. In one instance the boy's father was the owner of his house and lot and was earning $5 a day. He also had several hundred dollars in the bank. In only a few instances did the family, as a family, make any considerable gain, for the purposes of household expenses, from the child's labor.

Some fathers, it is true (notably the one who owned his house and lot), used the child selfishly and cruelly as a worker who required no wages and whose total earnings could be appropriated as soon as he came home. It was the same system as that to which "Jelly" had been subjected from ten to fifteen. But these cases were exceptional.

One of the boys was working in order to get the money for the installment payments on a violin, and another was working in order to pay for lessons on a violin of which he was already the complete and enthusiastic owner.

One little girl was selling late editions in the saloons on Van Buren Street in order to have white shoes for her first communion. Another little girl needed shoes of the same color for Easter. Still a third was working in order that after a while she might have clothes just as good as those of the girl who lived next door.

In at least ten of Mr. Wengierski's cases, the reason for earning money on the street at night was the penny arcade and the five-cent theater. The passion for these amusements among children is intense. They will, some of them, work until they have a nickel, expend it on a moving-picture performance, and then start in and work again until they have another nickel to be spent for the same purpose at another "theatorium."

The earnings of these children, according to the Hull House investigation, which is the only authoritative investigation on record, vary from ten cents a day when the children are five years old up to ninety cents a day when they are sixteen. This is the average, but of course there are many children who make less and many who, because of superior skill, make more. Among these latter is "Jelly."

"Jelly's" high average, which used to reach almost $2 a day, was due partly to his own personal power and partly to the fact that on Saturday night he employed the services of his little sister.

Saturday night was "Jelly's" big time. On other nights he went home by ten o'clock. He had to get up by four and it was necessary for even him to take some sleep. But on Saturday night he gave himself up with almost complete abandon to the opportunities of the street.

On that night he used to close up his stand by eight o'clock and then go down to the river and sell his few remaining papers to the passengers on the lake boats. "Last chanst ter git yer *Murrikin*!" "Only one *Choinal* left! De only *Choinal* on de dock!" "Buy a *Post,* mister! Youse won't be able ter sleep ter-night on de boat! De only paper fer only two cents!" "Here's yer *Noose*! Only one cent! No more *Nooses* till youse comes back! Last chanst! Dey will cost yer ten cents apiece on de boat!" "Git yer *Murrikin*. No papers sold on de boat!" "Git yer *Post*. Dey charges yer five cents w'en youse gits 'em on de boat!"

Slightly contradictory those statements of his used to be, but they attained their object. They sold the papers. And as soon as the boats had swung away from their moorings "Jelly" would come back to the region of the five-cent theaters and the penny arcades and resume his nocturnal inquiries into the state of cheap art.

At half past ten he went to an elevated railway station to meet his little sister. She was ten years old. She had dressed herself for the part. From her ragged and scanty wardrobe she had chosen her most ragged and her scantiest clothes.

Accompanied by his sister, "Jelly" then went to a flower shop and bought a bundle of carnations at closing prices. With these carnations he took his sister to the entrance of the Grand Opera House. There she sold the whole bundle to the people coming out from the performance. Her appearance was picturesque and pitiful. Her net profit from the sale of her flowers was usually about thirty-five cents.

As soon as the flowers were sold and the people had gone away, "Jelly" took his sister back to the elevated station. There he counted the money she had made and put it in his pocket. He then handed her out a nickel for carfare and, in addition, a supplementary nickel for herself. "Jelly" was being rapidly Americanized. If he had remained exactly like his father, he would have surrendered only the nickel for carfare.

It was time now to go to the office of the *American* and get the early morning Sunday editions. "Jelly" began selling these editions at about twelve o'clock. He sold them to stragglers in the downtown streets till two. It was then exactly twenty-two hours since he had left his bed. He began to feel a little bit sleepy. He therefore went down to the river and slept on a dock, next to an old berry crate, till four. At four he rose and took the elevated train to the South Side. There he reached his own news stand and opened it up at about five o'clock. This was his Saturday, Saturday-night, and Sunday-morning routine for a long time. On the other nights "Jelly" slept five hours. On Saturday nights he found that two hours was quite enough. And his ability to get along without sleep is characteristic of newsboys and messenger boys rather than exceptional among them.

The reason why "Jelly" used to dodge Mr. Wengierski is now explainable. To begin with, his opinion of all probation officers is unfavorable. He classes them with truant officers. They are not "on the level." They discriminate between different classes of boys. "Jelly" was once accosted by a probation officer at about ten o'clock at night on Clark Street. He gave this probation officer a good tip about a lot of boys who were staying out nights attending services in the old First Methodist Church. These boys had been seen by "Jelly" going home as late as half past ten. The probation officer took no action in their case while at the same time he advised "Jelly" to stop selling papers at an early hour.

Incidents like this had convinced "Jelly" that probation officers were certainly not on the level and were possibly "on the make." But in Mr. Wengierski's case he had an additional reason. Mr. Wengierski was looking for boys of fourteen and under, and, while "Jelly" was entitled by age to escape Mr. Wengierski's notice, he was not so entitled by size. He was sixteen, but he looked not more than thirteen. The street had given him a certain superficial knowledge, but it had dwarfed his body just as surely as it had dwarfed his mind.

Mr. J. J. Sloan, when he was superintendent of the John Worthy School (which is the local municipal juvenile reformatory), reported that the newsboys committed to his care were, on the average, one-third below the stature and one-third below the strength of average ordinary boys of the same age. In the face of testimony of this kind, which could be duplicated from every city in the United States, it seems absurd to talk about the educative influence of the street. That it has a certain educative influence is undeniable, but it is equally undeniable that the boys who are exposed to this influence should be prevented, by proper legislation, from exposing themselves to it too many hours a day and should especially be prevented from exposing themselves to it for even a single hour after seven o'clock in the evening.

"Jelly" has now become a messenger boy and has been given a new name by his new associates. He will some day go back to the newspaper business because there is more money in it, and "Jelly" is fundamentally commercial. But there seems to be, after all, a certain struggling, unruly bubble of romanticism in his nature and it had to rise to the surface and explode.

"Jelly" first thought of the messenger service when he was attending a five-cent theater. "Jelly" went in. The fleeting pictures on the screen at the farther end of the room were telling a story that filled him with swelling interest. A messenger boy is run over by an automobile. He is taken to the hospital. He regains consciousness in his bed. He remembers his message. He calls for a portable telephone. He phones the message to the young man to whom it was addressed. The young man comes at once to the hospital. The young woman who had sent the message also comes. She wants to find out what has happened to the message. The young man and the young woman meet at the bedside of the messenger boy. They fall into each other's arms and the messenger boy sinks back on his pillow and dies. And it is a mighty good story even if the rough points are not rubbed off.

"Jelly" determined at once to be a messenger boy, without delay. [. . .]

Peter Homans / The Western: The Legend and the Cardboard Hero

Look, March 13, 1962

One way to look at the heroes and heroines of popular culture is to see them as reflections of age-old myths. This is the perspective Peter Homans adopts in the following essay, which originally appeared in Look *magazine on March 13, 1962. By analyzing all of the characteristic elements of the typical Western, Homans demonstrates what all Westerns have in common.*

Peter Homans was born in New York in 1930 and has earned degrees at Princeton and the University of Chicago. He is the author of Theology after Freud: An Interpretive Inquiry *(1970) and has written on popular culture, psychology, and theology.*

Along with Life *and the* Saturday Evening Post, Look *was one of the giant-circulation general magazines that died as a weekly in the 1970s. "The power of* Look,*" the magazine's publisher once said, "is that it spans the whole universe of interests. It is a platform of all Americans to turn to, to learn about the basic issues, the real gut issues of the day. . . . It is information and entertainment for the whole family."*

He is the Law West of Tombstone, he is The Virginian at High Noon. He is Frontier Marshal, Knight of the Range, Rider of the Purple Sage. He Has Gun, Will Travel, and his name is Matt Dillon, Destry, Shane.

He is the hero of every Western that ever thundered out of the movies or TV screen, this Galahad with a Colt .45 who stalks injustice on the dusty streets of Dodge. Or Carson City. Or Virginia City.

Once he accomplishes his mission, he vanishes into the mists, as do all true heroes of all true legends. But where Hercules goes to Olympus and King Arthur to Avalon, this galoot rides Old Paint into the sunset.

With few variations, the movies have been telling this story for more than half a century. There have, in fact, been Western movies as long as there have been movies; the first American narrative film was a Western, *The Great Train Robbery,* made in 1903. Without the Westerns, it would be hard to imagine television today. Far outstripping the rowdy little boys who were its first enraptured audience, the Western has gone round the globe to become the youngest of the world's mythologies.

For each of us, even the word "Western" brings to mind an ordered sequence of character, event and detail. There may, of course, be variations within the pattern—but the basic outline remains constant. Details often vary, especially between movie and television Westerns, because the latter are essentially continued stories. Nonetheless, from the endless number of Westerns we have all seen, a basic concept emerges:

The Western takes place in a desolate, abandoned land. The desert, as a place without life, is indispensable. The story would not be credible were it set in a jungle, a fertile lowland or an arctic wasteland. We are dealing with a form of existence deprived of vitality.

This desert effect is contradicted by the presence of a town. Among the slapped-together buildings with false fronts, lined awkwardly along a road forever thick with dust, only three stand out—the saloon, the bank and the marshal's office (the hero's dwelling).

The saloon is the most important building in the Western. It is the only place in the story where people can be seen together time after time. It thereby functions as a meetinghouse, social center, church. More important, it is the setting for the climax of the story, the gunfight. No matter where the fight ends, it starts in the saloon.

The bank is a hastily constructed, fragile affair. Its only protection consists of a sniveling, timid clerk, with a mustache and a green eyeshade, who is only too glad to hand over the loot. Has there ever been a Western in which a robber wondered whether he could pull off his robbery?

The marshal's office appears less regularly. Most noticeable is the absence of any evidence of domesticity. We rarely see a bed, a place for clothes or any indication that a person actually makes his home here. There is not even a mirror. The overall atmosphere is that of austerity, which, we are led to suspect, is in some way related to our hero's virtue, and not to his finances.

The town as a whole has no business or industry. People have money, but we rarely see them make it. Homelife is conspicuous by its absence. There are no families, children, dogs. The closest thing to a home is a hotel, and this is rarely separated from the saloon.

One of the most interesting people in the town is the "derelict professional." He was originally trained in one of the usual Eastern professions (law, medicine, letters, ministry), but since his arrival in the West, he has become corrupted by drink, gambling, sex or violence. The point is that the traditional mentors of society (counselor, healer, teacher, shepherd) cannot exist in an uncorrupted state under the pressure of Western life. Somewhat similar is the "nonviolent Easterner." He often appears as a well-dressed business man, or as a very recent graduate of Harvard. In the course of the plot's development, this character is either humiliated or killed. The East, we soon note, is incapable of action when action is most needed.

The "good girl" is another supporting type in the cast of characters. Pale and without appetite, she, too, is from the East and is classically represented as the new schoolmarm. The "bad girl" is alone in the world and usually works for her living in the saloon as a waitress or dancer. Both girls have their eye on the hero.

The bartender observes the action, but rarely becomes involved in it. "The boys," those bearded, grimy people who are always "just there" drinking and gambling in the saloon, function as an audience. No hero ever shot it out with his adversary without these people watching.

Then we come to the principals. We meet the hero in the opening phase of the action. He is, above all, a transcendent figure, originating beyond the town. He rides into the town from nowhere; even if he is the marshal, his identity is disassociated from the people he must save. We know nothing of any past activities, relationships, future plans or ambitions. There are no friends, relatives, family, mistresses—not even a dog or cat—and even with his horse, he has a strangely formal relationship.

At first, the hero is lax to the point of laziness. Take his hat, for example. It sits exactly where it was placed—no effort has been made to align it. With feet propped up on the porch rail, frame balanced on a chair or stool tilted back on its rear legs, hat pushed slightly over the eyes, hands clasped over the buckle of his gun belt, he is a study in contrived indolence. Now he has time on his hands, but he knows his time is coming, and so do we.

The hero indicates no desire for women. He appears somewhat bored with the whole business. He never blushes, or betrays any enthusiasm. His monosyllabic stammer and brevity of speech clearly indicate an intended indifference.

In the drinking scenes, we are likely to see the hero equipped with the traditional shot glass and bottle. We seldom see him pay for more than one drink. He gulps his drink, rarely enjoys it and is impatient to be off. In the gambling scenes, his poker face veils any inner feelings of greed, enthusiasm or apprehension. We note, however, that he always wins or refuses to play. Similarly, he is utterly unimpressed by and indifferent to money.

There are hundreds of variations of the villain, but each is unshaven, darkly clothed and from the West. Like the hero, he is from beyond the town. He is inclined to cheat at cards, get drunk, lust after women who do not return the compliment, rob banks and, finally, shoot people he does not care for, especially heroes.

The impact of this evil one on the town is electric, suddenly animating it with vitality and purpose. Indeed, it is evil, rather than good, that actually gives meaning to the lives of these people. Nevertheless, they all know (as we do) that they are of themselves ultimately powerless to meet this evil. What is required is the hero—a transcendent power originating from beyond the town.

Notice what has happened to this power. Gone are the hero's indolence and lack of intention. Now, he is infused with vitality, direction and seriousness, in order to confront this ultimate threat. Once the radical shift has been accomplished, the hero (like the audience) is ready for the final conflict.

While the fight can take many forms (fistfight, fight with knives or whips, even a scowling match in which the hero successfully glares down the evil one), the classic and most popular form is the encounter with six-guns. It is a built-up and drawn-out affair, always allowing enough time for an audience to gather. The two men must adhere to an elaborate and well-defined casuistry as to who draws first, when it is proper to draw, etc. Although the hero's presence makes the fight possible—i.e., he insists on obstructing the evil one in some way; it is the latter who invariably attacks first. Were the hero ever to draw first, the story would no longer be a Western. With the destruction of the evil one, the action phase is completed.

In the closing phase, the town and its hero return to their preaction ways. One more event must take place, however, before the story can conclude. The hero must renounce any further involvement with the town. Traditionally, the hero marries the heroine and settles down. The Western hero always refuses—at least on television. He cannot identify himself with the situation he has influenced. When this has been made clear, the story is over.

The Western is, as most people by this time are willing to acknowledge, a popular myth that sets forth certain meanings about what is good and bad, right and wrong. Evil, according to the myth, is the failure to resist temptation. Temptation consists of five activities: drinking, gambling, moneymaking, sex and violence. In the drinking scenes, the hero is offered not one drink, but a whole bottle. He has at his disposal the opportunity for unlimited indulgence and its consequent loss of self-control. Gambling is a situation over which one has rather limited control—one loses, but the hero does not lose. He wins, thereby remaining in control. Wealth is not seized, although it is available to him through the unguarded bank. And both good girl and bad girl seek out the hero, to no avail—he remains a hero.

We perceive in the evil one a terrible power, which he has acquired at a great price; he has forfeited the control and resistance that sustain and make the hero what he is. The villain is the embodiment of the failure to resist temptation; he is the failure of denial. This is the real meaning of evil in the myth of the Western, and it is this that makes the evil one truly evil. He threatens the hero's resistance; each taunt and baiting gesture is a lure to the forfeiture of control and leads to the one temptation that the hero cannot afford to resist: the temptation to destroy temptation.

But why must the hero wait to be attacked? Why must he refrain from drawing first? The circumstances are contrived in order to make the violent destruction of the evil one appear just and virtuous. This process whereby desire is at once indulged and veiled is the "inner dynamic." It is the key to the Western, explaining not only the climax of the story, but everything else uniquely characteristic of it. What is required is that temptation be indulged while providing the appearance of having been resisted. Each of the minor-temptation episodes—drink, cards, moneymaking and sex—takes its unique shape from this need and is a climaxless Western in itself.

The derelict professional is derelict, and the nonviolent Easterner is weak, precisely because they have failed to resist temptation in the manner characteristic of the hero. Because these two types originate in the East, they have something in common with the good girl. Everything Eastern in the Western is weak, emotional, feminine. This covers family life, intellectual life, professional life. Only by becoming Westernized can the East be redeemed. The Western therefore is more a myth about the East than it is about the West; it is a secret and bitter parody of Eastern ways.

In summary, then, the Western is a myth in which evil appears as a series of temptations to be resisted by the hero. When faced with the embodiment of these temptations, he destroys the threat. But the story is so structured that the responsibility for the act falls upon the adversary, permitting the hero to destroy while appearing to save.

The Western bears a significant relationship to puritanism, in which it is the proper task of the will to rule and contain the spontaneous, vital aspects of life. Whenever vitality becomes too pressing, and the dominion of the will becomes threatened, the self must find some other mode of control. The puritan will seek a situation that allows him to express vitality while appearing to resist it. The Western provides just this opportunity, for the entire myth is shaped by the inner dynamic of apparent control and veiled expression. Indeed, in the gunfight, the hero's heightened gravity and dedicated exclusion of all other loyalties present a study in puritan virtue, while the evil one presents nothing more or less than the old New England Protestant devil—strangely costumed, to be sure—the traditional tempter whose horrid lures never allow the good puritan a moment's peace. In the gunfight, there are deliverance and redemption.

Here, then, is the real meaning of the Western: It is a puritan morality tale in which the savior-hero redeems the community from the temptations of the devil. Tall in the saddle, he rides straight from Plymouth Rock to a dusty frontier town, and though he be the fastest gun this side of Laramie, his Colt .45 is on the side of the angels.

DISCUSSION QUESTIONS

1. Read Homans's essay in connection with Gretel Ehrlich's "The Solace of Open Spaces." How are the images of the West in each essay similar? How are they different?

2. Could Homans's analysis be applied to other popular forms? For example, how might someone using Homans's method of interpretation read Edgar Rice Burroughs's *Tarzan of the Apes* or Mario Puzo's *The Godfather* (see "Best-Sellers")?

Time Staff / Death of a Maverick Mafioso

[On the Shooting of Joey Gallo] *Time*, April 1972

For many years, the slogan of Time *magazine was "curt, concise, complete." Founded in 1923 by Henry Luce and Briton Hadden,* Time, the Weekly News Magazine, *was intended to appeal to the growing number of American college graduates. Its title was meant to suggest both the scope of the magazine's coverage of current events and its sensitivity to the limited time which "busy men are able to spend on simply keeping informed." Luce and Hadden rejected the conventional format of objective news reporting and promoted instead a highly idiosyncratic, self-consciously lively narrative and a somewhat subjective, though corporate, journalistic style.*

Joey Gallo's murder received national attention. Inevitable were the comparisons with Mario Puzo's The Godfather *(see "Best-Sellers") to show how ruthlessly life imitates art.*

The scene could have been lifted right out of that movie. First, a night of champagne and laughter at Manhattan's Copacabana as Mobster Joseph ("Crazy Joe") Gallo, one of New York's most feared Mafiosi, celebrated his 43rd birthday. Then on to a predawn Italian breakfast at a gleaming new restaurant in the city's Little Italy area. Seated at his left at a rear table in Umbertos Clam House was his brawny bodyguard, Pete ("The Greek") Diopioulis; at Gallo's right, his sister Carmella. Across the table sat Gallo's darkly attractive bride of just three weeks, Sina, 29, and her daughter Lisa, 10. Quietly, a lone gunman stepped through a rear door and strode toward the table.

Both Gallo and Diopioulis were carelessly facing the wall instead of the door. The triggerman opened fire with a .38-caliber revolver. Women screamed. Joey and Pete were hit instantly. The Greek drew his own gun, began shooting back. So did one Gallo ally, seated at the front clam bar. Within 90 seconds, 20 shots ripped through the restaurant. Tables crashed over, hurling hot sauce and ketchup across the blue-tiled floor to mix with the blood of the wounded. The gunman whirled, ran out the same rear door and into a waiting car.

Gallo, wounded in a buttock, an elbow and his back, staggered toward the front of the café. He lurched through a front door and collapsed, bleeding, on the street. Carmella's screams attracted officers in a passing police car. They rushed Gallo to a hospital, but he died before reaching it.

MUSCLING

That melodramatic end to the short, brutal life of Joey Gallo surprised no one in New York's increasingly fratricidal underworld. There had been a contract out on his life ever since Mafia Boss Joe Colombo had been shot at an Italian Day rally in New York last June (TIME cover, July 12). Police do not believe that Gallo plotted that murder attempt, but friends of Colombo, who remains unable to talk or walk, thought he had. Gallo had been counted among the walking dead ever since he also aroused the anger of the biggest boss of them all, aging Carlo Gambino. Told to stop muscling into Gambino's operations, including the lucrative narcotics traffic in East Harlem, the cocky Gallo hurled the ultimate Mafia insult at Gambino: he spat at him.

If that act seemed foolhardy, it was nevertheless typical of Gallo, who never had the sense to play by the rigid rules of the brotherhood. He grew up with his brothers Larry and Albert in Brooklyn's Bath Beach, where mobsters often dumped their victims. One of his neighbors recalled Joey as "the kind of guy who wanted to grow up to be George Raft. He would stand on the corner when he was 15, flipping a half-dollar, and practice talking without moving his lips."

Joey first witnessed a gang murder in his early teens. After the victim was hauled away, he studied the scene, counted the bullet holes and took notes on how the killing must have been done. He began packing a pistol about the same time. Later, he affected the black shirt and white tie of Killer Richard Widmark in the movie *Kiss of Death.* He saw the movie so many times he knew all its lines. He spent hours in front of a mirror, trying to look as tough as Widmark—and he succeeded. He had a mercurial temper and acted out his movie fantasies as the cruelest of the Gallo brothers.

By the time Joey was 21, he was in trouble with the law, and a court-appointed psychiatrist found him insane. Other mobsters started calling him "Crazy Joe" but never to his face. He was too mean. Joey took pleasure in breaking the arm of one of his clients who was sluggish about paying protection money. He punctured an enemy with ice picks. He had gained his status by serving as one member (Colombo was another) of a five-man execution squad of Mafia Boss Joe Profaci in the late '50s. Police claim they had scored 40 hits. By then he and his brothers had carved out a chunk of the Brooklyn rackets; they turned against Profaci, touching off a gang war in which nine mobsters died and three disappeared.

Over the years, Gallo developed a wise-guy kind of humor that led some naive acquaintances to consider him a sort of folk hero. He was summoned to Robert Kennedy's office in 1959 when Kennedy was counsel to a Senate rackets investigating committee, looked at the rug and said, "Hey, this would be a great spot for a crap game." He once told a courtroom: "The cops say I've been picked up 15, maybe 17 times. That's junk. It was 150 times. I been worked over for nothing until my hat sits on my head like it belongs on a midget." Someone in 1961 overheard him trying to shake down a Brooklyn restaurant owner for a share of the profits. The proprietor asked for time to think about it. "Sure," said Gallo, "take three months in the hospital on me."

That quip cost Gallo nine years for extortion. In Attica state prison, Gallo earned a reputation as a civil rights leader of sorts. He helped lead an inmate drive to force white prison barbers to cut the hair of blacks; he had his own hair cut by a black barber to show his lack of prejudice. Actually, his motive seemed to be to recruit black toughs for his gang. When he got out of prison in March of 1971, he began hiring blacks as "button men" (musclemen)—pricking the ethnic sensibilities of other Mafiosi. He had openly toured Little Italy with four black henchmen a few days before he was hit. Some officials think that may have hastened execution of the contract.

HEARTY HOOD

Gallo's defiance of Mafia tradition did not mark him as particularly savvy. Neither did his open claim that he was about to write his memoirs. Other gangsters do not appreciate such literature. There was, for example, a $100,000 contract—for his death, not his papers—out on Joseph Valachi, who wrote in detail of his life with the Mob (he died of natural causes in prison). But Author Marta Curro, the wife of Actor Jerry Orbach, eagerly agreed to help write the book because she had discovered that Joey was "a great person, brilliant, absolutely charming."

It was at the Orbach apartment that Gallo married Sina Essary, a dental assistant he had met eleven years ago, before he went to jail. He and his first wife Jeffie Lee were divorced a few months ago. Joey and Sina, whose young daughter opened in the Broadway play *Voices* last week, soon became a part of the theatergoing, nightclubbing celebrity set. Crazy Joe, the killer, had become Pal Joey, the hearty hood. That, too, did not go down well with various godfathers.

SCRIPTS

Gallo kept telling his new found friends that he had gone straight. He told Celebrity Columnist Earl Wilson: "I'll never go back there—I think there is nothing out there for me but death." Police insist that Gallo was gulling others; that he actually was as much involved in the rackets as ever.

The truth seems to be that Gallo was leading a schizophrenic life in those last days: a steel-tough gunman in racket circles; a philosophic, warm conversationalist outside the Mob. Whether he was really at home in both roles, or just a good actor, he was clearly convincing. Actress Joan Hackett found him fascinating well before she knew of his Mafia connections. "I liked him completely apart from any grotesque glamorization of the underworld," she recalls. "I thought his attempt to leave that life was genuine. He was the brightest person I've ever known." But Gallo also conceded that "I'll never make it in the straight world."

With the slaying of two other lesser mobsters in New York last week, full gang warfare seemed imminent. The new image of Mafiosi as soft-spoken, smart-dressing businessmen, who shun such crudities as murder and torture as old-fashioned, seemed to be fading. Perhaps the Mob was taking those gory movie scripts about itself too seriously. At any rate, it was exposing the cruelty and ruthlessness of racketeering. Off-screen, murder is brutally final. Indeed, Gallo did not like parts of the *The Godfather*. He told a friend that he thought the death scenes seemed "too flashy."

N. Scott Momaday / A First American Views His Land

National Geographic, July 1976

The National Geographic *magazine was founded in 1888 under the auspices of the National Geographic Society as a professional journal devoted to technical essays on exploration and earth sciences. As the society invested more and more heavily in expeditions that would capture the popular imagination, the editors decided to alter the magazine's contents in the hope of attracting a larger, nonspecialized audience. Over the years, the* National Geographic *has become a popular forum for travel, adventure, anthropology, and geographical research. Its consistently high standard of color photography has been a major factor in the magazine's enormous circulation, now more than nine million.*

N. Scott Momaday's "A First American Views His Land" clearly fulfills the National Geographic*'s announced criteria for publication:*

> *First person narratives, making it easy for the reader to share the author's experience and observations. Writing should include plenty of human-interest incident, authentic direct quotation, and a bit of humor where appropriate. Accuracy is fundamental. Contemporary problems such as those of pollution and ecology are treated on a factual basis. The magazine is especially seeking short American place pieces with a strong regional "people" flavor.*

Born in Lawton, Oklahoma, in 1934, Momaday received his B.A. from the University of New Mexico, his M.A. and Ph.D. from Stanford. A professor of English at the University of Arizona in Tucson, Momaday won the Pulitzer Prize for fiction in 1969 for his novel House of Dawn. *He regularly contributes articles, fiction, and poetry to numerous periodicals and frequently reviews work on American Indian culture. The poem woven into the selection printed below is drawn from his book* The Gourd Dancer *(1976).*

First Man
behold:
the earth
glitters
with leaves;
the sky
glistens
with rain.
Pollen
is borne
on winds
that low
and lean
upon
mountains.
Cedars
blacken
the slopes—
and pines.

One hundred centuries ago. There is a wide, irregular landscape in what is now northern New Mexico. The sun is a dull white disk, low in the south; it is a perfect mystery, a deity whose coming and going are inexorable. The gray sky is curdled, and it bears very close upon the earth. A cold wind runs along the ground, dips and spins, flaking drift from a pond in the bottom of a ravine. Beyond the wind the silence is acute. A man crouches in the ravine, in the darkness there, scarcely visible. He moves not a muscle; only the wind lifts a lock of his hair and lays it back along his neck. He wears skins and carries a spear. These things in particular mark his human intelligence and distinguish him as the lord of the universe. And for him the universe is especially *this* landscape; for him the landscape is an element like the air. The vast, virgin wilderness is by and large his whole context. For him there is no possibility of existence elsewhere.

Directly there is a blowing, a rumble of breath deeper than the wind, above him, where some of the hard clay of the bank is broken off and the clods roll down into the water. At the same time there appears on the skyline the massive head of a long-horned bison, then the hump, then the whole beast, huge and black on the sky, standing to a height of seven feet at the hump, with horns that extend six feet across the shaggy crown. For a moment it is poised there; then it lumbers obliquely down the bank to the pond. Still the man does not move, though the beast is now only a few steps upwind. There is no sign of what is about to happen; the beast meanders; the man is frozen in repose.

Then the scene explodes. In one and the same instant the man springs to his feet and bolts forward, his arm cocked and the spear held high, and the huge animal lunges in panic, bellowing, its whole weight thrown violently into the bank, its hooves churning and chipping earth into the air, its eyes gone wide and wild and white. There is a moment in which its awful, frenzied motion is wasted, and it is mired and helpless in its fear, and the man hurls the spear with his whole strength, and the point is driven into the deep, vital flesh, and the bison in its agony staggers and crashes down and dies.

This ancient drama of the hunt is enacted again and again in the landscape. The man is preeminently a predator, the most dangerous of all. He hunts in order to survive; his very existence is simply, squarely established upon that basis. But he hunts also because he can, because he has the means; he has the ultimate weapon of his age, and his prey is plentiful. His relationship to the land has not yet become a moral equation.

But in time he will come to understand that there is an intimate, vital link between the earth and himself, a link that implies an intricate network of rights and responsibilities. In some unimagined future he will understand that he has the ability to devastate and perhaps destroy his environment. That moment will be one of extreme crisis in his evolution.

The weapon is deadly and efficient. The hunter has taken great care in its manufacture, especially in the shaping of the flint point, which is an extraordinary thing. A larger flake has been removed from each face, a groove that extends from the base nearly to the tip. Several hundred pounds of pressure, expertly applied, were required to make these grooves. The hunter then is an artisan, and he must know how to use rudimentary tools. His skill, manifest in the manufacture of this artifact, is unsurpassed for its time and purpose. By means of this weapon is the Paleo-Indian hunter eminently able to exploit his environment.

Thousands of years later, about the time that Columbus begins his first voyage to the New World, another man, in the region of the Great Lakes, stands in the forest shade on the edge of a sunlit brake. In a while a deer enters into the pool of light. Silently the man fits an arrow to a bow, draws aim, and shoots. The arrow zips across the distance and strikes home. The deer leaps and falls dead.

But this latter-day man, unlike his ancient predecessor, is only incidentally a hunter; he is also a fisherman, a husbandman, even a physician. He fells trees and builds canoes; he grows corn, squash, and beans, and he gathers fruits and nuts; he uses hundreds of species of wild plants for food, medicine, teas, and dyes. Instead of one animal, or two or three, he hunts many, none to extinction as the Paleo-Indian may have done. He has fitted himself far more precisely into the patterns of the wilderness than did his ancient predecessor. He lives on the land; he takes his living from it; but he does not destroy it. This distinction supports the fundamental ethic that we call conservation today. In principle, if not yet in name, this man is a conservationist.

These two hunting sketches are far less important in themselves than is that long distance between them, that whole possibility within the dimension of time. I believe that in that interim there grew up in the mind of man an idea of the land as sacred.

At dawn
eagles
lie and
hover
above
the plain
where light
gathers
in pools.
Grasses
shimmer
and shine.

Shadows
withdraw
and lie
away
like smoke.

"The earth is our mother. The sky is our father." This concept of nature, which is at the center of the Native American world view, is familiar to us all. But it may well be that we do not understand entirely what that concept is in its ethical and philosophical implications.

I tell my students that the American Indian has a unique investment in the American landscape. It is an investment that represents perhaps thirty thousand years of habitation. That tenure has to be worth something in itself—a great deal, in fact. The Indian has been here a long time; he is at home here. That simple and obvious truth is one of the most important realities of the Indian world, and it is integral in the Indian mind and spirit.

How does such a concept evolve? Where does it begin? Perhaps it begins with the recognition of beauty, the realization that the physical world *is* beautiful. We don't know much about the ancient hunter's sensibilities. It isn't likely that he had leisure in his life for the elaboration of an aesthetic ideal. And yet the weapon he made was beautiful as well as functional. It has been suggested that much of the minute chipping along the edges of his weapon served no purpose but that of aesthetic satisfaction.

A good deal more is known concerning that man of the central forests. He made beautiful boxes and dishes out of elm and birch bark, for example. His canoes were marvelous, delicate works of art. And this aesthetic perception was a principle of the whole Indian world of his time, as indeed it is of our time. The contemporary Native American is a man whose strong aesthetic perceptions are clearly evident in his arts and crafts, in his religious ceremonies, and in the stories and songs of his rich oral tradition. This, in view of the pressures that have been brought to bear upon the Indian world and the drastic changes that have been effected in its landscape, is a blessing and an irony.

Consider for example the Navajos of the Four Corners area. In recent years an extensive coal-mining operation has mutilated some of their most sacred land. A large power plant in that same region spews a contamination into the sky that is visible for many miles. And yet, as much as any people of whom I have heard, the Navajos perceive and celebrate the beauty of the physical world.

There is a Navajo ceremonial song that celebrates the sounds that are made in the natural world, the particular voices that beautify the earth:

Voice above,
Voice of thunder,
Speak from the
dark of clouds;
Voice below,
Grasshopper voice,
Speak from the
green of plants;
So may the earth
be beautiful.

There is in the motion and meaning of this song a comprehension of the world that is peculiarly native, I believe, that is integral in the Native American mentality. Consider: The singer stands at the center of the natural world, at the source of its sound, of its motion, of its life. Nothing of that world is inaccessible to him or lost upon him. His song is filled with reverence, with wonder and delight, and with confidence as well. He knows something about himself and about the things around him—and he knows that he knows. I am interested in what he sees and hears; I am interested in the range and force of his perception. Our immediate impression may be that his perception is narrow and deep—vertical. After all, "voice above . . . voice below," he sings. But is it vertical only? At each level of his expression there is an extension of his awareness across the whole landscape. The voice above is the voice of thunder, and thunder rolls. Moreover, it issues from the impalpable dark clouds and runs upon their horizontal range. It is a sound that integrates the whole of the atmosphere. And even so, the voice below, that of the grasshopper, issues from the broad plain and multiplicity of plants. And of course the singer is mindful of much more than thunder and insects; we are given in his song the wide angle of his vision and his hearing—and we are given the testimony of his dignity, his trust, and his deep belief.

This comprehension of the earth and air is surely a matter of morality, for it brings into account not only man's instinctive reaction to his environment but the full realization of his humanity as well, the achievement of his intellectual and spiritual development as an individual and as a race.

In my own experience I have seen numerous examples of this regard for nature. My grandfather Mammedaty was a farmer in his mature years; his grandfather was a buffalo hunter. It was not easy for Mammedaty to be a farmer; he was a Kiowa, and the Kiowas never had an agrarian tradition. Yet he had to make his living, and the old, beloved life of roaming the plains and hunting the buffalo was gone forever. Even so, as much as any man before him, he fitted his mind and will and spirit to the land; there was nothing else. He could not have conceived of living apart from the land.

In *The Way to Rainy Mountain* I set down a small narrative that belongs in the oral tradition of my family. It indicates something essential about the Native American attitude toward the land:

"East of my grandmother's house, south of the pecan grove, there is buried a woman in a beautiful dress. Mammedaty used to know where she is buried, but now no one knows. If you stand on the front porch of the house and look eastward towards Carnegie, you know that the woman is buried somewhere within the range of your vision. But her grave is unmarked. She was buried in a cabinet, and she wore a beautiful dress. How beautiful it was! It was one of those fine buckskin dresses, and it was decorated with elk's teeth and beadwork. That dress is still there, under the ground."

It seems to me that this statement is primarily a declaration of love for the land, in which the several elements—the woman, the dress, and this plain—are at last become one reality, one expression of the beautiful in nature. Moreover, it seems to me a peculiarly Native American expression in this sense: that the concentration of things that are explicitly remembered—the general landscape, the simple, almost abstract nature of the burial, above all the beautiful dress, which is wholly singular in kind (as well as in its function within the narrative)—is especially Indian in character. The things that are *not* explicitly remembered—the woman's name, the exact location of her grave—are the things that matter least in the special view of the storyteller. What matters here is the translation of the woman into the landscape, a translation particularly signified by means of the beautiful and distinctive dress, an *Indian* dress.

When I was a boy, I lived for several years at Jemez Pueblo, New Mexico. The Pueblo Indians are perhaps more obviously invested in the land than are other people. Their whole life is predicated upon a thorough perception of the physical world and its myriad aspects. When I first went there to live, the cacique, or chief, of the Pueblos was a venerable old man with long, gray hair and bright, deep-set eyes. He was entirely dignified and imposing—and rather formidable in the eyes of a boy. He excited my imagination a good deal. I was told that this old man kept the calendar of the tribe, that each morning he stood on a certain spot of ground near the center of the town and watched to see where the sun appeared on the skyline. By means of this solar calendar did he know and announce to his people when it was time to plant, to harvest, to perform this or that ceremony. This image of him in my mind's eye—the old man gazing each morning after the ranging sun—came to represent for me the epitome of that real harmony between man and the land that signifies the Indian world.

One day when I was riding my horse along the Jemez River, I looked up to see a long caravan of wagons and people on horseback and on foot. Men, women, and children were crossing the river ahead of me, moving out to the west, where most of the cultivated fields were, the farmland of the town. It was a wonderful sight to see, this long procession, and I was immediately deeply curious. I wanted to investigate, but it was not in me to do so at once, for that racial reserve, that sense of propriety that is deep-seated in Native American culture, stayed me, held me up. Then I saw someone coming toward me on horseback, galloping. It was a friend of mine, a boy of my own age. "Come on," he said. "Come with us." "Where are you going?" I asked casually. But he would not tell me. He simply laughed and urged me to come along, and of course I was very glad to do so. It was a bright spring morning, and I had a good horse under me, and the prospect of adventure was delicious. We moved far out across the eroded plain to the farthest fields at the foot of a great red mesa, and there we planted two large fields of corn. And afterward, on the edge of the fields, we sat on blankets and ate a feast in the shade of a cottonwood grove. Later I learned it was the cacique's fields we planted. And this is an ancient tradition at Jemez. The people of the town plant and tend and harvest the cacique's fields, and in the winter the hunters give to him a portion of the meat that they bring home from the mountains. It is as if the cacique is himself the translation of man, every man, into the landscape.

I have not forgotten that day, nor shall I forget it. I remember the warm earth of the fields, the smooth texture of seeds in my hands, and the brown water moving slowly and irresistibly among the rows. Above all I remember the spirit in which the procession was made, the work was done, and the feasting was enjoyed. It was a spirit of communion, of the life of each man in relation to the life of the planet and of the infinite distance and silence in which it moves. We made, in concert, an appropriate expression of that spirit.

One afternoon an old Kiowa woman talked to me, telling me of the place in Oklahoma in which she had lived for a hundred years. It was the place in which my grandparents, too, lived; and it is the place where I was born. And she told me of a time even further back, when the Kiowas came down from the north and centered their culture in the red earth of the southern plains. She told wonderful stories, and as I listened, I began to feel more and more sure that her voice proceeded from the land itself. I asked her many things concerning the Kiowas, for I wanted to understand all that I could of my heritage. I told the old woman that I had come there to learn from her and from people like her, those in whom the old ways were preserved. And she said simply: "It is good that you have come here." I believe that her word "good" meant many things; for one thing it meant *right,* or *appropriate.* And indeed it was appropriate that she should speak of the land. She was eminently qualified to do so. She had a great reverence for the land, and an ancient perception of it, a perception that it acquired only in the course of many generations.

It is this notion of the appropriate, along with that of the beautiful, that forms the Native American perspective on the land. In a sense these considerations are indivisible; Native American oral tradition is rich with songs and tales that celebrate natural beauty, the beauty of the natural world. What is more appropriate to our world than that which is beautiful:

At noon
turtles
enter
slowly
into
the warm
dark loam.
Bees hold
the swarm.
Meadows
recede
through planes
of heat
and pure
distance.

Very old in the Native American world view is the conviction that the earth is vital, that there is a spiritual dimension to it, a dimension in which man rightly exists. It follows logically that there are ethical imperatives in this matter. I think: Inasmuch as I am in the land, it is appropriate that I should affirm myself in the spirit of the land. I shall celebrate my life in the world and the world in my life. In the natural order man invests himself in the landscape and at the same time incorporates the landscape into his own most fundamental experience. This trust is sacred.

The process of investment and appropriation is, I believe, preeminently a function of the imagination. It is accomplished by means of an act of the imagination that is especially ethical in kind. We are what we imagine ourselves to be. The Native American is someone who thinks of himself, imagines himself in a particular way. By virtue of his experience his idea of himself comprehends his relationship to the land.

And the quality of this imagining is determined as well by racial and cultural experience. The Native American's attitudes toward this landscape have been formulated over a long period of time, a span that reaches back to the end of the Ice Age. The land, *this* land, is secure in his racial memory.

In our society as a whole we conceive of the land in terms of ownership and use. It is a lifeless medium of exchange; it has for most of us, I suspect, no more spirituality than has an automobile, say, or a refrigerator. And our laws confirm us in this view, for we can buy and sell the land, we can exclude each other from it, and in the context of ownership we can use it as we will. Ownership implies use, and use implies consumption.

But this way of thinking of the land is alien to the Indian. His cultural intelligence is opposed to these concepts; indeed, for him they are all but inconceivable quantities. This fundamental distinction is easier to understand with respect to ownership than to use, perhaps. For obviously the Indian does use, and has always used, the land and the available resources in it. The point is that *use* does not indicate in any real way his idea of the land. "Use" is neither his word nor his idea. As an Indian I think: "You say that I *use* the land, and I reply, yes, it is true; but it is not the first truth. The first truth is that I *love* the land; I see that it is beautiful; I delight in it; I am alive in it."

In the long course of his journey from Asia and in the realization of himself in the New World, the Indian has assumed a deep ethical regard for the earth and sky, a reverence for the natural world that is antipodal to that strange tenet of modern civilization that seemingly has it that man must destroy his environnment. It is this ancient ethic of the Native American that must shape our efforts to preserve the earth and the life upon and within it.

At dusk
the gray
foxes
stiffen
in cold;
blackbirds
are fixed
in white
branches.
Rivers
follow
the moon,
the long
white track
of the
full moon.

Toni Morrison / Cinderella's Stepsisters *Ms.*, September 1979

Born in Lorain, Ohio, in 1931, Toni Morrison has emerged over the past decade as one of the most admired and accomplished voices in black American literature. After receiving a master's degree in English from Cornell University in 1955, Morrison taught for a number of years until she was hired as a senior editor at Random House in 1968. Since then, she has also taught classes in black literature and techniques of fiction at Yale and Bard colleges, although writing remains her primary occupation. Her novels include The Bluest Eye *(1970),* Sula *(1973)* Song of Solomon *(1977), which won that year's National Book Award,* Tar Baby *(1981),* Beloved *(1987), and* Jazz *(1992).*

Instead of dealing with the conflict between races, Morrison's work focuses on the difficulties among people from various backgrounds within the black community. Combining elements of harsh reality with images and fairy tales, her novels show how men and women attempt to hold on to love, beauty, and a belief in miracles in a world "where we are all of us, in some measure victims of something." In the following article, adapted from a speech delivered at Barnard College, Morrison uses the Cinderella story as a metaphor for exhorting her fellow sisters to a greater vigilance on each other's behalf.

Ms. *was founded in 1972 as a monthly magazine featuring articles on politics and contemporary social developments, particularly those that most directly affect the women's movement.*

Let me begin by taking you back a little. Back before the days at college. To nursery school, probably, to a once-upon-a-time time when you first heard, or read, or, I suspect, even saw "Cinderella." Because it is Cinderella that I want to talk about; because it is Cinderella who causes me a feeling of urgency. What is unsettling about that fairy tale is that it is essentially the story of household—a world, if you please—of women gathered together and held together in order to abuse another woman. There is, of course, a rather vague absent father and a nick-of-time prince with a foot fetish. But neither has much personality. And there are the surrogate "mothers," of course (god- and step-), who contribute both to Cinderella's grief and to her release and happiness. But it is her stepsisters who interest me. How crippling it must have been for those young girls to grow up with a mother, to watch and imitate that mother, enslaving another girl.

I am curious about their fortunes after the story ends. For contrary to recent adaptations, the stepsisters were not ugly, clumsy, stupid girls with outsize feet. The Grimm collection describes them as "beautiful and fair in appearance." When we are introduced to them they are beautiful, elegant, women of status, and clearly women of power. Having watched and participated in the violent dominion of another woman, will they be any less cruel when it comes their turn to enslave other children, or even when they are required to take care of their own mother?

It is not a wholly medieval problem. It is quite a contemporary one: feminine power when directed at other women has historically been wielded in what has been described as a "masculine" manner. Soon you will be in a position to do the very same thing. Whatever your background—rich or poor—whatever the history of education in your family—five generations or one—you have taken advantage of what has been available to you at Barnard and you will therefore have both the economic and social status of the stepsisters *and* you will have their power.

I want not to *ask* you but to *tell* you not to participate in the oppression of your sisters. Mothers who abuse their children are women, and another woman, not an agency, has to be willing to stay their hands. Mothers who set fire to school buses are women, and another woman, not an agency, has to tell them to stay their hands. Women who stop the promotion of other women in careers are women, and another woman must come to the victim's aid. Social and welfare workers who humiliate their clients may be women, and other women colleagues have to deflect their anger.

I am alarmed by the violence that women do to each other: professional violence, competitive violence, emotional violence. I am alarmed by the willingness of women to enslave other women. I am alarmed by a growing absence of decency on the killing floor of professional women's worlds. You are the women who will take your place in the world where *you* can decide who shall flourish and who shall wither; you will make distinctions between the deserving poor and the undeserving poor; where you can yourself determine which life is expendable and which is indispensable. Since you will have the power to do it, you may also be persuaded that you have the right to do it. As educated women the distinction between the two is first-order business.

I am suggesting that we pay as much attention to our nurturing sensibilities as to our ambition. You are moving in the direction of freedom and the function of freedom is to free somebody else. You are moving toward self-fulfillment, and the consequences of that fulfillment should be to discover that there is something just as important as you are and that just-as-important thing may be Cinderella—or your stepsister.

In your rainbow journey toward the realization of personal goals, don't make choices based only on your security and your safety. Nothing is safe. That is not to say that anything ever was, or that anything worth achieving ever should be. Things of value seldom are. It is not safe to have a child. It is not safe to challenge the status quo. It is not safe to choose work that has not been done before. Or to do old work in a new way. There will always be someone there to stop you. But in pursuing your highest ambitions, don't let your personal safety diminish the safety of your stepsister. In wielding the power that is deservedly yours, don't permit it to enslave your stepsisters. Let your might and your power emanate from that place in you that is nurturing and caring.

Women's rights is not only an abstraction, a cause; it is also a personal affair. It is not only about "us"; it is also about me and you. Just the two of us.

Gretel Ehrlich / The Solace of Open Spaces

Atlantic, May 1981

One of the most prevalent topics of contemporary nonfiction is outdoor life—essays and articles on natural history, the wilderness, the environment, ranching and farming, camping, and travel. The writers who work best with this theme, such as Annie Dillard, Barry Lopez, Edward Hoagland, Edward Abbey, and Gretel Ehrlich, are writers who have learned to see nature in both its ordinary details and its breathtaking surprises. They are also writers who have masterfully combined two kinds of composition: the subjectively personal and the objectively descriptive.

Gretel Ehrlich's essays have appeared in Harper's, Atlantic, Time, *the* New York Times, New Age Journal, *and* Antaeus. *She is the author of* Wyoming Stories, The Solace of Open Spaces, Heart Mountain, *and* Islands, the Universe, Home. *She lives on a ranch in Shell, Wyoming.*

The Atlantic *is one of the oldest literary magazines in the country. Established in 1857, it regularly publishes fiction, poetry, and essays as well as serious articles devoted to education, science, politics, the arts, and general culture.*

It's May and I've just awakened from a nap, curled against sagebrush the way my dog taught me to sleep—sheltered from wind. A front is pulling the huge sky over me, and from the dark a hailstone has hit me on the head. I'm trailing a band of two thousand sheep across a stretch of Wyoming badlands, a fifty-mile trip that takes five days because sheep shade up in hot sun and won't budge until it's cool. Bunched together now, and excited into a run by the storm, they drift across dry land, tumbling into draws like water and surge out again onto the rugged, choppy plateaus that are the building blocks of this state.

The name Wyoming comes from an Indian word meaning "at the great plains," but the plains are really valleys, great arid valleys, sixteen hundred square miles, with the horizon bending up on all sides into mountain ranges. This gives the vastness a sheltering look.

Winter lasts six months here. Prevailing winds spill snowdrifts to the east, and new storms from the northwest replenish them. This white bulk is sometimes dizzying, even nauseating, to look at. At twenty, thirty, and forty degrees below zero, not only does your car not work, but neither do your mind and body. The landscape hardens into a dungeon of space. During the winter, while I was riding to find a new calf, my jeans froze to the saddle, and in the silence that such cold creates I felt like the first person on earth, or the last.

Today the sun is out—only a few clouds billowing. In the east, where the sheep have started off without me, the benchland tilts up in a series of eroded red-earthed mesas, planed flat on top by a million years of water; behind them, a bold line of muscular scarps rears up ten thousand feet to become the Big Horn Mountains. A tidal pattern is engraved into the ground, as if left by the sea that once covered this state. Canyons curve down like galaxies to meet the oncoming rush of flat land.

To live and work in this kind of open country, with its hundred-mile views, is to lose the distinction between background and foreground. When I asked an older ranch hand to describe Wyoming's openness, he said, "It's all a bunch of nothing—wind and rattlesnakes—and so much of it you can't tell where you're going or where you've been and it don't make much difference." John, a sheepman I know, is tall and handsome and has an explosive temperament. He had a perfect intuition about people and sheep. They call him "Highpockets," because he's so long-legged; his graceful stride matches the distances he has to cover. He says, "Open space hasn't affected me at all. It's all the people moving in on it." The huge ranch he was born on takes up much of one county and spreads into another state; to put 100,000 miles on his pickup in three years and never leave home is not unusual. A friend of mine has an aunt who ranched on Powder River and didn't go off her place for eleven years. When her husband died, she quickly moved to town, bought a car, and drove around the States to see what she'd been missing.

Most people tell me they've simply driven through Wyoming, as if there were nothing to stop for. Or else they've skied in Jackson Hole, a place Wyomingites acknowledge uncomfortably because its green beauty and chic affluence are mismatched with the rest of the state. Most of Wyoming has a "lean-to" look. Instead of big, roomy barns and Victorian houses, there are dugouts, low sheds, log cabins, sheep camps, and fence lines that look like driftwood blown haphazardly into place. People here still feel pride because they live in such a harsh place, part of the glamorous cowboy past, and they are determined not to be the victims of a mining-dominated future.

Most characteristic of the state's landscape is what a developer euphemistically describes as "indigenous growth right up to your front door"—a reference to waterless stands of salt sage, snakes, jack rabbits, deerflies, red dust, a brief respite of wildflowers, dry washes, and no trees. In the Great Plains the vistas look like music, like Kyries of grass, but Wyoming seems to be the doing of a mad architect—tumbled and twisted, ribboned with faded, deathbed colors, thrust up and pulled down as if the place had been startled out of a deep sleep and thrown into a pure light.

I came here four years ago. I had not planned to stay, but I couldn't make myself leave. John, the sheepman, put me to work immediately. It was spring, and shearing time. For fourteen days of fourteen hours each, we moved thousands of sheep through sorting corrals to be sheared, branded, and deloused. I suspect that my original motive for coming here was to "lose myself" in new and unpopulated territory. Instead of producing the numbness I thought I wanted, life on the sheep ranch woke me up. The vitality of the people I was working with flushed out what had become a hallucinatory rawness inside me. I threw away my clothes and bought new ones; I cut my hair. The arid country was a clean slate. Its absolute indifference steadied me.

Sagebrush covers 58,000 square miles of Wyoming. The biggest city has a population of fifty thousand, and there are only five settlements that could be called cities in the whole state. The rest are towns, scattered across the expanse with as much as sixty miles between them, their populations two thousand, fifty, or ten. They are fugitive-looking, perched on a barren, windblown bench, or tagged onto a river or a railroad, or laid out straight in a farming valley with implement stores and a block-long Mormon church. In the eastern part of the state, which slides down into the Great Plains, the new mining settlements are boomtowns, trailer cities, metal knots on flat land.

Despite the desolate look, there's a coziness to living in this state. There are so few people (only 470,000) that ranchers who buy and sell cattle know one another statewide; the kids who choose to go to college usually go to the state's one university, in Laramie; hired hands work their way around Wyoming in a lifetime of hirings and firings. And despite the physical separation, people stay in touch, often driving two or three hours to another ranch for dinner.

Seventy-five years ago, when travel was by buckboard or horseback, cowboys who were temporarily out of work rode the grub line—drifting from ranch to ranch, mending fences or milking cows, and receiving in exchange a bed and meals. Gossip and messages traveled this slow circuit with them, creating an intimacy between ranchers who were three and four weeks' ride apart. One old-time couple I know, whose turn-of-the-century homestead was used by an outlaw gang as a relay station for stolen horses, recall that if you were traveling, desperado or not, any lighted ranch house was a welcome sign. Even now, for someone who lives in a remote spot, arriving at a ranch or coming to town for supplies is cause for celebration. To emerge from isolation can be disorienting. Everything looks bright, new, vivid. After I had been herding sheep for only three days, the sound of the camp tender's pickup flustered me. Longing for human company, I felt a foolish grin take over my face; yet I had to resist an urgent temptation to run and hide.

Things happen suddenly in Wyoming, the change of seasons and weather; for people, the violent swings in and out of isolation. But good-naturedness is concomitant with severity. Friendliness is a tradition. Strangers passing on the road wave hello. A common sight is two pickups stopped side by side far out on a range, on a dirt track winding through the sage. The drivers will share a cigarette, uncap their thermos bottles, and pass a battered cup, steaming with coffee, between windows. These meetings summon up the details of several generations, because, in Wyoming, private histories are largely public knowledge.

Because ranch work is a physical and, these days, economic strain, being "at home on the range" is a matter of vigor, self-reliance, and common sense. A person's life is not a series of dramatic events for which he or she is applauded or exiled but a slow accumulation of days, seasons, years, fleshed out by the generational weight of one's family and anchored by a land-bound sense of place.

In most parts of Wyoming, the human population is visibly outnumbered by the animal. Not far from my town of fifty, I rode into a narrow valley and startled a herd of two hundred elk. Eagles look like small people as they eat car-killed deer by the road. Antelope, moving in small, graceful bands, travel at sixty miles an hour, their mouths open as if drinking in the space.

The solitude in which westerners live makes them quiet. They telegraph thoughts and feelings by the way they tilt their heads and listen; pulling their Stetsons into a steep dive over their eyes, or pigeon-toeing one boot over the other, they lean against a fence with a fat wedge of Copenhagen beneath their lower lips and take in the whole scene. These detached looks of quiet amusement are sometimes cynical, but they can also come from a dry-eyed humility as lucid as the air is clear.

Conversation goes on in what sounds like a private code; a few phrases imply a complex of meanings. Asking directions, you get a curious list of details. While trailing sheep I was told to "ride up that that kinda upturned rock, follow the pink wash, turn left at the dump, and then you'll see the water hole." One friend told his wife on roundup to "turn at the salt lick and the dead cow," which turned out to be a scattering of bones and no salt lick at all.

Sentence structure is shortened to the skin and bones of a thought. Descriptive words are dropped, even verbs; a cowboy looking over a corral full of horses will say to a wrangler, "Which one needs rode?" People hold back their thoughts in what seems to be a dumbfounded silence, then erupt with an excoriating, perceptive remark. Language, so compressed, becomes metaphorical. A rancher ended a relationship with one remark: "You're a bad check," meaning bouncing in and out was intolerable, and even coming back would be no good.

What's behind this laconic style is shyness. There is no vocabulary for the subject of feelings. It's not a hangdog shyness, or anything coy—always there's a robust spirit in evidence behind the restraint, as if the earth-dredging wind that pulls across Wyoming had carried its people's voices away but everything else in them had shouldered confidently into the breeze.

I've spent hours riding to sheep camp at dawn in a pickup when nothing was said; eaten meals in the cookhouse when the only words spoken were a mumbled "Thank you, ma'am" at the end of dinner. The silence is profound. Instead of talking, we seem to share one eye. Keenly observed, the world is transformed. The landscape is engorged with detail, every movement on it chillingly sharp. The air between people is charged. Days unfold, bathed in their own music. Nights become hallucinatory; dreams, prescient.

Spring weather is capricious and mean. It snows, then blisters with heat. There have been tornadoes. They lay their elephant trunks out in the sage until they find houses, then slurp everything up and leave. I've noticed that melting snowbanks hiss and rot, viperous, then drip into calm pools where ducklings hatch and livestock, being trailed to summer range, drink. With the ice cover gone, rivers churn a milkshake brown, taking culverts and small bridges with them. Water in such an arid place (the average annual rainfall where I live is less than eight inches) is like blood. It festoons drab land with green veins; a line of cottonwoods following a stream; a strip of alfalfa; and, on ditch banks, wild asparagus growing.

I've moved to a small cattle ranch owned by friends. It's at the foot of the Big Horn Mountains. A few weeks ago, I helped them deliver a calf who was stuck halfway out of his mother's body. By the time he was freed, we could see a heartbeat, but he was straining against a swollen tongue for air. Mary and I held him upside down by his back feet, while Stan, on his hands and knees in the blood, gave the calf mouth-to-mouth resuscitation. I have a vague memory of being pneumonia-choked as a child, my mother giving me her air, which may account for my romance with this wind-swept state.

If anything is endemic to Wyoming, it is wind. This big room of space is swept out daily, leaving a bone yard of fossils, agates, and carcasses in every stage of decay. Though it was water that initially shaped the state, wind is the meticulous gardener, raising dust and pruning the sage.

I try to imagine a world in which I could ride my horse across uncharted land. There is no wilderness left; wildness, yes, but true wilderness has been gone on this continent since the time of Lewis and Clark's overland journey.

Two hundred years ago, the Crow, Shoshone, Arapaho, Cheyenne, and Sioux roamed the intermountain West, orchestrating their movements according to hunger, season, and warfare. Once they acquired horses, they traversed the spines of all the big Wyoming ranges—the Absarokas, the Wind Rivers, the Tetons, the Big Horns—and wintered on the unprotected plains that fan out from them. Space was life. The world was their home.

What was life-giving to Native Americans was often nightmarish to sodbusters who had arrived encumbered with families and ethnic pasts to be transplanted in nearly uninhabitable land. The great distances, the shortage of water and trees, and the loneliness created unexpected hardships for them. In her book *O Pioneers!,* Willa Cather gives a settler's version of the bleak landscape:

> The little town behind them had vanished as if it had never been, had fallen behind the swell of the prairie, and the stern frozen country received them into its bosom. The homesteads were few and far apart; here and there a windmill gaunt against the sky, a sod house crouching in a hollow.

The emptiness of the West was for others a geography of possibility. Men and women who amassed great chunks of land and struggled to preserve unfenced empires were, despite their self-serving motives, unwitting geographers. They understood the lay of the land. But by the 1850s the Oregon and Mormon trials sported bumper-to-bumper traffic. Wealthy landowners, many of them aristocratic absentee landlords, known as remittance men because they were paid to come West and get out of their families' hair, overstocked the range with more than a million head of cattle. By 1885 the feed and water were desperately short, and the winter of 1886 laid out the gaunt bodies of dead animals so closely together that when the thaw came, one rancher from Kaycee claimed to have walked on cowhide all the way to Crazy Woman Creek, twenty miles away.

Territorial Wyoming was a boy's world. The land was generous with everything but water. At first there was room enough, food enough, for everyone. And, as with all beginnings, an expansive mood set in. The young cowboys, drifters, shopkeepers, schoolteachers, were heroic, lawless, generous, rowdy, and tenacious. The individualism and optimism generated during those times have endured.

John Tisdale rode north with the trail herds from Texas. He was a college-educated man with enough money to buy a small outfit near the Powder River. While driving home from the town of Buffalo with a buckboard full of Christmas toys for his family and a winter's supply of food, he was shot in the back by an agent of the cattle barons who resented the encroachment of small-time stockmen like him. The wealthy cattlemen tried to control all the public grazing land by restricting membership in the Wyoming Stock Growers Association, as if it were a country club. They ostracized from roundups and brandings cowboys and ranchers who were not members, then denounced them as rustlers. Tisdale's death, the second such cold-blooded murder, kicked off the Johnson County cattle war, which was no simple good-guy-bad-guy shoot-out but a complicated class struggle between landed gentry and less affluent settlers—a shocking reminder that the West was not an egalitarian sanctuary after all.

Fencing ultimately enforced boundaries, but barbed wire abrogated space. It was stretched across the beautiful valleys, into the mountains, over desert badlands, through buffalo grass. The "anything is possible" fever—the lure of any new place—was constricted. The integrity of the land as a geographical body, and the freedom to ride anywhere on it, were lost.

I punched cows with a young man named Martin, who is the great-grandson of John Tisdale. His inheritance is not the open land that Tisdale knew and prematurely lost but a rage against restraint.

Wyoming tips down as you head northeast; the highest ground—the Laramie Plains—is on the Colorado border. Up where I live, the Big Horn River leaks into difficult, arid terrain. In the basin where it's dammed, sandhill cranes gather and, with delicate legwork, slice through the stilled water. I was driving by with a rancher one morning when he commented that cranes are "old-fashioned." When I asked why, he said, "Because they mate for life." Then he looked at me with a twinkle in his eyes, as if to say he really did believe in such things but also understood why we break our own rules.

In all this open space, values crystalize quickly. People are strong on scruples but tenderhearted about quirky behavior. A friend and I found one ranch hand, who's "not quite right in the head," sitting in front of the badly decayed carcass of a cow, shaking his finger and saying, "Now, I don't want you to do this ever again!" when I asked what was wrong with him, I was told, "He's goofier than hell, just like the rest of us." Perhaps because the West is historically new, conventional morality is still felt to be less important than rock-bottom truths. Though there's always a lot of teasing and sparring, people are blunt with one another, sometimes even cruel, believing honesty is stronger medicine than sympathy, which may console but often conceals.

The formality that goes hand in hand with the rowdiness is known as the Western Code. It's a list of practical do's and don'ts, faithfully observed. A friend, Cliff, who runs a trap-line in the winter, cut off half his foot while chopping a hole in the ice. Alone, he dragged himself to his pickup and headed for town, stopping to open the ranch gate as he left, and getting out to close it again, thus losing, in his observance of rules, precious time and blood. Later, he commented, "How would it look, them having to come to the hospital to tell me their cows had gotten out?"

Accustomed to emergencies, my friends doctor each other from the vet's bag with relish. When one old-timer suffered a heart attack in hunting camp, his partner quickly stirred up a brew of red horse liniment and hot water and made the half-conscious victim drink it, then tied him onto a horse and led him twenty miles to town. He regained consciousness and lived.

The roominess of the state has affected political attitudes as well. Ranchers keep up with world politics and the convulsions of the economy but are basically isolationists. Being used to running their own small empires of land and livestock, they're suspicious of big government. It's a "don't fence me in" holdover from a century ago. They still want the elbow room their grandfathers had, so they're strongly conservative, but with a populist twist.

Summer is the season when we get our "cowboy tans"—on the lower parts of our faces and on three fourths of our arms. Excessive heat, in the nineties and higher, sends us outside with the mosquitoes. In winter we're tucked inside our houses, and the white wasteland outside appears to be expanding, but in summer all the greenery abridges space. Summer is a go-ahead season. Every living thing is off the block and in the race: battalions of bugs in flight and biting; bats swinging around my log cabin as if the bases were loaded and someone had hit a home run. Some of summer's high-speed growth is ominous: larkspur, death camas, and green greasewood can kill sheep—an ironic idea, dying in this desert from eating what is too verdant. With sixteen hours of daylight, farmers and ranchers irrigate feverishly. There are first, second, and third cuttings of hay, some crews averaging only four hours of sleep a night for weeks. And, like the cowboys who in summer ride the night rodeo circuit, night-hawks make daredevil dives at dusk with an eerie whirring sound like a plane going down on the shimmering horizon.

In the town where I live, they've had to board up the dance-hall windows because there have been so many fights. There's so little to do except work that people wind up in a state of idle agitation that becomes fatalistic, as if there were nothing to be done about all this untapped energy. So the dark side to the grandeur of these spaces is the small-mindedness that seals people in. Men become hermits; women go mad. Cabin fever explodes into suicides, or into grudges and lifelong family feuds. Two sisters in my area inherited a ranch but found they couldn't get along. They fenced the place in half. When one's cows got up and mixed with the other's, the women went at each other with shovels. They ended up in the same hospital room but never spoke a word to each other for the rest of their lives.

After the brief lushness of summer, the sun moves south. The range grass is brown. Livestock is trailed back down from the mountains. Water holes begin to frost over at night. Last fall Martin asked me to accompany him on a pack trip. With five horses, we followed a river into the mountains behind the tiny Wyoming town of Meeteetse. Groves of aspen, red and orange, gave off a light that made us look toasted. Our hunting camp was so high that clouds skidded across our foreheads, then slowed to sail out across the warm valleys. Except for a bull moose who wandered into our camp and mistook our black gelding for a rival, we shot at nothing.

One of our evening entertainments was to watch the night sky. My dog, a dingo bred to herd sheep, also came on the trip. He is so used to the silence and empty skies that when an airplane flies over he always looks up and eyes the distant intruder quizzically. The sky, lately, seems to be much more crowded than it used to be. Satellites make their silent passes in the dark with great regularity. We counted eighteen in one hour's viewing. How odd to think that while they circumnavigated the planet, Martin and I had moved only six miles into our local wilderness and had seen no other human for the two weeks we stayed there.

At night, by moonlight, the land is whittled to slivers—a ridge, a river, a strip of grassland stretching to the mountains, then the huge sky. One morning a full moon was setting in the west just as the sun was rising. I felt precariously balanced between the two as I loped across a meadow. For a moment, I could believe that the stars, which were still visible, work like cooper's bands, holding together everything above Wyoming.

Space has a spiritual equivalent and can heal what is divided and burdensome in us. My grandchildren will probably use space shuttles for a honeymoon trip or to recover from heart attacks, but closer to home we might also learn how to carry space inside ourselves in the effortless way we carry our skins. Space represents sanity, not a life purified, dull, or "spaced out" but one that might accommodate intelligently any idea or situation.

From the clayey soil of northern Wyoming is mined bentonite, which is used as a filler in candy, gum, and lipstick. We Americans are great on fillers, as if what we have, what we are, is not enough. We have a cultural tendency toward denial, but, being affluent, we strangle ourselves with what we can buy. We have only to look at the houses we build to see how we build *against* space, the way we drink against pain and loneliness. We fill up space as if it were a pie shell, with things whose opacity further obstructs our ability to see what is already there.

DISCUSSION QUESTIONS

1. Compare "The Solace of Open Spaces" to N. Scott Momaday's "A First American Views His Land" in this section and Barry Lopez's "Arctic Dreams" in "Best-Sellers." Explain how each writer responds to landscape. What differences and similarities can you find among the selections?

2. Read Peter Homans's "The Western: The Legend and the Cardboard Hero" in this section in connection with Ehrlich's essay. Does Ehrlich endorse or reject the cowboy myth? Explain.

Stephen King / Now You Take "Bambi" or "Snow White"—*That's* Scary!

TV Guide, June 13, 1981

Before the commercial success of Carrie *in 1973, Stephen King had worked as a schoolteacher and a gas-station attendant and even pressed sheets in an industrial laundry. Author of a succession of best-selling novels, including* Salem's Lot *(1975),* The Shining *(1977),* The Stand *(1978; 1990),* The Dead Zone *(1979),* Firestarter *(1980),* Cujo *(1981),* Christine *(1983),* Pet Sematary *(1983),*

> It *(1986),* Misery *(1987), and* Needful Things *(1991), King has more than forty million copies of his books in print and is the first author in literary history to have three books simultaneously on the* New York Times *hard- and soft-cover best-seller list.*
>
> *Few contemporary writers can match King's gift for combining essentially normal—almost mundane—descriptions of everyday life with disturbingly believable depictions of paranormal events. His characters gain our sympathy because their surroundings, cluttered with cereal boxes, battered household appliances, popular rock-and-roll songs, and other elements of our modern society, seem so familiar.*
>
> TV Guide *has the largest weekly circulation of any magazine in the world. It publishes, along with local and cable television listings, articles about TV celebrities and programs.*

Read the story synopsis below and ask yourself if it would make the sort of film you'd want your kids watching on the Friday- or Saturday-night movie:

A good but rather weak man discovers that, because of inflation, recession and his second wife's fondness for overusing his credit cards, the family is tottering on the brink of financial ruin. In fact, they can expect to see the repossession men coming for the car, the almost new recreational vehicle and the two color TVs any day; and a pink warning-of-foreclosure notice has already arrived from the bank that holds the mortgage on their house.

The wife's solution is simple but chilling: kill the two children, make it look like an accident and collect the insurance. She browbeats her husband into going along with this homicidal scheme. A wilderness trip is arranged, and while wifey stays in camp, the father leads his two children deep into the Great Smoky wilderness. In the end, he finds he cannot kill them in cold blood; he simply leaves them to wander around until, presumably, they will die of hunger and exposure.

The two children spend a horrifying three days and two nights in the wilderness. Near the end of their endurance, they stumble upon a back-country cabin and go to it, hoping for rescue. The woman who lives alone there turns out to be a cannibal. She cages the two children and prepares to roast them in her oven as she has roasted and eaten other wanderers before them. The boy manages to get free. He creeps up behind the woman as she stokes her oven and pushes her in, where she burns to death in her own fire.

You're probably shaking your head no, even if you have already recognized the origin of this bloody little tale (and if you didn't, ask your kids: they probably will) as "Hansel and Gretel," a so-called "fairy tale" that most kids are exposed to even before they start kindergarten. In addition to this story, with its grim and terrifying images of child abandonment, children lost in the woods and imprisoned by an evil woman, cannibalism and justifiable homicide, small children are routinely exposed to tales of mass murder and mutilation ("Bluebeard"), the eating of a loved one by a monster ("Little Red Riding-Hood"), treachery and deceit ("Snow White") and even the specter of a little boy who must face a black-hooded, ax-wielding headsman ("The 500 Hats of Bartholomew Cubbins," by Dr. Seuss).

I'm sometimes asked what I allow my kids to watch on the tube, for two reasons: first, my three children, at 10, 8 and 4, are still young enough to be in the age group that opponents of TV violence and horror consider to be particularly impressionable and at risk; and second, my seven novels have been popularly classified as "horror stories." People tend to think those two facts contradictory. But . . . I'm not sure that they are.

Three of my books have been made into films, and at this writing, two of them have been shown on TV. In the case of "Salem's Lot," a made-for-TV movie, there was never a question of allowing my kids to watch it on its first run on CBS; it began at 9 o'clock in our time zone, and all three children go to bed earlier than that. Even on a weekend, and even for the oldest, an 11 o'clock bedtime is just not negotiable. A previous TV GUIDE article about children and frightening programs mentioned a 3-year-old who watched "Lot" and consequently suffered night terrors. I have no wish to question any responsible parent's judgment—all parents raise their children in different ways—but it did strike me as passingly odd that a 3-year-old should have been allowed to stay up that late to get scared.

But in my case, the hours of the telecast were not really a factor, because we have one of those neat little time-machines, a videocassette recorder. I taped the program and, after viewing it myself, decided my children could watch it if they wanted to. My daughter had no interest; she's more involved with stories of brave dogs and loyal horses these days. My two sons, Joe, 8, and Owen, then 3, did watch. Neither of them seemed to have any problems either while watching it or in the middle of the night—when those problems most likely turn up.

I also have a tape of "Carrie," a theatrical film first shown on TV about two and a half years ago. I elected to keep this one on what my kids call "the high shelf" (where I put the tapes that are forbidden to them), because I felt that its depiction of children turning against other children, the lead character's horrifying embarrassment at a school dance and her later act of matricide would upset them. "Lot," on the contrary, is a story that the children accepted as a fairy tale in modern dress.

Other tapes on my "high shelf" include "Night of the Living Dead" (cannibalism), "The Brood" (David Cronenberg's film of intergenerational breakdown and homicidal "children of rage" who are set free to murder and rampage) and "The Exorcist." They are all up there for the same reason: they contain elements that I think might freak the kids out.

Not that it's possible to keep kids away from everything on TV (or in the movies, for that matter) that will freak them out; the movies that terrorized my own nights most thoroughly as a kid were not those through which Frankenstein's monster or the Wolfman lurched and growled, but the Disney cartoons. I watched Bambi's mother shot and Bambi running frantically to escape being burned up in a forest fire. I watched, appalled, dismayed and sweaty with fear, as Snow White bit into the poisoned apple while the old crone giggled in evil ecstasy. I was similarly terrified by the walking brooms in "Fantasia" and the big, bad wolf who chased the fleeing pigs from house to house with such grim and homicidal intensity. More recently, Owen, who just turned 4, crawled into bed with my wife and me, "Cruella DeVille is in my room," he said. Cruella DeVille is, of course, the villainess of "101 Dalmatians," and I suppose Owen had decided that a woman who would want to turn puppies into dogskin coats might also be interested in little boys. All these films would certainly get G-ratings if they were produced today, and frightening excerpts of them have been shown on TV during "the children's hour."

Do I believe that all violent or horrifying programming should be banned from network TV? No, I do not. Do I believe it should be telecast only in the later evening hours, TV's version of the "high shelf"? Yes, I do. Do I believe that children should be forbidden all violent or horrifying programs? No, I do not. Like their elders, children have a right to experience the entire spectrum of drama, from such warm and mostly unthreatening programs as *Little House on the Prairie* and *The Waltons* to scarier fare. It's been suggested again and again that such entertainment offers us a catharsis—a chance to enter for a little while a scary and yet controllable world where we can express our fears, aggressions and possibly even hostilities. Surely no one would suggest that children do not have their own fears and hostilities to face and overcome; those dark feelings are the basis of many of the fairy tales children love best.

Do I think a child's intake of violent or horrifying programs should be limited? Yes, I do, and that's why I have a high shelf. But the pressure groups who want to see all horror (and anything smacking of sex, for that matter) arbitrarily removed from television make me both uneasy and angry. The element of Big Brotherism inherent in such an idea causes the unease; the idea of a bunch of people I don't even know presuming to dictate what is best for my children causes the anger. I feel that deciding such things myself is my right—and my responsibility.

Responsibility is the bottom line, I guess. If you are going to have that magic window in your living room, you have to take a certain amount of responsibility for what it will show kids when they push the ON button. And when your children ask to stay up to watch something like "The Shining" (when it is shown on cable TV this month), here are some ideas on how you might go about executing your responsibility to your children—from a guy who's got kids of his own and who also wears a fright wig from time to time.

If it's a movie you've seen yourself, you should have no problem. It is not possible to know *everything* that will frighten a child—particularly a small one—but there are certain plot elements that can be very upsetting. These include physical mutilation, the death of an animal the child perceives as "good," the murder of a parent, a parent's treachery, blood in great quantities, drowning, being locked in a tight place and endings that offer no hope—and no catharsis.

If it's a movie you haven't seen, check the listings carefully for the elements listed above, or for things you know upset your children in particular (if, for instance, you have a child who was once lost and was badly shaken by the experience, you may want to skip even such a mild film as "Mountain Family Robinson").

If you're not getting a clear fix on the program from the listings, call the station. They'll be happy to help you; in fact, the station managers I queried said they fall all over themselves trying to help parents who request such information, but usually end up fielding complaints from adults who couldn't be bothered to call until after the offending program.

If the listing is marked *Meant for mature audiences only,* don't automatically give up. What may not be suitable for some families (or for some younger children) may be perfectly OK for your children.

If you do elect to let your children watch a frightening TV program, discuss it with them afterward. Ask them what frightened them and why. Ask them what made them feel good, and why. In most cases, you'll find that kids handle frightening make-believe situations quite well; most of them can be as tough as they need to be. And "talking it through" gives a parent a better idea of where his or her child's private fear button is located—which means a better understanding of the child and the child's mind.

If you think it's too scary, don't let them watch it. Period. The end. Remind yourself that you are bigger than they are, if that's what it takes. Too much frightening programming is no good for anyone, child or adult.

Most of all, try remembering that television spreads out the most incredible smorgasbord of entertainment in the history of the world, and it does so *every day.* Your child wants to taste a little of everything, even as you do yourself. But it would be wrong to let him or her eat only one single dish, particularly one as troublesome and as potentially dangerous as this one. Parenting presumes high shelves of all kinds, and that applies to some TV programs as well as to dangerous medicines or household cleaners.

One last word: when the scary program comes and you've decided that your children may watch, try to watch *with* them. Most children have to walk through their own real-life version of Hansel and Gretel's "dark wood" from time to time, as we did ourselves. The tale of terror can be a dress rehearsal for those dark times.

But if we remember our own scary childhood experiences, we'll probably remember that it was easier to walk through that dark wood with a friend.

Bob Greene / Fifteen — *Esquire,* August 1982

When asked which of his columns he thought were his favorites, Bob Greene responded, "The ones I like are the ones that people don't remember, just the little stories I find while traveling around the country that don't get a whole lot of letters or a whole lot of response; the kind of column where I'll go into a town and meet someone who has a small story to tell, but whose story might never have appeared in the newspaper otherwise."

Born in 1947, Greene became a professional writer by the age of twenty-three, reporting for the Chicago Sun-Times. *Later, as a syndicated columnist and contributing correspondent to ABC-TV's "Nightline" as well as the author of the "American Beat" column for* Esquire, *Greene had earned much critical acclaim as a writer dedicated to the human-interest story. In the following piece, Greene investigates—with a writer's knack for detail—the cruising habits of two bored fifteen-year-old boys whose only source of entertainment is the local shopping mall.*

Esquire *first appeared in October 1933, during the middle of the Depression. Developed as a men's fashion and literary quarterly dedicated to "The Art of Living and The New Leisure," the magazine was an immediate commercial success, thanks in large part to contributions by Ernest Hemingway, Dashiell Hammett, John Dos Passos, and Ring Lardner, among others. Now a monthly,* Esquire *has a circulation of 750,000 and continues to publish talented contemporary writers.*

"This would be excellent, to go in the ocean with this thing," says Dave Gembutis, fifteen.

He is looking at a $170 Sea Cruiser raft.

"Great," says his companion, Dan Holmes, also fifteen.

This is at Herman's World of Sporting Goods, in the middle of the Woodfield Mall in Schaumburg, Illinois.

The two of them keep staring at the raft. It is unlikely that they will purchase it. For one thing, Dan has only twenty dollars in his pocket, Dave five dollars. For another thing—ocean voyages aside—neither of them is even old enough to drive. Dave's older sister, Kim, has dropped them off at the mall. They will be taking the bus home.

Fifteen. What a weird age to be male. Most of us have forgotten about it, or have idealized it. But when you are fifteen . . . well, things tend to be less than perfect.

You can't drive. You are only a freshman in high school. The girls your age look older than you and go out with upperclassmen who have cars. You probably don't shave. You have nothing to do on the weekends.

So how do you spend your time? In 1982, most likely at a mall. Woodfield is an enclosed shopping center sprawling over 2.25 million square feet in northern Illinois. There are 230 stores at Woodfield, and on a given Saturday those stores are cruised in and out of by thousands of teenagers killing time. Today two of those teenagers are Dave Gembutis and Dan Holmes.

Dave is wearing a purple Rolling Meadows High School Mustangs Windbreaker over a gray M*A*S*H T-shirt, jeans, and Nike running shoes. He has a red plastic spoon in his mouth, and will keep it there for most of the afternoon. Dan is wearing a white Ohio State Buckeyes T-shirt, jeans, and Nike running shoes.

We are in the Video Forum store. Paul Simon and Art Garfunkel are singing "Wake Up Little Susie" from their Central Park concert on four television screens. Dave and Dan have already been wandering around Woodfield for an hour.

"There's not too much to do at my house," Dan says to me.

"Here we can at least look around," Dave says. "At home I don't know what we'd do."

"Play catch or something," Dan says. "Here there's lots of things to see."

"See some girls or something, start talking," Dave says.

I ask them how they would start a conversation with girls they had never met.

"Ask them what school they're from," Dan says. "Then if they say Arlington Heights High School or something, you can say, 'Oh, I know somebody from there.' "

I ask them how important meeting girls is to their lives.

"About forty-five percent," Dan says.

"About half your life," Dave says.

"Half is girls," Dan says. "Half is going out for sports."

An hour later, Dave and Dan have yet to meet any girls. They have seen a girl from their own class at Rolling Meadows High, but she is walking with an older boy, holding his hand. Now we are in the Woodfield McDonald's. Dave is eating a McRib sandwich, a small fries, and a small Coke. Dan is eating a cheeseburger, a small fries, and a medium root beer.

In here, the dilemma is obvious. The McDonald's is filled with girls who are precisely as old as Dave and Dan. The girls are wearing eye shadow, are fully developed, and generally look as if they could be dating the Green Bay Packers. Dave and Dan, on the other hand . . . well, when you're a fifteen-year-old boy, you look like a fifteen-year-old boy.

"They go with the older guys who have the cars," Dan says.

"It makes them more popular," Dave says.

"My ex-girlfriend is seeing a junior," Dan says.

I ask him what happened.

"Well, I was in Florida over spring vacation," he says. "And when I got back I heard that she was at Cinderella Rockefella one night, and she was dancing with this guy, and she liked him, and he drove her home and stuff."

"She two-timed him," Dave says.

"The guy's on the basketball team," Dan says.

I ask Dan what he did about it.

"I broke up with her," he says, as if I had asked the stupidest question in the world.

I ask him how he did it.

"Well, she was at her locker," he says. "She was working the combination. And I said, 'Hey, Linda, I want to break up.' And she was opening her locker door and she just nodded her head yes. And I said, 'I hear you had a good time while I was gone, but I had a better time in Florida.' "

I ask him if he feels bad about it.

"Well, I feel bad," he says. "But a lot of guys told me, 'I heard you broke up with her. Way to be.' "

"It's too bad the Puppy Palace isn't open," Dan says.

"They're remodeling," Dave says.

We are walking around the upper level of Woodfield. I ask them why they would want to go to the Puppy Palace.

"The dogs are real cute and you feel sorry for them," Dan says.

We are in a fast-food restaurant called the Orange Bowl. Dave is eating a frozen concoction called an O-Joy. They still have not met any girls.

"I feel like I'd be wasting my time if I sat at home," Dan says. "If it's Friday or Saturday and you sit home, it's considered . . . low."

"Coming to the mall is about all there is," Dave says. "Until we can drive."

"Then I'll cruise," Dan says. "Look for action a little farther away from my house, instead of just riding my bike around."

"When you're sixteen, you can do anything," Dave says. "You can go all the way across town."

"When you have to ride your bike . . ." Dan says. "When it rains, it ruins everything."

In the J.C. Penney store, the Penney Fashion Carnival is under way. Wally the Clown is handing out favors to children, but Dave and Dan are watching the young female models parade onto a stage in bathing suits.

"Just looking is enough for me," Dan says.

Dave suggests that they head out back into the mall and pick out some girls to wave to. I ask why.

"Well, see, even if they don't wave back, you might see them later in the day," Dan says. "And then they might remember that you waved at them, and you can meet them."

We are at the Cookie Factory. These guys eat approximately every twenty minutes.

It is clear that Dan is attracted to the girl behind the counter. He walks up, and his voice is slower and about half an octave lower than before.

The tone of voice is going to have to carry the day, because the words are not all that romantic:

"Can I have a chocolate-chip cookie?"

The girl does not even look up as she wraps the cookie in tissue paper.

Dan persists. The voice might be Clark Gable's:

"What do they cost?"

The girl is still looking down.

"Forty-seven," she says and takes his money, still looking away, and we move on.

Dave and Dan tell me that there are lots of girls at Woodfield's indoor ice-skating rink. It costs money to get inside, but they lead me to an exit door, and when a woman walks out we slip into the rink. It is chilly in here, but only three people are on the ice.

"It's not time for open skating yet," Dan says. "This is all private lessons."

"Not much in here," Dave says.

We sit on benches. I ask them if they wish they were older.

"Well," Dan says, "when you get there, you look back and you remember. Like I'm glad that I'm not in the fourth or fifth grade now. But I'm glad I'm not twenty-five, either."

"Once in a while I'm sorry I'm not twenty-one," Dave says. "There's not much you can do when you're fifteen. This summer I'm going to caddy and try to save some money."

"Yeah," Dan says. "I want to save up for a dirt bike."

"Right now, being fifteen is starting to bother me a little bit," Dave says. "Like when you have to get your parents to drive you to Homecoming with a girl."

I ask him how that works.

"Well, your mom is in the front seat driving," he says. "And you're in the back seat with your date."

I ask him how he feels about that.

"It's embarrassing," he says. "Your date understands that there's nothing you can do about it, but it's still embarrassing."

Dave says he wants to go to Pet World.

"I think they closed it down," Dan says, but we head in that direction anyway.

I ask them what the difference is between Pet World and the Puppy Palace.

"They've got snakes and fish and another assortment of dogs," Dan says. "But not as much as the Puppy Palace."

When we arrive, Pet World is, indeed, boarded up.

We are on the upper level of the mall. Dave and Dan have spotted two girls sitting on a bench directly below them, on the mall's main level.

"Whistle," Dan says. Dave whistles, but the girls keep talking.

"Dave, wave to them and see if they look," Dan says.

"They aren't looking," Dave says.

"There's another one over there," Dan says.

"Where?" Dave says.

"Oh, that's a mother," Dan says. "She's got her kid with her."

They return their attention to the two downstairs.

Dan calls to them: "Would you girls get the dollar I just dropped?"

The girls look up.

"Just kidding," Dan says.

The girls resume their conversation.

"I think they're laughing." Dan says.

"What are you going to do when the dumb girls won't respond," Dave says.

"At least we tried," Dan says.

I ask him what response would have satisfied him.

"The way we would have known that we succeeded," he says, "they'd have looked up here and started laughing."

The boys keep staring at the two girls.

"Ask her to look up," Dan says. "Ask her what school they go to."

"I did," Dave says. "I did."

The two boys lean over the railing.

"Bye, girls," Dave yells.

"See you later," Dan yells.

The girls do not look up.

"Too hard," Dan says. "Some girls are stuck on themselves, if you know what I mean by that."

We go to a store called the Foot Locker, where all the salespeople are dressed in striped referee's shirts.

"Dave!" Dan says. "Look at this! Seventy bucks!" He holds up a pair of New Balance running shoes. Both boys shake their heads.

We move on to a store called Passage to China. A huge stuffed tiger is placed by the doorway. There is a PLEASE DO NOT TOUCH sign attached to it. Dan rubs his hand over the tiger's back. "This would look so great in my room," he says.

We head over to Alan's TV and Stereo. Two salesmen ask the boys if they are interested in buying anything, so they go back outside and look at the store's window. A color television set is tuned to a baseball game between the Chicago Cubs and the Pittsburgh Pirates.

They watch for five minutes. The sound is muted, so they cannot hear the announcers.

"I wish they'd show the score," Dave says.

They watch for five minutes more.

"Hey, Dave," Dan says. "You want to go home?"

"I guess so," Dave says.

They do. We wave goodbye. I watch them walk out of the mall toward the bus stop. I wish them girls, dirt bikes, puppies, and happiness.

THE SPACE SHUTTLE DISASTER

The explosion of the space shuttle Challenger *shortly after takeoff on January 28, 1986, was one of the leading news stories of that year. Both* Time *and* Newsweek *prepared lengthy articles on the event, and both ran identical covers with photographs of the fiery explosion. The magazines prefaced their reports with the following brief reflective essays by senior staff writers Lance Morrow* (Time) *and Jerry Adler* (Newsweek).

Thomas J. C. Martyn, the first foreign news editor of Time *magazine, started* News-Week *in early 1933 as a simpler, less interpretive digest of the week's major events than* Time *had been in its first ten years. Although a merger with* Today *magazine in 1937 changed its title to* Newsweek, The Magazine of News Significance, *the periodical remained uncompetitive with* Time *until it was taken over by the* Washington Post *in the early 1960s. Ever since, the two magazines have competed fiercely at the newsstand and for subscriptions. For additional information on* Time *magazine,* *see p. 268.*

Lance Morrow / A Nation Mourns

Time, February 10, 1986

The eye accepted what the mind could not: a sudden burst of white and yellow fire, then white trails streaming up and out from the fireball to form a twisted Y against a pure heaven, and the metal turning to rags, dragging white ribbons into the ocean. A terrible beauty exploded like a primal event of physics—the birth of a universe; the death of a star; a fierce, enigmatic violence out of the blue. The mind recoiled in sheer surprise. Then it filled with horror.

One thought first of the teacher and her children—her own and her students. One wanted to snatch them away from the sight and rescind the thing they had seen. But the moment was irrevocable. Over and over, the bright extinction played on the television screen, almost ghoulishly repeated until it had sunk into the collective memory. And there it will abide, abetted by the weird metaphysics of videotape, which permits the endless repetition of a brute finality.

In last week's grief, some people rebelled, a little brusquely, and asked whether the nation would be pitched into such mourning if, say, a 747 went down with 300 Americans. Chuck Yeager, protohero of the space age, observed, "I don't see any difference, except for the public exposure of the shuttle, between this accident and one involving a military or a commercial airplane."

That had the machismo of matter-of-factness. It is true that the tragedy played itself out to maximum dramatic effect: the shuttle, now boringly routine, lifting off and then annihilating itself in full view of the world. It is true that television pitched itself fervently into what has become its sacramental role in national tragedies—first wounding with its vivid repetitions of the event, then consoling, grieving, reconciling, administering the anchor's unctions. It is true that Christa McAuliffe, a teacher representing all the right things in America, rode as a nonprofessional, an innocent, into space, and her death therefore seemed doubly poignant and unfair.

But the loss of the shuttle was a more profound event than that suggests. It inflicted upon Americans the purest pain that they have collectively felt in years. It was a pain uncontaminated by the anger and hatred and hungering for revenge that come in the aftermath of terrorist killings, for example. It was pain uncomplicated by the divisions, political, racial, moral, that usually beset American tragedies (Viet Nam and Watergate, to name two). The shuttle crew, spectacularly democratic (male, female, black, white, Japanese American, Catholic, Jewish, Protestant), was the best of us, Americans thought, doing the best of things Americans do. The mission seemed symbolically immaculate, the farthest reach of a perfectly American ambition to cross frontiers. And it simply vanished in the air.

Jerry Adler / We Mourn Seven Heroes

Newsweek, February 10, 1986

Long after the wind had swept the last traces of Shuttle Mission 51-L from the skies, the mission clocks all around the launch site kept counting up the seconds since liftoff, as if holding out hope that it had all been a mistake, and the orbiter might at any minute pop up on a radar screen halfway around the globe, the pilot laconically apologizing for a glitch in the downlink. The machinery, like the nation itself, seemed unprepared to cope with a mission that went up and didn't come back down. As the cameras gaped at the roiling cloud where three contrails converged, terminals at mission control were displaying mute electronic puzzlement, the computers frozen in contemplation of those last bits of data that had escaped the doomed ship, as if they, like us, were reluctant to believe the evidence of their senses.

So swift, so sudden was the catastrophe that it appeared to elude even the computers' comprehension, yet on another level it was a disaster that could be grasped by a six-year-old, or almost so: on being told that the astronauts had been blown up over the ocean, one second grader in an Idaho school hopefully asked his teacher: "Can they swim?" The nation's schoolchildren, of course, were linked to this flight by the ebullient presence of Christa McAuliffe, who was to achieve immortality by going where no social-studies teacher had dared go before, and teach two lessons when she got there. It seemed natural—to one Brooklyn youngster, anyway—to ask how long it would be before children themselves went up into space: to which the answer is, a lot longer than it was a week ago.

If the disaster was a humiliating failure of rocket technology, it was at best an equivocal success of technology for the dissemination and amplification of grief. There was something at once dreadful and compelling in watching the footage of the families assembled in the spectator's gallery at Cape Canaveral, trying to spot on individual faces the exact moment when excitement turned to doubt, doubt to shock and horror. Ronald Reagan, who has had much practice in the role of chief national mourner, spoke movingly and well that same afternoon; yet even as his somber words sounded across a darkening land, an unruly horde was descending with lights and cameras on Concord, N.H., in hopes of illuminating an authentic tear from a genuine member of the same community as Christa McAuliffe. Some there thought they should be allowed to grieve in peace, but the organs of mourning, once brought to full sepulchral voice, are not so easily muffled; by the weekend we knew everything of interest about the lives, families and careers of the seven. Except why they died.

Why did they die? We won't know for sure, even after we answer the related, but separate, question of why Challenger blew up barely a minute into its 10th flight at 11:39 last Tuesday morning. A weld, a bolt, an icicle—somewhere in the volumes of data NASA has impounded is the clue to the anomaly that brought hydrogen and oxygen into catastrophic contact. Precautions will be ordered and the shuttle will fly again; if it flies long enough, it will probably have another accident. "We always knew there would be a day like this," former astronaut, now senator, John Glenn said last week—a fine time to tell us, one might say, but a point worth keeping in mind.

One is tempted to say that they died because, as long as there are frontiers to cross, there will be men and women to whom the challenge is worth the risk of their lives. A noble generalization—although presumably the weighing of risk was different for the professional pilots who flew the shuttle than for Christa McAuliffe, teacher and the mother of two young children. This much, though, we can say of them all: that they died in the service of their country, and in the cause of professions they believed in; and that having died, they can live forever in our memories, poised in the clear blue sky almost 10 miles up and climbing, in that perfect instant before holocaust.

DISCUSSION QUESTIONS

1. Both of the essays on the shuttle disaster are five paragraphs long, and both respond to the same event. Can you find other similarities in style and approach?
2. Which essay strikes you as more emotional? Which seems more interested in the technical details of the disaster? How are these emphases reflected in the words and images of each writer?

Martin Gottfried / Rambos of the Road

Newsweek, September 8, 1986

There is one category of everyday conduct that etiquette books rarely cover—driving. Yet it is hard to think of another activity that makes people more sensitive and prone to insult than driving an automobile. On the American road, otherwise decent and well-mannered people can be suddenly transformed into hostile, ill-tempered brutes, cursing, leaning on horns, flinging obscene gestures, and—as recent events on the California freeways have shown—ready for murderous violence. Everyday, all across America, people swap horror stories about savagery on the highways.

A drama critic, Martin Gottfried wrote the following essay for Newsweek. *He is the author of* In Person: The Great Entertainers. *(1985), and* All His Jazz: The Life & Death of Bob Fosse *(1990).* Newsweek, *founded in 1933 by a former foreign news editor for* Time *magazine, was purchased by the* Washington Post *in the early 1960s. Ever since, it has been one of our nation's most-read news magazines.*

The car pulled up and its driver glared at us with such sullen intensity, such hatred, that I was truly afraid for our lives. Except for the Mohawk haircut he didn't have, he looked like Robert DeNiro in "Taxi Driver," the sort of young man who, delirious for notoriety, might kill a president.

He was glaring because we had passed him and for that affront he pursued us to the next stoplight so as to express his indignation and affirm his masculinity. I was with two women and, believe it, was afraid for all three of us. It was nearly midnight and we were in a small, sleeping town with no other cars on the road.

When the light turned green, I raced ahead, knowing it was foolish and that I was not in a movie. He didn't merely follow, he chased, and with his headlights turned off. No matter what sudden turn I took, he followed. My passengers were silent. I knew they were alarmed, and I prayed that I wouldn't be called upon to protect them. In that cheerful frame of mind, I turned off my own lights so I couldn't be followed. It was lunacy. I was responding to a crazy *as* a crazy.

"I'll just drive to the police station," I finally said, and as if those were the magic words, he disappeared.

ELBOWING FENDERS

It seems to me that there has recently been an epidemic of auto macho—a competition perceived and expressed in driving. People fight it out over parking spaces. They bully into line at the gas pump. A toll booth becomes a signal for elbowing fenders. And beetle-eyed drivers hunch over their steering wheels, squeezing the rims, glowering, preparing the excuse of not having seen you as they muscle you off the road. Approaching a highway on an entrance ramp recently, I was strong-armed by a trailer tuck, so immense that its driver all but blew me away by blasting his horn. The behemoth was just inches from my hopelessly mismatched coupe when I fled for the safety of the shoulder.

And this is happening on city streets, too. A New York taxi driver told me that "intimidation is the name of the game. Drive as if you're deaf and blind. You don't hear the other guy's horn and you sure as hell don't see him."

The odd thing is that long before I was even able to drive, it seemed to me that people were at their finest and most civilized when in their cars. They seemed so orderly and considerate, so reasonable, staying in the right-hand lane unless passing, signaling all intentions. In those days you really eased into highway traffic, and the long, neat rows of cars seemed mobile testimony to the sanity of most people. Perhaps memory fails, perhaps there were always testy drivers, perhaps—but everyone didn't give you the finger.

A most amazing example of driver rage occurred recently at the Manhattan end of the Lincoln Tunnel. We were four cars abreast, stopped at a traffic light. And there was no moving even when the light had changed. A bus had stopped in the cross traffic, blocking our paths: it was a normal-for-New-York-City gridlock. Perhaps impatient, perhaps late for important appointments, three of us nonetheless accepted what, after all, we could not alter. One, however, would not. He would not be helpless. He would go where he was going even if he couldn't get there. A Wall Street type in suit and tie, he got out of his car and strode toward the bus, rapping smartly on its doors. When they opened, he exchanged words with the driver. The doors folded shut. He then stepped in front of the bus, took hold of one of its large windshield wipers and broke it.

The bus doors reopened and the driver appeared, apparently giving the fellow a good piece of his mind. If so, the lecture was wasted, for the man started his car and proceeded to drive directly *into the bus*. He rammed it. Even though the point at which he struck the bus, the folding doors, was its most vulnerable point, ramming the side of a bus with your car has to rank very high on a futility index. My first thought was that it had to be a rented car.

LANE MERGER

To tell the truth, I could not believe my eyes. The bus driver opened his doors as much as they could be opened and he stepped directly onto the hood of the attacking car, jumping up and down with both his feet. He then retreated into the bus, closing the doors behind him. Obviously a man of action, the car driver backed up and rammed the bus again. How this exercise in absurdity would have been resolved none of us will ever know for at that point the traffic unclogged and the bus moved on. And the rest of us, we passives of the world, proceeded, our cars crossing a field of battle as if nothing untoward had happened.

It is tempting to blame such belligerent, uncivil and even neurotic behavior on the nuts of the world, but in our cars we all become a little crazy. How many of us speed up when a driver signals his intention of pulling in front of us? Are we resentful and anxious to pass him? How many of us try to squeeze in, or race along the shoulder at a lane merger? We may not jump on hoods, but driving the gantlet, we seethe, cursing not so silently in the safety of our steel bodies on wheels—fortresses for cowards.

What is it within us that gives birth to such antisocial behavior and why, all of a sudden, have so many drivers gone around the bend? My friend Joel Katz, a Manhattan psychiatrist, calls it, "a Rambo pattern. People are running around thinking the American way is to take the law into your own hands when anyone does anything wrong. And what constitutes 'wrong'? Anything that cramps your style."

It seems to me that it is a new America we see on the road now. It has the mentality of a hoodlum and the backbone of a coward. The car is its weapon and hiding place, and it is still a symbol even in this. Road Rambos no longer bespeak a self-reliant, civil people tooling around in family cruisers. In fact, there aren't families in these machines that charge headlong with their brights on in broad daylight, demanding we get out of their way. Bullies are loners, and they have perverted our liberty of the open road into drivers' license. They represent an America that derides the values of decency and good manners, then roam the highways riding shotgun and shrieking freedom. By allowing this to happen, the rest of us approve.

DISCUSSION QUESTIONS

1. Consider some of your own experiences with hostile, uncivil drivers. Are they similar to Gottfried's? Think carefully about how these experiences made you feel. Did these feelings stay with you afterward?
2. Do you feel that Gottfried's experiences are very widely shared? Do you think that he exaggerates the conditions? Can you think of evidence other than personal experience that can be brought in to support his generalization?
3. Why does Gottfried choose the image of "Rambo" to characterize the kind of driving he describes? What reasons does he provide for the craziness of American drivers? Can you think of other reasons for an increase in antisocial behavior on our roadways?

Sallie Tisdale / We Do Abortions Here: A Nurse's Story

Harper's, October 1987

The issue of abortion continues to evoke heated responses from nearly every sector of society. People who condemn abortion claim that it interferes with natural processes of conception; for these, abortion is the equivalent of murder. There are others, however, who believe that laws prohibiting abortion preclude a woman's right to control her own life. For these, abortion becomes an unfortunate, but sometimes necessary, aspect of modern culture. Sallie Tisdale, a writer and former nurse, worked at an abortion clinic at the time she wrote this essay. She is the author of several books, including The Sorcerer's Apprentice: Medical Miracles and Other Disasters *(1986),* Lot's Wife: Salt and the Human Condition *(1988), and* Stepping Westward: The Long Search for Home in the Pacific Northwest *(1991).*

We do abortions here; that is all we do. There are weary, grim moments when I think I cannot bear another basin of bloody remains, utter another kind phrase of reassurance. So I leave the procedure room in the back and reach for a new chart. Soon I am talking to an eighteen-year-old woman pregnant for the fourth time. I push up her sleeve to check her blood pressure and find row upon row of needle marks, neat and parallel and discolored. She has been so hungry for her drug for so long that she has taken to using the loose skin of her upper arms; her elbows are already a permanent ruin of bruises. She is surprised to find herself nearly four months pregnant. I suspect she is often surprised, in a mild way, by the blows she is dealt. I prepare myself for another basin, another brief and chafing loss.

"How can you stand it?" Even the clients ask. They see the machine, the strange instruments, the blood, the final stroke that wipes away the promise of pregnancy. Sometimes I see that too: I watch a woman's swollen abdomen sink to softness in a few stuttering moments and my own belly flip-flops with sorrow. But all it takes for me to catch my breath is another interview, one more story that sounds so much like the last one. There is a numbing sameness lurking in this job: the same questions, the same answers, even the same trembling tone in the voices. The worst is the sameness of human failure, of inadequacy in the face of each day's dull demands.

In describing this work, I find it difficult to explain how much I enjoy it most of the time. We laugh a lot here, as friends and as professional peers. It's nice to be with women all day. I like the sudden, transient bonds I forge with some clients: moments when I am in my strength, remembering weakness, and a woman in weakness reaches out for my strength. What I offer is not power, but solidness, offered almost eagerly. Certain clients waken in me every tender urge I have—others make me wince and bite my tongue. Both challenge me to find a balance. It is a sweet brutality we practice here, a stark and loving dispassion.

I look at abortion as if I am standing on a cliff with a telescope, gazing at some great vista. I can sweep the horizon with both eyes, survey the scene in all its distance and size. Or I can put my eye to the lens and focus on the small details, suddenly so close. In abortion the absolute must always be tempered by the contextual, because both are real, both valid, both hard. How can we do this? How can we refuse? Each abortion is a measure of our failure to protect, to nourish our own. Each basin I empty is a promise—but a promise broken a long time ago.

I grew up on the great promise of birth control. Like many women my age, I took the pill as soon as I was sexually active. To risk pregnancy when it was so easy to avoid seemed stupid, and my contraceptive success, as it were, was part of the promise of social enlightenment. But birth control fails, far more frequently than laboratory trials predict. Many of our clients take the pill; its failure to protect them is a shocking realization. We have clients who have been sterilized, whose husbands have had vasectomies; each one is a statistical misfit, fine print come to life. The anger and shame of these women I hold in one hand, and the basin in the other. The distance between the two, the length I pace and try to measure, is the size of an abortion.

The procedure is disarmingly simple. Women are surprised, as though the mystery of conception, a dark and hidden genesis, requires an elaborate finale. In the first trimester of pregnancy, it's a mere few minutes of vacuuming, a neat tidying up. I give a woman a small yellow Valium, and when it has begun to relax her, I lead her into the back, into bareness, the stirrups. The doctor reaches in her, opening the narrow tunnel to the uterus with a succession of slim, smooth bars of steel. He inserts a plastic tube and hooks it to a hose on the machine. The woman is framed against white paper that crackles as she moves, the light bright in her eyes. Then the machine rumbles low and loud in the small windowless room; the doctor moves the tube back and forth with an efficient rhythm, and the long tail of it fills with blood that spurts and stumbles along into a jar. He is usually finished in a few minutes. They are long minutes for the woman; her uterus frequently reacts to its abrupt emptying with a powerful, unceasing cramp, which cuts off the blood vessels and enfolds the irritated, bleeding tissue.

I am learning to recognize the shadows that cross the faces of the women I hold. While the doctor works between her spread legs, the paper drape hiding his intent expression, I stand beside the table. I hold the woman's hand in mine, resting them just below her ribs. I watch her eyes, finger her necklace, stroke her hair. I ask about her job, her family; in a haze she answers me; we chatter, faces close, eyes meeting and sliding apart.

I watch the shadows that creep up unnoticed and suddenly darken her face as she screws up her features and pushes a tear out each side to slide down her cheeks. I have learned to anticipate the quiver of chin, the rapid intake of breath, and the surprising sobs that rise soon after the machine starts to drum. I know this is when the cramp deepens, and the tears are partly the tears that follow pain—the sharp, childish crying when one bumps one's head on a cabinet door. But a well of woe seems to open beneath many women when they hear that thumping sound. The anticipation of the moment has finally come to fruit; the moment has arrived when the loss is no longer an imagined one. It has come true.

I am struck by the sameness and I am struck every day by the variety here—how this commonplace dilemma can so display the differences of women. A twenty-one-year old woman, unemployed, uneducated, without family, in the fifth month of her fifth pregnancy. A forty-two-year-old mother of teenagers, shocked by her condition, refusing to tell her husband. A twenty-three-year-old mother of two having her seventh abortion, and many women in their thirties having their first. Some are stoic, some hysterical, a few giggle uncontrollably, many cry.

I talk to a sixteen-year-old uneducated girl who was raped. She has gonorrhea. She describes blinding headaches, attacks of breathlessness, nausea. ''Sometimes I feel like two different people,'' she tells me with a calm smile, ''and I talk to myself.''

I pull out my plastic models. She listens patiently for a time, and then holds her hands wide in front of her stomach.

''When's the baby going to go up into my stomach?'' she asks.

I blink. ''What do you mean?'

''Well,'' she says, still smiling, ''when women get so big, isn't the baby in your stomach? Doesn't it hatch out of an egg there?''

My first question in an interview is always the same. As I walk down the hall with the woman, as we get settled in chairs and I glance through her files, I am trying to gauge her, to get a sense of the words, and the tone, I should use. With some I joke, with others I chat, sometimes I fall into a brisk, business-like patter. But I ask every woman, ''Are you sure you want to have an abortion?'' Most nod with grim knowing smiles. ''Oh, yes,'' they sigh. Some seek forgiveness, offer excuses. Occasionally a woman will flinch and say, ''Please don't use that word.''

Later I describe the procedure to come, using care with my language. I don't say ''pain'' any more than I would say ''baby.'' So many are afraid to ask how much it will hurt. ''My sister told me—'' I hear. ''A friend of mine said—'' and the dire expectations unravel. I prick the index finger of a woman for a drop of blood to test, and as the tiny lancet approaches the skin she averts her eyes, holding her trembling hand out to me and jumping at my touch.

It is when I am holding a plastic uterus in one hand, a suction tube in the other, moving them together in imitation of the scrubbing to come, that women ask the most secret question. I am speaking in a matter-of-fact voice about ''the tissue'' and ''the contents'' when the woman suddenly catches my eye and asks, ''How big is the baby now?'' These words suggest a quiet need for a definition of the boundaries being drawn. It isn't so odd, after all, that she feels relief when I describe the growing bud's bulbous shape, its miniature nature. Again I gauge, and sometimes lie a little, weaseling around in its infantile features until its clinging power slackens.

But when I look in the basin, among the curdlike blood clots, I see an elfin thorax, attenuated, its pencilline ribs all in parallel rows with tiny knobs of spine rounding upwards. A translucent arm and hand swim beside.

A sleepy-eyed girl, just fourteen, watched me with a slight and goofy smile all through her abortion. ''Does it have little feet and little fingers and all?'' she'd asked earlier. When the suction was over she sat up woozily at the end of the table and murmured, ''Can I see it?'' I shook my head firmly.

"It's not allowed," I told her sternly, because I knew she didn't really want to see what was left. She accepted this statement of authority, and a shadow of confused relief crossed her plain, pale face.

Privately, even grudgingly, my colleagues might admit the power of abortion to provoke emotion. But they seem to prefer the broad view and disdain the telescope. Abortion is a matter of choice, privacy, control. Its uncertainty lies in specific cases: retarded women and girls too young to give consent for surgery, women who are ill or hostile or psychotic. Such common dilemmas are met with both compassion and impatience; they slow things down. We are too busy to chew over ethics. One person might discuss certain concerns, behind closed doors, or describe a particularly disturbing dream. But generally there is to be no ambivalence.

Every day I take calls from women who are annoyed that we cannot see them, cannot do their abortion today, this morning, now. They argue the price, demand that we stay after hours to accommodate their job or class schedule. Abortion is so routine that one expects it to be like a manicure; quick, cheap, and painless.

Still, I've cultivated a certain disregard. It isn't negligence, but I don't always pay attention. I couldn't be here if I tried to judge each case on its merits; after all, we do over a hundred abortions a week. At some point each individual in this line of work draws a boundary and adheres to it. For one physician the boundary is a particular week of gestation; for another, it is a certain number of repeated abortions. But these boundaries can be fluid too: one physician overruled his own limit to abort a mature but severely malformed fetus. For me, the limit is allowing my clients to carry their own burden, shoulder the responsibility themselves. I shoulder the burden of trying not to judge them.

This city has several "crisis pregnancy centers" advertised in the Yellow Pages. They are small offices staffed by volunteers, and they offer free pregnancy testing, glossy photos of dead fetuses, and movies. I had a client recently whose mother is active in the anti-abortion movement. The young woman went to the local crisis center and was told that the doctor would be the most horrible she could imagine, and that she might, after an abortion, never be able to have children. All lies. They called her at home and at work, over and over and over, but she had been wise enough to give a false name. She came to us a fugitive. We who do abortions are marked, by some, as impure. It's dirty work.

When a deliveryman comes to the sliding glass window by the reception desk and tilts a box toward me, I hesitate. I read the packing slip, assess the shape and weight of the box in the light of its supposed contents. We request familiar faces. The doors are carefully locked; I have learned to half glance around at bags and boxes, looking for a telltale sign. I register with security when I arrive, and I am careful not to bang a door. We are a little on edge here.

Concern about size and shape seem to be natural, and so is the relief that follows. We make the powerful assumption that the fetus is different from us, and even when we admit the similarities, it is too simplistic to be seduced by form alone. But the form is enormously potent—humanoid, powerless, palm-sized, and pure, it evokes an almost fierce tenderness when viewed simply as what it appears to be. But appearance, and even potential, aren't enough. The fetus, in becoming itself, can ruin others; its utter dependence has a sinister side. When I am struck in the moment by the contents in the basin, I am careful to remember the context, to note the tearful teenager and the woman sighing with something more than relief. One kind of question, though, I find considerably trickier.

"Can you tell what it is?" I am asked, and this means gender. This question is asked by couples, not women alone. Always couples would abort a girl and keep a boy. I have been asked about twins, and even if I could tell what race the father was.

An eighteen-year-old woman with three daughters brought her husband to the interview. He glared first at me, then at his wife, as he sank lower and lower in the chair, picking his teeth with a toothpick. He interrupted a conversation with his wife to ask if I could tell whether the baby would be a boy or a girl. I told him I could not.

"Good," he replied in a slow and strangely malevolent voice, " 'cause if it was a boy I'd wring her neck."

In a literal sense, abortion exists because we are able to ask such questions, able to assign a value to the fetus which can shift with changing circumstances. If the human bond to a child were as primitive and unflinchingly narrow as that of other animals, there would be no abortion. There would be no abortion because there would be nothing more important than caring for the young and perpetuating the species, no reason for sex but to make babies. I sense this sometimes, this wordless organic duty, when I do ultrasounds.

We do ultrasound, a sound-wave test that paints a faint, gray picture of the fetus, whenever we're uncertain of gestation. Age is measured by the width of the skull and confirmed by the length of the femur or thighbone; we speak of a pregnancy as being a certain "femur length" in weeks. The usual concern is whether a pregnancy is within the legal limit for an abortion. Women this far along have bellies which swell out round and tight like trim muscles. When they lie flat, the mound rises softly above the hips, pressing the umbilicus upward.

It takes practice to read an ultrasound picture, which is grainy and etched as though in strokes of charcoal. But suddenly a rapid rhythmic motion appears—the beating heart. Nearby is a soft oval, scratched with lines—the skull. The leg is harder to find, and then suddenly the fetus moves, bobbing in the surf. The skull turns away, an arm slides across the screen, the torso rolls. I know the weight of a baby's head on my shoulder, the whisper of lips on ears, the delicate curve of a fragile spine in my hand. I know how heavy and correct a newborn cradled feels. The creature I watch in secret requires nothing from me but to be left alone, and that is precisely what won't be done.

These inadvertently made beings are caught in a twisting web of motive and desire. They are at least inconvenient, sometimes quite literally dangerous in the womb, but most often they fall somewhere in between—consequences never quite believed in come to roost. Their virtue rises and falls outside their own nature: they become only what we make them. A fetus created by accident is the most absolute kind of surprise. Whether the blame lies in a failed IUD, a slipped condom, or a false impression of safety, that fetus is a thing whose creation has been actively worked against. Its existence is an error. I think this is why so few women, even late in a pregnancy, will consider giving up for adoption. To do so means making the fetus real—imagining it as something whole and outside oneself. The decision to terminate a pregnancy is sometimes so difficult and confounding that it creates an enormous demand for immediate action. The decision is a rejection; the pregnancy has become something to be rid of, a condition to be ended. It is a burden, a weight, a thing separate.

Women have abortions because they are too old, and too young, too poor, and too rich, too stupid, and too smart. I see women who berate themselves with violent emotions for their first and only abortion, and other who return three times, five times, hauling two or three children, who cannot remember to take a pill or where they put the diaphragm. We talk glibly about choice. But the choice for what? I see all the broken promises in lives lived like a series of impromptu obstacles. There are the sweet, light promises of love and intimacy, the glittering promise of education and progress, the warm promise of safe families, long years of innocence and community. And there is the promise of freedom: freedom from failure, from faithlessness. Freedom from biology. The early feminist defense of abortion asked many questions, but the one I remember is this: is biology destiny? And the answer is yes, sometimes it is. Women who have the fewest choices of all exercise their right to abortion the most.

Oh, the ignorance. I take a woman to the back room and ask her to undress; a few minutes later I return and find her positioned discreetly behind a drape, still wearing underpants. "Do I have to take these off too?" she asks, a little shocked. Some swear they have not had sex, many do not know what a uterus is, how sperm and egg meet, how sex makes babies. Some late seekers do not believe themselves pregnant; they believes themselves *impregnable*. I was chastised when I began this job for referring to some clients as girls: it is a feminist heresy. They come so young, snapping gum, sockless and sneakered, and their shakily applied eyeliner smears when they cry. I call them girls with maternal benignity. I cannot imagine them as mothers.

The doctor seats himself between the woman's thighs and reaches into the dilated opening of a five-month pregnant uterus. Quickly he grabs and crushes the fetus in several places, and the room is filled with a low clatter and snap of forceps, the click of the tanaculum,[1] and a pulling, sucking sound. The paper crinkles as the drugged and sleepy woman shifts, the nurse's low, honey-brown voice explains each step in delicate words.

I have fetus dreams, we all do here: dreams of abortions one after the other; of buckets of blood splashed on the walls; trees full of crawling fetuses. I dreamed that two men grabbed me and began to drag me away: "Let's do an abortion," they said with a sickening leer, and I began to scream, plunged into a vision of sucking, scraping pain, of being spread and torn by impartial instruments that do only what they are bidden. I woke from this dream barely able to breathe and thought of kitchen tables and coat hangers, knitting needles striped with blood, and women all alone clutching a pillow in their teeth to keep the screams from piercing the apartment-house walls. Abortion is the narrowest edge between kindness and cruelty. Done as well as it can be, it is still violence—merciful violence, like putting a suffering animal to death.

Maggie, one of the nurses, received a call at midnight not long ago. It was a woman in her twentieth week of pregnancy; the necessarily gradual process of cervical dilation begun the day before had stimulated labor, as it sometimes does. Maggie and one of the doctors met the woman at the office in the night. Maggie helped her onto the table, and as she lay down the fetus was delivered into Maggie's hands. When Maggie told me about it the next day, she cupped her hands into a small bowl—"It was just like a little kitten," she said softly, wonderingly. "Everything was still attached."

At the end of the day I clean out the suction jars, pouring blood into the sink, splashing the sides with flecks of tissue. From the sink rises a rich and humid smell, hot, earthy, and moldering; it is the smell of something recently alive beginning to decay. I take care of the plastic tub on the floor, filled with pieces too big to be trusted to the trash. The law defines the contents of the bucket I hold protectively against my chest as "tissue." Some would say my complicity in filling that bucket gives me no right to call it anything else. I slip the tissue gently into a bag and place it in the freezer, to be burned at another time. Abortion requires of me an entirely new set of assumptions. It requires a willingness to live with conflict, fearlessness, and grief. As I close the freezer door, I imagine a world where this won't be necessary, and then return to the world where it is.

[1] Type of sharp forceps used on bleeding arteries.

DISCUSSION QUESTIONS

1. What is Sallie Tisdale's opinion about abortion? What was her goal in writing the essay? Does her essay imply that she is conflicted about her job?
2. Do you feel Tisdale should have provided the graphic description of an abortion that she does? How does this account affect your own views on abortion? What does its inclusion suggest about Tisdale's own stance?
3. According to Tisdale, to what extent do the workers at her clinic engage the ethical issues related to abortion on a day-to-day basis? How does their work affect their lives?

Randy Shilts / Talking AIDS to Death *Esquire,* March 1989

While the number of reported cases of AIDS (acquired immune deficiency syndrome) continues to rise steadily, the amount of media coverage of the epidemic has declined over the last several years. Our response as a society to this disease will determine the future of millions of Americans, both those who have tested positive for AIDS and those who might avert infection if properly educated. The nature of this response will, in turn, be determined by the amount and accuracy of press stories related to AIDS. ''Talking AIDS to Death'' raises grave questions about the current state of the media and their ineffectiveness in reporting on the deadly disease.

Randy Shilts is national correspondent of the San Francisco Chronicle. *His book,* And the Band Played On: Politics, People, and the AIDS Epidemic, *(1987), was an internationally acclaimed bestseller which documented the inability of government, public health organizations, and the scientific establishment to deal effectively with the crisis. ''Talking AIDS to Death'' first appeared in* Esquire.

I'M TALKING TO my friend Kit Herman when I notice a barely perceptible spot on the left side of his face. Slowly, it grows up his cheekbone, down to his chin, and forward to his mouth. He talks on cheerfully, as if nothing is wrong, and I'm amazed that I'm able to smile and chat on, too, as if nothing were there. His eyes become sunken; his hair turns gray; his ear is turning purple now, swelling into a carcinomatous cauliflower, and still we talk on. He's dying in front of me. He'll be dead soon if nothing is done.

Dead soon if nothing is done.

''Excuse me, Mr. Shilts, I asked if you are absolutely sure, if you can categorically state that you definitely can*not* get AIDS from a mosquito.''

I forget the early-morning nightmare and shift into my canned response. All my responses are canned now. I'm an AIDS talk-show jukebox. Press the button, any button on the AIDS question list, and I have my canned answer ready. Is this Chicago or Detroit?

''Of course you can get AIDS from a mosquito,'' I begin.

Here I pause for dramatic effect. In that brief moment, I can almost hear the caller murmur, ''I *knew* it.''

"If you have unprotected anal intercourse with an infected mosquito, you'll get AIDS," I continue. "Anything short of that and you won't."

The talk-show host likes the answer. All the talk-show hosts like my answers because they're short, punchy, and to the point. Not like those boring doctors with long recitations of scientific studies so overwritten with maybes and qualifiers that they frighten more than they reassure an AIDS-hysteria public. I give good interview, talk-show producers agree. It's amazing, they say, how I always stay so cool and never lose my temper.

"Mr. Shilts, has there ever been a case of anyone getting AIDS from a gay waiter?"

"In San Francisco, I don't think they allow heterosexuals to be waiters. This fact proves absolutely that if you could get AIDS from a gay waiter, all northern California would be dead by now."

I gave that same answer once on a Bay Area talk show, and my caller, by the sound of her a little old lady, quickly rejoined, "What if that gay waiter took my salad back into the kitchen and ejaculated into my salad dressing? Couldn't I get AIDS then?"

I didn't have a pat answer for that one, and I still wonder at what this elderly caller thought went on in the kitchens of San Francisco restaurants. Fortunately, this morning's phone-in—in Chicago, it turned out—is not as imaginative.

"You know, your question reminds me of a joke we had in California a couple of years back," I told the caller. "How many heterosexual waiters in San Francisco does it take to screw in a light bulb? The answer is both of them."

The host laughs, the caller is silent. Next comes the obligatory question about whether AIDS can be spread through coughing.

I had written a book to change the world, and here I was on talk shows throughout America, answering questions about mosquitoes and gay waiters.

This wasn't exactly what I had envisioned when I began writing *And the Band Played On*. I had hoped to effect some fundamental changes. I really believed I could alter the performance of the institutions that had allowed AIDS to sweep through America unchecked.

AIDS had spread, my book attested, because politicians, particularly those in charge of federal-level response, had viewed the disease as a political issue, not an issue of public health—they deprived researchers of anything near the resources that were needed to fight it. AIDS had spread because government health officials consistently lied to the American people about the need for more funds, being more concerned with satisfying their political bosses and protecting their own jobs than with telling the truth and protecting the public health. And AIDS had spread because indolent news organizations shunned their responsibility to provide tough, adversarial reportage, instead basing stories largely on the Official Truth of government press releases. The response to AIDS was never even remotely commensurate with the scope of the problem.

I figured the federal government, finally exposed, would stumble over itself to accelerate the pace of AIDS research and put AIDS prevention programs on an emergency footing. Once publicly embarrassed by the revelations of its years of shameful neglect, the media would launch serious investigative reporting on the epidemic. Health officials would step forward and finally lay bare the truth about how official disregard had cost this country hundreds of thousands of lives. And it would never happen again.

I was stunned by the "success" of my book. I quickly acquired all the trappings of bestsellerdom: *60 Minutes* coverage of my "startling" revelations, a Book-of-the-Month Club contract, a miniseries deal with NBC, translation into six languages, book tours on three continents, featured roles in movie-star-studded AIDS fund raisers, regular appearances on network news shows, and hefty fees on the college lecture circuit. A central figure in my book became one of *People* magazine's "25 Most Intriguing People of 1987," even though he had been dead for nearly four years, and the *Los Angeles Herald Examiner* pronounced me one of the "in" authors of 1988. The mayor of San Francisco even proclaimed my birthday last year "Randy Shilts Day."

And one warm summer day as I was sunning at a gay resort in the redwoods north of San Francisco, a well-toned, perfectly tanned young man slid into a chaise next to me and offered the ultimate testimony to my fifteen minutes of fame. His dark eyelashes rising an falling shyly, he whispered, "When I saw you on *Good Morning America* a couple weeks ago, I wondered what it would be like to go to bed with you."

"You're the world's first AIDS celebrity," enthused a friend at the World Health Organization, after hearing one of WHO's most eminent AIDS authorities say he would grant me an interview on one condition—that I autograph his copy of my book. "It must be great," he said.

It's not so great.

The bitter irony is, my role as an AIDS celebrity just gives me a more elevated promontory from which to watch the world make the same mistakes in the handling of the AIDS epidemic that I had hoped my work would help to change. When I return from network tapings and celebrity glad-handing, I come back to my home in San Francisco's gay community and see friends dying. The lesions spread from their cheeks to cover their faces, their hair falls out, they die slowly, horribly, and sometimes suddenly, before anybody has a chance to know they're sick. They die in my arms and in my dreams, and nothing at all has changed.

Never before have I succeeded so well; never before have I failed so miserably.

I gave my first speech on the college lecture circuit at the University of California at Los Angeles in January 1988. I told the audience that there were 50,000 diagnosed AIDS cases in the United States as of that week and that within a few months there would be more people suffering from this deadly disease in the United States than there were Americans killed during the Vietnam War. There were audible gasps. During the question-and-answer session, several students explained that they had heard that the number of AIDS cases in America was leveling off.

In the next speech, at the University of Tennessee, I decided to correct such misapprehension by adding the federal government's projection—the 270,000 expected to be dead or dying from AIDS in 1991, when the disease would kill more people than any single form of cancer, more than car accidents. When I spoke at St. Cloud State University in Minnesota three months later, I noted that the number of American AIDS cases had that week surpassed the Vietnam benchmark. The reaction was more a troubled murmur than a gasp.

By the time I spoke at New York City's New School for Social Research in June and there were 65,000 AIDS cases nationally, the numbers were changing so fast that the constant editing made my notes difficult to read. By then as many 1,000 Americans a week were learning that they, too, had AIDS, or on the average, about one every fourteen minutes. There were new government projections to report, too: by 1993, some 450,000 Americans would be diagnosed with AIDS. In that year, one American will be diagnosed with the disease every thirty-six seconds. Again, I heard the gasps.

For my talks at a hospital administrators' conference in Washington in August, I started using little yellow stick-ons to update the numbers on my outline. That made it easier to read; there were now 72,000 AIDS cases. Probably this month, or next, I'll tell another college audience that the nation's AIDS case load has topped 100,000, and there will be gasps again.

The gasps always amaze me. Why are they surprised? In epidemics, people get sick and die. That's what epidemics do to people and that's why epidemics are bad.

When Kit Herman was diagnosed with AIDS on May 13, 1986, his doctor leaned over his hospital bed, took his hand, and assured him, "Don't worry, you're in time for AZT." The drug worked so well that all Kit's friends let themselves think he might make it. And we were bolstered by the National Institutes of Health's assurance that AZT was only the first generation of AIDS drugs, and that the hundreds of millions of federal dollars going into AIDS treatment research meant there would soon be a second and third generation of treatments to sustain life beyond AZT's effectiveness. Surely nothing was more important, considering the federal government's own estimates that between 1 and 1.5 million Americans were infected with the Human Immunodeficiency Virus (HIV), and virtually all would die within the next decade if nothing was done. The new drugs, the NIH assured everyone, were "in the pipeline," and government scientists were working as a fast as they possibly could.

Despite my nagging, not one of dozens of public-affairs-show producers chose to look seriously into the development of those long-sought second and third generations of AIDS drugs. In fact, clinical trials of AIDS drugs were hopelessly stalled in the morass of bureaucracy at the NIH, but this story tip never seemed to cut it with producers. Clinical trials were not sexy. Clinical trials were boring.

I made my third *Nightline* appearance in January 1988 because new estimates had been released revealing that one in sixty-one babies born in New York City carried antibodies to the AIDS virus. And the link between those babies and the disease was intravenous drug use by one or both parents. Suddenly, junkies had become the group most likely to catch and spread AIDS through the heterosexual community. Free needles to junkies—now there was a sizzling television topic. I told the show's producers I'd talk about that, but that I was much more interested in the issue of AIDS treatments—which seemed most relevant to the night's program, since Ted Koppel's other guest was Dr. Anthony Fauci, associate NIH director for AIDs, and the Reagan administration's most visible AIDS official.

After fifteen minutes of talk on the ins and outs and pros and cons of free needles for intravenous drug users, I raised the subject of the pressing need for AIDS treatments. Koppel asked Fauci what was happening. The doctor launched into a discussion of treatments "in the pipeline" and how government scientists were working as fast as they possibly could.

I'd heard the same words from NIH officials for three years: drugs were in the pipeline. Maybe it was true, but when were they going to come out of their goddamn pipeline? Before I could formulate a polite retort to Fauci's stall, however, the segment was over, Ted was thanking us, and the red light on the camera had blipped off. Everyone seemed satisfied that the government was doing everything it possibly could to develop AIDS treatments.

Three months later, I was reading a week-old *New York Times* in Kit's room in the AIDS ward at San Francisco General Hospital. It was April, nearly two years after my friend's AIDS diagnosis. AZT had given him two years of nearly perfect health, but now its effect was wearing off, and Kit had suffered his first major AIDS related infection since his original bout with pneumonia—cryptococcal meningtitis. The meningitis could be treated, we all knew, but the discovery of this insidious brain infection meant more diseases were likely to follow. And the long-promised second and third generations of AIDS drugs were still nowhere on the horizon.

While perusing the worn copy of the *Times,* I saw a story about Dr. Fauci's testimony at a congressional hearing. After making Fauci swear an oath to tell the truth, a subcommittee headed by Congressman Ted Weiss of New York City asked why it was taking so long to get new AIDS treatments into testing at a time when Congress was putting hundreds of millions of dollars into NIH budgets for just such purposes. At first Fauci talked about unavoidable delays. He claimed government scientists were working as fast as they could. Pressed harder, he finally admitted that the problem stemmed ''almost exclusively'' from the lack of staffing in his agency. Congress had allocated funds, it was true, but the Reagan administration had gotten around spending the money by stingily refusing to let Fauci hire anybody. Fauci had requested 127 positions to speed the development of AIDS treatments; the administration had granted him eleven. And for a year, he had not told anyone. For a year, this spokesman for the public health answered reporters that AIDS drugs were in the pipeline and that government scientists had all the money they needed. It seemed that only when faced with the penalty of perjury would one of the administration's top AIDS officials tell the truth. That was the real story, I thought, but for some reason nobody else had picked up on it.

At the international AIDS conference in Stockholm two months later, the other reporters in ''the AIDS pack'' congratulated me on my success and asked what I was working on now. I admitted that I was too busy promoting the British and German release of my book to do much writing myself, and next month I had the Australian tour. But if I *were* reporting, I added with a vaguely conspiratorial tone, *I'd* look at the *scandal* in the NIH. Nobody had picked up that *New York Times* story from a few months ago about staffing shortages on AIDS clinical trials. The lives of 1.5 million HIV-infected Americans hung in the balance, and the only way you could get a straight answer out of an administration AIDS official was to put him under oath and make him face the charge of perjury. Where I went to journalism school, *that* was a news story.

One reporter responded to my tip with the question ''But who's going to play *you* in the miniseries?''

A few minutes later, when Dr. Fauci came into the press room, the world's leading AIDS journalists got back to the serious business of transcribing his remarks. Nobody asked him if he was actually telling the truth, or whether they should put him under oath to ensure a candid response to questions about when we'd get AIDS treatments. Most of the subsequent news accounts of Dr. Fauci's comments faithfully reported that many AIDS treatments were in the pipeline. Government scientists, he said once more, were doing all they possibly could.

The producer assured my publisher that Morton Downey, Jr., would be ''serious'' about AIDS. ''He's not going to play games on this issue,'' the producer said, adding solemnly, ''His brother has AIDS. He understands the need for compassion.'' The abundance of Mr. Downey's compassion was implicit in the night's call-in poll question: ''Should all people with AIDS be quarantined?''

Downey's first question to me was, ''You *are* a homosexual, aren't you?''

He wasn't ready for my canned answer: ''Why do you ask? Do you want a date or something?''

The show shifted into an earnest discussion of quarantine. In his television studio, Clearasil-addled high school students from suburban New Jersey held up MORTON DOWNEY FAN CLUB signs and cheered aggressively when the truculent, chain-smoking host appeared to favor a kind of homespun AIDS Auschwitz. The youths shouted down any audience member who stepped forward to defend the rights of AIDS sufferers, their howls growing particularly vitriolic if the speakers were gay. These kids were the ilk from which Hitler drew his Nazi youth. In the first commercial break, the other guest, an AIDS activist, and I told Downey we would walk off the show if he didn't tone down his gay-baiting rhetoric. Smiling amiably, Downey took a long drag on his cigarette and assured us, ''Don't worry, I have a fallback position.''

That comment provided one of the most lucid moments in my year as an AIDS celebrity. Downey's ''fallback position,'' it was clear, was the opposite of what he was promoting on the air. Of course, he didn't *really* believe that people with AIDS, people like his brother, should all be locked up. This was merely a deliciously provocative posture to exploit the working-class resentments of people who needed someone to hate. AIDS sufferers and gays would do for this week. Next week, if viewership dropped and Downey needed a new whipping boy, maybe he'd move on to Arabs, maybe Jews. It didn't seem to matter much to him, since he didn't believe what he was saying anyway. For Morton Downey, Jr., talking about AIDS was not an act of conscience; it was a ratings ploy. He knew it, he let his guests know it, his producers certainly knew it, and his television station knew it. The only people left out of the joke were his audience.

The organizers of the Desert AIDS Project had enlisted actor Kirk Douglas and CBS morning anchor Kathleen Sullivan to be honorary co-chairs of the Palm Springs fund raiser. The main events would include a celebrity tennis match pitting Douglas against Mayor Sonny Bono, and a $1,500-a-head dinner at which I would receive a Lucite plaque for my contributions to the fight against AIDS. The next morning I would fly to L.A. to speak at still another event, this one with Shirley MacLaine, Valerie Harper, and Susan Dey of *L.A. Law*.

The desert night was exquisite. There were 130 dinner guests, the personification of elegance and confidence, who gathered on a magnificent patio of chocolate-brown Arizona flagstone at the home of one of Palm Spring's most celebrated interior designers. A lot of people had come simply to see what was regarded as one of the most sumptuous dwellings in this sumptuous town.

When I was called to accept my reward, I began with the same lineup of jokes I use on talk shows and on the college lecture circuit. They work every time.

I told the crowd about how you get AIDS from a mosquito.

Kirk Douglas laughed; everybody laughed.

Next, I did the how-many-gay-waiters joke.

Kirk Douglas laughed; everybody laughed.

Then I mentioned the woman who asked whether she could get AIDS from a waiter ejaculating in her salad dressing.

That one always has my college audiences rolling in the aisles, so I paused for the expected hilarity.

But in the utter stillness of the desert night air, all that could be heard was the sound of Kirk Douglas's steel jaw dropping to the magnificent patio of chocolate-brown Arizona flagstone. The rest was silence.

''You've got to remember that most of these people came because they're my clients,'' the host confided later. ''You said that, and all I could think was how I'd have to go back to stitching slipcovers when this was done.''

It turned out that there was more to my lead-balloon remark than a misjudged audience. Local AIDS organizers told me that a year earlier, a rumor that one of Palm Springs's most popular restaurants was owned by a homosexual, and that most of its waiters were gay, had terrified the elite community. Patronage at the eatery quickly plummeted, and it had nearly gone out of business. Fears that I dismissed as laughable were the genuine concerns of my audience, I realized. My San Francisco joke was a Palm Springs fable.

As I watched the busboys clear the tables later that night, I made a mental note not to tell that joke before dinner again. Never had I seen so many uneaten salads, so much wasted iceberg lettuce.

• • •

A friend had just tested antibody positive, and I was doing my best to cheer him up as we ambled down the sidewalk toward a Castro Street restaurant a few blocks from where I live in San Francisco. It seems most of my conversations now have to do with who has tested positive or lucked out and turned up negative, or who is too afraid to be tested. We had parked our car near Coming Home, the local hospice for AIDS patients and others suffering from terminal illnesses, and as we stepped around a nondescript, powder-blue van that blocked our path, two men in white uniforms emerged from the hospice's side door. They carried a stretcher, and on the stretcher was a corpse, neatly wrapped in a royal-blue blanket and secured with navy-blue straps. My friend and I stopped walking. The men quickly guided the stretcher into the back of the van, climbed in the front doors, and drove away. We continued our walk but didn't say anything.

I wondered if the corpse was someone I had known. I'd find out Thursday when the weekly gay paper came out. Every week there are at least two pages filled with obituaries of the previous week's departed. Each week, when I turn to those pages, I hold my breath, wondering whose picture I'll see. It's the only way to keep track, what with so many people dying.

Sometimes I wonder if an aberrant mother or two going to mass at the Most Holy Redeemer Church across the street from Coming Home Hospice has ever warned a child, "That's where you'll end up if you don't obey God's law." Or whether some youngster, feeling that first awareness of a different sexuality, has looked at the doorway of this modern charnel house with an awesome, gnawing dread of annihilation.

"Is the limousine here? Where are the dancers?"

The room fell silent. Blake Rothaus had sounded coherent until that moment, but he was near death now and his brain was going. We were gathered around his bed in a small frame house on a dusty street in Oklahoma City. The twenty-four-year-old was frail and connected to life through a web of clear plastic tubing. He stared up at us and seemed to recognize from our looks that he had lapsed into dementia. A friend broke the uncomfortable silence.

"Of course, we all brought our dancing shoes," he said. "Nice fashionable pumps at that. I wouldn't go out without them."

Everyone laughed and Blake Rothaus was lucid again.

Blake had gone to high school in a San Francisco suburb. When he was a sophomore, he told us, he and his best friend sometimes skipped school, sneaking to the city to spend their afternoons in the gay neighborhood around Castro Street.

It's a common sight, suburban teenagers playing hooky on Castro Street. I could easily imagine him standing on a corner not far from my house. But back in 1982, when he was eighteen, I was already writing about a mysterious, unnamed disease that had claimed 330 victims in the United States.

Blake moved back to Oklahoma City with his family after he graduated from high school. When he fell ill with AIDS, he didn't mope. Instead, he started pestering Oklahoma health officials with demands to educate people about this disease and to provide services for the sick. The state health department didn't recoil. At the age of twenty-two, Blake Rothaus had become the one-man nucleus for Oklahoma's first AIDS patient services. He was the hero of the Sooner State's AIDS movement and something of a local legend.

Though the state had reported only 250 AIDS cases, Oklahoma City had a well-coordinated network of religious leaders, social workers, health-care providers, gay-rights advocates, state legislators, and businessmen, all committed to providing a sane and humane response to this frightening new disease.

"I think it's the old Dust Bowl mentality," suggested one AIDS organizer. "When the hard times come, people pull together."

My past year's travels to twenty-nine states and talks with literally thousands of people have convinced me of one thing about this country and AIDS: most Americans want to do the right thing about this epidemic. Some might worry about mosquitoes and a few may be suspicious of their salad dressing. But beyond these fears is a reservoir of compassion and concern that goes vastly underreported by a media that needs conflict and heartlessness to fashion a good news hook.

In Kalamazoo, Michigan, when I visited my stepmother, I was buttonholed by a dozen middle-aged women who wondered anxiously whether we were any closer to a vaccine or a long-term treatment. One mentioned a hemophiliac nephew. Another had a gay brother in Chicago. A third went to a gay hairdresser who, she quickly added, was one of the finest people you'd ever meet. When I returned to my conservative hometown of Aurora, Illnois, nestled among endless fields of corn and soy, the local health department told me they receive more calls than they know what to do with from women's groups, parishes, and community organizations that want to do something to help. In New Orleans, the archconservative, pro-nuke, anti-gay bishop had taken up the founding of an AIDS hospice as a personal mission because, he said, when people are sick, you've got to help them out.

Scientists, reporters, and politicians privately tell me that of course *they* want to do more about AIDS, but they have to think about the Morton Downeys of the world, who argue that too much research or too much news space or too much official sympathy is being meted out to a bunch of miscreants. They do as much as they can, they insist; more would rile the resentments of the masses. So the institutions fumble along, convinced they must pander to the lowest common denominator, while the women and men of America's heartland pull me aside to fret about a dying cousin or co-worker and to plead, "When will there be a cure? When will this be over?"

"I think I'll make it through this time," Kit said to me, "but I don't have it in me to go through it again."

We were in room 3 in San Francisco General Hospital's ward 5A, the AIDS ward. The poplar trees outside Kit's window were losing their leaves, and the first winter's chill was settling over the city. I was preparing to leave for my fourth and, I hoped, final media tour, this time for release of the book in paperback and on audiocassette; Kit was preparing to die.

The seizures had started a week earlier, indicating he was suffering either from toxoplasmosis, caused by a gluttonous protozoa that sets up housekeeping in the brain; or perhaps it was a relapse of cryptococcal meningitis; or, another specialist guessed, it could be one of those other nasty brain infections that nobody had seen much of until the past year. Now that AIDS patients were living longer, they fell victim to even more exotic infections than in the early days. But the seizures were only part of it. Kit had slowly been losing the sight in his left eye to a herpes infection. And the Kaposi's sarcoma lesions that had scarred his face were beginning to coat the inside of his lungs. When Kit mentioned he'd like to live until Christmas, the doctors said he might want to consider having an early celebration this year, because he wasn't going to be alive in December.

"I can't take another infection," Kit said.

"What does that mean?"

"Morphine," Kit answered, adding mischievously, "lots of it."

We talked briefly about the mechanics of suicide. We both knew people who'd made a mess of it, and people who had done it right. It was hardly the first time the subject had come up in conversation for either of us. Gay men facing AIDS now exchange formulas for suicide as casually as housewives swap recipes for chocolate-chip cookies.

Kit was released from the hospital a few days later. He had decided to take his life on a Tuesday morning. I had to give my first round of interviews in Los

Angeles that day, so I stopped on the way to the airport to say goodbye on Monday. All day Tuesday, while I gave my perfectly formed sound bites in a round of network radio appearances, I wondered: Is this the moment he's slipping out of consciousness and into that perfect darkness? When I called that night, it turned out he'd delayed his suicide until Thursday to talk to a few more relatives. I had to give a speech in Portland that day, so on the way to the airport I stopped again. He showed me the amber-brown bottle with the bubble-gum-pink morphine syrup, and we said another goodbye.

The next morning, Kit drank his morphine and fell into a deep sleep. That afternoon, he awoke and drowsily asked what time it was. When told it was five hours later, he murmured, "That's amazing. I should have been dead hours ago."

And then he went back to sleep.

That night, Kit woke up again.

"You know what they say about near-death experiences?" he asked. "Going toward the light?"

Shaking his head, he sighed, "No light. Nothing."

His suicide attempt a failure, Kit decided the timing of his death would now be up to God. I kept up on the bizarre sequence of events by phone and called as soon as I got back to San Francisco. I was going to tell Kit that his theme song should be "Never Can Say Goodbye," but then the person on the other end of the phone told me that Kit had lapsed into a coma.

The next morning, he died.

Kit's death was like everything about AIDS—anticlimactic. By the time he actually did die, I was almost beyond feeling.

The next day, I flew to Boston for the start of the paperback tour, my heart torn between rage and sorrow. All week, as I was chauffeured to my appearances on *Good Morning America, Larry King Live,* and various CNN shows, I kept thinking, it's all going to break. I'm going to be on a TV show with some officious government health spokesman lying to protect his job, and I'm going to start shouting, "You lying son of a bitch. Don't you know there are people, real people, people I love out there dying?" Or I'll be on a call-in show and another mother will phone about her thirty-seven-year-old son who just died and it will hit me all at once, and I'll start weeping.

But day after day as the tour went on, no matter how many official lies I heard and how many grieving mothers I talked to, the crack-up never occurred. All my answers came out rationally in tight little sound bites about institutional barriers to AIDS treatments and projections about 1993 case loads.

By the last day of the tour, when a limousine picked me up at my Beverly Hills hotel for my last round of satellite TV interviews, I knew I had to stop. In a few weeks I'd return to being national correspondent for the *Chronicle,* and it was time to get off the AIDS celebrity circuit, end the interviews and decline the invitations to the star-studded fund raisers, and get back to work as a newspaper reporter. That afternoon, there was just one last radio interview to a call-in show in the San Fernando Valley, and then it would be over.

The first caller asked why his tax money should go toward funding an AIDS cure when people got the disease through their own misdeeds.

I used my standard jukebox answer about how most cancer cases are linked to people's behavior but that nobody ever suggested we stop trying to find a cure for cancer.

A second caller phoned to ask why her tax money should go to finding an AIDS cure when these people clearly deserved what they got.

I calmly put a new spin on the same answer, saying in America you usually don't sentence people to die for having a different lifestyle from yours.

Then a third caller phoned in to say that he didn't care if all those queers and junkies died, as did a fourth and fifth and sixth caller. By then I was shouting. "You stupid bigot. You just want to kill off everybody you don't like. You goddamn Nazi."

The talk-show host sat in stunned silence. She'd heard I was so *reasonable*. My anger baited the audience further, and the seventh and eighth callers began talking about "you guys," as if only a faggot like myself could give a shit about whether AIDS patients all dropped dead tomorrow.

In their voices, I heard the reporters asking polite questions of NIH officials. Of course, they had to be polite to the government doctors; dying queers weren't anything to lose your temper over. I heard the dissembling NIH researchers go home to their wives at night, complain about the lack of personnel, and shrug; this was just how it was going to have to be for a while. They'd excuse their inaction by telling themselves that if they went public and lost their jobs, worse people would replace them. It was best to go along. But how would they feel if *their* friends, *their* daughters, were dying of this disease? Would they be silent—or would they shout? Maybe they'll forgive me for suspecting they believed that ultimately a bunch of fags weren't worth losing a job over. And when I got home, I was going to have to watch my friends get shoved into powder-blue vans, and it wasn't going to change.

The history of the AIDS epidemic, of yesterday and of today, was echoing in the voices of those callers. And I was screaming at them, and the show host just sat there stunned, and I realized I had rendered my self utterly and completely inarticulate.

I stopped, took a deep breath, and returned to compound-complex sentences about the American tradition of compassion and the overriding need to overcome institutional barriers to AIDS treatments.

When I got home to San Francisco that night, I looked over some notes I had taken from a conversation I'd had with Kit during his last stay in the hospital. I was carping about how frustrated I was at the prospect of returning to my reporting job. If an internationally acclaimed best seller hadn't done shit to change the world, what good would mere newspaper stories do?

"The limits of information," Kit said. "There's been a lot written on it."

"Oh," I said.

Kit closed his eyes briefly and faded into sleep while plastic tubes fed him a cornucopia of antibiotics. After five minutes, he stirred, looked up, and added, as if we had never stopped talking, "But you don't really have a choice. You've got to keep on doing it. What else are you going to do?"

DISCUSSION QUESTIONS

1. What factors, according to Randy Shilts, are responsible for the spread of AIDS in the United States? Why did the U.S. government not provide greater funding for AIDS research once the disease had become an epidemic?
2. Account for the difference between the two statements made by Dr. Anthony Fauci of the National Institutes of Health before a congressional committee and on "Nightline," respectively? Why, according to Shilts, was the *New York Times* the only major newspaper to pick up the story about Fauci's testimony?
3. Consider Shilts's recollection of his appearance on the "Morton Downey, Jr., Show." What was the host's attitude toward the AIDS epidemic? Is Downey's attitude representative of a more general attitude existing within the American media?

Ann Hodgman / No Wonder They Call Me a Bitch

Spy, June 1989

A contributing editor at the irreverent humor magazine Spy, *Ann Hodgman also writes a food column for* Eating Well. *Besides having written more than twenty children's books, she has published several volumes of humor. "No Wonder They Call Me a Bitch" is one of many humor pieces Hodgman has written for* Spy; *it was selected by Justin Kaplan for* The Best American Essays *1990. One of the nation's funniest and most satirical magazines,* Spy *was founded in 1986.*

I've always wondered about dog food. Is a Gaines-burger really like a hamburger? Can you fry it? Does dog food "cheese" taste like real cheese? Does Gravy Train actually make gravy in the dog's bowl, or is that brown liquid just dissolved crumbs? And exactly what *are* by-products?

Having spent the better part of a week eating dog food, I'm sorry to say that I now know the answers to these questions. While my dachshund, Shortie, watched in agonies of yearning, I gagged my way through can after can of stinky, white-flecked mush and bag after bag of stinky, fat-drenched nuggets. And now I understand exactly why Shortie's breath is so bad.

Of course, Gaines-burgers are neither mush nor nuggets. They are, rather, a miracle of beauty and packaging—or at least that's what I thought when I was little. I used to beg my mother to get them for our dogs, but she always said they were too expensive. When I finally bought a box of cheese-flavored Gaines-burgers—after twenty years of longing—I felt deliciously wicked.

"Dogs love real beef," the back of the box proclaimed proudly. "That's why Gaines-burgers is the only beef burger for dogs with real beef and no meat by-products!" The copy was accurate: meat by-products did not appear in the list of ingredients. Poultry by-products did, though—right there next to preserved animal fat.

One Purina spokesman told me that poultry by-products consists of necks, intestines, undeveloped eggs and other "carcass remnants," but not feathers, heads, or feet. When I told him I'd been eating dog food, he said, "Oh, you're kidding! Oh, *no!*" (I came to share his alarm when, weeks later, a second Purina spokesman said that Gaines-burgers *do* contain poultry heads and feet—but *not* undeveloped eggs.)

Up close my Gaines-burger didn't much resemble chopped beef. Rather, it looked—and felt—like a single long, extruded piece of redness that had been chopped into segments and formed into a patty. You could make one at home if you had a Play-Doh Fun Factory.

I turned on the skillet. While I waited for it to heat up I pulled out a shred of cheese-colored material and palpated it. Again, like Play-Doh, it was quite malleable. I made a little cheese bird out of it; then I counted to three and ate the bird.

There was a horrifying rush of cheddar taste, followed immediately by the dull tang of soybean flour—the main ingredient in Gaines-burgers. Next I tried a piece of red extrusion. The main difference between the meat-flavored and cheese-flavored extrusions is one of texture. The "cheese" chews like fresh Play-Doh, whereas the "meat" chews like Play-Doh that's been sitting out on a rug for a couple of hours.

Frying only turned the Gaines-burger black. There was no melting, no sizzling, no warm meat smells. A cherished childhood illusion was gone. I flipped the patty into the sink, where it immediately began leaking rivulets of red dye.

As alarming as the Gaines-burgers were, their soy meal began to seem like an old friend when the time came to try some *canned* dog foods. I decided to try the Cycle foods first. When I opened them, I thought about how rarely I use can openers these days, and I was suddenly visited by a long-forgotten sensation of can-opener distaste. *This* is the kind of unsavory place can openers spend their time when you're not watching! Every time you open a can of, say, Italian plum tomatoes, you infect them with invisible particles of by-product.

I had been expecting to see the usual homogeneous scrapple inside, but each can of Cycle was packed with smooth, round, oily nuggets. As if someone at Gaines had been tipped off that a human would be tasting the stuff, the four Cycles really were different from one another. Cycle-1, for puppies, is wet and soyish. Cycle-2, for adults, glistens nastily with fat, but it's passably edible—a lot like some canned Swedish meatballs I once got in a care package at college. Cycle-3, the "lite" one, for fatties, had no specific flavor; it just tasted like dog food. But at least it didn't make me fat.

Cycle-4, for senior dogs, had the smallest nuggets. Maybe old dogs can't open their mouths as wide. This kind was far sweeter than the other three Cycles—almost like baked beans. It was also the only one to contain "dried beef digest," a mysterious substance that the Purina spokesman defined as "enzymes" and my dictionary defined as "the products of digestion."

Next on the menu was a can of Kal Kan Pedigree with Chunky Chicken. Chunky *chicken?* There were chunks in the can, certainly—big, purplish-brown chunks. I forked one chunk out (by now I was becoming more callous) and found that while it had no discernible chicken flavor, it wasn't bad except for its texture—like meat load with ground-up chicken bones.

In the world of canned dog food, a smooth consistency is a sign of low quality—lots of cereal. A lumpy, frightening, bloody, stringy horror is a sign of high quality—lots of meat. Nowhere in the world of wet dog foods was this demonstrated better than in the fanciest I tried—Kal Kan's Pedigree Select Dinners. These came not in a can but in a tiny foil packet with a picture of an imperious Yorkie. When I pulled open the container, juice spurted all over my hand, and the first chunk I speared was trailing a long gray vein. I shrieked and went instead for a plain chunk, which I was able to swallow only after taking a break to read some suddenly fascinating office equipment catalogues. Once again, though, it tasted no more alarming than, say, canned hash.

Still, how pleasant it was to turn to *dry* dog food! Gravy Train was the first I tried, and I'm happy to report that it really does make a "thick, rich, real beef gravy" when you mix it with water. Thick and rich, anyway. Except for a lingering rancid-fat flavor, the gravy wasn't beefy, but since it tasted primarily like tap water, it wasn't nauseating either.

My poor dachshund just gets plain old Purina Dog Chow, but Purina also makes a dry food called Butcher's Blend that comes in Beef, Bacon & Chicken flavor. Here we see dog food's arcane semiotics at its best: a red triangle with a *T* stamped into it is supposed to suggest beef; a tan curl, chicken; and a brown *S,* a piece of bacon. Only dogs understand these messages. But Butcher's Blend does have an endearing slogan: "Great Meaty Tastes—without bothering the Butcher!" *You know, I wanted to buy some meat, but I just couldn't bring myself to bother the butcher. . . .*

Purina O.N.E. ("Optimum Nutritional Effectiveness") is targeted at people who are unlikely ever to worry about bothering a tradesperson. "We chose chicken as a primary ingredient in Purina O.N.E. for several reasonings,'' the long, long essay on the back of the bag announces. Chief among these reasonings, I'd guess, is the fact that chicken appeals to people who are—you know—*like us*. Although our dogs do nothing but spend eighteen-hour days alone in the apartment, we still want them to be *premium* dogs. We want them to cut down on red meat, too. We also want dog food that comes in a bag with an attractive design, a subtle type face, and no kitschy pictures of slobbering golden retrievers.

Besides that, we want a list of the Nutritional Benefits of our dog food—and we get it on O.N.E. One thing I especially like about this list is its constant references to a dog's ''hair coat,'' as in ''Beef tallow is good for the dog's skin and hair coat.'' (On the other hand, beef tallow merely provides palatability, while the dried beef digest in Cycle provides palatability *enhancement.)*

I hate to say it, but O.N.E. was pretty palatable. Maybe that's because it has about 100 percent more fat than, say, Butcher's Blend. Or maybe I'd been duped by the packaging; that's been known to happen before.

As with people food, dog snacks taste much better than dog meals. They're better looking too. Take Milk-Bone Flavor Snacks. The loving-hands-at-home prose describing each flavor is colorful; the writers practically choke on their own exuberance. Of bacon they say, ''It's so good, your dog will think it's hot off the frying pan.'' Of liver: ''The only taste your dog wants more than liver—is even more liver!'' Of poultry: ''All those farm fresh flavors deliciously mixed in one biscuit. Your dog will bark with delight!'' And of vegetable: ''Gardens of taste! Specially blended to give your dog that vegetable flavor he wants—but can rarely get!''

Well, I may be a sucker, but advertising *this* emphatic just doesn't convince me. I lined up all seven flavors of Milk-Bone Flavor Snacks on the floor. Unless my dog's palate is a lot more sensitive than mine—and considering that she steals dirty diapers out of the trash and eats them, I'm loath to think it is—she doesn't detect any more difference in the seven flavors than I did when I tried them.

I much preferred Bonz, the hard-baked, bone-shaped snack stuffed with simulated marrow. I liked the bone part, that is; it tasted almost exactly like the cornmeal it was made of. The mock marrow inside was a bit more problematic: in addition to looking like the sludge that collects in the treads of my running shoes, it was bursting with tiny hairs.

I'm sure you have a few dog food questions of your own. To save us time, I've answered them in advance.

Q. Are those little cans of Mighty Dog actually branded with the sizzling word BEEF, *the way they show in the commercials?*

A. You should know by now that that kind of thing never happens.

Q. Does chicken-flavored dog food taste like chicken-flavored cat food?

A. To my surprise, chicken cat food was actually a little better—more chickeny. It tasted like inferior canned pâté.

Q. Was there any dog food that you just couldn't bring yourself to try?

A. Alas, it was a can of Mighty Dog called Prime Entree with Bone Marrow. The meat was dark, dark brown, and it was surrounded by gelatin that was almost black. I knew I would die if I tasted it, so I put it outside for the raccoons.

DISCUSSION QUESTIONS

1. A good humorist likes to have many targets. How many things is Ann Hodgman making fun of in this essay?
2. Though the piece is comic through and through, can you detect any serious side to Hodgman's intentions? Who or what is being satirized?

Elizabeth F. Brown, M.D. and William R. Hendee, Ph.D. / Adolescents and Their Music

Journal of the American Medical Association, September 22/29, 1989

America's most popular music has come under attack once again. Rock music is under fire from religious groups, angry parents, social critics, and even the United States government. It has been charged with contributing to problems ranging from drug addiction to teen suicide, from illiteracy to criminal behavior in young adults. While these accusations are difficult to prove, few of us would disagree with the position that rock music plays an important role in the daily lives of adolescents.

Elizabeth F. Brown, M.D. and William R. Hendee, Ph.D., provide a survey of many recent studies devoted to the effects of rock music on teens. They appeal to physicians to consider carefully rock's influence on their adolescent patients. Dedicated to keeping physicians and other health professionals informed about advances in medicine and alerting them to new health problems, the Journal of American Medical Association *is the most widely read periodical of its kind.*

During adolescence, teenagers are expected to develop standards of behavior and reconcile them with their perceptions of adult standards. In this context, music, a powerful medium in the lives of adolescents, offers conflicting values. The explicit sexual and violent lyrics of some forms of music often clash with the themes of abstinence and rational behavior promoted by adult society. Identification with rock music, particularly those styles that are rejected by adults, functions to separate adolescents from adult society. Some forms of rock musics extended well beyond respectability in fulfilling this definitional role. Total immersion into a rock subculture, such as heavy metal, may be both a portrait of adolescent alienation and an unflattering reflection of an adolescent's perception of the moral and ethical duplicity of adult society. Physicians should be aware of the role of music in the lives of adolescents and use music preferences as clues to the emotional and mental health of adolescents.

(*JAMA.* 1989;262:1659–1663)

Traditionally the role of physicians has been to conquer disease and promote health. For physicians who treat adolescents, this role has become increasingly challenging. Often an adolescent presents with a seemingly trivial physical complaint that, after questioning by the physician, expands into a set of complex problems related to the teenager's psychosocial environment. Frequently the tragic health problems of teenagers, such as unplanned teen pregnancies, accidents, and violence, have strong roots in the psychosocial environment. Prevention and intervention in these health problems require the physician to be more sensitive and knowledgeable about the environment of adolescents.[1]

Health promotion and disease prevention in the adolescent encompass multiple dimensions of health care. They go beyond the traditional advocacy of a healthy diet, exercise, and avoidance of health risks such as tobacco, drugs, and excess alcohol to an understanding of the sociocultural forces that influence adolescents as they experience the transition into adulthood. Appreciation of this environment not only yields insights into the challenges facing adolescents but also enables the physician to identify adverse psychosocial problems and intervene before their consequences are expressed as health problems. One aspect of the adolescent environment that has been a source of concern since its appearance in the 1950s has been the role of rock music, specifically its lyrics. This concern has been enhanced by the visual imagery of rock music videos.

The term *rock music* is frequently used generically to encompass any type of music listened to by teenagers. However, the music associated with adolescents has, over the years, splintered into a wide variety of styles, including punk, heavy metal, rap, hip-hop, and house music, to name a few. The latter three styles are particularly identified with black adolescents. In this article, we have chosen to define rock music more narrowly, as music that might also be referred to as popular music and is typically played on the top-40 radio stations. This type of rock music is most often listened to by white adolescents. Much of the communications research has focused on this type of rock music and consequently on its effects on white adolescents. This article reviews and analyzes the recent communications literature on the impact of rock music on the lives of adolescents.

THE ROLE OF ROCK MUSIC

Music long has been recognized as a powerful communicative force that affects attitude, mood, emotions, and behavior. Anthropologist A. P. Merriam in his book *The Anthropology of Music* says, "The importance of music, as judged by the sheer ubiquity of its presence is enormous . . . there is probably no other human cultural activity which is so all pervasive and which reaches into, shapes and often controls so much of human behavior."[2]

For today's adolescents, music is particularly ubiquitous. During the early years of rock music, radios were heavy, bulky, and essentially stationary. Music became portable with the advent of transistor radios. Recent innovations in miniaturization and the development of light high-quality headphones have made it possible for teenagers to envelop themselves constantly in rock music. Between the seventh and 12th grades, the average teenager listens to 10,500 hours of rock music, just slightly less than the entire number of hours spent in the classroom from kindergarten through high school.[3] During this period, television viewing decreases and music becomes an increasingly powerful medium in an adolescent's life.[4]

Unlike television, for which the patterns of viewing are often subject to family discussion and parental control, music is largely uncensored. Parents frequently do not appreciate the sound of rock music and therefore ignore it. In the home, teenagers often listen to music in the privacy of their bedrooms,[5] and the ideas presented in the music are interpreted privately, without modulation or guidance by parents. Unlike television, music is controlled by the user; a song can be replayed anytime, anywhere, any number of times.

Music is important to adolescents in many ways. For example, music plays a large role in adolescent socialization. As adolescents gain independence, they turn to music as an information source about sexuality and alternative lifestyles, subjects that are largely taboo in both home and school.[6,7] Music can also introduce adolescents to political topics via the various concerts organized around political causes—for example, Amnesty International, Live Aid, or Farm Aid.

For young people, music is an important symbol in their search for independence and autonomy. Identification with a particular musical style may indicate resistance to authority, provide an outlet for personal troubles or conflicts with parents, or yield a sense of relaxation, release, and security in new environments. Music can be used to heighten emotions and encourage movement, such as dancing or clapping, or can be used to soothe emotions and provide relaxation. Music can be used alone, as background for other activities, or as the focus of events such as concerts.[8–10]

While rock music may generally symbolize adolescent rebellion and search for autonomy, the forms it takes differ among different cultures—the preference of black adolescents for rap or house music has already been mentioned—and also between sexes. For example, heavy metal music with its loud beat and performers with aggressive and startling stage antics attracts primarily white male adolescents. On the other hand, adolescent girls tend to be more attracted to soft, romantic, nonthreatening music. Weinstein[11] proposes that these musical preferences reflect the different types of struggles that boys and girls face as they make the transition to adulthood. As children, boys are typically allowed more freedom, to behave more aggressively, and to be slightly naughty. In contrast, as an adult, strict conformity and supervision is the rule. Heavy metal music then, though an extreme example and certainly not appealing to all boys, represents this conflict. A salient struggle for adolescent girls is the emergence of sexuality and the initiation, or at least contemplation, of sexual activity, Soft, romantic music serves to ease tensions about sexual activity in a nonthreatening way.[11]

Knowledge of rock music is used as a criterion of expertise by many adolescents, and music and musical personalities are often the subject of adolescent conversations. Shared enjoyment of music can be the basis of new friendships and form the basis of peer groups. Rock music has spawned many ''cultural accessories'' such as T-shirts, posters, and dress styles that are a prominent part of the adolescent's life.[6] Some youth subcultures such as punk rockers and heavy metal stylists can be immediately identified by music and sartorial preferences that imply a common bond with other devotees of the same musical genre.

In some cases, identifying features of adolescent preferences transmit a strong message of adolescent alienation. For example, Roe[10] proposes that there is a causal link between school performance and music preference. Specifically, academic performance defines status; negative status can lead to antischool activities, which then in turn result in alignment with an adolescent subculture. Therefore, students who perform well in school will be more likely to embrace the values taught in school, while those who perform poorly are more likely to react negatively toward the institution that labeled them failures. A heavy involvement in rock music by low achievers may be an adaptive reaction to their failures as students and an expression of their alienation from school and the learning experience. Affiliation with a particular teen subculture provides these youngsters with an identity and reputation that has been unattainable through academic performance.[10]

A longitudinal study of the academic performance and music preference of Swedish youths from age 11 to 15 years support this hypothesis. Successful students, including those from low socioeconomic backgrounds, exhibited a preference for mainstream music, less interest in punk and rock music, and less involvement in peer groups. Lower school achievement was indirectly related to a preference for rock music through an intervening factor of greater involvement with peer groups. In addition, a negative commitment to school, identified on a questionnaire, was directly related to a preference for punk and rock music.[10]

Roe[10] states that ''the findings unequivocally support the argument that music preferences are dependent on earlier levels of school achievement.'' This analysis challenges the widely held assumption that music, as a competitor for the time and commitment of young people, has a deleterious effect on school. It also suggests that teenage immersion into a rock subculture may be primarily symptomatic of alienation and hostility toward adult society.

Television is the entertainment medium for mainstream America, whereas rock music represents the adolescent peer culture. A study by Larson and Kubey[5] revealed that adolescents who preferred to watch television spent more time with their families and were reasonably well integrated into mainstream American culture. Similarly, heavy involvement with rock music is associated with a greater commitment to peer groups and less association with family.

ROCK MUSIC LYRICS AND VIDEOS

Against a backdrop of the pervasive presence of music, its multiple roles, and its power in communicating messages, the lyrics and images of rock music have been a persistent controversy. As a reflection of its origin in rhythm and blues, rock music espouses the themes of rebellion and sex. Even the words ''rock 'n' roll'' have strong sexual connotations. Attempts at censorship have occurred since the inception of rock music. For example, the BBC banned the line ''I'd love to turn you on'' in the Beatles song, ''A Day in the Life.'' To appear on the *Ed Sullivan Show* the Rolling Stones were required to change the lyrics and title of their song from ''Let's spend the night together'' to ''Let's spend some time together'' (*New Republic*. August 12, 1985;19:14–16).[12]

Such concerns seem quaint in light of the explicitness of the lyrics of current rock music. Parents groups and other concerned citizens have characterized many rock lyrics as sexually explicit and violent. For example, the song ''Darling Nikki'' by rock star Prince (which sold 10 million copies) speaks crudely of masturbation, and other songs by this artist refer to fellatio and incest. Ozzy Osborne's ''Suicide Solution'' distinctly advocates suicide.

Heavy metal music, a musical style more rebellious than mainstream rock music, features a loud pulsating rhythm and abounds with lyrics that glorify hatred, abuse, sexual deviancy, and occasionally satanism. While rock and roll has always symbolized rebellion, it has only recently embraced outright hatred and rejection through the style of heavy metal.[13] In earlier music that preceded rock and roll, connotations were implicit, often using the word ''it'' as an euphemism for sexual experiences, such as in Cole Porter's ''Birds do it, bees do it.'' Even the Beatles proposed, ''Why don't we do it in the road?'' In the 1980s the word ''it'' is no longer needed; the most deviant sexual activities can be described.[3]

Preteens and teenagers are highly impressionable and many have speculated that they may be particularly sensitive to the messages of rock music. In *The Closing of the American Mind,* Bloom[14] calls music the ''medium of the human soul.'' He finds rock music barren and a ''junk food for the human soul.'' Young teenagers with emerging concepts of sensuality and sexuality are not nurtured slowly and carefully by rock music; they are bombarded with messages about adult sexuality and perversities at an age when they have immature concepts of love, caring, and commitment. According to Bloom, the pervasiveness of rock music undermines parental control over a child's moral education.

In 1985, there were well-publicized discussions about the sexual and violent content of lyrics, prompted in part by a citizens group, The Parents' Music Research Center, which culminated in hearings before the Senate Commerce Committee in September 1985. Much of the discussion and controversy centered on adults' perceptions of the meanings of rock music. However, several studies indicate that an adult's interpretation of rock lyrics might be entirely different from that of a teenager.[15] A complete understanding of rock lyrics that is consonant with an adult's interpretation of the lyrics often requires sophistication beyond the reach of young persons. The symbolic meaning of a song, represented more by the rhythm of the music and personalities of the artists, may transcend any explicit appreciation or interpretation of its lyrics and may be the primary attraction for adolescents. For example, few teenagers in a survey of Southern California high schools correctly identified sex, drugs, or violence as subjects of their favorite songs. In 37% of songs listed as their favorites, the students were unable to identify any theme. Sex, drugs, or violence were identified in only 7% of the songs and even then the students' interpretations of the lyrics were frequently quite literal and unsophisticated; the teenagers very infrequently understood the symbolic meanings of the lyrics. The most prevalent items identified by the students were love and friendship and other themes that generally reflected experiences of teenage life.[15]

In a study of upper-middle-class 4th 8th, and 12th grade and college students, Greenfield et al[16] found that a surprisingly few number of students correctly interpreted the general theme of Bruce Springsteen's song "Born in the U.S.A.," even though the song was familiar to most students and the students were questioned directly after listening to it. The "correct" interpretation of alienation vs the common "incorrect" interpretation of "Born in the U.S.A." as a patriotic song increased with the age of the students, but still barely 50% of the college students identified the "correct" theme.[16]

Even though adolescents' understanding of the lyrics might be unsophisticated, their individual appeal and symbolic importance cannot be discounted. These young persons may be responding more to the themes of independence and rebellion against parental authority symbolized by rock music than to its actual verbal messages, for music is more than lyrics, rhythm, and melody. It is an interaction of these attributes with the listener's personality and receptivity and includes a perception of attitudes and style manifested by the performer.[17]

The visual dimensions of rock music have also been an enduring concern from the era of Elvis Presley's swiveling hips to the frankly sexual or violent stage antics of today's performers such as Prince and Ozzy Osborne. Music videos have added yet another visual dimension to rock music. Typically, rock videos have a surreal, dreamlike quality with dramatic visual effects.[18] There is concern that the marriage between television and music is powerful and synergistic. Multisensory input reinforces any message, specifically by enhancing learning and recall.[13] As an example, one study of music video found that individual meanings for a music video version of a song were more favorable and potent than the audio version alone.[19]

The violent and sexual content of the video images are disturbing to many. In one content analysis of 200 concept videos (distinguished from performance videos in which the predominant theme is a studio or concert performance), violence occurred in 57% of the samples and sexual intimacy in 75%. Of the videos containing violence, 81% also contained sexual references. Half of all women who appeared in the video were dressed provocatively.[20] Another study showed that 59.7% of a random sample of rock videos had sexual themes, and 53.2% had violent themes.[21] In an analysis of sexism in a sample of rock videos, 57% of those depicting women portrayed them in a condescending manner while only 14% depicted women as fully equal to men.[22]

Studies of the effects of television violence may also apply to music videos. These studies strongly suggest, but do not verify, that there is a causal connection between television violence and subsequent aggressive behavior.[23] Gerbner and coworkers[24,25] argue that television violence also may have a more subtle influence on social relationships. They hypothesize that the violent world of television portrays a pattern of domination, sexism, and inequality that colors viewers' perceptions of the real world. Those who view an excessive amount of television tend to regard the world as mean and hostile.

However, television and music videos may not be strictly comparable. For example, the negative imagery in the visuals of music videos may be mediated by their surrealistic and abstract qualities. Burns and Thompson[26] suggest that music videos may help young people to confront the real problems of adolescents growing up in our society. The frequent themes of holocaust and apocalypse presented in music videos, while irrational and dreamlike, may offer a subjective way of addressing these threatening problems in contrast to the depressing and sometimes complacent presentation by the news media of the threat of nuclear war.

Walker[27,28] argues that the total media profile of a viewer must be assessed before the influence of any one medium can be analyzed. High levels of violence on videos would be a significant concern, for example, only if they are associated with high levels of violence on the television programs watched by the viewer. However, Walker found that music video exposure is negatively related to watching televised crime and action programs.[27,28]

Some researchers have suggested that music videos, by supplying a visual image, inhibit the imagination. When a listener hears a song previously seen on a music video, the video image comes to mind instead of an individual and personally meaningful one. In this way music videos destroy the potential of music to evoke special feelings and memories for the viewers.[29] In an informal empirical study of the effect of music videos on the imagination of fifth and sixth graders, Greenfield and coworkers[16] found that those students who had watched a music video had less imaginative responses to a series of questions than those students who had only heard an audio version of the same song. The students themselves commented that seeing a music video before hearing the song on the radio inhibited their imaginative thinking about the song. In their studies of 587 high school students, however, Sun and Lull[30] found that although students enjoyed the visual images of music videos and used them in interpreting the music, they also were actively involved in selecting the music and had some perspective on music videos' content.

THE EFFECTS OF ROCK MUSIC

The lyrics and images in rock music and rock music videos are certainly disturbing. However, there have been few studies of the effects of these new trends in music. Such a study is methodologically very difficult. Rock music audiences are not totally passive, uncritically absorbing the lyrics and images of rock music. That is, adolescents are active participants in the rock music experience and are not "victims" of rock music.[9] Rock music, or any music for that matter, is processed through several complex steps in each individual. The listener first chooses certain music to satisfy a specific need. Then the message of the music is interpreted by the individual and assimilated and applied to the listener's daily life. In this way interpretation and use of a particular message provided by music are intervening variables between the verbatim lyrics and any possible effects.

In addition both the choice of the music and the way in which it is used by its fans are heavily influenced by such variables as social class, age, education, race, religion, or gender. While both a 13-year-old girl and a blue-collar worker both might enjoy the music of Prince, for example, their interpretation of the music and the way it fits into their lives is probably very different. Music can also be but one component of an immersion into an adolescent subculture. For example, the subculture represented by punk and heavy metal music is intimately linked with distinct dress codes, language, and attitudes.[8] Quite simply, music can mean different things to different people at different times. Music is a very individual and complex experience and thus resistant to traditional research.

The effects of music and its lyrics on teenagers are subtle and cumulative and could only be definitely studied in a carefully controlled longitudinal study. This type of study is unrealistic. Therefore, it is also unrealistic to expect that any direct causal role of music on the behavior of teenagers can be easily identified.

The evidence of possible effects of explicit rock music, specifically heavy metal, has so far been anecdotal and circumstantial. Heavy metal music is of particular concern since it is such a strong expression of rebellion and sometimes alienation. For example, several murders have been correlated with a fascination for heavy metal music. The ''Night Stalker,'' a serial murderer on the West Coast, was said to be obsessed with the heavy metal band AC/DC. A 14-year-old girl, also fascinated with heavy metal music, stabbed her mother to death (*US News World Rep.* October 28, 1985:46–49). In a study of chemically dependent adolescents, 60% named heavy metal as their first choice of music, leading the author to suggest that such music is associated with and may promote destructive behavior in susceptible individuals.[31] Healthy well-adjusted teenagers, on the other hand, may be minimally affected by explicit rock music.[22]

In a laboratory study of the effect of music television (MTV), Greeson and Williams[33] found that 7th and 10th graders, after watching 1 hour of selected musics videos, were more likely to approve of premarital sex compared with a control group of adolescents. Whether there were any long-term effects or whether the music videos actually changed the behavior of the adolescents was unknown. Another behavioral study found that violent music videos desensitized viewers to violence immediately after viewing.[34] Lack of human effects studies on heavy users of music videos and rock music, particularly heavy metal, leaves a major gap in our current knowledge.

An obvious question to ask is why there has been such an upsurge in the violent and sexual imagery of rock music. The explicitness of rock music today may be due in part to the aging of rock and roll. Rock music has always functioned to define the adolescent culture as distinct from adult society. As it has aged, however, much of the rock-and-roll culture has been absorbed into the mainstream and no longer separates ''them'' from ''us.'' Former hippies and baby boomers are now parents of adolescents and many rock stars have become accepted if not embraced by the establishment. Rock music has become the voice of corporate America.[35] Eric Clapton, Phil Collins, and Steve Winwood endorse beer, the song ''Revolution'' by the Beatles is used to promote tennis shoes, and Michael Jackson is seen shaking hands with President Reagan. The album ''Purple Rain'' by rock star Prince, which contained the offensive song ''Darling Nikki,'' has won both an Oscar and a Grammy.

The sexual freedom and recreational drug use that once were the exclusive property of young people have become an accepted part of adult behavior. The lyrics of rock and roll in the 1960s, which once so shocked parents, today seem quite tame. Adult society is already sexually and behaviorally explicit, and in order for rock music to express rebellion and autonomy, the explicitness must be taken to a higher level (*New Republic.* August 12, 1985;19:14–16).

For teenagers who identify with an alienated youth subculture, rock music must go beyond respectability to fulfill its definitional role. For these teenagers, nihilistic, violent, and at times sadistic music may express their reaction to the adult world in which they see no consistent and logical set of moral values. The music may be both a portrait of their alienation and an unflattering reflection of their perception of moral and ethical duplicity of adult society.

CONCLUSION

Adolescence is a challenging period under any circumstances. Young people are expected to develop a set of moral values and reconcile them with their perceptions of adult standards and behaviors. In this context, music, a prominent medium in the lives of adolescents, sends conflicting messages. Rock music, reflective of the adolescent peer culture, symbolizes the adolescent themes of rebellion and autonomy. Increasingly it does so with disturbing lyrics that connote violence and pornographic sexual imagery. In contrast to these media messages are the themes of abstinence and reasoned, responsible behavior promoted by authority figures such as parents, teachers, and government officials. At the very least, commitment to a rock subculture is symptomatic of adolescent alienation from these authority figures.

Whether, in addition to revealing adolescent alienation, explicit lyrics are also a lasting influence on adolescent values remains to be seen. Research into the effects of media messages has been problematic because of the very pervasiveness of music and its individual appeal and meaning. The effects of rock music, particularly heavy metal music, have not yet been studied extensively. As an important agent of adolescent socialization, however, the negative messages of rock music should not be dismissed.

In interactions with adolescents and their parents, physicians should be aware, and promote awareness, of the messages of music, and should nurture and encourage alternative responsible sources of information about sexuality and responsible behavior. Physicians should also educate parents about the potential influence of both music and music videos and encourage parental awareness of an adolescent's exposure to media.[32] Inasmuch as music can be representative of an adolescent subculture, questions about music preference can be corroborating evidence when other affective behavior of the adolescent suggests potentially destructive alienation. An extreme example is total immersion into a heavy metal subculture with total identification with such bands as Slayer and Metallica. Evidence, although anecdotal, suggests that these adolescents may be at risk for drug abuse[31] or even participation in satanic activities.

At the other end of the spectrum may be parents who are concerned about the explicit rock music that their well-adjusted adolescent child is listening to. Although perhaps not entirely comforting, the physician can point out that so far there is no evidence that this music has any deleterious effect on the behavior of adolescents. As a measure of its potential effect, physicians can encourage parents to question their children, in a very nonjudgmental way, about their interpretation of the music and what role it plays in their lives.

REFERENCES

1. Blum RW. Contemporary threats to adolescent health in the United States. *JAMA*. 1987;257:3390–3395.

2. Merriam AP. *The Anthropology of Music*. Chicago, Ill: Northwestern University Press; 1964:218.

3. Davis S. Pop lyrics: a mirror and molder of society. *Et cetera*. Summer 1985:167–169.

4. Avery R. Adolescents' use of the mass media. *Am Behav Scientist*. 1979;23:53–70.

5. Larson R, Kubey R. Television and music: contrasting media in adolescent life. *Youth Soc*. 1983;15:13–31.

6. Lull J. Listeners communicative uses of popular music. In: Lull J, ed. *Popular Music and Communication*. Beverly Hills, Calif: Sage Publications; 1987:212–230.

7. Lull J. On the communicative properties of music. *Comm Res*. 1985;12:363–372.

8. Grossberg L. Is there rock after punk? *Crit Stud Mass Comm*. 1986;3:50–70.

9. Grossberg L. Rock and roll in search of an audience. In: Lull J, ed. *Popular Music and Communication*. Beverly Hills, Calif: Sage Publications; 1987:175–197.

10. Roe K. The school and music and adolescent socialization. In: Lull J, ed. *Popular Music and Communication*. Beverly Hills, Calif: Sage Publications; 1987:212–230.

11. Weinstein D. Rock: youth and its music. *Pop Music Soc*. 1983;9:2–16.

12. MacDonald JR. Censoring rock lyrics: a historical analysis of the debate. *Youth Soc*. 1988;19:294–313.

13. Steussy J. *Testimony for the United States Senate Commerce Committee*. September 19, 1985.

14. Bloom A. *The Closing of the American Mind*. New York, NY: Simon & Schuster; 1987:68–81.

15. Prinsky L, Rosenbaum J. 'Leer-ics' or lyrics: teenage impressions of rock 'n' roll. *Youth Soc*. 1987;18:384–396.

16. Greenfield PM, Bruzzone L, Koyamatsu K, et al. What is rock music doing to the minds of our youth? a first experimental look at the effects of rock music. *J Early Adolesc*. 1987;7:315–329.

17. Hyden C, McCandless N J. Men and women as portrayed in the lyrics of contemporary music. *Pop Music Soc*. 1983;9:19–25.

18. Aufderheide P. Music videos, the look of the sound. *J Comm*. 1986;36:57–77.

19. Rubin RB, Rubin AM, Perse EM, et al. Media use and meaning of music video. *Journalism Q*. 1986;63:353–359.

20. Sherman RL, Dominick JR. Violence and sex in music videos: TV and rock 'n' roll. *J Comm*. 1986;36:79–93.

21. Baxter RL, DeRiemer C, Laudini A, et al. A content analysis of music videos. *J Broadcast Electron Media*. 1985;29:333–340.

22. Vincent RC, Davis DK, Bronszkowski LA. Sexism in MTV: the portrayal of women in rock videos. *Journalism Q*. 1987;64:750–755,941.

23. National Institute of Mental Health. *Television and Behavior: Ten Years of Scientific Progress and Implication for the Eighties. Summary Report*. Washington, DC: Dept of Health and Human Services; 1982. Publication 82–1195;1.

24. Gerbner G, Gross L, Signiorelli N, Morgan M, Jackson-Beech M. The demonstration of power: violence profile No. 10. *J Comm*. 1978;28:176–207.

25. Gerbner G, Gross L, Morgan M, Signiorelli N. The 'mainstreaming' of America: violence profile No. 11. *J Comm*. 1980;30:10–29.

26. Burns G, Thompson R. Music, television and video: historical and aesthetic considerations. *Pop Music Soc*. 1987;11:79–89.

27. Walker JR. How viewing of MTV relates to exposure of other media violence. *Journalism Q*. 1987;64:756–762.

28. Walker JR. The context of MTV: adolescent media use and music television. *Pop Music Soc*. 1987;18:177–189.

29. Abt D. Music video: impact of the visual dimension. In: Lull J, ed. *Popular Music and Communication*. Beverly Hills, Calif: Sage Publications; 1987:96–109.

30. Sun SW, Lull J. The adolescent audience for music videos and why they watch. *J Comm*. 1986;36:115–125.

31. King P. Heavy metal music and drug use in adolescents. *Postgrad Med*. 1988;83:295–304.

32. Frith S. *The Sociology of Rock*. London, England: Constable; 1978.

33. Greeson LE, Williams RA. Social implications of music videos for youth: an analysis of the contents and effects of MTV. *Youth Soc*. 1986;18:177–189.

34. Rehman S, Reilly S. Music videos: a new dimension of televised violence. *Penn Speech Comm Ann*. 1985;41:61–64.

35. Frith S. Trends in the music industry. In: Lull J, ed. *Popular Music and Communications*. Beverly Hills, Calif: Sage Publications; 1987:75, 76.

36. Committee on Communications, American Academy of Pediatrics. The impact of rock lyrics and music videos on children and youth. *Pediatrics*. 1989;83:314–315.

DISCUSSION QUESTIONS

1. What special problems does the treatment of adolescents present for physicians? According to the authors, what is the nature of the relation between a teenager's mental health and physical well-being?

2. What technological advances have made the presence of rock music in adolescent lives more pervasive? What are the negative effects associated with these advances? Why has the advent of music video exacerbated these effects?

3. Do you agree with the study that accounts for difference in musical taste by appealing to gender distinctions? What other factors besides gender and race might contribute to a person's preference for one kind of music over another?

4. How does the attitude toward popular music taken in this article differ from the ones taken in "The Case of 2 Live Crew" in "Press" and Allan Bloom's essay in "Best-Sellers"?

Lillian S. Robinson / What Culture Should Mean

The Nation, September 25, 1989

One of the most controversial academic issues affecting students and teachers alike is the debate over required reading. Traditionally, college and university officials have had a relatively easy time creating curriculums from the landmark books of Western civilization. In recent years, however, the task has grown more difficult as faculty and administrators try to create courses that reflect the greater attention being given to issues of gender, race, and class. Many educators doubt the need for alterations, while others feel the changes are necessary to prevent intellectual stagnation.

Lillian S. Robinson is a professor of English at the University of Hawaii. The editors of The Nation, *a weekly, remain "committed to reporting on issues of labor, national politics, consumer affairs, environment, civil liberties, and foreign affairs."*

Once upon a time the introduction of writings by women and people of color, both American and Third World, was called "politicizing the curriculum." Only *we* had politics, you see (and its nasty litter-mate, ideology), whereas *they* had standards. But nowadays, former Education Secretary William Bennett equates the modification of Stanford's Western Civilization (the required course) with the destruction of Western civilization (the social phenomenon); Lynne Cheney, chair of the National Endowment for the Humanities, sneers at universities that require students to take ethnic literature seriously; and the outgoing President devotes his last moments in office to excoriating the present approach to teaching history, with its trendy preference for critical thinking over mindless nationalism. Meanwhile, Christopher Clausen, head of the Pennsylvania State University English department, deplores the (dubious) fact that more undergraduates are required to read *The Color Purple* than the works of Shakespeare. And a winner of the Nobel Prize for Literature inquires rhetorically about the whereabouts of "the African Proust," apparently determined to bypass all African novelists until that one materializes.

Moreover—and notwithstanding elective and appointive offices, Nobel Prizes and university chairs—these assaults are couched in a discourse of marginality to some perceived radical hegemony. It is this claim to outsider, even guerrilla, status that underlies the aggressiveness of the attack. Now that those on the other side have so blatantly revealed that they have politics, dare we hope they'll recognize that we have standards? Apparently not, for we continue to be accused of adopting "sociological" criteria while they defend "universal values," the rhetorical weapons of choice being the compound verb "to throw out" and the pseudo-explanatory "simply because."

That is, those of us who want to expand (though I prefer to say enrich) the canon of great books and the curriculum based on it are accused of wanting *to throw out* the classics and replace them with works chosen *simply because* their authors are female, nonwhite or non-Western. The debate might be more effectively engaged if there were in fact a tendency in the reformist camp that proposed throwing out the entire received tradition. But as far as I know, the furthest we've gone is to propose adding to it and reading the whole tradition from a perspective informed by our sense of what is usually omitted and what that omission itself teaches.

''Throwing out'' is, in any event, a rather abstract notion when it comes to the canon, which has no prescribed number of places within it. The curriculum, however, is indeed susceptible to ''throwing out''; there, adding new material does entail squeezing or even eliminating other material. Well, *isn't* this ''throwing out'' the great books? I think not, because the real challenge is to their nature as required reading, and hence to the view that ''every educated person'' must be familiar with a certain set of texts in preference to other texts.

Accompanying the accusation of abandoning the great works is the charge that we are practicing a kind of literary affirmative action, a policy understood in this context to meaning hiring or promoting the un- and underqualified. The application of the affirmative action concept and its concomitant ''quotas'' to this debate is apparently based on the assumption that no claim is being made for the new material as literature, and that certainly none could be sustained. We are said to be proposing the addition of new voices ''simply because'' of their gender, race or nationality, with no regard for the aesthetic values that had hitherto defined and (as it happens) closed the curriculum. A different aesthetic is presumed to be no aesthetic. And the female, black, working-class or homosexual experience is uncritically assumed to be, at best, an unlikely candidate for canonization, precisely because it is the marked variant, whereas the experience of straight white men has a unique claim to universality.

In fact, however, we have always maintained that the new material has literary resonance, acknowledging the power of literature to move, stimulate and transform human consciousness. So the actual difference between our respective positions is that we assume such literary power can come from a wide range of places in the culture and a wide set of social experiences, whereas they assume we are evoking values and power external to the workings of literature.

Meanwhile, can Saul Bellow really be waiting for the African Proust to materialize before he reads African fiction? If so, he's going to have to wait a lot longer and he'll be missing a great deal of wonderful writing. In the process, he denies to the African writer the very privilege he arrogates to himself of selecting a literary form and model appropriate to the enterprise. Despite all Moses Herzog's letters to the great male thinkers of Europe, Bellow's representation of the accumulation of the past in the individual consciousness is very different from that found in *A la recherche du temps perdu.* And surely (surely!) he knows that and believes it's acceptable. Or does he secretly think he's the Chicago Proust?

Even leaving Bellow's own fiction out of the equation, one might argue that Proust dealt with certain issues quite familiar to the contemporary African writer—the operation, for instance, of modernization upon an essentially tribal society. And it is as natural for an African writer to center a narrative on the installation or the aftermath of colonization as it was for Proust to focus on the Dreyfus affair. If it made sense for Proust as a Jew and a homosexual to dissect the invented Swann and the historical Dreyfus or the various inhabitants of Sodom and Gomorrah, it also makes sense for Chinua Achebe, Bessie Head, Ngugi wa Thiong'o,

Mariama Bâ, Amos Tutuola or Buchi Emecheta to tell us about the range of economic, cultural and sexual confrontations between the native peoples and Europeans. As with opening up the American tradition, it is not because we owe it to the poor benighted Africans to give them some representation in an expanded definition of the literary tradition. Rather, we owe it to literature.

Well, maybe Bellow doesn't want to know from colonialism and neocolonialism and Third World debt peonage, even filtered through the inner life and sensibility of a single tormented individual. Arguably, he doesn't want to know about this stuff any more than the denizens of the Guermantes' drawing room or even the Verdurins' wanted to hear about Captain Dreyfus. But if Bellow grants French literature the right to have had a Zola as well as a Proust—and how can he fail in this retroactive courtesy?—it seems strange, to say the least, to deny an equivalent range to the emerging literatures of Africa. An equivalent range, but not an identical one. Africa doesn't necessarily need its Proust.

In the early 1960s, during the struggle over a national language for Tanzania, President Julius Nyerere translated *The Merchant of Venice* and *Julius Caesar* into Swahili. Critic Stephen Arnold maintains that Nyerere's translations assisted "the meteoric rise of literature in Swahili to its stature as a national literature today [while] . . . cautiously asserting that some things in the colonialist's culture might be of value in the formation of Tanzanian national culture." But most educated Westerners would smile rather than gasp at Arnold's notion of a "meteoric rise," and Bellow would remind us that there has certainly been no Tanzanian Shakespeare anyway, and that life is too short to bother with anything else, which is automatically understood as anything less.

Moreover, when a Third World writer does make use of symbols, myths and imagery from the dominant Western tradition, the variations are as important as the theme. It seems to me, for instance, that the Nigerian playwright Wole Soyinka may be seen as the African Brecht, although in the process of reinventing the filiation from John Gay to Brecht to himself, Soyinka proves a rather more refractory son of his literary father than Brecht was. A greater degree of deviation is required by his condition as a Western-educated black man in neocolonial Africa.

As someone with a grounding in the literary tradition, I confess I think the story about Nyerere translating Shakespeare into Swahili is rather charming. (Although I wish there were an audience for English translations of the Swahili literature his gesture inspired.) But I am also convinced that it is dangerous to proceed from there to fetishizing Shakespeare's purported universality at the expense of what might come from a black speaker of Swahili or English. There is no reason to assume that Shakespeare was any less grounded in his own history, with its particular opportunities and limits, than today's writers are. And we know that his history included not only the class, national and cultural experience of Elizabethan England but also his membership in the male sex. For Virginia Woolf has told us what would have happened to that brilliant failed poet, his sister.

Some argue that Shakespeare is so universal we don't need the others, with their gender, race and national blinders. The professor who complained about *The Color Purple* being taught in more required courses than Shakespeare thinks it's a shame because the Bard shows us a greater human range then Walker does. I am not prepared to concede even that, but if it were so, it there no value in being exposed to what Shakespeare leaves out of the range? Is there no point on the register of human experience where his approach is less than adequate? After all, his exploration of domestic violence, one of Walker's central themes, is *The Taming of the Shrew.* His victim of colonialism is the monster Caliban. His black man is the Prince of Morocco or Othello. His black woman, aside from a single nasty remark in *Love's Labour's Lost,* is nonexistent. Doesn't Alice Walker have something to tell us about "incestuous sheets" that *Hamlet* hasn't already covered?

The problem is, the universality argument is not usually made in terms of the range of human types and experiences the gentleman from Penn State invoked. The universality claimed for the classics is more often thought to reside in their general themes—where states of mind and spirit are understood as more universal than physical commonality—and the broad sympathy they express. This is the approach Lynne Cheney takes in her 1988 report *Humanities in America.* At one point, Cheney cites the passage in Maya Angelou's *I Know Why the Caged Bird Sings* in which the memoirist describes her childhood feelings about Shakespeare. She was eager to memorize one of his poems to recite at a church function, but she knew that her grandmother, with whom she was living in a small Arkansas town, would insist her piece be something by Langston Hughes or Countee Cullen, poets who spoke from the black experience. The words Angelou wished she could use to explain it to her formidable grandmother derive from this notion of universal sympathy. The adult writer, looking back, wishes she had been able to plead, "But I *know* that William Shakespeare was a black woman!"

I am not sure if this quotation from Angelou—the report's only reference to a noncanonical text—is a monumental misreading or an equally stunning example of bad faith. For the story as Angelou tells it actually begins with her rape at age 8 by her mother's lover. At the man's trial, she tells a lie to cover her sense of complicity in a previous incident of sexual molestation. As a result, the rapist is acquitted, and then murdered by the child's vengeful male relatives. Maya, packed off to stay with her grandmother in the South, learns the distorted lesson that her speech could bring about a death. So she remains silent for a year, talking only to her brother, until a sympathetic older woman lends her some poems of Shakespeare. The sonnet beginning "When in disgrace with fortune and men's eyes" speaks to the condition of the abused, aphonic 9-year-old. That's what she feels *she* is, in disgrace with fortune and men's eyes. The recognition of herself in those words makes her want to speak again and recite the words of this man who'd understood her. But she knows her grandmother will never understand wherein Shakespeare, too, was a black woman.

This story certainly has multiple meanings. It does not seem to me that one of them is that Shakespeare the great writer could read the heart of this black child, but rather that Maya Angelou, at 9 and through all her pain, was an extraordinary *reader.* The incident hardly lends itself to the use to which it was put by the N.E.H. chair, which was to suggest that, although reading Shakespeare helped make the scarred child a speaker and eventually a poet herself, it is superfluous for us or our students to read Angelou—except to pick out specious morals about the timeless, placeless, personless value of the great books.

If we have to read black women's literature for moral lessons, I prefer the scene in Gloria Naylor's *The Women of Brewster Place* in which a community organizer takes a single mother and her too many children to the park to see an all-black production of *A Midsummer Night's Dream.* As they walk home after the enchanting event, one of the children asks, "Mama . . . Shakespeare's black?" And she replies, "Not yet." It's a nice idea, a black theater group performing Shakespeare for the children of Brewster Place, and it's also fitting that the militant organizer, who has adopted the African name Kiswana and whose boyfriend directs the troupe, is the one who encourages them to go. But Naylor is hardly telling us that exposing those kids to Shakespeare is the beginning or the end of what "culture" should mean to them. Shakespeare's not black *yet.* And when he is, it will not be because of the protean universality of a single white male born in Stratford-on-Avon 425 years ago, but because we all understand that although Shakespeare is dead, great poetry can still be written.

Most students will not turn out to be Shakespeare, whatever reading list their institutions enshrine. But the educational event we call empowerment is the same for both readers and writers. It is one that replaces a fetishized respect for culture as a stagnant secular religion with respect for culture as a living historical process, in which one's own experience is seen as an authentic part.

DISCUSSION QUESTIONS

1. What charges does Lillian Robinson's essay attempt to refute? How does she respond to them? Do you think she argues successfully against her opponents? What do you find are her most persuasive points?

2. Do you think there is an inherent conflict between Robinson's attempt to redefine the canon and her attempt to label works she deems important literature? What does the term "literature" imply?

3. Why does Robinson believe that Lynne Cheney misreads Maya Angelou's narrative? In what important ways does her own reading differ from Cheney's? Why does she prefer Gloria Naylor's tale to Maya Angelou's as a way of talking about canonical texts?

Sidney Hook / Civilization and Its Malcontents

National Review, October 13, 1989

When Stanford University recently decided to scrap its popular first-year course entitled "Western Culture," critics of the move saw the university's decision as a sign of the deterioration of our intellectual heritage. Supporters of a revised curriculum charged that many of the classic texts had either lost their relevance for today's students or, even worse, that these works encouraged racism and sexism. The issues that emerged from the Stanford decision have sparked a lively intellectual debate that will profoundly affect future generations of American students.

Before his death in 1989, Sidney Hook was one of the nation's leading social and political philosophers. A member of the American Academy of Arts and Sciences, Hook served on the faculties of New York University and the New School for Social Research. The National Review, *founded by William F. Buckley, Jr., in 1955, is a biweekly political and cultural journal of conservative opinion.*

The current crisis of education in the United States may legitimately be characterized as an attempt to politicize the curriculum itself. Those who have provoked it contend that the existing curriculum in the humanities is already politicized in virtue of the fact that its basic texts have been composed by Western white males and that, in consequence, the required courses are intrinsically infected with racism, sexism, and imperialism. The remedy proposed for this deplorable situation is that the traditional texts be partly replaced and supplemented by books composed by women and people of color and by representatives of the oppressed classes of the past and present, and, further, that the study of foreign cultures in depth be required. To ensure that these texts be properly taught, it is urged that additional personnel of instruction, wherever possible, be recruited from minorities and women, if there is any doubt abut the willingness or capacity of existing faculties to do so.

This transformation or revision (call it what you will) has been carried out fully at Stanford University, and criticized in some educational circles as a politicizing of a curriculum designed for other purposes. Such criticism has provoked the rejoinder from the architects of the new curriculum that the criticism is itself politically oriented—indeed, an expression of the same repressive politics embodied in the canonic texts of the course in Western culture. Even before these developments, in a Report to Congress on *The Humanities in America,* Lynne Cheney, the present chair of the National Endowment for the Humanities, had deplored the fact that, in the teaching of the humanities on every level, "viewing humanities texts as though they were primarily political documents is the most noticeable trend in academic study of the humanities today. Truth and beauty and excellence are regarded as irrelevant, questions of aesthetic and intellectual quality dismissed." Her report has been subjected to strong criticism by a committee of the American Council of Learned Societies as itself a political document.

I am going to devote my main analysis to the concept of the "political" in this discussion, and to the way its different connotations are being employed to obfuscate the issues. Before doing this, I wish to state a few assumptions, which I am prepared to defend if challenged, that relate to the humanities curriculum.

We acknowledge or assume that what differentiates the disciplines in the humanities, as they are understood today, from other disciplines is their central concern with human values, their interconnection with an imaginative representation in human experience. We acknowledge the desirability of including a broadly based course in the humanities as a curricular *requirement* to provide all students with the legacy of their culture, and with an understanding of the conflicting cultural traditions of the past that have shaped the present. The materials in such study have provided us in part with the basic categories of our thought and language, the conceptual tools, sentiments, and dispositions with which we approach the central problems of reflective life, whatever our geography or region. We acknowledge that such study for many reasons cannot constitute the whole of the school's curriculum—that at most it will be confined to one year, preferably at the outset of the students' careers, before specialization begins. We acknowledge that there cannot be, in a decentralized educational system such as ours, only one program, however ideal, or a set of syllabi for a course of this character, whatever it is called, and that the diversification will reflect local resources, capacities, and opportunities. Finally, we acknowledge that whatever texts are selected for a course of this character, they are not eternally fixed; they can be varied from time to time, reflecting available talents and shifting interests, without affecting the overall goal of providing students from all backgrounds a unitary, but not uniform, educational experience whose existence can be built on whatever educational and vocational differentiation follows.

The first point I want to make, on the basis of a survey of courses in Western culture or civilization more or less like those previously offered at Stanford, is that, despite what their detractors have claimed, they are *not* a glorification of the status quo. On the contrary, the required reading gives an understanding of how the status quo has come into being, presents some of the revolutionary ideas that helped it come into being, and explores the struggle and debate among the great maps of personal and social salvation whose promises and dangers still engage our interest. As a matter of fact, it is from a curriculum of similar studies in Paris or London that some leaders of Third World countries absorbed the ideas and ideals they used to rally their peoples against colonialism. In truth, since the standard texts express conflicting ideals, they could hardly lend themselves coherently to any one point of view. But their grasp and analysis is required by anyone who seeks intelligently to transform or conserve our society. Whether it is the ideals of tolerance, the limitations of ethnocentrism, the visions of Utopia without which Wilde said no map of the world is complete—all are contained in every well-tailored course in the humanities. Any intelligent student who has completed such a course, if and when he acquaints himself with other cultures, can hardly help concluding that of all cultures of which we have any record, Western culture has been the most critical of itself, that its history has largely been a succession of heresies, and that it has been freer of the blind spots of ethnocentrism than any other.

More directly, addressing myself to the charge that courses in Western culture have been racist, sexist, and imperialistic, despite renewed requests, no one has ever cited *specific* evidence that any of the basic texts has been systematically taught in the spirit and attitude of invidious discrimination that these terms currently have. There was certainly no evidence of this in any of the tracks of the course at Stanford, although, like all courses, they invited improvement. Of course, in discussing Greek drama, we cannot but become aware of how different the status of women was in the classical world from what is is in our own. But we would be guilty of the grossest distortion of scholarship if we denied the fact. Effective teaching can take one of its points of exploration from it whether we are reading the *Medea* or discussing the startling feminist views in Plato's *Republic*. Indeed, Plato's *Republic* in the hands of a good teacher lends itself to the exciting counterposition of arguments and themes on a whole variety of subjects that possess contemporary vibrancy, like the temptations of censorship, the defects of democracy, and the snares of totalitarianism. Nor should we forget for a moment that no text imposes one reading on all interpreters of its meaning.

At this point we are likely to hear that the absence of women and people of color among the authors of the basic texts is evidence of the inherent bias with which such courses are infected. Where, it is asked, is the imaginative presentation of the life of the common people—the spear-carriers, the hewers of wood and drawers of water—of the victimization of women from Biblical days, of the mute and inglorious lives of slaves, especially the black slaves? The texts of courses in Western culture, it is asserted, were written by elite members of Western society for the elite, and they therefore slight the contributions of women and minority groups, without whom there would be no culture at all.

The naiveté of the complaint reflects the political commitment of those who level it, not their historical judgment. Of course the culture of the past was created by the elites of the past! Who else could have created it at a time when literacy itself was the monopoly of the elite classes? It was that creation, winnowed by the criticism of successive elites, that produced our culture. And the quality of that creation is not affected by its origins. It was none other than Karl Marx himself, steeped to his very pores in the elite classical culture of the West, who declared that although Greek art and epics are products of a class society, "they still constitute a source of aesthetic enjoyment and in certain respects prevail as the standard and model beyond attainment." He was not looking for a proletarian or slave art that did not exist, but wanted to make the best of art and culture developed in every society part of the cultural birthright of the working classes. To be sure, we may be curious to know how and why the masses and women were excluded from the creative cultural institutions of the past, and why they were confined to the kitchens and workplaces and denied the light of learning. These are legitimate questions explored in a wide variety of other courses in sociology, politics, the sciences, economic history, and anthropology open to inquiring student minds. But to introduce all of these studies into a course in the *humanities* is to dilute it into a very thin soup of social smatter.

The notion that the course in Western culture can be enriched by adding, to its core list of readings, books by women and persons of color not because they are the best or most appropriate for the subject in hand, but because of the race or sex or class of the author—a kind of affirmative-action program in scholarship—is both patronizing and ludicrous from the standpoint of honest scholarship. And it compounds the folly when tacked onto this is a mandate to recruit "women and people of color" to teach the ideas and aspects of culture that involve them. This is nothing more than a sophisticated revival of the old folk fantasy, and just as absurd, that only like can understand like. Does one have to be French to study or understand Napoleon, Russian to understand Lenin, Greek to read Homer or enjoy the figures of Praxiteles? As well argue that men cannot be good gynecologists, that only women with children can understand and administer family law, that only fat physicians can study obesity and hungry ones the physiology of starvation, as to assert or imply that people of color or women are uniquely qualified to do justice to the place, achievements, and oppressions of minorities and their culture. Was it not a white male and, to boot, a foreigner, a Swede, who in *An American Dilemma* moved the conscience of this country in recent times on the race question more than any other person before the appearance of Martin Luther King?

There is only one genuine educational question broached by the situation at Stanford, which, unfortunately, had little to do with the actual decision made there but which has occasionally been asked and discussed elsewhere, notably at a national conference at Michigan State University a few years ago. Granted that Western culture is now operating in a world of global issues enveloping the entire world, should the required basic course we have been proposing be taught as a course in world culture or world civilization rather than as one in Western culture or civilization? If so, its core list would have to contain the great works of different peoples and cultures, the kind of literature, art, and history that denizens of these foreign cultures have been nurtured in. But could that be done in an educationally fruitful way? There are many reasons to doubt this. A great work that has exercised its influence on a culture is approached with a mindset that in part has been determined by the influence of that work. The Japanese student reading *The Tale of the Genji,* the Chinese student reading Confucius's *Analects,* or the Indian the *Bhagavad Gita,* has a knowledge of its symbols and world view that is certainly not beyond the grasp or comprehension of the American student, but which manifestly would take him years to acquire. He hasn't the background with which he approaches the Gospels or even Shakespeare. He cannot unmake himself and grow into these other cultures as he did in his own. So although he can contrast and compare the way the Golden Rule is formulated positively and negatively in Rabbi Hillel, the New Testament, Buddha, and Lao Tze, it cannot serve in any formulation as a key to the whole culture without the student knowing much more than even his teachers are likely to know. The point of building bridges of understanding to other cultures is to prepare students, using familiar examples, for the encounter of visiting them and imaginatively empathizing with them, not for living in them. Whatever the global future will be, it is not likely to result in a homogeneous global culture. There will not be one global village but a plurality of global villages.

The study and history of humanities in the West certainly touches the borders of other cultures. But it is the humanists themselves, in pursuit of their pedagogical and research tasks, who know what is to be studied and when. The motivation of those who legislated that concerns for race, sex, and class be made central in the study of humanities at Stanford and elsewhere was not pedagogical but political. It was stated, often explicitly, that justice or fairness required that the needs of the exploited, oppressed, and hitherto unheard be recognized, that their voices be amplified and their separateness overcome. All worthy objectives of an enlightened political agenda. But however desirable this agenda is, its sphere of activity is the public and legislative forum, not the institutions for the dissemination of wisdom, let alone the curriculum of the humanities. In the study of the humanities, we can legitimately inquire into the influence of political decisions in the past on the ideals and models conceived to represent the best and most enduring in art and literature. But that is quite different from selecting readings in a course or teaching them in order to reshape the politics of the present or future.

This immediately brings the retort that the refusal to orient a course in the humanities politically is itself to take a political position. And so, if we are not careful to make and abide by the proper distinctions, the question of whether a work of art or literature exhibits a political aspect (the answer to which, if we know it, is yes or no) is transformed into the political question of whether we should study a subject at all (the answer to which depends on whether you are a liberal or a conservative, a reformer or a revolutionary).

Let us meet this position head on. Is it true that the refusal to take a stand is itself a political stand? No, unless we are dealing with an explicit political problem, where the act of not taking a stand—say, proclaiming neutrality between an aggressor and his victim—has political consequences affecting everyone. But outside the sphere of partisan political issues, the refusal to take a stand on a disputed issue may mean nothing more than a decision to suspend judgment until more evidence is in. If I refuse to come down on one side or the other of the question of whether Lord Bacon or the Earl of Oxford wrote the plays attributed to Shakespeare, or whether whoever write the play *Hamlet* portrayed Hamlet, the character, as genuinely mad or feigning madness or Polonius as a figure of fun or as genuinely a sage, my answer is decidedly *not* political in any ordinary sense of the term. It may be that in the light of overwhelming or preponderant evidence, my continued suspension of judgment could be warrantably called unscholarly, but not political.

It is often said that the choice of any set of books or writings in a course in the humanities is a political choice. What makes it political? That it is a choice? But how arbitrary that would be! Would the choice of textbooks in a course in mathematics be political, too? Certainly not. Even in the case where a teacher was prescribing his own book instead of a clearly better one because of the anticipated royalties, his choice is not political but unethical and unprofessional. It certainly would be odd if anyone characterized the choice of musical works to be studied in a course on music appreciation as "political." There could be all sorts of differences among the architects of such a course—or of any course in the humanities—about the justification for including each or any item, but unless one can show, and not merely assert, that there was a political reason for the selection, it is a plain abuse of what Charles Peirce called the ethics of words to call the choice political.

Why, then, comes the renewed complaint, are there no books by women, workers, people of color in the canon of the standard humanities courses? Does not that express a value judgment? To which the manifest answer is that, yes, it does express a value judgment, but *not* a political value judgment about women, workers, and minorities. It is a judgment about which books have had the greatest influence on the culture of our time and of past times, which books have been the sources of renewed delight, intellectual stimulation, and challenge, and which works of literature and art help us best understand our own contemporary culture, related as it is in thousands of ways to the cultural achievements of the past.

Political passion still sustains the argument. It asks whether the standards of excellence themselves, the criticisms of judgment, even the so-called "eternal values," do not "reflect" the social and class structure of the time. The word "reflect" is one of the most ambiguous terms in the vocabulary of criticism. If a writer or artist accepts the society of his time, his values "reflect" it; if he rejects the society, his action and values necessarily reflect it by his very negation. The question for scholarship is *how* do his values specifically reflect it? And the question whether his work is to be included in the canon of the humanities is answered by considering not whether it reflects *his* society, as in some way it necessarily does, but whether it has something to say of abiding significance to other times and other societies as well. We don't have to use the rhetoric of eternal values to make the point that whatever makes a claim to eternal value must establish its validity as an *enduring* value here and now—that, of course, since all things have a history, values have a history, and that all we can ever mean by intrinsic, perennial, or eternal value is that the book, painting, or musical composition that embodies it *still works its attractive power on us today,* regardless of our political partisanship.

What is basically objectionable in the contemporary movement to politicize the humanities is that it conflates different meanings of the term "political." It goes from a sense of "political" that is synonymous with a basic choice in any field—so broad that it lacks an intelligible opposite, so that to be is to be political—to the transparent, conventional sense of the term. In order to conceal that fact, and its relation to its overt political antecedents in the Sixties, those who hold this view fall back on the comprehensive, confusing usage of the term "political" as meaning any choice. Sometimes the exemplars of this movement frankly proclaim they want to reform the humanities program *in order* to shape the political future of the nation. But, *logically,* these goals have nothing to do with each other. One can be for or against the Equal Rights Amendment or the welfare state, regardless of the sex or color of the authors of the books studied. At this point the question, they seem to imply, is one of power, not logic. The situation is accurately characterized by Richard Rorty, who although critical is not himself unsympathetic to some of the social goals of this movement. "A new American cultural Left," he said in a public address at George Mason University (March 1, 1989), "has come into being made of deconstructionists, new historicists, people in gender studies, ethnic studies, media studies, a few left-over Marxists, and so on. This Left would like to use the English, French, and Comparative Literature Departments of the universities as staging areas for political action."

A more representative, and in a sense official, view is expressed by Professor Linda K. Kerber, recent past president of the American Studies Association, in the *Chronicle of Higher Education* (March 29, 1989):

> We have celebrated the speed with which we have discovered diversity—of race, class, gender, and ethnicity. But for all the skepticism, irony, and critical perspectives upon which we pride ourselves, we have remained too much part of the status quo we deplore.
>
> Freed from the defensive constraints of cold-war ideology, empowered by our new sensitivity to the distinctions of race, class, and gender, we are ready to begin to understand difference as a series of power relationships involving domination and subordination, and to use our understanding of power relations to reconceptualize both our interpretation and our teaching of American culture.

Associated with this view and outlook is an attitude which gives me profound concern because it challenges the very notion of objective truth on the ground that the quest for truth is itself affected by interests, which are ultimately tied up with the class structure of society. Accused of reading their own political bias into the interpretation and evaluation of events to further the indoctrination of their students, members of the New Left respond that their critics are themselves biased, that "objectivity" exists in the eye of the beholder, since no one is free from bias. It is not difficult to show that such a position is incoherent, flawed by its own assertions. It is true that no one can claim to know the whole truth about anything, but it by no means follows that all assertions are equally true or false, that we cannot ground some statements on the basis of evidence, as better or truer than others. Indeed, to hold that objectivity is a myth is tantamount to denying the distinction between fiction and history, guilt and innocence, in relation to the admitted evidence.

It is safe to predict that if such modes of thinking take over in the humanities, before long we will be hearing their echoes in medicine and the natural sciences, too. It was a mere fifty years ago that we were hearing about Aryan and Jewish physics and proletarian biology. Today once more there is talk of race, gender, and class not as a subject of scientific study but as characterizing the scientific approach itself. Nonsense, the literature reader will say. To be sure—but we have learned that nonsense, if unchecked, will kill.

DISCUSSION QUESTIONS

1. How does Sidney Hook define the term "political" as it relates to the canon? What is Hook's opinion of those who advocate the "politicization" of the canon?

2. Why, according to Hook, is it difficult to locate a single political agenda in the classic texts of Western culture? Does your own reading tend to support this view? If these works do conflict, how then is it possible to talk about the existence of a tradition?

3. Why does Hook disagree with the premise that all choices about the curriculum are political choices? Consider his argument about the use of classics in fields other than literature and philosophy. Could the choice to study particular works of mathematics or music be political?

Ishmael Reed / Antihero

Spin, May 1990

Although newscasters and networks claim that they provide balanced and accurate coverage of today's events, many media critics have come to believe that the evening news is not quite as objective as its writers and producers claim it to be. Some critics, like Ishmael Reed, go even further and accuse news programs of proliferating racist stereotypes. Reed is a prolific writer of fiction, poetry, essays, and drama. His works include The Free-Lance Pallbearers *(1967),* Yellow Back Radio Broke-Down *(1969),* Mumbo-Jumbo *(1972), and* New and Collected Poetry *(1988).* Spin *magazine offers its readers the most up-to-date coverage of the contemporary music and entertainment scenes as well as pieces of cultural and social criticism.*

Edward R. Murrow's broadcasts from Europe provided me with one of my earliest introductions to the modern writing style. His crisp, dramatic narratives brought the war home to thousands of American radio listeners. After witnessing how the Nazi propaganda machine fictionalized reality and used psychological warfare against unpopular groups, Murrow returned to America vowing to prevent such abuses of media power here. Since his death, Murrow has come to epitomize the great journalist. His documentary, *Harvest of Shame,* about the oppression of migrant workers, became model for the muckraking journalism of the 1960s. Today's muckraker, perhaps working for a think tank financed by the growers, would probably blame the migrant workers' plight on their personal behavior.

I often wonder what Murrow would think of today's media, with its performance-oriented newsmen, docudramas, instant analyses, and its manipulation by political candidates who are packaged and promoted through media sound bites and guided by media consultants. I wonder what his response would be to a government that manipulates the media so that we may never get all of the facts regarding the Iran-Contra affair, or the invasion of Panama. I wonder what he would think of technology that Joseph Goebbels would find awe-inspiring and that's often used as a weapon against unpopular groups. It's my impression that the media often behave as though blacks are members of an enemy nation and that they, the media, are a propaganda bureau for a nation at war.

For *Time* magazine, Gorbachev was the man of the decade. For me it was Willie Horton, the prisoner who committed a rape while he was on furlough from a Massachusetts prison. Mr. Horton seemed to epitomize the image of the black male projected by the media in the 1980s—that of a roving, irresponsible predator. It is clear to me that Bush's Willie Horton ad campaign was successful because it was created after a decade of black male bashing by the mass media. "The enemy wants to do something awful to 'our' women," is a classic image used in war propaganda. An ancestor of this campaign was a famous World War II poster depicting a grinning, sinister, buck-toothed Japanese soldier with a nude European woman slung over his shoulder.

As an African-American, I regularly become angry as I watch the racist stereotypes portrayed on television news. Unlike the print media, where one at least has an opportunity to reply with a letter, it's difficult to document the lies and half-truths that are perpetuated about minorities on the Big Tube—they fly by so fast, and it's far more difficult to challenge them. I find myself diving for sheets of paper, the backs of envelopes, napkins, or matchbook covers in order to document these abuses.

Why are black faces and bodies used to illustrate most social pathologies—illegitimacy, crime, illiteracy, alcoholism, drug addiction, spousal abuse, prostitution, AIDS, family abandonment, and abuse of the elderly—when there are millions more whites involved in these activities than blacks?

The media often portray the single black female parent as the source of all the country's poverty problems. Terry K. Adams and Greg J. Duncan challenge that myth in a paper they wrote for the University of Michigan's Survey Research Center in 1988. They write: "Media images of urban poverty often present households headed by young, never-married black women. . . . Data show that this image does not fit most, or even a substantial minority, of the persistently poor living in urban areas."

NBC News even illustrated a story about a white-collar crime with footage depicting blacks, when blacks usually don't commit white-collar crime of the sort that figured in the savings and loan scandals, scandals that may cost the American taxpayers $500 billion, many times the $40 billion spent on welfare and farm subsidies each year.

But of all social "pathologies," none has been attached to blacks in recent years as much as crack—the distribution, possession, and addiction to the substance. When several networks did their video montages summarizing the 1980s, whites were shown doing positive things—blacks were shown smoking crack pipes.

Both the government and the media have made crack a black issue, even though its consumption is more prevalent among whites than among blacks. Jack Anderson and others have been reporting on how crack has reached the suburbs and small towns for at least three years now. He says that in many of these white peach-cobbler communities, parents don't know where their children are, but I doubt these parents will be threatened with jail as was a Los Angeles black mother whose sons were engaged in illegal drug activities, nor will middle- and upper-class pregnant white women who use cocaine be threatened.

George Bush, so as not to embarrass what he views as a white middle-class constituency, and his drug czar William Bennett continue to portray crack addiction as a black problem, making appearances in black neighborhoods and at institutions that are predominantly black. These appearances are obediently covered by the media. Mr. Bush even went along with the staging of a drug buy from a black dealer so that he could say on television that the crack was bought across the street from the White House.

Hodding Carter, appearing on the David Brinkley show the weekend this strange prank was discovered, said you didn't have to go that far from the White House to buy coke. I wonder if the authorities who go around entrapping black politicians interviewed Hodding Carter for an elaboration of his remark, or if two-way mirrors and hidden cameras are set up in those parties in Georgetown frequented by the political elite, where Fawn Hall said she snorted coke on weekends.

The day after his cynical stunt, Mr. Bush posed with a black crack baby and later he was shown on the site of a public housing project in Alexandria, Virginia.

Will Mr. Bush ever pose with a white cocaine baby? Why doesn't he pose in front of the Los Angeles bank that was found to have raised its profits over 2000 percent in ten years to total assets of ten billion dollars through money laundering, or how about before a gun store that sells sophisticated weapons to black youths, no questions asked. Or on Wall Street, where cocaine sales and distribution were the subjects of a long piece published in the *New York Times*. Or better still, will he ever reveal whether he looked the other way as tons of cocaine were dumped into this country by his anticommunist allies? Or, will anybody in the administration ever explain its ties to Craig Spence, a right-wing socialite who was under investigation by the secret service and FBI at the time of his death a few months ago? Mr. Spence had been arrested for cocaine possession and weapons charges in New York on August 15, indicating that the refreshments served to the Washington, D.C., establishment at his million-dollar apartment, where he entertained "key officials of the Reagan and Bush administrations, military officers, congressional aides and US and foreign business people with close ties to Washington's political elite," included more than herbal tea.

And so the administration and the media have successfully used blacks as scapegoats for the crack problem.

The media continued to perpetuate the story that crack is black, even after evidence of widespread cocaine use among whites was supported by a study late last year by the Parents Resource Institute for Drug Education, Inc., which revealed that white teenagers are more prone to drug addiction than are blacks. On the Sunday, January 13, edition of *This Week with David Brinkley,* Mr. Brinkley asked General Clayton Powell about the drug problem as though it were an exclusively inner-city problem.

I decided that something had to be done when I saw one of those pompous, campy, incoherent Roger Rosenblatt essays, carried on the *MacNeil/Lehrer*

NewsHour, which associated black youth, as a class, with "evil." This convinced me that television had gone too far. Granted, the alleged attack and rape of a Central Park jogger was cruel, but was this an act on the same level as the Holocaust, the genocide committed by the Khmer Rouge, or the My Lai massacre as Mr. Rosenblatt suggested? And why accompany an essay about the alleged misdeeds of a few black youth with a graphic depicting a nonspecific, dark youthful figure and a commentary about Satanism? And why emphasize the Central Park incident as though it were even worse than those other colossal tragedies? There was a reference to the rape of a disabled child by some middle-class white youth—an event that has since disappeared from public consciousness—that had occurred in New Jersey the week before the commentary, but this was referred to only in passing during Jim Lehrer's introduction to Rosenblatt's essay. And unlike the case of the black youth, no photo of the white youth was shown, another practice of the television networks—concealing the faces of whites who are associated with pathologies.

Unlike the other hit-and-run TV spots that harass black people, I was able to record this commentary on videotape. I showed it to eleven young black professional people a few weeks later, during a meeting about television stereotypes in San Francisco. They were the sort of people who call my generation bitter, but even they agreed with me that something had to be done, and plans for a boycott of television and opinion programs were under way.

You would think commentators and reporters for government-supported television and radio would be less likely to rely on racist stereotypes, but in my monitoring of the media I've found that some of the most careless notions about black life are perpetuated by reporters and commentators on National Public Radio and the Public Broadcasting System.

Typical was the coverage of blacks by NPR's *Weekend Edition* on Saturday, January 12, and Sunday, January 13, during which there were at least four stories connecting blacks to crack, one about blacks and illiteracy, one about black teenage fathers who abandon their children, and one about homeless blacks, even though most homeless people are white. Sixty percent of the homeless found dead during San Francisco's most recent winter were white males in their forties.

On August 30, 1989, the day the *Times* revealed the extent of cocaine pregnancies among middle-class white women, this shocking story received one line on television news, while the drug addiction of Lawrence Taylor, a black football player, was featured.

Lack of motivation on the part of journalists to dig for the facts accounts in part for the unbalanced view that American audiences receive of black life. One gets the impression that they spend most of their time under the drier, or getting made up, or engaging in such lofty decisions as whether to stand or sit down while delivering the news. I told Mary Beth Grover, who called me to write an article for the Op-Ed page of the *New York Times* about whether there was a conspiracy to dump drugs in the black neighborhood—a notion that was treated with sarcasm and incredulity by Lianne Hansen on NPR's *Weekend Edition*—that it was up to the press to discover whether one exists, rather than dismiss the opinion held by large numbers of blacks as being based upon paranoia. Certainly there's far more evidence—some of which has appeared in her newspaper—than the quoted lines from *The Godfather:* "Let's give it to the [blacks]; they're animals anyway, they're going to lose their souls." And just because those lines were said in a movie doesn't mean that they were untrue. She said that she wanted a ghetto black to say conclusively that there was a white conspiracy. I wasn't her kind of ghetto black, I guess. Howard Kurtz, the journalist who began this debate in the *Washington Post,* erred when he wrote that crack was largely a problem in black communities. He must be getting all his news from television.

Another reason for the stereotypes of blacks in the white media may be that white journalists find it difficult to divorce themselves from cherished myths about black life even though the facts are right in front of their eyes. I'm constantly amazed that my primitive data base—strewn about the room as though some hurricane just blew through, and bookshelves still in disrepair from a recent earthquake—constantly proves to be superior to those of the most sophisticated newsgathering organizations in the world, with millions of dollars' worth of technology at their disposal.

Tom Brokaw seemed jubilant as he celebrated what he called the wresting away of the media by the people from the Communist state in Czechoslovakia. We're not even calling for the wresting away of the media from anybody, and as writers we would be the last to interfere with the First Amendment rights of anybody. We're calling for balance, which is what the minority critics have always called for. Balance. The best and the worst, the brightest and the stupidest, and all gradations in between, of black, Hispanic, and Asian-American life.

When the electronic media, which have the power to topple presidents, arbitrarily, as it turns out, become smug and arrogant and unresponsive to the people, this presents a danger in a democracy. A Reagan appointee even did away with the Fairness Doctrine, which at least pretended to give those with opposing points of view some time to respond to class slander.

If these electronic Leviathans, which have more power than most political institutions, were governments, they would have been toppled long ago.

DISCUSSION QUESTIONS

1. Why, according to Reed, are blacks "used to illustrate social pathologies"? What other reasons can you offer for the phenomenon he observes?

2. Do you agree with Reed that the media have portrayed drug use as a black issue? Why might he have arrived at this conclusion? Is the evidence that he provides enough to substantiate this claim? What other kinds of evidence might he have provided?

3. What does Reed mean by the term "balance" as it relates to the news media? Do you think his evaluation of the news as lacking balance is justified? How can "balance" be achieved?

Josh Ozersky / TV's Anti-Families: Married . . . with Malaise

Tikkun, January/February 1991

Has the decline of the American family so often commented on by our leaders finally reached the airwaves? The Simpsons, *a cartoon sitcom that has enthralled our nation's viewing public, presents the family unit at its most dysfunctional. Children take pleasure in imitating the caustic remarks and bad manners of Bart Simpson, while parents are either amused or angered by the irreverence being directed at the most basic unit of human society. Does this popular show merely offer a broad satire of the family, or does it raise more serious questions about American life?*

Josh Ozersky is a media critic working in New York City. While Tikkun, *published by the Institute for Labor and Mental Health, is a progressive magazine primarily concerned with Jewish life, culture, and politics, a surprisingly large number of its readers are non-Jews. This fact may be attributed to the rather wide-range of issues and viewpoints the magazine offers.*

It's an odd thing when a cartoon series is praised as one of the most trenchant and "realistic" programs on TV, but there you are. Never mind the Cosby-size ratings: if merchandising says anything about American culture, and it does, then America was utterly infatuated with "The Simpsons" in 1990. "Utterly," because unlike other big winners in the industry such as the Teenage Mutant Ninja Turtles and the New Kids on the Block, the Simpsons graced not only t-shirts for the clamoring young, but t-shirts (and sweatshirts and posters and mugs) that went out in droves to parents, who rivaled kids for viewer loyalty.

The animated series chronicles the life of the Simpson family: father Homer, who works in a nuclear power plant and reads bowling-ball catalogs; mother Marge, with her blue beehive hairdo and raspy voice; misunderstood-bohemian daughter Lisa; baby Maggie; and bratty son Bart, the anti-everything star of the series. Bart appeals to kids, who see a flattering image of themselves, and to their parents, who, even as they identify with Bart against his lumpkin parents, enjoy Bart's caricature of their own children, with his incomprehensible sloganeering ("Don't have a cow, man!") and bad manners. Nor, tellingly, has the popularity of the show stopped with the white mainstream: a black Bart soon began to turn up in unlicensed street paraphernalia.

In the first of the unauthorized shirts, Bart was himself, only darkened. The novelty soon wore off, however, and in successive generations Bart found himself ethnicized further: "Air Bart" had him flying toward a basketball hoop exclaiming "In your face, home boy." Another shirt had Bart leering at zaftig black women, loutishly yelling "Big Ole Butt!" at their retreating figures. And in later versions, Bart has a gold tooth, a razor cut, and an angry snarl—the slogan "I got the power!" juts overhead in an oversized balloon.

The "I got the power!" Bart is barely recognizable, disfigured by rancor. But even more jarring than his appearance is his vitriol, so out of keeping with the real Bart's laid-back, ironic demeanor—an endemic condition among TV characters. The naked discontent on that shirt is jarring, disturbing. It lacks the light touch. TV does not—but then the playful suppression of unhappiness has always been one of TV's great strengths; and in its latest, ugliest form, it subtly discourages alarm at the decline of the family, its own complicity in that decline, and the resulting effects on a disintegrating society.

The success in the last few seasons of new, "anti-family" sitcoms, such as Fox's "Married . . . with Children" and "The Simpsons" and ABC's "Roseanne," began a trend that has made waves in television. "Whether it's the influence of Bart Simpson and those cheeky sitcoms from Fox," write *TV Guide* in September, "or ABC's artsy anti-soap 'Twin Peaks,' unconventionality is in; slick and safe are out." The "cheeky sitcoms" began that trend. "Roseanne," about an obese and abrasive proletarian mom, and "Married . . . with Children," a half hour of pure viciousness, represented along with "The Simpsons" a new development of the situation comedy, TV's definitive genre. Each program (as well as its inevitable imitators) focuses on a family marked by visual styles and characterization as bleak and miserable as those of former TV families had been handsome or cheerful.

The innovation received a lot of attention in the mass media, most of it favorable. Richard Zoglin in *Time* hailed the "real-world grit these shows provide," produced psychological authorities, and quoted Barbara Ehrenreich's wide-eyed

''Zeitgeist Goddess'' piece in the *New Republic*. The *New York Times*'s Caryl Rivers wrote approvingly of the new realism, although she noted perfunctorily that gays, minorities, and women were less visible than they should have been. What all sides had in common, however, was a willingness to point out the improvement over other forms of TV. ''The anti-family shows aren't against the family, exactly, just scornful of the romantic picture TV has often painted of it,'' Zoglin pointed out. ''We're like a mutant Ozzie and Harriet,'' Simpsons creator Matt Groening boasted in *Newsweek,* which went on to point out that the show was ''hardly the stuff of Saturday-morning children's programming.'' ''Thankfully, we are past the days of perfect Mom and all-wise Dad and their twin beds,'' wrote the *New York Times*'s Rivers, speaking for reviewers and feature writers everywhere. And this was prior to the advent of the ''unconventional'' mystery serial ''Twin Peaks,'' which still has feature writers striving for superlatives to describe its ''innovations'' and ''departures.''

This unanimous juxtaposition of the ''anti-families'' to the stern TV households of yesteryear is a specious comparison designed to amuse and flatter. Not as the result of any conspiracy—writers in the commercial mass media generally write to please, and what they say is true enough if you have as your entire frame of reference the past and present of TV. But far from the ''authenticity'' it pretends to, the ''grit'' for the new shows is merely an improved artifice, a challenge only to the verisimilitude of art directors and casting companies. By pretending to realism, TV only extends its own hegemony, in which every standard of comparison points back to another sham. ''Gosh,'' gushed *TV Guide* of Bart, ''can you imagine Bud Anderson being so . . . *disrespectful* to Dad?'' As if the lead of ''Father Knows Best'' had only recently become a figure of fun.

It is through this sort of pseudo–self-deprecation that TV tries to ingratiate itself with Americans, who in an age marked by pervasive irony want to run with the hare and hunt with the hound—to feel superior to TV and yet keep watching it. TV offers this target audience an abundance of self-images that will permit them this trick. The target viewers may be enlightened, making the ''choice of a new generation'' by seeing through ''My Little Margie,'' or avant-garde, on the cutting edge, for watching ''Twin Peaks,'' which, like ''Hill Street Blues'' before it, supposedly ''breaks all the rules.'' They are in utter harmony with the very mechanics of TV production, which has no secrets from us, as we know from David Letterman's insider gags, such as the ''Late Night Danger Cam.''

As for discrediting paternalistic authority figures, Mark Crispin Miller has pointed out that the imperious Dads of the fifties TV, now such a rich source of burlesque, were overturned by a maturing medium very early on. The ''grim old abstinence'' of the Puritan patriarch stood in the way of the ''grim new self-indulgence'' of consumer culture and was hence banished. Dads turned into ''pleasant nullities,'' like Dick York in ''Bewitched'' and Timothy Busfield in ''thirtysomething,'' or unenlightened butts of knowing and self-flattering jokes, like Archie Bunker and Homer Simpson.

The downfall of Dad, however, saw no concomitant rise of Mom or the kids. Rather, it was advertisers and corporations that benefited from the free-spending self-indulgence of all parties, liberated from patriarchal discipline. And the networks, of course, cashed in and sold advertisers airtime. In the world beyond the screen, the family has disintegrated into epidemic divorces and deteriorating marriages, latchkey children, and working parents reduced to spending ''quality time'' with their children, as though they were hospital visitors or the lovelorn spouses of soldiers on leave. Meanwhile, the TV world—not only in sitcoms but in endless ''special reports'' and talk shows and (particularly) commercials—insists again and again that we are hipper, more ''open,'' more enlightened, and facing changing ''relationships'' in a new and better way. Mom, often divorced and underpaid, has her new ''independence,'' a standard theme of programming, and Dad and the kids, faced with other losses and hardships, are offered the bold new ''grittiness'' of prime-time entertainment. TV has absorbed the American family's increasing sense of defeat and estrangement and presented it as an ironic in-joke.

This dynamic is seldom noted, although the mere *fact* of watching is noted by critics and commentators everywhere, and nowhere more visibly than on TV itself. The opening credits of ''The Simpsons'' end with the family, assembled at the end of the day, jumping mutely into fixed position on the sofa and clicking on the TV set. This absorption of criticism is and has been, except for sheer distraction, TV's greatest weapon against criticism. The transformation of the hearth into an engine of negation, after all, should have caused *some* stir. And so it would have, if TV were no more than the yammering salesman it has caricatured itself as in satirical moments. But, as Miller demonstrates, TV has never shown us TV; rather, it shows itself to us as a laughable, absurd, and harmless entity, much like the characters on its shows.

When not played for background noise—whooping Indians in older shows, unctuous game-show hosts or newsmen in newer ones—depictions of the TV set on TV itself render it invisible and omnipresent. TV itself, its conventions and production, may be the crucial point of reference for the sophisticated appeal it enjoys today, but the set as household centerpiece is seldom seen, and then only as a joke, as on ''The Simpsons.'' Instead, the set most often poses as a portal to the outer world: hence its constant stream of images that tease us with alluring beaches, blue waters, busy city streets. Even in its living rooms, where we know its presence to be inescapable, the TV is often missing. This effect is accomplished by a simple trick of photography: when the family watches TV in ''All in the Family,'' in ''Good Times,'' in ''Married . . . with Children,'' etc., the scene is shot from behind the TV set. As the family sits facing us, with the screen nowhere in sight, the illusion exists for a moment that the TV really is, if not a portal, then a mirror or reflection of us. A close look at these families, and at our own, soon banishes this impression. We are not like these TV families at all; and the TV set is obtrusive, ideological, and tendentious.

When speaking of the ''anti-family'' sitcoms, most of the commentators seem to have in mind ''Married . . . with Children.'' No other show so luridly plays up the sheer negativity of the current ''authenticity'' trend, nor does any other show do so with such predictable regularity. The series portrays the Bundys, a lower-middle-class family with two children and a dog. Father Al (Ed O'Neill) only has ''knotted bowels'' to show for his life supporting the family. Peg (Katey Sagal) is Al's castrating wife. There is also the inevitable sharp-tongued teenage son, who singles out for special heckling his brainless and sleazy sister. The relentlessly ironic quality of a happy family turned thoroughly upside-down flatters the audience for their enlightenment (no ''Donna Reed,'' this) even as it invites them to enjoy the ongoing frenzy of spite in which the show indulges. And frenzy is indeed the word. Every member of the family despises everyone else, and any given program consists of little more than continuous insults, interspersed with snide loathing or occasional expressions of despair.

Father (to son): Did I ever tell you not to get married?
Son: Yeah, Dad.
Father: Did I ever tell you not to become a shoe salesman?
Son: Yeah, Dad.
Father: Well, then I've told you everything I know.

This sort of resigned and paralytic discontent dominates the tone of ''Married . . . with Children''; it lacks even the dim rays of hope that occasionally lifted

Ralph Kramden's or Riley's gloomy existence. Every show is devoted to a new kind of humiliation: to earn extra money, Al becomes a burger-flipper; when son Bud falls victim to a practical joke perpetrated by an old flame his slutty sister Kelly comes to his defense by crucifying the girl against a locker; wife Peg belittles Al's manhood in front of strangers. Again and again, the unrelenting negativity of the show finds new ways to expand, purifying itself of any nonironic, positive content. Lovebird neighbors intended for contrast in the first season soon divorce, adding to the show's already vast reserve of bitterness. Christina Applegate, the young actress who plays Kelly, filled out during the first two years, adding a missing element of nasty prurience to the show.

The result of this hermetic exclusion of all warmth, say a number of apologists for the show, is positive: "With these new programs," says Barbara Cadow, a psychologist at USC, "we see we're doing all right by comparison." Yet at the same time, it is the very "realism" of these shows that won them praise again and again. This "realism" appeals to a cynical element in us—no one would ever admit to resembling Roseanne Barr or her family, but they are eminently "realistic" portraits of the losers next door. Roseanne Barr is shrewish and miserable to the point of self-parody, and this is seen as the great strength of her series. "Mom" (who Roseanne, it is assumed, represents) "is no longer interested in being a human sacrifice on the altar of 'pro-family' values," says Barbara Ehrenreich in the *New Republic*.

The praise of the same style of TV both for its realism and for its horrific exaggeration, while apparently contradictory, is based on a common assumption. In each case, the pervasive unhappiness and derision on TV sitcoms is assumed to be a reflection, albeit a negative one, of the unhappiness of real families. Cadow assumes that it is caricature, and Ehrenreich that it is a manifesto, but neither woman doubts that both shows offer some kind of corrective to real life for their viewers, and that this explains their popularity. This congratulatory view of hit TV shows contains a fundamental error: the old network executive's rationale that TV "gives people what they want," in response to their Nielsen-measured "choice."

The concentration of mass media into a few corporate hands invalidates that idea even more today than in the past. Given TV's entirely corporate nature, it is unreasonable to assume that the channels are referenda, since almost every channel, at least until recently, offered almost identical options. What succeeds with the public makes it, yes. But that "success" is determined by TV's agenda—which now, as always, is more than selling dog biscuits. Consumption must be encouraged psychologically; sectors and tendencies in American society have to be identified and exploited. "Since the major broadcasters are no longer winning the big numbers," observes *TV Guide,* "they're now fighting for the youthful demographics that bring in the highest revenues. That's why everyone is hyping bold, hip shows."

Of course, the success of a culture based on mass consumption depends on the creation of boundless needs; boundless needs presuppose boundless discontent. Boundless discontent must begin with the family, where social patterns are first internalized. If, latchkey in hand, TV can flatter a kinless and dispossessed child into adulthood and at the same time kid his or her parents about it, perfect consumers are thereby made. The family becomes a breeding ground for easygoing and independent citizens of the marketplace, transported beyond the inner struggle and deep feeling of family life, and bound in their place by the laws of supply and demand, consumer "choices," and a continual negation of their truest selves.

By presenting unhappy families to viewers, TV achieves many gains. First, as Cadow rightly points out, mocking the traditional family does flatter the distorted family of our times. However, this does not necessarily lift spirits. On the contrary, it lowers expectations; it stupefies discontent instead of healing it. "Married . . . with Children" is the prototype of this strategy. The petty or profound resentments of real families do not rival those of the Bundys, but then neither does their ability to punish and humiliate each other. By making our problems "seem all right by comparison," the series trivializes them rather than taking them seriously. It in fact worsens them by its counsel of despair.

Secondly, the dysfunctional TV family aids advertisers in their perennial quest for credibility by creating a supersaturated atmosphere of irony, which atrophies our ability to believe in anything. Commercials themselves work on a principle of pseudo-rebelliousness. Burger King—now officially touted by the Simpsons—proudly sports the "radical" motto, "Sometimes you've gotta break the rules." Swallowing these giant absurdities relies not on credulity, but on an ironic, self-assured disbelief. "Roseanne," with its trademark sarcasm, and "Twin Peaks," with its tongue-in-cheek grotesqueries, are good examples.

Third, and most insidious, is the stability of TV's dysfunctional families, and their passive acceptance of their fate. A successful cast is the source of "ensemble acting," which has been the formula for success for some time now on TV. Since TV characters now move in herds, they do not get divorced, move out, have devastating affairs, or anything else that would disrupt the fabric of the show's format. Implicitly, these shows assure us that family life is largely a nightmare, but one that is self-perpetuating and only requires handling with a deft, protective irony. This irony, the antithesis of deep feeling, is the essential assault on the family and on all human relationships, reducing them to problems of managerial acumen. Thus, while remaining intact in their own impoverished world, sitcom families undermine the stability of real families, discrediting the embarrassingly earnest, often abject bonds of kind while hermetically sealing themselves off from the possibility of familial collapse. And this while they consume the increasingly rare time in which American families are actually together.

"The Simpsons," the most popular of the group and certainly the least ironic and "anti-family," is TV's most effective reinforcer. This paradox begins with the fact that the show is a cartoon: with their yellow skin, bulging eyes, and comical motions, the Simpsons are funny just to look at, and hence relieve the audience of the need to continually jeer at them. The Bundy family of "Married . . . with Children," like all sitcom characters, aspire to the televisual purity of cartoon characters, but are stuck in rubbery bags of protoplasm with nothing but one-liners and a laugh track to hide behind. The Simpsons, oddly, are freer than other TV families to act human.

And so they do. There is an element of family loyalty and principle to be found in the Simpsons, often combined with witty and valid social criticism. Brother Bart and sister Lisa petulantly demand of baby Maggie to "come to the one you love most," to which the infant responds by crawling lovingly to the TV. Or again, when father Homer's sinister boss inquires disbelievingly, "You'd give up a job and a raise for your principles?" Homer responds (with almost none of the usual sitcom character's irony), "When you put it that way, it does sound far-fetched—but that's the lunk you're lookin' at!" "Hmm," the boss replies. "You're not as dumb as you look. Or sound. Or as our best testing indicates."

With pointed jokes such as these, "The Simpsons" might prompt us to conclude the same about its vast audience. The harmlessness of these jokes can be taken for granted; no one who watches TV is going to stop because they see TV criticized. We criticize it ourselves as a matter of course. On the contrary, we feel flattered, and less inclined to stop watching.

And we are that much less inclined to object to the continuing presence of unsafe workplaces, vast corporations, the therapy racket, and all the other deserving targets of the Simpsons' harmless barbs. The genial knowingness of shows like "The Simpsons" subverts criticism through an innocuous pseudo-criticism, just as the familial discontents of TV shows subvert alarm at graver discontents in real life. Criticism is further weakened by the show's irony, which although less than some other programs is still pervasive and fundamental to its humor. No one in an ironic show can get too far out of line. For example, in one episode, misunderstood Lisa meets that well-worn figure of Caucasian lore, the wise and virtuous old colored bluesman, ever ready to act as mentor to young white people in their search for self-knowledge. "The Simpsons" is far too hip to hand us such a hackneyed cliché. The Virtuous Old Blues Man is as empty a conceit as the Perfect Family—so on the show, he is named "Bleeding Gums Murphy." (Why? "I haven't brushed my teeth in thirty years, that's why.") In place of the usual soulful laments, he sings the "I Don't Have an Italian Suit Blues."

Such undercutting is typical of TV as a whole; attempts to transcend the flattened-out emotional landscape of TV are almost invariably punished by some droll comeuppance. But since as bizarre cartoons there is little need to belittle them, the Simpsons get a little more than most, and are occasionally allowed moments of earnestness unmitigated by the selfishness of "thirtysomething," the weirdness of "Twin Peaks," or the inevitable "comic relief"—the stock entrances of deadpan tots and witty oldsters, etc.—used to terminate the maudlin embraces of non-animated sitcomites. None of this is to be had on "The Simpsons," but the picture it presents is still fundamentally hopeless. The Simpsons are basically boobs, and their occasional bursts of tenderness or insight are buried under biting irony and superior, if affectionate, mockery. More than any of the other "anti-family" shows, "The Simpsons" seems to come close to our lives; more than any of the other shows, as a result, it commits us to a shared vision of pessimism and self-deprecation.

Because the TV screen is neither a mirror, reflecting ourselves paralyzed in chairs in front of it, nor a window, through which we observe the antics of distant players, it is an implicit invitation to participate in a vision of "society" largely designed to flatter us in sinister ways, manipulate our attention, and commit us to the status quo. In discrediting "yesterday's" family values in its various "breakthrough" shows (ostensibly defining "A Different World" for us, as the title of one series has it), TV seeks only to impose its own values—which is to say, the values of the marketplace. Bart Simpson, master sneerer, is the prototype of the modern series character who—by the social scripts of TV—reflects us. Small, ridiculous, and at the same time admirable for his sarcasm and enlightened self-interest, Bart is the child of the culture of TV, his parents mere intermediaries.

Paradoxically, that is why the most powerless sector of American society has adopted him, fitting him with their own wishful slogan—"I got the power!" Though black Bart's anger may be incongruous with TV, his proclamation is not, since TV is so successful an invitation to impotent posturing. At the moment, the rage of the underclass cannot be appropriated by TV, yet in black Bart, in the fatal joining of ironic hipness and earnest wrath, we see perhaps a glimpse of the future (and in fact there are already a spate of new black shows—e.g., "Fresh Prince of Bel Air," "In Living Color"). "I got the power!" says black Bart. But in the world of the TV family, no one has power. Empty fantasies of might, like cynical, knowing giggles, are terminal symptoms of our capitulation to TV's vision.

Life outside of that vision *is* ugly and is becoming uglier as ties, familial and societal, dissolve and decay. But the only power we do have is the power of our own real selves to reject the defensive posture of materialist or ironist or cynic, and the soullessness of TV's "hip, bold," anti-life world. Bart and his aspirants exist in that world, and their example serves only to impoverish us.

DISCUSSION QUESTIONS

1. Ozersky makes his own view of the recent developments on television known almost immediately. What aspects of his tone and style alert us to his opinion almost from the start? Do you think his analysis of this recent trend in sitcoms is any less valid due to its subjective nature?

2. To what extent does Ozersky feel that TV itself is responsible for the degeneration of family values? Do you agree with his argument, or do you hold other factors responsible for this phenomenon?

3. According to Ozersky, what gains does television achieve by its presentation of unhappy families? Does he believe that there is enough other programming on TV to counteract the negative effects of shows like *The Simpsons?* In your opinion, what kinds of images currently on TV act to counter these effects?

4. In what ways does *The Simpsons* resemble *Roseanne* (see "Scripts") in its depiction of the American family? In what ways does it differ?

John Updike / The Mystery of Mickey Mouse

Art & Antiques, November 1991

One of America's most respected and versatile writers, John Updike was born in 1932 in Shillington, Pennsylvania, the setting for many of his early stories. He graduated from Harvard in 1954 and continued his studies at Oxford University and the Ruskin School of Drawing and Fine Art. After working for two years on the staff of the New Yorker *(to which he still regularly contributes fiction and reviews), Updike moved to Massachusetts and began practicing his "solitary trade" full time. He has published many volumes of short stories (see "Classics"), numerous novels, and several collections of poetry and essays. Among his most recent books are a memoir,* Self-Consciousness *(1989), a novel,* Rabbit at Rest *(1990), and a collection of essays and criticism,* Odd Jobs *(1991).*

"The Mystery of Mickey Mouse" was adapted by Art & Antiques *from Updike's introduction to* The Art of Mickey Mouse, *a volume edited by Craig Yoe and Janet Morra-Yoe.*

It's all in the ears. When Mickey Mouse was born, in 1927, the world of early cartoon animation was filled with two-legged zoomorphic humanoids, whose strange half-black faces were distinguished one from another chiefly by the ears. Felix the Cat had pointed triangular ears and Oswald the Rabbit—Walt Disney's first successful cartoon creation, which he abandoned when his New York distributor, Charles Mintz, attempted to swindle him—had long floppy ears, with a few notches in the end to suggest fur. Disney's Oswald films, and the Alice animations that preceded them, had mice in them, with linear limbs, wiry tails, and ears that are oblong, not yet round. On the way back to California from New York by train, having left Oswald enmeshed for good in the machinations of Mr. Mintz, Walt and his wife Lillian invented another character based—the genesis legend claims—on the tame fieldmice that used to wander into Disney's old studio in Kansas City. His first thought was to call the mouse Mortimer; Lillian proposed instead the less pretentious name Mickey. Somewhere between Chicago and Los Angeles, the young couple concocted the plot of Mickey's first cartoon short, *Plane Crazy,* co-starring Minnie and capitalizing on 1927's Lindbergh craze. The next short produced by Disney's fledgling studio—which included, besides himself and Lillian, his brother Roy, and his old Kansas City associate, Ub Iwerks—was *Gallopin' Gaucho,* and introduced a fat and wicked cat who did not yet wear the prosthesis that would give him his name of Pegleg Pete. The third short, *Steamboat Willie,* incorporated that brand-new novelty, a sound track, and was released first, in 1928. Mickey Mouse entered history, as the most persistent and pervasive figment of American popular culture in this century.

His ears are two solid black circles, no matter the angle at which he holds his head. Three-dimensional images of Mickey Mouse—toy dolls, or the papier-mâché heads the grotesque Disneyland Mickeys wear—make us uneasy, since the ears inevitably exist edgewise as well as frontally. These ears properly belong not to three-dimensional space but to an ideal realm of notation, of symbolization, of cartoon resilience and indestructibility. In drawings, when Mickey is in profile, one ear is at the back of his head like a spherical ponytail, or like a secondary bubble in a computer-generated Mandelbrot set. We accept it, as we accepted Li'l Abner's hair always being parted on the side facing the viewer. A surreal optical consistency is part of the cartoon world, halfway between our world and the plane of pure signs, of alphabets and trademarks.

In the sixty-four years since Mickey Mouse's image was promulgated, the ears, though a bit more organically irregular and flexible than the classic 1930s appendages, have not been essentially modified. Many other modifications have, however, overtaken that first crude cartoon, born of an era of starker stylizations. White gloves, like the gloves worn in minstrel shows, appeared after those first, to cover the black hands. The infantile bare chest and shorts with two buttons were phased out in the '40s. The eyes have undergone a number of changes, most drastically in the late '30s, when, some historians mistakenly claimed, they acquired pupils. Not so: the old eyes, the black oblongs that acquired a nick of reflection in the sides, *were* the pupils; the eye whites filled the entire space beneath Mickey's cap of black, its widow's peak marking the division between these enormous oculi. This can be seen clearly in the face of the classic Minnie; when she bats her eyelids, their lashed shades cover over the full width of what might be thought to be her brow. But all the old animated animals were built this way from Felix the Cat on; Felix had lower lids, and the Mickey of *Plane Crazy* also. So it was an evolutionary misstep that beginning in 1938, replaced the shiny black pupils with entire oval eyes, containing pupils of their own. No such mutation has overtaken Pluto, Goofy, or Donald Duck. The change brought Mickey closer to us humans, but also took away something of his vitality, his alertness, his bug-eyed cartoon readiness for adventure. It made him less abstract, less iconic, more merely cute and dwarfish. The original Mickey, as he scuttles and bounces through those early animated shorts, was angular and wiry, with much of the impudence and desperation of a true rodent. He was gradually rounded to the proportions of a child, a regression sealed by his '50s manifestation as the genius of the children's television show, *The Mickey Mouse Club,* with its live Mouseketeers. Most of the artists who depict Mickey today, though too young to have grown up, as I did, with his old form, have instinctively reverted to it; it is the bare-chested basic Mickey, with his yellow shoes and oval buttons on his shorts, who is the icon, beside whom his modified later version is a mere mousy trousered pipsqueak.

His first, iconic manifestation had something of Chaplin to it; he was the little guy, just over the border of the respectable. His circular ears, like two minimal cents, bespeak the smallest economic unit, the overlookable democratic man. His name has passed into the language as a byword for the small, the weak—a "Mickey Mouse operation" means an undercapitalized company or minor surgery. Children of my generation—wearing our Mickey Mouse watches, prying pennies from our Mickey Mouse piggy banks (I won one in a third-grade spelling bee, my first intellectual triumph), following his running combat with Pegleg Pete in the daily funnies, going to the local movie-house movies every Saturday afternoon and cheering when his smiling visage burst onto the screen to introduce a cartoon—felt Mickey was one of us, a bridge to the adult world of which Donald Duck was, for all of his childish sailor suit, an irascible, tyrannical member. Mickey didn't seek trouble, and he didn't complain; he rolled with the punches, and surprised himself as much as us when, as in *The Little Tailor,* he showed warrior resourcefulness and won, once again, a blushing kiss from dear, all but identical Minnie. His minimal, decent nature meant that he would yield, in the Disney animated cartoons, the starring role to combative, sputtering Donald Duck and even to Goofy, with his "gawshes" and Gary Cooper-like gawkiness. But for an occasional comeback like the "Sorcerer's Apprentice" episode of *Fantasia,* and last year's rather souped-up *The Prince and the Pauper,* Mickey was through as a star by 1940. But, as with Marilyn Monroe when her career was over, his life as an icon gathered strength. The America that is not symbolized by that imperial Yankee Uncle Sam is symbolized by Mickey Mouse. He is America as it feels to itself—plucky, put-on, inventive, resilient, good-natured, game.

Like America, Mickey has a lot of black blood. This fact was revealed to me in conversation by Saul Steinberg, who, in attempting to depict the racially mixed reality of New York streets for the supersensitive and race-blind *New Yorker* of the '60s and '70s, hit upon scribbling numerous Mickeys as a way of representing what was jauntily and scruffily and unignorably there. From just the way Mickey swings along in his classic, trademark pose, one three-fingered gloved hand held on high, he is jiving. Along with round black ears and yellow shoes, Mickey has soul. Looking back to such early animations as the early Looney Tunes' Bosko and Honey series (1930–36) and the Arab figures in Disney's own *Mickey in Arabia* of 1932, we see that blacks were drawn much like cartoon animals, with round button noses and great white eyes creating the double arch of the curious peaked skullcaps. Cartoon characters' rubberiness, their jazziness, their cheerful buoyance and idleness, all chimed with popular images of African Americans, earlier embodied in minstrel shows and in Joel Chandler Harris's tales of Uncle Remus, which Disney was to make into an animated feature, *Song of the South,* in 1946.

Up to 1950, animated cartoons, like films in general, contained caricatures of blacks that would be unacceptable now; in fact, *Song of the South* raised objections from the NAACP when it was released. In recent reissues of *Fantasia,* two Nubian centaurettes and a pickaninny centaurette who shines the others' hooves have been edited out. Not even the superb crows section of *Dumbo* would be made now. But there is a sense in which all animated cartoon characters are more or less black. Steven Spielberg's hectic tribute to animation, *Who Framed Roger Rabbit?,* has them all, from the singing trees of Silly Symphonies to Daffy Duck and Woody Woodpecker, living in a Los Angeles ghetto, Toonville. As blacks were second-class citizens with entertaining qualities, so the animated shorts were second-class movies, with unreal actors, who mocked and illuminated from underneath the real world, the live-actor cinema. Of course, even in a ghetto there are class distinctions. Porky Pig and Bugs Bunny have homes that they tend and defend, whereas Mickey started out, like those other raffish stick figures and dancing blots from the '20s, as a free spirit, a wanderer. As Richard Schickel has pointed out, "The locales of his adventures throughout the 1930s ranged from the

South Seas to the Alps to the deserts of Africa. He was, at various times, a gaucho, teamster, explorer, swimmer, cowboy, fireman, convict, pioneer, taxi driver, castaway, fisherman, cyclist, Arab, football player, inventor, jockey, storekeeper, camper, sailor, Gulliver, boxer,'' and so forth. He was, in short, a rootless vaudevillian who would play any part that the bosses at Disney Studios assigned him. And though the comic strip, which still persists, has fitted him with all of a white man's household comforts and headaches, it is as an unencumbered drifter whistling along on the road of hard knocks, ready for whatever adventure waits at the next turning, that he lives in our minds.

Cartoon characters have soul as Carl Jung defined it in his *Archetypes and the Collective Unconscious:* ''soul is a life-giving demon who plays his elfin game above and below human existence.'' Without the ''leaping and twinkling of the soul,'' Jung says, ''man would rot away in his greatest passion, idleness.'' The Mickey Mouse of the '30s shorts was a whirlwind of activity, with a host of unsuspected skills and a reluctant heroism that rose to every occasion. Like Chaplin and Douglas Fairbanks and Fred Astaire, he acted out our fantasies of endless nimbleness, of perfect weightlessness. Yet, withal, there was nothing aggressive or self-promoting about him, as there was about Popeye. Disney, interviewed in the '30s, said, ''Sometimes I've tried to figure out why Mickey appealed to the whole world. Everybody's tried to figure it out. So far as I know, nobody has. He's a pretty nice fellow who never does anybody any harm, who gets into scrapes through no fault of his own, but always manages to come up grinning.'' This was perhaps Disney's image of himself: for twenty years he did Mickey's voice in the films, and would often say, ''There's a lot of the Mouse in me.'' Mickey was a character created with his own pen, and nurtured on Disney's memories of his mouse-ridden Kansas City studio and of the Missouri farm where his struggling father tried for a time to make a living. Walt's humble, scrambling beginnings remained embodied in the mouse, whom the Nazis, in a fury against the Mickey-inspired Allied legions (the Allied code word on D-Day was ''Mickey Mouse''), called ''the most miserable ideal ever revealed . . . mice are dirty.''

But was Disney, like Mickey, just ''a pretty nice fellow?'' He was until crossed in his driving perfectionism, his Napoleonic capacity to marshal men and take risks in the service of an artistic and entrepreneurial vision. He was one of those great Americans, like Edison and Henry Ford, who invented themselves in terms of a new technology. The technology—in Disney's case, film animation—would have been there anyway, but only a few driven men seized the full possibilities, and made empires. In the dozen years between *Steamboat Willie* and *Fantasia,* the Disney studios took the art of animation to heights of ambition and accomplishment it would never have reached otherwise, and Disney's personal zeal was the animating force. He created an empire of the mind, and its emperor was Mickey Mouse.

The '30s were Mickey's conquering decade. His image circled the globe. In Africa, tribesmen painfully had tiny mosaic Mickey Mouses inset into their front teeth, and a South African tribe refused to buy soap unless the cakes were embossed with Mickey's image, and a revolt of some native bearers was quelled when the safari masters projected some Mickey Mouse cartoons for them. Nor were the high and mighty immune to Mickey's elemental appeal—King George V and Franklin Delano Roosevelt insisted that all film showings they attended include a dose of Mickey Mouse. But other popular phantoms, like Felix the Cat, have faded, where Mickey has settled into the national collective consciousness. The television program revived him for my children's generation, and the theme parks make him live for my grandchildren's. Yet survival cannot be imposed through weight of publicity; Mickey's persistence springs from something unhyped, something timeless in the image that has allowed it to pass in status from a fad to an icon.

To take a bite out of our imaginations, an icon must be simple. The ears, the wiggly tail, the red shorts, give us a Mickey. Donald Duck and Goofy, Bugs Bunny and Woody Woodpecker are inextricably bound up with the draftsmanship of the artists who make them move and squawk, but Mickey floats free. It was Claes Oldenburg's pop art that first alerted me to the fact that Mickey Mouse had passed out of the realm of commercially generated image into that of artifact. A new Disney gadget, advertised on television, is a cameralike box that spouts bubbles when a key is turned; the key consists of three circles, two mounted on a larger one, and the image is unmistakably Mickey. Like yin and yang, like the Christian cross and the star of Israel, Mickey can be seen everywhere—a sign, a rune, a hieroglyphic trace of a secret power, an electricity we want to plug into. Like totem poles, like African masks, Mickey stands at that intersection of abstraction and representation where magic connects.

Usually, cartoon figures do not age, and yet their audience does age, as generation succeeds generation, so that a weight of allusion and sentimental reference increases. To the movie audiences of the early '30s, Mickey Mouse was a piping-voiced live wire, the latest thing in entertainment; by the time of *Fantasia* he was already a sentimental figure, welcomed back. *The Mickey Mouse Show,* with its slightly melancholy pack leader Jimmie Dodd, created a Mickey more removed and marginal than in his first incarnation. The generation that watched it grew up into the rebels of the '60s, to whom Mickey became camp, a symbol of U.S. cultural fast food, with a touch of the old rodent raffishness. Politically, Walt, stung by the studio strike of 1940, moved to the right, but Mickey remains one of the '30s proletariat, not uncomfortable in the cartoon-rickety, cheerfully verminous crash pads of the counterculture. At the Florida and California theme parks, Mickey manifests himself as a short real person wearing an awkward giant head, costumed as a ringmaster; he is in a danger, in these '90s, of seeming not merely venerable kitsch but part of the great trash problem, one more piece of visual litter being moved back and forth by the bulldozers of consumerism.

But never fear, his basic goodness will shine through. Beyond recall, perhaps, is the simple love felt by us of the generation that grew up with him. He was five years my senior and felt like a playmate. I remember crying when the local newspaper, cutting down its comic pages to help us win World War II, eliminated the Mickey Mouse strip. I was old enough, nine or ten, to write an angry letter to the editor. In fact, the strips had been eliminated by the votes of a readership poll, and my indignation and sorrow stemmed from my incredulous realization that not everybody loved Mickey Mouse as I did. In an account of my boyhood written over thirty years ago, "The Dogwood Tree," I find these sentences concerning another boy, a rival: "When we both collected Big Little Books, he outbid me for my supreme find (in the attic of a third boy), the first Mickey Mouse. I can still see that book. I wanted it so badly, its paper tan with age and its drawings done in Disney's primitive style, when Mickey's black chest is naked like a child's and his eyes are two nicked oblongs." And I once tried to write a short story called "A Sensation of Mickey Mouse," trying to superimpose on adult experience, as a shiver-inducing revenant, that indescribable childhood sensation—a rubbery taste, a licorice smell, a feeling of supernatural clarity and close-in excitation that Mickey Mouse gave me, and gives me, much dimmed by the years, still. He is a "genius" in the primary dictionary sense of "an attendant spirit," with his vulnerable bare black chest, his touchingly big yellow shoes, the mysterious place at the back of his shorts where his tail came out, the little cleft cushion of a tongue, red as a valentine and glossy as candy, always peeping though the catenary curves of his undiscourageable smile. Not to mention his ears.

DISCUSSION QUESTIONS

1. Updike states: "The America that is not symbolized by that imperial Yankee Uncle Sam is symbolized by Mickey Mouse." In what sense do these two American symbols differ? To Updike, what does Mickey Mouse most symbolize about America? What does Mickey symbolize to you?
2. Updike concentrates on Mickey Mouse's physical appearance. What is it about Mickey's ears that he finds fascinating? What symbolic value or significance do Mickey's ears possess?

Robert Hughes / The Fraying of America

Time, February 3, 1992

Is America coming apart at the seams? Have we become a nation of victims, each individual with a unique complaint, each group with its own grievance? In the following Time *essay, Robert Hughes takes what the magazine's cover called "a scorching look" at a country on the edge of social breakdown. Challenging many cultural and educational trends, such as multiculturalism, ethnocentrism, and political correctness, Hughes finds a "society obsessed with therapies and filled with distrust of formal politics, skeptical of authority and prey to superstition, its political language corroded by fake pity and euphemism."*

Born and educated in Sydney, Australia, Robert Hughes lives in New York City and is a senior writer for Time *magazine, where he began working as an art critic in 1970. He is the author of an outstanding study of modern art,* The Shock of the New *(1980), a best-selling book about Australia,* The Fatal Shore *(1987), and* Barcelona *(1992), a social and cultural history of that Spanish city. "The Fraying of America" was adapted from a series of lectures entitled* The Culture of Complaint.

Just over 50 years ago, the poet W. H. Auden achieved what all writers envy: Making a prophecy that would come true. It is embedded in a long work called *For the Time Being,* where Herod muses about the distasteful task of massacring the Innocents. He doesn't want to, because he is at heart a liberal. But still, he predicts, if that Child is allowed to get away, "Reason will be replaced by Revelation. Instead of Rational Law, objective truths perceptible to any who will undergo the necessary intellectual discipline, Knowledge will degenerate into a riot of subjective visions . . . Whole cosmogonies will be created out of some forgotten personal resentment, complete epics written in private languages, the daubs of schoolchildren ranked above the greatest masterpieces. Idealism will be replaced by Materialism. Life after death will be an eternal dinner party where all the guests are 20 years old . . . The New Aristocracy will consist exclusively of hermits, bums and permanent invalids. The Rough Diamond, the Consumptive Whore, the bandit who is good to his mother, the epileptic girl who has a way with animals will be the heroes and heroines of the New Age, when the general, the statesman, and the philosopher have become the butt of every farce and satire."

What Herod saw was America in the late 1980s and early '90s, right down to that dire phrase "New Age." A society obsessed with therapies and filled with distrust of formal politics, skeptical of authority and prey to superstition, its political language corroded by fake pity and euphemism. A nation like late Rome in its long imperial reach, in the corruption and verbosity of its senators, in its reliance on sacred geese (those feathered ancestors of our own pollsters and spin doctors) and in its submission to senile, deified Emperors controlled by astrologers and extravagant wives. A culture that has replaced gladiatorial games, as a means of pacifying the mob, with high-tech wars on television that cause immense slaughter and yet leave the Mesopotamian satraps in full power over their wretched subjects.

Mainly it is women who object, for due to the prevalence of their mystery-religions, the men are off in the woods, affirming their manhood by sniffing one another's armpits and listening to third-rate poets rant about the moist, hairy satyr that lives inside each one of them. Meanwhile, artists vacillate between a largely self-indulgent expressiveness and a mainly impotent politicization, and the contest between education and TV—between argument and persuasion by spectacle—has been won by TV, a medium now more debased in America than ever before, and more abjectly self-censoring than anywhere in Europe.

The fundamental temper of America tends toward an existential ideal that can probably never be reached but can never be discarded: equal rights to variety, to construct your life as you see fit, to choose your traveling companions. It has always been a heterogeneous country, and its cohesion, whatever cohesion it has, can only be based on mutual respect. There never was a core America in which everyone looked the same, spoke the same language, worshipped the same gods and believed the same things.

America is a construction of mind, not of race or inherited class or ancestral territory. It is a creed born of immigration, of the jostling of scores of tribes that become American to the extent to which they can negotiate accommodations with one another. These negotiations succeed unevenly and often fail: you need only to glance at the history of racial relations to know that. The melting pot never melted. But American mutuality lives in recognition of difference. The fact remains that America is a collective act of the imagination whose making never ends, and once that sense of collectivity and mutual respect is broken, the possibilities of American-ness begin to unravel.

If they are fraying now, it is at least in part due to the prevalence of demagogues who wish to claim that there is only one path to virtuous Americanness: paleoconservatives like Jesse Helms and Pat Robertson who think this country has one single ethic, neoconservatives who rail against a bogey called multiculturalism—as though this culture was ever anything *but* multi!—and pushers of political correctness who would like to see grievance elevated into automatic sanctity.

BIG DADDY IS TO BLAME

Americans are obsessed with the recognition, praise and, when necessary, the manufacture of victims, whose one common feature is that they have been denied parity with that Blond Beast of the sentimental imagination, the heterosexual, middle-class white male. The range of victims available 10 years ago—blacks, Chicanos, Indians, women, homosexuals—has now expanded to include every permutation of the halt, the blind and the short, or, to put it correctly, the vertically challenged.

Forty years ago, one of the epic processes in the assertion of human rights started unfolding in the U.S.: the civil rights movement. But today, after more than a decade of government that did its best to ignore the issues of race when it was not trying to roll back the gains of the '60s, the usual American response to inequality is to rename it, in the hope that it will go away. We want to create a sort of linguistic Lourdes, where evil and misfortune are dispelled by a dip in the waters of euphemism. Does the cripple rise from his wheelchair, or feel better about being stuck in it, because someone back in the early days of the Reagan Administration decided that, for official purposes, he was ''physically challenged''?

Because the arts confront the sensitive citizen with the difference between good artists, mediocre ones and absolute duffers, and since there are always more of the last two than the first, the arts too must be politicized; so we cobble up critical systems to show that although we know what we mean by the quality of the environment, the idea of quality in aesthetic experience is little more than a paternalist fiction designed to make life hard for black, female and gay artists.

Since our newfound sensitivity decrees that only the victim shall be the hero, the white American male starts bawling for victim status too. Hence the rise of cult therapies teaching that we are all the victims of our parents, that whatever our folly, venality or outright thuggishness, we are not to be blamed for it, since we come from ''dysfunctional families.'' The ether is jammed with confessional shows in which a parade of citizens and their role models, from LaToya Jackson to Roseanne Arnold, rise to denounce the sins of their parents. The cult of the abused Inner Child has a very important use in modern America: it tells you that nothing is your fault, that personal grievance transcends political utterance.

The all-pervasive claim to victimhood tops off America's long-cherished culture of therapeutics. Thus we create a juvenile culture of complaint in which Big Daddy is always to blame and the expansion of rights goes on without the other half of citizenship: attachment to duties and obligations. We are seeing a public recoil from formal politics, from the active, reasoned exercise of citizenship. It comes because we don't trust anyone. It is part of the cafard the '80s induced: Wall Street robbery, the savings and loan scandal, the wholesale plunder of the economy, an orgy released by Reaganomics that went on for years with hardly a peep from Congress—events whose numbers were so huge as to be beyond the comprehension of most people.

Single-issue politics were needed when they came, because they forced Washington to deal with, or at least look at, great matters of civic concern that it had scanted: first the civil rights movement, and then the environment, women's reproductive rights, health legislation, the educational crisis. But now they too face dilution by a trivialized sense of civic responsibility. What are your politics? Oh, I'm antismoking. And yours? Why, I'm starting an action committee to have the suffix *-man* removed from every word in every book in the Library of Congress. And yours, sir? Well, God told me to chain myself to a fire hydrant until we put a fetus on the Supreme Court.

In the past 15 years the American right has had a complete, almost unopposed success in labeling as left-wing ordinary agendas and desires that, in a saner polity, would be seen as ideologically neutral, an extension of rights implied in the Constitution. American feminism has a large repressive fringe, self-caricaturing and often abysmally trivial, like the academic thought police who recently managed to get a reproduction of Goya's *Naked Maja* removed from a classroom at Pennsylvania State University; it has its loonies who regard all sex with men, even with consent, as a politicized form of rape. But does this in any way devalue the immense shared desire of millions of American women to claim the right of equality to men, to be free from sexual harassment in the workplace, to be accorded the reproductive rights to be individuals first and mothers second?

The '80s brought the retreat and virtual disappearance of the American left as a political, as distinct from a cultural, force. It went back into the monastery—that is, to academe—and also extruded out into the art world, where it remains even more marginal and impotent. Meanwhile, a considerable and very well-subsidized industry arose, hunting the lefty academic or artist in his or her retreat.

Republican attack politics turned on culture, and suddenly both academe and the arts were full of potential Willie Hortons. The lowbrow form of this was the ire of figures like Senator Helms and the Rev. Donald Wildmon directed against national Endowment subventions for art shows they thought blasphemous and obscene, or the trumpetings from folk like David Horowitz about how PBS should be demolished because it's a pinko-liberal-anti-Israel bureaucracy.

THE BATTLES ON CAMPUS

The middle-to-highbrow form of the assault is the ongoing frenzy about political correctness, whose object is to create the belief, or illusion, that a new and sinister McCarthyism, this time of the left, has taken over American universities and is bringing free thought to a stop. This is flatly absurd. The comparison to McCarthyism could be made only by people who either don't know or don't wish to remember what the Senator from Wisconsin and his pals actually did to academe in the '50s: the firings of tenured profs in mid-career, the inquisitions by the House Committee on Un-American Activities on the content of libraries and courses, the campus loyalty oaths, the whole sordid atmosphere of persecution, betrayal and paranoia. The number of conservative academics fired by the lefty thought police, by contrast, is zero. There has been heckling. There have been baseless accusations of racism. And Certainly there is no shortage of the zealots, authoritarians and scramblers who view PC as a shrewd career move or as a vent for their own frustrations.

In cultural matters we can hardly claim to have a left and a right anymore. Instead we have something more akin to two puritan sects, one masquerading as conservative, the other posing as revolutionary but using academic complaint as a way of evading engagement in the real world. Sect A borrows the techniques of Republican attack politics to show that if Sect B has its way, the study of Milton and Titian will be replaced by indoctrination programs in the works of obscure Third World authors and West Coast Chicano subway muralists, and the pillars of learning will forthwith collapse. Meanwhile, Sect B is so stuck in the complaint mode that it can't mount a satisfactory defense, since it has burned most of its bridges to the culture at large.

In the late '80s, while American academics were emptily theorizing that language and the thinking subject were dead, the longing for freedom and humanistic culture was demolishing European tyranny. Of course, if the Chinese students had read their Foucault, they would have known that repression is inscribed in all language, their own included, and so they could have saved themselves the trouble of facing the tanks in Tiananmen Square. But did Vaclav Havel and his fellow playwrights free Czechoslovakia by quoting Derrida or Lyotard on the inscrutability of texts? Assuredly not: they did it by placing their faith in the transforming power of thought—by putting their shoulders to the immense wheel of the world. The world changes more deeply, widely, thrillingly than at any moment since 1917, perhaps since 1848, and the American academic left keeps fretting about how phallocentricity is inscribed in Dickens' portrayal of Little Nell.

The obsessive subject of our increasingly sterile confrontation between the two PCs—the politically and the patriotically correct—is something clumsily called multiculturalism. America is a place filled with diversity, unsettled histories, images impinging on one another and spawning unexpected shapes. Its poloyphony of voices, its constant eddying of claims to identity, is one of the things that make America America. The gigantic, riven, hybridizing, multiracial republic each year receives a major share of the world's emigration, legal or illegal.

To put the argument for multiculturalism in merely practical terms of self-interest:

though élites are never going to go away, the composition of those élites is not necessarily static. The future of American ones, in a globalized economy without a cold war, will rest with people who can think and act with informed grace across ethnic, cultural, linguistic lines. And the first step in becoming such a person lies in acknowledging that we are not one big world family, or ever likely to be; that the differences among races, nations, cultures and their various histories are at least as profound and as durable as the similarities; that these differences are not divagations from a European norm but structures eminently worth knowing about for their own sake. In the world that is coming, if you can't navigate difference, you've had it.

Thus if multiculturalism is about learning to see through borders, one can be all in favor of it. But you do not have to listen to the arguments very long before realizing that, in quite a few people's minds, multiculturalism is about something else. Their version means cultural separatism within the larger whole of America. They want to Balkanize culture.

THE AUTHORITY OF THE PAST

This reflects the sense of disappointment and frustration with formal politics, which has caused many people to look to the arts as a field of power, since they have power nowhere else. Thus the arts become an arena for complaint about rights. The result is a gravely distorted notion of the political capacity of the arts, just at the moment when—because of the pervasiveness of mass media—they have reached their nadir of real political effect.

One example is the inconclusive debate over "the cannon," that oppressive Big Bertha whose muzzle is trained over the battlements of Western Civ at the black, the gay and the female. The canon, we're told, is a list of books by dead Europeans—Shakespeare and Dante and Tolstoy and Stendhal and John Donne and T. S. Eliot . . . you know, *them,* the pale, patriarchal penis people. Those who complain about the canon think it creates readers who will never read anything else. What they don't want to admit, at least not publicly, is that most American students don't read much anyway and quite a few, left to their own devices, would not read at all. Their moronic national baby-sitter, the TV set, took care of that. Before long, Americans will think of the time when people sat at home and read books for their own sake, discursively and sometimes even aloud to one another, as a lost era—the way we now see rural quilting bees in the 1870s.

The quarrel over the canon reflects the sturdy assumption that works of art are, or ought to be, therapeutic. Imbibe the *Republic* or *Phaedo* at 19, and you will be one kind of person; study *Jane Eyre* or *Mrs. Dalloway,* and you will be another. For in the literary zero-sum game of canon-talk, if you read *X,* it means that you don't read *Y.* This is a simple fancy.

So is the distrust of the dead, as in "dead white male." Some books are deeper, wider, fuller than others, and more necessary to an understanding of our culture and ourselves. They remain so long after their authors are dead. Those who parrot slogans like "dead white male" might reflect that, in writing, death is relative: Lord Rochester is as dead as Sappho, but not so moribund as Bret Easton Ellis or Andrea Dworkin. Statistically, most authors *are* dead, but some continue to speak to us with a vividness and urgency that few of the living can rival. And the more we read, the more writers we find who do so, which is why the canon is not a fortress but a permeable membrane.

The sense of quality, of style, of measure, is not an imposition bearing on literature from the domain of class, race or gender. All writers or artists carry in their mind an invisible tribunal of the dead, whose appointment is an imaginative act and not merely a browbeaten response to some notion of authority. This tribunal sits in judgment on their work. They intuit their standards from it. From its verdict there is no appeal. None of the contemporary tricks—not the fetishization of the personal, not the attempt to shift the aesthetic into the political, not the exhausted fictions of avant-gardism—will make it go away. If the tribunal weren't there, every first draft would be a final manuscript. You can't fool Mother Culture.

That is why one rejects the renewed attempt to judge writing in terms of its presumed social virtue. Through it, we enter a Marxist never-never land, where all the most retrograde phantoms of Literature as Instrument of Social Utility are trotted forth. Thus the *Columbia History of the American Novel* declares Harriet Beecher Stowe a better novelist than Herman Melville because she was "socially constructive" and because *Uncle Tom's Cabin* helped rouse Americans against slavery, whereas the captain of the *Pequod* was a symbol of laissez-faire capitalism with a bad attitude toward whales.

With the same argument you can claim that an artist like William Gropper, who drew those stirring cartoons of fat capitalists in top hats for the *New Masses* 60 years ago, may have something over an artist like Edward Hopper, who didn't care a plugged nickel for community and was always painting figures in lonely rooms in such a way that you can't be sure whether he was criticizing alienation or affirming the virtues of solitude.

REWRITING HISTORY

It's in the area of history that PC has scored its largest successes. The reading of history is never static. There is no such thing as the last word. And who could doubt that there is still much to revise in the story of the European conquest of North and South America that historians inherited? Its basic scheme was imperial: the epic advance of civilization against barbarism; the conquistador bringing the cross and the sword; the red man shrinking back before the cavalry and the railroad. Manifest Destiny. The notion that all historians propagated this triumphalist myth uncritically is quite false; you have only to read Parkman or Prescott to realize that. But after it left the histories and sank deep into popular culture, it became a potent myth of justification for plunder, murder and enslavement.

So now, in reaction to it, comes the manufacture of its opposite myth. European man, once the hero of the conquest of the Americas, now becomes its demon; and the victims, who cannot be brought back to life, are sanctified. On either side of the divide between Euro and native, historians stand ready with tarbrush and gold leaf, and instead of the wicked *old* stereotypes, we have a whole outfit of equally misleading new ones. Our predecessors made a hero of Christopher Columbus. To Europeans and white Americans in 1892, he was Manifest Destiny in tights, whereas a current PC book like Kirkpatrick Sale's *The Conquest of Paradise* makes him more like Hitler in a caravel, landing like a virus among the innocent people of the New World.

The need for absolute goodies and absolute baddies runs deep in us, but it drags history into propaganda and denies the humanity of the dead: their sins, their virtues, their failures. To preserve complexity, and not flatten it under the weight of anachronistic moralizing, is part of the historian's task.

You cannot remake the past in the name of affirmative action. But you can find narratives that haven't been written, histories of people and groups that have been distorted or ignored, and refresh history by bringing them in. That is why, in the past 25 years, so much of the vitality of written history has come from the left. When you read the work of the black Caribbean historian C. L. R. James, you see a part of the world break its long silence: a silence not of its own choosing but imposed on it by earlier imperialist writers. You do not have to be a Marxist to appreciate the truth of Eric Hobsbawm's claim that the most widely recognized achievement of radical history "has been to win a place for the history of ordinary people, common men and women." In America this work necessarily includes the histories of its minorities, which tend to break down complacent nationalist readings of the American past.

By the same token, great changes have taken place in the versions of American history taught to schoolchildren. The past 10 years have brought enormous and hard-won gains in accuracy, proportion and sensitivity in the textbook treatment of American minorities, whether Asian, native, black or Hispanic. But this is not enough for some extremists, who take the view that only blacks can write the history of slavery, only Indians that of pre-European America, and so forth.

That is the object of a bizarre document called the Portland African-American Baseline Essays, which has never been published as a book but, in photocopied form, is radically changing the curriculums of school systems all over the country. Written by an undistinguished group of scholars, these essays on history, social studies, math, language and arts and science are meant to be a charter of Afrocentrist history for young black Americans. They have had little scrutiny in the mainstream press. But they are popular with bureaucrats like Thomas Sobol, the education commissioner in New York State—people who are scared of alienating black voters or can't stand up to thugs like City College professor Leonard Jeffries. Their implications for American education are large, and mostly bad.

WAS CLEOPATRA BLACK?

The Afrocentrist claim can be summarized quite easily. It says the history of the cultural relations between Africa and Europe is bunk—a prop for the fiction of white European supremacy. Paleohistorians agree that intelligent human life began in the Rift Valley of Africa. The Afrocentrist goes further: the African was the *cultural* father of us all. European culture derives from Egypt, and Egypt is part of Africa, linked to its heart by the artery of the Nile. Egyptian civilization begin in sub-Saharan Africa, in Ethiopia and the Sudan.

Hence, argued the founding father of Afrocentrist history, the late Senegalese writer Cheikh Anta Diop, whatever is Egyptian is African, part of the lost black achievement; Imhotep, the genius who invented the pyramid as a monumental form in the 3rd millennium B.C., was black, and so were Euclid and Cleopatra in Alexandria 28 dynasties later. Blacks in Egypt invented hieroglyphics, and monumental stone sculpture, and the pillared temple, and the cult of the Pharaonic sun king. The habit of European and American historians of treating the ancient Egyptians as other than black is a racist plot to conceal the achievements of black Africa.

No plausible evidence exists for these claims of Egyptian negritude, though it is true that the racism of traditional historians when dealing with the cultures of Africa has been appalling. Most of them refused to believe African societies had a history that was worth telling. Here is Arnold Toynbee in *A Study of History:* "When we classify mankind by color, the only one of the primary races . . . which has not made a single creative contribution to any of our 21 civilizations is the black race."

No black person—indeed, no modern historian of any race—could read such bland dismissals without disgust. The question is, How to correct the record? Only by more knowledge. Toynbee was writing more than 50 years ago, but in the past 20 years, immense strides have been made in the historical scholarship of both

Africa and African America. But the upwelling of research, the growth of Black Studies programs, and all that goes with the long-needed expansion of the field seem fated to be plagued by movements like Afrocentrism, just as there are always cranks nattering about flying saucers on the edges of Mesoamerican archaeology.

To plow through the literature of Afrocentrism is to enter a world of claims about technological innovation so absurd that they lie beyond satire, like those made for Soviet science in Stalin's time. Afrocentrists have at one time or another claimed that Egyptians, alias Africans, invented the wet-cell battery by observing electric eels in the Nile; and that late in the 1st millennium B.C., they took to flying around in gliders. (This news is based not on the discovery of an aircraft in an Egyptian tomb but on a silhouette wooden votive sculpture of the god Horus, a falcon, that a passing English businessman mistook some decades ago for a model airplane.) Some also claim that Tanzanians 1,500 years ago were smelting steel with semiconductor technology. There is nothing to prove these tales, but nothing to disprove them either—a common condition of things that didn't happen.

THE REAL MULTICULTURALISM

Nowhere are the weaknesses and propagandistic nature of Afrocentrism more visible than in its version of slave history. Afrocentrists wish to invent a sort of remedial history in which the entire blame for the invention and practice of black slavery is laid at the door of Europeans. This is profoundly unhistorical, but it's getting locked in popular consciousness through the new curriculums.

It is true that slavery had been written into the basis of the classical world. Periclean Athens was a slave state, and so was Augustan Rome. Most of their slaves were Caucasian. The word slave meant a person of Slavic origin. By the 13th century slavery spread to other Caucasian peoples. But the African slave trade as such, the black traffic, was an Arab invention, developed by traders with the enthusiastic collaboration of black African ones, institutionalized with the most unrelenting brutality, centuries before the white man appeared on the African continent, and continuing long after the slave market in North America was finally crushed.

Naturally this is a problem for Afrocentrists, especially when you consider the recent heritage of Black Muslim ideas that many of them espouse. Nothing in the writings of the Prophet forbids slavery, which is why it became such an Arab-dominated business. And the slave traffic could not have existed without the wholehearted cooperation of African tribal states, built on the supply of captives generated by their relentless wars. The image promulgated by pop-history fictions like *Roots*—white slavers bursting with cutlass and musket into the settled lives of peaceful African villages—is very far from the historical truth. A marketing system had been in place for centuries, and its supply was controlled by Africans. Nor did it simply vanish with Abolition. Slave markets, supplying the Arab emirates, were still operating in Djibouti in the 1950s; and since 1960, the slave trade has flourished in Mauritania and the Sudan. There are still reports of chattel slavery in northern Nigeria, Rwanda and Niger.

But here we come up against a cardinal rule of the PC attitude to oppression studies. Whatever a white European male historian or witness has to say must be suspect; the utterances of an oppressed person or group deserve instant credence, even if they're the merest assertion. The claims of the victim do have to be heard, because they may cast new light on history. But they have to pass exactly the same tests as anyone else's or debate fails and truth suffers. The PC cover for this is the idea that all statements about history are expressions of power; history is written only by the winners, and truth is political and unknowable.

The word self-esteem has become one of the obstructive shibboleths of education. Why do black children need Afrocentrist education? Because, its promoters say, it will create self-esteem. The children live in a world of media and institutions whose images and values are created mainly by whites. The white tradition is to denigrate blacks. Hence blacks must have models that show them that they matter. Do you want your children to love themselves? Then change the curriculum. Feed them racist claptrap à la Leonard Jeffires, about how your intelligence is a function of the amount of melanin in your skin, and how Africans were sun people, open and cooperative, whereas Europeans were ice people, skulking pallidly in caves.

It is not hard to see why these claims for purely remedial history are intensifying today. They are symbolic. Nationalism always wants to have myths to prop itself up; and the newer the nationalism, the more ancient its claims. The invention of tradition, as Eric Hobsbawm has shown in detail, was one of the cultural industries of 19th century Europe. But the desire for self-esteem does not justify every lie and exaggeration and therapeutic slanting of evidence that can be claimed to alleviate it. The separatism it fosters turns what ought to be a recognition of cultural diversity, or real multiculturalism, tolerant on both sides, into a pernicious symbolic program. Separatism is the opposite of diversity.

The idea that European culture is oppressive in and of itself is a fallacy that can survive only among the fanatical and the ignorant. The moral and intellectual conviction that inspired Toussaint-Louverture to focus the rage of the Haitian slaves and lead them to freedom in 1791 came from his reading of Rousseau and Mirabeau. When thousands of voteless, propertyless workers the length and breadth of England met in their reading groups in the 1820s to discuss republican ideas and discover the significance of Shakespeare's *Julius Caesar,* they were seeking to unite themselves by taking back the meanings of a dominant culture from custodians who didn't live up to them.

Americans can still take courage from their example. Cultural separatism within this republic is more a fad than a serious proposal; it is not likely to hold. If it did, it would be a disaster for those it claims to help: the young, the poor and the black. Self-esteem comes from doing things well, from discovering how to tell a truth from a lie and from finding out what unites us as well as what separates us. The posturing of the politically correct is no more a guide to such matters than the opinions of Simon Legree.

DISCUSSION QUESTIOINS

1. Though Hughes has lived in the United States for many years, he is not an American native. Do you think this affects his critique in any way? Do you think there are aspects of American culture he doesn't understand? Or does his nonnative status permit him to look at the nation more objectively?

2. Hughes attacks many current cultural and political attitudes in this essay. Does he deal with these attitudes as isolated features of the American scene, or does he find any unifying foundation for them? Explain.

BEST-SELLERS

I concluded at length that the People were the best Judges of my Merit; for they buy my Works . . .

BENJAMIN FRANKLIN

FEW scenes in best-selling fiction can compare with the one from *Tarzan of the Apes* (1914) in which Tarzan, the son of a shipwrecked British aristocrat, raised from infancy by a tribe of apes in the African jungle, rescues Jane, the comely daughter of an American professor, from the evil clutches of the cruel and capricious ape-king Terkoz:

> Jane—her lithe, young form flattened against the trunk of a great tree, her hands tight pressed against her rising and falling bosom, and her eyes wide with mingled horror, fascination, fear, and admiration—watched the primordial ape battle with the primeval man for possession of a woman—for her.
>
> As the great muscles of the man's back and shoulders knotted beneath the tension of his efforts, and the huge biceps and forearm held at bay those mighty tusks, the veil of centuries of civilization and culture was swept from the blurred vision of the Baltimore girl.

Passion, violence, vengeance, and a melodramatic rescue—the passage is a paradigm of popular fiction.

After killing Terkoz, Tarzan carries off the reluctantly yielding Jane "deeper and deeper into the savage fastness of the untamed forest" to the security of his bower of bliss. What does he do when they get there?

> Tarzan had long since reached a decision as to what his future procedure should be. He had had time to recollect all that he had read of the ways of men and women in the books at the cabin. He would act as he imagined the men in the books would have acted were they in his place.

Apparently, even a situation so geographically and imaginatively far-fetched as that depicting an ape-man entertaining a captivating young woman from Baltimore cannot be entirely free from the guidance, if not the directions, of literature. In a moment obviously more threatening for him than any of his daily adventures in the uncharted jungle, Tarzan can offer no instinctive, spontaneous response. Instead, the "natural" man rescues himself by ponderously turning to the lessons of fiction. Though Tarzan does not tell us what books he had in his cabin library, he will undoubtedly model his future social behavior on the same late-nineteenth-century popular romances from which his creator, Edgar Rice Burroughs, derived his literary style.

Burroughs, like most best-selling novelists, knew what a reading public wanted. In the Tarzan books he satisfied a contemporary interest in imperialistic adventures and a psychological need for violent, bestial conflicts. A large part of his continuing success is attributable also to his grasp of a fundamental mythic element—that the popular masculine ideal of the twentieth century would be a sensitive brute, a natural aristocrat, a killer with a tender heart. As a type of masculine hero, Tarzan is intended to be not only alluringly primitive (a "woodland demi-god") but also the kind of man that heroines of American fiction have conventionally desired—a cultivated gentleman, preferably a foreign aristocrat.

The image—with variations, of course—dominates twentieth-century popular fiction and advertising. Michael Rossi, the hero of Grace Metalious's *Peyton Place* (1956), is "a massive boned man with muscles that seemed to quiver every time he moved. . . . His arms, beneath sleeves rolled above the elbow, were knotted powerfully, and the buttons of his work shirts always seemed about to pop off under the strain of trying to cover his chest." Though built like Tarzan, Michael Rossi is not going to wrestle wild beasts. Instead, he arrives in Peyton Place a stranger about to take on the job of headmaster at the local high school, for he "had a mind as analytical as a mathematician's and as curious as a philosopher's."

Styles and idioms may change (though in these passages it may not seem so), but a successful formula for fiction is hard to let go of.

Not all best-sellers, of course, are so masculinely aggressive, though even a predominately sentimental book like Harriet Beecher Stowe's *Uncle Tom's Cabin* (1852) contains its whip-wielding Simon Legree. Moreover, *Tarzan of the Apes* and *Peyton Place,* for all their self-conscious primitivsm and casual disregard for "centuries of civilization and culture," never really stray very far from the unassailable proprieties and the cozy gentility to which their authors and readers finally subscribe. At the end of *Peyton Place,* Michael Rossi is a vigorous, comfortable, middle-aged married man. And the final scene in *Tarzan of the Apes* finds an educated, love-lorn "demi-god" in conversation at a train station in Wisconsin: " 'I am Monsieur Tarzan,' said the ape-man."

One reason readers respond so positively to a best-selling novel is that it invariably reaffirms in easily accessible language its audience's attitudes, values, and collective fantasies and identifies reassuringly with its anxieties. Novels such as *Tarzan of the Apes* and *Peyton Place* become best-sellers, then, because, along with excursions into fantasy, they return to what are essentially nonnegotiable domestic standards. In that sense they resemble many other American best-sellers that have insisted on the inviolability of family bonds. Consider, for instance, the best-seller by Mario Puzo, *The Godfather* (1969), in which a world of official corruption, blurred loyalties, and misdirected justice is contrasted with a closely knit patriarchal "family" carrying out its obligations and vendettas in a style that ensures the dignity and personal honor of all its members. Another best-seller, *Uncle Tom's Cabin,* fiercely opposes the institution of slavery, not entirely on political or legal grounds but because it mercilessly breaks up the home by separating children from their parents, husbands from their wives.

Best-selling nonfiction also corroborates its readers' collective values. Many very successful volumes of nonfiction have taken the form of ready-reference compilations of practical advice. Dale Carnegie's *How to Win Friends and Influence People* (1936), Wilfred Funk and Norman Lewis's *Thirty Days to a More Powerful Vocabulary* (1942), and Benjamin Spock's *The Common Sense Book of Baby Care* (1946) exemplify the kinds of self-improvement and "how-to-do-it" books that offer their readers guidance that will presumably help them deal successfully with their feelings of ineptitude, confusion, and inferiority and reaffirm their yearnings for an uncomplicated life. Most best-sellers offer their characters, and vicariously their readers, a way out of public and private dilemmas by providing them with the possibilities of wealth, sexual gratification, justice or vengeance, romance and adventure, a hard-won optimistic philosophy, or a return to traditional loyalties and uncomplicated codes of behavior.

Like advertisements, newspapers, and magazines, best-sellers are frequently written in response to the pressures of contemporary events, issues, and tastes. They capitalize on the public's interests. Some best-selling authors "hit on" or invent something (practical advice for self-improvement, a timely exposé, or an extraordinary private eye) that many people want to read about. Others design their books to attract readers predisposed to certain kinds of material by news coverage and magazine articles. Stowe, a dedicated abolitionist, recognized that the much debated issue of slavery, or, more precisely, the Fugitive Slave Law, was a suitable subject for fiction and wrote what became America's first major best-selling novel. The enormous popularity of Puzo's *The Godfather,* one of the fastest-selling novels in the history of American publishing, can be partly explained by pointing to a reading public fascinated by the news coverage of the personalities, stratagems, and violence of organized crime.

Yet books like *Uncle Tom's Cabin* and *The Godfather* did not become best-sellers merely because of their responsiveness to newsworthy public events. If readers were interested only in the events or issues detailed in these books, they could have satisfied that need more easily and less expensively by reading newspapers and magazines. But these best-sellers, like many of the others included here, offer readers something more than reportage or polemics; they combine an awareness of topical subjects with the conventions and techniques of fiction. Readers can feel that they are learning about the management of the slave trade in the South or the operations of organized crime while at the same time being entertained by the invented characters, situations, and plots that give factual information the shape of fiction.

The excerpts from best-sellers appearing in this section are meant to characterize the kinds of writing that millions of readers have found and still find informative, entertaining, or both.[1] Perhaps the best way to read the following passages is to imagine yourself in a role opposite that of an editor who examines a piece of writing to try to decide whether it will be commercially successful. Instead, you have material that has been demonstrably successful, and you want to try to account for that success. What is it about the *writing* that has made it so popular? To what extent is the book's success attributable to the quality of its prose? To the types of characters rendered? To the kinds of themes dramatized? To the information proposed? To the particular psychological, social, or political issues involved? These and similar questions can, of course, be asked about any literary work, popular or unpopular, significant or insignificant. But because a best-seller attracts such a large audience, the answers to questions about its compositional strategies and its overall verbal performance suggest a great deal about the nature of popular writing and the characteristics of the people who read it.

You are being invited to look closely at the following selections from what might be called a socio-aesthetic point of view. That is, you are being asked to infer from the distinctive features of the author's prose the kind of people he or she expects will attend to his or her writing. By doing so, you will establish the identity of the book's "ideal reader"—the type of person you imagine the writer would feel most comfortable talking to. You will have also constructed a criterion against which you can measure your own response to the work. Whatever your final judgment about the relative worth of the material you have read, your criticism will be more attuned to the particular verbal characteristics of the work the more carefully you can determine how *you,* as the reader and individual you imagine yourself to be, are taken into account by the author's act of writing.

The audience presupposed by the author's style can become, if the book is a best-seller, the critical justification of his or her creative efforts. Mickey Spillane, author of the extraordinarily successful Mike Hammer detective novels, made this point clear when asked in an interview what he thought of the literary criticism of his fiction: "The public is the only critic. And the only *literature* is what the public reads. The first printing of my last book was more than two million copies—that's the kind of opinion that interests me." This tough talk is characteristic of Spillane's literary manner. It is a style he worked out before he became a celebrity, so his assurance is not necessarily the result of his having sold more than seventy-five million copies of his novels. In fact, the Spillane we hear speaking as a professional writer in the interview quoted above is most likely being playfully imitative of the Spillane who talks to us in the guise of his detective-narrator, Mike Hammer, in the following passage from *I, the Jury* (1947):

1. Margaret Mitchell's *Gone with the Wind,* one of America's most important best-selling novels, has been omitted because the author's estate refuses to allow the book to be excerpted.

> I said no more. I just sat there and glowered at the wall. Someday I'd trigger the bastard that shot Jack. In my time I've done it plenty of times. No sentiment. That went out with the first. After the war I've been almost anxious to get to some of the rats that make up the section of humanity that prey on people. People. How incredibly stupid they could be sometimes. A trial by law for a killer. A loophole in the phrasing that lets a killer crawl out. But in the end the people have their justice. They get it through guys like me once in a while. They crack down on society and I crack down on them. I shoot them like the mad dogs they are and society drags me to court to explain the whys and wherefores of the extermination. They investigate my past, check my fingerprints and throw a million questions my way. The papers make me look like a kill-crazy shamus, but they don't bear down too hard because Pat Chambers [Hammer's police detective friend] keeps them off my neck. Besides, I do my best to help the boys out and they know it. And I'm usually good for a story when I wind up a case.

In this angry interior monologue, Hammer does not talk to himself any differently from the way he talks to anyone else in the novel. This is his characteristic voice: tough, vindictive, self-assured. It is the voice of a man (rarely do women talk like this in fiction) who refuses to mince his words, who thinks that a more complicated way of talking would invariably associate him with the legalistic language that permits those loopholes through which killers are allowed to escape justice.

The language in this passage carries with it an authority that would gratify those readers who feel that their own lives are helplessly trapped in bureaucratic labyrinths and compromising civilities and who consequently seldom, if ever, have the occasion to talk to anybody the way Mike Hammer does. If Hammer recognizes in this passage that he is forced occasionally to make concessions to the police, the courts, and the press, he does so without compromising his role as a self-appointed arbiter of social justice. He does so also without ever having to modify unwillingly his deliberately aggressive, hard-boiled tone to suit the different types of characters he is obliged to confront. Hammer's is a voice that never interrupts itself to reconsider what it has said. It is a language without hesitations or unnecessary qualifications.

Hammer's style disassociates him from the official language of law enforcement, a language traditionally dependent on a complicated system of qualifications and constraints. By taking the law into his own hands, Hammer essentially transforms the law into his own language. If, as the self-assertion of the title indicates, Hammer *is* the jury, then he symbolically embodies the "People," whose expectations of justice he considers it is his mission in life to fulfill. The overwhelming public approval that Spillane confidently refers to as the most legitimate criticism of his fiction has been anticipated in the public approbation he has allowed his most successful character to take for granted.

It is not unusual for best-selling authors to find a confirmation of their talent in sales figures. Stowe, an author whose literary intentions differ radically from Spillane's and who would have been offended even by his idiom, acknowledged her enthusiasm for the public's approval of America's first major best-selling novel in terms Spillane would surely understand. Writing in the third person for an introduction to one of the many editions of *Uncle Tom's Cabin,* she remarks:

> The despondency of the author as to the question whether anybody would read or attend to her appeal was soon dispelled. Ten thousand copies were sold in a few days, and over three hundred thousand within a year; and eight power-presses, running day and night, were barely able to keep pace with the demand for it. It was read everywhere, apparently, and by everybody; and she soon began to hear echoes of sympathy all over the

> land. The indignation, the pity, the distress, that had long weighed upon her soul seemed to pass off from her into the readers of the book.

It would be difficult to find a more apt description of the merger of writer and reader in the collective enterprise that makes a book a best-seller.

Harriet Beecher Stowe / *Uncle Tom's Cabin* 1852

The daughter of a New England Congregational pastor, Harriet Beecher Stowe (1811–96) moved to Cincinnati when her father was appointed head of the Lane Theological Seminary. She began writing sketches for magazines, but after her marriage to Calvin Ellis Stowe, a professor of biblical literature at her father's seminary, she abandoned the idea of a literary career. At the time, Lane Theological Seminary was a center of antislavery sentiment. In this environment, and also through occasional visits to the slave state of Kentucky, Stowe gradually formed the abolitionist opinions that were given full expression in Uncle Tom's Cabin. *After a successful serialization in a Washington, D.C., antislavery weekly,* The National Era, *the novel was brought out in two volumes in 1852. It was a momentous publishing event: three hundred thousand copies were sold in the first year, and by 1856 the sales in England alone were well over a million. Translations were worldwide. Stowe, then living in Brunswick, Maine, where her husband had a teaching position at Bowdoin, found herself the most famous literary figure in America and an international celebrity. Though she continued to write (averaging nearly a book a year for the next thirty years), none of her later novels ever attained the success of her first.*

SELECT INCIDENT OF LAWFUL TRADE

> *"In Ramah there was a voice heard,—weeping, and lamentation, and great mourning; Rachel weeping for her children, and would not be comforted."*
>
> —Jeremiah, 31:15

Mr. Haley and Tom jogged onward in their wagon, each, for a time, absorbed in his own reflections. Now, the reflections of two men sitting side by side are a curious thing,—seated on the same seat, having the same eyes, ears, hands and organs of all sorts, and having pass before their eyes the same objects,—it is wonderful what a variety we shall find in these same reflections!

As, for example, Mr. Haley: he thought first of Tom's length, and breadth, and height, and what he would sell for, if he was kept fat and in good case till he got him into market. He thought of how he should make out his gang; he thought of the respective market value of certain supposititious men and women and children who were to compose it, and other kindred topics of the business; then he thought of himself, and how humane he was, that whereas other men chained their "niggers" hand and foot both, he only put fetters on the feet, and left Tom the use of his hands, as long as he behaved well; and he sighed to think how ungrateful human nature was, so that there was even room to doubt whether Tom appreciated his mercies. He had been taken in so by "niggers" whom he had favored; but still he was astonished to consider how good-natured he yet remained!

As to Tom, he was thinking over some words of an unfashionable old book, which kept running through his head, again and again, as follows: "We have here no continuing city, but we seek one to come; wherefore God himself is not ashamed to be called our God; for he hath prepared for us a city.'' These words of an ancient volume, got up principally by ''ignorant and unlearned men,'' have, through all time, kept up, somehow, a strange sort of power over the minds of poor, simple fellows, like Tom. They stir up the soul from its depths, and rouse, as with trumpet call, courage, energy, and enthusiasm, where before was only the blackness of despair.

Mr. Haley pulled out of his pocket sundry newspapers, and began looking over their advertisements, with absorbed interest. He was not a remarkably fluent reader, and was in the habit of reading in a sort of recitative half-aloud, by way of calling in his ears to verify the deductions of his eyes. In this tone he slowly recited the following paragraph:

''EXECUTOR'S SALE,—NEGROES!—*Agreeably to order of court, will be sold, on Tuesday, February 20, before the Court-house door, in the town of Washington, Kentucky, the following negroes: Hagar, aged 60; John, aged 30; Ben, aged 21; Saul, aged 25; Albert, aged 14. Sold for the benefit of the creditors and heirs of the estate of Jesse Blutchford, Esq.*

SAMUEL MORRIS,
THOMAS FLINT,
Executors''

''This yer I must look at,'' said he to Tom, for want of somebody else to talk to.

''Ye see, I'm going to get up a prime gang to take down with ye, Tom; it'll make it sociable and pleasant like,—good company will, ye know. We must drive right to Washington first and foremost, and then I'll clap you into jail, while I does the business.''

Tom received this agreeable intelligence quite meekly; simply wondering, in his own heart, how many of these doomed men had wives and children, and whether they would feel as he did about leaving them. It is to be confessed, too, that the naïve, off-hand information that he was to be thrown into jail by no means produced an agreeable impression on a poor fellow who had always prided himself on a strictly honest and upright course of life. Yes, Tom, we must confess it, was rather proud of his honesty, poor fellow,—not having very much else to be proud of;—if he had belonged to some of the higher walks of society, he, perhaps, would never have been reduced to such straits. However, the day wore on, and the evening saw Haley and Tom comfortably accommodated in Washington,—the one in a tavern, and the other in a jail.

About eleven o'clock the next day, a mixed throng was gathered around the court-house steps,—smoking, chewing, spitting, swearing, and conversing, according to their respective tastes and turns,—waiting for the auction to commence. The men and women to be sold sat in a group apart, talking in a low tone to each other. The woman who had been advertised by the name of Hagar was a regular African in feature and figure. She might have been sixty, but was older than that by hard work and disease, was partially blind, and somewhat crippled with rheumatism. By her side stood her only remaining son, Albert, a bright-looking little fellow of fourteen years. The boy was the only survivor of a large family, who had been successively sold away from her to a southern market. The mother held on to him with both her shaking hands, and eyed with intense trepidation every one who walked up to examine him.

''Don't be feared, Aunt Hagar,'' said the oldest of the men, ''I spoke to Mas'r Thomas 'bout it, and he thought he might manage to sell you in a lot both together.''

''Dey needn't call me worn out yet,'' said she, lifting her shaking hands. ''I can cook yet, and scrub, and scour,—I'm wuth a buying, if I come cheap;—tell em dat ar,—you *tell* em,'' she added, earnestly.

Haley here forced his way into the group, walked up to the old man, pulled his mouth open and looked in, felt of his teeth, made him stand and straighten himself, bend his back, and perform various evolutions to show his muscles; and then passed on to the next, and put him through the same trial. Walking up last to the boy, he felt of his arms, straightened his hands, and looked at his fingers, and made him jump, to show his agility.

''He an't gwine to be sold widout me!'' said the old woman, with passionate eagerness; ''he and I goes in a lot together; I 's rail strong yet, Mas'r and can do heaps o' work,—heaps on it, Mas'r.''

''On plantation?'' said Haley, with a contemptuous glance. ''Likely story!'' and, as if satisfied with his examination, he walked out and looked, and stood with his hands in his pocket, his cigar in his mouth, and his hat cocked on one side, ready for action.

''What think of 'em?'' said a man who had been following Haley's examination, as if to make up his own mind from it.

''Wal,'' said Haley, spitting, ''I shall put in, I think, for the youngerly ones and the boy.''

''They want to sell the boy and the old woman together,'' said the man.

''Find it a tight pull;—why, she's an old rack o'bones,—not worth her salt.''

''You wouldn't then?'' said the man.

''Anybody 'd be a fool 't would. She's half blind, crooked with rheumatis, and foolish to boot.''

''Some buys up these yer old critturs, and ses there's a sight more wear in 'em than a body 'd think,'' said the man, reflectively.

''No go, 't all,'' said Haley; ''wouldn't take her for a present,—fact,—I've *seen,* now.''

''Wal, 't is kinder pity, now, not to buy her with her son,—her heart seems so sot on him,—s'pose they fling her in cheap.''

''Them that's got money to spend that ar way, it's all well enough. I shall bid off on that ar boy for a plantation-hand;—wouldn't be bothered with her, no way,—not if they'd give her to me,'' said Haley.

''She'll take on desp't,'' said the man.

''Nat'lly, she will,'' said the trader, coolly.

The conversation was here interrupted by a busy hum in the audience; and the auctioneer, a short, bustling, important fellow, elbowed his way into the crowd. The old woman drew in her breath, and caught instinctively at her son.

''Keep close to yer mammy, Albert,—close,—dey'll put us up togedder,'' she said.

''O, mammy, I'm feard they won't,'' said the boy.

''Dey must, child; I can't live, no ways, if they don't,'' said the old creature, vehemently.

The stentorian tones of the auctioneer, calling out to clear the way, now announced that the sale was about to commence. A place was cleared, and the bidding began. The different men on the list were soon knocked off at prices which showed a pretty brisk demand in the market; two of them fell to Haley.

''Come, now, young un,'' said the auctioneer, giving the boy a touch with his hammer, ''be up and show your springs, now.''

''Put us two up togedder, togedder,—do please, Mas'r,'' said the old woman, holding fast to her boy.

''Be off,'' said the man, gruffly, pushing her hands away; ''you come last. Now, darkey, spring;'' and, with the word, he pushed the boy toward the block, while a deep, heavy groan rose behind him. The boy paused, and looked back; but there was no time to stay, and dashing the tears from his large, bright eyes, he was up in a moment.

His fine figure, alert limbs, and bright face, raised an instant competition, and half a dozen bids simultaneously met the ear of the auctioneer. Anxious, half-frightened, he looked from side to side, as he heard the clatter of contending bids,—now here, now there,—till the hammer fell. Haley had got him. He was pushed from the block toward his new master, but stopped one moment, and looked back, when his poor old mother, trembling in every limb, held out her shaking hands toward him.

"Buy me too, Mas'r, for de dear Lord's sake!—buy me,—I shall die if you don't!"

"You'll die if I do, that's the kink of it," said Haley,—"no!" And he turned on his heel.

The bidding for the poor old creature was summary. The man who had addressed Haley, and who seemed not destitute of compassion, bought her for a trifle, and the spectators began to disperse.

The poor victims of the sale, who had been brought up in one place together for years, gathered round the despairing old mother, whose agony was pitiful to see.

"Couldn't dey leave me one? Mas'r allers said I should have one,—he did," she repeated over and over, in heart-broken tones.

"Trust in the Lord, Aunt Hagar," said the oldest of the men, sorrowfully.

"What good will it do?" said she, sobbing passionately.

"Mother, mother,—don't! don't!" said the boy. "They say you's got a good master."

"I don't care—I don't care. O, Albert! oh, my boy! you's my last baby. Lord, how ken I?"

"Come, take her off, can't some of ye?" said Haley, dryly; "don't do no good for her to go on that ar way."

The old men of the company, partly by persuasion and partly by force, loosed the poor creature's last despairing hold, and, as they led her off to her new master's wagon, strove to comfort her.

"Now!" said Haley, pushing his three purchases together, and producing a bundle of handcuffs, which he proceeded to put on their wrists; and fastening each handcuff to a long chain, he drove them before him to the jail.

A few days saw Haley, with his possessions, safely deposited on one of the Ohio boats. It was the commencement of his gang, to be augmented, as the boat moved on, by various other merchandise of the same kind, which he, or his agent, had stored for him in various points along shore.

The La Belle Rivière, as brave and beautiful a boat as ever walked the waters of her namesake river, was floating gayly down the stream, under a brilliant sky, the stripes and stars of free America waving and fluttering over head; the guards crowded with well-dressed ladies and gentlemen walking and enjoying the delightful day. All was full of life, buoyant and rejoicing;—all but Haley's gang, who were stored, with other freight, on the lower deck, and who, somehow, did not seem to appreciate their various privileges, as they sat in a knot, talking to each other in low tones.

"Boys," said Haley, coming up, briskly, "I hope you keep up good heart, and are cheerful. Now, no sulks, ye see; keep stiff upper lip, boys; do well by me, and I'll do well by you."

The boys addressed responded the invariable "Yes, Mas'r," for ages the watchword of poor Africa; but it's to be owned they did not look particularly cheerful; they had their various little prejudices in favor of wives, mothers, sisters, and children, seen for the last time,—and though "they that wasted them required of them mirth," it was not instantly forthcoming.

"I've got a wife," spoke out the article enumerated as "John, aged thirty," and he laid his chained hand on Tom's knee,—"and she don't know a word about this, poor girl!"

"Where does she live?" said Tom.

"In a tavern a piece down here," said John; "I wish, now, I *could* see her once more in this world," he added.

Poor John! It *was* rather natural; and the tears that fell, as he spoke, came as naturally as if he had been a white man. Tom drew a long breath from a sore heart, and tried, in his poor way, to comfort him.

And over head, in the cabin, sat fathers and mothers, husbands and wives; and merry, dancing children moved round among them, like so many little butterflies, and everything was going on quite easy and comfortable.

"O, mamma," said a boy, who had just come up from below, "there's a negro trader on board, and he's brought four or five slaves down there."

"Poor creatures!" said the mother, in a tone between grief and indignation.

"What's that?" said another lady.

"Some poor slaves below," said the mother.

"And they've got chains on," said the boy.

"What a shame to our country that such sights are to be seen!" said another lady.

"O, there's a great deal to be said on both sides of the subject," said a genteel woman, who sat at her state-room door sewing, while her little girl and boy were playing round her. "I've been south, and I must say I think the negroes are better off than they would be to be free."

"In some respects, some of them are well off, I grant," said the lady to whose remark she had answered. "The most dreadful part of slavery, to my mind, is its outrages on the feelings and affections,—the separating of families, for example."

"That *is* a bad thing, certainly," said the other lady, holding up a baby's dress she had just completed, and looking intently on its trimmings; "but then, I fancy, it don't occur often."

"O, it does," said the first lady, eagerly; "I've lived many years in Kentucky and Virginia both, and I've seen enough to make any one's heart sick. Suppose, ma'am, your two children, there, should be taken from you, and sold?"

"We can't reason from our feelings to those of this class of persons," said the other lady, sorting out some worsteds on her lap.

"Indeed, ma'am, you can know nothing of them, if you say so," answered the first lady, warmly. "I was born and brought up among them. I know they *do* feel, just as keenly,—even more so, perhaps,—as we do."

The lady said "Indeed!" yawned, and looked out the cabin window, and finally repeated, for a finale, the remark with which she had begun,—"After all, I think they are better off than they would be to be free."

"It's undoubtedly the intention of Providence that the African race should be servants,—kept in a low condition," said a grave-looking gentleman in black, a clergyman, seated by the cabin door. " 'Cursed be Canaan; a servant of servants shall he be,' the Scripture says."

"I say, stranger, is that ar what that text means?" said a tall man, standing by.

"Undoubtedly. It pleased Providence, for some inscrutable reason, to doom the race to bondage, ages ago; and we must not set up our opinion against that."

"Well, then, we'll all go ahead and buy up niggers," said the man, "if that's the way of Providence,—won't we, Squire?" said he, turning to Haley, who had been standing, with his hands in his pockets, by the stove and intently listening to the conversation.

"Yes," continued the tall man, "we must all be resigned to the decrees of Providence. Niggers must be sold, and trucked round, and kept under; it's what they's made for. 'Pears like this yer view 's quite refreshing, ain't it, stranger?" said he to Haley.

"I never thought on 't," said Haley. "I couldn't have said as much, myself; I ha'nt no larning. I took up the trade just to make a living; if 'tan't right, I calculated to 'pent on 't in time, *ye* know."

"And now you'll save yerself the trouble, won't ye?" said the tall man. "See what 't is, now, to know scripture. If ye'd only studied yer Bible, like this yer good man, ye might have know'd it before, and saved ye a heap o' trouble. Ye could jist have said, 'Cussed be'—what's his name?—'and 't would all have come right.' " And the stranger, who was no other than the honest drover whom we introduced to our readers in the Kentucky tavern, sat down, and began smoking, with a curious smile on his long, dry face.

A tall, slender young man, with a face expressive of great feeling and intelligence, here broke in, and repeated the words, " 'All things whatsoever ye would that men should do unto you, do ye even so unto them.' I suppose," he added, "*that* is scripture, as much as 'Cursed be Canaan.' "

"Wal, it seems quite *as* plain a text, stranger," said John the drover, "to poor fellows like us, now;" and John smoked on like a volcano.

The young man paused, looked as if he was going to say more, when suddenly the boat stopped, and the company made the usual steamboat rush, to see where they were landing.

"Both them ar chaps parsons?" said John to one of the men, as they were going out.

The man nodded.

As the boat stopped, a black woman came running wildly up the plank, darted into the crowd, flew up to where the slave gang sat, and threw her arms round that unfortunate piece of merchandise before enumerated—"John, aged thirty," and with sobs and tears bemoaned him as her husband.

But what needs tell the story, told too oft,—every day told,—of heart-strings rent and broken,—the weak broken and torn for the profit and convenience of the strong! It needs not to be told;—every day is telling it,—telling it, too, in the ear of One who is not deaf, though he be long silent.

The young man who had spoken for the cause of humanity and God before stood with folded arms, looking on this scene. He turned, and Haley was standing at his side. "My friend," he said, speaking with thick utterance, "how can you, how dare you, carry on a trade like this? Look at those poor creatures! Here I am, rejoicing in my heart that I am going home to my wife and child; and the same bell which is a signal to carry me onward towards them will part this poor man and his wife forever. Depend upon it, God will bring you into judgment for this."

The trader turned away in silence.

"I say, now," said the drover, touching his elbow, "there's differences in parsons, an't there? 'Cussed be Cannan' don't seem to go down with this 'un, does it?"

Haley gave an uneasy growl.

"And that ar an't the worst on 't," said John; "mabbee it won't go down with the Lord, neither, when ye come to settle with Him, one o' these days, as all on us must, I reckon."

Haley walked reflectively to the other end of the boat.

"If I make pretty handsomely on one or two next gangs," he thought, "I reckon I'll stop off this yer; it's really getting dangerous." And he took out his pocket-book, and began adding over his accounts,—a process which many gentlemen besides Mr. Haley have found a specific for an uneasy conscience.

The boat swept proudly away from the shore, and all went on merrily, as before. Men talked, and loafed, and read, and smoked. Women sewed, and children played, and the boat passed on her way.

One day, when she lay to for a while at a small town in Kentucky, Haley went up into the place on a little matter of business.

Tom, whose fetters did not prevent his taking a moderate circuit, had drawn near the side of the boat, and stood listlessly gazing over the railing. After a time, he saw the trader returning, with an alert step, in company with a colored woman, bearing in her arms a young child. She was dressed quite respectably, and a colored man followed her, bringing along a small trunk. The woman came cheerfully onward, talking, as she came, with the man who bore her trunk, and so passed up the plank into the boat. The bell rung, the steamer whizzed, the engine groaned and coughed, and away swept the boat down the river.

The woman walked forward among the boxes and bales of the lower deck, and, sitting down, busied herself with chirruping to her baby.

Haley made a turn or two about the boat, and then, coming up, seated himself near her, and began saying something to her in an indifferent undertone.

Tom soon noticed a heavy cloud passing over the woman's brow; and that she answered rapidly, and with great vehemence.

"I don't believe it,—I won't believe it!" he heard her say. "You're jist a foolin with me."

"If you won't believe it, look here!" said the man, drawing out a paper; "this yer 's the bill of sale, and there's your master's name to it; and I paid down good solid cash for it, too, I can tell you,—so, now!"

"I don't believe Mas'r would cheat me so; it can't be true!" said the woman, with increasing agitation.

"You can ask any of these men here, that can read writing. Here!" he said, to a man that was passing by, "jist read this yer, won't you! This yer gal won't believe me, when I tell her what 't is."

"Why, it's a bill of sale, signed by John Fosdick," said the man, "making over to you the girl Lucy and her child. It's all straight enough, for aught I see."

The woman's passionate exclamations collected a crowd around her, and the trader briefly explained to them the cause of the agitation.

"He told me that I was going down to Louisville, to hire out as cook to the same tavern where my husband works,—that's what Mas'r told me, his own self; and I can't believe he'd lie to me," said the woman.

"But he has sold you, my poor woman, there's no doubt about it," said a good-natured looking man, who had been examining the papers; "he has done it, and no mistake."

"Then it's no account talking," said the woman, suddenly growing quite calm; and, clasping her child tighter in her arms, she sat down on her box, turned her back round, and gazed listlessly into the river.

"Going to take it easy, after all!" said the trader. "Gal's got grit, I see."

The woman looked calm, as the boat went on; and a beautiful soft summer breeze passed like a compassionate spirit over her head,—the gentle breeze, that never inquires whether the brow is dusky or fair that it fans. And she saw sunshine sparkling on the water, in golden ripples, and heard gay voices, full of ease and pleasure, talking around her everywhere; but her heart lay as if a great stone had fallen on it. Her baby raised himself up against her, and stroked her cheeks with his little hands; and, springing up and down, crowing and chatting, seemed determined to arouse her. She strained him suddenly and tightly in her arms, and slowly one tear after another fell on his wondering, unconscious face; and gradually she seemed, and little by little, to grow calmer, and busied herself with tending and nursing him.

The child, a boy of ten months, was uncommonly large and strong of his age, and very vigorous in his limbs. Never, for a moment, still, he kept his mother constantly busy in holding him, and guarding his springing activity.

"That's a fine chap!" said a man, suddenly stopping opposite to him, with his hands in his pockets. "How old is he?"

"Ten months and a half," said the mother.

The man whistled to the boy, and offered him part of a stick of candy, which he eagerly grabbed at, and very soon had it in a baby's general depository, to wit, his mouth.

"Rum fellow!" said the man. "Knows what's what!" and he whistled, and walked on. When he had got to the other side of the boat, he came across Haley, who was smoking on top of a pile of boxes.

The stranger produced a match, and lighted a cigar, saying, as he did so,

"Decentish kind o' wench you've got round there, stranger."

"Why, I reckon she *is* tol'able fair," said Haley, blowing the smoke out of his mouth.

"Taking her down south?" said the man.

Haley nodded, and smoked on.

"Plantation hand?" said the man.

"Wal," said Haley, "I'm fillin' out an order for a plantation, and I think I shall put her in. They telled me she was a good cook; and they can use her for that, or set her at the cotton-picking. She's got the right fingers for that; I looked at 'em. Sell well, either way;" and Haley resumed his cigar.

"They won't want the young 'un on the plantation," said the man.

"I shall sell him, first chance I find," said Haley, lighting another cigar.

"S'pose you'd be selling him tol'able cheap," said the stranger, mounting the pile of boxes, and sitting down comfortably.

"Don't know 'bout that," said Haley; "he's a pretty smart young 'un,—straight, fat, strong; flesh as hard as a brick!"

"Very true, but then there's the bother and expense of raisin'."

"Nonsense!" said Haley; "they is raised as easy as any kind of critter there is going; they an't a bit more trouble than pups. This yer chap will be running all around, in a month."

"I've got a good place for raisin', and I thought of takin' in a little more stock," said the man. "One cook lost a young 'un last week,—got drownded in a wash-tub while she was a hangin' out clothes,—and I reckon it would be well enough to set her to raisin' this yer."

Haley and the stranger smoked a while in silence, neither seeming willing to broach the test question of the interview. At last the man resumed:

"You wouldn't think of wantin' more than ten dollars for that ar chap, seeing you *must* get him off yer hand, any how?"

Haley shook his head, and spit impressively.

"That won't do, no ways," he said, and began his smoking again.

"Well, stranger, what will you take?"

"Well, now," said Haley, "I *could* raise that ar chap myself, or get him raised; he's oncommon likely and healthy, and he'd fetch a hundred dollars, six months hence; and, in a year or two, he'd bring two hundred, if I had him in the right spot;—so I shan't take a cent less nor fifty for him now."

"O, stranger! that's rediculous, altogether," said the man.

"Fact!" said Haley, with a decisive nod of his head.

"I'll give thirty for him," said the stranger, "but not a cent more."

"Now, I'll tell ye what I will do," said Haley, spitting again, with renewed decision. "I'll split the difference, and say forty-five; and that's the most I will do."

"Well, agreed!" said the man, after an interval.

"Done!" said Haley, "Where do you land?"

"At Louisville," said the man.

"Louisville," said Haley. "Very fair, we get there about dusk. Chap will be asleep,—all fair,—get him off quietly, and no screaming,—happens beautiful,—I like to do everything quietly,—I hates all kind of agitation and fluster.'' And so, after a transfer of certain bills had passed from the man's pocket-book to the trader's, he resumed his cigar.

It was a bright, tranquil evening when the boat stopped at the wharf at Louisville. The woman had been sitting with her baby in her arms, now wrapped in a heavy sleep. When she heard the name of the place called out, she hastily laid the child down in a little cradle formed by the hollow among the boxes, first carefully spreading under it her cloak; and then she sprung to the side of the boat, in hopes that, among the various hotel-waiters who thronged the wharf, she might see her husband. In this hope, she pressed forward to the front rails, and, stretching far over them, strained her eyes intently on the moving heads on the shore, and the crowd pressed in between her and the child.

''Now's your time,'' said Haley, taking the sleeping child up, and handing him to the stranger. ''Don't wake him up, and set him to crying, now; it would make a devil of a fuss with the gal.'' The man took the bundle carefully, and was soon lost in the crowd that went up the wharf.

When the boat, creaking, and groaning, and puffing, had loosed from the wharf, and was beginning slowly to strain herself along, the woman returned to her old seat. The trader was sitting there,—the child was gone!

''Why, why,—where?'' she began, in bewildered surprise.

''Lucy,'' said the trader, ''your child's gone; you may as well know it first as last. You see, I know'd you couldn't take him down south; and I got a chance to sell him to a first-rate family, that'll raise him better than you can.''

The trader had arrived at that stage of Christian and political perfection which has been recommended by some preachers and politicians of the north, lately, in which he had completely overcome every humane weakness and prejudice. His heart was exactly where yours, sir, and mine could be brought, with proper effort and cultivation. The wild look of anguish and utter despair that the woman cast on him might have disturbed one less practised; but he was used to it. He had seen that same look hundreds of time. You can get used to such things, too, my friend; and it is the great object of recent efforts to make our whole northern community used to them, for the glory of the Union. So the trader only regarded the mortal anguish which he saw working in those dark features, those clenched hands, and suffocating breathings, as necessary incidents of the trade, and merely calculated whether she was going to scream, and get up a commotion on the boat; for, like other supporters of our peculiar institution, he decidedly disliked agitation.

But the woman did not scream. The shot had passed too straight and direct through the heart, for cry or tear.

Dizzily she sat down. Her slack hands fell lifeless by her side. Her eyes looked straight forward, but she saw nothing. All the noise and hum of the boat, the groaning of the machinery, mingled dreamily to her bewildered ear; and the poor, dumb-stricken heart had neither cry nor tear to show for its utter misery. She was quite calm.

The trader, who, considering his advantages, was almost as humane as some of our politicians, seemed to feel called on to administer such consolation as the case admitted of.

''I know this yer comes kinder hard, at first, Lucy,'' said he; ''but such a smart, sensible gal as you are, won't give way to it. You see it's *necessary,* and can't be helped!''

''O! don't, Mas'r, don't!'' said the woman, with a voice like one that is smothering.

''You're a smart wench, Lucy,'' he persisted; ''I mean to do well by ye, and get ye a nice place down river; and you'll soon get another husband,—such a likely gal as you—''

"O! Mas'r, if you *only* won't talk to me now," said the woman, in a voice of such quick and living anguish that the trader felt that there was something at present in the case beyond his style of operation. He got up, and the woman turned away, and buried her head in her cloak.

The trader walked up and down for a time, and occasionally stopped and looked at her.

"Takes it hard, rather," he soliloquized, "but quiet, tho';—let her sweat a while; she'll come right, by and by!"

Tom had watched the whole transaction from first to last, and had a perfect understanding of its results. To him, it looked like something unutterably horrible and cruel, because, poor, ignorant black soul! he had not learned to generalize, and to take enlarged views. If he had only been instructed by certain ministers of Christianity, he might have thought better of it, and seen in it an every-day incident of a lawful trade; a trade which is the vital support of an institution which an American divine [1] tells us has *"no evils but such as are inseparable from any other relations in social and domestic life."* But Tom, as we see, being a poor, ignorant fellow, whose reading had been confined entirely to the New Testament, could not comfort and solace himself with views like these. His very soul bled within him for what seemed to him the *wrongs* of the poor suffering thing that lay like a crushed reed on the boxes; the feeling, living, bleeding, yet immortal *thing,* which American state law coolly classes with the bundles, and bales, and boxes, among which she is lying.

Tom drew near, and tried to say something; but she only groaned. Honestly, and with tears running down his own cheeks, he spoke of a heart of love in the skies, of a pitying Jesus, and an eternal home; but the ear was deaf with anguish, and the palsied heart could not feel.

Night came on,—night calm, unmoved, and glorious, shining down with her innumerable and solemn angel eyes, twinkling, beautiful, but silent. There was no speech nor language, no pitying voice or helping hand, from that distant sky. One after another, the voices of business or pleasure died away; all on the boat were sleeping, and the ripples at the prow were plainly heard. Tom stretched himself out on a box, and there, as he lay, he heard, ever and anon, a smothered sob or cry from the prostrate creature,—"O! what shall I do? O Lord! O good Lord, do help me!" and so, ever and anon, until the murmur died away in silence.

At midnight, Tom waked, with a sudden start. Something black passed quickly by him to the side of the boat, and he heard a splash in the water. No one else saw or heard anything. He raised his head,—the woman's place was vacant! He got up, and sought about him in vain. The poor bleeding heart was still, at last, and the river rippled and dimpled just as brightly as if it had not closed above it.

Patience! patience! ye whose hearts swell indignant at wrongs like these. Not one throb of anguish, not one tear of the oppressed, is forgotten by the Man of Sorrows, the Lord of Glory. In his patient, generous bosom he bears the anguish of a world. Bear thou, like him, in patience, and labor in love; for sure as he is God, "the year of his redeemed *shall* come."

The trader waked up bright and early, and came out to see to his live stock. It was now his turn to look about in perplexity.

"Where alive is that gal?" he said to Tom.

Tom, who had learned the wisdom of keeping counsel, did not feel called upon to state his observations and suspicions, but said he did not know.

"She surely couldn't have got off in the night at any of the landings, for I was awake, and on the look-out, whenever the boat stopped. I never trust these yer things to other folks."

1. Dr. Joel Parker of Philadelphia.

This speech was addressed to Tom quite confidentially, as if it was something that would be specially interesting to him. Tom made no answer.

The trader searched the boat from stem to stern, among boxes, bales and barrels, around the machinery, by the chimneys, in vain.

"Now, I say, Tom, be fair about this yer," he said, when, after a fruitless search, he came where Tom was standing. "You know something about it, now. Don't tell me,—I know you do. I saw the gal stretched out here about ten o'clock, and ag'in at twelve, and ag'in between one and two; and then at four she was gone, and you was a sleeping right there all the time. Now, you know something,—you can't help it."

"Well, Mas'r," said Tom, "towards morning something brushed by me, and I kinder half woke; and then I hearn a great splash, and then I clare woke up, and the gal was gone. That's all I know on 't."

The trader was not shocked nor amazed; because, as we said before, he was used to a great many things that you are not used to. Even the awful presence of Death struck no solemn chill upon him. He had seen Death many times,—met him in the way of trade, and got acquainted with him,—and he only thought of him as a hard customer, that embarrassed his property operations very unfairly; and so he only swore that the gal was a baggage, and that he was devilish unlucky, and that, if things went on in this way, he should not make a cent on the trip. In short, he seemed to consider himself an ill-used man, decidedly; but there was no help for it, as the woman had escaped into a state which *never will* give up a fugitive,—not even at the demand of the whole glorious Union. The trader, therefore, sat discontentedly down, with his little account-book, and put down the missing body and soul under the head of *losses!*

"He's a shocking creature, isn't he,—this trader? so unfeeling! It's dreadful, really!"

"O, but nobody thinks anything of these traders! They are universally despised,—never received into any decent society."

But who, sir makes the trader? Who is most to blame? the enlightened, cultivated, intelligent man, who supports the system of which the trader is the inevitable result, or the poor trader himself? You make the public statement that calls for his trade, that debauches and depraves him, till he feels no shame in it; and in what are you better than he?

Are you educated and he ignorant, you high and he low, you refined and he coarse, you talented and he simple?

In the day of a future Judgment, these very considerations may make it more tolerable for him than for you.

In concluding these little incidents of lawful trade, we must beg the world not to think that American legislators are entirely destitute of humanity, as might, perhaps, be unfairly inferred from the great efforts made in our national body to protect and perpetuate this species of traffic.

Who does not know how our great men are outdoing themselves, in declaiming against the *foreign* slave-trade. There are a perfect host of Clarksons and Wilberforces risen up among us on that subject, most edifying to hear and behold. Trading negroes from Africa, dear reader, is so horrid! It is not to be thought of! But trading them from Kentucky,—that's quite another thing!

P. T. Barnum / *Struggles and Triumphs of P. T. Barnum*

1855

"There's a sucker born every minute." So goes the adage fairly or unfairly attributed to Phineas Taylor Barnum (1810–91), who became, in his time, America's most famous showman. Throughout his career, Barnum was accused of constructing elaborate hoaxes to fool an unsuspecting public. He is best remembered, however, as the founder of the circus that still bears his name, one that he proudly regarded as the "Greatest Show on Earth." While presenting many of the most celebrated attractions in history, Barnum developed methods of advertising and promotion that continue to exert their influence in the worlds of business and entertainment. We have reprinted the first chapter of his memoir, Struggles and Triumphs, *which appeared in 1855.*

EARLY LIFE

I was born in the town of Bethel, in the State of Connecticut, July 5, 1810. My name, Phineas Taylor, is derived from my maternal grandfather, who was a great wag in his way, and who, as I was his first grandchild, gravely handed over to my mother at my christening a gift-deed, in my behalf, of five acres of land situated in that part of the parish of Bethel known as the "Plum Trees." I was thus a real estate owner almost at my very birth; and of my property, "Ivy Island," something shall be said anon.

My father, Philo Barnum, was the son of Ephraim Barnum, of Bethel, who was a captain in the revolutionary war. My father was a tailor, a farmer, and sometimes a tavern-keeper, and my advantages and disadvantages were such as fall to the general run of farmers' boys. I drove cows to and from the pasture, shelled corn, weeded the garden; as I grew larger, I rode horse for ploughing, turned and raked hay; in due time I handled the shovel and the hoe, and when I could do so I went to school.

I was six years old when I began to go to school, and the first date I remember inscribing upon my writingbook was 1818. The ferule,[1] in those days, was the assistant school-master; but in spite of it, I was a willing, and, I think, a pretty apt scholar; at least, I was so considered by my teachers and schoolmates, and as the years went on there were never more than two or three in the school who were deemed my superiors. In arithmetic I was unusually ready and accurate, and I remember, at the age of twelve years, being called out of bed one night by my teacher who had wagered with a neighbor that I could calculate the correct number of feet in a load of wood in five minutes. The dimensions given, I figured out the result in less than two minutes, to the great delight of my teacher and to the equal astonishment of his neighbor.

My organ of "acquisitiveness"[2] was manifest at an early age. Before I was five years of age, I began to accumulate pennies and "four-pences," and when I was six years old my capital amounted to a sum sufficient to exchange for a silver dollar, the possession of which made me feel far richer and more independent than I have ever since felt in the world.

Nor did my dollar long remain alone. As I grew older I earned ten cents a day

[1] A cane or ruler used by schoolmasters to punish students.

[2] Barnum refers to phrenology, a practice popular in his time in which "experts" could determine personality by examining the contours of the human head.

for riding the horse which led the ox team in ploughing, and on holidays and ''training days,'' instead of spending money, I earned it. I was a small peddler of molasses candy (of home make), ginger-bread, cookies and cherry rum, and I generally found myself a dollar or two richer at the end of a holiday than I was at the beginning. I was always ready for a trade, and by the time I was twelve years old, besides other property, I was the owner of a sheep and a calf, and should soon, no doubt, have become a small Croesus, had not my father kindly permitted me to purchase my own clothing, which somewhat reduced my little store.

When I was nearly twelve years old I made my first visit to the metropolis. It happened in this wise: Late one afternoon in January, 1822, Mr. Daniel Brown, of Southbury, Connecticut, arrived at my father's tavern, in Bethel, with some fat cattle he was driving to New York to sell. The cattle were put into our large barnyard, the horses were stabled, and Mr. Brown and his assistant were provided with a warm supper and lodging for the night. After supper I heard Mr. Brown say to my father that he intended to buy more cattle, and that he would be glad to hire a boy to assist in driving the cattle. I immediately besought my father to secure the situation for me, and he did so. My mother's consent was also gained, and at daylight next morning, after a slight breakfast, I started on foot in the midst of a heavy snow storm to help drive the cattle. Before reaching Ridgefield, I was sent on horseback after a stray ox, and, in galloping, the horse fell and my ankle was sprained. I suffered severely, but did not complain lest my employer should send me back. But he considerately permitted me to ride behind him on his horse; and, indeed, did so most of the way to New York, where we arrived in three or four days.

We put up at the Bull's Head Tavern, where we were to stay a week while the drover was disposing of his cattle, and we were then to return home in a sleigh. It was an eventful week for me. Before I left home my mother had given me a dollar which I supposed would supply every want that heart could wish. My first outlay was for oranges which I was told were four pence apiece, and as ''four-pence'' in Connecticut was six cents, I offered ten cents for two oranges which was of course readily taken; and thus, instead of saving two cents, as I thought, I actually paid two cents more than the price demanded. I then bought two more oranges, reducing my capital to eighty cents. Thirty-one cents was the ''charge'' for a small gun which would ''go off'' and send a stick some little distance, and this gun I bought. Amusing myself with this toy in the barroom of the Bull's Head, the arrow happened to hit the barkeeper, who forthwith came from behind the counter and shook me and soundly boxed my ears, telling me to put that gun out of the way or he would put it into the fire. I sneaked to my room, put my treasure under the pillow, and went out for another visit to the toy shop.

There I invested six cents in ''torpedoes,'' with which I intended to astonish my schoolmates in Bethel. I could not refrain, however, from experimenting upon the guests of the hotel, which I did when they were going in to dinner. I threw two of the torpedoes against the wall of the hall through which the guests were passing, and the immediate results were as follows: two loud reports,—astonished guests,—irate landlord,—discovery of the culprit, and summary punishment—for the landlord immediately floored me with a single blow with his open hand, and said:

''There, you little greenhorn, see if that will teach you better than to explode your infernal fire crackers in my house again.''

The lesson was sufficient if not entirely satisfactory. I deposited the balance of the torpedoes with my gun, and as a solace for my wounded feelings I again visited the toy shop, where I bought a watch, breastpin and top, leaving but eleven cents of my original dollar.

The following morning found me again at the fascinating toy shop, where I saw a beautiful knife with two blades, a gimlet, and a corkscrew,—a whole carpenter shop in miniature, and all for thirty-one cents. But, alas! I had only eleven cents. Have that knife I must, however, and so I proposed to the shop woman to take back the top and breastpin at a slight deduction, and with my eleven cents to let me have the knife. The kind creature consented, and this makes memorable my first "swap." Some fine and nearly white molasses candy then caught my eye, and I proposed to trade the watch for its equivalent in candy. The transaction was made and the candy was so delicious that before night my gun was absorbed in the same way. The next morning the torpedoes "went off" in the same direction, and before night even my beloved knife was similarly exchanged. My money and my goods all gone I traded two pocket handkerchiefs and an extra pair of stockings I was sure I should not want for nine more rolls of molasses candy, and then wandered about the city disconsolate, sighing because there was no more molasses candy to conquer.

I doubt not that in these first wanderings about the city I often passed the corner of Broadway and Ann Street—never dreaming of the stir I was destined at a future day to make in that locality as proprietor and manager of the American Museum.

After wandering, gazing and wondering, for a week, Mr. Brown took me in his sleigh and on the evening of the following day we arrived in Bethel. I had a thousand questions to answer, and then and for a long time afterwards I was quite a lion among my mates because I had seen the great metropolis. My brothers and sisters, however, were much disappointed at my not bringing them something from my dollar, and when my mother examined my wardrobe and found two pocket handkerchiefs and one pair of stockings missing she whipped me and sent me to bed. Thus ingloriously terminated my first visit to New York.

Previous to my visit to New York, I think it was in 1820, when I was ten years of age, I made my first expedition to my landed property, "Ivy Island." This, it will be remembered, was the gift of my grandfather, from whom I derived my name. From the time when I was four years old I was continually hearing of this "property." My grandfather always spoke of me (in my presence) to the neighbors and to strangers as the richest child in town, since I owned the whole of "Ivy Island," one of the most valuable farms in the State. My father and mother frequently reminded me of my wealth and hoped I would do something for the family when I attained my majority. The neighbors professed fear that I might refuse to play with their children because I had inherited so large a property.

These constant allusions, for several years, to "Ivy Island" excited at once my pride and my curiosity and stimulated me to implore my father's permission to visit my property. At last, he promised I should do so in a few days, as we should be getting some hay near "Ivy Island." The wished for day at length arrived and my father told me that as we were to mow an adjoining meadow, I might visit my property in company with the hired man during the "nooning." My grandfather reminded me that it was to his bounty I was indebted for this wealth, and that had not my name been Phineas I might never have been proprietor of "Ivy Island." To this my mother added:

"Now, Taylor, don't become so excited when you see your property as to let your joy make you sick, for remember, rich as you are, that it will be eleven years before you can come into possession of your fortune."

She added much more good advice, to all of which I promised to be calm and reasonable and not to allow my pride to prevent me from speaking to my brothers and sisters when I returned home.

When we arrived at the meadow, which was in that part of the "Plum Trees" know as the "East Swamp," I asked my father where "Ivy Island" was.

"Yonder, at the north end of this meadow, where you see those beautiful trees rising in the distance."

All the forenoon I turned grass as fast as two men could cut it, and after a hasty repast at noon, one of our hired men, a good natured Irishman, named Edmund, took an axe on his shoulder and announced that he was ready to accompany me to "Ivy Island." We started, and as we approached the north end of the meadow we found the ground swampy and wet and were soon obliged to leap from bog to bog on our route. A misstep brought me up to my middle in water. To add to the dilemma a swarm of hornets attacked me. Attaining the altitude of another bog I was cheered by the assurance that there was only a quarter of a mile of this kind of travel to the edge of my property. I waded on. In about fifteen minutes more, after floundering through the morass, I found myself half-drowned, hornet-stung, mud-covered, and out of breath, on comparatively dry land.

"Never mind, my boy," said Edmund, "we have only to cross this little creek, and ye'll be upon your own valuable property."

We were on the margin of a stream, the banks of which were thickly covered with alders. I now discovered the use of Edmund's axe, for he felled a small oak to form a temporary bridge to my "Island" property. Crossing over, I proceeded to the centre of my domain; I saw nothing but a few stunted ivies and straggling trees. The truth flashed upon me. I had been the laughing-stock of the family and neighborhood for years. My valuable "Ivy Island" was an almost inaccessible, worthless bit of barren land, and while I stood deploring my sudden downfall, a huge black snake (one of my tenants) approached me with upraised head. I gave one shriek and rushed for the bridge.

This was my first, and, I need not say, my last visit to "Ivy Island." My father asked me "how I liked my property?" and I responded that I would sell it pretty cheap. My grandfather congratulated me upon my visit to my property as seriously as if it had been indeed a valuable domain. My mother hoped its richness had fully equalled my anticipations. The neighbors desired to know if I was not now glad I was named Phineas, and for five years forward I was frequently reminded of my wealth in "Ivy Island."

As I grew older, my settled aversion to manual labor, farm or other kind, was manifest in various ways, which were set down to the general score of laziness. In despair of doing better with me, my father concluded to make a merchant of me. He erected a building in Bethel, and with Mr. Hiram Weed as a partner, purchased a stock of dry goods, hardware, groceries, and general notions and installed me as clerk in this country store.

Of course I "felt my oats." It was condescension on my part to talk with boys who did out-door work. I stood behind the counter with a pen over my ear, was polite to the ladies, and was wonderfully active in waiting upon customers. We kept a cash, credit and barter store, and I drove some sharp bargains with women who brought butter, eggs, beeswax and feathers to exchange for dry goods, and with men who wanted to trade oats, corn, buckwheat, axe-helves, hats, and other commodities for tenpenny nails, molasses, or New England rum. But it was a drawback upon my dignity that I was obliged to take down the shutters, sweep the store, and make the fire. I received a small salary for my services and the perquisite of what profit I could derive from purchasing candies on my own account to sell to our younger customers, and, as usual, my father stipulated that I should clothe myself.

There is a great deal to be learned in a country store, and principally this—that sharp trades, tricks, dishonesty, and deception are by no means confined to the city. More than once, in cutting open bundles of rags, brought to be exchanged for goods, and warranted to be all linen and cotton, I have discovered in the interior worthless woolen trash and sometimes stones, gravel or ashes. Sometimes, too, when measuring loads of oats, corn or rye, declared to contain a specified number of bushels, say sixty, I have found them four or five bushels short. In such cases, some one else was always to blame, but these happenings were frequent enough to make us watchful of our customers. In the evenings and on wet days trade was always dull, and at such times the story-telling and joke-playing wits and wags of the village used to assemble in our store, and from them I derived considerable amusement, if not profit. After the store was closed at night, I frequently joined some of the village boys at the houses of their parents, where, with story-telling and play, a couple of hours would soon pass by, and then as late, perhaps, as eleven o'clock, I went home and slyly crept up stairs so as not to waken my brother with whom I slept, and who would be sure to report my late hours. He made every attempt, and laid all sorts of plans to catch me on my return, but as sleep always overtook him, I managed easily to elude his efforts.

Like most people in Connecticut in those days, I was brought up to attend church regularly on Sunday, and long before I could read I was a prominent scholar in the Sunday school. My good mother taught me my lessons in the New Testament and the Catechism, and my every effort was directed to win one of those "Rewards of Merit," which promised to pay the bearer one mill, so that ten of these prizes amounted to one cent, and one hundred of them, which might be won by faithful assiduity every Sunday for two years, would buy a Sunday school book worth ten cents. Such were the magnificent rewards held out to the religious ambition of youth.

There was but one church or "meeting-house" in Bethel, which all attended, sinking all differences of creed in the Presbyterian faith. The old meeting-house had neither steeple nor bell and was a plain edifice, comfortable enough in the summer, but my teeth chatter even now when I think of the dreary, cold, freezing hours we passed in that place in winter. A stove in a meeting-house in those days would have been a sacrilegious innovation. The sermons were from an hour and one half to two hours long, and through these the congregation would sit and shiver till they really merited the title the profane gave them of "blue skins." Some of the women carried a "foot-stove" consisting of a small square tin box in a wooden frame, the sides perforated, and in the interior there was a small square iron dish, which contained a few live coals covered with ashes. These stoves were usually replenished just before meeting time at some neighbor's near the meeting-house.

After many years of shivering and suffering, one of the brethren had the temerity to propose that the church should be warmed with a stove. His impious proposition was voted down by an overwhelming majority. Another year came around, and in November the stove question was again brought up. The excitement was immense. The subject was discussed in the village stores and in the juvenile debating club; it was prayed over in conference; and finally in general "society's meeting," in December, the stove was carried by a majority of one and was introduced into the meeting-house. On the first Sunday thereafter, two ancient maiden ladies were so oppressed by the dry and heated atmosphere occasioned by the wicked innovation, that they fainted away and were carried out into the cool air where they speedily returned to consciousness, especially when they were informed that owing to the lack of two lengths of pipe, no fire had yet been made in the stove. The next Sunday was a bitter cold day, and the stove, filled with well-seasoned hickory, was a great gratification to the many, and displeased only a few. After the benediction, an old deacon rose and requested the congregation to remain, and called upon them to witness that he had from the first raised his voice against the introduction of a stove into the house of the Lord; but the majority had been against him and he had submitted; now, if they *must* have a stove, he insisted upon having a large one, since the present one did not heat the whole house, but drove the cold to the back outside pews, making them three times as cold as they were before! In the course of the week, this deacon was made to comprehend that, unless on unusually severe days, the stove was sufficient to warm the house, and, at any rate, it did not drive all the cold in the house into one corner.

During the Rev. Mr. Lowe's ministrations at Bethel, he formed a Bible class, of which I was a member. We used to draw promiscuously from a hat a text of scripture and write a composition on the text, which compositions were read after service in the afternoon, to such of the congregation as remained to hear the exercises of the class. Once, I remember, I drew the text, Luke x. 42: "But one thing is needful; and Mary hath chosen that good part which shall not be taken away from her." *Question,* "What is the one thing needful?" My answer was nearly as follows:

"This question 'what is the one thing needful?' is capable of receiving various answers, depending much upon the persons to whom it is addressed. The merchant might answer that 'the one thing needful' is plenty of customers, who buy liberally, without beating down and pay cash for all their purchases. The farmer might reply, that 'the one thing needful is large harvests and high prices.' The physician might answer that 'it is plenty of patients.' The lawyer might be of opinion that 'it is an unruly community, always engaged in bickerings and litigations.' The clergyman might reply, 'It is a fat salary with multitudes of sinners seeking salvation and paying large pew rents.' The bachelor might exclaim, 'It is a pretty wife who loves her husband, and who knows how to sew on buttons.' The maiden might answer, 'It is a good husband, who will love, cherish and protect me while life shall last.' But the most proper answer, and doubtless that which applied to the case of Mary, would be, 'The one thing needful is to believe in the Lord Jesus Christ, follow in his footsteps, love God and obey His commandments, love our fellow-man, and embrace every opportunity of administering to his necessities.' In short, 'the one thing needful' is to live a life that we can always look back upon with satisfaction, and be enabled ever to contemplate its termination with trust in Him who has so kindly vouchsafed it to us, surrounding us with innumerable blessings, if we have but the heart and wisdom to receive them in proper manner."

The reading of a portion of this answer occasioned some amusement in the congregation, in which the clergyman himself joined, and the name of "Taylor Barnum" was whispered in connection with composition; but at the close of the reading I had the satisfaction of hearing Mr. Lowe say that it was a well written and truthful answer to the question, "What is the one thing needful?"

DISCUSSION QUESTIONS

1. Why does Barnum in his opening paragraph choose to include the statement that he was a property owner almost from the time of his birth? In what ways does this fact grow in significance as his narrative unfolds?

2. What types of activity are most often related in Barnum's account of his first visit to New York City? What does the metropolis represent for the young Barnum?

3. What effect does the visit to "Ivy Island" have on its future owner? Before the visit, what kinds of expectations had his family and neighbors created about the property? Consider why Barnum views this event as an important one. In what ways does this event inform Barnum's successes as a showman?

Ernest Laurence Thayer / Casey at the Bat 1888

Ernest Laurence Thayer (1863–1940) published the humorous poem "Casey at the Bat" in the June 3, 1888, San Francisco Examiner, *using the pseudonym "Phin." The poem became famous when a well-known entertainer of the time, DeWolf Hopper, made it part of his vaudeville act. So compellingly does "Casey at the Bat" document the drama and idiom of the game that poet-critic Louis Untermeyer has called it "the acknowledged classic of baseball, its anthem and theme song."*

The outlook wasn't brilliant for the Mudville nine that day:
The score stood four to two with but one inning more to play.
And then when Cooney died at first, and Barrows did the same,
A sickly silence fell upon the patrons of the game.

A straggling few got up to go in deep despair. The rest
Clung to that hope which springs eternal in the human breast;
They thought if only Casey could but get a whack at that—
We'd put up even money now with Casey at the bat.

But Flynn preceded Casey, as did also Jimmy Blake,
And the former was a lulu and the latter was a cake;
So upon that stricken multitude grim melancholy sat,
For there seemed but little chance of Casey's getting to the bat..

But Flynn let drive a single, to the wonderment of all,
And Blake, the much despis-ed, tore the cover off the ball;
And when the dust had lifted, and the men saw what had occurred,
There was Jimmy safe at second and Flynn a-hugging third.

Then from 5,000 throats and more there rose a lusty yell;
It rumbled through the valley, it rattled in the dell;
It knocked upon the mountain and recoiled upon the flat,
For Casey, mighty Casey, was advancing to the bat.

There was ease in Casey's manner as he stepped into his place;
There was pride in Casey's bearing and a smile on Casey's face.
And when, responding to the cheers, he lightly doffed his hat,
No stranger in the crowd could doubt 'twas Casey at the bat.

Ten thousand eyes were on him as he rubbed his hands with dirt;
Five thousand tongues applauded when he wiped them on his shirt.
Then while the writhing pitcher ground the ball into his hip,
Defiance gleamed in Casey's eye, a sneer curled Casey's lip.

And now the leather-covered sphere came hurtling through the air,
And Casey stood a-watching it in haughty grandeur there.
Close by the sturdy batsman the ball unheeded sped—
"That ain't my style," said Casey. "Strike one," the umpire said.

From the benches back with people, there went up a muffled roar,
Like the beating of the storm-waves on a stern and distant shore.
"Kill him! Kill the umpire!" shouted some one on the stand;
And it's likely they'd have killed him had not Casey raised his hand.

With a smile of Christian charity great Casey's visage shone;
He stilled the rising tumult; he bade the game go on;
He signaled to the pitcher, and once more the spheroid flew;
But Casey still ignored it, and the umpire said, "Strike two."

"Fraud!" cried the maddened thousands, and echo answered fraud;
But one scornful look from Casey and the audience was awed.
They saw his face grow stern and cold, they saw his muscles strain,
And they knew that Casey wouldn't let that ball go by again.

The sneer is gone from Casey's lip, his teeth are clenched in hate;
He pounds with cruel violence his bat upon the plate.
And now the pitcher holds the ball, and now he lets it go,
And now the air is shattered by the force of Casey's blow.

Oh, somewhere in this favored land the sun is shining bright;
The band is playing somewhere, and somewhere hearts are light,
And somewhere men are laughing, and somewhere children shout;
But there is no joy in Mudville—mighty Casey has struck out.

Edgar Rice Burroughs / *Tarzan of the Apes*

[Tarzan Meets Jane; or Girl Goes Ape] 1914

A one-time soldier, policeman, cowboy, Sears Roebuck department store manager, advertising copywriter, gold miner, salesman, and business failure, Edgar Rice Burroughs (1875–1950) began one of the most successful writing careers in the history of popular literature with the publication of Tarzan of the Apes. *The first of a series of twenty-six novels,* Tarzan of the Apes *initially appeared in the* All Story *magazine for October 1912 and, when no publisher would touch it, was serialized in the* New York Evening World. *The newspaper serialization triggered a demand for the story in book form, and* Tarzan of the Apes *was finally published in 1914.*

Tarzan provided exactly the kind of material the new movie industry was looking for. The first Tarzan film was released in 1918, and the series remained popular until the 1960s. Burroughs's fantasies posed a challenge to "realism" that Hollywood must have delighted in, as the following description of the technical efforts that went into producing Tarzan's barbaric yawp so perfectly demonstrates:

> *M-G-M spared no expense on the Tarzan yell. Miles of sound track of human, animal and instrument sounds were tested in collecting the ingredients of an unearthly howl. The cry of a mother camel robbed of her young was used until still more mournful sounds were found. A combination of five different sound tracks is used today for the Tarzan yell. There are: 1. Sound track of Weissmuller yelling amplified. 2. Track of hyena howl, run backward and volume diminished. 3. Soprano note sung by Lorraine Bridges, recording on sound track at reduced*

> *speed; then rerecorded at varying speeds to give a "flutter" in sound. 4. Growl of dog, recorded very faintly. 5. Raspy note of violin G-string, recorded very faintly. In the experimental stage the five sound tracks were played over five different loud speakers. From time to time the speed of each sound track was varied and the volume amplified or diminished. When the orchestration of the yell was perfected, the five loudspeakers were played simultaneously and the blended sounds recorded on the master sound track. By constant practice Weissmuller is now able to let loose an almost perfect imitation of the sound track.*

From the time Tarzan left the tribe of great anthropoids in which he had been raised, it was torn by continual strife and discord. Terkoz proved a cruel and capricious king, so that, one by one, many of the older and weaker apes, upon whom he was particularly prone to vent his brutish nature, took their families and sought the quiet and safety of the far interior.

But at last those who remained were driven to desperation by the continued truculence of Terkoz, and it so happened that one of them recalled the parting admonition of Tarzan:

"If you have a chief who is cruel, do not do as the other apes do, and attempt, any one of you, to pit yourself against him alone. But, instead, let two or three or four of you attack him together. Then, if you will do this, no chief will dare to be other than he should be, for four of you can kill any chief who may ever be over you."

And the ape who recalled this wise counsel repeated it to several of his fellows, so that when Terkoz returned to the tribe that day he found a warm reception awaiting him.

There were no formalities. As Terkoz reached the group, five huge, hairy beasts sprang upon him.

At heart he was an arrant coward, which is the way with bullies among apes as well as among men; so he did not remain to fight and die, but tore himself away from them as quickly as he could and fled into the sheltering boughs of the forest.

Two more attempts he made to rejoin the tribe, but on each occasion he was set upon and driven away. At last he gave it up, and turned, foaming with rage and hatred, into the jungle.

For several days he wandered aimlessly, nursing his spite and looking for some weak thing on which to vent his pent anger.

It was in this state of mind that the horrible, man-like beast, swinging from tree to tree, came suddenly upon two women in the jungle.

He was right above them when he discovered them. The first intimation Jane Porter had of his presence was when the great hairy body dropped to the earth beside her, and she saw the awful face and the snarling, hideous mouth thrust within a foot of her.

One piercing scream escaped her lips as the brute hand clutched her arm. Then she was dragged toward those awful fangs which yawned at her throat. But ere they touched that fair skin another mood claimed the anthropoid.

The tribe had kept his women. He must find others to replace them. This hairless white ape would be the first of his new household, and so he threw her roughly across his broad, hairy shoulders and leaped back into the trees, bearing Jane away.

Esmeralda's scream of terror had mingled once with that of Jane, and then, as was Esmeralda's manner under stress of emergency which required presence of mind, she swooned.

But Jane did not once lose consciousness. It is true that that awful face, pressing close to hers, and the stench of the foul breath beating upon her nostrils, paralyzed her with terror; but her brain was clear, and she comprehended all that transpired.

With what seemed to her marvelous rapidity the brute bore her through the forest, but still she did not cry out or struggle. The sudden advent of the ape had confused her to such an extent that she thought now that he was bearing her toward the beach.

For this reason she conserved her energies and her voice until she could see that they had approached near enough to the camp to attract the succor she craved.

She could not have known it, but she was being borne farther and farther into the impenetrable jungle.

The scream that had brought Clayton and the two older men stumbling through the undergrowth had led Tarzan of the Apes straight to where Esmeralda lay, but it was not Esmeralda in whom his interest centered, though pausing over her he saw that she was unhurt.

For a moment he scrutinized the ground below and the trees above, until the ape that was in him by virtue of training and environment, combined with the intelligence that was his by right of birth, told his wondrous woodcraft the whole story as plainly as though he had seen the thing happen with his own eyes.

And then he was gone again into the swaying trees, following the high-flung spoor which no other human eye could have detected, much less translated.

At boughs' ends, where the anthropoid swings from one tree to another, there is most to mark the trail, but least to point the direction of the quarry; for there the pressure is downward always, toward the small end of the branch, whether the ape be leaving or entering a tree. Nearer the center of the tree, where the signs of passage are fainter, the direction is plainly marked.

Here, on this branch, a caterpillar has been crushed by the fugitive's great foot, and Tarzan knows instinctively where that same foot would touch in the next stride. Here he looks to find a tiny particle of the demolished larva, ofttimes not more than a speck of moisture.

Again, a minute bit of bark has been upturned by the scraping hand, and the direction of the break indicates the direction of the passage. Or some great limb, or the stem of the tree itself has been brushed by the hairy body, and a tiny shred of hair tells him by the direction from which it is wedged beneath the bark that he is on the right trail.

Nor does he need to check his speed to catch these seemingly faint records of the fleeing beast.

To Tarzan they stand out boldly against all the myriad other scars and bruises and signs upon the leafy way. But strongest of all is the scent, for Tarzan is pursuing up the wind, and his trained nostrils are as sensitive as a hound's.

There are those who believe that the lower orders are specially endowed by nature with better olfactory nerves than man, but it is merely a matter of development.

Man's survival does not hinge so greatly upon the perfection of his senses. His power to reason has relieved them of many of their duties, and so they have, to some extent, atrophied, as have the muscles which move the ears and scalp, merely from disuse.

The muscles are there, about the ears and beneath the scalp, and so are the nerves which transmit sensations to the brain, but they are under-developed because they are not needed.

Not so with Tarzan of the Apes. From early infancy his survival had depended upon acuteness of eyesight, hearing, smell, touch, and taste far more than upon the more slowly developed organ of reason.

The least developed of all in Tarzan was the sense of taste, for he could eat luscious fruits, or raw flesh, long buried with almost equal appreciation; but in that he differed but slightly from more civilized epicures.

Almost silently the ape-man sped on in the track of Terkoz and his prey, but the sound of his approach reached the ears of the fleeing beast and spurred it on to greater speed.

Three miles were covered before Tarzan overtook them, and then Terkoz, seeing that further flight was futile, dropped to the ground in a small open glade, that he might turn and fight for his prize or be free to escape unhampered if he saw that the pursuer was more than a match for him.

He still grasped Jane in one great arm as Tarzan bounded like a leopard into the arena which nature had provided for this primeval-like battle.

When Terkoz saw that it was Tarzan who pursued him, he jumped to the conclusion that this was Tarzan's woman, since they were of the same kind—white and hairless—and so he rejoiced at this opportunity for double revenge upon his hated enemy.

To Jane the strange apparition of this god-like man was as wine to sick nerves.

From the description which Clayton and her father and Mr. Philander had given her, she knew that it must be the same wonderful creature who had saved them, and she saw in him only a protector and a friend.

But as Terkoz pushed her roughly aside to meet Tarzan's charge, and she saw the great proportions of the ape and the mighty muscles and the fierce fangs, her heart quailed. How could any vanquish such a mighty antagonist?

Like two charging bulls they came together, and like two wolves sought each other's throat. Against the long canines of the ape was pitted the thin blade of the man's knife.

Jane—her lithe, young form flattened against the trunk of a great tree, her hands tight pressed against her rising and falling bosom, and her eyes wide with mingled horror, fascination, fear, and admiration—watched the primordial ape battle with the primeval man for possession of a woman—for her.

As the great muscles of the man's back and shoulders knotted beneath the tension of his efforts, and the huge biceps and forearm held at bay those mighty tusks, the veil of centuries of civilization and culture was swept from the blurred vision of the Baltimore girl.

When the long knife drank deep a dozen times of Terkoz' heart's blood, and the great carcass rolled lifeless upon the ground, it was a primeval woman who sprang forward with outstretched arms toward the primeval man who had fought for her and won her.

And Tarzan?

He did what no red-blooded man needs lessons in doing. He took his woman in his arms and smothered her upturned, panting lips with kisses.

For a moment Jane lay there with half-closed eyes. For a moment—the first in her young life—she knew the meaning of love.

But as suddenly as the veil had been withdrawn it dropped again, and an outraged conscience suffused her face with its scarlet mantle, and a mortified woman thrust Tarzan of the Apes from her and buried her face in her hands.

Tarzan had been surprised when he had found the girl he had learned to love after a vague and abstract manner a willing prisoner in his arms. Now he was surprised that she repulsed him.

He came close to her once more and took hold of her arm. She turned upon him like a tigress, striking his great breast with her tiny hands.

Tarzan could not understand it.

A moment ago and it had been his intention to hasten Jane back to her people, but that little moment was lost now in the dim and distant past of things which were but can never be again, and with it the good intention had gone to join the impossible.

Since then Tarzan of the Apes had felt a warm, lithe form close pressed to his. Hot, sweet breath against his cheek and mouth had fanned a new flame to life within his breast, and perfect lips had clung to his in burning kisses that had seared a deep brand into his soul—a brand which marked a new Tarzan.

Again he laid his hand upon her arm. Again she repulsed him. And then Tarzan of the Apes did just what his first ancestor would have done.

He took his woman in his arms and carried her into the jungle. . . .

When Jane realized that she was being borne away a captive by the strange forest creature who had rescued her from the clutches of the ape she struggled desperately to escape, but the strong arms that held her as easily as though she had been but a day-old babe only pressed a little more tightly.

So presently she gave up the futile effort and lay quietly, looking through half-closed lids at the face of the man who strode easily through the tangled undergrowth with her.

The face above her was one of extraordinary beauty.

A perfect type of the strongly masculine, unmarred by dissipation, or brutal or degrading passions. For, though Tarzan of the Apes was a killer of men and of beasts, he killed as the hunter kills, dispassionately, except on those rare occasions when he had killed for hate—though not the brooding, malevolent hate which marks the features of its own with hideous lines.

When Tarzan killed he more often smiled than scowled, and smiles are the foundation of beauty.

One thing the girl had noticed particularly when she had seen Tarzan rushing upon Terkoz—the vivid scarlet band upon his forehead, from above the left eye to the scalp; but now as she scanned his features she noticed that it was gone, and only a thin white line marked the spot where it had been.

As she lay more quietly in his arms Tarzan slightly relaxed his grip upon her.

Once he looked down into her eyes and smiled, and the girl had to close her own to shut out the vision of that handsome, winning face.

Presently Tarzan took to the trees, and Jane, wondering that she felt no fear, began to realize that in many respects she had never felt more secure in her whole life than now as she lay in the arms of this strong, wild creature, being borne, God alone knew where or to what fate, deeper and deeper into the savage fastness of the untamed forest.

When, with closed eyes, she commenced to speculate upon the future, and terrifying fears were conjured by a vivid imagination, she had but to raise her lids and look upon that noble face so close to hers to dissipate the last remnant of apprehension.

No, he could never harm her; of that she was convinced when she translated the fine features and the frank, brave eyes above her into the chivalry which they proclaimed.

On and on they went through what seemed to Jane a solid mass of verdure, yet ever there appeared to open before this forest god a passage, as by magic, which closed behind them as they passed.

Scarce a branch scraped against her, yet above and below, before and behind, the view presented naught but a solid mass of inextricably interwoven branches and creepers.

As Tarzan moved steadily onward his mind was occupied with many strange and new thoughts. Here was a problem the like of which he had never encountered, and he felt rather than reasoned that he must meet it as a man and not as an ape.

The free movement through the middle terrace, which was the route he had followed for the most part, had helped to cool the ardor of the first fierce passion of his new found love.

Now he discovered himself speculating upon the fate which would have fallen to the girl had he not rescued her from Terkoz.

He knew why the ape had not killed her, and he commenced to compare his intentions with those of Terkoz.

True, it was the order of the jungle for the male to take his mate by force; but could Tarzan be guided by the laws of the beasts? Was not Tarzan a Man? But what did men do? He was puzzled; for he did not know.

He wished that he might ask the girl, and then it came to him that she had already answered him in the futile struggle she had made to escape and to repulse him.

But now they had come to their destination, and Tarzan of the Apes with Jane in his strong arms, swung lightly to the turf of the arena where the great apes held their councils and danced the wild orgy of the Dum-Dum.

Though they had come many miles, it was still but midafternoon, and the amphitheater was bathed in the half light which filtered through the maze of encircling foliage.

The green turf looked soft and cool and inviting. The myriad noises of the jungle seemed far distant and hushed to a mere echo of blurred sounds, rising and falling like the surf upon a remote shore.

A feeling of dreamy peacefulness stole over Jane as she sank down upon the grass where Tarzan had placed her, and as she looked up at his great figure towering above her, there was added a strange sense of perfect security.

As she watched him from beneath half-closed lids, Tarzan crossed the little circular clearing toward the trees upon the further side. She noted the graceful majesty of his carriage, the perfect symmetry of his magnificent figure and the poise of his well-shaped head upon his broad shoulders.

What a perfect creature! There could be naught of cruelty or baseness beneath that godlike exterior. Never, she thought had such a man strode the earth since God created the first in his own image.

With a bound Tarzan sprang into the trees and disappeared. Jane wondered where he had gone. Had he left her there to her fate in the lonely jungle?

She glanced nervously about. Every vine and bush seemed but the lurking-place of some huge and horrible beast waiting to bury gleaming fangs into her soft flesh. Every sound she magnified into the stealthy creeping of a sinuous and malignant body.

How different now that he had left her!

For a few minutes that seemed hours to the frightened girl, she sat with tense nerves waiting for the spring of the crouching thing that was to end her misery of apprehension.

She almost prayed for the cruel teeth that would give her unconsciousness and surcease from the agony of fear.

She heard a sudden, slight sound behind her. With a cry she sprang to her feet and turned to face her end.

There stood Tarzan, his arms filled with ripe and luscious fruit.

Jane reeled and would have fallen, had not Tarzan, dropping his burden, caught her in his arms. She did not lose consciousness, but she clung tightly to him, shuddering and trembling like a frightened deer.

Tarzan of the Apes stroked her soft hair and tried to comfort and quiet her as Kala had him, when, as a little ape, he had been frightened by Sabor, the lioness, or Histah, the snake.

Once he pressed his lips lightly upon her forehead, and she did not move, but closed her eyes and sighed.

She could not analyze her feelings, nor did she wish to attempt it. She was satisfied to feel the safety of those strong arms, and to leave her future to fate; for the last few hours had taught her to trust this strange wild creature of the forest as she would have trusted but few of the men of her acquaintance.

As she thought of the strangeness of it, there commenced to dawn upon her the realization that she had, possibly, learned something else which she had never really known before—love. She wondered and then she smiled.

And still smiling, she pushed Tarzan gently away; and looking at him with a half-smiling, half-quizzical expression that made her face wholly entrancing, she pointed to the fruit upon the ground, and seated herself upon the edge of the earthen drum of the anthropoids, for hunger was asserting itself.

Tarzan quickly gathered up the fruit, and, bringing it, laid it at her feet; and then he, too, sat upon the drum beside her, and with his knife opened and prepared the various fruits for her meal.

Together and in silence they ate, occasionally stealing sly glances at one another, until finally Jane broke into a merry laugh in which Tarzan joined.

"I wish you spoke English," said the girl.

Tarzan shook his head, and an expression of wistful and pathetic longing sobered his laughing eyes.

Then Jane tried speaking to him in French, and then in German; but she had to laugh at her own blundering attempt at the latter tongue.

"Anyway," she said to him in English, "you understand my German as well as they did in Berlin."

Tarzan had long since reached a decision as to what his future procedure should be. He had had time to recollect all that he had read of the ways of men and women in the books at the cabin. He would act as he imagined the men in the books would have acted were they in his place.

Again he rose and went into the trees, but first he tried to explain by means of signs that he would return shortly, and he did so well that Jane understood and was not afraid when he had gone.

Only a feeling of loneliness came over her and she watched the point where he had disappeared, with longing eyes, awaiting his return. As before, she was appraised of his presence by a soft sound behind her, and turned to see him coming across the turf with a great armful of branches.

Then he went back again into the jungle and in a few minutes reappeared with a quantity of soft grasses and ferns. Two more trips he made until he had quite a pile of material at hand.

Then he spread the ferns and grasses upon the ground in a soft flat bed, and above it leaned many branches together so that they met a few feet over its center. Upon these he spread layers of huge leaves of the great elephant's ear, and with more branches and more leaves he closed one end of the little shelter he had built.

Then they sat down together again upon the edge of the drum and tried to talk by signs.

The magnificent diamond locket which hung about Tarzan's neck, had been a source of much wonderment to Jane. She pointed to it now, and Tarzan removed it and handed the pretty bauble to her.

She saw that it was the work of a skilled artisan and that the diamonds were of great brilliancy and superbly set, but the cutting of them denoted that they were of a former day.

She noticed too that the locket opened, and, pressing the hidden clasp, she saw the two halves spring apart to reveal in either section an ivory miniature.

One was of a beautiful woman and the other might have been a likeness of the man who sat beside her, except for a subtle difference of expression that was scarcely definable.

She looked up at Tarzan to find him leaning toward her gazing on the miniatures with an expression of astonishment. He reached out his hand for the locket and took it away from her, examining the likenesses within with unmistakable signs of surprise and new interest. His manner clearly denoted that he had never before seen them, nor imagined that the locket opened.

This fact caused Jane to indulge in further speculation, and it taxed her imagination to picture how this beautiful ornament came into the possession of a wild and savage creature of the unexplored jungles of Africa.

Still more wonderful was how it contained the likeness of one who might be a brother, or, more likely, the father of this woodland demi-god who was even ignorant of the fact that the locket opened.

Tarzan was still gazing with fixity at the two faces. Presently he removed the quiver from his shoulder, and emptying the arrows upon the ground reached into the bottom of the bag-like receptacle and drew forth a flat object wrapped in many soft leaves and tied with bits of long grass.

Carefully he unwrapped it, removing layer after layer of leaves until at length he held a photograph in his hand.

Pointing to the miniature of the man within the locket he handed the photograph to Jane, holding the open locket beside it.

The photograph only served to puzzle the girl still more, for it was evidently another likeness of the same man whose picture rested in the locket beside that of the beautiful young woman.

Tarzan was looking at her with an expression of puzzled bewilderment in his eyes as she glanced up at him. He seemed to be framing a question with his lips.

The girl pointed to the photograph and then to the miniature and then to him, as though to indicate that she thought the likenesses were of him, but he only shook his head, and then shrugging his great shoulders, he took the photograph from her and having carefully rewrapped it, placed it again in the bottom of his quiver.

For a few moments he sat in silence, his eyes bent upon the ground, while Jane held the little locket in her hand, turning it over and over in an endeavor to find some further clue that might lead to the identity of its original owner.

At length a simple explanation occurred to her.

The locket had belonged to Lord Greystoke, and the likenesses were of himself and Lady Alice.

This wild creature had simply found it in the cabin by the beach. How stupid of her not to have thought of that solution before.

But to account for the strange likeness between Lord Greystoke and this forest god—that was quite beyond her, and it is not strange that she could not imagine that this naked savage was indeed an English nobleman.

At length Tarzan looked up to watch the girl as she examined the locket. He could not fathom the meaning of the faces within, but he could read the interest and fascination upon the face of the live young creature by his side.

She noticed that he was watching her and thinking that he wished his ornament again she held it out to him. He took it from her and taking the chain in his two hands he placed it about her neck, smiling at her expression of surprise at his unexpected gift.

Jane shook her head vehemently and would have removed the golden links from about her throat, but Tarzan would not let her. Taking her hands in his, when she insisted upon it, he held them tightly to prevent her.

At last she desisted and with a little laugh raised the locket to her lips.

Tarzan did not know precisely what she meant, but he guessed correctly that it was her way of acknowledging the gift, and so he rose, and taking the locket in his hand, stooped gravely like some courtier of old, and pressed his lips upon it where hers had rested.

It was a stately and gallant little compliment performed with the grace and dignity of utter unconsciousness of self. It was the hall-mark of his aristocratic birth, the natural out-cropping of many generations of fine breeding, an hereditary instinct of graciousness which a lifetime of uncouth and savage training and environment could not eradicate.

It was growing dark now, and so they ate again of the fruit which was both food and drink for them; then Tarzan rose, and leading Jane to the little bower he had erected, motioned her to go within.

For the first time in hours a feeling of fear swept over her, and Tarzan felt her draw away as though shrinking from him.

Contact with this girl for half a day had left a very different Tarzan from the one on whom the morning's sun had risen.

Now, in every fiber of his being, heredity spoke louder than training.

He had not in one swift transition become a polished gentleman from a savage ape-man, but at last the instincts of the former predominated, and over all was the desire to please the woman he loved, and to appear well in her eyes.

So Tarzan of the Apes did the only thing he knew to assure Jane of her safety. He removed his hunting knife from its sheath and handed it to her hilt first, again motioning her into the bower.

The girl understood, and taking the long knife she entered and lay down upon the soft grasses while Tarzan of the Apes stretched himself upon the ground across the entrance.

And thus the rising sun found them in the morning.

When Jane awoke, she did not at first recall the strange events of the preceding day, and so she wondered at her odd surroundings—the little leafy bower, the soft grasses of her bed, the unfamiliar prospect from the opening at her feet.

Slowly the circumstances of her position crept one by one into her mind. And then a great wonderment arose in her heart—a mighty wave of thankfulness and gratitude that though she had been in such terrible danger, yet she was unharmed.

She moved to the entrance of the shelter to look for Tarzan. He was gone; but this time no fear assailed her for she knew that he would return.

In the grass at the entrance to her bower she saw the imprint of his body where he had lain all night to guard her. She knew that the fact that he had been there was all that had permitted her to sleep in such peaceful security.

With him near, who could entertain fear? She wondered if there was another man on earth with whom a girl could feel so safe in the heart of this savage African jungle. Even the lions and panthers had no fears for her now.

She looked up to see his lithe form drop softly from a near-by tree. As he caught her eyes upon him his face lighted with that frank and radiant smile that had won her confidence the day before.

As he approached her Jane's heart beat faster and her eyes brightened as they had never done before at the approach of any man.

He had again been gathering fruit and this he laid at the entrance of her bower. Once more they sat down together to eat.

Jane commenced to wonder what his plans were. Would he take her back to the beach or would he keep her here? Suddenly she realized that the matter did not seem to give her much concern. Could it be that she did not care!

She began to comprehend, also, that she was entirely contented sitting here by the side of this smiling giant eating delicious fruit in a sylvan paradise far within the remote depths of an African jungle—that she was contented and very happy.

She could not understand it. Her reason told her that she should be torn by wild anxieties, weighted by dread fears, cast down by gloomy forebodings; but instead, her heart was singing and she was smiling into the answering face of the man beside her.

When they had finished their breakfast Tarzan went to her bower and recovered his knife. The girl had entirely forgotten it. She realized that it was because she had forgotten the fear that prompted her to accept it.

Motioning her to follow, Tarzan walked toward the trees at the edge of the arena, and taking her in one strong arm swung to the branches above.

The girl knew that he was taking her back to her people, and she could not understand the sudden feeling of loneliness and sorrow which crept over her.

For hours they swung slowly along.

Tarzan of the Apes did not hurry. He tried to draw out the sweet pleasure of that journey with those dear arms about his neck as long as possible, and so he went far south of the direct route to the beach.

Several times they halted for brief rests, which Tarzan did not need, and at noon they stopped for an hour at a little brook, where they quenched their thirst, and ate.

So it was nearly sunset when they came to the clearing, and Tarzan, dropping to the ground beside a great tree, parted the tall jungle grass and pointed out the little cabin to her.

She took him by the hand to lead him to it, that she might tell her father that this man had saved her from death and worse than death, that he had watched over her as carefully as a mother might have done.

But again the timidity of the wild thing in the face of human habitation swept over Tarzan of the Apes. He drew back, shaking his head.

The girl came close to him, looking up with pleading eyes. Somehow she could not bear the thought of his going back into the terrible jungle alone.

Still he shook his head, and finally he drew her to him very gently and stooped to kiss her, but first he looked into her eyes and waited to learn if she were pleased, or if she would repulse him.

Just an instant the girl hesitated, and then she realized the truth, and throwing her arms about his neck she drew his face to hers and kissed him—unashamed.

"I love you—I love you," she murmured.

From far in the distance came the faint sound of many guns. Tarzan and Jane raised their heads.

From the cabin came Mr. Philander and Esmeralda.

From where Tarzan and the girl stood they could not see the two vessels lying at anchor in the harbor.

Tarzan pointed toward the sounds, touched his breast and pointed again. She understood. He was going, and something told her that it was because he thought her people were in danger.

Again he kissed her.

"Come back to me," she whispered. "I shall wait for you—always."

Dale Carnegie / *How to Win Friends and Influence People* 1936

One of the most successful nonfiction books in the history of American publishing, How to Win Friends and Influence People *was the culmination of Dale Carnegie's experiences in training thousands of business and professional people in the art of public speaking and the techniques of "handling people." A compilation of popular psychology, etiquette rules, and after-dinner speech anecdotes,* How to Win Friends and Influence People *suggests that the fuzzy areas of social relationships and human discourse can be gotten through effectively and profitably with elocutionary acumen, a little shrewdness, and the application of proper procedures.*

FUNDAMENTAL TECHNIQUES IN HANDLING PEOPLE

CHAPTER 1: "IF YOU WANT TO GATHER HONEY, DON'T KICK OVER THE BEEHIVE"

On May 7, 1931, New York City witnessed the most sensational man-hunt the old town had ever known. After weeks of search, "Two Gun" Crowley—the killer, the gunman who didn't smoke or drink—was at bay, trapped in his sweetheart's apartment on West End Avenue.

One hundred and fifty policemen and detectives laid siege to his top-floor hideaway. Chopping holes in the roof, they tried to smoke out Crowley, the "cop killer," with tear gas. Then they mounted their machine guns on surrounding buildings, and for more than an hour one of New York's fine residential sections reverberated with the crack of pistol fire and the rat-tat-tat of machine guns. Crowley, crouching behind an overstuffed chair, fired incessantly at the police. Ten thousand excited people watched the battle. Nothing like it had ever been seen before on the sidewalks of New York.

When Crowley was captured, Police Commissioner Mulrooney declared that the two-gun desperado was one of the most dangerous criminals ever encountered in the history of New York. "He will kill," said the Commissioner, "at the drop of a feather."

But how did "Two Gun" Crowley regard himself? We know, because while the police were firing into his apartment, he wrote a letter addressed "To whom it may concern." And, as he wrote, the blood flowing from his wounds left a crimson trail on the paper. In this letter Crowley said: "Under my coat is a weary heart, but a kind one—one that would do nobody any harm."

A short time before this, Crowley had been having a necking party on a country road out on Long Island. Suddenly a policeman walked up to the parked car and said: "Let me see your license."

Without saying a word, Crowley drew his gun, and cut the policeman down with a shower of lead. As the dying officer fell, Crowley leaped out of the car, grabbed the officer's revolver, and fired another bullet into the prostrate body. And that was the killer who said: "Under my coat is a weary heart, but a kind one—one that would do nobody any harm."

Crowley was sentenced to the electric chair. When he arrived at the death house at Sing Sing, did he say, "This is what I get for killing people?" No, he said: "This is what I get for defending myself."

The point of the story is this: "Two Gun" Crowley didn't blame himself for anything.

Is that an unusual attitude among criminals? If you think so, listen to this:

"I have spent the best years of my life giving people the lighter pleasures, helping them have a good time, and all I get is abuse, the existence of a hunted man."

That's Al Capone speaking. Yes, America's erstwhile Public Enemy Number One—the most sinister gang leader who ever shot up Chicago. Capone doesn't condemn himself. He actually regards himself as a public benefactor—an unappreciated and misunderstood public benefactor.

And so did Dutch Schultz before he crumpled up under gangster bullets in Newark. Dutch Schultz, one of New York's most notorious rats, said in a newspaper interview that he was a public benefactor. And he believed it.

I have had some interesting correspondence with Warden Lawes of Sing Sing on this subject, and he declares that "few of the criminals in Sing Sing regard themselves as bad men. They are just as human as you and I. So they rationalize, they explain. They can tell you why they had to crack a safe or be quick on the trigger finger. Most of them attempt by a form of reasoning, fallacious or logical, to justify their anti-social acts even to themselves, consequently stoutly maintaining that they should never have been imprisoned at all."

If Al Capone, "Two Gun" Crowley, Dutch Schultz, the desperate men behind prison walls don't blame themselves for anything—what about the people with whom you and I come in contact?

The late John Wanamaker once confessed: "I learned thirty years ago that it is foolish to scold. I have enough trouble overcoming my own limitations without fretting over the fact that God has not seen fit to distribute evenly the gift of intelligence.''

Wanamaker learned this lesson early; but I personally had to blunder through this old world for a third of a century before it even began to dawn upon me that ninety-nine times out of a hundred, no man ever criticizes himself for anything, no matter how wrong he may be.

Criticism is futile because it puts a man on the defensive, and usually makes him strive to justify himself. Criticism is dangerous, because it wounds a man's precious pride, hurts his sense of importance, and arouses his resentment.

The German army won't let a soldier file a complaint and make a criticism immediately after a thing has happened. He has to sleep on his grudge first and cool off. If he files his complaint immediately, he is punished. By the eternals, there ought to be a law like that in civil life too—a law for whining parents and nagging wives and scolding employers and the whole obnoxious parade of fault-finders.

You will find examples of the futility of criticism bristling on a thousand pages of history. Take, for example, the famous quarrel between Theodore Roosevelt and President Taft—a quarrel that split the Republican Party, put Woodrow Wilson in the White House, and wrote bold, luminous lines across the World War and altered the flow of history. Let's review the facts quickly: When Theodore Roosevelt stepped out of the White House in 1908, he made Taft president, and then went off to Africa to shoot lions. When he returned, he exploded. He denounced Taft for his conservatism, tried to secure the nomination for a third term himself, formed the Bull Moose Party, and all but demolished the G.O.P. In the election that followed, William Howard Taft and the Republican Party carried only two states—Vermont and Utah. The most disastrous defeat the old party had ever known.

Theodore Roosevelt blamed Taft; but did President Taft blame himself? Of course not. With tears in his eyes, Taft said: ''I don't see how I could have done any differently from what I have.''

Who was to blame? Roosevelt or Taft? Frankly, I don't know, and I don't care. The point I am trying to make is that all of Theodore Roosevelt's criticism didn't persuade Taft that he was wrong. It merely made Taft strive to justify himself and to reiterate with tears in his eyes: ''I don't see how I could have done any differently from what I have.''

Or, take the Teapot Dome Oil scandal. Remember it? It kept the newspapers ringing with indignation for years. It rocked the nation! Nothing like it had ever happened before in American public life within the memory of living men. Here are the bare facts of the scandal: Albert Fall, Secretary of the Interior in Harding's cabinet, was entrusted with the leasing of government oil reserves at Elk Hill and Teapot Dome—oil reserves that had been set aside for the future use of the Navy. Did Secretary Fall permit competitive bidding? No sir. He handed the fat, juicy contract outright to his friend, Edward L. Doheny. And what did Doheny do? He gave Secretary Fall what he was pleased to call a ''loan'' of one hundred thousand dollars. Then, in a high-handed manner, Secretary Fall ordered United States Marines into the district to drive off competitors whose adjacent wells were sapping oil out of the Elk Hill reserves. These competitors, driven off their ground at the ends of guns and bayonets, rushed into court—and blew the lid off the hundred million dollar Teapot Dome scandal. A stench arose so vile that it ruined the Harding administration, nauseated an entire nation, threatened to wreck the Republican Party, and put Albert B. Fall behind prison bars.

Fall was condemned viciously—condemned as few men in public life have ever been. Did he repent? Never! Years later Herbert Hoover intimated in a public speech that President Harding's death had been due to mental anxiety and worry because a friend had betrayed him. When Mrs. Fall heard that, she sprang from her chair, she wept, she shook her fists at fate, and screamed: "What! Harding betrayed by Fall? No! My husband never betrayed anyone. This whole house full of gold would not tempt my husband to do wrong. He is the one who has been betrayed and led to the slaughter and crucified."

There you are; human nature in action, the wrong-doer blaming everybody but himself. We are all like that. So when you and I are tempted to criticize someone tomorrow, let's remember Al Capone, "Two Gun" Crowley, and Albert Fall. Let's realize that criticisms are like homing pigeons. They always return home. Let's realize that the person we are going to correct and condemn will probably justify himself, and condemn us in return; or, like the gentle Taft, he will say: "I don't see how I could have done any differently from what I have."

On Saturday morning, April 15, 1865, Abraham Lincoln lay dying in a hall bedroom of a cheap lodging house directly across the street from Ford's Theatre, where Booth had shot him. Lincoln's long body lay stretched diagonally across a sagging bed that was too short for him. A cheap reproduction of Rosa Bonheur's famous painting, "The Horse Fair," hung above the bed, and a dismal gas jet flickered yellow light.

As Lincoln lay dying, Secretary of War Stanton said, "There lies the most perfect ruler of men that the world has ever seen."

What was the secret of Lincoln's success in dealing with men? I studied the life of Abraham Lincoln for ten years, and devoted all of three years to writing and rewriting a book entitled *Lincoln the Unknown*. I believe I have made as detailed and exhaustive a study of Lincoln's personality and home life as it is possible for any human being to make. I made a special study of Lincoln's method of dealing with men. Did he indulge in criticism? Oh, yes. As a young man in the Pigeon Creek Valley of Indiana, he not only criticized but he wrote letters and poems ridiculing people and dropped these letters on the country roads where they were sure to be found. One of these letters aroused resentments that burned for a lifetime.

Even after Lincoln had become a practicing lawyer in Springfield, Illinois, he attacked his opponents openly in letters published in the newspapers. But he did this just once too often.

In the autumn of 1842, he ridiculed a vain, pugnacious Irish politician by the name of James Shields. Lincoln lampooned him through an anonymous letter published in the *Springfield Journal*. The town roared with laughter. Shields, sensitive and proud, boiled with indignation. He found out who wrote the letter, leaped on his horse, started after Lincoln, and challenged him to fight a duel. Lincoln didn't want to fight. He was opposed to dueling; but he couldn't get out of it and save his honor. He was given the choice of weapons. Since he had very long arms, he chose cavalry broad swords, took lessons in sword fighting from a West Point graduate; and, on the appointed day, he and Shields met on a sand bar in the Mississippi River, prepared to fight to the death; but, at the last minute, their seconds interrupted and stopped the duel.

That was the most lurid personal incident in Lincoln's life. It taught him an invaluable lesson in the art of dealing with people. Never again did he write an insulting letter. Never again did he ridicule anyone. And from that time on, he almost never criticized anybody for anything.

Time after time, during the Civil War, Lincoln put a new general at the head of the Army of the Potomac, and each one in turn—McClellan, Pope, Burnside, Hooker, Meade—blundered tragically, and drove Lincoln to pacing the floor in despair. Half the nation savagely condemned these incompetent generals, but Lincoln, "with malice towards none, with charity for all," held his peace. One of his favorite quotations was "Judge not, that ye be not judged."

And when Mrs. Lincoln and others spoke harshly of the Southern people, Lincoln replied: "Don't criticize them; they are just what we would be under similar circumstances."

Yet, if any man ever had occasion to criticize, surely it was Lincoln. Let's take just one illustration:

The Battle of Gettysburg was fought during the first three days of July, 1863. During the night of July 4, Lee began to retreat southward while storm clouds deluged the country with rain. When Lee reached the Potomac with his defeated army, he found a swollen, impassable river in front of him, and a victorious Union army behind him. Lee was in a trap. He couldn't escape. Lincoln saw that. Here was a golden, heaven-sent opportunity—the opportunity to capture Lee's army and end the war immediately. So, with a surge of high hope, Lincoln ordered Meade not to call a council of war but to attack Lee immediately. Lincoln telegraphed his orders and then sent a special messenger to Meade demanding immediate action.

And what did General Meade do? He did the very opposite of what he was told to do. He called a council of war in direct violation of Lincoln's orders. He hesitated. He procrastinated. He telegraphed all manner of excuses. He refused point blank to attack Lee. Finally the waters receded and Lee escaped over the Potomac with his forces.

Lincoln was furious. "What does this mean?" Lincoln cried to his son Robert. "Great God! What does this mean? We had them within our grasp, and had only to stretch forth our hands and they were ours; yet nothing that I could say or do could make the army move. Under the circumstances, almost any general could have defeated Lee. If I had gone up there, I could have whipped him myself."

In bitter disappointment, Lincoln sat down and wrote Meade this letter. And remember, at this period of his life he was extremely conservative and restrained in his phraseology. So this letter coming from Lincoln in 1863 was tantamount to the severest rebuke.

"My dear General,

"I do not believe you appreciate the magnitude of the misfortune involved in Lee's escape. He was within our easy grasp, and to have closed upon him would, in connection with our other late successes, have ended the war. As it is, the war will be prolonged indefinitely. If you could not safely attack Lee last Monday, how can you possibly do so south of the river, when you can take with you very few—no more than two-thirds of the force you then had in hand? It would be unreasonable to expect and I do not expect that you can now effect much. Your golden opportunity is gone, and I am distressed immeasurably because of it."

What do you suppose Meade did when he read that letter?

Meade never saw that letter. Lincoln never mailed it. It was found among Lincoln's papers after his death.

My guess is—and this is only a guess—that after writing that letter, Lincoln looked out of the window and said to himself, "Just a minute. Maybe I ought not to be so hasty. It is easy enough for me to sit here in the quiet of the White House and order Meade to attack; but if I had been up at Gettysburg, and if I had seen as much blood as Meade has seen during the last week, and if my ears had been pierced with the screams and shrieks of the wounded and dying, maybe I wouldn't be so anxious to attack either. If I had Meade's timid temperament, perhaps I would have done just what he has done. Anyhow, it is water under the bridge now. If I send this letter, it will relieve my feelings but it will make Meade try to justify himself. It will make him condemn me. It will arouse hard feelings, impair all his further usefulness as a commander, and perhaps force him to resign from the army."

So, as I have already said, Lincoln put the letter aside, for he had learned by bitter experience that sharp criticisms and rebukes almost invariably end in futility.

Theodore Roosevelt said that when he, as President, was confronted with some perplexing problem, he used to lean back and look up at a large painting of Lincoln that hung above his desk in the White House and ask himself, "What would Lincoln do if he were in my shoes? How would he solve this problem?"

The next time we are tempted to give somebody "hail Columbia," let's pull a five-dollar bill out of our pocket, look at Lincoln's picture on the bill, and ask, "How would Lincoln handle this problem if he had it?"

Do you know someone you would like to change and regulate and improve? Good! That is fine. I am all in favor of it. But why not begin on yourself? From a purely selfish standpoint, that is a lot more profitable than trying to improve others—yes, and a lot less dangerous.

"When a man's fight begins within himself," said Browning, "he is worth something." It will probably take from now until Christmas to perfect yourself. You can then have a nice long rest over the holidays and devote the New Year to regulating and criticizing other people.

But perfect yourself first.

"Don't complain about the snow on your neighbor's roof," said Confucius, "when your own doorstep is unclean."

When I was still young and trying hard to impress people, I wrote a foolish letter to Richard Harding Davis, an author who once loomed large on the literary horizon of America. I was preparing a magazine article about authors; and I asked Davis to tell me about his method of work. A few weeks earlier, I had received a letter from someone with this notation at the bottom: "Dictated but not read." I was quite impressed. I felt the writer must be very big and busy and important. I wasn't the slightest bit busy; but I was eager to make an impression on Richard Harding Davis so I ended my short note with the words: "Dictated but not read."

He never troubled to answer the letter. He simply returned it to me with this scribbled across the bottom: "Your bad manners are exceeded only by your bad manners." True, I had blundered, and perhaps I deserved his rebuke. But, being human, I resented it. I resented it so sharply that when I read of the death of Richard Harding Davis ten years later, the one thought that still persisted in my mind—I am ashamed to admit—was the hurt he had given me.

If you and I want to stir up a resentment tomorrow that may rankle across the decades and endure until death, just let us indulge in a little stinging criticism—no matter how certain we are that it is justified.

When dealing with people, let us remember we are not dealing with creatures of logic. We are dealing with creatures of emotion, creatures bristling with prejudices and motivated by pride and vanity.

And criticism is a dangerous spark—a spark that is liable to cause an explosion in the powder magazine of pride—an explosion that sometimes hastens death. For example, General Leonard Wood was criticized and not allowed to go with the army to France. That blow to his pride probably shortened his life.

Bitter criticism caused the sensitive Thomas Hardy, one of the finest novelists that ever enriched English literature, to give up the writing of fiction forever. Criticism drove Thomas Chatterton, the English poet, to suicide.

Benjamin Franklin, tactless in his youth, became so diplomatic, so adroit at handling people that he was made American Ambassador to France. The secret of his success? "I will speak ill of no man," he said, ". . . and speak all the good I know of everybody."

Any fool can criticize, condemn, and complain—and most fools do.

But it takes character and self-control to be understanding and forgiving.

"A great man shows his greatness," said Carlyle, "by the way he treats little men."

Instead of condemning people, let's try to understand them. Let's try to figure out why they do what they do. That's a lot more profitable and intriguing than criticism; and it breeds sympathy, tolerance, and kindness. "To know all is to forgive all."

As Dr. Johnson said: "God Himself, sir, does not propose to judge man until the end of his days."

Why should you and I?

DISCUSSION QUESTIONS

1. Discuss whether Carnegie's prose style is an implementation of his contention that "When dealing with people, let us remember we are not dealing with creatures of logic. We are dealing with creatures of emotion, creatures bristling with prejudices and motivated by pride and vanity." How does Carnegie try to convince his audience of the benefits to be gained by refraining from personal criticism?
2. Compare the sense of an audience implicit in *How to Win Friends and Influence People* with the audience imagined for Funk and Lewis's *Thirty Days to a More Powerful Vocabulary*. What characteristics are common to the audiences anticipated by these writers? What distinctions can you make between these audiences? Show how the writer's particular ways of talking are indicative of the readers they imagine for their prose. How does the fact that these writers achieved a great deal of success affect the voices they adopt when addressing their readers?

Wilfred Funk and Norman Lewis / *Thirty Days to a More Powerful Vocabulary* 1942

Written in 1942 by Wilfred Funk, lexicographer, publisher, and author, and Norman Lewis, instructor in English at the City College of New York and New York University, Thirty Days to a More Powerful Vocabulary *has been one of the most widely used "how-to-do-it" books published in this country. As an introductory pep talk, "Give Us 15 Minutes a Day" started millions of students and adults off on a self-improvement regimen that promised nothing less than success and personal fulfillment when the exercises were completed.*

FIRST DAY: GIVE US 15 MINUTES A DAY

Your boss has a bigger vocabulary than you have.

That's one good reason why he's your boss.

This discovery has been made in the word laboratories of the world. Not by theoretical English professors, but by practical, hard-headed scholars who have been searching for the secrets of success.

After a host of experiments and years of testing they have found out:

> That if your vocabulary is limited your chances of success are limited.
>
> That one of the easiest and quickest ways to get ahead is by consciously building up your knowledge of words.

That the vocabulary of the average person almost stops growing by the middle twenties.

And that from then on it is necessary to have an intelligent plan if progress is to be made. No haphazard hit-or-miss methods will do.

It has long since been satisfactorily established that a high executive does not have a large vocabulary merely because of the opportunities of his position. That would be putting the cart before the horse. Quite the reverse is true. His skill in words was a tremendous help in getting him his job.

Dr. Johnson O'Connor of the Human Engineering Laboratory of Boston and of the Stevens Institute of Technology in Hoboken, New Jersey, gave a vocabulary test to 100 young men who were studying to be industrial executives.

Five years later those who had passed in the upper ten per cent *all,* without exception, had executive positions, while *not a single young man of the lower twenty-five per cent had become an executive.*

You see, there are certain factors in success that can be measured as scientifically as the contents of a test-tube, and it has been discovered that the most common characteristic of outstanding success is "an extensive knowledge of the exact meaning of English words."

The extent of your vocabulary indicates the degree of your intelligence. Your brain power will increase as you learn to know more words. Here's the proof.

Two classes in a high school were selected for an experiment. Their ages and their environment were the same. Each class represented an identical cross-section of the community. One, the control class, took the normal courses. The other class was given special vocabulary training. At the end of the period the marks of the latter class surpassed those of the control group, not only in English, but in every subject, including mathematics and the sciences.

Similarly it has been found by Professor Lewis M. Terman, of Stanford University, that a vocabulary test is as accurate a measure of intelligence as any three units of the standard and accepted Stanford-Binet I. Q. tests.

The study of words is not merely something that has to do with literature. Words are your tools of thought. *You can't even think at all without them.* Try it. If you are planning to go down town this afternoon you will find that you are saying to yourself: "I think I will go down town this afternoon." You can't make such a simple decision as this without using words.

Without words you could make no decisions and form no judgments whatsoever. A pianist may have the most beautiful tunes in his head, but if he had only five keys on his piano he would never get more than a fraction of these tunes out.

Your words are *your* keys for *your* thoughts. And the more words you have at your command the deeper, clearer and more accurate will be your thinking.

A command of English will not only improve the processes of your mind. It will give you assurance; build your self-confidence; lend color to your personality; increase your popularity. Your words are your personality. Your vocabulary is you.

Your words are all that we, your friends, have to know and judge you by. You have no other medium for telling us your thoughts—for convincing us, persuading us, giving us orders.

Words are explosive. Phrases are packed with TNT. A simple word can destroy a friendship, land a large order. The proper phrases in the mouths of clerks have quadrupled the sales of a department store. The wrong words used by a campaign orator have lost an election. For instance, on one occasion the four unfortunate words, "Rum, Romanism and Rebellion" used in a Republican campaign speech threw the Catholic vote and the presidential victory to Grover Cleveland. Wars are won by words. Soldiers fight for a phrase. "Make the world safe for Democracy." "All out for England." "V for Victory." The "Remember the Maine" of Spanish war days has now been changed to "Remember Pearl Harbor."

Words have changed the direction of history. Words can also change the direction of your life. They have often raised a man from mediocrity to success.

If you consciously increase your vocabulary you will unconsciously raise yourself to a more important station in life, and the new and higher position you have won will, in turn, give you a better opportunity for further enriching your vocabulary. It is a beautiful and successful cycle.

It is because of this intimate connection between words and life itself that we have organized this small volume in a new way. We have not given you mere lists of unrelated words to learn. We have grouped the words around various departments of your life.

This book is planned to enlist your active cooperation. The authors wish you to read it with a pencil in your hand, for you will often be asked to make certain notations, to write answers to particular questions. The more you use your pencil, the more deeply you will become involved, and the deeper your involvement the more this book will help you. We shall occasionally ask you to use your voice as well as your pencil—to say things out loud. You see, we really want you to keep up a running conversation with us.

It's fun. And it's so easy. And we've made it like a game. We have filled these pages with a collection of devices that we hope will be stimulating. Here are things to challenge you and your friends. Try these tests on your acquaintances. They will enjoy them and it may encourage them to wider explorations in this exciting field of speech. There are entertaining verbal calisthenics here, colorful facts about language, and many excursions among the words that keep our speech the rich, flexible, lively means of communication that it is.

Come to this book every day. Put the volume by your bedside, if you like. A short time spent on these pages before you turn the lights out each night is better than an irregular hour now and then. If you can find the time to learn only two or three words a day—we will still promise you that at the end of thirty days you will have found a new interest. Give us *fifteen minutes a day,* and we will guarantee, at the end of a month, when you have turned over the last page of this book, that your words and your reading and your conversation and your life will all have a new and deeper meaning for you.

For words can make you great!

Ogden Nash / Kindly Unhitch That Star, Buddy 1945

Few writers, especially in the twentieth century, have been able to earn a living exclusively by writing poetry. Ogden Nash is one who has. The Pocket Book of Ogden Nash *(1935) ranks among the top ten poetry best-sellers of the last eighty years, and nearly every volume of his poetry from* Free Wheeling *(1931) to* Boy Is a Boy *(1960) has found a highly receptive audience.*

Nash (1902–71) is a master of what is usually termed "light verse"—poetry that is witty, humorous, often sophisticated, and not without a slight sting of satire. Nash brought to light verse an exceptionally playful imagination, one that enjoyed challenging the conventions of language and poetry without surrendering a stroke of technical virtuosity. Like the Depression film comedies that were popular just around the time his first volumes began to appear, Nash's verse succeeded in striking a fine balance between tough talk and innocence, urbanity and absurdity.

The following poem, which takes its lead from Ralph Waldo Emerson's advice that we "hitch our wagon to a star," appeared in Many Long Years Ago *(1945).*

I hardly suppose I know anybody who wouldn't rather be a success than a failure,
Just as I suppose every piece of crabgrass in the garden would much rather be an azalea,
And in celestial circles all the run-of-the-mill angels would rather be archangels or at least cherubim and seraphim,
And in the legal world all the little process-servers hope to grow up into great big bailiffim and sheriffim.
Indeed, everybody wants to be a wow,
But not everybody knows exactly how.
Some people think they will eventually wear diamonds instead of rhinestones
Only by everlastingly keeping their noses to their ghrine-stones,
And other people think they will be able to put in more time at Palm Beach and the Ritz
By not paying too much attention to attendance at the office but rather in being brilliant by starts and fits.
Some people after a full day's work sit up all night getting a college education by correspondence,
While others seem to think they'll get just as far by devoting their evenings to the study of the difference in temperament between brunettance and blondance.
In short, the world is filled with people trying to achieve success,
And half of them think they'll get it by saying No and half of them by saying Yes,
And if all the ones who say No said Yes, and vice versa, such is the fate of humanity that ninety-nine per cent of them still wouldn't be any better off than they were before,
Which perhaps is just as well because if everybody was a success nobody could be contemptuous of anybody else and everybody would start in all over again trying to be a bigger success than everybody else so they would have somebody to be contemptuous of and so on forevermore,
Because when people start hitching their wagons to a star,
That's the way they are.

Mickey Spillane / *I, the Jury*

[Mike Hammer Plots Revenge] 1947

Born in 1918 in Brooklyn, the son of an Irish bartender, Mickey Spillane grew up in what he calls a "very tough neighborhood in Elizabeth, New Jersey." He attended Kansas State College, worked summers as captain of lifeguards at Breezy Point, New York, and supplemented his income by writing comic books. In 1935, Spillane began selling stories to detective magazines, and after flying fighter missions in World War II, he worked as a trampoline artist for the Ringling Brothers Circus. Since his first novel, I, the Jury, *published in 1947, Spillane's books have had extraordinary sales. At one time seven of his novels were included in a list of the top ten best-selling fiction works of the last fifty years. Many of the novels have been turned into movies, a few with Spillane playing the role of Mike Hammer.*

CHAPTER ONE

I shook the rain from my hat and walked into the room. Nobody said a word. They stepped back politely and I could feel their eyes on me. Pat Chambers was standing by the door to the bedroom trying to steady Myrna. The girl's body was racking with dry sobs. I walked over and put my arms around her.

"Take it easy, kid," I told her. "Come on over here and lie down." I led her to a studio couch that was against the far wall and sat her down. She was in pretty bad shape. One of the uniformed cops put a pillow down for her and she stretched out.

Pat motioned me over to him and pointed to the bedroom. "In there, Mike," he said.

In there. The words hit me hard. In there was my best friend lying on the floor dead. The body. Now I could call it that. Yesterday it was Jack Williams, the guy that shared the same mud bed with me through two years of warfare in the stinking slime of the jungle. Jack, the guy who said he'd give his right arm for a friend and did when he stopped a bastard of a Jap from slitting me in two. He caught the bayonet in the biceps and they amputated his arm.

Pat didn't say a word. He let me uncover the body and feel the cold face. For the first time in my life I felt like crying. "Where did he get it, Pat?"

"In the stomach. Better not look at it. The killer carved the nose off a forty-five and gave it to him low."

I threw back the sheet anyway and a curse caught in my throat. Jack was in shorts, his one hand still clutching his belly in agony. The bullet went in clean, but where it came out left a hole big enough to cram a fist into.

Very gently I pulled the sheet back and stood up. It wasn't a complicated setup. A trail of blood led from the table beside the bed to where Jack's artificial arm lay. Under him the throw rug was ruffled and twisted. He had tried to drag himself along with his one arm, but never reached what he was after.

His police positive, still in the holster, was looped over the back of the chair. That was what he wanted. With a slug in his gut he never gave up.

I pointed to the rocker, overbalanced under the weight of the .38. "Did you move the chair, Pat?"

"No, why?"

"It doesn't belong there. Don't you see?"

Pat looked puzzled. "What are you getting at?"

"That chair was over there by the bed. I've been here often enough to remember that much. After the killer shot Jack, he pulled himself toward the chair. But the killer didn't leave after the shooting. He stood here and watched him grovel on the floor in agony. Jack was after that gun, but he never reached it. He could have if the killer didn't move it. The trigger-happy bastard must have stood by the door laughing while Jack tried to make his last play. He kept pulling the chair back, inch by inch, until Jack gave up. Tormenting a guy who's been through all sorts of hell. Laughing. This was no ordinary murder, Pat. It's as cold-blooded and as deliberate as I ever saw one. I'm going to get the one that did this."

"You dealing yourself in, Mike?"

"I'm in. What did you expect?"

"You're going to have to go easy."

"Uh-uh. Fast, Pat. From now on it's a race. I want the killer for myself. We'll work together as usual, but in the homestretch, I'm going to pull the trigger."

"No, Mike, it can't be that way. You know it."

"Okay, Pat," I told him. "You have a job to do, but so have I. Jack was about the best friend I ever had. We lived together and fought together. And by Christ, I'm not letting the killer go through the tedious process of the law. You know what happens, damn it. They get the best lawyer there is and screw up the whole thing and wind up a hero! The dead can't speak for themselves. They can't tell what happened. How could Jack tell a jury what it was like to have his insides ripped out by a dumdum? Nobody in the box would know how it felt to be dying or have your own killer laugh in your face. One arm. Hell, what does that mean? So he has the Purple Heart. But did they ever try dragging themselves across a floor to a gun with that one arm, their insides filling up with blood, so goddamn mad to be shot they'd do anything to reach the killer. No, damn it. A jury is cold and impartial like they're supposed to be, while some snotty lawyer makes them pour tears as he tells how his client was insane at the moment or had to shoot in self-defense. Swell. The law is fine. But this time I'm the law and I'm not going to be cold and impartial. I'm going to remember all those things."

I reached out and grabbed the lapels of his coat. "And something more, Pat. I want you to hear every word I say. I want you to tell it to everyone you know. And when you tell it, tell it strong, because I mean every word of it. There are ten thousand mugs that hate me and you know it. They hate me because if they mess with me I shoot their damn heads off. I've done it and I'll do it again."

There was so much hate welled up inside me I was ready to blow up, but I turned and looked down at what was once Jack. Right then I felt like saying a prayer, but I was too mad.

"Jack, you're dead now. You can't hear me any more. Maybe you can. I hope so. I want you to hear what I'm about to say. You've known me a long time, Jack. My word is good just as long as I live. I'm going to get the louse that killed you. He won't sit in the chair. He won't hang. He will die exactly as you died, with a .45 slug in the gut, just a little below the belly button. No matter who it is, Jack, I'll get the one. Remember, no matter who it is, I promise."

When I looked up, Pat was staring at me strangely. He shook his head. I knew what he was thinking. "Mike, lay off. For God's sake don't go off half-cocked about this. I know you too well. You'll start shooting up anyone connected with this and get in a jam you'll never get out of."

"I'm over it now, Pat. Don't get excited. From now on I'm after one thing, the killer. You're a cop, Pat. You're tied down by rules and regulations. There's someone over you. I'm alone. I can slap someone in the puss and they can't do a damn thing. No one can kick me out of my job. Maybe there's nobody to put up a huge fuss if I get gunned down, but then I still have a private cop's license with the privilege to pack a rod, and they're afraid of me. I hate hard, Pat. When I latch on to the one behind this they're going to wish they hadn't started it. Some day, before long, I'm going to have my rod in my mitt and the killer in front of me. I'm going to watch the killer's face. I'm going to plunk one right in his gut, and when he's dying on the floor I may kick his teeth out.

"You couldn't do that. You have to follow the book because you're a Captain of Homicide. Maybe the killer will wind up in the chair. You'd be satisfied, but I wouldn't. It's too easy. That killer is going down like Jack did."

There was nothing more to say. I could see by the set of Pat's jaw that he wasn't going to try to talk me out of it. All he could do was to try to beat me to him and take it from there. We walked out of the room together. The coroner's men had arrived and were ready to carry the body away.

I didn't want Myrna to see that. I sat down on the couch beside her and let her sob on my shoulder. That way I managed to shield her from the sight of her fiancé being carted off in a wicker basket. She was a good kid. Four years ago, when Jack was on the force, he had grabbed her as she was about to do a Dutch over the Brooklyn

Bridge. She was a wreck then. Dope had eaten her nerve ends raw. But he had taken her to his house and paid for a full treatment until she was normal. For the both of them it had been a love that blossomed into a beautiful thing. If it weren't for the war they would have been married long ago.

When Jack came back with one arm it had made no difference. He no longer was a cop, but his heart was with the force. She had loved him before and she still loved him. Jack wanted her to give up her job, but Myrna persuaded him to let her hold it until he really got settled. It was tough for a man with one arm to find employment, but he had many friends.

Before long he was part of the investigating staff of an insurance company. It had to be police work. For Jack there was nothing else. Then they were happy. Then they were going to be married. Now this.

Pat tapped me on the shoulder. ''There's a car waiting downstairs to take her home.''

I rose and took her by the hand. ''Come on, kid. There's no more you can do. Let's go.''

She didn't say a word, but stood up silently and let a cop steer her out the door. I turned to Pat. ''Where do we start?'' I asked him.

''Well, I'll give you as much as I know. See what you can add to it. You and Jack were great buddies. It might be that you can add something that will make some sense.''

Inwardly I wondered. Jack was such a straight guy that he never made an enemy. Even while on the force. Since he'd gotten back, his work with the insurance company was pretty routine. But maybe an angle there, though.

''Jack threw a party last night,'' Pat went on. ''Not much of an affair.''

''I know,'' I cut in, ''he called me and asked me over, but I was pretty well knocked out. I hit the sack early. Just a group of old friends he knew before the army.''

''Yeah. We got their names from Myrna. The boys are checking on them now.''

''Who found the body?'' I asked.

''Myrna did. She and Jack were driving out to the country today to pick a building site for their cottage. She got here at eight A.M. or a little after. When Jack didn't answer, she got worried. His arm had been giving him trouble lately and she thought it might have been that. She called the super. He knew her and let her in. When she screamed the super came running back and called us. Right after I got the story about the party from her, she broke down completely. Then I called you.''

''What time did the shooting occur?''

''The coroner places it about five hours before I got here. That would make it about three fifteen. When I get an autopsy report we may be able to narrow it down even further.''

''Anyone hear a shot?''

''Nope. It probably was a silenced gun.''

''Even with a muffler, a .45 makes a good-sized noise.''

''I know, but there was a party going on down the hall. Not loud enough to cause complaints, but enough to cover up any racket that might have been made here.''

''What about those that were here?'' Pat reached in his pocket and pulled out a pad. He ripped a leaf loose and handed it to me.

''Here's a list Myrna gave me. She was the first to arrive. Got here at eight thirty last night. She acted as hostess, meeting the others at the door. The last one came about eleven. They spent the evening doing some light drinking and dancing, then left as a group about one.''

I looked at the names Pat gave me. A few of them I knew well enough, while a couple of the others were people of whom Jack had spoken, but I had never met.

''Where did they go after the party, Pat?''

"They took two cars. The one Myrna went in belonged to Hal Kines. They drove straight up to Westchester, dropping Myrna off on the way. I haven't heard from any of the others yet."

Both of us were silent for a moment, then Pat asked, "What about a motive, Mike?"

I shook my head. "I don't see any yet. But I will. He wasn't killed for nothing. I'll bet this much, whatever it was, was big. There's a lot here that's screwy. You got anything?"

"Nothing more than I gave you, Mike. I was hoping you could supply some answers."

I grinned at him, but I wasn't trying to be funny. "Not yet. Not yet. They'll come though. And I'll relay them on to you, but by that time I'll be working on the next step."

"The cops aren't exactly dumb, you know. We can get our own answers."

"Not like I can. That's why you buzzed me so fast. You can figure things out as quickly as I can, but you haven't got the ways and means of doing the dirty work. That's where I come in. You'll be right behind me every inch of the way, but when the pinch comes I'll get shoved aside and you slap the cuffs on. That is, if you can shove me aside. I don't think you can."

"Okay, Mike, call it your own way. I want you in all right. But I want the killer, too. Don't forget that. I'll be trying to beat you to him. We have every scientific facility at our disposal and a lot of men to do the leg work. We're not short in brains, either," he reminded me.

"Don't worry, I don't underrate the cops. But cops can't break a guy's arm to make him talk, and they can't shove his teeth in with the muzzle of a .45 to remind him that you aren't fooling. I do my own leg work, and there are a lot of guys who will tell me what I want to know because they know what I'll do to them if they don't. My staff is strictly ex officio, but very practical."

That ended the conversation. We walked out into the hall where Pat put a patrolman on the door to make sure things stayed as they were. We took the self-operated elevator down four flights to the lobby and I waited while Pat gave a brief report to some reporters.

My car stood at the curb behind the squad car. I shook hands with Pat and climbed into my jalopy and headed for the Hackard Building, where I held down a two-room suite to use for operation.

CHAPTER TWO

The office was locked when I got there. I kicked on the door a few times and Velda clicked the lock back. When she saw who it was she said, "Oh, it's you."

"What do you mean—'Oh, it's you'! Surely you remember me, Mike Hammer, your boss."

"Poo! You haven't been here in so long I can't tell you from another bill collector." I closed the door and followed her into my sanctum sanctorum. She had million-dollar legs, that girl, and she didn't mind showing them off. For a secretary she was an awful distraction. She kept her coal-black hair long in a page-boy cut and wore tight-fitting dresses that made me think of the curves in the Pennsylvania Highway every time I looked at her. Don't get the idea that she was easy, though. I've seen her give a few punks the brush off the hard way. When it came to quick action she could whip off a shoe and crack a skull before you could bat an eye.

Not only that, but she had a private op's ticket and on occasions when she went out with me on a case, packed a flat .32 automatic—and she wasn't afraid to use it. In the three years she worked for me I never made a pass at her. Not that I didn't want to, but it would be striking too close to home.

Velda picked up her pad and sat down. I plunked myself in the old swivel chair, then swung around facing the window. Velda threw a thick packet on my desk.

"Here's all the information I could get on those that were at the party last night." I looked at her sharply.

"How did you know about Jack? Pat only called my home." Velda wrinkled that pretty face of hers up into a cute grin.

"You forget that I have an in with a few reporters. Tom Dugan from the *Chronicle* remembered that you and Jack had been good friends. He called here to see what he could get and wound up by giving me all the info he had—and I didn't have to sex him, either." She put that in as an afterthought. "Most of the gang at the party were listed in your files. Nothing sensational. I got a little data from Tom who had more personal dealings with a few of them. Mostly character studies and some society reports. Evidently they were people whom Jack had met in the past and liked. You've even spoken about several yourself."

I tore open the package and glanced at a sheaf of photos. "Who are these?" Velda looked over my shoulder and pointed them out.

"Top one is Hal Kines, a med student from a university upstate. He's about twenty-three, tall, and looks like a crew man. At least that's the way he cuts his hair." She flipped the page over. "These two are the Bellemy twins. Age, twenty-nine, unmarried. In the market for husbands. Live off the fatta the land with dough their father left them. A half interest in some textile mills someplace down South."

"Yeah," I cut in, "I know them. Good lookers, but not very bright. I met them at Jack's place once and again at a dinner party."

She pointed to the next one. A newspaper shot of a middle-aged guy with a broken nose. George Kalecki. I knew him pretty well. In the roaring twenties he was a bootlegger. He came out of the crash with a million dollars, paid up his income tax, and went society. He fooled a lot of people but he didn't fool me. He still had his finger in a lot of games just to keep in practice. Nothing you could pin on him though. He kept a staff of lawyers on their toes to keep him clean and they were doing a good job. "What about him?" I asked her.

"You know more than I do. Hal Kines is staying with him. They live about a mile above Myrna in Westchester." I nodded. I remembered Jack talking about him. He had met George through Hal. The kid had been a friend of George ever since the older man had met him through some mutual acquaintance. George was the guy that was putting him through college, but why, I wasn't sure.

The next shot was one of Myrna with a complete history of her that Jack had given me. Included was a medical record from the hospital when he had made her go cold turkey, which is dope-addict talk for an all-out cure. They cut them off from the stuff completely. It either kills them or cures them. In Myrna's case, she made it. But she made Jack promise that he would never try to get any information from her about where she got the stuff. The way he fell for the girl, he was ready to do anything she asked, and so far as he was concerned, the matter was completely dropped.

I flipped through the medical record. Name, Myrna Devlin. Attempted suicide while under the influence of heroin. Brought to emergency ward of General Hospital by Detective Jack Williams. Admitted 3-15-40. Treatment complete 9-21-40. No information available on patient's source of narcotics. Released into custody of Detective Jack Williams 9-30-40. Following this was a page of medical details which I skipped.

"Here's one you'll like, chum," Velda grinned at me. She pulled out a full-length photo of a gorgeous blonde. My heart jumped when I saw it. The picture was taken at a beach, and she stood there tall and languid-looking in a white bathing suit. Long solid legs. A little heavier than the movie experts consider good form, but the kind that make you drool to look at. Under the suit I could see the muscles of her stomach. Incredibly wide shoulders for a woman, framing breasts that jutted out, seeking freedom from the restraining fabric of the suit. Her hair looked white in the picture, but I could tell that it was a natural blonde. Lovely, lovely yellow hair. But her face was what got me. I thought Velda was a good looker, but this one was even lovelier. I felt like whistling.

"Who is she?"

"Maybe I shouldn't tell you. That leer on your face could get you into trouble, but it's all there. Name's Charlotte Manning. She's a female psychiatrist with offices on Park Avenue, and very successful. I understand she caters to a pretty ritzy clientele."

I glanced at the number and made up my mind that right here was something that made this business a pleasurable one. I didn't say that to Velda. Maybe I'm being conceited, but I've always had the impression that she had designs on me. Of course she never mentioned it, but whenever I showed up late in the office with lipstick on my shirt collar, I couldn't get two words out of her for a week.

I stacked the sheaf back on my desk and swung around in the chair. Velda was leaning forward ready to take notes. "Want to add anything, Mike?"

"Don't think so. At least not now. There's too much to think about first. Nothing seems to make sense."

"Well, what about motive? Could Jack have had any enemies that caught up with him?"

"Nope. None I know of. He was square. He always gave a guy a break if he deserved it. Then, too, he never was wrapped up in anything big."

"Did he own anything of any importance?"

"Not a thing. The place was completely untouched. He had a few hundred dollars in his wallet that was lying on the dresser. The killing was done by a sadist. He tried to reach his gun, but the killer pulled the chair it hung on back slowly, making him crawl after it with a slug in his gut, trying to keep his insides from falling out with his hand."

"Mike, please."

I said no more. I just sat there and glowered at the wall. Someday I'd trigger the bastard that shot Jack. In my time I've done it plenty of times. No sentiment. That went out with the first. After the war I've been almost anxious to get to some of the rats that make up the section of humanity that prey on people. People. How incredibly stupid they could be sometimes. A trial by law for a killer. A loophole in the phrasing that lets a killer crawl out. But in the end the people have their justice. They get it through guys like me once in a while. They crack down on society and I crack down on them. I shoot them like the mad dogs they are and society drags me to court to explain the whys and wherefores of the extermination. They investigate my past, check my fingerprints and throw a million questions my way. The papers make me look like a kill-crazy shamus, but they don't bear down too hard because Pat Chambers keeps them off my neck. Besides, I do my best to help the boys out and they know it. And I'm usually good for a story when I wind up a case.

Velda came back into the office with the afternoon edition of the sheets. The kill was spread all over the front page, followed by a four-column layout of what details were available. Velda was reading over my shoulder and I heard her gasp.

"Did you come in for a blasting! Look." She was pointing to the last paragraph. There was my tie-up with the case, but what she was referring to was the word-for-word statement that I had made to Jack. My promise. My word to a dead friend that I would kill this murderer as he had killed him. I rolled the paper into a ball and threw it viciously at the wall.

"The louse! I'll break his filthy neck for printing that. I meant what I said when I made that promise. It's sacred to me, and they make a joke out of it. Pat did that. And I thought he was a friend. Give me the phone."

Velda grabbed my arm. "Take it easy. Suppose he did. After all, Pat's still a cop. Maybe he saw a chance of throwing the killer your way. If the punk knows you're after him for keeps he's liable not to take it standing still and make a play for you. Then you'll have him."

"Thanks, kid," I told her, "but your mind's too clean. I think you got the first part right, but your guess on the last part smells. Pat doesn't want me to have any part of him because he knows the case is ended right there. If he can get the killer to me you can bet your grandmother's uplift bra that he'll have a tail on me all the way with someone ready to step in when the shooting starts."

"I don't know about that, Mike. Pat knows you're too smart not to recognize when you're being tailed. I wouldn't think he'd do that."

"Oh, no? He isn't dumb by any means. I'll bet you a sandwich against a marriage license he's got a flatfoot downstairs covering every exit in the place ready to pick me up when I leave. Sure, I'll shake them, but it won't stop there. A couple of experts will take up where they leave off."

Velda's eyes were glowing like a couple of hot brands. "Are you serious about that? About the bet, I mean?"

I nodded. "Dead serious. Want to go downstairs with me and take a look?" She grinned and grabbed her coat. I pulled on my battered felt and we left the office, but not before I had taken a second glance at the office address of Charlotte Manning.

Pete, the elevator operator, gave me a toothy grin when we stepped into the car. "Evening, Mr. Hammer," he said.

I gave him an easy jab in the short ribs and said, "What's new with you?"

"Nothing much, 'cepting I don't get to sit down much on the job anymore." I had to grin. Velda had lost the bet already. That little piece of simple repartee between Pete and myself was a code system we had rigged up years ago. His answer meant that I was going to have company when I left the building. It cost me a fin a week but it was worth it. Pete could spot a flatfoot faster than I can. He should. He had been a pickpocket until a long stretch up the river gave him a turn of mind.

For a change I decided to use the front entrance. I looked around for my tail but there was none to be seen. For a split second my heart leaped into my throat. I was afraid Pete had gotten his signals crossed. Velda was a spotter, too, and the smile she was wearing as we crossed the empty lobby was a thing to see. She clamped onto my arm ready to march me to the nearest justice of the peace.

But when I went through the revolving doors her grin passed as fast as mine appeared. Our tail was walking in front of us. Velda said a word that nice girls don't usually use, and you see scratched in the cement by some evil-minded guttersnipe.

This one was smart. We never saw where he came from. He walked a lot faster than we did, swinging a newspaper from his hand against his leg. Probably, he spotted us through the windows behind the palm, then seeing what exit we were going to use, walked around the corner and came past us as we left. If we had gone the other way, undoubtedly there was another ready to pick us up.

But this one had forgotten to take his gun off his hip and stow it under his shoulder, and guns make a bump look the size of a pumpkin when you're used to looking for them.

When I reached the garage he was nowhere to be seen. There were a lot of doors he could have ducked behind. I didn't waste time looking for him. I backed the car out and Velda crawled in beside me. "Where to now?" she asked.

"The automat, where you're going to buy me a sandwich."

Grace Metalious / *Peyton Place*
[Michael Rossi Comes to Peyton Place] 1956

One of the greatest-selling novels in American publishing history was written by a New Hampshire housewife with little formal education and no literary background or cultural advantages. Born in Manchester, New Hampshire, in 1924, Grace Marie Antoinette Jeanne d'Arc de Repentigny was the daughter of parents who had not much more to give her than her fancy name. At seventeen she married George Metalious, a mill worker, who later put himself through college to become a schoolteacher only to lose his job as a result of the public scandal caused by his wife's novel. What is perhaps most remarkable about Peyton Place, *for all its faults of gracelessness and composition, is not that the book became a best-seller so unexpectedly and rapidly, but that a generally uneducated young woman, with three small children and very little money, had the literary ambition and steady application needed to write publishable fiction.*

Metalious was a tough-talking, hard-working, hard-drinking woman. Like many authors of best-sellers, she was often defensive about her work. "If I'm a lousy writer," she once said, "a hell of a lot of people have got lousy taste." She died at the age of thirty-nine of a severe liver ailment.

A few days later, Michael Rossi stepped off the train in front of the Peyton Place railroad station. No other passenger got off with him. He paused on the empty platform and looked around thoroughly, for it was a habit with him to fix a firm picture of a new place in his mind so that it could never be erased nor forgotten. He stood still, feeling the two heavy suitcases that he carried pulling at his arm muscles, and reflected that there wasn't much to see, nor to hear, for that matter. It was shortly after seven o'clock in the evening, but it might have been midnight or four in the morning for all the activity going on. Behind him there was nothing but the two curving railroad tracks and from a distance came the long-drawn-out wail of the train as it made the pull across the wide Connecticut River. And it was cold.

For April, thought Rossi, shrugging uncomfortably under his topcoat, it was damned cold.

Straight ahead of him stood the railroad station, a shabby wooden building with a severely pitched roof and several thin, Gothic-looking windows that gave it the air of a broken-down church. Nailed to the front of the building, at the far left of the front door, was a blue and white enameled sign. PEYTON PLACE, it read. POP. 3675.

Thirty-six seventy-five, thought Rossi, pushing open the railroad station's narrow door. Sounds like the price of a cheap suit.

The inside of the building was lit by several dim electric light bulbs suspended from fixtures which obviously had once burned gas, and there were rows of benches constructed of the most hideous wood obtainable, golden oak. No one was sitting on them. The brown, roughly plastered walls were trimmed with the same yellow wood and the floor was made of black and white marble. There was an iron-barred cage set into one wall and from behind this a straight, thin man with a pinched-looking nose, steel-rimmed glasses and a string tie stared at Rossi.

"Is there a place where I can check these?" asked the new principal, indicating the two bags at his feet.

"Next room," said the man in the cage.

"Thank you," said Rossi and made his way through a narrow archway into another, smaller room. It was a replica of the main room, complete with golden oak, marble and converted gas fixtures, but with the addition of two more doors. These were clearly labeled. MEN, said one. WOMEN, said the other. Against one wall there was a row of pale gray metal lockers, and to Rossi, these looked almost friendly. They were the only things in the station even faintly resembling anything he had ever seen in his life.

"Ah," he murmured, "shades of Grand Central," and bent to push his suitcases into one of the lockers. He deposited his dime, withdrew his key and noticed that his was the only locker in use.

Busy town, he thought, and walked back to the main room. His footsteps rang disquietingly on the scrubbed marble floor.

Leslie Harrington had instructed Rossi to call him at his home as soon as he got off the train, but Rossi by-passed the solitary telephone booth in the railroad station. He wanted to look at the town alone first, to see it through no one's eyes but his own. Besides, he had decided the night that Harrington had called long-distance that the chairman of the Peyton Place School Board sounded like a man puffed up with his own importance, and must therefore be a pain in the ass.

"Say, Dad," began Rossi, addressing the man in the cage.

"Name's Rhodes," said the old man.

"Mr. Rhodes," began Rossi again, "could you tell me how I can get into town from here? I noticed a distressing lack of taxicabs outside."

"Be damned peculiar if I couldn't."

"If you couldn't what?"

"Tell you how to get uptown. Been living here for over sixty years."

"That's interesting."

"You're Mr. Rossi, eh?"

"Admitted."

"Ain't you goin' to call up Leslie Harrington?"

"Later. I'd like to get a cup of coffee first. Listen, isn't there a cab to be had anywhere around here?"

"No."

Michael Rossi controlled a laugh. It was beginning to look as if everything he had ever heard about these sullen New Englanders was true. The old man in the cage gave the impression that he had been sucking lemons for years. Certainly sourness had not been one of the traits in that little Pittsburgh secretary who claimed to be from Boston, but she said herself that she was East Boston Irish, and therefore not reliably representative of New England.

"Do you mind, then, telling me how I can walk into town from here, Mr. Rhodes?" asked Rossi.

"Not at all," said the stationmaster, and Rossi noticed that he pronounced the three words as one: Notatall. "Just go out this front door, walk around the depot to the street and keep on walking for two blocks. That will bring you to Elm Street."

"Elm Street? Is that the main street?"

"Yes."

"I had the idea that the main streets of all small New England towns were named Main Street."

"Perhaps," said Mr. Rhodes, who prided himself, when annoyed, on enunciating his syllables, "it is true that the main streets of all *other* small towns are named Main Street. Not, however, in Peyton Place. Here the main street is called Elm Street."

Period. Paragraph, thought Rossi. Next question. "Peyton Place is an odd name," he said. "How did anyone come to pick that one?"

Mr. Rhodes drew back his hand and started to close the wooden panel that backed the iron bars of his cage.

"I am closing now, Mr. Rossi," he said. "And I suggest that you be on your way if you want to obtain a cup of coffee. Hyde's Diner closes in half an hour."

"Thank you," said Rossi to the wooden panel which was suddenly between him and Mr. Rhodes.

Friendly bastard, he thought, as he left the station and began to walk up the street labeled Depot.

Michael Rossi was a massively boned man with muscles that seemed to quiver every time he moved. In the steel mills of Pittsburgh he had looked, so one smitten secretary had told him, like a color illustration of a steelworker. His arms, beneath sleeves rolled above the elbow, were knotted powerfully, and the buttons of his work shirts always seemed about to pop off under the strain of trying to cover his chest. He was six feet four inches tall, weighed two hundred and twelve pounds, stripped, and looked like anything but a schoolteacher. In fact, the friendly secretary in Pittsburgh had told him that in his dark blue suit, white shirt and dark tie, he looked like a steelworker disguised as a schoolteacher, a fact which would not inspire trust in the heart of any New Englander.

Michael Rossi was a handsome man, in a dark-skinned, black-haired, obviously sexual way, and both men and women were apt to credit him more with attractiveness than intellect. This was a mistake, for Rossi had a mind as analytical as a mathematician's and as curious as a philosopher's. It was his curiosity which had prompted him to give up teaching for a year to go to work in Pittsburgh. He had learned more about economics, labor and capital in that one year than he had learned in ten years of reading books. He was thirty-six years old and totally lacking in regret over the fact that he had never stayed in one job long enough to "get ahead," as the Pittsburgh secretary put it. He was honest, completely lacking in diplomacy, and the victim of a vicious temper which tended to loosen a tongue that had learned to speak on the lower East Side of New York City.

Rossi was halfway through the second block on Depot Street, leading to Elm, when Parker Rhodes, at the wheel of an old sedan, passed him. The stationmaster looked out of the window on the driver's side of his car and looked straight through Peyton Place's new headmaster.

Sonofabitch, thought Rossi. Real friendly sonofabitch to offer me a lift in his junk heap of a car.

Then he smiled and wondered why Mr. Rhodes had been so sensitive on the subject of his town's name. He would ask around and see if everyone in this godforsaken place reacted the same way to his question. He had reached the corner of Elm Street and paused to look about him. On the corner stood a white, cupola-topped house with stiff lace curtains at the windows. Silhouetted against the light inside, he could see two women sitting at a table with what was obviously a checkerboard between them. The women were big, saggy bosomed and white haired, and Rossi thought that they looked like a pair who had worked too long at the same girls' school.

I wonder who they are? he asked himself, as he looked in at the Page Girls. Maybe they're the town's two Lizzies.

Reluctantly, he turned away from the white house and made his way west on Elm Street. When he had walked three blocks, he came to a small, clean-looking and well-lighted restaurant. *Hyde's Diner* said a polite neon sign, and Rossi opened the door and went in. The place was empty except for one old man sitting at the far end of the counter, and another man who came out of the kitchen at the sound of the door opening.

"Good evening, sir," said Corey Hyde.

"Good evening," said Rossi. "Coffee, please, and a piece of pie. Any kind."

"Apple, sir?"

"Any kind is O.K."

"Well, we have pumpkin, too."

"Apple is fine."

"I think there's a piece of cherry left, also."

"Apple," said Rossi, "will be fine."

"You're Mr. Rossi, aren't you?"

"Yes."

"Glad to meet you, Mr. Rossi. My name is Hyde. Corey Hyde."

"How do you do?"

"Quite well, as a rule," said Corey Hyde. "I'll keep on doing quite well, as long as no one starts up another restaurant."

"Look, could I have my coffee now?"

"Certainly. Certainly, Mr. Rossi."

The old man at the end of the counter sipped his coffee from a spoon and looked surreptitiously at the newcomer to town. Rossi wondered if the old man could be the village idiot.

"Here you are, Mr. Rossi," said Corey Hyde. "The best apple pie in Peyton Place."

"Thank you."

Rossi stirred sugar into his coffee and sampled the pie. It was excellent.

"Peyton Place," he said Corey Hyde, "is the oddest name for a town I've ever heard. Who is it named for?"

"Oh, I don't know," said Corey, making unnecessary circular motions with a cloth on his immaculate counter. "There's plenty of towns have funny names. Take that Baton Rouge, Louisiana. I had a kid took French over to the high school. Told me Baton Rouge means Red Stick. Now ain't that a helluva name for a town? Red Stick, Louisiana. And what about that Des Moines, Iowa? What a crazy name that is."

"True," said Rossi. "But for whom is Peyton Place named, or for what?"

"Some feller that built a castle up here back before the Civil War. Feller by the name of Samuel Peyton," said Corey reluctantly.

"A castle!" exclaimed Rossi.

"Yep. A real, true, honest-to-God castle, transported over here from England, every stick and stone of it."

"Who was this Peyton?" asked Rossi. "An exiled duke?"

"Nah," said Corey Hyde. "Just a feller with money to burn. Excuse me, Mr. Rossi. I got things to do in the kitchen."

The old man at the end of the counter chuckled. "Fact of the matter, Mr. Rossi," said Clayton Frazier in a loud voice, "is that this town was named for a friggin' nigger. That's what ails Corey. He's delicate like, and just don't want to spit it right out."

While Michael Rossi sipped his coffee and enjoyed his pie and conversation with Clayton Frazier, Parker Rhodes arrived at his home on Laurel Street. He parked his ancient sedan and entered the house where, without first removing his coat and hat, he went directly to the telephone.

"Hello," he said, as soon as the party he had called answered. "That you, Leslie? Well, he's here, Leslie. Got off the seven o'clock, checked his suitcases and walked uptown. He's sitting down at Hyde's right now. What's that? No, he can't get his bags out of the depot until morning, you know that. What? Well, goddamn it, he didn't ask me, that's why. He didn't ask for information about when he could get them out. He just wanted to know where he could check his bags, so I told him. What'd you say, Leslie? No, I did not tell him that no one has used those lockers since they were installed five years ago. What? Well, goddamn it, he didn't ask me, that's why. Yes. Yes, he is, Leslie. *Real* dark, and big. Sweet Jesus, he's as big as the side of a barn. Yes. Down at Hyde's. Said he wanted a cup of coffee.''

If Michael Rossi had overheard this conversation, he would have noticed again that Rhodes pronounced his last three words as one: Kupakawfee. But at the moment, Rossi was looking at the tall, silver-haired man who had just walked through Hyde's front door.

My God! thought Rossi, awed. This guy looks like a walking ad for a Planter's Punch. A goddamned Kentucky colonel in this place!

''Evenin', Doc,'' said Corey Hyde, who had put his head out of the kitchen at the sound of the door, looking, thought Rossi, rather like a tired turtle poking his head out of his shell.

''Evenin', Corey,'' and Rossi knew as soon as the man spoke, that this was no fugitive Kentucky colonel but a native.

''Welcome to Peyton Place, Mr. Rossi,'' said the white-haired native. ''It's nice to have you with us. My name is Swain. Matthew Swain.''

''Evenin', Doc,'' said Clayton Frazier. ''I just been tellin' Mr. Rossi here some of our local legends.''

''Make you want to jump on the next train out, Mr. Rossi?'' asked the doctor.

''No, sir,'' said Rossi, thinking that there was, after all, one goddamned face in this godforsaken town that looked human.

''I hope you'll enjoy living here,'' said the doctor. ''Maybe you'll let me show you the town after you get settled a little.''

''Thank you, sir. I'd enjoy that,'' said Rossi.

''Here comes Leslie Harrington,'' said Clayton Frazier.

The figure outside the glass door of the restaurant was clearly visible to those inside. The doctor turned to look.

''It's Leslie, all right,'' he said. ''Come to fetch you home, Mr. Rossi.''

Harrington strode into the restaurant, a smile like one made of molded ice cream on his face.

''Ah, Mr. Rossi,'' he cried jovially, extending his hand. ''It is indeed a pleasure to welcome you to Peyton Place.''

He was thinking, Oh, Christ, he's worse and more of it than I'd feared.

''Hello, Mr. Harrington,'' said Rossi, barely touching the extended hand. ''Made any long-distance calls lately?''

The smile on Harrington's face threatened to melt and run together, but he rescued it just in time.

''Ha, ha, ha,'' he laughed. ''No, Mr. Rossi, I haven't had much time for telephoning these days. I've been too busy looking for a suitable apartment for our new headmaster.''

''I trust you were successful,'' said Rossi.

''Yes. Yes, I was, as a matter of fact. Well, come along. I'll take you over in my car.''

''As soon as I finish my coffee,'' said Rossi.

''Certainly, certainly,'' said Harrington. ''Oh, hello, Matt. 'Lo, Clayton.''

''Coffee, Mr. Harrington?'' asked Corey Hyde.

''No, thanks,'' said Harrington.

When Rossi had finished, everyone said good night carefully, all the way around, and he and Harrington left the restaurant. As soon as the door had closed behind them, Dr. Swain began to laugh.

''Goddamn it,'' he roared, ''I'll bet my sweet young arse that Leslie has met his match this time!''

''There's one schoolteacher that Leslie ain't gonna shove around,'' observed Clayton Frazier.

Corey Hyde, who owed money at the bank where Leslie Harrington was a trustee, smiled uncertainly.

"The textile racket must be pretty good," said Rossi, as he opened the door of Leslie Harrington's new Packard.

"Can't complain," said Harrington. "Can't complain," and the mill-owner shook himself angrily at this sudden tendency to repeat all his words.

Rossi stopped in the act of getting into the car. A woman was walking toward them, and as she stepped under the street light on the corner, Rossi got a quick glimpse of blond hair and a swirl of dark coat.

"Who's that?" he demanded.

Leslie Harrington peered through the darkness. As the figure drew nearer, he smiled.

"That's Constance MacKenzie," he said. "Maybe you two will have a lot in common. She used to live in New York. Nice woman; good looking, too. Widow."

"Introduce me," said Rossi, drawing himself up to his full height.

"Certainly. Certainly, be glad to. Oh, Connie!"

"Yes, Leslie?"

The woman's voice was rich and husky, and Rossi fought down the urge to straighten the knot in his tie.

"Connie," said Harrington, "I'd like you to meet our new headmaster, Mr. Rossi. Mr. Rossi, Constance MacKenzie."

Constance extended her hand and while he held it, she gazed at him full in the eyes.

"How do you do?" she said at last, and Michael Rossi was puzzled, for something very much like relief showed through her voice.

"I'm glad to know you, Mrs. MacKenzie," said Rossi, and he thought, Very glad to know you, baby. I want to know you a lot better, on a bed, for instance, with that blond hair spread out on a pillow.

Vance Packard / *The Hidden Persuaders* 1957

With the publication of The Hidden Persuaders, *Vance Packard, a former columnist for the* Boston Daily Record *and a staff writer for* American Magazine *and* Collier's, *became the most widely read analyst of America's shopping habits. Based on motivational research and the techniques of depth psychology, Packard's findings served as a popular exposé of the manipulations of Madison Avenue. In "Babes in Consumerland," he focuses on how the goods are packaged and positioned in supermarkets to ensure impulse buying.*

BABES IN CONSUMERLAND

"You have to have a carton that attracts and hypnotizes this woman, like waving a flashlight in front of her eyes."

—Gerald Stahl, executive vice-president, Package Designers Council

For some years the DuPont company has been surveying the shopping habits of American housewives in the new jungle called the supermarket. The results have been so exciting in the opportunities they suggest to marketers that hundreds of leading food companies and ad agencies have requested copies. Husbands fretting over the high cost of feeding their families would find the results exciting, too, in a dismaying sort of way.

The opening statement of the 1954 report exclaimed enthusiastically in display type: "Today's shopper in the supermarket is more and more guided by the buying philosophy—'If somehow your product catches my eye—and for some reason it looks especially good—I WANT IT.' " That conclusion was based on studying the shopping habits of 5,338 shoppers in 250 supermarkets.

DuPont's investigators have found that the mid-century shopper doesn't bother to make a list or at least not a complete list of what she needs to buy. In fact less than one shopper in five has a complete list, but still the wives always manage to fill up their carts, often while exclaiming, according to DuPont: "I certainly never intended to get that much!" Why doesn't the wife need a list? DuPont gives this blunt answer: "Because seven out of ten of today's purchases are decided in the store, where the shoppers buy on impulse!!!"

The proportion of impulse buying of groceries has grown almost every year for nearly two decades, and DuPont notes that this rise in impulse buying has coincided with the growth in self-service shopping. Other studies show that in groceries where there are clerks to wait on customers there is about half as much impulse buying as in self-service stores. If a wife has to face a clerk she thinks out beforehand what she needs.

The impulse buying of pungent-odored food such as cheese, eye-appealing items like pickles or fruit salad in glass jars, and candy, cake, snack spreads, and other "self-gratifying items" runs even higher than average, 90 per cent of all purchases. Other investigators have in general confirmed the DuPont figures on impulse buying. The Folding Paper Box Association found that two-thirds of all purchases were completely or partially on impulse; the *Progressive Grocer* put the impulse figure about where DuPont does: seven out of ten purchases. And *Printer's Ink* observed with barely restrained happiness that the shopping list had become obsolescent if not obsolete.

One motivational analyst who became curious to know why there had been such a great rise in impulse buying at supermarkets was James Vicary. He suspected that some special psychology must be going on inside the women as they shopped in supermarkets. His suspicion was that perhaps they underwent an increase in tension when confronted with so many possibilities that they were forced into making quick purchases. He set out to find out if this was true. The best way to detect what was going on inside the shopper was a galvanometer or lie detector. That obviously was impractical. The next best thing was to use a hidden motion-picture camera and record the eye-blink rate of the women as they shopped. How fast a person blinks his eyes is a pretty good index of his state of inner tension. The average person, according to Mr. Vicary, normally blinks his eyes about thirty-two times a minute. If he is tense he blinks them more frequently, under extreme tension up to fifty or sixty times a minute. If he is notably relaxed on the other hand his eye-blink rate may drop to a subnormal twenty or less.

Mr. Vicary set up his cameras and started following the ladies as they entered the store. The results were startling, even to him. Their eye-blink rate, instead of going up to indicate mounting tension, went down and down, to a very subnormal fourteen blinks a minute. The ladies fell into what Mr. Vicary calls a hypnoidal trance, a light kind of trance that, he explains, is the first stage of hypnosis. Mr. Vicary has decided that the main cause of the trance is that the supermarket is packed with products that in former years would have been items that only kings and queens could afford, and here in this fairyland they were available. Mr. Vicary theorizes: "Just in this generation, anyone can be a king or queen and go through these stores where the products say 'Buy me, buy me.' "

Interestingly many of these women were in such a trance that they passed by neighbors and old friends without noticing or greeting them. Some had a sort of glassy stare. They were so entranced as they wandered about the store plucking things off shelves at random that they would bump into boxes without seeing them and did not even notice the camera although in some cases their face would pass within a foot and a half of the spot where the hidden camera was clicking away. When the wives had filled their carts (or satisfied themselves) and started toward the check-out counter their eye-blink rate would start rising up to a slightly subnormal twenty-five blinks per minute. Then, at the sound of the cash-register bell and the voice of the clerk asking for money, the eye-blink rate would race up past normal to a high abnormal of forty-five blinks per minute. In many cases it turned out that the women did not have enough money to pay for all the nice things they had put in the cart.

In this beckoning field of impulse buying psychologists have teamed up with merchandising experts to persuade the wife to buy products she may not particularly need or even want until she happens to see it invitingly presented. The 60,000,000 American women who go into supermarkets every week are getting "help" in their purchases and "splurchases" from psychologists and psychiatrists hired by the food merchandisers. On May 18, 1956, *The New York Times* printed a remarkable interview with a young man named Gerald Stahl, executive vice-president of the Package Designers Council. He stated: "Psychiatrists say that people have so much to choose from that they want help—they will like the package that hypnotizes them into picking it." He urged food packers to put more hypnosis into their package designing, so that the housewife will stick out her hand for it rather than one of many rivals.

Mr. Stahl has found that it takes the average woman exactly twenty seconds to cover an aisle in a supermarket if she doesn't tarry; so a good package design should hypnotize the woman like a flashlight waved in front of her eyes. Some colors such as red and yellow are helpful in creating hypnotic effects. Just putting the name and maker of the product on the box is old-fashioned and, he says, has absolutely no effect on the mid-century woman. She can't read anything, really, until she has picked the box up in her hands. To get the woman to reach and get the package in her hands designers, he explained, are now using "symbols that have a dreamlike quality." To cite examples of dreamlike quality, he mentioned the mouth-watering frosted cakes that decorate the packages of cake mixes, sizzling steaks, mushrooms frying in butter. The idea is to sell the sizzle rather than the meat. Such illustrations make the woman's imagination leap ahead to the end product. By 1956 package designers had even produced a box that, when the entranced shopper picked it up and began fingering it, would give a soft sales talk, or stress the brand name. The talk is on a strip that starts broadcasting when a shopper's finger rubs it.

The package people understandably believe that it is the package that makes or breaks the impulse sale, and some more objective experts agree. A buyer for a food chain told of his experience in watching women shopping. The typical shopper, he found, "picks up one, two, or three items, she puts them back on the shelf, then she picks up one and keeps it. I ask her why she keeps it. She says, 'I like the package.' " (This was a buyer for Bohack.)

The Color Research Institute, which specializes in designing deep-impact packages, won't even send a package out into the field for testing until it has been given ocular or eye-movement tests to show how the consumer's eye will travel over the package on the shelf. This is a gauge of the attention-holding power of the design.

According to some psychologists a woman's eye is most quickly attracted to items wrapped in red; a man's eye to items wrapped in blue. Students in this field have speculated on the woman's high vulnerability to red. One package designer, Frank Gianninoto, has developed an interesting theory. He has concluded that a majority of women shoppers leave their glasses at home or will never wear glasses in public if they can avoid it so that a package to be successful must stand out "from the blurred confusion."

Other merchandisers, I should add, have concluded that in the supermarket jungle the all-important fact in impulse buying is shelf position. Many sharp merchandisers see to it that their "splurge" items (on which their profit margin is highest) tend to be at eye level.

Most of the modern supermarkets, by the mid-fifties, were laid out in a carefully calculated manner so that the high-profit impulse items would be most surely noticed. In many stores they were on the first or only aisle the shopper could enter. Among the best tempters, apparently, are those items in glass jars where the contents can be seen, or where the food is actually out in the open, to be savored and seen. Offering free pickles and cubes of cheese on toothpicks has proved to be reliable as a sales booster. An Indiana supermarket operator nationally recognized for his advanced psychological techniques told me he once sold a half ton of cheese in a few hours, just by getting an enormous half-ton wheel of cheese and inviting customers to nibble slivers and cut off their own chunks for purchase. They could have their chunk free if they could guess its weight within an ounce. The mere massiveness of the cheese, he believes, was a powerful influence in making the sales. "People like to see a lot of merchandise," he explained. "When there are only three or four cans of an item on a shelf, they just won't move." People don't want the last package. A test by *The Progressive Grocer* showed that customers buy 22 per cent more if the shelves are kept full. The urge to conformity, it seems, is profound with many of us.

People also are stimulated to be impulsive, evidently, if they are offered a little extravagance. A California supermarket found that putting a pat of butter on top of each of its better steaks caused sales to soar 15 per cent. The Jewel Tea Company set up "splurge counters" in many of its supermarkets after it was found that women in a just-for-the-heck-of-it mood will spend just as freely on food delicacies as they will on a new hat. The Coca-Cola Company made the interesting discovery that customers in a supermarket who paused to refresh themselves at a soft-drink counter tended to spend substantially more. The Coke people put this to work in a test where they offered customers free drinks. About 80 per cent accepted the Cokes and spent on an average $2.44 more than the store's average customer had been spending.

Apparently the only people who are more prone to splurging when they get in a supermarket than housewives are the wives' husbands and children. Supermarket operators are pretty well agreed that men are easy marks for all sorts of impulse items and cite cases they've seen of husbands who are sent to the store for a loaf of bread and depart with both their arms loaded with their favorite snack items. Shrewd supermarket operators have put the superior impulsiveness of little children to work in promoting sales. The Indiana supermarket operator I mentioned has a dozen little wire carts that small children can push about the store while their mothers are shopping with big carts. People think these tiny carts are very cute; and the operator thinks they are very profitable. The small children go zipping up and down the aisles imitating their mothers in impulse buying, only more so. They reach out, hypnotically I assume, and grab boxes of cookies, candies, dog food, and everything else that delights or interests them. Complications arise, of course, when mother and child come out of their trances and together reach the check-out counter. The store operator related thus what happens: "There is usually a wrangle when the mother sees all the things the child has in his basket and she tries to make him take the stuff back. The child will take back items he doesn't particularly care about such as coffee but will usually bawl and kick before surrendering cookies, candy, ice cream, or soft drinks, so they usually stay for the family."

All these factors of sly persuasion may account for the fact that whereas in past years the average American family spent about 23 per cent of its income for food it now spends nearly 30 per cent. The Indiana operator I mentioned estimates that any supermarket shopper could, by showing a little old-fashioned thoughtfulness and preplanning, save 25 per cent easily on her family's food costs.

The exploration of impulse buying on a systematic basis began spreading in the mid-fifties to many other kinds of products not available in food stores. Liquor stores began organizing racks so that women could browse and pick up impulse items. This idea was pioneered on New York's own "ad alley," Madison Avenue, and spread to other parts of the country. Department and specialty stores started having counters simply labeled, "Why Not?" to promote the carefree, impulsive purchasing of new items most people had never tried before. One store merchandiser was quoted as saying: "Just give people an excuse to try what you are selling and you'll make an extra sale."

One of the most daring ventures into impulse selling was that launched by a Chicago insurance firm, Childs and Wood, which speculated that perhaps even insurance could be sold as an impulse item. So it set up a counter to sell insurance to passers-by at the department store Carson Pirie Scott and Company. Women who happened to be in that area, perhaps to shop for fur coats or a bridal gown, could buy insurance (life, automobile, household, fire, theft, jewelry, hospital) from an assortment of firms. The experiment was successful and instituted on a permanent basis. Auto, household, and fire insurance were reported to be the most popular impulse items.

Social scientists at the Survey Research Center at the University of Michigan made studies of the way people make their decisions to buy relatively expensive durable items such as TV sets, refrigerators, washing machines, items that are usually postponable. It concluded: "We did *not* find that all or most purchases of large household goods are made after careful consideration or deliberation . . . that much planning went into the purchasing . . . nor much seeking of information. About a quarter of these purchases of large household goods were found to lack practically all features of careful deliberation."

In a study that was made on the purchasing of homes in New London, Connecticut,[1] investigators were amazed that even with this, the most important purchase a family is likely to make in the year if not the decade, the shopping was lethargic and casual. On an average the people surveyed looked at less than a half-dozen houses before making a decision; 10 per cent of the home buyers looked at only one house before deciding; 19 per cent looked at only two houses before choosing one of them.

Dr. Warren Bilkey, of the University of Connecticut, and one of the nation's authorities on consumer behavior, systematically followed a large (sixty-three) group of families for more than a year as they wrestled with various major purchasing decisions. He learned that he could chart after each visit the intensity of two opposing factors, "desire" and "resistance." When one finally overwhelmed the other, the decision, pro or con, was made. He found that these people making major decisions, unlike the ladies in the supermarket, did build up a state of tension within themselves. The longer they pondered the decision, the higher the tension. He found that very often the people became so upset by the indecision that they often threw up their hands and decided to make the purchase just to find relief from their state of tension.

1. Ruby T. Norris, "Processes and Objectives in the New London Area," *Consumer Behavior*, ed. Lincoln Clark (New York: New York University Press, 1954), pp. 25–29.

DISCUSSION QUESTIONS

1. What are the sources of Packard's data on consumerism? Does personal observation play any role in the development of his argument? Explain how his attitudes toward the data are different from the attitudes of those who supply the data. What means does Packard use to suggest these differences?

2. What is the effect of calling the supermarket a "new jungle"? One source Packard cites calls it a "fairyland." Which metaphor seems closest to the data that Packard is using? Which image do you agree with?

3. What image of women is conveyed by the title of Packard's essay? Compare his attitude toward women with the images of women in the "Advertising" section.

Mario Puzo / *The Godfather*
[The Shooting of Don Corleone] 1969

Mario Puzo was born in New York City and educated at City College, Columbia, and the New School for Social Research. In two novels before The Godfather—The Dark Arena *(1955) and* The Passionate Pilgrim *(1965)—both of which he claims are better books, Puzo explored generational conflicts and the New York Italian community. Puzo disclaims any Mafia connections:*

> *I'm ashamed to admit that I wrote* The Godfather *entirely from research. I never met a real honest-to-god gangster. I knew the gambling world pretty good, but that's all. After the book became "famous," I was introduced to a few gentlemen related to the material. They were flattering. They refused to believe that I had never been in the rackets. They refused to believe that I had never had the confidence of a Don. But all of them loved the book.*

That evening, Hagen went to the Don's house to prepare him for the important meeting the next day with Virgil Sollozzo. The Don had summoned his eldest son to attend, and Sonny Corleone, his heavy Cupid-shaped face drawn with fatigue, was sipping at a glass of water. He must still be humping that maid of honor, Hagen thought. Another worry.

Don Corleone settled into an armchair puffing his Di Nobili cigar. Hagen kept a box of them in his room. He had tried to get the Don to switch to Havanas but the Don claimed they hurt his throat.

"Do we know everything necessary for us to know?" the Don asked.

Hagen opened the folder that held his notes. The notes were in no way incriminating, merely cryptic reminders to make sure he touched on every important detail. "Sollozzo is coming to us for help," Hagen said. "He will ask the family to put up at least a million dollars and to promise some sort of immunity from the law. For that we get a piece of the action, nobody knows how much. Sollozzo is vouched for by the Tattaglia family and they may have a piece of the action. The action is narcotics. Sollozzo has the contacts in Turkey, where they grow the poppy. From there he ships to Sicily. No trouble. In Sicily he has the plant to process into heroin. He has safety-valve operations to bring it down to morphine and bring it up to heroin if necessary. But it would seem that the processing plant in Sicily is protected in every way. The only hitch is bringing it into this country, and then distribution. Also initial capital. A million dollars cash doesn't grow on trees." Hagen saw Don Corleone grimace. The old man hated unnecessary flourishes in business matters. He went on hastily.

"They call Sollozzo the Turk. Two reasons. He's spent a lot of time in Turkey and is supposed to have a Turkish wife and kids. Second. He's supposed to be very quick with the knife, or was, when he was young. Only in matters of business, though, and with some sort of reasonable complaint. A very competent man and his own boss. He has a record, he's done two terms in prison, one in Italy, one in the United States, and he's known to the authorities as a narcotics man. This could be a plus for us. It means that he'll never get immunity to testify, since he's considered the top and, of course, because of his record. Also he has an American wife and three children and he is a good family man. He'll stand still for any rap as long as he knows that they will be well taken care of for living money."

The Don puffed on his cigar and said, "Santino, what do you think?"

Hagen knew what Sonny would say. Sonny was chafing at being under the Don's thumb. He wanted a big operation of his own. Something like this would be perfect.

Sonny took a long slug of scotch. "There's a lot of money in that white powder," he said. "But it could be dangerous. Some people could wind up in jail for twenty years. I'd say that if we kept out of the operations end, just stuck to protection and financing, it might be a good idea."

Hagen looked at Sonny approvingly. He had played his cards well. He had stuck to the obvious, much the best course for him.

The Don puffed on his cigar. "And you, Tom, what do you think?"

Hagen composed himself to be absolutely honest. He had already come to the conclusion that the Don would refuse Sollozzo's proposition. But what was worse, Hagen was convinced that for one of the few times in his experience, the Don had not thought things through. He was not looking far enough ahead.

"Go ahead, Tom," the Don said encouragingly. "Not even a Sicilian *Consigliori* always agrees with the boss." They all laughed.

"I think you should say yes," Hagen said. "You know all the obvious reasons. But the most important one is this. There is more money potential in narcotics than in any other business. If we don't get into it, somebody else will, maybe the Tattaglia family. With the revenue they earn they can amass more and more police and political power. Their family will become stronger than ours. Eventually they will come after us to take away what we have. It's just like countries. If they arm, we have to arm. If they become stronger economically, they become a threat to us. Now we have the gambling and we have the unions and right now they are the best things to have. But I think narcotics is the coming thing. I think we have to have a piece of that action or we risk everything we have. Not now, but maybe ten years from now."

The Don seemed enormously impressed. He puffed on his cigar and murmured, "That's the most important thing of course." He sighed and got to his feet. "What time do I have to meet this infidel tomorrow?"

Hagen said hopefully, "He'll be here at ten in the morning." Maybe the Don would go for it.

"I'll want you both here with me," the Don said. He rose, stretching, and took his son by the arm. "Santino, get some sleep tonight, you look like the devil himself. Take care of yourself, you won't be young forever."

Sonny, encouraged by this sign of fatherly concern, asked the question Hagen did not dare to ask. "Pop, what's your answer going to be?"

Don Corleone smiled. "How do I know until I hear the percentages and other details? Besides I have to have time to think over the advice given here tonight. After all, I'm not a man who does things rashly." As he went out the door he said casually to Hagen, "Do you have in your notes that the Turk made his living from prostitution before the war? As the Tattaglia family does now. Write that down before you forget.'' There was just a touch of derision in the Don's voice and Hagen flushed. He had deliberately not mentioned it, legitimately so since it really had no bearing, but he had feared it might prejudice the Don's decision. He was notoriously straitlaced in matters of sex.

Virgil ''the Turk'' Sollozzo was a powerfully built, medium-sized man of dark complexion who could have been taken for a true Turk. He had a scimitar of a nose and cruel black eyes. He also had an impressive dignity.

Sonny Corleone met him at the door and brought him into the office where Hagen and the Don waited. Hagen thought he had never seen a more dangerous-looking man except for Luca Brasi.

There were polite handshakings all around. If the Don ever asks me if this man has balls, I would have to answer yes, Hagen thought. He had never seen such force in one man, not even the Don. In fact the Don appeared at his worst. He was being a little too simple, a little too peasantlike in his greeting.

Sollozzo came to the point immediately. The business was narcotics. Everything was set up. Certain poppy fields in Turkey had pledged him certain amounts every year. He had a protected plant in France to convert into morphine. He had an absolutely secure plant in Sicily to process into heroin. Smuggling into both countries was as positively safe as such matters could be. Entry into the United States would entail about five percent losses since the FBI itself was incorruptible, as they both knew. But the profits would be enormous, the risk nonexistent.

''Then why do you come to me?'' the Don asked politely. ''How have I deserved your generosity?''

Sollozzo's dark face remained impassive. ''I need two million dollars cash,'' he said. ''Equally important, I need a man who has powerful friends in the important places. Some of my couriers will be caught over the years. That is inevitable. They will all have clean records, that I promise. So it will be logical for judges to give light sentences. I need a friend who can guarantee that when my people get in trouble they won't spend more than a year or two in jail. Then they won't talk. But if they get ten and twenty years, who knows? In this world there are many weak individuals. They may talk, they may jeopardize more important people. Legal protection is a must. I hear, Don Corleone, that you have as many judges in your pocket as a bootblack has pieces of silver.''

Don Corleone didn't bother to acknowledge the compliment. ''What percentage for my family?'' he asked.

Sollozzo's eyes gleamed. ''Fifty percent.'' He paused and then said in a voice that was almost a caress, ''In the first year your share would be three or four million dollars. Then it would go up.''

Don Corleone said, ''And what is the percentage of the Tattaglia family?''

For the first time Sollozzo seemed to be nervous. ''They will receive something from my share. I need some help in the operations.''

''So,'' Don Corleone said, ''I receive fifty percent merely for finance and legal protection. I have no worries about operations, is that what you tell me?''

Sollozzo nodded. ''If you think two million dollars in cash is 'merely finance,' I congratulate you, Don Corleone.''

The Don said quietly, ''I consented to see you out of my respect for the Tattaglias and because I've heard you are a serious man to be treated also with respect. I must say no to you but I must give you my reasons. The profits in your business are huge but so are the risks. Your operation, if I were part of it, could damage my other interests. It's true I have many, many friends in politics, but they would not be so friendly if my business were narcotics instead of gambling. They think gambling is something like liquor, a harmless vice, and they think narcotics a dirty business.

No, don't protest. I'm telling you their thoughts, not mine. How a man makes his living is not my concern. And what I am telling you is that this business of yours is too risky. All the members of my family have lived well the last ten years, without danger, without harm. I can't endanger them or their livelihoods out of greed."

The only sign of Sollozzo's disappointment was a quick flickering of his eyes around the room, as if he hoped Hagen or Sonny would speak in his support. Then he said, "Are you worried about security for your two million?"

The Don smiled coldly. "No," he said.

Sollozzo tried again. "The Tattaglia family will guarantee your investment also."

It was then that Sonny Corleone made an unforgivable error in judgment and procedure. He said eagerly, "The Tattaglia family guarantees the return of our investment without any percentage from us?"

Hagen was horrified at this break. He saw the Don turn cold, malevolent eyes on his eldest son, who froze in uncomprehending dismay. Sollozzo's eyes flickered again but this time with satisfaction. He had discovered a chink in the Don's fortress. When the Don spoke his voice held a dismissal. "Young people are greedy," he said. "And today they have no manners. They interrupt their elders. They meddle. But I have a sentimental weakness for my children and I have spoiled them. As you see. Signor Sollozzo, my no is final. Let me say that I myself wish you good fortune in your business. It has no conflict with my own. I'm sorry that I had to disappoint you."

Sollozzo bowed, shook the Don's hand and let Hagen take him to his car outside. There was no expression on his face when he said good-bye to Hagen.

Back in the room, Don Corleone asked Hagen, "What did you think of that man?"

"He's a Sicilian," Hagen said dryly.

The Don nodded his head thoughtfully. Then he turned to his son and said gently, "Santino, never let anyone outside the family know what you are thinking. Never let them know what you have under your fingernails. I think your brain is going soft from all that comedy you play with that young girl. Stop it and pay attention to business. Now get out of my sight."

Hagen saw the surprise on Sonny's face, then anger at his father's reproach. Did he really think the Don would be ignorant of his conquest, Hagen wondered. And did he really not know what a dangerous mistake he had made this morning? If that were true, Hagen would never wish to be the *Consigliori* to the Don of Santino Corleone.

Don Corleone waited until Sonny had left the room. Then he sank back into his leather armchair and motioned brusquely for a drink. Hagen poured him a glass of anisette. The Don looked up at him. "Send Luca Brasi to see me," he said.

Three months later, Hagen hurried through the paper work in his city office hoping to leave early enough for some Christmas shopping for his wife and children. He was interrupted by a phone call from a Johnny Fontane bubbling with high spirits. The picture had been shot, the rushes, whatever the hell they were, Hagen thought, were fabulous. He was sending the Don a present for Christmas that would knock his eyes out, he'd bring it himself but there were some little things to be done in the movie. He would have to stay out on the Coast. Hagen tried to conceal his impatience. Johnny Fontane's charm had always been lost on him. But his interest was aroused. "What is it?" he asked. Johnny Fontane chuckled and said, "I can't tell, that's the best part of a Christmas present." Hagen immediately lost all interest and finally managed, politely, to hang up.

Ten minutes later his secretary told him that Connie Corleone was on the phone and wanted to speak to him. Hagen sighed. As a young girl Connie had been nice, as a married woman she was a nuisance. She made complaints about her husband. She kept going home to visit her mother for two or three days. And Carlo Rizzi was turning out to be a real loser. He had been fixed up with a nice little business and was running it into the ground. He was also drinking, whoring around, gambling and beating his wife up occasionally. Connie hadn't told her family about that but she had told Hagen. He wondered what new tale of woe she had for him now.

But the Christmas spirit seemed to have cheered her up. She just wanted to ask Hagen what her father would really like for Christmas. And Sonny and Fred and Mike. She already knew what she would get her mother. Hagen made some suggestions, all of which she rejected as silly. Finally she let him go.

When the phone rang again, Hagen threw his papers back into the basket. The hell with it. He'd leave. It never occurred to him to refuse to take the call, however. When his secretary told him it was Michael Corleone he picked up the phone with pleasure. He had always liked Mike.

"Tom," Michael Corleone said, "I'm driving down to the city with Kay tomorrow. There's something important I want to tell the old man before Christmas. Will he be home tomorrow night?"

"Sure," Hagen said. "He's not going out of town until after Christmas. Anything I can do for you?"

Michael was as closemouthed as his father. "No," he said. "I guess I'll see you Christmas, everybody is going to be out at Long Beach, right?"

"Right," Hagen said. He was amused when Mike hung up on him without any small talk.

He told his secretary to call his wife and tell her he would be home a little late but to have some supper for him. Outside the building he walked briskly downtown toward Macy's. Someone stepped in his way. To his surprise he saw it was Sollozzo.

Sollozzo took him by the arm and said quietly, "Don't be frightened. I just want to talk to you." A car parked at the curb suddenly had its door open. Sollozzo said urgently, "Get in, I want to talk to you."

Hagen pulled his arm loose. He was still not alarmed, just irritated. "I haven't got time," he said. At that moment two men came up behind him. Hagen felt a sudden weakness in his legs. Sollozzo said softly, "Get in the car. If I wanted to kill you you'd be dead now. Trust me."

Without a shred of trust Hagen got into the car.

Michael Corleone had lied to Hagen. He was already in New York, and he had called from a room in the Hotel Pennsylvania less than ten blocks away. When he hung up the phone, Kay Adams put out her cigarette and said, "Mike, what a good fibber you are."

Michael sat down beside her on the bed. "All for you, honey; if I told my family we were in town we'd have to go there right away. Then we couldn't go out to dinner, we couldn't go to the theater, and we couldn't sleep together tonight. Not in my father's house, not when we're not married." He put his arms around her and kissed her gently on the lips. Her mouth was sweet and he gently pulled her down on the bed. She closed her eyes, waiting for him to make love to her and Michael felt an enormous happiness. He had spent the war years fighting in the Pacific, and on those bloody islands he had dreamed of a girl like Kay Adams. Of a beauty like hers. A fair and fragile body, milky-skinned and electrified by passion. She opened her eyes and then pulled his head down to kiss him. They made love until it was time for dinner and the theater.

After dinner they walked past the brightly lit department stores full of holiday shoppers and Michael said to her, "What shall I get you for Christmas?"

She pressed against him. "Just you," she said. "Do you think your father will approve of me?"

Michael said gently, "That's not really the question. Will your parents approve of me?"

Kay shrugged. "I don't care," she said.

Michael said, "I even thought of changing my name, legally, but if something happened, that wouldn't really help. You sure you want to be a Corleone?" He said it only half-jokingly.

"Yes," she said without smiling. They pressed against each other. They had decided to get married during Christmas week, a quiet civil ceremony at City Hall with just two friends as witnesses. But Michael had insisted he must tell his father. He had explained that his father would not object in any way as long as it was not done in secrecy. Kay was doubtful. She said she could not tell her parents until after the marriage. "Of course they'll think I'm pregnant," she said. Michael grinned. "So will my parents," he said.

What neither of them mentioned was the fact that Michael would have to cut his close ties with his family. They both understood that Michael had already done so to some extent and yet they both felt guilty about this fact. They planned to finish college, seeing each other weekends and living together during summer vacations. It seemed like a happy life.

The play was a musical called *Carousel* and its sentimental story of a braggart thief made them smile at each other with amusement. When they came out of the theater it had turned cold. Kay snuggled up to him and said, "After we're married, will you beat me and then steal a star for a present?"

Michael laughed. "I'm going to be a mathematics professor," he said. Then he asked, "Do you want something to eat before we go to the hotel?"

Kay shook her head. She looked up at him meaningfully. As always he was touched by her eagerness to make love. He smiled down at her, and they kissed in the cold street. Michael felt hungry, and he decided to order sandwiches sent up to the room.

In the hotel lobby Michael pushed Kay toward the newsstand and said, "Get the papers while I get the key." He had to wait in a small line; the hotel was still short of help despite the end of the war. Michael got his room key and looked around impatiently for Kay. She was standing by the newsstand, staring down at a newspaper she held in her hand. He walked toward her. She looked up at him. Her eyes were filled with tears. "Oh, Mike," she said, "oh, Mike." He took the paper from her hands. The first thing he saw was a photo of his father lying in the street, his head in a pool of blood. A man was sitting on the curb weeping like a child. It was his brother Freddie. Michael Corleone felt his body turning to ice. There was no grief, no fear, just cold rage. He said to Kay, "Go up to the room." But he had to take her by the arm and lead her into the elevator. They rode up together in silence. In their room, Michael sat down on the bed and opened the paper. The headlines said, VITO CORLEONE SHOT. ALLEGED RACKET CHIEF CRITICALLY WOUNDED. OPERATED ON UNDER HEAVY POLICE GUARD. BLOODY MOB WAR FEARED.

Michael felt the weakness in his legs. He said to Kay, "He's not dead, the bastards didn't kill him." He read the story again. His father had been shot at five in the afternoon. That meant that while he had been making love to Kay, having dinner, enjoying the theater, his father was near death. Michael felt sick with guilt.

Kay said, "Shall we go down to the hospital now?"

Michael shook his head. "Let me call the house first. The people who did this are crazy and now that the old man's still alive they'll be desperate. Who the hell knows what they'll pull next."

Both phones in the Long Beach house were busy and it was almost twenty minutes before Michael could get through. He heard Sonny's voice saying, "Yeah."

"Sonny, it's me," Michael said.

He could hear the relief in Sonny's voice. "Jesus, kid, you had us worried. Where the hell are you? I've sent people to that hick town of yours to see what happened."

"How's the old man?" Michael said. "How bad is he hurt?"

"Pretty bad," Sonny said. "They shot him five times. But he's tough." Sonny's voice was proud. "The doctors said he'll pull through. Listen, kid, I'm busy, I can't talk, where are you?"

"In New York," Michael said. "Didn't Tom tell you I was coming down?"

Sonny's voice dropped a little. "They've snatched Tom. That's why I was worried about you. His wife is here. She don't know and neither do the cops. I don't want them to know. The bastards who pulled this must be crazy. I want you to get out here right away and keep your mouth shut. OK?"

"OK," Mike said, "do you know who did it?"

"Sure," Sonny said. "And as soon as Luca Brasi checks in they're gonna be dead meat. We still have all the horses."

"I'll be out in a hour," Mike said. "In a cab." He hung up. The papers had been on the streets for over three hours. There must have been radio news reports. It was almost impossible that Luca hadn't heard the news. Thoughtfully Michael pondered the question. Where was Luca Brasi? It was the same question that Hagen was asking himself at that moment. It was the same question that was worrying Sonny Corleone out in Long Beach.

At a quarter to five that afternoon, Don Corleone had finished checking the papers the office manager of his olive oil company had prepared for him. He put on his jacket and rapped his knuckles on his son Freddie's head to make him take his nose out of the afternoon newspaper. "Tell Gatto to get the car from the lot," he said. "I'll be ready to go home in a few minutes."

Freddie grunted. "I'll have to get it myself. Paulie called in sick this morning. Got a cold again."

Don Corleone looked thoughtful for a moment. "That's the third time this month. I think maybe you'd better get a healthier fellow for this job. Tell Tom."

Fred protested. "Paulie's a good kid. If he says he's sick, he's sick. I don't mind getting the car." He left the office. Don Corleone watched out the window as his son crossed Ninth Avenue to the parking lot. He stopped to call Hagen's office but there was no answer. He called the house at Long Beach but again there was no answer. Irritated, he looked out the window. His car was parked at the curb in front of his building. Freddie was leaning against the fender, arms folded, watching the throng of Christmas shoppers. Don Corleone put on his jacket. The office manager helped him with his overcoat. Don Corleone grunted his thanks and went out the door and started down the two flights of steps.

Out in the street the early winter light was failing. Freddie leaned casually against the fender of the heavy Buick. When he saw his father come out of the building Freddie went out into the street to the driver's side of the car and got in. Don Corleone was about to get in on the sidewalk side of the car when he hesitated and then turned back to the long open fruit stand near the corner. This had been his habit lately, he loved the big out-of-season fruits, yellow peaches and oranges, that glowed in their green boxes. The proprietor sprang to serve him. Don Corleone did not handle the fruit. He pointed. The fruit man disputed his decisions only once, to show him that one of his choices had a rotten underside. Don Corleone took the paper bag in his left hand and paid the man with a five-dollar bill. He took his change and, as he turned to go back to the waiting car, two men stepped from around the corner. Don Corleone knew immediately what was to happen.

The two men wore black overcoats and black hats pulled low to prevent identification by witnesses. They had not expected Don Corleone's alert reaction. He dropped the bag of fruit and darted toward the parked car with startling quickness for a man of his bulk. At the same time he shouted, "Fredo, Fredo." It was only then that the two men drew their guns and fired.

The first bullet caught Don Corleone in the back. He felt the hammer shock of its impact but made his body move toward the car. The next two bullets hit him in the buttocks and sent him sprawling in the middle of the street. Meanwhile the two gunmen, careful not to slip on the rolling fruit, started to follow in order to finish him off. At that moment, perhaps no more than five seconds after the Don's call to his son, Frederico Corleone appeared out of his car, looming over it. The gunmen fired two more hasty shots at the Don lying in the gutter. One hit him in the fleshy part of his arm and the second hit him in the calf of his right leg. Though these wounds were the least serious they bled profusely, forming small pools of blood beside his body. But by this time Don Corleone had lost consciousness.

Freddie had heard his father shout, calling him by his childhood name, and then he had heard the first two loud reports. By the time he got out of the car he was in shock, he had not even drawn his gun. The two assassins could easily have shot him down. But they too panicked. They must have known the son was armed, and besides too much time had passed. They disappeared around the corner, leaving Freddie alone in the street with his father's bleeding body. Many of the people thronging the avenue had flung themselves into doorways or on the ground, others had huddled together in small groups.

Freddie still had not drawn his weapon. He seemed stunned. He stared down at his father's body lying face down on the tarred street, lying now in what seemed to him a blackish lake of blood. Freddie went into physical shock. People eddied out again and someone, seeing him start to sag, led him to the curbstone and made him sit down on it. A crowd gathered around Don Corleone's body, a circle that shattered when the first police car sirened a path through them. Directly behind the police was the *Daily News* radio car and even before it stopped a photographer jumped out to snap pictures of the bleeding Don Corleone. A few moments later an ambulance arrived. The photographer turned his attention to Freddie Corleone, who was now weeping openly, and this was a curiously comical sight, because of his tough, Cupid-featured face, heavy nose and thick mouth smeared with snot. Detectives were spreading through the crowd and more police cars were coming up. One detective knelt beside Freddie, questioning him, but Freddie was too deep in shock to answer. The detective reached inside Freddie's coat and lifted his wallet. He looked at the identification inside and whistled to his partner. In just a few seconds Freddie had been cut off from the crowd by a flock of plainclothesmen. The first detective found Freddie's gun in its shoulder holster and took it. Then they lifted Freddie off his feet and shoved him into an unmarked car. As that car pulled away it was followed by the *Daily News* radio car. The photographer was still snapping pictures of everybody and everything.

DISCUSSION QUESTIONS

1. How does Puzo go about making Don Corleone an attractive figure? For example, compare the characterization of Don Corleone to that of Sollozzo the Turk. In what ways are the Don's criminal activities given a kind of legiti-

macy? In this sense, how do Don Corleone's activities compare with those of Joey Gallo (see "Magazines")?

2. What is the literary effect of having Don Corleone's shooting first reported in the newspapers? How do the newspapers determine Puzo's description of the shooting? Compare his description with the account of Joey Gallo's death in "Magazines."

Alex Haley / *Roots*
[What Are Slaves?] 1976

A former magazine writer and Coast Guard chief journalist, Alex Haley had a modest reputation until the publication of his mammoth worth, Roots: The Saga of an American Family, *first condensed in* Reader's Digest *in 1974 and then published in its entirety by Doubleday in 1976. Twelve years in the making,* Roots *won for Haley international fame and personal fortune. An eight-part ABC television dramatization of* Roots *drew 130 million viewers. The last episode attracted 80 million alone, making it one of the most popular television programs ever aired.*

Kunta Kinte, Haley's African ancestor, born in Gambia in 1750 and carried to America as a slave in 1767, is the most vividly portrayed character in Roots. *His story fills more than half of the book's 688 pages. In the following selection, young Kunta Kinte and his brother, Lamin, learn from their father, Omoro, the meaning of slavery. Haley died in 1992.*

"What are slaves?" Lamin asked Kunta one afternoon. Kunta grunted and fell silent. Walking on, seemingly lost in thought, he was wondering what Lamin had overheard to prompt that question. Kunta knew that those who were taken by toubob became slaves, and he had overheard grown-ups talking about slaves who were owned by people in Juffure. But the fact was that he really didn't know what slaves *were*. As had happened so many other times, Lamin's question embarrassed him into finding out more.

The next day, when Omoro was getting ready to go out after some palm wood to build Binta a new food storehouse, Kunta asked to join his father; he loved to go off anywhere with Omoro. But neither spoke this day until they had almost reached the dark, cool palm grove.

Then Kunta asked abruptly, "Fa, what are slaves?"

Omoro just grunted at first, saying nothing, and for several minutes moved about in the grove, inspecting the trunks of different palms.

"Slaves aren't always easy to tell from those who aren't slaves," he said finally. Between blows of his bush ax against the palm he had selected, he told Kunta that slaves' huts were roofed with nyantang jongo and free people's huts with nyantang foro, which Kunta knew was the best quality of thatching grass.

"But one should never speak of slaves in the presence of slaves," said Omoro, looking very stern. Kunta didn't understand why, but he nodded as if he did.

When the palm tree fell, Omoro began chopping away its thick, tough fronds. As Kunta plucked off for himself some of the ripened fruits, he sensed his father's mood of willingness to talk today. He thought happily how now he would be able to explain to Lamin all about slaves.

"Why are some people slaves and others not?" he asked.

Omoro said that people became slaves in different ways. Some were born of slave mothers—and he named a few of those who lived in Juffure, people whom Kunta knew well. Some of them were the parents of some of his own kafo mates. Others, said Omoro, had once faced starvation during their home villages' hungry season, and they had come to Juffure and begged to become the slaves of someone who agreed to feed and provide for them. Still others—and he named some of Juffure's older people—had once been enemies and been captured as prisoners. "They become slaves, being not brave enough to die rather than be taken," said Omoro.

He had begun chopping the trunk of the palm into sections of a size that a strong man could carry. Though all he had named were slaves, he said, they were all respected people, as Kunta well knew. "Their rights are guaranteed by the laws of our forefathers," said Omoro, and he explained that all masters had to provide their slaves with food, clothing, a house, a farm plot to work on half shares, and also a wife or husband.

"Only those who permit themselves to be are despised," he told Kunta—those who had been made slaves because they were convicted murderers, thieves, or other criminals. These were the only slaves whom a master could beat or otherwise punish as he felt they deserved.

"Do slaves have to remain slaves always?" asked Kunta.

"No, many slaves buy their freedom with what they save from farming on half share with their masters." Omoro named some in Juffure who had done this. He named others who had won their freedom by marrying into the family that owned them.

To help him carry the heavy sections of palm, Omoro made a stout sling out of green vines, and as he worked, he said that some slaves, in fact, prospered beyond their masters. Some had even taken slaves for themselves, and some had become very famous persons.

"Sundiata was one!" exclaimed Kunta. Many times, he had heard the grandmothers and the griots speaking of the great forefather slave general whose army had conquered so many enemies.

Omoro grunted and nodded, clearly pleased that Kunta knew this, for Omoro also had learned much of Sundiata when he was Kunta's age. Testing his son, Omoro asked, "And who was Sundiata's mother?"

"Sogolon, the Buffalo Woman!" said Kunta proudly.

Omoro smiled, and hoisting onto his strong shoulders two heavy sections of the palm pole within the vine sling, he began walking. Eating his palm fruits, Kunta followed, and nearly all the way back to the village, Omoro told him how the great Mandinka Empire had been won by the crippled, brilliant slave general whose army had begun with runaway slaves found in swamps and other hiding places.

"You will learn much more of him when you are in manhood training," said Omoro—and the very thought of that time sent a fear through Kunta, but also a thrill of anticipation.

Omoro said that Sundiata had run away from his hated master, as most slaves did who didn't like their masters. He said that except for convicted criminals, no slaves could be sold unless the slaves approved of the intended master.

"Grandmother Nyo Boto also is a slave," said Omoro, and Kunta almost swallowed a mouthful of palm fruit. He couldn't comprehend this. Pictures flashed across his mind of beloved old Nyo Boto squatting before the door of her hut, tending the village's twelve or fifteen naked babies while weaving baskets of twigs, and giving the sharp side of her tongue to any passing adult—even the elders, if she felt like it. "That one is nobody's slave," he thought.

The next afternoon, after he had delivered his goats to their pens, Kunta took Lamin home by a way that avoided their usual playmates, and soon they squatted silently before the hut of Nyo Boto. Within a few moments the old lady appeared in her doorway, having sensed that she had visitors. And with but a glance at Kunta, who had always been one of her very favorite children, she knew that something special was on his mind. Inviting the boys inside her hut, she set about the brewing of some hot herb tea for them.

"How are your papa and mama?" she asked.

"Fine. Thank you for asking," said Kunta politely. "And you are well, Grandmother?"

"I'm quite fine, indeed," she replied.

Kunta's next words didn't come until the tea had been set before him. Then he blurted, "Why are you a slave, Grandmother?"

Nyo Boto looked sharply at Kunta and Lamin. Now it was she who didn't speak for a few moments. "I will tell you," she said finally.

"In my home village one night, very far from here and many rains ago, when I was a young woman and wife," Nyo Boto said, she had awakened in terror as flaming grass roofs came crashing down among her screaming neighbors. Snatching up her own two babies, a boy and a girl, whose father had recently died in a tribal war, she rushed out among the others—and awaiting them were armed white slave raiders with their black slatee helpers. In a furious battle, all who didn't escape were roughly herded together, and those who were too badly injured or too old or too young to travel were murdered before the others' eyes. Nyo Boto began to sob, "—including my own two babies and my aged mother."

As Lamin and Kunta clutched each other's hands, she told them how the terrified prisoners, bound neck-to-neck with thongs, were beaten and driven across the hot, hard inland country for many days. And every day, more and more of the prisoners fell beneath the whips that lashed their backs to make them walk faster. After a few days, yet more began to fall of hunger and exhaustion. Some struggled on, but those who couldn't were left for the wild animals to get. The long line of prisoners passed other villages that had been burned and ruined, where the skulls and bones of people and animals lay among the burned-out shells of thatch and mud that had once been family huts. Fewer than half of those who had begun the trip reached the village of Juffure, four days from the nearest place on the Kambi Bolongo where slaves were sold.

"It was here that one young prisoner was sold for a bag of corn," said the old woman. "That was me. And this was how I came to be called Nyo Boto," which Kunta knew meant "bag of corn." The man who bought her for his own slave died before very long, she said, "and I have lived here ever since."

Lamin was wriggling in excitement at the story, and Kunta felt somehow ever greater love and appreciation than he had before for old Nyo Boto, who now sat smiling tenderly at the two boys, whose father and mother, like them, she had once dandled on her knee.

"Omoro, your papa, was of the first kafo when I came to Juffure," said Nyo Boto, looking directly at Kunta. "Yaisa, his mother, who was your grandmother, was my very good friend. Do you remember her?" Kunta said that he did and added proudly that he had told his little brother all about their grandma.

"That is good!" said Nyo Boto. "Now I must get back to work. Run along, now."

Thanking her for the tea, Kunta and Lamin left and walked slowly back to Binta's hut, each deep in his own private thoughts.

The next afternoon, when Kunta returned from his goatherding, he found Lamin filled with questions about Nyo Boto's story. Had any such fire ever burned in Juffure? he wanted to know. Well, he had never heard of any, said Kunta, and the village showed no signs of it. Had Kunta ever seen one of those white people? "Of course not!" he exclaimed. But he said that their father had spoken of a time when he and his brothers had seen the toubob and their ships at a point along the river.

Kunta quickly changed the subject, for he knew very little about toubob, and he wanted to think about them for himself. He wished that he could *see* one of them—from a safe distance, of course, since everything he'd ever heard about them made it plain that people were better off who never got too close to them.

Only recently a girl out gathering herbs—and before her two grown men out hunting—had disappeared, and everyone was certain that toubob had stolen them away. He remembered, of course, how when drums of other villages warned that toubob had either taken somebody or was known to be near, the men would arm themselves and mount a double guard while the frightened women quickly gathered all of the children and hid in the bush far from the village—sometimes for several days—until the toubob was felt to be gone.

Kunta recalled once when he was out with his goats in the quiet of the bush, sitting under his favorite shade tree. He had happened to look upward and there, to his astonishment, in the tree overhead, were twenty or thirty monkeys huddled along the thickly leaved branches as still as statues, with their long tails hanging down. Kunta had always thought of monkeys rushing noisily about, and he couldn't forget how quietly they had been watching his every move. He wished that now *he* might sit in a tree and watch some toubob on the ground below him.

The goats were being driven homeward the afternoon after Lamin had asked him about toubob when Kunta raised the subject among his fellow goatherds—and in no time they were telling about the things they had heard. One boy, Demba Conteh, said that a very brave uncle had once gone close enough to *smell* some toubob, and they had a peculiar stink. All of the boys had heard that toubob took people away to eat them. But some had heard that the toubob claimed the stolen people were not eaten, only put to work on huge farms. Sitafa Silla spat out his grandfather's answer to that: "White man's lie!"

The next chance he had, Kunta asked Omoro, "Papa, will you tell me how you and your brothers saw the toubob at the river?" Quickly, he added, "The matter needs to be told correctly to Lamin." It seemed to Kunta that his father nearly smiled, but Omoro only grunted, evidently not feeling like talking at that moment. But a few days later, Omoro casually invited both Kunta and Lamin to go with him out beyond the village to collect some roots he needed. It was the naked Lamin's first walk anywhere with his father, and he was overjoyed. Knowing that Kunta's influence had brought this about, he held tightly onto the tail of his big brother's dundiko.

Omoro told his sons that after their manhood training, his two older brothers Janneh and Saloum had left Juffure, and the passing of time brought news of them as well-known travelers in strange and distant places. Their first return home came when drumtalk all the way from Juffure told them of the birth of Omoro's first son. They spent sleepless days and nights on the trail to attend the naming ceremony. And gone from home so long, the brothers joyously embraced some of their kafo mates of boyhood. But those few sadly told of others gone and lost—some in burned villages, some killed by fearsome firesticks, some kidnaped, some missing while farming, hunting, or traveling—and all because of toubob.

Omoro said that his brothers had then angrily asked him to join them on a trip to see what the toubob were doing, to see what might be done. So the three brothers trekked for three days along the banks of the Kamby Bolongo, keeping carefully concealed in the bush, until they found what they were looking for. About twenty great toubob canoes were moored in the river, each big enough that its insides might hold all the people of Juffure, each with a huge white cloth tied by ropes to a treelike pole as tall as ten men. Nearby was an island, and on the island was a fortress.

Many toubob were moving about, and black helpers were with them, both on the fortress and in small canoes. The small canoes were taking such things as dried indigo, cotton, beeswax, and hides to the big canoes. More terrible than he could describe, however, said Omoro, were the beatings and other cruelties they saw being dealt out to those who had been captured for the toubob to take away.

For several moments, Omoro was quiet, and Kunta sensed that he was pondering something else to tell him. Finally he spoke: ''Not as many of our people are being taken away now as then.'' When Kunta was a baby, he said, the King of Barra, who ruled this part of The Gambia, had ordered that there would be no more burning of villages and the capturing or killing of all their people. And soon it did stop, after the soldiers of some angry kings had burned the big canoes down to the water, killing all the toubob on board.

''Now,'' said Omoro, ''nineteen guns are fired in salute to the King of Barra by every toubob canoe entering the Kamby Bolongo.'' He said that the King's personal agents now supplied most of the people whom the toubob took away—usually criminals or debtors, or anyone convicted for suspicion of plotting against the king—often for little more than whispering. More people seemed to get convicted of crimes, said Omoro, whenever toubob ships sailed in the Kamby Bolongo looking for slaves to buy.

''But even a king cannot stop the stealings of some people from their villages,'' Omoro continued. ''You have known some of those lost from our village, three from among us just within the past few moons, as you know, and you have heard the drumtalk from other villages.'' He looked hard at his sons, and spoke slowly. ''The things I'm going to tell you now, you must hear with more than your ears—for not to do what I say can mean your being stolen away forever!'' Kunta and Lamin listened with rising fright. ''Never be alone when you can help it,'' said Omoro. ''Never be out at night when you can help it. And day or night, when you're alone, keep away from any high weeds or bush if you can avoid it.''

For the rest of their lives, ''even when you have come to be men,'' said their father, they must be on guard for toubob. ''He often shoots his firesticks, which can be heard far off. And wherever you see much smoke away from any villages, it is probably his cooking fires, which are too big. You should closely inspect his signs to learn which way the toubob went. Having much heavier footsteps than we do, he leaves signs you will recognize as not ours: he breaks twigs and grasses. And when you get close where he has been, you will find that his scent remains there. It's like a wet chicken smells. And many say a toubob sends forth a nervousness that we can feel. If you feel that, become quiet, for often he can be detected at some distance.''

But it's not enough to know the toubob, said Omoro. ''Many of our own people work for him. They are slatee *traitors*. But without knowing them, there is no way to recognize them. In the bush, therefore, trust *no* one you don't know.''

Kunta and Lamin sat frozen with fear. ''You cannot be told these things strongly enough,'' said their father. ''You must know what your uncles and I saw happening to those who had been stolen. It is the difference between slaves among ourselves and those whom toubob takes away to be slaves for him.'' He said that they saw stolen people chained inside long, stout, heavily guarded bamboo pens along the shore of the river. When small canoes brought important-acting toubob from the big canoes, the stolen people were dragged outside their pens onto the sand.

''Their heads had been shaved, and they had been greased until they shined all over. First they were made to squat and jump up and down,'' said Omoro. ''And then, when the toubob had seen enough of that, they ordered the stolen people's mouths forced open for their teeth and their throats to be looked at.''

Swiftly, Omoro's finger touched Kunta's crotch, and as Kunta jumped, Omoro said, ''Then the men's foto was pulled and looked at. Even the women's private parts were inspected.'' And the toubob finally made the people squat again and stuck burning hot irons against their backs and shoulders. Then, screaming and struggling, the people were shipped toward the water, where small canoes waited to take them out to the big canoes.

''My brothers and I watched many fall onto their bellies, clawing and eating the sand, as if to get one last hold and bite of their own home,'' said Omoro. ''But they were dragged and beaten on.'' Even in the small canoes out in the water, he told Kunta and Lamin, some kept fighting against the whips and the clubs until they jumped into the water among terrible long fish with gray backs and white bellies and curved mouths full of thrashing teeth that reddened the water with their blood.

Kunta and Lamin had huddled close to each other, each gripping the other's hands. ''It's better that you know these things than that your mother and I kill the white cock one day for you.'' Omoro looked at his sons. ''Do you know what that means?''

Kunta managed to nod, and found his voice. ''When someone is missing, Fa?'' He had seen families frantically chanting to Allah as they squatted around a white cock bleeding and flapping with its throat slit.

''Yes,'' said Omoro. ''If the white cock dies on its breast, hope remains. But when a white cock flaps to death on its back, then *no* hope remains, and the whole village joins the family in crying to Allah.''

''Fa—'' Lamin's voice, squeaky with fear, startled Kunta, ''where do the big canoes take the stolen people?''

''The elders say to Jong Sang Doo,'' said Omoro, ''a land where slaves are sold to huge cannibals called toubabo koomi, who eat us. No man knows any more about it.''

Benjamin Spock / *The Common Sense Book of Baby Care*

1976

Pediatrician, psychiatrist, former columnist for Ladies' Home Journal *and* Redbook, *and Vietnam antiwar activist, Dr. Benjamin Spock became America's most influential authority on child care soon after the publication of* The Common Sense Book of Baby Care *in 1945. The book was meant to counter some of the absurd notions promulgated by Spock's predecessors, including Dr. John B. Watson who had asserted in his widely distributed text,* Psychological Care of Infant and Child (1928): *''Never, never kiss your child. Never hold it on your lap. Never rock its carriage.'' Spock's reassuring ''common sense,'' evident in the selection reprinted below, encourages a more relaxed approach to the difficulties of parenthood. Millions of Americans have been raised according to Spock's principles. The book has enjoyed greater total sales than any other work except the Bible and Shakespeare's plays.*

The following selection on gun play—showing Spock's change of mind on the subject—is taken from the 1976 edition of his best-selling book.

SHOULD CHILDREN PLAY WITH GUNS?

Is gun play good or bad for children? For many years I emphasized its harmlessness. When thoughtful parents expressed doubt about letting their children have pistols and other warlike toys, because they didn't want to encourage them in the slightest degree to become delinquents or militarists, I would explain how little connection there was. In the course of growing up, children have a natural tendency to bring their aggressiveness more and more under control provided their parents encourage this. One- to 2-year-olds, when they're angry with another child, may bite the child's arm without hesitation. But by 3 or 4 they have already learned that crude aggression is not right. However, they like to pretend to shoot a pretend bad buy. They may pretend to shoot their mother or father, but grinning to assure them that the gun and the hostility aren't to be taken seriously.

In the 6- to 12-year-old period, children will play an earnest game of war, but it has lots of rules. There may be arguments and roughhousing, but real fights are relatively infrequent. At this age children don't shoot at their mother or father, even in fun. It's not that the parents have turned stricter; the children's own conscience has. They say, "Step on a crack; break your mother's back," which means that even the thought of wishing harm to their parents now makes them uncomfortable. In adolescence, aggressive feelings become much stronger, but well-brought-up children sublimate them into athletics and other competition or into kidding their pals.

In other words, I'd explain that playing at war is a natural step in the disciplining of the aggression of young children; that most clergymen and pacifists probably did the same thing; that an idealistic parent doesn't really need to worry about producing a scoundrel; that the aggressive delinquent was not distorted in personality by being allowed to play bandit at 5 or 10, he was neglected and abused in his first couple of years, when his character was beginning to take shape; that he was doomed before he had any toys worthy of the name.

But nowadays I'd give parents much more encouragement in their inclination to guide their child away from violence. A number of occurrences have convinced me of the importance of this.

One of the first things that made me change my mind, several years ago, was an observation that an experienced nursery school teacher told me about. Her children were crudely bopping each other much more than previously, without provocation. When she remonstrated with them, they would protest, "But that's what the Three Stooges do." (This was a children's TV program full of violence and buffoonery which had recently been introduced and which immediately became very popular.) This attitude of the children showed me that watching violence can lower a child's standards of behavior. Recent psychological experiments have shown that being shown brutality on film stimulates cruelty in adults, too.

What further shocked me into reconsidering my point of view was the assassination of President Kennedy, and the fact that some schoolchildren cheered about this. (I didn't so much blame the children as I blamed the kind of parents who will say about a President they dislike, "I'd shoot him if I got the chance!")

These incidents made me think of other evidences that Americans have often been tolerant of harshness, lawlessness, and violence. We were ruthless in dealing with the Indians. In some frontier areas we slipped into the tradition of vigilante justice. We were hard on the later waves of immigrants. At times we've denied justice to groups with different religions or political views. We have crime rates way above those of other, comparable nations. A great proportion of our adult as well as our child population has been endlessly fascinated with dramas of Western violence and with brutal crime stories, in movies and on television. We have had a shameful history of racist lynchings and murders, as well as regular abuse and humiliation. In recent years it has been realized that infants and small children are being brought to hospitals with severe injuries caused by gross parental brutality.

Of course, some of these phenomena are characteristic of only a small percentage of the population. Even the others that apply to a majority of people don't necessarily mean that we Americans on the average have more aggressiveness inside us than the people of other nations. I think rather that the aggressiveness we have is less controlled, from childhood on.

To me it seems very clear that in order to have a more stable and civilized national life we should bring up the next generation of Americans with a greater respect for law and for other people's rights and sensibilities than in the past. There are many ways in which we could and should teach these attitudes. One simple opportunity we could utilize in the first half of childhood is to show our disapproval of lawlessness and violence in television programs and in children's gun play.

I also believe that the survival of the world now depends on a much greater awareness of the need to avoid war and to actively seek peaceful agreements. There are enough nuclear arms to utterly destroy all civilization. One international incident in which belligerence or brinkmanship was carried a small step too far could escalate into annihilation within a few hours. This terrifying situation demands a much greater stability and self-restraint on the part of national leaders and citizens than they have ever shown in the past. We owe it to our children to prepare them very deliberately for this awesome responsibility. I see little evidence that this is being done now.

When we let people grow up feeling that cruelty is all right provided they know it is make-believe, or provided they sufficiently disapprove of certain individuals or groups, or provided the cruelty is in the service of their country (whether the country is right or wrong), we make it easier for them to go berserk when the provocation comes.

But can we imagine actually depriving American children of their guns or of watching their favorite Western or crime programs? I think we should consider it—to at least a partial degree.

I believe that parents should firmly stop children's war play or any other kind of play that degenerates into deliberate cruelty or meanness. (By this I don't mean they should interfere in every little quarrel or tussle.)

If I had a 3- or 4-year-old son who asked me to buy him a gun, I'd tell him—with a friendly smile, not a scowl—that I don't want to give him a gun for even pretend shooting because there is too much meanness and killing in the world, that we must all learn how to get along in a friendly way together. I'd ask him if he didn't want some other present instead.

If I saw him, soon afterward, using a stick for a pistol in order to join a gang that was merrily going "bang-bang" at each other, I wouldn't rush out to remind him of my views. I'd let him have the fun of participating as long as there was no cruelty. If his uncle gave him a pistol or a soldier's helmet for his birthday, I myself wouldn't have the nerve to take it away from him. If when he was 7 or 8 he decided he wanted to spend his own money for battle equipment, I wouldn't forbid him. I'd remind him that I myself don't want to buy war toys or give them as presents; but from now on he will be playing more and more away from home and making more of his own decisions; he can make this decision for himself. I wouldn't give this talk in such a disapproving manner that he wouldn't dare decide against my policy. I would feel I'd made my point and that he had been inwardly influenced by my viewpoint as much as I could influence him. Even if he should buy weapons then, he would be likely to end up—in adolescence and adulthood—as thoughtful about the problems of peace as if I'd prohibited his buying them, perhaps more so.

One reason I keep backing away from a flat prohibition is that it would have its heaviest effect on the individuals who need it least. If all the parents of America became convinced and agreed on a toy-weapons ban on the first of next month, this would be ideal from my point of view. But this isn't going to happen for a long time, unless one nuclear missile goes off by accident and shocks the world into a banning of all weapons, real and pretend. A small percentage of parents—those most thoughtful and conscientious—will be the first ones who will want to dissuade their children from war toys; but their children will be most apt to be the sensitive, responsible children anyway. So I think it's carrying the issue unnecessarily far for those of us who are particularly concerned about peace and kindliness to insist that our young children demonstrate a total commitment to our cause while all their friends are gun toters. (It might be practical in a neighborhood where a majority of parents had the same conviction.) The main ideal is that children should grow up with a fond attitude toward all humanity. That will come about basically from the general atmosphere of our families. It will be strengthened by the attitude that we teach specifically toward other nations and groups. The elimination of war play would have some additional influence, but not as much as the two previous factors.

I feel less inclined to compromise on brutality on television and in movies. The sight of a real human face being apparently smashed by a fist has a lot more impact on children than what they imagine when they are making up their own stories. I believe that parents should flatly forbid programs that go in for violence. I don't think they are good for adults either. Young children can only partly distinguish between dramas and reality. Parents can explain, "It isn't right for people to hurt each other or kill each other and I don't want you to watch them do it."

Even if children cheat and watch such a program in secret, they'll know very well that their parents disapprove, and this will protect them to a degree from the coarsening effect of the scenes.

Ron Kovic / *Born on the Fourth of July* [Wounded] 1976

Ron Kovic was born on July 4, 1946, on Long Island, New York. While serving in Vietnam, Kovic received the injury that would confine him to a wheelchair for the rest of his life. For his sacrifice, he was awarded the Purple Heart. Upon returning to America, he became a major figure in the antiwar movement. His autobiographical account of a soldier's experience in Vietnam became a best-seller soon after its publication in 1976 and was made into a popular film in 1989. What follows is the opening chapter of this important book.

The Blood is still rolling off my flak jacket from the hole in my shoulder and there are bullets cracking into the sand all around me. I keep trying to move my legs but I cannot feel them. I try to breathe but it is difficult. I have to get out of this place, make it out of here somehow.

Someone shouts from my left now, screaming for me to get up. Again and again he screams, but I am trapped in the sand.

Oh get me out of here, get me out of here, please someone help me! Oh help me, please help me. Oh God oh Jesus! "Is there a corpsman?" I cry. "Can you get a corpsman?"

There is a loud crack and I hear the guy begin to sob. "They've shot my fucking finger off! Let's go, sarge! Let's get outta here!"

"I can't move," I gasp. "I can't move my legs! I can't feel anything!"

I watch him go running back to the tree line.

"Sarge, are you all right?" Someone else is calling to me now and I try to turn around. Again there is the sudden crack of a bullet and a boy's voice crying. "Oh Jesus! Oh Jesus Christ!" I hear his body fall in back of me.

I think he must be dead but I feel nothing for him, I just want to live. I feel nothing.

And now I hear another man coming up from behind, trying to save me. "Get outta here!" I scream. "Get the fuck outta here!"

A tall black man with long skinny arms and enormous hands picks me up and throws me over his shoulder as bullets begin cracking over our heads like strings of firecrackers. Again and again they crack as the sky swirls around us like a cyclone. "Motherfuckers motherfuckers!" he screams. And the rounds keep cracking and the sky and the sun on my face and my body all gone, all twisted up dangling like a puppet's, diving again and again into the sand, up and down, rolling and cursing, gasping for breath. "Goddamn goddamn motherfuckers!"

And finally I am dragged into a hole in the sand with the bottom of my body that can no longer feel, twisted and bent underneath me. The black man runs from the hole without ever saying a thing. I never see his face. I will never know who he is. He is gone. And others now are in the hole helping me. They are bandaging my wounds. There is fear in their faces.

"It's all right," I say to them. "Everything is fine."

Someone has just saved my life. My rifle is gone and I don't feel like finding it or picking it up ever again. The only thing I can think of, the only thing that crosses my mind, is living. There seems to be nothing in the world more important than that.

Hundreds of rounds begin to crash in now. I stare up at the sky because I cannot move. Above the hole men are running around in every direction. I see their legs and frightened faces. They are screaming and dragging the wounded past me. Again and again the rounds crash in. They seem to be coming in closer and closer. A tall man jumps in, hugging me to the earth.

"Oh God!" he is crying. "Oh God please help us!"

The attack is lifted. They are carrying me out of the hole now—two, three, four men—quickly they are strapping me to a stretcher. My legs dangle off the sides until they realize I cannot control them. "I can't move them," I say, almost in a whisper. "I can't move them." I'm still carefully sucking the air, trying to calm myself, trying not to get excited, not to panic. I want to live. I keep telling myself, Take it slow now, as they strap my legs to the stretcher and carry my wounded body into an Amtrac packed with other wounded men. The steel trapdoor of the Amtrac slowly closes as we begin to move to the northern bank and back across the river to the battalion area.

Men are screaming all around me. "Oh God get me out of here!" "Please help!" they scream. Oh Jesus, like little children now, not like marines, not like the posters, not like that day in the high school, this is for real. "Mother!" screams a man without a face. "Oh I don't want to die!" screams a young boy cupping his intestines with his hands. "Oh please, oh no, oh God, oh help! Mother!" he screams again.

We are moving slowly through the water, the Amtrac rocking back and forth. We cannot be brave anymore, there is no reason. It means nothing now. We hold on to ourselves, to things around us, to memories, to thoughts, to dreams. I breathe slowly, desperately trying to stay awake.

The steel trapdoor is opening. I see faces. Corpsmen, I think. Others, curious, looking in at us. Air, fresh, I feel, I smell. They are carrying me out now. Over wounded bodies, past wounded screams. I'm in a helicopter now lifting above the battalion area. I'm leaving the war. I'm going to live. I am still breathing, I keep thinking over and over, I'm going to live and get out of here.

They are shoving tubes and needles in my arms. Now we are being packed into planes. I begin to believe more and more as I watch the other wounded packed around me on shelves that I am going to live.

I still fight desperately to stay awake. I am in an ambulance now rushing to some place. There is a man without any legs screaming in pain, moaning like a little baby. He is bleeding terribly from the stumps that were once his legs, thrashing his arms wildly about his chest, in a semiconscious daze. It is almost too much for me to watch.

I cannot take much more of this. I must be knocked out soon, before I lose my mind. I've seen too much today, I think. But I hold on, sucking the air. I shout then curse for him to be quiet. "My wound is much worse than yours!" I scream. "You're lucky," I shout, staring him in the eyes. "I can feel nothing from my chest down. You at least still have part of your legs. Shut up!" I scream again. "Shut the fuck up, you goddamned baby!" He keeps thrashing his arms wildly above his head and kicking his bleeding stumps toward the roof of the ambulance.

The journey seems to take a very long time, but soon we are at the place where the wounded are sent. I feel a tremendous exhilaration inside me. I have made it this far. I have actually made it this far without giving up and now I am in a hospital where they will operate on me and find out why I cannot feel anything from my chest down anymore. I know I am going to make it now. I am going to make it not because of any god, or any religion, but because *I* want to make it, *I* want to live. And I leave the screaming man without legs and am brought to a room that is very bright.

"What's your name?" the voice shouts.

"Wh-wh-what?" I say.

"What's your name?" the voice says again.

"K-K-Kovic." I say.

"No!" says the voice. "I want your name, rank and service number. Your date of birth, the name of your father and mother."

"Kovic. Sergeant. Two-oh-three-oh-two-six-one, uh, when are you going to . . ."

"Date of birth!" the voice shouts.

"July fourth, nineteen forty-six. I was born on the Fourth of July. I can't feel . . ."

"What religion are you?"

"Catholic," I say.

"What outfit did you come from?"

"What's going on? When are you going to operate?" I say.

"The doctors will operate," he says. "Don't worry," he says confidently. "They are very busy and there are many wounded but they will take care of you soon."

He continues to stand almost at attention in front of me with a long clipboard in his hand, jotting down all the information he can. I cannot understand why they are taking so long to operate. There is something very wrong with me, I think, and they must operate as quickly as possible. The man with the clipboard walks out of the room. He will send the priest in soon.

I lie in the room alone staring at the walls, still sucking the air, determined to live more than ever now.

The priest seems to appear suddenly above my head. With his fingers he is gently touching my forehead, rubbing it slowly and softly. "How are you," he says.

"I'm fine, Father." His face is very tired but it is not frightened. He is almost at ease, as if what he is doing he has done many times before.

"I have come to give you the Last Rites, my son."

"I'm ready, Father," I say.

And he prays, rubbing oils on my face and placing the crucifix to my lips. "I will pray for you," he says.

"When will they operate?" I say to the priest.

"I do not know," he says. "The doctors are very busy. There are many wounded. There is not much time for anything here but trying to live. So you must try to live my son, and I will pray for you."

Soon after that I am taken to a long room where there are many doctors and nurses. They move quickly around me. They are acting very competent. "You will be fine," says one nurse calmly.

"Breathe deeply into the mask," the doctor says.

"Are you going to operate?" I ask.

"Yes. Now breathe deeply into the mask." As the darkness of the mask slowly covers my face I pray with all my being that I will live through this operation and see the light of day once again. I want to live so much. And even before I go to sleep with the blackness still swirling around my head and the numbness of sleep, I begin to fight as I have never fought before in my life.

I awake to the screams of other men around me. I have made it. I think that maybe the wound is my punishment for killing the corporal and the children. That now everything is okay and the score is evened up. And now I am packed in this place with the others who have been wounded like myself, strapped into a strange circular bed. I feel tubes going into my nose and hear the clanking, pumping sound of a machine. I still cannot feel any of my body but I know I am alive. I feel a terrible pain in my chest. My body is so cold. It has never been this weak. It feels so tired and out of touch, so lost and in pain. I can still barely breathe. I look around me, at people moving in shadows of numbness. There is the man who had been in the ambulance with me, screaming louder than ever, kicking his bloody stumps in the air, crying for his mother, crying for his morphine.

Directly across from me there is a Korean who has not even been in the war at all. The nurse says he was going to buy a newspaper when he stepped on a booby trap and it blew off both his legs and his arm. And all that is left now is this slab of meat swinging one arm crazily in the air, moaning like an animal gasping for its last bit of life, knowing that death is rushing toward him. The Korean is screaming like a madman at the top of his lungs. I cannot wait for the shots of morphine. Oh, the morphine feels so good. It makes everything dark and quiet. I can rest. I can leave this madness. I can dream of my back yard once again.

When I wake they are screaming still and the lights are on and the clock, the clock on the wall, I can hear it ticking to the sound of their screams. I can hear the dead being carted out and the new wounded being brought in to the beds all around me. I have to get out of this place.

"Can I call you by your first name?" I say to the nurse.

"No. My name is Lieutenant Wiecker."

"Please, can I . . ."

"No," she says. "It's against regulations."

I'm sleeping now. The lights are flashing. The black pilot is next to me. He says nothing. He stares at the ceiling all day long. He does nothing but that. But something is happening now, something is going wrong over there. The nurse is shouting for the machine, and the corpsman is crawling on the black man's chest, he has his knees on his chest and he's pounding it with his fists again and again.

''His heart has stopped!'' screams the nurse.

Pounding, pounding, he's pounding his fist into his chest. ''Get the machine!'' screams the corpsman.

The nurse is pulling the machine across the hangar floor as quickly as she can now. They are trying to put curtains around the whole thing, but the curtains keep slipping and falling down. Everyone, all the wounded who can still see and think, now watch what is happening to the pilot, and it is happening right next to me. The doctor hands the corpsman a syringe, they are laughing as the corpsman drives the syringe into the pilot's chest like a knife. They are talking about the Green Bay Packers and the corpsman is driving his fist into the black man's chest again and again until the black pilot's body begins to bloat up, until he doesn't look like a body at all anymore. His face is all puffy like a balloon and saliva rolls slowly from the sides of his mouth. He keeps staring at the ceiling and saying nothing. ''The machine! The machine!'' screams the doctor, now climbing on top of the bed, taking the corpsman's place. ''Turn on the machine!'' screams the doctor.

He grabs a long suction cup that is attached to the machine and places it carefully against the black man's chest. The black man's body jumps up from the bed almost arcing into the air from each bolt of electricity, jolting and arcing, bloating up more and more.

''I'll bet on the Packers,'' says the corpsman.

''Green Bay doesn't have a chance,'' the doctor says, laughing.

The nurse is smiling now, making fun of both the doctor and the corpsman. ''I don't understand football,'' she says.

They are pulling the sheet over the head of the black man and strapping him onto the gurney. He is taken out of the ward.

The Korean civilian is still screaming and there is a baby now at the end of the ward. The nurse says it has been napalmed by our own jets. I cannot see the baby but it screams all the time like the Korean and the young man without any legs I had met in the ambulance.

I can hear a radio. It is the Armed Forces radio. The corpsman is telling the baby to shut the hell up and there is a young kid with half his head blown away. They have brought him in and put him where the black pilot has just died, right next to me. He has thick bandages wrapped all around his head till I can hardly see his face at all. He is like a vegetable—a nineteen-year-old vegetable, thrashing his arms back and forth, babbling and pissing in his clean white sheets.

''Quit pissin' in your sheets!'' screams the corpsman. But the nineteen-year-old kid who doesn't have any brains anymore makes the corpsman very angry. He just keeps pissing in the sheets and crying like a little baby.

There is a Green Beret sergeant calling for his mother. Every night now I hear him. He has spinal meningitis. He will be dead before this evening is over.

The Korean civilian does not moan anymore. He does not wave his one arm and two fingers above his head. He is dead and they have taken him away too.

There is a nun who comes through the ward now with apples for the wounded and rosary beads. She is very pleasant and smiles at all of the wounded. The corpsman is reading a comicbook, still cursing at the baby. The baby is screaming and the Armed Forces radio is saying that troops will be home soon. The kid with the bloody stumps is getting a morphine shot.

There is a general walking down the aisles now, going to each bed. He's marching down the aisles, marching and facing each wounded man in his bed. A skinny private with a Polaroid camera follows directly behind him. The general is dressed in an immaculate uniform with shiny shoes. ''Good afternoon, marine,'' the general says. ''In the name of the President of the United States and the United States

Marine Corps, I am proud to present you with the Purple Heart, and a picture,'' the general says. Just then the skinny man with the Polaroid camera jumps up, flashing a picture of the wounded man. ''And a picture to send to your folks.''

He comes up to my bed and says exactly the same thing he has said to all the rest. The skinny man jumps up, snapping a picture of the general handing the Purple Heart to me. ''And here,'' says the general, ''here is a picture to send home to your folks.'' The general makes a sharp left face. He is marching to the bed next to me where the nineteen-year-old kid is still pissing in his pants, babbling like a little baby.

''In the name of the President of the United States,'' the general says. The kid is screaming now almost tearing the bandages off his head, exposing the parts of his brain that are still left. ''. . . I present you with the Purple Heart. And here,'' the general says, handing the medal to the nineteen-year-old vegetable, the skinny guy jumping up and snapping a picture, ''here is a picture . . . ,'' the general says, looking at the picture the skinny guy has just pulled out of the camera. The kid is still pissing in his white sheets. ''. . . And here is a picture to send home. . . .'' The general does not finish what he is saying. He stares at the nineteen-year-old for what seems a long time. He hands the picture back to his photographer and as sharply as before marches to the next bed.

''Good afternoon, marine,'' he says.

The kid is still pissing in his clean white sheets when the general walks out of the room.

I am in this place for seven days and seven nights. I write notes on scraps of paper telling myself over and over that I will make it out of here, that I am going to live. I am squeezing rubber balls with my hands to try to get strong again. I write letters home to Mom and Dad. I dictate them to a woman named Lucy who is with the USO. I am telling Mom and Dad that I am hurt pretty bad but I have done it for America and that it is worth it. I tell them not to worry. I will be home soon.

The day I am supposed to leave has come. I am strapped in a long frame and taken from the place of the wounded. I am moved from hangar to hangar, then finally put on a plane, and I leave Vietnam forever.

DISCUSSION QUESTIONS

1. The opening chapter of Ron Kovic's *Born on the Fourth of July* is an example of first-person narration. How would you describe Kovic's tone of voice throughout this selection? What does it tell you about the narrator? Does Kovic sound like a professional writer? How does your answer to this question affect your response to the selection?

2. One literary device Kovic employs in his account is that of repetition. How does this device enhance the effectiveness of the passage? What other devices does Kovic use in telling his story? Are all of these devices equally effective?

3. Consider the passage of time in the narrative. How does Kovic let the reader know that time is moving ahead? Does time seem to speed up or slow down at different points in the story? How does Kovic manage this effect and why is time an important factor in his account of being wounded?

William Least Heat Moon / *Blue Highways* 1982

One of the most enduring traditions in American culture is the literature of the open road. From Walt Whitman and Henry David Thoreau to John Steinbeck and Jack Kerouac, American writers have eloquently expressed our collective fascination with wandering through the nation's landscape and meeting its people. A recent—and deservedly celebrated—contribution to this literary tradition is William Least Heat Moon's Blue Highways *(1982), a finely crafted narrative and cultural commentary on a fourteen-thousand-mile trek across the nation on rural back roads, those colored blue on our maps.*

The author, whose legal name is William Trogdon, derives his pseudonym from his Osage Indian blood. Released from his job teaching English at a small college in Missouri and separated from his wife (whom he calls simply "The Cherokee") at the age of thirty-eight, Heat Moon decided that if he couldn't make things go right he could at least go. He felt "a nearly desperate sense of isolation and a growing suspicion that I had lived in an alien land." Setting out in the small van he named "Ghost Dancer" and accompanied by volumes of Whitman and Nietzsche, Heat Moon drove America's back roads in search of "places where change did not mean ruin and where time and men and deeds connected." Citing Daniel Boone, who "moved at the sight of smoke from a new neighbor's chimney," Heat Moon kept "moving from the sight of my own."

Heat Moon writes evocatively of the land, the weather, and the dazzling array of American originals he meets along the way: Kentuckians rebuilding log cabins, a Brooklyn cop turned Trappist monk in Georgia, the boys in the barbershop in Dime Box, Texas, the drinkers in a roadside brothel in Nevada. And in each instance, Heat Moon's copious note taking allows these characters to tell their own stories in their own words.

In an interview, Heat Moon noted, "If writing isn't a process of discovery, then I can't imagine why anyone would write." In the following selection, he takes us to a seemingly nondescript town in eastern Tennessee. And in presenting the characters and stories of Nameless, Tennessee, Heat Moon helps us recognize the inadequacy of the generalizations we turn to when we describe who we are as Americans and where we are headed.

NAMELESS, TENNESSEE

Had it not been raining hard that morning on the Livingston square, I never would have learned of Nameless, Tennessee. Waiting for the rain to ease, I lay on my bunk and read the atlas to pass time rather than to see where I might go. In Kentucky were towns with fine names like Boreing, Bear Wallow, Decoy, Subtle, Mud Lick, Mummie, Neon; Belcher was just down the road from Mouthcard, and Minnie only ten miles from Mousie.

I looked at Tennessee. Turtletown eight miles from Ducktown. And also: Peavine, Wheel, Milky Way, Love Joy, Dull, Weakly, Fly, Spot, Miser Station, Only, McBurg, Peeled Chestnut, Clouds, Topsy, Isoline. And the best of all, Nameless. The logic! I was heading east, and Nameless lay forty-five miles west. I decided to go anyway.

The rain stopped, but things looked saturated, even bricks. In Gainesboro, a hill town with a square of businesses around the Jackson County Courthouse, I stopped for directions and breakfast. There is one almost infallible way to find honest food at just prices in blue-highway America: count the wall calendars in a cafe.

No calendar: Same as an interstate pit stop.
One calendar: Preprocessed food assembled in New Jersey.
Two calendars: Only if fish trophies present.
Three calendars: Can't miss on the farm-boy breakfasts.
Four calendars: Try the ho-made pie too.
Five calendars: Keep it under your hat, or they'll franchise.

One time I found a six-calendar cafe in the Ozarks, which served fried chicken, peach pie, and chocolate malts, that left me searching for another ever since. I've never seen a seven-calendar place. But old-time travelers—road men in a day when cars had running boards and lunchroom windows said AIR COOLED in blue letters with icicles dripping from the tops—those travelers have told me the golden legends of seven-calendar cafes.

To the rider of back roads, nothing shows the tone, the voice of a small town more quickly than the breakfast grill or the five-thirty tavern. Much of what the people do and believe and share is evident then. The City Cafe in Gainesboro had three calendars that I could see from the walk. Inside were no interstate refugees with full bladders and empty tanks, no wild-eyed children just released from the glassy cell of a stationwagon backseat, no longhaul truckers talking in CB numbers. There were only townspeople wearing overalls, or catalog-order suits with five-and-dime ties, or uniforms. That is, here were farmers and mill hands, bank clerks, the dry goods merchant, a policeman, and chiropractor's receptionist. Because it was Saturday, there were also mothers and children.

I ordered my standard on-the-road breakfast: two eggs up, hashbrowns, tomato juice. The waitress, whose pale, almost translucent skin shifted hue in the gray light like a thin slice of mother of pearl, brought the food. Next to the eggs was a biscuit with a little yellow Smiley button stuck in it. She said, "You from the North?"

"I guess I am." A Missourian gets used to Southerners thinking him a Yankee, a Northerner considering him a cracker, a Westerner sneering at his effete Easternness, and the Easterner taking him for a cowhand.

"So whata you doin' in the mountains?"

"Talking to people. Taking some pictures. Looking mostly."

"Lookin' for what?"

"A three-calendar cafe that serves Smiley buttons on the biscuits."

"You needed a smile. Tell me really."

"I don't know. Actually, I'm looking for some jam to put on this biscuit now that you've brought one."

She came back with grape jelly. In a land of quince jelly, apple butter, apricot jam, blueberry preserves, pear conserves, and lemon marmalade, you always get grape jelly.

"Whata you lookin' for?"

Like anyone else, I'm embarrassed to eat in front of a watcher, particularly if I'm getting interviewed. "Why don't you have a cup of coffee?"

"Cain't right now. You gonna tell me?"

"I don't know how to describe it to you. Call it harmony."

She waited for something more. "Is that it?" Someone called her to the kitchen. I had managed almost to finish by the time she came back. She sat on the edge of the booth. "I started out in life not likin' anything, but then it grew on me. Maybe that'll happen to you." She watched me spread the jelly. "Saw your van." She watched me eat the biscuit. "You sleep in there?" I told her I did. "I'd love to do that, but I'd be scared spitless."

"I don't mind being scared spitless. Sometimes."

"I'd love to take off cross country. I like to look at different license plates. But I'd take a dog. You carry a dog?"

"No dogs, no cats, no budgie birds. It's a one-man campaign to show Americans a person can travel alone without a pet."

"Cain't travel without a dog!"

"I like to do things the hard way."

"Shoot! I'd take me a dog to talk to. And for protection."

"It isn't traveling to cross the country and talk to your pug instead of people along the way. Besides, being alone on the road makes you ready to meet someone when you stop. You get sociable traveling alone."

She looked out toward the van again. "Time I get the nerve to take a trip, gas'll cost five dollars a gallon."

"Could be. My rig might go the way of the steamboat." I remembered why I'd come to Gainesboro. "You know the way to Nameless?"

"Nameless? I've heard of Nameless. Better ask the amlance driver in the corner booth." She pinned the Smiley on my jacket. "Maybe I'll see you on the road somewhere. His name's Bob, by the way."

"The ambulance driver?"

"The Smiley. I always name my Smileys—otherwise they all look alike. I'd talk to him before you go."

"The Smiley?"

"The amlance driver."

And so I went looking for Nameless, Tennessee, with a Smiley button named Bob.

"I don't know if I got directions for where you're goin'," the ambulance driver said. "I *think* there's a Nameless down the Shepardsville Road."

"When I get to Shepardsville, will I have gone too far?"

"Ain't no Shepardsville."

"How will I know when I'm there?"

"Cain't say for certain."

"What's Nameless look like?"

"Don't recollect."

"Is the road paved?"

"It's possible."

Those were the directions. I was looking for an unnumbered road named after a nonexistent town that would take me to a place called Nameless that nobody was sure existed.

Clumps of wild garlic lined the county highway that I hoped was the Shepardsville Road. It scrimmaged with the mountain as it tried to stay on top of the ridges; the hillsides were so steep and thick with oak, I felt as if I were following a trail through the misty treetops. Chickens, doing more work with their necks than legs, ran across the road, and, with a battering of wings, half leapt and half flew into the lower branches of oaks. A vicious pair of mixed-breed German shepherds raced along trying to eat the tires. After miles, I decided I'd missed the town—assuming there truly *was* a Nameless, Tennessee. It wouldn't be the first time I'd qualified for the Ponce de Leon Believe Anything Award.

I stopped beside a big man loading tools in a pickup. "I may be lost."

"Where'd you lose the right road?"

"I don't know. Somewhere around nineteen sixty-five."

"Highway fifty-six, you mean?"

"I came down fifty-six. I think I should've turned at the last junction."

"Only thing down that road's stumps and huckleberries, and the berries ain't there in March. Where you tryin' to get to?"

"Nameless. If there is such a place."

"You might not know Thurmond Watts, but he's got him a store down the road.

That's Nameless at his store. Still there all right, but I might not vouch you that tomorrow.'' He came up to the van. ''In my Army days, I wrote Nameless, Tennessee, for my place of birth on all the papers, even though I lived on this end of the ridge. All these ridges and hollers got names of their own. That's Steam Mill Holler over yonder. Named after the steam engine in the gristmill. Miller had him just one arm but done a good business.''

''What business you in?''

''I've always farmed, but I work in Cookeville now in a heatin' element factory. Bad back made me go to town to work.'' He pointed to a wooden building not much bigger than his truck. By the slanting porch, a faded Double Cola sign said J M WHEELER STORE. ''That used to be my business. That's me—Madison Wheeler. Feller came by one day. From Detroit. He wanted to buy the sign because he carried my name too. But I didn't sell. Want to keep my name up.'' He gave a cigarette a good slow smoking. ''Had a decent business for five years, but too much of it was in credit. Then them supermarkets down in Cookeville opened, and I was buyin' higher than they was sellin'. With these hard roads now, everybody gets out of the hollers to shop or work. Don't stay up in here anymore. This tar road under my shoes done my business in, and it's likely to do Nameless in.''

''Do you wish it was still the old way?''

''I got no debts now. I got two boys raised, and they never been in trouble. I got a brick house and some corn and tobacco and a few Hampshire hogs and Herefords. A good bull. Bull's pumpin' better blood than I do. Real generous man in town let me put my cow in with his stud. I couldna paid the fee on that specimen otherwise.'' He took another long, meditative pull on his filtertip. ''If you're satisfied, that's all they are to it. I'll tell you, people from all over the nation—Florida, Mississippi—are comin' in here to retire because it's good country. But our young ones don't stay on. Not much way to make a livin' in here anymore. Take me. I been beatin' on these stumps all my life, tryin' to farm these hills. They don't give much up to you. Fightin' rocks and briars all the time. One of the first things I recollect is swingin' a briar blade—filed out of an old saw it was. Now they come in with them crawlers and push out a pasture in a day. Still, it's a grudgin' land—like the gourd. Got to hard cuss gourd seed, they say, to get it up out of the ground.''

The whole time, my rig sat in the middle of the right lane while we stood talking next to it and wiped at the mist. No one else came or went. Wheeler said, ''Factory work's easier on the back, and I don't mind it, understand, but a man becomes what he does. Got to watch that. That's why I keep at farmin', although the crops haven't ever throve. It's the doin' that's important.'' He looked up suddenly. ''My apologies. I didn't ask what you do that gets you into these hollers.''

I told him. I'd been gone only six days, but my account of the trip already had taken on some polish.

He nodded. ''Satisfaction is doin' what's important to yourself. A man ought to honor other people, but he's got to honor what he believes in too.''

As I started the engine, Wheeler said, ''If you get back this way, stop in and see me. Always got beans and taters and a little piece of meat.''

Down along the ridge, I wondered why it's always those who live on little who are the ones to ask you to dinner.

Nameless, Tennessee, was a town of maybe ninety people if you pushed it, a dozen houses along the road, a couple of barns, same number of churches, a general merchandise store selling Fire Chief gasoline, and a community center with a lighted volleyball court. Behind the center was an open-roof, rusting metal privy with PAINT ME on the door; in the hollow of a nearby oak lay a full pint of Jack Daniel's Black Label. From the houses, the odor of coal smoke.

Next to a red tobacco barn stood the general merchandise with a poster of Senator Albert Gore, Jr., smiling from the window. I knocked. The door opened partway. A tall, thin man said, "Closed up. For good," and started to shut the door.

"Don't want to buy anything. Just a question for Mr. Thurmond Watts."

The man peered through the slight opening. He looked me over. "What question would that be?"

"If this is Nameless, Tennessee, could he tell me how it got that name?"

The man turned back into the store and called out, "Miss Ginny! Somebody here wants to know how Nameless come to be Nameless."

Miss Ginny edged to the door and looked me and my truck over. Clearly, she didn't approve. She said, "You know as well as I do, Thurmond. Don't keep him on the stoop in the damp to tell him." Miss Ginny, I found out, was Mrs. Virginia Watts, Thurmond's wife.

I stepped in and they both began telling the story, adding a detail here, the other correcting a fact there, both smiling at the foolishness of it all. It seems the hilltop settlement went for years without a name. Then one day the Post Office Department told the people if they wanted mail up on the mountain they would have to give the place a name you could properly address a letter to. The community met; there were only a handful, but they commenced debating. Some wanted patriotic names, some names from nature, one man recommended in all seriousness his own name. They couldn't agree, and they ran out of names to argue about. Finally, a fellow tired of the talk; he didn't like the mail he received anyway. "Forget the durn Post Office," he said. "This here's a nameless place if I ever seen one, so leave it be." And that's just what they did.

Watts pointed out the window. "We used to have signs on the road, but the Halloween boys keep tearin' them down."

"You think Nameless is a funny name," Miss Ginny said. "I see it plain in your eyes. Well, you take yourself up north a piece to Difficult or Defeated or Shake Rag. Now them are silly names."

The old store, lighted only by three fifty-watt bulbs, smelled of coal oil and baking bread. In the middle of the rectangular room, where the oak floor sagged a little, stood an iron stove. To the right was a wooden table with an unfinished game of checkers and a stool made from an apple-tree stump. On shelves around the walls sat earthen jugs with corncob stoppers, a few canned goods, and some of the two thousand old clocks and clockworks Thurmond Watts owned. Only one was ticking; the others he just looked at. I asked how long he'd been in the store.

"Thirty-five years, but we closed the first day of the year. We're hopin' to sell it to a churchly couple. Upright people. No athians."

"Did you build this store?"

"I built this one, but it's the third general store on the ground. I fear it'll be the last. I take no pleasure in that. Once you could come in here for a gallon of paint, a pickle, a pair of shoes, and a can of corn."

"Or horehound candy," Miss Ginny said. "Or corsets and salves. We had cough syrups and all that for the body. In season, we'd buy and sell blackberries and walnuts and chestnuts, before the blight got them. And outside, Thurmond milled corn and sharpened plows. Even shoed a horse sometimes."

"We could fix up a horse or a man or a baby," Watts said.

"Thurmond, tell him we had a doctor on the ridge in them days."

"We had a doctor on the ridge in them days. As good as any doctor alivin'. He'd cut a crooked toenail or deliver a woman. Dead these last years."

"I got some bad ham meat one day," Miss Ginny said, "and took to vomitin'. All day, all night. Hangin' on the drop edge of yonder. I said to Thurmond, 'Thurmond, unless you want shut of me, call the doctor.' "

"I studied on it," Watts said.

"You never did. You got him right now. He come over and put three drops of iodeen in half a glass of well water. I drank it down and the vomitin' stopped with the last swallow. Would you think iodeen could do that?''

''He put Miss Ginny on one teaspoon of spirits of ammonia in well water for her nerves. Ain't nothin' works better for her to this day.''

''Calms me like the hand of the Lord.''

Hilda, the Wattses' daughter, came out of the backroom. ''I remember him,'' she said. ''I was just a baby. Y'all were talkin' to him, and he lifted me up on the counter and gave me a stick of Juicy Fruit and a piece of cheese.''

''Knew the old medicines,'' Watts said. ''Only drugstore he needed was a good kitchen cabinet. None of them antee-beeotics that hit you worsen your ailment. Forgotten lore now, the old medicines, because they ain't profit in iodeen.''

Miss Ginny started back to the side room where she and her sister Marilyn were taking apart a duck-down mattress to make bolsters. She stopped at the window for another look at Ghost Dancing. ''How do you sleep in that thing? Ain't you all cramped and cold?''

''How does the clam sleep in his shell?'' Watts said in my defense.

''Thurmond, get the boy a piece of buttermilk pie afore he goes on.''

''Hilda, get him some buttermilk pie.'' He looked at me. ''You like good music?'' I said I did. He cranked up an old Edison phonograph, the kind with the big morning-glory blossom for a speaker, and put on a wax cylinder. ''This will be 'My Mother's Prayer,' '' he said.

While I ate buttermilk pie, Watts served as disc jockey of Nameless, Tennessee. ''Here's 'Mountain Rose.' '' It was one of those moments that you know at the time will stay with you to the grave: the sweet pie, the gaunt man playing the old music, the coals in the stove glowing orange, the scent of kerosene and hot bread. ''Here's 'Evening Rhapsody.' '' The music was so heavily romantic we both laughed. I thought: It is for this I have come.

Feathered over and giggling, Miss Ginny stepped from the side room. She knew she was a sight. ''Thurmond, give him some lunch. Still looks hungry.''

Hilda pulled food off the woodstove in the backroom: home-butchered and canned whole-hog sausage, home-canned June apples, turnip greens, cole slaw, potatoes, stuffing, hot cornbread. All delicious.

Watts and Hilda sat and talked while I ate. ''Wish you would join me.''

''We've ate,'' Watts said. ''Cain't beat a woodstove for flavorful cookin'.''

He told me he was raised in a one-hundred-fifty-year-old cabin still standing in one of the hollows. ''How many's left,'' he said, ''that grew up in a log cabin? I ain't the last surely, but I must be climbin' on the list.''

Hilda cleared the table. ''You Watts ladies know how to cook.''

''She's in nursin' school at Tennessee Tech. I went over for one of them football games last year there at Coevul.'' To say *Cookeville,* you let the word collapse in upon itself so that it comes out ''Coevul.''

''Do you like football?'' I asked.

''Don't know. I was so high up in that stadium, I never opened my eyes.''

Watts went to the back and returned with a fat spiral notebook that he set on the table. His expression had changed. ''Miss Ginny's *Deathbook.*''

The thing startled me. Was it something I was supposed to sign? He opened it but said nothing. There were scads of names written in a tidy hand over pages incised to crinkliness by a ballpoint. Chronologically, the names had piled up: wives, grandparents, a stillborn infant, relatives, friends close and distant. Names, names. After each, the date of *the* unknown finally known and transcribed. The last entry bore yesterday's date.

''She's wrote out twenty years' worth. Ever day she listens to the hospital report on the radio and puts the names in. Folks come by to check a date. Or they just turn through the books. Read them like a scrapbook.''

Hilda said, ''Like Saint Peter at the gates inscribin' the names.''

Watts took my arm. ''Come along.'' He led me to the fruit cellar under the store. As we went down, he said, ''Always take a newborn baby upstairs afore you take him downstairs, otherwise you'll incline him downwards.''

The cellar was dry and full of cobwebs and jar after jar of home-canned food, the bottles organized as a shopkeeper would: sausage, pumpkin, sweet pickles, tomatoes, corn relish, blackberries, peppers, squash, jellies. He held a hand out toward the dusty bottles. ''Our tomorrows.''

Upstairs again, he said, ''Hope to sell the store to the right folk. I see now, though, it'll be somebody offen the ridge. I've studied on it, and maybe it's the end of our place.'' He stirred the coals. ''This store could give a comfortable livin', but not likely get you rich. But just gettin' by is dice rollin' to people nowadays. I never did see my day guaranteed.''

When it was time to go, Watts said, ''If you find anyone along your way wants a good store—on the road to Cordell Hull Lake—tell them about us.''

I said I would. Miss Ginny and Hilda and Marilyn came out to say goodbye. It was cold and drizzling again. ''Weather to give a man the weary dismals,'' Watts grumbled. ''Where you headed from here?''

''I don't know.''

''Cain't get lost then.''

Miss Ginny looked again at my rig. It had worried her from the first as it had my mother. ''I hope you don't get yourself kilt in that durn thing gallivantin' around the country.''

''Come back when the hills dry off,'' Watts said. ''We'll go lookin' for some of them round rocks all sparkly inside.''

I thought a moment. ''Geodes?''

''Them's the ones. The county's properly full of them.''

Letitia Baldridge / *Letitia Baldridge's Complete Guide to Executive Manners* 1985

For many years, Letitia Baldridge has been considered one of our nation's foremost authorities on etiquette. Besides writing numerous books on the subject, she served as First Lady Jacqueline Kennedy's chief of staff at the White House and has been a consultant to United States embassies throughout the world. This selection from a recent book may be read alongside Susan Jacoby's ''Unfair Game'' (See ''Press''). Together these pieces provide an interesting commentary on the problems facing a woman alone.

A WOMAN TRAVELING ALONE

A woman alone doesn't mean an available woman. A woman on her own is often afraid of being perceived as an easy pickup or, even worse, as a hooker. To some men, ''alone'' signifies ''available,'' which is sexual discrimination in its worst form.

If you, a woman alone, are unpleasantly accosted by a stranger in your hotel who has the wrong idea, of course you tell him to ''get lost fast.'' But you certainly don't need to spend your evenings imprisoned in your mustard yellow and poison green motel room because of an occasional unpleasant experience. You should summon enough courage to have your drink in the hotel bar as well as eat your dinner in the hotel dining room, if that's what you want to do. It may take a little practice to enter public eating and drinking places by yourself and, of course, they must be selected with care. After a few times, being alone in a restaurant on your travels becomes very natural.

There are some things to remember, of course. First of all, *you should look like a professional* at all times when traveling for your company. Your conservative, business image is conveyed by the way you dress as well as by the way you behave.

Enter the bar with your briefcase or some files (a symbol of your status in life). Hold your head high, with a pleasant expression on your face, and without any embarrassment tell the person seating you, "Yes, a table for one, please." After you have ordered your drink, shuffle through a paper or two, to further establish yourself as someone who is stopping in this hotel on business.

Look elsewhere if you find a man staring at you; don't put on an expression either of panic or of extreme distaste. Both are signs of uneasiness. If he comes over uninvited and seats himself at your table, call the waiter and ask, "Is there a free table for this gentleman?" The interloper should get the message and leave you alone. If he does not, leave the table and report him to the management; they will handle it from there.

If an attractive man comes over to your table and politely asks if he can join you, you may say yes, if you feel like it. Explain to him at the beginning, however, that you have only a few more minutes before you have to leave. This gives you a chance to desert him if you find his company less than satisfactory.

If he then offers to pay for your drink, it is proper for you to accept. If you both order a second round, make it clear that you are going to pay for *this* round. As for the third round of drinks, finesse it. This is the round that one (or both) will have been sorry to have ordered.

If your companion invites you to join him for dinner, if you wish to accept, make it clear that you will charge your dinner to your own bill and that you do not wish to leave the premises. By not becoming indebted to him, he and everyone else will know you are a no-nonsense woman who does not pick up men. Mention something like "Dinner will have to be a pretty speedy one, because I have a lot of work to prepare before the meetings tomorrow." With this statement you are emitting a clear signal that you will not continue through the night as his companion.

There have been some very unpleasant stories about what has happened to businesswomen who left their hotels or motels with strangers who invited them out to dinner. This is why you should stay where you are to dine. It is wise to be safe.

A woman often feels self-conscious dining in a good restaurant without an escort or a friend. Yet when she is on the road on business it is enjoyable to try out the restaurants for which that city is famous. If you wish to dine in a particular restaurant in another city, be sure to book a reservation beforehand. (Make certain your choice is not the night club–cabaret kind of place, because if you are typical, a woman sitting alone while a floor show is in progress can feel uncomfortable.) When you reserve your table, give your name, your title, and company. It helps impress management of the restaurant. If you are fussed over and shown special attention, remember to be generous with your tips when you leave.

On rare occasions a maître d'hôtel will discriminate against solitary woman guests. If this happens to you, ask for a better table. If you have booked a reservation well in advance and you arrive early in the dining hour, you should be shown to a good table, not to one directly in front of the kitchen, where you are in danger of being hit each time the door opens.

If you are shy about having others see you dining alone, you might pass some time by making notes in your office diary or by jotting down some notes on a pad. It doesn't look very nice—or appetizing—if you read your newspaper, because dirty newsprint means dirty fingers on a clean white tablecloth. An exception to this rule is of course the breakfast meal, when most people are too tired or sleepy to care about inky fingers, and the cuisine is not subtle enough to worry about what newsprint might do to the food.

You might take a small book to the table to peruse occasionally. Don't stick your nose in it the entire time, or others might think you have an inferiority complex and are afraid to be looked at. Glance up from your reading every so often; put a pleasant expression on your face. If you find someone staring at you, ignore it—unless you want to try staring the other person down (I've found it always works). You have a right to be there, to enjoy your meal and your surroundings without your privacy being invaded. Besides, it is much more enjoyable to dine alone than to share your meal with someone who is unpleasant or even boring. (Keep reminding yourself of this, and it will help you combat any possible shyness about being alone.)

One night a very attractive young woman traveling for Procter & Gamble was absorbedly reading a book through part of her dinner in a hotel dining room. An executive at a nearby table asked the waiter to find out discreetly what book was holding her interest so completely. When the headwaiter returned to give him the name of a book on Elizabethan England, the executive smiled broadly. He had written his college thesis on the subject. He had a very legitimate entree with which to begin a conversation. There was an immediate exchange of notes between the two tables; there were glasses of champagne shared after dinner; and there was a wedding six months later, which goes to prove that not all business trips are boring!

DISCUSSION QUESTIONS

1. The above selection begins firmly with the statement: "A woman alone doesn't mean an available woman." To whom does this statement seem to be directed? Why would Baldridge direct this statement to the woman traveling alone as well as to male readers?

2. How would Baldridge react to the position that a woman's privacy while dining or drinking alone lies solely with the woman? How would Susan Jacoby (in "Press") react to such a remark?

3. Baldridge concludes the selection by relating an anecdote about a young businesswoman who met her future husband as the result of his approaching her while she was dining alone at her hotel. What comment does Baldridge make about this story? What other message might be derived from this story?

Garrison Keillor / *Lake Wobegon Days* 1985

"Smart doesn't count for so much" in Lake Wobegon, the imaginary small town in Minnesota invented by Garrison Keillor in 1974 as the setting of his weekly monologue for his popular radio show, "A Prairie Home Companion." Lake Wobegon is the quintessence of the American small town, just as Keillor's comic style contains the essence of American humor—the tall tale, the exaggerated regionalism, the deadpan understatement. "Sumus Quod Sumus" means "We are what we are"; it is the town's motto.

Born in Anoka, Minnesota, in 1942, Keillor graduated from the University of Minnesota in 1966. His first book, Happy to Be Here, *was also a best-seller.*

SUMUS QUOD SUMUS

Why isn't my town on the map?—Well, back before cartographers had the benefit of an aerial view, when teams of surveyors tramped from one town to the next, mistakes were made. Sometimes those towns were farther apart than they should have been. Many maps were drawn by French explorers in the bows of canoes bucking heavy rapids, including Sieur Marine de St. Croix, who was dizzy and nauseated when he penciled in the river that bears his name. He was miles off in some places, but since the river formed the Minnesota-Wisconsin border, revision was politically impossible and the mistakes were inked in, though it left thousands of people sitting high and dry on the other side.

A worse mistake was made by the Coleman Survey of 1866, which omitted fifty square miles of central Minnesota (including Lake Wobegon), an error that lives on in the F.A.A.'s Coleman Course Correction, a sudden lurch felt by airline passengers as they descend into Minnesota air space on flights from New York or Boston.

Why the state jobbed out the survey to drunks is a puzzle. The Coleman outfit, headed by Lieutenant Michael Coleman, had been attached to Grant's army, which they misdirected time and again so that Grant's flanks kept running head-on into Lee's rear until Union officers learned to make "right face" a 120-degree turn. Governor Marshall, however, regarded the 1866 survey as preliminary—"It will provide us a good general idea of the State, a foundation upon which we can build in the future," he said—though of course it turned out to be the final word.

The map was drawn by four teams of surveyors under the direction of Finian Coleman, Michael having left for the Nebraska gold rush, who placed them at the four corners of the state and aimed them inward. The southwest and northwest contingents moved fast over level ground, while the eastern teams got bogged down in the woods, so that, when they met a little west of Lake Wobegon, the four quadrants didn't fit within the boundaries legislated by Congress in 1851. Nevertheless, Finian mailed them to St. Paul, leaving the legislature to wrestle with the discrepancy.

The legislature simply reproportioned the state by eliminating the overlap in the middle, the little quadrangle that is Mist County. "The soil of that region is unsuited to agriculture, and we doubt that its absence would be much noticed," Speaker of the House Randolph remarked.

In 1933, a legislative interim commission proposed that the state recover the lost county by collapsing the square mileage of several large lakes. The area could be removed from the centers of the lakes, elongating them slightly so as not to lose valuable shoreline. Opposition was spearheaded by the Bureau of Fisheries, which pointed out the walleye breeding grounds to be lost; and the State Map Amendment was attached as a rider to a bill requiring the instruction of evolution in all secondary schools and was defeated by voice vote.

Proponents of map change, or "accurates" as they were called, were chastised by their opponents, the so-called "moderates," who denied the existence of Mist County on the one hand—"Where is it?" a moderate cried one day on the Senate floor in St. Paul. "Can you show me one scintilla of evidence that it exists?"—and, on the other hand, denounced the county as a threat to property owners everywhere. "If this county is allowed to rear its head, then no boundary is sacred, no deed is certain," the moderates said. "We might as well reopen negotiations with the Indians."

Wobegonians took the defeat of inclusion with their usual calm. "We felt that we were a part of Minnesota by virtue of the fact that when we drove more than a few miles in any direction, we were in Minnesota," Hjalmar Ingqvist says. "It didn't matter what anyone said."

In 1980, Governor Al Quie became the first governor to set foot in Mist County, slipping quietly away from his duties to attend a ceremony dedicating a plaque attached to the Statue of the Unknown Norwegian. "We don't know where he is. He was here, then he disappeared," his aides told reporters, all the time the Governor was enjoying a hearty meatball lunch in the company of fellow Lutherans. In his brief remarks, he saluted Lake Wobegon for its patience in anonymity. "Seldom has a town made such a sacrifice in remaining unrecognized so long," he said, though other speakers were quick to assure him that it had been no sacrifice, really, but a true pleasure.

"Here in 1867 the first Norwegian settlers knelt to thank God for bringing them to this place," the plaque read, "and though noting immediately the rockiness of the soil, remained, sowing seeds of Christian love."

What's special about this town, it's pretty much like a lot of towns, isn't it? There is a perfectly good answer to that question, it only takes a moment to think of it.

For one thing, the Statue of the Unknown Norweigan. If other towns have one, we don't know about it. Sculpted by a man named O'Connell or O'Connor in 1896, the granite youth stands in a small plot at a jog in the road where a surveyor knocked off for lunch years ago and looks down Main Street to the lake. A proud figure, his back is erect, his feet are on the ground on account of no money remained for a pedestal, and his eyes—well, his eyes are a matter of question. Probably the artist meant him to exude confidence in the New World, but his eyes are set a little deep so that dark shadows appear in the late afternoon and by sunset he looks worried. His confident smile turns into a forced grin. In the morning, he is stepping forward, his right hand extended in greeting, but as the day wears on, he hesitates, and finally he appears to be about to turn back. The right hand seems to say, Wait here. I think I forgot something.

Nevertheless, he is a landmark and an asset, so it was a shame when the tornado of 1947 did damage to him. That tornado skipped in from the northeast; it blew away one house except for a dresser mirror that wasn't so much as cracked—amazing; it's in the historical society now, and people still bring their relatives to look at it. It also picked up a brand-new Chevy pickup and set it down a quarter-mile away. *On a road. In the right-hand lane.* In town, it took the roof off the Lutheran church, where nobody was, and missed the Bijou, which was packed for *Shame,* starring Cliff DeCarlo. And it blew a stalk of quackgrass about six inches into the Unknown Norweigan, in an unusual place, a place where you wouldn't expect to find grass in a person, a part of the body where you've been told to insert nothing bigger than your finger in a washcloth.

Bud, our municipal employee, pulled it out, of course, but the root was imbedded in the granite, so it keeps growing out. Bud has considered using a preemergent herbicide on him but is afraid it will leave a stain on the side of his head, so, when he mows, simply reaches up to the Unknown's right ear and snips off the blade with his fingernails. It's not so noticeable, really; you have to look for it to see it.

The plaque that wouldn've been on the pedestal the town couldn't afford was bolted to a brick and set in the ground until Bud dug it out because it was dinging up his mower blade. Now in the historical society museum in the basement of the town hall, it sits next to the Lake Wobegon runestone, which proves that Viking explorers were here in 1381. Unearthed by a Professor Oftedahl or Ostenwald around 1921 alongside County Road 2, where the professor, motoring from Chicago to Seattle, had stopped to bury garbage, the small black stone is covered with Viking runic characters which read (translated by him): "8 of [us] stopped & stayed awhile to visit & have [coffee] & a short nap. Sorry [you] weren't here. Well, that's about [it] for now."

Every Columbus Day, the runestone is carried up to the school and put on a card-table in the lunchroom for the children to see, so they can know their true heritage. It saddens Norwegians that America still honors this Italian, who arrived late in the New World and by accident, who wasn't even interested in New Worlds but only in spices. Out on a spin in search of curry powder and hot peppers—a man on a voyage to the grocery—he stumbled onto the land of heroic Vikings and proceeded to get the credit for it. And then to name it *America* after Amerigo Vespucci, an Italian who never saw the New World but only sat in Italy and drew incredibly inaccurate maps of it. By rights, it should be called Erica, after Eric the Red, who did the work five hundred years earlier. The United States of Erica. Erica the Beautiful. The Erican League.

Not many children come to see the runestone where it spends the rest of the year. The museum is a locked door in the town hall, down the hall and to the left by the washroom. Viola Tordahl the clerk has the key and isn't happy to be bothered for it. "I don't know why I ever agreed to do it. You know, they don't pay me a red cent for this," she says as she digs around in a junk drawer for it.

The museum is in the basement. The light switch is halfway down the steps, to your left. The steps are concrete, narrow and steep. It's going to be very interesting, you think, to look at these many objects from olden days, and then when you put your hand on the switch, you feel something crawl on it. Not a fly. You brush the spider off, and then you smell the must from below, like bilgewater, and hear a slight movement as if a man sitting quietly in the dark for several hours had just risen slowly and the chair scraped a quarter-inch. He sighs a faint sigh, licks his upper lip, and shifts the axe from his left to his right hand so he can scratch his nose. He is left-handed, evidently. No need to find out any more about him. You turn off the light and shut the door.

What's so special about this town is not the food, though Ralph's Pretty Good Grocery has got in a case of fresh cod. Frozen, but it's fresher than what's been in his freezer for months. In the grocery business, you have to throw out stuff sometimes, but Ralph is Norwegian and it goes against his principles. People bend down and peer into the meat case. "Give me a pork loin," they say. "One of those in the back, one of the pink ones." "These in front are better," he says. "They're more aged. You get better flavor." But they want a pink one, so Ralph takes out a pink one, bites his tongue. This is the problem with being in retail; you can't say what you think.

More and more people are sneaking off to the Higgledy-Piggledy in St. Cloud, where you find two acres of food, a meat counter a block long with huge walloping roasts and steaks big enough to choke a cow, and exotic fish lying on crushed ice. Once Ralph went to his brother Benny's for dinner and Martha put baked swordfish on the table. Ralph's face burned. His own sister-in-law! "It's delicious," said Mrs. Ralph. "Yeah," Ralph said, "if it wasn't for the mercury poisoning, I'd take swordfish every day of the week." Cod, he pointed out, is farther down in the food chain, and doesn't collect the mercury that the big fish do. Forks paused in midair. He would have gone on to describe the effects of mercury on the body, how it lodges in the brain, wiping the slate clean until you wind up in bed attached to tubes and can't remember your own Zip Code, but his wife contacted him on his ankle. Later, she said, "You had no business saying that."

"I'll have no business, period," he said, "if people don't wake up."

"Well, it's a free country, and she has a perfect right to go shop where she wants to."

"Sure she does, and she can go live there, too."

When the Thanatopsis Club hit its centennial in 1982 and Mrs. Hallberg wrote to the White House and asked for an essay from the President on small-town life, she got one, two paragraphs that extolled Lake Wobegon as a model of free enterprise and individualism, which was displayed in the library under glass, although the truth is that Lake Wobegon survives to the extent that it does on a form of voluntary socialism with elements of Deism, fatalism, and nepotism. Free enterprise runs on self-interest.[1] This is socialism, and it runs on loyalty. You need a toaster, you buy it at Co-op Hardware even though you can get a deluxe model with all the toaster attachments for less money at K-Mart in St. Cloud. You buy it at Co-op because you know Otto. Glasses you will find at Clifford's which also sells shoes and ties and some gloves. (It is trying to be the department store it used to be when it was The Mercantile, which it is still called by most people because the old sign is so clear on the brick facade, clearer than the "Clifford's" in the window.) Though you might rather shop for glasses in a strange place where they'll encourage your vanity, though Clifford's selection of frames is clearly based on Scripture ("Take no thought for what you shall wear. . . .") and you might put a hideous piece of junk on your face and Clifford would say, "I think you'll like those" as if you're a person who looks like you don't care what you look like—nevertheless you should think twice before you get the Calvin Klein glasses from Vanity Vision in the St. Cloud Mall. Calvin Klein isn't going to come with the Rescue Squad and he isn't going to teach your children about redemption by grace. You couldn't find Calvin Klein to save your life.

If people were to live by comparison shopping, the town would go bust. It cannot compete with other places item by item. Nothing in town is quite as good as it appears to be somewhere else. If you live there, you have to take it as a whole. That's loyalty.

This is why Judy Ingqvist does not sing "Holy City" on Sunday morning, although everyone says she sounds great on "Holy City"—it's not her wish to sound great, though she is the leading soprano; it's her wish that all the sopranos sound at least okay. So she sings quietly. One Sunday when the Ingqvists went to the Black Hills on vacation, a young, white-knuckled seminarian filled in; he gave a forty-five minute sermon and had a lot of sermon left over when finally three deacons cleared their throats simultaneously. They sounded like German shepherds barking, and their barks meant that the congregation now knew that he was bright and he had nothing more to prove to them. The young man looked on the sermon as free enterprise.[2] You work like hell on it and come up a winner. He wanted to give it all the best what was in him, of which he had more than he needed. He was opening a Higgledy-Piggledy of theology, and the barks were meant to remind him where he was: in Lake Wobegon, where smart doesn't count for so much. A minister has to be able to read a clock. At noon, it's time to go home and turn up the pot roast and get the peas out of the freezer. Everybody gets their pot roast at Ralph's. It's not the tenderest meat in the Ninth Federal Reserve District, but after you bake it for four hours until it falls apart in shreds, what's the difference?

So what's special about this town is not smarts either. It counted zero when you worked for Bud on the road crew, as I did one summer. He said, "Don't get smart with me," and he meant it. One week I was wrestling with great ideas in

[1] The smoke machine at the Sidetrack Tap, if you whack it about two inches below the Camels, will pay off a couple packs for free, and some enterprising patrons find it in their interest to use this knowledge. Past a certain age, you're not supposed to do this sort of thing anymore. You're supposed to grow up. Unfortunately, that is just the age when many people start to smoke.

[2] He is no longer in the ministry. He is vice-president for sales at Devotional Systems, Inc., maker of quadraphonic sanctuary speakers for higher fidelity sermons, home devotional programs on floppy disks, and individual biofeedback systems in the pews. Two wires with electrodes hang from each hymnal rack, which the faithful press to their temples as they pray, attempting to bring the needle on the biometer into the reverence zone. For some reason, prayer doesn't accomplish that so well as, say, thinking about food, but DSI is working on it and thinks this may be a breakthrough in the worship of the future.

dimly-lit college classrooms, the next I was home shoveling gravel in the sun, just another worker. I'd studied the workers in humanities class, spent a whole week on the labor movement as it related to ideals of American individualism, and I thought it was pretty funny to sing "Soldiarity Forever" while patching potholes, but he didn't, he told me to quit smarting off. Work was serious business, and everybody was supposed to do it—*hard* work, unless of course you thought you were too good for it, in which case to hell with you. Bud's wife kept telling him to retire, he said, but he wasn't going to; all the geezers he'd known who decided to take it easy were flat on their backs a few months later with all their friends commenting on how natural they looked. Bud believed that when you feel bad, you get out of bed and put your boots on. "A little hard work never killed anybody," he told us, I suppose, about fifteen thousand times. Lean on your shovel for one second to straighten your back, and there was Bud to remind you. It would have been satisfying to choke him on the spot. We had the tar right there, just throw the old coot in and cook him and use him for fill. But he was so strong he might have taken the whole bunch of us. Once he said to me, "Here, take the other end of this." It was the hoist for the backhoe. I lifted my end, and right then I went from a 34- to a 36-inch sleeve. I thought my back was going to break. "Heavy?" he said. *Nooo.* "Want to set her down?" *Nooo. That's okay.* "Well, better set her down, cause this is where she goes." *Okay.* All my bones had been reset, making me a slightly curved person. "Next time try lifting with your legs," he said.

People who visit Lake Wobegon come to see somebody, otherwise they missed the turn on the highway and are lost. *Ausländers,* the Germans call them. They don't come for Toast 'n Jelly Days, or the Germans' quadrennial Gesuffa Days, or Krazy Daze, or the Feast Day of St. Francis, or the three-day Mist County Fair with its exciting Death Leap from the top of the grandstand to the arms of the haystack for only ten cents. What's special about here isn't special enough to draw a major crowd, though Flag Day—you could drive a long way on June 14 to find another like it.

Flag Day, as we know it, was the idea of Herman Hochstetter, Rollie's dad, who ran the dry goods store and ran Armistice Day, the Fourth of July, and Flag Day. For the Fourth, he organized a double-loop parade around the block which allowed people to take turns marching and watching. On Armistice Day, everyone stepped outside at 11 A.M. and stood in silence for two minutes as Our Lady's bell tolled eleven times.

Flag Day was his favorite. For a modest price, he would install a bracket on your house to hold a pole to hang your flag on, or he would drill a hole in the sidewalk in front of your store with his drill gun powered by a .22 shell. *Bam!* And in went the flag. On patriotic days, flags flew all over; there were flags on the tall poles, flags on the short, flags in the brackets on the pillars and the porches, and if you were flagless you could expect to hear from Herman. His hairy arm around your shoulder, his poochlike face close to yours, he would say how proud he was that so many people were proud of their country, leaving you to see the obvious, that you were a gap in the ranks.

In June 1944, the day after D-Day, a salesman from Fisher Hat called on Herman and offered a good deal on red and blue baseball caps. "Do you have white also?" Herman asked. The salesman thought that white caps could be had for the same wonderful price. Herman ordered two hundred red, two hundred white, and one hundred blue. By the end of the year, he still had four hundred and eighty-six caps. The inspiration of the Living Flag was born from that overstock.

On June 14, 1945, a month after V-E Day, a good crowd assembled in front of the Central Building in response to Herman's ad in the paper:

> Honor ''AMERICA'' June 14 AT 4 p.m. Be proud of ''Our Land & People''. Be part of the ''LIVING FLAG''. Don't let it be said that Lake Wobegon was ''Too Busy''. Be on time. 4 p.m. ''Sharp''.

His wife Louise handed out the caps, and Herman stood on a stepladder and told people where to stand. He lined up the reds and whites into stripes, then got the blues into their square. Mr. Hanson climbed up on the roof of the Central Building and took a photograph, they sang the national anthem, and then the Living Flag dispersed. The photograph appeared in the paper the next week. Herman kept the caps.

In the flush of victory, people were happy to do as told and stand in place, but in 1946 and 1947, dissension cropped up in the ranks: people complained about the heat and about Herman—what gave *him* the idea he could order *them* around? ''People! Please! I need your attention! You blue people, keep your hats on! Please! Stripe No. 4, you're sagging! You reds, you're up here! We got too many white people, we need more red ones! Let's do this without talking, people! I can't get you straight if you keep moving around! Some of you are not paying attention! Everybody shut up! Please!''

One cause of resentment was the fact that none of them got to see the Flag they were in; the picture in the paper was black and white. Only Herman and Mr. Hanson got to see the real Flag, and some boys too short to be needed down below. People wanted a chance to go up to the roof and witness the spectacle for themselves.

''How can you go up there if you're supposed to be down here?'' Herman said. ''You go up there to look, you got nothing to look at. Isn't it enough to know that you're doing your part?''

On Flag Day, 1949, just as Herman said, ''That's it! Hold it now!'' one of the reds made a break for it—dashed up four flights of stairs to the roof and leaned over and had a long look. Even with the hole he left behind, it was a magnificent sight. The Living Flag filled the street below. A perfect Flag! The reds so brilliant! He couldn't take his eyes off it. ''Get down here! We need a picture!'' Herman yelled up to him. ''How does it look?'' people yelled up to him. ''Unbelievable! I can't describe it!'' he said.

So then everyone had to have a look. ''No!'' Herman said, but they took a vote and it was unanimous. One by one, members of the Living Flag went up to the roof and admired it. It *was* marvelous! It brought tears to the eyes, it made one reflect on this great country and on Lake Wobegon's place in it. One wanted to stand up there all afternoon and just drink it in. So, as the first hour passed, and only forty of the five hundred had been to the top, the others got more and more restless. ''Hurry up! Quite dawdling! *You've* seen it! Get down here and give someone else a chance!'' Herman sent people up in groups of four, and then ten, but after two hours, the Living Flag became the Sitting Flag and then began to erode, as the members who had had a look thought about heading home to supper, which infuriated the ones who hadn't. ''Ten more minutes!'' Herman cried, but ten minutes became twenty and thirty, and people snuck off and the Flag that remained for the last viewer was a Flag shot through by cannon fire.

In 1950, the Sons of Knute took over Flag Day. Herman gave them the boxes of caps. Since then, the Knutes have achieved several good Flags, though most years the attendance was poor. You need at least four hundred to make a good one. Some years the Knutes made a ''no-look'' rule, other years they held a lottery. One year they experimented with a large mirror held by two men over the edge of the roof, but when people leaned back and looked up, the Flag disappeared, of course.

DISCUSSION QUESTIONS

1. Why does Garrison Keillor spend the first part of his story on "maps"? What is he making fun of? What is the relation of maps to reality?
2. In what way is the story about maps at the beginning of the essay similar to the story "Flag Day" at the end? What do these stories tell us about human accuracy? The "Flag Day" incident almost reads like a parable. How do you interpret its larger meaning?
3. Compare Keillor's humorous attitude toward his imaginary hometown with Mark Twain's attitude toward his real hometown in "Old Times on the Mississippi" (see "Classics").

Barry Lopez / *Arctic Dreams* [The Arctic Hunters] 1986

The Arctic has long beckoned American writers: Edgar Allan Poe wrote a novel about an imaginary voyage to the region; Jack London set many of his stories there; and John McPhee explored it recently in one of his most successful books, Coming into the Country. *In* Arctic Dreams, *Barry Lopez investigates how our fascination with the region is intimately linked to the wonders of its landscape. The following section of his best-selling book examines the connections between the Arctic landscape and the spiritual nature of the Eskimo hunting culture.*

Lopez was born in Port Chester, New York, in 1945. After receiving his B.A. and M.A. in English from Notre Dame, he studied folklore and anthropology at the University of Oregon. He began writing full-time in 1970 and is the author of several books, including Of Wolves and Men, Winter Count, *and a collection of essays,* Crossing Open Ground. *He has published essays and stories in a wide variety of periodicals.* Arctic Dreams *won an American Book Award in 1986.*

There is a small village in the central Brooks Range today called Anaktuvuk Pass. The Eskimos there are called Nunamiut, a group that until recently subsisted largely on caribou, Dall sheep, and moose. Originally nomadic, they spent winters in the Brooks Range and summers with relatives on the Beaufort Sea coast, trading caribou skins for sealskins and blubber. Their initial experience with modern trade goods was with such things as Russian tobacco in the eighteenth century, which they obtained from Eskimos living around the mouth of the Colville River, who had traded for it with Bering Sea Eskimos. After 1850 American whalers brought in large quantities of flour, tea, coffee, sugar, and tobacco, as well as guns, ammunition, and alcohol to the northwest coast of Alaska. The Nunamiut were less directly involved in this trade than their coastal relations, but they were profoundly affected nevertheless. The caribou herds they depended on were decimated to feed the whaling crews, and the Nunamiut were forced to abandon their life in the mountains. They shifted away from an economy based on hunting toward one based on trade. A few found seasonal employment on the coast, and most began trapping for furs in earnest.

A change came over the Nunamiut in the 1930s when the market for fur collapsed and the trading posts were closed, distant effects of economic depression in the United States. In 1934 a handful of families, knowing the caribou population had recovered and was again migrating through the mountains, sought to return to an earlier, more satisfying way of life. They set up a camp that first year at the junction of the Anaktuvuk and Colville rivers. For a few years they continued to travel regularly to the coast, where they fished and hunted seals, but in 1939, after this short period of readjustment, they returned to their homeland in the Brooks Range.

Ten years later the promise of trade goods to be brought into the mountains by airplane and the services of a temporary teacher in the summer induced several bands of Nunamiut to gather at a place called Tulugak Lake. In 1951 this group of sixty-five people moved a few miles farther south and a United States post office was established at Anaktuvuk Pass at the skin tent of a hunter named Homer Mekiana. A permanent school was built in 1961, by which time many of the Nunamiut were staying in or near the village year-round. Today about 180 people live there. There is a village store; satellites provide both telephone and television service; and there is a new school with sauna baths and a swimming pool, built with royalty money from Alaskan oil discoveries.

This story has been repeated many times in the same sequence across the Arctic in the past fifty years. Nomadic hunters are consolidated in one place for purposes of trade; radical changes are made in the native way of life in order to adapt to a trade-based or cash-based economy; some make strenuous efforts to return to a semblance of the older way of life; and, finally, large segments of the native language are lost, and the deep erosion of social, religious, political, and dietary customs occurs under intense pressure from missionaries, bureaucrats, and outside entrepreneurs. Hunting expertise, the ability of a man and a woman to keep a family going, the kind of knowledge of life that grew from patience and determination—such attributes were not as highly regarded by the interlopers, who sought to instill other virtues: promptness, personal cleanliness, self-improvement, and a high degree of orderliness and scheduling in daily life.*

Among those in the outside culture whom the Nunamiut have counted as friends in modern times are several anthropologists and biologists who recognized a repository of knowledge in the Nunamiut, particularly about the natural history of the local landscape, and who honored them for it. Some of the Nunamiut men and women who have led balanced and dignified lives through all the changes they have had to face have become symbols of unpretentious wisdom to visiting scientists. The situation, of course, is not unique to Anaktuvuk Pass. Many scientists comment in their papers and books and in private conversation about the character of their Eskimo companions. They admire their humble intelligence, their honesty, and their humor. They find it invigorating to be in the presence of people who, when they do speak, make so few generalized or abstract statements, who focus instead on the practical, the specific, the concrete.

I visited Anaktuvuk Pass in 1978 with a friend, a wolf biologist who had made a temporary home there and who was warmly regarded for his tact, his penchant for listening, and his help during an epidemic of flu in the village. We spent several days watching wolves and caribou in nearby valleys and visiting at several homes. The men talked a lot about hunting. The evenings were full of stories.

*It is easy to impugn the worth of such nebulous virtues, and to find among the interlopers venal and self-aggrandizing people. But it disparages Eskimos to see them as helpless in this situation. Most Eskimos are not opposed to changing their way of life, but they want the timing and the direction of change to be of their own choosing. "There is no insistence," a man once told me, "on living as hard a life as possible." In passing, it should be noted that many people have offered genuine assistance to Eskimos. One frequently hears praise in the Canadian Arctic, for example, for Catholic missionaries, because of their long-term commitment to a single village, their practice of learning to speak the language and to hunt, and their emphasis on good schooling.

There were moments of silence when someone said something very true, peals of laughter when a man told a story expertly at his own expense. One afternoon we left and traveled far to the west to the headwaters of the Utukok River.

The Alaska Department of Fish and Game had a small field camp on the Utukok, at the edge of a gravel-bar landing strip. Among the biologists there were men and women studying caribou, moose, tundra grizzly, wolverine, and, now that my companion had arrived, wolves. The country around the Utukok and the headwaters of the Kokolik River is a wild and serene landscape in summer. Parts of the Western Arctic caribou herd are drifting over the hills, returning from the calving grounds. The sun is always shining, somewhere in the sky. For a week or more we had very fine, clear weather. Golden eagles circled high over the tundra, hunting. Snowy owls regarded us from a distance from their tussock perches. Short-eared owls, a gyrfalcon. Familiar faces.

A few days after we arrived, my companion and I went south six or seven miles and established a camp from which we could watch a distant wolf den. In that open, rolling country without trees, I had the feeling, sometimes, that nothing was hidden. It was during those days that I went for walks along Ilingnorak Ridge and started visiting ground-nesting birds, and developed the habit of bowing to them out of regard for what was wonderful and mysterious in their lives.

The individual animals we watched tested their surroundings, tried things they had not done before, or that possibly no animal like them had ever done before—revealing their capacity for the new. The preservation of this capacity to adapt is one of the central mysteries of evolution.

We watched wolves hunting caribou, and owls hunting lemmings. Arctic ground squirrel eating *irok,* the mountain sorrel. I thought a great deal about hunting. In 1949, Robert Flaherty told an amazing story, which Edmund Carpenter was later successful in getting published, It was about a man named Comock. In 1902, when he and his family were facing starvation, Comock decided to travel over the sea ice to an island he knew about, where he expected they would be able to find food (a small island off Cape Wolstenholme, at the northern tip of Quebec's Ungava Peninsula). On the journey across, they lost nearly all their belongings—all of Comock's knives, spears, and harpoons, all their skins, their stone lamps, and most of their dogs—when the sea ice suddenly opened one night underneath their camp. They were without hunting implements, without a stone lamp to melt water to drink, without food or extra clothing. Comock had left only one sled, several dogs, his snow knife, with which he could cut snow blocks to build a snow house, and stones to make sparks for a fire.

They ate their dogs. The dogs they kept ate the other dogs, which were killed for them. Comock got his family to the island. He fashioned, from inappropriate materials, new hunting weapons. He created shelter and warmth. He hunted successfully. He reconstructed his entire material culture, almost from scratch, by improvising and, where necessary, inventing. He survived. His family survived. His dogs survived and multiplied.

Over the years they carefully collected rare bits of driftwood and bone until Comock had enough to build the frame for an umiak. They saved bearded-seal skins, from which Comock's wife made a waterproof hull. And one summer day they sailed away, back toward Ungava Peninsula. Robert Flaherty, exploring along the coast, spotted Comock and his family and dogs approaching across the water. When they came close, Flaherty, recognizing the form of an umiak and the cut of Eskimo clothing but, seeing that the materials were strange and improvised, asked the Eskimo who he was. He said his name was Comock. "Where in the world have you come from?" asked Flaherty. "From far away, from big island, from far over there," answered Comock, pointing. Then he smiled and made a joke about how poor the umiak must appear, and his family burst into laughter.

I think of this story because at its heart is the industry and competence, the determination and inventiveness of a human family. And because it is about people who lived resolutely in the heart of every moment they found themselves in, disastrous and sublime.

During those days I spent on Ilingnorak Ridge, I did not know what I know now about hunting; but I had begun to sense the outline of what I would learn in the years ahead with Eskimos and from being introduced, by various people, to situations I could not have easily found my way to alone. The insights I felt during those days had to do with the nature of hunting, with the movement of human beings over the land, and with fear. The thoughts grew out of watching the animals.

The evidence is good that among all northern aboriginal hunting peoples, the hunter saw himself bound up in a sacred relationship with the larger animals he hunted. The relationship was full of responsibilities—to the animals, to himself, and to his family. Among the great and, at this point, perhaps tragic lapses in the study of aboriginal hunting peoples is a lack of comprehension about the role women played in hunting. We can presume, I think, that in the same way the hunter felt bound to the animals he hunted, he felt the contract incomplete and somehow even inappropriate if his wife was not part of it. In no hunting society could a man hunt successfully alone. He depended upon his wife for obvious reasons—for the preparation of food and clothing, companionship, humor, subtle encouragement—and for things we can only speculate about, things of a religious nature, bearing on the mutual obligations and courtesies with which he approached the animals he hunted.

Hunting in my experience—and by hunting I simply mean being out on the land—is a state of mind. All of one's faculties are brought to bear in an effort to become fully incorporated into the landscape. It is more than listening for animals or watching for hoofprints or a shift in the weather. It is more than an analysis of what one *senses*. To hunt means to have the land around you like clothing. To engage in a wordless dialogue with it, one so absorbing that you cease to talk with your human companions. It means to release yourself from rational images of what something "means" and to be concerned only that it "is." And then to recognize that things exist only insofar as they can be related to other things. These relationships—fresh drops of moisture on top of rocks at a river crossing and a raven's distant voice—become patterns. The patterns are always in motion. Suddenly the pattern—which includes physical hunger, a memory of your family, and memories of the valley you are walking through, these particular plants and smells—takes in the caribou. There is a caribou standing in front of you. The release of the arrow or bullet is like a word spoken out loud. It occurs at the periphery of your concentration.

The mind we know in dreaming, a nonrational, nonlinear comprehension of events in which slips in time and space are normal, is, I believe, the conscious working mind of an aboriginal hunter. It is a frame of mind that redefines patience, endurance, and expectation.

The focus of a hunter in a hunting society was not killing animals but attending to the myriad relationships he understood bound him into the world he occupied with them. He tended to those duties carefully because he perceived in them everything he understood about survival. This does not mean, certainly, that every man did this, or that good men did not starve. Or that shamans whose duty it was to intercede with the forces that empowered these relationships weren't occasionally thinking of personal gain or subterfuge. It only means that most men understood how to behave.

A fundamental difference between our culture and Eskimo culture, which can be felt even today in certain situations, is that we have irrevocably separated ourselves from the world that animals occupy. We have turned all animals and elements of the natural world into objects. We manipulate them to serve the complicated ends of our destiny. Eskimos do not grasp this separation easily, and have difficulty imagining themselves entirely removed from the world of animals. For many of them, to make this separation is analogous to cutting oneself off from light or water. It is hard to imagine how to do it.

A second difference is that, because we have objectified animals, we are able to treat them impersonally. This means not only the animals that live around us but animals that live in distant lands. For Eskimos, most relationships with animals are local and personal. The animals one encounters are part of one's community, and one has obligations to them. A most confusing aspect of Western culture for Eskimos to grasp is our depersonalization of relationships with the human and animal members of our communities. And it is compounded, rather than simplified, by their attempting to learn how to objectify animals.

Eskimos do not maintain this intimacy with nature without paying a certain price. When I have thought about the ways in which they differ from people in my own culture, I have realized that they are more afraid than we are. On a day-to-day basis, they have more fear. Not of being dumped into cold water from an umiak, not a debilitating fear. They are afraid because they accept fully what is violent and tragic in nature. It is a fear tied to their knowledge that sudden, cataclysmic events are as much a part of life, of really living, as are the moments when one pauses to look at something beautiful. A Central Eskimo shaman named Aua, queried by Knud Rasmussen about Eskimo beliefs, answered, "We do not believe. We fear."

To extend these thoughts, it is wrong to think of hunting cultures like the Eskimo's as living in perfect harmony or balance with nature. Their regard for animals and their attentiveness to nuance in the landscape were not rigorous or complete enough to approach an idealized harmony. No one knew that much. No one would say they knew that much. They faced nature with fear, with *ilira* (nervous awe) and *kappia* (apprehension). And with enthusiasm. They accepted hunting as a way of life—its violence, too, though they did not seek that out. They were unsentimental, so much so that most outsiders thought them cruel, especially in their treatment of dogs. Nor were they innocent. There is murder and warfare and tribal vendetta in their history; and today, in the same villages I walked out of to hunt, are families shattered by alcohol, drugs, and ambition. While one cannot dismiss culpability in these things, any more than one can hold to romantic notions about hunting, it is good to recall what a *struggle* it is to live with dignity and understanding, with perspicacity or grace, in circumstances far better than these. And it is helpful to imagine how the forces of life must be construed by people who live in a world where swift and fatal violence, like *ivu,* the suddenly leaping shore ice, is inherent in the land. The land, in a certain, very real way, compels the minds of the people.

A good reason to travel with Eskimo hunters in modern times is that, beyond nettlesome details—foods that are not to one's liking, a loss of intellectual conversation, a consistent lack of formal planning—in spite of these things, one feels the constant presence of people who know something about surviving. At their best they are resilient, practical, and enthusiastic. They pay close attention in realms where they feel a capacity for understanding. They have a quality of *nuannaarpoq,* of taking extravagant pleasure in being alive; and they delight in finding it in other people. Facing as we do our various Armageddons, they are a good people to know.

In the time I was in the field with Eskimos I wondered at the basis for my admiration. I admired an awareness in the men of providing for others, and the soft tone of voice they used around bloodshed. I never thought I could understand, from their point of view, that moment of preternaturally heightened awareness, and the peril inherent in taking a life; but I accepted it out of respect for their seriousness toward it. In moments when I felt perplexed, that I was dealing with an order outside my own, I discovered and put to use a part of my own culture's wisdom, the formal divisions of Western philosophy—metaphysics, epistemology, ethics, aesthetics, and logic—which pose, in order, the following questions. What is real? What can we understand? How should we behave? What is beautiful? What are the patterns we can rely upon?

As I traveled, I would say to myself, What do my companions see where I see death? Is the sunlight beautiful to them, the way it sparkles on the water? Which for the Eskimo hunter are the patterns to be trusted? The patterns, I know, could be different from ones I imagined were before us. There could be other, remarkably different insights.

Those days on Ilingnorak Ridge, when I saw tundra grizzly tearing up the earth looking for ground squirrels, and watched wolves hunting, and horned lark sitting so resolutely on her nest, and caribou crossing the river and shaking off the spray like diamonds before the evening sun, I was satisfied only to watch. This was the great drift and pause of life. These were the arrangements that made the land ring with integrity. Somewhere downriver, I remembered, a scientist named Edward Sable had paused on a trek in 1947 to stare at a Folsom spear point, a perfectly fluted object of black chert resting on a sandstone ledge. People, moving over the land.

DISCUSSION QUESTIONS

1. In what ways do the Eskimo hunters differ from hunters in our culture? Why are these differences critical to our understanding of the Eskimo? How are these differences related to the Eskimo's sense of the land?

2. Lopez is asking us to see connections between the landscape and our imagination. What are some of these connections? Compare his view of the land with that of N. Scott Momaday and Gretel Ehrlich (see ''Magazines''). What do all of these writers have in common?

Allan Bloom / *The Closing of the American Mind* [Music]

1987

The appearance of Allan Bloom's The Closing of the American Mind *was one of the major publishing events of the 1980s. This influential study of higher education in America, the work of a University of Chicago scholar, condemned rock music and argued that it ''provides models that have no relation to any life the young people who go to universities can possibly lead, or to the kinds of admiration encouraged by liberal studies.'' Clearly, Bloom takes rock music as a serious cultural phenomenon, but you might consider whether he is concerned about rock music's effects on aspects of human life other than higher education.*

Allan Bloom was born in 1930. A professor in the Committee on Social Thought at the University of Chicago, Bloom has coauthored a book on Shakespeare and has translated Plato's Republic *and Jean-Jacques Rousseau's* Emile.

Though students do not have books, they most emphatically do have music. Nothing is more singular about this generation than its addiction to music. This is the age of music and the states of soul that accompany it. To find a rival to this enthusiasm, one would have to go back at least a century to Germany and the passion for Wagner's operas. They had the religious sense that Wagner was creating the meaning of life and that they were not merely listening to his works but experiencing that meaning. Today, a very large proportion of young people between the ages of ten and twenty live for music. It is their passion; nothing else excites them as it does; they cannot take seriously anything alien to music. When they are in school and with their families, they are longing to plug themselves back into their music. Nothing surrounding them—school, family, church—has anything to do with their musical world. At best that ordinary life is neutral, but mostly it is an impediment, drained of vital content, even a thing to be rebelled against. Of course, the enthusiasm for Wagner was limited to a small class, could be indulged only rarely and only in a few places, and had to wait on the composer's slow output. The music of the new votaries, on the other hand, knows neither class nor nation. It is available twenty-four hours a day, everywhere. There is the stereo in the home, in the car; there are concerts; there are music videos, with special channels exclusively devoted to them, on the air nonstop; there are the Walkmans so that no place—not public transportation, not the library—prevents students from communing with the Muse, even while studying. And, above all, the musical soil has become tropically rich. No need to wait for one unpredictable genius. Now there are many geniuses, producing all the time, two new ones rising to take the place of every fallen hero. There is no dearth of the new and the startling.

The power of music in the soul—described to Jessica marvelously by Lorenzo in the *Merchant of Venice*—has been recovered after a long period of desuetude. And it is rock music alone that has effected this restoration. Classical music is dead among the young. This assertion will, I know, be hotly disputed by many who, unwilling to admit tidal changes, can point to the proliferation on campuses of classes in classical music appreciation and practice, as well as performance groups of all kinds. Their presence is undeniable, but they involve not more than 5 to 10 percent of the students. Classical music is now a special taste, like Greek language or pre-Columbian archeology, not a common culture of reciprocal communication and psychological shorthand. Thirty years ago, most middle-class families made some of the old European music a part of the home, partly because they liked it, partly because they thought it was good for the kids. University students usually had some early emotive association with Beethoven, Chopin and Brahms, which was a permanent part of their makeup and to which they were likely to respond throughout their lives. This was probably the only regularly recognizable class distinction between educated and uneducated in America. Many, or even most, of the young people of that generation also swung with Benny Goodman, but with an element of self-consciousness—to be hip, to prove they weren't snobs, to show solidarity with the democratic ideal of a pop culture out of which would grow a new high culture. So there remained a class distinction between high and low, although private taste was beginning to create doubts about whether one really liked the high very much. But all that has changed. Rock music is as unquestioned and unproblematic as the air the students breathe, and very few have any acquaintance at all with classical music. This is a constant surprise to me. And one of the strange aspects of my relations with good students I come to know well is that I frequently introduce them to Mozart. This is a pleasure for me, inasmuch as it is always pleasant to give people gifts that please them. It is interesting to see whether and in what ways their studies are complemented by such music. But this is something utterly new to me as a teacher; formerly my students usually knew much more classical music than I did.

Music was not all that important for the generation of students preceding the current one. The romanticism that had dominated serious music since Beethoven appealed to refinements—perhaps overrefinements—of sentiments that are hardly to be found in the contemporary world. The lives people lead or wish to lead and their prevailing passions are of a different sort than those of the highly educated German and French bourgeoisie, who were avidly reading Rousseau and Baudelaire, Goethe and Heine, for their spiritual satisfaction. The music that had been designed to produce, as well as to please, such exquisite sensibilities had a very tenuous relation to American lives of any kind. So romantic musical culture in America had had for a long time the character of a veneer, as easily susceptible to ridicule as were Margaret Dumont's displays of coquettish chasteness, so aptly exploited by Groucho Marx in *A Night At The Opera*. I noticed this when I first started teaching and lived in a house for gifted students. The "good" ones studied their physics and then listened to classical music. The students who did not fit so easily into the groove, some of them just vulgar and restive under the cultural tyranny, but some of them also serious, were looking for things that really responded to their needs. Almost always they responded to the beat of the newly emerging rock music. They were a bit ashamed of their taste, for it was not respectable. But I instinctively sided with this second group, with real, if coarse, feelings as opposed to artificial and dead ones. Then their musical sans-culotteism won the revolution and reigns unabashed today. No classical music has been produced that can speak to this generation.

Symptomatic of this change is how seriously students now take the famous passages on musical education in Plato's *Republic*. In the past, students, good liberals that they always are, were indignant at the censorship of poetry, as a threat to free inquiry. But they were really thinking of science and politics. They hardly paid attention to the discussion of music itself and, to the extent that they even thought about it, were really puzzled by Plato's devoting time to rhythm and melody in a serious treatise on political philosophy. Their experience of music was as an entertainment, a matter of indifference to political and moral life. Students today, on the contrary, know exactly why Plato takes music so seriously. They know it affects life very profoundly and are indignant because Plato seems to want to rob them of their most intimate pleasure. They are drawn into argument with Plato about the experience of music, and the dispute centers on how to evaluate it and deal with it. This encounter not only helps to illuminate the phenomenon of contemporary music, but also provides a model of how contemporary students can profitably engage with a classic text. The very fact of their fury shows how much Plato threatens what is dear and intimate to them. They are little able to defend their experience, which had seemed unquestionable until questioned, and it is most resistant to cool analysis. Yet if a student can—and this is most difficult and unusual—draw back, get a critical distance on what he clings to, come to doubt the ultimate value of what he loves, he has taken the first and most difficult step toward the philosophic conversion. Indignation is the soul's defense against the wound of doubt about its own; it reorders the cosmos to support the justice of its cause. It justifies putting Socrates to death. Recognizing indignation for what it is constitutes knowledge of the soul, and is thus an experience more philosophic than the study of mathematics. It is Plato's teaching that music, by its nature, encompasses all that is today most resistent to philosophy. So it may well be that through the thicket of our greatest corruption runs the path to awareness of the oldest truths.

Plato's teaching about music is, put simply, that rhythm and melody, accompanied by dance, are the barbarous expression of the soul. Barbarous, not animal.

Music is the medium of the *human* soul in its most ecstatic condition of wonder and terror. Nietzsche, who in large measure agrees with Plato's analysis, says in *The Birth of Tragedy* (not to be forgotten is the rest of the title, *Out of the Spirit of Music*) that a mixture of cruelty and coarse sensuality characterized this state, which of course was religious, in the service of gods. Music is the soul's primitive and primary speech and it is *alogon,* without articulate speech or reason. It is not only not reasonable, it is hostile to reason. Even when articulate speech is added, it is utterly subordinate to and determined by the music and the passions it expresses.

Civilization or, to say the same thing, education is the taming or domestication of the soul's raw passions—not suppressing or excising them, which would deprive the soul of its energy—but forming and informing them as art. The goal of harmonizing the enthusiastic part of the soul with what develops later, the rational part, is perhaps impossible to attain. But without it, man can never be whole. Music, or poetry, which is what music becomes as reason emerges, always involves a delicate balance between passion and reason, and, even in its highest and most developed forms—religious, warlike and erotic—that balance is always tipped, if ever so slightly, toward the passionate. Music, as everyone experiences, provides an unquestionable justification and a fulfilling pleasure for the activities it accompanies: the soldier who hears the marching band is enthralled and reassured; the religious man is exalted in his prayer by the sound of the organ in the church; and the lover is carried away and his conscience stilled by the romantic guitar. Armed with music, man can damn rational doubt. Out of the music emerge the gods that suit it, and they educate men by their example and their commandments.

Plato's Socrates disciplines the ecstasies and thereby provides little consolation or hope to men. According to the Socratic formula, the lyrics—speech and, hence, reason—must determine the music—harmony and rhythm. Pure music can never endure this constraint. Students are not in a position to know the pleasures of reason; they can only see it as a disciplinary and repressive parent. But they do see, in the case of Plato, that that parent has figured out what they are up to. Plato teaches that, in order to take the spiritual temperature of an individual or a society, one must "mark the music." To Plato and Nietzsche, the history of music is a series of attempts to give form and beauty to the dark, chaotic, premonitory forces in the soul—to make them serve a higher purpose, an ideal, to give man's duties a fullness. Bach's religious intentions and Beethoven's revolutionary and humane ones are clear enough examples. Such cultivation of the soul uses the passions and satisfies them while sublimating them and giving them an artistic unity. A man whose noblest activities are accompanied by a music that expresses them while providing a pleasure extending from the lowest bodily to the highest spiritual, is whole, and there is no tension in him between the pleasant and the good. By contrast a man whose business life is prosaic and unmusical and whose leisure is made up of coarse, intense entertainments, is divided, and each side of his existence is undermined by the other.

Hence, for those who are interested in psychological health, music is at the center of education, both for giving the passions their due and for preparing the soul for the unhampered use of reason. The centrality of such education was recognized by all the ancient educators. It is hardly noticed today that in Aristotle's *Politics* the most important passages about the best regime concern musical education, or that the *Poetics* is an appendix to the *Politics*. Classical philosophy did not censor the singers. It persuaded them. And it gave them a goal, one that was understood by them, until only yesterday. But those who do not notice the role of music in Aristotle and despise it in Plato went to school with Hobbes, Locke and Smith, where such considerations have become unnecessary. The triumphant Enlightenment rationalism thought that it had discovered other ways to deal with the irrational part of the soul, and that reason needed less support from it. Only in those great critics of Enlightenment and rationalism, Rousseau and Nietzsche, does music return, and they were the most musical of philosophers. Both thought that the passions—and along with them their ministerial arts—had become thin under the rule of reason and that, therefore, man himself and what he sees in the world have become correspondingly thin. They wanted to cultivate the enthusiastic states of the soul and to re-experience the Corybantic possession deemed a pathology by Plato. Nietzsche, particularly, sought to tap again the irrational sources of vitality, to replenish our dried-up stream from barbaric sources, and thus encouraged the Dionysian and the music derivative from it.

This is the significance of rock music. I do not suggest that it has any high intellectual sources. But it has risen to its current heights in the education of the young on the ashes of classical music, and in an atmosphere in which there is no intellectual resistance to attempts to tap the rawest passions. Modern-day rationalists, such as economists, are indifferent to it and what it represents. The irrationalists are all for it. There is no need to fear that ''the blond beasts'' are going to come forth from the bland souls of our adolescents. But rock music has one appeal only, a barbaric appeal, to sexual desire—not love, not *eros,* but sexual desire undeveloped and untutored. It acknowledges the first emanations of children's emerging sensuality and addresses them seriously, eliciting them and legitimating them, not as little sprouts that must be carefully tended in order to grow into gorgeous flowers, but as the real thing. Rock gives children, on a silver platter, with all the public authority of the entertainment industry, everything their parents always used to tell them they had to wait for until they grew up and would understand later.

Young people know that rock has the beat of sexual intercourse. That is why Ravel's *Bolero* is the one piece of classical music that is commonly known and liked by them. In alliance with some real art and a lot of pseudo-art, an enormous industry cultivates the taste for the orgiastic state of feeling connected with sex, providing a constant flood of fresh material for voracious appetites. Never was there an art form directed so exclusively to children.

Ministering to and according with the arousing and cathartic music, the lyrics celebrate puppy love as well as polymorphous attractions, and fortify them against traditional ridicule and shame. The words implicitly and explicitly describe bodily acts that satisfy sexual desire and treat them as its only natural and routine culmination for children who do not yet have the slightest imagination of love, marriage or family. This has a much more powerful effect than does pornography on youngsters, who have no need to watch others do grossly what they can so easily do themselves. Voyeurism is for old perverts; active sexual relations are for the young. All they need is encouragement.

The inevitable corollary of such sexual interest is rebellion against the parental authority that represses it. Selfishness thus becomes indignation and then transforms itself into morality. The sexual revolution must overthrow all the forces of domination, the enemies of nature and happiness. From love comes hate, masquerading as social reform. A worldview is balanced on the sexual fulcrum. What were once unconscious or half-conscious childish resentments become the new Scripture. And then comes the longing for the classless, prejudice-free, conflictless, universal society that necessarily results from liberated consciousness—''We Are the World,'' a pubescent version of *Alle Menschen werden Brüder,* the fulfillment of which has been inhibited by the political equivalents of Mom and Dad. These are the three great lyrical themes: sex, hate and a smarmy, hypocritical version of brotherly love. Such polluted sources issue in a muddy stream where only monsters can swim. A glance at the videos that project images on the wall of Plato's cave since MTV took it over suffices to prove this. Hitler's image recurs frequently enough in exciting contexts to give one pause. Nothing noble, sublime, profound, delicate, tasteful or even decent can find a place in such tableaux. There is room only for the intense, changing, crude and immediate, which Tocqueville warned us would be the character of democratic art, combined with a pervasiveness, importance and content beyond Tocqueville's wildest imagination.

Picture a thirteen-year-old boy sitting in the living room of his family home doing his math assignment while wearing his Walkman headphones or watching MTV. He enjoys the liberties hard won over centuries by the alliance of philosophic genius and political heroism, consecrated by the blood of martyrs; he is provided with comfort and leisure by the most productive economy ever known to mankind; science has penetrated the secrets of nature in order to provide him with the marvelous, lifelike electronic sound and image reproduction he is enjoying. And in what does progress culminate? A pubescent child whose body throbs with orgasmic rhythms; whose feelings are made articulate in hymns to the joys of onanism or the killing of parents; whose ambition is to win fame and wealth in imitating the drag-queen who makes the music. In short, life is made into a nonstop, commercially prepackaged masturbational fantasy.

This description may seem exaggerated, but only because some would prefer to regard it as such. The continuing exposure to rock music is a reality, not one confined to a particular class or type of child. One need only ask first-year university students what music they listen to, how much of it and what it means to them, in order to discover that the phenomenon is universal in America, that it begins in adolescence or a bit before and continues through the college years. It is *the* youth culture and, as I have so often insisted, there is now no other countervailing nourishment for the spirit. Some of this culture's power comes from the fact that it is so loud. It makes conversation impossible, so that much of friendship must be without the shared speech that Aristotle asserts is the essence of friendship and the only true common ground. With rock, illusions of shared feelings, bodily contact and grunted formulas, which are supposed to contain so much meaning beyond speech, are the basis of association. None of this contradicts going about the business of life, attending classes and doing the assignments for them. But the meaningful inner life is with the music.

This phenomenon is both astounding and indigestible, and is hardly noticed, routine and habitual. But it is of historic proportions that a society's best young and their best energies should be so occupied. People of future civilizations will wonder at this and find it as incomprehensible as we do the caste system, witch-burning, harems, cannibalism and gladiatorial combats. It may well be that a society's greatest madness seems normal to itself. The child I described has parents who have sacrificed to provide him with a good life and who have a great stake in his future happiness. They cannot believe that the musical vocation will contribute very much to that happiness. But there is nothing they can do about it. The family spiritual void has left the field open to rock music, and they cannot possibly forbid their children to listen to it. It is everywhere; all children listen to it; forbidding it would simply cause them to lose their children's affection and obedience. When they turn on the television, they will see President Reagan warmly grasping the daintily proffered gloved hand of Michael Jackson and praising him enthusiastically. Better to set the faculty of denial in motion—avoid noticing what the words say, assume the kid will get over it. If he has early sex, that won't get in the way of his having stable relationships later. His drug use will certainly stop at pot. School is providing real values. And popular historicism provides the final salvation: there are new life-styles for new situations, and the older generation is there not to impose its values but to help the younger one to find its own. TV, which compared to music plays a comparatively small role in the formation of young people's character and taste, is a consensus monster—the Right monitors its content for sex, the Left for violence, and many other interested sects for many other things. But the music has hardly been touched, and what efforts have been made are both ineffectual and misguided about the nature and extent of the problem.

The result is nothing less than parents' loss of control over their children's moral education at a time when no one else is seriously concerned with it. This has been achieved by an alliance between the strange young males who have the gift of divining the mob's emergent wishes—our versions of Thrasymachus, Socrates' rhetorical adversary—and the record-company executives, the new robber barons, who mine gold out of rock. They discovered a few years back that children are one of the few groups in the country with considerable disposable income, in the form of allowances. Their parents spend all they have providing for the kids. Appealing to them over their parents' heads, creating a world of delight for them, constitutes one of the richest markets in the postwar world. The rock business is perfect capitalism, supplying to demand and helping to create it. It has all the moral dignity of drug trafficking, but it was so totally new and unexpected that nobody thought to control it, and now it is too late. Progress may be made against cigarette smoking because our absence of standards or our relativism does not extend to matters of bodily health. In all other things the market determines the value. (Yoko Ono is among America's small group of billionaires, along with oil and computer magnates, her late husband having produced and sold a commodity of worth comparable to theirs.) Rock is very big business, bigger than the movies, bigger than professional sports, bigger than television, and this accounts for much of the respectability of the music business. It is difficult to adjust our vision to the changes in the economy and to see what is really important. McDonald's now has more employees than U.S. Steel, and likewise the purveyors of junk food for the soul have supplanted what still seem to be more basic callings.

This change has been happening for some time. In the late fifties, De Gaulle gave Brigitte Bardot one of France's highest honors. I could not understand this, but it turned out that she, along with Peugeot, was France's biggest export item. As Western nations became more prosperous, leisure, which had been put off for several centuries in favor of the pursuit of property, the means to leisure, finally began to be of primary concern. But, in the meantime, any notion of the serious life of leisure, as well as men's taste and capacity to live it, had disappeared. Leisure became entertainment. The end for which they had labored for so long became entertainment. The end for which they had labored for so long has turned out to be amusement, a justified conclusion if the means justify the ends. The music business is peculiar only in that it caters almost exclusively to children, treating legally and naturally imperfect human beings as though they were ready to enjoy the final or complete satisfaction. It perhaps thus reveals the nature of all our entertainment and our loss of a clear view of what adulthood or maturity is, and our incapacity to conceive ends. The emptiness of *values* results in the acceptance of the natural *facts* as the ends. In this case infantile sexuality is the end, and I suspect that, in the absence of other ends, many adults have come to agree that it is.

It is interesting to note that the Left, which prides itself on its critical approach to "late capitalism" and is unrelenting and unsparing in its analysis of our other cultural phenomena, has in general given rock music a free ride. Abstracting from the capitalist element in which it flourishes, they regard it as a people's art, coming from beneath the bourgeoisie's layers of cultural repression. Its antinomianism and its longing for a world without constraint might seem to be the clarion of the proletarian revolution, and Marxists certainly do see that rock music dissolves the beliefs and morals necessary for liberal society and would approve of it for that alone. But the harmony between the young intellectual Left and rock is probably profounder than that. Herbert Marcuse appealed to university students in the sixties with a combination of Marx and Freud. In *Eros and Civilization* and *One Dimensional Man* he promised that the overcoming or capitalism and its false consciousness will result in a society where the greatest satisfactions are sexual, of a sort that the bourgeois moralist Freud called polymorphous and infantile. Rock music touches the same chord in the young. Free sexual expression, anarchism, mining of the irrational unconscious and giving it free rein are what they have in common. The high intellectual life I shall describe in Part Two and the low rock world are partners in the same entertainment enterprise. They must both be interpreted as parts of the cultural fabric of late capitalism. Their success comes for the bourgeois' need to feel that he is not bourgeois, to have undangerous experiments with the unlimited. He is willing to pay dearly for them. The Left is better interpreted by Nietzsche than by Marx. The critical theory of late capitalism is at once late capitalism's subtlest and crudest expression. Anti-bourgeois ire is the opiate of the Last Man.

This strong stimulant, which Nietzsche called Nihiline, was for a very long time, almost fifteen years, epitomized in a single figure, Mick Jagger. A shrewd, middle-class boy, he played the possessed lower-class demon and teen-aged satyr up until he was forty, with one eye on the mobs of children of both sexes whom he stimulated to a sensual frenzy and the other eye winking at the unerotic, commercially motivated adults who handled the money. In his act he was male and female, heterosexual and homosexual; unencumbered by modesty, he could enter everyone's dreams, promising to do everything with everyone; and, above all, he legitimated drugs, which were the real thrill that parents and policemen conspired to deny his youthful audience. He was beyond the law, moral and political, and thumbed his nose at it. Along with all this, there were nasty little appeals to the suppressed inclinations toward sexism, racism and violence, indulgence in which is not now publicly respectable. Nevertheless, he managed not to appear to contradict the rock ideal of a universal classless society founded on love, with the distinction between brotherly and bodily blurred. He was the hero and the model for countless young persons in universities, as well as elsewhere. I discovered that students who boasted of having no heroes secretly had a passion to be like Mick Jagger, to live his life, have his fame. They were ashamed to admit this in a university, although I am not certain that the reason has anything to do with a higher standard of taste. It is probably that they are not supposed to have heroes. Rock music itself and talking about it with infinite seriousness are perfectly respectable. It has proved to be the ultimate leveler of intellectual snobbism. But it is not respectable to think of it as providing weak and ordinary persons with a fashionable behavior, the imitation of which will make others esteem them and boost their own self-esteem. Unaware and unwillingly, however, Mick Jagger played the role in their lives that Napoleon played in the lives of ordinary young Frenchmen throughout the nineteenth century. Everyone else was so boring and unable to charm youthful passions. Jagger caught on.

In the last couple of years, Jagger has begun to fade. Whether Michael Jackson, Prince or Boy George can take his place is uncertain. They are even weirder than he is, and one wonders what new strata of taste they have discovered. Although each differs from the others, the essential character of musical entertainment is not changing. There is only a constant search for variations on the theme. And this gutter phenomenon is apparently the fulfillment of the promise made by so much psychology and literature that our weak and exhausted Western civilization would find refreshment in the true source, the unconscious, which appeared to the late romantic imagination to be identical to Africa, the dark and unexplored continent. Now all has been explored; light has been cast everywhere; the unconscious has been made conscious, the repressed expressed. And what have we found? Not creative devils, but show business glitz. Mick Jagger tarting it up on the stage is all that we brought back from the voyage to the underworld.

My concern here is not with the moral effects of this music—whether it leads to sex, violence or drugs. The issue here is its effect on education, and I believe it ruins the imagination of young people and makes it very difficult for them to have a passionate relationship to the art and thought that are the substance of liberal education. The first sensuous experiences are decisive in determining the taste for the whole of life, and they are the link between the animal and spiritual in us. The period of nascent sensuality has always been used for sublimation, in the sense of making sublime, for attaching youthful inclinations and longings to music, pictures and stories that provide the transition to the fulfillment of the human duties and the enjoyment of the human pleasures. Lessing, speaking of Greek sculpture, said "beautiful men made beautiful statues, and the city had beautiful statues in part to thank for beautiful citizens." This formula encapsulates the fundamental principle of the esthetic education of man. Young men and women were attracted by the beauty of heroes whose very bodies expressed their nobility. The deeper understanding of the meaning of nobility comes later, but is prepared for by the sensuous experience and is actually contained in it. What the senses long for as well as what reason later sees as good are thereby not at tension with one another. Education is not sermonizing to children against their instincts and pleasures, but providing a natural continuity between what they feel and what they can and should be. But this is a lost art. Now we have come to exactly the opposite point. Rock music encourages passions and provides models that have no relation to any life the young people who go to universities can possibly lead, or to the kinds of admiration encouraged by liberal studies. Without the cooperation of the sentiments, anything other than technical education is a dead letter.

Rock music provides premature ecstasy and, in this respect, is like the drugs with which it is allied. It artificially induces the exaltation naturally attached to the completion of the greatest endeavors—victory in a just war, consummated love, artistic creation, religious devotion and discovery of the truth. Without effort, without talent, without virtue, without exercise of the faculties, anyone and everyone is accorded the equal right to the enjoyment of their fruits. In my experience, students who have had a serious fling with drugs—and gotten over it—find it difficult to have enthusiasms or great expectations. It is as though the color has been drained out of their lives and they see everything in black and white. The pleasure they experienced in the beginning was so intense that they no longer look for it at the end, or as the end. They may function perfectly well, but dryly, routinely. Their energy has been sapped, and they do not expect their life's activity to produce anything but a living, whereas liberal education is supposed to encourage the belief that the good life is the pleasant life and that the best life is the most pleasant life. I suspect that the rock addiction, particularly in the absence of strong counterattractions, has an effect similar to that of drugs. The students will get over this music, or at least the exclusive passion for it. But they will do so in the same way Freud says that men accept the reality principle—as something harsh, grim and essentially unattractive, a mere necessity. These students will assiduously study economics or the professions and the Michael Jackson costume will slip off to reveal a Brooks Brothers suit beneath. They will want to get ahead and live comfortably. But this life is as empty and false as the one they left behind. The choice is not between quick fixes and dull calculation. This is what liberal education is meant to show them. But as long as they have the Walkman on, they cannot hear what the great tradition has to say. And, after its prolonged use, when they take it off, they find they are deaf.

DISCUSSION QUESTIONS

1. Do you find Bloom's arguments about the dangers of rock music persuasive? Which elements of his argument do you find the most convincing? Which elements do you find the least convincing?

2. Do you think that Bloom is correct in writing that rock music "has one appeal only"? What does he believe is the nature of that appeal? What other kinds of appeal does rock music have for its listeners?

3. How would you describe Bloom's language throughout the essay? What audience does he seem to have in mind for this essay? How does Bloom's argument differ from other arguments you have read or heard made against rock?

4. How does Bloom's view of rock music resemble the view presented in "Adolescents and Their Music" (in "Magazines")? In what ways do the arguments differ?

Amy Tan / *The Joy Luck Club* 1989

Amy Tan was born in Oakland, California, in 1952 shortly after her parents emigrated to the United States from China. In 1987 Tan traveled to China for the first time, an experience that helped her to better understand her identity as both American and Chinese. Her best-selling first novel, The Joy Luck Club, *from which the following selection is excerpted, appeared in 1989.* The Kitchen God's Wife *was published in 1991.*

TWO KINDS

My mother believed you could be anything you wanted to be in America. You could open a restaurant. You could work for the government and get good retirement. You could buy a house with almost no money down. You could become rich. You could become instantly famous.

"Of course, you can be prodigy, too," my mother told me when I was nine. "You can be best anything. What does Auntie Lindo know? Her daughter, she is only best tricky."

America was where all my mother's hopes lay. She had come to San Francisco in 1949 after losing everything in China: her mother and father, her family home, her first husband, and two daughters, twin baby girls. But she never looked back with regret. Things could get better in so many ways.

We didn't immediately pick the right kind of prodigy. At first my mother thought I could be a Chinese Shirley Temple. We'd watch Shirley's old movies on TV as though they were training films. My mother would poke my arm and say, *"Ni kan.* You watch." And I would see Shirley tapping her feet, or singing a sailor song, or pursing her lips into a very round O while saying "Oh, my goodness."

"Ni kan," my mother said, as Shirley's eyes flooded with tears. "You already know how. Don't need talent for crying!"

Soon after my mother got this idea about Shirley Temple, she took me to the beauty training school in the Mission District and put me in the hands of a student who could barely hold the scissors without shaking. Instead of getting big fat curls, I emerged with an uneven mass of crinkly black fuzz. My mother dragged me off to the bathroom and tried to wet down my hair.

"You look like Negro Chinese," she lamented, as if I had done this on purpose.

The instructor of the beauty training school had to lop off these soggy clumps to make my hair even again. "Peter Pan is very popular these days," the instructor assured my mother. I now had hair the length of a boy's, with curly bangs that hung at a slant two inches above my eyebrows. I liked the haircut, and it made me actually look forward to my future fame.

In fact, in the beginning I was just as excited as my mother, maybe even more so. I pictured this prodigy part of me as many different images, and I tried each one on for size. I was a dainty ballerina girl standing by the curtain, waiting to hear the music that would send me floating on my tiptoes. I was like the Christ child lifted out of the straw manger, crying with holy indignity. I was Cinderella stepping from her pumpkin carriage with sparkly cartoon music filling the air.

In all my imaginings I was filled with a sense that I would soon become perfect. My mother and father would adore me. I would be beyond reproach. I would never feel the need to sulk, or to clamor for anything.

But sometimes the prodigy in me became impatient. "If you don't hurry up and get me out of here, I'm disappearing for good," it warned. "And then you'll always be nothing."

Every night after dinner my mother and I would sit at the Formica-topped kitchen table. She would present new tests, taking her examples from stories of amazing children that she had read in *Ripley's Believe It or Not* or *Good Housekeeping, Reader's Digest,* or any of a dozen other magazines she kept in a pile in our bathroom. My mother got these magazines from people whose houses she cleaned. And since she cleaned many houses each week, we had a great assortment. She would look through them all, searching for stories about remarkable children.

The first night she brought out a story about a three-year-old boy who knew the capitals of all the states and even of most of the European countries. A teacher was quoted as saying that the little boy could also pronounce the names of the foreign cities correctly. "What's the capital of Finland?" my mother asked me, looking at the story.

All I knew was the capital of California, because Sacramento was the name of the street we lived on in Chinatown. "Nairobi!" I guessed, saying the most foreign word I could think of. She checked to see if that might be one way to pronounce *Helsinki* before showing me the answer.

The tests got harder—multiplying numbers in my head, finding the queen of hearts in a deck of cards, trying to stand on my head without using my hands, predicting the daily temperatures in Los Angeles, New York, and London. One night I had to look at a page from the Bible for three minutes and then report everything I could remember. "Now Jehoshaphat had riches and honor in abundance and . . . that's all I remember, Ma," I said.

And after seeing, once again, my mother's disappointed face, something inside me began to die. I hated the tests, the raised hopes and failed expectations. Before going to bed that night I looked in the mirror above the bathroom sink, and when I saw only my face staring back—and understood that it would always be this ordinary face—I began to cry. Such a sad, ugly girl! I made high-pitched noises like a crazed animal, trying to scratch out the face in the mirror.

And then I saw what seemed to be the prodigy side of me—a face I had never seen before. I looked at my reflection, blinking so that I could see more clearly. The girl staring back at me was angry, powerful. She and I were the same. I had new thoughts, willful thoughts—or, rather, thoughts filled with lots of won'ts. I won't let her change me, I promised myself. I won't be what I'm not.

So now when my mother presented her tests, I performed listlessly, my head propped on one arm. I pretended to be bored. And I was. I got so bored that I started counting the bellows of the foghorns out on the bay while my mother drilled me in other areas. The sound was comforting and reminded me of the cow jumping over the moon. And the next day I played a game with myself, seeing if my mother would give up on me before eight bellows. After a while I usually counted only one bellow, maybe two at most. At last she was beginning to give up hope.

Two or three months went by without any mention of my being a prodigy. And then one day my mother was watching the *Ed Sullivan Show* on TV. The TV was old and the sound kept shorting out. Every time my mother got halfway up from the sofa to adjust the set, the sound would come back on and Sullivan would be talking. As soon as she sat down, Sullivan would go silent again. She got up—the TV broke into loud piano music. She sat down—silence. Up and down, back and forth, quiet and loud. It was like a stiff, embraceless dance between her and the TV set. Finally, she stood by the set with her hand on the sound dial.

She seemed entranced by the music, a frenzied little piano piece with a mesmerizing quality, which alternated between quick, playful passages and teasing, lilting ones.

''Ni kan,'' my mother said, calling me over with hurried hand gestures. ''Look here.''

I could see why my mother was fascinated by the music. It was being pounded out by a little Chinese girl, about nine years old, with a Peter Pan haircut. The girl had the sauciness of a Shirley Temple. She was proudly modest, like a proper Chinese child. And she also did a fancy sweep of a curtsy, so that the fluffy skirt of her white dress cascaded to the floor like the petals of a large carnation.

In spite of these warning signs, I wasn't worried. Our family had no piano and we couldn't afford to buy one, let alone reams of sheet music and piano lessons. So I could be generous in my comments when my mother badmouthed the little girl on TV.

''Play note right, but doesn't sound good!'' my mother complained. ''No singing sound.''

''What are you picking on her for?'' I said carelessly. ''She's pretty good. Maybe she's not the best, but she's trying hard.'' I knew almost immediately that I would be sorry I had said that.

''Just like you,'' she said. ''Not the best. Because you are not trying.'' She gave a little huff as she let go of the sound dial and sat down on the sofa.

The little Chinese girl sat down also, to play an encore of ''Anitra's Tanz,'' by Grieg. I remember the song, because later on I had to learn how to play it.

Three days after watching the *Ed Sullivan Show* my mother told me what my schedule would be for piano lessons and piano practice. She had talked to Mr. Chong, who lived on the first floor of our apartment building. Mr. Chong was a retired piano teacher, and my mother had traded housecleaning services for weekly lessons and a piano for me to practice on every day, two hours a day, from four until six.

When my mother told me this, I felt as though I had been sent to hell. I whined, and then kicked my foot a little when I couldn't stand it anymore.

''Why don't you like me the way I am?'' I cried. ''I'm *not* a genius! I can't play the piano. And even if I could, I wouldn't go on TV if you paid me a million dollars!''

My mother slapped me. ''Who ask you to be genius?'' she shouted. ''Only ask you be your best. For you sake. You think I want you to be genius? Hnnh! What for! Who ask you!''

''So ungrateful,'' I heard her mutter in Chinese.. ''If she had as much talent as she has temper, she'd be famous now.''

Mr. Chong, whom I secretly nicknamed Old Chong, was very strange, always tapping his fingers to the silent music of an invisible orchestra. He looked ancient in my eyes. He had lost most of the hair on the top of his head, and he wore thick glasses and had eyes that always looked tired. But he must have been younger than I thought, since he lived with his mother and was not yet married.

I met Old Lady Chong once, and that was enough. She had a peculiar smell, like a baby that had done something in its pants, and her fingers felt like a dead person's, like an old peach I once found in the back of the refrigerator; its skin just slid off the flesh when I picked it up.

I soon found out why Old Chong had retired from teaching piano. He was deaf. ''Like Beethoven!'' he shouted to me. ''We're both listening only in our head!'' And he would start to conduct his frantic silent sonatas.

Our lessons went like this. He would open the book and point to different things, explaining their purpose: ''Key! Treble! Bass! No sharps or flats! So this is C major! Listen now and play after me!''

And then he would play the C scale a few times, a simple chord, and then, as if inspired by an old unreachable itch, he would gradually add more notes and running trills and a pounding bass until the music was really something quite grand.

I would play after him, the simple scale, the simple chord, and then just play some nonsense that sounded like a cat running up and down on top of garbage cans. Old Chong would smile and applaud and say,''Very good! But now you must learn to keep time!''

So that's how I discovered that Old Chong's eyes were too slow to keep up with the wrong notes I was playing. He went through the motions in half time. To help me keep rhythm, he stood behind me and pushed down on my right shoulder for every beat. He balanced pennies on top of my wrists so that I would keep them still as I slowly played scales and arpeggios. He had me curve my hand around an apple and keep that shape when playing chords. He marched stiffly to show me how to make each finger dance up and down, staccato, like an obedient little soldier.

He taught me all these things, and that was how I also learned I could be lazy and get away with mistakes, lots of mistakes. If I hit the wrong notes because I hadn't practiced enough, I never corrected myself. I just kept playing in rhythm. And Old Chong kept conducting his own private reverie.

So maybe I never really gave myself a fair chance. I did pick up the basics pretty quickly, and I might have become a good pianist at that young age. But I was so determined not to try, not to be anybody different, that I learned to play only the most ear-splitting preludes, the most discordant hymns.

Over the next year I practiced like this, dutifully in my own way. And then one day I heard my mother and her friend Lindo Jong both talking in a loud, bragging tone of voice so that others could hear. It was after church, and I was leaning against a brick wall, wearing a dress with stiff white petticoats. Aunti Lindo's daughter, Waverly, who was my age, was standing farther down the wall, about five feet away. We had grown up together and shared all the closeness of two sisters, squabbling over crayons and dolls. In other words, for the most part, we hated each other. I thought she was snotty. Waverly Jong had gained a certain amount of fame as ''Chinatown's Littlest Chinese Chess Champion.''

''She bring home too many trophy,'' Auntie Lindo lamented that Sunday. ''All day she play chess. All day I have no time do nothing but dust off her winnings." She threw a scolding look at Waverly, who pretended not to see her.

"You lucky you don't have this problem," Auntie Lindo said with a sigh to my mother.

And my mother squared her shoulders and bragged: "Our problem worser than yours. If we ask Jing-mei wash dish, she hear nothing but music. It's like you can't stop this natural talent."

And right then I was determined to put a stop to her foolish pride.

A few weeks later Old Chong and my mother conspired to have me play in a talent show that was to be held in the church hall. By then my parents had saved up enough to buy me a secondhand piano, a black Wurlitzer spinet with a scarred bench. It was the showpiece of our living room.

For the talent show I was to play a piece called "Pleading Child," from Schumann's *Scenes From Childhood.* It was a simple, moody piece that sounded more difficult than it was. I was supposed to memorize the whole thing. But I dawdled over it, playing a few bars and then cheating, looking up to see what notes followed. I never really listened to what I was playing. I daydreamed about being somewhere else, about being someone else.

The part I liked to practice best was the fancy curtsy: right foot out, touch the rose on the carpet with a pointed foot, sweep to the side, bend left leg, look up, and smile.

My parents invited all the couples from their social club to witness my debut. Aunti Lindo and Uncle Tin were there. Waverly and her two older brothers had also come. The first two rows were filled with children either younger or older than I was. The littlest ones got to go first. They recited simple nursery rhymes, squawked out tunes on miniature violins, and twirled hula hoops in pink ballet tutus, and when they bowed or curtsied, the audience would sigh in unison, *"Awww,"* and then clap enthusiastically.

When my turn came, I was very confident. I remember my childish excitement. It was as if I knew, without a doubt, that the prodigy side of me really did exist. I had no fear whatsoever, no nervousness. I remember thinking. This is it! This is it! I looked out over the audience, at my mother's blank face, my father's yawn, Aunti Lindo's stiff-lipped smile, Waverly's sulky expression. I had on a white dress, layered with sheets of lace, and a pink bow in my Peter Pan haircut. As I sat down, I envisioned people jumping to their feet and Ed Sullivan rushing up to introduce me to everyone on TV.

And I started to play. Everything was so beautiful. I was so caught up in how lovely I looked that I wasn't worried about how I would sound. So I was surprised when I hit the first wrong note. And then I hit another, and another. A chill started at the top of my head and began to trickle down. Yet I couldn't stop playing, as though my hands were bewitched. I kept thinking my fingers would adjust themselves back, like a train switching to the right track. I played this strange jumble through to the end, the sour notes staying with me all the way.

When I stood up, I discovered my legs were shaking. Maybe I had just been nervous, and the audience, like Old Chong, had seen me go through the right motions and had not heard anything wrong at all. I swept my right foot out, went down on my knee, looked up, and smiled. The room was quiet, except for Old Chong, who was beaming and shouting. "Bravo! Bravo! Well done!" But then I saw my mother's face, her stricken face. The audience clapped weakly, and as I walked back to my chair, with my whole face quivering as I tried not to cry, I heard a little boy whisper loudly to his mother, "That was awful," and the mother whispered back, "Well, she certainly tried."

And now I realized how many people were in the audience—the whole world, it seemed. I was aware of eyes burning into my back. I felt the shame of my mother and father as they sat stiffly through the rest of the show.

We could have escaped during intermission. Pride and some strange sense of honor must have anchored my parents to their chairs. And so we watched it all: The eighteen-year-old boy with a fake moustache who did a magic show and juggled flaming hoops while riding a unicycle. The breasted girl with white makeup who sang an aira from *Madame Butterfly* and got an honorable mention. And the eleven-year-old boy who won first prize playing a tricky violin song that sounded like a busy bee.

After the show the Hsus, the Jongs, and the St. Clairs, from the Joy Luck Club, came up to my mother and father.

''Lots of talented kids,'' Auntie Lindo said vaguely, smiling broadly.

''That was somethin' else, '' my father said, and I wondered if he was referring to me in a humorous way, or whether he even remembered what I had done.

Waverly looked at me and shrugged her shoulders. ''You aren't a genius like me,'' she said matter-of-factly. And if I hadn't felt so bad, I would have pulled her braids and punched her stomach.

But my mother's expression was what devastated me: a quiet, blank look that said she had lost everything. I felt the same way, and everybody seemed now to be coming up, like gawkers at the scene of an accident, to see what parts were actually missing.

When we got on the bus to go home, my father was humming the busy-bee tune and my mother was silent. I kept thinking she wanted to wait until we got home before shouting at me. But when my father unlocked the door to our apartment, my mother walked in and went straight to the back, into the bedroom. No accusations. No blame. And in a way, I felt disappointed. I had been waiting for her to start shouting, so that I could shout back and cry and blame her for all my misery.

I had assumed that my talent-show fiasco meant that I would never have to play the piano again. But two days later, after school, my mother came out of the kitchen and saw me watching TV.

''Four clock,'' she reminded me, as if it were any other day. I was stunned, as though she were asking me to go through the talent-show torture again. I planted myself more squarely in front of the TV.

''Turn off TV,'' she called from the kitchen five minutes later.

I didn't budge. And then I decided. I didn't have to do what my mother said anymore. I wasn't her slave. This wasn't China. I had listened to her before, and look what happened. She was the stupid one.

She came out from the kitchen and stood in the arched entryway of the living room. ''Four clock,'' she said once again, louder.

''I'm not going to play anymore,'' I said nonchalantly. ''Why should I? I'm not a genius.''

She stood in front of the TV. I saw that her chest was heaving up and down in an angry way.

''No!'' I said, and I now felt stronger, as if my true self had finally emerged. So this was what had been inside me all along.

''No! I won't!'' I screamed.

She snapped off the TV, yanked me by the arm and pulled me off the floor. She was frighteningly strong, half pulling, half carrying me toward the piano as I kicked the throw rugs under my feet. She lifted me up and onto the hard bench. I was sobbing by now, looking at her bitterly. Her chest was heaving even more and her mouth was open, smiling crazily as if she were pleased that I was crying.

''You want me to be someone that I'm not!'' I sobbed. ''I'll never be the kind of daughter you want me to be!''

"Only two kinds of daughters," she shouted in Chinese. "Those who are obedient and those who follow their own mind! Only one kind of daughter can live in this house. Obedient daughter!"

"Then I wish I weren't your daughter. I wish you weren't my mother," I shouted. As I said these things I got scared. It felt like worms and toads and slimy things crawling out of my chest, but it also felt good that this awful side of me had surfaced, at last.

"Too late change this," my mother said shrilly.

And I could sense her anger rising to its breaking point. I wanted to see it spill over. And that's when I remembered the babies she had lost in China, the ones we never talked about. "Then I wish I'd never been born!" I shouted. "I wish I were dead! Like them."

It was as if I had said magic words. Alakazam!—her face went blank, her mouth closed, her arms went slack, and she backed out of the room, stunned, as if she were blowing away like a small brown leaf, thin, brittle, lifeless.

It was not the only disappointment my mother felt in me. In the years that followed, I failed her many times, each time asserting my will, my right to fall short of expectations. I didn't get straight As. I didn't become class president. I didn't get into Stanford. I dropped out of college.

Unlike my mother, I did not believe I could be anything I wanted to be. I could only be me.

And for all those years we never talked about the disaster at the recital or my terrible declarations afterward at the piano bench. Neither of us talked about it again, as if it were a betrayal that was now unspeakable. So I never found a way to ask her why she had hoped for something so large that failure was inevitable.

And even worse, I never asked her about what frightened me the most: Why had she given up hope? For after our struggle at the piano, she never mentioned my playing again. The lessons stopped. The lid to the piano was closed, shutting out the dust, my misery, and her dreams.

So she surprised me. A few years ago she offered to give me the piano, for my thirtieth birthday. I had not played in all those years. I saw the offer as a sign of forgiveness, a tremendous burden removed.

"Are you sure?" I asked shyly. "I mean, won't you and Dad miss it?"

"No, this your piano," she said firmly. "Always your piano. You only one can play."

"Well, I probably can't play anymore," I said. "It's been years."

"You pick up fast," my mother said, as if she knew this was certain. "You have natural talent. You could be genius if you want to."

"No, I couldn't."

"You just not trying," my mother said. And she was neither angry nor sad. She said it as if announcing a fact that could never be disproved. "Take it," she said.

But I didn't at first. It was enough that she had offered it to me. And after that, every time I saw it in my parents' living room, standing in front of the bay window, it made me feel proud, as if it were a shiny trophy that I had won back.

Last week I sent a tuner over to my parents' apartment and had the piano reconditioned, for purely sentimental reasons. My mother had died a few months before, and I had been getting things in order for my father, a little bit at a time. I put the jewelry in special silk pouches. The sweaters she had knitted in yellow, pink, bright orange—all the colors I hated—I put in mothproof boxes. I found some old Chinese silk dresses, the kind with little slits up the sides. I rubbed the old silk against my skin, and then wrapped them in tissue and decided to take them home with me.

After I had the piano tuned, I opened the lid and touched the keys. It sounded even richer than I remembered. Really, it was a very good piano. Inside the bench were the same exercise notes with handwritten scales, the same secondhand music books with their covers held together with yellow tape.

I opened up the Schumann book to the dark little piece I had played at the recital. It was on the left-hand page, "Pleading Child." It looked more difficult than I remembered. I played a few bars, surprised at how easily the notes came back to me.

And for the first time, or so it seemed, I noticed the piece on the right-hand side. It was called "Perfectly Contented." I tried to play this one as well. It had a lighter melody but with the same flowing rhythm and turned out to be quite easy. "Pleading Child" was shorter but slower; "Perfectly Contented" was longer but faster. And after I had played them both a few times, I realized they were two halves of the same song.

DISCUSSION QUESTIONS

1. From whose point of view is the story told? Do you feel for the purposes of this story that it is necessary to distinguish between the point of view of the author and that of the narrator? Can the point of view be said to shift as the story unfolds? Describe the shift.
2. Though it is clear in the story that the mother has ambitions for her daughter, it is not clear that the daughter has ambitions of her own. What does the daughter have in mind for herself in the future?
3. What does the mother's use of the words "prodigy" and "genius" represent for her daughter? How do these words create a thematic focus for the first part of the story?

Susan Faludi / *Backlash, the Undeclared War against American Women* 1991

When Betty Friedan's groundbreaking book on women, The Feminine Mystique, *hit the best-seller charts in 1963, it proved that a sizable audience existed for the serious discussion of feminist issues. Since then, many books on feminism (both supportive and antagonistic, both fiction and nonfiction) have continued the discussion, helping to make the movement one of the most provocative issues in the American media. In the following essay from a recent feminist best-seller,* Backlash, the Undeclared War against American Women, *Susan Faludi contends that the media industries have launched a "counterassault" against women's rights, an attack largely premised on the unfounded assumption that women today have achieved full equality and that their currently reported dissatisfactions are—paradoxically—a direct result of their political gains. Her book reached the best-seller list within one month after its publication.*

A Pulitzer Prize-winning reporter for the Wall Street Journal, *Susan Faludi has written extensively on political issues. Her articles frequently appear in such progressive magazines as* Mother Jones, *where this selection also appeared.*

BLAME IT ON FEMINISM

To be a woman in America at the close of the twentieth century—what good fortune. That's what we keep hearing, anyway. The barricades have fallen, politicians assure us. Women have "made it," Madison Avenue cheers. Women's fight for equality has "largely been won," *Time* magazine announces. Enroll at any university, join any law firm, apply for credit at any bank. Women have so many opportunities now, corporate leaders say, that they don't really need opportunity policies. Women are so equal now, lawmakers say, that they no longer need an Equal Rights Amendment. Woman have "so much," former president Ronald Reagan says, that the White House no longer needs to appoint them to high office. Even American Express ads are saluting a woman's right to charge it. At last, women have received their full citizenship papers. And yet . . .

Behind this celebration of the American woman's victory, behind the news, cheerfully and endlessly repeated, that the struggle for women's rights is won, another message flashes: You may be free and equal now, but you have never been more miserable.

This bulletin of despair is posted everywhere—at the newsstand, on the TV set, at the movies, in advertisements and doctors' offices and academic journals. Professional women are suffering "burnout" and succumbing to an "infertility epidemic." Single women are grieving from a "man shortage." The *New York Times* reports: Childless women are "depressed and confused" and their ranks are swelling. *Newsweek* says: Unwed women are "hysterical" and crumbling under a "profound crisis of confidence." The health-advice manuals inform: High-powered career women are stricken with unprecedented outbreaks of "stress-induced disorders," hair loss, bad nerves, alcoholism, and even heart attacks. The psychology books advise: Independent women's loneliness represents "a major mental-health problem today." Even founding feminist Betty Friedan has been spreading the word: She warns that women now suffer from "new problems that have no name."

How can American women be in so much trouble at the same time that they are supposed to be so blessed? If women got what they asked for, what could possibly be the matter now?

The prevailing wisdom of the past decade has supported one, and only one, answer to this riddle: It must be all that equality that's causing all that pain. Women are unhappy precisely because they are free. Women are enslaved by their own liberation. They have grabbed at the gold ring of independence, only to miss the one ring that really matters. They have gained control of their fertility, only to destroy it. They have pursued their own professional dreams—and lost out on romance, the greatest female adventure. "Our generation was the human sacrifice" to the women's movement, writer Elizabeth Mehren contends in a *Time* cover story. Baby-boom women, like her, she says, have been duped by feminism: "We believed the rhetoric." In *Newsweek,* writer Kay Ebeling dubs feminism the "Great Experiment That Failed" and asserts, "Women in my generation, its perpetrators, are the casualties."

In the eighties, publications from the *New York Times* to *Vanity Fair* to *The Nation* have issued a steady stream of indictments against the women's movement, with such headlines as "WHEN FEMINISM FAILED" or "THE AWFUL TRUTH ABOUT WOMEN'S LIB." They hold the campaign for women's equality responsible for nearly every woe besetting women, from depression to meager savings accounts, from teenage suicides to eating disorders to bad complexions. The *Today* show says women's liberation is to blame for bag ladies. A guest columnist in the *Baltimore Sun* even proposes that feminists produced the rise in slasher movies. By making the "violence" of abortion more acceptable, the author reasons, women's-rights activists made it all right to show graphic murders on screen.

At the same time, other outlets of popular culture have been forging the same connection: In Hollywood films, of which *Fatal Attraction* is only the most famous, emancipated women with condominiums of their own slink wild-eyed between bare walls, paying for their liberty with an empty bed, a barren womb. "My biological clock is ticking so loud it keeps me awake at night," Sally Field cries in the film *Surrender,* as, in an all-too-common transformation in the cinema of the eighties, an actress who once played scrappy working heroines is now showcased groveling for a groom. In prime-time television shows, from *thirtysomething* to *Family Man,* single, professional, and feminist women are humiliated, turned into harpies, or hit by nervous breakdowns; the wise ones recant their independent ways by the closing sequence. In popular novels, from Gail Parent's *A Sign of the Eighties* to Stephen King's *Misery,* unwed women shrink to sniveling spinsters or inflate to fire-breathing she-devils; renouncing all aspirations but marriage, they beg for wedding bands from strangers or swing axes at reluctant bachelors. Even Erica Jong's high-flying independent heroine literally crashes by the end of the decade, as the author supplants *Fear of Flying's* saucy Isadora Wing, an exuberant symbol of female sexual emancipation in the seventies, with an embittered careerist-turned-recovering-"codependent" in *Any Woman's Blues*—a book that is intended, as the narrator bluntly states, "to demonstrate what a dead end the so-called sexual revolution had become and how desperate so-called free women were in the last few years of our decadent epoch."

Popular psychology manuals peddle the same diagnosis for contemporary female distress. "Feminism, having promised her a stronger sense of her own identity, has given her little more than an identity *crisis,*" the best-selling advice manual *Being a Woman* asserts. The authors of the era's self-help classic, *Smart Women/Foolish Choices,* proclaim that women's distress was "an unfortunate consequence of feminism" because "it created a myth among women that the apex of self-realization could be achieved only through autonomy, independence, and career."

In the Reagan and Bush years, government officials have needed no prompting to endorse this thesis. Reagan spokeswoman Faith Ryan Whittlesey declared feminism a "straitjacket" for women, in one of the White House's only policy speeches on the status of the American female population—entitled "Radical Feminism in Retreat." The U.S. attorney general's Commission on Pornography even proposed that women's professional advancement might be responsible for rising rape rates: With more women in college and at work now, the commission members reasoned in their report, women just have more opportunities to be raped.

Legal scholars have railed against the "equality trap." Sociologists have claimed that "feminist-inspired" legislative reforms have stripped women of special "protections." Economists have argued that well-paid working women have created a "less stable American family." And demographers, with greatest fanfare, have legitimated the prevailing wisdom with so-called neutral data on sex ratios and fertility trends; they say they actually have the numbers to prove that equality doesn't mix with marriage and motherhood.

Finally, some "liberated" women themselves have joined the lamentations. In *The Cost of Loving: Women and the New Fear of Intimacy,* Megan Marshall, a Harvard-pedigreed writer, asserts that the feminist "Myth of Independence" has turned her generation into unloved and unhappy fast-trackers, "dehumanized" by careers and "uncertain of their gender identity." Other diaries of mad Superwomen charge that "the hard-core feminist viewpoint," as one of them puts it, has relegated educated executive achievers to solitary nights of frozen dinners and closet drinking. The triumph of equality, they report, has merely given women hives, stomach cramps, eye "twitching" disorders, even comas.

But what "equality" are all these authorities talking about?

If American women are so equal, why do they represent two-thirds of all poor adults? Why are more than 70 percent of full-time working women making less than twenty-five thousand dollars a year, nearly double the number of men at that level? Why are they still far more likely than men to live in poor housing, and twice as likely to draw no pension? If women "have it all," then why don't they have the most basic requirements to achieve equality in the work force: unlike that of virtually all other industrialized nations, the U.S. government still has no family-leave and child-care programs.

If women are so "free," why are their reproductive freedoms in greater jeopardy today than a decade earlier? Why, in their own homes, do they still shoulder 70 percent of the household duties—while the only major change in the last fifteen years is that now men *think* they do more around the house? In thirty states, it is still generally legal for husbands to rape their wives; and only ten states have laws mandating arrest for domestic violence—even though battering is the leading cause of injury to women (greater than rapes, muggings, and auto accidents combined).

The word may be that women have been "liberated," but women themselves seem to feel otherwise. Repeatedly in national surveys, majorities of women say they are still far from equality. In poll after poll in the decade, overwhelming majorities of women said they need equal pay and equal job opportunities, they need an Equal Rights Amendment, they need the right to an abortion without government interference, they need a federal law guaranteeing maternity leave, they need decent child-care services. They have none of these. So how exactly have women "won" the war for women's rights?

Seen against this background, the much ballyhooed claim that feminism is responsible for making women miserable becomes absurd—and irrelevant. The afflictions ascribed to feminism, from "the man shortage" to "the infertility epidemic" to "female burnout" to "toxic day care," have had their origins not in the actual conditions of women's lives but rather in a closed system that starts and ends in the media, popular culture, and advertising—an endless feedback loop that perpetuates and exaggerates its own false images of womanhood. And women don't see feminism as their enemy, either. In fact, in national surveys, 75 to 95 percent of women credit the feminist campaign with *improving* their lives, and a similar proportion say that the women's movement should keep pushing for change.

If the many ponderers of the Women Question really wanted to know what is troubling the American female population, they might have asked their subjects. In public-opinion surveys, women consistently rank their own *inequality,* at work and at home, among their most urgent concerns. Over and over, women complain to pollsters of a lack of economic, not marital, opportunities; they protest that working men, not working women, fail to spend time in the nursery and the kitchen. It is justice for their gender, not wedding rings and bassinets, that women believe to be in desperately short supply.

As the last decade ran its course, the monitors that serve to track slippage in women's status have been working overtime. Government and private surveys are showing that women's already vast representation in the lowliest occupations is rising, their tiny presence in high-paying trade and craft jobs stalled or backsliding, their minuscule representation in upper management posts stagnant or falling, and their pay dropping in the very occupations where they have made the most "progress."

In national politics, the already small numbers of women in both elective posts and political appointments fell during the eighties. In private life, the average amount that a divorced man paid in child support fell by about 25 percent from the late seventies to the mid-eighties (to a mere $140 a month). And government records chronicled a spectacular rise in sexual violence against women. Reported rapes more than doubled from the early seventies—at nearly twice the rate of all other violent crimes and four times the overall crime rate in the United States.

The truth is that the last decade has seen a powerful counterassault on women's rights, a backlash, an attempt to retract the handful of small and hard-won victories that the feminist movement did manage to win for women. This counterassault is largely insidious: in a kind of pop-culture version of the big lie, it stands the truth boldly on its head and proclaims that the very steps that have elevated women's position have actually led to their downfall.

The backlash is at once sophisticated and banal, deceptively "progressive" and proudly backward. It deploys both the "new" findings of "scientific research" and the dime-store moralism of yesteryear; it turns into media sound bites both the glib pronouncements of pop-psych trend-watchers and the frenzied rhetoric of New Right preachers. The backlash has succeeded in framing virtually the whole issue of women's rights in it own language. Just as Reaganism shifted political discourse far to the right and demonized liberalism, so the backlash convinced the public that women's "liberation" was the true contemporary American scourge—the source of an endless laundry list of personal, social, and economic problems.

But what has made women unhappy in the last decade is not their "equality"—which they don't yet have—but the rising pressure to halt, and even reverse, women's quest for that equality. The "man shortage" and the "infertility epidemic" are not the price of liberation; in fact, they do not even exist. But these chimeras are part of a relentless whittling-down process—much of it amounting to outright propaganda—that has served to stir women's private anxieties and break their political wills. Identifying feminism as women's enemy only furthers the ends of a backlash against women's equality by simultaneously deflecting attention from the backlash's central role and recruiting women to attack their own cause.

Some social observers may well ask whether the current pressures on women actually constitute a backlash—or just a continuation of American society's long-standing resistance to women's equal rights. Certainly hostility to female independence has always been with us. But if fear and loathing of feminism is a sort of perpetual viral condition in our culture, it is not always in an acute stage; its symptoms subside and resurface periodically. And it is these episodes of resurgence, such as the one we face now, that can accurately be termed "backlashes" to women's advancement. If we trace these occurrences in American history, we find such flare-ups are hardly random; they have always been triggered by the perception—accurate or not—that women are making great strides. These outbreaks are backlashes because they have always arisen in reaction to women's "progress," caused not simply by a bedrock of misogyny but by the specific efforts of contemporary women to improve their status, efforts that have been interpreted time and again by men—especially men grappling with real threats to their economic and social well-being on other fronts—as spelling their own masculine doom.

The most recent round of backlash first surfaced in the late seventies on the fringes, among the evangelical Right. By the early eighties, the fundamentalist ideology had shouldered its way into the White House. By the mid-eighties, as resistance to women's rights acquired political and social acceptability, it passed into the popular culture. And in every case, the timing coincided with signs that women were believed to be on the verge of a breakthrough.

Just when women's quest for equal rights seemed closest to achieving its objectives, the backlash struck it down. Just when a "gender gap" at the voting booth surfaced in 1980, and women in politics began to talk of capitalizing on it, the Republican party elevated Ronald Reagan and both political parties began to shunt women's rights off their platforms. Just when support for feminism and the Equal Rights Amendment reached a record high in 1981, the amendment was defeated the following year. Just when women were starting to mobilize against battering and sexual assaults, the federal government cut funding for battered-women's programs, defeated bills to fund shelters, and shut down its Office of Domestic Violence—only two years after opening it in 1979. Just when record numbers of younger women were supporting feminist goals in the mid-eighties (more of them, in fact, than older women) and a majority of all women were calling themselves feminists, the media declared the advent of a younger "postfeminist generation" that supposedly reviled the women's movement. Just when women racked up their largest percentage ever supporting the right to abortion, the U.S. Supreme Court moved toward reconsidering it.

In other words, the antifeminist backlash has been set off not by women's achievement of full equality but by the increased possibility that they might win it. It is a preemptive strike that stops women long before they reach the finish line. "A backlash may be an indication that women really have had an effect," feminist psychiatrist Dr. Jean Baker Miller has written, "but backlashes occur when advances have been small, before changes are sufficient to help many people. . . . It is almost as if the leaders of backlashes use the fear of change as a threat before major change has occurred." In the last decade, some women did make substantial advances before the backlash hit, but millions of others were left behind, stranded. Some women now enjoy the right to legal abortion—but not the forty-four million women, from the indigent to the military worker, who depend on the federal government for their medical care. Some women can now walk into high-paying professional careers—but not the millions still in the typing pools or behind the department-store sales counters. (Contrary to popular myth about the "have-it-all" baby-boom women, the largest percentage of women in this generation remain in office support roles.)

As the backlash has gathered force, it has cut off the few from the many—and the few women who have advanced seek to prove, as a social survival tactic, that they aren't so interested in advancement after all. Some of them parade their defection from the women's movement, while their working-class peers founder and cling to the splintered remains of the feminist cause. While a very few affluent and celebrity women who are showcased in news stories boast about going home to "bake bread," the many working-class women appeal for their economic rights—flocking to unions in record numbers, striking on their own for pay equity, and establishing their own fledgling groups for working-women's rights. In 1986, while 41 percent of upper-income women were claiming in the Gallup poll that they were not feminists, only 26 percent of low-income women were making the same claim.

Women's advances and retreats are generally described in military terms: battles won, battles lost, points and territory gained and surrendered. The metaphor of combat is not without its merits in this context, and, clearly, the same sort of martial accounting and vocabulary is already surfacing here. But by imagining the conflict as two battalions neatly arrayed on either side of the line, we miss the entangled nature, the locked embrace, of a "war" between women and the male culture they inhabit. We miss the reactive nature of a backlash, which, by definition, can exist only in response to another force.

In times when feminism is at a low ebb, women assume the reactive role—privately and, most often, covertly struggling to assert themselves against the dominant cultural tide. But when feminism itself becomes the tide, the opposition doesn't simply go along with the reversal: it digs in its heels, brandishes its fists, builds walls and dams. And its resistance creates countercurrents and treacherous undertows.

The force and furor of the backlash churn beneath the surface, largely invisible to the public eye. On occasion in the last decade, they have burst into view. We have seen New Right politicians condemn women's independence, antiabortion protesters firebomb women's clinics, fundamentalist preachers damn feminists as "whores." Other signs of the backlash's wrath, by their sheet brutality, can push their way into public consciousness for a time—the sharp increase in rape, for example, or the rise in pornography that depicts extreme violence against women.

More subtle indicators in popular culture may receive momentary, and often bemused, media notice, then quickly slip from social awareness: A report, for instance, that the image of women on prime-time TV shows has suddenly degenerated. A survey of mystery fiction finding the numbers of tortured and mutilated female characters mysteriously multiplying. The puzzling news that, as one commentator put it, "so many hit songs have the B word [bitch] to refer to women that some rap music seems to be veering toward rape music." The ascendancy of violently misogynist comics like Andrew Dice Clay, who calls women "pigs" and "sluts," or radio hosts like Rush Limbaugh, whose broadsides against "femi-Nazi" feminists helped make his syndicated program the most popular radio talk show in the nation. Or word that, in 1987, the American Women in Radio and Television couldn't award its annual prize to ads that feature women positively: it could find no ad that qualified.

These phenomena are all related, but that doesn't mean they are somehow coordinated. The backlash is not a conspiracy, with a council dispatching agents from some central control room, nor are the people who serve its ends often aware of their role; some even consider themselves feminists. For the most part, its workings are encoded and internalized, diffuse and chameleonic. Not all of the manifestations of the backlash are of equal weight or significance, either; some are mere ephemera thrown up by a culture machine that is always scrounging for a "fresh" angle. Taken as a whole, however, these codes and cajolings, these whispers and threats and myths, move overwhelmingly in one direction: they try to push women back into their "acceptable" roles—whether as Daddy's girl or fluttery romantic, active nester or passive love object.

Although the backlash is not an organized movement, that doesn't make it any less destructive. In fact, the lack of orchestration, the absence of a single stringpuller, only makes it harder to see—and perhaps more effective. A backlash against women's rights succeeds to the degree that it appears *not* to be political, that it appears not to be a struggle at all. It is most powerful when it goes private, when it lodges inside a woman's mind and turns her vision inward, until she imagines the pressure is all in her head, until she begins to enforce the backlash, too—on herself.

In the last decade, the backlash has moved through the culture's secret chambers, traveling through passageways of flattery and fear. Along the way, it has adopted disguises: a mask of mild derision or the painted face of deep "concern." Its lips profess pity for any woman who won't fit the mold, while it tries to clamp the mold around her ears. It pursues a divide-and-conquer strategy: single versus married women, working women versus homemakers, middle versus working class. It manipulates a system of rewards and punishments, elevating women who follow its rules, isolating those who don't. The backlash remarkets old myths about women as new facts and ignores all appeals to reason. Cornered, it denies its own existence, points an accusatory finger at feminism, and burrows deeper underground.

Backlash happens to be the title of a 1947 Hollywood movie in which a man frames his wife for a murder he's committed. The backlash against women's rights works in much the same way: its rhetoric charges feminists with all the crimes it perpetrates. The backlash line blames the women's movement for the "feminization of poverty"—while the backlash's own instigators in Washington have pushed through the budget cuts that have helped impoverish millions of women, have fought pay-equity proposals, and undermined equal-opportunity laws. The backlash line claims the women's movement cares nothing for children's rights—while its own representatives in the capital and state legislatures have blocked one bill after another to improve child care, slashed billions of dollars in aid for children, and relaxed state licensing standards for day-care centers. The backlash line accuses the women's movement of creating a generation of unhappy single and childless women—but its purveyors in the media are the ones guilty of making single and childless women feel like circus freaks.

To blame feminism for women's "lesser life" is to miss its point entirely, which is to win women a wider range of experience. Feminism remains a pretty simple concept, despite repeated—and enormously effective—efforts to dress it up in greasepaint and turn its proponents into gargoyles. As Rebecca West wrote sardonically in 1913, "I myself have never been able to find out precisely what feminism is: I only know that people call me a feminist whenever I express sentiments that differentiate me from a doormat."

The meaning of the word feminism has not really changed since it first appeared in a book review in *The Athenaeum* on April 27, 1895, describing a woman who "has in her the capacity of fighting her way back to independence." It is the basic proposition that, as Nora put it in Ibsen's *A Doll's House* a century ago, "Before everything else I'm a human being." It is the simply worded sign hoisted by a little girl in the 1970 Women's Strike for Equality: "I AM NOT A BARBIE DOLL." Feminism asks the world to recognize at long last that women aren't decorative ornaments, worthy vessels, members of a "special-interest group." They are half (in fact, now more than half) of the national population, and just as deserving of rights and opportunities, just as capable of participting in the world's events, as the other half. Feminism's agenda is basic: It asks that women not be forced to "choose" between public justice and private happiness. It asks that women be free to define themselves—instead of having their identity defined for them, time and again, by their culture and their men.

The fact that these are still such incendiary notions should tell us that American women have a way to go before they enter the promised land of equality.

DISCUSSION QUESTIONS

1. Note the numerous references to books, magazine articles, television shows, and films throughout Faludi's piece. What do most of the references have in common? Why are these citations important to her argument?

2. In an otherwise favorable review of the book for the *New York Times Book Review*, Ellen Goodman noted that *Backlash* is "sometimes guilty of the sort of trend reporting that it criticizes." Do you think this objection is fair? Can you detect any instances of it in the selection?

CLASSICS

Literature is news that stays news.

EZRA POUND

IN its popular sense, *classic* means something that remains in style. The word often comes up in talk about a particular cut of clothing, the movements of dancers and athletes, someone's features, the lines of a building or an automobile, and even the preparation of food. *Classic,* in such instances, describes certain qualities of craftsmanship, performance, or appearance that remain constant despite changes in fashion, taste, doctrine, or government. Unlike most of the ads, best-sellers, articles, and journalism you have read in previous sections of this book, the prose and poetry reprinted in the following pages represent the work of many writers who have been read continuously over the years, writers who have remained in style. A classic is durable; it is writing that stays in print.

Why do some works preserve a lively reputation for generations while others are forgotten by the end of a season? Surely it is not because the writers of what eventually become classics attend to different subjects than do the authors of even those best-sellers whose popularity does not endure very much beyond their arrival in paperback at local bookstores. Adventure and romance, love and death, individual freedom and social order, innocence and experience, success and failure are, for example, often themes of classics and best-sellers as well as, for that matter, most journalism and advertising. If what makes a work a classic is not simply the author's choice of material—all material is, strictly speaking, in the public domain—then the best place to find the reason for a work's continuing success is in the quality of its writing.

In general, our selections from American classics will provide you with more complicated uses of language than most of the other forms of writing you have encountered in earlier sections of this book. It should be added, however, that the authors of classics are not necessarily hostile to those other, less complicated forms of writing. If anything, they are probably more willing to incorporate the multiplicity of styles and voices surrounding them than are writers who must, because of a greater commercial investment, appeal to quite specific audiences. Journalists, for example, may be reluctant to record the interferences and intrusions they may have encountered in their attempted news coverage. (They have copy editors to satisfy and only a limited amount of newspaper space for their stories.) So too, authors of best-sellers may not want to, may not know how to, or may not even dare to risk unsettling their readers with sudden shifts in tone or point of view or subtle maneuvers into irony or parody.

From the philosophical manner of Henry David Thoreau to the Beat poetics of Allen Ginsberg, the writing collected here is meant to suggest the variety and complexity of classic American literature. It is literature whose authors, for the most part, have been receptive, at times competitively responsive, to whatever environment of language they chose to work in. Mark Twain, who told many good stories in his own lifetime, makes it clear that telling a story well is a performance of tone and nuance that ought to rival the most successful forms of contemporary entertainment. Twain wants his audience to delight, as he does, in the art of mimicry and parody. "How to Tell a Story" is much more than an enjoyable training manual for delivering effective jokes; it is also a fine critical statement reminding us that the art of reading well is also the art of listening attentively. Kate Chopin in "The Dream of an Hour," John Updike in "A & P," Tillie Olsen in "I Stand Here Ironing," and Allen Ginsberg in "A Supermarket in California" expect (as Twain does) their audiences to be fully attuned to the ways their styles embody the nonliterary idioms and intonations of American advertising, popular music, and film.

Along with Mark Twain, such writers as Stephen Crane, Ernest Hemingway, and Norman Mailer are competitively aware of how the techniques and verbal formulations of journalism can be exploited and even parodied in their own efforts to render events distinctively. Having been reporters themselves, they have experienced firsthand the advantages and limitations of writing the kind of prose that newspapers consistently promote. For example, a comparison of Mailer's account with the newspaper report of the astronauts' walk on the moon will demonstrate what a major novelist considers to be the obligations of a literary consciousness contending with an event that is surrounded, if not dominated, by the machinery of news coverage. In Crane's "The Open Boat," we can observe how a writer transforms the raw data of a journalist scoop (see "Stephen Crane's Own Story" in "Press") into the complex arrangements of classic fiction.

It should be clear from the following selections that the writers of classics use language in the most demanding and selective ways possible. Theirs is a prose that requires its audience to have attained a more highly developed reading aptitude than that needed to respond to much of the writing appearing earlier in this book. A classic expects its readers to be more than simply literate. Readers of classics are obliged to engage in difficult, sometimes highly complicated verbal experiences and, at the same time, are encouraged in the act of reading to refer these verbal experiences to a wide network of accumulated literary responses. In fact, the writers of classic prose (whether it be fiction or nonfiction) very often imagine for themselves readers who take delight in having such demands made on them.

Few authors are more exacting in the demands their writing makes on their audience than William Faulkner. Take, for example, the following passage from *The Bear,* in which Faulkner describes the culmination of young Ike McCaslin's nearly obsessive, increasingly solitary search for the elusive, indomitable bear, Old Ben:

> Then he saw the bear. It did not emerge, appear: it was just there, immobile, fixed in the green and windless noon's hot dappling, not as big as he had dreamed it but as big as he had expected, bigger, dimensionless against the dappled obscurity, looking at him. Then it moved. It crossed the glade without haste, walking for an instant into the sun's full glare and out of it, and stopped again and looked back at him across one shoulder. Then it was gone. It didn't walk into the woods. It faded, sank back into the wilderness without motion as he had watched a fish, a huge old bass, sink back into the dark depths of its pool and vanish without even any movement of its fins.

Faulkner allows Ike his long-awaited confrontation with the bear only after the boy has willingly surrendered himself to the woods by relinquishing his gun, watch, and compass. Bereft of weapon and instruments, those "tainted" items of civilization, Ike can *know* the wilderness in ways that permit him to go further than even his mastery of the technique of woodmanship could take him. When Ike finally encounters Old Ben, it is because he has entered into a new relation with the woods, one that has superseded the boundaries set up by the rules and rituals of hunting and tracking.

As a factual account of a hunting incident, this passage is rather unremarkable, surely anticlimactic. Nothing much seems to happen. The boy sees the bear. The bear sees the boy. The bear disappears into the woods. There is no kill, no breathtaking capture or escape. Furthermore, the reader is given few of the details that might be anticipated in such an encounter. Nothing is told of the bear's size, color, or smell; there is none of the usual metaphorical approximations hunters like to make of an animal's brute power. What is perhaps even more surprising, the reader is told nothing at all about the boy's emotional response to the one moment he has trained and waited for through so many hunting seasons.

If the reader cannot easily picture this episode within the frame of a glossy photograph from *Field and Stream* or *True,* it is because Faulkner's writing resists the kind of imagination that would want to reduce the scene to one more clearly and conventionally focused. The total effect produced by the blurring of the bear and woods, the amorphous presence of the boy, the uncertainty of movement, and the confusing shifts of sunlight and shadow is not the result of a verbal or pictorial incompetence but, on the contrary, is the consequence of a deliberate and complex effort of intelligence. Faulkner's style demands that the reader participate in that complexity. The reliance on negatives (''It did not emerge . . . not as big . . . It didn't walk''), the sudden modification of syntax (''but as big as he had expected, bigger, dimensionless''), the struggle to find adequate verbs or adjectives (''emerge, appear . . . immobile, fixed . . . faded, sank''), the process of expansion (''a fish, a huge old bass''), and the apparently reluctant concessions to narrative sequence (''Then he saw the bear . . . Then it moved . . . Then it was gone.'') force the reader into suspending temporarily his expectations of the dimensions of an experience and the conduct of sentences. The style, in effect, compels the reader to experience a dislocation and conversion analogous to those that made Ike McCaslin's initiation into the wilderness possible.

A writer's style attests to the quality of his perceptions. Though Faulkner's verbal expansiveness in *The Bear* may seem difficult, even discouragingly so, the demands he makes on his readers are not necessarily any greater than those of writers like Thoreau, Crane, Wright, or Hemingway whose difficulties may seem, at first, much less apparent. The writing in ''Soldier's Home'' certainly looks easy, but that does not mean the tale is a simple one. Hemingway's stylistic reticence, his self-conscious artistic control, is the consequence of a literary acuity that is perhaps only slightly less remarkable than Faulkner's. If the styles of writers like Hemingway and Faulkner are based on perceptions that happen to be intricate, even unsettling, that is only because each writer struggles to master in his own way the countless verbal options at his disposal. Such writing presupposes an energetic reader, one who is willing to work almost as hard at reading as the author worked at writing. The readers imagined by the writers of the selections that follow would not be intimidated by the kind of rigorous training that, according to Thoreau, they must undergo if they are to read proficiently:

> To read well, that is, to read books in a true spirit, is a noble exercise, and one that will task the reader more than any exercise which the customs of the day esteem. It requires a training such as the athletes underwent, the steady intention almost of the whole life to this object. Books must be read as deliberately and reservedly as they were written. (''Reading,'' from *Walden.*)

Thoreau's metaphor is an appropriate one. By comparing the exertion of reading to the exercise of athletics, Thoreau converts what is ordinarily regarded as an idle occasion into a tough and invigorating practice. To read well is to do something more than just be a spectator to what Robert Frost terms ''the feat of words.''

Christopher Columbus / Michele de Cuneo's Letter on Columbus' Second Voyage* 1495

During the course of a decade of voyages to the New World, Christopher Columbus was convinced that he could find a passage to the Orient by sailing west. The first of those four voyages resulted in Columbus's reaching the island of San Salvador, and from that point he explored what are now the Bahamas, Cuba, and Haiti, naming that island Hispaniola. Certain that he had found the Indies, he named the people of those islands "Indians." The journal he kept on that voyage was lost.

Columbus set out on a second voyage in 1493 and explored Puerto Rico, Jamaica, portions of Cuba, the Virgin Islands, and the Lesser Antilles. No journal account of this expedition in Columbus's hand survives, although an aristocratic friend of Columbus who accompanied him on the expedition, Michele de Cuneo, did keep an informal record of the voyage. This account underscores how rapidly relations between the Europeans and the natives deteriorated into bloody conflict.

As the conquest of the Americas is reassessed in light of ethnic and Native American voices, the "official" story many of us learned in grade school begins to decay. One aspect of reconsidering the Columbus myth involves rereading history, with particular attention to the primary documents available from the time of the voyages. This excerpt from a letter by de Cuneo provides a graphic early account of the dynamics of discovery and imperialism.

In the name of Jesus and of his glorious mother Mary from whom all good things come. On the 25th of September, 1493, we left Cadiz under 17 sails and all in good order—15 square and 2 lateen sails—and on the 2nd of October we anchored at the Grand Canary Island; the following night we set sail and on the 5th we anchored at Gomera, one of the Canary Islands; and it would take too long to tell you about the glorious reception we were given, the rounds fired by cannons and flame-throwers, all ordered by the lady who governs the island and with whom our admiral was once somewhat in love.[1] Here we refreshed ourselves as much as we needed and on October 10th we set out on our voyage, but due to unfavorable weather we stayed around the Canary Islands three days. On the morning of October 13th, a Sunday, we left the Island of Ferro [Hierro], the last of the Canaries and we headed southwest. On the 25th of October, the eve of Saints Simon and Jude, at approximately 1600 we hit a storm of such force you wouldn't believe it and we thought our time was up. It lasted all night and 'til day and was so bad we couldn't see one another; at the end, as it pleased God, we found each other, and on November 3rd, a Sunday, we sighted land—five unknown islands. Our admiral named the first Santo Domingo since it was discovered on the Lord's day; the second he called Santa Maria la Gallante out of love for his ship, which was called Maria la Gallante. These two were not very large islands; nevertheless the admiral mapped them. If I remember correctly, it took us 22 days to get from the Island of Ferro to Santa Maria la Gallante, but I think one could well make the trip in 16 days of good wind.

*No official journal or abstract of the second voyage has survived. This account was written by Michele de Cuneo, an aristocratic friend who accompanied Columbus on the expedition. The translation here was prepared especially for this volume by Elissa Weaver.

[1]Although Cuneo is the only source of this information, Columbus apparently had fallen in love with the woman who ruled the island of Gomera.

On the island of Santa Maria la Gallante we got water and wood. The island is uninhabited even though it's full of trees and plains. We set sail from there that day and arrived at a large island inhabited by Cannibals,[2] who fled immediately to the mountains when they saw us. We landed on this island and stayed about 6 days since eleven of our men, who had banded together in order to steal, went 5 or 6 miles into the deserted area by such a route that when they wanted to return, they were unable to find their way, even though they were all sailors and could follow the sun, which they couldn't see well for the thick and full woods. When the admiral saw that these men had not returned and were nowhere to be found, he sent 200 men divided into 4 squadrons with trumpets, horns and lanterns, but even they were unable to find the lost men, and there was a time when we were worried about the 200 men than the others before them. But, as it pleased God, the 200 returned with great difficulty and greater hunger; we judged that the eleven had been eaten by the Cannibals as they are wont to do. However, after 5 or 6 days, the eleven men, as it pleased God, when there remained little hope of ever finding them, built a fire on a cape; seeing the fire, we judged it to be them and we sent a boat and in that way recovered them. Had it not been that an old woman showed them the way back with gestures they'd have been done for since we had planned to set sail on the following day.

On that island we took 12 very beautiful and fat females about 15 or 16 years old and 2 boys of the same age whose genital member had been cut off down to their belly; and we judged that this had been done to keep them from mixing with their women or at least to fatten them and then eat them. These boys and girls had been picked by the Cannibals for us to send to Spain to the king as an exhibit. The admiral named this island Santa Maria di Guadalupe.[3]

We set sail from this island of Santa Maria di Guadalupe, the Island of Cannibals, on November 10th and on the 14th we reached another beautiful and fertile island[4] of Cannibals and we came to a very beautiful port. When the Cannibals caught sight of us they fled, as the others had, to the mountains and abandoned their houses where we went and took what we liked. In these few days we found many islands where we didn't disembark, but others where we did—for the night. When we didn't leave the ship we kept it tied, and this we did so we wouldn't travel on and out of fear of running aground. Because these islands were closely adjoining, the admiral called them the Eleven Thousand Virgins,[5] and the previous one, Santa Croce.

We had anchored and gone ashore one day when we saw, coming from a cape, a canoe, that is, a boat, for so it is called in their speech, and it was beating oars as though it were a well-armed brigantine. On it there were three or four male Cannibals with two female Cannibals and two captured Indian slaves—so the Cannibals call their other neighbors from those other islands; they had also just cut off their genital member down to their belly and so they were still sick. Since we had the captain's boat ashore with us, when we saw this canoe we quickly jumped into the boat and gave chase to the canoe. As we approached it, the Cannibals shot hard at us with their bows, and if we had not had our Pavian shields[6] we would have been half destroyed. I must also tell you that a companion who had a shield in his hand got hit by an arrow which went through the shield and into his chest 3 inches causing him to die within a few days. We captured this canoe with all the men. One Cannibal was wounded by a lance-blow and thinking him dead we left him in the sea. Suddenly we saw him begin to swim away; therefore we

[2] In the original manuscript the word is *Camballi;* it means either "Carib Indians" or "cannibals."
[3] Guadeloupe, named after the famous Spanish shrine.
[4] Now St. Croix.
[5] The Virgin Islands, named for the legend of St. Ursula and the 11,000 virgin martyrs of Cologne.
[6] Large, rectangular shields from the northern Italian city of Pavia.

caught him and with a long hook we pulled him aboard where we cut off his head with an axe. We sent the other Cannibals together with the two slaves to Spain. When I was in the boat, I took a beautiful Cannibal girl and the admiral gave her to me. Having her in my room and she being naked as is their custom, I began to want to amuse myself with her. Since I wanted to have my way with her and she was not willing, she worked me over so badly with her nails that I wished I had never begun. To get to the end of the story, seeing how things were going, I got a rope and tied her up so tightly that she made unheard of cries which you wouldn't have believed. At the end, we got along so well that, let me tell you, it seemed she had studied at a school for whores. The admiral named the cape on that island the Cape of the Arrow for the man who was killed by the arrow.

On the 14th of November we set sail from the island in bad weather. On the 19th we anchored at a large and beautiful island of Indians called, in their language, Boluchen, which the admiral named St. John the Baptist.[7] As we sailed these 5 days both on the right and on the left we saw many islands all of which the admiral has had clearly mapped. At the island mentioned above we stopped to refresh ourselves and on the 21st we sailed; on the 25th, in the name of God, we anchored at Hispaniola,[8] an island discovered earlier by the admiral, where we want ashore at an excellent port called Monte Christo. In these few days we had more bad weather and we saw about 10 islands. We judged the distance from the island of Santo Domingo to Monte Christo to be 300 leagues. We were not able to keep a straight course for the shallows.

On the 27th of November we set sail to go to Monte Santo where the admiral on his last voyage left 38 men, and that same night we anchored at that very place.[9] On the 28th we went ashore, where we found all of our above-mentioned men dead and still stretched out there on the ground; their eyes were gone and we judged they had been eaten since when the Cannibals decapitate someone they immediately take out his eyes and eat them. They could have been dead 15 to 20 days. We were with the ruler of the place whose name was Goachanari, who, with tears running down his chest, and his men likewise, told us that the ruler of the mountain area named Goacanaboa had come with 3 thousand men and killed them together with some of their own people and robbed them out of spite. We found none of the things the admiral had left there, and having heard this story, we took it to be true. We spent 10 days on this business and on the 8th of December we left the place since it was not healthful because of its swamps, and we went to another place on the same island to an excellent port where we went ashore. There we built 200 houses which are small, like the huts we build at home for hunting birds, and they are covered with grass.

When we had built the settlement[10] for ourselves, the inhabitants of the island, who lived between one and two leagues from us, came to visit, as though we were brothers, saying that we were men of God come down from the sky, and many stood in awe watching us. They brought us some of their food to eat and we gave them some of ours since they behaved like brothers. And here we arrive at the end of our voyage, although I will say more below of another voyage I made later with the admiral when he decided to find terra firma; but now we will speak of other things and first about the search for gold on the island of Hispaniola.

[7] Now Puerto Rico.

[8] The large island that Columbus called Hispaniola is the present-day Haiti and the Dominican Republic.

[9] The fortress of Navidad, which Columbus had constructed on his first voyage.

[10] Isabella, the first European attempt at a permanent settlement in the New World.

Tom Wolfe / Columbus and the Moon 1979

Some writers have a magnetic sense about their generation's zeitgeist. Their works, from the very words they use to the stories they tell, capture the anxieties, pleasures, and hopes of their time so vividly that they come to define the moments they describe. During the 1960s, Tom Wolfe was such a writer. "The me decade," "radical chic," "the right stuff"—these are a few of the phrases that Tom Wolfe has introduced into the American vocabulary. A genius at deciphering an attitude or an entire ideology from the slightest stylistic quirk or idiom, Wolfe is without a doubt one of the major interpreters of contemporary American culture.

Born in 1931, Wolfe grew up in Richmond, Virginia. He graduated from Washington and Lee University and then went on to receive a Ph.D. in American studies at Yale. He spent several years as a newspaper reporter and in 1980 received the Columbia Journalism Award for distinguished service in the field of journalism. Wolfe's first book, The Kandy-Kolored Tangerine-Flake Streamline Baby, *appeared in 1964 and established him at once as a leading commentator on popular culture. His other books include* The Electric Kool-Aid Acid Test *(1968),* The Pump House Gang *(1968),* Radical Chic and Mau-Mauing the Flak Catchers *(1970),* The Painted Word *(1975),* The Right Stuff *(1979), and* From Bauhaus to Our House *(1981). His first novel,* Bonfire of the Vanities, *was published in 1985.*

The following essay, reprinted from the July 20, 1979, edition of the New York Times, *uses wry humor to compare the NASA project to land humans on the moon with the voyages of Columbus to the New World. Wolfe manages to deflate both the myth of our nation's origins and the mystique surrounding space exploration by recounting the numerous failures of the adventurers in charge of these journeys and the evasive measures they took to protect their reputations. In doing so, Wolfe shows up the dreams and foibles involved in any act of territorial expansion.*

The National Aeronautics and Space Administration's moon landing 10 years ago today was a Government project, but then so was Columbus's voyage to America in 1492. The Government, in Columbus's case, was the Spanish Court of Ferdinand and Isabella. Spain was engaged in a sea race with Portugal in much the same way that the United States would be caught up in a space race with the Soviet Union four and a half centuries later.

The race in 1492 was to create the first shipping lane to Asia. The Portuguese expeditions had always sailed east, around the southern tip of Africa. Columbus decided to head due west, across open ocean, a scheme that was feasible only thanks to a recent invention—the magnetic ship's compass. Until then ships had stayed close to the great land masses even for the longest voyages. Likewise, it was only thanks to an invention of the 1940's and early 1950's, the high-speed electronic computer, that NASA would even consider propelling astronauts out of the Earth's orbit and toward the moon.

But NASA and Columbus made not one but a series of voyages. NASA landed men on six different parts of the moon. Columbus made four voyages to different parts of what he remained convinced was the east coast of Asia. As a result both NASA and Columbus had to keep coming back to the Government with their hands out, pleading for refinancing. In each case the reply of the Government became, after a few years: "This is all very impressive, but what earthly good is it to anyone back home?"

Columbus was reduced to making the most desperate claims. When he first reached land in 1492 at San Salvador, off Cuba, he expected to find gold, or at least spices. The Arawak Indians were awed by the strangers and their ships, which they believed had descended from the sky, and they presented them with their most prized possessions, live parrots and balls of cotton. Columbus soon set them digging for gold, which didn't exist. So he brought back reports of fabulous riches in the form of manpower; which is to say, slaves. He was not speaking of the Arawaks, however. With the exception of criminals and prisoners of war, he was supposed to civilize all natives and convert them to Christianity. He was talking about the Carib Indians, who were cannibals and therefore qualified as criminals. The Caribs would fight down to the last unbroken bone rather than endure captivity, and few ever survived the voyages back to Spain. By the end of Columbus's second voyage, in 1496, the Government was becoming testy. A great deal of wealth was going into voyages to Asia, and very little was coming back. Columbus made his men swear to return to Spain saying that they had not only reached the Asian mainland, they had heard Japanese spoken.

Likewise by the early 1970's, it was clear that the moon was in economic terms pretty much what it looked like from Earth, a gray rock. NASA, in the quest for appropriations, was reduced to publicizing the "spinoffs" of the space program. These included Teflon-coated frying pans, a ballpoint pen that would write in a weightless environment, and a computerized biosensor system that would enable doctors to treat heart patients without making house calls. On the whole, not a giant step for mankind.

In 1493, after his first voyage, Columbus had ridden through Barcelona on the side of King Ferdinand in the position once occupied by Ferdinand's late son, Juan. By 1500, the bad-mouthing of Columbus had reached the point where he was put in chains at the conclusion of his third voyage and returned to Spain in disgrace. NASA suffered no such ignominy, of course, but by July 20, 1974, the fifth anniversary of the landing of Apollo 11, things were grim enough. The public had become gloriously bored by space exploration. The fifth anniversary celebration consisted mainly of about 200 souls, mostly NASA people, sitting on folding chairs underneath a camp meeting canopy on the marble prairie outside the old Smithsonian Air Museum in Washington listening to speeches by Neil Armstrong, Michael Collins, and Buzz Aldrin and watching the caloric waves ripple.

Extraordinary rumors had begun to circulate about the astronauts. The most lurid said that trips to the moon, and even into earth orbit, had so traumatized the men, they had fallen victim to religious and spiritualist manias or plain madness. (Of the total 73 astronauts chosen, one, Aldrin, is known to have suffered from depression, rooted, as his own memoir makes clear, in matters that had nothing to do with space flight. Two teamed up in an evangelical organization, and one set up a foundation for the scientific study of psychic phenomena—interests the three of them had developed long before they flew in space.) The NASA budget, meanwhile, had been reduced to the light-bill level.

Columbus died in 1509, nearly broke and stripped of most of his honors as Spain's Admiral of the Ocean, a title he preferred. It was only later that history began to look upon him not as an adventurer who had tried and failed to bring home gold—but as a man with a supernatural sense of destiny, whose true glory was his willingness to plunge into the unknown, including the remotest parts of the universe he could hope to reach.

NASA still lives, albeit in reduced circumstances, and whether or not history will treat NASA like the admiral is hard to say.

The idea that the exploration of the rest of the universe is its own reward is not very popular, and NASA is forced to keep talking about things such as bigger communications satellites that will enable live television transmission of European soccer games at a fraction of the current cost. Such notions as ''building a bridge to the stars for mankind'' do not light up the sky today—but may yet.

DISCUSSION QUESTIONS

1. Wolfe's piece uses the image of Christopher Columbus as a basis for looking at some of America's historic ideas of progress and accomplishment. How does this piece comment on the one by Michele de Cuneo? In what specific ways is Wolfe's interest akin to—and different from—de Cuneo's?
2. Examine the use of stereotypical images in these two pieces on Columbus. How are we able to critique the racist tendencies of the de Cuneo excerpt while retaining some respect for the text as it was written? How does the Wolfe excerpt play on stereotypes? Consider, for example, the images of masculinity that run throughout the piece.

Thomas Jefferson / The Declaration of Independence 1776

Thomas Jefferson's life as a writer is bound together with his remarkable career as a diplomat, statesman, architect, scientist, politician, as well as educational and political theorist. As we approach the end of the twentieth century and move deeper into an age of increasing specialization, the range and depth of Thomas Jefferson's intelligence and imagination remain truly remarkable. An aristocrat by upbringing, Jefferson remained a democrat in his intellectual interests and ideals.

In 1774 Jefferson participated in the First Continental Congress and earned praise and respect for his eloquent defense of colonial rights, published in pamphlet form as A Summary View of the Rights of British America. *By 1776, political events in the American colonies had moved rapidly toward revolution, and Jefferson was appointed to a committee to prepare a document declaring the separation of the colonies from England. Although the committee and the Congress edited the draft, the Declaration of Independence clearly had his conceptual and stylistic stamp indelibly impressed on it.*

Jefferson reported, concerning the preparation of the document, ''I turned to neither book nor pamphlet. . . . I did not consider it as any part of my charge to invent new ideas, but to place before mankind the common sense of the subject.'' He considered the Declaration of Independence—as do subsequent generations of Americans—an ''expression of the American mind.''

When in the course of human events, it becomes necessary for one people to dissolve the political bands which have connected them with another, and to assume among the Powers of the earth, the separate and equal station to which the Laws of Nature and of Nature's God entitle them, a decent respect to the opinions of mankind requires that they should declare the causes which impel them to the separation.

We hold these truths to be self-evident, that all men are created equal, that they are endowed by their Creator with certain unalienable Rights, that among these are Life, Liberty and the pursuit of Happiness.

That to secure these rights, Governments are instituted among Men, deriving their just powers from the consent of the governed.

That whenever any Form of Government becomes destructive of these ends, it is the Right of the People to alter or to abolish it, and to institute a new Government, laying its foundation on such principles and organizing its powers in such form, as to them shall seem most likely to effect their Safety and Happiness. Prudence, indeed, will dictate that Governments long established should not be changed for light and transient causes; and accordingly all experience hath shown that mankind are more disposed to suffer, while evils are sufferable, than to right themselves by abolishing the forms to which they are accustomed. But when a long train of abuses and usurpations pursuing invariably the same Object evinces a design to reduce them under absolute Despotism, it is their right, it is their duty, to throw off such government, and to provide new Guards for their future security.

Such has been the patient sufferance of these Colonies; and such is now the necessity which constrains them to alter their former Systems of Government. The history of the present King of Great Britain is a history of repeated injuries and usurpations, all having in direct object the establishment of an absolute Tyranny over these States. To prove this, let Facts be submitted to a candid world.

He has refused his Assent to Laws, the most wholesome and necessary for the public good.

He has forbidden his Governors to pass Laws of immediate and pressing importance, unless suspended in their operation till his Assent should be obtained: and when so suspended, he has utterly neglected to attend to them.

He has refused to pass other Laws for the accommodation of large districts of people, unless those people would relinquish the right of Representation in the Legislature, a right inestimable to them and formidable to tyrants only.

He has called together legislative bodies at places unusual, uncomfortable, and distant from the depository of their Public Records, for the sole purpose of fatiguing them into compliance with his measures.

He has dissolved Representative Houses repeatedly, for opposing with manly firmness his invasions on the rights of the people.

He has refused for a long time, after such dissolutions, to cause others to be elected; whereby the Legislative Powers, incapable of Annihilation, have returned to the People at large for their exercise; the State remaining in the mean time exposed to all the dangers of invasion from without, and convulsions within.

He has endeavored to prevent the population of these States, for that purpose obstructing the Laws of Naturalization of Foreigners; refusing to pass others to encourage their migration hither, and raising the conditions of new Appropriations of Lands.

He has obstructed the Administration of Justice, by refusing his Assent to Laws for establishing Judiciary Powers.

He has made Judges dependent on his Will alone, for the tenure of their offices, and the amount and payment of their salaries.

He has erected a multitude of New Offices, and sent hither swarms of Officers to harass our People, and eat out their substance.

He has kept among us, in time of peace, Standing Armies without the consent of our Legislature.

He has affected to render the Military independence of and superior to the Civil Power.

He has combined with others to subject us to jurisdictions foreign to our constitution, and unacknowledged by our laws; giving his Assent to their acts of pretended Legislation:

For quartering large bodies of armed troops among us:

For protecting them, by a mock Trial, from Punishment for any Murders which they should commit on the Inhabitants of these States:

For cutting off our Trade with all parts of the world:

For imposing Taxes on us without our Consent:

For depriving us in many cases, of the benefits of Trial by Jury:

For transporting us beyond Seas to be tried for pretended offenses:

For abolishing the free System of English Laws in a Neighbouring Province, establishing therein an Arbitrary government, and enlarging its boundaries so as to render it at once an example and fit instrument for introducing the same absolute rule into these Colonies:

For taking away our Charters, abolishing our most valuable Laws, and altering fundamentally the Forms of our Governments.

For suspending our own Legislatures, and declaring themselves invested with Power to legislate for us in all cases whatsoever.

He has abdicated Government here, by declaring us out of his Protection and waging War against us.

He has plundered our seas, ravaged our Coasts, burnt our towns and destroyed the Lives of our people.

He is at this time transporting large Armies of foreign Mercenaries to compleat the works of death, desolation and tyranny, already begun with circumstances of Cruelty & perfidy scarcely paralleled in the most barbarous ages, and totally unworthy the Head of a civilized nation.

He has constrained our fellow Citizens taken Captive on the high Seas to bear Arms against their Country, to become the executioners of their friends and Brethren, or to fall themselves by their Hands.

He has excited domestic insurrections amongst us, and has endeavored to bring on the inhabitants of our frontiers, the merciless Indian Savages, whose known rule of warfare, is an undistinguished destruction of all ages, sexes and conditions.

In every stage of these Oppressions We Have Petitioned for Redress in the most humble terms: Our repeated petitions have been answered only by repeated injury. A Prince, whose character is thus marked by every act which may define a Tyrant, is unfit to be the ruler of a free People.

Nor have We been wanting in attention to our British brethren. We have warned them from time to time of attempts by their legislature to extend an unwarrantable jurisdiction over us. We have reminded them of the circumstances of our emigration and settlement here. We have appealed to their native justice and magnanimity and we have conjured them by the ties of our common kindred to disavow these usurpations, which would inevitably interrupt our connections and consanguinity. We must, therefore, acquiesce in the necessity, which denounces our Separation, and hold them, as we hold the rest of mankind, Enemies in War, in Peace Friends.

We, therefore, the Representatives of the United States of America, in General Congress, Assembled, appealing to the Supreme Judge of the world for the rectitude of our intentions, do, in the Name, and by Authority of the good People of these Colonies, solemnly publish and declare. That these United Colonies are, and of Right ought to be, Free and Independent States; that they are Absolved from all Allegiance to the British Crown, and that all political connection between them and the State of Great Britain, is and ought to be totally dissolved; and that as Free and Independent States, they have full power to levy War, conclude Peace, contract Alliances, establish Commerce, and to do all other Acts and Things which Independent States may of right do. And for the support of this Declaration, with a firm reliance on the protection of Divine Providence, we mutually pledge to each other our lives, our Fortunes, and our sacred Honor.

Nathaniel Hawthorne / My Kinsman, Major Molineux 1832

Throughout his literary career, Nathaniel Hawthorne (1804–64) was acutely conscious of his Puritan ancestors, one of whom presided at the infamous Salem witchcraft trials. After graduating from Bowdoin College in 1825, Hawthorne spent the next twelve years in relative seclusion at his home in Salem, researching and brooding over the chronicles and annals of New England local history that were to supply him with material for sketches and tales he published continually in the popular periodicals of the day. In 1836, Hawthorne went to Boston, where he edited the American Magazine of Useful and Entertaining Knowledge. *Three years later he was offered a political appointment in the Boston Custom House, where he was able to support himself for a number of years while writing short stories and his first novel,* The Scarlett Letter *(1850).*

First published in 1832, "My Kinsman, Major Molineux" was included in Hawthorne's Twice-Told Tales *(1837). The story offers a special perspective on the events swirling around America's Declaration of Independence.*

After the kings of Great Britain had assumed the right of appointing the colonial governors,[1] the measures of the latter seldom met with the ready and general approbation which had been paid to those of their predessors, under the original charters. The people looked with most jealous scrutiny to the exercise of power which did not emanate from themselves, and they usually rewarded their rulers with slender gratitude for the compliances by which, in softening their instructions from beyond the sea, they had incurred the reprehension of those who gave them. The annals of Massachusetts Bay will inform us, that of six governors in the space of about forty years from the surrender of the old charter, under James II, two were imprisoned by a popular insurrection; a third, as Hutchinson[2] inclines to believe, was driven from the province by the whizzing of a musket-ball; a fourth, in the opinion of the same historian, was hastened to his grave by continual bickerings with the House of Representatives; and the remaining two, as well as their ancestors, till the Revolution, were favored with few and brief intervals of peaceful sway. The inferior members of the court party,[3] in times of high political excitement, led scarcely a more desirable life. These remarks may serve as a preface to the following adventures, which chanced upon a summer night, not far from a hundred years ago. The reader, in order to avoid a long and dry detail of colonial affairs, is requested to dispense with an account of the train of circumstances that had caused much temporary inflammation of the popular mind.

It was near nine o'clock of a moonlight evening, when a boat crossed the ferry with a single passenger, who had obtained his conveyance at that unusual hour by the promise of an extra fare. While he stood on the landing-place, searching in either pocket for the means of fulfilling his agreement, the ferryman lifted a lantern, by the aid of which, and the newly risen moon, he took a very accurate survey of the stranger's figure. He was a youth of barely eighteen years, evidently country-bred, and now, as it should seem, upon his first visit to town. He was clad in a coarse gray coat, well worn, but in excellent repair; his under garments

[1]The first royal governor of Massachusetts was appointed in 1685 by James II, after the Massachusetts Charter had been annulled.

[2]Thomas Hutchinson (1711–1780), the last royal governor of Massachusetts, was also a historian and author of *The History of the Colony and Province of Massachusetts-Bay* (1764, 1767).

[3]The pro-royal party.

were durably constructed of leather, and fitted tight to a pair of serviceable and well-shaped limbs; his stockings of blue yarn were the incontrovertible work of a mother or a sister; and on his head was a three-cornered hat, which in its better days had perhaps sheltered the graver brow of the lad's father. Under his left arm was a heavy cudgel formed of an oak sapling, and retaining a part of the hardened root; and his equipment was completed by a wallet,[4] not so abundantly stocked as to incommode the vigorous shoulders on which it hung. Brown, curly hair, well-shaped features, and bright, cheerful eyes were nature's gifts, and worth all that art could have done for his adornment.

The youth, one of whose names was Robin, finally drew from his pocket the half of a little province bill[5] of five shillings, which, in the depreciation in that sort of currency, did but satisfy the ferryman's demand, with the surplus of a sexangular piece of parchment, valued at three pence. He then walked forward into the town, with as light a step a if his day's journey had not already exceeded thirty miles, and with as eager an eye as if he were entering London city, instead of the little metropolis of a New England colony. Before Robin had proceeded far, however, it occurred to him that he knew not whither to direct his steps; so he paused, and looked up and down the narrow street, scrutinizing the small and mean wooden buildings that were scattered on either side.

''This low hovel cannot be my kinsman's dwelling,'' thought he, ''nor yonder old house, where the moonlight enters at the broken casement; and truly I see none hereabouts that might be worthy of him. It would have been wise to inquire my way of the ferryman, and do bootless he would have gone with me, and earned a shilling from the Major for his pains. But the next man I meet will do as well.''

He resumed his walk, and was glad to perceive that the street now became wider, and the houses more respectable in their appearance. He soon discerned a figure moving on moderately in advance, and hastened his steps to overtake it. As Robin drew nigh, he saw that the passenger was a man in years, with a full periwig of gray hair, a wide-skirted coat of dark cloth, and silk stockings rolled above his knees. He carried a long and polished cane, which he struck down perpendicularly before him at every step; and at regular intervals he uttered two successive hems, of a peculiarly solemn and sepulchral intonation. Having made these observations, Robin laid hold of the skirt of the old man's coat, just when the light from the open door and windows of a barber's shop fell upon both their figures.

''Good evening to you,'' honored sir, said he, making a low bow, and still retaining his hold of the skirt. ''I pray you tell me whereabouts is the dwelling of my kinsman, Major Molineux.''

The youth's question was uttered very loudly; and one of the barbers, whose razor was descending on a well-soaped chin, and another who was dressing a Ramillies wig,[6] left their occupations, and came to the door. The citizen, in the mean time, turned a long-favored countenance upon Robin, and answered him in a tone of excessive anger and annoyance. His two sepulchral hems, however, broke into the very centre of his rebuke, with most singular effect, like a thought of the cold grave obtruding among wrathful passions.

''Let go my garment, fellow! I tell you, I know not the man you speak of. What! I have authority, I have—hem, hem—authority; and if this be the respect you show for your betters, your feet shall be brought acquainted with the stocks[7] by daylight, tomorrow morning!''

[4]Knapsack.

[5]Colonial paper money.

[6]Elaborately braided wig named for a British victory at Ramillies, Belgium.

[7]Heavy wooden instruments, used for public punishment, that lock around the ankles and sometimes the wrists.

Robin released the old man's skirt, and hastened away, pursued by an ill-mannered roar of laughter from the barber's shop. He was at first considerably surprised by the result of his question, but, being a shrewd youth, soon thought himself able to account for the mystery.

"This is some country representative," was his conclusion, "who has never seen the inside of my kinsman's door, and lacks the breeding to answer a stranger civilly. The man is old, or verily—I might be tempted to turn back and smite him on the nose. Ah, Robin, Robin! even the barber's boys laugh at you for choosing such a guide! You will be wider in time, friend Robin."

He now became entangled in a succession of crooked and narrow streets, which crossed each other, and meandered at no great distance from the water-side. The smell of tar was obvious to his nostrils, the masts of vessels pierced the moonlight above the tops of the buildings, and the numerous signs, which Robin paused to read, informed him that he was near the centre of business. But the streets were empty, the shops were closed, and lights were visible only in the second stories of a few dwelling-houses. At length, on the corner of a narrow lane, through which he was passing, he beheld the broad countenance of a British hero swinging before the door[8] of an inn, whence proceeded the voices of many guests. The casement of one of the lower windows was thrown back, and a very thin curtain permitted Robin to distinguish a party at supper, round a well-furnished table. The fragrance of the good cheer steamed forth into the outer air, and the youth could not fail to recollect that the last remnant of his travelling stock of provision had yielded to his morning appetite, and that noon had found and left him dinnerless.

"Oh, that a parchment three-penny might give me a right to sit down at yonder table!" said Robin, with a sigh. "But the Major will make me welcome to the best of his victuals; so I will even step boldly in, and inquire my way to his dwelling."

He entered the tavern, and was guided by the murmur of voices and the fumes of tobacco to the public-room. It was a long and law apartment, with oaken walls, grown dark in the continual smoke, and a floor which was thickly sanded, but of no immaculate purity. A number of persons—the larger part of whom appeared to be mariners, or in some way connected with the sea—occupied the wooden benches, or leather-bottomed chairs, conversing on various matters, and occasionally lending their attention to some topic of general interest. Three or four little groups were draining as many bowls of punch, which the West India trade had long since made a familiar drink in the colony. Others, who had the appearance of men who lived by regular and laborious handicraft, preferred the insulated bliss of an unshared potation, and became more taciturn under its influence. Nearly all, in short, evinced a predilection for the Good Creature[9] in some of its various shapes, for this is a vice to which, as Fast Day[10] sermons of a hundred years ago will testify, we have a long hereditary claim. The only guests to whom Robin's sympathies inclined him were two or three sheepish countrymen, who were using the inn somewhat after the fashion of a Turkish caravansary,[11] they had gotten themselves into the darkest corner of the room, and heedless of the Nicotian[12] atmosphere, were supping on the bread of their own ovens, and the bacon cured in their own chimney-smoke. But though Robin felt a sort of brotherhood with these strangers, his eyes were attracted from them to a person who stood near the door, holding whispered conversation with a group of ill-dressed associates. His features were

[8] I.e., on a signboard.

[9] I Timothy 4:4: "For every creature of God is good and nothing to be refused, if it be received with Thanksgiving."

[10] A day for public pentence.

[11] Inn built to accommodate caravans.

[12] Smoke-filled from tobacco. Jean Nicot (hence "nicotine") brought the first tobacco to France from Lisbon.

separately striking almost to grotesqueness, and the whole face left a deep impression on the memory. The forehead bulged out into a double prominence, with a vale between; the nose came boldly forth in an irregular curve, and its bridge was of more than a finger's breadth; the eyebrows were deep and shaggy, and the eyes glowed beneath them like fire in a cave.

While Robin deliberated of whom to inquire respecting his kinsman's dwelling, he was accosted by the innkeeper, a little man in a stained white apron, who had come to pay his professional welcome to the stranger. Being in the second generation from a French Protestant, he seemed to have inherited the courtesy of his parent nation; but no variety of circumstances was ever known to change his voice from the one shrill note in which he now addressed Robin.

''From the country, I presume, sir?'' said he, with a profound bow. ''Beg leave to congratulate you on your arrival, and trust you intend a long stay with us. Fine town here, sir, beautiful buildings, and much that may interest a stranger. May I hope for the honor of your commands in respect to supper?''

''The man sees a family likeness! the rogue has guessed that I am related to the Major!'' thought Robin, who had hitherto experienced little superfluous civility.

All eyes were now turned on the country lad, standing at the door, in his worn three-cornered hat, gray coat, leather breeches, and blue yarn stockings, leaning on an oaken cudgel, and bearing a wallet on his back.

Robin replied to the courteous innkeeper, with such an assumption of confidence as befitted the Major's relative. ''My honest friend,'' he said, ''I shall make it a point to patronize your house on some occasion, when''—here he could not help lowering his voice—''when I may have more than a parchment three-pence in my pocket. My present business,'' continued he, speaking with lofty confidence, ''is merely to inquire my way to the dwelling of my kinsman, Major Molineux.''

There was a sudden and general movement in the room, which Robin interpreted as expressing the eagerness of each individual to become his guide. But the innkeeper turned his eyes to a written paper on the wall, which he read, or seemed to read, with occasional recurrencies to the young man's figure.

''What have we here?'' said he, breaking his speech into little dry fragments.'' 'Left the house of the subscriber, bounden servant,[13] Hezekiah Mudge,—had on, when he went away, gray coat, leather breeches, master's third-best hat. One pound currency reward to whosoever shall lodge him in any jail of the province.' Better trudge, boy; better trudge!''

Robin had begun to draw his hand towards the lighter end of the oak cudgel, but a strange hostility in every countenance induced him to relinquish his purpose of breaking the courteous innkeeper's head. As he turned to leave the room, he encountered a sneering glance from the bold-featured personage whom he had before noticed; and no sooner was he beyond the door, than he heard a general laugh, in which the innkeeper's voice might be distinguished, like the dropping of small stones into a kettle.

''Now, is it not strange,'' thought Robin, with his usual shrewdness,—''is it not strange that the confession of an empty pocket should outweigh the name of my kinsman, Major Molineux? Oh, if I had one of those grinning rascals in the woods, where I and my oak sapling grew up together, I would teach him that my arm is heavy through my purse be light!''

On turning the corner of the narrow lane, Robin found himself in a spacious street, with an unbroken line of lofty houses on each side, and a steepled building at the upper end, whence the ringing of a bell announced the hour of nine. The

[13] Person bound to servitude (indentured) for a specific period, usually in exchange for transportation to the colonies.

light of the moon, and the lamps from the numerous shop-windows, discovered people promenading on the pavement, and amongst them Robin hoped to recognize his hitherto inscrutable relative. The result of his former inquiries made him unwilling to hazard another, in a scene of such publicity, and he determined to walk slowly and silently up the street, thrusting his face close to that of every elderly gentleman, in search of the Major's lineaments. In his progress, Robin encountered many gay and gallant figures. Embroidered garments of showy colors, enormous periwigs, gold-laced hats, and silver-hilted swords glided past him and dazzled his optics. Travelled youths, imitators of the European fine gentlemen of the period, trod jauntily along, half dancing to the fashionable tunes which they hummed, and making poor Robin ashamed of his quiet and natural gait. At length, after many pauses to examine the gorgeous display of goods in the shop-windows, and after suffering some rebukes for the impertinence of his scrutiny into people's faces, the Major's kinsman found himself near the steepled building, still unsuccessful in his search. As yet, however, he had seen only one side of the thronged street; so Robin crossed, and continued the same sort of inquisiton down the opposite pavement, with stronger hopes than the philosopher seeking an honest man,[14] but with no better fortune. He had arrived about midway towards the lower end, from which his course began, when he overheard the approach of some one who struck down a cane on the flag-stones at every step, uttering, at regular intervals, two sepulchral hems.

"Mercy on us!" quoth Robin, recognizing the sound.

Turning a corner, which chanced to be close at his right hand, he hastened to pursue his researches in some other part of the town. His patience now was wearing low, and he seemed to feel more fatigue from his rambles since he crossed the ferry, than from his journey of several days on the other side. Hunger also pleaded loudly within him, and Robin began to balance the propriety of demanding, violently, and with lifted cudgel, the necessary guidance from the first solitary passenger whom he should meet. While a resolution to this effect was gaining strength, he entered a street of mean appearance, on either side of which a row of ill-built houses was straggling towards the harbor. The moonlight fell upon no passenger along the whole extent, but in the third domicile which Robin passed there was a half-opened door, and his keen glance detected a woman's garment within.

"My luck may be better here," said he to himself.

Accordingly, he approached the door, and beheld it shut closer as he did so; yet an open space remained, sufficing for the fair occupant to observe the stranger, without a corresponding display on her part. All that Robin could discern was a strip of scarlet petticoat, and the occasional sparkle of an eye, as if the moonbeams were trembling on some bright thing.

"Pretty mistress," for I may call her so with a good conscience, thought the shrewd youth, since I know nothing to the contrary,—"my sweet pretty mistress, will you be kind enough to tell me whereabouts I must seek the dwelling of my kinsman, Major Molineux?"

Robin's voice was plaintive and winning, and the female, seeing nothing to be shunned in the handsome country youth, thrust open the door, and came forth into the moonlight. She was a dainty little figure, with a white neck, round arms, and a slender waist, at the extremity of which her scarlet petticoat jutted out over a hoop, as if she were standing on a balloon. Moreover, her face was oval and pretty, her hair dark beneath the little cap, and her bright eyes possessed a sly freedom, which triumphed over those of Robin.

[14]Diogenes, Greek Cynic philosopher (412?–323 B.C.), supposedly roamed the world in search of an honest man.

''Major Molineux dwells here,'' said this fair woman.

Now, her voice was the sweetest Robin had heard that night, the airy counterpart of a stream of melted silver; yet he could not help doubting whether that sweet voice spoke Gospel truth. He looked up and down the mean street, and then surveyed the house before which they stood. It was a small, dark edifice of two stories, the second of which projected over the lower floor, and the front apartment had the aspect of a shop for petty commodities.

''Now, truly, I am in luck,'' replied Robin, cunningly, ''and so indeed is my kinsman, the Major, in having so pretty a housekeeper. But I prithee trouble him to step to the door; I will deliver him a message from his friends in the country, and then go back to my lodgings at the inn.''

''Nay, the Major has been abed this hour or more,'' said the lady of the scarlet petticoat; ''and it would be to little purpose to disturb him to-night, seeing his evening draught was of the strongest. But he is a kind-hearted man, and it would be as much as my life's worth to let a kinsman of his turn away from the door. You are the good old gentleman's very picture, and I could swear that was his rainy-weather hat. Also, he has garments very much resembling those leather small-clothes. But come in, I pray, for I bid you hearty welcome in his name.''

So saying, the fair and hospitable dame took our hero by the hand; and the touch was light, and the force was gentleness, and though Robin read in her eyes what he did not hear in her words, yet the slender-waisted woman in the scarlet petticoat proved stronger than the athletic country youth. She had drawn his half-willing footsteps nearly to the threshold, when the opening of a door in the neighborhood startled the Major's housekeeper, and, leaving the Major's kinsman, she vanished speedily into her own domicile. A heavy yawn preceded the appearance of a man, who, like the Moonshine of Pyramus and Thisbe,[15] carried a lantern, needlessly aiding his sister luminary in the heavens. As he walked sleepily up the street, he turned his broad, dull face on Robin, and displayed a long staff, spiked at the end.

''Home, vagabond, home!'' said the watchman, in accents that seemed to fall asleep as soon as they were uttered. ''Home, or we'll set you in the stocks by peep of day!''

''This is the second hint of the end,'' thought Robin. ''I wish they would end my difficulties, by setting me there to-night.''

Nevertheless, the youth felt an instinctive antipathy towards the guardian of midnight order, which at first prevented him from asking his usual question. But just when the man was about to banish behind the corner, Robin resolved not to lose the opportunity, and shouted lustily after him,—

''I say, friend! will you guide me to the house of my kidsman, Major Molineux?''

The watchman made no reply, but turned the corner and was gone; yet Robin seemed to hear the sound of drowsy laughter stealing along the solitary street. At that moment, also, a pleasant titter saluted him from the open window above his head; he looked up, and caught the sparkle of a saucy eye; a round arm beckoned to him, and next he heard light footsteps descending the staircase within. But Robin, being of the household of a New England clergyman, was a good youth, as well as a shrewd one; so he resisted temptation, and fled away.

He now roamed desperately, and at random, through the town, almost ready to believe that a spell was on him, like that by which a wizard of his country had once kept three pursuers wandering, a whole winter night, within twenty paces of the cottage which they sought. The streets lay before him, strange and desolate,

[15] Moonshine appears in a bumbling enactment of the story of Pyramus and Thisbe by characters in Shakespeare's play *A Midsummer Night's Dream*.

and the lights were extinguished in almost every house. Twice, however, little parties of men, among whom Robin distinguished individuals in outlandish attire, came hurrying along; but, though on both occasions they paused to address him, such intercourse did not at all enlighten his perplexity. They did but utter a few words in some language of which Robin knew nothing, and perceiving his inability to answer, bestowed a curse upon him in plain English and hastened away. Finally, the lad determined to knock at the door of every mansion that might appear worthy to be occupied by his kinsman, trusting that perseverance would overcome the fatality that had hitherto thwarted him. Firm in this resolve, he was passing beneath the walls of a church, which formed the corner of two streets, when, as he turned into the shade of its steeple, he encountered a bulky stranger, muffled in a cloak. The man was proceeding with the speed of earnest business, but Robin planted himself full before him, holding the oak cudgel with both hands across his body as a bar to further passage.

"Halt, honest man, and answer me a question," said he, very resolutely. "Tell me, this instant, whereabouts is the dwelling of my kinsman, Major Molineux!"

"Keep your tongue between your teeth, fool, and let me pass!" said a deep, gruff voice, which Robin partly remembered. "Let me pass, I say, or I'll strike you to the earth!"

"No, no neighbor!" cried Robin, flourishing his cudgel, and then thrusting its larger end close to the man's muffled face. "No, no, I'm not the fool you take me for, nor do you pass till I have an answer to my question. Whereabouts is the dwelling of my kinsman, Major Molineux?"

The stranger, instead of attempting to force his passage, stepped back into the moonlight, unmuffled his face, and stared full into that of Robin.

"Watch here an hour, and the Major Molineux will pass by," said he.

Robin gazed with dismay and astonishment on the unprecedented physiognomy of the speaker. The forehead with its double prominence, the broad hooked nose, the shaggy eyebrows, and fiery eyes were those which he had noticed at the inn, but the man's complexion had undergone a singular, or, more properly, a twofold change. One side of the face blazed an intense red, while the other was black as midnight, the division line being in the broad bridge of the nose; and a mouth which seemed to extend from ear to ear was black or red, in contrast to the color of the cheek. The effect was as if two individual devils, a fiend of fire and a fiend of darkness, had united themselves to form this infernal visage. The stranger grinned in Robin's face, muffled his party-colored features, and was out of sight in a moment.

"Strange things we travellers see!" ejaculated Robin.

He seated himself, however, upon the steps of the church-door, resolving to wait the appointed time for his kinsman. A few moments were consumed in philosophical speculations upon the species of man who had just left him; but having settled this point shrewdly, rationally, and satisfactorily, he was compelled to look elsewhere for his amusement. And first he threw his eyes along the street. It was of more respectable appearance than most of those into which he had wandered; and the moon, creating, like the imaginative power, a beautiful strangeness in familiar objects, gave something of romance to a scene that might not have possessed it in the light of day. The irregular and often quaint architecture of the houses, some of whose roofs were broken into numerous little peaks, while others ascended, steep and narrow, into a single point, and others again were square; the pure snow-white of some of their complexions, the aged darkness of others, and the thousand sparklings, reflected from bright substances in the walls of many; these matters engaged Robin's attention for a while, and then began to grow wearisome. Next he endeavored to define the forms of distant objects, starting away, with almost ghostly indistinctiveness, just as his eye appeared to grasp them; and finally he took a minute survey of an edifice which stood on the opposite side of the street, directly in front of the church-door, where he was stationed. It was a large, square mansion, distinguished from its neighbors by a balcony, which rested on tall pillars, and by an elaborate Gothic window, communicating therewith.

"Perhaps this is the very house I have been seeking," thought Robin.

Then he strove to speed away the time, by listening to a murmur which swept continually along the street, yet was scarcely audible, except to an unaccustomed ear like his; it was a low, dull, dreamy sound, compounded of many noises, each of which was at too great a distance to be separately heard. Robin marvelled at this snore of a sleeping town, and marvelled more whenever its continuity was broken by now and then a distant shout, apparently loud where it originated. But altogether it was a sleep-inspiring sound, and, to shake off its drowsy influence, Robin arose, and climbed a window-frame, that he might view the interior of the church. There the moonbeams came trembling in, and fell down upon the deserted pews, and extended along the quiet aisles. A fainter yet more awful radiance was hovering around the pulpit, and one solitary ray had dared to rest upon the open page of the great Bible. Had nature, in that deep hour, become a worshipper in the house which man had builded? Or was that heavenly light the visible sanctity of the place,—visible because no earthly and impure feet were within the walls? The scene made Robin's heart shiver with a sensation of loneliness stronger than he had ever felt in the remotest depths of his native woods; so he turned away and sat down again before the door. There were graves around the church, and now an uneasy thought obtruded into Robin's breast. What if the object of his search, which had been so often and so strangely thwarted, were all the time mouldering in his shroud? What if his kinsman should glide through yonder gate, and nod and smile to him in dimly passing by?

"Oh that any breathing thing were here with me!" said Robin.

Recalling his thoughts from this uncomfortable track, he sent them over forest, hill, and stream, and attempted to imagine how that evening of ambiguity and weariness had been spent by his father's household. He pictured them assembled at the door, beneath the tree, the great old tree, which had been spared for its huge twisted trunk and venerable shade, when a thousand leafy brethren fell. There, at the going down of the summer sun, it was his father's custom to perform domestic worship, that the neighbors might come and join with him like brothers of the family, and that the wayfaring man might pause to drink at that fountain, and keep his heart pure by freshening the memory of home. Robin distinguished the seat of every individual of the little audience; he saw the good man in the midst, holding the Scriptures in the golden light that fell from the western clouds; he beheld him close the book and all rise up to pray. He heard the old thanksgivings for daily mercies, the old supplications for their continuance, to which he had so often listened in weariness, but which were now among his dear remembrances. He perceived the slight inequality of his father's voice to the broad and knotted trunk; how his elder brother scorned, because the beard was rough upon his upper lip, to permit his features to be moved; how the younger sister drew down a low hanging branch before her eyes; and how the little one of all, whose sports had hitherto broken the decorum of the scene, understood the prayer for her playmate, and burst into clamorous grief. Then he saw them go in at the door; and when Robin would have entered also, the latch tinkled into its place, and he was excluded from his home.

"Am I here, or there?" cried Robin, starting; for all at once, when his thoughts had become visible and audible in a dream, the long, wide, solitary street shone out before him.

He aroused himself, and endeavored to fix his attentions steadily upon the large edifice which he had surveyed before. But still his mind kept vibrating between fancy and reality; by turns, the pillars of the balcony lengthened into the tall, bare stems of pines, dwindled down to human figures, settled again into their true shape and size, and then commenced a new succession of changes. For a single moment, when he deemed himself awake, he could have sworn that a visage—one which he seemed to remember, yet could not absolutely name as his kinsman's—was looking towards him from the Gothic window. A deeper sleep wrestled with and nearly overcame him, but fled at the sound of footsteps along the opposite pavement. Robin rubbed his eyes, discerned a man passing at the foot of the balcony, and addressed him in a loud, peevish, and lamentable cry.

"Hallo, friend! must I wait here all night for my kinsman, Major Molineux?"

The sleeping echoes awoke, and answered the voice; and the passenger, barely able to discern a figure sitting in the oblique shade of the steeple, traversed the street to obtain a nearer view. He was himself a gentleman in his prime, of open, intelligent, cheerful, and altogether prepossessing countenance. Perceiving a country youth, apparently homeless and without friends, he accosted him in a tone of real kindness, which had become strange to Robin's ears.

"Well, my good lad, who are you sitting here?" inquired he. "Can I be of service to you in any way?"

"I am afraid not, sir," replied Robin, despondingly; "yet I shall take it kindly, if you'll answer me a single question. I've been searching, half the night, for one Major Molineux; now, sir, is there really such a person in these parts, or am I dreaming?"

"Major Molineux! The name is not altogether strange to me," said the gentleman, smiling. "Have you any objection to telling me the nature of your business with him?"

Then Robin briefly related that his father was a clergyman, settled on a small salary, at a long distance back in the country, and that he and Major Molineux were brothers' children. The Major, having inherited riches, and acquired civil and military rank, had visited his cousin, in great pomp, a year or two before; had manifested much interest in Robin and an elder brother, and, being childless himself, had thrown out hints respecting the future establishment of one of them in life. The elder brother was destined to succeed to the farm which his father cultivated in the interval of sacred duties; it was therefore determined that Robin should profit by his kinsman's generous intentions, especially as he seemed to be rather the favorite, and was thought to possess other necessary endowments.

"For I have the name of being a shrewd youth," observed Robin, in this part of his story.

"I doubt not you deserve it," replied his new friend, good-naturedly; "but pray proceed."

"Well, sir, being nearly eighteen years old, and well grown, as you see," continued Robin, drawing himself up to his full height, "I thought it high time to begin the world. So my mother and sister put me in handsome trim, and my father gave me half the remnant of his last year's salary, and five days ago I started for this place, to pay the Major a visit. But, would you believe it, sir! I crossed the ferry a little after dark, and have yet found nobody that would show me the way to his dwelling; only, an hour or two since, I was told to wait here, and Major Molineux would pass by."

"Can you describe the man who told you this?" inquired the gentleman.

"Oh, he was a very ill-favored fellow, sir," replied Robin," with two great bumps on his forehead, a hook nose, fiery eyes; and, what struck me as the strangest, his face was of two different colors. Do you happen to know such a man, sir?"

"Not intimately," answered the stranger, "but I chanced to meet him a little time previous to your stopping me. I believe you may trust his word, and that the

Major will very shortly pass through this street. In the mean time, as I have a singular curiosity to witness your meeting, I will sit down here upon the steps and bear you company.''

He seated himself accordingly, and soon engaged his companion in animated discourse. It was but of brief continuance, however, for a noise of shouting, which had long been remotely audible, drew so much nearer that Robin inquired its cause.

''What may be the meaning of this uproar?'' asked he. ''Truly, if your town be always as noisy, I shall find little sleep while I am an inhabitant.''

''Why, indeed, friend Robin, there do appear to be three or four riotious fellows abroad to-night,'' replied the gentleman. ''You must not expect all the stillness of your native woods here in our streets. But the watch will shortly be at the heels of these lads and''—

''Ay, and set them in the stocks by peep of day,'' interrupted Robin, recollecting his own encounter with the drowsy lantern-bearer. ''But, dear sir, if I may trust my ears, an army of watchmen would never make head against such a multitude of rioters. There were at least a thousand voices went up to make that one shout.''

''May not a man have several voices, Robin, as well as two complexions?'' said his friend.

''Perhaps a man may; but Heaven forbid that a woman should!'' responded the shrewd youth, thinking of the seductive tones of the Major's housekeeper.

The sounds of a trumpet in some neighboring street now became so evident and continual, that Robin's curiosity was strongly excited. In addition to the shouts, he heard frequent bursts from many instruments of discord, and a wild and confused laughter filled up the intervals. Robin rose from the steps, and looked wistfully towards a point whither people seemed to be hastening.

''Surely some prodigious merry-making is going on,'' exclaimed he. ''I have laughed very little since I left home, sir, and should be sorry to lose an opportunity. Shall we step round the corner by that darkish house, and take our share of the fun?''

''Sit down again, sit down, good Robin,'' replied the gentleman, laying his hand on the skirt of the gray coat. ''You forget that we must wait here for your kinsman; and there is reason to believe that he will pass by, in the course of a very few moments.''

The near approach of the uproar had now disturbed the neighborhood; windows flew open on all sides: and many heads, in the attire of the pillow, and confused by sleep suddenly broken, were protruded to the gaze of whoever had leisure to observe them. Eager voices hailed each other from house to house, all demanding the explanation, which not a soul could give. Half-dressed men hurried towards the unknown commotion, stumbling as they went over the stone steps that thrust themselves into the narrow foot-walk. The shouts, the laughter, and the tuneless bray, the antipodes of music, came onwards with increasing din, till scattered individuals, and then denser bodies, began to appear round a corner at the distance of a hundred yards.

''Will you recognize your kinsman, if he passes in this crowd?'' inquired the gentleman.

''Indeed, I can't warrant it, sir; but I'll take my stand here, and keep a bright lookout,'' answered Robin, descending to the outer edge of the pavement.

A mighty stream of people now emptied into the street, and came rolling slowly towards the church. A single horseman wheeled the corner in the midst of them, and close behind him came a band of fearful wind-instruments, sending forth a fresher discord now that no intervening buildings kept it from the ear. Then a redder light disturbed the moonbeams, and a dense multitude of torches shone along the street, concealing, by their glare, whatever object they illuminated. The single horseman, clad in a military dress, and bearing a drawn sword, rode onward as the leader, and, by his fierce and variegated countenance, appeared like war personified; the red of one cheek was an emblem of fire and sword; the blackness of the other betokened the mourning that attends them. In his train were wild figures in the Indian dress, and many fantastic shapes without a model, giving the whole march a visionary air, as if a dream had broken forth from some feverish brain, and were sweeping visibly through the midnight streets. A mass of people, inactive, except as applauding spectators, hemmed the procession in; and several women ran along the sidewalk, piercing the confusion of heavier sounds with their shrill voices of mirth or terror.

"The double-faced fellow has his eye upon me," muttered Robin, with an indefinite but an uncomfortable idea that he was himself to bear a part in the pageantry.

The leader turned himself in the saddle, and fixed his glance full upon the country youth, as the steed went slowly by. When Robin had freed his eyes from those fiery ones, the musicians were passing before him, and the torches were close at hand; but the unsteady brightness of the latter formed a veil which he could not penetrate. The rattling of wheels over the stones sometimes found its way to his ear, and confused traces of a human form appeared at intervals, and then melted into the vivid light. A moment more, and the leader thundered a command to halt: the trumpets vomited a horrid breath, and then held their peace; the shouts and laughter of the people died away, and there remained only a universal hum, allied to silence. Right before Robin's eyes was an uncovered cart. There the torches blazed the brightest, there the moon shone out like day, and there, in tar-and-feathery dignity, sat his kinsman, Major Molineux!

He was an elderly man, of large and majestic person, and strong, square features, betokening a steady soul; but steady as it was, his enemies had found means to shake it. His face was pale as death, and far more ghastly; the broad forehead was contracted in his agony, so that his eyebrows formed one grizzled line; his eyes were red and wild, and the foam hung white upon his quivering lip. His whole frame was agitated by a quick and continual tremor, which his pride strove to quell, even in those circumstances of overwhelming humiliation. But perhaps the bitterest pang of all was when his eyes met those of Robin; for he evidently knew him on the instant, as the youth stood witnessing the foul disgrace of a head grown gray in honor. They stared at each other in silence, and Robin's knees shook, and his hair bristled, with a mixture of pity and terror. Soon, however, a bewildering excitement began to seize upon his mind; the preceding adventures of the night, the unexpected appearance of the crowd, the torches, the confused din and the hush that followed, the spectre of his kinsman reviled by that great multitude,—all this, and, more than all, a perception of tremendous ridicule in the whole scene, affected him with a sort of mental inebrity. At that moment a voice of sluggish merriment saluted Robin's ears; he turned instinctively, and just behind the corner of the church stood the lantern-bearer, rubbing his eyes, and drowsily enjoying the lad's amazement. Then he heard a peal of laughter like the ringing of silvery bells; a woman twitched his arm, a saucy eye met his, and he saw the lady of the scarlet petticoat. A sharp, dry cachinnation[16] appealed to his memory, and, standing on tiptoe in the crowd, with his white apron over his head, he beheld the courteous little innkeeper. And lastly, there sailed over the heads of the multitude a great, broad laugh, broken in the midst by two sepulchral hems; thus, "Haw, haw, haw,—hem, hem,—haw, haw, haw, haw!"

The sound proceeded from the balcony of the opposite edifice, and thither Robin

[16]Laugh.

turned his eyes. In front of the Gothic window stood the old citizen, wrapped in a wide gown, his gray periwig exchanged for a nightcap, which was thrust back from his forehead, and his silk stockings hanging about his legs. He supported himself on his polished cane in a fit of convulsive merriment, which manifested itself on his solemn old features like a funny inscription on a tomb-stone. Then Robin seemed to hear the voices of the barbers, of the guests of the inn, and of all who had made sport of him that night. The contagion was spreading among the multitude, when all at once, it seized upon Robin, and he sent forth a shout of laughter that echoed through the street,—every man shook his sides, every man emptied his lungs, but Robin's shout was the loudest there. The cloud-spirits peeped from their silvery islands, as the congregated mirth went roaring up the sky! The Man in the Moon heard the far bellow. "Oho," quoth he, "the old earth is frolicsome to-night!"

When there was a momentary calm in that tempestuous sea of sound, the leader gave the sign, the procession resumed its march. On they went, like fiends that throng in mockery around some dead potentate, mighty no more, but majestic still in his agony. On they went, in counterfeited pomp, in senseless uproar, in frenzied merriment, trampling all on an old man's heart. On swept the tumult, and left a silent street behind. . . .

"Well, Robin, are you dreaming?" inquired the gentleman, laying his hand on the youth's shoulder.

Robin started, and withdrew his arm from the stone post to which he had instinctively clung, as the living stream rolled by him. His cheek was somewhat pale, and his eye not quite as lively as in the earlier part of the evening.

"Will you be kind enough to show me the way to the ferry?" said he, after a moment's pause.

"You have, then, adopted a new subject of inquiry?" observed his companion, with a smile.

"Why, yes, sir," replied Robin, rather dryly. "Thanks to you, and to my other friends, I have at least met my kinsman, and he will scarce desire to see my face again. I begin to grow weary of a town life, sir. Will you show me the way to the ferry?"

"No, my good friend Robin—not to-night, at least," said the gentleman. "Some few days hence, if you wish it, I will speed you on your journey. Or, if you prefer to remain with us, perhaps, as you are a shrewd youth, you may rise in the world without the help of your kinsman, Major Molineux."

Frederick Douglass / *Narrative of the Life of Frederick Douglass*

1845

Born a slave in Tuckahoe, Maryland, Frederick Augustus Washington Bailey (1817–95) assumed the name Frederick Douglass after he escaped to New York City in 1838. He married a free black woman and moved to New Bedford, Massachusetts, where he worked as a common laborer. In 1841 he became involved with the Massachusetts Anti-Slavery Society. A powerful orator, Douglass soon won national recognition as a leading figure in the New England abolitionist movement. His moving autobiography, the Narrative of the Life of Frederick Douglass *(1845), dispelled a prevailing doubt that Douglass was an educated black man pretending slave origins for propagandistic purposes. After a few years in England where he lectured on slavery, Douglass returned to Rochester, New York, and established a newspaper,* The North Star, *which he published for seventeen years. Throughout his successful public career he spoke ardently on behalf of educational improvements, civil rights, and women's suffrage.*

I have already intimated that my condition was much worse, during the first six months of my stay at Mr. Covey's, than in the last six. The circumstances leading to the change in Mr. Covey's course toward me form an epoch in my humble history. You have seen how a man was made a slave; you shall see how a slave was made a man. On one of the hottest days of the month of August, 1833, Bill Smith, William Hughes, a slave named Eli, and myself, were engaged in fanning wheat. Hughes was clearing the fanned wheat from before the fan. Eli was turning, Smith was feeding, and I was carrying wheat to the fan. The work was simple, requiring strength rather than intellect; yet, to one entirely unused to such work, it came very hard. About three o'clock of that day, I broke down; my strength failed me; I was seized with a violent aching of the head, attended with extreme dizziness; I trembled in every limb. Finding what was coming, I nerved myself up, feeling it would never do to stop work. I stood as long as I could stagger to the hopper with grain. When I could stand no longer, I fell, and felt as if held down by an immense weight. The fan of course stopped; every one had his own work to do; and no one could do the work of the other, and have his own go on at the same time.

Mr. Covey was at the house, about one hundred yards from the treading-yard where we were fanning. On hearing the fan stop, he left immediately, and came to the spot where we were. He hastily inquired what the matter was. Bill answered that I was sick, and there was no one to bring wheat to the fan. I had by this time crawled away under the side of the post and rail-fence by which the yard was enclosed, hoping to find relief by getting out of the sun. He then asked where I was. He was told by one of the hands. He came to the spot, and, after looking at me awhile, asked me what was the matter. I told him as well as I could, for I scarce had strength to speak. He then gave me a savage kick in the side, and told me to get up. I tried to do so, but fell back in the attempt. He gave me another kick, and again told me to rise. I again tried, and succeeded in gaining my feet; but, stooping to get the tub with which I was feeding the fan, I again staggered and fell. While down in this situation, Mr. Covey took up the hickory slat with which Hughes had been striking off the half-bushel measure, and with it gave me a heavy blow upon the head, making a large wound, and the blood ran freely; and with this again told me to get up. I made no effort to comply, having now made up my mind to let him do his worst. In a short time after receiving this blow, my head grew better. Mr. Covey had now left me to my fate. At this moment I resolved, for the first time, to go to my master, enter a complaint, and ask his protection. In order to do this, I must that afternoon walk seven miles; and this, under the circumstances, was truly a severe undertaking. I was exceedingly feeble; made so as much by the kicks and blows which I received, as by the severe fit of sickness to which I had been subjected. I, however, watched my chance, while Covey was looking in an opposite direction, and started for St. Michael's: I succeeded in getting a considerable distance on my way to the woods, when Covey discovered me, and called after me to come back, threatening what he would do if I did not come. I disregarded both his calls and his threats, and made my way to the woods as fast as my feeble state would allow, and thinking I might be overhauled by him if I kept the road, I walked through the woods, keeping far enough from the road to avoid detection, and near enough to prevent losing my way. I had not gone far before my little strength again failed me. I could go no farther. I fell down, and lay for a considerable time. The blood was yet oozing from the wound on my head. For a time I thought I should bleed to death; and think now that I should have done so, but that the blood so matted my hair as to stop the wound. After lying there about three quarters of an hour, I nerved myself up again, and started on my way, through bogs and briers, barefooted and bareheaded, tearing my feet sometimes at nearly every step; and after a journey of about seven miles, occupying some five hours to perform it, I arrived at my master's store. I then presented an appearance enough to affect any but a heart of iron. From the crown of my head to my feet, I was covered with blood. My hair was all clotted with dust and blood; my shirt was stiff with blood. My legs and feet were torn in sundry places with briers and thorns, and were also covered with blood. I suppose I looked like a man who had escaped a den of wild beasts, and barely escaped them. In this state I appeared before my master, humbly entreating him to interpose his authority for my protection. I told him all the circumstances as well as I could, and it seemed, as I spoke, at times to affect him. He would then walk the floor, and seek to justify Covey by saying he expected I deserved it. He asked me what I wanted. I told him, to let me get a new home; that as sure as I lived with Mr. Covey again, I should live with but to die with him; that Covey would surely kill me; he was in a fair way for it. Master Thomas ridiculed the idea that there was any danger of Mr. Covey's killing me, and said that he knew Mr. Covey, that he was a good man, and that he could not think of taking me from him; that, should he do so, he would lose the whole year's wages; that I belonged to Mr. Covey for one year, and that I must go back to him, come what might; and that I must not trouble him with any more stories, or that he would himself *get hold of me.* After threatening me thus, he gave me a very large dose of salts, telling me that I might remain in St. Michael's that night, (it being quite late) but that I must be off back to Mr. Covey's early in the morning; and that if I did not, he would *get hold of me,* which meant that he would whip me. I remained all night, and, according to his orders, I started off to Covey's in the morning, (Saturday morning,) wearied in body and broken in spirit. I got no supper that night, or breakfast that morning. I reached Covey's about nine o'clock; and just as I was getting over the fence that divided Mrs. Kemp's fields from ours, out ran Covey with his cowskin, to give me another whipping. Before he could reach me, I succeeded in getting to the cornfield; and as the corn was very high, it afforded me the means of hiding. He seemed very angry, and searched for me for a long time. My behavior was altogether unaccountable. He finally gave up the chase, thinking, I suppose, that I must come home for something to eat; he would give himself no further trouble in looking for me. I spent that day mostly in the woods, having the alternative before me—to go home and be whipped to death, or stay in the woods and be starved to death. That night, I fell in with Sandy Jenkins, a slave with whom I was somewhat acquainted. Sandy had a free wife who lived about four miles from Mr. Covey's; and it being Saturday, he was on his way to see her. I told him my circumstances, and he very kindly invited me to go home with him. I went home with him, and talked this whole matter over, and got his advice as to what course it was best for me to pursue. I found Sandy an odd adviser. He told me, with great solemnity, I must go back to Covey; but that before I went, I must go with him into another part of the woods, where there was a certain *root,* which, if I would take some of it with me, carrying it *always on my right side,* would render it impossible for Mr. Covey, or any other white man, to whip me. He said he had carried it for years; and since he had done so, he had never received a blow, and never expected to while he carried it. I at first rejected the idea, that the simple carrying of a root in my pocket would have any such effect as he had said, and was not disposed to take it; but Sandy impressed the necessity with much earnestness, telling me it could do no harm, if it did no good. To please him, I at length took the root, and, according to his direction, carried it upon my right side. This was Sunday morning, I immediately started for home; and upon entering the yard gate, out came Mr. Covey on his way to meeting. He spoke to me very kindly, bade me drive the pigs from a lot near by, and passed on towards the church. Now, this singular conduct of Mr. Covey really made me begin to think that there was something in the *root* which Sandy had given me; and had it been on any other day than Sunday, I could have attributed the conduct to no other cause than the influence of that root; and as it was, I was half inclined to think the *root* to be something more than I at first had taken it to be. All went well till Monday morning. On this morning, the virtue of the *root* was fully tested. Long before daylight, I was called to go and rub, curry, and feed, the horses. I obeyed, and was glad to obey. But whilst thus engaged, whilst in the act of throwing down some blades from the loft, Mr. Covey entered the stable with a long rope; and just as I was half out of the loft, he caught hold of my legs, and was about tying me. As soon as I found what he was up to, I gave a sudden spring, and as I did so, he holding to my legs, I was brought sprawling on the stable floor. Mr. Covey seemed now to think he had me, and could do what he pleased; but at this moment—from whence came the spirit I don't know—I resolved to fight; and, suiting my action to the resolution, I seized Covey hard by the throat; and as I did so, I rose. He held on to me, and I to him. My resistance was so entirely unexpected, that Covey seemed all taken aback. He trembled like a leaf. This gave me assurance, and I held him uneasy, causing the blood to run where I touched him with the ends of my fingers. Mr. Covey soon called out to Hughes for help. Hughes came, and, while Covey held me, attempted to tie my right hand. While he was in the act of doing so, I watched my chance, and gave him a heavy kick close under the ribs. This kick fairly sickened Hughes, so that he left me in the hands of Mr. Covey. This kick had the effect of not only weakening Hughes, but Covey also. When he saw Hughes bending over with pain, his courage quailed. He asked me if I meant to persist in my resistance. I told him I did, come what might; that he had used me like a brute for six months, and that I was determined to be used so no longer. With that, he strove to drag me to a stick that was lying just out of the stable door. He meant to knock me down. But just as he was leaning over to get the stick, I seized him with both hands by his collar, and brought him by a sudden snatch to the ground. By this time, Bill came. Covey called upon him for assistance. Bill wanted to know what he could do. Covey said, "Take hold of him, take hold of him!" Bill said his master hired him out to work, and not to help to whip me; so he left Covey and myself to fight our own battle out. We were at it for nearly two hours. Covey at length let me go, puffing and blowing at a great rate, saying that if I had not resisted, he would not have whipped me half so much. The truth was that he had not whipped me at all. I considered him as getting entirely the worst end of the bargain; for he had drawn no blood from me, but I had from him. The whole six months afterwards, that I spent with Mr. Covey, he never laid the weight of his finger upon me in anger. He would occasionally say he didn't want to get hold of me again. "No," thought I, "you need not; for you will come off worse than you did before."

This battle with Mr. Covey was the turning-point in my career as a slave. It rekindled the few expiring embers of freedom, and revived within me a sense of my own manhood. It recalled the departed self-confidence, and inspired me again with a determination to be free. The gratification afforded by the triumph was a full compensation for whatever else might follow, even death itself. He only can understand the deep satisfaction which I experienced, who has himself repelled by force the bloody arm of slavery. I felt as I never felt before. It was a glorious resurrection, from the tomb of slavery, to the heaven of freedom. My long-crushed spirit rose, cowardice departed, bold defiance took its place; and I now resolved that, however long I might remain a slave in form, the day had passed forever when I could be a slave in fact. I did not hesitate to let it be known of me, that the white man who expected to succeed in whipping, must also succeed in killing me.

From this time I was never again what might be called fairly whipped, though I remained a slave four years afterwards. I had several fights, but was never whipped.

It was for a long time a matter of surprise to me why Mr. Covey did not immediately have me taken by the constable to the whipping-post, and there regularly whipped for the crime of raising my hand against a white man in defence of myself. And the only explanation I can now think of does not entirely satisfy me; but such as it is, I will give it. Mr. Covey enjoyed the most unbounded reputation for being a first-rate overseer and negro-breaker. It was of considerable importance to him. That reputation was at stake; and had he sent me—a boy about sixteen years old—to the public whipping-post, his reputation would have been lost; so, to save his reputation, he suffered me to go unpunished.

Henry David Thoreau / *Walden* 1854

Although Henry David Thoreau participated very deeply in American political and cultural life, his name has become synonymous with the archetypal voluntary exile who rejects a crass, materialistic world in favor of a rugged, self-reliant outdoor existence and a career as an amateur naturalist. The image is partly true: Thoreau consistently endorses a simple, independent, organic life. But it is important to remember that Thoreau was also an outspoken abolitionist, a defender of John Brown even after the bloody raid on Harper's Ferry, and a conscientious dissenter who devised a highly influential philosophy of civil disobedience.

Born in Concord, Massachusetts, son of a pencil manufacturer, Thoreau graduated from Harvard having mastered Greek in 1837. He was also a master of many trades, though all his life he worked only sporadically—at chores, at surveying, at tutoring, at his father's shop, at lecturing, at odd jobs. He never made a good living, although he apparently lived a good life. Only two of his books were published in his lifetime: A Week on the Concord and Merrimack Rivers *(1849) and* Walden *(1854). He never married; he left parties early; he seldom traveled beyond Concord. He died of tuberculosis, a disappointment to his family and friends, when he was forty-four.*

At a time in American history when thousands voluntarily exiled themselves in tiny cabins on the slopes of western mountains to search for gold, Thoreau searched for a different kind of wealth along the gentle edges of a small Massachusetts pond. The book he wrote describing his twenty-six-month retreat has long been considered a classic account of a peculiarly American consciousness. The following section, "Where I Lived, and What I Lived For," is an excerpt from the second chapter of Walden.

WHERE I LIVED, AND WHAT I LIVED FOR

I went to the woods because I wished to live deliberately, to front only the essential facts of life, and see if I could not learn what it had to teach, and not, when I came to die, discover that I had not lived. I did not wish to live what was not life, living is so dear; nor did I wish to practise resignation, unless it was quite necessary. I wanted to live deep and suck out all the marrow of life, to live so sturdily and Spartan-like as to put to rout all that was not life, to cut a broad swath and shave close, to drive life into a corner, and reduce it to its lowest terms, and, if it proved to be mean, why then to get the whole and genuine meanness of it, and publish its meanness to the world; or if it were sublime, to know it by experience, and be able to give a true account of it in my next excursion. For most men, it appears to me, are in a strange uncertainty about it, whether it is of the devil or of God, and have *somewhat hastily* concluded that it is the chief end of man here to "glorify God and enjoy him forever."

Still we live meanly, like ants; though the fable tells us that we were long ago changed into men; like pygmies we fight with cranes; it is error upon error, and clout upon clout, and our best virtue has for its occasion a superfluous and evitable wretchedness. Our life is frittered away by detail. An honest man has hardly need to count more than his ten fingers, or in extreme cases he may add his ten toes, and lump the rest. Simplicity, simplicity, simplicity! I say, let your affairs be as two or three, and not a hundred or a thousand; instead of a million count half a dozen, and keep your accounts on your thumb-nail. In the midst of this chopping sea of civilized life, such are the clouds and storms and quicksands and thousand-and-one items to be allowed for, that a man has to live, if he would not founder and go to the bottom and not make his port at all, by dead reckoning, and he must be a great calculator indeed who succeeds. Simplify, simplify. Instead of three meals a day, if it be necessary eat but one; instead of a hundred dishes, five; and reduce other things in proportion. Our life is like a German Confederacy, made up of petty states, with its boundary forever fluctuating, so that even a German cannot tell you how it is bounded at any moment. The nation itself, with all its so-called internal improvements, which, by the way, are all external and superficial, is just such an unwieldy and overgrown establishment, cluttered with furniture and tripped up by its own traps, ruined by luxury and heedless expense, by want of calculation and a worthy aim, as the million households in the land· and the only cure for it, as for them, is in a rigid economy, a stern and more than Spartan simplicity of life and elevation of purpose. It lives too fast. Men think that it is essential that the *Nation* have commerce, and export ice, and talk through a telegraph, and ride thirty miles an hour, without a doubt, whether *they* do or not; but whether we should live like baboons or like men, is a little uncertain. If we do not get out sleepers, and forge rails, and devote days and nights to the work, but go to tinkering upon our *lives* to improve *them,* who will build railroads? And if railroads are not built, how shall we get to Heaven in season? But if we stay at home and mind our business, who will want railroads? We do not ride on the railroad; it rides upon us. Did you ever think what those sleepers are that underlie the railroad? Each one is a man, an Irishman, or a Yankee man. The rails are laid on them, and they are covered with sand, and the cars run smoothly over them. They are sound sleepers, I assure you. And every few years a new lot is laid down and run over; so that, if some have the pleasure of riding on a rail, others have the misfortune to be ridden upon. And when they run over a man that is walking in his sleep, a supernumerary sleeper in the wrong position, and wake him up, they suddenly stop the cars, and make a hue and cry about it as if this were an exception. I am glad to know that it takes a gang of men for every five miles to keep the sleepers down and level in their beds as it is, for this is a sign that they may sometime get up again.

Why should we live with such hurry and waste of life? We are determined to be starved before we are hungry. Men say that a stitch in time saves nine, and so they take a thousand stitches to-day to save nine tomorrow. As for *work,* we haven't any of any consequence. We have the Saint Vitus' dance, and cannot possibly keep our heads still. If I should only give a few pulls at the parish bell-rope, as for a fire, that is, without setting the bell, there is hardly a man on his farm in the outskirts of Concord, notwithstanding that press of engagements which was his excuse so many times this morning, nor a boy, nor a woman, I might almost say, but would forsake all and follow that sound, not mainly to save property from the flames, but, if we will confess the truth, much more to see it burn, since burn it must, and we, be it known, did not set it on fire,—or to see it put out, and have a hand in it, if that is done as handsomely; yes, even if it were the parish church itself. Hardly a man takes a half-hour's nap after dinner, but when he wakes he holds up his head and asks, "What's the news?" as if the rest of mankind had stood his sentinels. Some give directions to be waked every half-hour, doubtless for no other purpose; and then, to pay for it, they tell what they have dreamed. After a night's sleep the news is as indispensable as the breakfast. "Pray tell me anything new that has happened to a man anywhere on this globe,"—and he reads it over his coffee and rolls, that a man has had his eyes gouged out this morning on the Wachito River; never dreaming the while that he lives in the dark unfathomed mammoth cave of this world, and has but the rudiment of an eye himself.

For my part, I could easily do without the post-office. I think that there are very few important communications made through it. To speak critically, I never received more than one or two letters in my life—I wrote this some years ago—that were worth the postage. The penny-post is, commonly, an institution through which you seriously offer a man that penny for his thoughts which is so often safely offered in jest. And I am sure that I never read any memorable news in a newspaper. If we read of one man robbed, or murdered, or killed by accident, or one house burned, or one vessel wrecked, or one steamboat blown up, or one cow run over on the Western Railroad, or one mad dog killed, or one lot of grasshoppers in the winter,—we never need read of another. One is enough. If you are acquainted with the principle, what do you care for a myriad instances and applications? To a philosopher all *news,* as it is called, is gossip and they who edit and read it are old women over their tea. Yet not a few are greedy after this gossip. There was such a rush, as I hear, the other day at one of the offices to learn the foreign news by the last arrival, that several large squares of plate glass belonging to the establishment were broken by the pressure,—news which I seriously think a ready wit might write a twelvemonth, or twelve years, beforehand with sufficient accuracy. As for Spain, for instance, if you know how to throw in Don Carlos and the Infanta, and Don Pedro and Seville and Granada, from time to time in the right proportions,—they may have changed the names a little since I saw the papers,—and serve up a bull-fight when other entertainments fail, it will be true to the letter, and give us as good an idea of the exact state or ruin of things in Spain as the most succinct and lucid reports under this head in the newspapers: and as for England, almost the last significant scrap of news from that quarter was the revolution of 1649; and if you have learned the history of her crops for an average year, you never need attend to that thing again, unless your speculations are of a merely pecuniary character. If one may judge who rarely looks into the newspapers, nothing new does ever happen in foreign parts, a French revolution not excepted.

What news! how much more important to know what that is which was never old! "Kieou-he-yu (great dignitary of the state of Wei) sent a man to Khoung-tseu to know his news. Khoung-tseu caused the messenger to be seated near him, and questioned him in these terms: What is your master doing? The messenger answered with respect: My master desires to diminish the number of his faults, but he cannot come to the end of them. The messenger being gone, the philosopher remarked: What a worthy messenger! What a worthy messenger!" The preacher, instead of vexing the ears of drowsy farmers on their day of rest at the end of the week,—for Sunday is the fit conclusion of an ill-spent week, and not the fresh and brave beginning of a new one,—with this one other draggle-tail of a sermon, should shout with thundering voice, "Pause! Avast! Why so seeming fast, but deadly slow?"

Shams and delusions are esteemed for soundest truths, while reality is fabulous. If men would steadily observe realities only, and not allow themselves to be deluded, life, to compare it with such things as we know, would be like a fairy tale and the Arabian Nights' Entertainments. If we respected only what is inevitable and has a right to be, music and poetry would resound along the streets. When we are unhurried and wise, we perceive that only great and worthy things have any permanent and absolute existence, that petty fears and petty pleasures are but the shadow of the reality. This is always exhilarating and sublime. By closing the eyes and slumbering, and consenting to be deceived by shows, men establish and confirm their daily life of routine and habit everywhere, which still is built on purely illusory foundations. Children, who play life, discern its true law and relations more clearly than men, who fail to live it worthily, but who think that they are wiser by experience, that is, by failure. I have read in a Hindoo book, that "there was a king's son, who, being expelled in infancy from his native city, was brought up by a forester, and, growing up to maturity in that state, imagined himself to belong to the barbarous race with which he lived. One of his father's ministers having discovered him, revealed to him what he was, and the misconception of his character was removed, and he knew himself to be a prince. So soul," continues the Hindoo philosopher, "from the circumstances in which it is placed, mistakes its own character, until the truth is revealed to it by some holy teacher, and then it knows itself to be *Brahme*." I perceive that we inhabitants of New England live this mean life that we do because our vision does not penetrate the surface of things. We think that this *is* which *appears* to be. If a man should walk through this town and see only the reality, where, think you, would the "Mill-dam" go to? If he should give us an account of the realities he beheld there, we should not recognize the place in his description. Look at a meeting-house, or a court-house, or a jail, or a shop, or a dwelling-house, and say what that thing really is before a true gaze, and they would all go to pieces in your account of them Men esteem truth remote, in the outskirts of the system, behind the farthest star, before Adam and after the last man. In eternity there is indeed something true and sublime. But all these times and places and occasions are now and here. God himself culminates in the present moment, and will never be more divine in the lapse of all the ages. And we are enabled to apprehend at all what is sublime and noble only by the perpetual instilling and drenching of the reality that surrounds us. The universe constantly and obediently answers to our conceptions; whether we travel fast or slow, the track is laid for us. Let us spend our lives in conceiving then. The poet or the artist never yet had so fair and noble a design but some of his posterity at least could accomplish it.

Let us spend one day as deliberately as Nature, and not be thrown off the track by every nutshell and mosquito's wing that falls on the rails. Let us rise early and fast, or break fast, gently and without perturbation; let company come and let company go, let the bells ring and the children cry,—determined to make a day of it. Why should we knock under and go with the stream? Let us not be upset and overwhelmed in that terrible rapid and whirlpool called a dinner, situated in the meridian shallows. Weather this danger and you are safe, for the rest of the way is down hill. With unrelaxed nerves, with morning vigor, sail by it, looking another way, tied to the mast like Ulysses. If the engine whistles, let it whistle till it is hoarse for its pains. If the bell rings, why should we run? We will consider what kind of music they are like. Let us settle ourselves, and work and wedge our feet downward through the mud and slush of opinion, and prejudice, and tradition, and delusion, and appearance, that alluvion which covers the globe, through Paris and London, through New York and Boston and Concord, through Church and State, through poetry and philosophy and religion, till we come to a hard bottom and rocks in place, which we can call *reality,* and say, This is, and no mistake; and then begin, having a *point d'appui,* below freshet and frost and fire, a place where you might found a wall or a state, or set a lamp-post safely, or perhaps a gauge, not a Nilometer, that future ages might know how deep a freshet of shams and appearances had gathered from time to time. If you stand right fronting and face to face to a fact, you will see the sun glimmer on both its surfaces, as if it were a cimeter, and feel its sweet edge dividing you through the heart and marrow, and so you will happily conclude your mortal career. Be it life or death we crave only reality. If we are really dying, let us hear the rattle in our throats and feel cold in the extremities; if we are alive, let us go about our business.

Time is but the stream I go a-fishing in. I drink at it; but while I drink I see the sandy bottom and detect how shallow it is. Its thin current slides away, but eternity remains. I would drink deeper; fish in the sky, whose bottom is pebbly with stars. I cannot count one. I know not the first letter of the alphabet. I have always been regretting that I was not as wise as the day I was born. The intellect is a cleaver; it discerns and rifts its way into the secret of things. I do not wish to be any more busy with my hands than is necessary. My head is hands and feet. I feel all my best faculties concentrated in it. My instinct tells me that my head is an organ for burrowing, as some creatures use their snout and fore paws, and with it I would mine and burrow my way through these hills. I think that the richest vein is somewhere hereabouts; so by the divining-rod and thin rising vapors I judge; and here I will begin to mine.

DISCUSSION QUESTIONS

1. Compare Thoreau's description of nature with N. Scott Momaday's "A First American Views His Land" (see "Magazines"). What perspective does each writer adopt in order to describe the natural world? What attitude does each express toward nature?

2. Which author attends more carefully to details in describing nature? Which uses the most figurative language? To what effect? Does each writer draw on the same kinds of experience? Explain.

3. In which description of nature does the personal life of the speaker play the most prominent role? Explain. Which writer goes to the natural world to seek adventure? To search for self-improvement? To enjoy an idyllic experience?

4. What are the reasons for each writer's excursion into the natural world? Do you find any of these unconvincing? For which writer is nature most associated with political controversy?

Walt Whitman

For most of his life, Walt Whitman (1819–92) lived in neighborly relation to poverty. He worked as an apprentice in a printing shop, as a journalist for New York City and Long Island newspapers, as editor of the Brooklyn Eagle, *as a teacher, as a building contractor, and as a clerk in the Bureau of Indian Affairs until the sullied reputation of his collection of poems,* Leaves of Grass, *provoked his hurried dismissal.*

Said to have been set in type by Whitman himself and published at his own expense, Leaves of Grass *attracted little critical attention and sold few copies when first published in 1855. Of all the editors and writers to whom Whitman sent copies, Ralph Waldo Emerson responded most readily and enthusiastically: "I find in it the most extraordinary piece of wit and wisdom that America has yet contributed." But Emerson was well ahead of his time in appreciating Whitman's verse. Its seeming formlessness, boasts, sexual overtones, and "vulgar" language stirred much controversy in the decades that followed. Several generations of critics characterized his work as "the poetry of barbarism" and admonished audiences that this was poetry "not to be read aloud to mixed audiences." The poet John Greenleaf Whittier went further. He condemned the poems as "loose, lurid, and impious" and tossed his copy into a fire.*

After service in Washington during the Civil War, Whitman suffered a paralytic stroke in 1873 and moved to his brother's home in Camden, New Jersey, where he spent his remaining years revising Leaves of Grass.

In Leaves of Grass, *an unprecedented mixture of a radically new poetic consciousness, commonplace subject matter, and distinctively colloquial rhythms, Whitman aspired to create nothing less than an epic of American democracy. But while his ambition to be known as "the bard of democracy" was never fully endorsed during his lifetime, Whitman's vision and innovative verse have cut a deepening course through which much of twentieth-century poetry has passed.*

"One's-Self I Sing" was written in 1867 and published in Leaves of Grass *in the 1871 edition of the poem. "I Hear America Singing" was written in 1860 and published in the 1860 edition of* Leaves of Grass *as No. 20 of "Chants Democratic." "A Noiseless Patient Spider" was written in 1868 and included in the "Whispers of Heavenly Death" section of* Leaves of Grass *in 1881. These poems offer a sample of Whitman's poetic themes as well as his single-handed attempt to introduce a new style and idiom into American literature. They also demonstrate Whitman's belief that the process of reading should be:*

> *a half-sleep, but . . . an exercise, a gymnast's struggle; that the reader is to do something for himself, must be on the alert, must . . . construct indeed the poem, argument, history, metaphysical essay—the text furnishing the hints, the clue, the start or frame-work.*

Walt Whitman / One's-Self I Sing 1867

One's-Self I sing, a simple separate person,
Yet utter the word Democratic, the word En-Masse.

Of physiology from top to toe I sing,
Not physiognomy alone not brain alone is worthy for the Muse, I say the
  Form complete is worthier far,
The Female equally with the Male I sing.
Of Life immense in passion, pulse, and power,
Cheerful, for freest action form'd under the laws divine,
The Modern Man I sing.

Walt Whitman / I Hear America Singing 1860

I hear America singing, the varied carols I hear,
Those of mechanics, each one singing his as it should be blithe and strong,

The carpenter singing his as he measures his plank or beam,
The mason singing his as he makes ready for work, or leaves off work,
The boatman singing what belongs to him in his boat, the deckhand singing on the steamboat deck,
The shoemaker singing as he sits on his bench, the hatter singing as he stands,
The wood-cutter's song, the ploughboy's on his way in the morning, or at noon intermission or at sundown,
The delicious singing of the mother, or of the young wife at work, or of the girl sewing or washing,
Each singing what belongs to him or her and to none else,
The day what belongs to the day—at night the party of young fellows, robust, friendly,
Singing with open mouths their strong melodious songs.

Walt Whitman / A Noiseless Patient Spider 1868

A noiseless patient spider,
I mark'd where on a little promonotory it stood isolated,
Mark'd how to explore the vacant vast surrounding,
It launch'd forth filament, filament, out of itself,
Ever unreeling them, ever tirelessly speeding them.

And you O my soul where you stand,
Surrounded, detached, in measureless oceans of space,
Ceaselessly musing, venturing, throwing, seeking the spheres to connect them,
Till the bridge you will need be form'd, till the ductile anchor hold,
Till the gossamer thread you fling catch somewhere, O my soul.

Harriet Jacobs / The Loophole of Retreat

from *Incidents in the Life of a Slave Girl* 1861

Harriet Jacobs took great risks in publishing an account of her experiences as a slave. While the story of her suffering (her efforts to elude her master's sexual advances, her years hiding in a cramped garret, her escape to the north, and her separation from her family) could win converts to the abolition movement, her failure to observe nineteenth-century sexual standards when she had children out of wedlock might prompt the Victorian women who would constitute her readership to condemn her in moral terms. Jacobs resolved this tension and explained her overall purpose in writing in a letter to her friend Amy Post:

> I have My dear friend—Striven faithfully to give a true and just account of my own life in Slavery—God knows I have tried to do it in a Christian spirit. . . . I ask nothing—I have placed myself before you

1. A reference to William Cowper's "The Task," IV.88–90:

> 'Tis pleasant, through the loopholes of retreat.
> To peep at such a world,—to see the stir
> Of the great Babel, and not feel the crowd.

Jacobs was not the first Afro-American to use Cowper's phrase. In 1838 the phrase "From the loopholes of Retreat" appeared as an epigraph to "The Curtain," a column in *Freedom's Journal* (New York).

> to be judged as a woman whether I deserve your pity or contempt—I have another object in view—it is to come to you just as I am a poor Slave Mother—not to tell you what I have heard but what I have seen—and what I have suffered—and if there is any sympathy to give—let it be given to the thousands—of Slave Mothers that are still in bondage . . . let it plead for their helpless children.

Jacobs' method of persuasion in her narrative is to draw on the popular language of sentimentalism and melodrama to dramatize her experiences; she then directs her audience's emotional response towards a political one on behalf of the abolitionist cause. Jacobs's narrator frequently steps back from the actual storytelling to analyze, explain, and criticize the corrupt system that created the unhappy circumstances of her life—though she is careful always to exonerate the northern women from guilt. In effect, Jacobs skillfully controls the meaning of the experiences she relates and leads her readers towards emphatic social activism. In the following passage, for example, Jacobs speaks directly to her readers, showing that the protagonist's sin is the result of a corrupt, evil system—that her fall, her lost chastity, could have been their own loss:

> O, ye happy women, whose purity has been sheltered from childhood, who have been free to choose the objects of your affection, whose homes are protected by law, do not judge the poor desolate slave girl too severely! If slavery had been abolished, I, also, could have married the man of my choice; I could have had a home shielded by the laws; and I should have been spared the painful task of confessing what I am now about to relate; but all my prospects had been blighted by slavery. I wanted to keep myself pure; and under the most adverse circumstances, I tried hard to preserve my self-respect; but I was struggling alone in the powerful grasp of the demon Slavery; and the monster proved too strong for me. I felt as if I was forsaken by God and man; as if all my efforst must be frustrated; and I became reckless in my despair.

Her experience becomes representative: the slave mother becomes a generic female protagonist—virtuous, delicate, innocent, up against a monster and a demon, feeling forsaken by a support system which should have been hers. As such, Jacobs' narrative is not only a moving autobiography but also a powerful political document.

In the following selection, Jacobs describes with the plight of a mother separated from her children, able to observe but not to speak to them or touch them. She also shows, however, the empowerment she found in her concealed vantage point; she discovers a reversal of power when she sees her master in a rage of helplessness to find her.

A small shed has been added to my grandmother's house years ago. Some boards were laid across the joists at the top, and between these boards and the roof was a very small garret, never occupied by any thing but rats and mice. It was a pent roof, covered with nothing but shingles, according to the southern custom for such buildings. The garret was only nine feet long and seven wide. The highest part was three feet high, and sloped down abruptly to the loose board floor. There was no admission for either light or air. My uncle Phillip, who was a carpenter, had very skilfully made a concealed trap-door, which communicated with the storeroom. He had been doing this while I was waiting in the swamp. The storeroom opened upon a piazza. To this hole I was conveyed as soon as I entered the house. The air was stifling; the darkness total. A bed had been spread on the floor. I could sleep quite comfortably on one side; but the slope was so sudden that I could not turn on the other without hitting the roof.[2] The rats and mice ran over my bed; but I was weary, and I slept such sleep as the wretched may, when a tempest has passed over them. Morning came. I knew it only by the noises I heard; for my small den day and night were all the same. I suffered for air even more than for light. But I was not comfortless. I heard the voices of my children. There was joy and there was sadness in the sound. It made my tears flow. How I longed to speak to them! I was eager to look on their faces; but there was no hole, no crack, through which I could peep. This continued darkness was oppressive. It seemed horrible to sit or lie in a cramped position day after day without one gleam of light. Yet I would have chosen this, rather than my lot as a slave, though white people considered it an easy one; and it was so compared with the fate of others. I was never cruelly over-worked; I was never lacerated with the whip from head to foot; I was never so beaten and bruised that I could not turn from one side to the other; I never had my heel-strings cut to prevent my running away; I was never chained to a log and forced to drag it about, while I toiled in the fields from morning till night; I was never branded with hot iron, or torn by bloodhounds. On the contrary, I had always been kindly treated, and tenderly cared for, until I came into the hands of Dr. Flint. I had never wished for freedom till then. But though my life in slavery was comparatively devoid of hardships, God pity the woman who is compelled to lead such a life!

My food was passed up to me through the trap-door my uncle had contrived; and my grandmother, my uncle Phillip, and aunt Nancy would seize such opportunities as they could, to mount up there and chat with me at the opening. But of course this was not safe in the daytime. It must all be done in darkness. It was impossible for me to move in an erect position, but I crawled about my den for exercise. One day I hit my head against something, and found it was a gimlet. My uncle had left it sticking there when he made the trap-door. I was as rejoiced as Robinson Crusoe could have been at finding such a treasure. It put a lucky thought into my head. I said to myself, "Now I will have some light. Now I will see my children." I did not dare to begin my work during the daytime, for fear of attracting attention. But I groped round; and having found the side next the street, where I could frequently see my children, I stuck the gimlet in and waited for evening. I bored three rows of holes, one above another; then I bored out the interstices between. I thus succeeded in making one hole about an inch long and an inch broad. I sat by it till late into the night, to enjoy the little whiff of air that floated in. In the morning I watched for my children. The first person I saw in the street was Dr. Flint.[3] I had a shuddering, superstitious feeling that it was a bad omen. Several familiar faces passed by. At last I heard the merry laugh of children, and presently two sweet little faces were looking up at me, as though they knew I was there, and were conscious of the joy they impaired. How I longed to *tell* them I was there!

My condition was now a little improved. But for weeks I was tormented by hundreds of little red insects, fine as a needle's point, that pierced through my

2. John S. Jacobs describes the hiding place as follows: "My grandmother's house had seven rooms—two upper rooms, and five on the lower floor: on the west side there was a piazza. On the east side there were two rooms, with a lobby leading to the centre of the house. The room on the left on entering the lobby was used as a store-room; the ceiling of this room was of boards, the roof was shingled; the space between the roof and ceiling was from three and a half to four feet in height, running off to a point. My uncle made a cupboard in one corner of this room, with the top attached to the ceiling. The part of the board that covered the top of the cupboard was cut and made into a trap-door; the whole of it was so small and neatly done that no one would have believed it to be what it was—the entrance to her hiding-place." "A True Tale of Slavery."

3. Jacobs had bored the "loophole" on the south side of the house, facing West King Street. Norcom's office was across Broad on East King Street, less than a block away; his home on Eden Alley was a block north of Molly Horniblow's house.

skin, and produced an intolerable burning. The good grandmother gave me herb teas and cooling medicines, and finally I got rid of them. The heat of my den was intense, for nothing but thin shingles protected me from the scorching summer's sun. But I had my consolations. Through my peeping-hole I could watch the children, and when they were near enough, I could hear their talk. Aunt Nancy brought me all the news she could hear at Dr. Flint's. From her I learned that the doctor had written to New York to a colored woman, who had been born and raised in our neighborhood, and had breathed his contaminating atmosphere. He offered her a reward if she could find out any thing about me. I know not what was the nature of her reply; but he soon after started for New York in haste, saying to his family that he had business of importance to transact.[4] I peeped at him as he passed on his way to the steamboat. It was a satisfaction to have miles of land and water between us, even for a little while; and it was a still greater satisfaction to know that he believed me to be in the Free States. My little den seemed less dreary than it had done. He returned, as he did from his former journey to New York, without obtaining any satisfactory information. When he passed our house next morning, Benny was standing at the gate. He had heard them say that he had gone to find me, and he called out, "Dr. Flint, did you bring my mother home? I want to see her." The doctor stamped his foot at him in a rage, and exclaimed, "Get out of the way, you little damned rascal! If you don't I'll cut off your head."

Benny ran terrified into the house, saying, "You can't put me in jail again. I don't belong to you now." It was well that the wind carried the words away from the doctor's ear. I told my grandmother of it, when we had our next conference at the trap-door; and begged of her not to allow the children to be impertinent to the irascible old man.

Autumn came, with a pleasant abatement of heat. My eyes had become accustomed to the dim light, and by holding my book or work in a certain position near the aperture I contrived to read and sew. That was a great relief to the tedious monotony of my life. But when winter came, the cold penetrated through the thin shingle roof, and I was dreadfully chilled. The winters there are not so long, or so severe, as in northern latitudes; but the houses are not built to shelter from cold, and my little den was peculiarly comfortless.[5] The kind grandmother brought me bed-clothes and warm drinks. Often I was obliged to lie in bed all day to keep comfortable; but with all my precautions, my shoulders and feet were frostbitten. O, those long, gloomy days, with no object for my eye to rest upon, and no thoughts to occupy my mind, except the dreary past and the uncertain future! I was thankful when there came a day sufficiently mild for me to wrap myself up and sit at the loophole to watch the passers by. Southerners have the habit of stopping and talking in the streets, and I heard many conversations not intended to meet my ears. I heard slave-hunters planning how to catch some poor fugitive. Several times I heard allusions to Dr. Flint, myself, and the history of my children, who, perhaps, were playing near the gate. One would say, "I wouldn't move my little finger to catch her, as old Flint's property." Another would say, "I'll catch *any* nigger for the reward. A man ought to have what belongs to him, if he *is* a damned brute." The opinion was often expressed that I was in the Free

4. Correspondence indicates that Norcom was traveling in August 1835. John Norcom to B. R. Norcom, M.D., NFP.

5. Meteorological data are not available for 1835–1842. From 1896–1913, the average mean temperature of Edenton was 60.65°F. Winters usually began after Christmas and were over by March 20. During the winter of 1896–97, the average mean temperature in January, the coldest month of the year, was 39.9°F. W. Scott Boyce, *Economic and Social History of Chowan County, North Carolina, 1880–1915*. Studies in History, Economics and Public Law, 76, no. 1 (New York: Columbus University Press, 1917), pp. 19–21; monthly reports from the Edenton Weather Station, 1896–1897, NCSA.

States. Very rarely did any one suggest that I might be in the vicinity. Had the least suspicion rested on my grandmother's house, it would have been burned to the ground. But it was the last place they thought of. Yet there was no place, where slavery existed, that could have afforded me so good a place of concealment.

Dr. Flint and his family repeatedly tried to coax and bribe my children to tell something they had heard said about me. One day the doctor took them into a shop, and offered them some bright little silver pieces and gay handkerchiefs if they would tell where their mother was. Helen shrank away from him, and would not speak; but Benny spoke up, and said, "Dr. Flint, I don't know where my mother is. I guess she's in New York; and when you go there again, I wish you'd ask her to come home, for I want to see her; but if you put her in jail, or tell her you'll cut her head off, I'll tell her to go right back."

Emily Dickinson

Born in Amherst, Massachusetts, in 1830, Emily Dickinson remained within the confines of her father's house in that small conservative village for most of her life. Her poems are marked by an acute awareness of psychological states and physical sensations as much as by their brilliant images and melodic blending of assonant and dissonant sounds. Only seven of Dickinson's many poems appeared in print before she died in 1886.

Emily Dickinson / After Great Pain, a Formal Feeling Comes—

ca. 1862

After great pain, a formal feeling comes—
The Nerves sit ceremonious, like Tombs—
The stiff Heart questions was it He, that bore,
And Yesterday, or Centuries before?

The Feet, mechanical, go round—
Of Ground, or Air, or Ought—
A Wooden way
Regardless grown,
A quartz contentment, like a stone—

This is the Hour of Lead—
Remembered, if outlived,
As Freezing persons, recollect the Snow—
First—Chill—then Stupor—then the letting go—

Emily Dickinson / One Need Not Be a Chamber—To Be Haunted—

ca. 1863

One need not be a Chamber—to be Haunted—
One need not be a House—
The Brain has Corridors—surpassing
Material Place—

Far safer, of a Midnight Meeting
External Ghost
Than its interior Confronting—
That Cooler Host.

Far safer, through an Abbey gallop,
The Stones a'chase—
Than Unarmed, one's a'self encounter—
In lonesome Place—

Ourself behind ourself, concealed—
Should startle most—
Assassin hid in our Apartment
Be Horror's least.

The Body—borrows a Revolver—
He bolts the Door—
O'erlooking a superior spectre—
Or More—

Emily Dickinson / I Felt a Cleaving in My Mind— ca. 1864

I felt a Cleaving in my Mind—
As if my Brain had split—
I tried to match it—Seam by Seam—
But could not make them fit.

The thought behind. I strove to join
Unto the thought before—
But Sequence ravelled out of Sound
Like Balls—upon a Floor.

Mark Twain / *Old Times on the Mississippi* 1875

Samuel Langhorne Clemens (Mark Twain), like many prominent American novelists, began his writing career as a journalist. He was born along the Mississippi River in Florida, Missouri, in 1835, and throughout his life that great river remained a vital presence. After briefly working on the Mississippi as a riverboat pilot and mining for silver in Nevada, Twain felt his energies would be better spent writing for newspapers. He learned early how to combine skillfully the official prose of news reporting with the folksy language of tall tales, and his work in this humorous vein began to attract literary attention. He traveled to Hawaii, then to the Middle East, and later turned these experiences into parodies of the then popular conventional guidebooks. In 1876 he wrote The Adventures of Tom Sawyer, *a best-selling nostalgic glance at his Missouri boyhood, and in 1885 he brought out his masterpiece,* The Adventures of Huckleberry Finn, *the book Ernest Hemingway claimed marked the origins of "all modern American literature."*

Twain's later career, though productive, was interrupted by a series of futile business ventures (he invested heavily in an aborted typesetting invention) and personal tragedies. The tone of much of his later work hinges on his own pessimistic answers to the question posed in one of his final essays, "What Is Man?"

Old Times on the Mississippi *was originally written as a series for* The Atlantic Monthly *and ran through seven installments in 1875.*

In "How to Tell a Story" (1897), Twain, by then a distinguished novelist and man of letters, explains why effective narrative styles need to be rooted in an oral tradition.

When I was a boy, there was but one permanent ambition among my comrades in our village[1] on the west bank of the Mississippi River. That was, to be a steamboatman. We had transient ambitions of other sorts, but they were only transient. When a circus came and went, it left us all burning to become clowns; the first negro minstrel show that came to our section left us all suffering to try that kind of life; now and then we had a hope that if we lived and were good, God would permit us to be pirates. These ambitions faded out, each in its turn; but the ambitions to be a steamboatman always remained.

Once a day a cheap, gaudy packet arrived upward from St. Louis, and another downward from Keokuk. Before these events had transpired, the day was glorious with expectancy; after they had transpired, the day was a dead and empty thing. Not only the boys, but the whole village, felt this. After all these years I can picture that old time to myself now, just as it was then: the white town drowsing in the sunshine of a summer's morning; the streets empty, or pretty nearly so; one or two clerks sitting in front of the Water Street stores, with their splint-bottomed chairs tilted back against the wall, chins on breasts, hats slouched over their faces, asleep—with shingle-shavings enough around to show what broke them down; a sow and a litter of pigs loafing along the sidewalk, doing a good business in watermelon rinds and seeds; two or three lonely little freight piles scattered about the "levee"; a pile of "skids" on the slope of the stone-paved wharf, and the fragrant town drunkard asleep in the shadow of them; two or three wood flats at the head of the wharf, but nobody to listen to the peaceful lapping of the wavelets against them; the great Mississippi, the majestic, the magnificent Mississippi, rolling its mile-wide tide along, shining in the sun; the dense forest away on the other side; the "point" above the town, and the "point" below, bounding the river-glimpse and turning it into a sort of sea, and withal a very still and brilliant and lonely one. Presently a film of dark smoke appears above one of those remote "points"; instantly a negro drayman, famous for his quick eye and prodigious voice, lifts up the cry, "S-t-e-a-m-boat a-comin!" and the scene changes! The town drunkard stirs, the clerks wake up, a furious clatter of drays follows, every house and store pours out a human contribution, and all in a twinkling the dead town is alive and moving. Drays, carts, men, boys, all go hurrying from many quarters to a common centre, the wharf. Assembled there, the people fasten their eyes upon the coming boat as upon a wonder they are seeing for the first time. And the boat *is* rather a handsome sight, too. She is long and sharp and trim and pretty; she has two tall, fancy-topped chimneys, with a gilded device of some kind swung between them; a fanciful pilot-house, all glass and "gingerbread," perched on top of the "texas" deck behind them; the paddle-boxes are gorgeous with a picture or with gilded rays above the boat's name; the boiler deck, the hurricane deck, and the texas deck are fenced and ornamented with clean white railings; there is a flag gallantly flying from the jack-staff; the furnace doors are open and the fires

1. Hannibal, Missouri.

glaring bravely; the upper decks are black with passengers; the captain stands by the big bell, calm, imposing, the envy of all; great volumes of the blackest smoke are rolling and tumbling out of the chimneys—a husbanded grandeur created with a bit of pitch pine just before arriving at a town; the crew are grouped on the forecastle; the broad stage is run far out over the port bow, and an envied deck-hand stands picturesquely on the end of it with a coil of rope in his hand; the pent steam is screaming through the gauge-cocks; the captain lifts his hand, a bell rings, the wheels stop; then they turn back, churning the water to foam, and the steamer is at rest. Then such a scramble as there is to get aboard, and to get ashore, and to take in freight and to discharge freight, all at once and the same time; and such a yelling and cursing as the mates facilitate it all with! Ten minutes later the steamer is under way again, with no flag on the jack-staff and no black smoke issuing from the chimneys. After ten more minutes the town is dead again, and the town drunkard asleep by the skids once more.

My father was a justice of the peace, and I supposed he possessed the power of life and death over all men and could hang anybody that offended him. This was distinction enough for me as a general thing; but the desire to be a steam-boatman kept intruding, nevertheless. I first wanted to be a cabin-boy, so that I could come out with a white apron on and shake a table-cloth over the side, where all my old comrades could see me; later I thought I would rather be the deck-hand who stood on the end of the stageplank with the coil of rope in his hand, because he was particularly conspicuous. But these were only daydreams—they were too heavenly to be contemplated as real possibilities. By and by one of our boys went away. He was not heard of for a long time. At last he turned up as apprentice engineer or "striker" on a steamboat. This thing shook the bottom out of all my Sunday-school teachings. That boy had been notoriously worldly, and I just the reverse; yet he was exalted to this eminence, and I left in obscurity and misery. There was nothing generous about this fellow in his greatness. He would always manage to have a rusty bolt to scrub while his boat tarried at our town, and he would sit on the inside guard and scrub it, where we could all see him and envy him and loathe him. And whenever his boat was laid up he would come home and swell around the town in his blackest and greasiest clothes, so that nobody could help remembering that he was a steamboatman; and he used all sorts of steamboat technicalities in his talk, as if he were so used to them that he forgot common people could not understand them. He would speak of the "labboard" side of a horse in an easy, natural way that would make one wish he was dead. And he was always talking about "St. Looy" like an old citizen; he would refer casually to occasions when he "was coming down Fourth Street," or when he was "passing by the Planter's House," or when there was a fire and he took a turn on the brakes of "the old Big Missouri"; and then he would go on and lie about how many towns the size of ours were burned down there that day. Two or three of the boys had long been persons of consideration among us because they had been to St. Louis once and had a vague general knowledge of its wonders, but the day of their glory was over now. They lapsed into a humble silence, and learned to disappear when the ruthless "cub"-engineer approached. This fellow had money, too, and hair oil. Also an ignorant silver watch and a showy brass watch chain. He wore a leather belt and used no suspenders. If ever a youth was cordially admired and hated by his comrades, this one was. No girl could with-stand his charms. He "cut out" every boy in the village. When his boat blew up at last, it diffused a tranquil contentment among us such as we had not known for months. But when he came home the next week, alive, renowned, and appeared in church all battered up and bandaged, a shining hero, stared at and wondered over by everybody, it seemed to us that the partiality of Providence for an unde-serving reptile had reached a point where it was open to criticism.

This creature's career could produce but one result, and it speedily followed. Boy after boy managed to get on the river. The minister's son became an engineer. The doctor's and the postmaster's sons became "mud clerks"; the wholesale liquor dealer's son became a bar-keeper on a boat; four sons of the chief merchant, and two sons of the county judge, became pilots. Pilot was the grandest position of all. The pilot, even in those days of trivial wages, had a princely salary—from a hundred and fifty to two hundred and fifty dollars a month, and no board to pay. Two months of his wages would pay a preacher's salary for a year. Now some of us were left disconsolate. We could not get on the river—at least four parents would not let us.

So by and by I ran away. I said I never would come home again till I was a pilot and could come in glory. But somehow I could not manage it. I went meekly aboard a few of the boats that lay packed together like sardines at the long St. Louis wharf, and very humbly inquired for the pilots, but got only a cold shoulder and short words from mates and clerks. I had to make the best of this sort of treatment for the time being, but I had comforting daydreams of a future when I should be a great and honored pilot, with plenty of money, and could kill some of these mates and clerks and pay for them.

Months afterward the hope within me struggled to a reluctant death, and I found myself without an ambition. But I was ashamed to go home. I was in Cincinnati, and I set to work to map out a new career. I had been reading about the recent exploration of the river Amazon by an expedition sent out by our government. It was said that the expedition, owing to difficulties, had not thoroughly explored a part of the country lying about the head-waters, some four thousand miles from the mouth of the river. It was only about fifteen hundred miles from Cincinnati to New Orleans, where I could doubtless get a ship. I had thirty dollars left; I would go and complete the exploration of the Amazon. This was all the thought I gave to the subject. I never was great in matters of detail. I packed my valise, and took passage on an ancient tub called the Paul Jones, for New Orleans. For the sum of sixteen dollars I had the scarred and tarnished splendors of "her" main saloon principally to myself, for she was not a creature to attract the eye of wiser travelers.

When we presently got under way and went poking down the broad Ohio, I became a new being, and the subject of my own admiration. I was a traveler! A word never had tasted so good in my mouth before. I had an exultant sense of being bound for mysterious lands and distant climes which I never have felt in so uplifting a degree since. I was in such a glorified condition that all ignoble feelings departed out of me, and I was able to look down and pity the untraveled with a compassion that had hardly a trace of contempt in it. Still, when we stopped at villages and wood-yards, I could not help lolling carelessly upon the railings of the boiler deck to enjoy the envy of the country boys on the bank. If they did not seem to discover me, I presently sneezed to attract their attention, or moved to a position where they could not help seeing me. And as soon as I knew they saw me I gaped and stretched, and gave other signs of being mightily bored with traveling.

I kept my hat off all the time, and stayed where the wind and the sun could strike me, because I wanted to get the bronzed and weather-beaten look of an old traveler. Before the second day was half gone, I experienced a joy which filled me with the purest gratitude; for I saw that the skin had begun to blister and peel off my face and neck. I wished that the boys and girls at home could see me now.

We reached Louisville in time—at least the neighborhood of it. We stuck hard and fast on the rocks in the middle of the river and lay there four days. I was now beginning to feel a strong sense of being a part of the boat's family, a sort of infant son to the captain and younger brother to the officers. There is no estimating the pride I took in this grandeur, or the affection that began to swell and grow in me for those people. I could not know how the lordly steamboatman scorns that sort of presumption in a mere landsman. I particularly longed to acquire the least trifle to notice from the big stormy mate, and I was on the alert for an opportunity to do him a service to that end. It came at last. The riotous powwow of setting a spar was going on down on the forecastle, and I went down there and stood around in the way—or mostly skipping out of it—till the mate suddenly roared a general order for somebody to bring him a capstan bar. I sprang to his side and said: "Tell me where it is—I'll fetch it!"

If a rag-picker had offered to do a diplomatic service for the Emperor of Russia, the monarch could not have been more astounded than the mate was. He even stopped swearing. He stood and stared down at me. It took him ten seconds to scrape his disjointed remains together again. Then he said impressively: "Well, if this don't beat hell!" and turned to his work with the air of a man who had been confronted with a problem too abstruse for solution.

I crept away, and courted solitude for the rest of the day. I did not go to dinner; I stayed away from supper until everybody else had finished. I did not feel so much like a member of the boat's family now as before. However, my spirits returned, in installments, as we pursued our way down the river. I was sorry I hated the mate so, because it was not in (young) human nature not to admire him. He was huge and muscular, his face was bearded and whiskered all over; he had a red woman and a blue woman tattooed on his right arm,—one on each side of a blue anchor with a red rope to it; and in the matter of profanity he was perfect. When he was getting out cargo at a landing, I was always where I could see and hear. He felt all the sublimity of his great position, and made the world feel it, too. When he gave even the simplest order, he discharged it like a blast of lightning, and sent a long, reverberating peal of profanity thundering after it. I could not help contrasting the way in which the average landsman would give an order, with the mate's way of doing it. If the landsman should wish the gangplank moved a foot farther forward, he would probably say: "James, or William, one of you push that plank forward, please;" but put the mate in his place, and he would roar out: "Here, now, start that gang-plank for'ard! Lively, now! *What*'re you about! Snatch it! *snatch* it! There! there! Aft again! aft again! Don't you hear me? Dash it to dash! are you going to *sleep* over it! *'Vast* heaving. 'Vast heaving, I tell you! Going to heave it clear astern? WHERE're you going with that barrel! *for'ard* with it 'fore I make you swallow it, you dash-dash-dash-*dashed* split between a tired mud-turtle and a crippled hearse-horse!"

I wished I could talk like that.

When the soreness of my adventure with the mate had somewhat worn off, I began timidly to make up to the humblest official connected with the boat—the night watchman. He snubbed my advances at first, but I presently ventured to offer him a new chalk pipe, and that softened him. So he allowed me to sit with him by the big bell on the hurricane deck, and in time he melted into conversation. He could not well have helped it, I hung with such homage on his words and so plainly showed that I felt honored by his notice. He told me the names of dim capes and shadowy islands as we glided by them in the solemnity of the night, under the winking stars, and by and by got to talking about himself. He seemed oversentimental for a man whose salary was six dollars a week—or rather he might have seemed so to an older person than I. But I drank in his words hungrily, and with a faith that might have moved mountains if it had been applied judiciously. What was it to me that he was soiled and seedy and fragrant with gin? What was it to me that his grammar was bad, his construction worse, and his profanity so void of art that it was an element of weakness rather than strength in his conversation? He was a wronged man, a man who had seen trouble, and that was enough for me. As he mellowed into his plaintive history his tears dripped upon the lantern in his lap, and I cried, too, from sympathy. He said he was the son of an English nobleman—either an earl or an alderman, he could not remember which, but believed he was both; his father, the nobleman, loved him, but his mother hated him from the cradle; and so while he was still a little boy he was sent to "one of them old, ancient colleges"—he couldn't remember which; and by and by his father died and his mother seized the property and "shook" him, as he phrased it. After his mother shook him, members of the nobility with whom he was acquainted used their influence to get him the position of "loblolly-boy in a ship"; and from that point my watchman threw off all trammels of date and locality and branched out into a narrative that bristled all along with incredible adventures; a narrative that was so reeking with bloodshed and so crammed with hair-breadth escapes and the most engaging and unconscious personal villainies, that I sat speechless, enjoying, shuddering, wondering, worshiping.

It was a sore blight to find out afterwards that he was a low, vulgar, ignorant, sentimental, half-witted humbug, an untraveled native of the wilds of Illinois, who had absorbed wildcat literature and appropriated its marvels, until in time he had woven odds and ends of the mess into this yarn, and then gone on telling it to fledgelings like me, until he had come to believe it himself.

Mark Twain / How to Tell a Story 1897

I do not claim that I can tell a story as it ought to be told. I only claim to know how a story ought to be told, for I have been almost daily in the company of the most expert story-tellers for many years.

There are several kinds of stories, but only one difficult kind—the humorous. I will talk mainly about that one. The humorous story is American, the comic story is English, the witty story is French. The humorous story depends for its effect upon the *manner* of the telling; the comic story and the witty story upon the *matter*.

The humorous story may be spun out to great length, and may wander around as much as it pleases, and arrive nowhere in particular; but the comic and witty stories must be brief and end with a point. The humorous story bubbles gently along, the others burst.

The humorous story is strictly a work of art—high and delicate art—and only an artist can tell it; but no art is necessary in telling the comic and the witty story; anybody can do it. The art of telling a humorous story—understand, I mean by word of mouth, not print—was created in America, and has remained at home.

The humorous story is told gravely; the teller does his best to conceal the fact that he even dimly suspects that there is anything funny about it; but the teller of the comic story tells you beforehand that it is one of the funniest things he has ever heard, then tells it with eager delight, and is the first person to laugh when he gets through. And sometimes, if he has had good success, he is so glad and happy that he will repeat the "nub" of it and glance around from face to face, collecting applause, and then repeat it again. It is a pathetic thing to see.

Very often, of course, the rambling and disjointed humorous story finishes with a nub, point, snapper, or whatever you like to call it. Then the listener must be alert, for in many cases the teller will divert attention from that nub by dropping it in a carefully casual and indifferent way, with the pretense that he does not know it is a nub.

Artemus Ward used that trick a good deal; then when the belated audience presently caught the joke he would look up with innocent surprise, as if wondering what they had found to laugh at. Dan Setchell used it before him, Nye and Riley and others use it to-day.

But the teller of the comic story does not slur the nub; he shouts it at you—every time. And when he prints it, in England, France, Germany, and Italy, he italicizes it, puts some whooping exclamation-points after it and sometimes explains it in a parenthesis. All of which is very depressing, and makes one want to renounce joking and lead a better life.

Let me set down an instance of the comic method, using an anecdote which has been popular all over the world for twelve or fifteen hundred years. The teller tells it in this way:

> *The Wounded Soldier*
>
> In the course of a certain battle a soldier whose leg had been shot off appealed to another soldier who was hurrying by to carry him to the rear, informing him at the same time of the loss which he had sustained; whereupon the generous son of Mars, shouldering the unfortunate, proceeded to carry out his desire. The bullets and cannon-balls were flying in all directions, and presently one of the latter took the wounded man's head off—without, however, his deliverer being aware of it. In no long time he was hailed by an officer, who said:
>
> "Where are you going with that carcass?"
>
> "To the rear, sir—he's lost his leg!"
>
> "His leg, forsooth?" responded the astonished officer, "you mean his head, you booby."
>
> Whereupon the soldier dispossessed himself of his burden, and stood looking down upon it in great perplexity. At length he said:
>
> "It is true, sir, just as you have said." Then after a pause he added. "***But he*** TOLD *me* IT WAS HIS LEG ! ! ! ! !"

Here the narrator bursts into explosion after explosion of thunderous horse-laughter, repeating that nub from time to time through his gaspings and shriekings and suffocatings.

It takes only a minute and a half to tell that in its comic-story form; and isn't worth the telling, after all. Put into the humorous-story form it takes ten minutes, and is about the funniest thing I have ever listened to—as James Whitcomb Riley tells it.

He tells it in the character of a dull-witted old farmer who has just heard it for the first time, thinks it is unspeakably funny, and is trying to repeat it to a neighbor. But he can't remember it; so he gets all mixed up and wanders helplessly round and round, putting in tedious details that don't belong in the tale and only retard it; taking them out conscientiously and putting in others that are just as useless; making minor mistakes now and then and stopping to correct them and explain how he came to make them; remembering things which he forgot to put in in their proper place and going back to put them in there; stopping his narrative a good while in order to try to recall the name of the soldier that was hurt, and finally remembering that the soldier's name was not mentioned, and remarking placidly that the name is of no real importance, anyway—better, of course if one knew it, but not essential, after all—and so on, and so on, and so on.

The teller is innocent and happy and pleased with himself, and has to stop every little while to hold himself in and keep from laughing outright; and does hold in, but his body quakes in a jelly-like way with interior chuckles; and at the end of the ten minutes the audience have laughed until they are exhausted, and the tears are running down their faces.

The simplicity and innocence and sincerity and unconsciousness of the old farmer are perfectly simulated, and the result is a performance which is thoroughly charming and delicious. This is art—and fine and beautiful, and only a master can compass it; but a machine could tell the other story.

To string incongruities and absurdities together in a wandering and sometimes purposeless way, and seem innocently unaware that they are absurdities, is the basis of the American art, if my position is correct. Another feature is the slurring of the point. A third is the dropping of a studied remark apparently without knowing it, as if one were thinking aloud. The fourth and last is the pause.

Artemus Ward dealt in numbers three and four a good deal. He would begin to tell with great animation something which he seemed to think was wonderful; then lose confidence, and after an apparently absent-minded pause add an incongruous remark in a soliloquizing way; and that was the remark intended to explode the mine—and it did.

For instance, he would say eagerly, excitedly, "I once knew a man in New Zealand who hadn't a tooth in his head"—here his animation would die out; a silent, reflective pause would follow, then he would say dreamily, and as if to himself, "and yet that man could beat a drum better than any man I ever saw."

The pause is an exceedingly important feature in any kind of story, and a frequently recurring feature, too. It is a dainty thing, and delicate, and also uncertain and treacherous; for it must be exactly the right length—no more and no less—or it fails of its purpose and makes trouble. If the pause is too short the impressive point is passed, and the audience have had time to divine that a surprise is intended—and then you can't surprise them, of course.

On the platform I used to tell a negro ghost story that had a pause in front of the snapper on the end, and that pause was the most important thing in the whole story. If I got it the right length precisely, I could spring the finishing ejaculation with effect enough to make some impressible girl deliver a startled little yelp and jump out of her seat—and that was what I was after. This story was called "The Golden Arm," and was told in this fashion. You can practise with it yourself—and mind you look out for the pause and get it right.

The Golden Arm

Once 'pon a time dey wuz a monsus mean man, en he live 'way out in de prairie all 'lone by hisself, 'cep'n he had a wife. En bimeby she died, en he tuck en toted her way out dah in de prairie en buried her. Well, she had a golden arm—all solid gold, fum de shoulder down. He wuz pow'ful mean—pow'ful; en dat night he couldn't sleep, caze he want dat golden arm so bad.

When it come midnight he couldn't stan' it no mo'; so he git up, he did, en tuck his lantern en shoved out thoo de storm en dug her up en got de golden arm; en he bent his head down 'gin de win', en plowed en plowed en plowed thoo de snow. Den all on a sudden he stop (make a considerable pause here, and look startled, and take a listening attitude) en say: "My *lan'*, what's dat?"

En he listen—en listen—en de win' say (set your teeth together and imitate the wailing and wheezing singsong of the wind), "Bzzz-z-zzz"—en den, way back yonder whah de grave is, he hear a *voice!*—he hear a voice all mix' up in de win'—can't hardly tell 'em 'part—"Bzzz—zzz—W-h-o—g-o-t—m-y—g-o-l-d-e-n *arm?*" (You must begin to shiver violently now.)

En he begin to shiver en shake, en say, "Oh, my! *Oh,* my lan'!" en de win' blow de lantern out, en de snow en sleet blow in his face en mos' choke him, en he start a-plowin' knee-deep towards home mos' dead, he so sk'yerd—en pooty soon he hear de voice agin, en (pause) it 'us comin' *after* him! "Bzzz—zzz—zzz—W-h-o—g-o-t—m-y—g-o-l-d-e-n—*arm?*"

When he git to de pasture he hear it agin—closter now, en a-*comin'!*—a-comin' back dah in de dark en de storm—(repeat the wind and the voice). When he git to de house he rush up-stairs en jump in de bed en kiver up, head and years, en lay dah shiverin' en shakin'—en den way out dah he hear it *agin!*—en a-*comin'!* En bimeby he hear (pause—awed, listening attitude)—pat—pat—pat—*hit's a-comin upstairs!* Den he hear de latch, en he *know* it's in de room!

Den pooty soon he know it's a-*stannin' by de bed!* (Pause.) Den—he know it's a-*bendin' down over him*—en he cain't skasely git his breath! Den—den—he seem to feel someth'n' *c-o-l-d*, right down 'most agin his head! (Pause.)

Den de voice say, *right at his year*—"W-h-o—g-o-t—m-y—g-o-l-d-e-n *arm?*" (You must wail it out very plaintively and accusingly; then you stare steddily and impressively into the face of the farthest-gone auditor—a girl, preferably—and let that awe-inspiring pause begin to build itself in the deep hush. When it has reached exactly the right length, jump suddenly at that girl and yell, "*You've* got it!")

If you've got the *pause* right, she'll fetch a dear little yelp and spring right out of her shoes. But you *must* get the pause right; and you will find it the most troublesome and aggravating and uncertain thing you ever undertook.

DISCUSSION QUESTION

1. How does Twain's advice about the proper methods of storytelling help you read the opening chapter of *Old Times on the Mississippi?* Does Twain put into practice his oral techniques for telling a story? Identify a few elements of his narrative style that are directly related to his methods of oral pacing and delivery.

Charlotte Perkins Gilman / The Yellow Wallpaper 1892

Contemporary feminism has its roots in the struggles of countless brave women from earlier generations. Charlotte Perkins Gilman is one such woman. She was a theorist, magazine editor, lecturer, and fiction writer whose works challenged the proprieties of her time and set forth a bold vision of a future based on gender equality. Born in 1860, Gilman realized the stresses placed upon women early; her father abandoned the family when Charlotte was still a child. After a difficult youth, Gilman married her first husband, the artist Charles Stetson. Soon after the marriage, she began to experience deep bouts of depression.

"The Yellow Wallpaper" is partly based on Gilman's own experience of psychological unrest and medical maltreatment. This short novella was inspired by Gilman's experiences with a "nerve cure" prescribed by Dr. S. Weir Mitchell, a restrictive program of inactivity and isolation that only served to drive Gilman deeper into despair. The story, while pertaining to the particulars of America in the 1890s, resonates today, as disturbed women continue to struggle against being labeled "mad" by an unsympathetic medical profession.

Charlotte Perkins Gilman authored numerous books, poems and articles, including an important treatise on the oppression of women, Women and Economics *(1898), and a utopian novel,* Herland *(1915). She died in 1935.*

It is very seldom that mere ordinary people like John and myself secure ancestral halls for the summer.

A colonial mansion, a hereditary estate, I would say a haunted house and reach the height of romantic felicity—but that would be asking too much of fate!

Still I will proudly declare that there is something queer about it.

Else, why should it be let so cheaply? And why have stood so long untenanted?

John laughs at me, of course, but one expects that.

John is practical in the extreme. He has no patience with faith, an intense horror of superstition, and he scoffs openly at any talk of things not to be felt and seen and put down in figures.

John is a physician, and *perhaps*—(I would not say it to a living soul, of course, but this is dead paper and a great relief to my mind)—*perhaps* that is one reason I do not get well faster.

You see, he does not believe I am sick! And what can one do?

If a physician of high standing, and one's own husband, assures friends and relatives that there is really nothing the matter with one but temporary nervous depression—a slight hysterical tendency—what is one to do?

My brother is also a physician, and also of high standing, and he says the same thing.

So I take phosphates or phosphites—whichever it is—and tonics, and air and exercise, and journeys, and am absolutely forbidden to "work" until I am well again.

Personally, I disagree with their ideas.

Personally, I believe that congenial work, with excitement and change, would do me good.

But what is one to do?

I did write for a while in spite of them; but it *does* exhaust me a good deal—having to be so sly about it, or else meet with heavy opposition.

I sometimes fancy that in my condition, if I had less opposition and more society and stimulus—but John says the very worst thing I can do is to think about my condition, and I confess it always makes me feel bad.

So I will let it alone and talk about the house.

The most beautiful place! It is quite alone, standing well back from the road, quite three miles from the village. It makes me think of English places that you read about, for there are hedges and walls and gates that lock, and lots of separate little houses for the gardeners and people.

There is a *delicious* garden! I never saw such a garden—large and shady, full of box-bordered paths, and lined with long grape-covered arbors with seats under them.

There were greenhouses, but they are all broken now.

There was some legal trouble, I believe, something about the heirs and co-heirs; anyhow, the place has been empty for years.

That spoils my ghostliness, I am afraid, but I don't care—there is something strange about the house—I can feel it.

I even said so to John one moonlight evening, but he said what I felt was a draught, and shut the window.

I get unreasonably angry with John sometimes. I'm sure I never used to be so sensitive. I think it is due to this nervous condition.

But John says if I feel so I shall neglect proper self-control; so I take pains to control myself—before him, at least, and that makes me very tired.

I don't like our room a bit. I wanted one downstairs that opened onto the piazza and had roses all over the window, and such pretty old-fashioned chintz hangings! But John would not hear of it.

He said there was only one window and not room for two beds, and no near room for him if he took another.

He is very careful and loving, and hardly lets me stir without special direction.

I have a schedule prescription of each hour in the day; he takes all care from me, and so I feel basely ungrateful not to value it more.

He said he came here solely on my account, that I was to have perfect rest and all the air I could get. "Your exercise depends on your strength, my dear," said he, "and your food somewhat on your appetite; but air you can absorb all the time." So we took the nursery at the top of the house.

It is a big, airy room, the whole floor nearly, with windows that look all ways, and air and sunshine galore. It was nursery first, and then playroom and gymnasium, I should judge, for the windows are barred for little children, and there are rings and things in the walls.

The paint and paper looks as if a boys' school had used it. It is stripped off—the paper—in great patches all around the head of my bed, about as far as I can reach, and in a great place on the other side of the room low down. I never saw a worse paper in my life. One of those sprawling, flamboyant patterns committing every artistic sin.

It is dull enough to confuse the eye in following, pronouned enough constantly to irritate and provoke study, and when you follow the lame uncertain curves for a little distance they suddenly commit suicide--plunge off at outrageous angles, destroy themselves in unheard-of contradictions.

The color is repellent, almost revolting: a smouldering unclean yellow, strangely faded by the slow-turning sunlight. It is a dull yet lurid orange in some places, a stickly sulphur tint in others.

No wonder the children hated it! I should hate it myself if I had to live in this room long.

There comes John, and I must put this away—he hates to have me write a word.

We have been here two weeks, and I haven't felt like writing before since that first day.

I am sitting by the window now, up in this atrocious nursery, and there is nothing to hinder my writings as much as I please, save lack of strength.

John is away all day, and even some nights when his cases are serious.

I am glad my case is not serious!

But these nervous troubles are dreadfully depressing.

John does not know how much I really suffer. He knows there is no reason to suffer, and that satisfies him.

Of course it is only nervousness. It does weigh on me so not to do my duty in any way!

I meant to be such a help to John, such a real rest and comfort, and here I am a comparative burden already!

Nobody would believe what an effort it is to do what little I am able—to dress and entertain, and order things.

It is fortunate Mary is so good with the baby. Such a dear baby!

And yet I *cannot* be with him, it makes me so nervous.

I suppose John never was nervous in his life. He laughs at me so about this wallpaper!

At first he meant to repaper the room, but afterward he said that I was letting it get the better of me, and that nothing was worse for a nervous patient than to give way to such fancies.

He said that after the wallpaper was changed it would be the heavy bedstead, and then the barred windows, and then that gate at the head of the stairs, and so on.

"You know the place is doing you good," he said, "and really, dear, I don't care to renovate the house just for a three months' rental."

"Then do let us go downstairs," I said. "There are such pretty rooms there.

Then he took me in his arms and called me a blessed little goose, and said he would go down cellar, if I wished, and have it whitewashed into the bargain.

But he is right enough about the beds and windows and things.

It is as airy and comfortable a room as anyone need wish, and, of course, I would not be so silly as to make him uncomfortable just for a whim.

I'm really getting quite fond of the big room, all but that horrid paper.

Out of one window I can see the garden—those mysterious deep-shaded arbors, the riotous old-fashioned flowers, and bushes and gnarly trees.

Out of another I get a lovely view of the bay and a little private wharf belonging to the estate. There is a beautiful shaded lane that runs down there from the house. I always fancy I see people walking in these numerous paths and arbors, but John has cautioned me not to give way to fancy in the least. He says that with my imaginative power and habit of story-making, a nervous weakness like mine is sure to lead to all manner of excited fancies, and that I ought to use my will and good sense to check the tendency. So I try.

I think sometimes that if I were only well enough to write a little it would relieve the press of ideas and rest me.

But I find I get pretty tired when I try.

It is so discouraging not to have any advice and companionship about my work. When I get really well, John says we will ask Cousin Henry and Julia down for a long visit; but he says he would as soon put fireworks in my pillow-case as to let me have those stimulating people about now.

I wish I could get well faster.

But I must not think about that. This paper looks to me as if it *knew* what a vicious influence it had!

There is a recurrent spot where the pattern lolls like a broken neck and two bulbous eyes stare at you upside down.

I get positively angry with the impertinence of it and the everlastingness. Up and down and sideways they crawl, and those absurd unblinking eyes are everywhere. There is one place where two breadths didn't match, and the eyes go all up and down the line, one a little higher than the other.

I never saw so much expression in an inanimate thing before, and we all know how much expression they have! I used to lie awake as a child and get more entertainment and terror out of blank walls and plain furniture than most children could find in a toy-store.

I remember what a kindly wink the knobs of our big old bureau used to have, and there was one chair that always seemed like a strong friend.

I used to feel that if any of the other things looked too fierce I could always hop into that chair and be safe.

The furniture in this room is no worse than inharmonious, however, for we had to bring it all from downstairs. I suppose when this was used as a playroom they had to take the nursery things out, and no wonder! I never saw such ravages as the children have made here.

The wallpaper, as I said before, is torn off in spots, and it sticketh closer than a brother—they must have had perseverance as well as hatred.

Then the floor is scratched and gouged and splintered, the plaster itself is dug out here and there, and this great heavy bed, which is all we found in the room, looks as if it had been through the wars.

But I don't mind it a bit—only the paper.

There comes John's sister. Such a dear girl as she is, and so careful of me! I must not let her find me writing.

She is a perfect and enthusiastic housekeeper, and hopes for no better profession. I verily believe she thinks it is the writing which made me sick!

But I can write when she is out, and see her a long way off from these windows.

There is one that commands the road, a lovely shaded winding road, and one that just looks off over the country. A lovely country, too, full of great elms and velvet meadows.

This wallpaper has a kind of subpattern in a different shade, a particularly irritating one, for you can only see it in certain lights, and not clearly then.

But in the places where it isn't faded and where the sun is just so—I can see a strange, provoking, formless sort of figure that seems to skulk about behind that silly and conspicuous front design.

There's sister on the stairs!

Well, the Fourth of July is over! The people are all gone, and I am tired out. John thought it might do me good to see a little company, so we just had Mother and Nellie and the children down for a week.

Of course I didn't do a thing. Jennie sees to everything now.

But it tired me all the same.

John says if I don't pick up faster he shall send me to Weir Mitchell[1] in the fall.

But I don't want to go there at all. I had a friend who was in his hands once, and she says he is just like John and my brother, only more so!

Besides, it is such an undertaking to go so far.

I don't feel as if it was worthwhile to turn my hand over for anything, and I'm getting dreadfully fretful and querulous.

I cry at nothing, and cry most of the time.

Of course I don't when John is here, or anybody else, but when I am alone.

And I am alone a good deal just now. John is kept in town very often by serious cases, and Jennie is good and lets me alone when I want her to.

So I walk a little in the garden or down that lovely lane, sit on the porch under the roses, and lie down up here a good deal.

I'm getting really fond of the room in spite of the wallpaper. Perhaps *because* of the wallpaper.

It dwells on my mind so!

I lie here on this great immovable bed—it is nailed down, I believe—and follow that pattern about by the hour. It is as good as gymnastics, I assure you. I start, we'll say, at the bottom, down in the corner over there where it has not been touched, and I determine for the thousandth time that I *will* follow that pointless pattern to some sort of a conclusion.

I know a little of the principle of design, and I know this thing was not arranged on any laws of radiation, or alternation, or repetition, or symmetry, or anything else that I ever heard of.

It is repeated, of course, by the breadths, but not otherwise.

Looked at in one way, each breadth stands alone; the bloated curves and flourishes—a kind of "debased Romanesque" with dilirium tremens go waddling up and down in isolated columns of fatuity.

But, on the other hand, they connect diagonally, and the sprawling outlines run off in great slanting waves of optic horror, like a lot of wallowing sea-weeds in full chase.

The whole thing goes horizontally, too, at least it seems so, and I exhaust myself trying to distinguish the order of its going in that direction.

They have used a horizontal breadth for a frieze, and that adds wonderfully to the confusion.

There is one end of the room where it is almost intact, and there, when the crosslights fade and the low sun shines directly upon it, I can almost fancy radiation after all—the interminable grotesque seems to form around a common center and rush off in headlong plunges of equal distraction.

It makes me tired to follow it. I will take a nap, I guess.

[1]Dr. S. Weir Mitchell (1829–1914) was an eminent Philadelphia neurologist who advocated "rest cures" for nervous disorders. He was the author of *Diseases of the Nervous System, Especially of Women* (1881).

I don't know why I should write this.

I don't want to.

I don't feel able.

And I know John would think it absurd. But I *must* say what I feel and think in some way—it is such a relief!

But the effort is getting to be greater than the relief.

Half the time now I am awfully lazy, and lie down ever so much. John says I mustn't lose my strength, and has me take cod liver oil and lots of tonics and things, to say nothing of ale and wines and rare meat.

Dear John! He loves me very dearly, and hates to have me sick. I tried to have a real earnest reasonable talk with him the other day, and tell him how I wish he would let me go and make a visit to Cousin Henry and Julia.

But he said I wasn't able to go, nor able to stand it after I got there; and I did not make out a very good case for myself, for I was crying before I had finished.

It is getting to be a great effort for me to think straight. Just this nervous weakness, I suppose.

And dear John gathered me up in his arms, and just carried me upstairs and laid me on the bed, and sat by me and read to me till it tired my head.

He said I was his darling and his comfort and all he had, and that I must take care of myself for his sake, and keep well.

He says no one but myself can help me out of it, and I must use my will and self-control and not let any silly fancies run away with me.

There's one comfort—the baby is well and happy, and does not have to occupy this nursery with the horrid wallpaper.

If we had not used it, that blessed child would have! What a fortunate escape! Why, I wouldn't have a child of mine, an impressionable little thing, living in such a room for worlds.

I never thought of it before, but it is lucky that John kept me here after all; I can stand it so much easier than a baby, you see.

Of course I never mention it to them any more—I am too wise—but I keep watch for it all the same.

There are things in the wallpaper that nobody knows about but me, or ever will.

Behind that outside pattern the dim shapes get clearer every day.

It is always the same shape, only very numerous.

And it is like a woman stooping down and creeping about behind that pattern. I don't like it a bit. I wonder—I begin to think—I wish John would take me away from here!

It is so hard to talk with John about my case, because he is so wise, and because he loves me so.

But I tried it last night.

It was moonlight. The moon shines in all around just as the sun does.

I hate to see it sometimes, it creeps so slowly, and always comes in by one window or another.

John was asleep and I hated to waken him, so I kept still and watched the moonlight on that undulating wallpaper till I felt creepy.

The faint figure behind seemed to shake the pattern, just as if she wanted to get out.

I got up softly and went to feel and see if the paper *did* move, and when I came back John was awake.

"What is it, little girl?" he said. "Don't go walking about like that—you'll get cold."

I thought it was a good time to talk, so I told him that I really was not gaining here, and that I wished he would take me away.

"Why darling!" said he. "Our lease will be up in three weeks, and I can't see how to leave before.

"The repairs are not done at home, and I cannot possibly leave town just now. Of course, if you were in any danger, I could and would, but you really are better, dear, whether you can see it or not. I am a doctor, dear, and I know. You are gaining flesh and color, your appetite is better, I feel really much easier about you."

"I don't weigh a bit more," said I, "nor as much; and my appetite may be better in the evening when you are here but it is worse in the morning when you are away!"

"Bless her little heart!" said he with a big hug. "She shall be as sick as she pleases! But now let's improve the shining hours by going to sleep, and talk about in the morning!"

"And you won't go away?" I asked gloomily.

"Why, how can I, dear? It is only three weeks more and then we will take a nice little trip for a few days while Jennie is getting the house ready. Really, dear, you are better!"

"Better in body perhaps—" I began, and stopped short, for he sat up straight and looked at me with such a stern, reproachful look that I could not say another word.

"My darling," said he, "I beg you, for my sake and for our child's sake, as well as for your own, that you will never for one instant let that idea enter your mind! There is nothing so dangerous, so fascinating, to a temperament like yours. It is a false and foolish fancy. Can you trust me as a physician when I tell you so?"

So of course I said no more on that score, and we went to sleep before long. He thought I was asleep first, but I wasn't, and lay there for hours trying to decide whether that front pattern and the back pattern really did move together or separately.

On a pattern like this, by daylight, there is a lack of sequence, a defiance of law, that is a constant irritant to a normal mind.

The color is hideous enough, and unreliable enough, and infuriating enough, but the pattern is torturing.

You think you have mastered it, but just as you get well under way in following, it turns a back-somersault and there you are. It slaps you in the face, knocks you down, and tramples upon you. It is like a bad dream.

The outside pattern is a florid arabesque, reminding one of a fungus. If you can imagine a toadstool in joints, an interminable string of toadstools, budding and sprouting in endless convolutions—why, that is something like it.

That is, sometimes!

There is one marked peculiarity about this paper, a thing nobody seems to notice but myself, and that is that it changes as the light changes.

When the sun shoots in through the east window—I always watch for that first long, straight ray—it changes so quickly that I never can quite believe it.

That is why I watch it always.

By moonlight—the moon shines in all night when there is a moon—I wouldn't know it was the same paper.

At night in any kind of light, in twilight, candlelight, lamplight, and worst of all by moonlight, it becomes bars! The outside pattern, I mean, and the woman behind it is as plain as can be.

I didn't realize for a long time what the thing was that showed behind, that dim subpattern, but now I am quite sure it is a woman.

By daylight she is subdued, quiet. I fancy it is the pattern that keeps her so still. It is so puzzling. It keeps me quiet by the hour.

I lie down ever so much now. John says it is good for me, and to sleep all I can.

It is a very bad habit, I am convinced, for you see, I don't sleep.

And that cultivates deceit, for I don't tell them I'm awake—oh, no!

The fact is I am getting a little afraid of John.

He seems very queer sometimes, and even Jennie has an inexplicable look.

It strikes me occasionally, just as a scientific hypothesis, that perhaps it is the paper!

I have watched John when he did not know I was looking, and come into the room suddenly on the most innocent excuses, and I've caught him several times *looking at the paper!* And Jennie too. I caught Jennie with her hand on it once.

She didn't know I was in the room, and when I asked her in a quiet, a very quiet voice, with the most restrained manner possible, what she was doing with the paper, she turned around as if she had been caught stealing, and looked quite angry—asked me why I should frighten her so!

Then she said that the paper stained everything it touched, that she had found yellow smooches on all my clothes and John's and she wished we would be more careful!

Did not that sound innocent? But I know she was studying that pattern, and I am determined that nobody shall find it out but myself!

Life is very much more exciting now than it used to be. You see, I have something more to expect, to look forward to, to watch. I really do eat better, and am more quiet than I was.

John is so pleased to see me improve! He laughed a little the other day, and said I seemed to be flourishing in spite of my wallpaper.

I turned it off with a laugh. I had no intention of telling him it was *because* of the wallpaper—he would make fun of me. He might even want to take me away.

I don't want to leave now until I have found it out. There is a week more, and I think that will be enough.

I'm feeling so much better!

I don't sleep much at night, for it is so interesting to watch developments; but I sleep a good deal during the daytime.

In the daytime it is tiresome and perplexing.

There are always new shoots on the fungus, and new shades of yellow all over it. I cannot keep count of them, though I have tried conscientiously.

It is the strangest yellow, that wallpaper! It makes me think of all the yellow things I ever saw—not beautiful ones like buttercups, but old, foul, bad yellow things.

But there is something else about the paper—the smell! I noticed it the moment we came into the room, but with so much air and sun it was not bad. Now we have had a week of fog and rain, and whether the windows are open or not, the smell is here.

It creeps all over the house.

I find it hovering in the dining-room, skulking in the parlor, hiding in the hall, lying in wait for me on the stairs.

It gets into my hair.

Even when I go to ride, if I turn my head suddenly and surprise it—there is that smell!

Such a peculiar odor, too! I have spent hours in trying to analyze it, to find what it smelled like.

It is not bad—at first—and very gentle, but quite the subtlest, most enduring odor I ever met.

In this damp weather it is awful. I wake up in the night and find it hanging over me.

It used to disturb me at first. I thought seriously of burning the house—to reach the smell.

But now I am used to it. The only thing I can think of that it is like is the *color* of the paper! A yellow smell.

There a very funny mark on this wall, low down, near the mopboard. A streak that runs round the room. It goes behind every piece of furniture, except the bed, a long straight, even *smooch,* as if it had been rubbed over and over.

I wonder how it was done and who did it, and what they did it for. Round and round and round—round and round and round—it makes me dizzy!

I really have discovered something at last.

Through watching so much at night, when it changes so, I have finally found out.

The front pattern *does* move—and no wonder! The woman behind shakes it!

Sometimes I think there are a great many women behind, and sometimes only one, and she crawls around fast, and her crawling shakes it all over.

Then in the very bright spots she keeps still, and in the very shady spots she just takes hold of the bars and shakes them hard.

And she is all the time trying to climb through. But nobody could climb through that pattern—it strangles so; I think that is why it has so many heads.

They get through and then the pattern strangles them off and turns them upside down, and makes their eyes white!

If those heads were covered or taken off it would not be half so bad.

I think that woman gets out in the daytime!

And I'll tell you why—privately—I've seen her!

I can see her out of every one of my windows!

It is the same woman,. I know, for she is always creeping, and most women do not creep by daylight.

I see her in that long shaded lane, creeping up and down. I see her in those dark grape arbors, creeping all round the garden.

I see her on that long road under the trees, creeping along, and when a carriage comes she hides under the blackberry vines.

I don't blame her a bit. It must be very humiliating to be caught creeping by daylight!

I always lock the doors when I creep by daylight. I can't do it at night, for I know John would suspect something at once.

And John is so queer now that I don't want to irritate him. I wish he would take another room! Besides, I don't want anybody to get that woman out at night but myself.

I often wonder if I could see her out of all the windows at once.

But, turn as fast as I can, I can only see out of one at one time.

And though I always see her, she *may* be able to creep faster than I can turn! I have watched her sometimes away off in the open country, creeping as fast as a cloud shadow in a wind.

If only that top pattern could be gotten off from the under one! I mean to try it, little by little.

I have found out another funny thing, but I shan't tell it this time! It does not do to trust people too much.

There are only two more days to get this paper off, and I believe John is beginning to notice. I don't like the look in his eyes.

And I heard him ask Jennie a lot of professional questions about me. She had a very good report to give.

She said I slept a good deal in the daytime.

John knows I don't sleep very well at night, for all I'm so quiet!

He asked me all sorts of questions too, and pretended to be very loving and kind.

As if I couldn't see through him!

Still, I don't wonder he acts so, sleeping under this paper for three months.

It only interests me, but I feel sure John and Jennie are affected by it.

Hurrah! This is the last day, but it is enough. John is to stay in town over night, and won't be out until this evening.

Jennie wanted to sleep with me—the sly thing; but I told her I should undoubtedly rest better for a night all alone.

That was clever, for really I wasn't alone a bit! As soon as it was moonlight and that poor thing began to crawl and shake the pattern, I got up and ran to help her.

I pulled and she shook. I shook and she pulled, and before morning we had peeled off yards of that paper.

A strip about as high as my head and half around the room.

And then when the sun came and that awful pattern began to laugh at me, I declared I would finish it today!

We go away tomorrow, and they are moving all my furniture down again to leave things as they were before.

Jennie looked at the wall in amazement, but I told her merrily that I did it out of pure spite at the vicious thing.

She laughed and said she wouldn't mind doing it herself, but I must not get tired.

How she betrayed herself that time!

But I am here, and no person touches this paper but Me—not *alive!*

She tried to get me out of the room—it was too patent! But I said it was so quiet and empty and clean now that I believed I would lie down again and sleep all I could, and not to wake me even for dinner—I would call when I woke.

So now she's gone, and the servants are gone, and the things are gone, and there is nothing left but that great bedstead nailed down, with the canvas mattress we found on it.

We shall sleep downstairs tonight, and take the boat home tomorrow.

I quite enjoy the room, now it is bare again.

How those children did tear about here!

This bedstead is fairly gnawed!

But I must get to work.

I have locked the door and thrown the key down the front path.

I don't want to go out, and I don't want to have anybody come in, till John comes.

I want to astonish him.

I've got a rope up here that even Jennie did not find. If that woman does get out, and tries to get away, I can tie her!

But I forgot I could not reach far without anything to stand on!

This bed will *not* move!

I tried to lift and push it until I was lame, and then I got so angry I bit off a little piece at one corner—but it hurt my teeth.

Then I peeled off all the paper I could reach standing on the floor. It sticks horribly and the pattern just enjoys it! All those strangled heads and bulbous eyes and waddling fungus growths just shriek with derision!

I am getting angry enough to do something desperate. To jump out of the window would be admirable exercise, but the bars are too strong even to try.

Besides I wouldn't do it. Of course not. I know well enough that a step like that is improper and might be misconstrued.

I don't like to *look* out of the windows even—there are so many of those creeping women, and they creep so fast.

I wonder if they all come out of that wallpaper as I did!

But I am securely fastened now by my well-hidden rope—you don't get *me* out in the road there!

I suppose I shall have to get back behind the pattern when it comes night, and that is hard!

It is so pleasant to be out in this great room and creep around as I please!

I don't want to go outside. I won't, even if Jennie asks me to.

For outside you have to creep on the ground, and everything is green instead of yellow.

But here I can creep smoothly on the floor, and my shoulder just fits in that long smooch around the wall, so I cannot lose my way.

Why, there's John at the door!

It is no use, young man, you can't open it!

How he does call and pound!

Now he's crying to Jennie for an axe.

It would be a shame to break down that beautiful door!

"John dear!" said I in the gentlest voice. "The key is down by the front steps, under a plantain leaf!"

That silenced him for a few moments.

Then he said, very quietly indeed, "Open the door, my darling!"

"I can't," said I. "The key is down by the front door under a plantain leaf!" And then I said it again, several times, very gently and slowly, and said it so often that he had to go and see, and he got it of course, and came in. He stopped short by the door.

"What is the matter?" he cried. "For God's sake, what are you doing!"

I kept on creeping just the same, but I looked at him over my shoulder.

"I've got out at last," said I, "in spite of you and Jane. And I've pulled off most of the paper, so you can't put me back!"

Now why should that man have fainted? But he did, and right across my path by the wall, so that I had to creep over him every time!

DISCUSSION QUESTIONS

1. Compare Charlotte Perkins Gilman's story with the poems of Emily Dickinson and the autobiographical writing of Harriet Jacobs. How do these works use images of isolation and confinement to critique the position of American women in the nineteenth century? Which of these excerpts makes you feel most angry? Which do you consider the easiest to relate to? What can women and people of color learn about their experiences today from these writings?

2. In some ways, Gilman's story resembles a tale of horror. Madness is often a theme in ghost stories and horror films; the average person is scared by images of people behaving erratically. What recent examples of texts from popular culture can you think of that use madness as a theme, either to frighten viewers or to drive home a point about social problems?

Kate Chopin / The Dream of an Hour 1894

Born Katherine O'Flaherty in St. Louis in 1851 to a wealthy Irish father and a Creole mother, Kate Chopin was raised in French, Southern, Catholic, aristocratic circumstances. After studies at a convent school, she entered and was soon bored with the fashionable social circle of St. Louis: "I am invited to a ball and I go.—I dance with people I despise; amuse myself with men whose only talent lies in their feet." At nineteen, she married a Creole cotton broker and moved first to New Orleans and then to the bayou country that forms a backdrop for many of her stories. A year after her husband died of swamp fever in 1883, Chopin returned to St. Louis with her six children and began composing short fiction, novels, and children's books. Writing in the midst of her children's activities, she obviously enjoyed the spontaneity such circumstances imposed:

> *I am completely at the mercy of unconscious selection. To such an extent is this true, that what is called the polishing up process always proved disastrous to my work, and I avoid it, preferring the integrity of crudities to artificialities.*

"The Dream of an Hour" appeared originally in Vogue *magazine in 1894. Chopin's stories were frequently published in such leading periodicals as* Atlantic Monthly, Harper's, *and* Century *and were subsequently collected in* Bayou Folk *(1894) and* A Night in Acadia *(1897). Demoralized by the severe criticism that attended the publication of her third novel,* The Awakening, *a tale of extramarital and interracial love, she wrote little more before her death in 1904.*

Knowing that Mrs. Mallard was afflicted with a heart trouble, great care was taken to break to her as gently as possible the news of her husband's death.

It was her sister Josephine who told her, in broken sentences; veiled hints that revealed in half concealing. Her husband's friend Richards was there, too, near her. It was he who had been in the newspaper office when intelligence of the railroad disaster was received, with Brently Mallard's name leading the list of "killed." He had only taken the time to assure himself of its truth by a second telegram, and had hastened to forestall any less careful, less tender friend in bearing the sad message.

She did not hear the story as many women have heard the same, with a paralyzed inability to accept its significance. She wept at once, with sudden, wild abandonment, in her sister's arms. When the storm of grief had spent itself she went away to her room alone. She would have no one follow her.

There stood, facing the open window, a comfortable, roomy armchair. Into this she sank, pressed down by a physical exhaustion that haunted her body and seemed to reach into her soul.

She could see in the open square before her house the tops of trees that were all aquiver with the new spring life. The delicious breath of rain was in the air. In the street below a peddler was crying his wares. The notes of a distant song which some one was singing reached her faintly, and countless sparrows were twittering in the eaves.

There were patches of blue sky showing here and there through the clouds that had met and piled one above the other in the west facing her window.

She sat with her head thrown back upon the cushion of the chair, quite motionless, except when a sob came up into her throat and shook her, as a child who has cried itself to sleep continues to sob in its dreams.

She was young, with a fair, calm face, whose lines bespoke repression and even a certain strength. But now there was a dull stare in her eyes, whose gaze was fixed away off yonder on one of those patches of blue sky. It was not a glance of reflection, but rather indicated a suspension of intelligent thought.

There was something coming to her and she was waiting for it, fearfully. What was it? She did not know; it was too subtle and elusive to name. But she felt it, creeping out of the sky, reaching toward her through the sounds, the scents, the color that filled the air.

Now her bosom rose and fell tumultuously. She was beginning to recognize this thing that was approaching to possess her, and she was striving to beat it back with her will—as powerless as her two white slender hands would have been.

When she abandoned herself a little whispered word escaped her slightly parted lips. She said it over and over under her breath: "free, free, free!" The vacant stare and the look of terror that had followed it went from her eyes. They stayed keen and bright. Her pulses beat fast, and the coursing blood warmed and relaxed every inch of her body.

She did not stop to ask if it were or were not a monstrous joy that held her: A clear and exalted perception enabled her to dismiss the suggestion as trivial.

She knew that she would weep again when she saw the kind, tender hands folded in death; the face that had never looked save with love upon her, fixed and gray and dead. But she saw beyond that bitter moment a long procession of years to come that would belong to her absolutely. And she opened and spread her arms out to them in welcome.

There would be no one to live for her during those coming years; she would live for herself. There would be no powerful will bending hers in that blind persistence with which men and women believe they have a right to impose a private will upon a fellow-creature. A kind intention or a cruel intention made the act seem no less a crime as she looked upon it in that brief moment of illumination.

And yet she had loved him—sometimes. Often she had not. What did it matter! What could love, the unsolved mystery, count for in face of this possession of self-assertion which she suddenly recognized as the strongest impulse of her being!

"Free! Body and soul free!" she kept whispering.

Josephine was kneeling before the closed door with her lips to the keyhole, imploring for admission. "Louise, open the door! I beg; open the door—you will make yourself ill. What are you doing, Louise? For heaven's sake open the door."

"Go away. I am not making myself ill." No; she was drinking in a very elixir of life through that open window.

Her fancy was running riot along those days ahead of her. Spring days, and summer days, and all sorts of days that would be her own. She breathed a quick prayer that life might be long. It was only yesterday she had thought with a shudder that life might be long.

She arose at length and opened the door to her sister's importunities. There was a feverish triumph in her eyes, and she carried herself unwittingly like a goddess of Victory. She clasped her sister's waist, and together they descended the stairs. Richards stood waiting for them at the bottom.

Some one was opening the front door with a latchkey. It was Brently Mallard who entered, a little travel-stained, composedly carrying his grip-sack and umbrella. He had been far from the scene of accident, and did not even know there had been one. He stood amazed at Josephine's piercing cry; at Richards' quick motion to screen him from the view of his wife.

But Richards was too late.

When the doctors came they said she had died of heart disease—of joy that kills.

DISCUSSION QUESTION

1. Robert Frost often argued that poetry exists "for griefs, not grievances." Do you think this distinction is applicable to Chopin's "The Dream of an Hour"? Explain. Locate other stories and essays in this collection to which this distinction may be applied.

Stephen Crane / The Open Boat 1897

"The Open Boat," written a few months after his report on the sinking of the Commodore *for the* New York Press *on January 7, 1897 (see "Stephen Crane's Own Story" in "Press"), was Crane's second attempt to fictionalize his near disaster at sea. According to a fellow journalist, Crane was so worried about accuracy that he wanted the captain of the wrecked vessel, Edward Murphy, to go over the manuscript. "Listen, Ed. I want to have this* right, *from your point of view. How does it sound so far?" "You've got it, Steve," said the other man. "That is just how it happened, and how it felt." Long regarded as a masterpiece of naturalistic fiction, "The Open Boat" is an early attempt by a major American writer to give literary certification to the ironic, jocularly resilient speech of average men trapped in difficult circumstances. (See, for example, the transcripts of the astronaut's conversations in "Press.") In his efforts to combine the crafts of journalism and literature, Crane helped to set a new tone for fiction, one that could express, as he puts it in "The Open Boat," "humour, contempt, tragedy, all in one."*

A TALE INTENDED TO BE AFTER THE FACT: BEING THE EXPERIENCE OF FOUR MEN FROM THE SUNK STEAMER COMMODORE

I

None of them knew the colour of the sky. Their eyes glanced level, and were fastened upon the waves that swept toward them. These waves were of the hue of slate, save for the tops, which were of foaming white, and all of the men knew the colours of the sea. The horizon narrowed and widened, and dipped and rose, and at all times its edge was jagged with waves that seemed thrust up in points like rocks.

Many a man ought to have a bathtub larger than the boat which here rode upon the sea. These waves were most wrongfully and barbarously abrupt and tall, and each froth-top was a problem in small-boat navigation.

The cook squatted in the bottom, and looked with both eyes at the six inches of gunwale which separated him from the ocean. His sleeves were rolled over his fat forearms, and the two flaps of his unbuttoned vest dangled as he bent to bail out the boat. Often he said, "Gawd! that was a narrow clip." As he remarked it he invariably gazed eastward over the broken sea.

The oiler, steering with one of the two oars in the boat, sometimes raised himself suddenly to keep clear of water that swirled in over the stern. It was a thin little oar, and it seemed often ready to snap.

The correspondent, pulling at the other oar, watched the waves and wondered why he was there.

The injured captain, lying in the bow, was at this time buried in that profound dejection and indifference which comes, temporarily at least, to even the bravest and most enduring when, willy-nilly, the firm fails, the army loses, the ship goes down. The mind of the master of a vessel is rooted deep in the timbers of her, though he command for a day or a decade; and this captain had on him the stern impression of a scene in the greys of dawn of seven turned faces, and later a stump of a topmast with a white ball on it, that slashed to and fro at the waves, went low and lower, and down. Thereafter there was something strange in his voice. Although steady, it was deep with mourning, and of a quality beyond oration or tears.

"Keep 'er a little more south, Billie," said he.

"A little more south, sir," said the oiler in the stern.

A seat in his boat was not unlike a seat upon a bucking broncho, and by the same token a broncho is not much smaller. The craft pranced and reared and plunged like an animal. As each wave came, and she rose for it, she seemed like a horse making at a fence outrageously high. The manner of her scramble over these walls of water is a mystic thing, and, moreover, at the top of them were ordinarily these problems in white water, the foam racing down from the summit of each wave requiring a new leap, and a leap from the air. Then, after scornfully bumping a crest, she would slide and race and splash down a long incline, and arrive bobbing and nodding in front of the next menace.

A singular disadvantage of the sea lies in the fact that after successfully surmounting one wave you discover that there is another behind it just as important and just as nervously anxious to do something effective in the way of swamping boats. In a ten-foot dinghy one can get an idea of the resources of the sea in the line of waves that is not probable to the average experience which is never at sea in a dinghy. As each slaty wall of water approached, it shut all else from the view of the men in the boat, and it was not difficult to imagine that this particular wave was the final outburst of the ocean, the last effort of the grim water. There was a terrible grace in the move of the waves, and they came in silence, save for the snarling of the crests.

In the wan light the faces of the men must have been grey. Their eyes must have glinted in strange ways as they gazed steadily astern. Viewed from a balcony, the whole thing would doubtless have been weirdly picturesque. But the men in the boat had no time to see it, and if they had had leisure, there were other things to occupy their minds. The sun swung steadily up the sky, and they knew it was broad day because the colour of the sea changed from slate to emerald green streaked with amber lights, and the foam was like tumbling snow. The process of the breaking day was unknown to them. They were aware only of this effect upon the colour of the waves that rolled toward them.

In disjointed sentences the cook and the correspondent argued as to the difference between a life-saving station and a house of refuge. The cook had said: "There's a house of refuge just north of the Mosquito Inlet Light, and as soon as they see us they'll come off in their boat and pick us up."

"As soon as who see us?" said the correspondent.

"The crew," said the cook.

"Houses of refuge don't have crews," said the correspondent. "As I understand them, they are only places where clothes and grub are stored for the benefit of shipwrecked people. They don't carry crews."

"Oh, yes, they do," said the cook.

"No, they don't," said the correspondent.

"Well, we're not there yet, anyhow," said the oiler, in the stern.

"Well," said the cook, "perhaps it's not a house of refuge that I'm thinking of as being near Mosquito Inlet Light; perhaps it's a life-saving station."

"We're not there yet," said the oiler in the stern.

II

As the boat bounced from the top of each wave the wind tore through the hair of the hatless men, and as the craft plopped her stern down again the spray slashed past them. The crest of each of these waves was a hill, from the top of which the men surveyed for a moment a broad tumultuous expanse, shining and wind-riven. It was probably splendid, it was probably glorious, this play of the free sea, wild with lights of emerald and white and amber.

"Bully good thing it's an on-shore wind," said the cook. "If not, where would we be? Wouldn't have a show."

"That's right," said the correspondent.

The busy oiler nodded his assent.

Then the captain, in the bow, chuckled in a way that expressed humour, contempt, tragedy, all in one. "Do you think we've got much of a show now, boys?" said he.

Whereupon the three were silent, save for a trifle of hemming and hawing. To express any particular optimism at this time they felt to be childish and stupid, but they all doubtless possessed this sense of the situation in their minds. A young man thinks doggedly at such times. On the other hand, the ethics of their condition was decidedly against any open suggestion of hopelessness. So they were silent.

"Oh, well," said the captain, soothing his children, "we'll get ashore all right."

But there was that in his tone which made them think; so the oiler quoth, "Yes! if this wind holds."

The cook was bailing. "Yes! if we don't catch hell in the surf."

Canton-flannel gulls flew near and far. Sometimes they sat down on the sea, near patches of brown seaweed that rolled over the waves with a movement like carpets on a line in a gale. The birds sat comfortably in groups, and they were envied by some in the dinghy, for the wrath of the sea was no more to them than it was to a covey of prairie chickens a thousand miles inland. Often they came very close and stared at the men with black bead-like eyes. At these times they were uncanny and sinister in their unblinking scrutiny, and the men hooted angrily at them, telling them to be gone. One came, and evidently decided to alight on the top of the captain's head. The bird flew parallel to the boat and did not circle, but made short sidelong jumps in the air in chicken-fashion. His black eyes were wistfully fixed upon the captain's head. "Ugly brute," said the oiler to the bird. "You look as if you were made with a jackknife." The cook and the correspondent swore darkly at the creature. The captain naturally wished to knock it away with the end of the heavy painter, but he did not dare do it, because anything resembling an emphatic gesture would have capsized this freighted boat; and so, with his open hand, the captain gently and carefully waved the gull away. After it had been discouraged from the pursuit the captain breathed easier on account of his hair, and others breathed easier because the bird struck their minds at this time as being somehow gruesome and ominous.

In the meantime the oiler and the correspondent rowed. And also they rowed. They sat together in the same seat, and each rowed an oar. Then the oiler took both oars; then the correspondent took both oars; then the oiler; then the correspondent. They rowed and they rowed. The very ticklish part of the business was when the time came for the reclining one in the stern to take his turn at the oars. By the very last star of truth, it is easier to steal eggs from under a hen than it was to change seats in the dinghy. First the man in the stern slid his hand along the thwart and moved with care, as if he were of Sevres. Then the man in the rowing-seat slid his hand along the other thwart. It was all done with the most extraordinary care. As the two sidled past each other, the whole party kept watchful eyes on the coming wave, and the captain cried: "Look out, now! Steady, there!"

The brown mats of seaweed that appeared from time to time were like islands, bits of earth. They were travelling, apparently, neither one way nor the other. They were, to all intents, stationary. They informed the men in the boat that it was making progress slowly toward the land.

The captain, rearing cautiously in the bow after the dinghy soared on a great swell, said that he had seen the lighthouse at Mosquito Inlet. Presently the cook remarked that he had seen it. The correspondent was at the oars then, and for some reason he too wished to look at the lighthouse; but his back was toward the far shore, and the waves were important, and for some time he could not seize an opportunity to turn his head. But at last there came a wave more gentle than the others, and when at the crest of it he swiftly scoured the western horizon.

"See it?" said the captain.

"No," said the correspondent, slowly; "I didn't see anything."

"Look again," said the captain. He pointed. "It's exactly in that direction."

At the top of another wave the correspondent did as he was bid, and this time his eyes chanced on a small, still thing on the edge of the swaying horizon. It was precisely like the point of a pin. It took an anxious eye to find a lighthouse so tiny.

"Think we'll make it, Captain?"

"If this wind holds and the boat don't swamp, we can't do much else," said the captain.

The little boat, lifted by each towering sea and splashed viciously by the crests, made progress that in the absence of seaweed was not apparent to those in her. She seemed just a wee thing wallowing, miraculously top up, at the mercy of five oceans. Occasionally a great spread of water, like white flames, swarmed into her.

"Bail her, cook," said the captain, serenely.

"All right, Captain," said the cheerful cook.

III

It would be difficult to describe the subtle brotherhood of men that was here established on the seas. No one said that it was so. No one mentioned it. But it dwelt in the boat, and each man felt it warm him. They were a captain, an oiler, a cook, and a correspondent, and they were friends—friends in a more curiously iron-bound degree than may be common. The hurt captain, lying against the water-jar in the bow, spoke always in a low voice and calmly; but he could never command a more ready and swiftly obedient crew than the motley three of the dinghy. It was more than a mere recognition of what was best for the common safety. There was surely in it a quality that was personal and heart-felt. And after this devotion to the commander of the boat, there was this comradeship, that the correspondent, for instance, who had been taught to be cynical of men, knew even at the time was the best experience of his life. But no one said that it was so. No one mentioned it.

"I wish we had a sail," remarked the captain. "We might try my overcoat on the end of an oar, and give you two boys a chance to rest." So the cook and the correspondent held the mast and spread wide the overcoat; the oiler steered; and the little boat made good way with her new rig. Sometimes the oiler had to scull sharply to keep a sea from breaking into the boat, but otherwise sailing was a success.

Meanwhile the lighthouse had been growing slowly larger. It had now almost assumed colour, and appeared like a little grey shadow on the sky. The man at the oars could not be prevented from turning his head rather often to try for a glimpse of this little grey shadow.

At last, from the top of each wave, the men in the tossing boat could see land. Even as the lighthouse was an upright shadow on the sky, this land seemed but a long black shadow on the sea. It certainly was thinner than paper. "We must be about opposite New Smyrna," said the cook, who had coasted this shore often in schooners. "Captain, by the way, I believe they abandoned that life-saving station there about a year ago."

"Did they?" said the captain.

The wind slowly died away. The cook and the correspondent were not now obliged to slave in order to hold high the oar. But the waves continued their old impetuous swooping at the dinghy, and the little craft, no longer under way, struggled woundily over them. The oiler or the correspondent took the oars again.

Shipwrecks are apropos of nothing. If men could only train for them and have them occur when the men had reached pink condition, there would be less drowning at sea. Of the four in the dinghy none had slept any time worth mentioning for two days and two nights previous to embarking in the dinghy, and in the excitement of clambering about the deck of a foundering ship they had also forgotten to eat heartily.

For these reasons, and for others, neither the oiler nor the correspondent was fond of rowing at this time. The correspondent wondered ingenuously how in the name of all that was sane could there be people who thought it amusing to row a boat. It was not an amusement; it was a diabolical punishment, and even a genius of mental aberrations could never conclude that it was anything but a horror to the muscles and a crime against the back. He mentioned to the boat in general how the amusement of rowing struck him, and the weary-faced oiler smiled in full sympathy. Previously to the foundering, by the way, the oiler had worked a double watch in the engine-room of the ship.

"Take her easy now, boys," said the captain. "Don't spend yourselves. If we have to run a surf you'll need all your strength, because we'll sure have to swim for it. Take your time."

Slowly the land arose from the sea. From a black line it became a line of black and a line of white—trees and sand. Finally the captain said that he could make out a house on the shore. "That's the house of refuge, sure," said the cook. "They'll see us before long, and come out after us."

The distant lighthouse reared high. "The keeper ought to be able to make us out now, if he's looking through a glass," said the captain. "He'll notify the life-saving people."

"None of those other boats could have got ashore to give word of this wreck," said the oiler, in a low voice, "else the life-boat would be out hunting us."

Slowly and beautifully the land loomed out of the sea. The wind came again. It had veered from the north-east to the south-east. Finally a new sound struck the ears of the men in the boat. It was the low thunder of the surf on the shore. "We'll never be able to make the lighthouse now," said the captain. "Swing her head a little more north, Billie."

"A little more north, sir," said the oiler.

Whereupon the little boat turned her nose once more down the wind, and all but the oarsman watched the shore grow. Under the influence of this expansion doubt and direful apprehension were leaving the minds of the men. The management of the boat was still most absorbing, but it could not prevent a quiet cheerfulness. In an hour, perhaps, they would be ashore.

Their backbones had become thoroughly used to balancing in the boat, and they now rode this wild colt of a dinghy like circus men. The correspondent thought that he had been drenched to the skin, but happening to feel in the top pocket of his coat, he found therein eight cigars. Four of them were soaked with sea-water; four were perfectly scatheless. After a search, somebody produced three dry matches; and thereupon the four waifs rode impudently in their little boat and, with an assurance of an impending rescue shining in their eyes, puffed at the big cigars, and judged well and ill of all men. Everybody took a drink of water.

IV

"Cook," remarked the captain, "there don't seem to be any signs of life about your house of refuge."

"No," replied the cook. "Funny they don't see us!"

A broad stretch of lowly coast lay before the eyes of the men. It was of low dunes topped with dark vegetation. The roar of the surf was plain, and sometimes they could see the white lip of a wave as it spun up the beach. A tiny house was blocked out black upon the sky. Southward, the slim lighthouse lifted its little grey length.

Tide, wind, and waves were swinging the dinghy northward. "Funny they don't see us," said the men.

The surf's roar was here dulled, but its tone was nevertheless thunderous and mighty. As the boat swam over the great rollers the men sat listening to this roar. "We'll swamp sure," said everybody.

It is fair to say here that there was not a life-saving station within twenty miles in either direction; but the men did not know this fact, and in consequence they made dark and opprobrious remarks concerning the eyesight of the nation's life-savers. Four scowling men sat in the dinghy and surpassed records in the invention of epithets.

"Funny they don't see us."

The light-heartedness of a former time had completely faded. To their sharpened minds it was easy to conjure pictures of all kinds of incompetency and blindness and, indeed, cowardice. There was the shore of the populous land, and it was bitter and bitter to them that from it came no sign.

"Well," said the captain, ultimately, "I suppose we'll have to make a try for ourselves. If we stay out here too long, we'll none of us have strength left to swim after the boat swamps."

And so the oiler, who was at the oars, turned the boat straight for the shore. There was a sudden tightening of muscles. There was some thinking.

"If we don't all get ashore," said the captain—"if we don't all get ashore, I suppose you fellows know where to send news of my finish?"

They then briefly exchanged some addresses and admonitions. As for the reflections of the men, there was a great deal of rage in them. Perchance they might be formulated thus: "If I am going to be drowned—if I am going to be drowned—if I am going to be drowned, why, in the name of the seven mad gods who rule the sea, was I allowed to come thus far and contemplate sand and trees? Was I brought here merely to have my nose dragged away as I was about to nibble the sacred cheese of life? It is preposterous. If this old ninny-woman, Fate, cannot do better than this, she should be deprived of the management of men's fortunes. She is an old hen who knows not her intention. If she has decided to drown me, why did she not do it in the beginning and save me all this trouble? The whole affair is absurd.—But no; she cannot mean to drown me. She dare not drown me. She cannot drown me. Not after all this work." Afterward the man might have had an impulse to shake his fist at the clouds. "Just you drown me, now, and then hear what I call you!"

The billows that came at this time were more formidable. They seemed always just about to break and roll over the little boat in a turmoil of foam. There was a preparatory and long growl in the speech of them. No mind unused to the sea would have concluded that the dinghy could ascend these sheer heights in time. The shore was still afar. The oiler was a wily surfman. "Boys," he said swiftly, "she won't live three minutes more, and we're too far out to swim. Shall I take her to sea again, Captain?"

"Yes; go ahead!" said the captain.

This oiler, by a series of quick miracles and fast and steady oarsmanship, turned the boat in the middle of the surf and took her safely to sea again.

There was a considerable silence as the boat bumped over the furrowed sea to deeper water. Then somebody in gloom spoke: "Well, anyhow, they must have seen us from the shore by now."

The gulls went in slanting flight up the wind toward the grey, desolate east. A squall, marked by dingy clouds and clouds brick-red like smoke from a burning building, appeared from the south-east.

"What do you think of those life-saving people? Ain't they peaches?"

"Funny they haven't seen us."

"Maybe they think we're out here for sport! Maybe they think we're fishin'. Maybe they think we're damned fools."

It was a long afternoon. A changed tide tried to force them southward, but wind and wave said northward. Far ahead, where coast-line, sea, and sky formed their mighty angle, there were little dots which seemed to indicate a city on the shore.

"St. Augustine?"

The captain shook his head. "Too near Mosquito Inlet."

And the oiler rowed, and then the correspondent rowed; then the oiler rowed. It was a weary business. The human back can become the seat of more aches and pains than are registered in books for the composite anatomy of a regiment. It is a limited area, but it can become the theatre of innumerable muscular conflicts, tangles, wrenches, knots, and other comforts.

"Did you ever like to row, Billie?" asked the correspondent.

"No," said the oiler; "hang it!"

When one exchanged the rowing-seat for a place in the bottom of the boat, he suffered a bodily depression that caused him to be careless of everything save an obligation to wiggle one finger. There was cold sea-water swashing to and fro in the boat, and he lay in it. His head, pillowed on a thwart, was within an inch of the swirl of a wave-crest, and sometimes a particularly obstreperous sea came inboard and drenched him once more. But these matters did not annoy him. It is almost certain that if the boat had capsized he would have tumbled comfortably out upon the ocean as if he felt sure that it was a great soft mattress.

"Look! There's a man on the shore!"

"Where?"

"There! See 'im? See 'im?"

"Yes, sure! He's walking along."

"Now he's stopped. Look! He's facing us!"

"He's waving at us!"

"So he is! By thunder!"

"Ah, now we're all right! Now we're all right! There'll be a boat out here for us in half an hour."

"He's going on. He's running. He's going up to that house there."

The remote beach seemed lower than the sea, and it required a searching glance to discern the little black figure. The captain saw a floating stick, and they rowed to it. A bath towel was by some weird chance in the boat, and, tying this on the stick, the captain waved it. The oarsman did not dare turn his head, so he was obliged to ask questions.

"What's he doing now?"

"He's standing still again. He's looking, I think.—There he goes again—toward the house.—Now he's stopped again."

"Is he waving at us?"

"No, not now; he was, though."

"Look! There comes another man!"

"He's running."

"Look at him go, would you!"

"Why, he's on a bicycle. Now he's met the other man. They're both waving at us. Look!"

"There comes something up the beach."

"What the devil is that thing?"

"Why, it looks like a boat."

"Why, certainly, it's a boat."

"No; it's on wheels."

"Yes, so it is. Well, that must be the life-boat. They drag them along shore on a wagon."

"That's the life-boat, sure."

"No, by God, it's—it's an omnibus."

"I tell you it's a life-boat."

"It is not! It's an omnibus. I can see it plain. See? One of these big hotel omnibuses."

"By thunder, you're right. It's an omnibus, sure as fate. What do you suppose they are doing with an omnibus? Maybe they are going around collecting the life-crew, hey?"

"That's it, likely. Look! There's a fellow waving a little black flag. He's standing on the steps of the omnibus. There come those other two fellows. Now they're all talking together. Look at the fellow with the flag. Maybe he ain't waving it!"

"That ain't a flag, is it? That's his coat. Why, certainly, that's his coat."

"So it is; it's his coat. He's taken it off and is waving it around his head. But would you look at him swing it!"

"Oh, say, there isn't any life-saving station there. That's just a winter-resort hotel omnibus that has brought over some of the boarders to see us drown."

"What's that idiot with the coat mean? What's he signalling, anyhow?"

"It looks as if he were trying to tell us to go north. There must be a life-saving station up there."

"No; he thinks we're fishing. Just giving us a merry hand. See? Ah, there, Willie!"

"Well, I wish I could make something out of those signals. What do you suppose he means?"

"He don't mean anything; he's just playing."

"Well, if he'd just signal us to try the surf again, or to go to sea and wait, or go north, or go south, or go to hell, there would be some reason in it. But look at him! He just stands there and keeps his coat revolving like a wheel. The ass!"

"There come more people."

"Now there's quite a mob. Look! Isn't that a boat?"

"Where? Oh, I see where you mean. No, that's no boat."

"That fellow is still waving his coat."

"He must think we like to see him do that. Why don't he quit it? It don't mean anything."

"I don't know. I think he is trying to make us go north. It must be that there's a life-saving station there somewhere."

"Say, he ain't tired yet. Look at 'im wave!"

"Wonder how long he can keep that up. He's been revolving his coat ever since he caught sight of us. He's an idiot. Why aren't they getting men to bring a boat out? A fishing-boat—one of those big yawls—could come out here all right. Why don't he do something?"

"Oh, it's all right now."

"They'll have a boat out here for us in less than no time, now that they've seen us."

A faint yellow tone came into the sky over the low land. The shadows on the sea slowly deepened. The wind bore coldness with it, and the men began to shiver.

"Holy smoke!" said one, allowing his voice to express his impious mood, "if we keep on monkeying out here! If we've got to flounder out here all night!"

"Oh, we'll never have to stay here all night! Don't you worry. They've seen us now, and it won't be long before they'll come chasing out after us."

The shore grew dusky. The man waving a coat blended gradually into this gloom, and it swallowed in the same manner the omnibus and the group of people. The spray, when it dashed uproariously over the side, made the voyagers shrink and swear like men who were being branded.

"I'd like to catch the chump who waved the coat. I feel like socking him one, just for luck."

"Why? What did he do?"

"Oh, nothing, but then he seemed so damned cheerful."

In the meantime the oiler rowed, and then the correspondent rowed, and then the oiler rowed. Grey-faced and bowed forward, they mechanically, turn by turn, plied the leaden oars. The form of the lighthouse had vanished from the southern horizon, but finally a pale star appeared, just lifting from the sea. The streaked saffron in the west passed before the all-merging darkness, and the sea to the east was black. The land had vanished, and was expressed only by the low and drear thunder of the surf.

"If I am going to be drowned—if I am going to be drowned—if I am going to be drowned, why, in the name of the seven mad gods who rule the sea, was I allowed to come thus far and contemplate sand and trees? Was I brought here merely to have my nose dragged away as I was about to nibble the sacred cheese of life?"

The patient captain, drooped over the water-jar, was sometimes obliged to speak to the oarsman.

"Keep her head up! Keep her head up!"

"Keep her head up, sir." The voices were weary and low.

This was surely a quiet evening. All save the oarsman lay heavily and listlessly in the boat's bottom. As for him, his eyes were just capable of noting the tall black waves that swept forward in a most sinister silence, save for an occasional subdued growl of a crest.

The cook's head was on a thwart, and he looked without interest at the water under his nose. He was deep in other scenes. Finally he spoke. "Billie," he murmured, dreamfully, "what kind of pie do you like best?"

V

"Pie!" said the oiler and the correspondent, agitatedly. "Don't talk about those things, blast you!"

"Well," said the cook, "I was just thinking about ham sandwiches and—"

A night on the sea in an open boat is a long night. As darkness settled finally, the shine of the light, lifting from the sea in the south, changed to full gold. On the northern horizon a new light appeared, a small bluish gleam on the edge of the waters. These two lights were the furniture of the world. Otherwise there was nothing but waves.

Two men huddled in the stern, and distances were so magnificent in the dinghy that the rower was enabled to keep his feet partly warm by thrusting them under his companions. Their legs indeed extended far under the rowing-seat until they touched the feet of the captain forward. Sometimes, despite the efforts of the tired oarsman, a wave came piling into the boat, an icy wave of the night, and the chilling water soaked them anew. They would twist their bodies for a moment and groan, and sleep the dead sleep once more, while the water in the boat gurgled about them as the craft rocked.

The plan of the oiler and the correspondent was for one to row until he lost the ability, and then arouse the other from his sea-water couch in the bottom of the boat.

The oiler plied the oars until his head drooped forward and the overpowering sleep blinded him; and he rowed yet afterward. Then he touched a man in the bottom of the boat, and called his name. "Will you spell me for a little while?" he said, meekly.

"Sure, Billie," said the correspondent, awaking and dragging himself to a sitting position. They exchanged places carefully, and the oiler, cuddling down in the sea-water at the cook's side, seemed to go to sleep instantly.

The particular violence of the sea had ceased. The waves came without snarling. The obligation of the man at the oars was to keep the boat headed so that the tilt of the rollers would not capsize her, and to preserve her from filling when the crests rushed past. The black waves were silent and hard to be seen in the darkness. Often one was almost upon the boat before the oarsman was aware.

In a low voice the correspondent addressed the captain. He was not sure that the captain was awake, although this iron man seemed to be always awake. "Captain, shall I keep her making for that light north, sir?"

The same steady voice answered him. "Yes. Keep it about two points off the port bow."

The cook had tied a life-belt around himself in order to get even the warmth which this clumsy cork contrivance could donate, and he seemed almost stove-like when a rower, whose teeth invariably chattered wildly as soon as he ceased his labour, dropped down to sleep.

The correspondent, as he rowed, looked down at the two men sleeping underfoot. The cook's arm was around the oiler's shoulders, and, with their fragmentary clothing and haggard faces, they were the babes of the sea—a grotesque rendering of the old babes in the wood.

Later he must have grown stupid at his work, for suddenly there was a growling of water, and a crest came with a roar and a swash into the boat, and it was a wonder that it did not set the cook afloat in his life-belt. The cook continued to sleep, but the oiler sat up, blinking his eyes and shaking with the new cold.

"Oh, I'm awful sorry, Billie," said the correspondent, contritely.

"That's all right, old boy," said the oiler, and lay down again and was asleep.

Presently it seemed that even the captain dozed, and the correspondent thought that he was the one man afloat on all the oceans. The wind had a voice as it came over the waves, and it was sadder than the end.

There was a long, loud swishing astern of the boat, and a gleaming trail of phosphorescence, like blue flame, was furrowed on the black waters. It might have been made by a monstrous knife.

Then there came a stillness, while the correspondent breathed with open mouth and looked at the sea.

Suddenly there was another swish and another long flash of bluish light, and this time it was alongside the boat, and might almost been reached with an oar. The correspondent saw an enormous fin speed like a shadow through the water, hurling the crystalline spray and leaving the long glowing trail.

The correspondent looked over his shoulder at the captain. His face was hidden, and he seemed to be asleep. He looked at the babes of the sea. They certainly were asleep. So, being bereft of sympathy, he leaned a little way to one side and swore softly into the sea.

But the thing did not then leave the vicinity of the boat. Ahead or astern, on one side or the other, at intervals long or short, fled the long sparkling streak, and there was to be heard the *whirroo* of the dark fin. The speed and power of the thing was greatly to be admired. It cut the water like a gigantic and keen projectile.

The presence of this biding thing did not affect the man with the same horror that it would if he had been a picnicker. He simply looked at the sea dully and swore in an undertone.

Nevertheless, it is true that he did not wish to be alone with the thing. He wished one of his companions to awake by chance and keep him company with it. But the captain hung motionless over the water-jar, and the oiler and the cook in the bottom of the boat were plunged in slumber.

VI

"If I am going to be drowned—if I am going to be drowned—if I am going to be drowned, why, in the name of the seven mad gods who rule the sea, was I allowed to come thus far and contemplate sand and trees?"

During this dismal night, it may be remarked that a man would conclude that it was really the intention of the seven mad gods to drown him, despite the abominable injustice of it. For it was certainly an abominable injustice to drown a man who had worked so hard, so hard. The man felt it would be a crime most unnatural. Other people had drowned at sea since galleys swarmed with painted sails, but still—

When it occurs to a man that nature does not regard him as important, and that she feels she would not maim the universe by disposing of him, he at first wishes to throw bricks at the temple, and he hates deeply the fact that there are no bricks and no temples. Any visible expression of nature would surely be pelleted with his jeers.

Then, if there be no tangible thing to hoot, he feels, perhaps, the desire to confront a personification and indulge in pleas, bowed to one knee, and with hands supplicant, saying, "Yes, but I love myself."

A high cold star on a winter's night is the word he feels that she says to him. Thereafter he knows the pathos of his situation.

The men in the dinghy had not discussed these matters, but each had, no doubt, reflected upon them in silence and according to his mind. There was seldom any expression upon their faces save the general one of complete weariness. Speech was devoted to the business of the boat.

To chime the notes of his emotion, a verse mysteriously entered the correspondent's head. He had even forgotten that he had forgotten this verse, but it suddenly was in mind.

A soldier of the Legion lay dying in Algiers;
There was lack of woman's nursing, there was dearth of woman's tears;
But a comrade stood beside him, and he took that comrade's hand,
And he said, "I never more shall see my own, my native land."

In his childhood the correspondent had been made acquainted with the fact that a soldier of the Legion lay dying in Algiers, but he had never regarded the fact as important. Myriads of his school-fellows had informed him of the soldier's plight, but the dinning had naturally ended by making him perfectly indifferent. He had never considered it his affair that a soldier of the Legion lay dying in Algiers, nor had it appeared to him as a matter for sorrow. It was less to him than the breaking of a pencil's point.

Now, however, it quaintly came to him as a human, living thing. It was no longer merely a picture of a few throes in the breast of a poet, meanwhile drinking tea and warming his feet at the grate; it was an actuality—stern, mournful, and fine.

The correspondent plainly saw the soldier. He lay on the sand with his feet out straight and still. While his pale left hand was upon his chest in an attempt to thwart the going of his life, the blood came between his fingers. In the far Algerian distance, a city of low square forms was set against a sky that was faint with the last sunset hues. The correspondent, plying the oars and dreaming of the slow and slower movements of the lips of the soldier, was moved by a profound and perfectly impersonal comprehension. He was sorry for the soldier of the Legion who lay dying in Algiers.

The thing which had followed the boat and waited had evidently grown bored at the delay. There was no longer to be heard the slash of the cutwater, and there was no longer the flame of the long trail. The light in the north still glimmered, but it was apparently no nearer to the boat. Sometimes the boom of the surf rang in the correspondent's ears, and he turned the craft seaward then and rowed harder.

Southward, some one had evidently built a watch-fire on the beach. It was too low and too far to be seen, but it made a shimmering, roseate reflection upon the bluff in back of it, and this could be discerned from the boat. The wind came stronger, and sometimes a wave suddenly raged out like a mountain cat, and there was to be seen the sheen and sparkle of a broken crest.

The captain, in the bow, moved on his water-jar and sat erect. "Pretty long night," he observed to the correspondent. He looked at the shore. "Those life-saving people take their time."

"Did you see that shark playing around?"

"Yes, I saw him. He was a big fellow, all right."

"Wish I had known you were awake."

Later the correspondent spoke into the bottom of the boat. "Billie!" There was a slow and gradual disentanglement. "Billie, will you spell me?"

"Sure," said the oiler.

As soon as the correspondent touched the cold, comfortable sea-water in the bottom of the boat and had huddled close to the cook's life-belt he was deep in sleep, despite the fact that his teeth played all the popular airs. This sleep was so good to him that it was but a moment before he heard a voice call his name in a tone that demonstrated the last stages of exhaustion. "Will you spell me?"

"Sure, Billie."

The light in the north had mysteriously vanished, but the correspondent took his course from the wide-awake captain.

Later in the night they took the boat farther out to sea, and the captain directed the cook to take one oar at the stern and keep the boat facing the seas. He was to call out if he should hear the thunder of the surf. This plan enabled the oiler and the correspondent to get respite together. "We'll give those boys a chance to get into shape again," said the captain. They curled down and, after a few preliminary chatterings and trembles, slept once more the dead sleep. Neither knew they had bequeathed to the cook the company of another shark, or perhaps the same shark.

As the boat caroused on the waves, spray occasionally bumped over the side and gave them a fresh soaking, but this had no power to break their repose. The ominous slash of the wind and the water affected them as it would have affected mummies.

"Boys," said the cook, with the notes of every reluctance in his voice, "she's drifted in pretty close. I guess one of you had better take her to sea again." The correspondent, aroused, heard the crash of the toppled crests.

As he was rowing, the captain gave him some whisky-and-water, and this steadied the chills out of him. "If I ever get ashore and anybody shows me even a photograph of an oar—"

At last there was a short conversation.

"Billie!—Billie, will you spell me?"

"Sure," said the oiler.

VII

When the correspondent again opened his eyes, the sea and the sky were each of the grey hue of the dawning. Later, carmine and gold was painted upon the waters. The morning appeared finally, in its splendour, with a sky of pure blue, and the sunlight flamed on the tips of the waves.

On the distant dunes were set many little black cottages, and a tall white windmill reared above them. No man, nor dog, nor bicycle appeared on the beach. The cottages might have formed a deserted village.

The voyagers scanned the shore. A conference was held in the boat. "Well," said the captain, "if no help is coming, we might better try a run through the surf right away. If we stay out here much longer we will be too weak to do anything for ourselves at all." The others silently acquiesced in this reasoning. The boat was headed for the beach. The correspondent wondered if none ever ascended the tall wind-tower, and if then they never looked seaward. This tower was a giant, standing with its back to the plight of the ants. It represented in a degree, to the correspondent, the serenity of nature amid the struggles of the individual—nature in the wind, and nature in the vision of men. She did not seem cruel to him then, nor beneficent, nor treacherous, nor wise. But she was indifferent, flatly indifferent. It is, perhaps, plausible that a man in this situation, impressed with the unconcern of the universe, should see the innumerable flaws of his life, and have them taste wickedly in his mind, and wish for another chance. A distinction between right and wrong seems absurdly clear to him, then, in this new ignorance of the grave-edge, and he understands that if he were given another opportunity he would mend his conduct and his words, and be better and brighter during an introduction or at a tea.

"Now, boys," said the captain, "she is going to swamp sure. All we can do is to work her in as far as possible, and then when she swamps, pile out and scramble for the beach. Keep cool now, and don't jump until she swamps sure."

The oiler took the oars. Over his shoulders he scanned the surf. "Captain," he said, "I think I'd better bring her about and keep her head-on to the seas and back her in."

"All right, Billie," said the captain. "Back her in." The oiler swung the boat then, and, seated in the stern, the cook and the correspondent were obliged to look over their shoulders to contemplate the lonely and indifferent shore.

The monstrous inshore rollers heaved the boat high until the men were again enabled to see the white sheets of water scudding up the slanted beach. "We won't get in very close," said the captain. Each time a man could wrest his attention from the rollers, he turned his glance toward the shore, and in the expression of the eyes during this contemplation there was a singular quality. The correspondent, observing the others, knew that they were not afraid, but the full meaning of their glances was shrouded.

As for himself, he was too tired to grapple fundamentally with the fact. He tried to coerce his mind into thinking of it, but the mind was dominated at this time by the muscles, and the muscles said they did not care. It merely occurred to him that if he should drown it would be a shame.

There were no hurried words, no pallor, no plain agitation. The men simply looked at the shore. "Now, remember to get well clear of the boat when you jump," said the captain.

Seaward the crest of a roller suddenly fell with a thunderous crash, and the long white comber came roaring down upon the boat.

"Steady now," said the captain. The men were silent. They turned their eyes from the shore to the comber and waited. The boat slid up the incline, leaped at the furious top, bounced over it, and swung down the long back of the wave. Some water had been shipped, and the cook bailed it out.

But the next crest crashed also. The tumbling, boiling flood of white water caught the boat and whirled it almost perpendicular. Water swarmed in from all sides. The correspondent had his hands on the gunwale at this time, and when the water entered at that place he swiftly withdrew his fingers, as if he objected to wetting them.

The little boat, drunken with this weight of water, reeled and snuggled deeper into the sea.

"Bail her out, cook! Bail her out!" said the captain.

"All right, Captain," said the cook.

"Now, boys, the next one will do for us sure," said the oiler. "Mind to jump clear of the boat."

The third wave moved forward, huge, furious, implacable. It fairly swallowed the dinghy, and almost simultaneously the men tumbled into the sea. A piece of life-belt had lain in the bottom of the boat, and as the correspondent went overboard he held this to his chest with his left hand.

The January water was icy, and he reflected immediately that it was colder than he had expected to find it off the coast of Florida. This appeared to his dazed mind as a fact important enough to be noted at the time. The coldness of the water was sad; it was tragic. This fact was somehow mixed and confused with his opinion of his own situation, so that it seemed almost a proper reason for tears. The water was cold.

When he came to the surface he was conscious of little but the noisy water. Afterward he saw his companions in the sea. The oiler was ahead in the race. He was swimming strongly and rapidly. Off to the correspondent's left, the cook's great white and corked back bulged out of the water; and in the rear the captain was hanging with his one good hand to the keel of the overturned dinghy.

There is a certain immovable quality to a shore, and the correspondent wondered at it amid the confusion of the sea.

It seemed also very attractive; but the correspondent knew that it was a long journey, and he paddled leisurely. The piece of life-preserver lay under him, and sometimes he whirled down the incline of a wave as if he were on a hand-sled.

But finally he arrived at a place in the sea where travel was beset with difficulty. He did not pause swimming to inquire what manner of current had caught him, but there his progress ceased. The shore was set before him like a bit of scenery on a stage, and he looked at it and understood with his eyes each detail of it.

As the cook passed, much farther to the left, the captain was calling to him, "Turn over on your back, cook! Turn over on your back and use the oar."

"All right, sir." The cook turned on his back, and, paddling with an oar, went ahead as if he were a canoe.

Presently the boat also passed to the left of the correspondent, with the captain clinging with one hand to the keel. He would have appeared like a man raising himself to look over a board fence if it were not for the extraordinary gymnastics of the boat. The correspondent marvelled that the captain could still hold to it.

They passed on nearer to shore—the oiler, the cook, the captain—and following them went the water-jar, bouncing gaily over the seas.

The correspondent remained in the grip of this strange new enemy—a current. The shore, with its white slope of sand and its green bluff topped with little silent cottages, was spread like a picture before him. It was very near to him then, but he was impressed as one who, in a gallery, looks at a scene from Brittany or Holland.

He thought: "I am going to drown? Can it be possible? Can it be possible? Can it be possible?" Perhaps an individual must consider his own death to be the final phenomenon of nature.

But later a wave perhaps whirled him out of this small deadly current, for he found suddenly that he could again make progress toward the shore. Later still he was aware that the captain, clinging with one hand to the keel of the dinghy, had his face turned away from the shore and toward him, and was calling his name. "Come to the boat! Come to the boat!"

In his struggle to reach the captain and the boat, he reflected that when one gets properly wearied drowning must really be a comfortable arrangement—a cessation of hostilities accompanied by a large degree of relief; and he was glad of it, for the main thing in his mind for some moments had been horror of the temporary agony. He did not wish to be hurt.

Presently he saw a man running along the shore. He was undressing with most remarkable speed. Coat, trousers, shirt, everything flew magically off him.

"Come to the boat!" called the captain.

"All right, Captain." As the correspondent paddled, he saw the captain let himself down to bottom and leave the boat. Then the correspondent performed his one little marvel of the voyage. A large wave caught him and flung him with ease and supreme speed completely over the boat and far beyond it. It struck him even then as an event in gymnastics and a true miracle of the sea. An overturned boat in the surf is not a plaything to a swimming man.

The correspondent arrived in water that reached only to his waist, but his condition did not enable him to stand for more than a moment. Each wave knocked him into a heap, and the undertow pulled at him.

Then he saw the man who had been running and undressing, and undressing and running, come bounding into the water. He dragged ashore the cook, and then waded toward the captain; but the captain waved him away and sent him to the correspondent. He was naked—naked as a tree in winter; but a halo was about his head, and he shone like a saint. He gave a strong pull, and a long drag, and a bully heave at the correspondent's hand. The correspondent, schooled in the minor formulae, said, "Thanks, old man." But suddenly the man cried, "What's that?" He pointed a swift finger. The correspondent said, "Go."

In the shallows, face downward, lay the oiler. His forehead touched sand that was periodically, between each wave, clear of the sea.

The correspondent did not know all that transpired afterward. When he achieved safe ground he fell, striking the sand with each particular part of his body. It was as if he had dropped from a roof, but the thud was grateful to him.

It seemed that instantly the beach was populated with men with blankets, clothes, and flasks, and women with coffee-pots and all the remedies sacred to their minds. The welcome of the land to the men from the sea was warm and generous; but a still and dripping shape was carried slowly up the beach, and the land's welcome for it could only be the different and sinister hospitality of the grave.

When it came night, the white waves paced to and fro in the moonlight, and the wind brought the sound of the great sea's voice to the men on the shore, and they felt that they could then be interpreters.

DISCUSSION QUESTIONS

1. How does the fictionalized tale "The Open Boat" differ from the newspaper report of the same event in "Stephen Crane's Own Story"? Have any incidents been changed or added? Has anything been distorted? Explain how Crane's role as a participant and writer changes as he turns from journalism to fiction.

2. How do Crane's tone and imagery change as he imagines a different form and audience for his writing? Point to specific examples.

Jack London / To Build a Fire 1908

One of America's most prolific and popular authors, Jack London was born in San Francisco in 1876. By the age of fourteen he had dropped out of school to take on risky jobs and hang around the Oakland saloons. His adventures did not interfere with his love of reading and thirst for knowledge, however, and for a time London studied at the University of California, Berkeley. In 1897, London joined the Klondike gold rush and lived for nearly a year on the Alaskan frontier. He found no gold but instead found the subjects for many stories and novels. His first collection of short stories, The Son of the Wolf, *appeared in 1900, and three years later London published his best-selling novel,* The Call of the Wild. *Over the next several years London wrote some of his most important novels—*The Sea Wolf *(1904),* White Fang *(1906), and the autobiographical* Martin Eden *(1909). London, who ran unsuccessfully in two Oakland mayoral elections as a Socialist, also wrote much social criticism. He died of an overdose of morphine in 1916.*

For more information on London, see "Magazines."

Day had broken cold and gray, exceedingly cold and gray, when the man turned aside from the main Yukon trail and climbed the high earth-bank, where a dim and little-travelled trail led eastward through the fat spruce timberland. It was a steep bank, and he paused for breath at the top, excusing the act to himself by looking at his watch. It was nine o'clock. There was no sun nor hint of sun, though there was not a cloud in the sky. It was a clear day, and yet there seemed an intangible pall over the face of things, a subtle gloom that made the day dark, and that was due to the absence of sun. This fact did not worry the man. He was used to the lack of sun. It had been days since he had seen the sun, and he knew that a few more days must pass before that cheerful orb, due south, would just peep above the sky line and dip immediately from view.

The man flung a look back along the way he had come. The Yukon lay a mile wide and hidden under three feet of ice. On top of this ice were as many feet of snow. It was all pure white, rolling in gentle undulations where the ice jams of the freeze-up had formed. North and south, as far as the eye could see, it was unbroken white, save for a dark hairline that curved and twisted from around the spruce-covered island to the south, and that curved and twisted away into the north, where it disappeared behind another spruce-covered island. This dark hairline was the trail—the main trail—that led south five hundred miles to the Chilcoot Pass, Dyea, and salt water; and that led north seventy miles to Dawson, and still on to the north a thousand miles to Nulato, and finally to St. Michael, on Bering Sea, a thousand miles and half a thousand more.

But all this—the mysterious, far-reaching hairline trail, the absence of sun from the sky, the tremendous cold, and the strangeness and weirdness of it all—made no impression on the man. It was not because he was long used to it. He was a newcomer in the land, a *chechaquo,* and this was his first winter. The trouble with him was that he was without imagination. He was quick and alert in the things of life, but only in the things, and not in the significances. Fifty degrees below zero meant eighty-odd degrees of frost. Such fact impressed him as being cold and uncomfortable, and that was all. It did not lead him to meditate upon his frailty as a creature of temperature, and upon man's frailty in general, able only to live within certain narrow limits of heat and cold; and from there on it did not lead him to the conjectural field of immortality and man's place in the universe. Fifty degrees below zero stood for a bite of frost that hurt and that must be guarded against by the use of mittens, ear flaps, warm moccasins, and thick socks. Fifty degrees below zero was to him just precisely fifty degrees below zero. That there should be anything more to it than that was a thought that never entered his head.

As he turned to go on, he spat speculatively. There was a sharp, explosive crackle that startled him. He spat again. And again, in the air, before it could fall to the snow, the spittle crackled. He knew that at fifty below spittle crackled on the snow, but this spittle had crackled in the air. Undoubtedly it was colder than fifty below—how much colder he did not know. But the temperature did not matter. He was bound for the old claim on the left fork of Henderson Creek, where the boys were already. They had come over across the divide from the Indian Creek country, while he had come the roundabout way to take a look at the possibilities of getting out logs in the spring from the islands in the Yukon. He would be in to camp by six o'clock; a bit after dark, it was true, but the boys would be there, a fire would be going, and a hot supper would be ready. As for lunch, he pressed his hand against the protruding bundle under his jacket. It was also under his shirt, wrapped up in a handkerchief and lying against the naked skin. It was the only way to keep the biscuits from freezing. He smiled agreeably to himself as he thought of those biscuits, each cut open and sopped in bacon grease, and each enclosing a generous slice of fried bacon.

He plunged in among the big spruce trees. The trail was faint. A foot of snow had fallen since the last sled had passed over, and he was glad he was without a sled, travelling light. In fact, he carried nothing but the lunch wrapped in the handkerchief. He was surprised, however, at the cold. It certainly was cold, he concluded, as he rubbed his numb nose and cheekbones with his mittened hand. He was a warm-whiskered man, but the hair on his face did not protect the high cheekbones and the eager nose that thrust itself aggressively into the frosty air.

At the man's heels trotted a dog, a big native husky, the proper wolf dog, gray-coated and without any visible or temperamental difference from its brother, the wild wolf. The animal was depressed by the tremendous cold. It knew that it was no time for travelling. Its instinct told it a truer tale than was told to the man by the man's judgment. In reality, it was not merely colder than fifty below zero; it was colder than sixty below, than seventy below. It was seventy-five below zero. Since the freezing point is thirty-two above zero, it meant that one hundred and seven degrees of frost obtained. The dog did not know anything about thermometers. Possibly in its brain there was no sharp consciousness of a condition of very cold such as was in the man's brain. But the brute had its instinct. It experienced a vague but menacing apprehension that subdued it and made it slink along at the man's heels, and that made it question eagerly every unwonted movement of the man as if expecting him to go into camp or to seek shelter somewhere and build a fire. The dog had learned fire, and it wanted fire, or else to burrow under the snow and cuddle its warmth away from the air.

The frozen moisture of its breathing had settled on its fur in a fine powder of frost, and especially were its jowls, muzzle, and eyelashes whitened by its crystalled breath. The man's red beard and mustache were likewise frosted, but more solidly, the deposit taking the form of ice and increasing with every warm, moist breath he exhaled. Also, the man was chewing tobacco, and the muzzle of ice held his lips so rigidly that he was unable to clear his chin when he expelled the juice. The result was that a crystal beard of the color and solidity of amber was increasing its length on his chin. If he fell down it would shatter itself, like glass, into brittle fragments. But he did not mind the appendage. It was the penalty all tobacco chewers paid in that country, and he had been out before in two cold snaps. They had not been so cold as this, he knew, but by the spirit thermometer at Sixty Mile he knew they had been registered at fifty below and at fifty-five.

He held on through the level stretch of woods for several miles, crossed a wide flat of nigger heads, and dropped down a bank to the frozen bed of a small stream. This was Henderson Creek, and he knew he was ten miles from the forks. He looked at his watch. It was ten o'clock. He was making four miles an hour, and he calculated that he would arrive at the forks at half-past twelve. He decided to celebrate that event by eating his lunch there.

The dog dropped in again at his heels, with a tail drooping discouragement, as the man swung along the creek bed. The furrow of the old sled trail was plainly visible, but a dozen inches of snow covered the marks of the last runners. In a month no man had come up or down that silent creek. The man held steadily on. He was not much given to thinking, and just then particularly he had nothing to think about save that he would eat lunch at the forks and that at six o'clock he would be in camp with the boys. There was nobody to talk to; and, had there been, speech would have been impossible because of the ice muzzle on his mouth. So he continued monotonously to chew tobacco and to increase the length of his amber beard.

Once in a while the thought reinterated itself that it was very cold and that he had never experienced such cold. As he walked along he rubbed his cheekbones and nose with the back of his mittened hand. He did this automatically, now and again changing hands. But, rub as he would, the instant he stopped his cheekbones went numb, and the following instant the end of his nose went numb. He was sure to frost his cheeks; he knew that, and experienced a pang of regret that he had not devised a nose strap of the sort Bud wore in cold snaps. Such a strap passed across the cheeks, as well, and saved them. But it didn't matter much, after all. What were frosted cheeks? A bit painful, that was all; they were never serious.

Empty as the man's mind was of thoughts, he was keenly observant, and he noticed the changes in the creek, the curves and bends and timber jams, and always he sharply noted where he placed his feet. Once, coming around a bend, he shied abruptly, like a startled horse, curved away from the place where he had been walking, and retreated several paces back along the trail. The creek he knew was frozen clear to the bottom—no creek could contain water in that arctic winter—but he knew also that there were springs that bubbled out from the hillsides and ran along under the snow and on top the ice of the creek. He knew that the coldest snaps never froze these springs, and he knew likewise their danger. They were traps. They hid pools of water under the snow that might be three inches deep, or three feet. Sometimes a skin of ice half an inch thick covered them, and in turn was covered by the snow. Sometimes there were alternate layers of water and ice skin, so that when one broke through he kept on breaking through for a while, sometimes wetting himself to the waist.

That was why he had shied in such panic. He had felt the give under his feet and heard the crackle of a snow-hidden ice skin. And to get his feet wet in such a temperature meant trouble and danger. At the very least it meant delay, for he would be forced to stop and build a fire, and under its protection to bare his feet while he dried his socks and moccasins. He stood and studied the creek bed and its banks, and decided that the flow of water came from the right. He reflected awhile, rubbing his nose and cheeks, then skirted to the left, stepping gingerly and testing the footing for each step. Once clear of the danger, he took a fresh chew of tobacco and swung along at his four-mile gait.

In the course of the next two hours he came upon several similar traps. Usually the snow above the hidden pools had a sunken, candied appearance that advertised the danger. Once again, however, he had a close call; and once, suspecting danger, he compelled the dog to go on in front. The dog did not want to go. It hung back until the man shoved it toward, and then it went quickly across the white, unbroken surface. Suddenly it broke through, floundered to one side, and got away to firmer footing. It had wet its forefeet and legs, and almost immediately the water that clung to it turned to ice. It made quick efforts to lick the ice off its legs, then dropped down in the snow and began to bite out the ice that had formed between the toes. This was matter of instinct. To permit the ice to remain would mean sore feet. It did not know this. It merely obeyed the mysterious prompting that arose from the deep crypts of its being. But the man knew, having achieved a judgment on the subject, and he removed the mitten from his right hand and helped tear out the ice particles. He did not expose his fingers more than a minute, and was astonished at the swift numbness that smote them. It certainly was cold. He pulled on the mitten hastily, and beat the hand savagely across the chest.

At twelve o'clock the day was at its brightest. Yet the sun was too far south on its winter journey to clear the horizon. The bulge of the earth intervened between it and Henderson Creek, where the man walked under a clear sky at noon and cast no shadow. At half-past twelve, to the minute, he arrived at the forks of the creek. He was pleased at the speed he had made. If he kept it up, he would certainly be with the boys by six. He unbuttoned his jacket and shirt and drew forth his lunch. The action consumed no more than a quarter of a minute, yet in that brief moment the numbness laid hold of the exposed fingers. He did not put the mitten on, but, instead, struck the fingers a dozen sharp smashes against his leg. Then he sat down on a snow-covered log to eat. The sting that followed upon the striking of his fingers against his leg ceased so quickly that he was startled. He had had no chance to take a bit of biscuit. He struck the fingers repeatedly and returned them to the mitten, baring the other hand for the purpose of eating. He tried to take a mouthful, but the ice muzzle prevented. He had forgotten to build a fire and thaw out. He chuckled at his foolishness, and as he chuckled he noted the numbness creeping into the exposed fingers. Also, he noted that the stinging which had first come to his toes when he sat down was already passing away. He wondered whether the toes were warm or numb. He moved them inside the moccasins and decided that they were numb.

He pulled the mitten on hurriedly and stood up. He was a bit frightened. He stamped up and down until the stinging returned into the feet. It certainly was cold, was his thought. That man from Sulphur Creek had spoken the truth when telling how cold it sometimes got in the country. And he had laughed at him at the time! That showed one must not be too sure of things. There was no mistake about it, it was cold. He strode up and down, stamping his feet and threshing his arms, until reassured by the returning warmth. Then he got out matches and proceeded to make a fire. From the undergrowth, where high water of the previous spring had lodged a supply of seasoned twigs, he got his firewood. Working carefully from a small beginning, he soon had a roaring fire, over which he thawed the ice from his face and in the protection of which he ate his biscuits. For the moment the cold of space was outwitted. The dog took satisfaction in the fire, stretching out close enough for warmth and far enough away to escape being singed.

When the man had finished, he filled his pipe and took his comfortable time over a smoke. Then he pulled on his mittens, settled the ear flaps of his cap firmly about his ears, and took the creek trail up the left fork. The dog was disappointed and yearned back toward the fire. This man did not know cold. Possibly all the generations of his ancestry had been ignorant of cold, of real cold, of cold one hundred and seven degrees below freezing point. But the dog knew; all its ancestry knew, and it had inherited the knowledge. And it knew that it was not good to walk abroad in such fearful cold. It was the time to lie snug in a hole in the snow and wait for a curtain of cloud to be drawn across the face of outer space whence this cold came. On the other hand, there was no keen intimacy between the dog and the man. The one was the toil slave of the other, and the only caresses it had ever received were the caresses of the whip lash and of harsh and menacing throat sounds that threatened the whip lash. So the dog made no effort to communicate its apprehension to the man. It was not concerned in the welfare of the man; it was for its own sake that it yearned back toward the fire. But the man whistled, and spoke to it with the sound of whip lashes, and the dog swung in at the man's heels and followed after.

The man took a chew of tobacco and proceeded to start a new amber beard. Also, his moist breath quickly powdered with white his mustache, eyebrows, and lashes. There did not seem to be so many springs on the left fork of the Henderson, and for half an hour the man saw no signs of any. And then it happened. At a place where there were no signs, where the soft, unbroken snow seemed to advertise solidity beneath, the man broke through. It was not deep. He wet himself halfway to the knees before he foundered out to the firm crust.

He was angry, and cursed his luck aloud. He had hoped to get into camp with the boys at six o'clock, and this would delay him an hour, for he would have to build a fire and dry out his footgear. This was imperative at that low temperature—he knew that much; and he turned aside to the bank, which he climbed. On top, tangled in the underbrush about the trunks of several small spruce trees, was a highwater deposit of dry firewood—sticks and twigs, principally, but also larger portions of seasoned branches and fine, dry, last year's grasses. He threw down several large pieces on top of the snow. This served for a foundation and prevented the young flame from drowning itself in the snow it otherwise would melt. The flame he got by touching a match to a small shred of birch bark that he took from his pocket. This burned even more readily than paper. Placing it on the foundation, he fed the young flame with wisps of dry grass and with the tiniest dry twigs.

He worked slowly and carefully, keenly aware of his danger. Gradually, as the flame grew stronger, he increased the size of the twigs with which he fed it. He squatted in the snow, pulling the twigs out from their entanglement in the brush and feeding directly to the flame. He knew there must be no failure. When it is seventy-five below zero, a man must not fail in his first attempt to build a fire—that is, if his feet are wet. If his feet are dry, and he fails, he can run along the trail for half a mile and restore his circulation. But the circulation of wet and freezing feet cannot be restored by running when it is seventy-five below. No matter how fast he runs, the wet feet will freeze the harder. All this the man knew. The old-timer on Sulphur Creek had told him about it the previous fall, and now he was appreciating the advice. Already all sensation had gone out of his feet. To build the fire he had been forced to remove his mittens, and the fingers had quickly gone numb. His pace of four miles an hour had kept his heart pumping blood to the surface of his body and to all the extremities. But the instant he stopped, the action of the pump eased down. The cold of space smote the unprotected tip of the planet, and he, being on that unprotected tip, received the full force of the blow. The blood of his body recoiled before it. The blood was alive, like the dog, and like the dog it wanted to hide away and cover itself up from the fearful cold. So long as he walked four miles an hour, he pumped that blood, willy-nilly, to the surface; but now it ebbed away and sank down into the recesses of his body. The extremities were the first to feel its absence. His wet feet froze the faster, and his exposed fingers numbed the faster, though they had not yet begun to freeze. Nose and cheeks were already freezing, while the skin of all his body chilled as it lost its blood.

But he was safe. Toes and nose and cheeks would be only touched by the frost, for the fire was beginning to burn with strength. He was feeding it with twigs the size of his finger. In another minute he would be able to feed it with branches the size of his wrist, and then he could remove his wet footgear, and, while it dried, he could keep his naked feet warm by the fire, rubbing them at first, of course, with snow. The fire was a success. He was safe. He remembered the advice of the old-timer on Sulphur Creek, and smiled. The old-timer had been very serious in laying down the law that no man must travel alone in the Klondike after fifty below. Well, here he was; he had had the accident, he was alone; and he had saved himself. Those old-timers were rather womanish, some of them, he thought. All a man had to do was to keep his head, and he was all right. Any man who was a man could travel alone. But it was surprising, the rapidity with which his cheeks and nose were freezing. And he had not thought his fingers could go lifeless in so short a time. Lifeless they were, for he could scarcely make them move together to grip a twig, and they seemed remote from his body and from him. When he touched a twig, he had to look and see whether or not he had hold of it. The wires were pretty well down between him and his finger ends.

All of which counted for little. There was the fire, snapping and crackling and promising life with every dancing flame. He started to untie his moccasins. They were coated with ice; the thick German socks were like sheaths of iron halfway to the knees; and the moccasin strings were like rods of steel all twisted and knotted as by some conflagration. For a moment he tugged with his numb fingers, then, realizing the folly of it, he drew his sheath knife.

But before he could cut the strings, it happened. It was his own fault or, rather, his mistake. He should not have built the fire under the spruce tree. He should have built it in the open. But it had been easier to pull the twigs from the brush and drop them directly on the fire. Now the tree under which he had done this carried a weight of snow on its boughs. No wind had blown for weeks, and each bough was fully freighted. Each time he had pulled a twig he had communicated a slight agitation to the tree—an imperceptible agitation, so far as he was concerned, but an agitation sufficient to bring about the disaster. High up in the tree one bough capsized its load of snow. This fell on the boughs beneath, capsizing them. This process continued, spreading out and involving the whole tree. It grew like an avalanche, and it descended without warning upon the man and the fire, and the fire was blotted out! Where it had burned was a mantle of fresh and disordered snow.

The man was shocked. It was as though he had just heard his own sentence of death. For a moment he sat and stared at the spot where the fire had been. Then he grew very calm. Perhaps the old-timer on Sulphur Creek was right. If he had only had a trail mate he would have been in no danger now. The trail mate could have built the fire. Well, it was up to him to build the fire over again, and this second time there must be no failure. Even if he succeeded, he would most likely lose some toes. His feet must be badly frozen by now, and there would be some time before the second fire was ready.

Such were his thoughts, but he did not sit and think them. He was busy all the time they were passing through his mind. He made a new foundation for a fire, this time in the open, where no treacherous tree could blot it out. Next he gathered dry grasses and tiny twigs from the highwater flotsam. He could not bring his fingers together to pull them out, but he was able to gather them by the handful. In this way he got many rotten twigs and bits of green moss that were undesirable, but it was the best he could do. He worked methodically, even collecting an armful of the larger branches to be used later when the fire gathered strength. And all the while the dog sat and watched him, a certain yearning wistfulness in its eyes, for it looked upon him as the fire provider, and the fire was slow in coming.

When all was ready, the man reached in his pocket for a second piece of birch bark. He knew the bark was there, and though he could not feel it with his fingers, he could hear its crisp rustling as he fumbled for it. Try as he would, he could not clutch hold of it. And all the time, in his consciousness, was the knowledge that each instant his feet were freezing. This thought tended to put him in a panic, but he fought against it and kept calm. He pulled on his mittens with his teeth, and threshed his arms back and forth, beating his hands with all his might against his sides. He did this sitting down, and he stood up to do it; and all the while the dog sat in the snow, its wolf brush of a tail curled around warmly over its forefeet, its sharp wolf ears pricked forward intently as it watched the man. And the man, as he beat and threshed with his arms and hands, felt a great surge of envy as he regarded the creature that was warm and secure in its natural covering.

After a time he was aware of the first faraway signals of sensation in his beaten fingers. The faint tingling grew stronger till it evolved into a stinging ache that was excruciating, but which the man hailed with satisfaction. He stripped the mitten from his right hand and fetched forth the birch bark. The exposed fingers were quickly going numb again. Next he brought out his bunch of sulphur matches. But the tremendous cold had already driven the life out of his fingers. In his effort to separate one match from the others, the whole bunch fell in the snow. He tried to pick it out of the snow, but failed. The dead fingers could neither touch nor clutch. He was very careful. He drove the thought of his freezing feet, and nose, and cheeks, out of his mind, devoting his whole soul to the matches. He watched, using the sense of vision in place of that of touch, and when he saw his fingers on each side the bunch, he closed them—that is, he willed to close them, for the wires were down, and the fingers did not obey. He pulled the mitten on the right hand, and beat it fiercely against his knee. Then, with both mittened hands, he scooped the bunch of matches, along with much snow, into his lap. Yet he was no better off.

After some manipulation he managed to get the bunch between the heels of his mittened hands. In this fashion he carried it to his mouth. The ice crackled and snapped when by a violent effort he opened his mouth. He drew the lower jaw in, curled the upper lip out of the way, and scraped the bunch with his upper teeth in order to separate a match. He succeeded in getting one, which he dropped on his lap. He was no better off. He could not pick it up. Then he devised a way. He picked it up in his teeth and scratched it on his leg. Twenty times he scratched before he succeeded in lighting it. As it flamed he held it with his teeth to the birch bark. But the burning brimstone went up his nostrils and into his lungs, causing him to cough spasmodically. The match fell into the snow and went out.

The old-timer on Sulphur Creek was right, he thought in the moment of controlled despair that ensued: after fifty below, a man should travel with a partner. He beat his hands, but failed in exciting any sensation. Suddenly he bared both hands, removing the mittens with his teeth. He caught the whole bunch between the heels of his hands. His arm muscles not being frozen enabled him to press the hand heels tightly against the matches. Then he scratched the bunch along his leg. It flared into flame, seventy sulphur matches at once! There was no wind to blow them out. He kept his head to one side to escape the strangling fumes, and held the blazing bunch to the birch bark. As he so held it, he became aware of sensation in his hand. His flesh was burning. He could smell it. Deep down below the surface he could feel it. The sensation developed into pain that grew acute. And still he endured it, holding the flame of the matches clumsily to the bark that would not light readily because his own burning hands were in the way, absorbing most of the flame.

At last, when he could endure no more, he jerked his hands apart. The blazing matches fell sizzling into the snow, but the birch bark was alight. He began laying dry grasses and the tiniest twigs on the flame. He could not pick and choose, for he had to lift the fuel between the heels of his hands. Small pieces of rotten wood and green moss clung to the twigs, and he bit them off as well as he could with his teeth. He cherished the flame carefully and awkwardly. It meant life, and it must not perish. The withdrawal of blood from the surface of his body now made him begin to shiver, and he grew more awkward. A large piece of green moss fell squarely on the little fire. He tried to poke it out with his fingers, but his shivering frame made him poke too far, and he disrupted the nucleus of the little fire, the burning grasses and tiny twigs separating and scattering. He tried to poke them together again, but in spite of the tenseness of the effort, his shivering got away with him, and the twigs were hopelessly scattered. Each twig gushed a puff of smoke and went out. The fire provider had failed. As he looked apathetically about him, his eyes chanced on the dog, sitting across the ruins of the fire from him, in the snow, making restless, hunching movements, slightly lifting one forefoot and then the other, shifting its weight back and forth on them with wistful eagerness.

The sight of the dog put a wild idea into his head. He remembered the tale of the man, caught in a blizzard, who killed a steer and crawled inside the carcass, and so was saved. He would kill the dog and bury his hands in the warm body until the numbness went out of them. Then he could build another fire. He spoke to the dog, calling it to him; but in his voice was a strange note of fear that frightened the animal, who had never known the man to speak in such way before. Something was the matter, and its suspicious nature sensed danger—it knew not what danger, but somewhere, somehow, in its brain arose an apprehension of the man. It flattened its ears down at the sound of the man's voice, and its restless, hunching movements and the liftings and shiftings of its forefeet became more pronounced; but it would not come to the man. He got on his hands and knees and crawled toward the dog. This unusual posture again excited suspicion, and the animal sidled mincingly away.

The man sat up in the snow for a moment and struggled for calmness. Then he pulled on is mittens, by means of his teeth, and got upon his feet. He glanced down at first in order to assure himself that he was really standing up, for the absence of sensation in his feet left him unrelated to the earth. His erect position in itself started to drive the webs of suspicion from the dog's mind; and when he spoke peremptorily, with the sound of whip lashes in his voice, the dog rendered its customary allegiance and came to him. As it came within reaching distance, the man lost his control. His arms flashed out to the dog, and he experienced genuine surprise when he discovered that his hands could not clutch, that there was neither bend nor feeling in the fingers. He had forgotten for the moment that they were frozen and that they were freezing more and more. All this happened quickly, and before the animal could get away, he encircled its body with his arms. He sat down in the snow, and in this fashion held the dog, while it snarled and whined and struggled.

But it was all he could do, hold its body encircled in his arms and sit there. He realized that he could not kill the dog. There was no way to do it. With his helpless hands he could neither draw nor hold his sheath knife nor throttle the animal. He released it, and it plunged wildly away, with tail between its legs, and still snarling. It halted forty feet away and surveyed him curiously, with ears sharply pricked forward.

The man looked down at his hands in order to locate them, and found them hanging on the ends of his arms. It struck him as curious that one should have to use his eyes in order to find out where his hands were. He began threshing his arms back and forth, beating the mittened hands against his sides. He did this for five minutes, violently, and his heart pumped enough blood up to the surface to put a stop to his shivering. But no sensation was aroused in the hands. He had an impression that they hung like weights on the ends of his arms, but when he tried to run the impression down, he could not find it.

A certain fear of death, dull and oppressive, came to him. This fear quickly became poignant as he realized that it was no longer a mere matter of freezing his fingers and toes, or of losing his hands and feet, but that it was a matter of life and death with the chances against him. This threw him into a panic, and he turned and ran up the creek bed along the old, dim trail. The dog joined in behind and kept up with him. He ran blindly, without intention, in fear such as he had never known in his life. Slowly as he plowed and floundered through the snow, he began to see things again—the banks of the creek, the old timber jams, the leafless aspens, and the sky. The running made him feel better. He did not shiver. Maybe, if he ran on, his feet would thaw out; and, anyway, if he ran far enough, he would reach camp and the boys. Without doubt he would lose some fingers and toes and some of his face; but the boys would take care of him, and save the rest of him when he got there. And at the same time there was another thought in his mind that said he would never get to the camp and the boys; that it was too many miles away, that the freezing had too great a start on him, and that he would soon be stiff and dead. This thought he kept in the background and refused to consider. Sometimes it pushed itself forward and demanded to be heard, but he thrust it back and strove to think of other things.

It struck him as curious that he could run at all on feet so frozen that he could not feel them when they struck the earth and took the weight of his body. He seemed to himself to skim along above the surface, and to have no connection with the earth. Somewhere he had once seen a winged Mercury, and he wondered if Mercury felt as he felt when skimming over the earth.

His theory of running until he reached camp and the boys had one flaw in it: he lacked the endurance. Several times he stumbled, and finally he tottered, crumpled up, and fell. When he tried to rise, he failed. He must sit and rest, he decided, and next time he would merely walk and keep on going. As he sat and regained his breath, he noted that he was feeling quite warm and comfortable. He was not shivering, and it even seemed that a warm glow had come to his chest and trunk. And yet, when he touched his nose or cheeks, there was no sensation. Running would not thaw them out. Nor would it thaw out his hands and feet. Then the thought came to him that the frozen portions of his body must be extending. He tried to keep this thought down, to forget it, to think of something else; he was aware of the panicky feeling that it caused, and he was afraid of the panic. But the thought asserted itself, and persisted, until it produced a vision of his body totally frozen. This was too much, and he made another wild run along the trail. Once he slowed down to a walk, but the thought of the freezing extending itself made him run again.

And all the time the dog ran with him, at his heels. When he fell down a second time, it curled its tail over its forefeet and sat in front of him, facing him, curiously eager and intent. The warmth and security of the animal angered him, and he cursed it till it flattened down its ears appeasingly. This time the shivering came more quickly upon the man. He was losing in his battle with the frost. It was creeping into his body from all sides. The thought of it drove him on, but he ran no more than a hundred feet, when he staggered and pitched headlong. It was his last panic. When he had recovered his breath and control, he sat up and entertained in his mind the conception of meeting death with dignity. However, the conception did not come to him in such terms. His idea of it was that he had been making a fool of himself, running around like a chicken with its head cut off—such was the simile that occurred to him. Well, he was bound to freeze anyway, and he might as well take it decently. With this new-found peace of mind came the first glimmerings of drowsiness. A good idea, he thought, to sleep off to death. It was like taking an anesthetic. Freezing was not so bad as people thought. There were lots worse ways to die.

He pictured the boys finding his body next day. Sudddenly he found himself with them, coming along the trail and looking for himself. And, still with them, he came around a turn in the trail and found himself lying in the snow. He did not belong with himself any more, for even then he was out of himself, standing with the boys and looking at himself in the snow. It certainly was cold, was his thought. When he got back to the States he could tell the folks what real cold was. He drifted on from this to a vision of the old-timer on Sulphur Creek. He could see him quite clearly, warm and comfortable, and smoking a pipe.

"You were right, old hoss; you were right," the man mumbled to the old-timer of Sulphur Creek.

Then the man drowsed off into what seemed to him the most comfortable and satisfying sleep he had ever known. The dog sat facing him and waiting. The brief day drew to a close in a long, slow twilight. There were no signs of a fire to be made, and, besides, never in the dog's experience had it known a man to sit like that in the snow and make no fire. As the twilight drew on, its eager yearning for the fire mastered it, and with a great lifting and shifting of forefeet, it whined softly, then flattened its ears down in anticipation of being chidden by the man. But the man remained silent. Later the dog whined loudly. And still later it crept close to the man and caught the scent of death. This made the animal bristle and back away. A little longer it delayed, howling under the stars that leaped and danced and shone brightly in the cold sky. Then it turned and trotted up the trail in the direction of the camp it knew, where were the other food providers and fire providers.

DISCUSSION QUESTIONS

1. Though London's Yukon stories are often full of action and suspense, they are nevertheless meant to convey a moral significance beyond narrative. How would you describe the philosophy of this story?
2. Compare "To Build a Fire" with Barry Lopez's *Arctic Dreams* (in "Best-Sellers"). Though their purposes are different, each writer is dealing in his own way with the relationship of landscape to human imagination. What similarities in the handling of this theme can you detect in both writers? What differences can you find?

Robert Frost

"There are tones of voice that mean more than words," wrote Robert Frost (1874–1963) in a letter:

> *Sentences may be so constructed as definitely to indicate these tones. Only when we are making sentences so shaped are we really writing. And that is flat. A sentence* must *convey a meaning by tone of voice and it must be the particular meaning the writer intended. The reader must have no choice in the matter. The tone of voice and its meaning must be in black and white on the page.*

Frost wanted to direct readers away from the conventional notion of syntax as a grammatical arrangement toward a new definition of a sentence as a cluster of sounds, "because to me a sentence is not interesting merely in conveying a meaning in words. It must do something more; it must convey a meaning by sound." But more often than not, it was the "meaning in words" that most of his large audience attended to, and more often than that to the image of Frost projected by the mass media: a kindly and wise old man, rugged in appearance yet homely and whimsical in the way he talked publicly. To the average citizen, Frost was the American representative of poetry. Yet his public image even today induces his readers to concentrate almost exclusively on paraphrasing the thought, the "meaning in words," of his poetry without paying adequate attention to the ways in which that thought comes into existence through the dynamics of voice, through the "meaning by sound."

Frost's poem "Design" first appeared in American Poetry *in 1922. "The Gift Outright" was first published in the* Virginia Quarterly Review *in 1942. The poem was also read by Frost at John F. Kennedy's inauguration in 1961.*

Robert Frost / Design 1922

I found a dimpled spider, fat and white,
On a white heal-all,[1] holding up a moth

[1] Plant thought to have medicinal value.

Like a white piece of rigid satin cloth—
Assorted characters of death and blight
Mixed ready to begin the morning right,
Like the ingredients of a witches' broth—
A snow-drop spider, a flower like a froth,
And dead wings carried like a paper kite.

What had that flower to do with being white,
The wayside blue and innocent heal-all?
What brought the kindred spider to that height,
Then steered the white moth thither in the night?
What but design of darkness to appall?—
If design govern in a thing so small.

Robert Frost / The Gift Outright 1942

The land was ours before we were the land's.
She was our land more than a hundred years
Before we were her people. She was ours
In Massachusetts, in Virginia,
But we were England's, still colonials,
Possessing what we still were unpossessed by,
Possessed by what we now no more possessed.
Something we were withholding made us weak
Until we found out that it was ourselves
We were withholding from our land of living,
And forthwith found salvation in surrender.
Such as we were we gave ourselves outright
(The deed of gift was many deeds of war)
To the land vaguely realizing westward,
But still unstoried, artless, unenhanced,
Such as she was, such as she would become.

Ernest Hemingway / Soldier's Home 1925

Ernest Hemingway (1899–1961) was first employed as a reporter for the Kansas City Star *in 1917. After serving in a Red Cross ambulance unit on the Italian front during World War I, Hemingway wrote for the* Toronto Star Weekly *and later worked briefly for a Chicago advertising firm. He gradually turned to free-lance journalism and published a good deal of short fiction characterized by a lean, understated prose style that he later partially attributed to the constraints of having to write cablegrams. With the encouragement of Sherwood Anderson and the promise of a job as foreign correspondent for the* Toronto Daily Star, *Hemingway left for Paris in 1921. There he met Gertrude Stein and gravitated toward her corps of literary expatriates.*

"Soldier's Home," the tale of a young man returning from World War I to the routines of his hometown and family, was collected in Hemingway's first major volume of short stories, In Our Time *(1925). For a film adaptation of this story, see "Scripts."*

Krebs went to the war from a Methodist college in Kansas. There is a picture which shows him among his fraternity brothers, all of them wearing exactly the same height and style collar. He enlisted in the Marines in 1917 and did not return to the United States until the second division returned from the Rhine in the summer of 1919.

There is a picture which shows him on the Rhine with two German girls and another corporal. Krebs and the corporal look too big for their uniforms. The German girls are not beautiful. The Rhine does not show in the picture.

By the time Krebs returned to his home town in Oklahoma the greeting of heroes was over. He came back much too late. The men from the town who had been drafted had all been welcomed elaborately on their return. There had been a great deal of hysteria. Now the reaction had set in. People seemed to think it was rather ridiculous for Krebs to be getting back so late, years after the war was over.

At first Krebs, who had been at Belleau Wood, Soissons, the Champagne, St. Mihiel and in the Argonne did not want to talk about the war at all. Later he felt the need to talk but no one wanted to hear about it. His town had heard too many atrocity stories to be thrilled by actualities. Krebs found that to be listened to at all he had to lie, and after he had done this twice he, too, had a reaction against the war and against talking about it. A distaste for everything that had happened to him in the war set in because of the lies he had told. All of the times that had been able to make him feel cool and clear inside himself when he thought of them; the times so long back when he had done the one thing, the only thing for a man to do, easily and naturally, when he might have done something else, now lost their cool, valuable quality and then were lost themselves.

His lies were quite unimportant lies and consisted in attributing to himself things other men had seen, done or heard of, and stating as facts certain apocryphal incidents familiar to all soldiers. Even his lies were not sensational at the pool room. His acquaintances, who had heard detailed accounts of German women found chained to machine guns in the Argonne forest and who could not comprehend, or were barred by their patriotism from interest in, any German machine gunners who were not chained, were not thrilled by his stories.

Krebs acquired the nausea in regard to experience that is the result of untruth or exaggeration, and when he occasionally met another man who had really been a soldier and they talked a few minutes in the dressing room at a dance he fell into the easy pose of the old soldier among other soldiers: that he had been badly, sickeningly frightened all the time. In this way he lost everything.

During this time, it was late summer, he was sleeping late in bed, getting up to walk down town to the library to get a book, eating lunch at home, reading on the front porch until he became bored and then walking down through the town to spend the hottest hours of the day in the cool dark of the pool room. He loved to play pool.

In the evening he practised on his clarinet, strolled down town, read and went to bed. He was still a hero to his two young sisters. His mother would have given him breakfast in bed if he had wanted it. She often came in when he was in bed and asked him to tell her about the war, but her attention always wandered. His father was non-committal.

Before Krebs went away to the war he had never been allowed to drive the family motor car. His father was in the real estate business and always wanted the car to be at his command when he required it to take clients out into the country to show them a piece of farm property. The car always stood outside the First National Bank building where his father had an office on the second floor. Now, after the war, it was still the same car.

Nothing was changed in the town except that the young girls had grown up. But they lived in such a complicated world of already defined alliances and shifting feuds that Krebs did not feel the energy or the courage to break into it. He liked to look at them, though. There were so many good-looking young girls. Most of them had their hair cut short. When he went away only little girls wore their hair like that or girls that were fast. They all wore sweaters and shirt waists with round Dutch collars. It was a pattern. He liked to look at them from the front porch as they walked on the other side of the street. He liked to watch them walking under the shade of the trees. He liked the round Dutch collars above their sweaters. He liked their silk stockings and flat shoes. He liked their bobbed hair and the way they walked.

When he was in town their appeal to him was not very strong. He did not like them when he saw them in the Greek's ice cream parlor. He did not want them themselves really. They were too complicated. There was something else. Vaguely he wanted a girl but he did not want to have to work to get her. He would have liked to have a girl but he did not want to have to spend a long time getting her. He did not want to get into the intrigue and the politics. He did not want to have to do any courting. He did not want to tell any more lies. It wasn't worth it.

He did not want any consequences. He did not want any consequences ever again. He wanted to live along without consequences. Besides he did not really need a girl. The army had taught him that. It was all right to pose as though you had to have a girl. Nearly everybody did that. But it wasn't true. You did not need a girl. That was the funny thing. First a fellow boasted how girls mean nothing to him, that he never thought of them, that they could not touch him. Then a fellow boasted that he could not get along without girls, that he had to have them all the time, that he could not go to sleep without them.

That was all a lie. It was all a lie both ways. You did not need a girl unless you thought about them. He learned that in the army. Then sooner or later you always got one. When you were really ripe for a girl you always got one. You did not have to think about it. Sooner or later it would come. He had learned that in the army.

Now he would have liked a girl if she had come to him and not wanted to talk. But here at home it was all too complicated. He knew he could never get through it all again. It was not worth the trouble. That was the thing about French girls and German girls. There was not all this talking. You couldn't talk much and you did not need to talk. It was simple and you were friends. He thought about France and then he began to think about Germany. On the whole he had liked Germany better. He did not want to leave Germany. He did not want to come home. Still, he had come home. He sat on the front porch.

He liked the girls that were walking along the other side of the street. He liked the look of them much better than the French girls or the German girls. But the world they were in was not the world he was in. He would like to have one of them. But it was not worth it. They were such a nice pattern. He liked the pattern. It was exciting. But he would not go through all the talking. He did not want one badly enough. He liked to look at them all, though. It was not worth it. Not now when things were getting good again.

He sat there on the porch reading a book on the war. It was a history and he was reading about all the engagements he had been in. It was the most interesting reading he had ever done. He wished there were more maps. He looked forward with a good feeling to reading all the really good histories when they would come out with good detail maps. Now he was really learning about the war. He had been a good soldier. That made a difference.

One morning after he had been home about a month his mother came into his bedroom and sat on the bed. She smoothed her apron.

"I had a talk with your father last night, Harold," she said, "and he is willing for you to take the car out in the evenings."

"Yeah?" said Krebs, who was not fully awake. "Take the car out? Yeah?"

"Yes. Your father has felt for some time that you should be able to take the car out in the evenings whenever you wished but we only talked it over last night."

"I'll bet you made him," Krebs said.

"No. It was your father's suggestion that we talk the matter over."

"Yeah. I'll bet you made him," Krebs sat up in bed.

"Will you come down to breakfast, Harold?" his mother said.

"As soon as I get my clothes on," Krebs said.

His mother went out of the room and he could hear her frying something downstairs while he washed, shaved and dressed to go down into the dining-room for breakfast. While he was eating breakfast his sister brought in the mail.

"Well, Hare," she said. "You old sleepy-head. What do you ever get up for?"

Krebs looked at her. He liked her. She was his best sister.

"Have you got the paper?" he asked.

She handed him *The Kansas City Star* and he shucked off its brown wrapper and opened it to the sporting page. He folded *The Star* open and propped it against the water pitcher with his cereal dish to steady it, so he could read while he ate.

"Harold," his mother stood in the kitchen doorway, "Harold, please don't muss up the paper. Your father can't read his *Star* if it's been mussed."

"I won't muss it," Krebs said.

His sister sat down at the table and watched him while he read.

"We're playing indoor over at school this afternoon," she said. "I'm going to pitch."

"Good," said Krebs. "How's the old wing?"

"I can pitch better than lots of the boys. I tell them all you taught me. The other girls aren't much good."

"Yeah?" said Krebs.

"I tell them all you're my beau. Aren't you my beau, Hare?"

"You bet."

"Couldn't your brother really be your beau just because he's your brother?"

"I don't know."

"Sure you know. Couldn't you be my beau, Hare, if I was old enough and if you wanted to?"

"Sure. You're my girl now."

"Am I really your girl?"

"Sure."

"Do you love me?"

"Uh, huh."

"Will you love me always?"

"Sure."

"Will you come over and watch me play indoor?"

"Maybe."

"Aw, Hare, you don't love me. If you loved me, you'd want to come over and watch me play indoor."

Kreb's mother came into the dining-room from the kitchen. She carried a plate with two fried eggs and some crisp bacon on it and a plate of buckwheat cakes.

"You run along, Helen," she said. "I want to talk to Harold."

She put the eggs and bacon down in front of him and brought in a jug of maple syrup for the buckwheat cakes. Then she sat down across the table from Krebs.

"I wish you'd put down the paper a minute, Harold," she said.

Krebs took down the paper and folded it.

"Have you decided what you are going to do yet, Harold?" his mother said, taking off her glasses.

"No," said Krebs.

"Don't you think it's about time?" His mother did not say this in a mean way. She seemed worried.

"I hadn't thought about it," Krebs said.

"God has some work for every one to do," his mother said. "There can be no idle hands in His Kingdom."

"I'm not in His Kingdom," Krebs said.

"We are all of us in His Kingdom."

Krebs felt embarrassed and resentful as always.

"I've worried about you so much, Harold," his mother went on. "I know the temptations you must have been exposed to. I know how weak men are. I know what your own dear grandfather, my own father, told us about the Civil War and I have prayed for you. I pray for you all day long, Harold."

Krebs looked at the bacon fat hardening on his plate.

"Your father is worried, too," his mother went on. "He thinks you have lost your ambition, that you haven't got a definite aim in life. Charley Simmons, who is just your age, has a good job and is going to be married. The boys are all settling down; they're all determined to get somewhere; you can see that boys like Charley Simmons are on their way to being really a credit to the community."

Krebs said nothing.

"Don't look that way, Harold," his mother said. "You know we love you and I want to tell you for your own good how matters stand. Your father does not want to hamper your freedom. He thinks you should be allowed to drive the car. If you want to take some of the nice girls out riding with you, we are only too pleased. We want you to enjoy yourself. But you are going to have to settle down to work, Harold. Your father doesn't care what you start in at. All work is honorable as he says. But you've got to make a start at something. He asked me to speak to you this morning and then you can stop in and see him at his office."

"Is that all?" Krebs said.

"Yes. Don't you love your mother, dear boy?"

"No," Krebs said.

His mother looked at him across the table. Her eyes were shiny. She started crying.

"I don't love anybody," Krebs said.

It wasn't any good. He couldn't tell her, he couldn't make her see it. It was silly to have said it. He had only hurt her. He went over and took hold of her arm. She was crying with her head in her hands.

"I didn't mean it," he said. "I was just angry at something. I didn't mean I didn't love you."

His mother went on crying. Krebs put his arm on her shoulder.

"Can't you believe me, mother?"

His mother shook her head.

"Please, please, mother. Please believe me."

"All right," his mother said chokily. She looked up at him. "I believe you, Harold."

Krebs kissed her hair. She put her face up to him.

"I'm your mother," she said. "I held you next to my heart when you were a tiny baby."

Krebs felt sick and vaguely nauseated.

"I know, Mummy," he said. "I'll try and be a good boy for you."

"Would you kneel and pray with me, Harold?" his mother asked.

They knelt down beside the dining-room table and Krebs's mother prayed.

"Now, you pray, Harold," she said.

"I can't," Krebs said.

"Try, Harold."

"I can't."

"Do you want me to pray for you?"

"Yes."

So his mother prayed for him and then they stood up and Krebs kissed his mother and went out of the house. He had tried so to keep his life from being complicated. Still, none of it had touched him. He had felt sorry for his mother and she had made him lie. He would go to Kansas City and get a job and she would feel all right about it. There would be one more scene maybe before he got away. He would not go down to his father's office. He would miss that one. He wanted his life to go smoothly. It had just gotten going that way. Well, that was all over now, anyway. He would go over to the schoolyard and watch Helen play indoor baseball.

DISCUSSION QUESTION

1. Hemingway's famous tale evokes the malaise of an America shaken to the core by its first world war. Since that time, our country has participated in many battles; bombings are broadcast over network news. Compare George Lakoff's reading of the Gulf War in the "Press" section with "Soldier's Home." What has changed in the public consciousness regarding war? What has stayed the same?

William Carlos Williams / The Use of Force 1933

Five minutes, ten minutes, can always be found. I had my typewriter in my office desk. All I needed to do was pull up the leaf to which it was fastened and I was ready to go. I worked at top speed. If a patient came in at the door while I was in the middle of a sentence, bang would go the machine—I was a physician. When the patient left, up would come the machine. My head developed a technique: something growing inside me demanded reaping. It had to be attended to. Finally, after eleven at night, when the last patient had been put to bed, I could always find time to bang out ten or twelve pages. In fact, I couldn't rest until I had freed my mind from the obsessions which had been tormenting me all day. Cleansed of that torment, having scribbled, I could rest.

As the above passage from his Autobiography *makes clear, William Carlos Williams worked hard all his life at two demanding careers. A busy pediatrician in a densely populated northern New Jersey area, Williams also attained a reputation as one of the leading figures in modern American poetry. In his best work he succeeds in giving literary form to the discordant, brittle, nonliterary idioms of an industrial civilization.*

Born in Rutherford, New Jersey, in 1883, Williams received a medical education at the University of Pennsylvania, where he became acquainted with the poet and critic Ezra Pound. After a year's study abroad, Williams returned to his home town to discipline himself in the arts of healing and writing. His first book of poems, published at his own expense in 1909, was followed by nearly forty volumes of poetry, short stories, novels, plays, history, biography, and criticism, in which he consistently demonstrates a special fondness for local subjects and his native grounds. His most ambitious effort, an epic of a modern industrial city, Paterson, *received the National Book Award in 1949. Williams died in Rutherford in 1963.*

"The Use of Force" documents in unsentimental terms an encounter between a determined physician and the seriously ill child of a poor, backward family–the kind of people Williams cared for all his life. It originally appeared in Blast, *a short-lived American literary magazine that, according to Williams, was started by an unemployed "tool designer living precariously over a garage in Brooklyn."*

They were new patients to me, all I had was the name, Olson. Please come down as soon as you can, my daughter is very sick.

When I arrived I was met by the mother, a big startled-looking woman, very clean and apologetic who merely said, Is this the doctor? and let me in. In the back, she added. You must excuse us, doctor, we have her in the kitchen where it is warm. It is very damp here sometimes.

The child was fully dressed and sitting on her father's lap near the kitchen table. He tried to get up, but I motioned for him not to bother, took off my overcoat and started to look things over. I could see that they were all very nervous, eyeing me up and down distrustfully. As often, in such cases, they weren't telling me more than they had to, it was up to me to tell them; that's why they were spending three dollars on me.

The child was fairly eating me up with her cold, steady eyes, and no expression to her face whatever. She did not move and seemed, inwardly, quiet; an unusually attractive little thing, and as strong as a heifer in appearance. But her face was flushed, she was breathing rapidly, and I realized that she had a high fever. She had magnificent blond hair, in profusion. One of those picture children often reproduced in advertising leaflets and the photogravure sections of the Sunday papers.

She's had a fever for three days, began the father and we don't know what it comes from. My wife has given her things, you know, like people do, but it don't do no good. And there's been a lot of sickness around. So we tho't you'd better look her over and tell us what is the matter.

As doctors often do I took a trial shot at it as a point of departure. Has she had a sore throat?

Both parents answered me together, No . . . No, she says her throat don't hurt her.

Does your throat hurt you? added the mother to the child. But the little girl's expression didn't change nor did she move her eyes from my face.

Have you looked?

I tried to, said the mother, but I couldn't see.

As it happens we had been having a number of cases of diphtheria in the school to which this child went during that month and we were all, quite apparently, thinking of that, though no one had as yet spoken of the thing.

Well, I said, suppose we take a look at the throat first. I smiled in my best professional manner and asking for the child's first name I said, come on, Mathilda, open your mouth and let's take a look at your throat.

Nothing doing.

Aw, come on, I coaxed, just open your mouth wide and let me take a look. Look, I said opening both hands wide, I haven't anything in my hands. Just open up and let me see.

Such a nice man, put in the mother. Look how kind he is to you. Come on, do what he tells you to. He won't hurt you.

At that I ground my teeth in disgust. If only they wouldn't use the word "hurt" I might be able to get someplace. But I did not allow myself to be hurried or disturbed but speaking quietly and slowly I approached the child again.

As I moved my chair a little nearer suddenly with one cat-like movement both her hands clawed instinctively for my eyes and she almost reached them too. In fact she knocked my glasses flying and they fell, though unbroken, several feet away from me on the kitchen floor.

Both the mother and father almost turned themselves inside out in embarrassment and apology. You bad girl, said the mother, taking her and shaking her by one arm. Look what you've done. The nice man . . .

For heaven's sake, I broke in. Don't call me a nice man to her. I'm here to look at her throat on the chance that she might have diphtheria and possibly die of it. But that's nothing to her. Look here, I said to the child, we're going to look at your throat. You're old enough to understand what I'm saying. Will you open it now by yourself or shall we have to open it for you?

Not a move. Even her expression hadn't changed. Her breaths however were coming faster and faster. Then the battle began. I had to do it. I had to have a throat culture for her own protection. But first I told the parents that it was entirely up to them. I explained the danger but said that I would not insist on a throat examination so long as they would take the responsibility.

If you don't do what the doctor says you'll have to go to the hospital, the mother admonished her severely.

Oh yeah? I had to smile to myself. After all, I had already fallen in love with the savage brat, the parents were contemptible to me. In the ensuing struggle they grew more and more abject, crushed, exhausted while she surely rose to magnificent heights of insane fury of effort bred of her terror of me.

The father tried his best, and he was a big man but the fact that she was his daughter, his shame at her behavior and his dread of hurting her made him release her just at the critical moment several times when I had almost achieved success, till I wanted to kill him. But his dread also that she might have diphtheria made him tell me to go on, go on though he himself was almost fainting, while the mother moved back and forth behind us raising and lowering her hands in an agony of apprehension.

Put her in front of you on your lap, I ordered, and hold both her wrists.

But as soon as he did the child let out a scream. Don't, you're hurting me. Let go of my hands. Let them go I tell you. Then she shrieked terrifyingly, hysterically. Stop it! Stop it! You're killing me!

Do you think she can stand it, doctor! said the mother.

You get out, said the husband to his wife. Do you want her to die of diphtheria?

Come on now, hold her, I said.

Then I grasped the child's head with my left hand and tried to get the wooden tongue depressor between her teeth. She fought, with clenched teeth, desperately! But now I also had grown furious—at a child. I tried to hold myself down but I couldn't. I know how to expose a throat for inspection. And I did my best. When finally I got the wooden spatula behind the last teeth and just the point of it into the mouth cavity, she opened up for an instant but before I could see anything she came down again and gripping the wooden blade between her molars she reduced it to splinters before I could get it out again.

Aren't you ashamed, the mother yelled at her. Aren't you ashamed to act like that in front of the doctor?

Get me a smooth-handled spoon of some sort, I told the mother. We're going through with this. The child's mouth was already bleeding. Her tongue was cut and she was screaming in wild hysterical shrieks. Perhaps I should have desisted and come back in an hour or more. No doubt it would have been better. But I have seen at least two children lying dead in bed of neglect in such cases, and feeling that I must get a diagnosis, now or never I went at it again. But the worst of it was that I too had got beyond reason. I could have torn the child apart in my own fury and enjoyed it. It was a pleasure to attack her. My face was burning with it.

The damned little brat must be protected against her own idiocy, one says to one's self at such times. Others must be protected against her. It is social necessity. And all these things are true. But a blind fury, a feeling of adult shame, bred of a longing for muscular release are the operatives. One goes on to the end.

In a final unreasoning assault I overpowered the child's neck and jaws. I forced the heavy silver spoon back on her teeth and down her throat till she gagged. And there it was—both tonsils covered with membrane. She had fought valiantly to keep me from knowing her secret. She had been hiding that sore throat for three days at least and lying to her parents in order to escape just such an outcome as this.

Now truly she *was* furious. She had been on the defensive before but now she attacked. Tried to get off her father's lap and fly at me while tears of defeat blinded her eyes.

E. B. White / Once More to the Lake *1941*

Perhaps the most respected twentieth-century American essayist, E. B. White once claimed that the essay writer is "sustained by the childish belief that everything he thinks about, everything that happens to him, is of general interest." In other words, the writer begins by being self-centered; only then can the writer's self imaginatively engage the centers of other selves.

White was born in Mt. Vernon, New York, in 1899. After graduating from Cornell in 1921, he worked as a journalist for several years and then landed a position with the newly formed New Yorker *magazine, where he contributed the "Talk of the Town" column. The winner of the National Institute of Arts and Letters gold medal in 1960. White is the author of nineteen books, including two classics for children,* Stuart Little *(1948) and* Charlotte's Web *(1952). Regarded as an eminent stylist, White revised his former teacher's brief writing manual,* The Elements of Style *(1959), and the tiny edition known as "Strunk and White" can probably be seen on the desks of more professional writers than any other book of its kind.*

"Once More to the Lake" is White's most famous essay.

One summer, along about 1904, my father rented a camp on a lake in Maine and took us all there for the month of August. We all got ringworm from some kittens and had to rub Pond's Extract on our arms and legs night and morning, and my father rolled over in a canoe with all his clothes on: but outside of that the vacation was a success and from then on none of us ever thought there was any place in the world like that lake in Maine. We returned summer after summer—always on August 1st for one month. I have since become a salt-water man, but sometimes in summer there are days when the restlessness of the tides and the fearful cold of the sea water and the incessant wind that blows across the afternoon and into the evening make me wish for the placidity of a lake in the woods. A few weeks ago this feeling got so strong I bought myself a couple of bass hooks and a spinner and returned to the lake where we used to go, for a week's fishing and to revisit old haunts.

I took along my son, who had never had any fresh water up his nose and who had seen lily pads only from train windows. On the journey over to the lake I began to wonder what it would be like. I wondered how time would have marred this unique, this holy spot—the coves and streams, the hills that the sun set behind, the camps and the paths behind the camps. I was sure that the tarred road would have found it out and I wondered in what other ways it would be desolated. It is strange how much you can remember about places like that once you allow your mind to return into the grooves that lead back. You remember one thing, and that suddenly reminds you of another thing. I guess I remembered clearest of all the early mornings, when the lake was cool and motionless, remembered how the bedroom smelled of the lumber it was made of and of the wet woods whose scent entered through the screen. The partitions in the camp were thin and did not extend clear to the top of the rooms, and as I was always the first up I would dress softly so as not to wake the others, and sneak out into the sweet outdoors and start out in the canoe, keeping close along the shore in the long shadows of the pines. I remembered being very careful never to rub my paddle against the gunwale for fear of disturbing the stillness of the cathedral.

That lake had never been what you would call a wild lake. There were cottages sprinkled around the shores, and it was in farming country although the shores of the lake were quite heavily wooded. Some of the cottages were owned by nearby farmers, and you would live at the shore and eat your meals at the farmhouse. That's what our family did. But although it wasn't wild, it was a fairly large and undisturbed lake and there were places in it which, to a child at least, seemed infinitely remote and primeval.

I was right about the tar; it led to within half a mile of the shore. But when I got back there, with my boy, and we settled into a camp near a farmhouse and into the kind of summertime I had known, I could tell that it was going to be pretty much the same as it had been before—I knew it, lying in bed the first morning, smelling the bedroom, and hearing the boy sneak quietly out and go off along the shore in a boat. I began to sustain the illusion that he was I, and therefore, by simple transposition, that I was my father. This sensation persisted, kept cropping up all the time we were there. It was not an entirely new feeling, but in this setting it grew much stronger. I seemed to be living a dual existence. I would be in the middle of some simple act, I would be picking up a bait box or laying down a table fork, or I would be saying something, and suddenly it would be not I but my father who was saying the words or making the gesture. It gave me a creepy sensation.

We went fishing the first morning. I felt the same damp moss covering the worms in the bait can, and saw the dragonfly alight on the tip of my rod as it hovered a few inches from the surface of the water. It was the arrival of this fly that convinced me beyond any doubt that everything was as it always had been, that the years were a mirage and there had been no years. The small waves were the same, chucking the rowboat under the chin as we fished at anchor, and the boat was the same boat, the same color green and the ribs broken in the same places, and under the floor-boards the same fresh-water leavings and debris—the dead hellgrammite, the wisps of moss, the rusty discarded fishhook, the dried blood from yesterday's catch. We stared silently at the tips of our rods, at the dragonflies that came and went. I lowered the tip of mine into the water, tentatively, pensively dislodging the fly, which darted two feet away, poised, darted two feet back, and came to rest again a little farther up the rod. There had been no years between the ducking of this dragonfly and the other one—the one that was part of memory. I looked at the boy, who was silently watching his fly, and it was my hands that held his rod, my eyes watching, I felt dizzy and didn't know which rod I was at the end of.

We caught two bass, hauling them in briskly as though they were mackerel, pulling them over the side of the boat in a businesslike manner without any landing net, and stunning them with a blow on the back of the head. When we got back for a swim before lunch, the lake was exactly where we had left it, the same number of inches from the dock, and there was only the merest suggestion of a breeze. This seemed an utterly enchanted sea, this lake you could leave to its own devices for a few hours and come back to, and find that it had not stirred, this constant and trustworthy body of water. In the shallows, the dark, watersoaked sticks and twigs, smooth and old, were undulating in clusters on the bottom against the clean ribbed sand, and the track of the mussel was plain. A school of minnows swam by, each minnow with its small individual shadow, doubling the attendance, so clear and sharp in the sunlight. Some of the other campers were in swimming, along the shore, one of them with a cake of soap, and the water felt thin and clear and unsubstantial. Over the years there had been this person with the cake of soap, the cultist, and here he was. There had been no years.

Up to the farmhouse to dinner through the teeming, dusty field, the road under our sneakers was only a two-track road. The middle track was missing, the one with the marks of the hooves and splotches of dried, flaky manure. There had always been three tracks to choose from in choosing which track to walk in: now the choice was narrowed down to two. For a moment I missed terribly the middle alternative. But the way led past the tennis court, and something about the way it lay there in the sun reassured me: the tape had loosened along the backline, the alleys were green with plantains and other weeds, and the net (installed in June and removed in September) sagged in the dry noon, and the whole place steamed with midday heat and hunger and emptiness. There was a choice of pie for dessert, and one was blueberry and one was apple, and the waitresses were the same country girls, there having been no passing of time, only the illusion of it as in a dropped curtain—the waitresses were still fifteen; their hair had been washed, that was the only difference—they had been to the movies and seen the pretty girls with the clean hair.

Summertime, oh summertime, pattern of life indelible, the fade-proof lake, the woods unshatterable, the pasture with the sweetfern and the juniper forever and ever, summer without end; this was the background, and the life along the shore was the design, the cottages with their innocent and tranquil design, their tiny docks with the flagpole and the American flag floating against the white clouds in the blue sky, the little paths over the roots of the trees leading from camp to camp and the paths leading back to the outhouses and the can of lime for sprinkling, and at the souvenir counters at the store the miniature birch-bark canoes and the post cards that showed things looking a little better than they looked. This was the American family at play, escaping the city heat, wondering whether the newcomers in the camp at the head of the cove were "common" or "nice," wondering whether it was true that the people who drove up for Sunday dinner at the farmhouse were turned away because there wasn't enough chicken.

It seemed to me, as I kept remembering all this, that those times and those summers had been infinitely precious and worth saving. There had been jollity and peace and goodness. The arriving (at the beginning of August) had been so big a business in itself, at the railway station the farm wagon drawn up, the first smell of the pine-laden air, the first glimpse of the smiling farmer, and the great importance of the trunks and your father's enormous authority in such matters, and the feel of the wagon under you for the long ten-mile haul, and at the top of the last long hill catching the first view of the lake after eleven months of not seeing this cherished body of water. The shouts and cries of the other campers when they saw you, and the trunks to be unpacked, to give up their rich burden. (Arriving was less exciting nowadays, when you sneaked up in your car and parked it under a tree near the camp and took out the bags and in five minutes it was all over, no fuss, no loud wonderful fuss about trunks.)

Peace and goodness and jollity. The only thing that was wrong now, really, was the sound of the place, an unfamiliar nervous sound of the outboard motors. This was the note that jarred, the one thing that would sometimes break the illusion and set the years moving. In those other summertimes all motors were inboard: and when they were at a little distance, the noise they made was a sedative, an ingredient of summer sleep. They were one-cylinder and two-cylinder engines, and some were shake-and-break and some were jump-spark, but they all made a sleepy sound across the lake. The one-lungers throbbed and fluttered, and the twin-cylinder ones purred and purred, and that was a quiet sound too. But now the campers all had outboards. In the daytime, in the hot mornings, these motors made a petulant, irritable sound; at night, in the still evening when the afterglow lit the water, they whined about one's ears like mosquitoes. My boy loved our rented outboard, and his great desire was to achieve single-handed mastery over it, and authority, and he soon learned the trick of choking it a little (but not too much), and the adjustment of the needle valve. Watching him I would remember the things you could do with the old one-cylinder engine with the heavy flywheel, how you could have it eating out of your hand if you got really close to it spiritually. Motor boats in those days didn't have clutches, and you would make a landing by shutting off the motor at the proper time and coasting in with a dead rudder. But there was a way of reversing them, if you learned the trick, by cutting the switch and putting it on again exactly on the final dying revolution of the flywheel, so that it would kick back against compression and begin reversing. Approaching a dock in a strong following breeze, it was difficult to slow up sufficiently by the ordinary coasting method, and if a boy felt he had complete mastery over his motor, he was tempted to keep it running beyond its time and then reverse it a few feet from the dock. It took a cool nerve, because if you threw the switch a twentieth of a second too soon you could catch the flywheel when it still had speed enough to go up past center, and the boat would leap ahead, charging bull-fashion at the dock.

We had a good week at the camp. The bass were biting well and the sun shone endlessly, day after day. We would be tired at night and lie down in the accumulated heat of the little bedrooms after the long hot day and the breeze would stir almost imperceptibly outside and the smell of the swamp drift in through the rusty screens. Sleep would come easily and in the morning the red squirrel would be on the roof, tapping out his gay routine. I kept remembering everything, lying in bed in the mornings—the small steamboat that had a long rounded stern like the lip of a Ubangi, and how quietly she ran on the moonlight sails, when the older boys played their mandolins and the girls sang and we ate doughnuts dipped in sugar, and how sweet the music was on the water in the shining night, and what it had felt like to think about girls then. After breakfast we would go up to the store and the things were in the same place—the minnows in a bottle, the plugs and spinners disarranged and pawed over by the youngsters from the boys' camp, the Fig Newtons and the Beeman's gum. Outside, the road was tarred and cars stood in front of the store. Inside, all was just as it had always been, except there was more Coca-Cola and not so much Moxie and root beer and birch beer and sarsaparilla. We would walk out with a bottle of pop apiece and sometimes the pop would backfire up our noses and hurt. We explored the streams, quietly, where the turtles slid off the sunny logs and dug their way into the soft bottom; and we lay on the town wharf and fed worms to the tame bass. Everywhere we went I had trouble making out which was I, the one walking at my side, the one walking in my pants.

One afternoon while we were there at that lake a thunderstorm came up. It was like the revival of an old melodrama that I had seen long ago with childish awe. The second-act climax of the drama of the electrical disturbance over a lake in America had not changed in any important respect. This was the big scene, still the big scene. The whole thing was so familiar, the first feeling of oppression and heat and a general air around camp of not wanting to go very far away. In mid-afternoon (it was all the same) a curious darkening of the sky, and a lull in everything that had made life tick; and then the way the boats suddenly swung the other way at their moorings with the coming of a breeze out of the new quarter, and the premonitory rumble. Then the kettle drum, then the snare, then the bass drum and cymbals, then crackling light against the dark, and the gods grinning and licking their chops in the hills. Afterward the calm, the rain steadily rustling in the calm lake, the return of light and hope and spirits, and the campers running out in joy and relief to go swimming in the rain, their bright cries perpetuating the deathless joke about how they were getting simply drenched, and the children screaming with delight at the new sensation of bathing in the rain, and the joke about getting drenched linking the generations in a strong indestructible chain. And the comedian who waded in carrying an umbrella.

When the others went swimming my son said he was going in too. He pulled his dripping trunks from the line where they had hung all through the shower, and wrung them out. Languidly, and with no thought of going in, I watched him, his hard little body, skinny and bare, saw him wince slightly as he pulled up around his vitals the small, soggy, icy garment. As he buckled the swollen belt suddenly my groin felt the chill of death.

William Faulkner / *The Bear* 1942

Sole owner, proprietor, historian, and inventor of the most turbulent 2,400 square miles in America, Yoknapatawpha County, Mississippi, William Faulkner (1897–1962) remains the most powerful American novelist of the first half of the twentieth century. The major portion of his life was spent in Oxford, Mississippi, except for a brief period during World War I with the British Flying Corps in Canada, a job in a bookstore in New York City, a stint writing sketches for the New Orleans Time-Picayune, *and an occasional acquiescence to the lure of Hollywood. We have reprinted the opening section of* The Bear, *a novella in five parts, which originally appeared (also excerpted) in the* Saturday Evening Post *in 1942 with the caption "Boy Meets Bear after Years of Stalking."*

PART I

There was a man and a dog too this time. Two beasts, counting Old Ben, the bear, and two men, counting Boon Hogganbeck, in whom some of the same blood ran which ran in Sam Fathers, even though Boon's was a plebeian strain of it and only Sam and Old Ben and the mongrel Lion were taintless and incorruptible.

He was sixteen. For six years now he had been a man's hunter. For six years now he had heard the best of all talking. It was of the wilderness, the big woods, bigger and older than any recorded document:—of white man fatuous enough to believe he had bought any fragment of it, of Indian ruthless enough to pretend that any fragment of it had been his to convey; bigger than Major de Spain and the scrap he pretended to, knowing better; older than old Thomas Sutpen of whom Major de Spain had had it and who knew better; older even than old Ikkemotubbe, the Chickasaw chief, of whom old Sutpen had had it and who knew better in his turn. It was of the men, not white nor black nor red but men, hunters, with the will and hardihood to endure and the humility and skill to survive, and the dogs and the bear and deer juxtaposed and reliefed against it, ordered and compelled by and within the wilderness in the ancient and unremitting contest according to the ancient and immitigable rules which voided all regrets and brooked no quarter;—the best game of all, the best of all breathing and forever the best of all listening, the voices quiet and weighty and deliberate for retrospection and recollection and exactitude among the concrete trophies—the racked guns and the heads and skins—in the libraries of town houses or the offices of plantation houses or (and best of all) in the camps themselves where the intact and still-warm meat yet hung, the men who had slain it sitting before the burning logs on hearths when there were houses and hearths or about the smoky blazing of piled wood in front of stretched tarpaulins when there were not. There was always a bottle present, so that it would seem to him that those fine fierce instants of heart and brain and courage and wiliness and speed were concentrated and distilled into that brown liquor which not women, not boys and children, but only hunters drank, drinking not of the blood they spilled but some condensation of the wild immortal spirit, drinking it moderately, humbly even, not with the pagan's base and baseless hope of acquiring thereby the virtues of cunning and strength and speed but in salute to them. Thus it seemed to him on this December morning not only natural but actually fitting that this should have begun with whisky.

He realised later that it had begun long before that. It had already begun on that day when he first wrote his age in two ciphers and his cousin McCaslin brought him for the first time to the camp, the big woods, to earn for himself from the wilderness the name and state of hunter provided he in his turn were humble and enduring enough. He had already inherited then, without ever having seen it, the big old bear with one trap-ruined foot that in an area almost a hundred miles square had earned for himself a name, a definite designation like a living man:—the long legend of corn-cribs broken down and rifled, of shoats and grown pigs and even calves carried bodily into the woods and devoured and traps and deadfalls overthrown and dogs mangled and slain and shotgun and even rifle shots delivered at point-blank range yet with no more effect than so many peas blown through a tube by a child—a corridor of wreckage and destruction beginning back before the boy was born, through which sped, not fast but rather with the ruthless and irresistible deliberation of a locomotive, the shaggy tremendous shape. It ran in his knowledge before he ever saw it. It loomed and towered in his dreams before he even saw the unaxed woods where it left its crooked print, shaggy, tremendous, red-eyed, not malevolent but just big, too big for the dogs which tried to bay it, for the horses which tried to ride it down, for the men and the bullets they fired into it; too big for the very country which was its constricting scope. It was as if the boy had already divined what his senses and intellect had not encompassed yet: that doomed wilderness whose edges were being constantly and punily gnawed at by men with plows and axes who feared it because it was wilderness, men myriad and nameless even to one another in the land where the old bear had earned a name, and through which ran not even a mortal beast but an anachronism indomitable and invincible out of an old dead time, a phantom, epitome and apotheosis of the old wild life which the little puny humans swarmed and hacked at in a fury of abhorrence and fear like pygmies about the ankles of a drowsing elephant;—the old bear, solitary, indomitable, and alone; widowered childless and absolved of mortality—old Priam reft of his old wife and outlived all his sons.

Still a child, with three years then two years then one year yet before he too could make one of them, each November he would watch the wagon containing the dogs and the bedding and food and guns and his cousin McCaslin and Tennie's Jim and Sam Fathers too until Sam moved to the camp to live, depart for the Big Bottom, the big woods. To him, they were going not to hunt bear and deer but to keep yearly rendezvous with the bear which they did not even intend to kill. Two weeks later they would return, with no trophy, no skin. He had not expected it. He had not even feared that it might be in the wagon this time with the other skins and heads. He did not even tell himself that in three years or two years or one year more he would be present and that it might even be his gun. He believed that only after he had served his apprenticeship in the woods which would prove him worthy to be a hunter, would he even be permitted to distinguish the crooked print, and that even then for two November weeks he would merely make another minor one, along with his cousin and Major de Spain and General Compson and Walter Ewell and Boon and the dogs which feared to bay it and the shotguns and rifles which failed even to bleed it, in the yearly pageant-rite of the old bear's furious immortality.

His day came at last. In the surrey with his cousin and Major de Spain and General Compson he saw the wilderness through a slow drizzle of November rain just above the ice point as it seemed to him later he always saw it or at least always remembered it—the tall and endless wall of dense November woods under the dissolving afternoon and the year's death, sombre, impenetrable (he could not even discern yet how, at what point they could possibly hope to enter it even though he knew that Sam Fathers was waiting there with the wagon), the surrey moving through the skeleton stalks of cotton and corn in the last of open country, the last trace of man's puny gnawing at the immemorial flank, until, dwarfed by that perspective into an almost ridiculous diminishment, the surrey itself seemed to have ceased to move (this too to be completed later, years later, after he had grown to a man and had seen the sea) as a solitary small boat hangs in lonely immobility, merely tossing up and down, in the infinite waste of the ocean while the water and then the apparently impenetrable land which it nears without appreciable progress, swings slowly and opens the widening inlet which is the anchorage. He entered it. Sam was waiting, wrapped in a quilt on the wagon seat behind the patient and steaming mules. He entered his novitiate to the true wilderness with Sam beside him as he had begun his apprenticeship in miniature to manhood after the rabbits and such with Sam beside him, the two of them wrapped in the damp, warm, negro-rank quilt while the wilderness closed behind his entrance as it had opened momentarily to accept him, opening before his advancement as it closed behind his progress, no fixed path the wagon followed but a channel nonexistent ten yards ahead of it and ceasing to exist ten yards after it had passed, the wagon progressing not by its own volition but by attrition of their intact yet fluid circumambience, drowsing, earless, almost lightless.

It seemed to him that at the age of ten he was witnessing his own birth. It was not even strange to him. He had experienced it all before, and not merely in dreams. He saw the camp—a paintless six-room bungalow set on piles above the spring highwater—and he knew already how it was going to look. He helped in the rapid orderly disorder of their establishment in it and even his motions were familiar to him, foreknown. Then for two weeks he ate the coarse, rapid food—the shapeless sour bread, the wild strange meat, venison and bear and turkey and coon which he had never tasted before—which men ate, cooked by men who were hunters first and cooks afterward; he slept in harsh sheetless blankets as hunters slept. Each morning the gray of dawn found him and Sam Fathers on the stand, the crossing, which had been allotted him. It was the poorest one, the most barren. He had expected that; he had not dared yet to hope even to himself that he would even hear the running dogs this first time. But he did hear them. It was on the third morning—a murmur, sourceless, almost indistinguishable, yet he knew what it was although he had never before heard that many dogs running at once, the murmur swelling into separate and distinct voices until he could call the five dogs which his cousin owned from among the others. "Now," Sam said, "slant your gun up a little and draw back the hammers and then stand still."

But it was not for him, not yet. The humility was there; he had learned that. And he could learn the patience. He was only ten, only one week. The instant had passed. It seemed to him that he could actually see the deer, the buck, smoke-colored, elongated with speed, vanished, the woods, the gray solitude still ringing even when the voices of the dogs had died away; from far away across the sombre woods and the gray half-liquid morning there came two shots. "Now let your hammers down," Sam said.

He did so. "You knew it too," he said.

"Yes," Sam said. "I want you to learn how to do when you didn't shoot. It's after the chance for the bear or the deer has done already come and gone that men and dogs get killed."

"Anyway, it wasn't him," the boy said. "It wasn't even a bear. It was just a deer."

"Yes," Sam said, "it was just a deer."

Then one morning, it was in the second week, he heard the dogs again. This time before Sam even spoke he readied the too-long, too-heavy, man-size gun as Sam had taught him, even though this time he knew the dogs and the deer were coming less close than ever, hardly within hearing even. They didn't sound like any running dogs he had ever heard before even. Then he found that Sam, who had taught him first of all to cock the gun and take position where he could see best in all directions and then never to move again, had himself moved up beside him. "There," he said. "Listen." The boy listened, to no ringing chorus strong and fast on a free scent but a moiling yapping an octave too high and with something more than indecision and even abjectness in it which he could not yet recognise, reluctant, not even moving very fast, taking a long time to pass out of hearing, leaving even then in the air that echo of thin and almost human hysteria, abject, almost humanly grieving, with this time nothing ahead of it, no sense of a fleeing unseen smoke-colored shape. He could hear Sam breathing at his shoulder. He saw the arched curve of the old man's inhaling nostrils.

"It's Old Ben!" he cried, whispering.

Sam didn't move save for the slow gradual turning of his head as the voices faded on and the faint steady rapid arch and collapse of his nostrils. "Hah," he said. "Not even running. Walking."

"But up here!" the boy cried. "Way up here!"

"He do it every year," Sam said. "Once. Ash and Boon say he comes up here to run the other little bears away. Tell them to get to hell out of here and stay out until the hunters are gone. Maybe." The boy no longer heard anything at all, yet still Sam's head continued to turn gradually and steadily until the back of it was toward him. Then it turned back and looked down at him—the same face, grave, familiar, expressionless until it smiled, the same old man's eyes from which as he watched there faded slowly a quality darkly and fiercely lambent, passionate and proud. "He dont care no more for bears than he does for dogs or men neither. He come to see who's here, who's new in camp this year, whether he can shoot or not, can stay or not. Whether we got the dog yet that can bay and hold him until a man gets there with a gun. Because he's the head bear. He's the man." It faded, was gone; again they were the eyes as he had known them all his life. "He'll let them follow him to the river. Then he'll send them home. We might as well go too; see how they look when they get back to camp."

The dogs were there first, ten of them huddled back under the kitchen, himself and Sam squatting to peer back into the obscurity where they crouched, quiet, the eyes rolling and luminous, vanishing, and no sound, only that effluvium which the boy could not quite place yet, of something more than dog, stronger than dog and not just animal, just beast even. Because there had been nothing in front of the abject and painful yapping except the solitude, the wilderness, so that when the eleventh hound got back about mid-afternoon and he and Tennie's Jim held the passive and still trembling bitch while Sam daubed her tattered ear and raked shoulder with turpentine and axle-grease, it was still no living creature but only the wilderness which, leaning for a moment, had patted lightly once her temerity. "Just like a man," Sam said. "Just like folks. Put off as long as she could having to be brave, knowing all the time that sooner or later she would have to be brave once so she could keep on calling herself a dog, and knowing beforehand what was going to happen when she done it."

He did not know just when Sam left. He only knew that he was gone. For the next three mornings he rose and ate breakfast and Sam was not waiting for him. He went to his stand alone; he found it without help now and stood on it as Sam had taught him. On the third morning he heard the dogs again, running strong and free on a true scent again, and he readied the gun as he had learned to do and heard the hunt sweep past on since he was not ready yet, had not deserved other yet in just one short period of two weeks as compared to all the long life which he had already dedicated to the wilderness with patience and humility; he heard the shot again, one shot, the single clapping report of Walter Ewell's rifle. By now he could not only find his stand and then return to camp without guidance, by using the compass his cousin had given him he reached Walter waiting beside the buck and the moiling of dogs over the cast entrails before any of the others except Major de Spain and Tennie's Jim on the horses, even before Uncle Ash arrived with the one-eyed wagon-mule which did not mind the smell of blood or even, so they said, of bear.

It was not Uncle Ash on the mule. It was Sam, returned. And Sam was waiting when he finished his dinner and, himself on the one-eyed mule and Sam on the other one of the wagon team, they rode for more than three hours through the rapid shortening sunless afternoon, following no path, no trail even that he could discern, into a section of country he had never seen before. Then he understood why Sam had made him ride the one-eyed mule which would not spook at the smell of blood, of wild animals. The other one, the sound one, stopped short and tried to whirl and bolt even as Sam got down, jerking and wrenching at the rein while Sam held it, coaxing it forward with his voice since he did not dare risk hitching it, drawing it forward while the boy dismounted from the marred one which would stand. Then, standing beside Sam in the thick great gloom of ancient woods and the winter's dying afternoon, he looked quietly down at the rotted log scored and gutted with claw-marks and, in the wet earth beside it, the print of the enormous warped two-toed foot. Now he knew what he had heard in the hounds' voices in the woods that morning and what he had smelled when he peered under the kitchen where they huddled. It was in him too, a little different because they were brute beasts and he was not, but only a little different—an eagerness, passive; an abjectness, a sense of his own fragility and impotence against the timeless woods, yet without doubt or dread; a flavor like brass in the sudden run of saliva in his mouth, a hard sharp constriction either in his brain or his stomach, he could not tell which and it did not matter; he knew only that for the first time he realised that the bear which had run in his listening and loomed in his dreams since before he could remember and which therefore must have existed in the listening and the dreams of his cousin and Major de Spain and even old General Compson before they began to remember in their turn, was a mortal animal and that they had departed for the camp each November with no actual intention of slaying it, not because it could not be slain but because so far they had no actual hope of being able to. "It will be tomorrow," he said.

"You mean we will try tomorrow," Sam said. "We aint got the dog yet."

"We've got eleven," he said. "They ran him Monday."

"And you heard them," Sam said. "Saw them too. We aint got the dog yet. It wont take but one. But he aint there. Maybe he aint nowhere. The only other way will be for him to run by accident over somebody that had a gun and knowed how to shoot it."

"That wouldn't be me," the boy said. "It would be Walter or Major or——"

"It might," Sam said. "You watch close tomorrow. Because he's smart. That's how come he has lived this long. If he gets hemmed up and has got to pick out somebody to run over, he will pick out you."

"How?" he said. "How will he know. . . ." He ceased. "You mean he already knows me, that I aint never been to the big bottom before, aint had time to find out yet whether I . . ." He ceased again, staring at Sam; he said humbly, not even amazed: "It was me he was watching. I don't reckon he did need to come but once."

"You watch tomorrow," Sam said. "I reckon we better start back. It'll be long after dark now before we get to camp."

The next morning they started three hours earlier than they had ever done. Even Uncle Ash went, the cook, who called himself by profession a camp cook and who did little else save cook for Major de Spain's hunting and camping parties, yet who had been marked by the wilderness from simple juxtaposition to it until he responded as they all did, even the boy who until two weeks ago had never even seen the wilderness, to a hound's ripped ear and shoulder and the print of a crooked foot in a patch of wet earth. They rode. It was too far to walk: the boy and Sam and Uncle Ash in the wagon with the dogs, his cousin and Major de Spain and General Compson and Boon and Walter and Tennie's Jim riding double on the horses; again the first gray light found him, as on that first morning two weeks ago, on the stand where Sam had placed and left him. With the gun which was too big for him, the breech-loader which did not even belong to him but to Major de Spain and which he had fired only once, at a stump on the first day to learn the recoil and how to reload it with the paper shells, he stood against a big gum tree beside a little bayou whose black still water crept without motion out of a cane-brake, across a small clearing and into the cane again, where, invisible, a bird, the big woodpecker called Lord-to-God by negroes, clattered at a dead trunk. It was a stand like any other stand, dissimilar only in incidentals to the one where he had stood each morning for two weeks; a territory new to him yet no less familiar than that other one which after two weeks he had come to believe he knew a little—the same solitude, the same loneliness through which frail and timorous man had merely passed without altering it, leaving no mark nor scar, which looked exactly as it must have looked when the first ancestor of Sam Fathers' Chickasaw predecessors crept into it and looked about him, club or stone axe or bone arrow drawn and ready, different only because, squatting at the edge of the kitchen, he had smelled the dogs huddled and cringing beneath it and saw the raked ear and side of the bitch that, as Sam had said, had to be brave once in order to keep on calling herself a dog, and saw yesterday in the earth beside the gutted log, the print of the living foot. He heard no dogs at all. He never did certainly hear them. He only heard the drumming of the woodpecker stop short off, and knew that the bear was looking at him. He never saw it. He did not know whether it was facing him from the cane or behind him. He did not move, holding the useless gun which he knew now he would never fire at it now or ever, tasting in his saliva that taint of brass which he had smelled in the huddled dogs when he peered under the kitchen.

Then it was gone. As abruptly as it had stopped, the woodpecker's dry hammering set up again, and after a while he believed he even heard the dogs—a murmur, scarce a sound even, which he had probably been hearing for a time, perhaps a minute or two, before he remarked it, drifting into hearing and then out again, dying away. They came nowhere near him. If it was dogs he heard, he could not have sworn to it; if it was a bear they ran, it was another bear. It was Sam himself who emerged from the cane and crossed the bayou, the injured bitch following at heel as a bird dog is taught to walk. She came and crouched against his leg, trembling. "I didn't see him," he said. "I didn't, Sam."

"I know it," Sam said. "He done the looking. You didn't hear him neither, did you?"

"No," the boy said. "I—"

"He's smart," Sam said. "Too smart." Again the boy saw in his eyes that quality of dark and brooding lambence as Sam looked down at the bitch trembling faintly and steadily against the boy's leg. From her raked shoulder a few drops of fresh blood clung like bright berries. "Too big. We aint got the dog yet. But maybe some day."

Because there would be a next time, after and after. He was only ten. It seemed to him that he could see them, the two of them, shadowy in the limbo from which time emerged and became time: the old bear absolved of mortality and himself who shared a little of it. Because he recognised now what he had smelled in the huddled dogs and tasted in his own saliva, recognised fear as a boy, a youth, recognises the existence of love and passion and experience which is his heritage but not yet his patrimony, from entering by chance the presence or perhaps even merely the bedroom of a woman who has loved and been loved by many men. *So I will have to see him,* he thought, without dread or even hope. *I will have to look at him.* So it was in June of the next summer. They were at the camp again, celebrating Major de Spain's and General Compson's birthdays. Although the one had been born in September and the other in the depth of winter and almost thirty years earlier, each June the two of them and McCaslin and Boon and Walter Ewell (and the boy too from now on) spent two weeks at the camp, fishing and shooting squirrels and turkey and running coons and wildcats with the dogs at night. That is, Boon and the negroes (and the boy too now) fished and shot squirrels and ran the coons and cats, because the proven hunters, not only Major de Spain and old General Compson (who spent those two weeks sitting in a rocking chair before a tremendous iron pot of Brunswick stew, stirring and tasting, with Uncle Ash to quarrel with about how he was making it and Tennie's Jim to pour whisky into the tin dipper from which he drank it) but even McCaslin and Walter Ewell who were still young enough, scorned such other than shooting the wild gobblers with pistols for wagers or to test their marksmanship.

That is, his cousin McCaslin and the others thought he was hunting squirrels. Until the third evening he believed that Sam Fathers thought so too. Each morning he would leave the camp right after breakfast. He had his own gun now, a new breech-loader, a Christmas gift; he would own and shoot it for almost seventy years, through two new pairs of barrels and locks and one new stock, until all that remained of the original gun was the silver-inlaid trigger-guard with his and McCaslin's engraved names and the date in 1878. He found the tree beside the little bayou where he had stood that morning. Using the compass he ranged from that point; he was teaching himself to be better than a fair woodsman without even knowing he was doing it. On the third day he even found the gutted log where he had first seen the print. It was almost completely crumbled now, healing with unbelievable speed, a passionate and almost visible relinquishment, back into the earth from which the tree had grown. He ranged the summer woods now, green with gloom, if anything actually dimmer than they had been in November's gray dissolution, where even at noon the sun fell only in windless dappling upon the earth which never completely dried and which crawled with snakes—moccasins and water-snakes and rattlers, themselves the color of the dappled gloom so that he would not always see them until they moved; returning to camp later and later and later, first day, second day, passing in the twilight of the third evening the little log pen enclosing the log barn where Sam was putting up the stock for the night. "You aint looked right yet," Sam said.

He stopped. For a moment he didn't answer. Then he said peacefully, in a peaceful rushing burst, as when a boy's miniature dam in a little brook gives way: "All right. Yes. But how? I went to the bayou. I even found that log again. I——"

"I reckon that was all right. Likely he's been watching you. You never saw his foot?"

"I . . ." the boy said. "I didn't . . . I never thought . . ."

"It's the gun," Sam said. He stood beside the fence, motionless, the old man, son of a negro slave and a Chickasaw chief, in the battered and faded overalls and the frayed five-cent straw hat which had been the badge of the negro's slavery and was now the regalia of his freedom. The camp—the clearing, the house, the barn and its tiny lot with which Major de Spain in his turn had scratched punily and evanescently at the wilderness—faded in the dusk, back into the immemorial darkness of the woods. *The gun,* the boy thought. *The gun.* "You will have to choose," Sam said.

He left the next morning before light, without breakfast, long before Uncle Ash would wake in his quilts on the kitchen floor and start the fire. He had only the compass and a stick for the snakes. He could go almost a mile before he would need to see the compass. He sat on a log, the invisible compass in his hand, while the secret night-sounds which had ceased at his movements, scurried again and then fell still for good and the owls ceased and gave over to the waking day birds and there was light in the gray wet woods and he could see the compass. He went fast yet still quietly, becoming steadily better and better as a woodsman without yet having time to realise it; he jumped a doe and a fawn, walked them out of the bed, close enough to see them—the crash of undergrowth, the white scut, the fawn scudding along behind her, faster than he had known it could have run. He was hunting right, upwind, as Sam had taught him, but that didn't matter now. He had left the gun; by his own will and relinquishment he had accepted not a gambit, not a choice, but a condition in which not only the bear's heretofore inviolable anonymity but all the ancient rules and balances of hunter and hunted had been abrogated. He would not even be afraid, not even in the moment when the fear would take him completely: blood, skin, bowels, bones, memory from the long time before it even became his memory—all save that thin clear quenchless lucidity which alone differed him from this bear and from all the other bears and bucks he would follow during almost seventy years, to which Sam had said: "Be scared. You cant help that. But dont be afraid. Aint nothing in the woods going to hurt you if you dont corner it or it dont smell that you are afraid. A bear or a deer has got to be scared of a coward the same as a brave man has got to be."

By noon he was far beyond the crossing on the little bayou, farther into the new and alien country than he had ever been, travelling now not only by the compass but by the old, heavy, biscuit-thick silver watch which had been his father's. He had left the camp nine hours ago; nine hours from now, dark would already have been an hour old. He stopped, for the first time since had had risen from the log when he could see the compass face at last, and looked about, mopping his sweating face on his sleeve. He had already relinquished, of his will, because of his need, in humility and peace and without regret, yet apparently that had not been enough, the leaving of the gun was not enough. He stood for a moment—a child, alien and lost in the green and soaring gloom of the markless wilderness. Then he relinquished completely to it. It was the watch and the compass. He was still tainted. He removed the linked chain of the one and the looped thong of the other from his overalls and hung them on a bush and leaned the stick beside them and entered it.

When he realised he was lost, he did as Sam had coached and drilled him: made a cast to cross his backtrack. He had not been going very fast for the last two or three hours, and he had gone even less fast since he left the compass and watch on the bush. So he went slower still now, since the tree could not be very far; in fact, he found it before he really expected to and turned and went to it. But there was no bush beneath it, no compass nor watch, so he did next as Sam had coached and drilled him: made this next circle in the opposite direction and much larger, so that the pattern of the two of them would bisect his track somewhere but crossing no trace nor mark anywhere of his feet or any feet, and now he was going faster though still not panicked, his heart beating a little more rapidly but strong and steady enough, and this time it was not even the tree because there was a down log beside it which he had never seen before and beyond the log a little swamp, a seepage of moisture somewhere between earth and water, and he did what Sam had coached and drilled him as the next and the last, seeing as he sat down on the log the crooked print, the warped indentation in the wet ground which while he looked at it continued to fill with water until it was level full and the water began to overflow and the sides of the print began to dissolve away. Even as he looked up he saw the next one, and, moving, the one beyond it; moving, not hurrying, running, but merely keeping pace with them as they appeared before him as though they were being shaped out of thin air just one constant pace short of where he would lose them forever and be lost forever himself, tireless, eager, without doubt or dread, panting a little above the strong rapid little hammer of his heart, emerging suddenly into a little glade and the wilderness coalesced. It rushed, soundless, and solidified—the tree, the bush, the compass and the watch glinting where a ray of sunlight touched them. Then he saw the bear. It did not emerge, appear: it was just there, immobile, fixed in the green and windless noon's hot dappling, not as big as he had dreamed it but as big as he had expected, bigger, dimensionless against the dappled obscurity, looking at him. Then it moved. It crossed the glade without haste, walking for an instant into the sun's full glare and out of it, and stopped again and looked back at him across one shoulder. Then it was gone. It didn't walk into the woods. It faded, sank back into the wilderness without motion as he had watched a fish, a huge old bass, sink back into the dark depths of its pool and vanish without even any movement of its fins.

Richard Wright / *Black Boy*
[Discovering Books] 1945

Born into a sharecropper family in Natchez, Mississippi, in 1908, Richard Wright spent his youth in Memphis, Tennessee, with relatives and, for a while, in an orphanage. His desultory formal education ended in the eighth grade but was augmented by the young man's own fervid program of extensive reading. Determined to be a writer but limited to menial employment, Wright broke from Depression-torn Memphis, working first in Chicago for the Federal Writers Project and then in New York where he compiled the government-sponsored Guide to Harlem *(1937).*

Though the five novellas comprising Uncle Tom's Children *(1938) were his first published works, Wright did not gain national prominence or financial security until the publication of his best-selling first novel,* Native Son *(1940). In the following chapter from his autobiography,* Black Boy, *Wright poignantly recounts his discovery of the freedom and influence exercised by writers and the inception of his own commitment to a literary career.*

Soon after the appearance of Black Boy, *Wright left for Paris, where he lived and wrote until his death in 1960.*

One morning I arrived early at work and went into the bank lobby where the Negro porter was mopping. I stood at a counter and picked up the Memphis *Commercial Appeal* and began my free reading of the press. I came finally to the editorial page and saw an article dealing with one H. L. Mencken. I knew by hearsay that he was the editor of the *American Mercury,* but aside from that I knew nothing about him. The article was a furious denunciation of Mencken, concluding with one, hot, short sentence: Mencken is a fool.

I wondered what on earth this Mencken had done to call down upon him the scorn of the South. The only people I had ever heard denounced in the South were Negroes, and this man was not a Negro. Then what ideas did Mencken hold that made a newspaper like the *Commercial Appeal* castigate him publicly? Undoubtedly he must be advocating ideas that the South did not like. Were there, then, people other than Negroes who criticized the South? I knew that during the Civil War the South had hated northern whites, but I had not encountered such hate during my life. Knowing no more of Mencken than I did at that moment, I felt a vague sympathy for him. Had not the South, which had assigned me the role of a non-man, cast at him its hardest words?

Now, how could I find out about this Mencken? There was a huge library near the riverfront, but I knew that Negroes were not allowed to patronize its shelves any more than they were the parks and playgrounds of the city. I had gone into the library several times to get books for the white men on the job. Which of them would now help me to get books? And how could I read them without causing concern to the white men with whom I worked? I had so far been successful in hiding my thoughts and feelings from them, but I knew that I would create hostility if I went about this business of reading in a clumsy way.

I weighed the personalities of the men on the job. There was Don, a Jew; but I distrusted him. His position was not much better than mine and I knew that he was uneasy and insecure; he had always treated me in an offhand, bantering way that barely concealed his contempt. I was afraid to ask him to help me to get books; his frantic desire to demonstrate a racial solidarity with the whites against Negroes might make him betray me.

Then how about the boss? No, he was a Baptist and I had the suspicion that he would not be quite able to comprehend why a black boy would want to read Mencken. There were other white men on the job whose attitudes showed clearly that they were Kluxers or sympathizers, and they were out of the question.

There remained only one man whose attitude did not fit into an anti-Negro category, for I had heard the white men refer to him as a "Pope lover." He was an Irish Catholic and was hated by the white Southerners. I knew that he read books, because I had got him volumes from the library several times. Since he, too, was an object of hatred, I felt that he might refuse me but would hardly betray me. I hesitated, weighing and balancing the imponderable realities.

One morning I paused before the Catholic fellow's desk.

"I want to ask you a favor," I whispered to him.

"What is it?"

"I want to read. I can't get books from the library. I wonder if you'd let me use your card?"

He looked at me suspiciously.

"My card is full most of the time," he said.

"I see," I said and waited, posing my question silently.

"You're not trying to get me into trouble, are you, boy?" he asked, staring at me.

"Oh, no, sir."

"What book do you want?"

"A book by H. L. Mencken."

"Which one?"

"I don't know. Has he written more than one?"

"He has written several."

"I didn't know that."

"What makes you want to read Mencken?"

"Oh, I just saw his name in the newspaper," I said.

"It's good of you to want to read," he said. "But you ought to read the right things."

I said nothing. Would he want to supervise my reading?

"Let me think," he said. "I'll figure out something."

I turned from him and he called me back. He stared at me quizzically.

"Richard, don't mention this to the other white men," he said.

"I understand," I said. "I won't say a word."

A few days later he called me to him.

"I've got a card in my wife's name," he said. "Here's mine."

"Thank you, sir."

"Do you think you can manage it?"

"I'll manage fine," I said.

"If they suspect you, you'll get in trouble," he said.

"I'll write the same kind of notes to the library that you wrote when you sent me for books," I told him. "I'll sign your name."

He laughed.

"Go ahead. Let me see what you get," he said.

That afternoon I addressed myself to forging a note. Now, what were the names of books written by H. L. Mencken? I did not know any of them. I finally wrote what I thought would be a foolproof note: *Dear Madam: Will you please let this nigger boy*—I used the word "nigger" to make the librarian feel that I could not possibly be the author of the note—*have some books by H. L. Mencken?* I forged the white man's name.

I entered the library as I had always done when on errands for whites, but I felt that I would somehow slip up and betray myself. I doffed my hat, stood a respectful distance from the desk, looked as unbookish as possible, and waited for the white patrons to be taken care of. When the desk was clear of people, I still waited. The white librarian looked at me.

"What do you want, boy?"

As though I did not possess the power of speech, I stepped forward and simply handed her the forged note, not parting my lips.

"What books by Mencken does he want?" she asked.

"I don't know, ma'am," I said, avoiding her eyes.

"Who gave you this card?"

"Mr. Falk," I said.

"Where is he?"

"He's at work, at the M—— Optical Company," I said. "I've been in here for him before."

"I remember," the woman said. "But he never wrote notes like this."

Oh, God, she's suspicious. Perhaps she would not let me have the books? If she had turned her back at that moment, I would have ducked out the door and never gone back. Then I thought of a bold idea.

"You can call him up, ma'am," I said, my heart pounding.

"You're not using these books, are you?" she asked pointedly.

"Oh, no, ma'am. I can't read."

"I don't know what he wants by Mencken," she said under her breath.

I knew now that I had won; she was thinking of other things and the race question had gone out of her mind. She went to the shelves. Once or twice she looked over her shoulder at me, as though she was still doubtful. Finally she came forward with two books in her hand.

"I'm sending him two books," she said. "But tell Mr. Falk to come in next time, or send me the names of the books he wants. I don't know what he wants to read."

I said nothing. She stamped the card and handed me the books. Not daring to glance at them, I went out of the library, fearing that the woman would call me back for further questioning. A block away from the library I opened one of the books and read a title: *A Book of Prefaces*. I was nearing my nineteenth birthday and I did not know how to pronounce the word "preface." I thumbed the pages and saw strange words and strange names. I shook my head, disappointed. I looked at the other book; it was called *Prejudices*. I knew what that word meant; I had heard it all my life. And right off I was on guard against Mencken's books. Why would a man want to call a book *Prejudices?* The word was so stained with all my memories of racial hate that I could not conceive of anybody using it for a title. Perhaps I had made a mistake about Mencken? A man who had prejudices must be wrong.

When I showed the books to Mr. Falk, he looked at me and frowned.

"That librarian might telephone you," I warned him.

"That's all right," he said. "But when you're through reading those books, I want you to tell me what you get out of them."

That night in my rented room, while letting the hot water run over my can of pork and beans in the sink, I opened *A Book of Prefaces* and began to read. I was jarred and shocked by the style, the clear, clean, sweeping sentences. Why did he write like that? And how did one write like that? I pictured the man as a raging demon, slashing with his pen, consumed with hate, denouncing everything American, extolling everything European or German, laughing at the weaknesses of people, mocking God, authority. What was this? I stood up, trying to realize what reality lay behind the meaning of the words . . . Yes, this man was fighting, fighting with words. He was using words as a weapon, using them as one would use a club. Could words be weapons? Well, yes, for here they were. Then, maybe, perhaps, I could use them as a weapon? No. It frightened me. I read on and what amazed me was not what he said, but how on earth anybody had the courage to say it.

Occasionally I glanced up to reassure myself that I was alone in the room. Who were these men about whom Mencken was talking so passionately? Who was Anatole France? Joseph Conrad? Sinclair Lewis, Sherwood Anderson, Dostoevski, George Moore, Gustave Flaubert, Maupassant, Tolstoy, Frank Harris, Mark Twain, Thomas Hardy, Arnold Bennett, Stephen Crane, Zola, Norris, Gorky, Bergson, Ibsen, Balzac, Bernard Shaw, Dumas, Poe, Thomas Mann, O. Henry, Dreiser, H. G. Wells, Gogol, T. S. Eliot, Gide, Baudelaire, Edgar Lee Masters, Stendhal, Turgenev, Huneker, Nietzsche, and scores of others? Were these men real? Did they exist or had they existed? And how did one pronounce their names?

I ran across many words whose meanings I did not know, and I either looked them up in a dictionary or, before I had a chance to do that, encountered the word in a context that made its meaning clear. But what strange world was this? I concluded the book with the conviction that I had somehow overlooked something terribly important in life. I had once tried to write, had once reveled in feeling, had let my crude imagination roam, but the impulse to dream had been slowly beaten out of me by experience. Now it surged up again and I hungered for books, new ways of looking and seeing. It was not a matter of believing or disbelieving what I read, but of feeling something new, of being affected by something that made the look of the world different.

As dawn broke I ate my pork and beans, feeling dopey, sleepy. I went to work, but the mood of the book would not die; it lingered, coloring everything I saw, heard, did. I now felt that I knew what the white men were feeling. Merely because I had read a book that had spoken of how they lived and thought, I identified myself with that book. I felt vaguely guilty. Would I, filled with bookish notions, act in a manner that would make the whites dislike me?

I forged more notes and my trips to the library became frequent. Reading grew into a passion. My first serious novel was Sinclair Lewis's *Main Street*. It made me see my boss, Mr. Gerald, and identify him as an American type. I would smile when I saw him lugging his golf bags into the office. I had always felt a vast distance separating me from the boss, and now I felt closer to him, though still distant. I felt now that I knew him, that I could feel the very limits of his narrow life. And this had happened because I had read a novel about a mythical man called George F. Babbitt.

The plots and stories in the novels did not interest me so much as the point of view revealed. I gave myself over to each novel without reserve, without trying to criticize it; it was enough for me to see and feel something different. And for me, everything was something different. Reading was like a drug, a dope. The novels created moods in which I lived for days. But I could not conquer my sense of guilt, my feeling that the white men around me knew that I was changing, that I had begun to regard them differently.

Whenever I brought a book to the job, I wrapped it in newspaper—a habit that was to persist for years in other cities and under other circumstances. But some of the white men pried into my packages when I was absent and they questioned me.

"Boy, what are you reading those books for?"

"Oh, I don't know, sir."

"That's deep stuff you're reading, boy."

"I'm just killing time, sir."

"You'll addle your brains if you don't watch out."

I read Dreiser's *Jennie Gerhardt* and *Sister Carrie* and they revived in me a vivid sense of my mother's suffering; I was overwhelmed. I grew silent, wondering about the life around me. It would have been impossible for me to have told anyone what I derived from these novels, for it was nothing less than a sense of life itself. All my life had shaped me for the realism, the naturalism of the modern novel, and I could not read enough of them.

Steeped in new moods and ideas, I bought a ream of paper and tried to write; but nothing would come, or what did come was flat beyond telling. I discovered that more than desire and feeling were necessary to write and I dropped the idea. Yet I still wondered how it was possible to know people sufficiently to write about them? Could I ever learn about life and people? To me, with my vast ignorance, my Jim Crow station in life, it seemed a task impossible of achievement. I now knew what being a Negro meant. I could endure the hunger. I had learned to live with hate. But to feel that there were feelings denied me, that the very breath of life itself was beyond my reach, that more than anything else hurt, wounded me. I had a new hunger.

In buoying me up, reading also cast me down, made me see what was possible, what I had missed. My tension returned, new, terrible, bitter, surging, almost too great to be contained. I no longer *felt* that the world about me was hostile, killing; I *knew* it. A million times I asked myself what I could do to save myself, and there were no answers. I seemed forever condemned, ringed by walls.

I did not discuss my reading with Mr. Falk, who had lent me his library card; it would have meant talking about myself and that would have been too painful. I smiled each day, fighting desperately to maintain my old behavior, to keep my disposition seemingly sunny. But some of the white men discerned that I had begun to brood.

"Wake up there, boy!" Mr. Olin said one day.

"Sir!" I answered for the lack of a better word.

"You act like you've stolen something," he said.

I laughed in the way I knew he expected me to laugh, but I resolved to be more conscious of myself, to watch my every act, to guard and hide the new knowledge that was dawning within me.

If I went north, would it be possible for me to build a new life then? But how could a man build a life upon vague, unformed yearnings? I wanted to write and I did not even know the English language. I bought English grammars and found them dull. I felt that I was getting a better sense of the language from novels than from grammars. I read hard, discarding a writer as soon as I felt that I had grasped his point of view. At night the printed page stood before my eyes in sleep.

Mrs. Moss, my landlady, asked me one Sunday morning:

"Son, what is this you keep on reading?"

"Oh, nothing. Just novels."

"What you get out of 'em?"

"I'm just killing time," I said.

"I hope you know your own mind," she said in a tone which implied that she doubted if I had a mind.

I knew of no Negroes who read the books I liked and I wondered if any Negroes ever thought of them. I knew that there were Negro doctors, lawyers, newspapermen, but I never saw any of them. When I read a Negro newspaper I never caught the faintest echo of my preoccupation in its pages. I felt trapped and occasionally, for a few days, I would stop reading. But a vague hunger would come over me for books, books that opened up new avenues of feeling and seeing, and again I would forge another note to the white librarian. Again I would read and wonder as only the naïve and unlettered can read and wonder, feeling that I carried a secret, criminal burden about with me each day.

That winter my mother and brother came and we set up housekeeping, buying furniture on the installment plan, being cheated and yet knowing no way to avoid it. I began to eat warm food and to my surprise found that regular meals enabled me to read faster. I may have lived through many illnesses and survived them, never suspecting that I was ill. My brother obtained a job and we began to save toward the trip north, plotting our time, setting tentative dates for departure. I told none of the white men on the job that I was planning to go north; I knew that the moment they felt I was thinking of the North they would change toward me. It would have made them feel that I did not like the life I was living, and because my life was completely conditioned by what they said or did, it would have been tantamount to challenging them.

I could calculate my chances for life in the South as a Negro fairly clearly now.

I could fight the southern whites by organizing with other Negroes, as my grandfather had done. But I knew that I could never win that way; there were many whites and there were but few blacks. They were strong and we were weak. Outright black rebellion could never win. If I fought openly I would die and I did not want to die. News of lynchings were frequent.

I could submit and live the life of a genial slave, but that was impossible. All of my life had shaped me to live by my own feelings and thoughts. I could make up to Bess and marry her and inherit the house. But that, too, would be the life of a slave; if I did that, I would crush to death something within me, and I would hate myself as much as I knew the whites already hated those who had submitted. Neither could I ever willingly present myself to be kicked, as Shorty had done. I would rather have died than do that.

I could drain off my restlessness by fighting with Shorty and Harrison. I had seen many Negroes solve the problem of being black by transferring their hatred of themselves to others with a black skin and fighting them. I would have to be cold to do that, and I was not cold and I could never be.

I could, of course, forget what I had read, thrust the whites out of my mind, forget them; and find release from anxiety and longing in sex and alcohol. But the memory of how my father had conducted himself made that course repugnant. If I did not want others to violate my life, how could I voluntarily violate it myself?

I had no hope whatever of being a professional man. Not only had I been so conditioned that I did not desire it, but the fulfillment of such an ambition was beyond my capabilities. Well-to-do Negroes lived in a world that was almost as alien to me as the world inhabited by whites.

What, then, was there? I held my life in my mind, in my consciousness each day, feeling at times that I would stumble and drop it, spill it forever. My reading had created a vast sense of distance between me and the world in which I lived and tried to make a living, and that sense of distance was increasing each day. My days and nights were one long, quiet, continuously contained dream of terror, tension, and anxiety. I wondered how long I could bear it.

Flannery O'Connor / The Life You Save May Be Your Own 1953

Born in Savannah, Georgia, in 1925, Flannery O'Connor was educated and spent most of her adult life in the small town of Milledgeville, Georgia. Her muse, like Hawthorne's, is lovingly provincial and, also like Hawthorne's, her grotesques, eccentrics, and spooks, though insistently local, live at the heart of the human condition. "My people," she said in an interview, "could come from anywhere, but naturally since I know the South they speak with a Southern accent."

"The Life You Save May Be Your Own" was originally published in the Spring 1953 issue of The Kenyon Review, *a quarterly periodical devoted to literature and criticism. As "The Life You Save," the story appeared in 1957 as a television play, ending, however, on a more positive note.*

The old woman and her daughter were sitting on their porch when Mr. Shiftlet came up their road for the first time. The old woman slid to the edge of her chair and leaned forward, shading her eyes from the piercing sunset with her hand. The daughter could not see far in front of her and continued to play with her fingers. Although the old woman lived in this desolate spot with only her daughter and she had never seen Mr. Shiftlet before, she could tell, even from a distance, that he was a tramp and no one to be afraid of. His left coat sleeve was folded up to show there was only half an arm in it and his gaunt figure listed slightly to the side as if the breeze were pushing him. He had on a black town suit and a brown felt hat that was turned up in the front and down in the back and he carried a tin tool box by a handle. He came on, at an amble, up her road, his face turned toward the sun which appeared to be balancing itself on the peak of a small mountain.

The old woman didn't change her position until he was almost into her yard; then she rose with one hand fisted on her hip. The daughter, a large girl in a short blue organdy dress, saw him all at once and jumped up and began to stamp and point and make excited speechless sounds.

Mr. Shiftlet stopped just inside the yard and set his box on the ground and tipped his hat at her as if she were not in the least afflicted; then he turned toward the old woman and swung the hat all the way off. He had long black slick hair that hung flat from a part in the middle to beyond the tips of his ears on either side. His face descended in forehead for more than half its length and ended suddenly with his features just balanced over a jutting steel-trap jaw. He seemed to be a young man but he had a look of composed dissatisfaction as if he understood life thoroughly.

"Good evening," the old woman said. She was about the size of a cedar fence post and she had a man's gray hat pulled down low over her head.

The tramp stood looking at her and didn't answer. He turned his back and faced the sunset. He swung both his whole and his short arm up slowly so that they indicated an expanse of sky and his figure formed a crooked cross. The old woman watched him with her arms folded across her chest as if she were the owner of the sun, and the daughter watched, her head thrust forward and her fat helpless hands hanging at the wrists. She had long pink-gold hair and eyes as blue as a peacock's neck.

He held the pose for almost fifty seconds and then he picked up his box and came on to the porch and dropped down on the bottom step. "Lady," he said in a firm nasal voice, "I'd give a fortune to live where I could see me a sun do that every evening."

"Does it every evening," the old woman said and sat back down. The daughter sat down too and watched him with a cautious sly look as if he were a bird that had come up very close. He leaned to one side, rooting in his pants pocket, and in a second he brought out a package of chewing gum and offered her a piece. She took it and unpeeled it and began to chew without taking her eyes off him. He offered the old woman a piece but she only raised her upper lip to indicate she had no teeth.

Mr. Shiftlet's pale sharp glance had already passed over everything in the yard—the pump near the corner of the house and the big fig tree that three or four chickens were preparing to roost in—and had moved to a shed where he saw the square rusted back of an automobile. "You ladies drive?" he asked.

"That car ain't run in fifteen year," the old woman said. "The day my husband died, it quit running."

"Nothing is like it used to be, lady," he said. "The world is almost rotten."

"That's right," the old woman said. "You from around here?"

"Name Tom T. Shiftlet," he murmured, looking at the tires.

"I'm pleased to meet you," the old woman said. "Name Lucynell Crater and daughter Lucynell Crater. What you doing around here, Mr. Shiftlet?"

He judged the car to be about a 1928 or '29 Ford. "Lady," he said, and turned and gave her his full attention, "lemme tell you something. There's one of these doctors in Atlanta that's taken a knife and cut the human heart—the human heart," he repeated, leaning forward, "out of a man's chest and held it in his hand," and he held his hand out, palm up, as if it were slightly weighted with the human heart, "and studied it like it was a day-old chicken, and lady," he said, allowing a long significant pause in which his head slid forward and his clay-colored eyes brightened, "he don't know no more about it than you or me."

"That's right," the old woman said.

"Why, if he was to take that knife and cut into every corner of it, he still wouldn't know no more than you or me. What you want to bet?"

"Nothing," the old woman said wisely. "Where you come from, Mr. Shiftlet?"

He didn't answer. He reached into his pocket and brought out a sack of tobacco and a package of cigarette papers and rolled himself a cigarette, expertly with one hand, and attached it in a hanging position to his upper lip. Then he took a box of wooden matches from his pocket and struck one on his shoe. He held the burning match as if he were studying the mystery of flame while it traveled dangerously toward his skin. The daughter began to make loud noises and to point to his hand and shake her finger at him, but when the flame was just before touching him, he leaned down with his hand cupped over it as if he were going to set fire to his nose and lit the cigarette.

He flipped away the dead match and blew a stream of gray into the evening. A sly look came over his face. "Lady," he said, "nowadays, people'll do anything anyways. I can tell you my name is Tom T. Shiftlet and I come from Tarwater, Tennessee, but you never have seen me before: how you know I ain't lying? How you know my name ain't Aaron Sparks, lady, and I come from Singleberry, Georgia, or how you know it's not George Speeds and I come from Lucy, Alabama, or how you know I ain't Thompson Bright from Toolafalls, Mississippi?"

"I don't know nothing about you," the old woman muttered, irked.

"Lady," he said, "people don't care how they lie. Maybe the best I can tell you is, I'm a man; but listen lady," he said and paused and made his tone more ominous still, "what is a man?"

The old woman began to gum a seed. "What you carry in that tin box, Mr. Shiftlet?" she asked.

"Tools," he said, put back. "I'm a carpenter."

"Well, if you come out here to work, I'll be able to feed you and give you a place to sleep but I can't pay. I'll tell you that before you begin," she said.

There was no answer at once and no particular expression on his face. He leaned back against the two-by-four that helped support the porch roof. "Lady," he said slowly, "there's some men that some things mean more to them than money." The old woman rocked without comment and the daughter watched the trigger that moved up and down in his neck. He told the old woman then that all most people were interested in was money, but he asked what a man was made for. He asked her if a man was made for money, or what. He asked her what she thought she was made for but she didn't answer, she only sat rocking and wondered if a one-armed man could put a new roof on her garden house. He asked a lot of questions that she didn't answer. He told her that he was twenty-eight years old and had lived a varied life. He had been a gospel singer, a foreman on the railroad, an assistant in an undertaking parlor, and he come over the radio for three months with Uncle Roy and his Red Creek Wranglers. He said he had fought and bled in the Arm Service of his country and visited every foreign land and that everywhere he had seen people that didn't care if they did a thing one way or another. He said he hadn't been raised thataway.

A fat yellow moon appeared in the branches of the fig tree as if it were going to roost there with the chickens. He said that a man had to escape to the country to see the world whole and that he wished he lived in a desolate place like this where he could see the sun go down every evening like God made it to do.

"Are you married or are you single?" the old woman asked.

There was a long silence. "Lady," he asked finally, "where would you find you an innocent woman today? I wouldn't have any of this trash I could just pick up."

The daughter was leaning very far down, hanging her head almost between her knees, watching him through a triangular door she had made in her overturned hair; and she suddenly fell in a heap on the floor and began to whimper. Mr. Shiftlet straightened her out and helped her get back in the chair.

"Is she your baby girl?" he asked.

"My only," the old woman said, "and she's the sweetest girl in the world. I would give her up for nothing on earth. She's smart too. She can sweep the floor, cook, wash, feed the chickens, and hoe. I wouldn't give her up for a casket of jewels."

"No," he said kindly, "don't ever let any man take her away from you."

"Any man come after her," the old woman said, "he'll have to stay around the place."

Mr. Shiftlet's eye in the darkness was focused on a part of the automobile bumper that glittered in the distance.

"Lady," he said, jerking his short arm up as if he could point with it to her house and yard and pump, "there ain't a broken thing on this plantation that I couldn't fix for you, one-arm jackleg or not. I'm a man,'' he said with a sullen dignity, ''even if I ain't a whole one. I got,'' he said, tapping his knuckles on the floor to emphasize the immensity of what he was going to say, ''a moral intelligence!'' and his face pierced out of the darkness into a shaft of doorlight and he stared at her as if he were astonished himself at this impossible truth.

The old woman was not impressed with the phrase. ''I told you you could hang around and work for food,'' she said, ''if you don't mind sleeping in that car yonder.''

''Why listen, lady,'' he said with a grin of delight, ''the monks of old slept in their coffins!''

''They wasn't as advanced as we are,'' the old woman said.

The next morning he began on the roof of the garden house while Lucynell, the daughter, sat on a rock and watched him work. He had not been around a week before the change he had made in the place was apparent. He had patched the front and back steps, built a new hog pen, restored a fence, and taught Lucynell, who was completely deaf and had never said a word in her life, to say the word ''bird.'' The big rosy-faced girl followed him everywhere, saying ''Burrttddt ddbirrrttdt,'' and clapping her hands. The old woman watched from a distance, secretly pleased. She was ravenous for a son-in-law.

Mr. Shiftlet slept on the hard narrow back seat of the car with his feet out the side window. He had his razor and a can of water on a crate that served him as a bedside table and he put up a piece of mirror against the back glass and kept his coat neatly on a hanger that he hung over one of the windows.

In the evenings he sat on the steps and talked while the old woman and Lucynell rocked violently in their chairs on either side of him. The old woman's three mountains were black against the dark blue sky and were visited off and on by various planets and by the moon after it had left the chickens. Mr. Shiftlet pointed out that the reason he had improved this plantation was because he had taken a personal interest in it. He said he was even going to make the automobile run.

He had raised the hood and studied the mechanism and he said he could tell that the car had been built in the days when cars were really built. You take now, he said, one man puts in one bolt and another man puts in another bolt and another man puts in another bolt so that it's a man for a bolt. That's why you have to pay so much for a car: you're paying all those men. Now if you didn't have to pay but one man, you could get you a cheaper car and one that had had a personal interest taken in it, and it would be a better car. The old woman agreed with him that this was so.

Mr. Shiftlet said that the trouble with the world was that nobody cared, or stopped and took any trouble. He said he never would have been able to teach Lucynell to say a word if he hadn't cared and stopped long enough.

''Teach her to say something else,'' the old woman said.

''What you want her to say next?'' Mr. Shiftlet asked.

The old woman's smile was broad and toothless and suggestive. ''Teach her to say 'sugarpie,' '' she said.

Mr. Shiftlet already knew what was on her mind.

The next day he began to tinker with the automobile and that evening he told her that if she would buy a fan belt, he would be able to make the car run.

The old woman said she would give him the money. ''You see that girl yonder?'' she asked, pointing to Lucynell who was sitting on the floor a foot away, watching him, her eyes blue even in the dark. ''If it was ever a man wanted to take her away, I would say, 'No man on earth is going to take that sweet girl of mine away from me!' but if he was to say, 'Lady, I don't want to take her away, I want her right here,' I would say, 'Mister, I don't blame you none. I wouldn't pass up a chance to live in a permanent place and get the sweetest girl in the world myself. You ain't no fool,' I would say."

"How old is she?" Mr. Shiftlet asked casually.

"Fifteen, sixteen," the old woman said. The girl was nearly thirty but because of her innocence it was impossible to guess.

"It would be a good idea to paint it too," Mr. Shiftlet remarked. "You don't want it to rust out."

"We'll see about that later," the old woman said.

The next day he walked into town and returned with the parts he needed and a can of gasoline. Late in the afternoon, terrible noises issued from the shed and the old woman rushed out of the house, thinking Lucynell was somewhere having a fit. Lucynell was sitting on a chicken crate, stamping her feet and screaming, "Burrddttt! bddurrddtttt!" but her fuss was drowned out by the car. With a volley of blasts it emerged from the shed, moving in a fierce and stately way. Mr. Shiftlet was in the driver's seat, sitting very erect. He had an expression of serious modesty on his face as if he had just raised the dead.

That night, rocking on the porch, the old woman began her business at once. "You want you an innocent woman, don't you?" she asked sympathetically. "You don't want none of this trash."

"No'm, I don't," Mr. Shiftlet said.

"One that can't talk," she continued, "can't sass you back or use foul language. That's the kind for you to have. Right there," and she pointed to Lucynell sitting cross-legged in her chair, holding both feet in her hands.

"That's right," he admitted. "She wouldn't give me any trouble."

"Saturday," the old woman said, "you and her and me can drive into town and get married."

Mr. Shiftlet eased his position on the steps.

"I can't get married right now," he said. "Everything you want to do takes money and I ain't got any."

"What you need with money?" she asked.

"It takes money," he said. "Some people'll do anything anyhow these days, but the way I think, I wouldn't marry no woman that I couldn't take on a trip like she was somebody. I mean take her to a hotel and treat her. I wouldn't marry the Duchesser Windsor," he said firmly, "unless I could take her to a hotel and giver something good to eat.

"I was raised thataway and there ain't a thing I can do about it. My old mother taught me how to do."

"Lucynell don't even know what a hotel is," the old woman muttered. "Listen here, Mr. Shiftlet," she said, sliding forward in her chair, "you'd be getting a permanent house and a deep well and the most innocent girl in the world. You don't need no money. Lemme tell you something: there ain't any place in the world for a poor disabled friendless drifting man."

The ugly words settled in Mr. Shiftlet's head like a group of buzzards in the top of a tree. He didn't answer at once. He rolled himself a cigarette and lit it and then he said in an even voice, "Lady, a man is divided into two parts, body and spirit."

The old woman clamped her gums together.

"A body and a spirit," he repeated. "The body, lady, is like a house: it don't go anywhere: but the spirit, lady, is like a automobile: always on the move, always . . ."

"Listen, Mr. Shiftlet," she said, "my well never goes dry and my house is always warm in the winter and there's no mortgage on a thing about this place. You can go to the courthouse and see for yourself. And yonder under that shed is a fine automobile." She laid the bait carefully. "You can have it painted by Saturday. I'll pay for the paint."

In the darkness, Mr. Shiftlet's smile stretched like a weary snake waking up by a fire. After a second he recalled himself and said, "I'm only saying a man's spirit means more to him than anything else. I would have to take my wife off for the week end without no regards at all for cost. I got to follow where my spirit says to go."

"I'll give you fifteen dollars for a week-end trip," the old woman said in a crabbed voice. "That's the best I can do."

"That wouldn't hardly pay for more than the gas and the hotel," he said. "It wouldn't feed her."

"Seventeen-fifty," the old woman said. "That's all I got so it isn't any use you trying to milk me. You can take a lunch."

Mr. Shiftlet was deeply hurt by the word "milk." He didn't doubt that she had more money sewed up in her mattress but he had already told her he was not interested in her money. "I'll make that do," he said and rose and walked off without treating with her further.

On Saturday the three of them drove into town in the car that the paint had barely dried on and Mr. Shiftlet and Lucynell were married in the Ordinary's office while the old woman witnessed. As they came out of the courthouse, Mr. Shiftlet began twisting his neck in his collar. He looked morose and bitter as if he had been insulted while someone held him. "That didn't satisfy me none," he said. "That was just something a woman in an office did, nothing but paper work and blood tests. What do they know about my blood? If they was to take my heart and cut it out," he said, "they wouldn't know a thing about me. It didn't satisfy me at all."

"It satisfied the law," the old woman said sharply.

"The law," Mr. Shiftlet said and spit. "It's the law that don't satisfy me."

He had painted the car dark green with a yellow band around it just under the windows. The three of them climbed in the front seat and the old woman said, "Don't Lucynell look pretty? Looks like a baby doll." Lucynell was dressed up in a white dress that her mother had uprooted from a trunk and there was a Panama hat on her head with a bunch of red wooden cherries on the brim. Every now and then her placid expression was changed by a sly isolated little thought like a shoot of green in the desert. "You got a prize!" the old woman said.

Mr. Shiftlet didn't even look at her.

They drove back to the house to let the old woman off and pick up the lunch. When they were ready to leave, she stood staring in the window of the car, with her fingers clenched around the glass. Tears began to seep sideways out of her eyes and run along the dirty creases in her face. "I ain't ever been parted with her for two days before," she said.

Mr. Shiftlet started the motor.

"And I wouldn't let no man have her but you because I seen you would do right. Good-by, Sugarbaby," she said, clutching at the sleeve of the white dress. Lucynell looked straight at her and didn't seem to see her there at all. Mr. Shiftlet eased the car forward so that she had to move her hands.

The early afternoon was clear and open and surrounded by pale blue sky. Although the car would go only thirty miles an hour, Mr. Shiftlet imagined a terrific climb and dip and swerve that went entirely to his head so that he forgot his morning bitterness. He had always wanted an automobile but he had never been able to afford one before. He drove very fast because he wanted to make Mobile by nightfall.

Occasionally he stopped his thoughts long enough to look at Lucynell in the seat beside him. She had eaten the lunch as soon as they were out of the yard and now she was pulling the cherries off the hat one by one and throwing them out the window. He became depressed in spite of the car. He had driven about a hundred miles when he decided that she must be hungry again and at the next small town they came to, he stopped in front of an aluminum-painted eating place called The Hot

Spot and took her in and ordered her a plate of ham and grits. The ride had made her sleepy and as soon as she got up on the stool, she rested her head on the counter and shut her eyes. There was no one in The Hot Spot but Mr. Shiftlet and the boy behind the counter, a pale youth with a greasy rag hung over his shoulder. Before he could dish up the food, she was snoring gently.

"Give it to her when she wakes up," Mr. Shiftlet said. "I'll pay for it now."

The boy bent over her and stared at the long pink-gold hair and the half-shut sleeping eyes. Then he looked up and stared at Mr. Shiftlet. "She looks like an angel of Gawd," he murmured.

"Hitch-hiker," Mr. Shiftlet explained. "I can't wait. I got to make Tuscaloosa."

The boy bent over again and very carefully touched his finger to a strand of the golden hair and Mr. Shiftlet left.

He was more depressed than ever as he drove on by himself. The late afternoon had grown hot and sultry and the country had flattened out. Deep in the sky a storm was preparing very slowly and without thunder as if it meant to drain every drop of air from the earth before it broke. There were times when Mr. Shiftlet preferred not to be alone. He felt too that a man with a car had a responsibility to others and he kept his eye out for a hitchhiker. Occasionally he saw a sign that warned: "Drive carefully. The life you save may be your own."

The narrow road dropped off on either side into dry fields and here and there a shack or a filling station stood in a clearing. The sun began to set directly in front of the automobile. It was a reddening ball that through his windshield was slightly flat on the bottom and top. He saw a boy in overalls and a gray hat standing on the edge of the road and he slowed the car down and stopped in front of him. The boy didn't have his hand raised to thumb the ride, he was only standing there, but he had a small cardboard suitcase and his hat was set on his head in a way to indicate that he had left somewhere for good. "Son," Mr. Shiftlet said, "I see you want a ride."

The boy didn't say he did or he didn't but he opened the door of the car and got in, and Mr. Shiftlet started driving again. The child held the suitcase on his lap and folded his arms on top of it. He turned his head and looked out the window away from Mr. Shiftlet. Mr. Shiftlet felt oppressed. "Son," he said after a minute, "I got the best old mother in the world so I reckon you only got the second best."

The boy gave him a quick dark glance and then turned his face back out the window.

"It's nothing so sweet," Mr. Shiftlet continued, "as a boy's mother. She taught him his first prayers at her knee, she gave him love when no other would, she told him what was right and what wasn't, and she seen that he done the right thing. Son," he said, "I never rued a day in my life like the one I rued when I left that old mother of mine."

The boy shifted in his seat but he didn't look at Mr. Shiftlet. He unfolded his arms and put one hand on the door handle.

"My mother was a angel of Gawd," Mr. Shiftlet said in a very strained voice. "He took her from heaven and giver to me and I left her." His eyes were instantly clouded over with a mist of tears. The car was barely moving.

The boy turned angrily in the seat. "You go to the devil!" he cried. "My old woman is a flea bag and yours is a stinking pole cat!" and with that he flung the door open and jumped out with his suitcase into the ditch.

Mr. Shiftlet was so shocked that for about a hundred feet he drove along slowly with the door still open. A cloud, the exact color of the boy's hat and shaped like a turnip, had descended over the sun, and another, worse looking, crouched behind the car. Mr. Shiftlet felt that the rottenness of the world was about to engulf him. He raised his arm and let it fall again to his breast. "Oh Lord!" he prayed. "Break forth and wash the slime from this earth!"

The turnip continued slowly to descend. After a few minutes there was a guffawing peal of thunder from behind and fantastic raindrops, like tin-can tops, crashed over the rear of Mr. Shiftlet's car. Very quickly he stepped on the gas and with his stump sticking out the window he raced the galloping shower into Mobile.

Tille Olsen / *Tell Me a Riddle* 1953–54

In Tell Me a Riddle, *Tillie Olsen ''found characters who could fully embody her vision of hope with hopelessness, of beauty in the midst of ugliness,'' in the view of one critic writing for the* New Republic. *Many of the stories in that collection have been anthologized and widely acclaimed. ''I Stand Here Ironing'' has been read on the radio and recorded in the Lamont Poetry Room at Harvard. Her most recent books are* Silences *(1979) and* Mothers and Daughters *(1987).*

Born in Omaha, Nebraska, in 1913, Olsen has worked in factories and as a typist-transcriber. She was awarded a Stanford University Creative Writing Fellowship (1955–56), a Ford Foundation Grant in Literature (1956), and a fellowship to the Radcliffe Institute for Independent Study (1962–64).

I STAND HERE IRONING

I stand here ironing, and what you asked me moves tormented back and forth with the iron.

''I wish you would manage the time to come in and talk with me about your daughter. I'm sure you can help me understand her. She's a youngster who needs help and whom I'm deeply interested in helping.''

''Who needs help.'' . . . Even if I came, what good would it do? You think because I am her mother I have a key, or that in some way you could use me as a key? She has lived for nineteen years. There is all that life that has happened outside of me, beyond me.

And when is there time to remember, to sift, to weigh, to estimate, to total? I will start and there will be an interruption and I will have to gather it all together again. Or I will become engulfed with all I did or did not do, with what should have been and what cannot be helped.

She was a beautiful baby. The first and only one of our five that was beautiful at birth. You do not guess how new and uneasy her tenancy in her now-loveliness. You did not know her all those years she was thought homely, or see her poring over her baby pictures, making me tell her over and over how beautiful she had been—and would be, I would tell her—and was now, to the seeing eye. But the seeing eyes were few or nonexistent. Including mine.

I nursed her. They feel that's important nowadays. I nursed all the children, but with her, with all the fierce rigidity of first motherhood, I did like the books then said. Though her cries battered me to trembling and my breasts ached with swollenness, I waited till the clock decreed.

Why do I put that first? I do not even know if it matters, or if it explains anything.

She was a beautiful baby. She blew shining bubbles of sound. She loved motion, loved light, loved color and music and textures. She would lie on the floor in her blue overalls patting the surface so hard in ecstasy her hands and feet would blur. She was a miracle to me, but when she was eight months old I had to leave her daytimes with the woman downstairs to whom she was no miracle at all, for I worked or looked for work and for Emily's father, who "could no longer endure" (he wrote in his good-bye note) "sharing want with us."

I was nineteen. It was the pre-relief, pre-WPA world of the depression. I would start running as soon as I got off the streetcar, running up the stairs, the place smelling sour, and awake or asleep to startle awake, when she saw me she would break into a clogged weeping that could not be comforted, a weeping I can hear yet.

After a while I found a job hashing at night so I could be with her days, and it was better. But it came to where I had to bring her to this family and leave her.

It took a long time to raise the money for her fare back. Then she got chicken pox and I had to wait longer. When she finally came, I hardly knew her, walking quick and nervous like her father, looking like her father, thin, and dressed in a shoddy red that yellowed her skin and glared at the pockmarks. All the baby loveliness gone.

She was two. Old enough for nursery school they said, and I did not know then what I know now—the fatigue of the long day, and the lacerations of group life in the kinds of nurseries that are only parking places for children.

Except that it would have made no difference if I had known. It was the only place there was. It was the only way we could be together, the only way I could hold a job.

And even without knowing, I knew. I knew the teacher that was evil because all these years it has curdled into my memory, the little boy hunched in the corner, her rasp, "why aren't you outside, because Alvin hits you? that's no reason, go out, scaredy." I knew Emily hated it even if she did not clutch and implore "don't go Mommy" like the other children, mornings.

She always had a reason why we should stay home. Momma, you look sick. Momma, I feel sick. Momma, the teachers aren't there today, they're sick. Momma, we can't go, there was a fire there last night. Momma, it's a holiday today, no school, they told me.

But never a direct protest, never rebellion. I think of our others in their three-, four-year-oldness—the explosions, the tempers, the denunciations, the demands—and I feel suddenly ill. I put the iron down. What in me demanded that goodness in her? And what was the cost, the cost to her of such goodness?

The old man living in the back once said in his gentle way: "You should smile at Emily more when you look at her." What *was* in my face when I looked at her? I loved her. There were all the acts of love.

It was only with the others I remembered what he said, and it was the face of joy, and not of care or tightness or worry I turned to them—too late for Emily. She does not smile easily, let alone almost always as her brothers and sisters do. Her face is closed and sombre, but when she wants, how fluid. You must have seen it in her pantomimes, you spoke of her rare gift for comedy on the stage that rouses a laughter out of the audience so dear they applaud and applaud and do not want to let her go.

Where does it come from, that comedy? There was none of it in her when she came back to me that second time, after I had had to send her away again. She had a new daddy now to learn to love, and I think perhaps it was a better time.

Except when we left her alone nights, telling ourselves she was old enough.

"Can't you go some other time, Mommy, like tomorrow?" she would ask. "Will it be just a little while you'll be gone? Do you promise?"

The time we came back, the front door open, the clock on the floor in the hall. She rigid awake. "It wasn't just a little while. I didn't cry. Three times I called you, just three times, and then I ran downstairs to open the door so you could come faster. The clock talked loud. I threw it away, it scared me what it talked."

She said the clock talked loud again that night I went to the hospital to have Susan. She was delirious with the fever that comes before red measles, but she was fully conscious all the week I was gone and the week after we were home when she could not come near the new baby or me.

She did not get well. She stayed skeleton thin, not wanting to eat, and night after night she had nightmares. She would call for me, and I would rouse from exhaustion to sleepily call back: "You're all right, darling, go to sleep, it's just a dream," and if she still called, in a sterner voice, "now go to sleep, Emily, there's nothing to hurt you." Twice, only twice, when I had to get up for Susan anyhow, I went in to sit with her.

Now when it is too late (as if she would let me hold and comfort her like I do the others) I get up and go to her at once at her moan or restless stirring. "Are you awake, Emily? Can I get you something?" And the answer is always the same: "No, I'm all right, go back to sleep, Mother."

They persuaded me at the clinic to send her away to a convalescent home in the country where "she can have the kind of food and care you can't manage for her, and you'll be free to concentrate on the new baby." They still send children to that place. I see pictures on the society page of sleek young women planning affairs to raise money for it, or dancing at the affairs, or decorating Easter eggs or filling Christmas stockings for the children.

They never have a picture of the children so I do not know if the girls still wear those gigantic red bows and the ravaged looks on the every other Sunday when parents can come to visit "unless otherwise notified"—as we were notified the first six weeks.

Oh it is a handsome place, green lawns and tall trees and fluted flower beds. High up on the balconies of each cottage the children stand, the girls in their red bows and white dresses, the boys in white suits and giant red ties. The parents stand below shrieking up to be heard and the children shriek down to be heard, and between them the invisible wall "Not To Be Contaminated by Parental Germs or Physical Affection."

There was a tiny girl who always stood hand in hand with Emily. Her parents never came. One visit she was gone. "They moved her to Rose Cottage" Emily shouted in explanation. "They don't like you to love anybody here."

She wrote once a week, the labored writing of a seven-year-old. "I am fine. How is the baby. If I write my leter nicly I will have a star. Love." There never was a star. We wrote every other day, letters she could never hold or keep but only hear read—once. "We simply do not have room for children to keep any personal possessions," they patiently explained when we pieced one Sunday's shrieking together to plead how much it would mean to Emily, who loved so to keep things, to be allowed to keep her letters and cards.

Each visit she looked frailer, "She isn't eating," they told us.

(They had runny eggs for breakfast or mush with lumps, Emily said later, I'd hold it in my mouth and not swallow. Nothing ever tasted good, just when they had chicken.)

It took us eight months to get her released home, and only the fact that she gained back so little of her seven lost pounds convinced the social worker.

I used to try to hold and love her after she came back, but her body would stay stiff, and after a while she'd push away. She ate little. Food sickened her, and I think much of life too. Oh she had physical lightness and brightness, twinkling by on skates, bouncing like a ball up and down up and down over the jump rope, skimming over the hill; but these were momentary.

She fretted about her appearance, thin and dark and foreign-looking at a time when every little girl was supposed to look or thought she should look a chubby blonde replica of Shirley Temple. The doorbell sometimes rang for her, but no one seemed to come and play in the house or be a best friend. Maybe because we moved so much.

There was a boy she loved painfully through two school semesters. Months later she told me how she had taken pennies from my purse to buy him candy. "Licorice was his favorite and I brought him some every day, but he still liked Jennifer better'n me. Why, Mommy?" The kind of question for which there is no answer.

School was a worry to her. She was not glib or quick in a world where glibness and quickness were easily confused with ability to learn. To her overworked and exasperated teachers she was an overconscientious "slow learner" who kept trying to catch up and was absent entirely too often.

I let her be absent, though sometimes the illness was imaginary. How different from my now-strictness about attendance with the others. I wasn't working. We had a new baby, I was home anyhow. Sometimes, after Susan grew old enough, I would keep her home from school, too, to have them all together.

Mostly Emily had asthma, and her breathing, harsh and labored, would fill the house with a curiously tranquil sound. I would bring the two old dresser mirrors and her boxes of collections to her bed. She would select beads and single earrings, bottle tops and shells, dried flowers and pebbles, old postcards and scraps, all sorts of oddments; then she and Susan would play Kingdom, setting up landscapes and furniture, peopling them with action.

Those were the only times of peaceful companionship between her and Susan. I have edged away from it, that poisonous feeling between them, that terrible balancing of hurts and needs I had to do between the two, and did so badly, those earlier years.

Oh there are conflicts between the others too, each one human, needing, demanding, hurting, taking—but only between Emily and Susan, no, Emily toward Susan that corroding resentment. It seems so obvious on the surface, yet it is not obvious. Susan, the second child, Susan, golden- and curly-haired and chubby, quick and articulate and assured, everything in appearance and manner Emily was not; Susan, not able to resist Emily's precious things, losing or sometimes clumsily breaking them; Susan telling jokes and riddles to company for applause while Emily sat silent (to say to me later: that was *my* riddle, Mother, I told it to Susan); Susan, who for all the five years' difference in age was just a year behind Emily in developing physically.

I am glad for that slow physical development that widened the difference between her and her contemporaries, though she suffered over it. She was too vulnerable for that terrible world of youthful competition, of preening and parading, of constant measuring of yourself against every other, of envy, "If I had that copper hair," "If I had that skin. . . ." She tormented herself enough about not looking like the others, there was enough of the unsureness, the having to be conscious of words before you speak, the constant caring—what are they thinking of me? without having it all magnified by the merciless physical drives.

Ronnie is calling. He is wet and I change him. It is rare there is such a cry now. That time of motherhood is almost behind me when the ear is not one's own but must always be racked and listening for the child cry, the child call. We sit for a while and I hold him, looking out over the city spread in charcoal with its soft aisles of light. *"Shoogily,"* he breathes and curls closer. I carry him back to bed, asleep. *Shoogily*. A funny word, a family word, inherited from Emily, invested by her to say: *comfort*.

In this and other ways she leaves her seal, I say aloud. And startle at my saying it. What do I mean? What did I start to gather together, to try and make coherent? I was at the terrible, growing years. War years. I do not remember them well. I was working, there were four smaller ones now, there was not time for her. She had to help be a mother, and housekeeper, and shopper. She had to set her seal. Mornings of crisis and near hysteria trying to get lunches packed, hair combed, coats and shoes found, everyone to school or Child Care on time, the baby ready for transportation. And always the paper scribbled on by a smaller one, the book looked at by Susan then mislaid, the homework not done. Running out to that huge school where she was one, she was lost, she was a drop; suffering over the unpreparedness, stammering and unsure of her classes.

There was so little time left at night after the kids were bedded down. She would struggle over books, always eating (it was in those years she developed her enormous appetite that is legendary in our family) and I would be ironing, or preparing food for the next day, or writing V-mail to Bill, or tending the baby. Sometimes, to make me laugh, or out of her despair, she would imitate happenings or types at school.

I think I said once: "Why don't you do something like this in the school amateur show?" One morning she phoned me at work, hardly understandable through the weeping: "Mother, I did it. I won, I won; they gave me first prize; they clapped and clapped and wouldn't let me go."

Now suddenly she was Somebody, and as imprisoned in her difference as she had been in anonymity.

She began to be asked to perform at other high schools, even in colleges, then at city and statewide affairs. The first one we went to, I only recognized her that first moment when thin, shy, she almost drowned herself into the curtains. Then: Was this Emily? The control, the command, the convulsing and deadly clowning, the spell, then the roaring, stamping audience, unwilling to let this rare and precious laughter out of their lives.

Afterwards: You ought to do something about her with a gift like that—but without money or knowing how, what does one do? We have left it all to her, and the gift has as often eddied inside, clogged and clotted, as been used and growing.

She is coming. She runs up the stairs two at a time with her light graceful step, and I know she is happy tonight. Whatever it was that occasioned your call did not happen today.

"Aren't you ever going to finish the ironing, Mother? Whistler painted his mother in a rocker. I'd have to paint mine standing over an ironing board." This is one of her communicative nights and she tells me everything and nothing as she fixes herself a plate of food out of the icebox.

She is so lovely. Why did you want me to come in at all? Why were you concerned? She will find her way.

She starts up the stairs to bed. "Don't get me up with the rest in the morning." "But I thought you were having midterms." "Oh, those," she comes back in, kisses me, and say quite lightly, "in a couple of years when we'll all be atom-dead they won't matter a bit."

She has said it before. She *believes* it. But because I have been dredging the past, and all that compounds a human being is so heavy and meaningful in me, I cannot endure it tonight.

I will never total it all. I will never come in to say: She was a child seldom smiled at. Her father left me before she was a year old. I had to work her first six years when there was work, or I sent her home and to his relatives. There were years she had care she hated. She was dark and thin and foreign-looking in a world where the prestige went to blondeness and curly hair and dimples, she was slow where glibness was prized. She was a child of anxious, not proud, love. We were poor and could not afford for her the soil of easy growth. I was a young mother, I was a distracted mother. There were the other children pushing up, demanding. Her younger sister seemed all that she was not. There were years she did not want me to touch her. She kept too much in herself, her life was such she had to keep too much in herself. My wisdom came too late. She has much to her and probably little will come of it. She is a child of her age, of depression, of war, of fear.

Let her be. So all that is in her will not bloom—but in how many does it? There is still enough left to live by. Only help her to know—help make it so there is cause for her to know—that she is more than this dress on the ironing board, helpless before the iron.

DISCUSSION QUESTIONS

1. Characterize the speaker in this piece. Whom is she addressing? How does she feel about her daughter? About her own life?

2. The piece ends with an appeal: "Only help her to know—help make it so there is cause for her to know—that she is more than this dress on the ironing board, helpless before the iron." Explain the significance of the image. Does the speaker seem to wish someone could have helped her to know the same thing earlier in her life? Does she still seem "helpless before the iron" herself? What do you think the author wants us to feel for the speaker? For the daughter? What specifically makes you think so?

Allen Ginsberg / A Supermarket in California 1955

The author of poetry regarded as "great," "strange," "angelic," "degenerate," "unsurpassed," and "apocalyptic," Allen Ginsberg remains one of the most celebrated and vilified literary figures of the past three decades. Born in Newark, New Jersey, in 1926, Ginsberg graduated from Columbia University in 1948 and spent several years on the road, supporting himself as a spot welder, reporter, dishwasher, porter, book reviewer, and seaman. Soon after his arrival in San Francisco, he launched an immediately successful career as a market research consultant. But a year of psychoanalysis prompted him, as he says, to "quit the job, my tie and suit, the apartment on Nob Hill . . . and do what I wanted"—write poetry. By the mid-1950s, Ginsberg was identified—along with, among others, Jack Kerouac, Lawrence Ferlinghetti, and William Burroughs—as a cofounder of the Beat Generation. Lionized for his experimentations with literary forms and unconventional life-styles, Ginsberg remains an ardent supporter of political and social causes. A late-1960s profile in The New Yorker *characterized him not only as a major American poet but also as a guru of the "amalgamated hippie-pacifist-activist-visionary-orgiastic-anarchist-Orientalist-psychedelic underground."*

Ginsberg's first volume of poetry, Howl *(1956), is also his most famous. It has gone through more than thirty printings, In a preface to the volume, William Carlos Williams cautions readers that Ginsberg's vision of contemporary America is like "going through hell" but also reminds us that Ginsberg "proves to us, in spite of the most debasing experiences that life can offer a man, the spirit of love survives to ennoble our lives if we have the wit and the courage and the faith—and the art! to persist."*

"A Supermarket in California" was included in Ginsberg's first controversial volume. The poem remains a pensive rendition of Walt Whitman's vision of America as a land of abundance.

What thoughts I have of you tonight, Walt Whitman, for I walked down the sidestreets under the trees with a headache self-conscious looking at the full moon.
In my hungry fatigue, and shopping for images, I went into the neon fruit supermarket, dreaming of your enumerations!
What peaches and what penumbras! Whole families shopping at night! Aisles full of husbands! Wives in the avocados, babies in the tomatoes!—and you, Garcia Lorca, what were you doing down by the watermelons?

I saw you, Walt Whitman, childless, lonely old grubber, poking among the meats in the refrigerator and eyeing the grocery boys.
I heard you asking questions of each: Who killed the pork chops? What price bananas? Are you my Angel?
I wandered in and out of the brilliant stacks of cans following you, and followed in my imagination by the store detective.
We strode down the open corridors together in our solitary fancy tasting artichokes, possessing every frozen delicacy, and never passing the cashier.

Where are we going, Walt Whitman? The doors close in an hour. Which way does your beard point tonight?
(I touch your book and dream of our odyssey in the supermarket and feel absurd.)
Will we walk all night through solitary streets? The trees add shade to shade, lights out in the houses, we'll both be lonely.
Will we stroll dreaming of the lost America of love past blue automobiles in driveways, home to our silent cottage?
Ah, dear father, graybeard, lonely old courage-teacher, what America did you have when Charon quit poling his ferry and you got out on a smoking bank and stood watching the boat disappear on the black waters of Lethe?

Sylvia Plath

Sylvia Plath (1932–63) was born in Boston, graduated from Smith College with honors, attended Newham College, Cambridge, on a fellowship, and lived in England during the last years of her life. While writing the stunning poetry that brought her posthumous acclaim, she longed to publish fiction in American magazines. "Poetry," she once wrote, "is an evasion from the real job of writing prose."

"Man in Black" and "The Detective" demonstrate her range and complexity as a poet.

Sylvia Plath / Man in Black 1959

Where the three magenta
Breakwaters take the shove
And suck of the grey sea

To the left, and the wave
Unfists against the dun
Barb-wired headland of

The Deer Island prison
With its trim piggeries,
Hen huts and cattle green

To the right, and March ice
Glazes the rock pools yet,
Snuff-colored sand cliffs rise

Over a great stone spit
Bared by each falling tide,
And you, across those white

Stones, strode out in your dead
Black coat, black shoes, and your
Black hair till there you stood,

Fixed vortex on the far
Tip, riveting stones, air,
All of it, together.

Sylvia Plath / The Detective 1962

What was she doing when it blew in
Over the seven hills, the red furrow, the blue mountain?
Was she arranging cups? It is important.
Was she at the window, listening?
In that valley the train shrieks echo like souls on hooks.

That is the valley of death, though the cows thrive.
In her garden the lies were shaking out their moist silks
And the eyes of the killer moving sluglike and sidelong,
Unable to face the fingers, those egotists.
The fingers were tamping a woman into a wall,

A body into a pipe, and the smoke rising.
This is the smell of years burning, here in the kitchen,
These are the deceits, tacked up like family photographs,
And this is a man, look at his smile,
The death weapon? No one is dead.

There is no body in the house at all.
There is the smell of polish, there are plush carpets.
There is the sunlight, playing its blades,
Bored hoodlum in a red room
Where the wireless talks to itself like an elderly relative.

Did it come like an arrow, did it come like a knife?
Which of the poisons is it?
Which of the nerve-curlers, the convulsors? Did it electrify?
This is a case without a body.
The body does not come into it at all.

It is a case of vaporization.
The mouth first, its absence reported
In the second year. It had been insatiable

And in punishment was hung out like brown fruit
To wrinkle and dry.

The breasts next.
There were harder, two white stones.
The milk came yellow, then blue and sweet as water.
There was no absence of lips, there were two children,
But their bones showed, and the moon smiled.

Then the dry wood, the gates,
The brown motherly furrows, the whole estate.
We walk on air, Watson.
There is only the moon, embalmed in phosphorus.
There is only a crow in a tree. Make notes.

DISCUSSION QUESTIONS

1. Three decades after her suicide, Sylvia Plath remains as famous as a "mad poet" as she is as a talented poet. Some feminists believe that Plath's bouts with psychic unrest were related to her experiences as a housewife and mother. Compare Plath's work with Charlotte Perkins Gilman's story "The Yellow Wallpaper." What emotions are evoked by the presence of mad characters in these works? Is there a difference between the way the two writers "use" madness as a theme?
2. After having read Plath's poems, consider those written by Emily Dickinson and reprinted earlier in this section. What thematic interests and stylistic features do these poems share? In what specific ways are they different?

John Updike / A & P 1962

After graduating from Harvard in 1954, where he was president of the Lampoon, *John Updike joined* The New Yorker *magazine as a reporter. Though he officially left the staff of that magazine in 1957 to concentrate on his fiction, issue after issue of* The New Yorker *declares Updike's presence in short stories, sketches, book reviews, and occasional light verse. "A & P," a tale of adolescent sensibility and one of the most widely anthologized short stories by a contemporary American writer, shows Updike's characteristic concern for the minutiae of sensory perceptions and the achievement of individual identity.*

In walks these three girls in nothing but bathing suits. I'm in the third checkout slot, with my back to the door, so I don't see them until they're over by the bread. The one that caught my eye first was the one in the plaid green two-piece. She was a chunky kid, with a good tan and a sweet broad soft-looking can with those two crescents of white just under it, where the sun never seems to hit, at the top of the backs of her legs. I stood there with my hand on a box of HiHo crackers trying to remember if I rang it up or not. I ring it up again and the customer starts giving me hell. She's one of these cash-register-watchers, a witch about fifty with rouge on her cheekbones and no eyebrows, and I know it made her day to trip me up. She'd been watching cash registers for fifty years and probably never seen a mistake before.

By the time I got her feathers smoothed and her goodies into a bag—she gives me a little snort in passing, if she'd been born at the right time they would have burned her over in Salem—by the time I get her on her way the girls had circled around the bread and were coming back, without a pushcart, back my way along the counters, in the aisle between the checkouts and the Special bins. They didn't even have shoes on. There was this chunky one, with the two-piece—it was bright green and the seams on the bra were still sharp and her belly was still pretty pale so I guessed she just got it (the suit)—there was this one, with one of those chubby berry-faces, the lips all bunched together under her nose, this one, and a tall one, with black hair that hadn't quite frizzed right, and one of these sunburns right across under the eyes, and a chin that was too long—you know, the kind of girl other girls think is very "striking" and "attractive" but never quite makes it, as they very well know, which is why they like her so much—and then the third one, that wasn't quite so tall. She was the queen. She kind of led them, the other two peeking around and making their shoulders round. She didn't look around, not this queen, she just walked straight on slowly, on those long white prima-donna legs. She came down a little hard on her heels, as if she didn't walk in her bare feet that much, putting down her heels and then letting the weight move along to her toes as if she was testing the floor with every step, putting a little deliberate extra action into it. You never know for sure how girls' minds work (do you really think it's a mind in there or just a little buzz like a bee in a glass jar?) but you got the idea she had talked the other two into coming in here with her, and now she was showing them how to do it, walk slow and hold yourself straight.

She had on a kind of dirty-pink—beige maybe, I don't know—bathing suit with a little nubble all over it and, what got me, the straps were down. They were off her shoulders looped loose around the cool tops of her arms, and I guess as a result the suit had slipped a little on her, so all around the top of the cloth there was this shining rim. If it hadn't been there you wouldn't have known there could have been anything whiter than those shoulders. With the straps pushed off, there was nothing between the top of the suit and the top of her head except just *her*, this clean bare plane of the top of her chest down from the shoulder bones like a dented sheet of metal tilted in the light. I mean, it was more than pretty.

She had sort of oaky hair that the sun and salt had bleached, done up in a bun that was unravelling, and a kind of prim face. Walking into the A & P with your straps down, I suppose it's the only kind of face you *can* have. She held her head so high her neck, coming up out of those white shoulders, looked kind of stretched, but I didn't mind. The longer her neck was, the more of her there was.

She must have felt in the corner of her eye me and over my shoulder Stokesie in the second slot watching, but she didn't tip. Not this queen. She kept her eyes moving across the racks, and stopped, and turned so slow it made my stomach rub the inside of my apron, and buzzed to the other two, who kind of huddled against her for relief, and then they all three of them went up the cat-and-dog-food-breakfast-cereal-macaroni-rice-raisons-seasonings-spreads-spaghetti-soft-drinks-crackers-and-cookies aisle. From the third slot I look straight up this aisle to the meat counter, and I watched them all the way. The fat one with the tan sort of fumbled with the cookies, but on second thought she put the package back. The sheep pushing their carts down the aisle—the girls were walking against the usual traffic (not that we have one-way signs or anything)—were pretty hilarious. You could see them, when Queenie's white shoulders dawned on them, kind of jerk, or hop, or hiccup, but their eyes snapped back to their own baskets and on they pushed. I bet you could set off dynamite in an A & P and the people would by and large keep reaching and checking oatmeal off their lists and muttering "Let me see, there was a third thing, began with A, asparagus, no, ah, yes, applesauce!" or whatever it is they do mutter. But there was no doubt, this jiggled them. A few houseslaves in pin curlers even looked around after pushing their carts past to make sure what they had seen was correct.

You know, it's one thing to have a girl in a bathing suit down on the beach, where what with the glare nobody can look at each other much anyway, and another thing in the cool of the A & P, under the fluorescent lights, against all those stacked packages, with her feet paddling along naked over our checkerboard green-and-cream rubber-tile floor.

"Oh Daddy," Stokesie said beside me. "I feel so faint."

"Darling," I said. "Hold me tight." Stokesie's married, with two babies chalked up on his fuselage already, but as far as I can tell that's the only difference. He's twenty-two, and I was nineteen this April.

"Is it done?" he asks, the responsible married man finding his voice. I forgot to say he thinks he's going to be manager some sunny day, maybe in 1990 when it's called the Great Alexandrov and Petrooshki Tea Company or something.

What he meant was, our town is five miles from a beach, with a big summer colony out on the Point, but we're right in the middle of town, and the women generally put on a shirt or shorts or something before they get out of the car into the street. And anyway these are usually women with six children and varicose veins mapping their legs and nobody, including them, could care less. As I say, we're right in the middle of town, and if you stand at our front doors you can see two banks and the Congregational church and the newspaper store and three real-estate offices and about twenty-seven old freeloaders tearing up Central Street because the sewer broke again. It's not as if we're on the Cape; we're north of Boston and there's people in this town haven't seen the ocean for twenty years.

The girls had reached the meat counter and were asking McMahon something. He pointed, they pointed, and they shuffled out of sight behind a pyramid of Diet Delight peaches. All that was left for us to see was old McMahon patting his mouth and looking after them sizing up their joints. Poor kids, I began to feel sorry for them, they couldn't help it.

Now here comes the sad part of the story, at least my family says it's sad, but I don't think it's so sad myself. The store's pretty empty, it being Thursday afternoon, so there was nothing much to do except lean on the register and wait for the girls to show up again. The whole store was like a pinball machine and I didn't know which tunnel they'd come out of. After a while they come around out of the far aisle, around the light bulbs, records at discount of the Caribbean Six or Tony Martin Sings or some such gunk you wonder they waste the wax on, sixpacks of candy bars, and plastic toys done up in cellophane that fall apart when a kid looks at them anyway. Around they come, Queenie still leading the way, and holding a little gray jar in her hand. Slots Three through Seven are unmanned and I could see her wondering between Stokes and me, but Stokesie with his usual luck draws an old party in baggy gray pants who stumbles up with four giant cans of pineapple juice (what do these bums *do* with all that pineapple juice? I've often asked myself) so the girls come to me. Queenie puts down the jar and I take it into my fingers icy cold. Kingfish Fancy Herring Snacks in Pure Sour Cream: 49¢. Now her hands are empty, not a ring or a bracelet, bare as God made them, and I wonder where the money's coming from. Still with that prim look she lifts a folded dollar bill out of the hollow at the center of her nubbled pink top. The jar went heavy in my hand. Really, I thought that was so cute.

Then everybody's luck begins to run out. Lengel comes in from haggling with a truck full of cabbages on the lot and is about to scuttle into that door marked MANAGER behind which he hides all day when the girls touch his eye. Lengel's pretty dreary, teaches Sunday school and the rest, but he doesn't miss that much. He comes over and says, "Girls, this isn't the beach."

Queenie blushes, though maybe it's just a brush of sunburn I was noticing for the first time, now that she was so close. "My mother asked me to pick up a jar of herring snacks." Her voice kind of startled me, the way voices do when you see the people first, coming out so flat and dumb yet kind of tony, too, the way it ticked over "pick up" and "snacks." All of a sudden I slid right down her voice into her living room. Her father and the other men were standing around in ice-cream coats and bow ties and the women were in sandals picking up herring snacks on toothpicks off a big glass plate and they were all holding drinks the color of water with olives and sprigs of mint in them. When my parents have somebody over they get lemonade and if it's a real racy affair Schlitz in tall glasses with "They'll Do It Every Time" cartoons stencilled on.

"That's all right," Lengel said. "But this isn't the beach." His repeating this struck me as funny, as if it had just occurred to him, and he had been thinking all these years the A & P was a great big dune and he was the head lifeguard. He didn't like my smiling—as I say he doesn't miss much—but he concentrates on giving the girls that sad Sunday-school-superintendent stare.

Queenie's blush is no sunburn now, and the plump one in plaid, that I liked better from the back—a really sweet can—pipes up, "We weren't doing any shopping. We just came in for the one thing."

"That makes no difference," Lengel tells her, and I could see from the way his eyes went that he hadn't noticed she was wearing a two-piece before. "We want you decently dressed when you come in here."

"We *are* decent," Queenie says suddenly, her lower lip pushing, getting sore now that she remembers her place, a place from which the crowd that runs the A & P must look pretty crummy. Fancy Herring Snacks flashed in her very blue eyes.

"Girls, I don't want to argue with you. After this come in here with your shoulders covered. It's our policy." He turns his back. That's policy for you. Policy is what the kingpins want. What the others want is juvenile delinquency.

All this while, the customers had been showing up with their carts but, you know, sheep, seeing a scene, they had all bunched up on Stokesie, who shook open a paper bag as gently as peeling a peach, not wanting to miss a word. I could feel in the silence everybody getting nervous, most of all Lengel, who asks me, "Sammy, have you rung up their purchase?"

I thought and said "No" but it wasn't about that I was thinking. I go through the punches, 4, 9, GROC, TOT—it's more complicated than you think, and after you do it often enough, it begins to make a little song, that you hear words to, in my case "Hello (*bing*) there, you (*gung*) hap-py *pee*-pul (*splat*)!"—the *splat* being the drawer flying out. I uncrease the bill, tenderly as you may imagine, it just having come from between the two smoothest scoops of vanilla I had ever known were there, and pass a half and a penny into her narrow pink palm, and nestle the herrings in a bag and twist its neck and hand it over, all the time thinking.

The girls, and who'd blame them, are in a hurry to get out, so I say "I quit" to Lengel quick enough for them to hear, hoping they'll stop and watch me, their unsuspected hero. They keep right on going, into the electric eye; the door flies open and they flicker across the lot to their car, Queenie and Plaid and Big Tall Goony-Goony (not that as raw material she was so bad), leaving me with Lengel and a kink in his eyebrow.

"Did you say something, Sammy?"

"I said I quit."

"I thought you did."

"You didn't have to embarrass them."

"It was they who were embarrassing us."

I started to say something that came out "Fiddle-de-doo." It's a saying of my grandmother's, and I know she would have been pleased.

"I don't think you know what you're saying," Lengel said.

"I know you don't," I said. "But I do." I pull the bow at the back of my apron and start shrugging it off my shoulders. A couple customers that had been heading for my slot begin to knock against each other, like scared pigs in a chute.

Lengel sighs and begins to look very patient and old and gray. He's been a friend of my parents for years. "Sammy, you don't want to do this to your Mom and Dad," he tells me. It's true, I don't. But it seems to me that once you begin a gesture it's fatal not to go through with it. I fold the apron, "Sammy" stitched in red on the pocket, and put it on the counter, and drop the bow tie on top of it. The bow tie is theirs, if you've ever wondered. "You'll feel this for the rest of your life," Lengel says, and I know that's true, too, but remembering how he made that pretty girl blush makes me so scrunchy inside I punch the No Sale tab and the machine whirls "pee-pul" and the drawer splats out. One advantage to this scene taking place in summer, I can follow this up with a clean exit, there's no fumbling around getting your coat and galoshes, I just saunter into the electric eye in my white shirt that my mother ironed the night before, and the door heaves itself open, and outside the sunshine is skating around on the asphalt.

I look around for my girls, but they're gone, of course. There wasn't anybody but some young married screaming with her children about some candy they didn't get by the door of a powder-blue Falcon station wagon. Looking back in the big windows, over the bags of peat moss and aluminum lawn furniture stacked on the pavement, I could see Lengel in my place in the slot, checking the sheep through. His face was dark gray and his back stiff, as if he'd just had an injection of iron, and my stomach kind of fell as I felt how hard the world was going to be to me hereafter.

Martin Luther King, Jr. / I Have a Dream 1963

Martin Luther King, Jr., accomplished a great deal in a short time. The son of a Baptist minister, King was himself ordained at the age of eighteen. At twenty-six he became nationally prominent as a spiritual and civil-rights leader when he led a successful boycott in 1955 of the segregated bus system in Montgomery, Alabama. He became the first president of the Southern Christian Leadership Conference and was awarded the Nobel Peace Prize in 1964, largely for his policy of nonviolent resistance to racial injustice. Along the way, he studied at Morehouse College, Crozer Theological Seminary, Boston University, and Chicago Theological Seminary.

One of the most eloquent speakers and charismatic leaders of modern times, King was assassinated in Memphis, Tennessee, in 1968, shortly before his fortieth birthday. He has become an American folk hero.

His "I Have a Dream" speech epitomizes King's vision of the future. He delivered his sermon from the steps of the Lincoln Memorial to more than 200,000 people who had come to Washington, D.C., to show their support of civil rights as an issue and of King as a man.

Five score years ago, a great American, in whose symbolic shadow we stand, signed the Emancipation Proclamation. This momentous decree came as a great beacon light of hope to millions of Negro slaves who had been seared in the flames of withering injustice. It came as a joyous daybreak to end the long night of captivity.

But one hundred years later, we must face the tragic fact that the Negro is still not free. One hundred years later, the life of the Negro is still sadly crippled by the manacles of segregation and the chains of discrimination. One hundred years later, the Negro lives on a lonely island of poverty in the midst of a vast ocean of material prosperity. One hundred years later, the Negro is still languishing in the corners of American society and finds himself an exile in his own land. So we have come here today to dramatize an appalling condition.

In a sense we have come to our nation's Capitol to cash a check. When the architects of our republic wrote the magnificent words of the Constitution and the Declaration of Independence, they were signing a promissory note to which every American was to fall heir. This note was a promise that all men would be guaranteed the unalienable rights of life, liberty, and the pursuit of happiness.

It is obvious today that America has defaulted on this promissory note insofar as her citizens of color are concerned. Instead of honoring this sacred obligation, America has given the Negro people a bad check; a check which has come back marked ''insufficient funds.'' But we refuse to believe that the bank of justice is bankrupt. We refuse to believe that there are insufficient funds in the great vaults of opportunity of this nation. So we have come to cash this check—a check that will give us upon demand the riches of freedom and the security of justice. We have also come to this hallowed spot to remind America of the fierce urgency of *now*. This is no time to engage in the luxury of cooling off or to take the tranquilizing drug of gradualism. *Now* is the time to make real the promises of Democracy. *Now* is the time to rise from the dark and desolate valley of segregation to the sunlit path of racial justice. *Now* is the time to open the doors of opportunity to all of God's children. *Now* is the time to lift our nation from the quicksands of racial injustice to the solid rock of brotherhood.

It would be fatal for the nation to overlook the urgency of the moment and to underestimate the determination of the Negro. This sweltering summer of the Negro's legitimate discontent will not pass until there is an invigorating autumn of freedom and equality. 1963 is not an end, but a beginning. Those who hope that the Negro needed to blow off steam and will now be content will have a rude awakening if the nation returns to business as usual. There will be neither rest nor tranquility in America until the Negro is granted his citizenship rights. The whirlwind of revolt will continue to shake the foundations of our nation until the bright day of justice emerges.

But there is something I must say to my people who stand on the warm threshold which leads into the palace of justice. In the process of gaining our rightful place we must not be guilty of wrongful deeds. Let us not seek to satisfy our thirst for freedom by drinking from the cup of bitterness and hatred. We must forever conduct our struggle on the high plane of dignity and discipline. We must not allow our creative protest to degenerate into physical violence. Again and again we must rise to the majestic heights of meeting physical force with soul force. The marvelous new militancy which has engulfed the Negro community must not lead us to a distrust of all white people, for many of our white brothers, as evidenced by their presence here today, have come to realize that their destiny is tied up with our destiny and their freedom is inextricably bound to our freedom. We cannot walk alone.

And as we walk, we must make the pledge that we shall march ahead. We cannot turn back. There are those who are asking the devotees of civil rights, ''When will you be satisfied?'' We can never be satisfied as long as the Negro is the victim of the unspeakable horrors of police brutality. We can never be satisfied as long as our bodies, heavy with the fatigue of travel, cannot gain lodging in the motels of the highways and the hotels of the cities. We cannot be satisfied as long as the Negro's basic mobility is from a smaller ghetto to a larger one. We can never be satisfied as long as a Negro in Mississippi cannot vote and a Negro in New York believes he has nothing for which to vote. No, no, we are not satisfied, and we will not be satisfied until justice rolls down like waters and righteousness like a mighty stream.

I am not unmindful that some of you have come here out of great trials and tribulations. Some of you have come fresh from narrow jail cells. Some of you have come from areas where your quest for freedom left you battered by the storms of persecution and staggered by the winds of police brutality. You have been the veterans of creative suffering. Continue to work with the faith that unearned suffering is redemptive.

Go back to Mississippi, go back to Alabama, go back to South Carolina, go back to Georgia, go back to Louisiana, go back to the slums and ghettoes of our northern cities, knowing that somehow this situation can and will be changed. Let us not wallow in the valley of despair.

I say to you today, my friends, that in spite of the difficulties and frustrations of the moment I still have a dream. It is a dream deeply rooted in the American dream.

I have a dream that one day this nation will rise up and live out the true meaning of its creed: "We hold these truths to be self-evident; that all men are created equal."

I have a dream that one day on the red hills of Georgia the sons of former slaves and the sons of former slave-owners will be able to sit down together at the table of brotherhood.

I have a dream that the state of Mississippi, a desert state sweltering with the heat of injustice and oppression, will be transformed into an oasis of freedom and justice.

I have a dream that my four little children will one day live in a nation where they will not be judged by the color of their skin but by the content of their character.

I have a dream today.

I have a dream that the state of Alabama, whose governor's lips are presently dripping with the words of interposition and nullification, will be transformed into a situation where little black boys and black girls will be able to join hands with little white boys and white girls and walk together as sisters and brothers.

I have a dream today.

I have a dream that one day every valley shall be exalted, every hill and mountain shall be made low, the rough place will be made plain, and the crooked places will be made straight, and the glory of the Lord shall be revealed, and all flesh shall see it together.

This is our hope. This is the faith with which I return to the South. With this faith we will be able to hew out of the mountain of despair a stone of hope. With this faith we will be able to transform the jangling discords of our nation into a beautiful symphony of brotherhood. With this faith we will be able to work together, to pray together, to struggle together, to go to jail together, to stand up for freedom together, knowing that we will be free one day.

This will be the day when all of God's children will be able to sing with new meaning:

> My country, 'tis of thee
> Sweet land of liberty
> Of thee I sing:
> Land where my fathers died,
> Land of the pilgrims' pride,
> From every mountainside
> Let freedom ring.

And if America is to be a great nation this must become true. So let freedom ring from the prodigious hilltops of New Hampshire! Let freedom ring from the heightening Alleghenies of Pennsylvania!

Let freedom ring from the snowcapped Rockies of Colorado!

Let freedom ring from the curvaceous peaks of California!

But not only that; let freedom ring from Stone Mountain of Georgia!

Let freedom ring from every hill and molehill of Mississippi. From every mountainside, let freedom ring.

When we let freedom ring, when we let it ring from every village and every hamlet, from every state and every city, we will be able to speed up that day when all of God's children, black men and white men, Jews and Gentiles, Protestants and Catholics, will be able to join hands and sing in the words of the old Negro spiritual, "Free at last! free at last! thank God almighty, we are free at last!"

Maya Angelou / *I Know Why the Caged Bird Sings* 1969

Maya Angelou was born Marguerite Johnson in St. Louis in 1928. After her turbulent youth ("from a broken family, raped at eight, unwed mother at sixteen"), she went on to study dance with the Pearl Primus company in New York, star in an off-Broadway show (The Blacks), *write three books of poetry, produce a series on Africa for PBS, serve as coordinator for the Southern Christian Leadership Conference at the request of Martin Luther King, Jr., and accept three honorary doctorates.*

As an author, actress, singer, dancer, songwriter, teacher, editor, and film director, Angelou has been a pioneer in furthering the role of the American black woman in the arts.

She is best known for her autobiography, I Know Why the Caged Bird Sings *(1969), from which the following reminiscence is taken. For another memory of Joe Louis, see Howie Evans's "Joe Louis: American Folk Hero" (in "Press").*

CHAMPION OF THE WORLD

The last inch of space was filled, yet people continued to wedge themselves along the walls of the Store. Uncle Willie had turned the radio up to its last notch so that youngsters on the porch wouldn't miss a word. Women sat on kitchen chairs, dining-room chairs, stools and upturned wooden boxes. Small children and babies perched on every lap available and men leaned on the shelves or on each other.

The apprehensive mood was shot through with shafts of gaiety, as a black sky is streaked with lightning.

"I ain't worried 'bout this fight. Joe's gonna whip that cracker like it's open season."

"He gone whip him till that white boy call him Momma."

At last the talking was finished and the string-along songs about razor blades were over and the fight began.

"A quick jab to the head." In the Store the crowd grunted. "A left to the head and a right and another left." One of the listeners cackled like a hen and was quieted.

"They're in a clinch, Louis is trying to fight his way out."

Some bitter comedian on the porch said, "That white man don't mind hugging that niggah now, I betcha."

"The referee is moving in to break them up, but Louis finally pushed the contender away and it's an uppercut to the chin. The contender is hanging on, now he's backing away. Louis catches him with a short left to the jaw."

A tide of murmuring assent poured out the doors and into the yard.

"Another left and another left. Louis is saving that mighty right . . ." The mutter in the Store had grown into a baby roar and it was pierced by the clang of a bell and the announcer's "That's the bell for round three, ladies and gentlemen."

As I pushed my way into the Store I wondered if the announcer gave any thought to the fact that he was addressing as "ladies and gentlemen" all the Negroes around the world who sat sweating and praying, glued to their "master's voice."[1]

There were only a few calls for R.C. Colas, Dr. Peppers, and Hires root beer. The real festivities would begin after the fight. Then even the old Christian ladies who taught their children and tried themselves to practice turning the other cheek would buy soft drinks, and if the Brown Bomber's victory was a particularly bloody one they would order peanut patties and Baby Ruths also.

Bailey and I laid the coins on top of the cash register. Uncle Willie didn't allow us to ring up sales during a fight. It was too noisy and might shake up the atmosphere. When the gong rang for the next round we pushed through the near-sacred quiet to the herd of children outside.

"He's got Louis against the ropes and now it's a left to the body and a right to the ribs. Another right to the body, it looks like it was low. . . . Yes, ladies and gentlemen, the referee is signaling but the contender keeps raining the blows on Louis. It's another to the body, and it looks like Louis is going down."

My race groaned. It was our people falling. It was another lynching, yet another Black man hanging on a tree. One more woman ambushed and raped. A Black boy whipped and maimed. It was hounds on the trail of a man running through slimy swamps. It was a white woman slapping her maid for being forgetful.

The men in the Store stood away from the walls and at attention. Women greedily clutched the babes on their laps while on the porch the shufflings and smiles, flirtings and pinching of a few minutes before were gone. This might be the end of the world. If Joe lost we were back in slavery and beyond help. It would all be true, the accusations that we were lower types of human beings. Only a little higher than apes. True that we were stupid and ugly and lazy and dirty and, unlucky and worst of all, that God Himself hated us and ordained us to be hewers of wood and drawers of water, forever and ever, world without end.

We didn't breathe. We didn't hope. We waited.

"He's off the ropes, ladies and gentlemen. He's moving towards the center of the ring." There was no time to be relieved. The worst might still happen.

"And now it looks like Joe is mad. He's caught Carnera with a left hook to the head and a right to the head. It's a left jab to the body and another left to the head. There's a left cross and a right to the head. The contender's right eye is bleeding and he can't seem to keep his block up. Louis is penetrating every block. The referee is moving in, but Louis sends a left to the body and it's an uppercut to the chin and the contender is dropping. He's on the canvas, ladies and gentlemen."

Babies slid to the floor as women stood up and men leaned toward the radio.

"Here's the referee. He's counting. One, two, three, four, five, six, seven . . . Is the contender trying to get up again?"

All the men in the store shouted, "NO."

"—eight, nine, ten." There were a few sounds from the audience, but they seemed to be holding themselves in against tremendous pressure.

"The fight is all over, ladies and gentlemen. Let's get the microphone over to the referee . . . Here he is. He's got the Brown Bomber's hand, he's holding it up . . . Here he is . . ."

Then the voice, husky and familiar, came to wash over us—"The winnah, and still heavyweight champeen of the world . . . Joe Louis."

1. A famous advertising slogan for RCA phonographs.

Champion of the world. A Black boy. Some Black mother's son. He was the strongest man in the world. People drank Coca-Colas like ambrosia and ate candy bars like Christmas. Some of the men went behind the Store and poured white lightning in their soft-drink bottles, and a few of the bigger boys followed them. Those who were not chased away came back blowing their breath in front of themselves like proud smokers.

It would take an hour or more before the people would leave the Store and head for home. Those who lived too far had made arrangements to stay in town. It wouldn't do for a Black man and his family to be caught on a lonely country road on a night when Joe Louis had proved that we were the strongest people in the world.

Norman Mailer / *Of a Fire on the Moon*
[The First Moon Walk] 1970

Born in New Jersey in 1923 and brought up in Brooklyn, Norman Mailer began writing while still an undergraduate at Harvard. In his fiction, essays, and highly personal journalism, Mailer has covered many significant phases of American life since the end of World War II. Part of his account of the Apollo XI *voyage first appeared in* Life *magazine and was later expanded into a book-length study of the astronauts,* Of a Fire on the Moon, *from which the following passage is excerpted. Always attracted to the action at the center of the arena, as his reporting of political conventions* (Miami and the Siege of Chicago) *and the peace movement of the sixties* (Armies of the Night) *testifies, Mailer finds himself during his coverage of the moon walk an unwilling nonparticipant on an assignment without a location.*

They had landed, there was jubilation in Mission Control, and a moment of fraternization between Armstrong and Aldrin, but in fact they were actually at work in the next instant. No one knew what would await them—there were even theories that most of the surface of the moon was as fragile as icing on a cake. If they landed, and the moon ground began to collapse, they were ready to blast off with the ascent stage even as the descent stage was sinking beneath. But no sound of crumbling came up through the pipes of the legs, no shudder of collapse. A minute passed. They received the order to Stay. The second Stay–No Stay would be on them nine minutes later, and they rushed through a checklist, testing specific instruments to make certain they were intact from the landing. The thirty-odd seconds of fuel they still had left when they touched down was vented from the descent stage, a hissing and steaming beneath the legs like a steed loosing water on icy ground. Verbs and Nouns were punched into the DSKY. Now came the second Stay. There would not be another Stay–No Stay until the Command Module had made a complete revolution of the moon and would be coming back toward them in good position for rendezvous. So, unless some mishap were suddenly to appear, they had at least another two hours on the satellite. It was time to unscrew their gloves at the wrist and take them off, time to unscrew their helmets at the neck, lift them off.

They gave their first description of the landing, and made a few general remarks about the view through the window, the variety of rocks. But there was too much work to look for long. After a few comments on the agreeableness of lunar gravity, after a conversation with Columbia and mutual congratulations, they were back at the computer. Now, in the time before the next Stay–No Stay, they had to simulate a countdown for a planned ascent and realign the Inertial Measurement Unit, that is, determine the vertical line of moon gravity, and install its index into the Inertial Measurement Unit, then level the table and gyroscope from which all navigation was computed. Star checks were taken. Meanwhile, Armstrong was readying the cameras and snapping photographs through the window. Now Aldrin aligned the Abort Guidance Section. Armstrong laid in the data for Program 12, the Powered Ascent Guidance. The Command Module came around again. The simulated countdown was over. They had another Stay. They powered down their systems.

In the transcript the work continues minute after minute, familiar talk of stars and Nouns, acronyms, E-memory dumps, and returns to POO where Pings may idle. They are at rest on the moon, but the dialogue is not unencumbered of pads, updata link switches and noise suppression devices on the Manned Space Flight Network relay.

Then in what is virtually their first pause in better than an hour on the moon, they request permission to do their EVA early, begin in fact in the next few hours rather than take a halt to sleep. For days there had been discussion in every newspaper of the world whether the astronauts could land on the moon and a few hours later go to sleep before they even stepped out of the Lem; now the question has been answered—they are impatient to go.

CAPCOM: *We will support it.*
ALDRIN: *Roger.*
CAPCOM: *You guys are getting prime time TV there.*
ARMSTRONG: *Hope that little TV set works, but we'll see.*

Now the astronauts stopped to eat and to relax. Over the radio came the dialogue of Mission Control talking to Collins in orbit overhead. Around them, through each pinched small window, were tantalizing views of the moon. They could feel themselves in one-sixth gravity. How light were their bodies. Yet they were not weightless. There was gravity beneath them, a faint sensuous tug at their limbs. If they dropped a pencil, it did not float before drifting slowly away. Rather, it dropped. Slowly it dropped, dropped indeed at the same leisurely speed with which Apollo-Saturn had risen off its launching pad four and a half days ago. What a balm for the muscles of the eye! One-sixth of earth gravity was agreeable, it was attractive, it was, said Aldrin, "less *lonesome*" than weightlessness. He had, at last, " a distinct feeling of being somewhere." Yes, the moon was beneath them, hardly more than the height of a ten-foot diving board beneath them—they were in the domain of a presence again. How much like magnetism must lunar gravity have felt.

ALDRIN: *This is the Lem pilot. I'd like to take this opportunity to ask every person listening in, whoever and wherever they may be, to pause for a moment and contemplate the events of the past few hours, and to give thanks in his or her way.*

In the silence, Aldrin took out the bread, the wine, and the chalice he had brought in his Personal Preference Kit, and he put them on the little table in front of the Abort Guidance Section computer. Then he read some passages from the Bible and celebrated Communion.

A strange picture of religious intensity: there is of course no clue in Aldrin's immediate words—they are by now tuned to precisely what one would expect.

"I would like to have observed just how the wine poured in that environment, but, it wasn't pertinent at that particular time. It wasn't important how it got in the cup. It was important only to get it there"—and not spill, we may assume, this most special blood of the Lord. "I offered some private prayers, but I find now that thoughts, feelings, come into my memory instead of words. I was not so selfish as to include my family in those prayers at the moment, nor so spacious as to include the fate of the world. I was thinking more about our particular task, and the challenge and the opportunity that had been given us. I asked people to offer thanks in their own way, and it is my hope that people will keep this whole event in their minds and see beyond minor details and technical achievements to a deeper meaning behind it all, challenge, a quest, the human need to do these things and the need to recognize that we are all one mankind under God.''

Yes, his recollections are near to comic in their banality, but one gets a picture of this strong-nosed strong-armed gymnast in his space suit, deep in prayer in the crowded closet space of the Lem, while Armstrong the mystic (with the statue of Buddha on his living room table) is next to him in who knows what partial or unwilling communion, Armstrong so private in his mind that when a stranger tried to talk to him one day on a bus, he picked up a book to read. There, before his partner, Aldrin prayed, light lunar gravity new in his limbs, eyes closed. Can we assume the brain of his inner vision expanded to the dimensions of a church, the loft of a cathedral, Aldrin, man of passions and disciplines, fatalist, all but open believer in predestination, agent of God's will, Aldrin, prodigy of effort on Gemini 12, whose pulse after hours of work in space had shot up only when he read a Veteran's Day message to the ground. Patriotism had the power of a stroke for Aldrin and invocation was his harmony. Tribal chief, first noble savage on the moon, he prayed to the powers who had brought him there, whose will he would fulfill—God, the earth, the moon and himself all for this instant part of the lofty engine of the universe, and in that eccentric giant of character, that conservative of all the roots in all the family trees, who now was ripping up the roots of the ages, that man whose mother's name was Moon, was there a single question whose lament might suggest that if the mission were ill-conceived or even a work of art designed by the Devil, then all the prayers of all good men were nothing but a burden upon the Lord, who in order to reply would be forced to work in the mills of Satan, or leave the prayers of his flock in space. Not likely. Aldrin did not seem a man for thoughts like that, but then his mind was a mystery wrapped in the winding-sheet of a computer with billions of bits.

Later, Armstrong would say, ''That first hour on the moon was hardly the time for long thoughts; we had specific jobs to do. Of course the sights were simply magnificent, beyond any visual experience that I had ever been exposed to,'' and Aldrin would describe it as ''a unique, almost mystical environment.'' In fact, there is an edge of the unexplained to their reactions. Their characteristic matter-of-fact response is overcome occasonally by swoops of hyperbole. And to everyone's slight surprise, they were almost two hours late for their EVA. Their estimate of time was off by close to fifty percent. For astronauts that was an error comparable to a carpenter mistaking an eight-foot stud for a twelve-foot piece. If a carpenter can look at a piece of wood and guess its length to the nearest quarter-inch, it is because he has been working with lengths all his life. Equally, people in some occupations have a close ability to estimate time.

With astronauts, whose every day in a simulator was a day laid out on the measure of a time-line, the estimate of time elapsed had to become acute. Armstrong and Aldrin had consistently fulfilled their tasks in less time than was allotted. Now, curiously, they fell behind, then further behind. There were unexpected problems of course—it took longer to bleed the pressure out of the Lunar Module than had been anticipated, and the cooling units in the backpacks were sluggish at first in operation, but whether from natural excitement and natural anxiety, or an unconscious preoccupation with lunar phenomena so subtle that it is just at the edge of their senses, any extract from the transcript at this point where they are helping to adjust the Portable Life Support System on each others' backs shows real lack of enunciation. Nowhere else do the NASA stenographers have as much difficulty with where one voice ends and another begins.

TRANQUILITY: *Got it (garbled) prime rows in.*
TRANQUILITY: *Okay.*
TRANQUILITY: *(garbled)*
TRANQUILITY: *Let me do that for you.*
TRANQUILITY: *(Inaudible)*
TRANQUILITY: *Mark I*
TRANQUILITY: *(garbled) valves*
TRANQUILITY: *(garbled)*
TRANQUILITY: *Okay*
TRANQUILITY: *All of the (garbled)*
TRANQUILITY: *(garbled) locked and double-locked.*
TRANQUILITY: *Did you put it—*
TRANQUILITY: *Oh, wait a minute*
TRANQUILITY: *Should be (garbled)*
TRANQUILITY: (garbled)
TRANQUILITY: *Roger. (garbled)*
TRANQUILITY: *I'll try it on the middle*
TRANQUILITY: *All right, check my (garbled) valves vertical*
TRANQUILITY: *Both vertical*
TRANQUILITY: *That's two vertical*
TRANQUILITY: *Okay*
TRANQUILITY: *(garbled)*
TRANQUILITY: *Locked and double-locked*
TRANQUILITY: *Okay*
TRANQUILITY: *Miss marked*
TRANQUILITY: *Sure wish I would have shaved last night.*
PAO: *That was a Buzz Aldrin comment.*

The hint is faint enough, but the hint exists—something was conceivably interfering with their sense of order. Could it have been the lunar gravity? Clock-time was a measure which derived from pendulums and spiral springs, clock-time was anchored right into the tooth of earth gravity—so a time might yet be coming when psychologists, not geologists, would be conducting experiments on the moon. Did lunar gravity have power like a drug to shift the sense of time?

Armstrong was connected at last to his PLSS. He was drawing oxygen from the pack he carried on his back. But the hatch door would not open. The pressure would not go low enough in the Lem. Down near a level of one pound per square inch, the last bit of man-created atmosphere in Eagle seemed to cling to its constituency, reluctant to enter the vacuums of the moon. But they did not know if they could get the hatch door open with a vacuum on one side and even a small pressure on the other. It was taking longer than they thought. While it was not a large concern since there would be other means to open it—redundancies pervaded throughout—nonetheless, a concern must have intruded: how intolerably comic they would appear if they came all the way and then were blocked before a door they could not crack. That thought had to put one drop of perspiration on the back of the neck. Besides, it must have been embarrassing to begin so late. The world of television was watching, and the astronauts had exhibited as much sensitivity to an audience as any bride on her way down the aisle.

It was not until nine-forty at night, Houston time, that they got the hatch open at last. In the heat of running almost two hours late, ensconced in the armor of a man-sized spaceship, could they still have felt an instant of awe as they looked out that open hatch at a panorama of theater: the sky is black, but the ground is brightly lit, bright as footlights on the floor of a dark theater. A black and midnight sky, yet on the moon ground, "you could almost go out in your shirt-sleeves and get a suntan," Aldrin would say. "I remember thinking, 'Gee, if I didn't know where I was, I could believe that somebody had created this environment somewhere out in the West and given us another simulation to work in.' " Everywhere on that pitted flat were shadows dark as the sky above, shadows dark as mine shafts.

What a struggle to push out from that congested cabin, now twice congested in their bulky-wham suits, no feeling of obstacle against their flesh, their sense of touch dead and numb, spaceman body manipulated out into the moon world like an upright piano turned by movers on the corner of the stairs.

"You're lined up on the platform. Put your left foot to the right a little bit. Okay, that's good. Roll left."

Armstrong was finally on the porch. Could it be with any sense of an alien atmosphere receiving the fifteen-layer encapsulations of the pack and suit on his back? Slowly, he climbed down the ladder. Archetypal, he must have felt, a boy descending the rungs in the wall of an abandoned well, or was it Jack down the stalk? And there he was on the bottom, on the footpad of the leg of the Lem, a metal plate perhaps three feet across. Inches away was the soil of the moon. But first he jumped up again to the lowest rung of the ladder. A couple of hours later, at the end of the EVA, conceivably exhausted, the jump from the ground to the rung, three feet up, might be difficult in that stiff and heavy space suit, so he tested it now. "It takes," said Armstrong, "a pretty good little jump."

Now, with television working, and some fraction of the world peering at the murky image of this instant, poised between the end of one history and the beginning of another, he said quietly, "I'm at the foot of the ladder. The Lem footpads are only depressed in the surface about one or two inches, although the surface appears to be very very fine-grained as you get close to it. It's almost like a powder." One of Armstrong's rare confessions of uneasiness is focused later on this moment. "I don't recall any particular emotion or feeling other than a little caution, a desire to be sure it was safe to put my weight on that surface outside Eagle's footpad."

Did his foot tingle in the heavy lunar overshoe? "I'm going to step off the Lem now."

Did something in him shudder at the touch of the new ground? Or did he draw a sweet strength from the balls of his feet? Nobody was necessarily going ever to know.

"That's one small step for a man," said Armstrong, "one giant leap for mankind." He had joined the ranks of the forever quoted. Patrick Henry, Henry Stanley and Admiral Dewey moved over for him.

Now he was out there, one foot on the moon, then the other foot on the moon, the powder like velvet underfoot. With one hand still on the ladder, he comments, "The surface is fine and powdery. I can . . . I can pick it up loosely with my toe." And as he releases his catch, the grains fall back slowly to the soil, a fan of feathers gliding to the floor. "It does adhere in fine layers like powdered charcoal to the sole and sides of my boots. I only go in a small fraction of an inch. Maybe an eighth of an inch. But I can see the footprints of my boots and the treads in the fine sand particles."

Capcom: "Neil, this is Houston. We're copying."

Yes, they would copy. He was like a man who goes into a wrecked building to defuse a new kind of bomb. He talks into a microphone as he works, for if a mistake is made, and the bomb goes off, it will be easier for the next man if every detail of his activities has been mentioned as he performed them. Now, he released his grip on the ladder and pushed off for a few steps on the moon, odd loping steps, almost thrust into motion like a horse trotting up a steep slope. It could have been a moment equivalent to the first steps he took as an infant for there was nothing to hold onto and he did not dare to fall—the ground was too hot, the rocks might tear his suit. Yet if he stumbled, he could easily go over for he could not raise his arms above his head nor reach to his knees, his arms in the pressure bladder stood out before him like sausages; so, if he tottered, the weight of the pack could twist him around, or drop him. They had tried to shape up simulations of lunar gravity while weighted in scuba suits at the bottom of a pool, but water was not a vacuum through which to move; so they had also flown in planes carrying two hundred pounds of equipment on their backs. The pilot would take the plane through a parabolic trajectory. There would be a period of twenty-two seconds at the top of the curve when a simulation of one-sixth gravity would be present, and the two hundred pounds of equipment would weigh no more than on the moon, no more than thirty-plus pounds, and one could take loping steps down the aisle of the plane, staggering through unforeseen wobbles or turbulence. Then the parabolic trajectory was done, the plane was diving, and it would have to pull out of the dive. That created the reverse of one-sixth gravity—it multiplied gravity by two and a half times. The two hundred pounds of equipment now weighed five hundred pounds and the astronauts had to be supported by other men straining to help them bear the weight. So simulations gave them time for hardly more than a clue before heavy punishment was upon them. But now he was out in the open endless lunar gravity, his body and the reflexes of his life obliged to adopt a new rhythm and schedule of effort, a new disclosure of grace.

Still, he seemed pleased after the first few steps. "There seems to be no difficulty in moving around as we suspected. It's even perhaps easier than the simulations . . ." He would run a few steps and stop, run a few steps and stop. Perhaps it was not unlike directing the Lem when it hovered over the ground. One moved faster than on earth and with less effort, but it was harder to stop—one had to pick the place to halt from several yards ahead. Yes, it was easier once moving, but awkward at the beginning and the end because of the obdurate plastic bendings of the suit. And once standing at rest, the sense of the vertical was sly. One could be leaning further forward than one knew. Or leaning backward. Like a needle on a dial one would have to oscillate from side to side of the vertical to find position. Conceivably the sensation was not unlike skiing with a child on one's back.

It was time for Aldrin to descend the ladder from the Lem to the ground, and Armstrong's turn to give directions: "The shoes are about to come over the sill. Okay, now drop your PLSS down. There you go. You're clear. . . . About an inch clearance on top of your PLSS."

Aldrin spoke for future astronauts: "Okay, you need a little bit of arching of the back to come down . . ."

When he reached the ground, Aldrin took a big and exuberant leap up the ladder again, as if to taste the pleasures of one-sixth gravity all at once. "Beautiful, beautiful," he exclaimed.

Armstrong: "Isn't that something. Magnificent sight out here."

Aldrin: "Magnificent desolation."

They were looking at a terrain which lived in a clarity of focus unlike anything they had ever seen on earth. There was no air, of course, and so no wind, nor clouds, nor dust, nor even the finest scattering of light from the smallest dispersal of microscopic particles on a clear day on earth, no, nothing visible or invisible moved in the vacuum before them. All light was pure. No haze was present, not even the invisible haze of the finest day—therefore objects did not go out of focus as they receded into the distance. If one's eyes were good enough, an object at a hundred yards was as distinct as a rock at a few feet. And their eyes were good enough. Just as one could not determine one's altitude above the moon, not from fifty miles up nor five, so now along the ground before them no distance was real, for all distances had the faculty to appear equally near if one peered at them through blinders and could not see the intervening details. Again the sense of being on a stage or on the lighted floor of a room so large one could not see where the dark ceiling began must have come upon them, for there were no hints of gathering evanescence in ridge beyond ridge; rather each outline was as severe as the one in front of it, and since the ground was filled with small craters of every size, from antholes to potholes to empty pools, and the horizon was near, four times nearer than on earth and sharp as the line drawn by a pencil, the moon ground seemed to slope and drop in all directions "like swimming in an ocean with six-foot or eight-foot swells and waves," Armstrong said later. "In that condition, you never can see very far away from where you are." But what they could see, they could see entirely—to the depth of their field of view at any instant their focus was complete. And as they swayed from side to side, so a sense of the vertical kept eluding them, the slopes of the craters about them seeming to tilt a few degrees to one side of the horizontal, then the other. On earth, one had only to incline one's body an inch or two and a sense of the vertical was gone, but on the moon they could lean over, then further over, lean considerably further over without beginning to fall. So verticals slid and oscillated. Rolling from side to side, they could as well have been on water, indeed their sense of the vertical was probably equal to the subtle uncertainty of the body when a ship is rolling on a quiet sea. "I say," said Aldrin, "the rocks are rather slippery."

They were discovering the powder of the moon soil was curious indeed, comparable in firmness and traction to some matter between sand and snow. While the Lem looked light as a kite, for its pads hardly rested on the ground and it appeared ready to lift off and blow away, yet their own feet sometimes sank for two or three inches into the soft powder on the slope of very small craters, and their soles would slip as the powder gave way under their boots. In other places the ground was firm and harder than sand, yet all of these variations were to be found in an area not a hundred feet out from the legs of the Lem. As he explored his footing, Aldrin sent back comments to Mission Control, reporting in the rapt professional tones of a coach instructing his team on the conditions of the turf in a new plastic football field.

Meanwhile Armstrong was transporting the television camera away from the Lem to a position where it could cover most of their activities. Once properly installed, he revolved it through a full panorama of their view in order that audiences on earth might have a clue to what he saw. But in fact the transmission was too rudimentary to give any sense of what was about them, that desert sea of rocks, rubble, small boulders, and crater lips.

Aldrin was now working to set up the solar wind experiment, a sheet of aluminum foil hung on a stand. For the next hour and a half, the foil would be exposed to the solar wind, and invisible, unfelt, but high-velocity flow of noble gases from the sun like argon, krypton, neon and helium. For the astronauts, it was the simplest of procedures, no more difficult than setting up a piece of sheet music on a music stand. At the end of the EVA, however, the aluminum foil would be rolled up, inserted in the rock box, and delivered eventually to a laboratory in Switzerland uniquely equipped for the purpose. There any nobles gases which had been trapped in the atomic lattice of the aluminum would be baked out in virtuoso procedures of quantitative analysis, and a closer knowledge of the components of the solar wind would be gained. Since the solar wind, it may be recalled, was diverted by the magnetosphere away from the earth it had not hitherto been available for casual study.

That was the simplest experiment to set up; the other two would be deployed about an hour later. One was a passive seismometer to measure erratic disturbances and any periodic vibrations, as well as moonquakes, and the impact of meteors in the weeks and months to follow; it was equipped to radio this information to earth, the energy for transmission derived from solar panels which extended out to either side, and thereby gave it the look of one of those spaceships of the future with thin extended paperlike wings which one sees in science fiction drawings. In any case it was so sensitive that the steps of the astronauts were recorded as they walked by. Finally there was a Laser Ranging Retro-Reflector, an LRRR (or LRQ, for L R-cubed), and that was a mirror whose face was a hundred quartz crystals, black as coal, cut to a precision never obtained before in glass—one-third of an arch/sec. Since each quartz crystal was a corner of a rectangle, any ray of light striking one of the three faces in each crystal would bounce off the other two in such a way that the light would return in exactly the same direction it had been received. A laser beam sent up from earth would therefore reflect back to the place from which it was sent. The time it required to travel this half-million miles from earth to moon round trip, a journey of less than three seconds, could be measured so accurately that physicists might then discern whether the moon was drifting away from the earth a few centimeters a year, or (by using two lasers) whether Europe and America might be drifting apart some comparable distance, or even if the Pacific Ocean were contracting. These measurements could then be entered into the caverns of Einstein's General Theory of Relativity, and new proof or disproof of the great thesis could be obtained.

We may be certain the equipment was remarkable. Still, its packaging and its ease of deployment had probably done as much to advance its presence on the ship as any clear priority over other scientific equipment; the beauty of these items from the point of view of NASA was that the astronauts could set them up in a few minutes while working in their space suits, even set them up with inflated gloves so insensitive that special silicone pads had to be inserted at the fingertips in order to leave the astronauts not altogether numb-fingered in their manipulations. Yet these marvels of measurement would soon be installed on the moon with less effort than it takes to remove a vacuum cleaner from its carton and get it operating.

It was at this point that patriotism, the corporation, and the national taste all came to occupy the same head of a pin, for the astronauts next proceeded to set up the flag. But that operation, as always, presented its exquisite problems. There was, we remind ourselves, no atmosphere for the flag to wave in. Any flag made of cloth would droop, indeed it would dangle. Therefore a species of starched plastic flag had to be employed, a flag which would stand out, there, out to the nonexistent breeze, flat as a slab of plywood. No, that would not do either. The flag was better crinkled and curled. Waves and billows were bent into it, and a full corkscrew of a curl at the end. There it stands for posterity, photographed in the twists of a high gale on the windless moon, curled up tin flag, numb as a pickled pepper.

Aldrin would hardly agree. "Being able to salute that flag was one of the more humble yet proud experiences I've ever had. To be able to look at the American flag and know how much so many people had put of themselves and their work into getting it where it was. We sensed—we really did—this almost mystical identification of all the people in the world at that instant."

Two minutes after the flag was up, the President of the United States put in his phone call. Let us listen one more time:

"Because of what you have done," said Nixon, "the heavens have become a part of man's world. And as you talk to us from the Sea of Tranquility, it inspires us to redouble our efforts to bring peace and tranquility to earth . . ."

"Thank you, Mr. President. It's a great honor and privilege for us to be here representing not only the United States, but men of peace of all nations . . ."

In such piety is the schizophrenia of the ages.

Immediately afterward, Aldrin practiced kicking moon dust, but he was somewhat broken up. Either reception was garbled, or Aldrin was temporarily incoherent. "They seem to leave," he said to the Capcom, referring to the particles, "and most of them have about the same angle of departure and velocity. From where I stand, a large portion of them will impact at a certain distance out. Several—the percentage is, of course, that will impact . . ."

Capcom: "Buzz this is Houston. You're cutting out on the end of your transmissions. Can you speak a little more forward into your microphone. Over."

Aldrin: "Roger. I'll try that."

Capcom: "Beautiful."

Aldrin: "Now I had that one inside my mouth that time."

Capcom: "It sounded a little wet."

And on earth, a handful of young scientists were screaming, "Stop wasting time with flags and presidents—collect some rocks!"

DISCUSSION QUESTIONS

1. How does the language of the astronauts, especially Aldrin's, affect Mailer? Why does Mailer use their words and NASA terminology so frequently? How are these transcripts and codes used by O'Toole in his account of the moon landing for the *Washington Post* (see "Press")?

2. Why does Mailer concentrate on a particular spot where the transcript is garbled? Why does he speculate on the length of time it takes the astronauts to step out onto the moon? How does his description of the "clarity of focus" on the moon suggest an environment that is different from the one described by the astronauts? For example, how does Aldrin's comparison of the moon landscape to "an environment somewhere out West" affect our response to what they are seeing? What does Mailer want us to see?

Joan Didion / On the Mall 1975

A former associate feature editor at Vogue *and contributing editor to the* National Review, The Saturday Evening Post, *and* Esquire, *Joan Didion has written for* Mademoiselle, Holiday, The American Scholar, *and* Life *magazines. Interviews and self-assertion are not her journalistic forte:*

> *My only advantage as a reporter is that I am so physically small, so temperamentally unobtrusive, and so neurotically inarticulate that people tend to forget that my presence runs counter to their best interests. And it always does. That is one last thing to remember: writers are always selling somebody out.*

The author of three novels—Run River, Play It as It Lays, *and* Democracy—*Didion has also published several collections of essays, including* Slouching Towards Bethlehem *(1968) and* The White Album *(1979), from which the following essay on shopping malls is taken. Her study of the politics and culture of Central America,* Salvador, *appeared in 1983.*

They float on the landscape like pyramids to the boom years, all those Plazas and Malls and Esplanades. All those Squares and Fairs. All those Towns and Dales, all those Villages, all those Forests and Parks and Lands. Stonestown. Hillsdale.

Valley Fair, Mayfair, Northgate, Southgate, Eastgate, Westgate. Gulfgate. They are toy garden cities in which no one lives but everyone consumes, profound equalizers, the perfect fusion of the profit motive and the egalitarian ideal, and to hear their names is to recall words and phrases no longer quite current. Baby Boom. Consumer Explosion. Leisure Revolution. Do-It-Yourself Revolution. Backyard Revolution. Suburbia. "The Shopping Center," the Urban Land Institute could pronounce in 1957, "is today's extraordinary retail business evolvement. . . . The automobile accounts for suburbia, and suburbia accounts for the shopping center."

It was a peculiar and visionary time, those years after World War II to which all the Malls and Towns and Dales stand as climate-controlled monuments. Even the word "automobile," as in "the automobile accounts for suburbia and suburbia accounts for the shopping center," no longer carries the particular freight it once did: as a child in the late Forties in California I recall reading and believing that the "freedom of movement" afforded by the automobile was "America's fifth freedom." The trend was up. The solution was in sight. The frontier had been reinvented, and its shape was the subdivision, that new free land on which all settlers could recast their lives *tabula rasa*. For one perishable moment there the American idea seemed about to achieve itself, via F.H.A. housing and the acquisition of major appliances, and a certain enigmatic glamour attached to the architects of this newfound land. They made something of nothing. They gambled and sometimes lost. They staked the past to seize the future. I have difficulty now imagining a childhood in which a man named Jere Strizek, the developer of Town and Country Village outside Sacramento (143,000 square feet gross floor area, 68 stores, 1000 parking spaces, the Urban Land Institute's "prototype for centers using heavy timber and tile construction for informality"), could materialize as a role model, but I had such a childhood, just after World War II, in Sacramento. I never met or even saw Jere Strizek, but at the age of 12 I imagined him a kind of frontiersman, a romantic and revolutionary spirit, and in the indigenous grain he was.

I suppose James B. Douglas and David D. Bohannon were too.

I first heard of James B. Douglas and David D. Bohannon not when I was 12 but a dozen years later, when I was living in New York, working for *Vogue*, and taking, by correspondence, a University of California Extension course in shopping-center theory. This did not seem to me eccentric at the time. I remember sitting on the cool floor in Irving Penn's studio and reading, in *The Community Builders Handbook*, advice from James B. Douglas on shopping-center financing. I recall staying late in my pale-blue office on the twentieth floor of the Graybar Building to memorize David D. Bohannon's parking ratios. My "real" life was to sit in this office and describe life as it was lived in Djakarta and Caneel Bay and in the great châteaux of the Loire Valley, but my dream life was to put together a Class-A regional shopping center with three full-line department stores as major tenants.

That I was perhaps the only person I knew in New York, let alone on the Condé Nast floors of the Graybar Building, to have memorized the distinctions among "A," "B," and "C" shopping centers did not occur to me (the defining distinction, as long as I have your attention, is that an "A," or "regional," center has as its major tenant a full-line department store which carries major appliances; a "B," or "community," center has as its major tenant a junior department store which does not carry major appliances; and a "C," or "neighborhood," center has as its major tenant only a supermarket): my interest in shopping centers was in no way casual. I did want to build them. I wanted to build them because I had fallen into the habit of writing fiction, and I had it in my head that a couple of good centers might support this habit less taxingly than a pale-blue office at *Vogue*.

I had even devised an original scheme by which I planned to gain enough capital and credibility to enter the shopping-center game: I would lease warehouses in, say, Queens, and offer Manhattan delicatessens the opportunity to sell competitively by buying cooperatively, from my trucks. I see a few wrinkles in this scheme now (the words ''concrete overcoat'' come to mind), but I did not then. In fact I planned to run it out of the pale-blue office.

James B. Douglas and David D. Bohannon. In 1950 James B. Douglas had opened Northgate, in Seattle, the first regional center to combine a pedestrian mall with an underground truck tunnel. In 1954 David D. Bohannon had opened Hillsdale, a forty-acre regional center on the peninsula south of San Francisco. That is the only solid bio I have on James B. Douglas and David D. Bohannon to this day, but many of their opinions are engraved on my memory. David D. Bohannon believed in preserving the integrity of the shopping center by not cutting up the site with any dedicated roads. David D. Bohannon believed that architectural setbacks in a center looked ''pretty on paper'' but caused ''customer resistance.'' James B. Douglas advised that a small-loan office could prosper in a center only if it were placed away from foot traffic, since people who want small loans do not want to be observed getting them. I do not now recall whether it was James B. Douglas or David D. Bohannon or someone else altogether who passed along this hint on how to paint the lines around the parking spaces (actually this is called ''striping the lot,'' and the spaces are ''stalls''): make each space a foot wider than it need be—ten feet, say, instead of nine—when the center first opens and business is slow. By this single stroke the developer achieves a couple of important objectives, the appearance of a popular center and the illusion of easy parking, and no one will really notice when business picks up and the spaces shrink.

Nor do I recall who first solved what was once a crucial center dilemma: the placement of the major tenant vis-à-vis the parking lot. The dilemma was that the major tenant—the draw, the raison d'être for the financing, the Sears, the Macy's, the May Company—wanted its customer to walk directly from car to store. The smaller tenants, on the other hand, wanted that same customer to *pass their stores* on the way from the car to, say, Macy's. The solution to this conflict of interests was actually very simple: *two major tenants,* one at each end of a mall. This is called ''anchoring the mall,'' and represents seminal work in shopping-center theory. One thing you will note about shopping-center theory is that you could have thought of it yourself, and a course in it will go a long way toward dispelling the notion that business proceeds from mysteries too recondite for you and me.

A few aspects of shopping-center theory do in fact remain impenetrable to me. I have no idea why the Community Builders' Council ranks ''Restaurant'' as deserving a Number One (or ''Hot Spot'') location but exiles ''Chinese Restaurant'' to a Number Three, out there with ''Power and Light Office'' and ''Christian Science Reading Room.'' Nor do I know why the Council approves of enlivening a mall with ''small animals'' but specifically, vehemently, and with no further explanation, excludes ''monkeys.'' If I had a center I would have monkeys, and Chinese restaurants, and Mylar kites and bands of small girls playing tambourine.

A few years ago at a party I met a woman from Detroit who told me that the Joyce Carol Oates novel with which she identified most closely was *Wonderland.*

I asked her why.

''Because,'' she said, ''my husband has a branch there.''

I did not understand.

''In Wonderland the center,'' the woman said patiently. ''My husband has a branch in Wonderland.''

I have never visited Wonderland but imagine it to have bands of small girls playing tambourine.

A few facts about shopping centers.

The ''biggest'' center in the United States is generally agreed to be Woodfield, outside Chicago, a ''super'' regional or ''leviathan'' two-million-square-foot center with four major tenants.

The ''first'' shopping center in the United States is generally agreed to be Country Club Plaza in Kansas City, built in the twenties. There were some other early centers, notably Edward H. Bouton's 1907 Roland Park in Baltimore, Hugh Prather's 1931 Highland Park Shopping Village in Dallas, and Hugh Potter's 1937 River Oaks in Houston, but the developer of Country Club Plaza, the late J. C. Nichols, is referred to with ritual frequency in the literature of shopping centers, usually as ''pioneering J. C. Nichols,'' ''trailblazing J. C. Nichols,'' or ''J. C. Nichols, of the center as we know it.''

Those are some facts I know about shopping centers because I still want to be Jere Strizek or James B. Douglas or David D. Bohannon. Here are some facts I know about shopping centers because I never will be Jere Strizek or James B. Douglas or David D. Bohannon: a good center in which to spend the day if you wake feeling low in Honolulu, Hawaii, is Ala Moana, major tenants Liberty House and Sears. A good center in which to spend the day if you wake feeling low in Oxnard, California, is The Esplanade, major tenants the May Company and Sears. A good center in which to spend the day if you wake feeling low in Biloxi, Mississippi, is Edgewater Plaza, major tenant Godchaux's. Ala Moana in Honolulu is larger than The Esplanade in Oxnard, and The Esplanade in Oxnard is larger than Edgewater Plaza in Biloxi. Ala Moana has carp pools. The Esplanade and Edgewater Plaza do not.

These marginal distinctions to one side, Ala Moana, The Esplanade, and Edgewater Plaza are the same place, which is precisely their role not only as equalizers but in the sedation of anxiety. In each of them one moves for a while in an aqueous suspension not only of light but of judgment, not only of judgment but of ''personality.'' One meets no acquaintances at The Esplanade. One gets no telephone calls at Edgewater Plaza. ''It's a hard place to run in to for a pair of stockings,'' a friend complained to me recently of Ala Moana, and I knew that she was not yet ready to surrender her ego to the idea of the center. The last time I went to Ala Moana it was to buy *The New York Times*. Because *The New York Times* was not in, I sat on the mall for a while and ate caramel corn. In the end I bought not *The New York Times* at all but two straw hats at Liberty House, four bottles of nail enamel at Woolworth's, and a toaster, on sale at Sears. In the literature of shopping centers these would be described as impulse purchases, but the impulse here was obscure. I do not wear hats, nor do I like caramel corn. I do not use nail enamel. Yet flying back across the Pacific I regretted only the toaster.

Maxine Hong Kingston / *The Woman Warrior* 1975

There is an autobiographical center to Maxine Hong Kingston's much celebrated fiction. Born in Stockton, California, in 1940, Maxine Hong Kingston earned her B.A. at the University of California, Berkeley, where she has recently returned to teach writing. Her first book, The Woman Warrior: Memoirs of a Girlhood among Ghosts, *received the National Book Critics Circle Award for nonfiction. Her second book,* China Men, *was awarded the 1981 American Book Award. Her most recent work is* Tripmaster Monkey: His Fake Book *(1990). In each of these remarkable books, Maxine Hong Kingston draws on her own life and the stories of her family and portrays with stunning sensitivity the intersections of three cultures: American, Chinese, and Chinese American. "I have no idea," she says, "how people who don't write can endure their lives."*

Maxine Hong Kingston describes The Woman Warrior *as not only "a family book or an American book or a woman's book but a world book, and, at the same moment, my book." The following selection also demonstrates that she has mastered the art of narration and blurred the distinction between fiction and nonfiction. "My characters are storytellers, and I suspect that some of them are telling me fiction. So when I write their lives down is it fiction or nonfiction?" For Kingston, the most reasonable response can be found in perspective. In addition to presenting verifiable representations of experience, Kingston draws freely on the emotions and impressions that color her—and her characters'—views of experience. And she doesn't hesitate to explain her purpose in doing so: "When I tell . . . all these versions, I'm actually giving the culture of these people in a very accurate way. You can see where the people make up these fictions about themselves, and it's not just for fun. It's a terrible necessity." The result is a remarkable blend of truth and beauty.*

NO NAME WOMAN

"You must not tell anyone," my mother said, "what I am about to tell you. In China your father had a sister who killed herself. She jumped into the family well. We say that your father has all brothers because it is as if she had never been born.

"In 1924 just a few days after our village celebrated seventeen hurry-up weddings—to make sure that every young man who went 'out on the road' would responsibly come home—your father and his brothers and your grandfather and his brothers and your aunt's new husband sailed for America, the Gold Mountain. It was your grandfather's last trip. Those lucky enough to get contracts waved good-bye from the decks. They fed and guarded the stowaways and helped them off in Cuba, New York, Bali, Hawaii. 'We'll meet in California next year,' they said. All of them sent money home.

"I remember looking at your aunt one day when she and I were dressing: I had not noticed before that she had such a protruding melon of a stomach. But I did not think. 'She's pregnant,' until she began to look like other pregnant women, her shirt pulling and the white tops of her black pants showing. She could not have been pregnant, you see, because her husband had been gone for years. No one said anything. We did not discuss it. In early summer she was ready to have the child, long after the time when it could have been possible.

"The village had also been counting. On the night the baby was to be born the villagers raided our house. Some were crying. Like a great saw, teeth strung with lights, files of people walked zigzag across our land, tearing the rice. Their lanterns doubled in the disturbed black water, which drained away through the broken bunds. As the villagers closed in, we could see that some of them, probably men and women we knew well, wore white masks. The people with long hair hung it over their faces. Women with short hair made it stand up on end. Some had tied white bands around their foreheads, arms, and legs.

"At first they threw mud and rocks at the house. Then they threw eggs and began slaughtering our stock. We could hear the animals scream their deaths—the roosters, the pigs, a last great roar from the ox. Familiar wild heads flared in our night windows: the villagers encircled us. Some of the faces stopped to peer at us, their eyes rushing like searchlights. The hands flattened against the panes, framed heads, and left red prints.

"The villagers broke in the front and the back doors at the same time, even though we had not locked the doors against them. Their knives dripped with the blood of our animals. They smeared blood on the doors and walls. One woman swung a chicken, whose throat she had split, splattering blood in red arcs about her. We stood together in the middle of our house, in the family hall with the pictures and tables of the ancestors around us, and looked straight ahead.

"At that time the house had only two wings. When the men came back, we would build two more to enclose our courtyard and a third one to begin a second courtyard. The villagers pushed through both wings, even your grandparents' rooms, to find your aunt's, which was also mine until the men returned. From this room a new wing for one of the younger families would grow. They ripped up her clothes and shoes and broke her combs, grinding them underfoot. They tore her work from the loom. They scattered the cooking fire and rolled the new weaving in it. We could hear them in the kitchen breaking our bowls and banging the pots. They overturned the great waist-high earthenware jugs; duck eggs, pickled fruits, vegetables burst out and mixed in acrid torrents. The old woman from the next field swept a broom through the air and loosed the spirits-of-the-broom over our heads. 'Pig.' 'Ghost.' 'Pig,'' they sobbed and scolded while they ruined our house.

"When they left, they took sugar and oranges to bless themselves. The cut pieces from the dead animals. Some of them took bowls that were not broken and clothes that were not torn. Afterward we swept up the rice and sewed it back up into sacks. But the smells from the spilled preserves lasted. Your aunt gave birth in the pigsty that night. The next morning when I went up for the water. I found her and the baby clugging up the family well.

"Don't let your father know that I told you. He denies her. Now that you have started to menstruate, what happened to her could happen to you. Don't humiliate us. You wouldn't like to be forgotten as if you had never been born. The villagers are watchful."

Whenever she had to warn us about life, my mother told stories that ran like this one, a story to grow up on. She tested our strength to establish realities. Those in the emigrant generations who could not reassert brute survival died young and far from home. Those of us in the first American generations have had to figure out how the invisible world the emigrants built around our childhoods fit in solid America.

The emigrants confused the gods by delivering their curse, misleading them with crooked streets and false names. They must try to confuse their offspring as well, who, I suppose, threaten them in similar ways—always trying to get things straight, always trying to name the unspeakable. The Chinese I know hide their names; sojourners take new names when their lives change and guard their real names with silence.

Chinese-Americans, when you try to understand what things in you are Chinese, how do you separate what is peculiar to childhood, to poverty, insanities, one family, your mother who marked your growing with stories, from what is Chinese? What is Chinese tradition and what is the movies?

If I want to learn what clothes my aunt wore, whether flashy or ordinary, I would have to begin, "Remember Father's drowned-in-the-well sister?" I cannot ask that. My mother has told me once and for all the useful parts. She will add nothing unless powered by Necessity, a riverbank that guides her life. She plants vegetable gardens rather than lawns: she carries the odd-shaped tomatoes home from the fields and eats food left for gods.

Whenever we did frivolous things, we used up energy; we flew high kites. We children came up off the ground over the melting cones our parents brought home from work and the American movie on New Year's Day—*Oh, You Beautiful Doll* with Betty Grable one year, and *She Wore a Yellow Ribbon* with John Wayne another year. After the one carnival ride each, we paid in guilt; our tired father counted his change on the dark walk home.

Adultery is extravagance. Could people who hatch their own chicks and eat the embryos and the heads for delicacies and boil the feet in vinegar for party food, leaving only the gravel, eating even the gizzard lining—could such people engender a prodigal aunt? To be a woman, to have a daughter in starvation time was a waste enough. My aunt could not have been the lone romantic who gave up everything for sex. Women in the old China did not choose. Some man had commanded her to lie with him and be his secret evil. I wonder whether he masked himself when he joined the raid on her family.

Perhaps she encountered him in the fields or on the mountain where the daughters-in-law collected fuel. Or perhaps he first noticed her in the marketplace. He was not a stranger because the village housed no strangers. She had to have dealings with him other than sex. Perhaps he worked an adjoining field, or he sold her the cloth for the dress she sewed and wore. His demand must have surprised, then terrified her. She obeyed him: she always did as she was told.

When the family found a young man in the next village to be her husband, she stood tractably beside the best rooster, his proxy, and promised before they met that she would be his forever. She was lucky that he was her age and she would be the first wife, an advantage secure now. The night she first saw him, he had sex with her. Then he left for America. She had almost forgotten what he looked like. When she tried to envision him, she only saw the black and white face in the group photograph the men had had taken before leaving.

The other man was not, after all, much different from her husband. They both gave orders: she followed. "If you tell your family, I'll beat you. I'll kill you. Be here again next week." No one talked sex, ever. And she might have separated the rapes from the rest of living if only she did not have to buy her oil from him or gather wood in the same forest. I want her fear to have lasted just as long as rape lasted so that the fear could have been contained. No drawn-out fear. But women at sex hazarded birth and hence lifetimes. The fear did not stop but permeated everywhere. She told the man, "I think I'm pregnant." He organized the raid against her.

On nights when my mother and father talked about their life back home, sometimes they mention an "outcast table" whose business they still seemed to be settling, their voices tight. In a commensal tradition, where food is precious, the powerful older people made wrongdoers eat alone. Instead of letting them start separate new lives like the Japanese, who could become samurais and geishas, the Chinese family, faces averted but eyes glowering sideways, hung on to the offenders and fed them leftovers. My aunt must have lived in the same house as my parents and eaten at an outcast table. My mother spoke about the raid as if she had seen it, when she and my aunt, a daughter-in-law to a different household, should not have been living together at all. Daughters-in-law lived with their husbands' parents, not their own; a synonym for marriage in Chinese is "taking a daughter-in-law." Her husband's parents could have sold her, mortgaged her, stoned her. But they had sent her back to her own mother and father, a mysterious act hinting at disgraces not told me. Perhaps they had thrown her out to deflect the avengers.

She was the only daughter: her four brothers went with her father, husband, and uncles "out on the road" and for some years became western men. When the goods were divided among the family, three of the brothers took land, and the youngest, my father, chose an education. After my grandparents gave their daughter away to her husband's family, they had dispensed all the adventure and all the property. They expected her alone to keep the traditional ways, which her brothers, now among the barbarians, could fumble without detection. The heavy, deep-rooted women were to maintain the past against the flood, safe for returning. But the rare urge west had fixed upon our family, and so my aunt crossed boundaries not delineated in space.

The work of preservation demands that the feelings playing about in one's guts not be turned into action. Just watch their passing like cherry blossoms. But perhaps my aunt, my forerunner, caught in a slow life, let dreams grow and fade and after some months or years went toward what persisted. Fear at the enormities of the forbidden kept her desires delicate, wire and bone. She looked at a man because she liked the way the hair was tucked behind his ears, or she liked the questionmark line of a long torso curving at the shoulder and straight at the hip. For warm eyes or a soft voice or a slow walk—that's all—a few hairs, a line, a brightness, a sound, a pace, she gave up family. She offered us up for a charm that vanished with tiredness, a pigtail that didn't toss when the wind died. Why, the wrong lighting could erase the dearest thing about him.

It could very well have been, however, that my aunt did not take subtle enjoyment of her friend, but, a wild woman, kept rollicking company. Imagining her free with sex doesn't fit, though. I don't know any women like that, or men either. Unless I see her life branching into mine, she gives me no ancestral help.

To sustain her being in love, she often worked at herself in the mirror, guessing at the colors and shapes that would interest him, changing them frequently in order to hit on the right combination. She wanted him to look back.

On a farm near the sea, a woman who tended her appearance reaped a reputation for eccentricity. All the married women blunt-cut their hair in flaps about their ears or pulled it back in tight buns. No nonsense. Neither style blew easily into heart-catching tangles. And at their weddings they displayed themselves in their long hair for the last time. "It brushed the backs of my knees," my mother tells me. "It was braided, and even so, it brushed the backs of my knees."

At the mirror my aunt combed individuality into her bob. A bun could have been contrived to escape into black streamers blowing in the wind or in quiet wisps about her face, but only the older women in our picture album wear buns. She brushed her hair back from her forehad, tucking the flaps behind her ears. She looped a piece of thread, knotted into a circle between her index fingers and thumbs, and ran the double strand across her forehead. When she closed her fingers as if she were making a pair of shadow geese bite, the string twisted together catching the little hairs. Then she pulled the thread away from her skin, ripping the hairs out neatly, her eyes watering from the needles of pain. Opening her fingers, she cleaned the thread, then rolled it along her hairline and the tops of her eyebrows. My mother did the same to me and my sisters and herself. I used to believe that the expression "caught by the short hairs" meant a captive held with a depilatory string. It especially hurt at the temples, but my mother said we were lucky we didn't have to have our feet bound when we were seven. Sisters used to sit on their beds and cry together, she said, as their mothers or their slave removed the bandages for a few minutes each night and let the blood gush back into their veins. I hope that the man my aunt loved appreciated a smooth brow, that he wasn't just a tits-and-ass man.

Once my aunt found a freckle on her chin, at a spot that the almanac said predestined her for unhappiness. She dug it out with a hot needle and washed the wound with peroxide.

More attention to her looks than these pullings of hairs and pickings at spots would have caused gossip among the villagers. They owned work clothes and good clothes, and they wore good clothes for feasting the new seasons. But since a woman combing her hair hexes beginnings, my aunt rarely found an occasion to look her best. Women looked like great sea snails—the corded wood, babies, and laundry they carried were the whorls on their backs. The Chinese did not admire a bent back; goddesses and warriors stood straight. Still there must have been a marvelous freeing of beauty when a worker laid down her burden and stretched and arched.

Such commonplace loveliness, however, was not enough for my aunt. She dreamed of a lover for the fifteen days of New Year's, the time for families to exchange visits, money, and food. She plied her secret comb. And sure enough she cursed the year, the family, the village, and herself.

Even as her hair lured her imminent lover, many other men looked at her. Uncles, cousins, nephews, brothers would have looked, too, had they been home between journeys. Perhaps they had already been restraining their curiosity, and they left, fearful that their glances, like a field of nesting birds, might be startled and caught. Poverty hurt, and that was their first reason for leaving. But another, final reason for leaving the crowded house was the never-said.

She may have been unusually beloved, the precious only daughter, spoiled and mirror-gazing because of the affection the family lavished on her. When her husband left, they welcomed the chance to take her back from the in-laws: she could live like the little daughter for just a while longer. There are stories that my grandfather was different from other people, "crazy ever since the little Jap bayoneted him in the head." He used to put his naked penis on the dinner table, laughing. And one day he brought home a baby girl, wrapped up inside his brown western-style greatcoat. He had traded one of his sons, probably my father, the youngest, for her. My grandmother made him trade back. When he finally got a daughter of his own, he doted on her. They must have all loved her, except perhaps my father, the only brother who never went back to China, having once been traded for a girl.

Brothers and sisters, newly men and women, had to efface their sexual color and present plain miens. Disturbing hair and eyes, a smile like no other, threatened the ideal of five generations living under one roof. To focus blurs, people shouted face to face and yelled from room to room. The immigrants I know have loud voices, unmodulated to American tones even after years away from the village where they called their friendships out across the fields. I have not been able to stop my mother's screams in public libraries or over telephones. Walking erect (knees straight, toes pointed forward, not pigeon-toed, which is Chinese-feminine) and speaking in an inaudible voice. I have tried to turn myself American-feminine. Chinese communication was loud, public. Only sick people had to whisper. But at the dinner table, where the family members came nearest one another, no one could talk, not the outcasts nor any eaters. Every word that falls from the mouth is a coin lost. Silently they gave and accepted food with both hands. A preoccupied child who took his bowl with one hand got a sideways glare. A complete moment of total attention is due everyone alike. Children and lovers have no singularity here, but my aunt used a secret voice, a separate attentiveness.

She kept the man's name to herself throughout her labor and dying; she did not accuse him that he be punished with her. To save her inseminator's name she gave silent birth.

He may have been somebody in her own household, but intercourse with a man outside the family would have been no less abhorrent. All the village were kinsmen, and the titles shouted in loud country voices never let kinship be forgotten. Any man within visiting distance would have been neutralized as a lover—"brother," "older brother"—115 relationship titles. Parents researched birth charts probably not so much to assure good fortune as to circumvent incest in a population that has but one hundred surnames. Everybody has eight million relatives. How useless than sexual mannerisms, how dangerous.

As if it came from an atavism deeper than fear, I used to add "brother" silently to boy's names. It hexed the boys, who would or would not ask me to dance, and made them less scary and as familiar and deserving of benevolence as girls.

But, of course, I hexed myself also—no dates. I should have stood up, both arms waving, and shouted out across libraries, "Hey, you! Love me back." I had no idea, though, how to make attraction selective, how to control its direction and magnitude. If I made myself American-pretty so that the five or six Chinese boys in the class fell in love with me, everyone else—the Caucasian, Negro, and Japanese boys—would too. Sisterliness, dignified and honorable, made much more sense.

Attraction eludes control so stubbornly that whole societies designed to organize relationships among people cannot keep order, not even when they bind people to one another from childhood and raise them together. Among the very poor and the wealthy, brothers married their adopted sisters, like doves. Our family allowed some romance, paying adult brides' prices and providing dowries so that their sons and daughters could marry strangers. Marriage promises to turn strangers into friendly relatives—a nation of siblings.

In the village structure, spirits shimmered among the live creatures, balanced and held in equilibrium by time and land. But one human being flaring up into violence could open up a black hole, a maelstrom that pulled in the sky. The frightened villages, who depended on one another to maintain the real, went to my aunt to show her a personal, physical representation of the break she made in the "roundness." Misallying couples snapped off the future, which was to be embodied in true offspring. The villagers punished her for acting as if she could have a private life, secret and apart from them.

If my aunt had betrayed the family at a time of large grain yields and peace, when many boys were born, and wings were being built on many houses, perhaps she might have escaped such severe punishment. But the men—hungry, greedy, tired of planting in dry soil, cuckolded—had been forced to leave the village in order to send food-money home. There were ghost plagues, bandit plagues, wars with the Japanese, floods. My Chinese brother and sister had died of an unknown sickness. Adultery, perhaps only a mistake during good times, became a crime when the village needed food.

The round moon cakes and round doorways, the round tables of graduated size that fit one roundness inside another, round windows and rice bowls—these talismans had lost their power to warn this family of the law: a family must be whole, faithfully keeping the descent line by having sons to feed the old and the dead who in turn look after the family. The villagers came to show my aunt and lover-in-hiding a broken house. The villagers were speeding up the circling of events because she was too shortsighted to see that her infidelity had already harmed the village, that waves of consequences would return unpredictably, sometimes in disguise, as now, to hurt her. This roundness had to be made coin-sized so that she would see its circumference: punish her at the birth of her baby. Awaken her to the inexorable. People who refuse fatalism because they could invent small resources insisted on culpability. Deny accidents and wrest fault from the stars.

After the villagers left, their lanterns now scattering in various directions toward home, the family broke their silence and cursed her. "Aiaa, we're going to die. Death is coming. Death is coming. Look what you've done. You've killed us. Ghost! Dead Ghost! You've never been born." She ran out into the fields, far enough from the house so that she could no longer hear their voices, and pressed herself against the earth, her own land no more. When she felt the birth coming, she thought that she had been hurt. Her body seized together. "They've hurt me too much," she thought. "This is gall, and it will kill me." With forehead and knees against the earth, her body convulsed and then relaxed. She turned on her back, lay on the ground. The black well of sky and stars went out and out forever: her body and her complexity seemed to disappear. She was one of the stars, a bright dot in blackness, without home, without a companion, in eternal cold and silence. An agoraphobia rose in her, speeding higher and higher, bigger and bigger: she would not be able to contain it: there would be no end to fear.

Flayed, unprotected against space, she felt pain return, focusing her body. This pain chilled her—a cold, steady kind of surface pain. Inside, spasmodically, the other pain, the pain of the child, heated her. For hours she lay on the ground, alternately body and space. Sometimes a vision of normal comfort obliterated reality: she saw the family in the evening gambling at the dinner table, the young people massaging their elders' backs. She saw them congratulating one another, high joy on the mornings the rice shoots came up. When these pictures burst, the stars drew yet further apart. Black space opened.

She got to her feet to fight better and remembered that old-fashioned women gave birth in their pigsties to fool the jealous, pain-dealing gods, who do not snatch piglets. Before the next spasms could stop her, she ran to the pigsty, each step a rushing out into emptiness. She climbed over the fence and knelt in the dirt. It was good to have a fence enclosing her, a tribal person alone.

Laboring, this woman who had carried her child as a foreign growth that sickened her every day, expelled it at last. She reached down to touch the hot, wet, moving mass, surely smaller than anything human, and could feel that it was human after all—fingers, toes, nails, nose. She pulled it up on to her belly, and it lay curled there, butt in the air, feet precisely tucked one under the other. She opened her loose shirt and buttoned the child inside. After resting, it squirmed and thrashed and she pushed it up to her breast. It turned its head this way and that until it found her nipple. There, it made little snuffling noises. She clenched her teeth at its preciousness, lovely as a young calf, a piglet, a little dog.

She may have gone to the pigsty as a last act of responsibility: she would protect this child as she had protected its father. It would look after her soul, leaving supplies on her grave. But how would this tiny child without family find her grave when there would be no marker for her anywhere, neither in the earth nor the family hall? No one would give her a family hall name. She had taken the child with her into the wastes. At its birth the two of them had felt the same raw pain of separation, a wound that only the family pressing tight could close. A child with no descent line would not soften her life but only trail after her, ghostlike, begging her to give it purpose. At dawn the villagers on their way to the fields would stand around the fence and look.

Full of milk, the little ghost slept. When it awoke, she hardened her breasts against the milk that crying loosens. Toward morning she picked up the baby and walked to the well.

Carrying the baby to the well shows loving. Otherwise abandon it. Turn its face into the mud. Mothers who love their children take them along. It was probably a girl: there is some hope of forgiveness for boys.

"Don't tell anyone you had an aunt. Your father does not want to hear her name. She has never been born." I have believed that sex was unspeakable and words so strong and fathers so frail that "aunt" would do my father mysterious harm. I have thought that my family, having settled among immigrants who had also been their neighbors in the ancestral land, needed to clean their name, and a wrong word would incite the kinspeople even here. But there is more to this silence: they want me to participate in her punishment. And I have.

In the twenty years since I heard this story I have not asked for details nor said my aunt's name: I do not know it. People who comfort the dead can also chase after them to hurt them further—a reverse ancestor worship. The real punishment was not the raid swiftly inflicted by the villagers, but the family's deliberately forgetting her. Her betrayal so maddened them, they saw to it that she would suffer forever, even after death. Always hungry, always needing, she would have to beg food from other ghosts, snatch and steal it from those whose living descendants give them gifts. She would have to fight the ghosts massed at crossroads for the buns a few thoughtful citizens leave to decoy her away from village and home so that the ancestral spirits could feast unharassed. At peace, they could act like gods, not ghosts, their descent lines providing them with paper suits and dresses, spirit money, paper houses, paper automobiles, chicken, meat, and rice into eternity—essences delivered up in smoke and flames, steam and incense rising from each rice bowl. In an attempt to make the Chinese care for people outside the family, Chairman Mao encourages us now to give our paper replicas to the spirits of outstanding soldiers and workers, no matter whose ancestors they may be. My aunt remains forever hungry. Goods are not distributed evenly among the dead.

My aunt haunts me—her ghost drawn to me because now, after fifty years of neglect, I alone devote pages of paper to her, though not origamied into houses and clothes. I do not think she always means me well, I am telling on her, and she was a spite suicide, drowning herself in the drinking water. The Chinese are always very frightened of the drowned one, whose weeping ghost, wet hair hanging and skin bloated, waits silently by the water to pull down a substitute.

Walker Percy / The Loss of the Creature 1975

Walker Percy's first novel, The Moviegoer *(1961), showed him to be a writer seriously interested in the effects of popular media on both the individual psyche and American society. His later books have further explored this theme, especially his use of science-fiction motifs in the companion novels* Love in the Ruins *(1971) and* The Thanatos Syndrome *(1986) and in the nonfiction work* Lost in the Cosmos: The Last Self-Help Book *(1983). Throughout his fiction and essays, Percy has proposed a disturbing message: "something has gone badly wrong with America and American life."*

Percy was born in Birmingham, Alabama, in 1916. He graduated from the University of North Carolina with a degree in chemistry and received a medical degree in 1941 from the Columbus University College of Physicians and Surgeons. A few years later, after a long recovery from tuberculosis, Percy converted to Catholicism. He lived in Covington, Louisiana, a small town outside of New Orleans, until his death in 1991. Besides fiction, Percy wrote numerous philosophical, linguistic, and critical essays, some of which have been collected in The Message in the Bottle *(1975). His final publication was* Signposts in a Strange Land *(1991).*

I

Every explorer names his island Formosa, beautiful. To him it is beautiful because, being first, he has access to it and can see it for what it is. But to no one else is it ever beautiful—except the rare man who manages to recover it, who knows that it has to be recovered.

Garcia López de Cárdenas discovered the Grand Canyon and was amazed at the sight. It can be imagined: One crosses miles of desert, breaks through the mesquite, and there it is at one's feet. Later the government set the place aside as a national park, hoping to pass along to millions the experience of Cárdenas. Does not one see the same sight from the Bright Angel Lodge that Cárdenas saw?

The assumption is that the Grand Canyon is a remarkably interesting and beautiful place and that if it had a certain value *P* for Cárdenas, the same value *P* may be transmitted to any number of sightseers—just as Banting's discovery of insulin can be transmitted to any number of diabetics. A counterinfluence is at work, however, and it would be nearer the truth to say that if the place is seen by a million sightseers, a single sightseer does not receive value *P* but a millionth part of value *P*.

It is assumed that since the Grand Canyon has the fixed interest value *P*, tours can be organized for any number of people. A man in Boston decides to spend his vacation at the Grand Canyon. He visits his travel bureau, looks at the folder, signs up for a two-week tour. He and his family take the tour, see the Grand Canyon, and return to Boston. May we say that this man has seen the Grand Canyon? Possibly he has. But it is more likely that what he has done is the one sure way not to see the canyon.

Why is it almost impossible to gaze directly at the Grand Canyon under these circumstances and see it for what it is—as one picks up a strange object from one's back yard and gazes directly at it? It is almost impossible because the Grand Canyon, the thing as it is, has been appropriated by the symbolic complex which has already been formed in the sightseer's mind. Seeing the canyon under approved circumstances is seeing the symbolic complex head on. The thing is no longer the thing as it confronted the Spaniard: it is rather that which has already been formulated—by picture postcard, geography book, tourist folders, and the words *Grand Canyon.* As a result of this preformulation, the source of the sightseer's pleasure undergoes a shift. Where the wonder and delight of the Spaniard arose from his penetration of the thing itself, from a progressive discovery of depths, patterns, colors, shadows, etc., now the sightseer measures his satisfaction *by the degree to which the canyon conforms to the preformed complex.* If it does so, if it looks just like the postcard, he is pleased: he might even say, "Why it is every bit as beautiful as a picture postcard!" He feels he has not been cheated. But if it does not conform, if the colors are somber, he will not be able to see it directly; he will only be conscious of the disparity between what it is and what it is supposed to be. He will say later that he was unlucky in not being there at the right time. The highest point, the term of the sightseer's satisfaction, is not the sovereign discovery of the thing before him: it is rather the measuring up of the thing to the criterion of the preformed symbolic complex.

Seeing the canyon is made even more difficult by what the sightseer does when the moment arrives, when sovereign knower confronts the thing to be known. Instead of looking at it, he photographs it. There is no confrontation at all. At the end of forty years of preformulation and with the Grand Canyon yawning at his feet, what does he do? He waives his right of seeing and knowing and records symbols for the next forty years. For him there is no present; there is only the past of what has been formulated and seen and the future of what has been formulated and not seen. The present is surrendered to the past and the future.

The sightseer may be aware that something is wrong. He may simply be bored; or he may be conscious of the difficulty: that the great thing yawning at his feet somehow eludes him. The harder he looks at it, the less he can see. It eludes everybody. The tourist cannot see it; the bellboy at the Angel Lodge cannot see it: For him it is only one side of the space he lives in, like one wall of a room; to the ranger it is a tissue of everyday signs relevant to his own prospects—the blue haze down there means that he will probably get rained on during the donkey ride.

How can the sightseer recover the Grand Canyon? He can recover it in any number of ways, all sharing in common the stratagem of avoiding the approved confrontation of the tour and the Park Service.

It may be recovered by leaving the beaten track. The tourist leaves the tour, camps in the back country. He arises before dawn and approaches the South Rim through a wild terrain where there are no trails and no railed-in lookout points. In other words, he sees the canyon by avoiding all the facilities for seeing the canyon. If the benevolent Park Service hears about this fellow and thinks he has a good idea and places the following notice in the Bright Angel Lodge: *Consult ranger for information on getting off the beaten track*—the end result will only be the closing of another access to the canyon.

It may be recovered by a dialectical movement which brings one back to the beaten track but at a level above it. For example, after a lifetime of avoiding the beaten track and guided tours, a man may deliberately seek out the most beaten track of all, the most commonplace tour imaginable: he may visit the canyon by a Greyhound tour in the company of a party from Terre Haute—just as a man who has lived in New York all his life may visit the Statue of Liberty. (Such dialectical savorings of *familiar* as the familiar are, of course, a favorite stratagem of *The New Yorker* magazine.) The thing is recovered from familiarity by means of an exercise in familiarity. Our complex friend stands behind the fellow tourists at the Bright Angel Lodge and sees the canyon through them and their predicament, their picture taking and busy disregard. In a sense, he exploits his fellow tourists; he stands on their shoulders to see the canyon.

Such a man is far more advanced in the dialectic than the sightseer who is trying to get off the beaten track—getting up at dawn and approaching the canyon through the mesquite. This stratagem is, in fact, for our complex man the weariest, most beaten track of all.

It may be recovered as a consequence of a breakdown of the symbolic machinery by which the experts present the experience to the consumer. A family visits the canyon in the usual way. But shortly after their arrival, the park is closed by an outbreak of typhus in the south. They have the canyon to themselves. What do they mean when they tell the home folks of their good luck: "We had the whole place to ourselves"? How does one see the thing better when the others are absent? Is looking like sucking: the more lookers, the less there is to see? They could hardly answer, but by saying this they testify to a state of affairs which is considerably more complex than the simple statement of the schoolbook about the Spaniard and the millions who followed him. It is a state in which there is a complex distribution of sovereignty, of zoning.

It may be recovered in a time of national disaster. The Bright Angel Lodge is converted into a rest home, a function that has nothing to do with the canyon a few yards away. A wounded man is brought in. He regains consciousness; there outside his window is the canyon.

The most extreme case of access by privilege conferred by disaster is the Huxleyan[1] novel of adventures of the surviving remnant after the great wars of the twentieth century. An expedition from Australia lands in Southern California and heads east. They stumble across the Bright Angel Lodge, now fallen into ruins. The trails are grown over, the guard rails fallen away, the dime telescope at Battleship Point rusted. But there is the canyon, exposed at last. Exposed by what? By the decay of those facilities which were designed to help the sightseer.

This dialectic of sightseeing cannot be taken into account by planners, for the

[1] A reference to the English novelist Aldous Huxley (1894–1963), best known for his anti-utopian novel. *Brave New World* (1932).—Eds.

object of the dialectic is nothing other than the subversion of the efforts of the planners.

The dialectic is not known to objective theorists, psychologists, and the like. Yet it is quite well known in the fantasy-consciousness of the popular arts. The devices by which the museum exhibit, the Grand Canyon, the ordinary thing, is recovered have long since been stumbled upon. A movie shows a man visiting the Grand Canyon. But the moviemaker knows something the planner does not know. He knows that one cannot take the sight frontally. The canyon must be approached by the stratagems we have mentioned: the inside Track, the Familiar Revisited, the Accidental Encounter. Who is the stranger at the Bright Angel Lodge? Is he the ordinary tourist from Terre Haute that he makes himself out to be? He is not. He has another objective in mind, to revenge his wronged brother, counterespionage, etc. By virtue of the fact that he has other fish to fry, he may take a stroll along the rim after supper and then we can see the canyon through him. The movie accomplishes its purpose by concealing it. Overtly the characters (the American family marooned by typhus) and we the onlookers experience pity for the sufferers, and the family experience anxiety for themselves; covertly and in truth they are the happiest of people and we are happy through them, for we have the canyon to ourselves. The movie cashes in on the recovery of sovereignty through disaster. Not only is the canyon now accessible to the remnant: the members of the remnant are now accessible to each other; a whole new ensemble of relations becomes possible—friendship, love, hatred, clandestine sexual adventures. In a movie when a man sits next to a woman on a bus, it is necessary either that the bus break down or that the woman lose her memory. (The question occurs to one: Do you imagine there are sightseers who see sights just as they are supposed to? a family who live in Terre Haute, who decide to take the canyon tour, who go there, see it, enjoy it immensely, and go home content? a family who are entirely innocent of all the barriers, zones, losses of sovereignty I have been talking about? Wouldn't most people be sorry if Battleship Point fell into the canyon, carrying all one's fellow passengers to their death, leaving one alone on the South Rim? I cannot answer this. Perhaps there are such people. Certainly a great many American families would swear they had no such problems, that they came, saw, and went away happy. Yet it is just these families who would be happiest if they had gotten the Inside Track and been among the surviving remnant.)

It is not apparent that as between the many measures which may be taken to overcome the opacity, the boredom, of the direct confrontation of the thing or creature in its citadel of symbolic investiture, some are less authentic than others. That is to say, some stratagems obviously serve other purposes than that of providing access to being—for example, various unconscious motivations which it is not necessary to go into here.

Let us take an example in which the recovery of being is ambiguous, where it may under the same circumstances contain both authentic and unauthentic components. An American couple, we will say, drives down into Mexico. They see the usual sights and have a fair time of it. Yet they are never without the sense of missing something. Although Taxco and Cuernavaca are interesting and picturesque as advertised, they fall short of "it." What do the couple have in mind by "it"? What do they really hope for? What sort of experience could they have in Mexico so that upon their return, they would feel that "it" had happened? We have a clue: Their hope has something to do with their own role as tourists in a foreign country and the way in which they conceive this role. It has something to do with other American tourists. Certainly they feel that they are very far from "it" when, after traveling five thousand miles, they arrive at the plaza in Guanajuato only to find themselves surrounded by a dozen other couples from the Midwest.

Already we may distinguish authentic and unauthentic elements. First, we see the problem the couple faces and we understand their efforts to surmount it. The problem is to find an "unspoiled" place. "Unspoiled" does not mean only that a place is left physically intact; it means also that it is not encrusted by renown and by the familiar (as in Taxco), that it has not been discovered by others. We understand that the couple really want to get at the place and enjoy it. Yet at the same time we wonder if there is not something wrong in their dislike of their compatriots. Does access to the place require the exclusion of others?

Let us see what happens.

The couple decide to drive from Guanajuato to Mexico City. On the way they get lost. After hours on a rocky mountain road, they find themselves in a tiny valley not even marked on the map. There they discover an Indian village. Some sort of religious festival is going on. It is apparently a corn dance in supplication of the rain god.

The couple know at once that this is "it." They are entranced. They spend several days in the village, observing the Indians and being themselves observed with friendly curiosity.

Now may we not say that the sightseers have at least come face to face with an authentic sight, a sight which is charming, quaint, picturesque, unspoiled, and that they see the sight and come away rewarded? Possibly this may occur. Yet it is more likely that what happens is a far cry indeed from an immediate encounter with being, that the experience, while masquerading as such, is in truth a rather desperate impersonation. I use the word *desperate* advisedly to signify an actual loss of hope.

The clue to the spuriousness of their enjoyment of the village and the festival is a certain restiveness in the sightseers themselves. It is given expression by their repeated exclamations that "this is too good to be true," and by their anxiety that it may not prove to be so perfect, and finally by their downright relief at leaving the valley and having the experience in the bag, so to speak—that is, safely embalmed in memory and movie film.

What is the source of their anxiety during the visit? Does it not mean that the couple are looking at the place with a certain standard of performance in mind? Are they like Fabre,[2] who gazed at the world about him with wonder, letting it be what it is; or are they not like the overanxious mother who sees her child as one performing, now doing badly, now doing well? The village is their child and their love for it is an anxious love because they are afraid that at any moment it might fail them.

We have another clue in their subsequent remark to an ethnologist friend. "How we wished you had been there with us! What a perfect goldmine of folkways! Every minute we would say to each other, if only you were here! You must return with us." This surely testifies to a generosity of spirit, a willingness to share their experience with others, not at all like their feelings toward their fellow Iowans on the plaza at Guanajuato!

I am afraid this is not the case at all. It is true that they longed for their ethnologist friend, but it was for an entirely different reason. They wanted him, not to share their experience, but to certify their experience as genuine.

"This is it" and "Now we are really living" do not necessarily refer to the sovereign encounter of the person with the sight that enlivens the mind and gladdens the heart. It means that now at least we are having the acceptable experience. The present experience is always measured by a prototype, the "it" of their dreams. "Now I am really living" means that now I am filling the role of sightseer and

[2] Jean-Henri Fabre (1823–1913). French scientist who wrote numerous books on insects (*The Life of the Fly, The Life of the Spider,* etc.) based on careful observations.

the sight is living up to the prototype of sights. This quaint and picturesque village is measured by a Platonic ideal of the Quaint and the Picturesque.

Hence their anxiety during the encounter. For at any minute something could go wrong. A fellow Iowan might emerge from a 'dobe hut; the chief might show them his Sears catalogue. (If the failures are "wrong" enough, as these are, they might still be turned to account as rueful conversation pieces: "There we were expecting the chief to bring us a churinga and he shows up with a Sears catalogue!") They have snatched a victory from disaster, but their experience always runs the danger of failure.

They need the ethnologist to certify their experience as genuine. This is borne out by their behavior when the three of them return for the next corn dance. During the dance, the couple do not watch the goings-on; instead they watch the ethnologist! Their highest hope is that their friend should find the dance interesting. And if he should show signs of true absorption, an interest in the goings-on so powerful that he becomes oblivious of his friends—then their cup is full. "Didn't we tell you?" they say at last. What they want from him is not ethnological explanations; all they want is his approval.

What has taken place is a radical loss of sovereignty over that which is as much theirs as it is the ethnologist's. The fault does not lie with the ethnologist. He has no wish to stake a claim to the village; in fact, he desires the opposite; he will bore his friends to death by telling them about the village and the meaning of the folkways. A degree of sovereignty has been surrendered by the couple. It is the nature of the loss, moreover, that they are not aware of the loss, beyond a certain uneasiness. (Even if they read this and admitted it, it would be very difficult for them to bridge the gap in their confrontation of the world. Their consciousness of the corn dance cannot escape their consciousness of their consciousness, so that with the onset of the first direct enjoyment, their higher consciousness pounces and certifies: "Now you are doing it! Now you are really living!' and, in certifying the experience, sets it at nought.)

Their basic placement in the world is such that they reorganize a priority of title of the expert over his particular department of being. The whole horizon of being is staked out by "them," the experts. The highest satisfaction of the sightseer (not merely the tourist but any layman seer of sights) is that his sight should be certified as genuine. The worst of this impoverishment is that there is no sense of impoverishment. The surrender of title is so complete that it never even occurs to one to reassert title. A poor man may envy the rich man, but the sightseer does not envy the expert. When a caste system becomes absolute, envy disappears. Yet the caste of layman-expert is not the fault of the expert. It is due altogether to the eager surrender of sovereignty by the layman so that he may take up the role not of the person but of the consumer.

I do not refer only to the special relation of layman to theorist. I refer to the general situation in which sovereignty is surrendered to a class of privileged knowers, whether these be theorists or artists. A reader may surrender sovereignty over that which has been written about, just as consumer may surrender sovereignty over a thing which has been theorized about. The consumer is content to receive an experience just as it has been presented to him by theorists and planners. The reader may also be content to judge life by whether it has or has not been formulated by those who know and write about life. A young man goes to France. He too has a fair time of it, sees the sights, enjoys the food. On his last day, in fact as he sits in a restaurant in Le Havre waiting for his boat, something happens. A group of French students in the restaurant get into an impassioned argument over a recent play. A riot takes place. Madame la concierge joins in, swinging her mop at the rioters. Our young American is transported. This is "it." And he had almost left France without seeing "it"!

But the young man's delight is ambiguous. On the one hand, it is a pleasure for him to encounter the same Gallic temperament he had heard about from Puccini and Rolland.[3] But on the other hand, the source of his pleasure testifies to a certain alienation. For the young man is actually barred from a direct encounter with anything French excepting only that which has been set forth, authenticated by Puccini and Rolland—those who know. If he had encountered the restaurant scene without reading Hemingway, without knowing that the performance was so typically, charmingly French, he would not have been delighted. He would only have been anxious at seeing things get out of hand. The source of his delight is the sanction of those who know.

This loss of sovereignty is not a marginal process, as might appear from my example of estranged sightseers. It is a generalized surrender of the horizon to those experts within whose competence a particular segment of the horizon is thought to lie. Kwakiutls are surrendered to Franz Boas;[4] decaying Southern mansions are surrendered to Faulkner and Tennessee Williams. So that, although it is by no means the intention of the expert to expropriate sovereignty—in fact he would not even know what sovereignty meant in this context—the danger of theory and consumption is a seduction and deprivation of the consumer.

In the New Mexico desert, natives occasionally come across strange-looking artifacts which have fallen from the skies and which are stenciled: *Return to U.S. Experimental Project, Alamogordo. Reward.* The finder returns the object and is rewarded. He knows nothing of the nature of the object has found and does not care to know. The sole role of the native, the highest role he can play, is that of finder and returner of the mysterious equipment.

The same is true of the layman's relation to *natural* objects in a modern technical society. No matter what the object or event is, whether it is a star, a swallow, a Kwakiutl, a "psychological phenomenon," the layman who confronts it does not confront it as a sovereign person, as Crusoe confronts a seashell he finds on the beach. The highest role he can conceive himself as playing is to be able to recognize the title of the object, to return it to the appropriate expert and have it certified as a genuine find. He does not even permit himself to see the thing—as Gerard Hopkins[5] could see a rock or a cloud or a field. If anyone asks him why he doesn't look, he may reply that he didn't take that subject in college (or he hasn't read Faulkner).

This loss of sovereignty extends even to oneself. There is the neurotic who asks nothing more of his doctor than that his symptoms should prove interesting. When all else fails, the poor fellow has nothing to offer but his own neurosis. But even this is sufficient if only the doctor will show interest when he says, "Last night I had a curious sort of dream; perhaps it will be significant to one who knows about such things. It seems I was standing in a sort of alley—" (I have nothing else to offer you but my own unhappiness. Please say that it, at least, measures up, that it is a *proper* sort of unhappiness.)

II

A young Falkland Islander walking along a beach and spying a dead dogfish and going to work on it with his jackknife has, in a fashion wholly unprovided in

[3]Giacomo Puccini (1853–1924), the Italian composer of such well-known operas as *La Bohème* (1896) and *Madame Butterfly* (1904); Romain Rolland (1866–1944), Nobel-Prize-winning French novelist and dramatist.

[4]Franz Boas (1858–1942), influential German-born American anthropologist who specialized in the languages of and cultures of Native Americans; in 1886 he began studying the Kwakiutl tribe of British Columbia.

[5]Gerard Manly Hopkins (1844–1889), English poet admired for his observations of nature and his innovative use of rhythm and metrics.

modern educational theory, a great advantage over the Scarsdale high-school pupil who finds the dogfish on his laboratory desk. Similarly the citizen of Huxley's *Brave New World* who stumbles across a volume of Shakespeare in some vine-grown ruins and squats on a potsherd to read it is in a fairer way of getting at a sonnet than the Harvard sophomore taking English Poetry II.

The educator whose business it is to teach students biology or poetry is unaware of a whole ensemble of relations which exist between the student and the dogfish and between the student and the Shakespeare sonnet. To put it bluntly: A student who has the desire to get at a dogfish or a Shakespeare sonnet may have the greatest difficulty in salvaging the creature itself from the educational package in which it is presented. The great difficulty is that he is not aware that there is a difficulty; surely, he thinks, in such a fine classroom, with such a fine textbook, the sonnet must come across! What's wrong with me?

The sonnet and the dogfish are obscured by two different processes. The sonnet is obscured by the symbolic package which is formulated not by the sonnet itself but by the *media* through which the sonnet is transmitted, the media which the educators believe for some reason to be transparent. The new textbook, the type, the smell of the page, the classroom, the aluminum windows and the winter sky, the personality of Miss Hawkins—these media which are supposed to transmit the sonnet may only succeed in transmitting themselves. It is only the hardiest and cleverest of students who can salvage the sonnet from this many-tissued package. It is only the rarest student who knows that the sonnet must be salvaged from the package. (The educator is well aware that something is wrong, that there is a fatal gap between the student's learning and the student's life: The student reads the poem, appears to understand it, and gives all the answers. But what does he recall if he should happen to read a Shakespeare sonnet twenty years later? Does he recall the poem or does he recall the smell of the page and the smell of Miss Hawkins?)

One might object, pointing out that Huxley's citizen reading his sonnet in the ruins and the Falkland Islander looking at his dogfish on the beach also receive them in a certain package. Yes, but the difference lies in the fundamental placement of the student in the world, a placement which makes it possible to extract the thing from the package. The pupil at Scarsdale High sees himself placed as a consumer receiving an experience-package; but the Falkland Islander exploring his dogfish is a person exercising the sovereign right of a person in his lordship and mastery of creation. He too could use an instructor and a book and a technique, but he would use them as his subordinates, just as he uses his jackknife. The biology student does not use his scalpel as an instrument; he uses it as a magic wand! Since it is a "scientific instrument," it should do "scientific things."

The dogfish is concealed in the same symbolic package as the sonnet. But the dogfish suffers an additional loss. As a consequence of this double deprivation, the Sarah Lawrence student who scores A in zoology is apt to know very little about a dogfish. She is twice removed from the dogfish, once by the spoliation of the dogfish by theory which renders it invisible. Through no fault of zoology instructors, it is nevertheless a fact that the zoology laboratory at Sarah Lawrence College is one of the few places in the world where it is all but impossible to see a dogfish.

The dogfish, the tree, the seashell, the American Negro, the dream, are rendered invisible by a shift of reality from concrete thing to theory which Whitehead[6] has called the fallacy of misplaced concreteness. It is the mistaking of an idea, a principle, an abstraction, for the real. As a consequence of the shift, the "specimen" is seen as less real than the theory of the specimen. As Kierkegaard[7] said,

[6] Alfred North Whitehead (1861–1947), prominent British philosopher and mathematician.

[7] Sören Aabye Kierkegaard (1813–1855), Danish philosopher and theologian.

once a person is seen as a specimen of a race or a species, at that very moment he ceases to be an individual. Then there are no more individuals but only specimens.

To illustrate: A student enters a laboratory which, in the pragmatic view, offers the student the optimum conditions under which an educational experience may be had. In the existential view, however—that view of the student in which he is regarded not as a receptacle of experience but as a knowing being whose peculiar property it is to see himself as being in a certain situation—the modern laboratory could not have been more effectively designed to conceal the dogfish forever.

The student comes to his desk. On it, neatly arranged by his instructor, he finds his laboratory manual, a dissecting board, instruments, and a mimeographed list:

Exercise 22: Materials

1 dissecting board

1 scalpel

1 forceps

1 probe

1 bottle india ink and syringe

1 specimen of *Squalus acanthias*

The clue to the situation in which the student finds himself is to be found in the last item: 1 specimen of *Squalus acanthias*.

The phrase *specimen of* expresses in the most succinct way imaginable the radical character of the loss of being which has occurred under his very nose. To refer to the dogfish, the unique concrete existent before him, as a "specimen of *Squalus acanthias*" reveals by its grammar the spoliation of the dogfish by the theoretical method. This phrase, *specimen of,* example of, instance of, indicates the ontological status of the individual creature in the eyes of the theorist. The dogfish itself is seen as a rather shabby expression of an ideal reality, the species *Squalus acanthias*. The result is the radical devaluation of the individual dogfish. (The *reductio ad absurdum*[8] of Whitehead's shift if Toynbee's[9] employment of it in his historical method. If a gram of NaCl is referred to by the chemist as a "sample of" NaCl, one may think of it as such and not much is missed by the oversight of the act of being of this particular pinch of salt, but when the Jews, and the Jewish religion are understood as—in Toynbee's favorite phrase—a "classical example of" such and such a kind of *Voelkerwanderung,*[10] we begin to suspect that something is being left out.)

If we look into the ways in which the student can recover the dogfish (or the sonnet), we will see that they have in common the stratagem of avoiding the educator's direct presentation of the object as a lesson to be learned and restoring access to sonnet and dogfish as beings to be known, reasserting the sovereignty of knower over known.

In truth, the biography of scientists and poets is usually the story of the discovery of the indirect approach, the circumvention of the educator's presentation—the young man who was sent to the *Technikum*[11] and on his way fell into the habit

[8]"A reduction to absurdity" (Latin); the argumentative method by which one shows that a statement carried to its logical conclusion leads to an absurdity.

[9]Arnold Toynbee (1889–1975), British historian who believed that civilizations were formed out of responses to adversity.

[10]Barbarian invasion (German).

[11]Technical school (German).

of loitering in book stores and reading poetry; or the young man dutifully attending law school who on the way became curious about the comings and goings of ants. One remembers the scene in *The Heart Is a Lonely Hunter*[12] where the girl hides in the bushes to hear the Capehart in the big house play Beethoven. Perhaps she was the lucky one after all. Think of the unhappy souls inside, who see the record, worry about scratches, and most of all worry about whether they are *getting it,* whether they are bona fide music lovers. What is the best way to hear Beethoven: sitting in a proper silence around the Capehart or eavesdropping from an azalea bush?

However it may come about, we notice two traits of the second situation: (1) an openness of the thing before one—instead of being an exercise to be learned according to an approved mode, it is a garden of delights which beckons to one; (2) a sovereignty of the knower—instead of being a consumer of a prepared experience, I am a sovereign wayfarer, a wanderer in the neighborhood of being who stumbles into the garden.

One can think of two sorts of circumstances through which the thing may be restored to the person. (There is always, of course, the direct recovery: A student may simply be strong enough, brave enough, clever enough to take the dogfish and the sonnet by storm, to wrest control of it from the educators and the educational package.) First by ordeal: The Bomb falls; when the young man recovers consciousness in the shambles of the biology laboratory, there not ten inches from his nose lies the dogfish. Now all at once he can see it, directly and without let, just as the exile or the prisoner or the sick man see the sparrow at his window in all its inexhaustibility; just as the commuter who has had a heart attack sees his own hand for the first time. In these cases, the simulacrum of everydayness and of consumption has been destroyed by disaster; in the case of the bomb, literally destroyed. Secondly, by apprenticeship to a great man: One day a great biologist walks into the laboratory; he stops in front of our student's desk; he leans over, picks up the dogfish, and ignoring instruments and procedure, probes with a broken fingernail into the little carcass. "Now here is a curious business," he says, ignoring also the proper jargon of the specialty. "Look here how this little duct reverses its direction and drops into the pelvis. Now if you would look into a coelacanth, you would see that it—" And all at once the student can see. The technician and the sophomore who loves his textbooks are always offended by the genuine research man because the latter is usually a little vague and always humble before the thing; he doesn't have much use for the equipment or the jargon. Whereas the technician is never vague and never humble before the thing; he holds the thing disposed of by the principle, the formula, the textbook outline; and he thinks a great deal of equipment and jargon.

But since neither of these methods of recovering the dogfish is pedagogically feasible—perhaps the great man even less so than the Bomb—I wish to propose the following educational technique which should prove equally effective for Harvard and Shreveport High School. I propose that English poetry and biology should be taught as usual, but that at irregular intervals, poetry students should find dogfishes on their desks and biology students should find Shakespeare sonnets on their dissection boards. I am serious in declaring that a Sarah Lawrence English major who began poking about in a dogfish with a bobby pin would learn more in thirty minutes than a biology major in a whole semester; and that the latter upon reading on her dissecting board

> That time of year Thou may'st in me behold
> When yellow leaves, or none, or few, do hang

[12] A 1940 novel by Carson McCullers (1917–1967).

> Upon those boughs which shake against the cold—
> Bare ruin'd choirs where late the sweet birds sang.[13]

might catch fire at the beauty of it.

The situation of the tourist at the Grand Canyon and the biology student are special cases of a predicament in which everyone finds himself in a modern technical society—a society, that is, in which there is a division between expert and layman, planner and consumer, in which experts and planners take special measures to teach and edify the consumer. The measures taken are measures appropriate to the consumer: The expert and the planner *know* and *plan,* but the consumer *needs* and *experiences*.

There is a double deprivation. First, the thing is lost through its packaging. The very means by which the thing is presented for consumption, the very techniques by which the thing is made available as an item of need-satisfaction, these very means operate to remove the thing from the sovereignty of the knower. A loss of title occurs. The measures which the museum curator takes to present the thing to the public are self-liquidating. The upshot of the curator's efforts are not that everyone can see the exhibit but that no one can see it. The curator protests: Why are they so indifferent? Why do they even deface the exhibit? Don't they know it is theirs? But it is not theirs. It is his, the curator's. By the most exclusive sort of zoning, the museum exhibit, the park oak tree, is part of an ensemble, a package, which is almost impenetrable to them. The archaeologist who puts his find in a museum so that everyone can see it accomplishes the reverse of his expectations. The result of his action is that no one can see it now but the archaeologist. He would have done better to keep it in his pocket and show it now and then to strangers.

The tourist who carves his initials in a public place, which is theoretically "his" in the first place, has good reasons for doing so, reasons which the exhibitor and planner know nothing about. He does so because in his role of consumer of an experience (a "recreational experience" to satisfy a "recreational need") he knows that he is disinherited. He is deprived of his title over being. He knows very well that he is in a very special sort of zone in which his only rights are the rights of a consumer. He moves like a ghost through schoolroom, city streets, trains, parks, movies. He carves his initials as a last desperate measure to escape his ghostly role of consumer. He is saying in effect: I am not a ghost after all; I am a sovereign person. And he establishes title the only way remaining to him, by staking his claim over one square inch of wood or stone.

Does this mean that we should get rid of museums? No, but it means that the sightseer should be prepared to enter into a struggle to recover a sight from a museum.

The second loss is the spoliation of the thing, the tree, the rock, the swallow, by the layman's misunderstanding of scientific theory. He believes that the thing is *disposed of* by theory, that it stands in the Platonic relation of being a *specimen of* such and such an underlying principle. In the transmission of scientific theory and from theorist to layman, the expectation of the theorist is reversed. Instead of the marvels of the universe being made available to the public, the universe is disposed of by theory. The loss of sovereignty takes this form: As a result of the science of botany, trees are not made available to every man. On the contrary. The tree loses its proper density and mystery as a concrete existent and, as merely another *specimen of* a species, becomes itself nugatory.

Does this mean that there is no use taking biology at Harvard and Shreveport High? No, but it means that the student should know what a fight he has on his

[13] The opening lines of William Shakespeare's Sonnet 73.

hands to rescue the specimen from the educational package. The educator is only partly to blame. For there is nothing the educator can do to provide for this need of the student. Everything the educator does only succeeds in becoming, for the student, part of the educational package. The highest role of the educator is the maieutic role of Socrates: to help the student come to himself not as a consumer of experience but as a sovereign individual.

The thing is twice lost to the consumer. First, sovereignty is lost: It is theirs, not his. Second, it is radically devalued by theory. This is a loss which has been brought about by science but through no fault of the scientist and through no fault of scientific theory. The loss has come about as a consequence of the seduction of the layman by science. The layman will be seduced as long as he regards beings as consumer items to be experienced rather than prizes to be won, and as long as he waives his sovereign rights as a person and accepts his role of consumer as the highest estate to which the layman can aspire.

As Mounier said, the person is not something one can study and provide for; he is something one struggles for. But unless he also struggles for himself, unless he knows that there is a struggle, he is going to be just what the planners think he is.

DISCUSSION QUESTIONS

1. Walker Percy uses the motif of discovery to lament the loss of spontaneity in our prefabricated urban world. Yet his evocation of Spanish conquistadors may seem problematic in light of recent critiques of the myths of Christopher Columbus and the New World. Reread Percy's essay in light of arguments such as those put forth in Patrick O'Connell's editorial ''Settlement of America: A Continuing Crime'' (see ''Press''). What is the effect when contemporary writers use these metaphors? Is there a way to use traditional mythology without forgetting the real events it ignores?

2. Contrast Percy's critique of American culture with Gretel Ehrlich's homage to the beauty of wide open spaces (see ''Magazines''). How do these two essayists employ different examples to come to similar conclusions? How do these pieces differ? Do you agree with Percy or Ehrlich on the subject of seeing?

Raymond Carver / What We Talk About When We Talk about Love 1981

The short story was a faded form in American literature at the beginning of the 1980s. Novels dominated the marketplace and the assessments of literary critics. While such short-story pioneers as Guy de Maupassant, Sherwood Anderson, and Eudora Welty were still read in literature classes, relatively few American contemporary writers reached out to a new audience using the form.

Enter Raymond Carver. Born in 1939 in a small town in Oregon, Carver had been raised in the Pacific Northwest and attended Chico State College in California and (briefly) the writers' workshop at the University of Iowa. He emerged as a significant writer in 1967, when his story ''Will You Please Be Quiet, Please?'' was selected for the Best American Short Stories *anthology. In 1976, that story became the title work in Carver's first published collection. Yet not until 1981, when he published* What We Talk About When We Talk about

Love, *did Carver reach a wide audience. With that book and the publication of* Cathedral *(1983), Carver almost single-handedly revitalized the short-story form. Now numerous authors publish collections of stories as first books, and many readers and writers remain dedicated to the genre.*

The distinguishing feature of Carver's work is nuance—he paints the smallest of pictures with delicate strokes, telling ordinary stories so vividly that they seem to emanate from the reader's own thoughts. He once said, "It's possible to write about commonplace things and objects using commonplace but precise language, and to endow these things—a chair, a window curtain, a fork, a stone, a woman's earring—with immense, even startling power. It is possible to write a line of seemingly innocuous dialogue and have it send a chill along the reader's spine." Carver achieves just this effect with the following tale of a rambling yet heartrending four-way conversation, the title story from his famous 1981 collection.

My friend Mel McGinnis was talking. Mel McGinnis is a cardiologist, and sometimes that gives him the right.

The four of us were sitting around his kitchen table drinking gin. Sunlight filled the kitchen from the big window behind the sink. There were Mel and me and his second wife, Teresa—Terri, we called her—and my wife, Laura. We lived in Albuquerque then. But we were all from somewhere else.

There was an ice bucket on the table. The gin and the tonic water kept going around, and we somehow got on the subject of love. Mel thought real love was nothing less than spiritual love. He said he's spent five years in a seminary before quitting to go to medical school. He said he still looked back on those years in the seminary as the most important years in his life.

Terri said the man she lived with before she lived with Mel loved her so much he tried to kill her. Then Terri said, "He beat me up one night. He dragged me around the living room by my ankles. He kept saying, 'I love you, I love you, you bitch.' He went on dragging me around the living room. My head kept knocking on things." Terri looked around the table. "What do you do with love like that?"

She was a bone-thin woman with a pretty face, dark eyes, and brown hair that hung down her back. She liked necklaces made of turquoise, and long pendant earrings.

"My God, don't be silly. That's not love, and you know it," Mel said. "I don't know what you'd call it, but I sure know you wouldn't call it love."

"Say what you want to, but I know it was," Terri said. "It may sound crazy to you, but it's true just the same. People are different, Mel. Sure, sometimes he may have acted crazy. Okay. But he loved me. In his own way maybe, but he loved me. There was love there, Mel. Don't say there wasn't."

Mel let out his breath. He held his glass and turned to Laura and me. "The man threatened to kill me," Mel said. He finished his drink and reached for the gin bottle. "Terri's a romantic. Terri's of the kick-me-so-I'll-know-you-love-me school. Terri, hon, don't look that way." Mel reached across the table and touched Terri's cheek with his fingers. He grinned at her.

"Now he wants to make up," Terri said.

"Make up what?" Mel said. "What is there to make up? I know what I know. That's all."

"How'd we get started on this subject, anyway?" Terri said. She raised her glass and drank from it. "Mel always has love on his mind," she said. "Don't you, honey?" She smiled, and I thought that was the last of it.

"I just wouldn't call Ed's behavior love. That's all I'm saying, honey," Mel said. ''What about you guys?'' Mel said to Laura and me. ''Does that sound like love to you?''

''I'm the wrong person to ask,'' I said. ''I didn't even know the man. I've only heard his name mentioned in passing. I wouldn't know. You'd have to know the particulars. But I think what you're saying is that love is an absolute.''

Mel said, ''The kind of love I'm talking about is. The kind of love I'm talking about, you don't try to kill people.''

Laura said, ''I don't know anything about Ed, or anything about the situation. But who can judge anyone else's situation?''

I touched the back of Laura's hand. She gave me a quick smile. I picked up Laura's hand. It was warm, the nails polished, perfectly manicured. I encircled the broad wrist with my fingers, and I held her.

''When I left, he drank rat poison,'' Terri said. She clasped her arms with her hands. ''They took him to the hospital in Santa Fe. That's where we lived then, about ten miles out. They saved his life. But his gums went crazy from it. I mean they pulled away from his teeth. After that, his teeth stood out like fangs. My God,'' Terri said. She waited a minute, then let go of her arms and picked up her glass.

''What people won't do!'' Laura said.

''He's out of the action now,'' Mel said. ''He's dead.''

Mel handed me the saucer of limes. I took a section, squeezed it over my drink, and stirred the ice cubes with my finger.

''It gets worse,'' Terri said. ''He shot himself in the mouth. But he bungled that too. Poor Ed,'' she said. Terri shook her head.

''Poor Ed nothing,'' Mel said. ''He was dangerous.''

Mel was forty-five years old. He was tall and rangy with curly soft hair. His face and arms were brown from the tennis he played. When he was sober, his gestures, all his movements, were precise, very careful.

''He did love me though, Mel. Grant me that,'' Terri said. ''That's all I'm asking. He didn't love me the way you love me. I'm not saying that. But he loved me. You can grant me that, can't you?''

''What do you mean, he bungled it?'' I said.

Laura leaned forward with her glass. She put her elbows on the table and held her glass in both hands. She glanced from Mel to Terri and waited with a look of bewilderment on her open face, as if amazed that such things happened to people you were friendly with.

''How'd he bungle it when he killed himself?'' I said.

''I'll tell you what happened,'' Mel said. ''He took this twenty-two pistol he bought to threaten Terri and me with. Oh, I'm serious, the man was always threatening. You should have seen the way we lived in those days. Like fugitives. I even bought a gun myself. Can you believe it? A guy like me? But I did. I bought one for self-defense and carried it in the glove compartment. Sometimes I'd have to leave the apartment in the middle of the night. To go to the hospital, you know? Terri and I weren't married then, and my first wife had the house and kids, the dog, everything, and Terri and I were living in this apartment here. Sometimes, as I say, I'd get a call in the middle of the night and have to go in to the hospital at two or three in the morning. It'd be dark out there in the parking lot, and I'd break into a sweat before I could even get to my car. I never knew if he was going to come up out of the shrubbery or from behind a car and start shooting. I mean, the man was crazy. He was capable of wiring a bomb, anything. He used to call my service at all hours and say he needed to talk to the doctor, and when I'd return the call, he'd say, 'Son of a bitch, your days are numbered.' Little things like that. It was scary, I'm telling you.''

''I still feel sorry for him,'' Terri said.

"It sounds like a nightmare," Laura said. "But what exactly happened after he shot himself?"

Laura is a legal secretary. We'd met in a professional capacity. Before we knew it, it was a courtship. She's thirty-five, three years younger than I am. In addition to being in love, we like each other and enjoy one another's company. She's easy to be with.

"What happened?" Laura said.

Mel said. "He shot himself in the mouth in his room. Someone heard the shot and told the manager. They came in with a passkey, saw what had happened, and called an ambulance. I happened to be there when they brought him in, alive but past recall. The man lived for three days. His head swelled up to twice the size of a normal head. I'd never seen anything like it, and I hope I never do again. Terri wanted to go in and sit with him when she found out about it. We had a fight over it. I didn't think she should see him like that. I didn't think she should see him, and I still don't.

"Who won the fight?" Laura said.

"I was in the room with him when he died," Terri said. "He never came up out of it. But I sat with him. He didn't have anyone else."

"He was dangerous," Mel said. "If you call that love, you can have it."

"It was love," Terri said. "Sure, it's abnormal in most people's eyes. But he was willing to die for it. He did die for it."

"I sure as hell wouldn't call it love," Mel said. "I mean, no one knows what he did it for. I've seen a lot of suicides, and I couldn't say anyone ever knew what they did it for."

Mel put his hands behind his neck and tilted his chair back. "I'm not interested in that kind of love," he said. "If that's love, you can have it."

Terri said, "We were afraid. Mel even made a will out and wrote to his brother in California who used to be a Green Beret. Mel told him who to look for if something happened to him."

Terri drank from her glass. She said, "But Mel's right—we lived like fugitives. We were afraid. Mel was, weren't you, honey? I even called the police at one point, but they were no help. They said they couldn't do anything until Ed actually did something. Isn't that a laugh?" Terri said.

She poured the last of the gin into her glass and waggled the bottle. Mel got up from the table and went to the cupboard. He took down another bottle.

"Well, Nick and I know what love is," Laura said. "For us, I mean," Laura said. She bumped my knee with her knee. "You're supposed to say something now," Laura said, and turned her smile on me.

For an answer, I took Laura's hand and raised it to my lips. I made a big production out of kissing her hand. Everyone was amused.

"We're lucky," I said.

"You guys," Terri said. "Stop that now. You're making me sick. You're still on the honeymoon, for God's sake. You're still gaga, for crying out loud. Just wait. How long have you been together now? How long has it been? A year? Longer than a year?"

"Going on a year and a half," Laura said, flushed and smiling.

"Oh, now," Terri said. "Wait awhile."

She held her drink and gazed at Laura.

"I'm only kidding," Terri said.

Mel opened the gin and went around the table with the bottle.

"Here, you guys," he said. "Let's have a toast. I want to propose a toast. A toast to love. To true love," Mel said.

We touched glasses.

''To love,'' we said.

Outside in the backyard, one of the dogs began to bark. The leaves of the aspen that leaned past the window ticked against the glass. The afternoon sun was like a presence in this room, the spacious light of ease and generosity. We could have been anywhere, somewhere enchanted. We raised our glasses again and grinned at each other like children who had agreed on something forbidden.

''I'll tell you what real love is,'' Mel said. ''I mean, I'll give you a good example. And then you can draw your own conclusions.'' He poured more gin into his glass. He added an ice cube and a sliver of lime. We waited and sipped our drinks. Laura and I touched knees again. I put a hand on her warm thigh and left it there.

''What do any of us really know about love?'' Mel said. ''It seems to me we're just beginners at love. We say we love each other and we do, I don't doubt it. I love Terri and Terri loves me, and you guys love each other too. You know the kind of love I'm talking about now. Physical love, that impulse that drives you to someone special, as well as love of the other person's being, his or her essence, as it were. Carnal love and, well, call it sentimental love, the day-to-day caring about the other person. But sometimes I have a hard time accounting for the fact that I must have loved my first wife too. But I did, I know I did. So I suppose I am like Terri in that regard. Terri and Ed.'' He thought about it and then he went on. ''There was a time when I thought I loved my first wife more than life itself. But now I hate her guts. I do. How do you explain that? What happened to that love? What happened to it, is what I'd like to know. I wish someone could tell me. Then there's Ed. Okay, we're back to Ed. He loves Terri so much he tries to kill her and he winds up killing himself.'' Mel stopped talking and swallowed from his glass. ''You guys have been together eighteen months and you love each other. It shows all over you. You glow with it. But you both loved other people before you met each other. You've both been married before, just like us. And you probably loved other people before that too, even. Terri and I have been together five years, been married for four. And the terrible thing, the terrible thing is, but the good thing too, the saving grace, you might say, is that if something happened to one of us—excuse me for saying this—but if something happened to one of us tomorrow I think the other one, the other person, would grieve for a while, you know, but then the surviving party would go out and love again, have someone else soon enough. All this, all of this love we're talking about, it would just be a memory. Maybe not even a memory. And I wrong? Am I way off base? Because I want you to set me straight if you think I'm wrong. I want to know. I mean, I don't know anything, and I'm the first one to admit it.''

''Mel, for God's sake,'' Terri said. She reached out and took hold of his wrist. ''Are you getting drunk? Honey? Are you drunk?''

''Honey, I'm just talking,'' Mel said. ''All right? I don't have to be drunk to say what I think. I mean, we're all just talking, right?'' Mel said. He fixed his eyes on her.

''Sweetie, I'm not criticizing,'' Terri said.

She picked up her glass.

''I'm not on call today,'' Mel said. ''Let me remind you of that. I am not on call,'' he said.

''Mel, we love you,'' Laura said.

Mel looked at Laura. He looked at her as if he could not place her, as if she was not the woman she was.

''Love you too, Laura,'' Mel said. ''And you, Nick, love you too. You know something?'' Mel said. ''You guys are our pals,'' Mel said.

He picked up his glass.

Mel said, "I was going to tell you about something. I mean, I was going to prove a point. You see, this happened a few months ago, but it's still going on right now, and it ought to make us feel ashamed when we talk like we know what we're talking about when we talk about love."

"Come on now," Terri said. "Don't talk like you're drunk if you're not drunk."

"Just shut up for once in your life," Mel said very quietly. "Will you do me a favor and do that for a minute? So as I was saying, there's this old couple who had this car wreck out on the interstate. A kid hit them and they were all torn to shit and nobody was giving them much chance to pull through."

Terri looked at us and then back at Mel. She seemed anxious, or maybe that's too strong a word.

Mel was handing the bottle around the table.

"I was on call that night," Mel said. "It was May or maybe it was June. Terri and I had just sat down to dinner when the hospital called. There'd been this thing out on the interstate. Drunk kid, teenager, plowed his dad's pickup truck into this camper with this old couple in it. They were up in their mid-seventies, that couple. The kid—eighteen, nineteen, something—he was DOA. Taken the steering wheel through his sternum. The old couple, they were alive, you understand. I mean, just barely. But they had everything. Multiple fractures, internal injuries, hemorrhaging, contusions, lacerations, the works, and they each of them had themselves concussions. They were in a bad way, believe me. And, of course, their age was two strikes against them. I'd say she was worse off than he was. Ruptured spleen along with everything else. Both kneecaps broken. But they'd been wearing their seatbelts and, God knows, that's what saved them for the time being."

"Folks, this is an advertisement for the National Safety Council," Terri said. "This is your spokesman, Dr. Melvin R. McGinnis, talking." Terri laughed. "Mel," she said, "sometimes you're just too much. But I love you, hon," she said.

"Honey, I love you," Mel said.

He leaned across the table. Terri met him halfway. They kissed.

"Terri's right," Mel said as he settled himself again. "Get those seatbelts on. But seriously, they were in some shape, those oldsters. By the time I got down there, the kid was dead, as I said. He was off in a corner, laid out on a gurney. I took one look at the old couple and told the ER nurse to get me a neurologist and an orthopedic man and a couple of surgeons down there right away."

He drank from his glass. "I'll try to keep this short," he said. "So we took the two of them up to the OR and worked like fuck on them most of the night. They had these incredible reserves, those two. You see that once in a while. So we did everything that could be done, and toward morning we're giving them a fifty-fifty chance, maybe less than that for her. So here they are, still alive the next morning. So, okay, we move them into the ICU, which is where they both kept plugging away at it for two weeks, hitting it better and better on all the scopes. So we transfer them out to their own room."

Mel stopped talking. "Here," he said, "let's drink this cheapo gin the hell up. Then we're going to dinner, right? Terri and I know a new place. That's where we'll go, to this new place we know about. But we're not going until we finish up this cut-rate, lousy gin."

Terri said, "We haven't actually eaten there yet. But it looks good. From the outside, you know."

"I like food," Mel said. "If I had to do all over again, I'd be a chef, you know? Right, Terri?" Mel said.

He laughed. He fingered the ice in his glass.

"Terri knows," he said. "Terri can tell you. But let me say this. If I could come back again in a different life, a different time and all, you know what? I'd like to come back as a knight. You were pretty safe wearing all that armor. It was all right being a knight until gunpowder and muskets and pistols came along."

"Mel would like to ride a horse and carry a lance," Terri said.

"Carry a woman's scarf with you everywhere," Laura said.

"Or just a woman," Mel said.

"Shame on you," Laura said.

Terri said, "Suppose you came back as a serf. The serfs didn't have it so good in those days," Terri said.

"The serfs never had it good," Mel said. "But I guess even the knights were vessels to someone. Isn't that the way it worked? But then everyone is always a vessel to someone. Isn't that right? Terri? But what I liked about knights, besides their ladies, was that they had that suit of armor, you know, and they couldn't get hurt very easy. No cars in those days, you know? No drunk teenagers to tear into your ass."

"Vassals." Terri said.

"What?" Mel said.

"Vassals," Terri said. "They were called vassals, not vessels."

"Vassals, vessels," Mel said, "what the fuck's the difference? You knew what I meant anyway. All right," Mel said. "So I'm not educated. I learned my stuff. I'm a heart surgeon, sure, but I'm just a mechanic. I go in and I fuck around and I fix things. Shit," Mel said.

"Modesty doesn't become you," Terri said.

"He's just a humble sawbones," I said. "But sometimes they suffocated in all that armor, Mel. They'd even have heart attacks if it got too hot and they were too tired and worn out. I read somewhere that they'd fall off their horses and not be able to get up because they were too tired to stand with all that armor on them. They got trampled by their own horses sometimes."

"That's terrible," Mel said. "That's a terrible thing, Nicky. I guess they'd just lay there and wait until somebody came along and made a shish kebab out of them."

"Some other vessel," Terri said.

"That's right," Mel said. "Some vassal would come along and spear the bastard in the name of love. Or whatever the fuck it was they fought over in those days."

"Same things we fight over these days," Terri said.

Laura said, "Nothing's changed."

The color was still high in Laura's cheeks. Her eyes were bright. She brought her glass to her lips.

Mel poured himself another drink. He looked at the label closely as if studying a long row of numbers. Then he slowly put the bottle down on the table and slowly reached for the tonic water.

"What about the old couple?" Laura said. "You didn't finish that story you started."

Laura was having a hard time lighting her cigarette. Her matches kept going out.

The sunshine inside the room was different now, changing, getting thinner. But the leaves outside the window were still shimmering, and I stared at the pattern they made on the panes and on the Formica counter. They weren't the same patterns, of course.

"What about the old couple?" I said.

"Older but wiser," Terri said.

Mel stared at her.

Terri said, "Go on with your story, hon. I was only kidding. Then what happened?"

"Terri, sometimes," Mel said.

"Please, Mel," Terri said. "Don't always be so serious, sweetie. Can't you take a joke?"

"Where's the joke?" Mel said.

He held his glass and gazed steadily at his wife.

"What happened?" Laura said.

Mel fastened his eyes on Laura. He said, "Laura, if I didn't have Terri and if I didn't love her so much, and if Nick wasn't my best friend, I'd fall in love with you. I'd carry you off, honey," he said.

"Tell your story," Terri said. "Then we'll go to that new place, okay?"

"Okay," Mel said. "Where was I?" he said. He stared at the table and then began again.

"I dropped in to see each of them every day, sometimes twice a day if I was up doing other calls anyway. Casts and bandages, head to foot, the both of them. You know, you've seen it in the movies. That's just the way they looked, just like in the movies. Little eye-holes and nose-holes and mouth-holes. And she had to have her legs slung up on top of it. Well, the husband was very depressed for the longest while. Even after he found out that his wife was going to pull through, he was still very depressed. Not about the accident, though. I mean, the accident was one thing, but it wasn't everything. I'd get up to his mouth-hole; you know, and he'd say no, it wasn't the accident exactly but it was because he couldn't see her through his eye-holes. He said that was what was making him feel so bad. Can you imagine? I'm telling you, the man's heart was breaking because he couldn't turn his goddamn head and *see* his goddamn wife."

Mel looked around the table and shook his head at what he was going to say.

"I mean, it was killing the old fart just because he couldn't *look* at the fucking woman."

We all looked at Mel.

"Do you see what I'm saying?" he said.

Maybe we were a little drunk by then. I know it was hard keeping things in focus. The light was draining out of the room, going back through the window where it had come from. Yet nobody made a move to get up from the table to turn on the overhead light.

"Listen," Mel said. "Let's finish this fucking gin. There's about enough left here for one shooter all around. Then let's go eat. Let's go to the new place."

"He's depressed," Terri said. "Mel, why don't you take a pill?"

Mel shook his head. "I've taken everything there is."

"We all need a pill now and then," I said.

"Some people are born needing them," Terri said.

She was using her finger to rub at something on the table. Then she stopped rubbing.

"I think I want to call my kids," Mel said. "Is that all right with everybody? I'll call my kids," he said.

Terri said, "What if Marjorie answers the phone? You guys, you've heard us on the subject of Marjorie? Honey, you know you don't want to talk to Marjorie. It'll make you feel even worse."

"I don't want to talk to Marjorie," Mel said. "But I want to talk to my kids."

"There isn't a day goes by that Mel doesn't say he wishes she'd get married again. Or else die," Terri said. "For one thing," Terri said, "she's bankrupting us. Mel says it's just to spite him that she won't get married again. She has a boyfriend who lives with her and the kids, so Mel is supporting the boyfriend too."

"She's allergic to bees," Mel said. "If I'm not praying she'll get married again, I'm praying she'll get herself stung to death by a swarm of fucking bees."

"Shame on you," Laura said.

"Bzzzzzzz," Mel said, turning his fingers into bees and buzzing them at Terri's throat. Then he let his hands drop all the way to his sides.

"She's vicious," Mel said. "Sometimes I think I'll go up there dressed like a beekeeper. You know, that hat that's like a helmet with the plate that comes down over your face, the big gloves, and the padded coat? I'll knock on the door and let loose a hive of bees in the house. But first I'd make sure the kids were out, of course."

He crossed one leg over the other. It seemed to take him a lot of time to do it. Then he put both feet on the floor and leaned forward, elbows on the table, his chin cupped in his hands.

"Maybe I won't call the kids, after all. Maybe it isn't such a hot idea. Maybe we'll just go eat. How does that sound?"

"Sounds fine to me," I said. "Eat or not eat. Or keep drinking. I could head right on out into the sunset."

"What does that mean, honey?" Laura said.

"It just means what I said," I said. "It means I could just keep going. That's all it means."

"I could eat something myself," Laura said. "I don't think I've ever been so hungry in my life. Is there something to nibble on?"

"I'll put out some cheese and crackers," Terri said.

But Terri just sat there. She did not get up to get anything.

Mel turned his glass over. He spilled it on the table.

"Gin's gone," Mel said.

Terri said, "Now what?"

I could hear my heart beating. I could hear everyone's heart. I could hear the human noise we sat there making, not one of us moving, not even when the room went dark.

Lewis Thomas / The World's Biggest Membrane 1982

"We have language and can build metaphors as skillfully and precisely as ribosomes make proteins," writes Lewis Thomas, a man who moves through language and the laboratory with energy and eloquence. In addition to being a doctor, researcher, professor, and director emeritus of the Memorial Sloan-Kettering Cancer Center in New York City, Thomas is a National Book Award winner in Arts and Letters whom Time *magazine has called, "quite possibly the best essayist on science now working anywhere in the world." His first book,* The Lives of a Cell *(1974), sold well over 300,000 copies, making it one of the most popular works of its kind. Although he began writing poetry during his college days at Princeton and has published over 200 scientific papers. Thomas did not begin his career as an essayist until 1970, when he was fifty-seven years old. Since then he has continued to write his monthly column for the* New England Journal of Medicine. *A second collection of essays,* The Medusa and the Snail, *was published in 1979 and quickly joined the best-seller list. Lewis Thomas's most recent collections of essays include* Late Night Thoughts on Listening to Mahler's 9th Symphony *(1983) and* Et cetera, et cetera *(1990).*

Viewed from the distance of the moon, the astonishing thing about the earth, catching the breath, is that it is alive. The photographs show the dry, pounded surface of the moon in the foreground, dead as an old bone. Aloft, floating free beneath the moist, gleaming membrane of bright blue sky, is the rising earth, the only exuberant thing in this part of the cosmos. If you could look long enough, you would see the swirling of the great drifts of white cloud, covering and uncovering the half-hidden masses of land. If you had been looking for a very long, geologic time, you could have seen the continents themselves in motion, drifting apart on their crustal plates, held afloat by the fire beneath. It has the organized, self-contained look of a live creature, full of information, marvelously skilled in handling the sun.

It takes a membrane to make sense out of disorder in biology. You have to be able to catch energy and hold it, storing precisely the needed amount and releasing it in measured shares. A cell does this, and so do the organelles inside. Each assemblage is poised in the flow of solar energy, tapping off energy from metabolic surrogates of the sun. To stay alive, you have to be able to hold out against equilibrium, maintain imbalance, bank against entropy, and you can only transact this business with membranes in our kind of world.

When the earth came alive it began constructing its own membrane, for the general purpose of editing the sun. Originally, in the time of prebiotic elaboration of peptides and nucleotides from inorganic ingredients in the water on the earth, there was nothing to shield out ultraviolet radiation except the water itself. The first thin atmosphere came entirely from the degassing of the earth as it cooled, and there was only a vanishingly small trace of oxygen in it. Theoretically, there could have been some production of oxygen by photodissociation of water vapor in ultraviolet light, but not much. This process would have been self-limiting, as Urey showed, since the wave lengths needed for photolysis are the very ones screened out selectively by oxygen; the production of oxygen would have been cut off almost as soon as it occurred.

The formation of oxygen had to await the emergence of photosynthetic cells, and these were required to live in an environment with sufficient visible light for photosynthesis but shielded at the same time against lethal ultraviolet. Berkner and Marshall calculate that the green cells must therefore have been about ten meters below the surface of water, probably in pools and ponds shallow enough to lack strong convection currents (the ocean could not have been the starting place).

You could say that the breathing of oxygen into the atmosphere was the result of evolution, or you could turn it around and say that evolution was the result of oxygen. You can have it either way. Once the photosynthetic cells had appeared, very probably counterparts of today's blue-green algae, the future respiratory mechanism of the earth was set in place. Early on, when the level of oxygen had built up to around 1 per cent of today's atmospheric concentration, the anaerobic life of the earth was placed in jeopardy, and the inevitable next stage was the emergence of mutants with oxidative systems and ATP.[1] With this, we were off to an explosive developmental stage in which great varieties of respiring life, including the multicellular forms, became feasible.

Berkner has suggested that there were two such explosions of new life, like vast embryological transformations, both dependent on threshold levels of oxygen. The first, at 1 per cent of the present level, shielded out enough ultraviolet radiation to permit cells to move into the surface layers of lakes, rivers, and oceans. This happened around 600 million years ago, at the beginning of the Paleozoic era,

[1] Adenosine triphosphate, a key chemical in living cells that is a source of energy for physiological reaction.

and accounts for the sudden abundance of marine fossils of all kinds in the record of this period. The second burst occurred when oxygen rose to 10 per cent of the present level. At this time, around 400 million years ago, there was a sufficient canopy to allow life out of the water and onto the land. From here on it was clear going, with nothing to restrain the variety of life except the limits of biologic inventiveness.

It is another illustration of our fantastic luck that oxygen filters out the very bands of ultraviolet light that are most devastating for nucleic acids and proteins, while allowing full penetration of the visible light needed for photosynthesis. If it had not been for this semipermeability, we could never have come along.

The earth breathes, in a certain sense. Berkner suggests that there may have been cycles of oxygen production and carbon dioxide consumption, depending on relative abundances of plant and animal life, with the ice ages representing periods of apnea. An overwhelming richness of vegetation may have caused the level of oxygen to rise above today's concentration, with a corresponding depletion of carbon dioxide. Such a drop in carbon dioxide may have impaired the ''greenhouse'' property of the atmosphere, which holds in the solar heat otherwise lost by radiation from the earth's surface. The fall in temperature would in turn have shut off much of living, and, in a long sigh, the level of oxygen may have dropped by 90 per cent. Berkner speculates that this is what happened to the great reptiles; their size may have been all right for a richly oxygenated atmosphere, but they had the bad luck to run out of air.

Now we are protected against lethal ultraviolet rays by a narrow rim of ozone, thirty miles out. We are safe, well ventilated, and incubated, provided we can avoid technologies that might fiddle with that ozone, or shift the levels of carbon dioxide. Oxygen is not a major worry for us, unless we let fly with enough nuclear explosives to kill off the green cells in the sea; if we do that, of course, we are in for strangling.

It is hard to feel affection for something as totally impersonal as the atmosphere, and yet there it is, as much a part and product of life as wine or bread. Taken all in all, the sky is a miraculous achievement. It works, and for what it is designed to accomplish it is as infallible as anything in nature. I doubt whether any of us could think of a way to improve on it, beyond maybe shifting a local cloud from here to there on occasion. The word ''chance'' does not serve to account well for structures of such magnificence. There may have been elements of luck in the emergence of chloroplasts, but once these things were on the scene, the evolution of the sky became absolutely ordained. Chance suggests alternatives, other possibilities, different solutions. This may be true for gills and swimbladders and forebrains, matters of detail, but not for the sky. There was simply no other way to go.

We should credit it for what it is: for sheer size and perfection of function, it is far and away the grandest product of collaboration in all of nature.

It breathes for us, and it does another thing for our pleasure. Each day, millions of meteorites fall against the outer limits of the membrane and are burned to nothing by the friction. Without out shelter, our surface would long since have become the pounded powder of the moon. Even though our receptors are not sensitive enough to hear it, there is comfort in knowing that the sound is there overhead, like the random noise of rain on the roof at night.

Annie Dillard / Total Eclipse 1982

In the midst of the last decade's resurgence of nostalgia for the outdoors, Annie Dillard distinguished herself through the clarity of her vision, the tenacity of her refusal to sentimentalize nature, and the forcefulness of her prose. Born Annie Doak in Pittsburgh in 1945, she took B.A. and M.A. degrees at Hollins College in Virginia's Roanoke Valley. A contributing editor to Harper's *magazine and a columnist for the Wilderness Society, Dillard has also written strikingly original essays for such publications as the* Christian Science Monitor, Atlantic Monthly, Cosmopolitan, Sports Illustrated, *and* American Scholar. *In 1974 she published* Pilgrim at Tinker Creek, *which collected much of her magazine work and won her a Pulitzer Prize for nonfiction. Her other books include* Holy the Firm *(1977),* Living by Fiction *(1978),* Teaching a Stone to Talk *(1982),* Encounters with Chinese Writers *(1984),* An American Childhood *(1987),* The Writing Life *(1989), and a novel,* The Living *(1992).*

The following account of a rare natural phenomenon and its effect on the ragtag community that witnesses it is pure Dillard: acute in observation, immediate in style; it rises to a crescendo that allows the reader some sense of the catharsis that must have come with witnessing the described event. As in all her works, Dillard here communicates a sense of the sacred nature of life on earth as well as the way people transcend their habits by paying attention to the random beauty of the natural world.

I

It had been like dying, the sliding down the mountain pass. It had been like the death of someone, irrational, that sliding down the mountain pass and into the region of dread. It was like slipping into fever, or falling down that hole in sleep from which you wake yourself whimpering. We had crossed the mountains that day, and now we were in a strange place—a hotel in central Washington, in a town near Yakima. The eclipse we had traveled here to see would occur early in the next morning.

I lay in bed. My husband, Gary, was reading beside me. I lay in bed and looked at the painting on the hotel room wall. It was a print of a detailed and lifelike painting of a smiling clown's head, made out of vegetables. It was a painting of the sort which you do not intend to look at, and which, alas, you never forgot. Some tasteless fate presses it upon you; it becomes part of the complex interior junk you carry with you wherever you go. Two years have passed since the total eclipse of which I write. During those years I have forgotten, I assume, a great many things I wanted to remember—but I have not forgotten that clown painting or its lunatic setting in the old hotel.

The clown was bald. Actually, he wore a clown's tight rubber wig, painted white; this stretched over the top of his skull, which was a cabbage. His hair was bunches of baby carrots. Inset in his white clown makeup, and in his cabbage skull, were his small and laughing human eyes. The clown's glance was like the glance of Rembrandt in some of the self-portraits: lively, knowing, deep, and loving. The crinkled shadows around his eyes were string beans. His eyebrows were parsley. Each of his ears was a broad bean. His thin, joyful lips were red chili peppers; between his lips were wet rows of human teeth and a suggestion of a real tongue. The clown print was framed in gilt and glassed.

To put ourselves in the path of the total eclipse, that day we had driven five hours inland from the Washington coast, where we lived. When we tried to cross the Cascades range, an avalanche had blocked the pass.

A slope's worth of snow blocked the road; traffic backed up. Had the avalanche buried any cars that morning? We could not learn. This highway was the only winter road over the mountains. We waited as highway crews bulldozed a passage through the avalanche. With two-by-fours and walls of plywood, they erected a one-way, roofed tunnel through the avalanche. We drove through the avalanche tunnel, crossed the pass, and descended several thousand feet into central Washington and the broad Yakima valley, about which we knew only that it was orchard country. As we lost altitude, the snows disappeared; our ears popped; the trees changed, and in the trees were strange birds. I watched the landscape innocently, like a fool, like a diver in the rapture of the deep who plays on the bottom while his air runs out.

The hotel lobby was a dark, derelict room, narrow as a corridor, and seemingly without air. We waited on a couch while the manager vanished upstairs to do something unknown to our room. Beside us on an overstuffed chair, absolutely motionless, was a platinum-blond woman in her forties wearing a black silk dress and a strand of pearls. Her long legs were crossed; she supported her head on her fist. At the dim far end of the room, their backs toward us, sat six bald men in their shirtsleeves, around a loud television. Two of them seemed asleep. They were drunks. "Number six!" cried the man on television. "Number six!"

On the broad lobby desk, lighted and bubbling, was a ten-gallon aquarium containing one large fish; the fish tilted up and down in its water. Against the long opposite wall sang a live canary in its cage. Beneath the cage, among spilled millet seeds on the carpet, were a decorated child's sand bucket and matching sand shovel.

Now the alarm was set for six. I lay awake remembering an article I had read downstairs in the lobby, in an engineering magazine. The article was about gold mining.

In South Africa, in India, and in South Dakota, the gold mines extend so deeply into the earth's crust that they are hot. The rock walls burn the miners' hands. The companies have to air-condition the mines; if the air conditioners break, the miners die. The elevators in the mine shafts run very slowly, down, and up, so the miners' ears will not pop in their skulls. When the miners return to the surface, their faces are deathly pale.

Early the next morning we checked out. It was February 26, 1979, a Monday morning. We would drive out of town, find a hilltop, watch the eclipse, and then drive back over the mountains and home to the coast. How familiar things are here; how adept we are; how smoothly and professionally we check out! I had forgotten the clown's smiling head and the hotel lobby as if they had never existed. Gary put the car in gear and off we went, as off we have gone to a hundred other adventures.

It was dawn when we found a highway out of town and drove into the unfamiliar countryside. By the growing light we could see a band of cirrostratus clouds in the sky. Later the rising sun would clear these clouds before the eclipse began. We drove at random until we came to a range of unfenced hills. We pulled off the highway, bundled up, and climbed one of these hills.

II

The hill was five hundred feet high. Long winter-killed grass covered it, as high as our knees. We climbed and rested, sweating in the cold; we passed clumps of bundled people on the hillside who were setting up telescopes and fiddling with cameras. The top of the hill stuck up in the middle of the sky. We tightened our scarves and looked around.

East of us rose another hill like ours. Between the hills, far below, was the highway which threaded south into the valley. This was the Yakima valley; I had never seen it before. It is justly famous for its beauty, like every planted valley. It extended south into the horizon, a distant dream of a valley, a Shangri-la. All its hundreds of low, golden slopes bore orchards. Among the orchards were towns, and roads, and plowed and fallow fields. Through the valley wandered a thin shining river; from the river extended fine, frozen irrigation ditches. Distance blurred and blued the sight, so that the whole valley looked like a thickness or sediment at the bottom of the sky. Directly behind us was more sky, and empty lowlands blued by distance, and Mount Adams. Mount Adams was an enormous, snow-covered volcanic cone rising flat, like so much scenery.

Now the sun was up. We could not see it; but the sky behind the band of clouds was yellow, and, far down the valley, some hillside orchards had lighted up. More people were parking near the highway and climbing the hills. It was the West. All of us rugged individuals were wearing knit caps and blue nylon parkas. People were climbing the nearby hills and setting up shop in clumps among the dead grasses. It looked as though we had gathered on hilltops to pray for the world on its last day. It looked as though we had all crawled out of spaceships and were preparing to assault the valley below. It looked as though we were scattered on hilltops at dawn to sacrifice virgins, make rain, set stone stelae in a ring. There was no place out of the wind. The straw grasses banged our legs.

Up in the sky where we stood the air was lusterless yellow. To the west the sky was blue. Now the sun cleared the clouds. We cast rough shadows on the blowing grass; freezing, we waved our arms. Near the sun, the sky was bright and colorless. There was nothing to see.

It began with no ado. It was odd that such a well-advertised public event should have no starting gun, no overture, no introductory speaker. I should have known right then that I was out of my depth. Without pause or preamble, silent as orbits, a piece of the sun went away. We looked at it through welders' goggles. A piece of the sun was missing; in its place we saw empty sky.

I had seen a partial eclipse in 1970. A partial eclipse is very interesting. It bears almost no relation to a total eclipse. Seeing a partial eclipse bears the same relation to seeing a total eclipse as kissing a man does to marrying him, or as flying in an airplane does to falling out of an airplane. Although the one experience precedes the other, it in no way prepares you for it. During a partial eclipse the sky does not darken—not even when 94 percent of the sun is hidden. Nor does the sun, seen colorless through protective devices, seem terribly strange. We have all seen a sliver of light in the sky; we have all seen the crescent moon by day. However, during a partial eclipse the air does indeed get cold, precisely as if someone were standing between you and the fire. And blackbirds do fly back to their roosts. I had seen a partial eclipse before, and here was another.

What you see in an eclipse is entirely different from what you know. It is especially different for those of us whose grasp of astronomy is so frail that, given a flashlight, a grapefruit, two oranges, and fifteen years, we still could not figure out which way to set the clocks for Daylight Saving Time. Usually it is a bit of a trick to keep your knowledge from blinding you. But during an eclipse it is easy. What you see is much more convincing than any wild-eyed theory you may know.

You may read that the moon has something to do with eclipses. I have never seen the moon yet. You do not see the moon. So near the sun, it is as completely invisible as the stars are by day. What you see before your eyes is the sun going through phases. It gets narrower and narrower, as the waning moon does, and, like the ordinary moon, it travels alone in the simply sky. The sky is of course background. It does not appear to eat the sun; it is far behind the sun. The sun simply shaves away; gradually, you see less sun and more sky.

The sky's blue was deepening, but there was no darkness. The sun was a wide crescent, like a segment of tangerine. The wind freshened and blew steadily over the hill. The eastern hill across the highway grew dusky and sharp. The towns and orchards in the valley to the south were dissolving into the blue light. Only the thin river held a trickle of sun.

Now the sky to the west deepened to indigo, a color never seen. A dark sky usually loses color. This as a saturated, deep indigo, up in the air. Stuck up into that unworldly sky was the cone of Mount Adams, and the alpenglow was upon it. The alpenglow is that red light of sunset which holds out on snowy mountain-tops long after the valleys and tablelands are dimmed. "Look at Mount Adams," I said, and that was the last sane moment I remember.

I turned back to the sun. It was going. The sun was going, and the world was wrong. The grasses were wrong; they were platinum. Their every detail of stem, head, and blade shone lightless and artificially distinct as an art photographer's platinum print. This color has never been seen on earth. The hues were metallic; their finish was matte. The hillside was a nineteenth-century tinted photograph from which the tints had faded. All the people you see in the photograph, distinct and detailed as their faces look, are now dead. The sky was navy blue. My hands were silver. All the distant hills' grasses were finespun metal which the wind laid down. I was watching a faded color print of a movie filmed in the Middle Ages; I was standing in it, by some mistake. I was standing in a movie of hillside grasses filmed in the Middle Ages. I missed my own century, the people I knew, and the real light of day.

I looked at Gary. He was in the film. Everything was lost. He was a platinum print, a dead artist's version of life. I saw on the skull the darkness of night mixed with the colors of day. My mind was going out; my eyes were receding the way galaxies recede to the rim of space. Gary was light-years away, gesturing inside a circle of darkness, down the wrong end of a telescope. He smiled as if he saw me; the stringy crinkles around his eyes moved. The sight of him, familiar and wrong, was something I was remembering from centuries hence, from the other side of death: yes, *that* is the way he used to look, when we were living. When it was our generation's turn to be alive. I could not hear him; the wind was too loud. Behind him the sun was going. We had all started down a chute of time. At first it was pleasant; now there was no stopping it. Gary was chuting away across space, moving and talking and catching my eye, chuting down the long corridor of separation. The skin on his face moved like thin bronze plating that would peel.

The grass at our feet was wild barley. It was the wild einkorn wheat which grew on the hilly flanks of the Zagros Mountains, above the Euphrates valley, above the valley of the river we call *River*. We harvested the grass with stone sickles, I remember. We found the grasses on the hillsides; we built our shelter beside them and cut them down. That is how he used to look then, that one, moving and living and catching my eye, with the sky so dark behind him, and the wind blowing. God save our life.

From all the hills came screams. A piece of sky beside the crescent sun was detaching. It was a loosened circle of evening sky, suddenly lighted from the back. It was an abrupt black body out of nowhere; it was a flat disk; it was almost over the sun. That is when there were screams. At once the disk of sky slid over the sun like a lid. The sky snapped over the sun like a lens cover. The hatch in the brain slammed. Abruptly it was dark night, on the land and in the sky. In the night sky was a tiny ring of light. The hole where the sun belongs is very small. A thin ring of light marked its place. There was no sound. The eyes dried, the arteries drained, the lungs hushed. There was no world. We were the world's dead people rotating and orbiting around and around, embedded in the planet's crust, while the earth rolled down. Our minds were light-years distant, forgetful of almost everything. Only an extraordinary act of will could recall to us our former, living selves and our contexts in matter and time. We had, it seems, loved the planet and loved our lives, but could no longer remember the way of them. We got the light wrong. In the sky was something that should not be there. In the black sky was a ring of light. It was a thin ring, an old, thin silver wedding band, an old, worn ring. It was an old wedding band in the sky, or a morsel of bone. There were stars. It was all over.

III

It is now that the temptation is strongest to leave these regions. We have seen enough; let's go. Why burn our hands any more than we have to? But two years have passed; the price of gold has risen. I return to the same buried alluvial beds and pick through the strata again.

I saw, early in the morning, the sun diminish against a backdrop of sky. I saw a circular piece of that sky appear, suddenly detached, blackened, and backlighted; from nowhere it came and overlapped the sun. It did not look like the moon. It was enormous and black. If I had not read that it was the moon, I could have seen the sight a hundred times and never thought of the moon once. (If, however, I had not read that it was the moon—if, like most of the world's people throughout time, I had simply glanced up and seen this thing—then I doubtless would not have speculated much, but would have, like Emperor Louis of Bavaria in 840, simply died of fright on the spot.) It did not look like a dragon, although it looked more like a dragon than the moon. It looked like a lens cover, or the lid of a pot. It materialized out of thin air—black, and flat, and sliding, outlined in flame.

Seeing this black body was like seeing a mushroom cloud. The heart screeched. The meaning of the sight overwhelmed its fascination. It obliterated meaning itself. If you were to glance out one day and see a row of mushroom clouds rising on the horizon, you would know at once that what you were seeing, remarkable as it was, was intrinsically not worth remarking. No use running to tell anyone. Significant as it was, it did not matter a whit. For what is significance? It is significance for people. No people, no significance. This is all I have to tell you.

In the deeps are the violence and terror of which psychology has warned us. But if you ride these monsters deeper down, if you drop with them farther over the world's rim, you find what our sciences cannot locate or name, the substate, the ocean or matrix or ether which buoys the rest, which gives goodness its power for good, and evil its power for evil, the unified field: our complex and inexplicable caring for each other, and for our life together here. This is given. It is not learned.

The world which lay under darkness and stillness following the closing of the lid was not the world we know. The event was over. Its devastation lay around about us. The clamoring mind and heart stilled, almost indifferent, certainly disembodied, frail, and exhausted. The hills were hushed, obliterated. Up in the sky, like a crater from some distant cataclysm, was a hollow ring.

You have seen photographs of the sun taken during a total eclipse. The corona fills the print. All of those photographs were taken through telescopes. The lenses of telescopes and cameras can no more cover the breadth and scale of the visual array than language can cover the breadth and simultaneity of internal experience. Lenses enlarge the sight, omit its context, and make of it a pretty and sensible picture, like something on a Christmas card. I assure you, if you send any shepherds a Christmas card on which is printed a three-by-three photograph of the angel of the Lord, the glory of the Lord, and a multitude of the heavenly host, they will not be sore afraid. More fearsome things can come in envelopes. More moving photographs than those of the sun's corona can appear in magazines. But I pray you will never see anything more awful in the sky.

You see the wide world swaddled in darkness; you see a vast breadth of hilly land, and an enormous, distant, blackened valley; you see towns' lights, a river's path, and blurred portions of your hat and scarf; you see your husband's face looking like an early black-and-white film; and you see a sprawl of black sky and blue sky together, with unfamiliar stars in it, some barely visible bands of cloud, and over there, a small white ring. The ring is as small as one goose in a flock of migrating geese—if you happen to notice a flock of migrating geese. It is one 360th part of the visible sky. The sun we see is less than half the diameter of a dime held at arm's length.

The Crab Nebula, in the constellation Taurus, looks, through binoculars, like a smoke ring. It is a star in the process of exploding. Light from its explosion first reached the earth in 1054; it was a supernova then, and so bright it shone in the daytime. Now it is not so bright, but it is still exploding. It expands at the rate of seventy million miles a day. It is interesting to look through binoculars at something expanding seventy million miles a day. It does not budge. Its apparent size does not increase. Photographs of the Crab Nebula taken fifteen years ago seem identical to photographs of it taken yesterday. Some lichens are similar. Botanists have measured some ordinary lichens twice, at fifty-year intervals, without detecting any growth at all. And yet their cells divide; they live.

The small ring of light was like these things—like a ridiculous lichen up in the sky, like a perfectly still explosion 4,200 light-years away: it was interesting, and lovely, and in witless motion, and it had nothing to do with anything.

It had nothing to do with anything. The sun was too small, and too cold, and too far away, to keep the world alive. The white ring was not enough. It was feeble and worthless. It was as useless as a memory; it was as off kilter and hollow and wretched as a memory.

When you try your hardest to recall someone's face, or the look of a place, you see in your mind's eye some vague and terrible sight such as this. It is dark; it is insubstantial; it is all wrong.

The white ring and the saturated darkness made the earth and the sky look as they must look in the memories of the careless dead. What I saw, what I seemed to be standing in, was all the wrecked light that the memories of the dead could shed upon the living world. We had all died in our boots on the hilltops of Yakima, and were alone in eternity. Empty space stopped our eyes and mouths; we cared for nothing. We remembered our living days wrong. With great effort we had remembered some sort of circular light in the sky—but only the outline. Oh, and then the orchard trees withered, the ground froze, the glaciers slid down the valleys and overlapped the towns. If there had ever been people on earth, nobody knew it. The dead had forgotten those they had loved. The dead were parted one from the other and could no longer remember the faces and lands they had loved in the light. They seemed to stand on darkened hilltops, looking down.

IV

We teach our children one thing only, as we were taught: to wake up. We teach our children to look alive there, to join by words and activities the life of human culture on the planet's crust. As adults we are almost all adept at waking up. We have so mastered the transition we have forgotten we ever learned it. Yet it is a transition we make a hundred times a day, as, like so many will-less dolphins, we plunge and surface, lapse and emerge. We live half our waking lives and all of our sleeping lives in some private, useless, and insensible waters we never mention or recall. Useless, I say. Valueless, I might add—until someone hauls their wealth up to the surface and into the wide-awake city, in a form that people can use.

I do not know how we got to the restaurant. Like Roethke, "I take my waking slow." Gradually I seemed more or less alive and already forgetful. It was now almost nine in the morning. It was the day of a solar eclipse in central Washington, and a fine adventure for everyone. The sky was clear; there was a fresh breeze out of the north.

The restaurant was a roadside place with tables and booths. The other eclipse-watchers were there. From our booth we could see their cars' California license plates, their University of Washington parking stickers. Inside the restaurant we were all eating eggs or waffles; people were fairly shouting and exchanging enthusiasms, like fans after a World Series game. Did you see . . .? Did you see . . .? Then somebody said something which knocked me for a loop.

A college student, a boy in a blue parka who carried a Hasselblad, said to us, "Did you see that little white ring? It looked like a Life Saver. It looked like a Life Saver up in the sky."

And so it did. The boy spoke well. He was a walking alarm clock. I myself had at that time no access to such a word. He could write a sentence, and I could not. I grabbed the Life Saver and rode it to the surface. And I had to laugh. I had been dumbstruck on the Euphrates River, I had been dead and gone and grieving, all over the sight of something which, if you could claw you way up to that level, you would grant looked very much like a Life Saver. It was good to be back among people so clever; it was good to have all the world's words at the mind's disposal, so the mind could begin its task. All those things for which we have no words are lost. The mind—the culture—has two little tools, grammar and lexicon: a decorated sand bucket and a matching shovel. With these we bluster about the continents and do all the world's work. With these we try to save our very lives.

There are a few more things to tell from this level, the level of the restaurant. One is the old joke about breakfast. "It can never be satisfied, the mind, never." Wallace Stevens wrote that, and in the long run he was right. The mind wants to live forever, or to learn a very good reason why not. The mind wants the world to return its love, or its awareness; the mind wants to know all the world, and all eternity, and God. The mind's sidekick, however, will settle for two eggs over easy.

The dear, stupid body is as easily satisfied as a spaniel. And, incredibly, the simple spaniel can lure the brawling mind to its dish. It is everlastingly funny that the proud, metaphysically ambitious, clamoring mind will hush if you give it an egg.

Further: while the mind reels in deep space, while the mind grieves or fears or exults, the workaday senses, in ignorance or idiocy, like so many computer terminals printing out market prices while the world blows up, still transcribe their little data and transmit them to the warehouse in the skull. Later, under the tranquilizing influence of fried eggs, the mind can sort through this data. The restaurant was a halfway house, decompression chamber. There I remembered a few things more.

The deepest, and more terrifying, was this: I have said that I heard screams. (I have since read that screaming, with hysteria, is a common reaction even to expected total eclipses.) People on all the hillsides, including, I think, myself, screamed when the black body of the moon detached from the sky and rolled over the sun. But something else was happening at that same instant, and it was this, I believe, which made us scream.

The second before the sun went out we saw a wall of dark shadow come speeding at us. We no sooner saw it than it was upon us, like thunder. It roared up the valley. It slammed our hill and knocked us out. It was the monstrous swift shadow cone of the moon. I have since read that this wave shadow moves 1,800 miles an hour. It was 195 miles wide. No end was in sight—you saw only the edge. It rolled at you across the land at 1,800 miles an hour, hauling darkness like plague behind it. Seeing it, and knowing it was coming straight for you, was like feeling a slug of anesthetic shoot up your arm. If you think very fast, you may have time to think, "Soon it will hit my brain." You can feel the deadness race up your arm; you can feel the appalling, inhuman speed of your own blood. We saw the wall of shadow coming, and screamed before it hit.

This was the universe about which we have read so much and never before felt: the universe as a clockwork of loose spheres flung at stupefying, unauthorized speeds. How could anything moving so fast not crash, not veer from its orbit amok like a car out of control on a turn?

Less than two minutes later, when the sun emerged, the trailing edge of the shadow cone sped away. It coursed down our hill and raced eastward over the plain, faster than the eye could believe; it swept over the plain and dropped over the planet's rim in a twinkling. It had clobbered us, and now it roared away. We blinked in the light. It was as though an enormous, loping god in the sky had reached down and slapped the earth's face.

Something else, something more ordinary, came back to me along about the third cup of coffee. During the moments of totality, it was so dark that drivers on the highway below turned on their cars' headlights. We could see the highway's route as a strand of lights. It was bumper-to-bumper down there. It was eight-fifteen in the morning. Monday morning, and people were driving into Yakima to work. That it was as dark as night, and eerie as hell, an hour after dawn, apparently meant that in order to *see* to drive to work, people had to use their headlights. Four or five cars pulled off the road. The rest, in a line at least five miles long, drove to town. The highway ran between hills; the people could not have seen any of the eclipsed sun at all. Yakima will have another total eclipse in 2086. Perhaps, in 2086, businesses will give their employees an hour off.

From the restaurant we drove back to the coast. The highway crossing the Cascades range was open. We drove over the mountain like old pros. We joined our places on the planet's thin crust; it held. For the time being, we were home free.

Early that morning at six, when we had checked out, the six bald men were sitting on folding chairs in the dim hotel lobby. The television was on. Most of them were awake. You might drown in your own spittle, God knows, at any time; you might wake up dead in a small hotel, a cabbage head watching TV while snows pile up in the passes, watching TV while the chili peppers smile and the moon passes over the sun and nothing changes and nothing is learned because you have lost your bucket and shovel and no longer care. What if you regain the surface and open your sack and find, instead of treasure, a beast which jumps at you? Or you may not come back at all. The winches may jam, the scaffolding buckle, the air conditioning collapse. You may glance up one day and see by your headlamp the canary keeled over in its cage. You may reach into a cranny for pearls and touch a moray eel. You yank on your rope; it is too late.

Apparently people share a sense of these hazards, for when the total eclipse ended, an odd thing happened.

When the sun appeared as a blinding bead on the ring's side, the eclipse was over. The black lens cover appeared again, backlighted, and slid away. At once the yellow light made the sky blue again; the black lid dissolved and vanished. The real world began there. I remember now: we all hurried away. We were born and bored at a stroke. We rushed down the hill. We found our car; we saw the other people streaming down the hillsides; we joined the highway traffic and drove away.

We never looked back. It was a general vamoose, and an odd one, for when we left the hill, the sun was still partially eclipsed—a sight rare enough, and one which, in itself, we would probably have driven five hours to see. But enough is enough. One turns at last even from glory itself with a sigh of relief. From the depths of mystery, and even from the heights of splendor, we bounce back and hurry for the latitudes of home.

Eudora Welty / The Little Store 1975

Eudora Welty was born in Jackson, Mississippi, in 1909 and attended Mississippi State College for Women, the University of Wisconsin, and the School of Business at Columbia University. During the Depression, while working for newspapers, radios, and the Works Progress Administration, she traveled throughout Mississippi taking numerous photographs which were later exhibited in New York. Her first collection of stories, A Curtain of Green, *appeared in 1941. Since that time, Welty has written several more story collections and novels including* The Robber Bridegroom *(1942),* The Ponder Heart *(1954),* Losing Battles *(1970), and the Pulitzer Prize-winning* The Optimist's Daughter *(1972). She is also regarded as a talented essayist and critic.*

Welty still resides in Jackson, and the following sketch recalls the flavor of her childhood years there.

My mother considered herself pretty well prepared in her kitchen and pantry for any emergency that, in her words, might choose to present itself. But if she should, all of a sudden, need another lemon or find she was out of bread, all she had to do was call out, "Quick! Who'd like to run to the Little Store for me?"

I would.

She'd count out the change into my hand, and I was away. I'll bet the nickel that would be left over that all over the country, for those of my day, the neighborhood grocery played a similar part in our growing up.

Our store had its name—it was that of the grocer who owned it, whom I'll call

Mr. Sessions—but "the Little Store" is what we called it at home. It was a block down our street toward the capitol and half a block further, around the corner, toward the cemetery. I knew even the sidewalk to it as well as I knew my own skin. I'd skipped my jumping-rope up and down it, hopped its length through mazes of hopscotch, played jacks in its islands of shade, serpentined along it on my Princess bicycle, skated it backward and forward. In the twilight I had dragged my steamboat by its string (this was home-made out of every new shoebox, with candle in the bottom lighted and shining through colored tissue paper pasted over windows scissored out in the shapes of the sun, moon and stars) across every crack of the walk without letting it bump or catch fire. I'd "played out" on that street after supper with my brothers and friends as long as "first-dark" lasted; I'd caught its lightning bugs. On the first Armistice Day (and this will set the time I'm speaking of) we made our own parade down that walk on a single velocipede—my brother pedaling, our little brother riding the handlebars, and myself standing on the back, all with arms wide, flying flags in each hand. (My father snapped that picture as we raced by. It came out blurred.) . . .

Our Little Store rose right up from the sidewalk; standing in a street of family houses, it alone hadn't any yard in front, any tree or flowerbed. It was a plain frame building covered over with brick. Above the door, a little railed porch ran across on an upstairs level and four windows with shades were looking out. But I didn't catch on to those.

Running in out of the sun, you met what seemed total obscurity inside. There were almost tangible smells—licorice recently sucked in a child's cheek, dill-pickle brine that had leaked through a paper sack in a fresh trail across the wooden floor, ammonia-loaded ice that had been hoisted from wet croker sacks and slammed into the icebox with its sweet butter at the door, and perhaps the smell of still-untrapped mice.

Then through the motes of cracker dust, cornmeal dust, the Gold Dust of the Gold Dust Twins that the floor had been swept out with, the realities emerged. Shelves climbed to high reach all the way around, set out with not too much of any one thing but a lot of things—lard, molasses, vinegar, starch, matches, kerosene, Octagon soap (about a year's worth of octagon-shaped coupons cut out and saved brought a signet ring addressed to you in the mail. Furthermore, when the postman arrived at your door, he blew a whistle). It was up to you to remember what you came for, while your eye traveled from cans of sardines to ice cream salt to harmonicas to flypaper (over your head, batting around on a thread beneath the blades of the ceiling fan, stuck with its testimonial catch).

Its confusion may have been in the eye of its beholder. Enchantment is cast upon you by all those things you weren't supposed to have need for, it lures you close to wooden tops you'd outgrown, boy's marbles and agates in little net pouches, small rubber balls that wouldn't bounce straight, frazzly kitestring, clay bubble-pipes that would snap off in your teeth, the stiffest scissors. You could contemplate those long narrow boxes of sparklers gathering dust while you waited for it to be the Fourth of July or Christmas, and noisemakers in the shape of tin frogs for somebody's birthday party you hadn't been invited to yet, and see that they were all marvelous.

You might not have even looked for Mr. Sessions when he came around his store cheese (as big as a doll's house) and in front of the counter looking for you. When you'd finally asked him for, and received from him in its paper bag, whatever single thing it was that you had been sent for, the nickel that was left over was yours to spend.

Down at a child's eye level, inside those glass jars with mouths in their sides through which the grocer could run his scoop or a child's hand might be invited to reach for a choice, were wineballs, all-day suckers, gumdrops, peppermints. Making a row under the glass of a counter were the Tootsie Rolls, Hershey Bars, Goo-Goo Clusters, Baby Ruths. And whatever was the name of those pastilles that came stacked in a cardboard cylinder with a cardboard lid? They were thin and dry, about the size of tiddlywinks, and in the shape of twisted rosettes. A kind of chocolate dust came out with them when you shook them out in your hand. Were they chocolate? I'd say rather they were brown. They didn't taste of anything at all, unless it was wood. Their attraction was the number you got for a nickel.

Making up your mind, you circled the store around and around, around the pickle barrel, around the tower of Cracker Jack boxes; Mr. Sessions had built it for us himself on top of a packing case, like a house of cards.

If it seemed too hot for Cracker Jacks, I might get a cold drink. Mr. Sessions might have already stationed himself by the cold-drinks barrel, like a mind reader. Deep in ice water that looked black as ink, murky shapes that would come up as Coca-Colas, Orange Crushes, and various flavors of pop, were all swimming around together. When you gave the word, Mr. Sessions plunged his bare arm in to the elbow and fished out your choice, first try. I favored a locally bottled concoction called Lake's Celery. (What else could it be called? It was made by a Mr. Lake out of celery. It was a popular drink here for years but was not known universally, as I found out when I arrived in New York and ordered one in the Astor bar.) You drank on the premises, with feet set wide apart to miss the drip, and gave him back his bottle.

But he didn't hurry you off. A standing scales was by the door, with a stack of iron weights and a brass slide on the balance arm, that would weigh you up to three hundred pounds. Mr. Sessions, whose hands were gentle and smelled of carbolic, would lift you up and set your feet on the platform, hold your loaf of bread for you, and taking his time while you stood still for him, he would make certain of what you weighed today. He could even remember what you weighed the last time, so you could subtract and announce how much you'd gained. That was goodbye.

June Jordan / Nobody Mean More to Me than You and the Future Life of Willie Jordan[1] 1985

June Jordan makes her position clear in the introduction to On Call, *the collection of political essays from which the following essay is reprinted: "I am a dissident American poet and writer," she writes, "completely uninterested to run away from my country, my home." As an African-American woman and radical activist, Jordan has fought to get her writings in print; she has experienced "American censorship" firsthand. "On the left, as well as in the mainstream, airborne orthodoxies attempt to identify the correct subject matters for discussion, as well as the correct points of view," Jordan writes. During a varied career as teacher, poet, essayist, public speaker, and activist, Jordan has made it her business to challenge those orthodoxies and develop a politics more attuned to people's real lives.*

The following essay chronicles one such effort. Its interweaving of two inextricably linked stories—one about the development of a Black English class at the State University of New York at Stony Brook, the other about the murder by

[1]Black English aphorism crafted by Monica Morris, a Junior at S.U.N.Y. at Stony Brook, October, 1984. [Jordan's note.]

police of a young black man and that killing's ramifications—demonstrates how language can empower and limit us in a racist society, and that in the face of the day-to-day brutality experienced by most African Americans, rhetoric is not enough.

June Jordan's collections of poetry and prose include Soulscript *(1970),* Some Changes *(1971),* Things That I Do in the Dark *(1977),* Civil Wars *(1981). and* On Call *(1985). Her most recent book is* Technical Difficulties *(1992). June Jordan currently divides her time as a teacher in the department of African American Studies and Women's Studies at the University of California, Berkeley.*

Black English is not exactly a linguistic buffalo; as children, most of the thirty-five million Afro-Americans living here depend on this language for our discovery of the world. But then we approach our maturity inside a larger social body that will not support our efforts to become anything other than the clones of those who are neither our mothers nor our fathers. We begin to grow up in a house where every true mirror shows us the face of somebody who does not belong there, whose walk and whose talk will never look or sound "right," because that house was meant to shelter a family that is alien and hostile to us. As we learn our way around this environment, either we hide our original word habits, or we completely surrender our own voice, hoping to please those who will never respect anyone different from themselves: Black English is not exactly a linguistic buffalo, but we should understand its status as an endangered species, as a perishing, irreplaceable system of community intelligence, or we should expect its extinction, and, along with that, the extinguishing of much that constitutes our own proud, and singular identity.

What we casually call "English," less and less defers to England and its "gentlemen." "English" is no longer a specific matter of geography or an element of class privilege; more than thirty-three countries use this tool as a means of "intranational communication."[2] Countries as disparate as Zimbabwe and Malaysia, or Israel and Uganda, use it as their non-native currency of convenience. Obviously, this tool, this "English," cannot function inside thirty-three discrete societies on the basis of rules and values absolutely determined somewhere else, in a thirty-fourth other country, for example.

In addition to that staggering congeries of non-native users of English, there are five countries, or 333,746,000 people, for whom this thing called "English" serves as a native tongue.[3] Approximately ten percent of these native speakers of "English" are Afro-American citizens of the U.S.A. I cite these numbers and varieties of human beings dependent on "English" in order, quickly, to suggest how strange and how tenuous is any concept of "Standard English." Obviously, numerous forms of English now operate inside a natural, an uncontrollable, continuum of development. I would suppose "the standard" for English in Malaysia is not the same as "the standard" in Zimbabwe. I know that standard forms of English for Black people in this country do not copy that of whites. And, in fact, the structural differences between these two kinds of English have intensified, becoming more Black, or less white, despite the expected homogenizing effects of television[4] and other mass media.

[2]*English Is Spreading, But What Is English?* A presentation by Professor S. N. Sridahr, Dept. of Linguistics, S.U.N.Y. at Stonybrook, April 9, 1985: Dean's Conversation Among the Disciplines. [Jordan's note.]

[3]Ibid. [Jordan's note.]

[4]*New York Times,* March 15, 1985, Section One, p. 14: Report on study by Linguistics at the University of Pennsylvania. [Jordan's note.]

Nonetheless, white standards of English persist, supreme and unquestioned, in these United States. Despite our multilingual population, and despite the deepening Black and white cleavage within that conglomerate, white standards control our official and popular judgments of verbal proficiency and correct, or incorrect, language skills, including speech. In contrast to India, where at least fourteen languages co-exist as legitimate Indian languages, in contrast to Nicaragua, where all citizens are legally entitled to formal school instruction in their regional or tribal languages, compulsory education in America compels accommodation to exclusively white forms of "English." White English, in America, is "Standard English."

This story begins two years ago. I was teaching a new course, "In Search of the Invisible Black Woman," and my rather large class seemed evenly divided between young Black women and men. Five or six white students also sat in attendance. With unexpected speed and enthusiasm we had moved through historical narratives of the 19th century to literature by and about Black women, in the 20th. I had assigned the first forty pages of Alice Walker's *The Color Purple,* and I came, eagerly, to class that morning:

"So!" I exclaimed, aloud. "What did you think? How did you like it?"

The students studied their hands, or the floor. There was no response. The tense, resistant feeling in the room fairly astounded me.

At last, one student, a young woman still not meeting my eyes, muttered something in my direction:

"What did you say?" I prompted her.

"Why she have them talk so funny. It don't sound right."

"You mean the language?"

Another student lifted his head: "It don't look right, neither. I couldn't hardly read it."

At this, several students dumped on the book. Just about unanimously, their criticisms targeted the language. I listened to what they wanted to say and silently marvelled at the similarities between their casual speech patterns and Alice Walker's written version of Black English.

But I decided against pointing to these identical traits of syntax; I wanted not to make them self-conscious about their own spoken language—not while they clearly felt it was "wrong." Instead I decided to swallow my astonishment. Here was a negative Black reaction to a prize winning accomplishment of Black literature that white readers across the country had selected as a best seller. Black rejection was aimed at the one irreducibly Black element of Walker's work: the language—Celie's Black English. I wrote the opening lines of *The Color Purple* on the blackboard and asked the students to help me translate these sentences into Standard English:

> *You better not never tell nobody but God. It'd kill your mammy.*
> Dear God,
> I am fourteen years old. I have always been a good girl. Maybe you can give me a sign letting me know what is happening to me.
> Last spring after Little Lucious come I heard them fussing. He was pulling on her arm. She say it too soon, Fonso. I aint well. Finally he leave her alone. A week go by, he pulling on her arm again. She say, Naw, I ain't gonna. Can't you see I'm already half dead, and all of the children.[5]

Our process of translation exploded with hilarity and even hysterical, shocked laughter: The Black writer, Alice Walker, knew what she was doing! If rudimen-

[5] Alice Walker, *The Color Purple,* p. 11, Harcourt Brace, N.Y. [Jordan's note.]

tary criteria for good fiction includes the manipulation of language so that the syntax and diction of sentences will tell you the identity of speakers, the probable age and sex and class of speakers, and even the locale—urban/rural/southern/western—then Walker had written perfectly. This is the translation into Standard English that our class produced:

> *Absolutely, one should never confide in anybody besides God. Your secrets could prove devastating to your mother.*
> Dear God,
> I am fourteen years old. I have always been good. But now, could you help me to understand what is happening to me?
> Last spring, after my little brother, Lucious, was born, I heard my parents fighting. My father kept pulling at my mother's arm. But she told him, "It's too soon for sex, Alfonso. I am still not feeling well." Finally, my father left her alone. A week went by, and then he began bothering my mother, again: Pulling her arm. She told him, "No, I won't! Can't you see I'm already exhausted from all of these children?"

(Our favorite line was "It's too soon for sex, Alphonso.")

Once we could stop laughing, once we could stop our exponentially wild improvisations on the theme of Translated Black English, the students pushed me to explain their own negative first reactions to their spoken language on the printed page. I thought it was probably akin to the shock of seeing yourself in a photograph for the first time. Most of the students had never before seen a written facsimile of the way they talk. None of the students had ever learned how to read and write their own verbal system of communication: Black English. Alternatively, this fact began to baffle or else bemuse and then infuriate my students. Why not? Was it too late? Could they learn how to do it, now? And, ultimately, the final test question, the one testing my sincerity: Could I teach them? Because I had never taught anyone Black English and, as far as I knew, no one, anywhere in the United States, had ever offered such a course, the best I could say was "I'll try."

He looked like a wrestler.

He sat dead center in the packed room and, every time our eyes met, he quickly nodded his head as though anxious to reassure, and encourage, me.

Short, with strikingly broad shoulders and long arms, he spoke with a surprisingly high, soft voice that matched the soft bright movement of his eyes. His name was Willie Jordan. He would have seemed even more unlikely in the context of Contemporary Women's Poetry, except that ten or twelve other Black men were taking the course, as well. Still, Willie was conspicuous. His extreme fitness, the muscular density of his presence underscored the riveted, gentle attention that he gave to anything anyone said. Generally, he did not join the loud and rowdy dialogue flying back and forth, but there could be no doubt about his interest in our discussions. And, when he stood to present an argument he'd prepared, overnight, that nervous smile of his vanished and an irregular stammering replaced it, as he spoke with visceral sincerity, word by word.

That was how I met Willie Jordan. It was in between "In Search of the Invisible Black Woman" and "The Art of Black English." I was waiting for Departmental approved and I supposed that Willie might be, so to speak, killing time until he, too, could study Black English. But Willie really did want to explore Contemporary Women's poetry and, to that end, volunteered for extra research and never missed a class.

Towards the end of that semester, Willie approached me for an independent study project on South Africa. It would commence the next semester. I thought Willie's writing needed the kind of improvement only intense practice will yield.

I knew his intelligence was outstanding. But he'd wholeheartedly opted for "Standard English" at a rather late age, and the results were stilted and frequently polysyllabic, simply for the sake of having more syllables. Willie's unnatural formality of language seemed to me consistent with the formality of his research into South African apartheid. As he projected his studies, he would have little time, indeed, for newspapers. Instead, more than 90 percent of his research would mean saturation in strictly historical, if not archival, material. I was certainly interested. It would be tricky to guide him into a more confident and spontaneous relationship both with language and apartheid. It was going to be wonderful to see what happened when he could catch up with himself, entirely, and talk back to the world.

September, 1984: Breezy fall weather and much excitement! My class, "The Art of Black English," was full to the limit of the fire laws. And, in Independent Study, Willie Jordan showed up, weekly, fifteen minutes early for each of our sessions. I was pretty happy to be teaching altogether!

I remember an early class when a young brother, replete with his ever present poke-pie hat, raised his hand and then told us that most of what he'd heard was "all right" except it was "too clean." "The brothers on the street," he continued, "they mix it up more. Like 'fuck' and 'motherfuck.' Or like 'shit.' " He waited. I waited. Then all of us laughed a good while, and we got into a brawl about "correct" and "realistic" Black English that led to Rule 1.

Rule 1: *Black English is about a whole lot more than mothafuckin.*

As a criterion, we decided, "realistic" could take you anywhere you want to go. Artful places. Angry places. Eloquent and sweetalkin places. Polemical places. Church. And the local Bar & Grill. We were checking out a language, not a mood or a scene or one guy's forgettable mouthing off.

It was hard. For most of the students, learning Black English required a fallback to patterns and rhythms of speech that many of their parents had beaten out of them. I mean *beaten.* And, in a majority of cases, correct Black English could be achieved only by striving for *incorrect* Standard English, something they were still pushing at, quite uncertainly. This state of affairs led to Rule 2.

Rule 2: *If it's wrong in Standard English it's probably right in Black English, or, at least, you're hot.*

It was hard. Roommates and family members ridiculed their studies, or remained incredulous, "You *studying* that shit? At school?" But we were beginning to feel the companionship of pioneers. And we decided that we needed another rule that would establish each one of us as equally important to our success. This was Rule 3.

Rule 3: *If it don't sound like something that come out somebody mouth then it don't sound right. If it don't sound right then it ain't hardly right. Period.*

This rule produced two weeks of compositions in which the students agonizingly tried to spell the sound of the Black English sentence they wanted to convey. But Black English is, preeminently, an oral/spoken means of communication. *And spelling don't talk.* So we needed Rule 4.

Rule 4: *Forget about the spelling. Let the syntax carry you.*

Once we arrived at Rule 4 we started to fly because syntax, the structure of an idea, leads you to the world view of the speaker and reveals her values. The syntax of a sentence equals the structure of your consciousness. If we insisted that the language of Black English adheres to a distinctive Black syntax, then we were postulating a profound difference between white and Black people, *per se.* Was it a difference to prize or to obliterate?

There are three qualities of Black English—the presence of life, voice, and clarity—that testify to a distinctive Black value system that we became excited about and self-consciously tried to maintain.

1. Black English has been produced by a pre-technocratic, if not anti-technological,

culture. More, our culture has been constantly threatened by annihilation or, at least, the swallowed blurring of assimilation. Therefore, our language is a system constructed by people constantly needing to insist that we exist, that we are present. Our language devolves from a culture that abhors all abstraction, or anything tending to obscure or delete the fact of the human being who is here and now/the truth of the person who is speaking or listening. Consequently, *there is no passive voice construction possible in Black English.* For example, you cannot say, "Black English is being eliminated." You must say, instead, "White people eliminating Black English." The assumption of the presence of live governs all of Black English. Therefore, overwhelmingly, *all action takes place in the language of the present indicative.* And every sentence assumes the living and active participation of at least two human beings, the speaker and the listener.

2. A primary consequence of the person-centered values of Black English is the delivery of voice. If you speak or write Black English, your ideas will necessarily possess that otherwise elusive attribute, *voice.*

3. One main benefit following from the person-centered values of Black English is that of *clarity.* If your idea, your sentence, assumes the presence of at least two living and active people, you will make it understandable because the motivation behind every sentence is the wish to say something real to somebody real.

As the weeks piled up, translation from Standard English into Black English or vice versa occupied a hefty part of our course work.

> Standard English (hereafter S.E.): "In considering the idea of studying Black English those questioned suggested—"
>
> (What's the subject? Where's the person? Is anybody alive in there, in that idea?)
>
> Black English (hereafter B.E.): "I been asking people what you think about somebody studying Black English and they answer me like this."

But there were interesting limits. You cannot "translate" instances of Standard English preoccupied with abstraction or with nothing/nobody evidently alive, into Black English. That would warp the language into uses antithetical to the guiding perspective of its community of users. Rather you must first change those Standard English sentences, themselves, into ideas consistent with the person-centered assumptions of Black English.

GUIDELINES FOR BLACK ENGLISH

1. Minimal number of words for every idea: This is the source for the aphoristic and/or poetic force of the language; eliminate every possible word.
2. Clarity: If the sentence is not clear it's not Black English.
3. Eliminate use of the verb *to be* whenever possible. This leads to the deployment of more descriptive and therefore, more precise verbs.
4. Use *be* or *been* only when you want to describe a chronic, ongoing state of things.

> He *be* at the office, by 9. (He is always at the office by 9.)
> He *been* with her since forever.

5. Zero copula: Always eliminate the verb *to be* whenever it would combine with another verb, in Standard English.

> S.E.: She is going out with him.
> B.E.: She going out with him.

6. Eliminate *do* as in:

S.E.: What do you think? What do you want?
B.E.: What you think? What you want?

Rules number 3, 4, 5, and 6 provide for the use of the minimal number of verbs per idea and, therefore, greater accuracy in the choice of verb.

7. In general, if you wish to say something really positive, try to formulate the idea using emphatic negative structure.

S.E.: He's fabulous.
B.E.: He bad.

8. Use double or triple negatives for dramatic emphasis.

S.E.: Tina Turner sings out of this world.
B.E.: Ain nobody sing like Tina.

9. Never use the *-ed* suffix to indicate the past tense of a verb.

S.E.: She closed the door.
B.E.: She close the door. Or, she have close the door.

10. Regardless of intentional verb time, only use the third person singular, present indicative, for use of the verb *to have,* as an auxiliary.

S.E.: He had his wallet then he lost it.
B.E.: He have him wallet then he lose it.
S.E.: He had seen that movie.
B.E.: We seen that movie. Or, we have see that movie.

11. Observe a minimal inflection of verbs. Particularly, never change from the first person singular forms to the third person singular.

S.E.: Present Tense Forms: He goes to the store.
B.E.: He go to the store.
S.E.: Past Tense Forms: He went to the store.
B.E.: He go to the store. Or, he gone to the store. Or, he been to the store.

12. The possessive case scarcely ever appears in Black English. Never use an apostrophe('s) construction. If you wander into a possessive case component of an idea, then keep logically consistent: *ours, his, theirs, mines.* But, most likely, if you bump into such a component, you have wandered outside the underlying world-view of Black English.

S.E.: He will take their car tomorrow.
B.E.: He taking they car tomorrow.

13. Plurality: Logical consistency, continued: If the modifier indicates plurality then the noun remains in the singular case.

S.E.: He ate twelve doughnuts.
B.E.: He eat twelve doughnut.
S.E.: She has many books.
B.E.: She have many book.

14. Listen for, or invent, special Black English forms of the past tense, such as: "He losted it. That what she felted." If they are clear and readily understood, then use them.

15. Do not hesitate to play with words, sometimes inventing them: e.g. "astropotomous" means huge like a hippo plus astronomical and, therefore, signifies real big.

16. In Black English, unless you keenly want to underscore the past tense na-

ture of an action, stay in the present tense and rely on the overall context of your ideas for the conveyance of time and sequence.

17. Never use the suffix *-ly* form of adverb in Black English.

> S.E.: The rain came down rather quickly.
> B.E.: The rain come down pretty quick.

18. Never use the indefinite article *an* in Black English.

> S.E.: He wanted to ride an elephant.
> B.E.: He want to ride him a elephant.

19. Invarient syntax: in correct Black English it is possible to formulate an imperative, an interogative, and a simple declarative idea with the same syntax:

> B.E.: You going to the store?
> You going to the store.
> You going to the store!

Where was Willie Jordan? We'd reached the mid-term of the semester. Students had formulated Black English guidelines, by consensus, and they were now writing with remarkable beauty, purpose, and enjoyment:

> *I ain hardly speakin for everybody but myself so understan that.*—Kim Parks

Samples from student writings.

> Janie have a great big ole hole inside her. Tea Cake the only thing that fit that hole . . .
>
> That pear tree beautiful to Janie, especial when bees fiddlin with the blossomin pear there growin large and lovely. But personal speakin, the love she get from starin at that tree ain the love what starin back at her in them relationship. (Monica Morris)

> Love is a big theme in, *They Eye Was Watching God.* Love show people new corners inside theyself. It pull out good stuff and stuff back bad stuff . . . Joe worship the doing uh his own hand and need other people to worship him too. But he ain't think about Janie that she a person and ought to live like anybody common do. Queen life not for Janie. (Monica Morris)

> In both life and writin, Black womens have varietous experience of love that be cold like a iceberg or fiery like a inferno. Passion got for the other partner involve, man or woman, seem as shallow, ankle-deep water or the most profoundest abyss. (Constance Evans)

> You know it really cold / When the friend you / Always get out the fire / Act like they don't know you / When you in the heat. (Constance Evans)

> Big classroom discussion bout love at this time. I never take no class where us have any long arguin for and against for two or three day. New to me and great. I find the class time talkin a million time more interestin than detail bout the book. (Kathy Esseks)

As these examples suggest, Black English no longer limited the students, in any way. In fact, one of them, Philip Garfield, would shortly "translate" a pivotal scene from Ibsen's *Doll House,* as his final term paper.

> NORA: I didn't gived no shit. I thinked you a asshole back then, too, you make it so hard for me save mines husband life.
>
> KROGSTAD: Girl, it clear you ain't any idea what you done. You done exact what once done, and I losed my reputation over it.
>
> NORA: You asks me believe you once act brave save you wife life?

> KROGSTAD: Law care less why you done it.
> NORA: Law must suck.
> KROGSTAD: Suck or no, if I wants, judge screw you wid dis paper.
> NORA: No way, man. (Philip Garfield)

But where was Willie? Compulsively punctual, and always thoroughly prepared with neatly typed compositions, he had disappeared. He failed to show up for our regularly scheduled conference, and I received neither a note nor a phone call of explanation. A whole week went by. I wondered if Willie had finally been captured by the extremely current happenings in South Africa: passage of a new constitution that did not enfranchise the Black majority, and militant Black South African reaction to that affront. I wondered if he'd been hurt, somewhere. I wondered if the serious workload of weekly readings and writings had overwhelmed him and changed his mind about independent study. Where was Willie Jordan?

One week after the first conference that Willie missed, he called: "Hello, Professor Jordan? This is Willie. I'm sorry I wasn't there last week. But something has come up and I'm pretty upset. I'm sorry but I really can't deal right now."

I asked Willie to drop by my office and just let me see that he was okay. He agreed to do that. When I saw him I knew something hideous had happened. Something had hurt him and scared him to the marrow. He was all agitated and stammering and terse and incoherent. At last, his sadly jumbled account let me surmise, as follows: Brooklyn police had murdered his unarmed, twenty-five-year-old brother, Reggie Jordan. Neither Willie nor his elderly parents knew what to do about it. Nobody from the press was interested. His folks had no money. Police ran his family around and around, to no point. And Reggie was really dead. And Willie wanted to fight, but he felt helpless.

With Willie's permission I began to try to secure legal counsel for the Jordan family. Unfortunately Black victims of police violence are truly numerous while the resources available to prosecute their killers are truly scarce. A friend of mine at the Center for Constitutional Rights estimated that just the preparatory costs for bringing the cops into court normally approaches $180,000. Unless the execution of Reggie Jordan became a major community cause for organizing, and protest, his murder would simply become a statistical item.

Again, with Willie's permission, I contacted every newspaper and media person I could think of. But the William Bastone feature article in *The Village Voice* was the only result from that canvassing.

Again, with Willie's permission, I presented the case to my class in Black English. We had talked about the politics of language. We had talked about love and sex and child abuse and men and women. But the murder of Reggie Jordan broke like a hurricane across the room.

There are few "issues" as endemic to Black life as police violence. Most of the students knew and respected and liked Jordan. Many of them came from the very neighborhood where the murder had occurred. All of the students had known somebody close to them who had been killed by police, or had known frightening moments of gratuitous confrontation with the cops. They wanted to do everything at once to avenge death. Number One: They decided to compose personal statements of condolence to Willie Jordan and his family written in Black English. Number Two: They decided to compose individual messages to the police, in Black English. These should be prefaced by an explanatory paragraph composed by the entire group. Number Three: These individual messages, with their lead paragraph, should be sent to *Newsday*.

The morning after we agreed on these objectives, one of the young women students appeared with an unidentified visitor, who sat through the class, smiling in a peculiar, comfortable way.

Now we had to make more tactical decisions. Because we wanted the messages published, and because we thought it imperative that our outrage be known by the police, the tactical question was this: Should the opening, group paragraph be written in Black English or Standard English?

I have seldom been privy to a discussion with so much heart at the dead heat of it. I will never forget the eloquence, the sudden haltings of speech, the fierce struggle against tears, the furious throwaway, and useless explosions that this question elicited.

That one question contained several others, each of them extraordinarily painful to even contemplate. How best to serve the memory of Reggie Jordan? Should we use the language of the killers—Standard English—in order to make our ideas acceptable to those controlling the killers? But wouldn't what we had to say be rejected, summarily, if we said it in our own language, the language of the victim, Reggie Jordan? But if we sought to express ourselves by abandoning our language wouldn't that mean our suicide on top of Reggie's murder? But if we expressed ourselves in our own language wouldn't that be suicidal to the wish to communicate with those who, evidently, did not give a damn about us/Reggie/police violence in the Black community?

At the end of one of the longest, most difficult hours of my own life, the students voted, unanimously, to preface their individual messages with a paragraph composed in the language of Reggie Jordan. *"At least we don't give up nothing else. At least we stick to the truth: Be who we been. And stay all the way with Reggie."*

It was heartbreaking to proceed, from that point. Everyone in the room realized that our decision in favor of Black English had doomed our writings, even as the distinctive reality of our Black lives always has doomed our efforts to "be who we been" in this country.

I went to the blackboard and took down this paragraph, dictated by the class:

> . . . YOU COPS!
>
> WE THE BROTHER AND SISTER OF WILLIE JORDAN, A FELLOW STONY BROOK STUDENT WHO THE BROTHER OF THE DEAD REGGIE JORDAN. REGGIE, LIKE MANY BROTHER AND SISTER, HE A VICTIM OF BRUTAL RACIST POLICE, OCTOBER 25, 1984. US APPALL, FED UP. BECAUSE THAT ANOTHER SENSELESS DEATH WHAT OCCUR IN OUR COMMUNITY. THIS WHAT WE FEEL. THIS, FROM OUR HEART, FOR WE AIN'T STAYIN' SILENT NO MORE:

With the completion of this introduction, nobody said anything. I asked for comments. At this invitation, the unidentified visitor, a young Black man, ceaselessly smiling, raised his hand. He was, it so happens, a rookie cop. He had just joined the force in September and, he said, he thought he should clarify a few things. So he came forward and sprawled easily into a posture of barroom, or fireside, nostalgia:

"See," Officer Charles enlightened us, "Most times when you out on the street and something come down you do one of two things. Over-react or under-react. Now, if you under-react then you can get yourself kilt. And if you over-react then maybe you kill somebody. Fortunately it's about nine times out of ten and you will over-react. So the brother got kilt. And I'm sorry about that, believe me. But what you have to understand is what kilt him: Over-reaction. That's all. Now you talk about Black people and white police but see, now, I'm a cop myself. And (big smile) I'm Black. And just a couple months ago I was on the other side. But see it's the same for me. You a cop, you the ultimate authority: the Ultimate Authority. And you on the street, most of the time you can only do one of two things: over-react or under-react. That's all it is with the brother. Over-reaction. Didn't have nothing to do with race.''

That morning Officer Charles had the good fortune to escape without being boiled alive. But barely. And I remember the pride of his smile when I read about the fate of Black policemen and other collaborators, in South Africa. I remember him, and I remember the shock and palpable feeling of shame that filled the room. It was as though that foolish, and deadly, young man had just relieved himself of his foolish, and deadly, explanation, face to face with the grief of Reggie Jordan's father and Reggie Jordan's mother. Class ended quietly. I copied the paragraph from the blackboard, collected the individual messages and left to type them up.

Newsday rejected the piece.

The Village Voice could not find room in their ''Letters'' section to print the individual messages from the students to the police.

None of the tv news reporters picked up the story.

Nobody raised $180,000 to prosecute the murder of Reggie Jordan.

Reggie Jordan is really dead.

I asked Willie Jordan to write an essay pulling together everything important to him from that semester. He was still deeply beside himself with frustration and amazement and loss. This is what he wrote, unedited, and in its entirety:

> Throughout the course of this semester I have been researching the effects of oppression and exploitation along racial lines in South Africa and its neighboring countries. I have become aware of South African police brutalization of native Africans beyond the extent of the law, even though the laws themselves are catalyst affliction upon Black men, women and children. Many Africans die each year as a result of the deliberate use of police force to protect the white power structure.
>
> Social control agents in South Africa, such as policemen, are also used to force compliance among citizens through both overt and covert tactics. It is not uncommon to find bold-faced coercion and cold-blooded killings of Blacks by South African police for undetermined and/or inadequate reasons. perhaps the truth is that the only reasons for this heinous treatment of Blacks rests in racial differences. We should also understand that what is conveyed through the media is not always accurate and may sometimes be construed as the tip of the iceberg at best.
>
> I recently received a painful reminder that racism, poverty, and the abuse of power are global problems which are by no means unique to South Africa. On October 25, 1984 at approximately 3:00 p.m. my brother, Mr. Reginald Jordan, was shot and killed by two New York City policemen from the 75th precinct in the East New York section of Brooklyn. His life ended at the age of twenty-five. Even up to this current point in time the Police Department has failed to provide my family, which consists of five brothers, eight sisters, and two parents, with a plausible reason for Reggie's death. Out of the many stories that were given to my family by the Police Department, not one of them seems to hold water. In fact, I honestly believe that the Police Department's assessment of my brother's murder is nothing short of ABSOLUTE BULLSHIT, and thus far no evidence had been produced to alter perception of the situation.
>
> Furthermore, I believe that one of three cases may have occurred in this incident. First, Reggie's death may have been the desired outcome of the police officer's action, in which case the killing was premeditated. Or, it was a case of mistaken identity, which clarifies the fact that the two officers who killed my brother and their commanding parties are all grossly incompetent. Or, both of the above cases are correct, i.e., Reggie's murderers intended to kill him and the Police Department behaved insubordinately.

Part of the argument of the officers who shot Reggie was that he had attacked one of them and took his gun. This was their major claim. They also said that only one of them had actually shot Reggie. The facts, however, speak for themselves. According to the Death Certificate and autopsy report, Reggie was shot eight times from point-blank range. The Doctor who performed the autopsy told me himself that two bullets entered the side of my brother's head, four bullets were sprayed into his back, and two bullets struck him in the back of his legs. It is obvious that unnecessary force was used by the police and that it is extremely difficult to shoot someone in his back when he is attacking or approaching you.

After experiencing a situation like this and researching South Africa I believe that to a large degree, justice may only exist as rhetoric. I find it difficult to talk of true justice when the oppression of my people both at home and abroad attests to the fact that inequality and injustice are serious problems whereby Blacks and Third World people are perpetually short-changed by society. Something has to be done about the way in which this world is set up. Although it is a difficult task, we do have the power to make a change.

—Willie J. Jordan, Jr.
EGL 487, Section 58, November 14, 1984

It is my privilege to dedicate this book to the future life of Willie J. Jordan, Jr.

SCRIPTS

A story can sound so good over lunch; it's so tough to get it to come out of the typewriter the same way.

CHARLTON HESTON

THE most popular writing in America is meant to be *heard,* not read. When we watch a situation comedy on television, or go to a movie, or tune in to a radio news program, we easily forget that the language we are listening to was originally *written.* Even with today's electronic media, the written word still precedes the performance; the most visually impressive movie probably started out as an idea in a scriptwriter's head. And much of what we hear on radio and television came out of a typewriter before it went over the air.

Scripts come in a variety of shapes and sizes. A filmscript, generally called a screenplay, is defined in a leading practical manual as "a written composition designed to serve as a sort of work diagram for the motion picture director."[1] Screenplays usually contain dialogue, along with a description of action and directions for camera and lighting setups. The final working script, incorporating all the changes, is often called the shooting script. Each media industry has its own script requirements and conventions. Because of time and budget constraints, television filmscripts, usually referred to as teleplays, frequently need to be more polished and "camera-ready" than movie scripts.

All scripts have one thing in common: they are intended to be read aloud. Scripts assume the primacy of the speaking voice. If a scripted word, phrase, idion, or speech rhythm sounds unnatural, a performer or director will change it. Thus, scripts are rarely treated as finished products but are constantly revised to conform as closely as possible to the inflections of the spoken voice. Of course, the voices will be affected by the particular setting or action. A movie script portraying, for example, the infantry in Kuwait talking about recent combat would sound very different from a television anchorperson's script reporting a similar battle. The rhythm, tone, emphasis, diction, and pacing would be dramatically different, though each script might be considered professionally well crafted with respect to its overall purpose.

Scriptwriting differs from most other kinds of writing because it is largely invisible. Movie scripts, for example, are rarely published, and when they are, they tend to be read by people who have already seen the film. A good script is so closely connected to the total effect of the film that in itself it may seem barely significant as a piece of writing. A well-crafted screenplay, in other words, should not be thought of as similar to a literary drama, which can often be rewardingly read without benefit of performance. In fact, many television and movie directors react skeptically to scripts that appear too polished, that sound too much like finished plays. Such scripts may read well but not translate easily into image and action. After all, most films consist of long stretches of action without any dialogue.

Radio scripts function differently. In radio, voice counts for everything, and any silence seems unendurably long. Radio stations select performers largely based on the quality of their voice. Most radio advertising, for example, depends almost entirely on the dramatic use of highly idiosyncratic and memorable voices. Disc jockeys, though they seldom use scripts for anything other than commercials or announcements, build reputations on unique styles of delivery. In the 1930s and 1940s—during the golden age of radio—people listened to soap operas with the same avidity with which they now watch them (the old daytime melodramas were mostly sponsored by soap products—hence their name). So identifiable were the voices on these programs that listeners could easily distinguish the good guys from the bad guys on the basis of speech char-

1. Lewis Herman, *A Practical Manual of Screen Playwriting for Theater and Television Films* (1952; 1974).

acteristics alone. In television, where someone can be quickly characterized by physical appearance and gesture, the individual voice plays a far less dramatic role. One has only to compare a radio and a television commercial for the same product to note how differently scripts are created for each medium.

Another way to appreciate differences in techniques between two media is to study the film adaptation of a work of literature. Though critics often praise a film that stays especially close to its original text, a literal, word-by-word translation of prose into visual image is seldom feasible and not always desirable. One author who has seen her fiction transferred to the screen, Joyce Carol Oates, wonders why there should be any "enmity" between authors and screenwriters. She argues that an adaptation is really a collaborative enterprise; it is "not only a perfectly legitimate and exciting activity, it is an artistic venture of its own." The great novelist Vladimir Nabokov, after trying to turn his own masterpiece, *Lolita,* into a screenplay, was finally forced to admire the "unfaithful" though "first-rate film with magnificent actors" that the director Stanley Kubrick managed to create: "he saw my novel in one way," said Nabokov, "I saw it in another."

This section on "Scripts" includes Robert Geller's film adaptation of Ernest Hemingway's well-known short story "Soldier's Home" (which appears in the "Classics" section). A comparison of the film adaptation with the original story provides an excellent opportunity to see how an experienced screenwriter works with material never intended for film. "Soldier's Home" seems at first to have little cinematic potential. The story is very short and lacks the full narrative development a film director might prefer. More importantly, the impact of the story occurs mainly in the narrator's voice and is not fully reflected in external activity. A film that tried to be a perfect visual enactment of the original story would certainly lack the imagery and action required for compelling drama.

As even a cursory reading shows, Geller's script differs sharply from Hemingway's story. The atmosphere, the psychological tone, and the moral nuance have been retained, but Geller has made significant changes. He has introduced new characters (the flirtatious Roselle Simmons) and developed others (Mr. Krebs, merely mentioned in the short story, is physically present in the screenplay). Geller has dramatized incidents that Hemingway only alludes to (Kreb's pool playing) and has created situations not in the original story (the scene in front of the "Greek's soda shop"). Though Geller retains nearly verbatim several crucial stretches of dialogue, most of the conversation in the script was invented expressly for the film.

Like many adaptations, Geller's version of Hemingway's story depends on the careful selection of detail. The screenwriter must be particularly alert to those parts of an original text not fully developed by the author. These implicit images, characters, locations, and incidents—elements of the literary work a reader may not always consciously attend to—frequently allow the scriptwriter to work around all of the noncinematic portions of a story. An experienced scriptwriter reads literature with a keen eye for barely noticeable descriptive details that can then be integrated into the overall visual texture of the film. In "Soldier's Home," for example, Geller turns Hemingway's brief reference to the town library into a separate scene that also helps establish character and moves the plot.

The striking contrasts between Geller's screenplay and the original short story reflect, of course, the fundamental differences between prose fiction and film. Hemingway expects a reader to *hear* silently the way the narrative voice imitates the nervous consciousness of the story's main character. To duplicate this central feature of the story, Geller resorts to the contrivance of a narrative voice-over, and he fabricates dialogue that clearly articulates in actual conversation Harold Krebs's inner thoughts. Film does not easily adapt to long stretches of private consciousness. Nor can film readily convey the complexity of the narrator's attitude toward the various characters—perhaps the essential drama of serious fiction—an attitude that can be identified from the behavior of the narrative voice as irony, sympathy, satire, parody, and so on. One of the most important critical questions to ask of Hemingway's "Soldier's Home" is, what does the narrator think of Harold Krebs? How you answer that question will most likely affect how you judge the success of Geller's adaptation.

Besides differing in basic techniques, film and literature often vary widely in their assumptions about their respective audiences. A screenwriter often makes major changes in a story's plot to satisfy popular demands or to clarify a deliberate ambiguity. When Flannery O'Connor's "The Life You Save May Be Your Own" (in the "Classics" section) was adapted for television in the 1950s, the conclusion was completely changed to end the story on a happier note. That change had nothing to do with the technical problems of translating literature to the screen but was entirely a matter of how the television network felt its audience would react to the story's original ending. In "Soldier's Home," Geller introduces no such major distortions, yet the consideration of an audience still plays a significant part in shaping the script. Why, for example, does the narrator at the end of the film repeat all of Hemingway's concluding paragraph *except* the final sentence?

Originally adapted for educational television, "Soldier's Home" was intended for a relatively small viewing audience. With scripts prepared for prime-time network television, however, audience becomes an extremely important commercial calculation. Television shows live or die according to audience ratings, and scriptwriters almost always need to shape their material with respect to elaborate guidelines and specifications so that the individual episodes of a series will follow a similar format and reflect consistent values. Networks spend small fortunes testing shows on sample audiences and using attitudinal research methods to develop the final program. For example, after assessing the preliminary audience reactions in 1976 to the pilot of the enormously popular series "Charlie's Angels," the ABC research department offered such advice as the following:

> 1. Develop the three female leading characters so that they can be made more distinctive, different, and recognizable from each other. Their motives for working for Charlie should be made clear with the emphasis on a moral desire to fight crime rather than what viewers felt was a "lust for money, clothes, or a sexual attachment to their boss." . . .
>
> 4. Improve future story lines by developing plots that are more plausible and straightforward, have greater mystery and suspense, are less corny and predictable and far less contrived.
>
> 5. Improve the dialogue in future story lines by avoiding "stock cops-and-robbers phrases" and "sexual allusions or cliches" in the talk with Charlie. . . .[1]

Scriptwriters would then be expected to adhere to such guidelines when constructing new episodes.

Prime-time television often toes a fine line between social controversy and dramatic convention. Popular new shows must appear lively and original without violating the values of mass audiences. Shows that present sharp opinions—the bigotry of an Archie Bunker, for example—are careful to neutralize those opinions by having other characters on the show tactfully express alternative ideas and attitudes. Unfortunately, the fear of offending any large group fre-

1. *Source:* Sally Bedell, *Up the Tube* (1981).

quently results in dramatic predictability. If an elderly person on a sitcom were to make a nasty crack about the behavior of today's teenagers, the next scene would more than likely show a teenager acting in a remarkably saintly manner. The elderly person would then be pleasantly surprised and the viewing public reassured that the show was sensitive and responsive to contemporary values. Later, if the same teenager happened to complain that old people had no energy, the audience could be fairly certain that within the next few scenes remarkably spry grandparents would bounce through several rugged sets of tennis—and, of course, thrash an exhausted teenager.

An actual example of how mass entertainment will sometimes take greater risks with an audience's presumed values can be seen in "The Blackout," Richard B. Eckhaus's award-winning script for the well-known television show "The Jeffersons." The writer chose a controversial subject: looting in a black neighborhood during a citywide power failure. The script dealt openly and even ironically with racism by having the main character, who is black, arrested as a looter while trying to protect his own store. The climax of the story occurred while a frustrated George Jefferson paced a crowded jail cell vehemently protesting his innocence:

> GEORGE: I own a chain of cleanin' stores. I made my way up BY MYSELF, and I don't need to steal. I ain't looted from nobody, and I don't belong in this dump . . . That's all I gotta say. *(George angrily sits down on the cell floor.)*
>
> SECOND INMATE *(looking down at George):* Man . . . you're really somethin'. You DO think you're too good for us, don't you?

Though George is legally in the right (he *has* been wrongfully arrested) and is morally in the right (he *is* innocent of stealing), he is nevertheless by the script's standards dramatically and culturally *wrong*. By assuming a proud, holier-than-thou stance (always a mistake in situation comedies), he has disassociated himself from his ethnic and neighborhood roots—a worse act, the script suggests, than the looting itself. The remainder of the episode shows how George must come to terms with his momentary violation of ethnic values that not everyone in the audience would necessarily share. The spectacular success of Alex Haley's *Roots* (see "Best-sellers"), however, which reached an unprecedented television audience in January 1977, the year before "The Blackout" was aired, quite clearly helped prepare viewers for George's final—though still cautious—understanding of the importance of his cultural origins.

Radio, television, and the movies entertain and instruct us daily, even hourly, yet rarely do they confront us with a single written word. Scripts are not intended for a reading audience. When you read the screenplay of "Soldier's Home" or "The Blackout" you should keep in mind that they were written with the sole purpose of being performed. They are not finished texts in the same sense as are most of the other selections in this book. The reader needs to supply—as did the actors and directors—the missing dimensions of sound, image, and movement to bring a script to life. It is one thing to read Abbott and Costello's famous "Who's on First" routine; it is quite another to see and hear the two great comedians perform it. Reading a script is like going behind the scenes; we see what was not intended to be seen. As the audience of a print advertisement, news item, essay, or story, you are doing exactly what the writer intended—reading it. Scripts, however, require that you put yourself in the role of two different audiences: the individual reader of the actual script and the larger, intended audience of the imagined performance.

Orson Welles / The War of the Worlds 1938

Born in Kenosha, Wisconsin, in 1915, Orson Welles had earned, by the age of twenty-six, an international reputation as an actor and director in radio, theater, and cinema. Welles's virtuosity included celebrated performances as a playwright, cartoonist, and journalist. He wrote several syndicated columns.

In 1937, Welles launched the Mercury Theatre on the Air to present a regular series of radio broadcasts of dramatic adaptations of famous novels. On October 31, 1938, Welles's "splendid purple-velvet voice" came on the radio to announce a story appropriate to a Halloween evening—H. G. Wells's The War of the Worlds, *written in 1898, depicting an invasion from Mars. Despite several reminders to the audience that they were listening to an adaptation of a novel, the authentic-sounding details and tones of the broadcast, as the following excerpts dramatize, threw much of the nation's population into mass hysteria.*

ANNOUNCER

Ladies and gentlemen, here is the latest bulletin from the Intercontinental Radio News, Toronto, Canada: Professor Morse of Macmillan University reports observing a total of three explosions on the planet Mars, between the hours of 7:45 p.m. and 9:20 p.m., eastern standard time. This confirms earlier reports received from American observatories. Now, nearer home, comes a special announcement from Trenton, New Jersey. It is reported that at 8:50 p.m. a huge, flaming object, believed to be a meteorite, fell on a farm in the neighborhood of Grovers Mill, New Jersey, twenty-two miles from Trenton. The flash in the sky was visible within a radius of several hundred miles and the noise of the impact was heard as far north as Elizabeth.

We have dispatched a special mobile unit to the scene, and we will have our commentator, Mr. Phillips, give you a word description as soon as he can reach there from Princeton. In the meantime, we take you to the Hotel Martinet in Brooklyn, where Bobby Millette and his orchestra are offering a program of dance music. (SWING BAND FOR 20 SECONDS . . . THEN CUT)

ANNOUNCER

We take you now to Grovers Mill, New Jersey.
(CROWD NOISES . . . POLICE SIRENS)

PHILLIPS

Ladies and gentlemen, this is Carl Phillips again, at the Wilmuth farm, Grovers Mill, New Jersey. Professor Pierson and myself made the eleven miles from Princeton in ten minutes. Well, I . . . I hardly know where to begin, to paint for you a word picture of the strange scene before my eyes, like something out of a modern Arabian Nights. Well, I just got here. I haven't had a chance to look around yet. I guess that's *it.* Yes, I guess that's the . . . *thing,* directly in front of me, half buried in a vast pit. Must have struck with terrific force. The ground is covered with splinters of a tree it must have struck on its way down. What I can see of the . . . object itself doesn't look very much like a meteor, at least not the meteors I've seen. It looks more like a huge cylinder. It has a diameter of . . . what would you say, Professor Pierson? . . .

ANNOUNCER

Ladies and gentlemen, I have a grave announcement to make. Incredible as it may seem, both the observations of science and the evidence of our eyes lead to the inescapable assumption that those strange beings who landed in the Jersey farmlands tonight are the vanguard of an invading army from the planet Mars. The battle which took place tonight at Grovers Mill has ended in one of the most startling defeats ever suffered by an army in modern times; seven thousand men armed with rifles and machine guns pitted against a single fighting machine of the invaders from Mars. One hundred and twenty known survivors. The rest strewn over the battle area from Grovers Mill to Plainsboro crushed and trampled to death under the metal feet of the monster, or burned to cinders by its heat-ray. The monster is now in control of the middle section of New Jersey and has effectively cut the state through its center. Communication lines are down from Pennsylvania to the Atlantic Ocean. Railroad tracks are torn and service from New York to Philadelphia discontinued except routing some of the trains through Allentown and Phoenixville. Highways to the north, south, and west are clogged with frantic human traffic. Police and army reserves are unable to control the mad flight. By morning the fugitives will have swelled Philadelphia, Camden and Trenton, it is estimated, to twice their normal population.

At this time martial law prevails throughout New Jersey and eastern Pennsylvania. We take you now to Washington for a special broadcast on the National Emergency . . . the Secretary of the Interior. . . .

ANNOUNCER

I'm speaking from the roof of Broadcasting Building, New York City. The bells you hear are ringing to warn the people to evacuate the city as the Martians approach. Estimated in last two hours three million people have moved out along the roads to the north, Hutchison River Parkway still kept open for motor traffic. Avoid bridges to Long Island . . . hopelessly jammed. All communication with Jersey shore closed ten minutes ago. No more defenses. Our army wiped out . . . artillery, air force, everything wiped out. This may be the last broadcast. We'll stay here to the end. . . . People are holding service below us . . . in the cathedral. (VOICES SINGING HYMN)

Now I look down the harbor. All manner of boats, overloaded with fleeing population, pulling out from docks. (SOUND OF BOAT WHISTLES)

Streets are all jammed. Noise in crowds like New Year's Eve in city. Wait a minute. . . . Enemy now in sight above the Palisades. Five great machines. First one is crossing river. I can see it from here, wading the Hudson like a man wading through a brook. . . . A bulletin's handed me. . . . Martian cylinders are falling all over the country. One outside Buffalo, one in Chicago, St. Louis . . . seem to be timed and spaced. . . . Now the first machine reaches the shore. He stands watching, looking over the city. His steel, cowlish head is even with the skyscrapers. He waits for the others. They rise like a line of new towers on the city's west side. . . . Now they're lifting their metal hands. This is the end now. Smoke comes out . . . black smoke, drifting over the city. People in the streets see it now. They're running towards the East River . . . thousands of them, dropping in like rats. Now the smoke's spreading faster. It's reached Times Square. People trying to run away from it, but it's no use. They're falling like flies. Now the smoke's crossing Sixth Avenue . . . Fifth Avenue . . . 100 yards away . . . it's fifty feet. . . .

Bud Abbott and Lou Costello / Who's on First 1945

The zany classic comedy routine "Who's on First," which might have been written by Samuel Beckett for the Theatre of the Absurd, had a long vaudeville history before Bud Abbott and Lou Costello gave it their special imprint. The routine—sometimes played long, sometimes short—moved with the two through radio, movies, and television. Often played live and laced with ad libs, the script clearly has no definitive text. The version printed below is a transcript from their film The Gay Nineties *(1945).*

Both comedians were born in New Jersey; Bud Abbott in Asbury Park in 1900 and Lou Costello in Paterson in 1908. They struggled through burlesque and vaudeville for nine years until 1938, when they brought their relentless corny bickering to radio and became overnight sensations.

LOU: Look, Abbott, if you're the coach, you must know all the players.

BUD: I certainly do.

LOU: Well, you know, I never met the guys, so you'll have to tell me their names and then I'll know who's playing on the team.

BUD: Oh, I'll tell you their names. But, you know, strange as it may seem, they give these ballplayers nowadays very peculiar names.

LOU: You mean funny names?

BUD: Strange names, pet names like Dizzy Dean.

LOU: And his brother Daffy.

BUD: Daffy Dean—

LOU: And their French cousin.

BUD: French?

LOU: Goofé.

BUD: Goofé Dean. Oh, I see. Well, let's see, we have on the bags, we have Who's on first, What's on second. I Don't Know is on third.

LOU: That's what I want to find out.

BUD: I say, Who's on first, What's on second, I Don't Know's on third.

LOU: Are you the manager?

BUD: Yes.

LOU: You're gonna be the coach, too?

BUD: Yes.

LOU: Do you know the fellas' names?

BUD: Well, I should.

LOU: Well, then who's on first?

BUD: Yes.

LOU: I mean the fella's name.

BUD: Who.

LOU: The guy on first.

BUD: Who!

LOU: The first baseman.

BUD: WHO!

LOU: The guy playing first.

BUD: Who is on first.

LOU: I'm asking *you* who's on first.

BUD: That's the man's name.

LOU: That's whose name?

BUD: Yes.

LOU: Well, go ahead and tell me.
BUD: That's it.
LOU: That's who?
BUD: Yes!
LOU: Look, you got a first baseman?
BUD: Certainly.
LOU: Who's playing first?
BUD: That's right.
LOU: When you pay off the first baseman every month, who gets the money?
BUD: Every dollar of it.
LOU: All I'm trying to find out is the fella's name on first base.
BUD: Who.
LOU: The guy that gets the money.
BUD: That's it.
LOU: Who gets the money?
BUD: He does, every dollar. Sometimes his wife comes down and collects it.
LOU: Whose wife?
BUD: Yes. What's wrong with that?
LOU: Look, all I wanna know is, when you sign up the first baseman, how does he sign his name to the contract?
BUD: Who.
LOU: The guy.
BUD: Who.
LOU: How does he sign his name?
BUD: That's how he signs it.
LOU: Who?
BUD: Yes.
LOU: All I'm trying to find out is what's the guy's name on first base?
BUD: No, What is on second base.
LOU: I'm not asking you who's on second.
BUD: Who's on first.
LOU: One base at a time!
BUD: Well, don't change the players around.
LOU: I'm not changing nobody.
BUD: Take it easy, buddy.
LOU: I'm only asking you, who's the guy on first base?
BUD: That's right.
LOU: Okay.
BUD: All right.
LOU: I mean, what's the guy's name on first base.
BUD: No, What is on second.
LOU: I'm not asking you who's on second.
BUD: Who's on first.
LOU: I don't know.
BUD: Oh, he's on third. We're not talking about him. Now let's get—
LOU: Now *how* did I get on third base?
BUD: Why, you mentioned his name.
LOU: If I mentioned the third baseman's name, who did I say was playing third?
BUD: No, Who's playing first.
LOU: What's on first?
BUD: What's on second.
LOU: I don't know.
BUD: *He's* on third.
LOU: There I go, back on third again.

BUD: I can't help it.

LOU: Now, will you stay on third base? And don't go off it..

BUD: All right, now what do you want to know?

LOU: Now, who's playing third base?

BUD: Why do you insist on putting Who on third base?

LOU: What am I putting on third?

BUD: No, What is on second.

LOU: You don't want *who* on second?

BUD: Who is on first.

LOU: I don't know!

BOTH: Third base!

LOU: Look, you got outfield?

BUD: Sure.

LOU: The left fielder's name?

BUD: Why.

LOU: I just thought I'd ask you.

BUD: Well, I just thought I'd tell you.

LOU: Then tell me who's playing left field.

BUD: Who is playing *first*.

LOU: I'm not—Stay out of the infield! I wanna know what's the guy's name in left field.

BUD: No, What is on second.

LOU: I'm not *asking* you who's on second.

BUD: Who's on first.

LOU: I don't know.

BOTH: Third base!

LOU: And the left fielder's name?

BUD: Why!

LOU: Because.

BUD: Oh, he's *center* field.

LOU: Bey-eeyh-echh

BUD: You know his name as well as I do.

LOU: Look, look, look you got a pitcher on the team?

BUD: Sure.

LOU: The pitcher's name?

BUD: Tomorrow.

LOU: You don't wanna tell me today?

BUD: I'm telling you today.

LOU: Then go ahead.

BUD: Tomorrow.

LOU: What time?

BUD: What time what?

LOU: What time tomorrow you going to tell me who's pitching.

BUD: Now listen, Who is not pitching. Who—

LOU: I'll break your arm you say "Who's on first." I want to know what's the pitcher's name.

BUD: What's on second.

LOU: I don't know.

BOTH: Third base!

LOU: You got a catcher?

BUD: Certainly.

LOU: The catcher's name?

BUD: Today.

LOU: Today. And tomorrow's pitching?

BUD: Now you've got it.

LOU: All we got is a couple of days of the week. You know, I'm a catcher, too.

BUD: So they tell me.

LOU: I get behind the plate, do some fancy catching, tomorrow's pitching on my team and the heavy hitter gets up.

BUD: Yes.

LOU: Now, the heavy hitter bunts the ball. When he bunts the ball, me being a good catcher, I'm going to throw the guy out at first base, so I pick up the ball and throw it to who?

BUD: Now, that's the first thing you've said right.

LOU: I don't even know what I'm *talking* about!

BUD: That's all you have to do.

LOU: Is to throw the ball to first base?

BUD: *Yes.*

LOU: Now, who's got it?

BUD: Naturally.

LOU: Look, if I throw the ball to first base, somebody's got to get it. Now, who has it?

BUD: Naturally.

LOU: Who?

BUD: Naturally.

LOU: Naturally?

BUD: Naturally.

LOU: So, I pick up the ball and I throw it to Naturally?

BUD: No, you don't. You throw the ball to Who!

LOU: Naturally.

BUD: That's different.

LOU: That's what I say.

BUD: You're not saying it—

LOU: I throw the ball to Naturally?

BUD: You throw it to Who.

LOU: Naturally.

BUD: That's it.

LOU: That's what I said.

BUD: Listen, you ask me.

LOU: I throw the ball to who?

BUD: Naturally.

LOU: Now you ask me.

BUD: You throw the ball to Who.

LOU: Naturally.

BUD: That's it.

LOU: Same as you!

BUD: Don't change them around.

LOU: Same as you!

BUD: Okay, now get it over with.

LOU: I throw the ball to who. Whoever it is drops the ball and the guy runs to second.

BUD: Yes.

LOU: Who picks up the ball and throws it to what. What throws it to I don't know. I don't know throws it back to tomorrow. Triple play.

BUD: Yes.

LOU: Another guy gets up and hits a long fly to because. Why? I don't know. He's on third and I don't *give* a darn.

BUD: —eh, what?

LOU: I said, "I don't *give* a darn."

BUD: Oh, that's our shortstop.

LOU: Ayeiiii!

Batten, Barton, Durstine, and Osborne / Ring around the Collar

ca. 1975

One of the most successful and long-running campaigns in television history, the "Ring around the Collar" commercials for Wisk were launched in 1969 by the advertising firm of Batten, Barton, Durstine, and Osborne (BBD&O). Though shoppers frequently complain about the commercials, their irritation apparently does not stand in the way of their buying the product.

Courtesy of Lever Brothers Co.

GONDOLIER: Of love I sing . . .

la-la-la-la.

ANNOUNCER: Those dirty rings . . . You tried scrubbing, even spraying, and still . . .

you've got ring-around-the-collar.

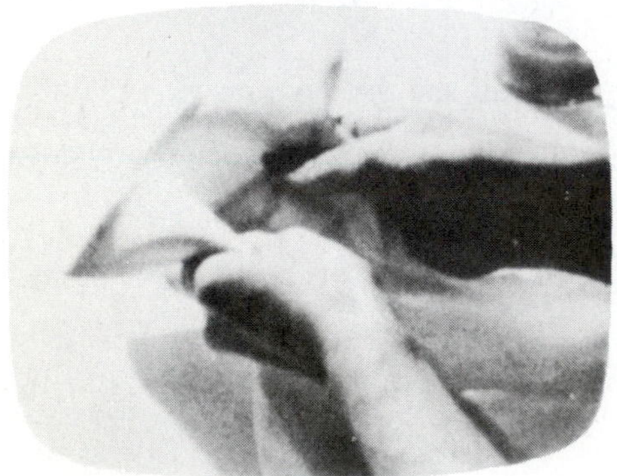

before you start to wash.

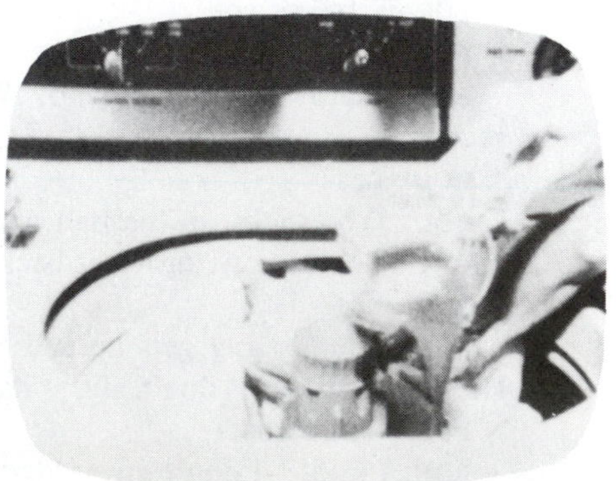

Then gets your whole wash really clean.

But you've got ring-around-the-collar-la-la.

WIFE: My powder didn't work.

Try Wisk.

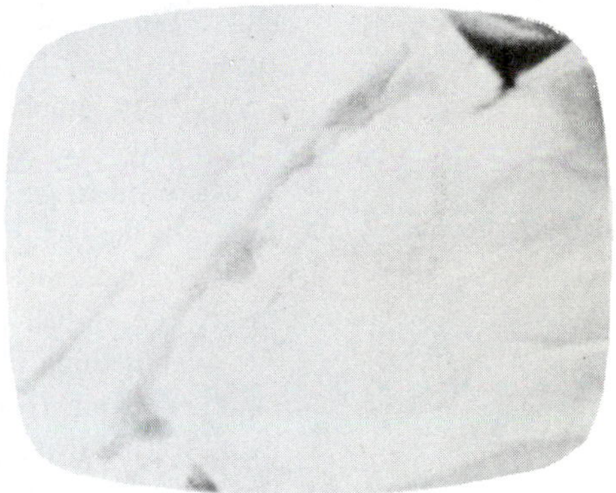
Wisk sinks in and starts to clean

HUSBAND: No more ring-around-the-collar-la-la!

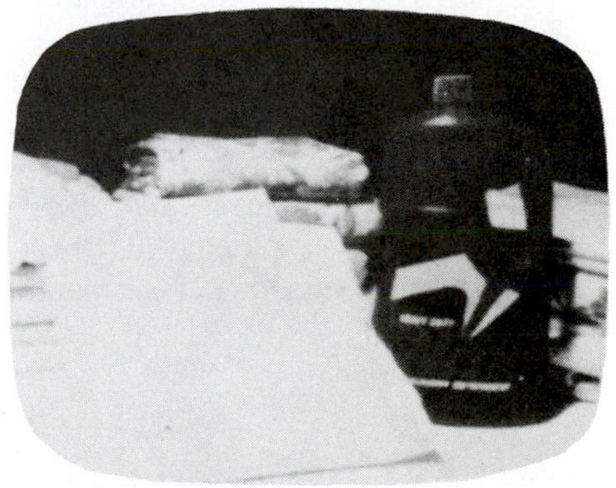
ANNOUNCER: Use Wisk around the collar for ring-around-the-collar.

Dick Orkin and Bert Berdis / Puffy Sleeves: A *Time* Magazine Commercial 1977

''Dick and Bert'' call their brand of radio advertising humor ''situation comedy commercials.'' Believing that advertising too often portrays ideal people in unreal situations, the team writes instead about an imperfect world:

> *People who dribble a little bit, people who get arrested for wearing their wife's housecoat to go out to buy a* Time *magazine, a guy that gets fired for reading* Time, *just the little stupid things that everyone does.*

Their radio campaign for Time *magazine aired in the mid-1970s; ''Puffy Sleeves'' was one of the most popular spots.*

BERT: Pardon me, sir, would you step over here to the patrol car please?

DICK: Oh, h-hello, officer.

BERT: Do you have business in this neighborhood, sir?

DICK: Yes, I live f-four blocks from here . . . It's the brick colonial with the crack in the driveway.

BERT: What are you doing out this time of night, sir?

DICK: Well, I got all ready for bed and darn it if I didn't forget to pick up a copy of *Time* magazine at the newsstand today.

BERT: What type of coat would you call that, sir?

DICK: Th-this? This is a h-housecoat. See, I spilled cocoa on mine and I just grabbed my wife's. I guess the puffy sleeves look a little silly . . . *(laugh)*. . . .

BERT: Want to get in the car, sir?

DICK: In the car . . .?

SOUND EFFECTS: *(door open)*

DICK: See, I just don't go to bed without a *Time* movie review or something from the modern living section . . .

BERT: Yes, sir. *(car pulls away)*

DICK: I tried reading something else, but there isn't anything like *Time*. Do you know, officer, how many editorial awards *Time* magazine has won?

BERT: No, sir.

DICK: And *Time* is so respected—and I'm a firm believer—along with Winston Churchill . . . that you are uh . . . what you read . . . *(pause)*. . . . Oh please don't send me up the river just for wearing puffy sleeves.

BERT: You're home, sir.

DICK: I'm home—oh . . . I thou—thank—God bless you. . . .

SOUND EFFECTS: *(door open)*

DICK: . . . Okay—bye.

ANNOUNCER: *Time* magazine makes everything more interesting, including you.

Robert Geller / Hemingway's "Soldier's Home": A Screenplay 1976

In the mid-1970s, Educational Television, with the support of the National Endowment for the Humanities, launched a series of films based on classic American short stories. Besides Ernest Hemingway's "Soldier's Home," the series offered remarkable film adaptations of such stories as John Cheever's "The Five-Forty-Eight," Sherwood Anderson's "I'm a Fool," Stephen Crane's "The Blue Hotel," and Richard Wright's "Almos' a Man." Much acclaimed, the short-story series is responsible for some of the finest television movies in the history of the medium.

Robert Geller is a scriptwriter and the author of numerous articles on film and television. He served as the executive producer of the "American Short Story" series.

1. Prologue. In sepia. Eight or ten young men are being huddled together for a fraternity picture. All dressed in high white collars. Most wear silver-rimmed glasses. Austere building in background. No laughter or chatter.

NARRATOR (*off camera*): Krebs went to the war from a Methodist college in Kansas. There is a picture which shows him among his fraternity brothers. . . .

Photographer motions them to close ranks, and sheep-like they shuffle closer. One young man, Harold Krebs, stands slightly to the side and moves just a fraction after the command "hold it."

NARRATOR (*off camera*): He enlisted in the Army in 1917. . . .

Cut to Photographer and "explosion" of his camera gun.

Cut to 2. Stock footage of WWI, expository in nature, and of returning veterans. Not meant to editorialize about the war.

NARRATOR (*off camera*): . . . and did not return to the United States until the second division returned from the Rhine in 1919.

3. Exterior. Dusk. Empty train depot in rural town. Krebs with duffle bag. Platform is deserted, with the exception of the station master and one passenger, neither of whom pays Krebs any attention.

Krebs crosses tracks deftly. Stops at depot to catch breath. Tattered signs flap in wind: "Buy U.S. Bonds," etc. At the front end of the platform a banner with "WELCOME HOME YANKS" droops limply from a worn cornice.

NARRATOR (*off camera*): By the time Krebs returned to his home town the greeting of heroes was over. He came back much too late.

4. Interior. Night. Dissolve to dining room of Krebs house. Dinner is over. Harold is still in uniform. Mr. and Mrs. Krebs and Marge hunt for words. There is no real jubilation or ease. Harold is lighting up. Faces of family watch.

MR. KREBS: Son . . . You smoke lots in battle? You seem to do it . . . naturally.

HAROLD: Not really . . . I just picked it up.

MARGE (*enthusiastic*): Did you actually smoke, in the war, Hare? Didn't they see you lighting up? The Germans?

HAROLD: Uh . . . uh. We smoked mostly when we were bored.

MRS. KREBS: Bored! Little chance you had to be bored . . .

HAROLD: We were. I was. A lot of the time.

(*Silence. Ticking of clock. It is after 11:00* P.M.)

MRS. KREBS: Harold, you must be tired . . . All that traveling. And we've asked so many questions.

HAROLD: I'm fine.

MR. KREBS: Well . . . it's gettin' late. I gotta go out in the county tomorrow. We'll get to talk . . . about what you wanna be doin'. Plenty of time.

HAROLD: Yes . . . I'll need a week or so . . .

MRS. KREBS: Of course. Let's just be thankful that you're home safe. Let us be thankful to our Dear Lord (*her eyes are raised*) that you're back home. Oh, Harold, we did pray for you. And each Sunday Reverend Nelson . . .

MR. KREBS (*interrupts with a yawn*): Folks . . . I'm goin' up. Welcome home, Harold.

(*Mr. Krebs extends his hand.*)

HAROLD: Night, Dad . . . It was a fine dinner . . . Guess I'll go up, too. (*He starts to follow Mr. Krebs out.*)

5. Interior. Hallway at foot of stairs.

MRS. KREBS (*to Harold at the foot of the stairs*): Son . . . Marjorie and I could fix up a special breakfast. Serve it to you in bed. Remember when you had those awful winter coughs and . . .

HAROLD: Not tomorrow, Mom . . . I'll want to get up early, and . . .

MRS. KREBS: Hare?

HAROLD: Mom?

MRS. KREBS (*moves to hug him*): Sleep well.

HAROLD (*stiffens, hugs her back*): I will . . . thanks . . . for everything.

Cut to 6. Interior. Night. Harold's room. Dimly lit. Flowered wallpaper. Pan to boyhood mementos, which are sparse save for some scouting medals and a trophy for track & field. Harold unpacks. Looks at photo of college fraternity at Methodist school. Considers replacing it with picture of himself and another soldier with two coarse, older German women. The military uniforms are too large.

Krebs moves around his smallish room. Picks up the trophy and buffs it. Takes out a clarinet from a book shelf and slowly assembles it. Tinkers tentatively with some scales. Begins to undress and neatly pile clothes on chair near his bed. Cranks up his phonograph. It still works. He smiles. Climbs into bed with a record playing.

Krebs lights cigarette and leans on elbow, staring out at the quiet, empty streets..

MR. KREBS (*off camera*) (*knocking at Harold's door*): Harold. Could you turn it down? It's late, and I need to be fresh and ginger tomorrow.

7. The following shots take place in one day, during which we get the feelings and rhythms of Harold being home contrasted against the rhythms of the town.

Exterior. Point of view Krebs House. Day. Harold's window. We see the shade, which is pulled half down with the tassle hanging. We hear the sound of footsteps on the porch and the rattling of bottles as the milkman puts the milk on the porch and takes the old bottles.

Cut to interior. Harold's bedroom. Day. Close-up of Harold's face. He's lying awake in bed listening to the sounds of the milkman. He's been up for a while.

Cut to interior/exterior. Harold's window. Day. Harold moves into frame, raises the shade, then looks down, out the window. Then Harold's face, close up. Then the sound of a factory whistle in the distance.

Exterior. Krebs house. Day. Harold's point of view. Looking down at the milkman walking away from the house carrying empty bottles away in a rack.

Exterior. Krebs porch and house. Day. Harold has a cup of coffee. He's wearing his army overcoat to protect him against the morning cold. Sits on the edge of the step and leans back against the pillar. Lights up a cigarette. The early morning sun comes through the trees.

Then the procession of men going to work begins. Through the bushes and through the empty spaces between the trees, Harold sees the working-class men of the town on their way to the factory. The procession begins with only a few, but builds in tempo as it gets closer to the hour to be in the factory. Then a few stragglers, and then it is quiet again.

Some of the images we see are two men walking carrying lunch pails. A third man behind them runs to catch up with them, and they then walk on together. Some of the figures are partially masked—seen through the screen of bushes—so we pan with them, seeing their lunch pails swinging and their footsteps on the pavement.

A car goes by carrying some workmen. The sounds of other cars are heard going to work and their image/presence is suggested in the movement of Harold's eyes as they go by up the street. As the procession ends, in the distance the sound of the factory whistle, which heralds the start of the day's work.

The newspaper boy throws the newspaper up the walk, and Harold picks it up.

Interior. Harold's bedroom. Day. Point of views. A series of images of Harold follow that suggest his day, to be punctuated with some activities that take place around him, such as:

A. Marge leaves for school, maybe picked up by another girl.
B. Mr. Krebs's car leaves the house. (Perhaps this could occur earlier.)
C. Two church ladies come and pick up Mrs. Krebs. We hear their voices and see them walk away from the house.

Interior. Harold's room. Day. Harold reads the sports page of the newspaper, smokes, rests, and plays his clarinet.

When Harold plays his clarinet, he plays some scales to reacquaint himself with the instrument. His playing at first is very tentative—he is feeling for the instrument and for his own voice, his own theme or melody. We would use his music as a means of expressing Harold's mood. The music creates a space for him separate from the world around him.

Exterior. Krebs house. Day. As the day grows late, the activities are reversed. The factory whistle blows late in the day, and then we see the tracking feet again, now worn, tired, the men slump-shouldered, trailing off to their homes.

8. Exterior. Bright morning. Harold walking to town. Is stopped by a prim old man.

MAN: Mornin', young Krebs. Welcome home. How long you back now?

HAROLD: It's two weeks, today.

MAN: Your folks said you had some very difficult times over there?

HAROLD: No . . . not that bad.

MAN: Anyhow, you must be glad to be home . . . Are you planning to go back to school?

HAROLD: No.

MAN: You going to be selling farm land with Dad? At the bank? It's a blessing when a man and his son can . . .

HAROLD (*edging away*): 'Scuse me.

(HAROLD *walks on down street.*)

MAN: Well, I'll be! You'd think he'd killed the Kaiser. Even as a young boy . . .

(*They exit; their voices trail.*)

9. Exterior. Day. Harold walks on to town. Nods back to few passersby who seem to remember him. Harold notices the young girls in town. He sees one through shop windows. He notices their pretty faces and the patterns that they make.

NARRATOR (*off camera*): Nothing was changed in the town except that the young girls had grown up. There were so many good-looking young girls.

10. Exterior. Day. Harold stops in front of bank where Mr. Krebs works as land agent.

NARRATOR (*off camera*): Before Krebs went away to the war he had never been allowed to drive the family motor car. The car always stood outside the First National Bank building where his father had an office. Now, after the war, it was still the same car.

Harold crosses the street, walks past the car to the window of his father's office. He looks in.

Reverse angle of Mr. Krebs amiably chatting with young customers Harold's age. Offers cigar. Laughter and clapping of each other's shoulders. Harold stares for several seconds and then turns away, crossing the street quickly.

11. Interior. Day. Signs indicate library room of YMCA. Harold is checking out books. Young male librarian, glasses, devoutly scrubbed, early 30s, is at checkout desk.

LIBRARIAN: Krebs. Are you Harold Krebs?

HAROLD (*startled*): Yes. That's me.

LIBRARIAN: Don't you remember me? I'm Mr. Phillips. I was your youth group advisor in the lower grades.

HAROLD: Sorry. I was involved with these books.

LIBRARIAN: Are you an avid reader? Have you tried the new Booth Tarkington? I try to encourage good reading. (*The* LIBRARIAN *begins to notice the books* KREBS *has checked out.*) My heavens. They're all books about the war. I should think that . . .

HAROLD: It helps to make sense out of things that happened. The maps and . . .

LIBRARIAN: But weren't you at Argonne? My Lord, the reports we received . . .

HAROLD (*eager to go*): Thanks . . . I'd like them for two weeks, or longer. All right?

LIBRARIAN (*stiffly*): Two weeks. That's all that's allowed. (*Pause.*) Krebs . . .

HAROLD (*begins to leave*): Sir?

LIBRARIAN: Krebs . . . you might want to check the social calendar on the way out of the building. We hold socials and dances so that you young vets can catch up with community activities. This Saturday . . .

HAROLD (*looks uninterested*): Thanks . . . I'll look. (HAROLD *exits.*)

Cut to 12. Interior. Late afternoon. Sitting room. Harold is absorbed in reading a book on the war. There is a map that he studies, trying to figure out the course of battle. Harold's mother comes in.

MRS. KREBS: I had a talk with your father last night, Harold, and he's willing for you to take the car out in the evenings.

HAROLD: Yeah? (*Still absorbed in his reading.*) Take the car out? Yeah?

MRS. KREBS: Yes. Your father has felt for some time you should be able to take the car out in the evenings whenever you wished but we only talked it over last night.

HAROLD: I'll bet you made him.

MRS. KREBS: No. It was your father's suggestion that we talk it over.

HAROLD: Yeah. I'll bet you made him.

MRS. KREBS: Harold . . . we'll be having dinner a little early this evening.

HAROLD: All right . . . Think I'll walk a little.

MRS. KREBS: Don't be late. I've cooked your favorite roast.

HAROLD (*mumbles*): All right. (*Looks back as he leaves.*)

13. Exterior. Day. Harold enters pool hall. (Close crop and only exterior of door is needed.)

Cut to 14. Interior. Pool hall. Cool and shaded. Proprietor is ex-pug. He and Harold shadow-box and exchange jabs. They say little. But Harold is at ease here as he picks up cue and chalks.

Harold looks relaxed and concentrates on each shot. Two younger boys admire his ease and relaxed style as he puts away each ball. He smokes casually.

FIRST BOY: Hey, Harold . . . betcha didn't get no time for pool in France . . . eh . . . didja?

(HAROLD *smiles benignly throughout their banter.*)

HAROLD: Nope, not much time for pool.

SECOND BOY: Hey . . . is it true you got home last 'cause they needed the best soldiers around to keep the Krauts in line?

(HAROLD *nods yes.* HAROLD *continues to pick off shots. Lets the ash on his cigarette grow precariously long. The younger boys edge closer, begging confidences. Smoke stings his eyes.*)

YOUNGER BOY: Hey, Harold . . . swear to the truth . . . Did you really kill Germans . . . right face to face . . . honest to God? With bayonets?

HAROLD (*nods*): That's what we went there for. Not to see the Eiffel Tower.

(*They are silent, not wanting to break his concentration.*)

PROPRIETOR (*off camera*): Gotta close up, Harold. Run 'em out—one, two, three—the way you always used ta . . .

NARRATOR (*off camera*): At first Krebs did not want to talk about the war at all. Later he felt the need to talk but no one wanted to hear about it. Krebs found that to be listened to at all he had to lie, and after he had done this twice he, too, had a reaction against the war and against talking about it.

(HAROLD *sizes up the last shot. The proprietor and the younger boys huddle close behind.* HAROLD'S *eyes open wide and . . . Cut to cue ball as it explodes into last remaining ball and pushes it deftly into far pockets. Ex-pug and younger boys nod in admiration.*)

15. Exterior. Late afternoon. Krebs walks tall and the younger boys follow as worshippers. All, as silhouettes, pass the same crisp, white houses. They pass war monument. Their questions are heard as echoes. No other sounds but their voices.

FIRST BOY: Harold, is it true that they chained Kraut women to their machine guns for GIs to . . . you know . . . to . . .

SECOND BOY: Hey, Harold, did you bring any of them pictures back . . . you know . . . the French ones . . .

FIRST BOY: Harold, are the German women all that great? Denny's brother said all they want to do is make love to Americans . . . Don't matter where they do it, or the time of day . . .

SECOND BOY: Hey, Harold, can you come to the dance at the Y Friday? Cripes . . . everybody wants to talk to you, and the girls in town are waiting for you to give them a tumble. Might even be some hard liquor if you're in the mood . . .

(*All through these questions, there are no other sounds or street noises. It is meant to be a parade, a parodied ceremony for* HAROLD KREBS'S *return. Shot almost as a dreamlike ceremony. The boys double-time like GIs to keep in step with their hero.*)

16. Same as preceding shot, but nearer to Krebs house. Harold begins to run. Close up as he feels the joy of movement. Knows he's late for dinner, too.

Harold collides abruptly with young man. They both struggle for balance. The man is Charlie Simmons, tall and bulky, dressed in prosperous attire of an older businessman.

CHARLIE SIMMONS: Ouch . . . Hey, what's goin on . . .

HAROLD: Sorry . . . I wasn't looking.

CHARLIE (*recovering*): Krebs! . . . Harold Krebs. When did you get back?

HAROLD: It's just two weeks now.

CHARLIE: You look fine, just fine.

HAROLD: Thanks.

CHARLIE: You workin' for your dad at the bank?

HAROLD (*hedging*): Not yet.

CHARLIE: You lookin' for a permanent line of work?

HAROLD: Might be . . .

CHARLIE (*blocking* HAROLD'S *path with his bulk*): I'm doing real well. Selling insurance. All the vets are interested and need the security. They know the future . . .

HAROLD: Makes sense.

CHARLIE: Think you'd be interested?

HAROLD: Buying some?

CHARLIE: Well . . . actually that, and maybe working with me on the selling part.

HAROLD: I'll think about it. I'm late for dinner. (*He begins to trot away.*)

CHARLIE: Hey . . . did you know I'm married now? Remember Edith Hanes? She was our class secretary and the prettiest gal in this whole town (*fishing for a compliment*).

HAROLD (*over his shoulder*): Good luck, Charlie.

17. Exterior. Night or very late afternoon. Krebs porch. Harold looks in window at his family at supper. All heads are bowed in grace. (The MOS[1] of grace exaggerates the piety.) They finally finish the prayer. Mrs. Krebs nervously eyes the clock. Harold, resigned, walks in.

18. Exterior. Greek's soda shop. Day. Car pulls up in front of soda shop with Krebs driving. Harold gets out of car and looks in window. Sees the interior, decorated with decor of period. Marge and friends are having ice-cream sodas. They are exuberant as they ''recreate'' some incident from school (*in pantomime*).

Harold looks in, raps on window, and beckons Marge to come outside. She signals to Harold that she'll be out in one minute.

BILL KENNER (*off camera*): Hey, Krebs . . . Harold Krebs . . .

(BILL KENNER: *early 20s. Dressed flamboyantly with bohemian dash. Sports cane with golden handle. He limps perceptibly into frame.*) Remember me? William Kenner. Your fellow sufferer in geometry and Latin. C'mere, my lovelies.

(KENNER *waves to two teenagers, who obediently follow.*)

HAROLD: Sure . . . Bill Kenner. I remember you. You all right?

BILL KENNER (*with bravura*): Sure . . . if losing a chunk of your knee on a mine is all right, then I'm just fine.

HAROLD (*embarrassed for the girls*): That's . . . that's too bad. You seem to be doin' well though.

KENNER: Well . . . with lovelies like these, *pourquoi s'en faire?* . . . Am I right?

1. A segment of film shot without sound.

HAROLD (*edgy*): I guess.

KENNER: You guess. Aren't we lucky to be alive? You know this little town had three killed? Lots of injured, too. In our graduating class alone . . .

HAROLD (*spots* MARGE): Here . . . Right here, Marge.

KENNER: Is that lovely mademoiselle a Krebs? (*Bows.*) May I introduce myself?

MARGE: Let's go, Hare . . .

HAROLD: Well . . . goodbye, Bill.

KENNER (*not dissuaded*): That your car?

HAROLD: My dad's.

KENNER: Splen-did work of art.

HAROLD: Thanks.

KENNER: Can you get it nights?

MARGE: (*impatient*): Har-old!

HAROLD: I guess so. Why.

KENNER: You busy this Friday?

HAROLD: Well . . . I'm not sure. Let me think about it . . .

KENNER: Think about it! About what? Let's you and I live it up, my friend. (*Girls giggle.*) There's a dance at the Y. I might even have some gen-u-ine cognac. Come by at 8:00.

HAROLD: All right . . . I'll try.

KENNER: I'll *expect* you. (*Winks.*) Bye now.

(*To* MARGE): Bye, lovely. See you on the Champs Elysées. (*Tips his hat and limps away dramatically.* HAROLD *and* MARGE *drive away.*)

19. Interior. Night. Large room of YMCA. Small crowd of fifteen to twenty is dwarfed by the place. Clusters of girls, some overly dressed and coiffed. Mr. Phillips, the librarian, and Mr. and Mrs. Charlie Simmons and chaperones are standing at punch bowl. Boys, some teenagers, busily sharing their own secrets and howling at their own jokes. Few couples are dancing.

Harold stands apart, remote from the activities, watching.

NARRATOR (*off camera*): Vaguely he wanted a girl, but he did not want to have to work to get her. He did not want to get into the intrigue and politics . . .

(*We see the usual behavior of a dance. Boys egg on one of their fellows to ask a girl to dance. A girl moves away from a boy as he approaches to ask her for a dance—as if she is too busy. Another boy approaches a girl and then veers to another girl—the first thinking he was going to ask her. All of the little intrigues of the dance.*)

NARRATOR (*off camera*): Besides, he did not really need a girl.

(KENNER *in dramatic cape and Tyrolian hat is "performing" for* ROSELLE SIMMONS, *who is flushed and heavily rouged.*)

NARRATOR (*off camera*): You did not need a girl unless you thought about them.

(*She looks toward* HAROLD, *who is obviously bored. He walks toward the door and into hallway.* ROSELLE *follows.* HAROLD *lights a cigarette.*)

NARRATOR (*off camera*): When you were really ripe for a girl you always got one. He had learned that in the army.

20. Interior. Hallway. Cases filled with trophies. Pictures of austere town philanthropist.

ROSELLE: Harold? Harold Krebs. (*For her, all conversation is a flirtation.*)

HAROLD: It's me.

ROSELLE: I'm Roselle, Roselle Simmons.

HAROLD: Charlie's sister . . . right?

ROSELLE: Why . . . heavens . . . have I changed all that much in two years?

HAROLD: Three years . . . actually.

ROSELLE: You don't seem to be having much fun at all. . . . You haven't danced once. I've been spying on you.

HAROLD: Well, I'm not up to the steps . . . or all the chatter . . .

ROSELLE: You need to be taught. . . . Didn't your little sister Marge ever try? There are lots of new steps . . . I could teach you . . . It's my war effort . . . Trade for a smoke?

HAROLD (*doesn't offer her a cigarette*): It's a waste of time. I never could get my feet straight . . .

ROSELLE: Silly . . . the feet are the easy part . . . it's the rest of your body . . . the way you lead . . . the way you hold your partner . . . I'll bet you like to command a girl . . .

HAROLD (*surprised*): Command a girl . . . Why?

ROSELLE (*she leads to music*): Command me, Mr. Harold Krebs . . .

HAROLD (*he responds slowly*): Like this?

(*These scenes should be played slowly—moving from awkwardness to* HAROLD'S *own arousal and assertion.*)

ROSELLE (*gently circling his arms around her. Emphasize physical aspects of their dancing*): Just move one, two, three, four . . . get closer . . . Did you ever dance like this, with those foreign women?

(*Cuts to* HAROLD *dancing closer. Stroking her as he would the women he has known in Europe. The music stops, and* HAROLD *continues to caress her with sureness.*)

ROSELLE (*scared now*): Don't . . . I've got to freshen up . . . I won't be long . . . All right? Wait out here . . . Don't!

HAROLD (*confused*): Hey . . . Where're you going? C'mon back here, Roselle.

ROSELLE (*vampishly over her shoulder*): Silly . . .

(ROSELLE *leaves.* HAROLD *continues to wait. The music begins. He is filled with a crushing sadness, a new confusion, a feeling of betrayal.*)

21. Exterior. Evening. Krebs and Kenner are in the Krebs car parked out front of Kenner house.

Krebs and Kenner are getting drunk. They try to whisper, but talk loudly. Kenner is much louder in his speech and more slurred. The only real sign of drunkenness for Harold is that he's talking louder than usual and trying to tell the truth to Kenner.

KENNER: We shouldn't have left. It would've gotten better.

HAROLD: You should have stayed.

KENNER: That tart Roselle is really somethin'. Know what we'd do to girls like her in France? (*Long pause as* HAROLD *says nothing.*) Christ. What do you want to do? Just mope around forever? I can't figure you. Whenever I want to forget things, I just drink. Drink and find a woman.

HAROLD: I want to *remember*—the *good* things.

KENNER: Like being over there. Scared to death. Watching guys screamin' and bleeding to death.

HAROLD: I wasn't scared . . . not like you tell it.

KENNER: Damn . . . everybody was. Didn't you ever wake up in sweats and shivers? I used to put my blanket in my mouth and . . .

HAROLD (*shakes his head, no.*)

KENNER: Well . . . I was scared. Everybody was.

HAROLD (*softly*): That's a lie.

KENNER (*pretends not to hear*): Everybody was. Only one thing is worth remembering over there.

HAROLD: Mmm . . .

KENNER: The damned women . . . No names or faces. Those white bodies, smelling like . . . like sweet apricots in those warm hotel rooms.

HAROLD: That isn't worth remembering.

KENNER: All right . . . all right. What is worth remembering?

HAROLD: Being a good soldier. Doing what you had to . . .

KENNER: Being a good soldier? You're crazy. You really are, Krebs.

HAROLD (*softly*): And you lie, Kenner, about everything.

KENNER: Don't call me a liar.

HAROLD: It's not worth it.

KENNER: Shut up.

(*Kenner pulls the bottle from Harold, and almost falls out car door.*)

HAROLD: Hey . . . You all right?

KENNER (*getting out of car*): Bastard . . . Crazy bastard. Stay away from me. I don't need a friend like you, Krebs. You spoil things.

(HAROLD *starts to follow Kenner.*)

HAROLD: Hey . . . wait! No! Go on. Go on, Kenner.

(KENNER *stumbles up front steps of his home.*)

22. Interior. Morning. Harold's bedroom. A knock on Harold's door. Harold wakes up. He feels miserable. His mother pokes her head in the door.

MRS. KREBS (*off camera*): Will you come down to breakfast, Harold?

HAROLD: As soon as I get my clothes on.

23. Interior. Dining room. Morning.

MARGE (*bringing in folded-up newspaper*): Well, Hare, you old sleepy-head. What do you ever get up for?

(HAROLD *removes brown wrapper of newspaper and opens it to the sporting page. He folds* The Star *open and props it against the water pitcher with his cereal dish to steady it, so he can read while he eats.*)

MRS. KREBS (*standing in the kitchen doorway*): Harold, please don't muss up the paper. Your father can't read his *Star* if it's been mussed.

HAROLD: I won't muss it.

MARGE (*sitting down*): We're playing indoor over at school this afternoon. I'm going to pitch.

HAROLD: Good. How's the old wing?

MARGE: I can pitch better than lots of the boys. I tell them all you taught me. I tell them all you're my beau. Aren't you my beau, Hare?

HAROLD: You bet.

MARGE: Could your brother really be your beau if he's your brother?

HAROLD: I don't know.

MARGE: Sure you know. Couldn't you be my beau, Hare, if I was old enough and if you wanted to?

HAROLD: Sure.

MARGE: Am I really your girl?

HAROLD: Sure.

MARGE: Do you love me?

HAROLD: Uh, huh.

MARGE: Will you love me always?

HAROLD (*by now becoming impatient with* MARGE): Sure.

MARGE: Will you come over and watch me play indoor?

HAROLD: Maybe.

MARGE: Aw, Hare, you don't love me. If you loved me, you'd definitely come over and watch me play indoor.

MRS. KREBS (*entering dining room*): You run along. I want to talk to Harold. Harold . . . I wish you'd put down the paper a minute, Harold.

HAROLD (*glances at her, hard*): Mmm . . .

MRS. KREBS: You acted shamefully last night. . . . The whole neighborhood could hear you, stumbling around out there.

HAROLD (*searches for the words*): Sorry . . .

MRS. KREBS: Why? You have so much . . . our love . . . You have a fine mind and a strong body . . . Have you decided what you're going to do yet, Harold?

HAROLD: No.

MRS. KREBS: Don't you think it's about time?

HAROLD: I hadn't decided yet . . .

MRS. KREBS (*stands*): God has some work for everyone to do . . . There can be no idle hands in His Kingdom. . . .

HAROLD (*without malice*): I'm not in His Kingdom. . . .

MRS. KREBS: We are all of us in His Kingdom. . . . Harold, please . . . I've worried about you so much . . . I know the temptations you must have suffered . . . I know how weak men are . . . I have prayed for you . . . I pray for you all day long, Harold . . .

(HAROLD *stares straight at his food.*)

MRS. KREBS: Harold . . . your father is worried, too . . . He thinks you've lost your ambition, that you have no definite aim in life. The Simmons boy is just your age, and he's doing so well . . . The boys are all settling down . . . They're all determined to get somewhere. Boys like Charlie Simmons are on the way to being a credit to the community . . . all of them . . . You, too, Harold . . .

(MRS. KREBS *starts to get up. Shaken, she sits back down.*)

MRS. KREBS: Don't look that way, Harold . . . You know we love you, and I want to tell you, for your own good, how matters stand . . . Your father doesn't want to hamper your freedom . . . He thinks you should be allowed to drive the car . . . We want you to enjoy yourself . . . but you are going to have to settle down to work, Harold. . . . Your father doesn't care what you start in at . . . All work is honorable as he says . . . but you've got to make a start at something . . . He didn't like . . . what you did last night . . . He asked me to speak to you this morning, and then you can stop in and see him at his office in the bank.

HAROLD (*gets up*): Is that all, Mother?

MRS. KREBS: Yes, don't you love your mother, dear?

HAROLD (*waits, not wanting to lie, just this once*): No.

MRS. KREBS (*her eyes grow shiny. She begins to cry*): Oh . . . Harold . . .

HAROLD: I don't love anybody . . .

(MRS. KREBS *sits down.*)

HAROLD: I didn't mean it . . . I was just angry at something . . . I didn't mean I didn't love you . . . Can't you believe me? Please, Mother . . . Please believe me.

MRS. KREBS (*shakes her head, chokily*): All right . . . I believe you, Harold. I'm your mother . . . I held you next to my heart when you were a tiny baby . . . (*She presses his hand against her bosom.*)

HAROLD (*sick and vaguely nauseated*): I know, Mom . . . I know . . . I'll try and be a good boy for you.

MRS. KREBS (*more controlled*): Would you kneel and pray with me, Harold?

(HAROLD *and* MRS. KREBS *kneel beside the table.*)

MRS. KREBS: Now, you pray, Harold . . .

HAROLD: I can't . . .

MRS. KREBS: Try, Harold . . .

HAROLD: I can't . . .

MRS. KREBS: Do you want me to pray for you? . . .

HAROLD: Yes . . .
MRS. KREBS: Our dear heavenly Father . . .

Cut to (*over continuing prayers*) (HAROLD *stares straight ahead. Dissolves of* HAROLD *packing his battered trunk. Waiting at deserted bus or train depot and riding with face against window. Looking at flat, open lands. Dusk. Tracking shots.*)

(*Clarinet music grows louder. Up with parodied version of "When Johnny Comes Marching Home Again."*)

(*Cut to reverse angle of* MRS. KREBS *monotonously droning her prayer and* HAROLD *continuing to stare into space. Music fades. Freeze on* HAROLD, *impassive.*)

NARRATOR (*off camera*): He had tried to keep his life from being complicated. He had felt sorry for his mother and she had made him lie. He would go to Kansas City and get a job and she would feel all right about it. There would be one more scene maybe before he got away. He would not go down to his father's office. He would miss that one. He wanted his life to go smoothly. Well, that was all over now, anyway.

DISCUSSION QUESTIONS

1. Read Geller's script in conjunction with Hemingway's original story (in "Classics"). Mark sections of the script that do not appear in the story. Do you think Geller's changes are substantial or trivial? Explain.

2. Discuss the nature of Geller's changes. Why were they made? What purpose do they serve? Do you think a perfectly faithful film version was possible? What would it have been like?

3. Does Geller's version of the story leave you with a different impression of its meaning? Why, for example, is the final sentence of the story omitted from the script. Point to other such changes or omissions and discuss how these affect interpretation.

Richard B. Eckhaus / *The Jeffersons:* "The Blackout" 1978

On Thursday evening, July 14, 1977, New York City was suddenly plunged into one of the worst electrical failures in recent urban history. The blackout continued through the night as thousands of looters and arsonists devastated entire neighborhoods. The New York Post *headline read, "24 Hours of Terror." More than 3,400 men and women were arrested in what the* Post *called the "worst outbreak of rioting in the city's history" and "the most expensive man-made [disaster] the nation has ever seen."*

*Though not a likely subject for television humor, the blackout nevertheless served as the situation for one comedy show—*The Jeffersons. *Written in November 1977 by Richard B. Eckhaus and produced the following year, "The Blackout" was nominated for a humanitarian award.* The Jeffersons, *which began airing in 1975, starred Sherman Hemsley as George Jefferson and Isabel Sanford as his wife, Louise. The show is still popular in reruns.*

ACT ONE

Fade in. Interior, Jefferson living room—night. (*Late evening. The drapes are closed, and the sofa is in a new position—perpendicular to the upstage wall. George and Louise are rearranging the furniture. George struggles to hold one of the chairs in the air, as Louise tries to decide its new location.*)

LOUISE (*pointing to a spot behind George*): Maybe over there . . .

(*George drops the chair with a thud and a gasp.*)

GEORGE: Weezy . . .

LOUISE (*looking at the chair*): Definitely not THERE.

GEORGE (*impatiently*): Weezy . . . that's the third time I moved that chair.

LOUISE: I know, George . . . but I want the room to look right when it's changed.

GEORGE: We've been through this before. (*lifting the chair again*) Ain't nothin' gonna' stay changed but my body.

(*Florence enters from the kitchen. She carries a coffee cup, and looks sleepy.*)

FLORENCE: Now, I'd call THAT "Urban Renewal."

GEORGE (*reacts and drops chair*): Where you been while I've been doin' your work?

FLORENCE (*yawns*): Makin' a cup of hot chocolate . . . and it ain't MY work. (*She calmly takes a sip from the cup.*)

GEORGE (*getting a bit ticked*): What do you think I'm payin' you for?

FLORENCE: Company . . . I guess.

GEORGE: You wanna' stay part of the company, you'd better help me with this chair.

(*Florence shrugs, places the cup on the dinette table, and crosses to help George.*) (*George bends over to pick up the chair, expecting Florence's help.*)

GEORGE (*grinning*): That's more like it . . .

(*Florence merely takes the cushion from the chair, and walks back to her hot chocolate.*)

GEORGE (*glaring at Florence*): You're pushin' . . .

FLORENCE: No . . . I'm drinkin' . . . (*She takes a sip from the cup.*)

SOUND EFFECTS: (*Doorbell.*)

GEORGE (*points to the door*): Florence . . . DOOR . . .

FLORENCE (*picking up the chair cushion, and pointing to it*): Mr. Jefferson . . . PILLOW . . . (*points to table*) . . . and that's a TABLE. (*George reacts, and glares at Florence.*) Ain't it amazin' what that child's learnin'?

LOUISE (*a bit impatient*): George . . . would you PLEASE get the door. I'd like to get this done TONIGHT.

(*Florence begins to exit to the kitchen.*)

GEORGE (*crossing to the door*): NOW, where do you think you're goin'?

FLORENCE: To get more cocoa. These cups are too darn small.

GEORGE (*to Florence, as he opens the door to reveal Marcus, who is carrying some cleaning*): So's your brai . . . MARCUS! (*George puts his arm around Marcus, and leads him into the apartment.*)

MARCUS: Hey, Mr. Jefferson . . . (*waving to Louise across the room, who is still studying the furniture arrangement*) . . . Mrs. Jefferson. We managed to get that gravy stain out of your suit, Mr. Jefferson.

LOUISE (*chuckling*): And he'll manage to get it back IN.

GEORGE (*forcing a laugh*): Hey, Weezy . . . you always said I needed a hobby.

LOUISE: Would you like to stay for coffee and dessert, Marcus?

MARCUS: I'd sure like to, Mrs. Jefferson, but I promised to be home early. (*He notices the half-changed furniture.*) Hey . . . you're re-doin' the living room.

GEORGE (*laughing*): Yeah . . . Mrs. Jefferson's playin' INFERIOR decorator . . . for the third time this week.

LOUISE: Funny, George. (*She starts to move one of the coffee tables.*)

MARCUS (*rushing across the room to help her*): That's too heavy for you, Mrs. Jefferson. Let me do it.

LOUISE: Oh . . . thank you, Marcus, but you'd better be going. You wanted to get home early, remember?

MARCUS: Aw, that's okay. I got a few minutes to kill . . . might as well work 'em to death. (*He lifts the table.*)

LOUISE: Marcus, you really don't have to . . .

GEORGE (*interrupting as he hangs the cleaning in the closet*): Sure he does. Marcus has got himself one good attitude . . . always ready to help people.

(*Louise points to a spot where Marcus then places the table. She turns to glare at George.*)

LOUISE: Marcus sure isn't like SOME people I know.

(*As Marcus and Louise move the other coffee table, George crosses from the hall closet, and plops into one of the armchairs.*)

GEORGE: That Florence sure is lazy . . . ain't she?

(*Louise reacts, and turns to stare at George.*)

LOUISE: And just what do you think you're doing?

GEORGE (*smiling*): Resting myself. Ain't you heard that middle-aged black men can get high blood-pressure?

LOUISE: That's ridiculous, George. In all the time we've been together, your blood pressure hasn't gone up two points.

(*Florence re-enters from the kitchen.*)

FLORENCE: If it ever does . . . SELL!!

(*Suddenly, the apartment lights begin to flicker.*)

LOUISE: What's that?

(*The lights now dim.*)

GEORGE: Just another power shortage, Weezy. The Arabs probably raised the prices again.

(*The lights go out completely. We can only hear voices.*)

LOUISE (*alarmed*): George . . . I'm scared.

GEORGE: Take it easy, Weezy. Must be a fuse. (*pause*) I'll get the flashlight . . .

(*A beat of silence, then Louise remembers something.*)

LOUISE (*urgently*): GEORGE . . . Don't forget we moved the . . .

SOUND EFFECTS: (*A crash, a thud, and a howl of pain.*)

LOUISE: . . . sofa.

(*The lights flicker on again, and we see George sprawled on the floor on the stage right side of the sofa.*)

GEORGE (*picking himself off the floor*): This all ain't REALLY happenin' . . .

LOUISE (*starting across to help George*): Are you alright, George?

(*The lights dim and go out again.*)

GEORGE (*voice in the dark*): It's happenin'. Weezy . . . you pay that damn bill?

LOUISE (*voice in the dark*): Of course, I paid it. George, I'm REALLY frightened.

(*A beat of silence.*)

GEORGE: There . . . there . . . Sugar. I've got you.

FLORENCE (*angry*): NO YOU DON'T . . . SUCKER!!

(*We hear a "thud," and George yells in pain.*)

(*Marcus lights a match, and we see Louise reach into the corner hutch. They light two candles which illuminate the room with a soft glow. George stands beside a glowering Florence. He holds his ribs in pain.*)

MARCUS: Must be some sort of bad short . . .

FLORENCE (*still frowning at poor George*): Damn right, it's a BAD SHORT!

(*Louise opens the drapes, and discovers that the entire area is dark.*)

LOUISE: Come here, George. It looks like we're not alone.

(*Still wincing, George crosses to the window, and looks out.*)

GEORGE: Just what this city needs . . . another blackout.

MARCUS: That means the subways ain't runnin'. How long you figure it'll last?

GEORGE: Long as it takes for the electric company to rook us outa' more money. Why d'ya think they're called CON Edison.

SOUND EFFECTS: (*a knock at the door.*)

(*Florence crosses, and opens the door to Harry Bentley, who carries an electric Coleman camping lantern.*)

BENTLEY: Greetings, everybody. I see you're as much in the dark about this as I am. (*He chuckles at his own pun.*)

GEORGE (*not amused*): What do you want, Bentley?

BENTLEY (*crossing into the living room*): Actually, I just popped over to borrow a few candles. I knew I'd be needing them this morning, but I forgot to stop by the store on the way home. Rather silly of me . . . wouldn't you say, Mr. J?

GEORGE: I woulda' said it, anyway. (*He thinks a beat.*) Wait a minute, Bentley. You tryin' to tell me you're psychic or somethin'?

BENTLEY (*puzzled*): How's that, Mr. J?

GEORGE: You said you knew this morning you'd be needin' candles for the blackout. Besides, you already got a lattern.

BENTLEY (*laughing*): Oh . . . I didn't know about the blackout . . . but I DID know about Susan.

GEORGE (*really puzzled*): Say what??

BENTLEY: I had already invited Susan over for a candle-light dinner. (*He looks down at his lantern.*) And as for this . . . who ever heard of a romantic FLASH-LIGHT dinner?

GEORGE (*suddenly alarmed, as he thinks of something*): OHMYGOSH!!

LOUISE: What's the matter, George?

BENTLEY: No need to get excited, Mr. J. We can use the lantern in a pinch . . . if we have to.

GEORGE: It's my mother. She's probably scared stiff in the dark.

LOUISE (*calmly*): Only if she can't find her Vodka.

GEORGE: That ain't funny, Weezy. I'd better call her. (*He crosses to the phone, and dials. Not able to get through, he hangs up, and tries again.*)

BENTLEY (*to Louise and Marcus*): You know, this reminds me of the big blackout back in 1966. There are so many similarities . . . except for Susan, of course. She doesn't look a thing like Gloria.

(*Louise listens to Bentley with an amused look.*)

MARCUS: How long did that one go for?

BENTLEY (*with a far-away look*): Gloria?

MARCUS: No, man . . . the BLACKOUT.

BENTLEY: Oh . . . that. It's hard to say. Gloria and I didn't notice for three days.

(*In the background, George has gotten through to his mother.*)

GEORGE (*on phone*): . . . that's so? Don't let it worry you, Momma. Oh you FOUND IT?! (*Embarrassed, he glances up at a smiling Louise, who has been listening to George's side of the conversation.*) Well not too much, now . . . sleep tight. (*He hangs up.*)

LOUISE: I'm sure she'll sleep tight as a drum.

GEORGE (*quickly changing the subject*): Momma heard on her radio that all of New York and part of Jersey are blacked out. (*He thinks a beat.*) We got a portable radio?

FLORENCE (*suddenly perking up*): Hey . . . I got one. (*She exits to her bedroom.*)

GEORGE: Huh . . . FINALLY we got a reason to keep Florence around. Weezy, remind me to buy a portable radio. (*He notices Bentley.*) You still here, Bentley?

BENTLEY: Actually, I haven't had a chance to ask Mrs. J if I might borrow some candles.

(*George starts to hustle Harry to the door.*)

GEORGE: There . . . you asked . . .

LOUISE: I'm sorry, Mr. Bentley, but these are our last two.

GEORGE (*as he opens the door*): You heard her, Bentley. You'll just have to have a FLASHLIGHT dinner.

BENTLEY (*smiling licentiously*): I suppose it shan't be too bad. Susan is . . . EVEREADY. (*Bentley chuckles at his own lousy pun, but George just stares at him.*)

GEORGE: Finished, Bentley?

BENTLEY: Just one more thing, Mr. J. How come they never have a blackout during the day?

GEORGE: 'Cause then they'd call it a "WHITE-OUT." Speakin' of which . . . (*George pushes Bentley out into the hall, and slams the door.*)

(*Florence re-enters carrying a portable radio.*)

FLORENCE: This is the best idea you ever had, Mr. Jefferson. (*Florence turns on her radio. It is tuned to a soul/rock station, and she begins to dance to the music.*)

GEORGE (*grabbing the radio from her*): Gimme that!! (*He tunes the radio into a news station.*)

VOICE ON RADIO: . . . pandemonium breaking out all over the city. Police report that looters are having a field day in Bedford-Stuyvesant and the South Bronx.

(*George quickly shuts off the radio. He looks very worried.*)

LOUISE: What's the matter, George?

MARCUS: You got a store in the South Bronx . . . don't you, Mr. Jefferson?

GEORGE (*looking very upset*): I sure do . . . and it's full of customers' cleaning. (*He begins to pace the floor.*) They'll clean ME out.

LOUISE (*putting a hand on George's shoulder*): Try not to get too upset about it, dear. You can't do anything now . . . and besides, your insurance'll cover any . . .

GEORGE: WHAT insurance?

LOUISE (*shocked*): You mean you don't have insurance??!!

GEORGE: Not on the South Bronx store. They wouldn't sell me none . . . said it was a bad risk.

LOUISE: But you've been in that store for fifteen years.

GEORGE: You know that, and I know that, Weezy . . . but the insurance companies don't CARE about stuff like that. They said the neighborhood's changed, and it ain't safe for a business no more. (*He crosses to the front closet.*)

LOUISE: Does that make us liable for our customers' property?

GEORGE (*He takes an old coat from the closet.*): It sure does.

MARCUS: That's gonna' cost you a fortune, Mr. Jefferson.

GEORGE: No it ain't, Marcus.

MARCUS (*confused*): Huh??

GEORGE: Me and you are gonna' take the truck, and high-tail it up there before they get everything.

MARCUS: We are?

GEORGE: Sure . . . and we'll bring the stuff down here where it's safe.

LOUISE (*incredulous*): You WILL??

GEORGE: Sure! It'll take us no time. (*He puts on the old coat.*) This old thing'll make me look inconspicuous.

FLORENCE (*as she picks up one of the candles, and crosses to the kitchen*): You don't need a costume for that.

(*George reacts.*)

GEORGE: Common, Marcus.

(*Marcus reluctantly crosses to join George by the door.*)

LOUISE (*worried*): George . . . don't go.

GEORGE: There ain't nothin' to worry about, Weezy. We'll be home before you know it.

MARCUS (*nervous*): It sure is dark out there . . .

(*George opens the door, and they step into the hall.*)

LOUISE: George . . .

GEORGE: I told you, Weezy . . . everything's gonna' be okay. I'll take care of Marcus.

(*George and Marcus exit.*)

LOUISE (*looking very worried*): It's not Marcus I'm worried about . . .

Dissolve to:

Interior, Jefferson South Bronx store—night. (*An hour later. The store is dark, and through the front window, we can see passers-by carrying T.V. sets, stereos, etc. From the back room of the store, we can see a faint light moving about, and we hear voices.*)

FIRST VOICE: Are you crazy, man? That ain't worth a damn thing.

SECOND VOICE: Yeah . . . but it'll look good on my old lady.

FIRST VOICE: Shooot! She puts on five more pounds, an' she'll look good in commercial plates.

SECOND VOICE: Hey man . . . watch your mouth!

(*George and Marcus appear at the front door, and begin to unlock it.*)

FIRST VOICE: SSSHHH . . . somebody's comin'.

(*George and Marcus enter the store.*)

GEORGE (*relieved, as he points his flashlight around*): Whew! It looks like we ain't been hit yet.

MARCUS: The rest of the neighborhood looks like a bomb hit it.

GEORGE: Well . . . that ain't our worry. Let's get all this stuff . . .

(*There is a crash in the back room.*)

MARCUS (*stunned*): WHAAZZAATT??!!

GEORGE (*very frightened*): Who's b..b..back there?

(*Two men slowly emerge from the back room.*)

FIRST LOOTER: You ain't the cops??!!

GEORGE: No . . . we ain't . . . but . . .

SECOND LOOTER: So, split, man! (*The two looters resume picking things from the racks.*)

GEORGE: SPLIT??!! You guys'd better split.

FIRST LOOTER (*calmly turning to face George and Marcus*): You still here?

GEORGE (*indignant*): You bet I'm still here. This is MY store.

SECOND LOOTER: Wrong, brother. We was here first . . .

FIRST LOOTER: . . . and that makes it OUR store.

GEORGE: Hey, man . . . I OWN this place.

(*The two looters look at each other, then break out laughing.*)

MARCUS: Yeah . . . this here's "Jefferson Cleaners," and he's George Jefferson.

FIRST LOOTER (*still smirking*): Not THE George Jefferson??

GEORGE (*dripping with pride*): That's right . . . THE George Jefferson.

SECOND LOOTER: In that case . . . (*He takes a gun from his pocket.*). . . STICK 'EM UP!!

(*George and Marcus look at each other, and break into a nervous chuckle.*)

GEORGE: Heh . . . heh . . . you guys are funny . . .

FIRST LOOTER (*frowning*): He said "STICK 'EM UP"!! (*George and Marcus put their hands in the air.*) Let's have your wallets. (*George and Marcus reach into their pockets, and hand over their wallets.*)

SECOND LOOTER (*examining George's wallet*): Hey . . . this cat really IS Jefferson . . . and he's loaded too.

FIRST LOOTER (*looking into the wallet*): WOW! He WAS loaded. This sure is our lucky day.

SECOND LOOTER: And you said we shoulda' hit the liquor store . . . HA!

FIRST LOOTER: Grab those leather coats, and let's split. (*The second looter exits to the back room for a beat, and returns carrying several leather garments.*) Well, Mr. Jefferson . . . it's been a pleasure doin' business with you . . . (*The two looters cross to the door.*) If you go out there tonight, be careful. This neighborhood's a jungle. (*The two looters exit.*)

GEORGE (*jumping up and down in anger*): Damn . . . damn . . . DAMN!

MARCUS: You gotta' admit . . . those guys had style.

GEORGE: Yeah . . . and now they got my wallet too.

(*Marcus steps behind the counter, and checks the register.*)

MARCUS: Empty . . .

GEORGE: It figures. (*He looks around.*) Well . . . let's get this stuff on the truck, and get outa' here.

(*George and Marcus begin to take garments from the hanging racks. Suddenly, the door bursts open, and two uniformed cops storm in with their guns drawn.*)

FIRST COP: HOLD IT . . . both of you!!

GEORGE (*stunned*): HUH??!!

SECOND COP: Drop what you're stealing, and get against the counter!

GEORGE: This ain't happenin' . . .

MARCUS (*frightened*): It's happenin', Mr. Jefferson . . . it's happenin'.

(*The cops force George and Marcus to spread-eagle against the counter, and then frisk them.*)

GEORGE: You dudes are makin' a mistake. I OWN this place.

FIRST COP: Sure, bud . . . and I'm Kojak.

GEORGE: If you guys'll just look in my wallet . . .

SECOND COP: I just frisked you, and you ain't got a wallet.

GEORGE (*remembering*): Oh yeah . . . that's right. Two guys just stole our wallets.

SECOND COP: Hey, you guys are REAL creative. The last bunch of looters just said they were takin' inventory. (*He chuckles as he handcuffs George and Marcus together.*)

GEORGE (*furious*): You guys can't do this.

(*They lead George and Marcus to the door.*)

FIRST COP: Pipe down, will ya'?

GEORGE (*as he is being dragged out the door*): I wanna' see my lawyer!!

SECOND COP: Sure . . . sure . . . good old Calhoun's out in the paddy wagon.

GEORGE (*howling*): WEEEEZZYYY. . . .

Fade out.

ACT TWO

Fade in: Interior, jail cell—night. (*A short time later. The cell is filled with surly-looking men. New York's power is still out, and the cell and hallway are only illuminated by emergency lanterns. Some of the inmates pace back and forth, others try to doze on cots or on the floor. Suddenly, the relative quiet is broken by the approaching sound of George's voice.*)

GEORGE (*off-screen*) (*angry as hell*): I'm tellin' you dudes . . . you're in BIG trouble.

FIRST COP (*off-screen*): Sure pal . . . sure.

(*George and Marcus now appear in the hallway, accompanied by the two cops.*)

GEORGE (*rubbing his hands on his old coat*): Damn ink all over my hands . . .

SECOND COP (*sarcastic, as he unlocks the cell door*): Aw, gee . . . I'm sorry. The manicurist won't be in till tomorrow.

(*George and Marcus step into the cell.*)

FIRST COP (*sarcastic, chuckling*): I do hope you find our accommodations to your liking.

GEORGE: I hope you find my lawyer to your likin'. When he gets done with you, you'll be poundin' a beat in Uganda.

SECOND COP (*slamming the cell door behind George and Marcus*): Yeah?! I could use a vacation. (*The two cops exit laughing.*)

FIRST COP: Can you believe that guy? He OWNS the place . . . the nerve of that turkey!

SECOND COP (*mocking*): YOU'LL BE POUNDING A BEAT IN UGANDA!! He probably knows Idi Amin personally.

(*Furious, George turns and looks around the cell. Upon seeing the surly inmates, who are quietly watching his performance, he panics, runs back to the bars and bellows after the cops.*)

GEORGE (*screaming*): What about my phone call??

FIRST COP (*off-screen*): Wait your turn, chump. Now . . . SHADDUP!!

MARCUS: I don't think they believed you, Mr. Jefferson.

GEORGE (*pacing the crowded floor*): They'll believe me when I sue their butts off. I'm gonna' fix Con Edison too.

MARCUS (*smiling proudly*): 'Atta' way, Mr. J! We're gonna fight City Hall.

GEORGE: No we ain't. Just the cops and Con Ed.

MARCUS: By the way . . . how come you're gonna' sue the electric company?

GEORGE (*pacing up a storm*): 'Cause if it wasn't for them turkeys, we wouldn't be here. I'll fix 'em.

(*Suddenly the cell's main lights come on. The blackout is over, and the other prisoners cheer. One of them, a raggedy-looking character, approaches George.*)

FIRST INMATE (*shaking George's hand*): Man . . . I don't know who you are, but keep talkin'. Maybe you can get us a steak dinner.

(*The other inmates now approach George and Marcus, and begin to size them up.*)

MARCUS (*aside to George*): Mr. Jefferson . . . I'm scared.

GEORGE (*trembling*): Stick close to me . . . I'll look after you.

MARCUS (*not reassured*): That's what you said right after "Let's get the truck an' go up to the Bronx."

(*A particularly tough-looking inmate stares George in the eye.*)

SECOND INMATE: What're you dudes in for? You looters?

GEORGE (*indignant*): We ain't done nothin'. It's a mistake.

SECOND INMATE (*smiling*): Sure . . . sure. We've all been framed. Don't let 'em bluff ya's. Just stick to that story . . .

GEORGE: It ain't no story. The cops picked us up in my own store.

(*The* SECOND INMATE *begins to laugh.*)

SECOND INMATE: Hey . . . that's rich! An' I was picked up carryin' my OWN air conditioner down the street.

FIRST INMATE (*rolling with laughter*): Yeah . . . and I wandered into that furniture factory by accident. I mean, it WAS dark.

(*All the inmates start to roar. George is frustrated and furious.*)

GEORGE (*shouting above the laughter*): I AIN'T JIVIN'!! (*The cell quiets down.*) I own a chain of cleanin' stores. I made my way up BY MYSELF, and I don't need to steal. I ain't looted from nobody, and I don't belong in this dump. (*One of the inmates, sitting on a cot, takes out a harmonica, and goes into some classic prison riff.*) That's all I gotta' say. (*George angrily sits down on the cell floor.*)

SECOND INMATE (*looking down at George*): Man . . . you're really somethin'. You DO think you're too good for us, don't you?

(*Marcus quickly steps between George and the burly inmate.*)

MARCUS (*shaking with fear*): He didn't mean nothin' by it . . . honest.

SECOND INMATE: Then what's he goin' around dumpin' that innocent jazz on us for?

MARCUS (*searching for an "out"*): Uh . . . 'cause he's a . . . he's a SMART hood, that's why. My boss always knows how to put on a front.

SECOND INMATE (*scoffing*): Boy . . . you take me for a fool?

MARCUS (*confused*): Uh . . . yeah . . . I mean . . . NO.

GEORGE: Forget it, Marcus. They ain't buyin' . . . and I ain't sellin'.

(*Frustrated, Marcus slides down onto the floor next to George.*)

MARCUS: I was just tryin' to help . . .

GEORGE (*patting Marcus on the back*): I know, man . . . but I ain't apologizin' 'cause I AIN'T a looter.

FIRST INMATE: Ya know . . . I think the runt is tellin' the truth. He ain't the lootin' type.

GEORGE: Damn right, I ain't.

(*Another voice comes out of the crowd of inmates. Jackson is a tall, black man. He rises from one of the bunk beds, and walks over to George.*)

JACKSON: Jefferson's telling the truth. He's no looter.

(*George stands up to face Jackson, but still has to look way up at the man.*)

GEORGE (*surprised*): You know me?

JACKSON: I've seen you around . . . with your fine clothes and your well-dressed wife.

GEORGE (*beaming*): Ha . . . see there? The man knows me.

JACKSON: Yeah . . . I've seen you. I've seen you strutting into your store to count up all the bread in your cash register. Year after year I'd see you coming by . . . getting fatter and fatter . . .

GEORGE (*self-consciously sucking in his gut*): That ain't fat . . . I slouch.

JACKSON (*looking George up and down*): Well . . . your head's sure gotten fat. Why, I bet you never REALLY noticed the change in the neighborhood . . . just the change in your pocket.

GEORGE: How could I MISS what was goin' down in that neighborhood?

JACKSON: Did you know WHY it was changing? (*George tries to answer, but can't.*) I used to be a welder at the Brooklyn Navy Yard. When I got laid-off, I found part time work for awhile . . . then nothing.

MARCUS: How'd you get in here?

JACKSON: Last night the cops caught Old Henry Jackson looting an appliance store.

GEORGE: I bet you feel like hell.

JACKSON: Sure I do . . . 'cause I got CAUGHT.

GEORGE (*puzzled*): Say what?

JACKSON: I'm not ashamed of trying to feed my family. I'm just ashamed of not being too good at it.

GEORGE: There ain't no excuse for stealin'.

SECOND INMATE: You ever been poor?

MARCUS (*jumping in to George's defense*): He was so poor . . . his folks couldn't afford a taller kid.

(*George reacts.*)

JACKSON: Then he doesn't REMEMBER what it's like to have to steal to eat. Man . . . that neighborhood's full of guys like me. You better believe that when the Man's pants are down, we're gonna' grab whatever we can get our hands on.

GEORGE (*not as forceful as before*): You tellin' me that nobody was lootin' just for the sake of doin' it?

JACKSON: Sure they were . . . some of them. (*He points to another man in the cell.*) Lewis over there's got a good job. He didn't have to do it. But when some guys see a crowd doing something . . .

GEORGE (*calling over to Lewis*): Hey Lewis . . . is that the truth?

LEWIS (*singing*): I LOVE A PARADE . . .

(*George reacts.*)

JACKSON: Point is . . . there is no right and wrong . . . no black and white . . .

GEORGE (*trying to make a joke*): Sure there is . . . the Willises . . . (*Nobody laughs—not even Marcus.*) Inside joke . . .

JACKSON: I don't know, Jefferson. Maybe you've just gotten out of touch . . . (*Jackson shakes his head, turns, and walks back to his cot. George leans on the bars, and looks blankly out. A weird-looking inmate now approaches George.*)

WEIRD INMATE (*in a loud whisper*): PSSST . . . Buddy . . .

(*George turns to look at the guy.*)

GEORGE: What do YOU want?

WEIRD INMATE: Just wanna' give you some advice . . . (*George listens intently.*) Keep an eye out in here . . . the place is full of crooks. (*George stares at the man in disbelief. The character rolls up his coat-sleeve, and displays a half-dozen watches to George.*) Wanna' buy an Omega watch . . .?

Dissolve to:

Interior, jail cell—night. (*Some time later. Most of the men in the cell are asleep. George dozes in a corner on the floor, his battered old coat covers him like a blanket. George tosses and turns in his sleep. Marcus is awake, and sits next to George, guarding him. The weird inmate sits by himself, wide awake and happily listening to his watches tick. We hear voices approaching off-stage. After a beat, Louise appears in the hallway outside the cell. She is accompanied by the First Cop.*)

FIRST COP (*quietly to Louise*): You see him in there?

(*She looks around the cell for a beat. As Louise's eyes search for George, Marcus happens to look up and see her. Overjoyed, he reaches over and shakes George.*)

GEORGE (*in his sleep*): Not now, Weezy . . .

MARCUS (*again shaking George*): Mr. Jefferson . . . wake up . . .

GEORGE (*turning over—still asleep*): I said not now, Weezy. I got a headache!

(*Louise spots George and Marcus, and points them out to the cop. Marcus still tries to awaken George.*)

MARCUS (*He thinks for a beat, then speaks very quietly.*): What do you mean Imperial Cleaners is cuttin' their prices again?

(*George's eyes open, and he sits up with a start. He is totally disoriented.*)

GEORGE: WHAZZAT?? Where am I? (*He looks around, sees the cell, then Marcus.*) Oh . . . yeah . . .

MARCUS (*excited*): Mrs. Jefferson's here.

(*George leaps to his feet, just as the cop unlocks the cell door.*)

FIRST COP: You sure that's him, Mrs. Jefferson??

LOUISE (*anxious*): I'm POSITIVE!

FIRST COP (*still baffled*): Gosh . . . I'm sorry for the mistake. He sure had us fooled. (*The cop unlocks the cell door.*)

LOUISE (*a bit angry*): Evidently.

(*George rushes to Louise. He is ecstatic.*)

GEORGE: WEEEEEEEZZZZZZZYYYYYYY!!!!!!!

(*They embrace, then George notices the cop standing there, and begins to glower at him.*)

FIRST COP (*nervous*): Jeez . . . I'm sorry for the mistake, Mr. Jefferson.

(*George and Marcus step into the hallway, and the cop re-locks the cell door.*)

GEORGE (*angry*): Not as sorry as you're gonna' be.

FIRST COP: We were just doing our jobs. If there were REAL looters in your store, you'd've wanted us there . . . wouldn't you?

GEORGE (*cooling down a bit*): Yeah . . . I guess so . . .

MARCUS: We were sort of askin' for it when we went up there.

GEORGE (*reluctantly*): Well, yeah . . .

LOUISE: And if they didn't let you finally make that call to me when the lines were cleared, you might have been in here all night.

FIRST COP: Next time remember, Mr. Jefferson . . . in an area like the South Bronx the only way to protect a store is steel-plated walls and iron bars. Even then there are no guarantees. The people up there are animals.

GEORGE: I dunno' . . . maybe you're right. (*yawning*) Who's got the time?

(*The weird inmate leans against the bars, and rolls up his sleeves.*)

WEIRD INMATE: What city?

GEORGE: Forget it. (*They walk down the hallway.*)

LOUISE: Let's go home and get some sleep.

GEORGE: Just a couple o' hours, Weezy. Then I gotta' go up to the South Bronx store.

MARCUS: Got some cleanin' up to do, I guess.

GEORGE (*as they exit*): No . . . I got some CLOSIN' up to do, Marcus.

Dissolve to:

Interior, Jefferson South Bronx store—morning. (*Early the next morning. The store is a disaster area. Every one of the customers' garments is missing, the shelves are empty, the windows are broken, and the floor is covered with debris. George and Louise stand sadly in the ruins.*)

GEORGE (*Looking around, he feels angry, hurt, and bitter.*): After so many years in this store, this is what I got left . . . damn!

(*Louise rummages around in the rubble.*)

LOUISE: They didn't leave much, did they?

GEORGE: The animals took EVERYTHING. I'm surprised they left the air.

LOUISE: I'm sorry Marcus had to see all this. It doesn't give him much of an outlook on things . . . does it, George? (*Louise sees something in the mess near the door.*) What's this?

GEORGE: Probably a roach . . . and the only reason they ain't stole him is 'cause they got enough of their own.

(*Louise bends down and picks up a wallet.*)

LOUISE: It's your wallet George.

GEORGE (*surprised*): You're jivin' . . .

LOUISE: No . . . it's here. (*He rushes over to look.*)

GEORGE: I'll be damned. I bet they took everything of any value.

LOUISE (*looking through the wallet*): You're right, George . . . your mother's picture's still here.

GEORGE (*He reacts, and is not amused.*): That ain't funny, Weezy.

LOUISE (*chuckling as she studies the picture*): Mother Jefferson sitting on a pony IS funny, George. (*looks through the wallet some more*) Your credit cards are still here.

GEORGE (*really surprised*): You GOTTA be kiddin'.

(*She shows him the credit cards.*)

GEORGE (*smiling*): What d'ya know . . . I got hit by dumb looters.

LOUISE: See, George? It's not all that bad.

GEORGE (*frowning*): Don't try to change my mind, Weezy. I'm not gonna' re-open this place . . . NEVER!

LOUISE: I'm not going to try . . .

GEORGE (*beginning to pace back and forth*): There's NO WAY I'm ever gonna' set foot in this neighborhood again. Give me one reason why I oughta' come back here.

LOUISE (*as she calmly resumes looking around for valuables*): I can't, George . . .

GEORGE: You heard the cop . . . they're animals up here now. We left the ghetto behind YEARS ago. (*rambling on*) I ain't got no insurance . . . I gotta' pay off all my customers for their stuff . . .

LOUISE: No question you're right, George.

GEORGE (*pacing up a storm*): . . . cop said I gotta' get steel-plated walls and iron bars to keep 'em out . . .

(*The door opens, and an elderly man enters the store.*)

LOUISE (*to the old man*): Can we help you?

OLD MAN (*sadly looking around at the damage*): They hit you pretty bad, huh?

GEORGE (*abruptly*): Yeah. Now what can we do for you?

OLD MAN: You the owners?

LOUISE: Yes . . . we're the Jeffersons.

OLD MAN: I've been a customer of yours for a long, long time. I had a suit being cleaned . . .

GEORGE (*snapping*): You'll get paid for it like everybody else . . . before we close up.

OLD MAN: No big deal. It was an old suit, anyway . . . still had pleats. (*thinks for a beat*) Did you say you're closing up?

GEORGE: You heard me. I'm shuttin' down. I got other stores to worry about.

OLD MAN (*sighing*): Can't say I blame you. You're a rich man.

(*In the background, Louise finds something.*)

GEORGE: Damn right I am . . . and I worked hard for it too.

OLD MAN: If I had what you had, I'd go too. Leave all this behind . . . that's your best bet. It's the same with all the merchants. They've gotten fat . . . (*Again George sucks in his gut, but then lets it out, thinking.*) . . . and don't need to be reminded of the old days. (*The old man looks around again.*) Well, I'll let you do your business. (*He turns and exits.*)

GEORGE (*pausing, then calling out after the man exits*): Hey . . . your suit . . .

LOUISE: George . . . look what I found. (*She holds a small, cracked picture frame.*)

GEORGE (*in thought*): Huh?

LOUISE: I found the first dollar this old store earned us. I'm surprised the looters didn't grab it.

(*George looks it over carefully.*)

GEORGE: That IS somethin', Weezy.

LOUISE: Well, at least you'll have a souvenir of your second store after we close it.

GEORGE (*stiffening his spine*): Close it? What do you mean CLOSE IT??

LOUISE (*shocked*): But George . . .

GEORGE: Ain't no "buts" about it, Weezy. I ain't no quitter. This store is more than just a business . . . it's a link to what WAS for us.

(*Louise grabs George and hugs him.*)

LOUISE: Oh, George . . . I'm so proud of you.

GEORGE (*smiling—proud of himself too*): Yeah . . . well . . . I learned a few things in the last couple o' days.

LOUISE: Like . . . ?

GEORGE: Like . . . just 'cause you're successful don't mean you ain't the same person you was.

LOUISE: And . . . ?

GEORGE: And . . . no matter what happens, you've gotta' have some trust left in people. (*She hugs him again.*) Now let's go home . . . I'm whipped. (*They walk to the door, and George turns back to look at the store again.*) Weezy . . . how much you figure steel-plated walls and iron bars'll run us?

(*Louise reacts, and stares at George, as we:*)

Fade out.

DISCUSSION QUESTIONS

1. Situation comedies require many one liners. Identify several of the jokes in this episode and examine what they have in common. Can you state the show's central joke; that is, the joke the comedy seems to revolve around, that all the jokes grow out of? For example, is there any joke inherent in the basic situation of this series that a scriptwriter can use over and over?

2. Discuss the moral problem of this episode. What is George's dilemma? Why is *he* arrested? Does the show have a moral? If so, can you state it in one sentence?

Matt Williams / *Roseanne:* "Life and Stuff" 1988

While the sitcom Roseanne *may not ultimately change the way we look at the American family, it has certainly contributed to changing the way that families are portrayed on television. As noted feminist critic Barbara Ehrenreich writes:* Roseanne "*. . . is a radical departure simply for featuring blue-collar Americans—and for depicting them as something other than half-witted greasers and low-life louts. The working class does not usually get much of a role in the American entertainment spectacle.*"

Roseanne *was created by comedienne Roseanne Arnold (formerly Barr) who developed the main character as part of a stand-up comedy routine. The popularity of the character with live audiences encouraged her to expand her original concept for television treatment. One of the most popular shows among college students,* Roseanne *first went on the air in 1988.*

ACT ONE

I

Fade in.

Int. kitchen—7:30 A.M. (day 1) (*Roseanne, Dan, Becky, Darlene, D.J.*)

(*Becky is on the phone, ad libbing, "What are you going to wear?" Etc.. Roseanne is at the toaster. She crosses to the pantry. D.J. enters, running. He crosses in front of Roseanne and exits into the utility room. Roseanne ignores him, crosses, and sets the cereal on the table.*) (*)

ROSEANNE (*calling off*): Breakfast!

(*Roseanne crosses to the refrigerator and takes out a gallon of milk. Becky, still talking on the phone, crosses to the table and grabs a handful of cereal. D.J. enters from the utility room, carrying his shoes. He crosses, sits in a chair, and starts to put on the shoes.*) (*)

DARLENE (*OS*): Mom! Mom!

(*Becky crosses to the toast.*)

BECKY: Do we have any jam?

ROSEANNE: No.

(*Roseanne crosses and starts putting sandwiches into bags.*)

DARLENE (*OS*): Mom!

(*Becky continues talking on the phone as she eats toast. Darlene enters and throws a bag of books on the floor.*)

DARLENE (*cont'd*): Mom, where's my English book?

ROSEANNE: I sold it.

DARLENE: Mom.

ROSEANNE: Top of the TV.

(*Darlene heads toward the living room.*)

BECKY (*into phone*): . . . Okay. I'll see you at school. Bye.

(*Darlene exits. Becky hangs up the telephone, crosses to the cupboard, and starts pulling out cans of food*).

D.J.: Mom?

ROSEANNE: What?

D.J. (*holding up the sneaker*): I got a knot in my shoe.

ROSEANNE: Wear loafers.

D.J.: Mom. Come on.

ROSEANNE: All right, Give it here.

(*Roseanne takes the shoe and unties the knot.*)

D.J.: Can I have pie for breakfast?

ROSEANNE: No, it's contaminated. Now, sit down and eat.

(*D.J. crosses to the table.*)

ROSEANNE (*cont'd*): And don't spill your milk today. Here.

(*Roseanne tosses the shoe to D.J. Becky exits to the utility room.*)

ROSEANNE (*cont'd*) (*To Becky*): What are you doing?

BECKY: Nothing.

(*Dan enters, dressed for work. Becky enters and crosses to the pantry.*)

DAN: Is there coffee?

ROSEANNE: Dan.

DAN: Yeah?

ROSEANNE: Isn't there coffee every morning?

DAN: Yes.

ROSEANNE: In the fifteen years we've been married, has there ever once been a morning when there wasn't coffee?

DAN: No.

ROSEANNE: Then why do you ask me if there's coffee every single morning?

(*Dan stares at her a beat, then*)

DAN: Is there toast?

(*Roseanne laughs and crosses to the table with the toast. Dan crosses to the coffee maker and pours a cup.*) (*)

ROSEANNE: Hold it. What is going on here?

BECKY: Mother. This is very important. My school is having a food drive for poor people.

ROSEANNE: Have them drive some of that food over here.

BECKY: Mother!

ROSEANNE: All right. You can take two cans.

DAN: Don't take the creamed corn.

SFX: (*telephone rings.*)

BECKY: I'll get it!

(*Becky races to the telephone. Darlene enters, carrying her history book. As she passes D.J., she smacks him on the back of his head with the book.*)

D.J.: Mom!

DARLENE: He started it.

D.J.: I did not.

DARLENE: You little creep.

D.J.: You pig face.

ROSEANNE: That's enough. Stop it. Stop it. Stop it.

DAN: Listen to your mother.

ROSEANNE: You heard your father.

(*Darlene and D.J. stop fighting. As Becky talks, she reaches around Roseanne for some cereal.*)

BECKY (*) (*into phone*): Connie, you can't tell him that.

ROSEANNE: Get off the phone.

BECKY: But, Mom . . .

ROSEANNE: Now.

BECKY: (*into phone*) Got to go. Bye.

(*Becky hangs up and exits.*)

D.J.: Dad, you know what would really be good for breakfast?

DAN: What?

D.J.: Pie.

ROSEANNE (*to Dan*): Tell him no.

DAN (*to D.J.*): No.

SFX: (*telephone rings.*)

(*Roseanne quickly snatches up the receiver.*)

ROSEANNE (*) (*into phone*): Oh, hi. I looked in the mirror. I'm getting boobs. He looked at me. He looked at me. Becky's not here.

(*Roseanne hangs up and crosses to the table. Darlene sits reading her history book.*)

DARLENE: Oh my gosh. I was supposed to give you this.

ROSEANNE: What is it?

(*Darlene pulls a folded piece of paper out of her history book and hands it to Roseanne.*) (*)

DARLENE (*): It's a note from my History teacher, Miss Crane. You got to meet with her at three-fifteen.

ROSEANNE: Today?

DARLENE: Uh-huh.

ROSEANNE: Why do you always wait until the last minute to tell me these things? I have a life, too, you know. It's not like I don't have anything to do.

DARLENE: I'm sorry. What do you want me to do, throw myself off a bridge?

ROSEANNE: Yeah, and take your brother and sister with you.

SFX: (*school bus horn.*)

(*The kids scramble, gathering their books. Roseanne quickly shoves sandwiches, apples, and chips into the brown paper bags.*)

ROSEANNE (*cont'd*): You didn't brush your teeth.

D.J.: We don't have time.

DARLENE: We'll miss the bus.

(*Roseanne hands D.J. and Darlene the lunch bags.*)

D.J.: Bye.

DARLENE: Bye.

DAN (*still reading*): Bye.

(*D.J. and Darlene exit on the run. Roseanne crosses to the table.*)

ROSEANNE: Okay, they're gone. Quick. Change the locks.

(*Roseanne notices Dan staring at the butter.*)

ROSEANNE (*cont'd*): All right, what is it?

DAN: Rose, I really don't mean to pick.

ROSEANNE: What?

DAN: I can't stand it when people leave toast crumbs on the butter.

ROSEANNE: What difference does it make? You're just going to smear it on your toast.

DAN: It's not right. You don't like it when there's jelly in the peanut butter jar.

ROSEANNE: That's sickening.

DAN: It's the same thing.

ROSEANNE: No, it's not.

DAN: Yes, it is.

ROSEANNE: Okay, forget it. Forget it.

(*She scrapes the crumbs off the butter and pushes it back toward Dan.*)

ROSEANNE (*cont'd*) (*): Here. Fresh butter. Knock yourself out.

DAN: I love you, darling.

ROSEANNE: Yeah, right. I love you, too.

SFX: (*car horn.*)

Save that detergent coupon.

(*calling off*) Becky!

(*Roseanne crosses to Becky's lunch bag, then notices the sink.*)

ROSEANNE (*cont'd*): Dan?

DAN: Yeah.

ROSEANNE: This sink is backed up again.

DAN: I'll plunge it right after breakfast. (*)

ROSEANNE: I don't want it plunged. I want it fixed.

DAN: You got it, babe.

ROSEANNE: This is the third time this week. I want it done today.

DAN: Absolutely.

(*Becky enters, carrying books, two cans of food, and a new, red bookbag.*)

BECKY: Mom? My bookbag fell apart.

(*Becky holds up the bookbag.*) (*)

ROSEANNE: I just bought it yesterday.

SFX: (*car horn.*)

BECKY: Mother. Please. You have to take it back.

ROSEANNE: Okay, okay. I'll go to the store after work.

(*Becky kisses Roseanne on the cheek.*)

BECKY: Thanks. Bye.

(*Becky grabs her lunch bag off the counter and exits.*)

(*Roseanne sits at the table. During the following, she picks up a piece of left-over toast and dunks it in Dan's coffee.*)

ROSEANNE: Can you meet with Darlene's teacher today? (*)

DAN: Can't do it, babe. Putting in a bid on a job. If I get it, me and Freddy'll start construction this afternoon.

ROSEANNE: Well, how about exchanging this bookbag? Can you squeeze that into your busy schedule?

DAN: It's either that or fix the sink.

ROSEANNE: Fix the sink. I'll do everything else, like I always do. I'll have to take off work early, lose an hour's pay, totally rearrange my day. But I don't mind. (*)

DAN: You ever sorry we got married?

ROSEANNE: Every day of my life.

DAN: Me, too.

ROSEANNE: You are? Really?

DAN: Nah.
ROSEANNE: Okay. Me neither, then.
(*a beat.*)
ROSEANNE (*cont'd*): Who would you've married if you didn't marry me?
DAN: Rosie . . .
ROSEANNE: Who?
DAN: No one.
ROSEANNE: I know. Beth Winchester.
DAN: Are you kidding?
ROSEANNE: Brenda Phillips?
DAN: Please.
ROSEANNE (*): Tell me. I won't get mad. Just say it. I just want to know.
DAN: Josephine Carter.
ROSEANNE: Josephine Carter! That little slut?
DAN: She had great toes.
ROSEANNE: Toes?
DAN: Oh, yeah. She'd sit with her legs crossed and dangle her shoe on the end of her toe. Drove me crazy.
ROSEANNE: You were going to marry her for that?
DAN: (*): Yes, ma'am.
ROSEANNE: Why didn't you?
DAN: The morning I was going to propose, I took her to this coffee shop—real quiet, out of the way place. Just as I started to pop the question, she smeared toast crumbs on the butter. That was it. I got up and left, didn't even pay the check.
(*a beat*)
ROSEANNE: You think you're pretty cute, don't you?
DAN (*): Pretty much.
(*Roseanne laughs and gives Dan a playful shove.*)
Dissolve to:

ACT ONE

II

Int. lunch room/factory—8:00 A.M. (day 1) (*Roseanne, Jackie, Crystal, Booker, Pete, Juanita, Vonda, Sylvia, Extras*)

(*Workers mingle around the vending machines or sit at tables. Crystal Anderson, Vonda Greene, and Sylvia Foster sit a a table, eating donuts and sipping coffee. Juanita lights a cigarette and crosses to the coffee.*) (*)
SYLVIA (*reading a tabloid*): Says here there's no PMS in Russia.
CRYSTAL: I don't believe anything they print about Russia.
(*Roseanne enters. Pete Wilkins approaches her.*)
PETE: There she is. The woman I dream about every night. Of course, I have nightmares.
(*Pete cracks up at his own joke. Roseanne grabs her timecard and punches in.*)
ROSEANNE: Yeah, boy. That's really funny, Pete.
PETE: Nightmares. (*)
ROSEANNE: You're like the funniest man that ever lived.
(*Robert "Booker" Brooks enters, crosses to the vending machine, and puts in a quarter. Roseanne continues across the room. Juanita Herrera passes by Roseanne.*) (*)

JUANITA: Hey, Slim.

ROSEANNE: Juanita, que tal?

JUANITA: Same crap, different day.

ROSEANNE: Tell me about it.

(*Juanita exits to the bathroom. Roseanne crosses to Booker at the vending machine. He pulls one of the knobs and hits the machine repeatedly.*)

ROSEANNE: (*cont'd*) Booker.

BOOKER: What?

(*Booker stops pounding.*)

ROSEANNE: It's not an employee. You don't have to beat it to get it to work.

(*Roseanne gently pulls the knob. A pack of gum drops into the chute. Roseanne picks it up.*)

BOOKER: Thanks. (*)

ROSEANNE: Listen. I have to take off an hour early today.

BOOKER: No way. We're two hundred cases behind on that Gelman order.

(*Booker crosses to the timecards. Roseanne follows.*) (*)

ROSEANNE: Booker, it's for one of my kids.

BOOKER: You have to understand my position.

ROSEANNE: And you have to understand mine. I've got to see a teacher today.

BOOKER: Roseanne, here at Wellman Plastics, we are a team. And I want us to be a winning team. All the players are equally important. The running backs aren't any more important than the pulling guards. The pulling guards—

ROSEANNE: Oh, I get it, I get it. It's kind of like a quilting bee.

BOOKER: What?

ROSEANNE: You know. Where all the barefoot women on the prairie get together and stitch like this one really big quilt. And each woman has her own patch. And no patch is more important than any other patch.

BOOKER (*trying to follow*): Uh-huh.

ROSEANNE: Well, the woman sewing *this* patch has to leave an hour early.

BOOKER: Look, Roseanne . . .

ROSEANNE: (*) I'm looking, Booker. Come on.

BOOKER: All right. I'll give you half an hour. But it's coming off your check.

ROSEANNE: There goes the Porsche.

(*Juanita enters from the bathroom as Roseanne crosses to the coffee counter.*)

JUANITA: Booker, can I have—

BOOKER (*authoritatively*): No!

(*Booker exits. Juanita mutters to herself and sits at the table. Roseanne holds up a packet of artificial sweetener and turns to the women at the table.*)

ROSEANNE: We got any actual sugar here?

(*Crystal holds up a packet of sugar.*)

CRYSTAL: I've got some.

ROSEANNE: Thanks.

(*Roseanne crosses to the table and takes the sugar.*)

VONDA: Was Booker giving you a hard time again

ROSEANNE: Nah. He was giving me the football speech.

VONDA: Oh, yeah. The running backs . . .

(*The other women join in.*)

ALL: . . . aren't any more important than the pulling guards . . .

(*The women ad lib, "Yeah," "Right," "We know," etc.*)

ROSEANNE (*): I love it when a guy talks sports. It does something to me. The only thing that's more exciting is when my Dan talks about hydraulic jacks and snow tires.

CRYSTAL: You can joke all you want. But you got yourself the ideal man.

ROSEANNE: Ideal, huh?

CRYSTAL: Sure. I'd give anything to have a man like Dan. He never runs around on you. He's good to the kids. And he's hygienic.

ROSEANNE: Crystal, you think he came that way? Fifteen years of fighting is what made him like that.

CRYSTAL: You are so full of it.

ROSEANNE (*): It's true. Good men don't just happen. They have to be created by us women.

(*The women ad lib: "Yeah," "I like it," etc.*)

CRYSTAL (*): Oh, you think you know everything.

ROSEANNE: It's true. You see, Crystal, a man is basically a lump. Like this donut. (*Roseanne picks up a donut.*) First, you got to get rid of all those things his mom did to him. (*She tears off two pieces of the donut and tosses them away.*) Then you got to take away all that macho crap they get from beer commercials. (*She tears off another piece and tosses it.*) And then there's my favorite . . . (*She tears off a large hunk of donut.*) The male ego.

(*She pops the piece into her mouth and chews. Some women cheer, others groan.*)

SFX: (*whistle blows.*)

(*As everyone exits to the factory, Roseanne's sister, Jackie Harris, enters, punches in, and crosses to Roseanne.*)

ROSEANNE (*): Hey, Sis.

JACKIE (*): Rose, do you realize that most people use only two percent of their mind's potential?

ROSEANNE (*): That much, huh?

JACKIE: How would you like to achieve success and realize your greatest dreams?

ROSEANNE: Nah.

JACKIE: Sure you would. Everybody would.

ROSEANNE: What's got into you?

JACKIE: Last night, I went to this incredible seminar.

ROSEANNE: What was it this time, "Dare to Be a Millionaire?"

JACKIE: "See It and Be It."

ROSEANNE: Be what?

(*Roseanne and Jackie head toward the swinging doors.*)

Cut to:

Reset

Int. factory

(*Crystal is at the workbench. Roseanne and Jackie enter.*)

CRYSTAL: Hi, Jackie.

JACKIE: Morning, Crystal. Roseanne, this guy, Doctor Jerry Macklin, teaches you how to tap into the hidden treasures of your unconscious mind.

ROSEANNE: He does, huh?

JACKIE: Yeah. It's so simple. He says, "If your mind can conceive it, and your heart can believe it, then you can achieve it."

CRYSTAL: Achieve what?

ROSEANNE: Sis, here, went to another "incredible" seminar.

CRYSTAL: Oh.

JACKIE: It was great.

CRYSTAL: Maybe I should go to one of these seminars with you.

JACKIE: "See It and Be It" is the one, Crystal. It'll change your life.

CRYSTAL: I'd love to change my life.

JACKIE: You can. For only thirty dollars. A one-night course. What you get are the basics of visualization.

CRYSTAL: Visualization?

JACKIE: Right. You use your mind's potential to get anything you want. If you want a brand new car, all you have to do is visualize it.

CRYSTAL: That sounds easy enough.

JACKIE: It is. You just create an image of the car in your unconscious mind.

ROSEANNE: You know, maybe you're on to something.

JACKIE: Get out of here.

ROSEANNE: No, really. I'm serious. I'm visualizing a clean house, kids who don't talk back, and a husband who waits on me hand and foot.

JACKIE: You can have it.

ROSEANNE: We're in Crystal's new car and we're driving up to the country . . .

JACKIE: That's the idea.

ROSEANNE: . . . to visit my sister at the nut barn.

Dissolve to:

ACT ONE

III

Int. Classroom—3:30 P.M. (day 1) (*Roseanne, Miss Crane*)

(*Miss Crane is at her desk, preparing to leave. She carries a briefcase and a sports bag with a squash racquet. Roseanne enters, out of breath.*)

ROSEANNE (*): Hi. Are you the History teacher?

MISS CRANE: Yes. I'm Ms. Crane.

ROSEANNE: I'm Darlene's mom.

MISS CRANE (*Checking her watch*): I'd given up on you. You're fifteen minutes late.

ROSEANNE: I know. I'm so sorry. I got here as soon as I could.

MISS CRANE: I don't think we can do this now.

ROSEANNE: What?

MISS CRANE: I have an another engagement.

ROSEANNE (*Indicating sports bag*): You going to go play tennis?

MISS CRANE: Squash. Could we do this another day?

ROSEANNE (*): No. You see, I had to get off work early. I got caught in traffic. And then—

MISS CRANE: All right. We'll do it today. Have a seat.

(*Roseanne sits.*)

MISS CRANE (*cont'd*): Darlene has been demonstrating behavorial problems.

ROSEANNE: What does that mean?

MISS CRANE: She's been barking in class.

ROSEANNE: Barking?

MISS CRANE: Like a dog.

ROSEANNE: (*) Did you tell her to stop?

MISS CRANE: I did.

ROSEANNE: What happened?

MISS CRANE: She stopped.

ROSEANNE: So, what's the problem?

MISS CRANE: I feel this barking is an aggressive manifestation of a deeper internal problem.

ROSEANNE: Huh?

MISS CRANE: Well, let me explain. We have found that when behavioral problems arise in the classroom, it usually indicates a problem at home.

ROSEANNE: Uh-huh.

MISS CRANE: How would you describe your relationship with your daughter?

ROSEANNE: I'd call it typical.

MISS CRANE: Typical? Not special?

ROSEANNE: Typical.

MISS CRANE: Do you feel you spend enough time with your daughter?

ROSEANNE: You mean like "quality" time?

MISS CRANE: Yes. Do you spend any free time with Darlene?

ROSEANNE: I work and I got three kids. I don't have any free time.

MISS CRANE: That may be the problem.

ROSEANNE: No. I think the problem is, there is no problem.

MISS CRANE: But your daughter barks.

ROSEANNE (*): Our whole family barks. (*Rising*) Now, if you'll excuse me, I'm going home to spend some "quality" time with little Darlene. Don't worry. I'll talk to my daughter.

(*Roseanne exits.*)

ROSEANNE (*os*) (*cont'd*): Grrrfff. Grrrfff.

Fade out.

END OF ACT ONE

ACT TWO

I

Fade in.

Int. kitchen/living room/utility room—4:45P.M. (day 1) (*Roseanne, Dan, Becky, Darlene, D.J.*)

(*The room is littered with jackets, shoes, school books, dirty dishes, and soda cans. D.J. is at the stove, eating the blueberry pie. He scoops out large bites with a spoon. From outside, we hear:*)

SFX: (*Car pulling into driveway.*)

(*D.J. crosses and quickly shoves the pie into the refrigerator. He crosses and sits at the table. Roseanne enters, struggling with several grocery bags.*)

D.J.: You want some help?

ROSEANNE: No, that's all right, D.J. I don't want you to strain yourself.

(*Roseanne sets the bags on the counter and notices the sink. She reaches into it and lifts out a filthy, sopping wet, dishtowel.*)

ROSEANNE (*cont'd*): Where's your father?

D.J.: Who?

ROSEANNE: The guy I'm married to.

D.J.: I don't know.

(*Roseanne spots the pie-smeared spoon. She picks it up and looks at D.J. He is the picture of innocence.*)

D.J. (*cont'd*): I'm going to go play with my trucks.

(*D.J. exits to the living room. Roseanne crosses to the refrigerator and pulls out the pie. A large section is missing. Roseanne heads toward the living room.*)

Cut to:

Reset.

Int. living room

(*Roseanne enters, crosses, and sits next to D.J., holding up the pie and the spoon. D.J. has pie crumbs and a gob of pie filling in the corner of his mouth.*)

ROSEANNE: You know anything about this?

D.J.: About what?

ROSEANNE: This pie. Did you eat it?

D.J.: Nope.

ROSEANNE: Not even a nibble?

D.J.: Nope.

(*Roseanne scrapes the gob of pie filling off D.J.'s mouth with her finger.*)

ROSEANNE: What is this?

D.J.: Dirt?

(*Roseanne licks her finger.*)

ROSEANNE: Tastes like blueberry dirt.

D.J.: Okay. I did it. I ate your pie. But it's not my fault.

ROSEANNE: Oh, really? Who's fault is it?

D.J.: Yours. When you tell me not to do something, it makes me want to do it.

ROSEANNE: Why is that?

D.J.: I don't know. It must be something inside my brain.

(*Roseanne laughs and grabs D.J.'s shoulders.*)

ROSEANNE: Well, let's shake it out.

(*Roseanne gives D.J. a playful shake. They both laugh. Darlene enters through the front door, wearing a baseball glove. Her clothes are dirty and grass-stained.*)

DARLENE (*Triumphantly*): I struck out Mark Winstead six times. He threw his bat at me and started crying. The wimp.

(*Darlene exits to the kitchen and grabs a can of soda out of the refrigerator.*)

D.J. (*): Mom, can I go over to Billy's?

ROSEANNE: No. You can't go anywhere for the rest of your life.

(*Roseanne heads toward the kitchen as Darlene enters the living room.*)

ROSEANNE (*cont'd*): You. Come here.

DARLENE: What?

Cut to:

Reset.

Int. kitchen

(*Roseanne and Darlene enter.*)

ROSEANNE (*): I talked to your History teacher.

DARLENE: Miss Crane, "The Pain."

ROSEANNE: Yeah, you're a real jokester, all right.

SFX: (*TV cartoons from living room.*)

ROSEANNE (*cont'd*) (*Calling off*): Turn that down! (*To Darlene*) Now what's going on? She says you've been barking in class.

DARLENE: Yeah.

ROSEANNE (*): Why would you do that?

DARLENE: Mom, she's so boring. If I don't bark, I'll fall asleep.

(*Becky enters from the living room.*)

BECKY: Mom. Did you get my bookbag?

ROSEANNE (*indicating the counter*): Over there. (*To Darlene*) Darlene, I want it to stop. No more barking.

DARLENE: But everyone makes fun of Miss Crane.

BECKY: Mom, this is blue.

DARLENE (*to Becky*): Hey, I'm talking to Mom.

BECKY: So am I.

DARLENE: Shut up.

BECKY: Don't tell me to shut up.

DARLENE: Shut up. Shut up. Shut up. You make me want to puke.

BECKY (*cont'd*): You are so immature. When are you ever going to grow up?

ROSEANNE: All right, quit it.

ROSEANNE (*cont'd*) (*): Knock it off! (*To Becky*) You are going to use that bag until you're thirty.

BECKY: Great. I'll just look like a freak, that's all.

DARLENE: What else is new?

BECKY: Shut up.

(*Becky exits to the living room.*)

ROSEANNE: This is why some animals eat their young. (*Indicating Darlene's things.*) Take this stuff up to your room.

(*As Darlene is picking up her books, baseball glove, and jacket, Dan enters through the back door, carrying an object wrapped in a towel. He sets the object on the table.*) (*)

DAN (*Crossing to the refrigerator*): Hi, babe.

DARLENE: Dad, guess what. I struck out Mark Winstead six times.

DAN: Yeah, I read about it in the sports page.

DARLENE: Dad.

DAN: Said something about him being your boyfriend.

DARLENE: He is not! He's not my boyfriend!

DAN: You always strike out the one you love, Mrs. Winstead.

DARLENE (*Heading toward the living room*): He's not my boyfriend. I can't stand him. He makes me sick.

(*Darlene exits.*)

DAN (*looking in the refrigerator*): You didn't get any beer?

ROSEANNE: On the counter.

DAN: Thank you, honey. You're a peach.

(*Dan crosses to the counter and pulls a can of beer off a six-pack.*)

DAN (*cont'd*): It's warm. (*A beat*) Ah, that's all right.

(*Dan pops open the beer, takes a sip, and sits on the counter.*)

ROSEANNE: Dan.

DAN: Yeah?

ROSEANNE: How come this sink ain't fixed?

DAN (*): I'm going to get right on it. But, first, check this out.

(*Dan unwraps a wooden figurehead.*)

DAN (*cont'd*): A genuine, handcarved figurehead.

ROSEANNE: Uh-huh. Yeah.

DAN: When I get the boat finished, I'm going to slap this baby right on the front.

ROSEANNE: You are, huh?

DAN: Isn't it a beaut? I can't believe Dwight was going to throw it out.

ROSEANNE: Oh, you were over at Dwight's?

DAN: Yeah. Me and Freddy went over to help him work on his truck.

ROSEANNE: I thought you were starting a job today.

DAN: I didn't get it. Somebody put in a lower bid.

ROSEANNE (*): So what you're saying is, you had the whole day off.

DAN: No, I didn't have the whole day off. I was busy. Making contacts.

ROSEANNE: With what, Dwight's truck and a six-pack?

DAN: Come on, Roseanne—

ROSEANNE: Come on, Dan.

DAN: I was hoping he'd kick a little work my way. Dwight got me my last two jobs.

ROSEANNE: Maybe he can get you your next wife.

DAN: Maybe.

ROSEANNE: Oooo, how would I ever get along without you? You just sit and drink your beer, hubby. I'll fix the sink.

DAN: The hell you will. I'll fix the sink.

(*Roseanne exits to the utility room. Dan follows her.*)

Cut to:

Reset.

Int. utility room

(*Dan enters.*)

ROSEANNE: Talk is cheap, Mister Fix-It.

DAN: Roseanne, fixing the sink is the husband's job. I am the husband.

ROSEANNE: And I am the wife. So, it's my job to do everything else. Right?

DAN: Don't give me that.

(*Roseanne grabs the plunger.*)

ROSEANNE: It's true. I put in eight hours a day at the factory, come home, and put in another eight hours.

(*Darlene enters from the kitchen.*)

ROSEANNE (*cont'd*): I'm running around like a maniac, fighting kids . . .

DARLENE: Mom, where's the tape?

ROSEANNE: Bathroom. Middle drawer.

(*Darlene exits.*)

ROSEANNE (*cont'd*) (*To Dan*): I'm talking to teachers, exchanging bookbags, and you don't do nothing.

(*Roseanne heads toward the kitchen. Dan follows.*)

Cut to:

Reset.

Int. kitchen

(*Roseanne enters carrying the plunger, followed by Dan.*)

DAN: Hey, I do lots of things around here.

ROSEANNE: Like what?

DAN: Clean out the gutters.

ROSEANNE: Oh, yeah. And?

(*A beat. Then*)

DAN: What's your point here, Roseanne?

ROSEANNE: There is no point. Okay? No point.

(*Roseanne plunges the sink for several beats.*)

ROSEANNE (*cont'd*): The point is, you act like this house is a magic kingdom where you just sit on your throne.

DAN: Oh, yeah?

ROSEANNE: Yeah. And everything gets done around here by some wonderful wizard. Poof! The laundry is folded. Poof! Dinner is on the table.

DAN: You want me to fix dinner? I'll fix dinner. I'm fixing it right now.

(*Dan crosses to the cupboard, pulls out several cans, crosses to the stove, and starts opening them.*)

ROSEANNE: Oh, but, honey, you just fixed dinner three years ago.

DAN: Think I can't cook? I can cook. I'm cooking.

ROSEANNE: Great. And I'll spend the rest of the night washing dishes.

DAN: Hey, I wash dishes.

ROSEANNE: When?

DAN: Thursday. Six forty-five. P.M.

ROSEANNE (*): Yeah, nineteen seventy-what?

(*Noticing Dan is struggling with the can.*)

ROSEANNE: (*cont'd*): We can't have a big can of corn for dinner. Get out of the way. I'll do it.

(*Roseanne pushes Dan away and grabs the can opener.*)

DAN: You see? I try to help.

(*Roseanne crosses to the pantry, grabs more food, then crosses back to the stove.*) (*)

ROSEANNE: Well, you better try harder. Get off your throne and start helping me out around here, because I'm fed up.

DAN (*): Oh, yeah? Well, I got a royal news flash for you.

(*From the living room, we hear:*)

DARLENE (*os*): Ahhh!

BECKY (*os*): Mom! Dad! (*Becky enters.*)

BECKY (*cont'd*): Darlene cut her finger off!

(*Roseanne, Dan, and Becky head toward the living room.*)

Cut to:

Reset.

Int. living room

(*The TV is still on. Darlene is holding her finger, crying. Roseanne, Dan, and Becky enter.*)

SFX: (*TV Cartoons.*)

ROSEANNE: What happened?

BECKY (*): She cut herself with the scissors. Take her to the emergency room.

DAN: Come on, let's go.

(*Dan carries Darlene toward the kitchen.*)

BECKY: Call an ambulance. She needs a tourniquet.

ROSEANNE: Shut up, honey.

(*Roseanne heads toward the kitchen.*)

Cut to:

Reset.

Int. kitchen

(*Dan enters with Darlene, who is still crying. He leads her to the sink and runs water over the finger.*)

DAN: It's going to be okay. We got to rinse it off.

(*Roseanne enters and crosses into the utility room.*)

DARLENE: Owww.

(*Dan wraps Darlene's finger in a paper towel.*)

DAN: It's okay. You're going to be all right. Now, you got to keep that finger above your head.

(*Dan holds Darlene's finger above her head and applies pressure. Roseanne enters with the first-aid kit and takes out a bandage.*)

DARLENE: It hurts.

DAN: Honey, don't think about your finger. Think about something else.

DARLENE: I can't.

DAN: Yes, you can. Think about . . . a flower.

ROSEANNE: A flower?

DAN: Yeah. Close your eyes. Go ahead, close them.

(*Darlene closes her eyes.*)

DAN (*cont'd*): Okay. Now, picture a real pretty flower. It's out in a field and the sun is shining on it. Can you see it?

DARLENE: No.

ROSEANNE: Okay, forget the flower. Think about . . . demolition derby.

DARLENE: What about it?

ROSEANNE (*): Remember that yellow station wagon? How it got clobbered?

DARLENE: Yeah. That was neat.

(*As Roseanne talks, Dan removes the towel, checks the finger. Roseanne applies a bandaid*)

ROSEANNE: How those two cars sandwiched him and slammed him into the wall.

DARLENE: Yeah.

DAN: And then Ricky Tornado came full speed and tore his whole back end off, flipped him over.

ROSEANNE: You remember that?

DARLENE (*getting into it*): That was a blast.

(*Roseanne finishes applying the bandaid.*)

DAN: Okay, darling. You're all done.

DARLENE (*opening her eyes)*: I am?

DAN: Yep.

DARLENE: I didn't even feel it.

ROSEANNE: Pretty cool, huh?

DARLENE: (*examining her finger*): Yeah. Thanks.

(*Darlene exits. Dan and Roseanne look at each other for a long beat. Then*)

ROSEANNE: You hungry?

DAN: Not really.

ROSEANNE: I'll fix dinner.

DAN: Great.

(*Dan crosses to the sink. Roseanne crosses to the stove.*)

Fade out.

END OF ACT TWO

TAG

Int. garage—twilight (day 1) (*Roseanne, Dan*)

(*Dan is working on his sailboat, which is in the early stages of construction. The figurehead is propped up against the frame. Roseanne enters, carrying a cup of coffee.*)

ROSEANNE: Here.

DAN: Thanks. Rosie, come here and feel this board. You won't believe how smooth it is. Go on. Run your hand along it.

(*Roseanne runs her hand along the board.*)

DAN (*cont'd*): Feels good, huh?

ROSEANNE: I'm trembling with excitement.

DAN: Just think, when you and I are retired, we're going to be cruising the Caribbean on this baby.

ROSEANNE (*): I ain't getting on that thing.

DAN (*): It'll be great. We'll spend our last years together sailing through paradise.

ROSEANNE (*): All that sailor stuff really turns you on, huh?

DAN: Absolutely. There's nothing more romantic than drifting on the open sea. We'll be all alone, cuddled up in bed. Moonlight dancing on the water. Every night will be a voyage to ecstasy.

ROSEANNE: You're turning me on.

DAN: I am?

(*A beat.*)

ROSEANNE: Let's do it.

DAN (*moving closer*): What about the sink?

ROSEANNE: Anywhere you want.

Fade out.

END OF SHOW

DISCUSSION QUESTIONS

1. *Roseanne* attempts to portray working-class America. Having read a sample episode, which aspects of the show do you believe accurately reflect this group? Which aspects do you find inaccurate?
2. How would you describe the language of the main characters in the show? In what ways is their dialogue reminiscent of conversations you've experienced?
3. Media critics have commented that *Roseanne* represents a new wave of feminism that focuses on the plight of blue-collar women with jobs and families. What form does Roseanne's rebellion against traditional domestic and workplace values take? Is this rebelliousness affirmed or negated in the show's final scene? Explain your position.